Shojo Beat

Skip·Beat!

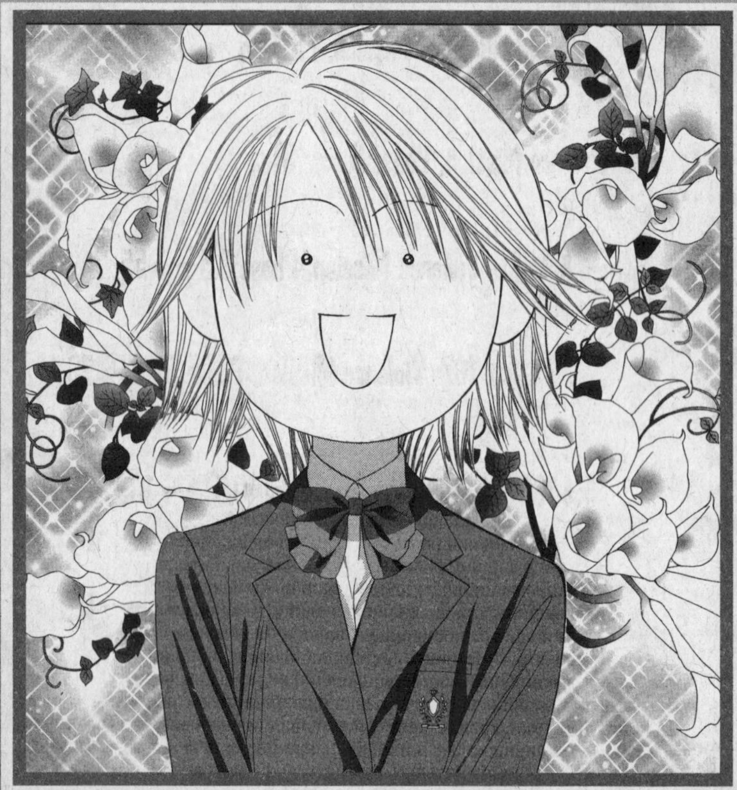

28

Story & Art by Yoshiki Nakamura

Skip·Beat!

Volume 28

CONTENTS

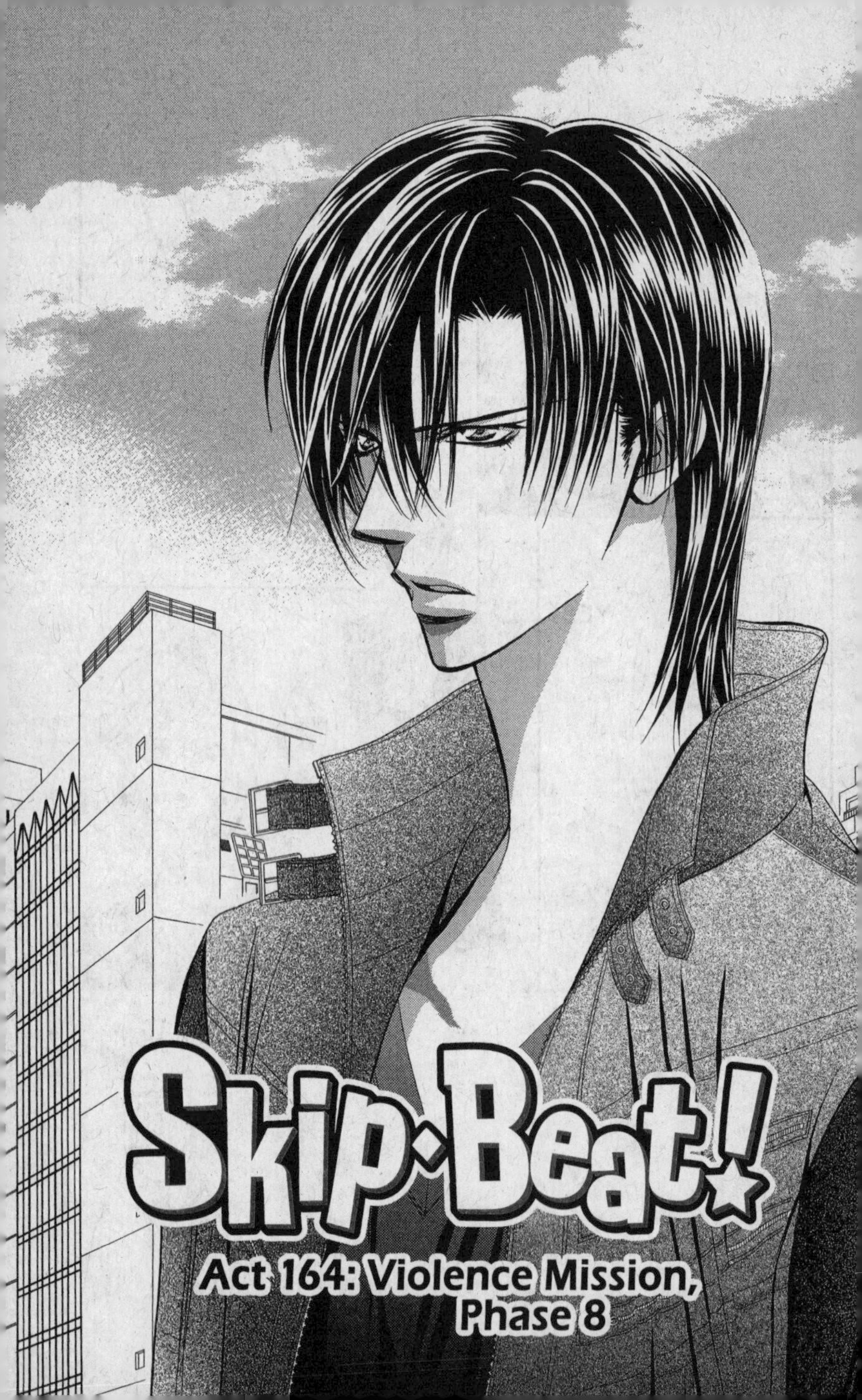
Skip·Beat!
Act 164: Violence Mission, Phase 8

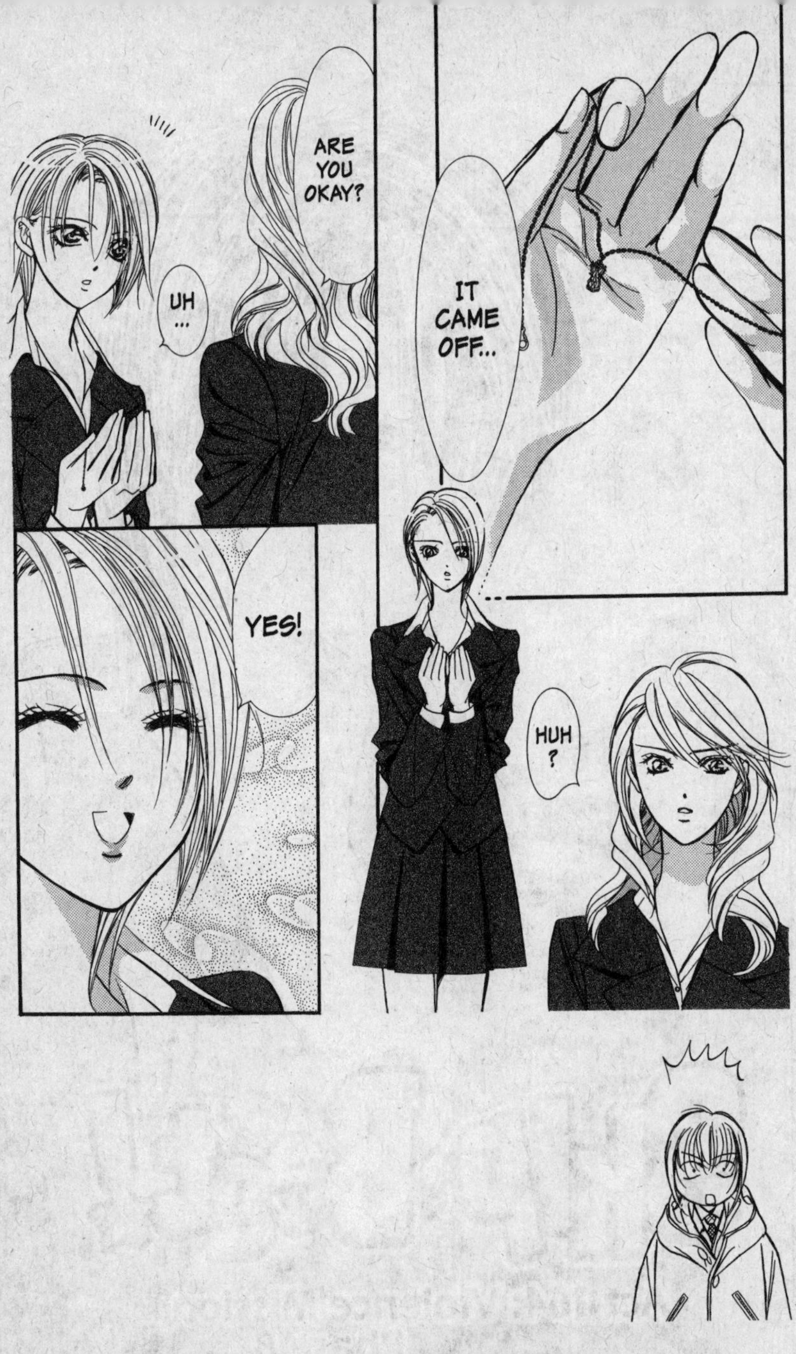
IT CAME OFF...
ARE YOU OKAY?
UH ...
HUH ?
YES!

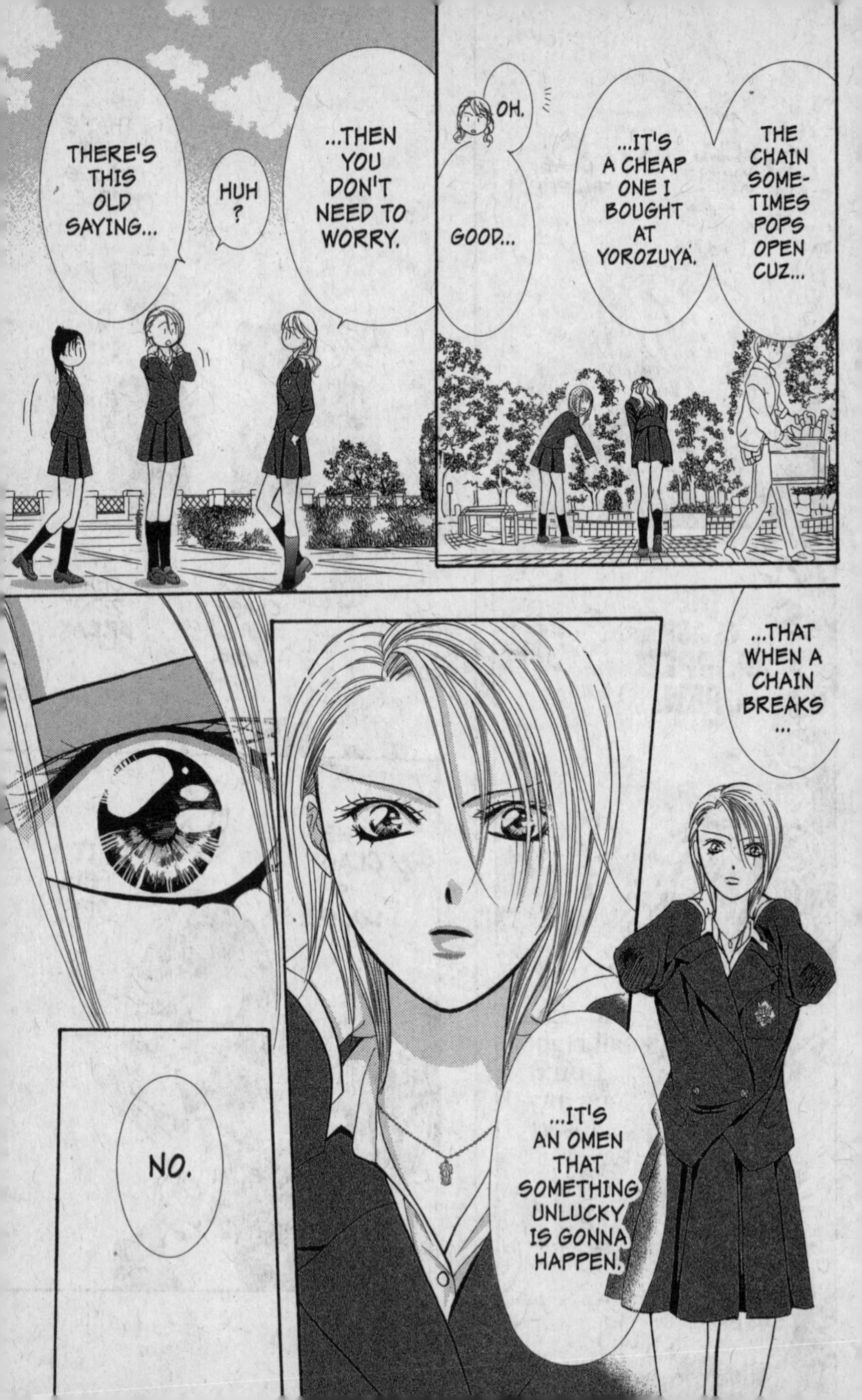
THE CHAIN SOMETIMES POPS OPEN CUZ...
...IT'S A CHEAP ONE I BOUGHT AT YOROZUYA.
OH.
GOOD...
...THEN YOU DON'T NEED TO WORRY.
HUH?
THERE'S THIS OLD SAYING...
...THAT WHEN A CHAIN BREAKS ...
...IT'S AN OMEN THAT SOMETHING UNLUCKY IS GONNA HAPPEN.
NO.

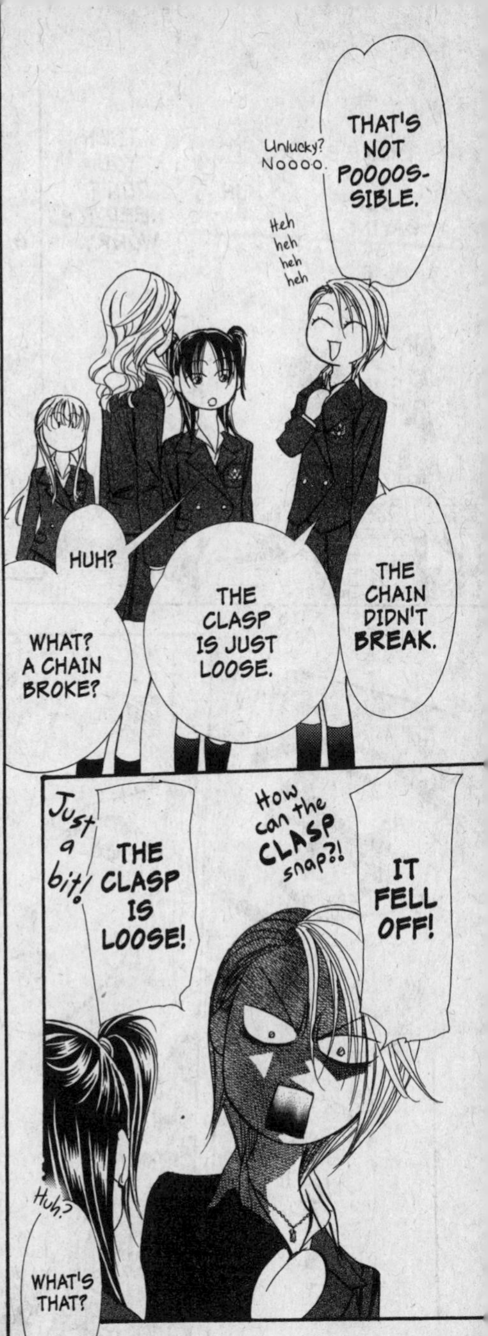
THAT'S NOT POOOOS-SIBLE.
Unlucky? Noooo.
Heh heh heh heh
THE CHAIN DIDN'T BREAK.
THE CLASP IS JUST LOOSE.
HUH?
WHAT? A CHAIN BROKE?
IT FELL OFF!
How can the CLASP snap?!
THE CLASP IS LOOSE!
Just a bit!
Huh?
WHAT'S THAT?

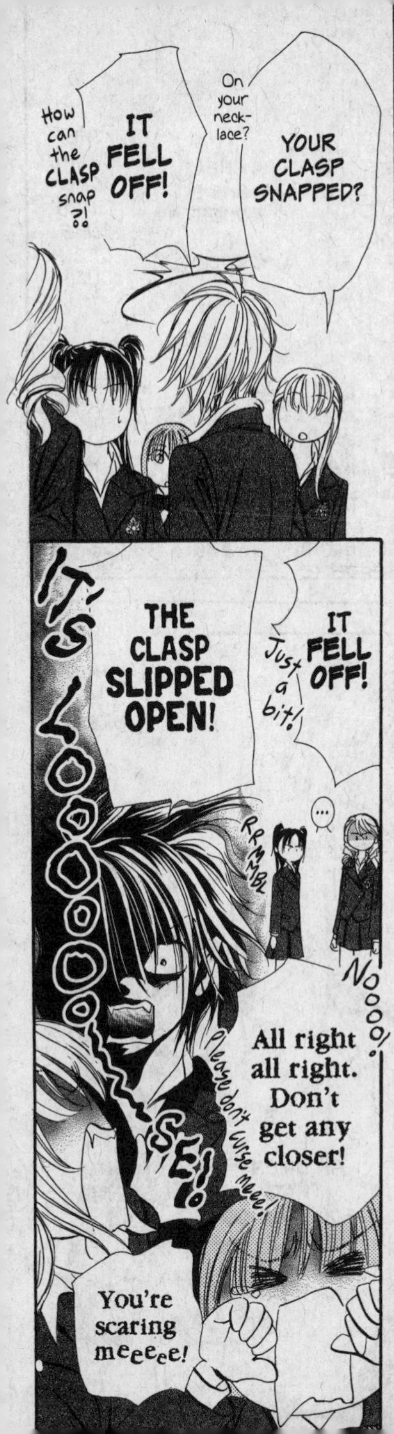
YOUR CLASP SNAPPED?
On your neck-lace?
IT FELL OFF!
How can the CLASP snap?!
IT FELL OFF!
Just a bit!
THE CLASP SLIPPED OPEN!
IT'S LOOOOOOOO~SE!
...
RRMMBL
Noooo!
All right all right. Don't get any closer!
Please don't curse meee!
You're scaring meeeee!

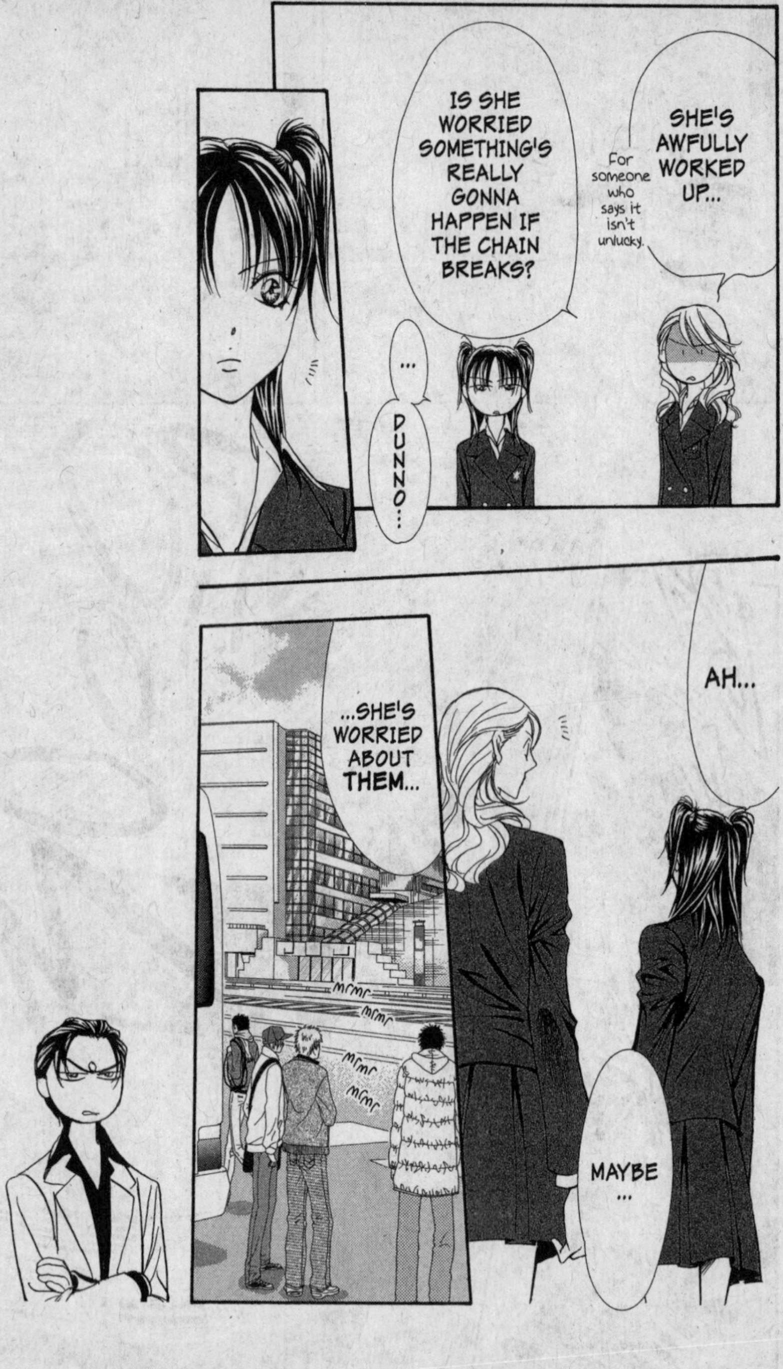
SHE'S AWFULLY WORKED UP...
For someone who says it isn't unlucky.
IS SHE WORRIED SOMETHING'S REALLY GONNA HAPPEN IF THE CHAIN BREAKS?
...
DUNNO...
AH...
...SHE'S WORRIED ABOUT THEM...
MAYBE ...
MMMM
MMMM
MMMM
MMMM

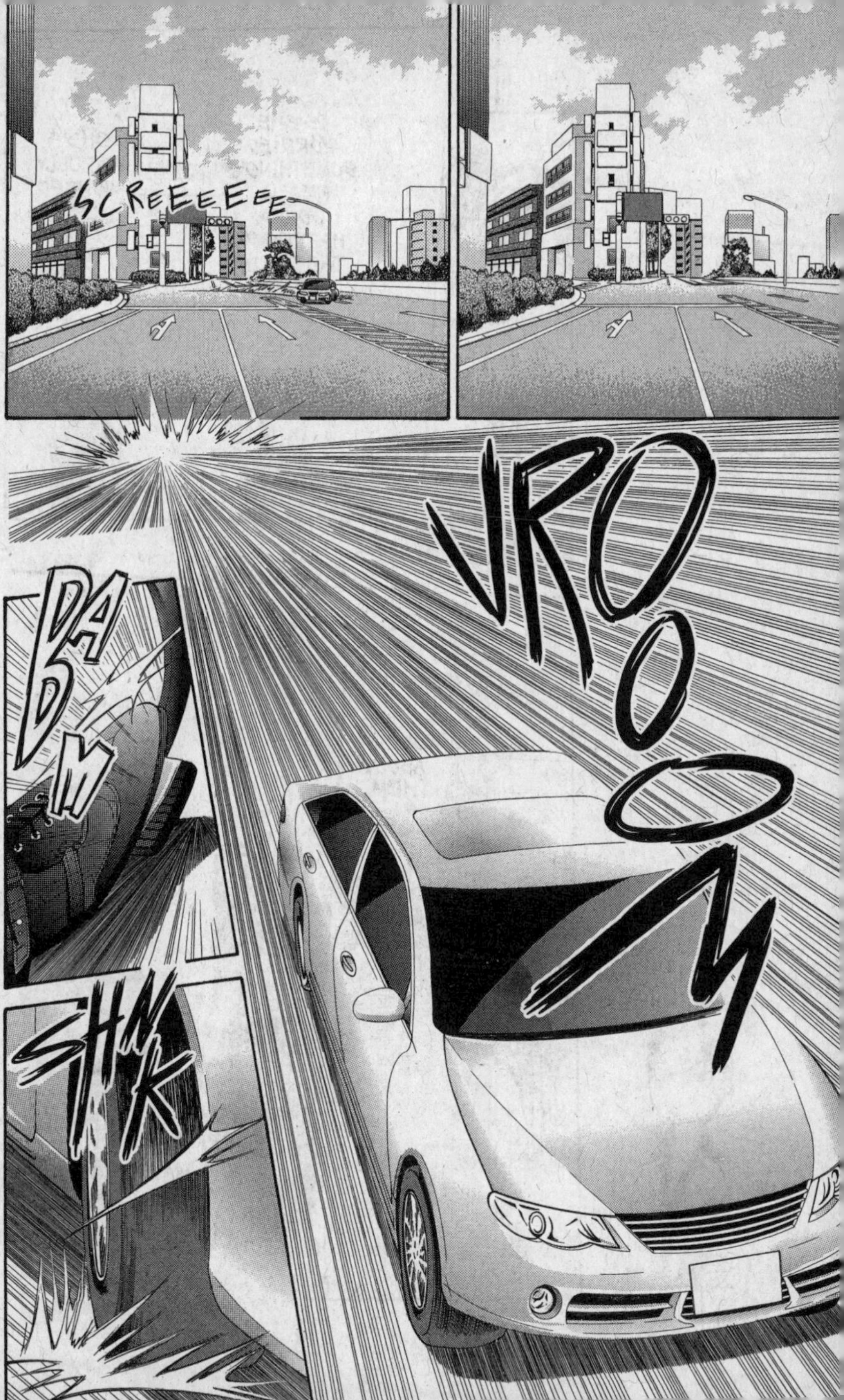
SCREEEEEEE
VROOOM
BAM
SHAK

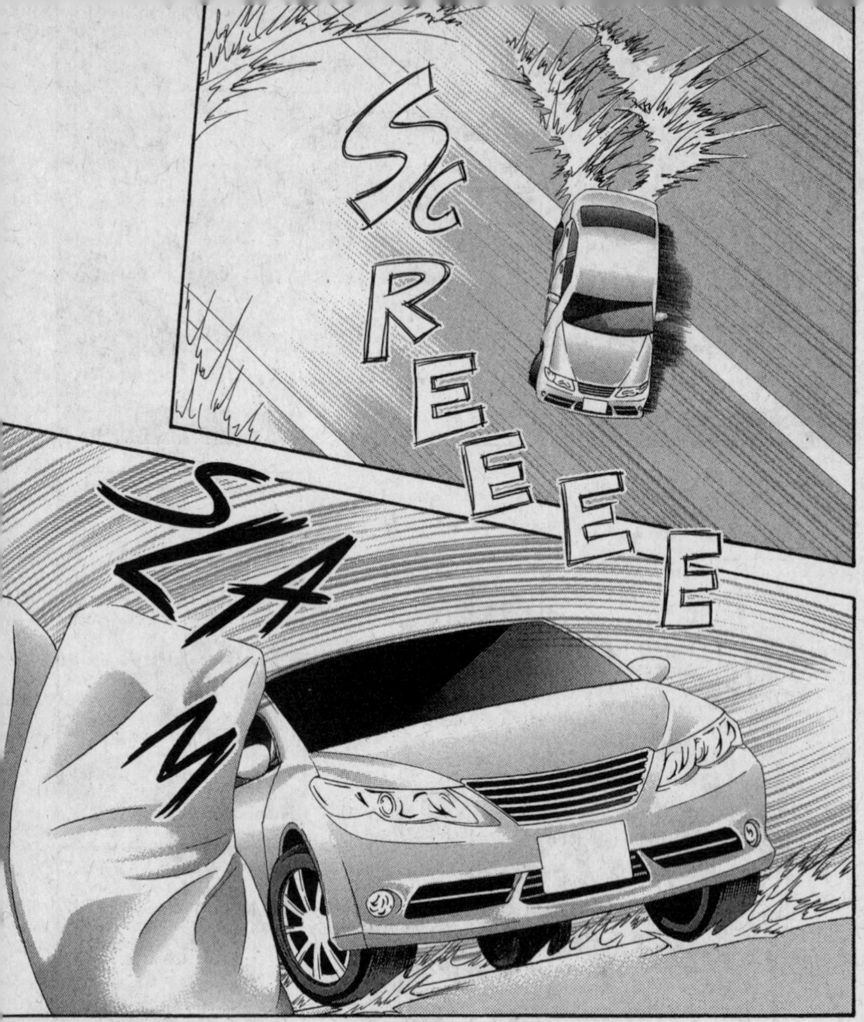
SCREEEE
SLAM

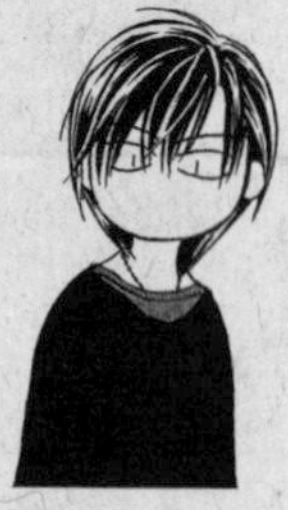

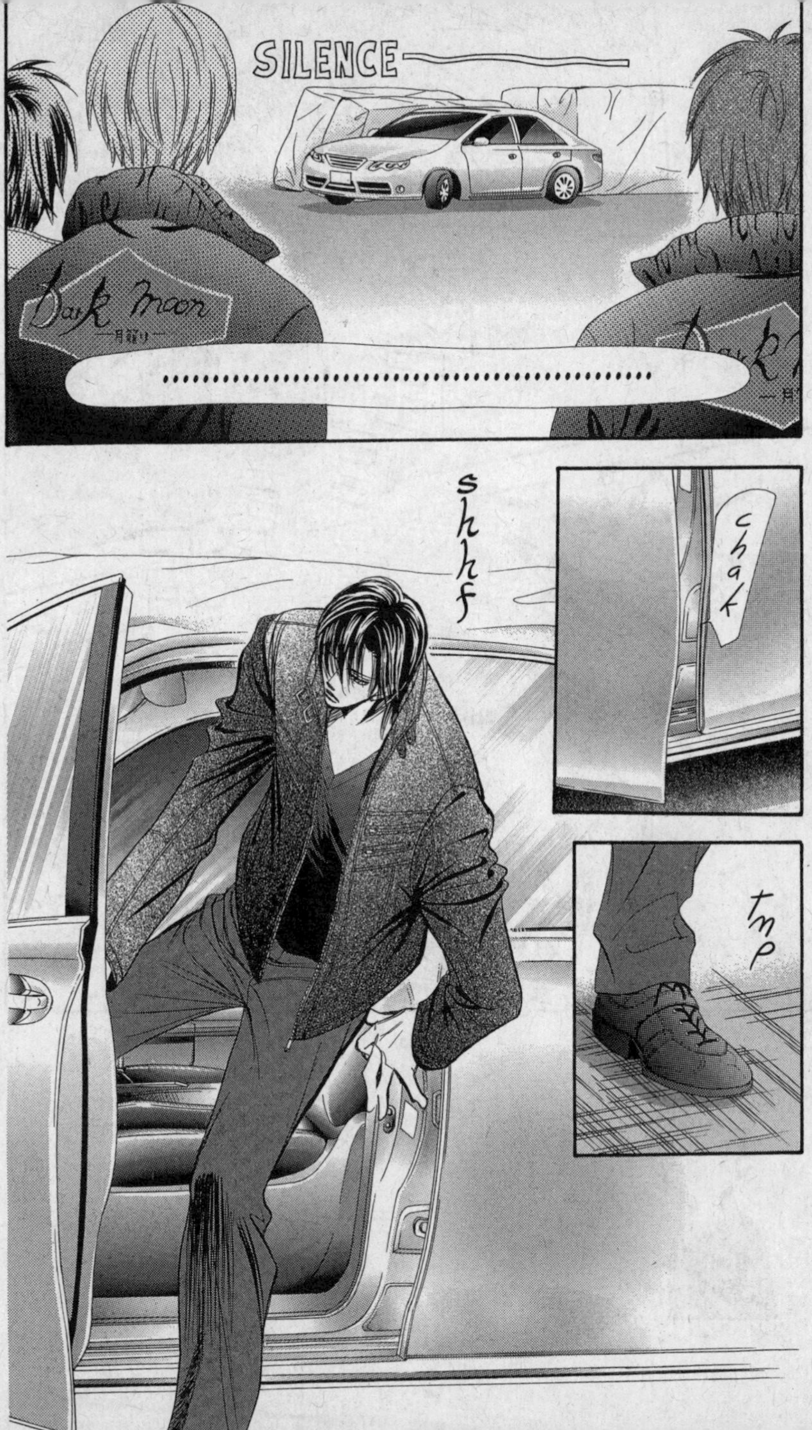
SILENCE
Dark moon
—月籠り—
....
chak
tmp
shhf

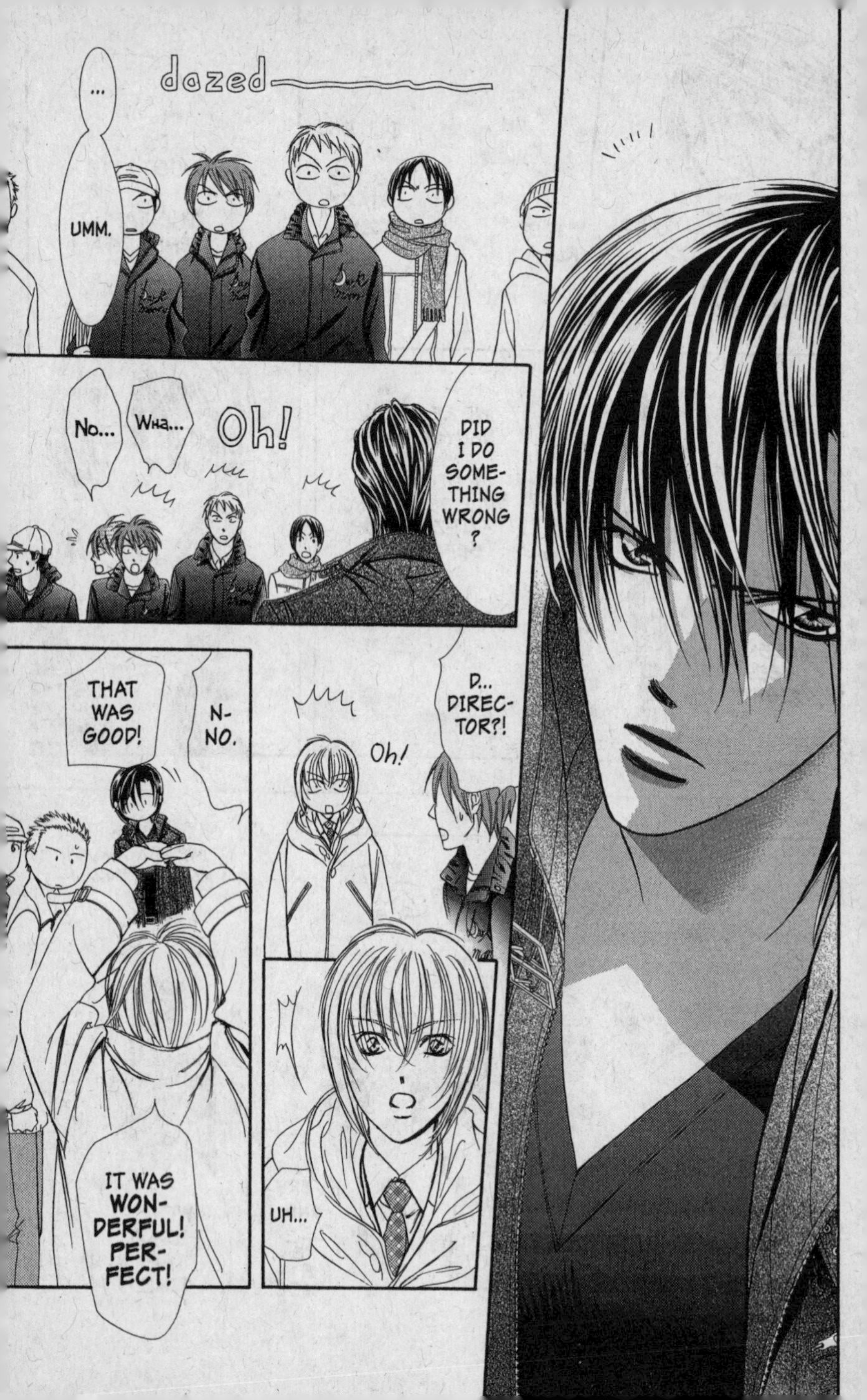

dazed
...
UMM.
DID I DO SOMETHING WRONG?
Oh!
Wha...
No...
D... DIRECTOR?!
Oh!
N-NO.
THAT WAS GOOD!
UH...
IT WAS WONDERFUL! PERFECT!

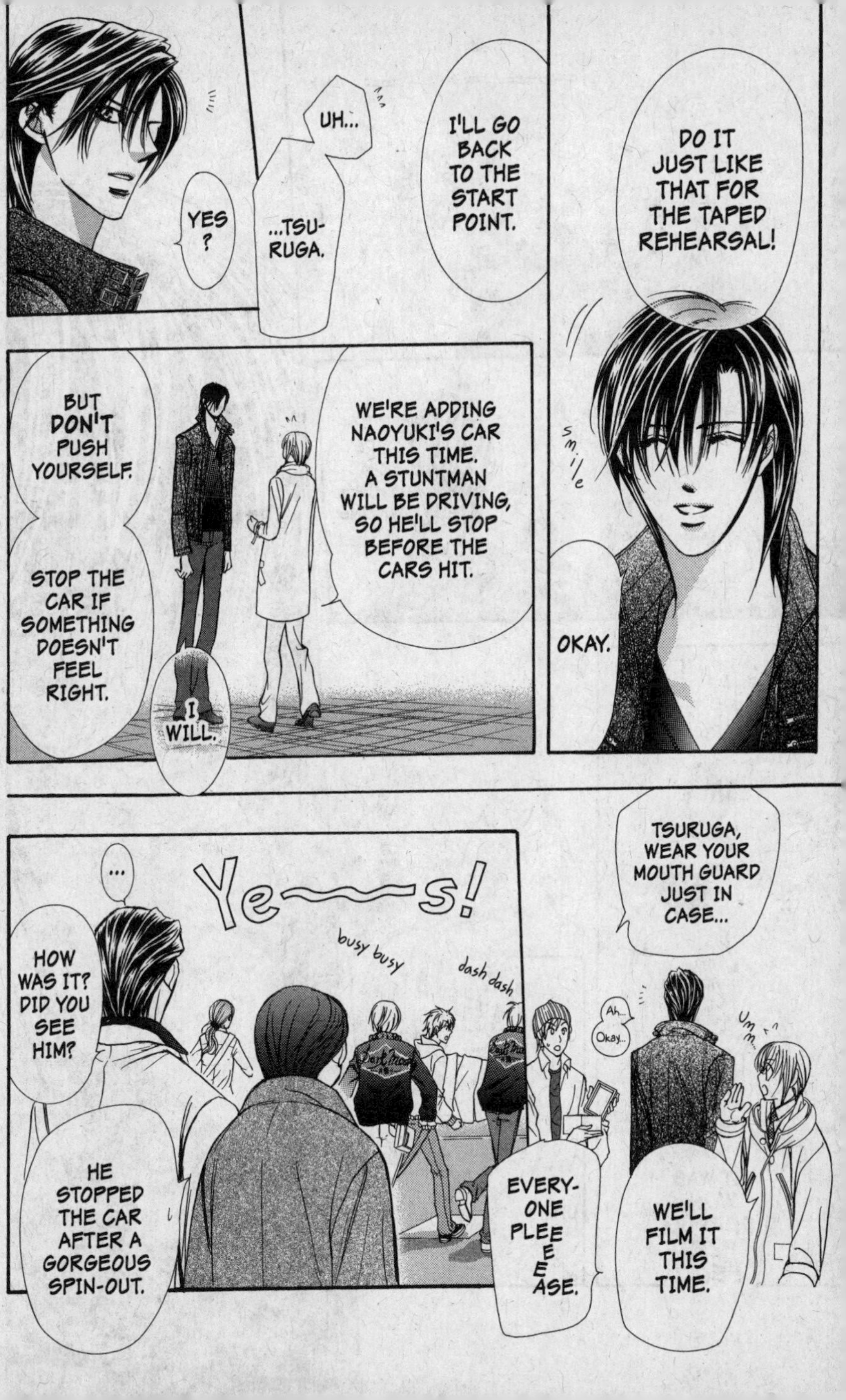
DO IT JUST LIKE THAT FOR THE TAPED REHEARSAL!
smile
OKAY.
I'LL GO BACK TO THE START POINT.
UH...
...TSURUGA.
YES?
WE'RE ADDING NAOYUKI'S CAR THIS TIME. A STUNTMAN WILL BE DRIVING, SO HE'LL STOP BEFORE THE CARS HIT.
BUT DON'T PUSH YOURSELF.
STOP THE CAR IF SOMETHING DOESN'T FEEL RIGHT.
I WILL.
TSURUGA, WEAR YOUR MOUTH GUARD JUST IN CASE...
Ah... Okay...
Umm
WE'LL FILM IT THIS TIME.
EVERYONE PLEEEEASE.
dash dash
busy busy
Ye——s!
...
HOW WAS IT? DID YOU SEE HIM?
HE STOPPED THE CAR AFTER A GORGEOUS SPIN-OUT.

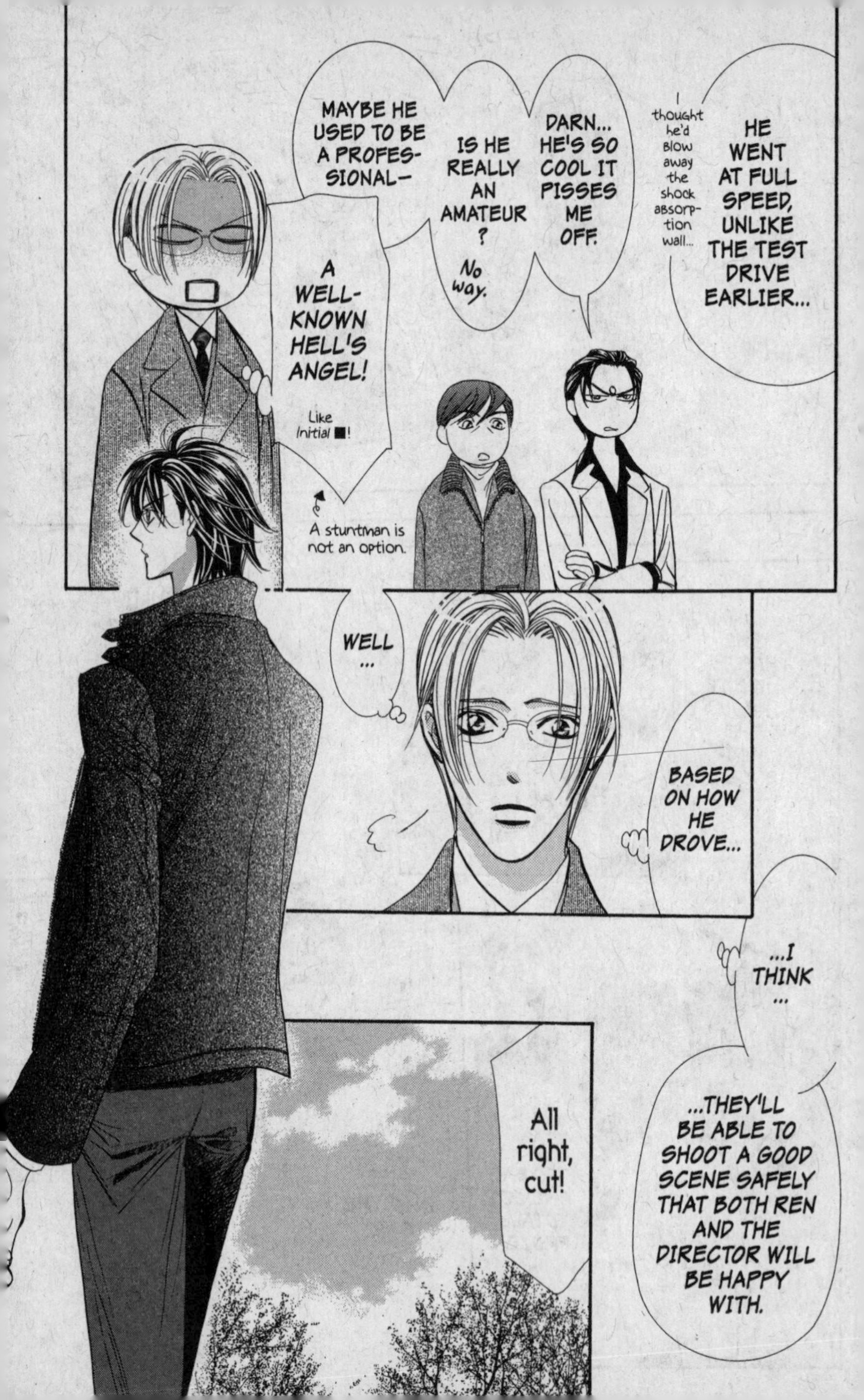
HE WENT AT FULL SPEED, UNLIKE THE TEST DRIVE EARLIER...
I thought he'd blow away the shock absorption wall...
DARN... HE'S SO COOL IT PISSES ME OFF.
IS HE REALLY AN AMATEUR?
No way.
MAYBE HE USED TO BE A PROFESSIONAL—
A WELL-KNOWN HELL'S ANGEL!
Like Initial [redacted]!
A stuntman is not an option.
WELL...
BASED ON HOW HE DROVE...
...I THINK...
...THEY'LL BE ABLE TO SHOOT A GOOD SCENE SAFELY THAT BOTH REN AND THE DIRECTOR WILL BE HAPPY WITH.
All right, cut!

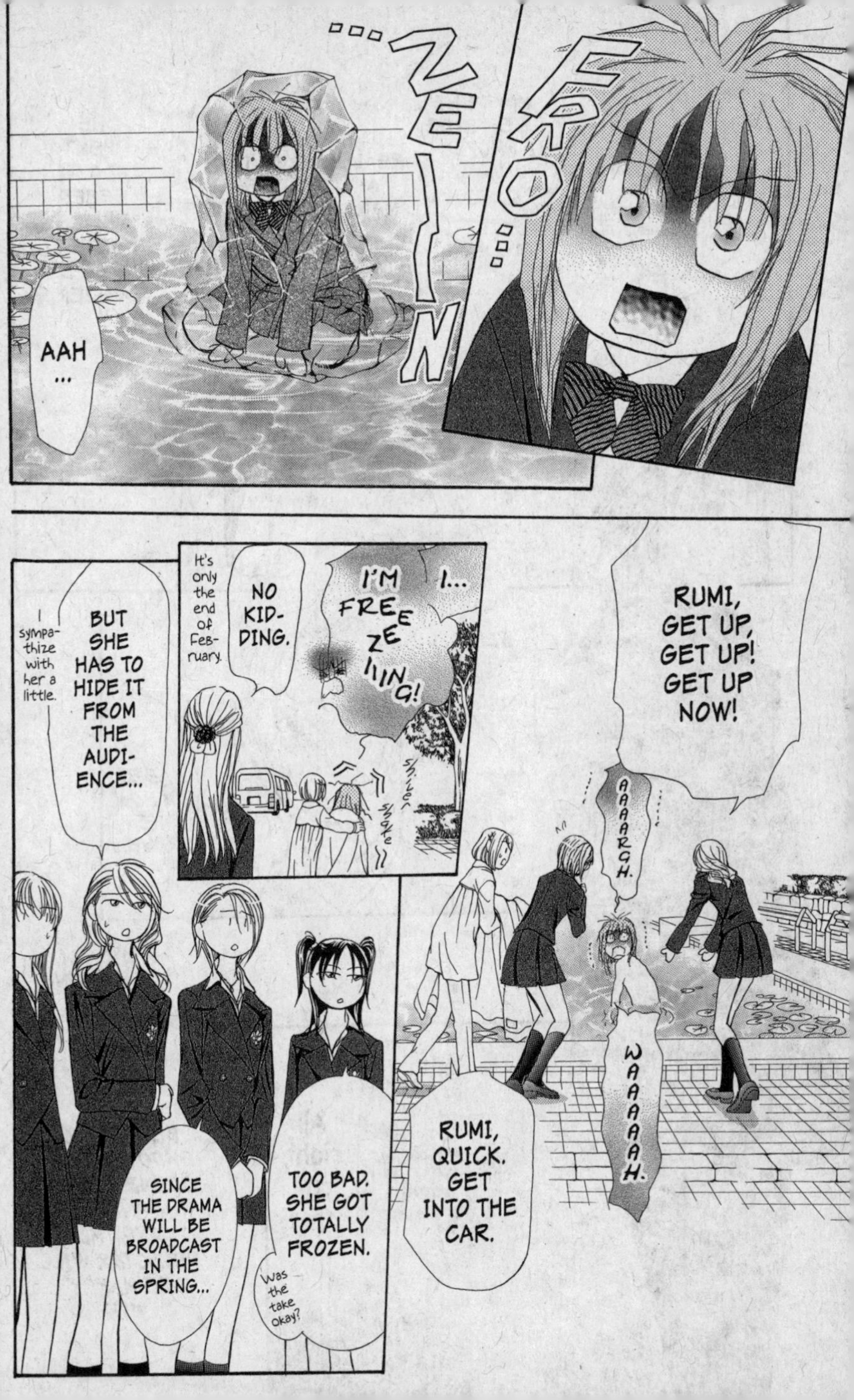
FRO...
...ZE——N
AAH ...
RUMI, GET UP, GET UP! GET UP NOW!
AAAARGH.
WAAAAAAH.
RUMI, QUICK. GET INTO THE CAR.
I...
I'M FREEZING!
NO KIDDING.
It's only the end of February.
shiver
shake
BUT SHE HAS TO HIDE IT FROM THE AUDIENCE...
I sympathize with her a little.
TOO BAD. SHE GOT TOTALLY FROZEN.
Was the take okay?
SINCE THE DRAMA WILL BE BROADCAST IN THE SPRING...

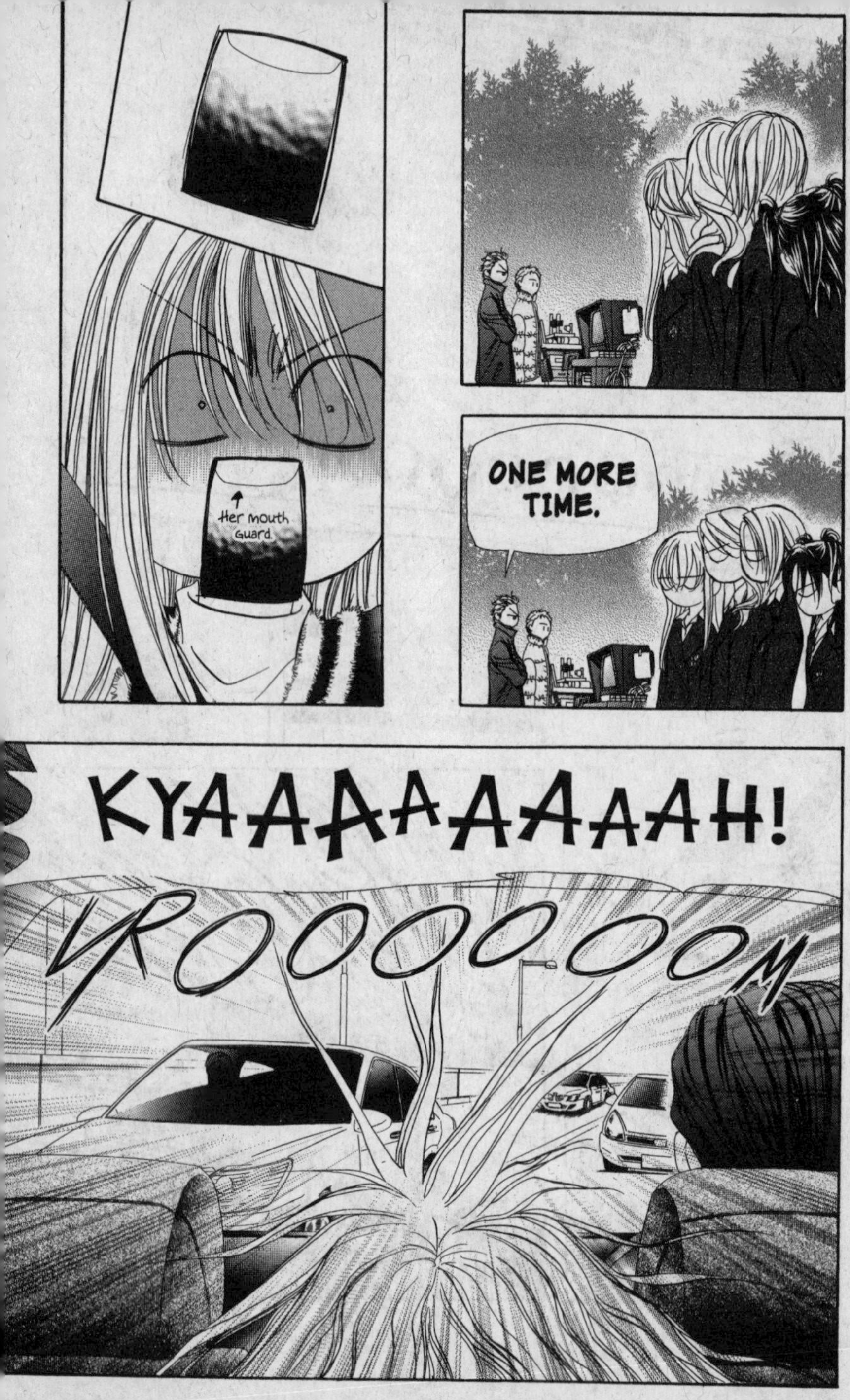
ONE MORE TIME.
Her mouth guard.
KYAAAAAAAAH!
VROOOOOOM

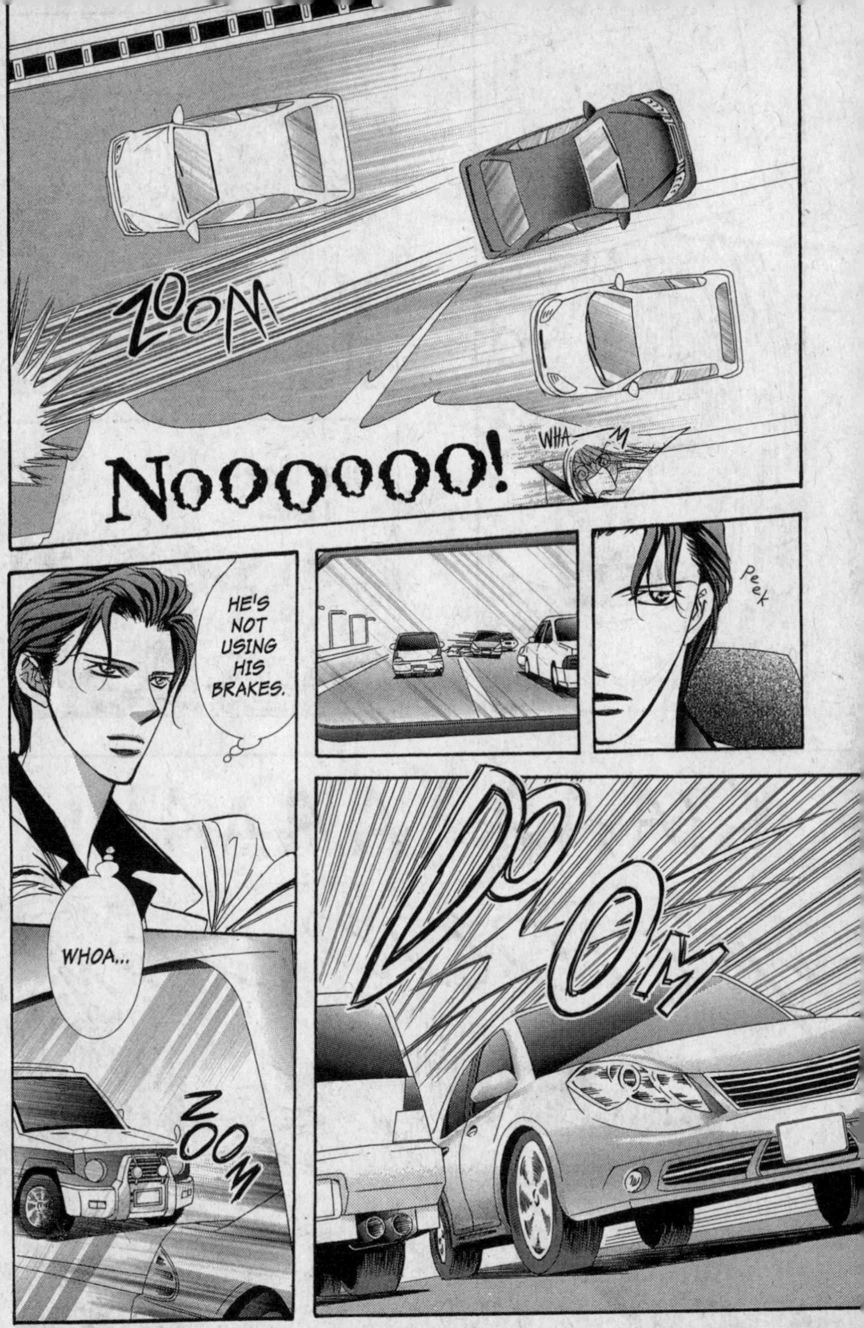
ZOOM
WHA—M
NOOOOOO!
Peek
DOOM
HE'S NOT USING HIS BRAKES.
WHOA...
ZOOM

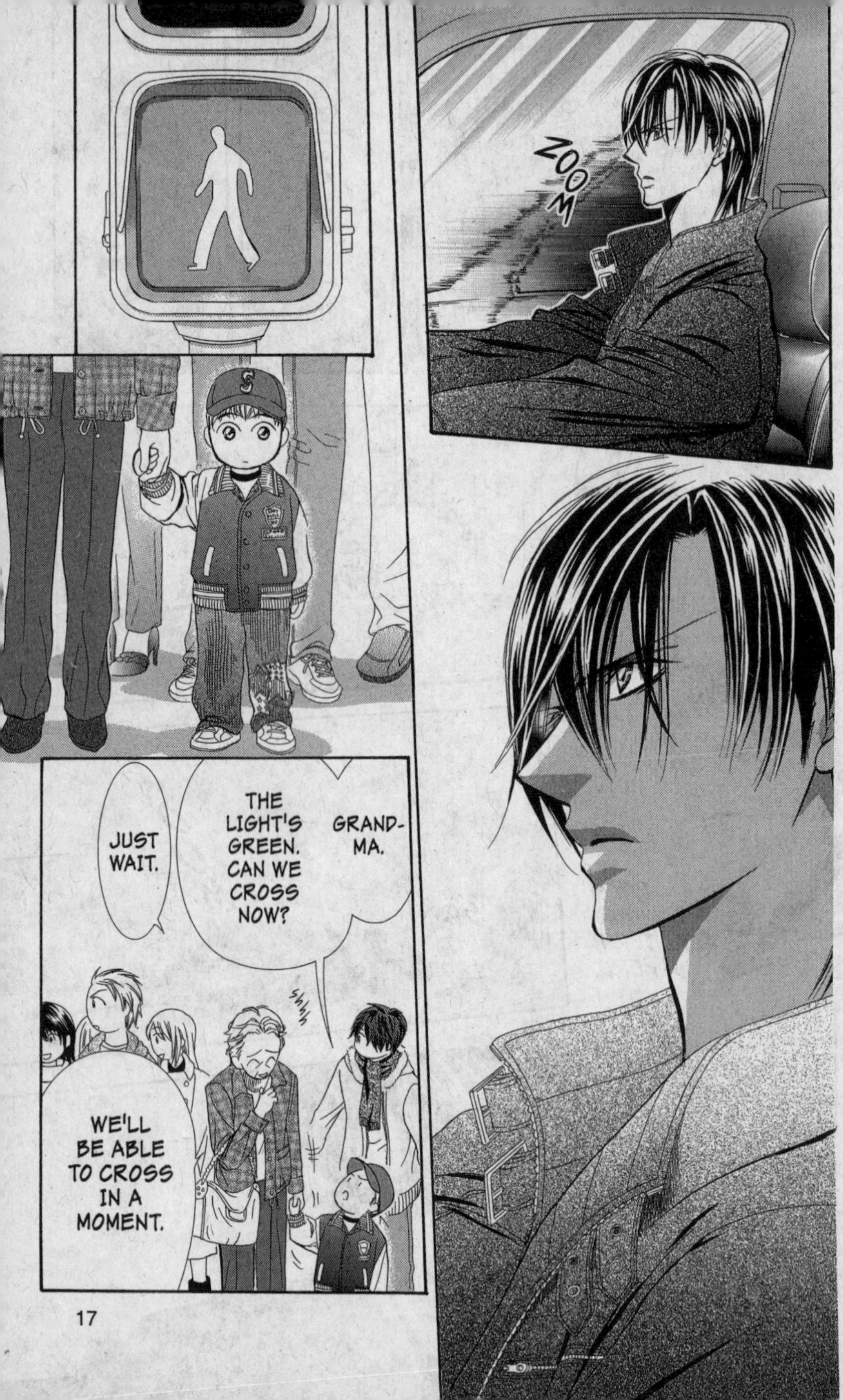
ZOOM
GRAND-MA.
THE LIGHT'S GREEN. CAN WE CROSS NOW?
JUST WAIT.
shhh
WE'LL BE ABLE TO CROSS IN A MOMENT.

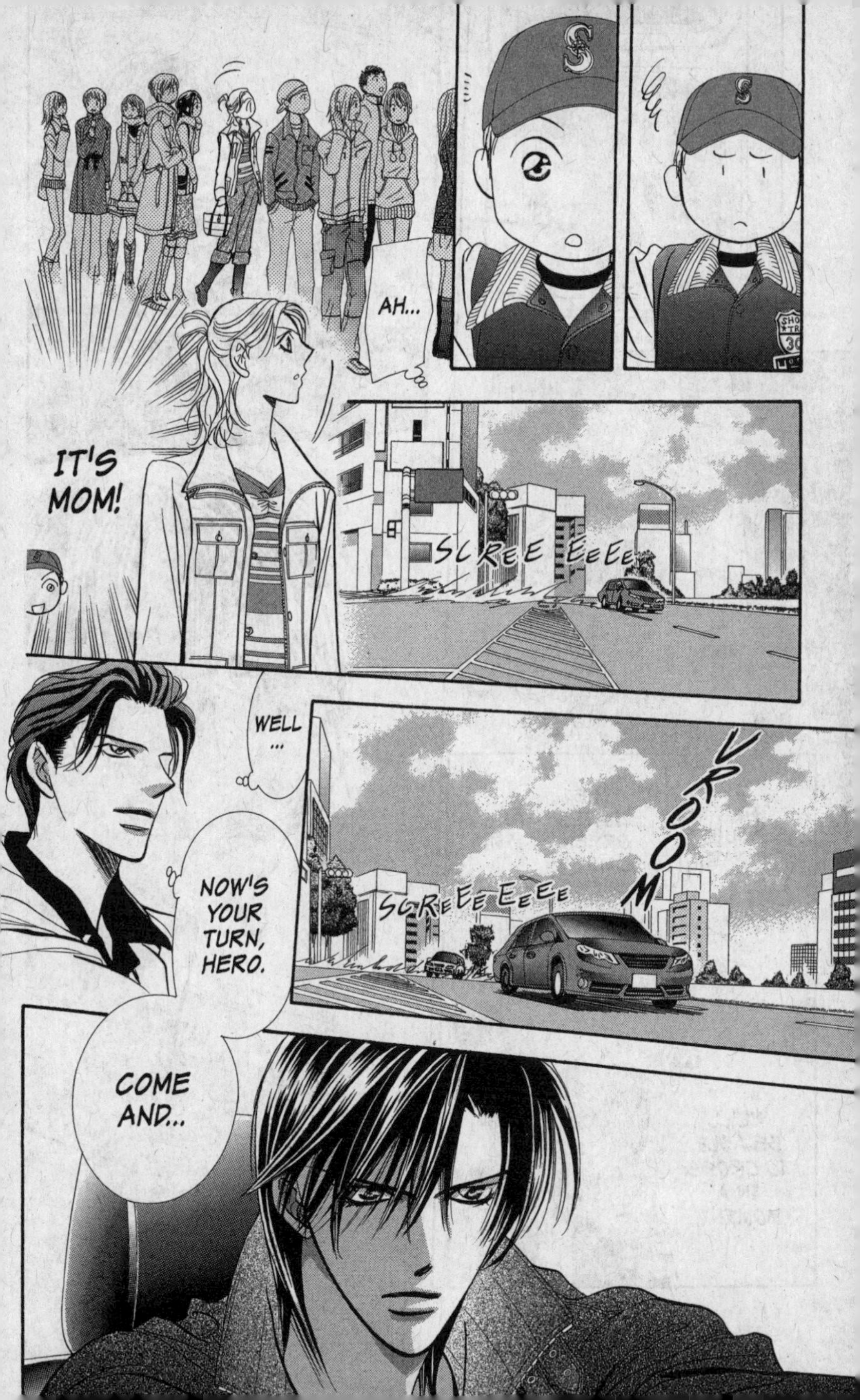
SCREEEEEEE
AH...
IT'S MOM!
VROOOM
SCREEEEEEE
WELL...
NOW'S YOUR TURN, HERO.
COME AND...

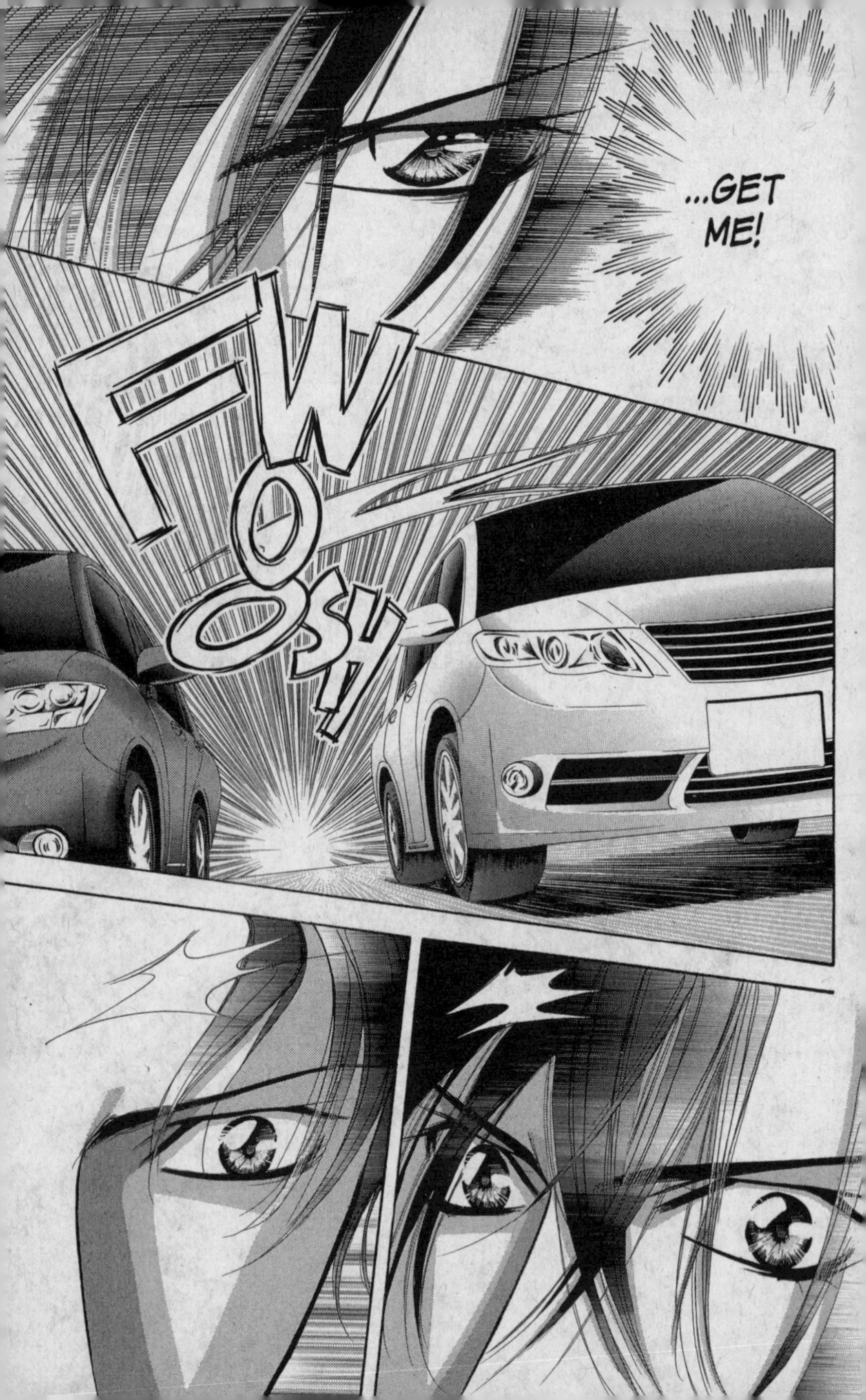
...GET ME!
FWOOSH

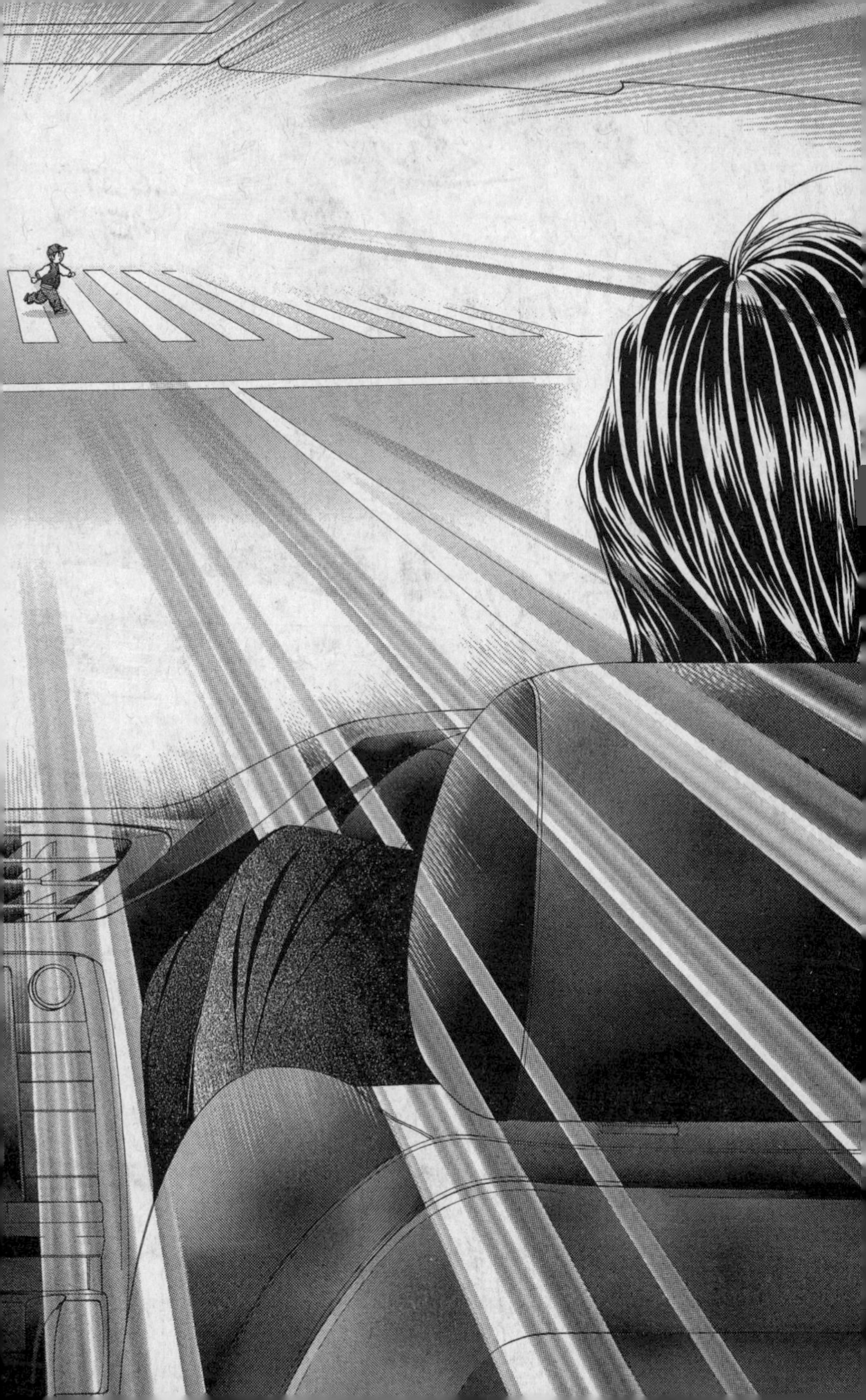

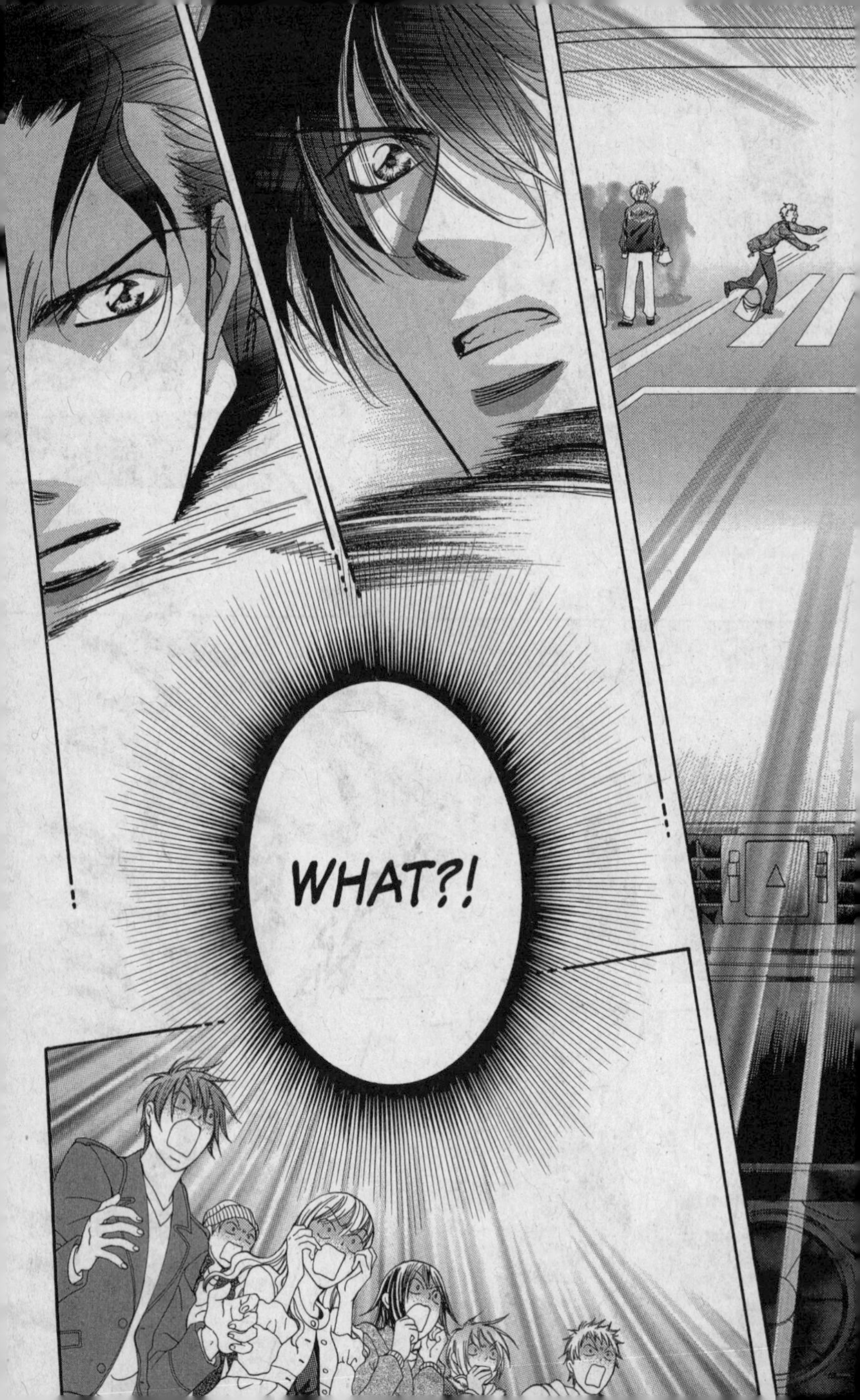
WHAT?!

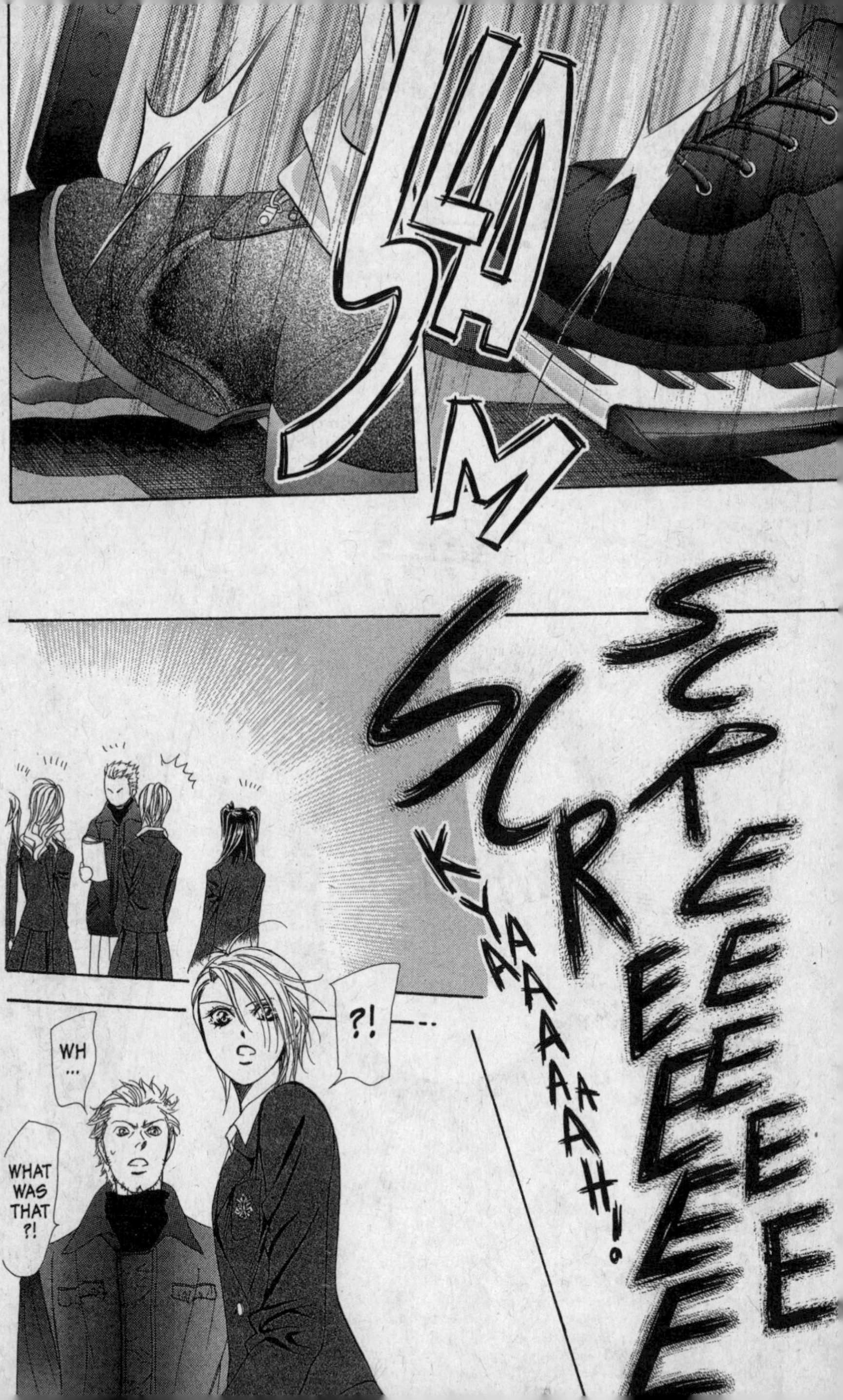

SLAM
SCREEEEEEE
SCREEEEEEE
KYAAAAAAAH!!
?!
WH...
WHAT WAS THAT?!

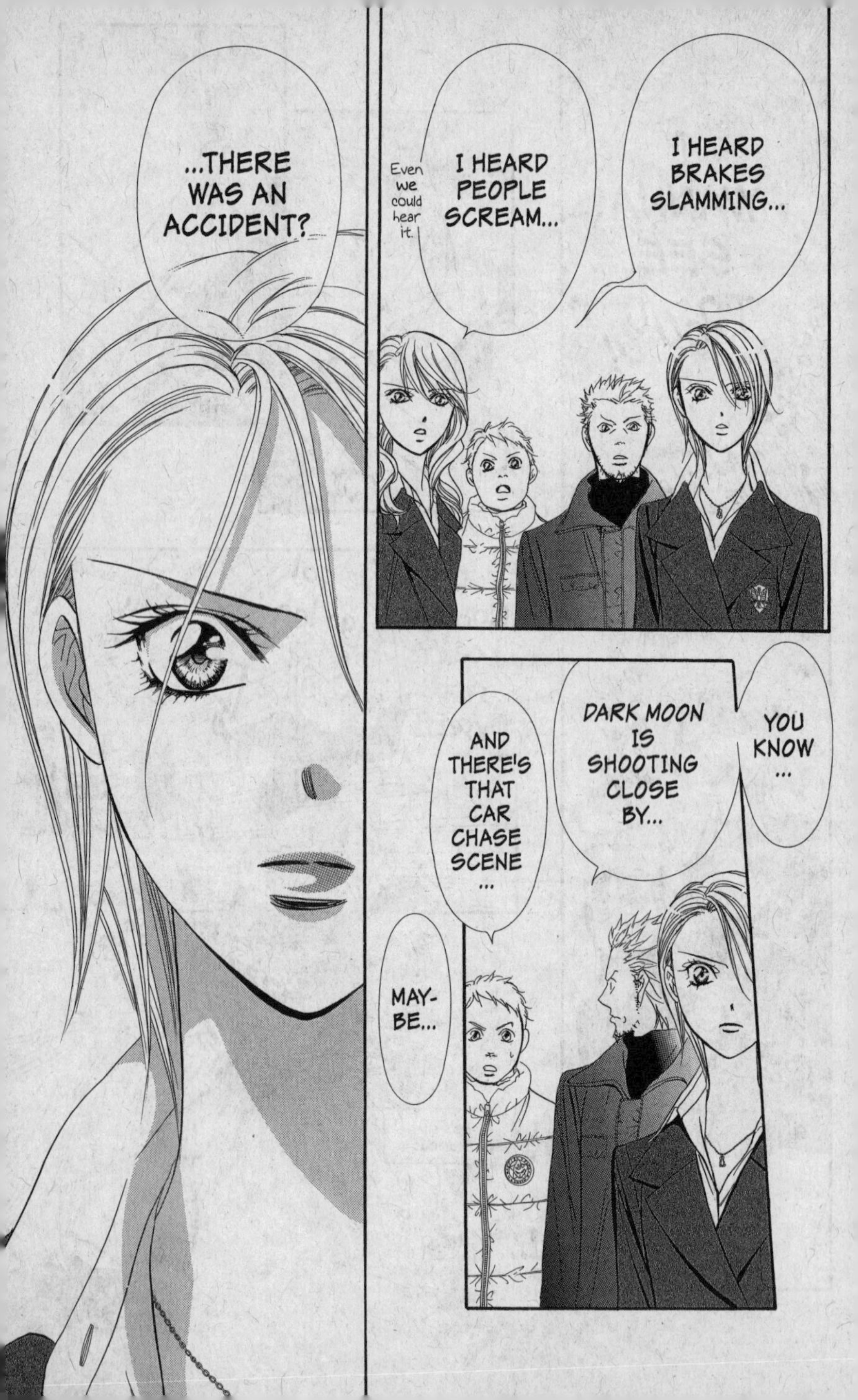
I HEARD BRAKES SLAMMING...
I HEARD PEOPLE SCREAM...
Even we could hear it.
YOU KNOW ...
DARK MOON IS SHOOTING CLOSE BY...
AND THERE'S THAT CAR CHASE SCENE ...
MAY-BE...
...THERE WAS AN ACCIDENT?

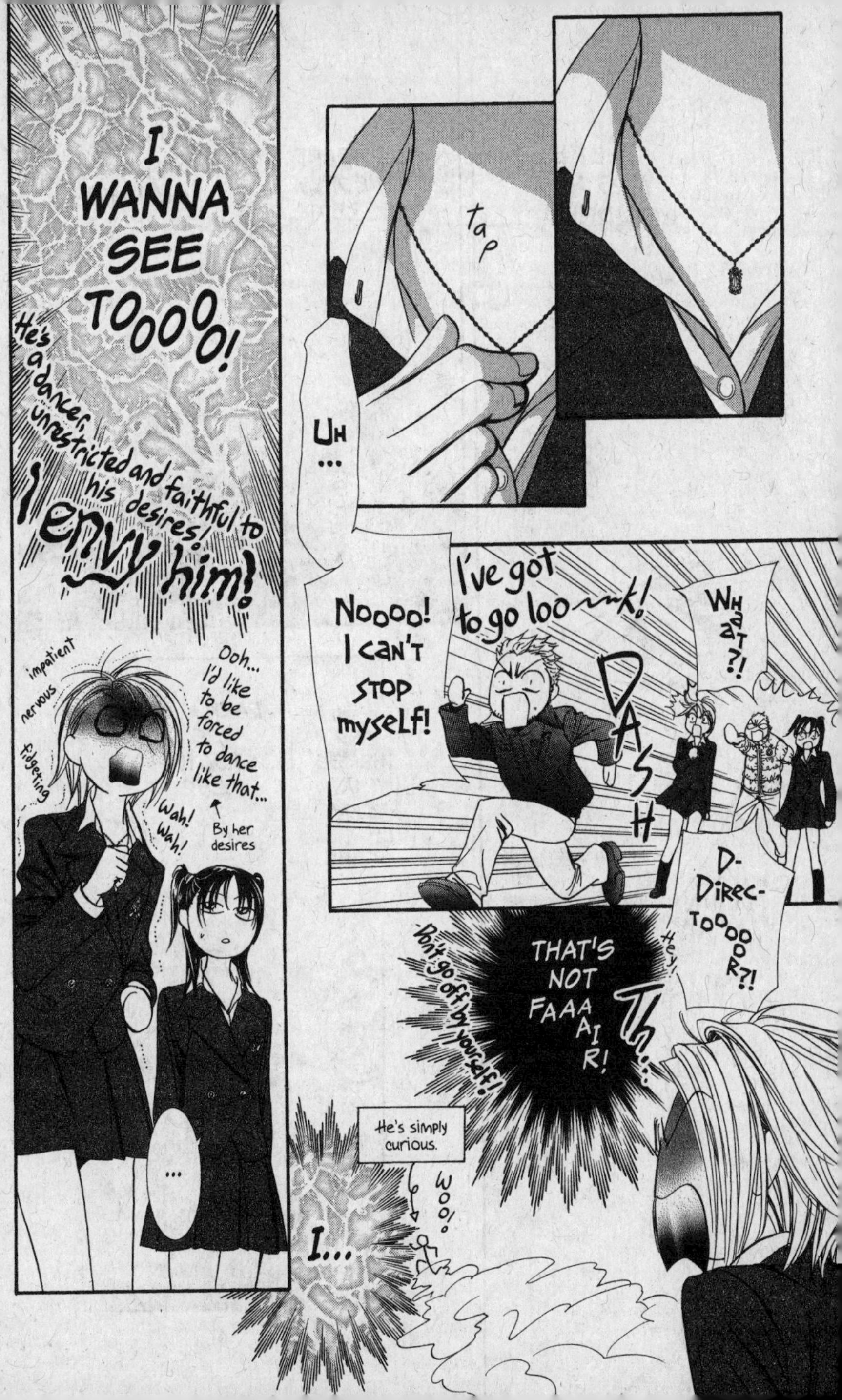
tap
UH...
WHAT?!
I've got to go loo~k!
Noooo! I can't stop myself!
DASH
D-DIREC-TOOOOOR?!
THAT'S NOT FAAAAIR!
Hey! Don't go off by yourself!
Th...
He's simply curious.
WOO!
I...
I WANNA SEE TOOOOO!
He's a dancer, unrestricted and faithful to his desires!
I envy him!
impatient
nervous
fidgeting
Ooh... I'd like to be forced to dance like that...
By her desires
Wah! Wah!
...

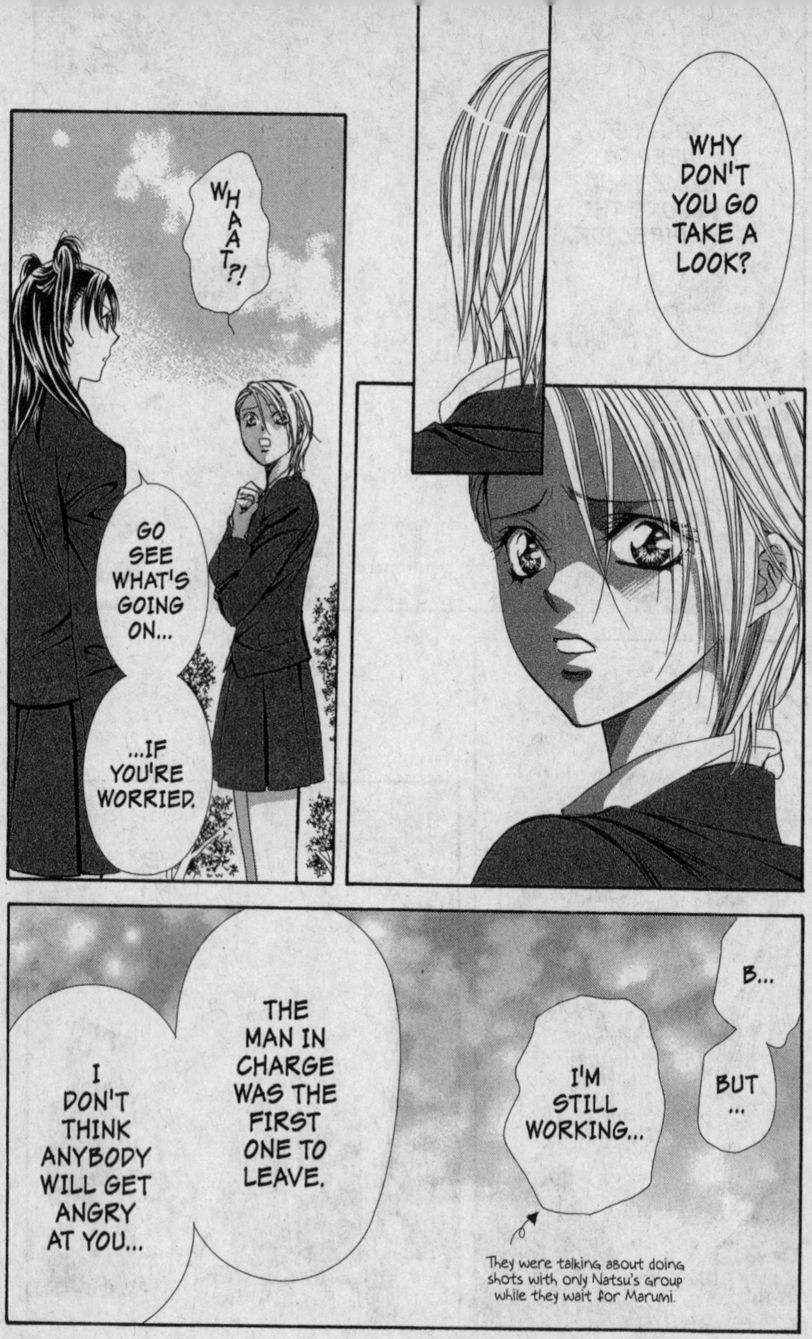
WHY DON'T YOU GO TAKE A LOOK?
WHAAAT?!
GO SEE WHAT'S GOING ON...
...IF YOU'RE WORRIED.
B...
BUT...
I'M STILL WORKING...
They were talking about doing shots with only Natsu's group while they wait for Marumi.
THE MAN IN CHARGE WAS THE FIRST ONE TO LEAVE.
I DON'T THINK ANYBODY WILL GET ANGRY AT YOU...

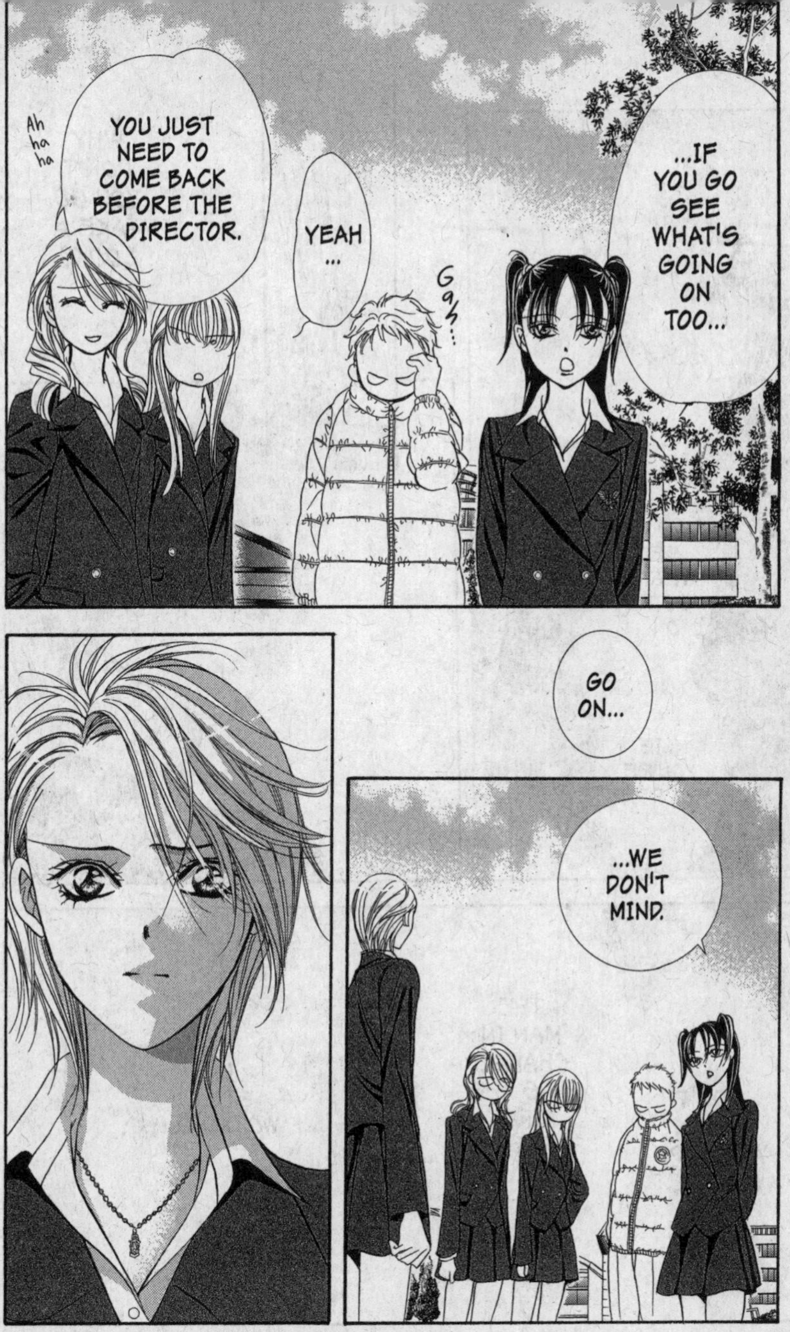
...IF YOU GO SEE WHAT'S GOING ON TOO...
Gah...
YEAH ...
YOU JUST NEED TO COME BACK BEFORE THE DIRECTOR.
Ah ha ha
GO ON...
...WE DON'T MIND.

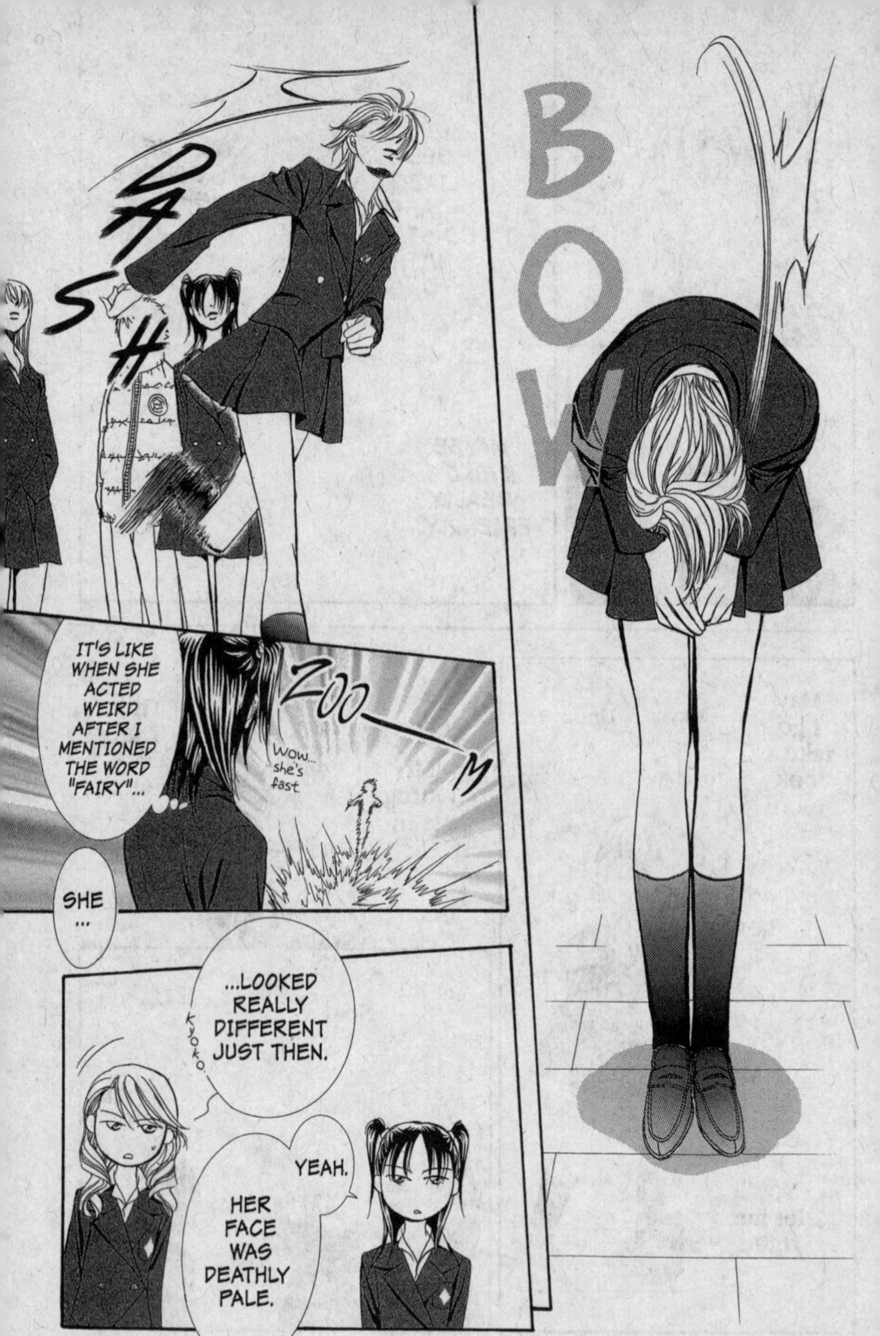
BOW
DASH
ZOOM
Wow... she's fast.
IT'S LIKE WHEN SHE ACTED WEIRD AFTER I MENTIONED THE WORD "FAIRY"...
SHE ...
...LOOKED REALLY DIFFERENT JUST THEN.
Kyoko...
YEAH.
HER FACE WAS DEATHLY PALE.

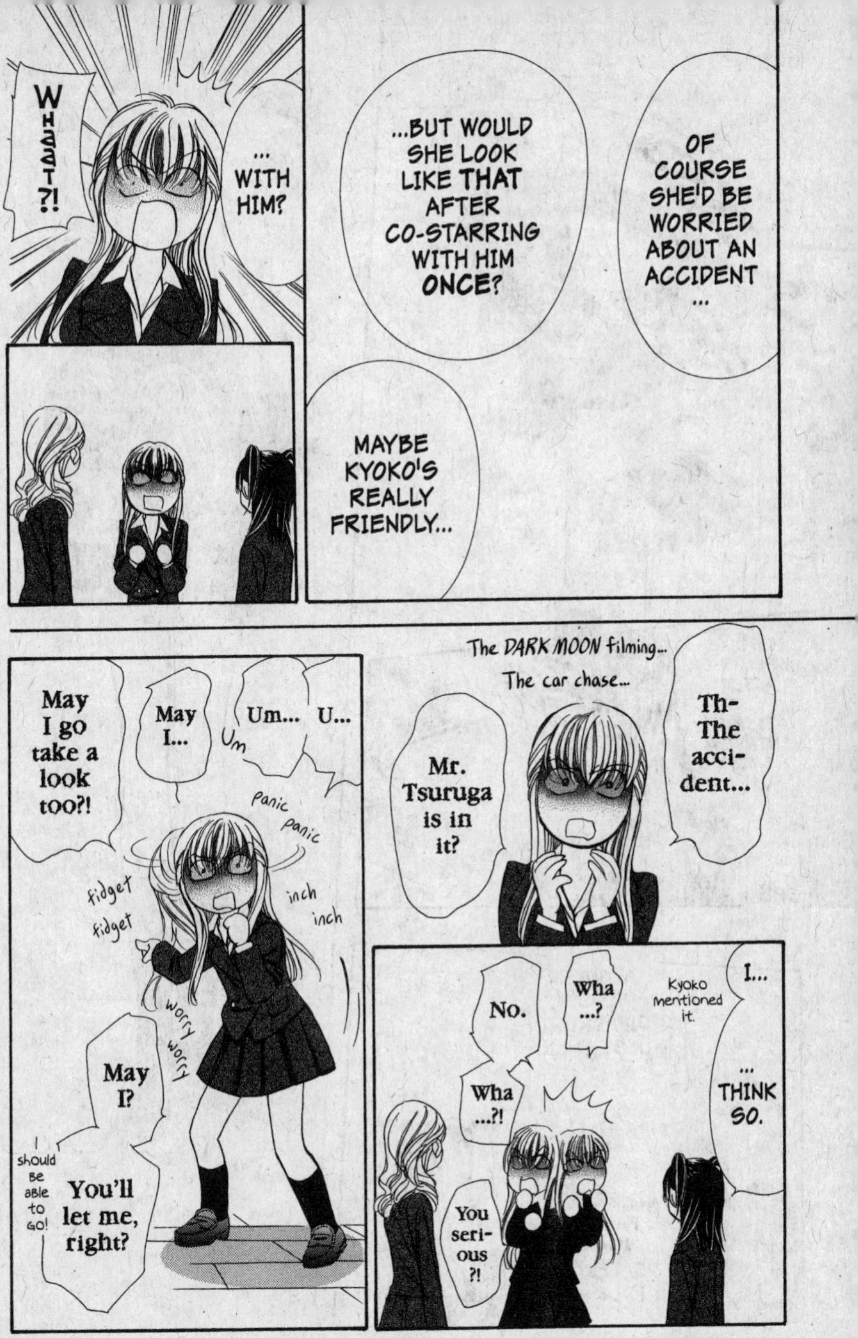

OF COURSE SHE'D BE WORRIED ABOUT AN ACCIDENT...
...BUT WOULD SHE LOOK LIKE THAT AFTER CO-STARRING WITH HIM ONCE?
MAYBE KYOKO'S REALLY FRIENDLY...
... WITH HIM?
WHAAT?!
The DARK MOON filming...
The car chase...
Th- The accident...
Mr. Tsuruga is in it?
I...
... THINK SO.
Kyoko mentioned it.
Wha ...?
No.
Wha ...?!
You serious?!
U...
Um...
Um
May I...
May I go take a look too?!
panic panic
inch inch
fidget fidget
worry worry
May I?
You'll let me, right?
I should be able to go!

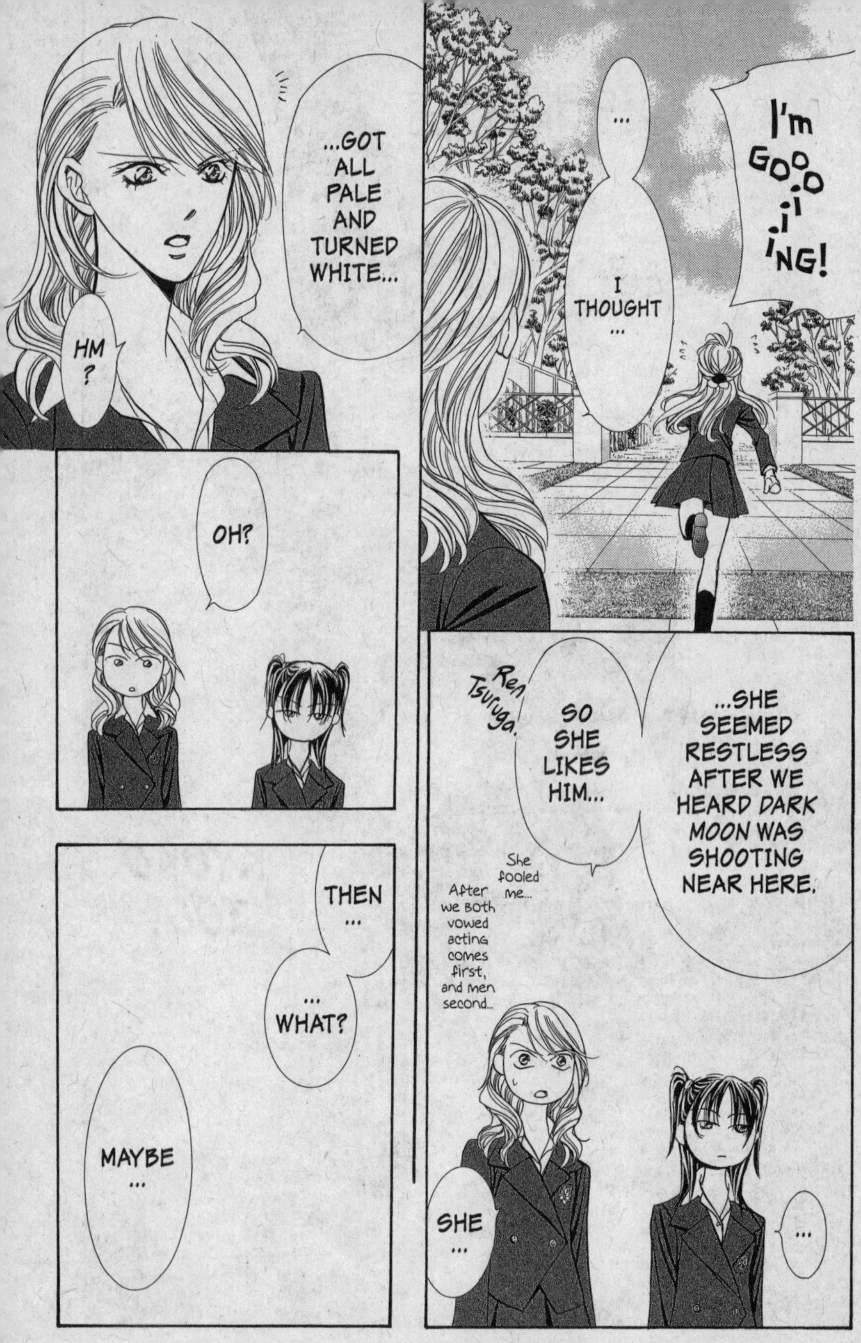

I'm GOOOOIIING!
...
I THOUGHT ...
...SHE SEEMED RESTLESS AFTER WE HEARD DARK MOON WAS SHOOTING NEAR HERE.
SO SHE LIKES HIM...
Ren Tsuruga.
She fooled me...
After we both vowed acting comes first, and men second...
...
SHE ...
...GOT ALL PALE AND TURNED WHITE...
HM ?
OH?
THEN ...
... WHAT?
MAYBE ...

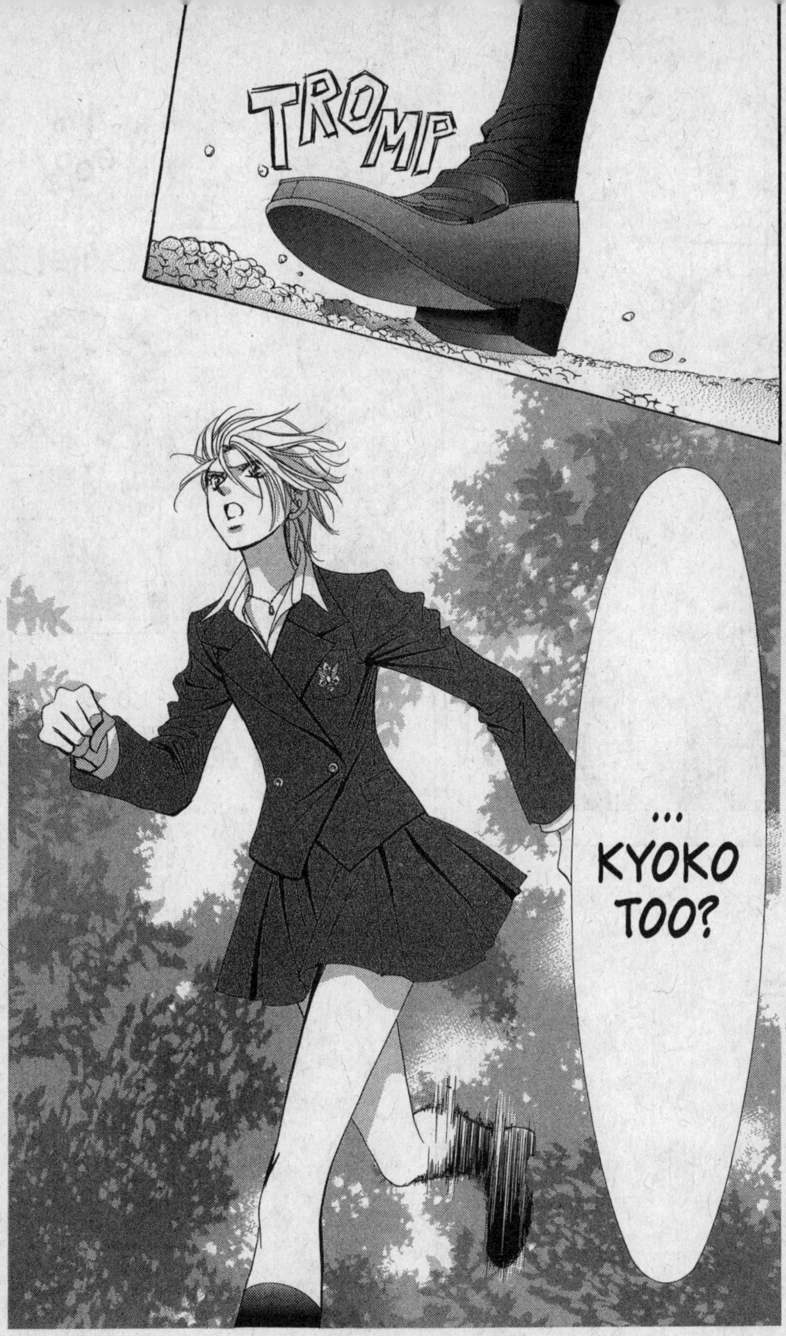
TROMP
...
KYOKO TOO?

End of Act 164

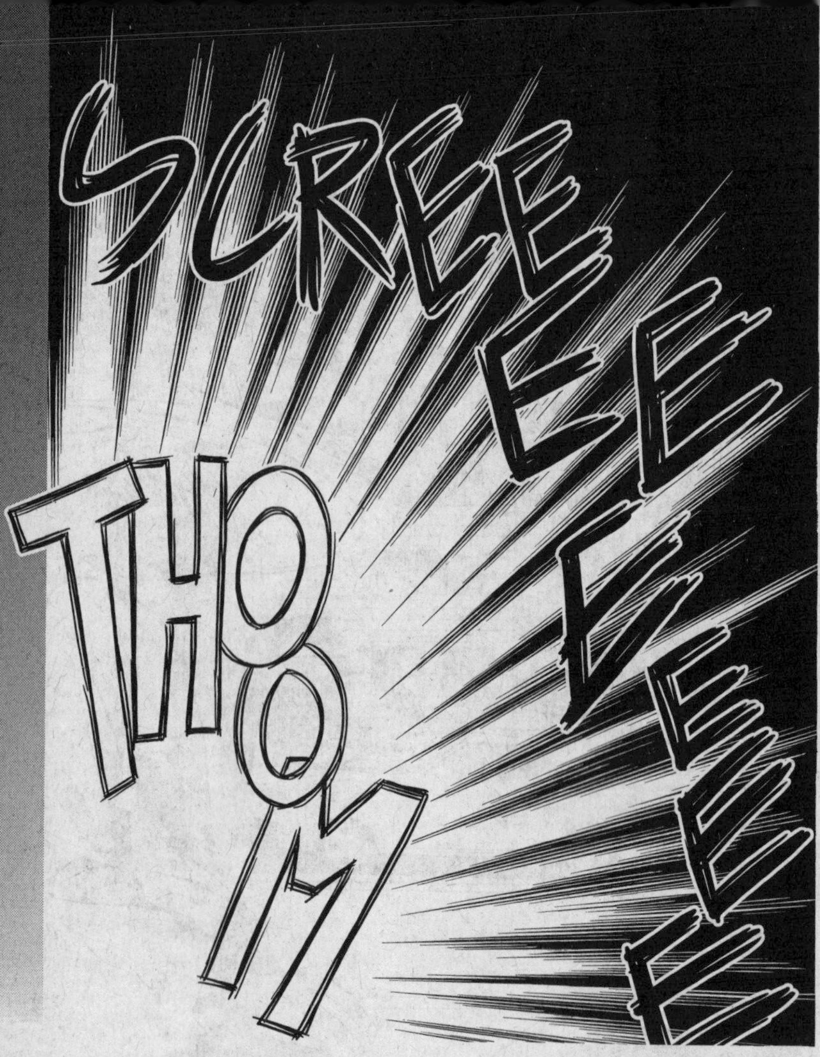
SCREEEEEEEEE
THOOM

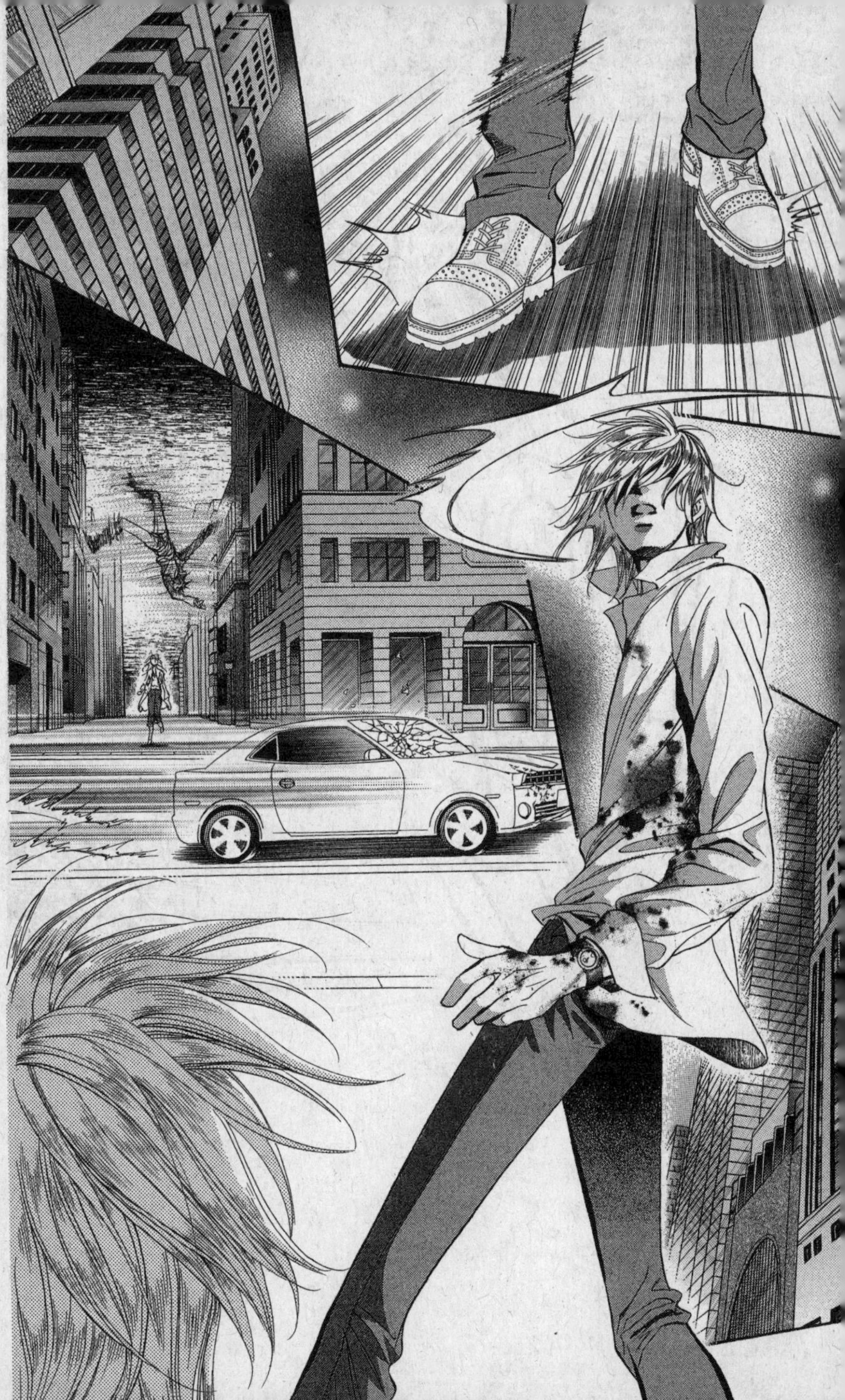

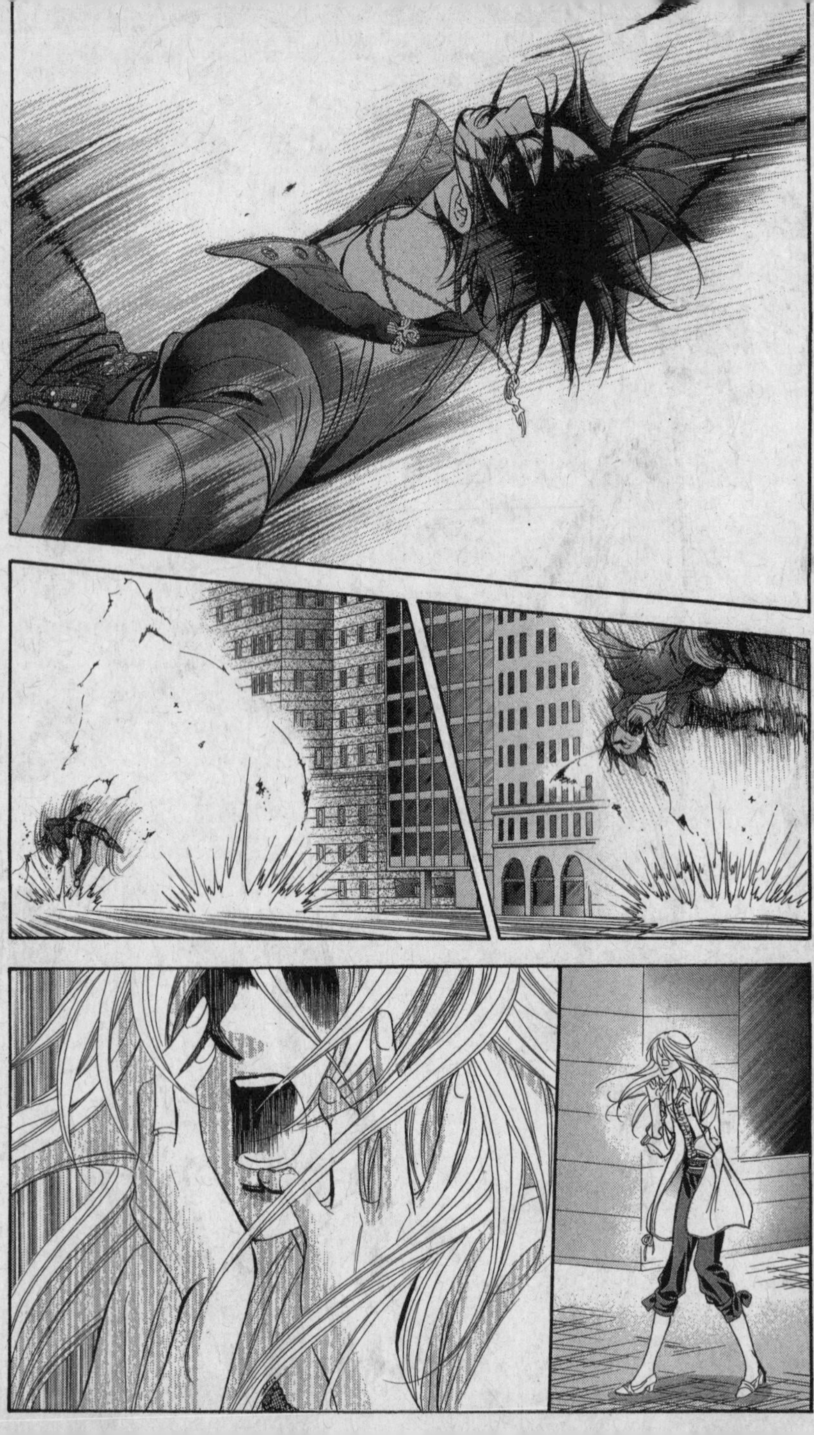

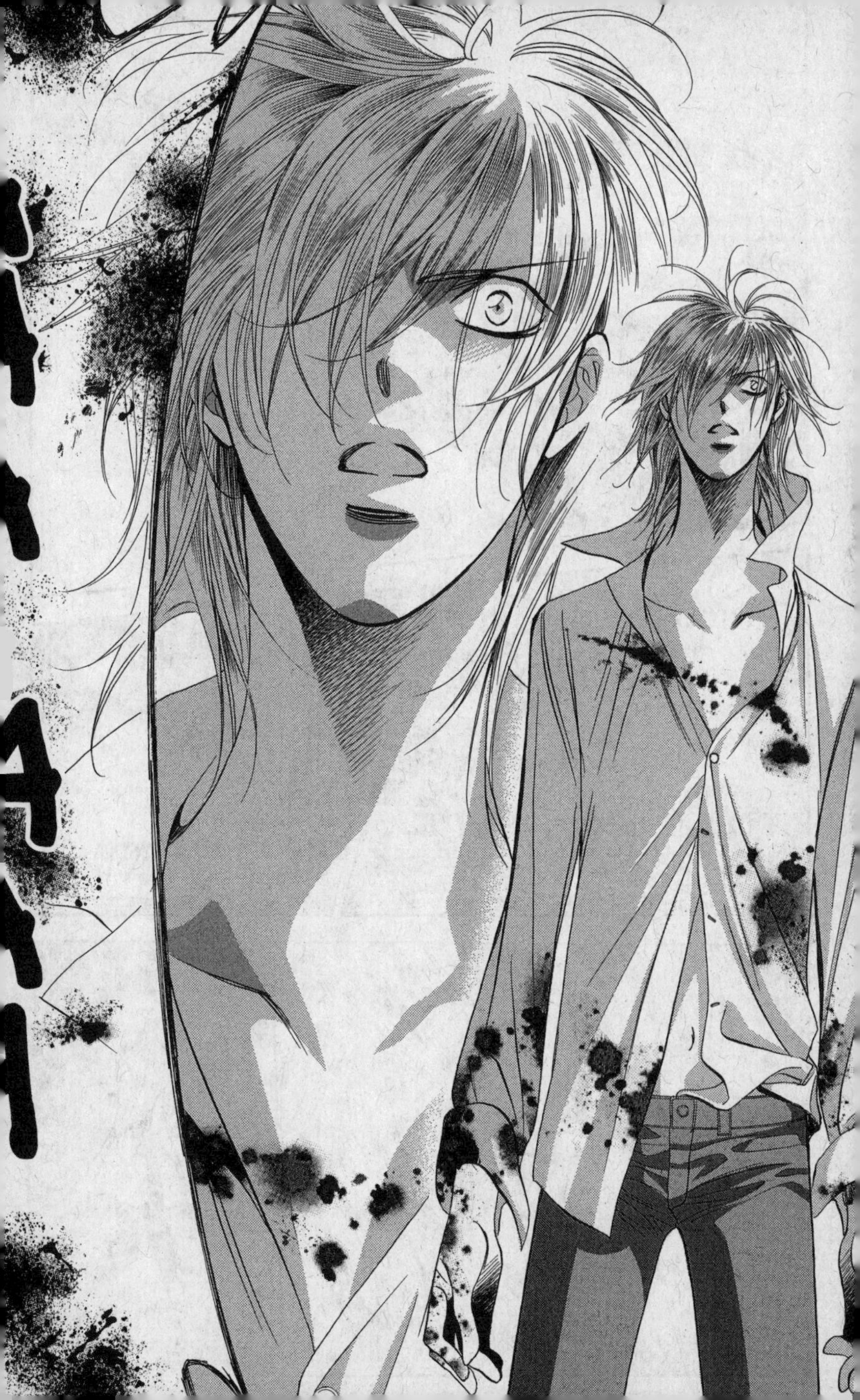

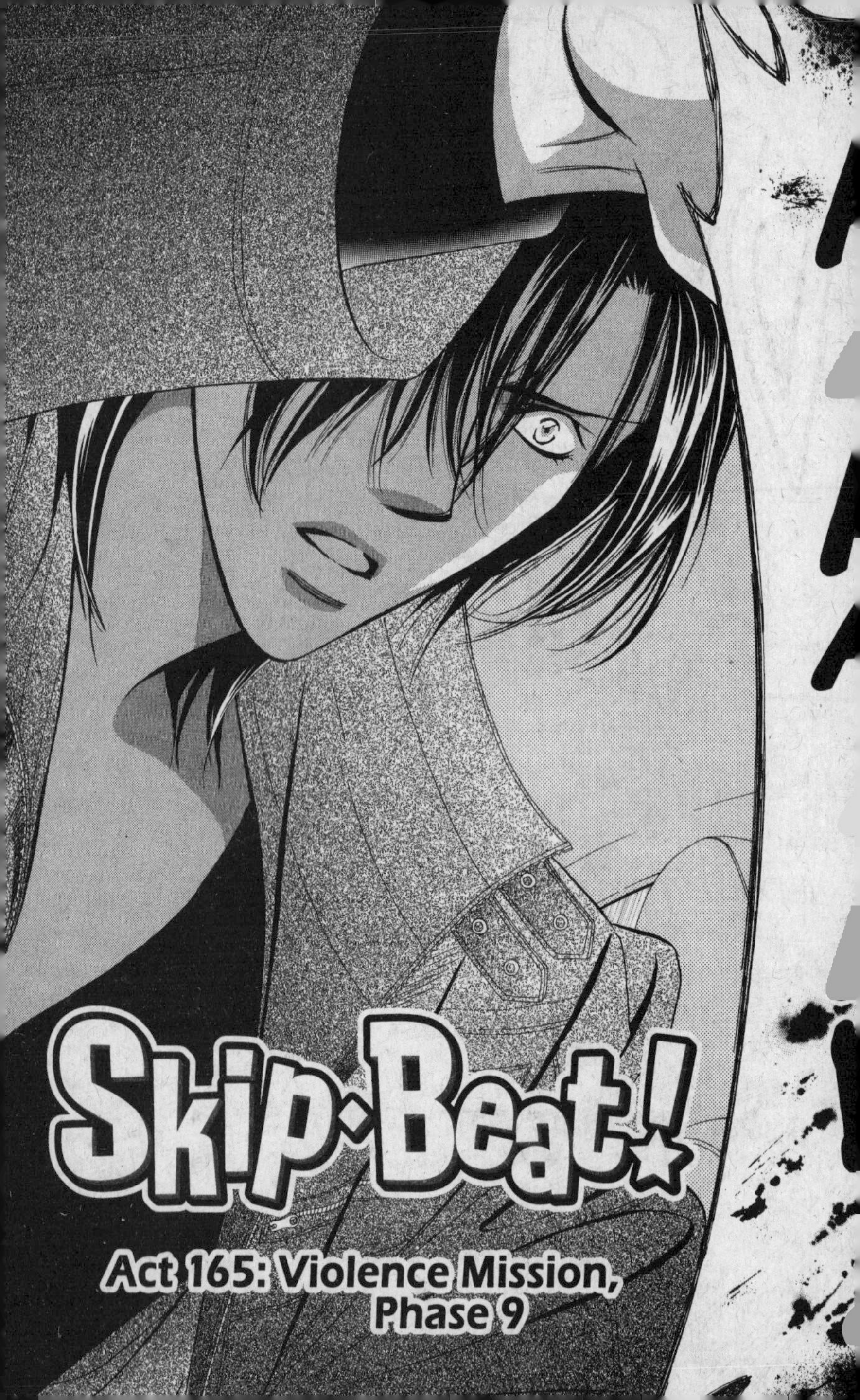
Skip·Beat!
Act 165: Violence Mission, Phase 9

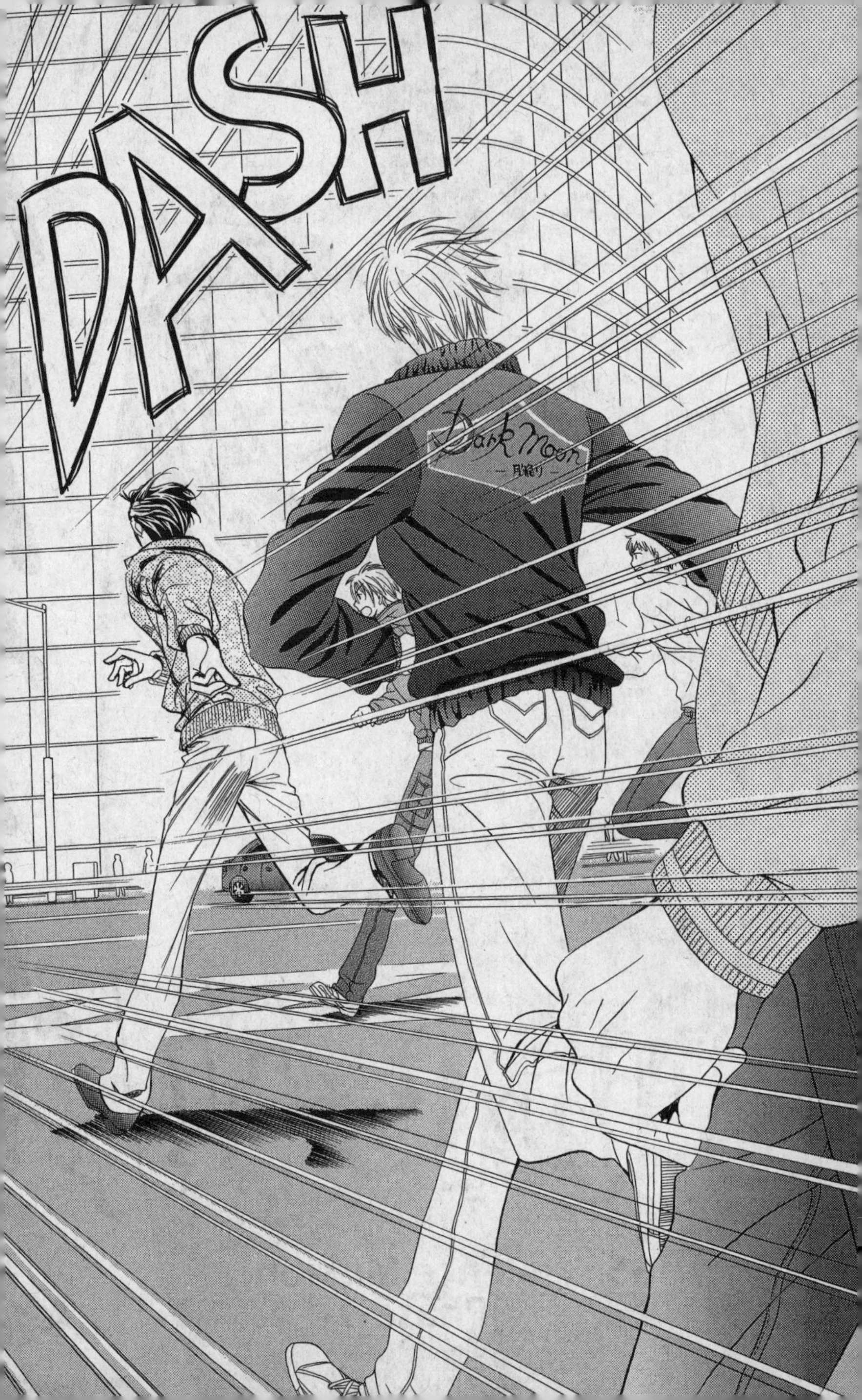
DASH
Dark Moon

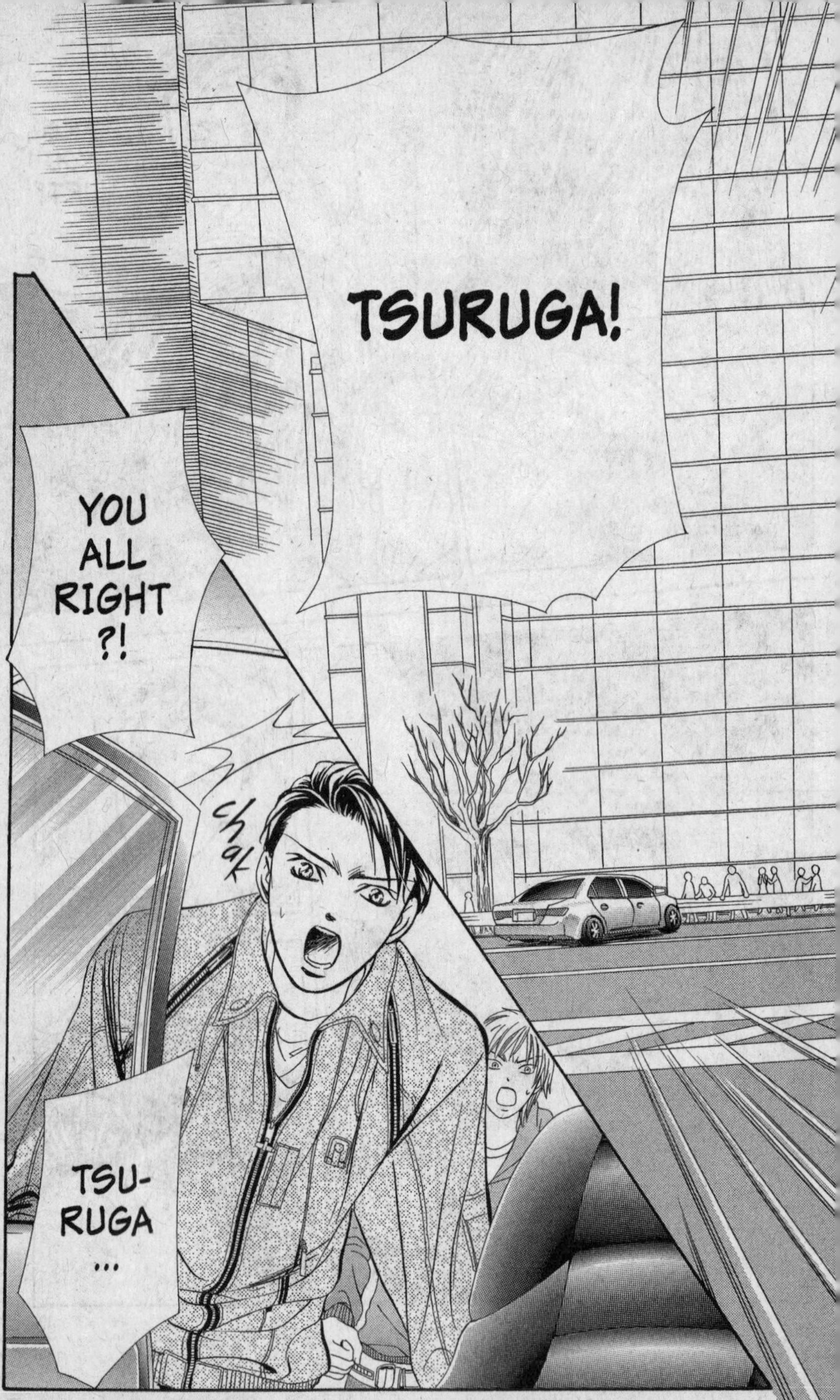
TSURUGA!
YOU ALL RIGHT ?!
chak
TSU-RUGA ...

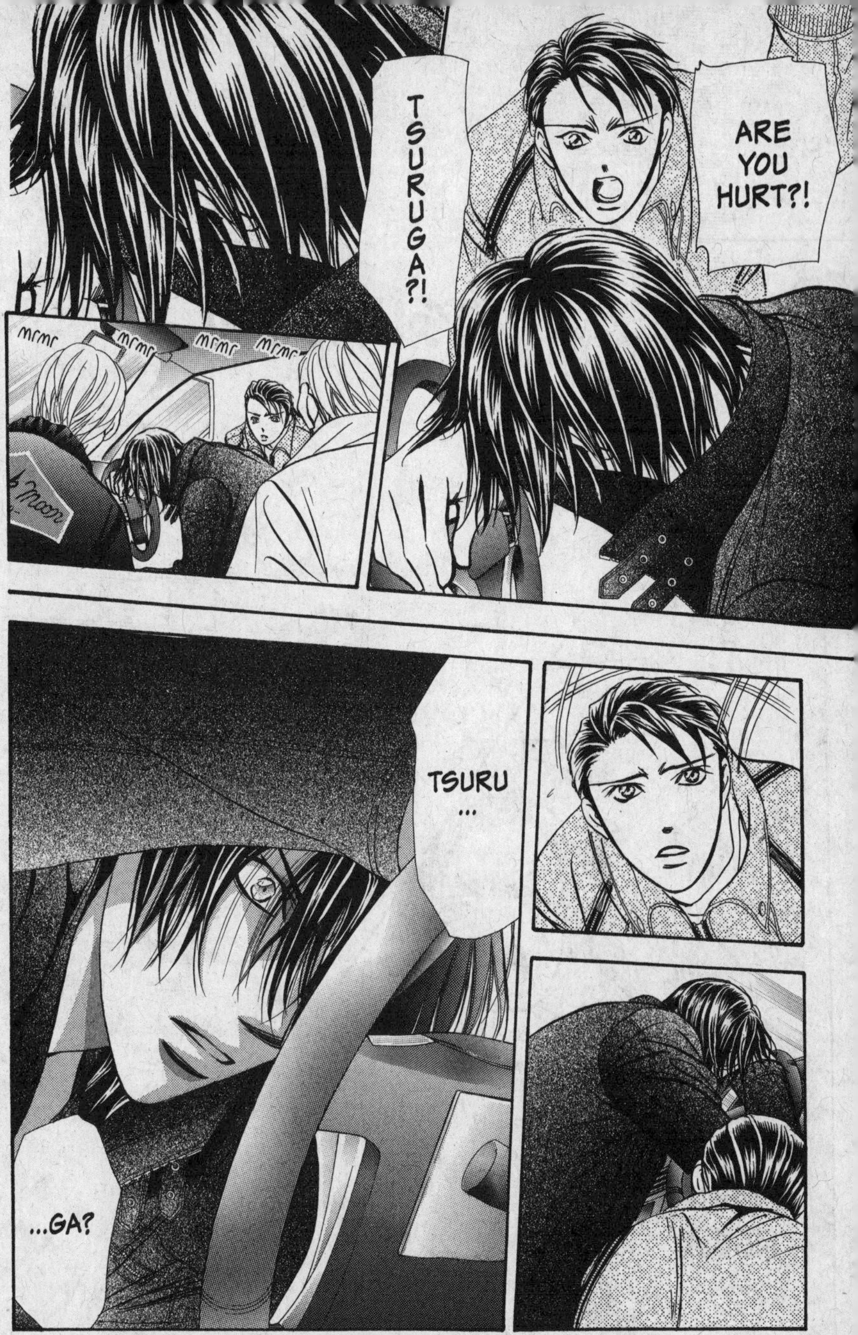
ARE YOU HURT?!
TSURUGA?!
mrmr
mrmr
mrmr
mrmr
TSURU ...
...GA?

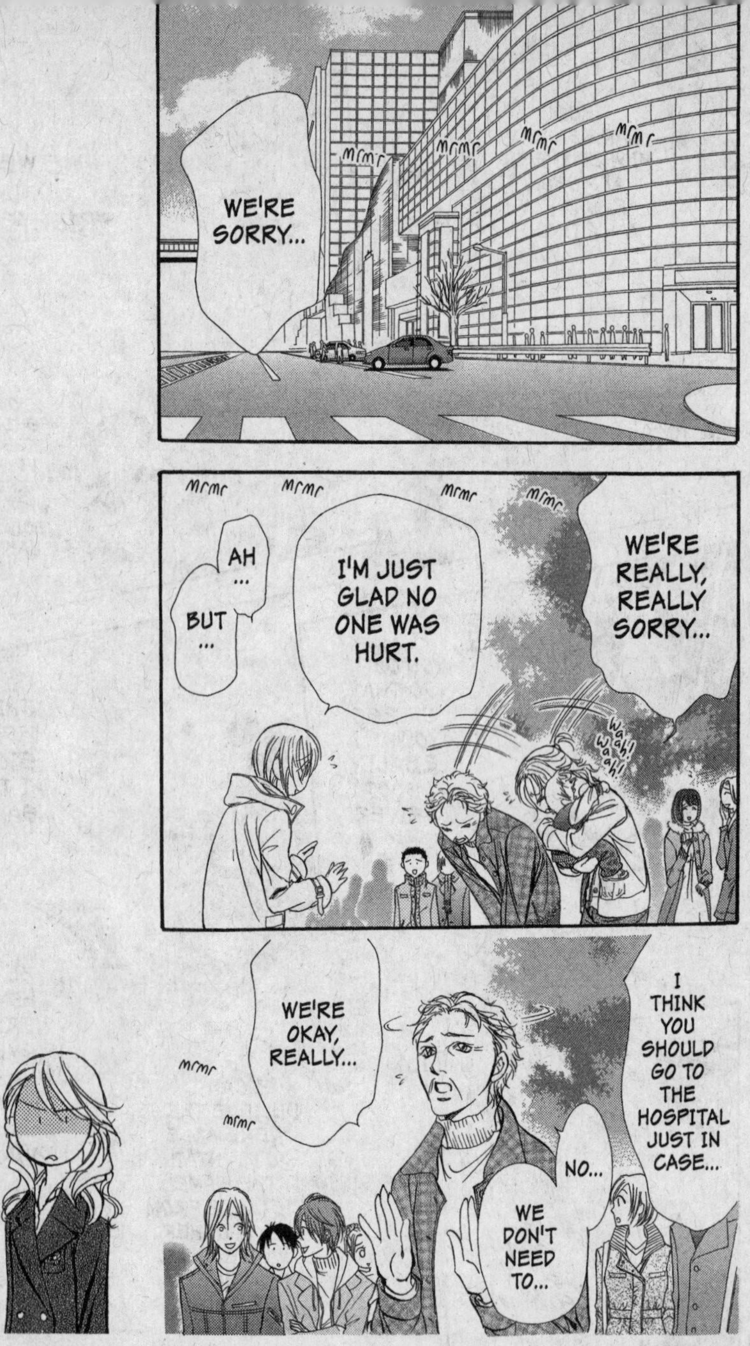
mrmr
mrmr
mrmr
mrmr
WE'RE SORRY...
mrmr
mrmr
mrmr
mrmr
WE'RE REALLY, REALLY SORRY...
Waah! Waah!
I'M JUST GLAD NO ONE WAS HURT.
AH... BUT...
I THINK YOU SHOULD GO TO THE HOSPITAL JUST IN CASE...
NO...
WE DON'T NEED TO...
WE'RE OKAY, REALLY...
mrmr
mrmr

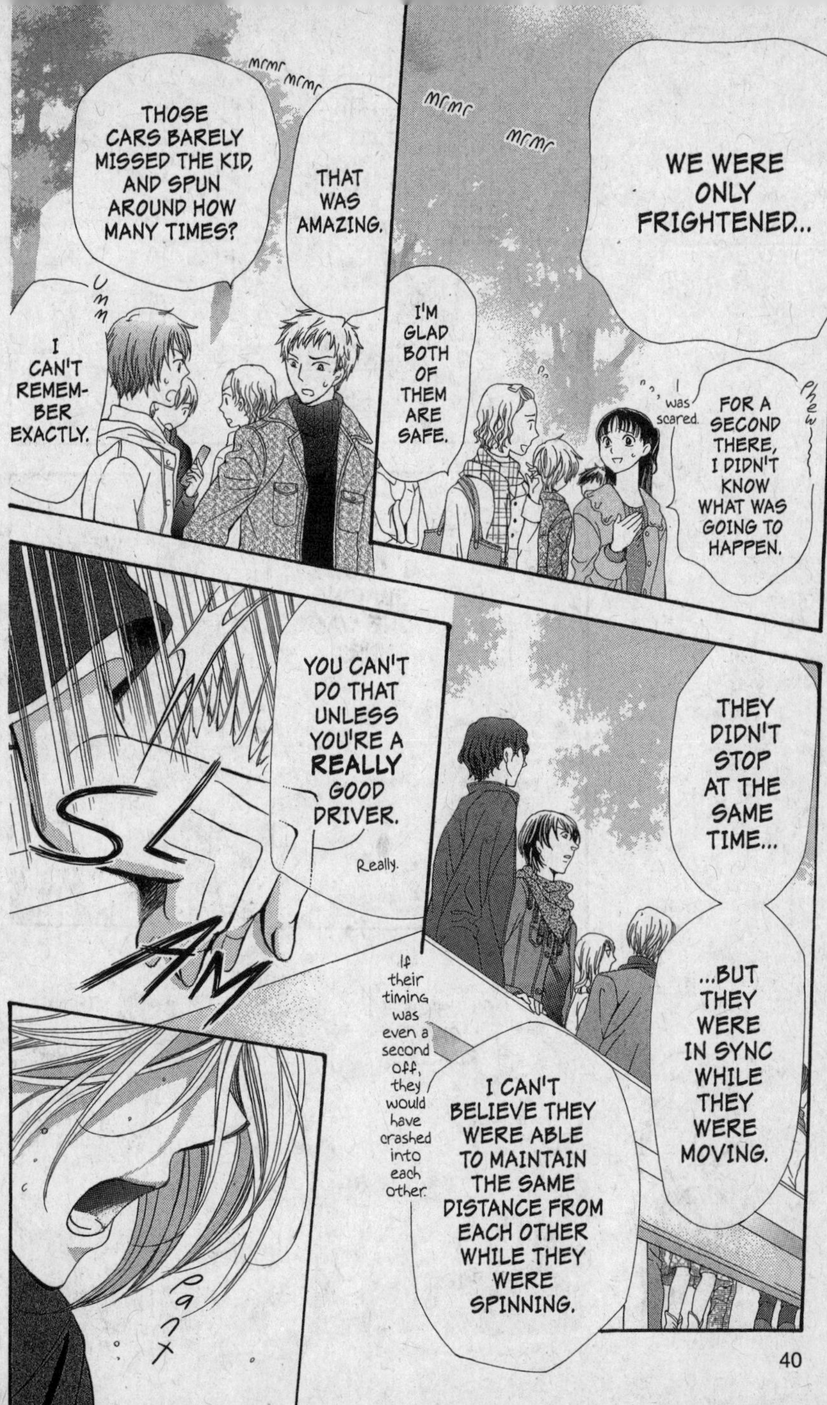
WE WERE ONLY FRIGHTENED...
mrmr
mrmr
Phew
FOR A SECOND THERE, I DIDN'T KNOW WHAT WAS GOING TO HAPPEN.
I was scared.
I'M GLAD BOTH OF THEM ARE SAFE.
mrmr mrmr
THAT WAS AMAZING.
THOSE CARS BARELY MISSED THE KID, AND SPUN AROUND HOW MANY TIMES?
Umm
I CAN'T REMEM-BER EXACTLY.
THEY DIDN'T STOP AT THE SAME TIME...
...BUT THEY WERE IN SYNC WHILE THEY WERE MOVING.
I CAN'T BELIEVE THEY WERE ABLE TO MAINTAIN THE SAME DISTANCE FROM EACH OTHER WHILE THEY WERE SPINNING.
If their timing was even a second off, they would have crashed into each other.
YOU CAN'T DO THAT UNLESS YOU'RE A REALLY GOOD DRIVER.
Really.
SLAM
pant

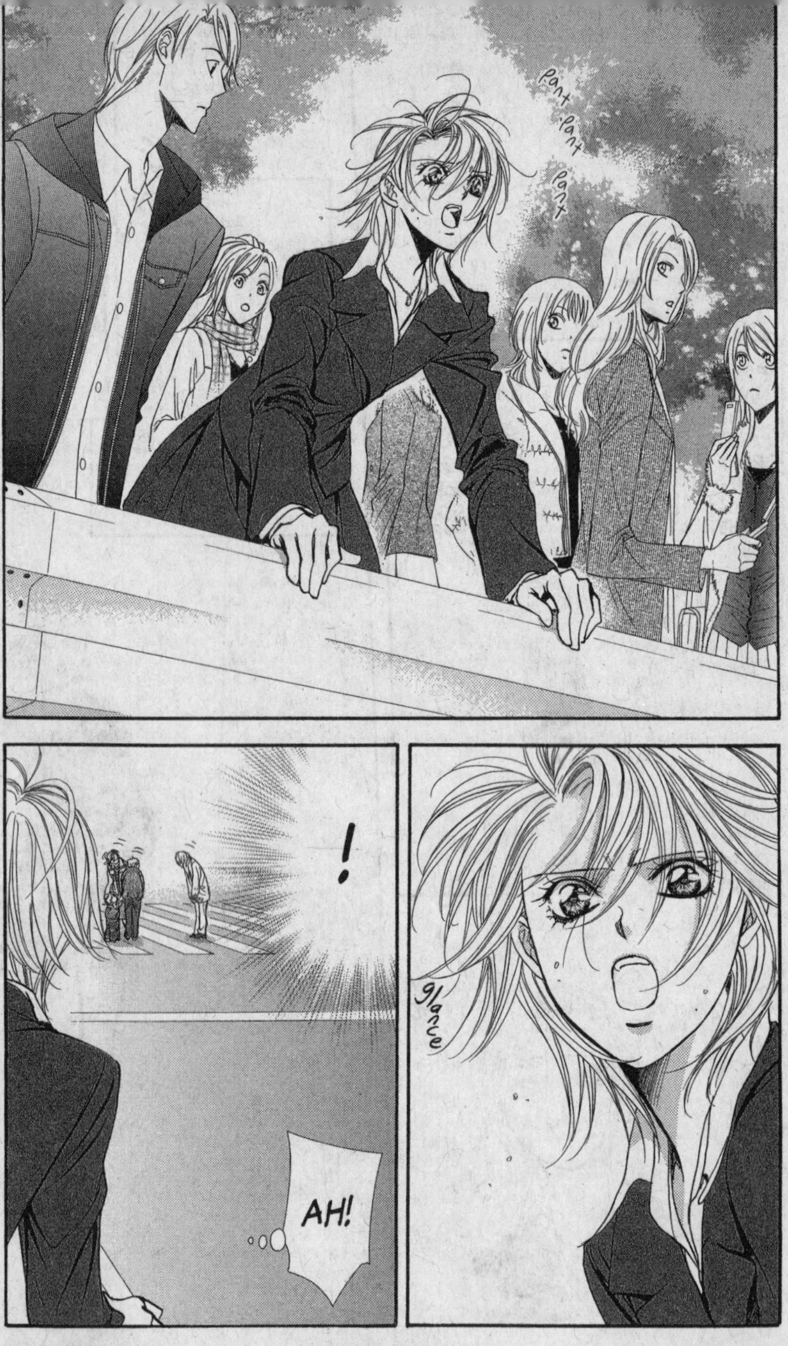
pant
pant
pant
glance
!
AH!

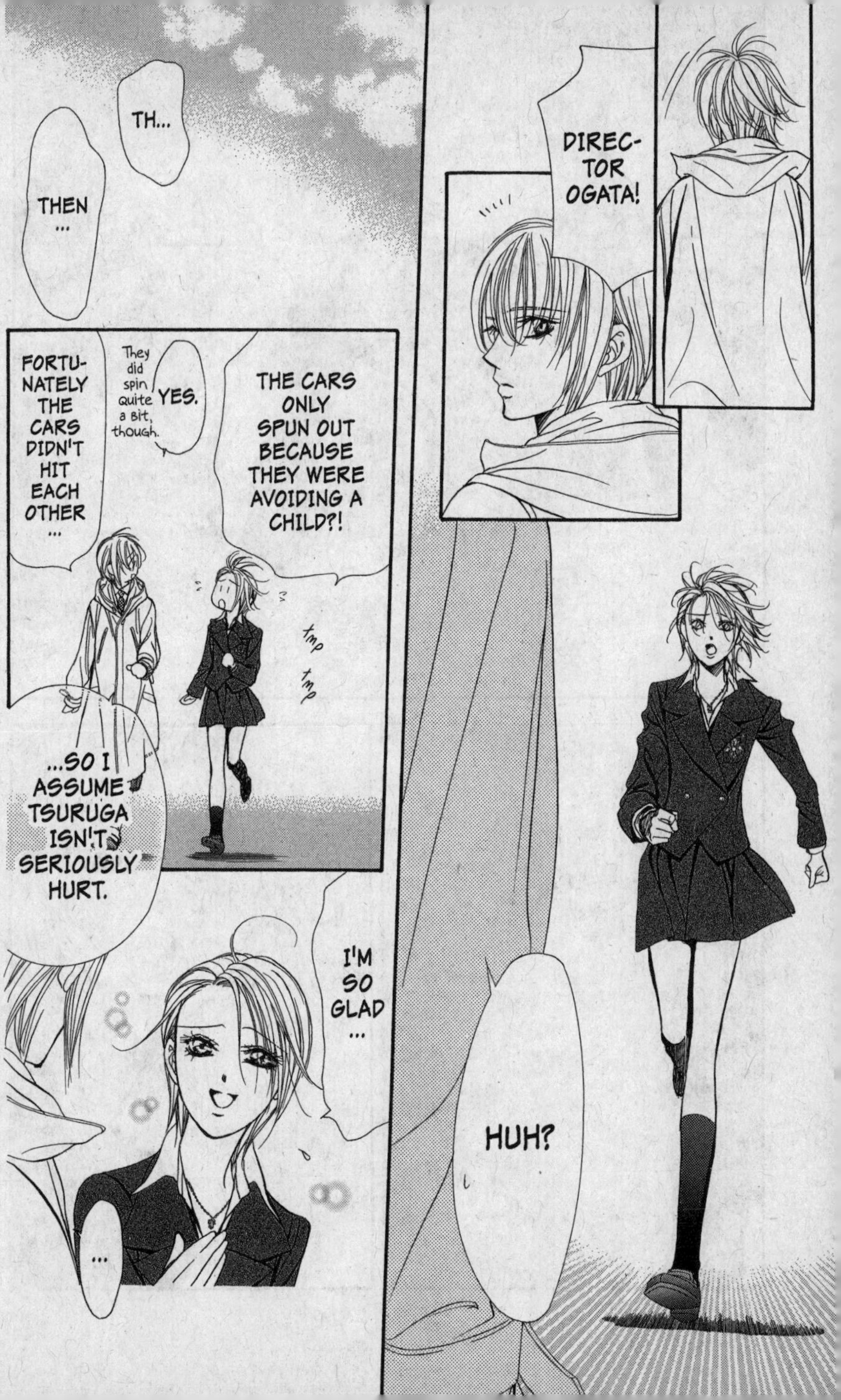
DIRECTOR OGATA!
HUH?
TH...
THEN...
THE CARS ONLY SPUN OUT BECAUSE THEY WERE AVOIDING A CHILD?!
tmp tmp
YES.
They did spin quite a bit, though.
FORTUNATELY THE CARS DIDN'T HIT EACH OTHER...
...SO I ASSUME TSURUGA ISN'T SERIOUSLY HURT.
I'M SO GLAD...
...

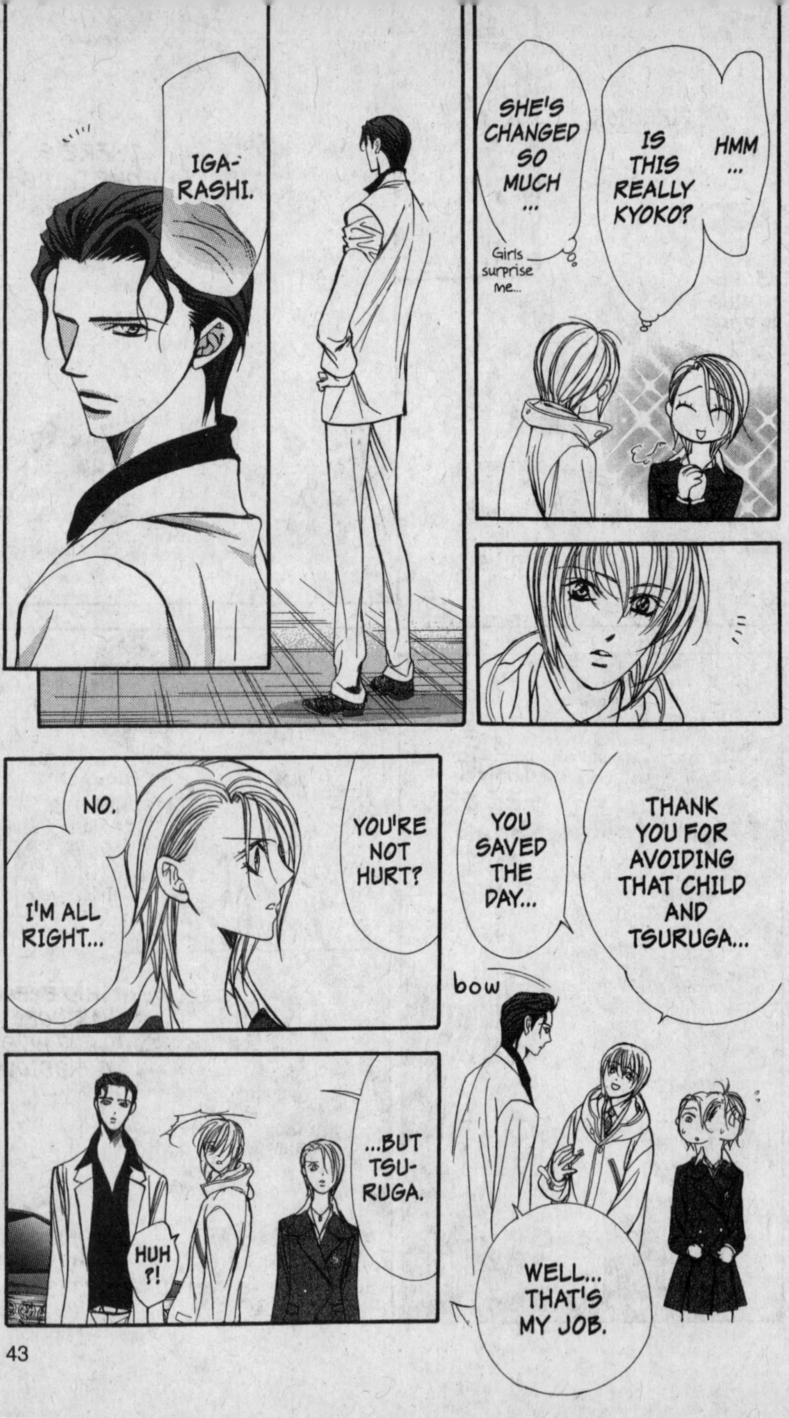
HMM...
IS THIS REALLY KYOKO?
SHE'S CHANGED SO MUCH...
Girls surprise me...
IGA-RASHI.
THANK YOU FOR AVOIDING THAT CHILD AND TSURUGA...
YOU SAVED THE DAY...
bow
WELL... THAT'S MY JOB.
YOU'RE NOT HURT?
NO.
I'M ALL RIGHT...
...BUT TSU-RUGA.
HUH?!

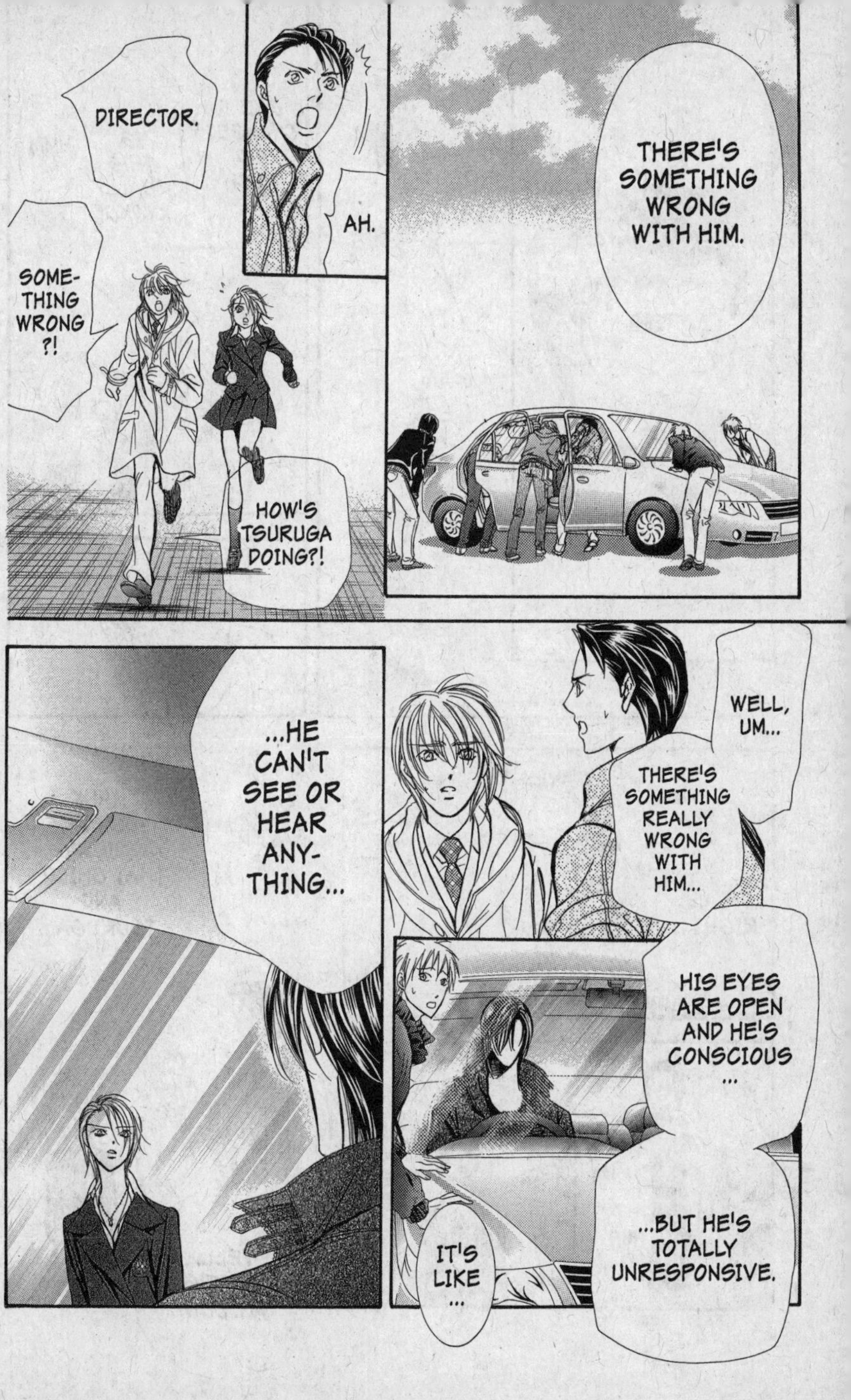
THERE'S SOMETHING WRONG WITH HIM.
AH.
DIRECTOR.
SOME-THING WRONG?!
HOW'S TSURUGA DOING?!
WELL, UM...
THERE'S SOMETHING REALLY WRONG WITH HIM...
HIS EYES ARE OPEN AND HE'S CONSCIOUS...
...BUT HE'S TOTALLY UNRESPONSIVE.
IT'S LIKE...
...HE CAN'T SEE OR HEAR ANY-THING...

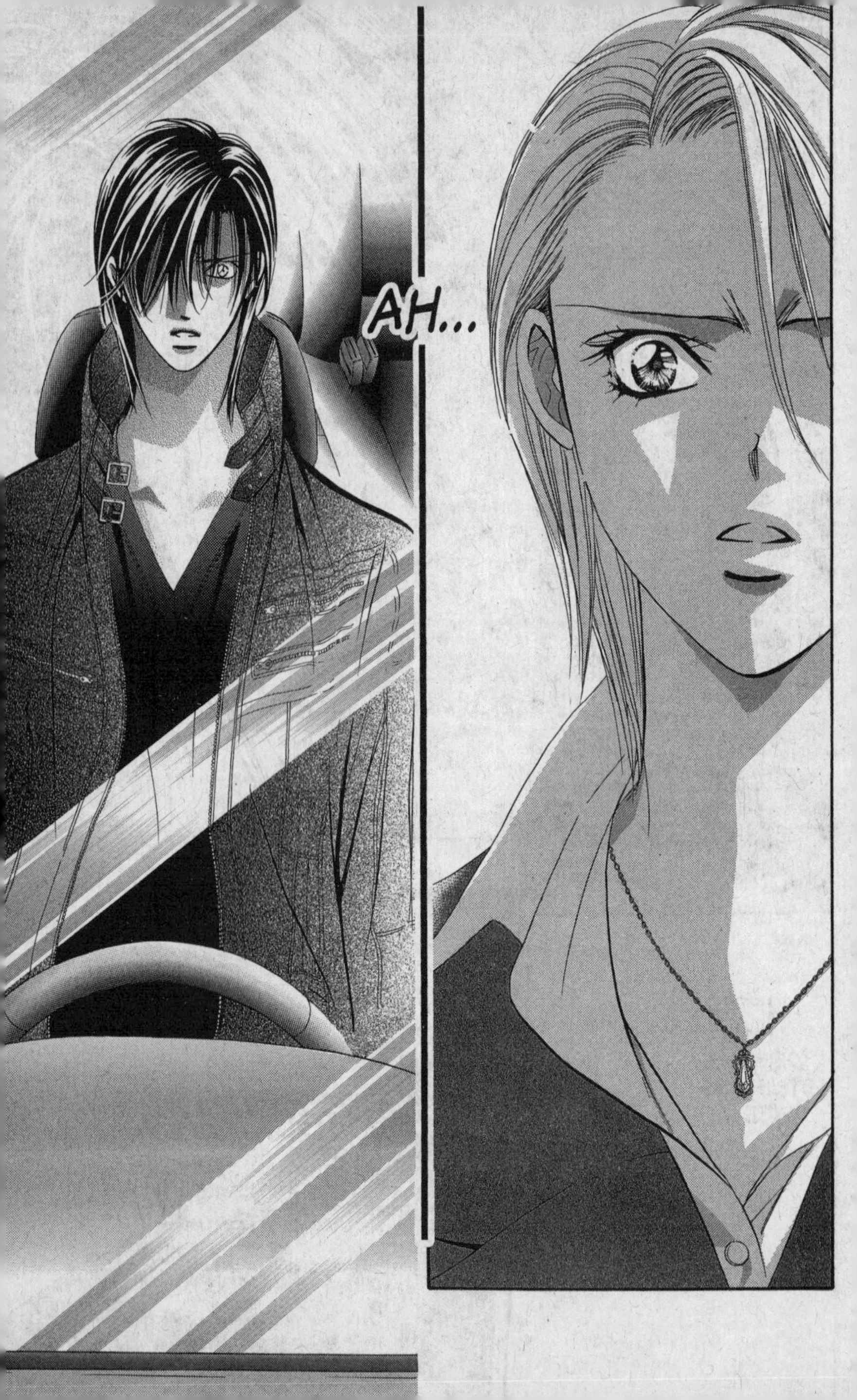
AH...

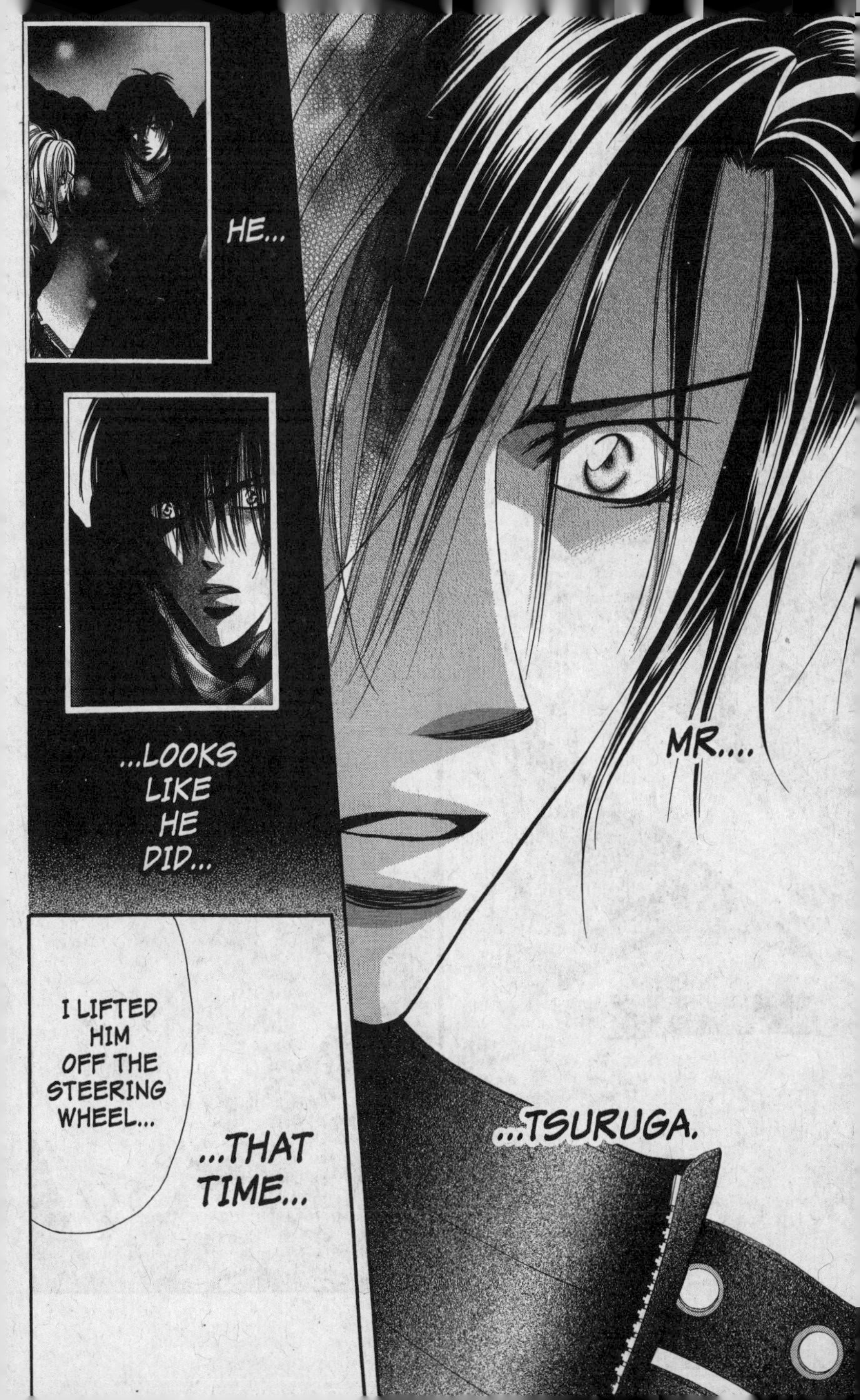
MR....
...TSURUGA.
HE...
...LOOKS LIKE HE DID...
I LIFTED HIM OFF THE STEERING WHEEL...
...THAT TIME...

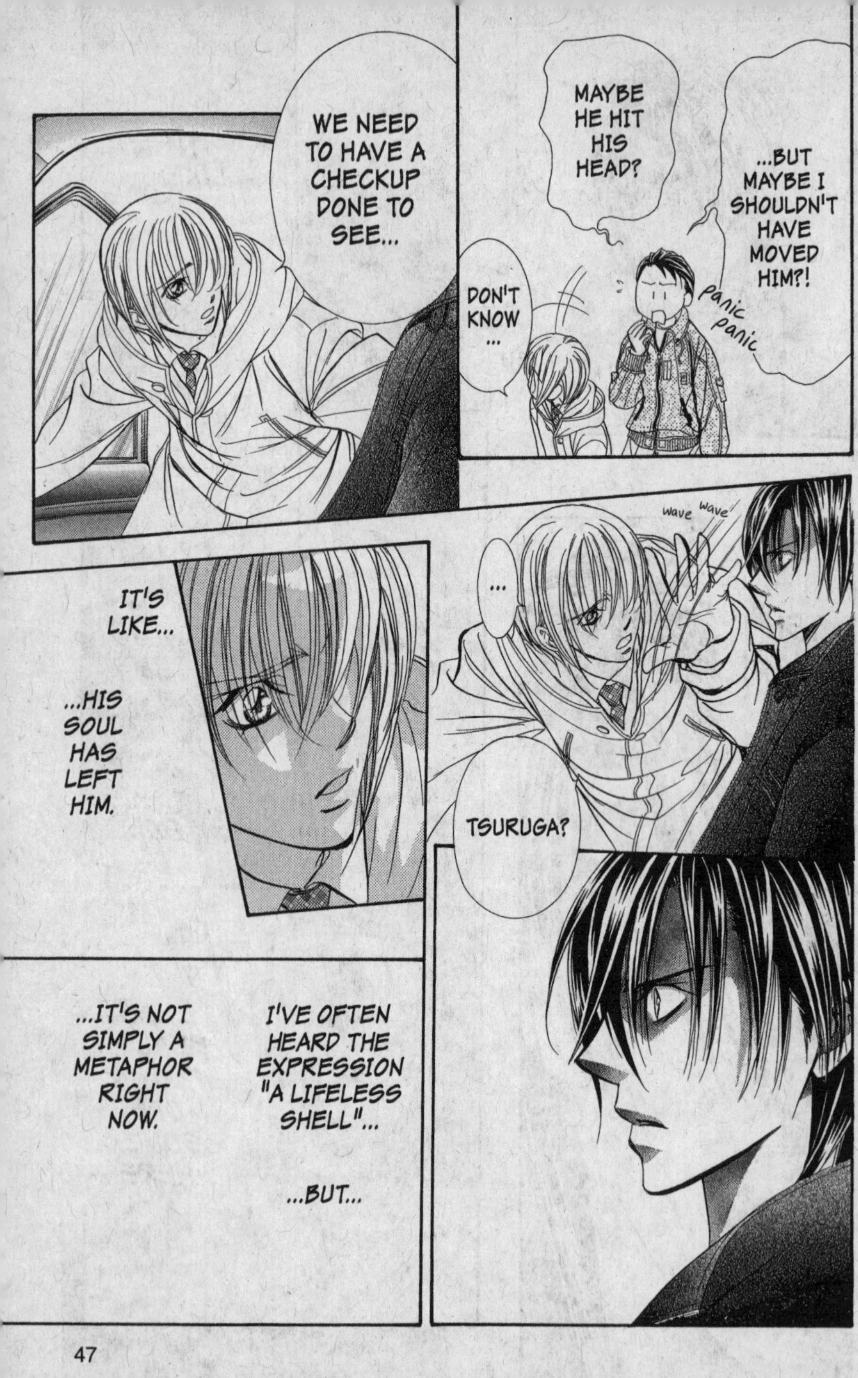
MAYBE HE HIT HIS HEAD?
...BUT MAYBE I SHOULDN'T HAVE MOVED HIM?!
panic panic
DON'T KNOW ...
WE NEED TO HAVE A CHECKUP DONE TO SEE...
...
wave wave
TSURUGA?
IT'S LIKE...
...HIS SOUL HAS LEFT HIM.
I'VE OFTEN HEARD THE EXPRESSION "A LIFELESS SHELL"...
...BUT...
...IT'S NOT SIMPLY A METAPHOR RIGHT NOW.

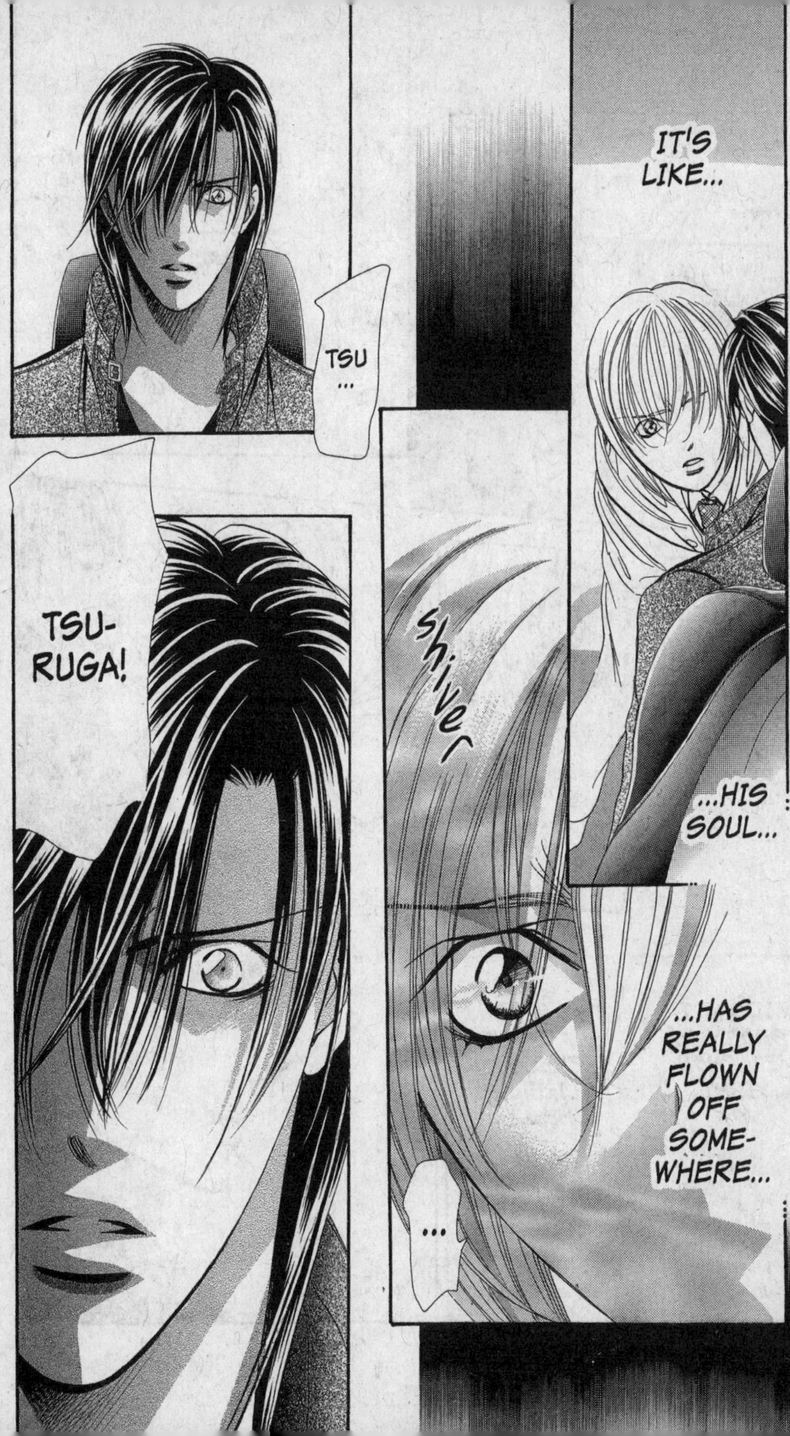
IT'S LIKE...
...HIS SOUL...
TSU ...
...HAS REALLY FLOWN OFF SOME-WHERE...
shiver
...
TSU-RUGA!

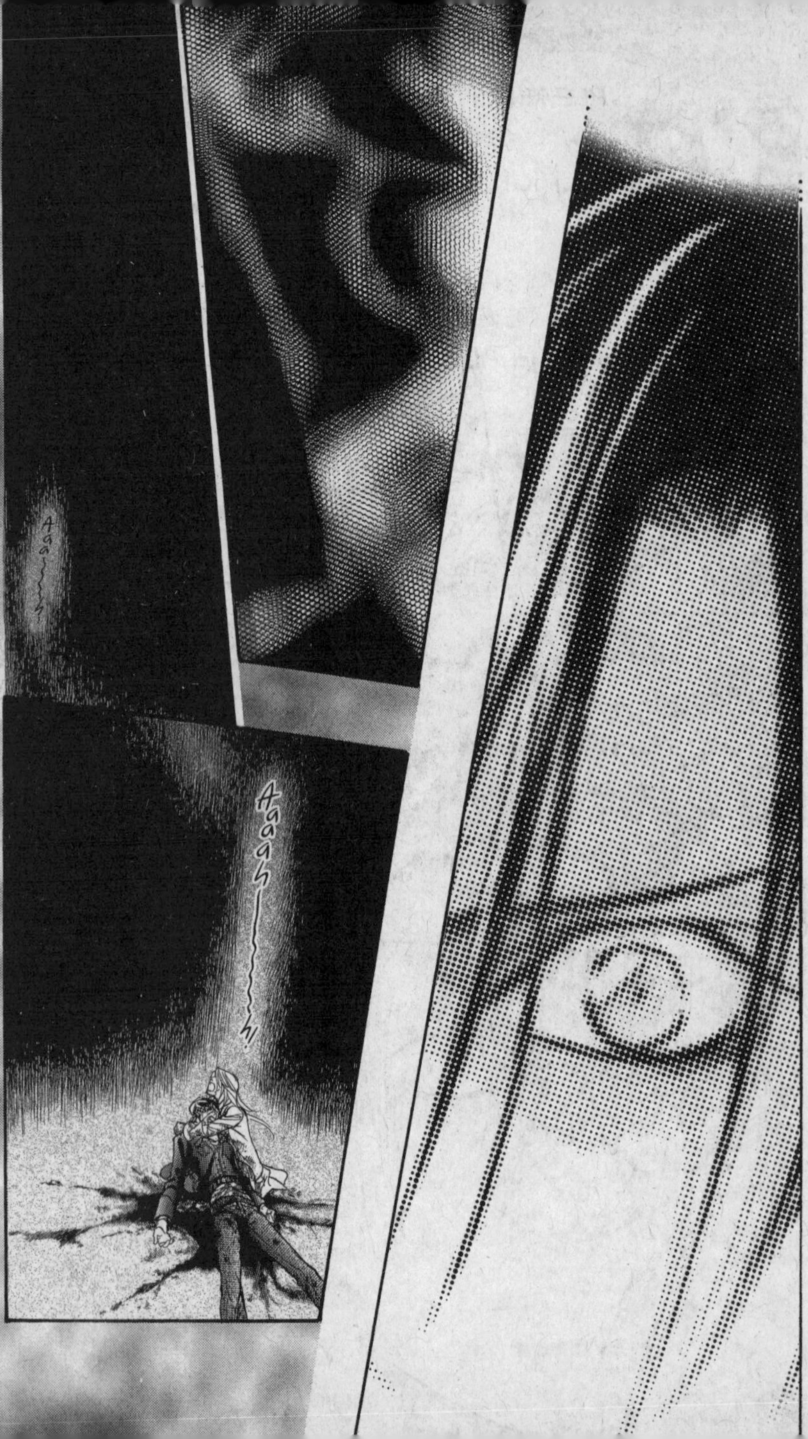
Aaa~~~h
Aaaah~~~~h!

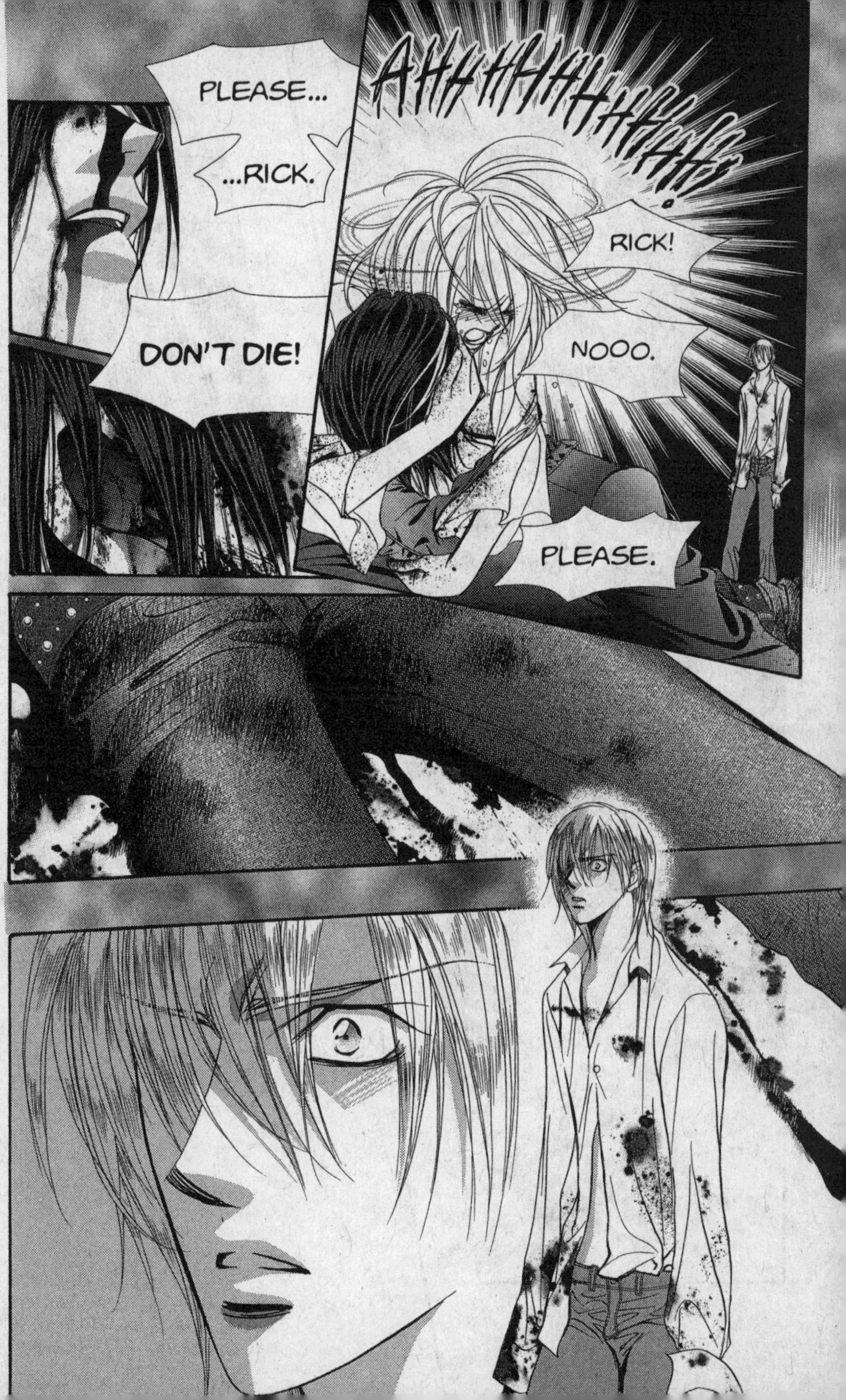
AHHHAAAHHHHHH!!
RICK!
NOOO.
PLEASE.
PLEASE...
...RICK.
DON'T DIE!

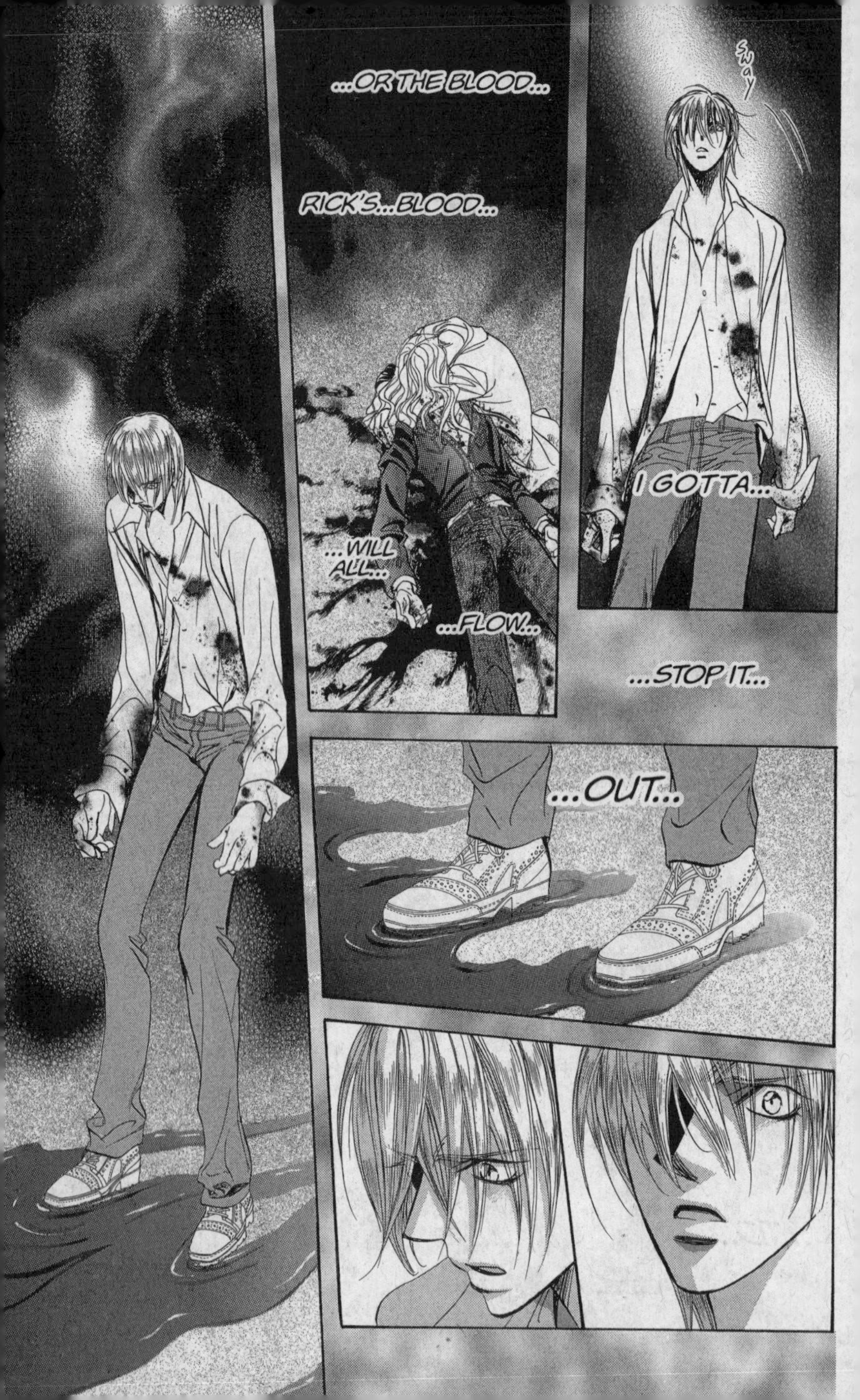
sway
I GOTTA...
...STOP IT...
...OR THE BLOOD...
RICK'S...BLOOD...
...WILL ALL...
...FLOW...
...OUT...

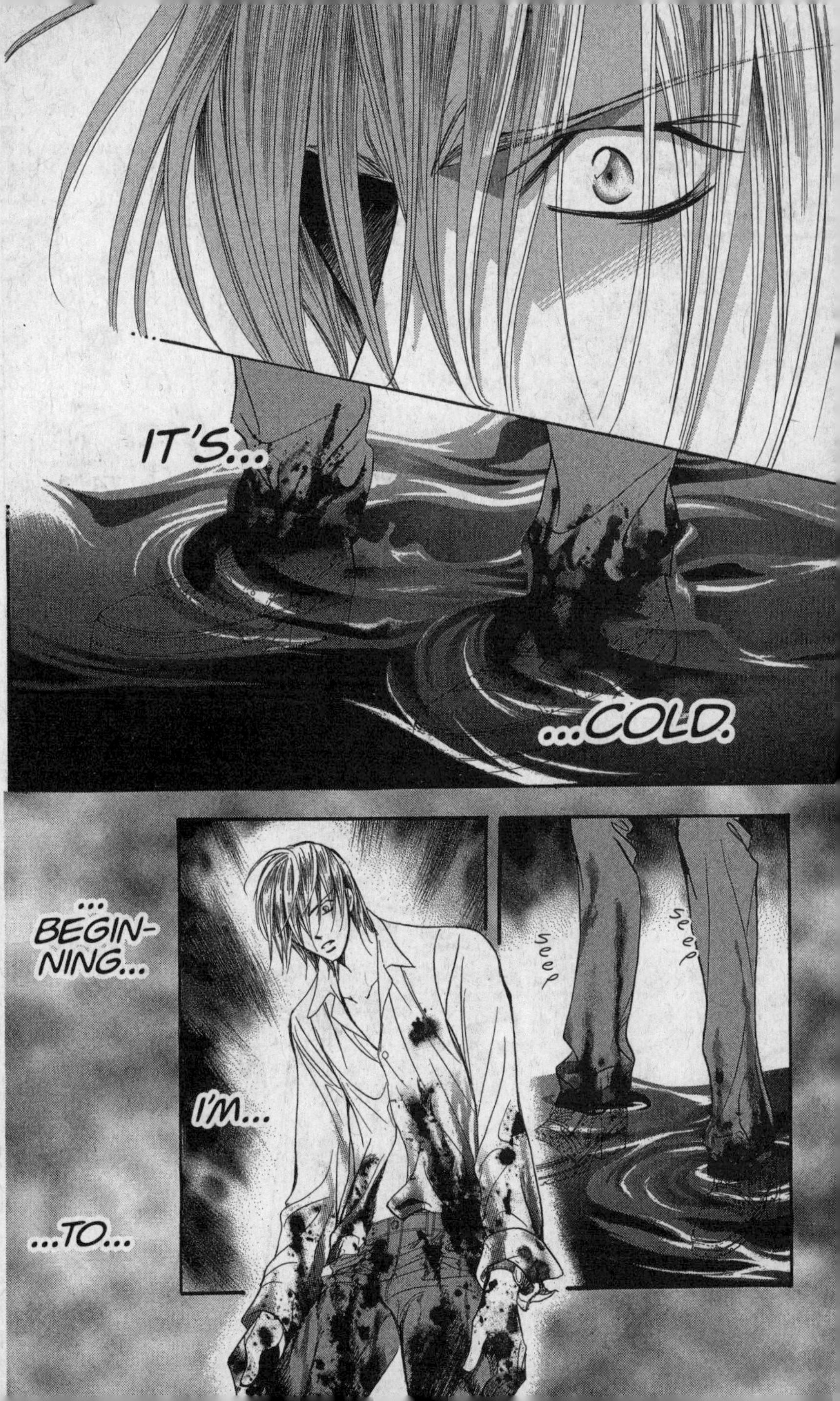
IT'S...
...COLD.
seep
seep
...BEGIN-NING...
I'M...
...TO...

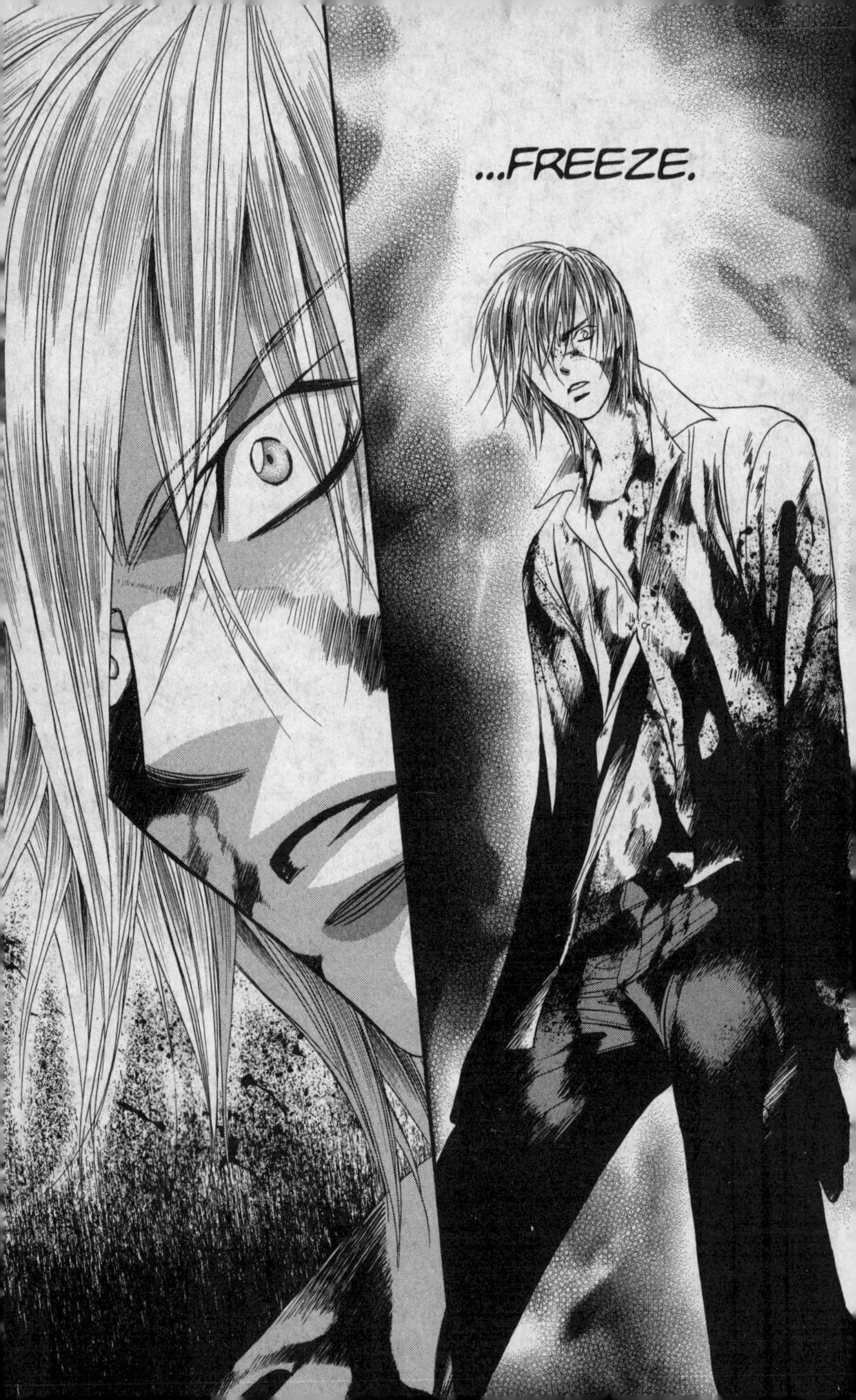
...FREEZE.

I...

...CAN'T MOVE...

End of Act 165

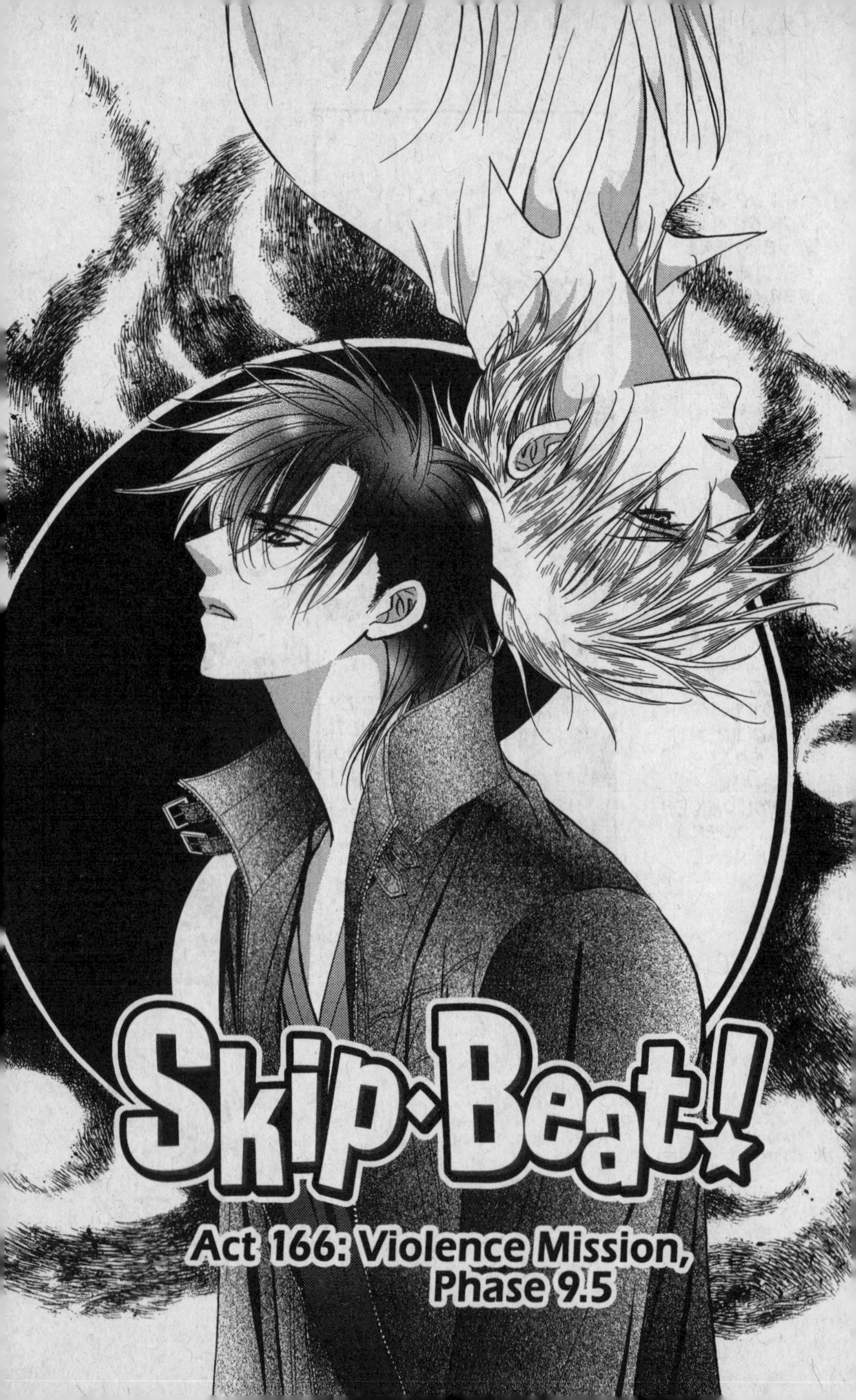
Skip·Beat!
Act 166: Violence Mission, Phase 9.5

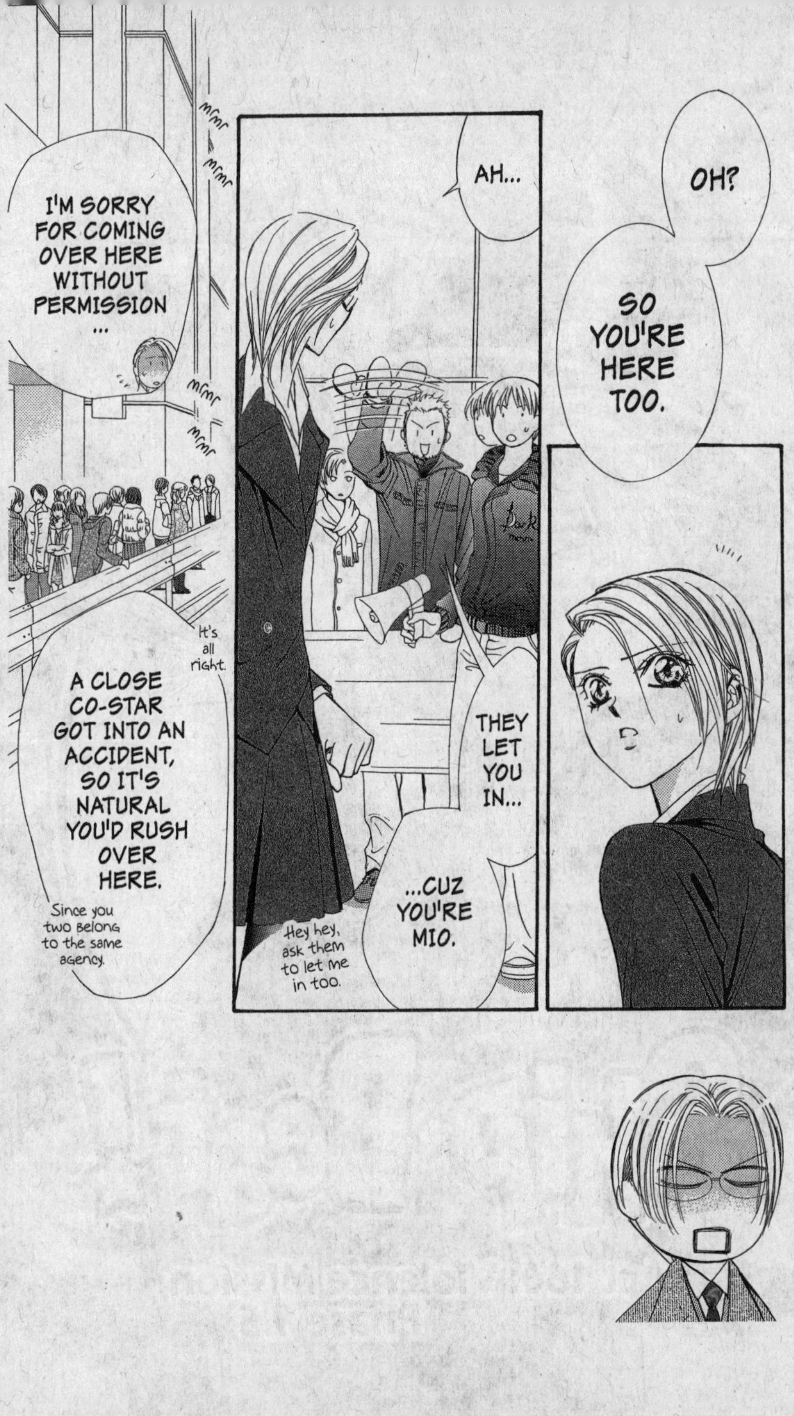
OH?
SO YOU'RE HERE TOO.
AH...
THEY LET YOU IN...
...CUZ YOU'RE MIO.
Hey hey, ask them to let me in too.
mrmr
mrmr
I'M SORRY FOR COMING OVER HERE WITHOUT PERMISSION...
mrmr
mrmr
It's all right.
A CLOSE CO-STAR GOT INTO AN ACCIDENT, SO IT'S NATURAL YOU'D RUSH OVER HERE.
Since you two belong to the same agency.

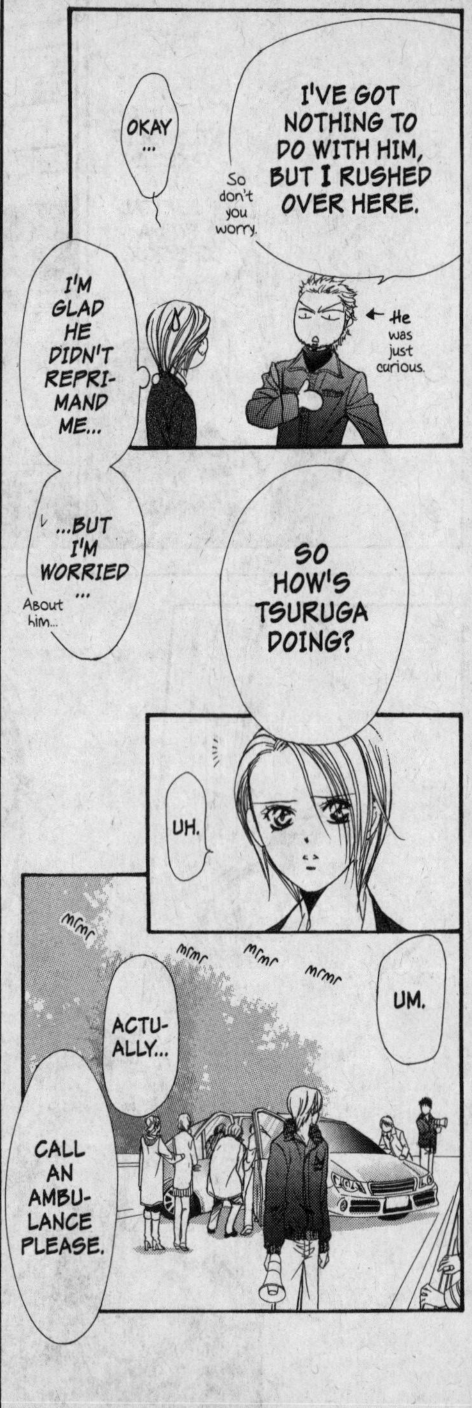
I'VE GOT NOTHING TO DO WITH HIM, BUT I RUSHED OVER HERE.
So don't you worry.
He was just curious.
OKAY...
I'M GLAD HE DIDN'T REPRIMAND ME...
...BUT I'M WORRIED...
About him...
SO HOW'S TSURUGA DOING?
UH.
UM.
mrmr
mrmr
mrmr
mrmr
ACTUALLY...
CALL AN AMBULANCE PLEASE.
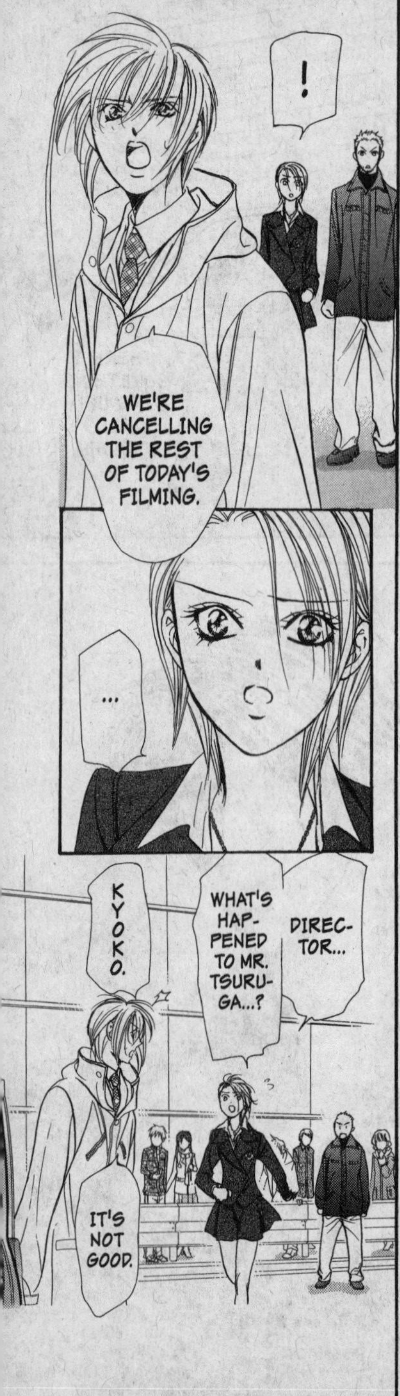
!
WE'RE CANCELLING THE REST OF TODAY'S FILMING.
...
DIRECTOR...
WHAT'S HAPPENED TO MR. TSURUGA...?
KYOKO.
IT'S NOT GOOD.

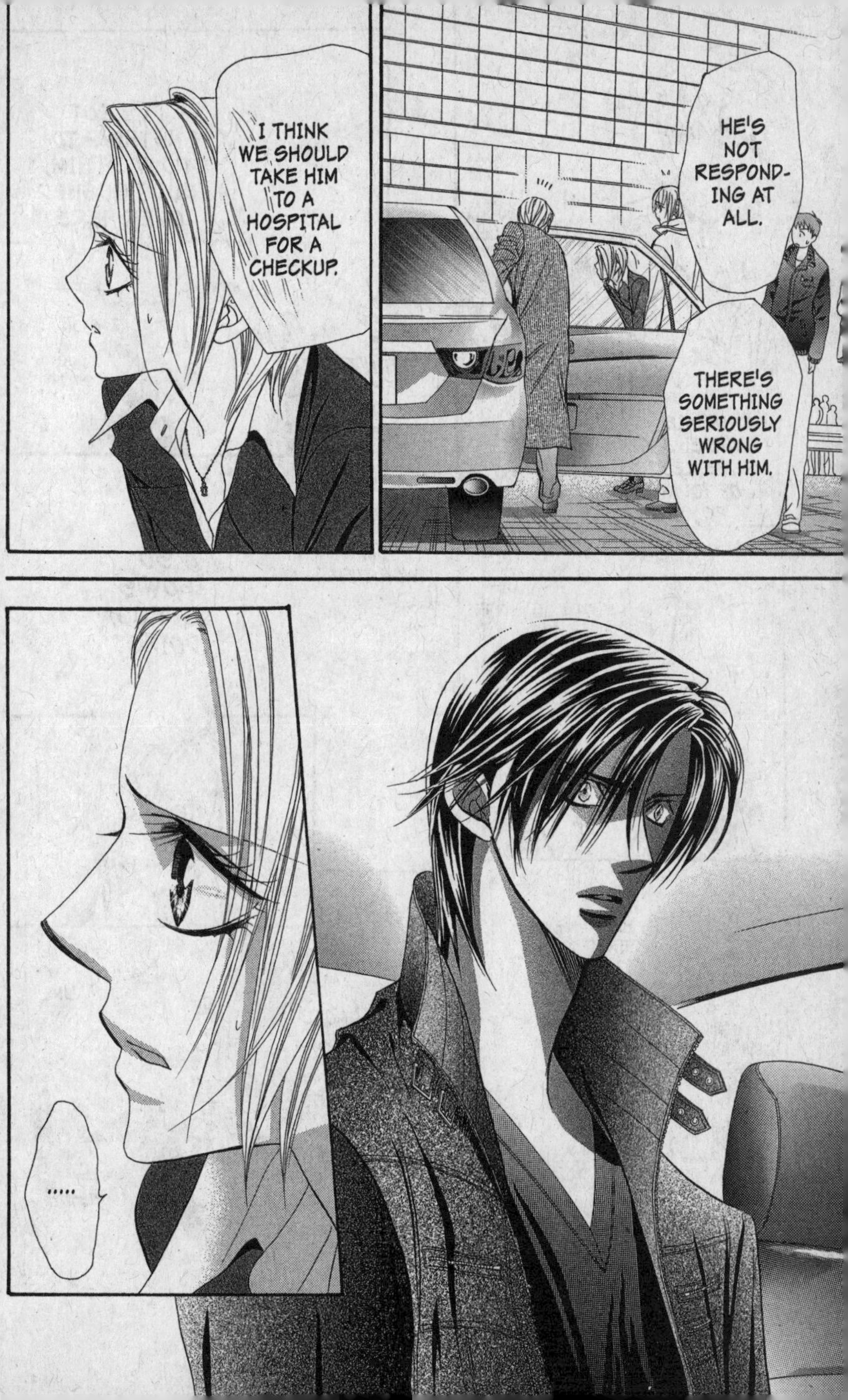
HE'S NOT RESPONDING AT ALL.
THERE'S SOMETHING SERIOUSLY WRONG WITH HIM.
I THINK WE SHOULD TAKE HIM TO A HOSPITAL FOR A CHECKUP.
.....

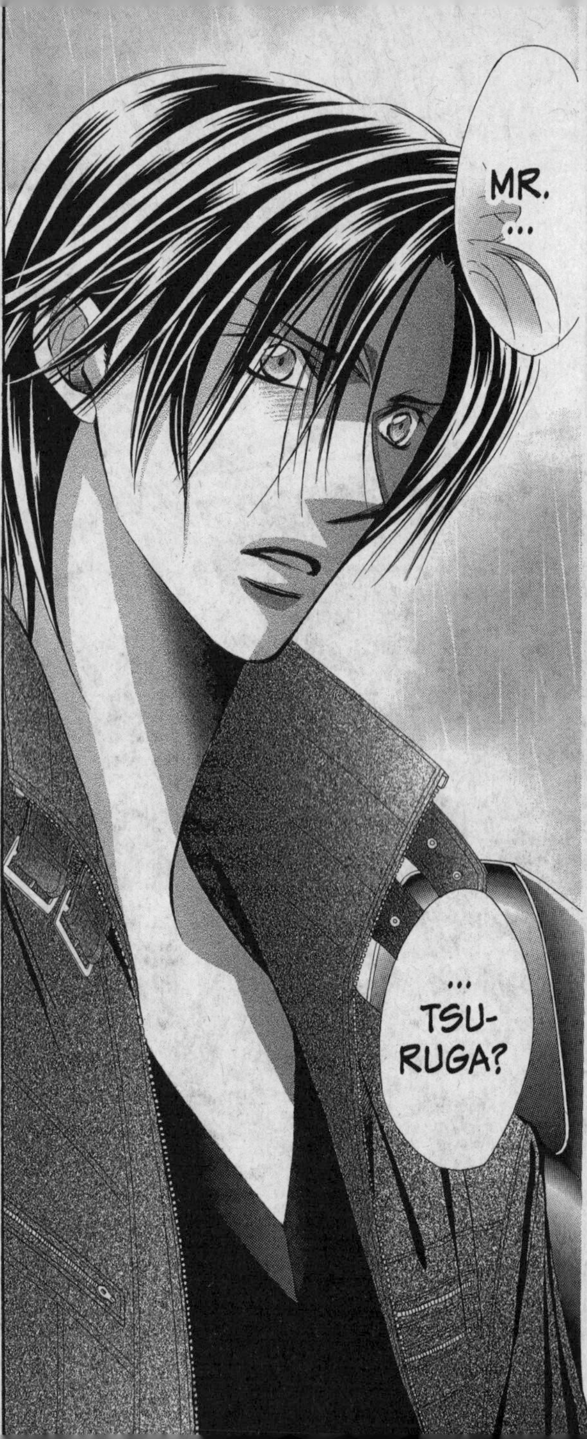
MR. ...
... TSU-RUGA?

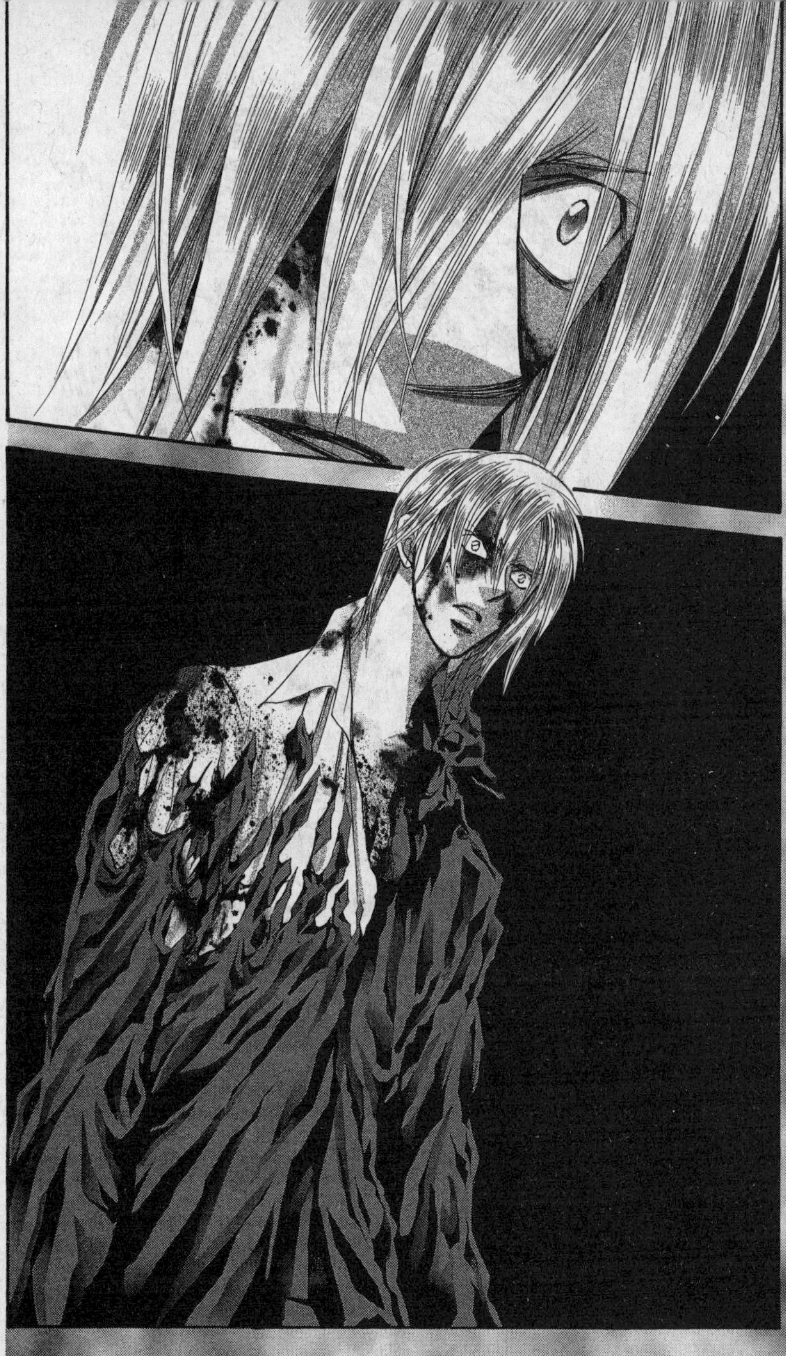

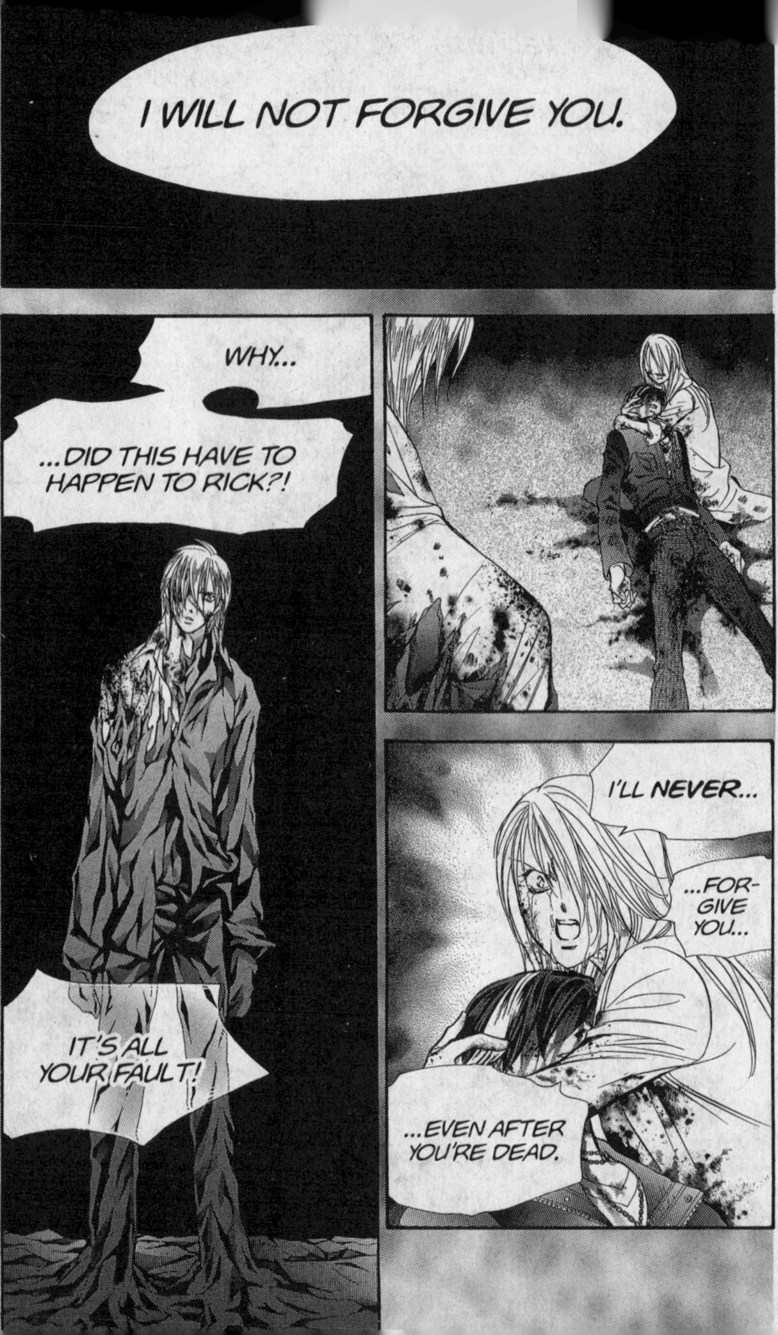
I WILL NOT FORGIVE YOU.
I'LL NEVER...
...FOR-GIVE YOU...
...EVEN AFTER YOU'RE DEAD.
WHY...
...DID THIS HAVE TO HAPPEN TO RICK?!
IT'S ALL YOUR FAULT!

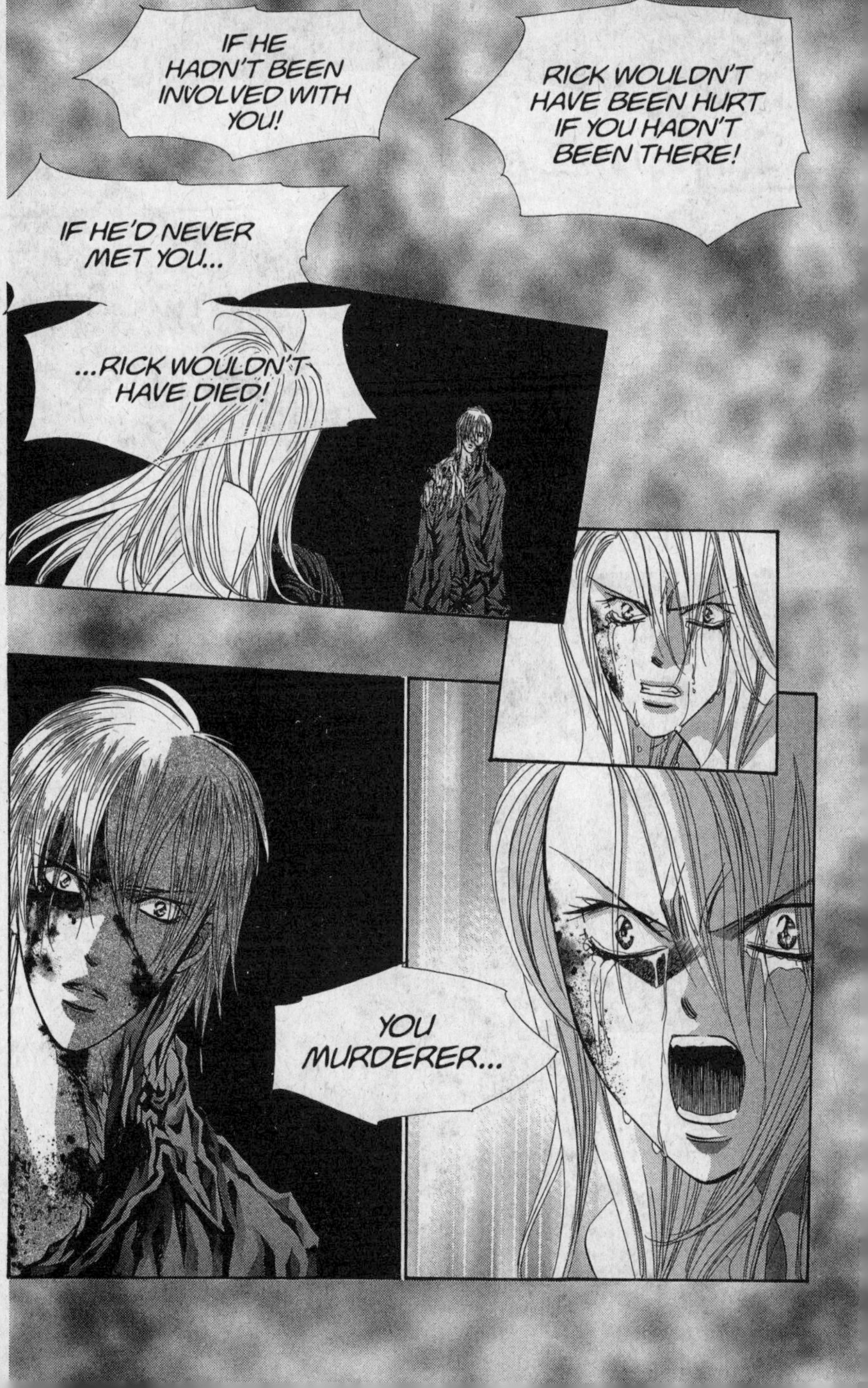
RICK WOULDN'T HAVE BEEN HURT IF YOU HADN'T BEEN THERE!
IF HE HADN'T BEEN INVOLVED WITH YOU!
IF HE'D NEVER MET YOU...
...RICK WOULDN'T HAVE DIED!
YOU MURDERER...

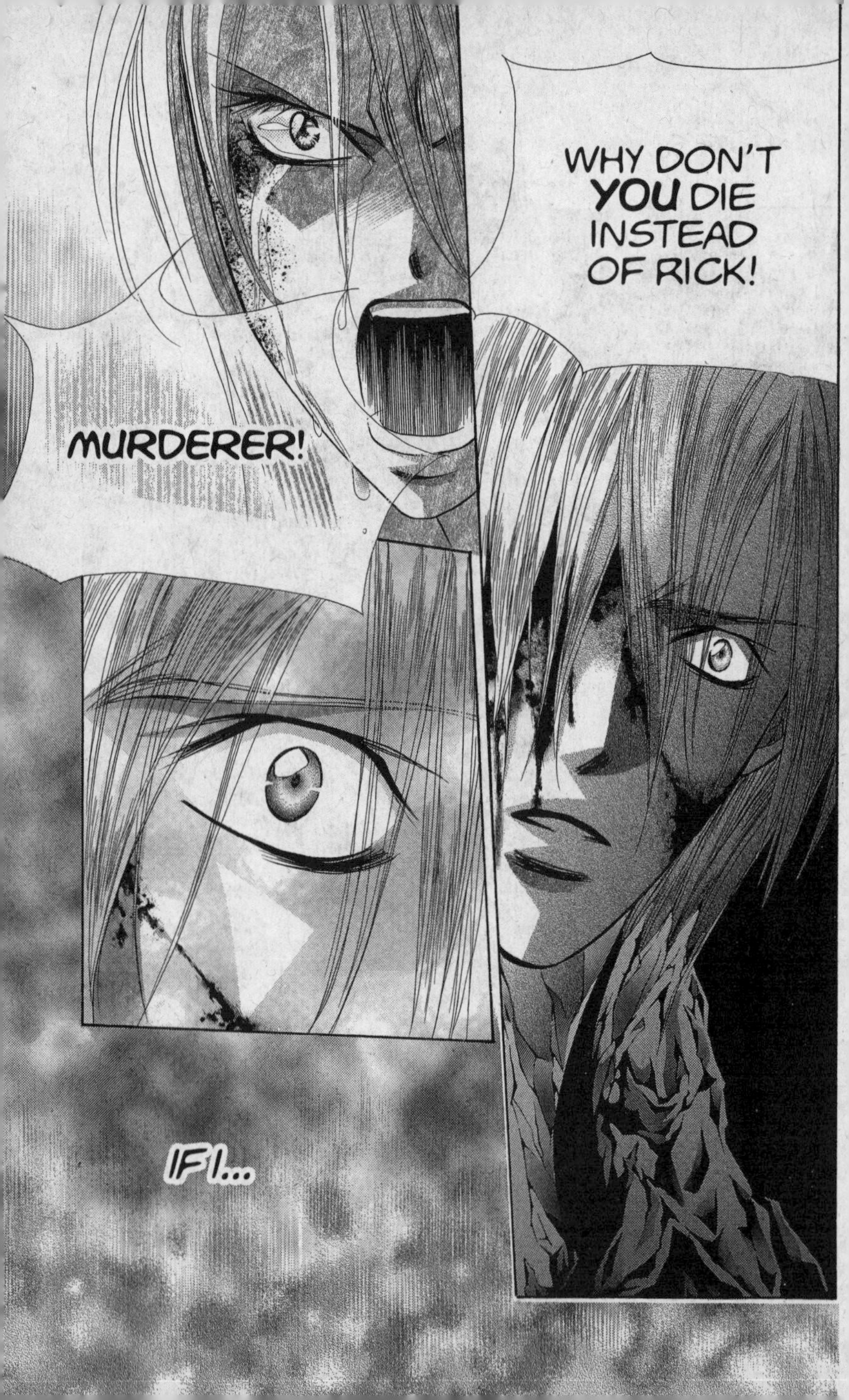
WHY DON'T YOU DIE INSTEAD OF RICK!
MURDERER!
IF I...

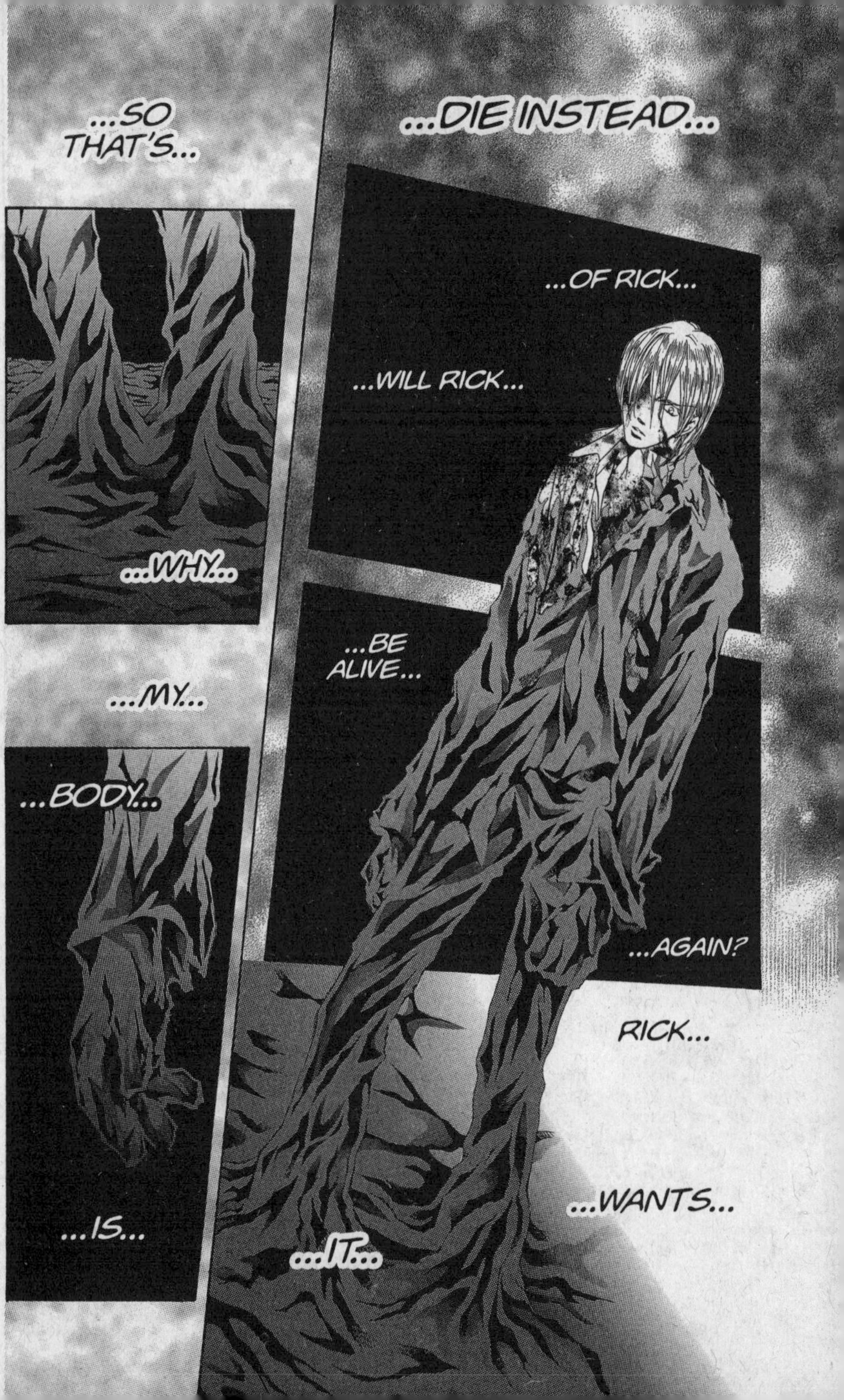
...DIE INSTEAD...
...OF RICK...
...WILL RICK...
...BE ALIVE...
...AGAIN?
RICK...
...WANTS...
...IT...
...SO THAT'S...
...WHY...
...MY...
...BODY...
...IS...

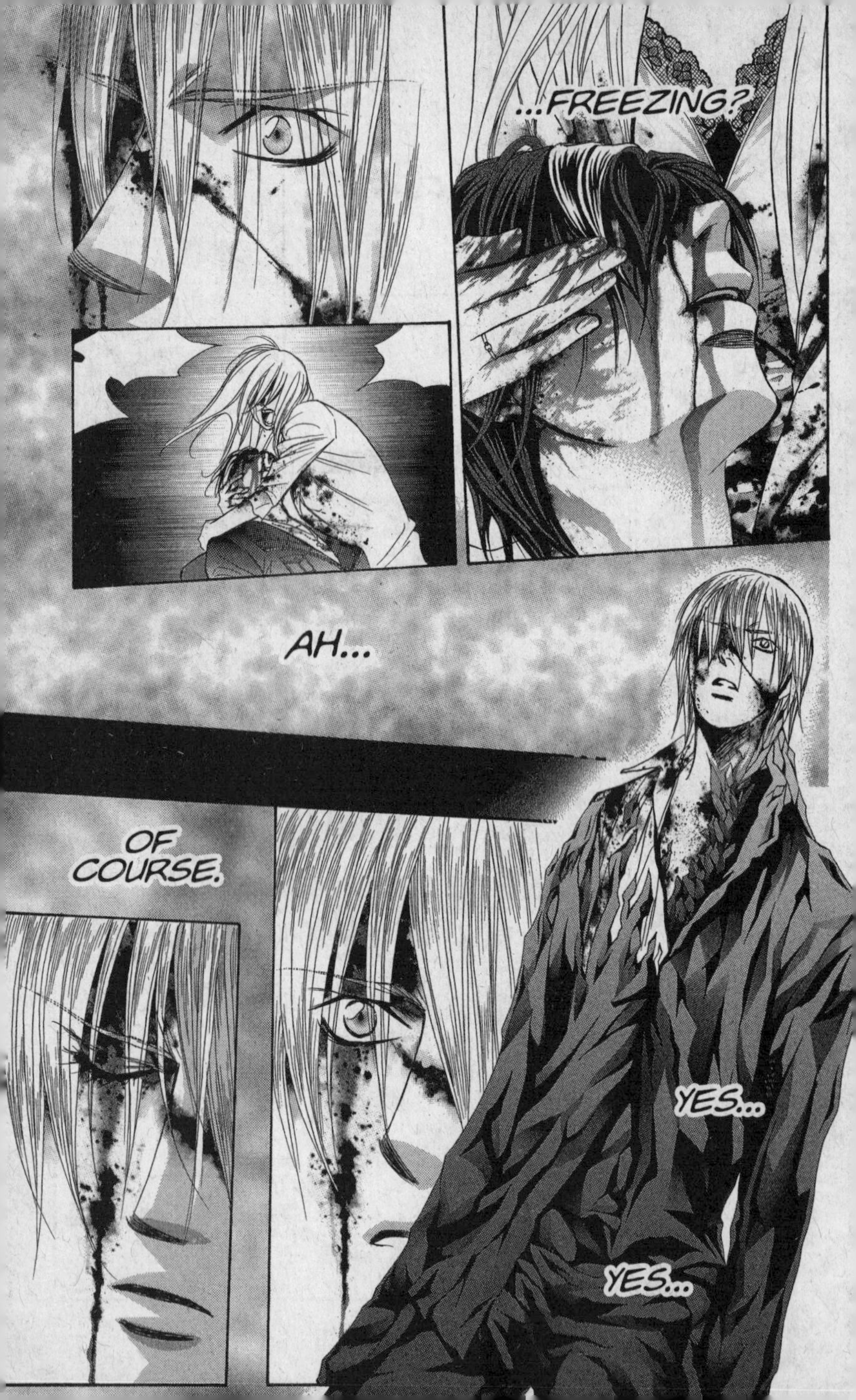
...FREEZING?
AH...
OF COURSE.
YES...
YES...

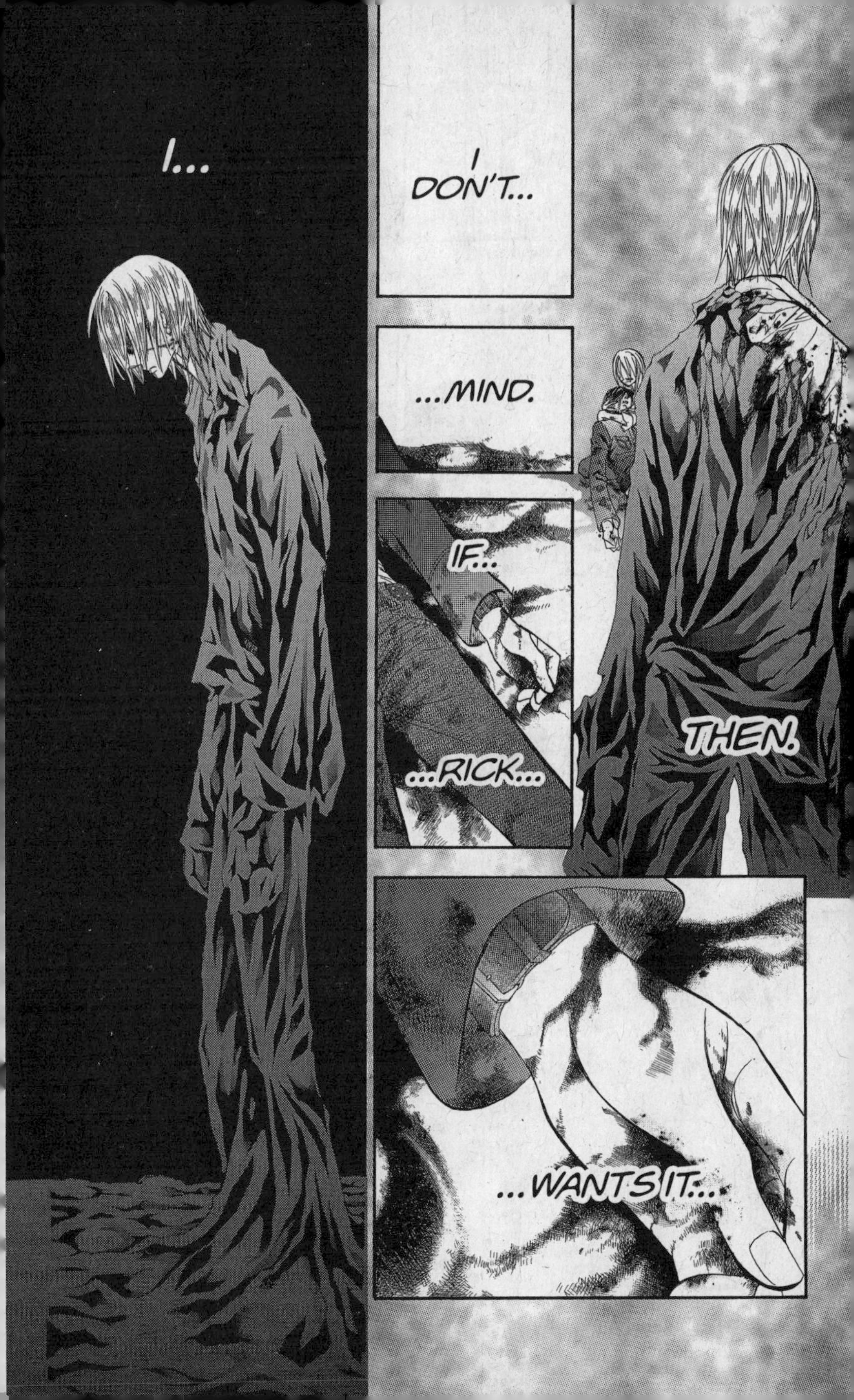
I...
I DON'T...
...MIND.
IF...
...RICK...
...WANTS IT...
THEN.

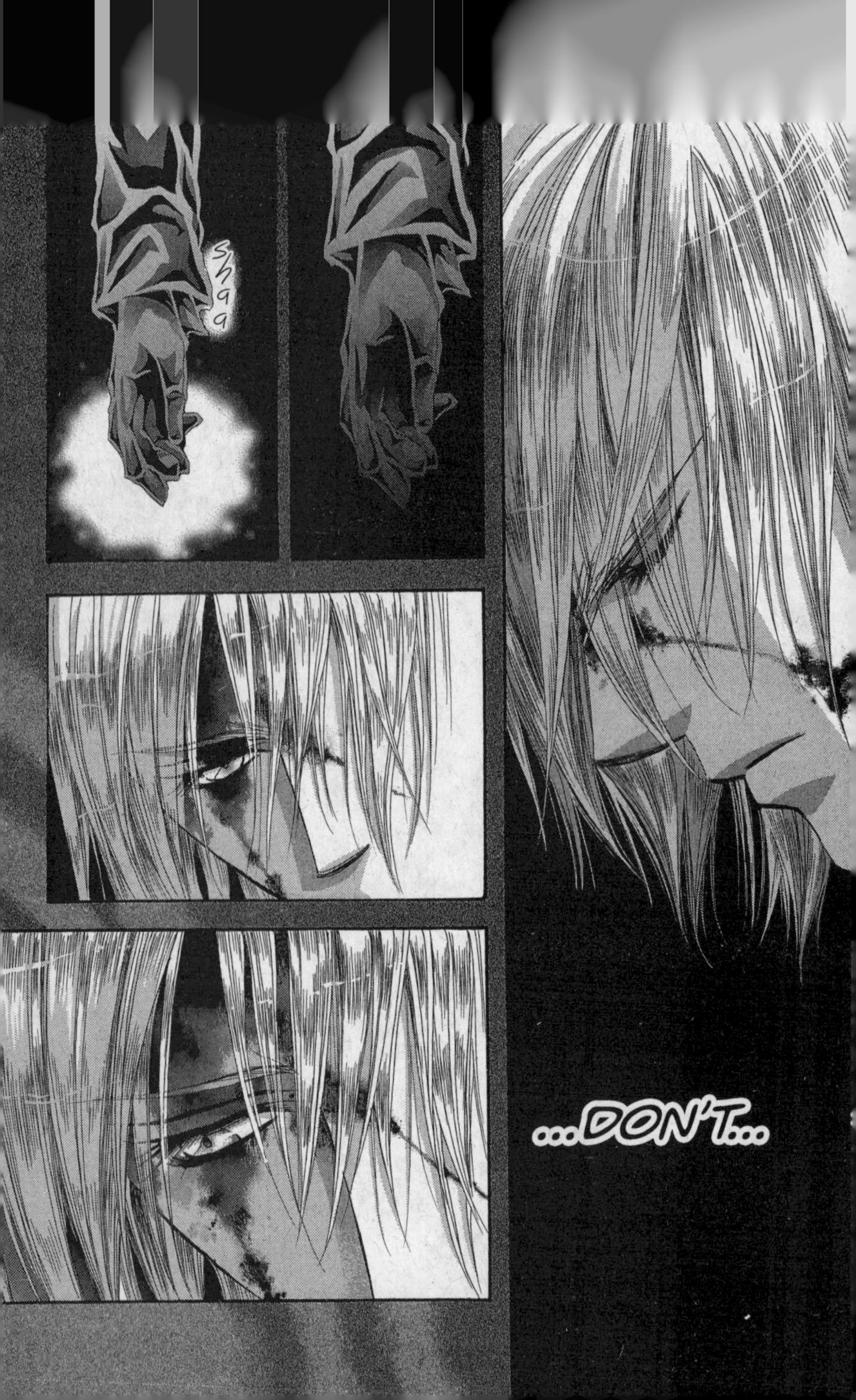
...DON'T...

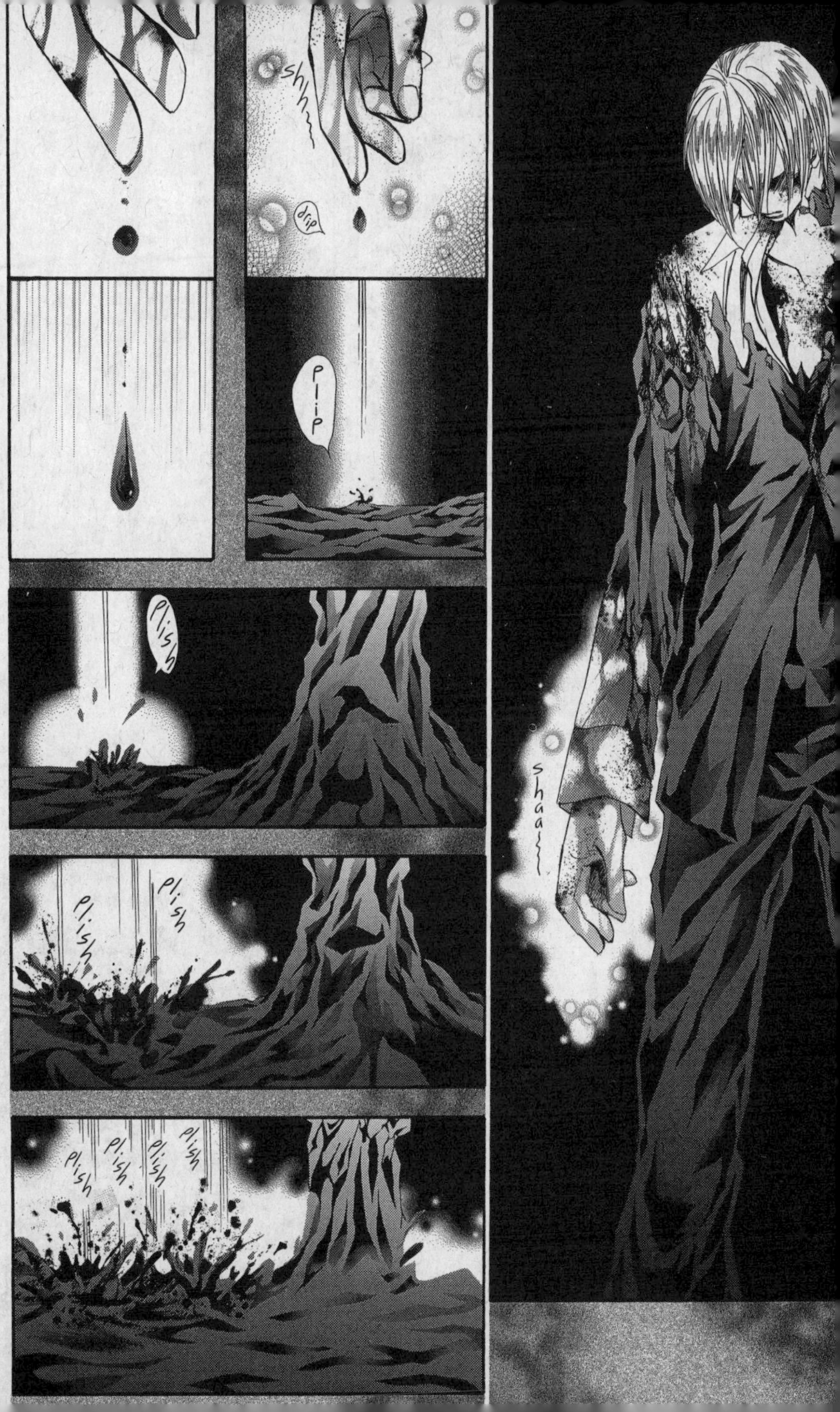
shaa
shh
drip
plip
plish
plish
plish
plish
plish
plish
plish

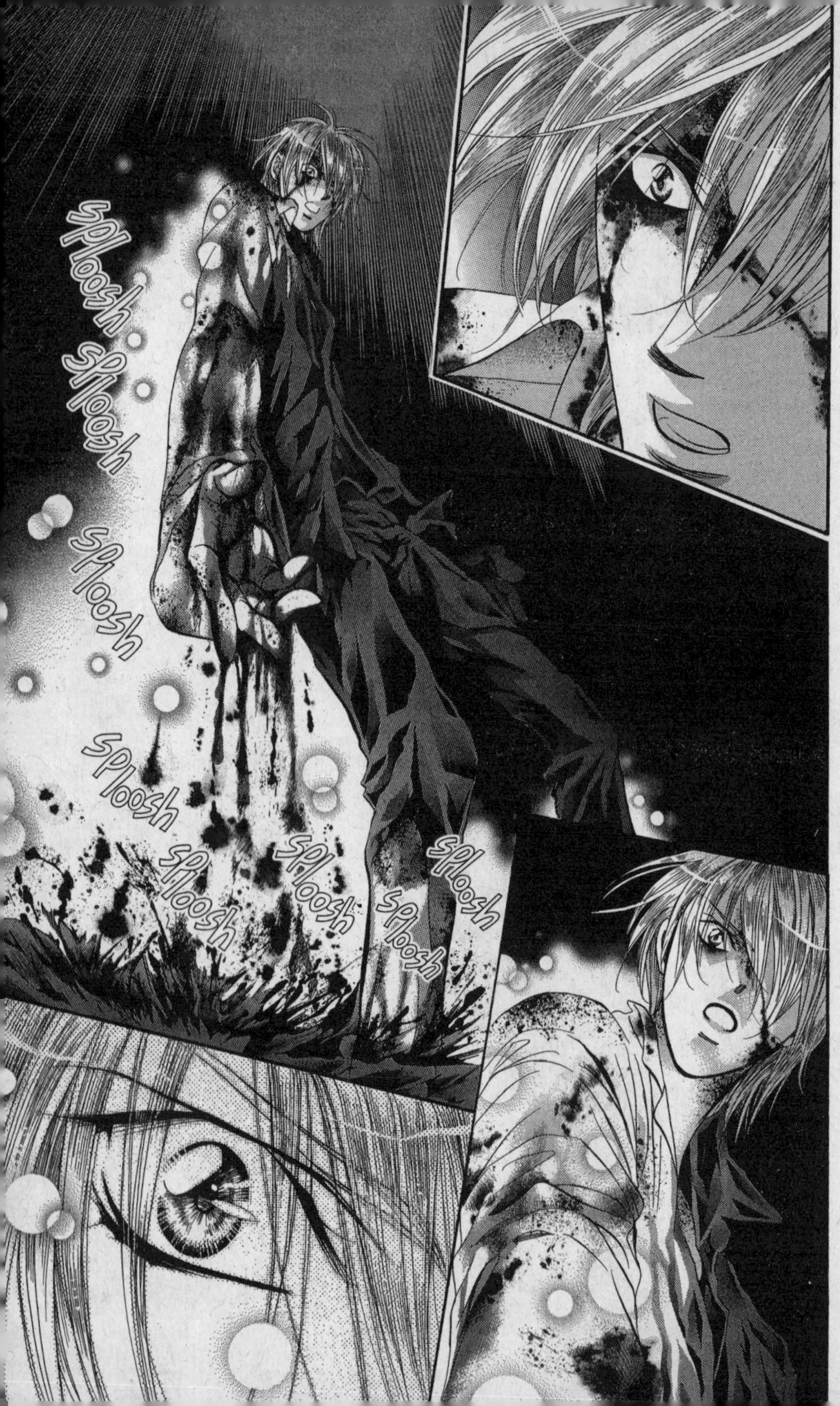
sploosh
sploosh
sploosh
sploosh
sploosh
sploosh
sploosh
sploosh

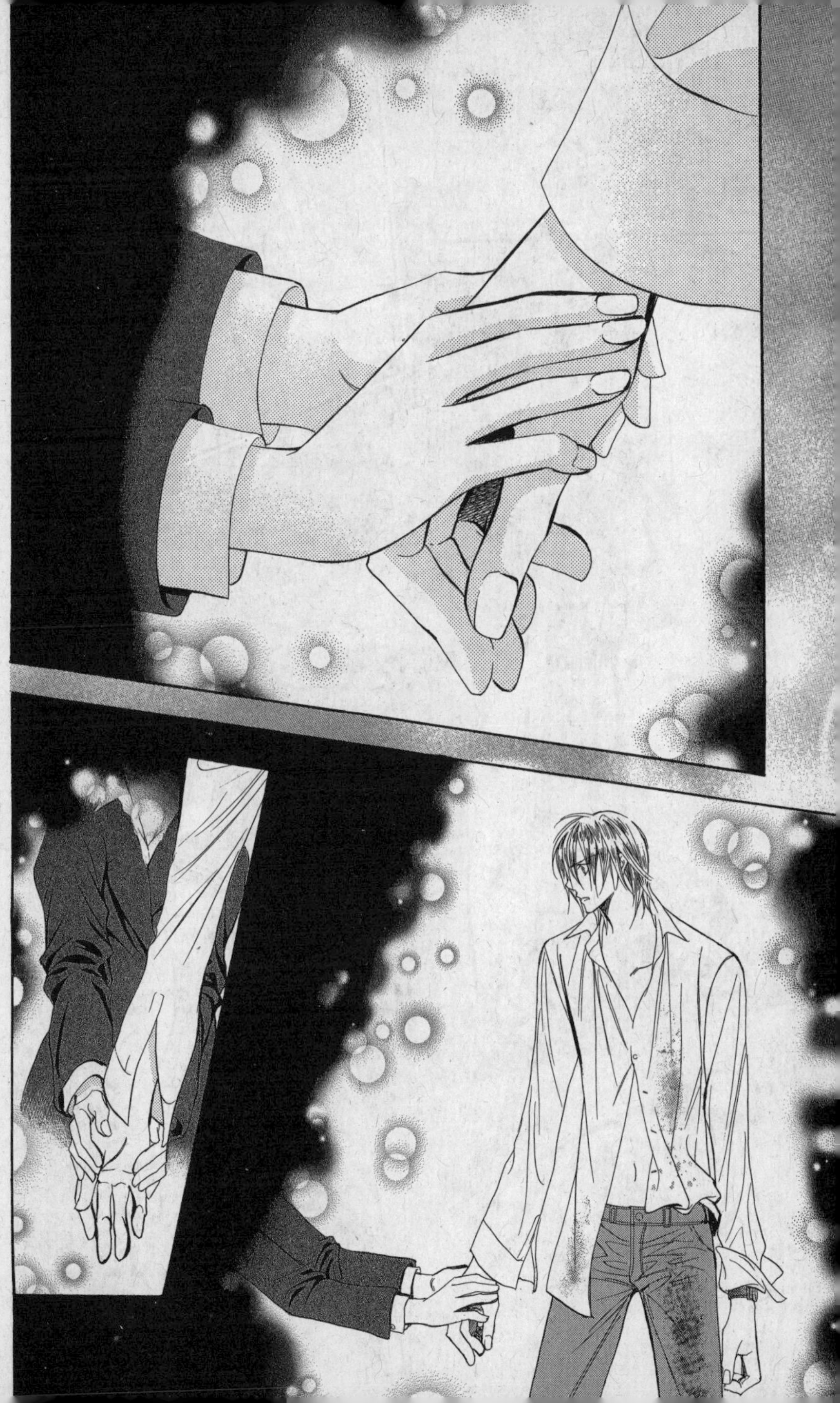

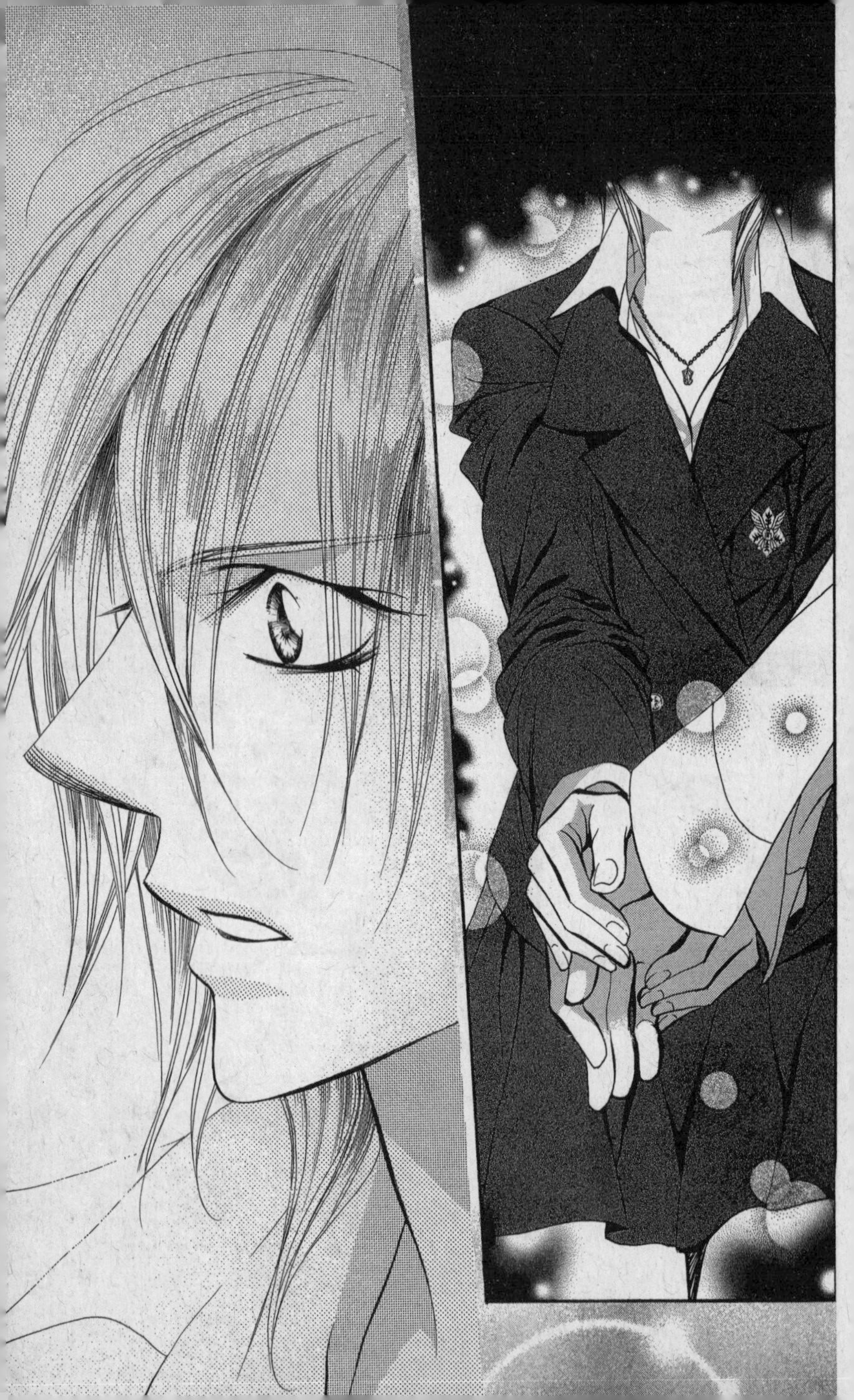

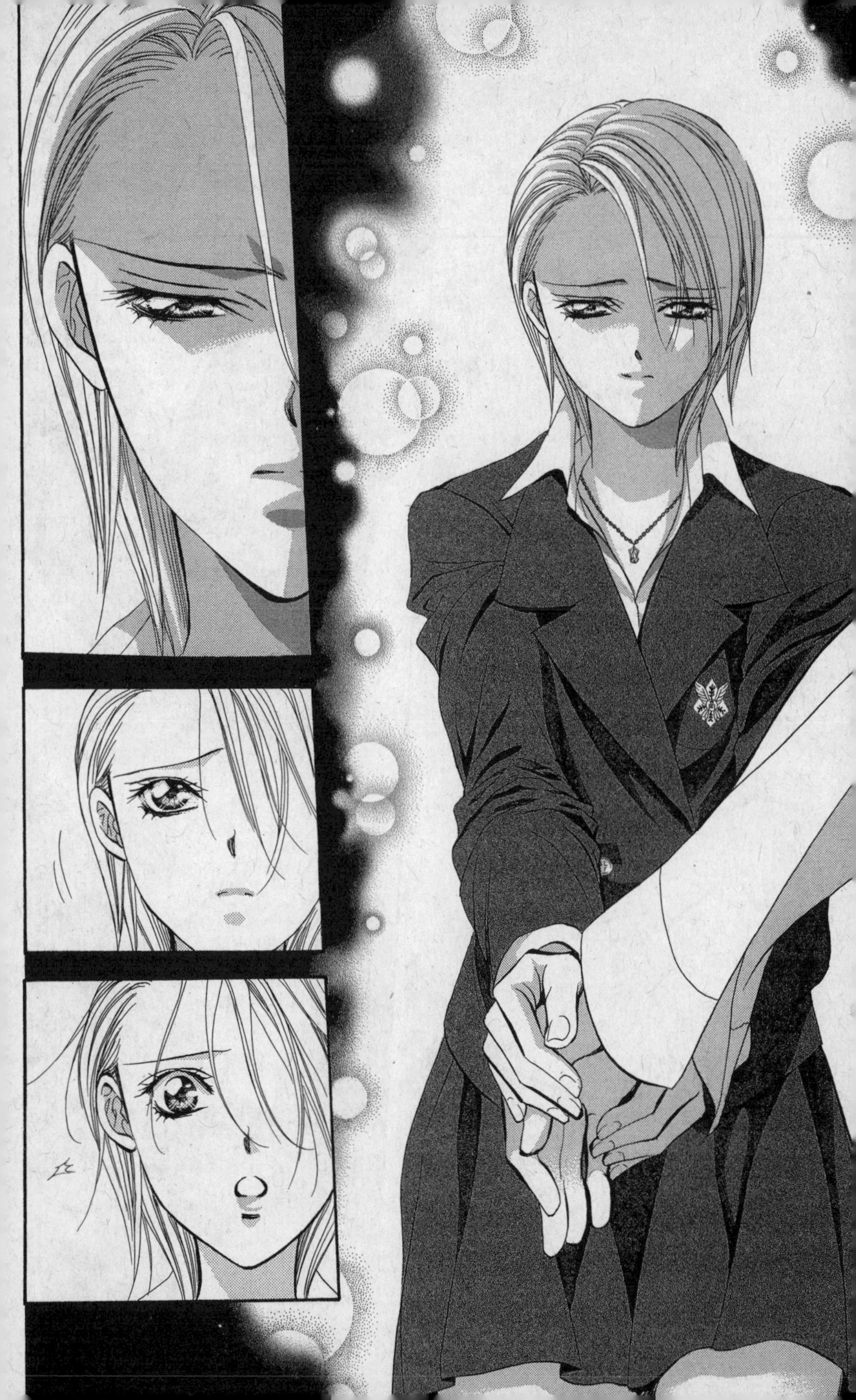

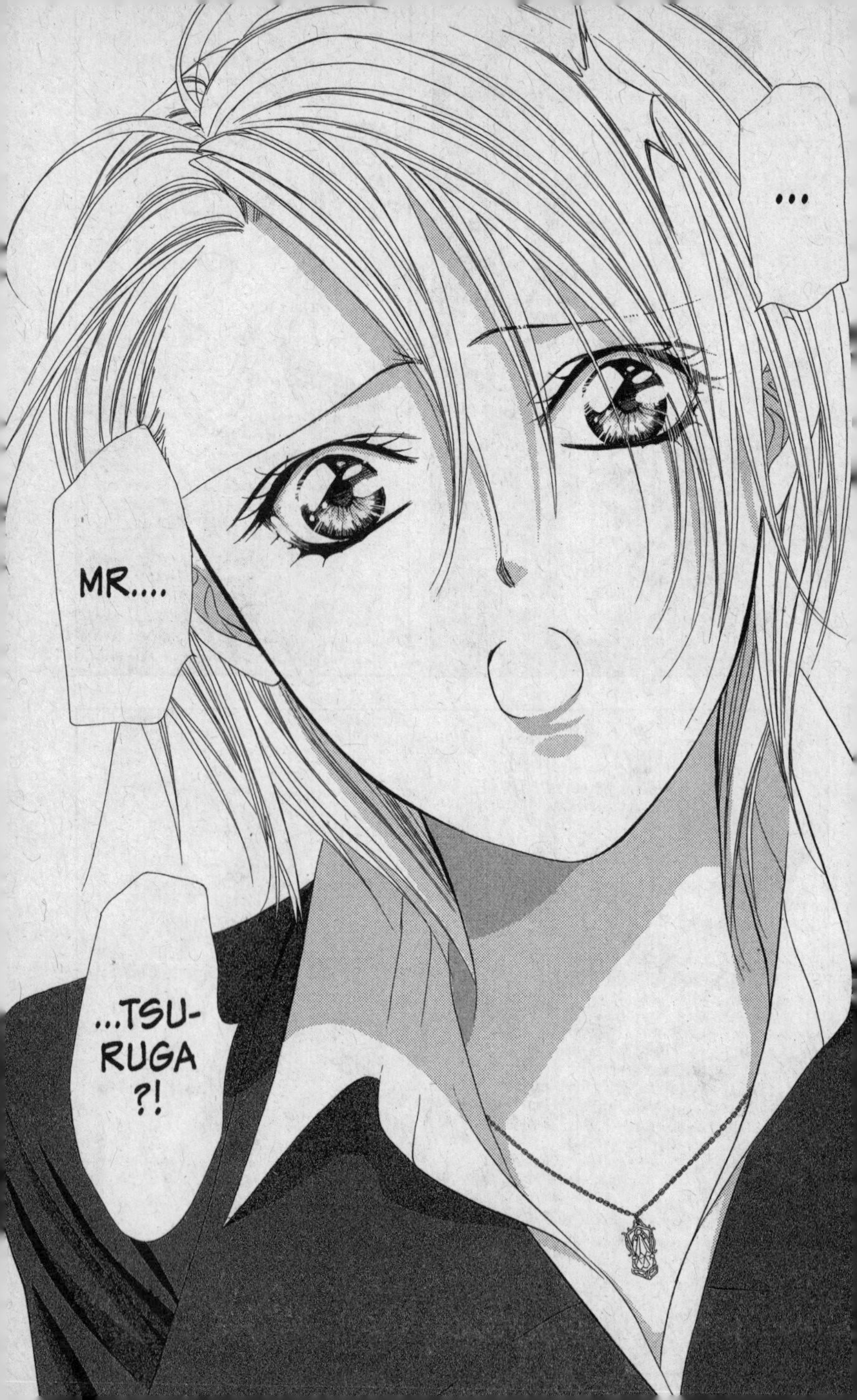
...
MR....
...TSU-RUGA ?!

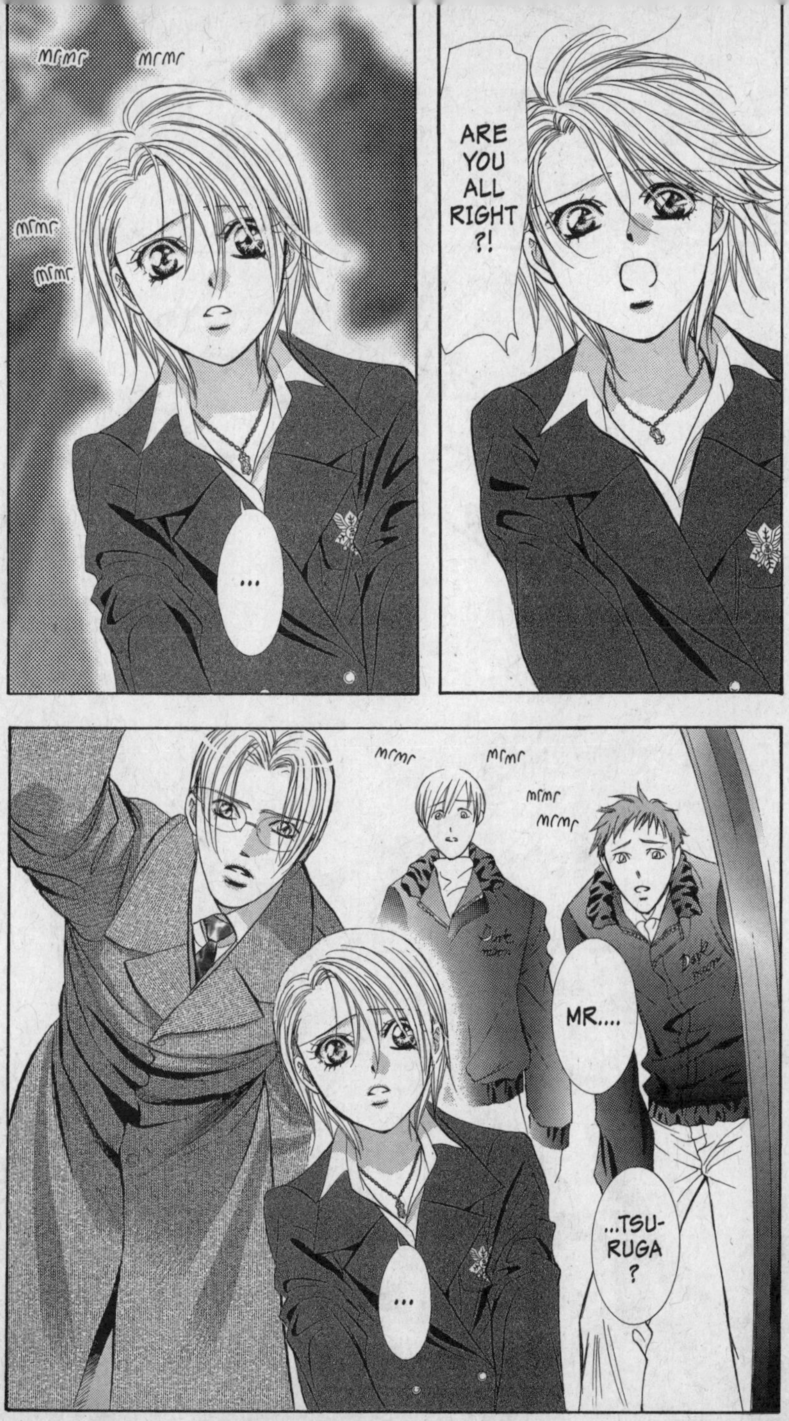
ARE YOU ALL RIGHT ?!
mrmr
mrmr
mrmr
mrmr
...
mrmr
mrmr
mrmr
mrmr
MR....
...TSU-RUGA ?
...

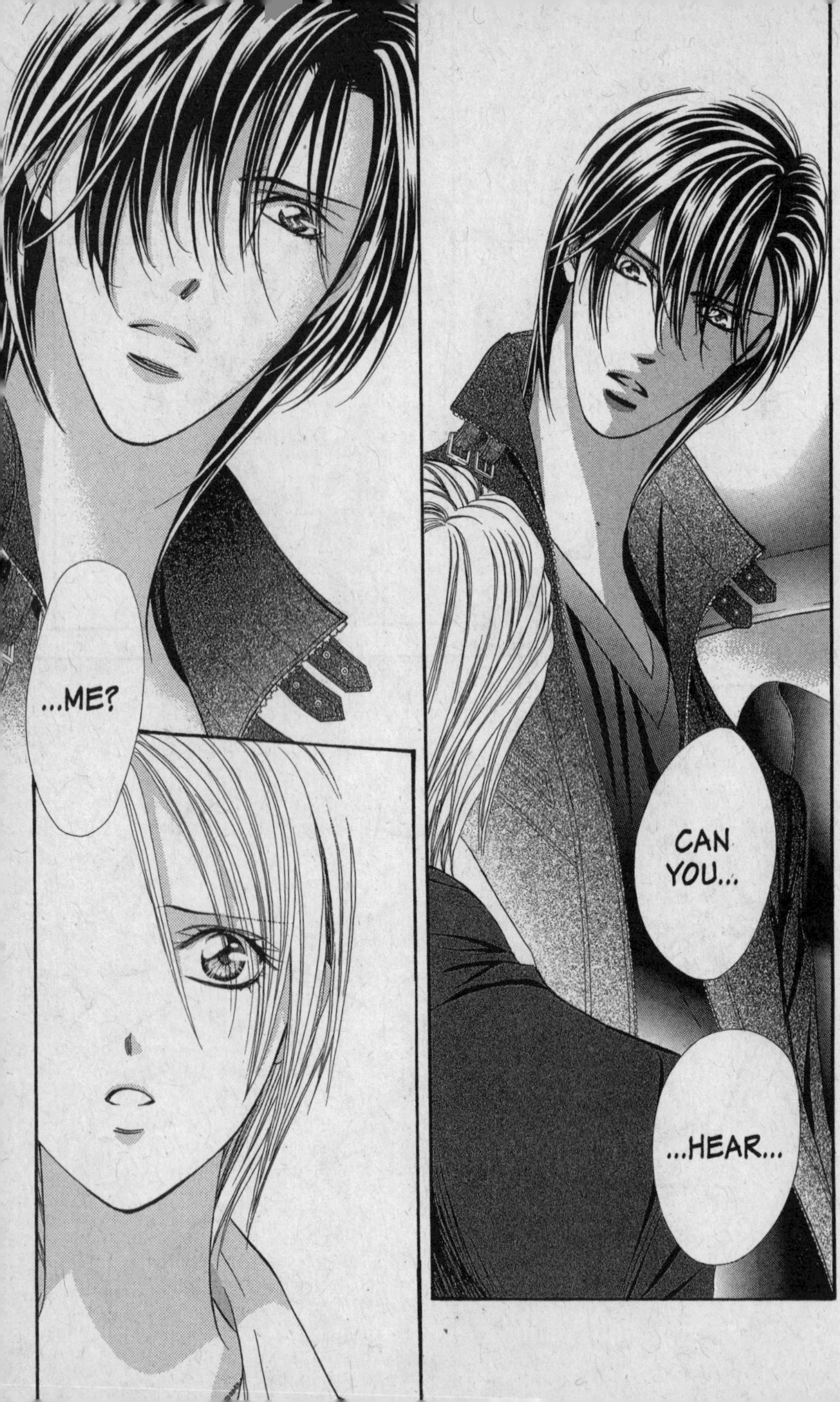
CAN YOU...
...HEAR...
...ME?

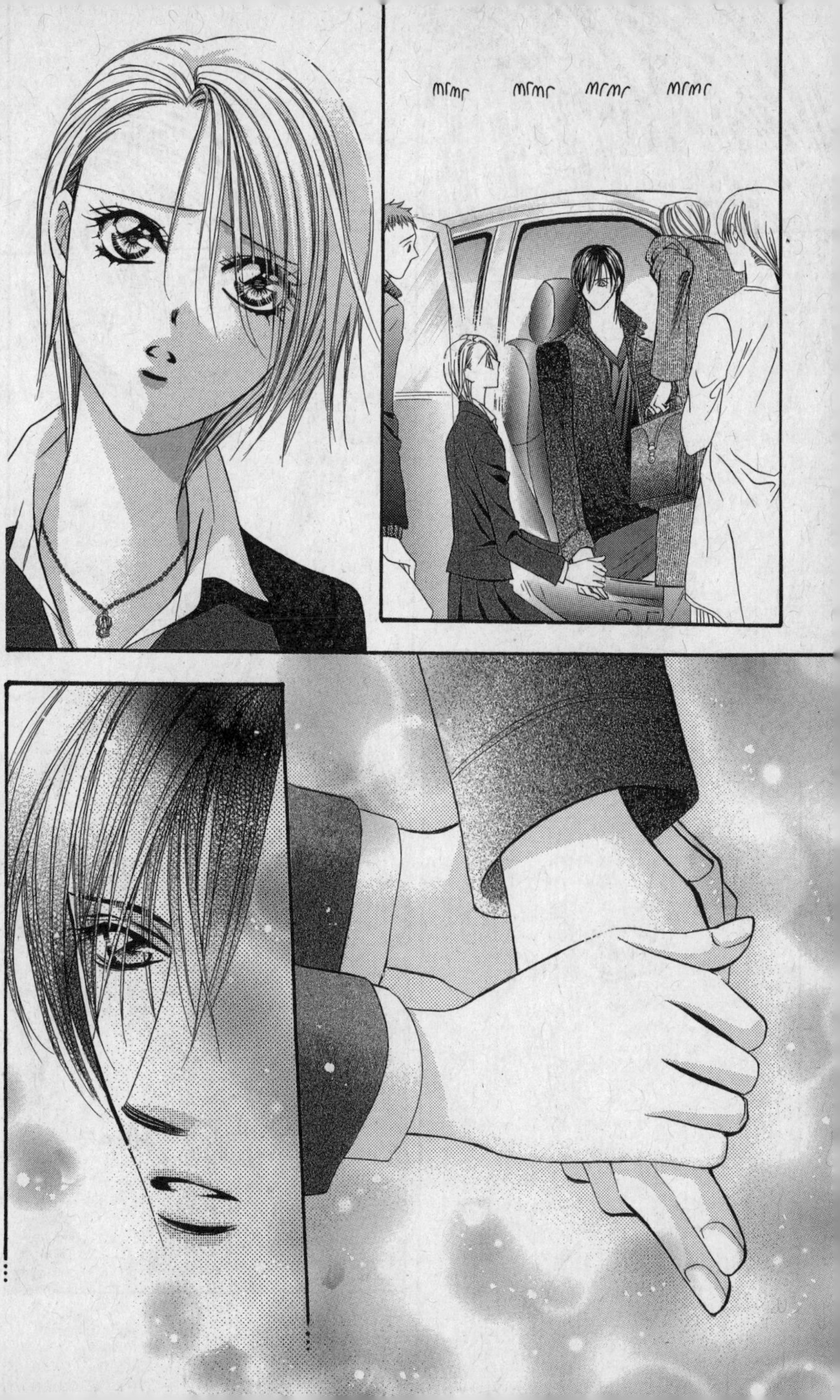
mrmr
mrmr
mrmr
mrmr

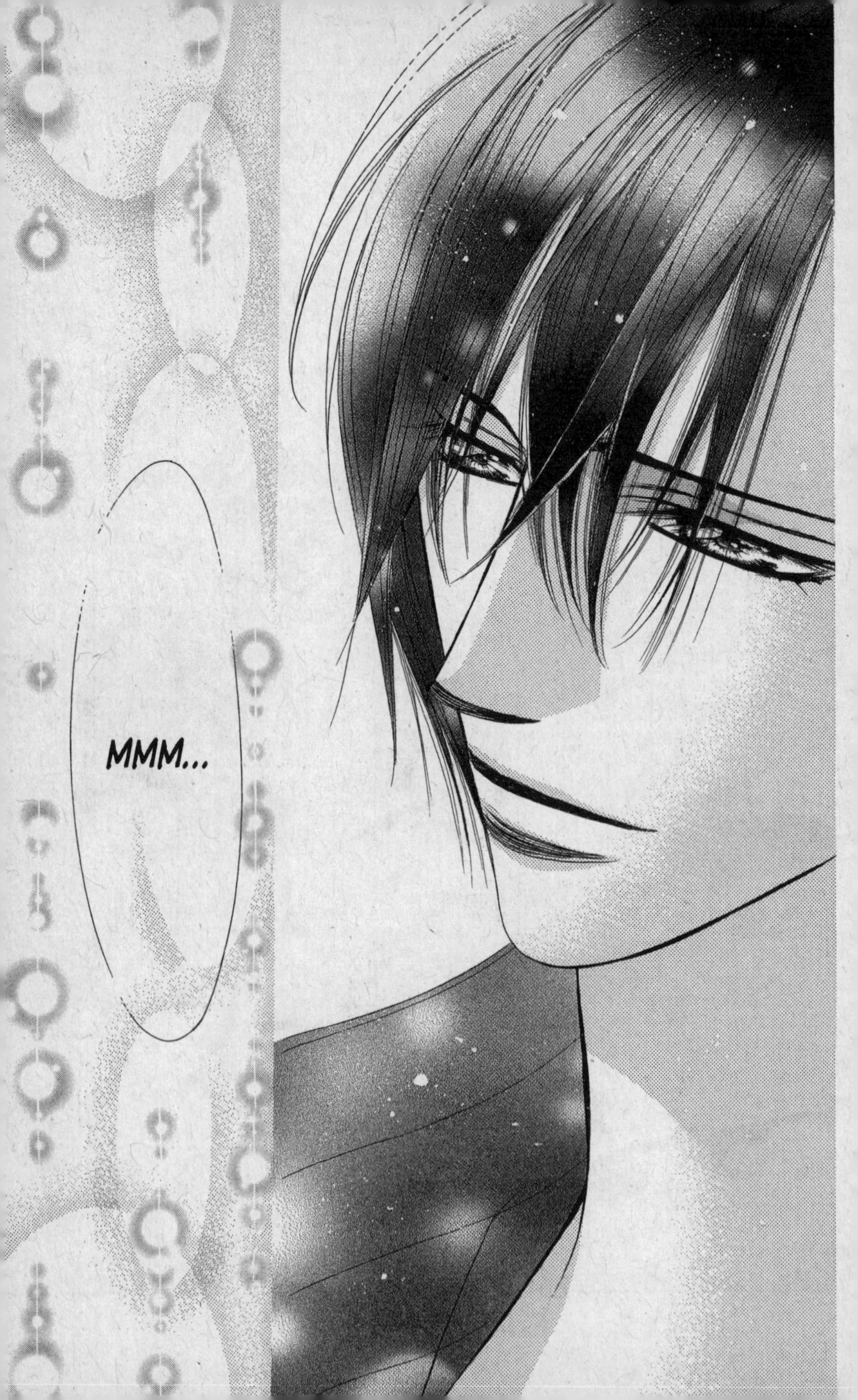
MMM...

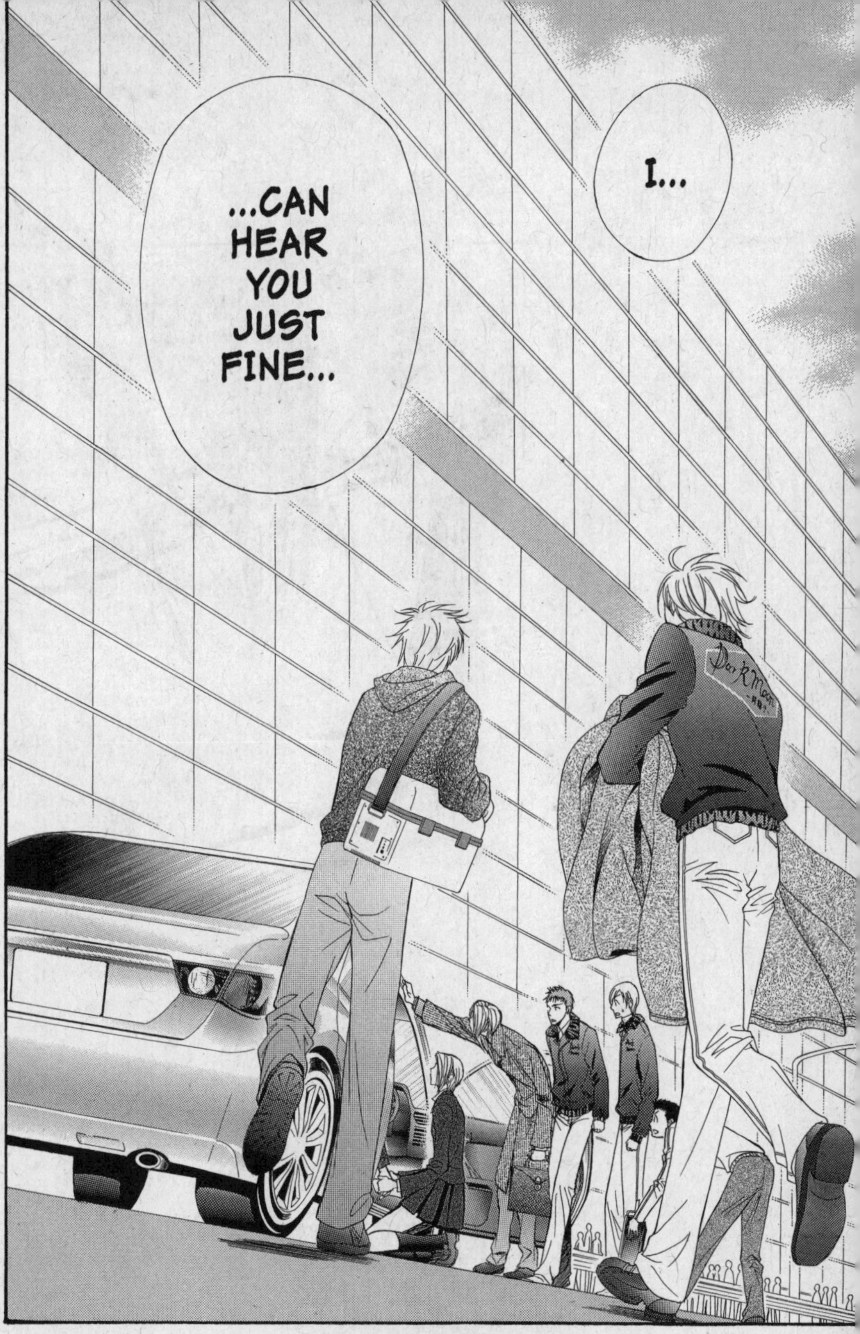
I...
...CAN HEAR YOU JUST FINE...

End of Act 166

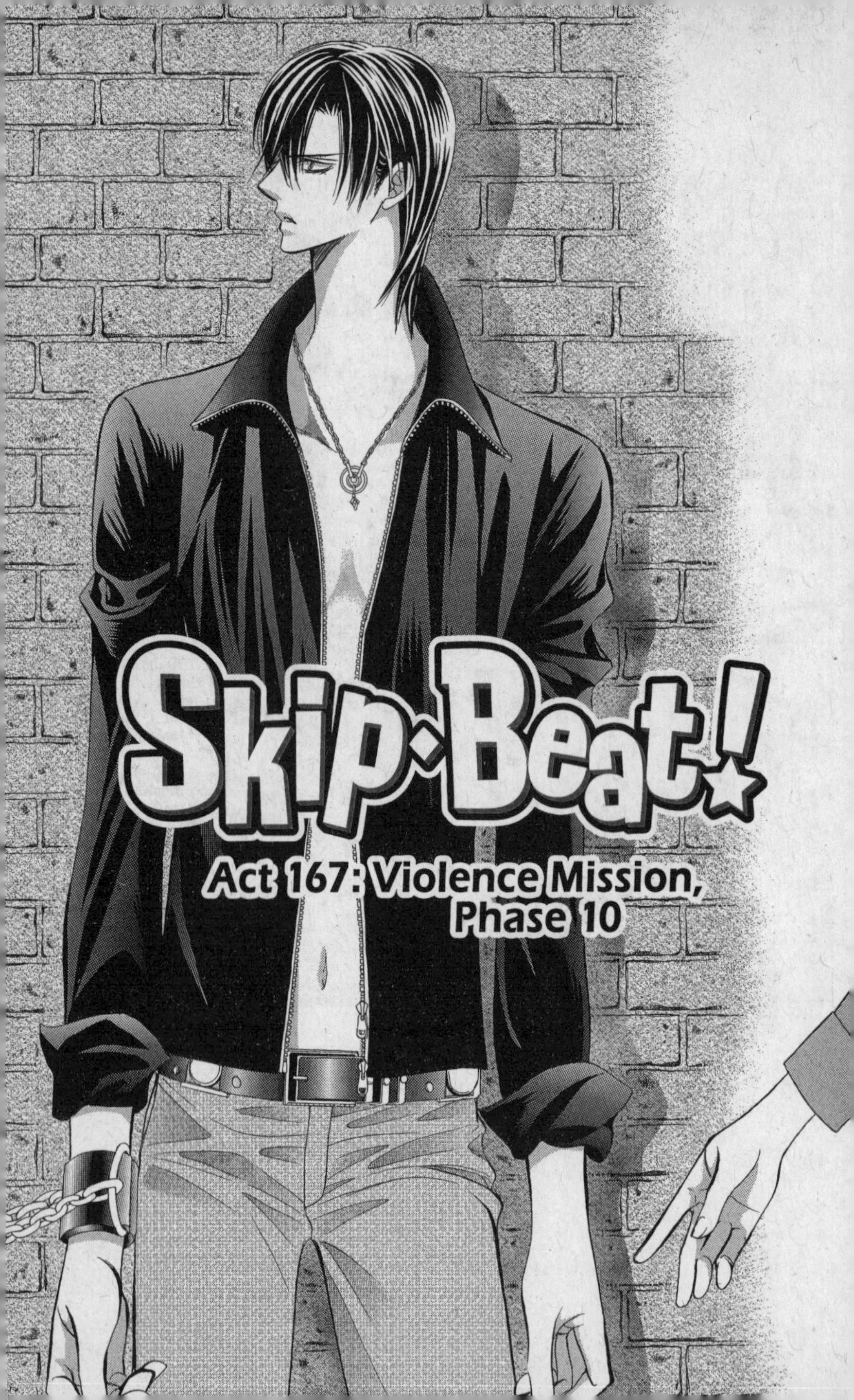
Skip·Beat!
Act 167: Violence Mission, Phase 10

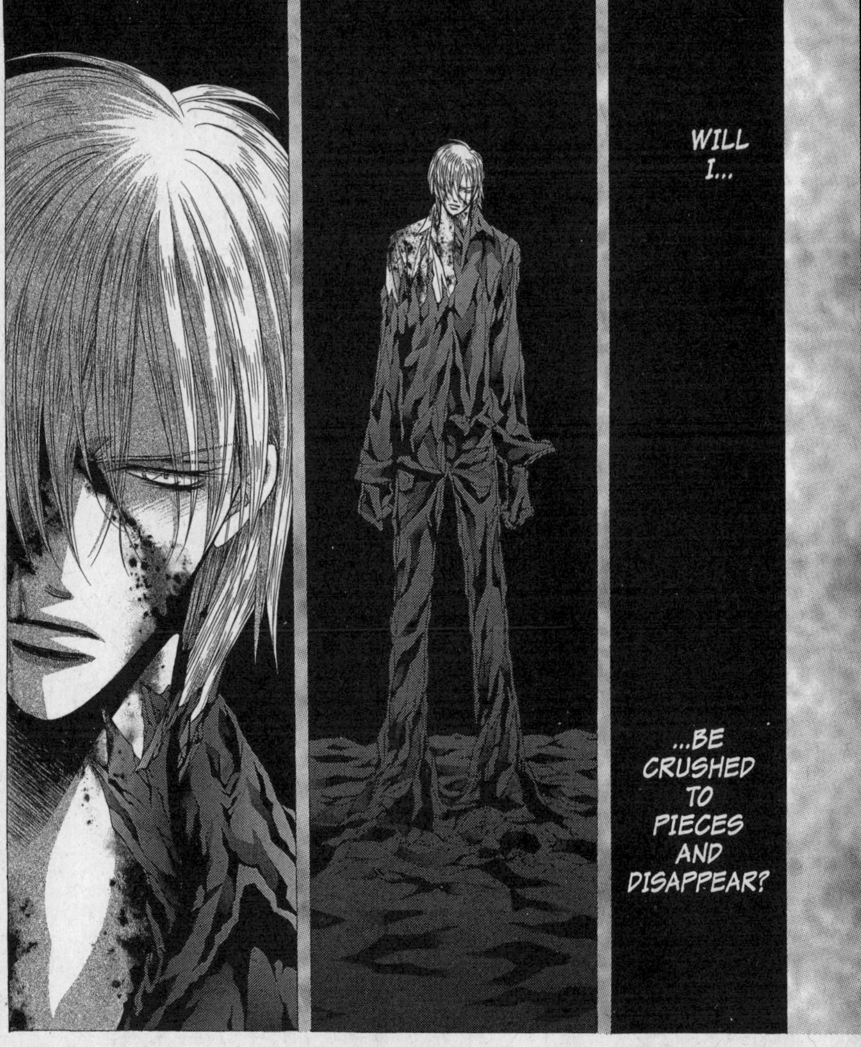
WILL I...
...BE CRUSHED TO PIECES AND DISAPPEAR?

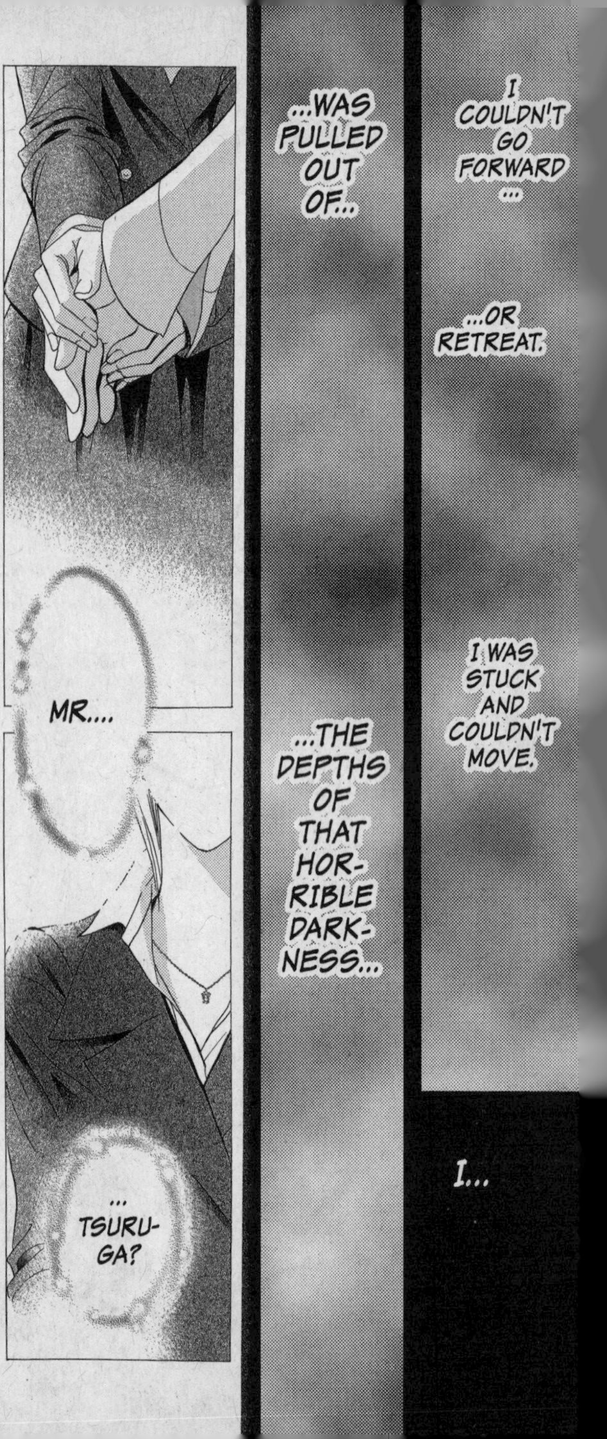
I COULDN'T GO FORWARD...
...OR RETREAT.
I WAS STUCK AND COULDN'T MOVE.
I...
...WAS PULLED OUT OF...
...THE DEPTHS OF THAT HORRIBLE DARKNESS...
MR....
...TSURUGA?

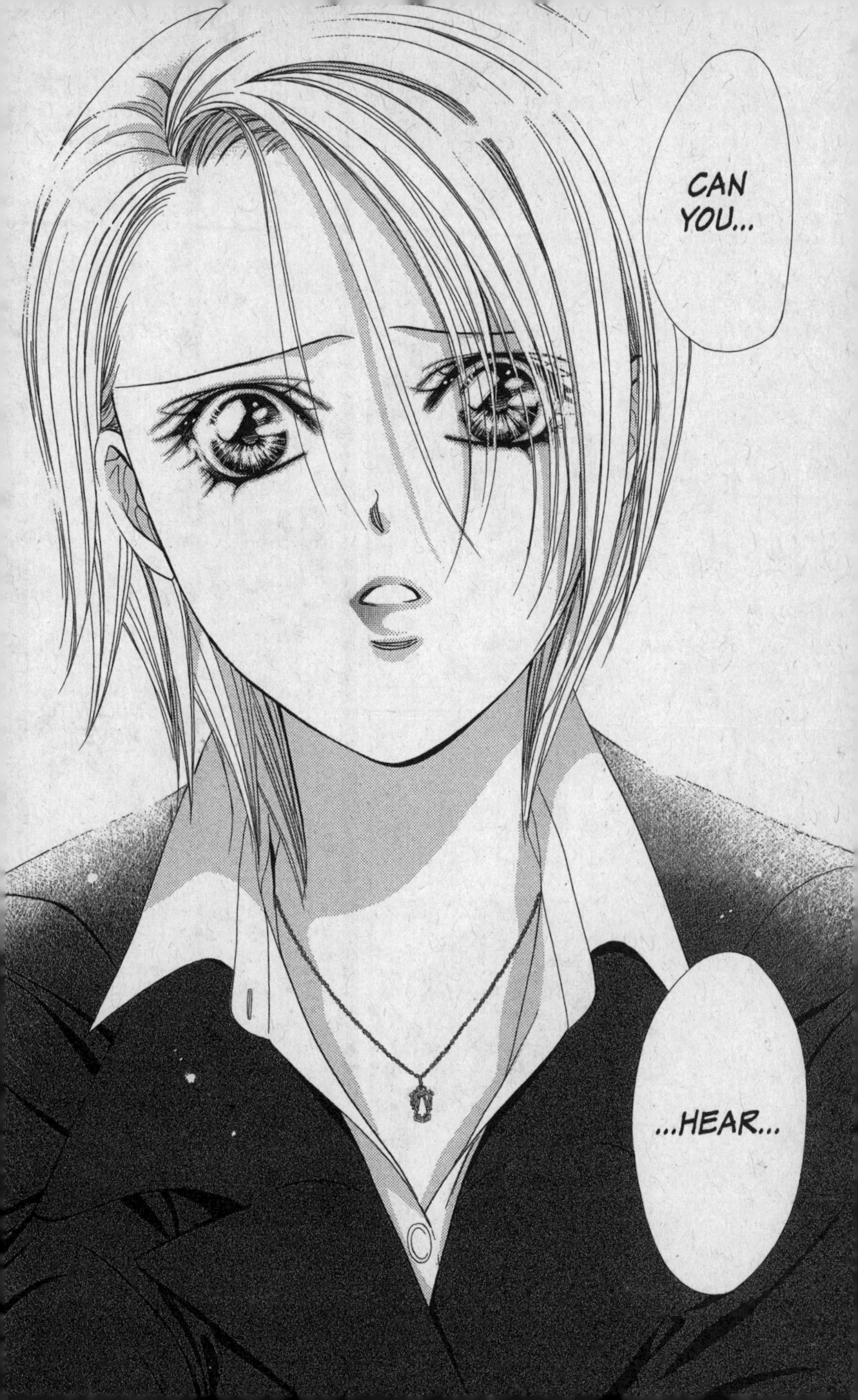
CAN YOU...
...HEAR...

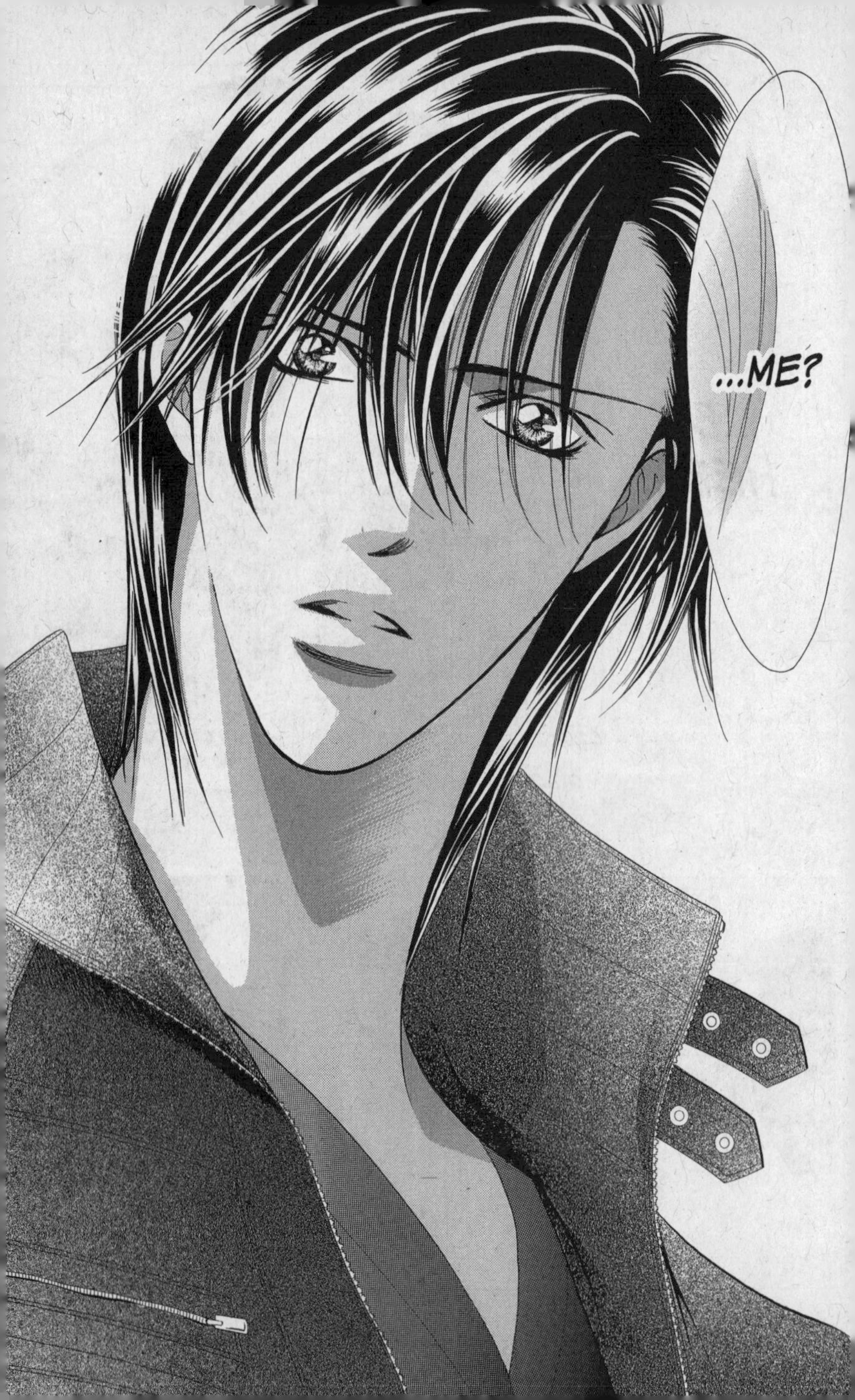
...ME?

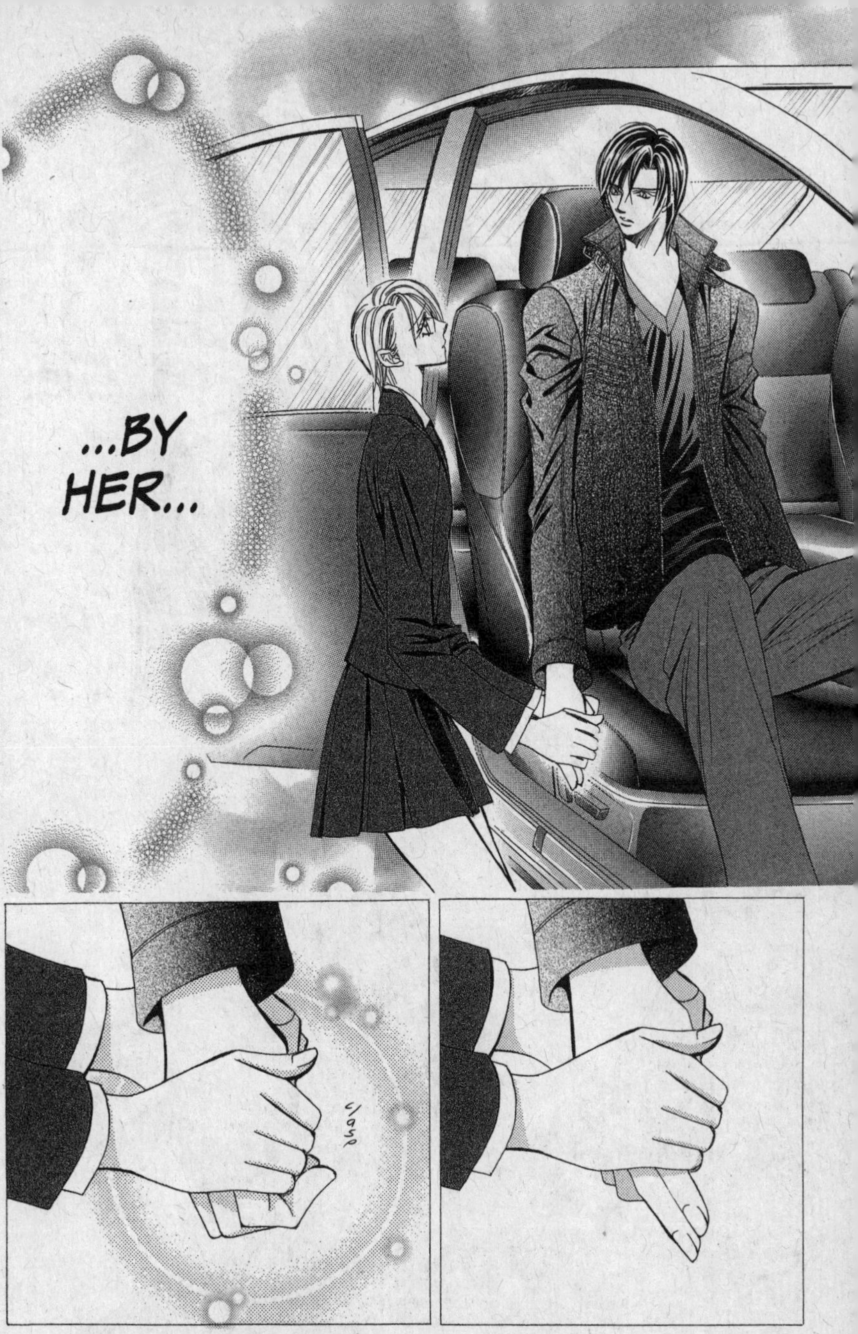
...BY HER...
clasp

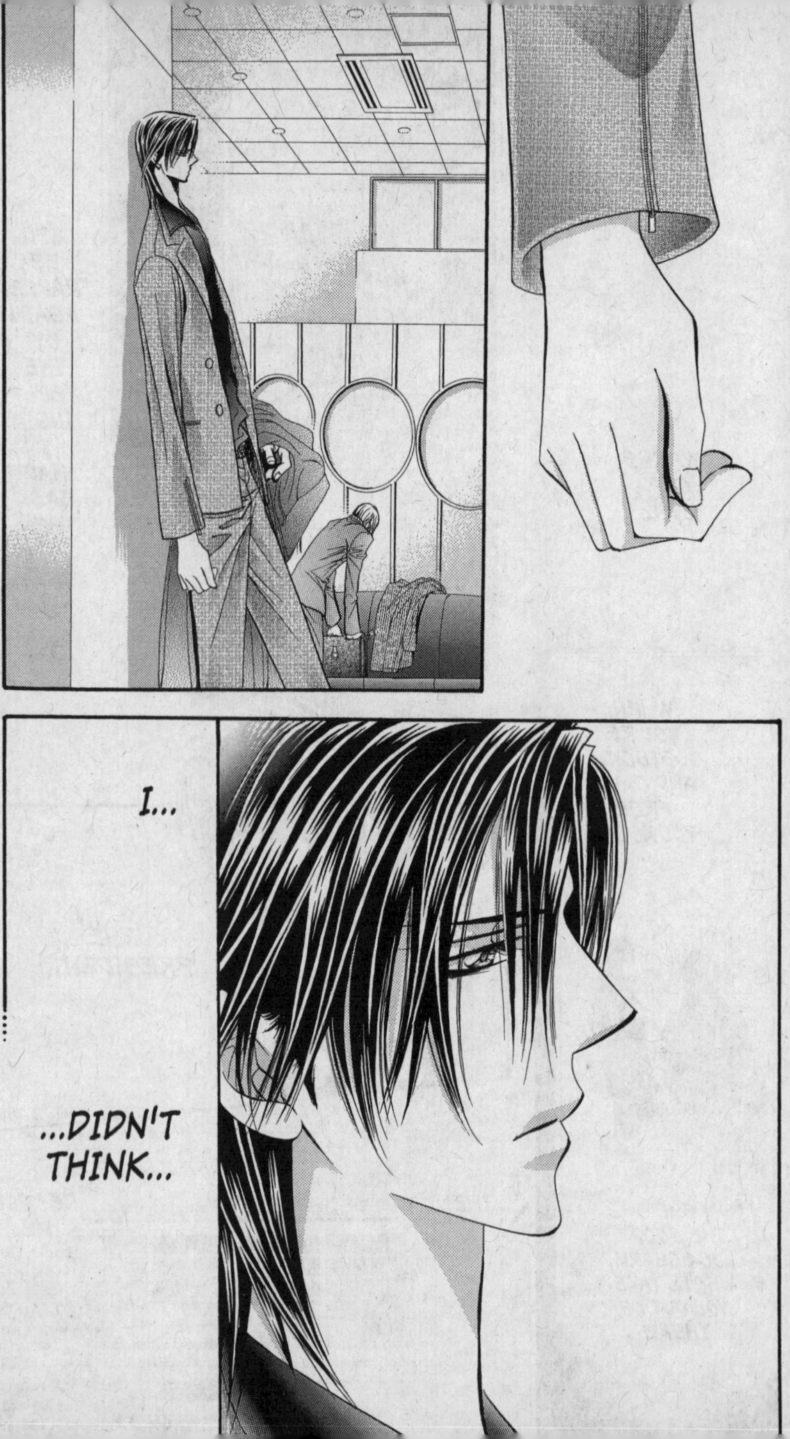
I...
...DIDN'T THINK...

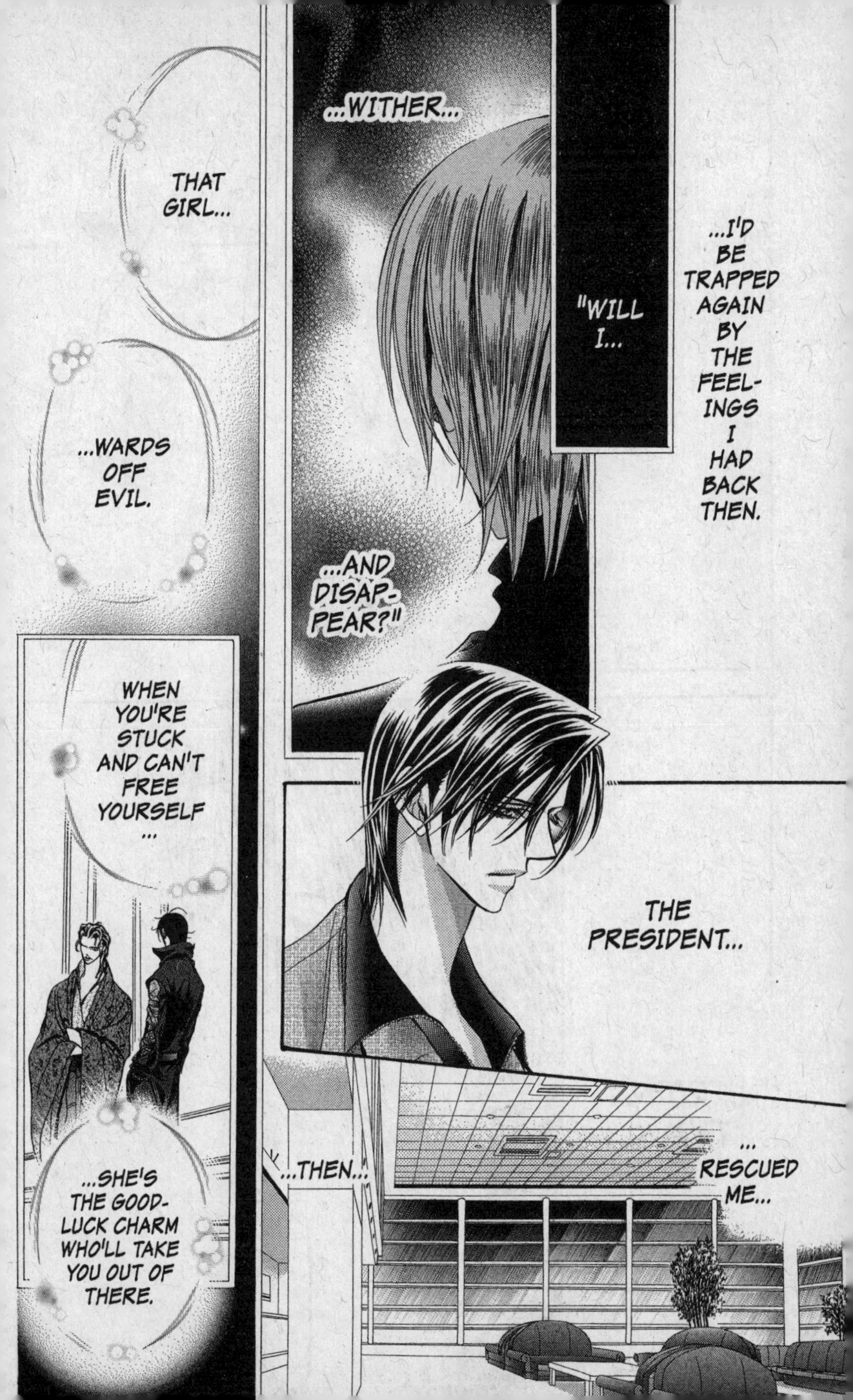
...I'D BE TRAPPED AGAIN BY THE FEELINGS I HAD BACK THEN.
"WILL I...
...WITHER...
...AND DISAP-PEAR?"
THE PRESIDENT...
...THEN...
...RESCUED ME...
THAT GIRL...
...WARDS OFF EVIL.
WHEN YOU'RE STUCK AND CAN'T FREE YOURSELF...
...SHE'S THE GOOD-LUCK CHARM WHO'LL TAKE YOU OUT OF THERE.

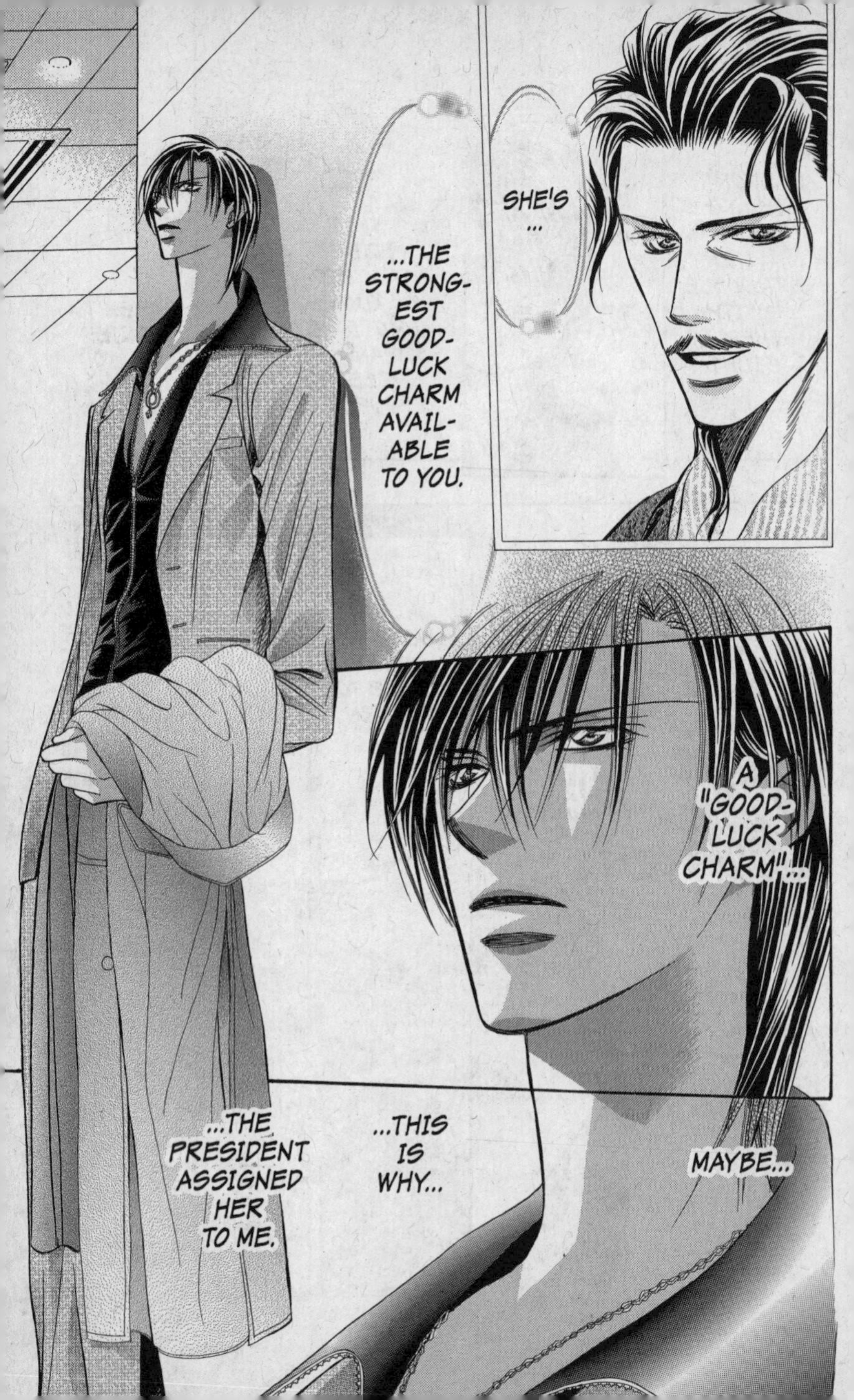
SHE'S ...
...THE STRONGEST GOOD-LUCK CHARM AVAILABLE TO YOU.
A "GOOD-LUCK CHARM"...
MAYBE...
...THIS IS WHY...
...THE PRESIDENT ASSIGNED HER TO ME.

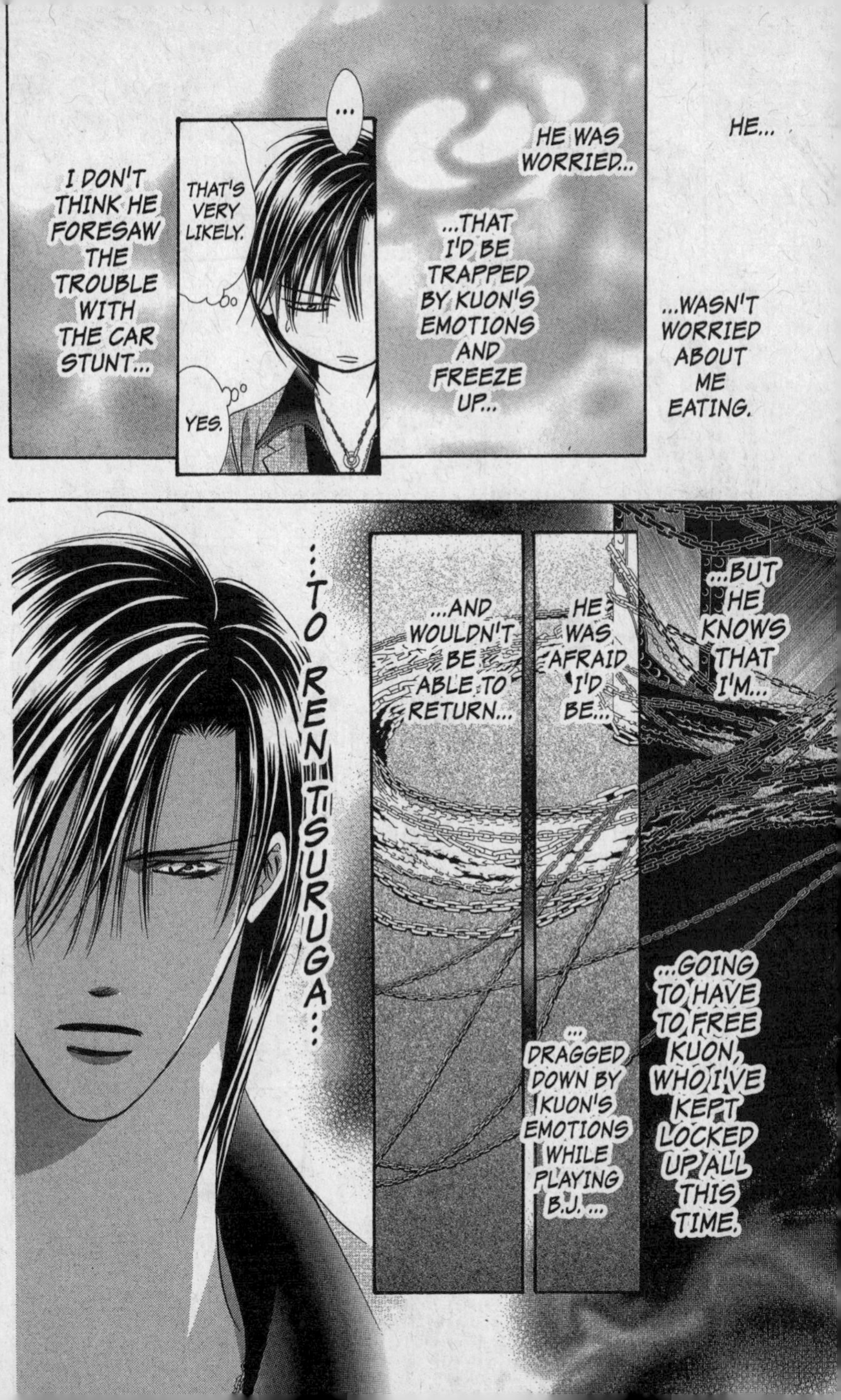
HE...
...WASN'T WORRIED ABOUT ME EATING.
HE WAS WORRIED...
...THAT I'D BE TRAPPED BY KUON'S EMOTIONS AND FREEZE UP...
...
THAT'S VERY LIKELY.
YES.
I DON'T THINK HE FORESAW THE TROUBLE WITH THE CAR STUNT...
...BUT HE KNOWS THAT I'M...
...GOING TO HAVE TO FREE KUON, WHO I'VE KEPT LOCKED UP ALL THIS TIME.
HE WAS AFRAID I'D BE...
...DRAGGED DOWN BY KUON'S EMOTIONS WHILE PLAYING B.J. ...
...AND WOULDN'T BE ABLE TO RETURN...
...TO REN TSURUGA...

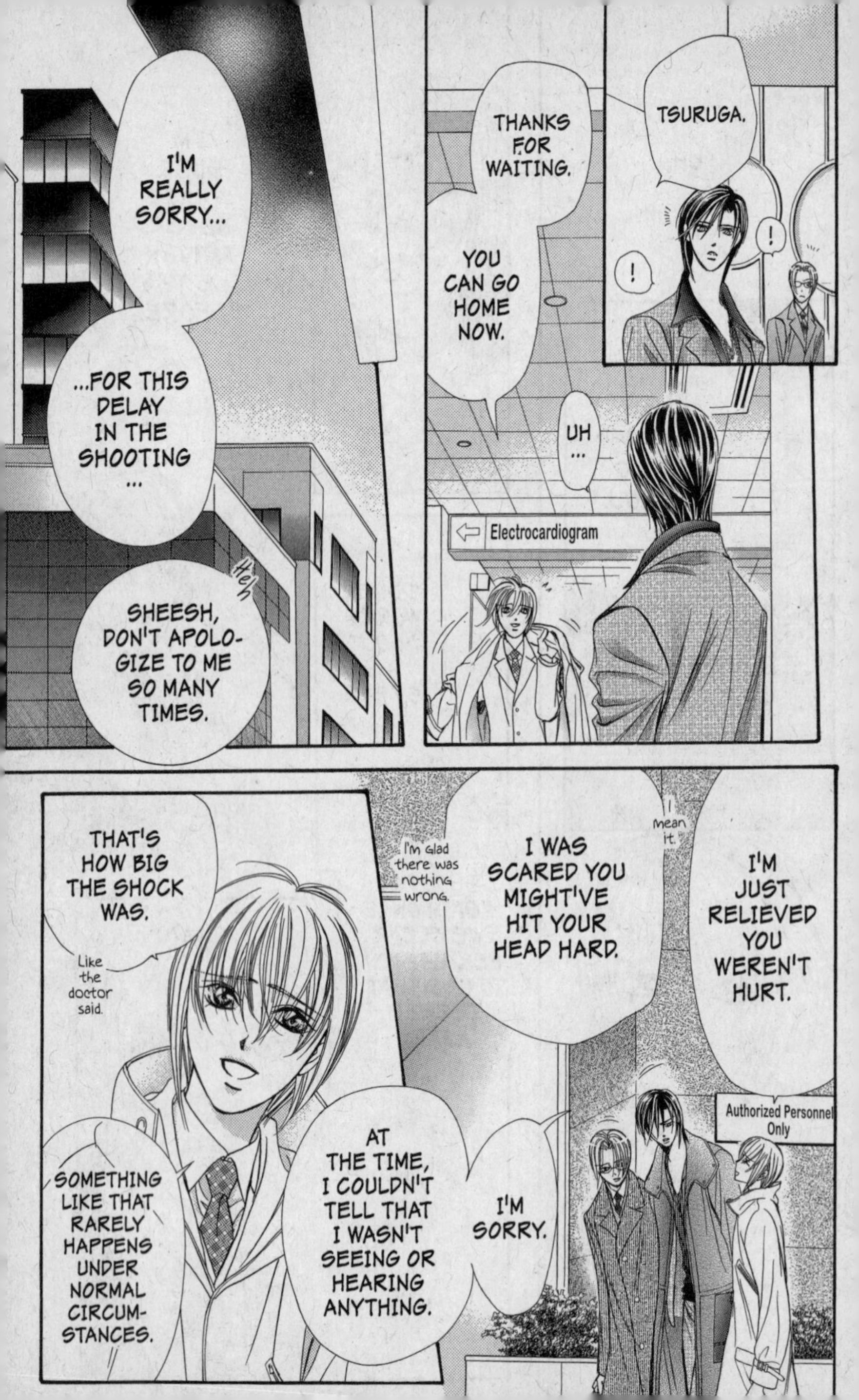
TSURUGA.
THANKS FOR WAITING.
YOU CAN GO HOME NOW.
UH...
Electrocardiogram
I'M REALLY SORRY...
...FOR THIS DELAY IN THE SHOOTING...
Heh
SHEESH, DON'T APOLOGIZE TO ME SO MANY TIMES.
I'M JUST RELIEVED YOU WEREN'T HURT.
I mean it.
I WAS SCARED YOU MIGHT'VE HIT YOUR HEAD HARD.
I'm glad there was nothing wrong.
Authorized Personnel Only
I'M SORRY.
AT THE TIME, I COULDN'T TELL THAT I WASN'T SEEING OR HEARING ANYTHING.
THAT'S HOW BIG THE SHOCK WAS.
Like the doctor said.
SOMETHING LIKE THAT RARELY HAPPENS UNDER NORMAL CIRCUM-STANCES.

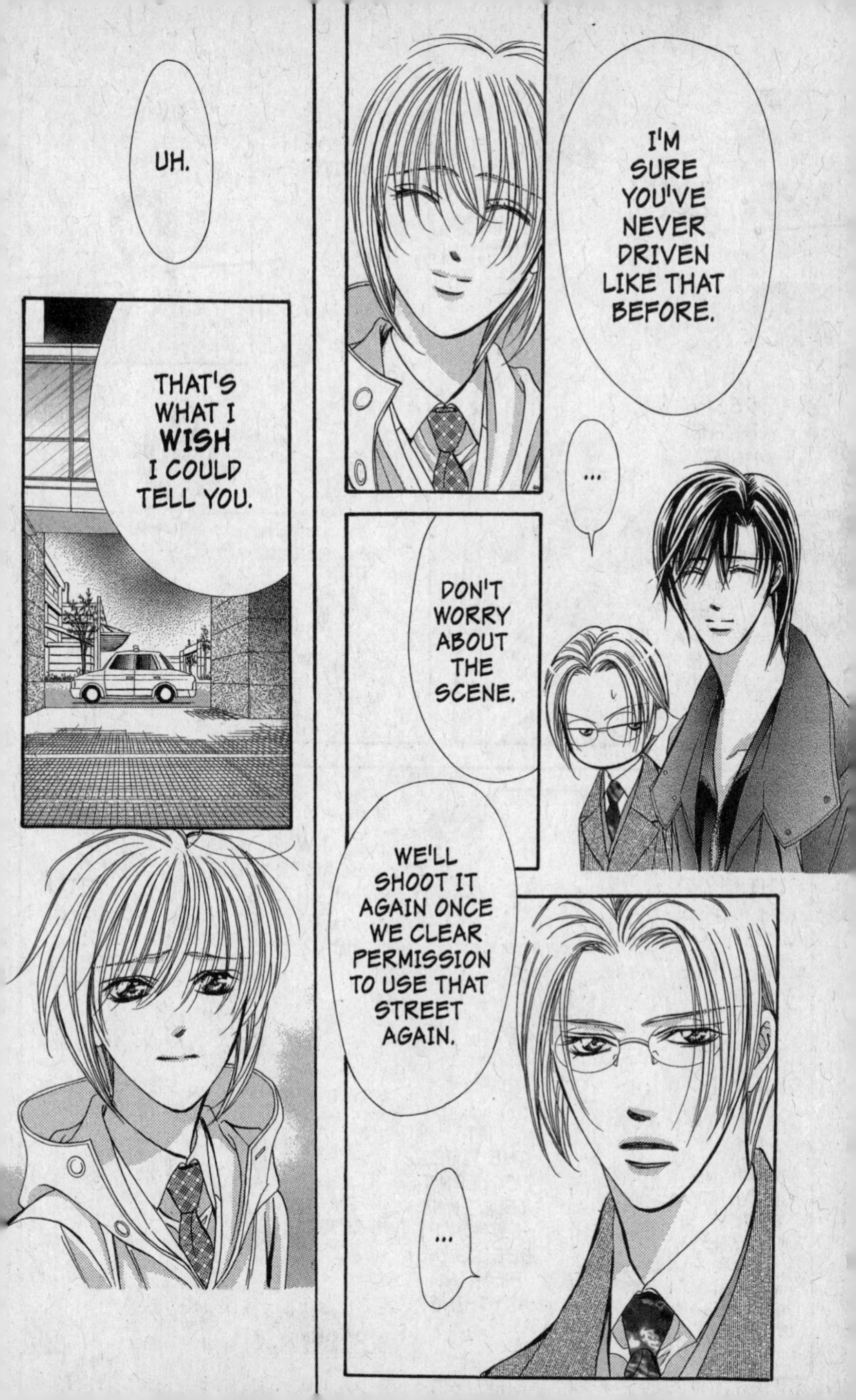
I'M SURE YOU'VE NEVER DRIVEN LIKE THAT BEFORE.
...
DON'T WORRY ABOUT THE SCENE.
WE'LL SHOOT IT AGAIN ONCE WE CLEAR PERMISSION TO USE THAT STREET AGAIN.
...
UH.
THAT'S WHAT I **WISH** I COULD TELL YOU.

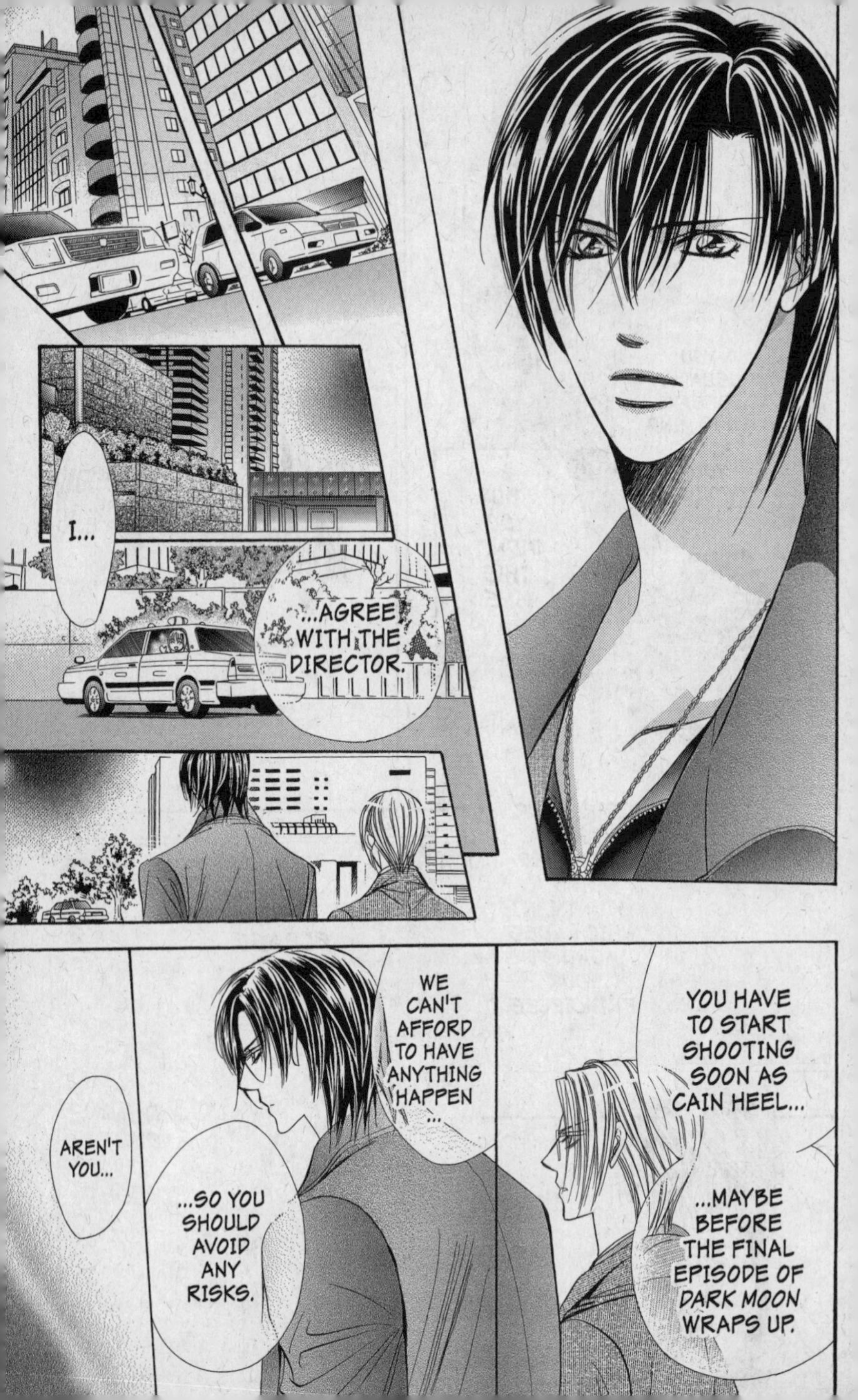
I...
...AGREE WITH THE DIRECTOR.
YOU HAVE TO START SHOOTING SOON AS CAIN HEEL...
...MAYBE BEFORE THE FINAL EPISODE OF DARK MOON WRAPS UP.
WE CAN'T AFFORD TO HAVE ANYTHING HAPPEN...
...SO YOU SHOULD AVOID ANY RISKS.
AREN'T YOU...

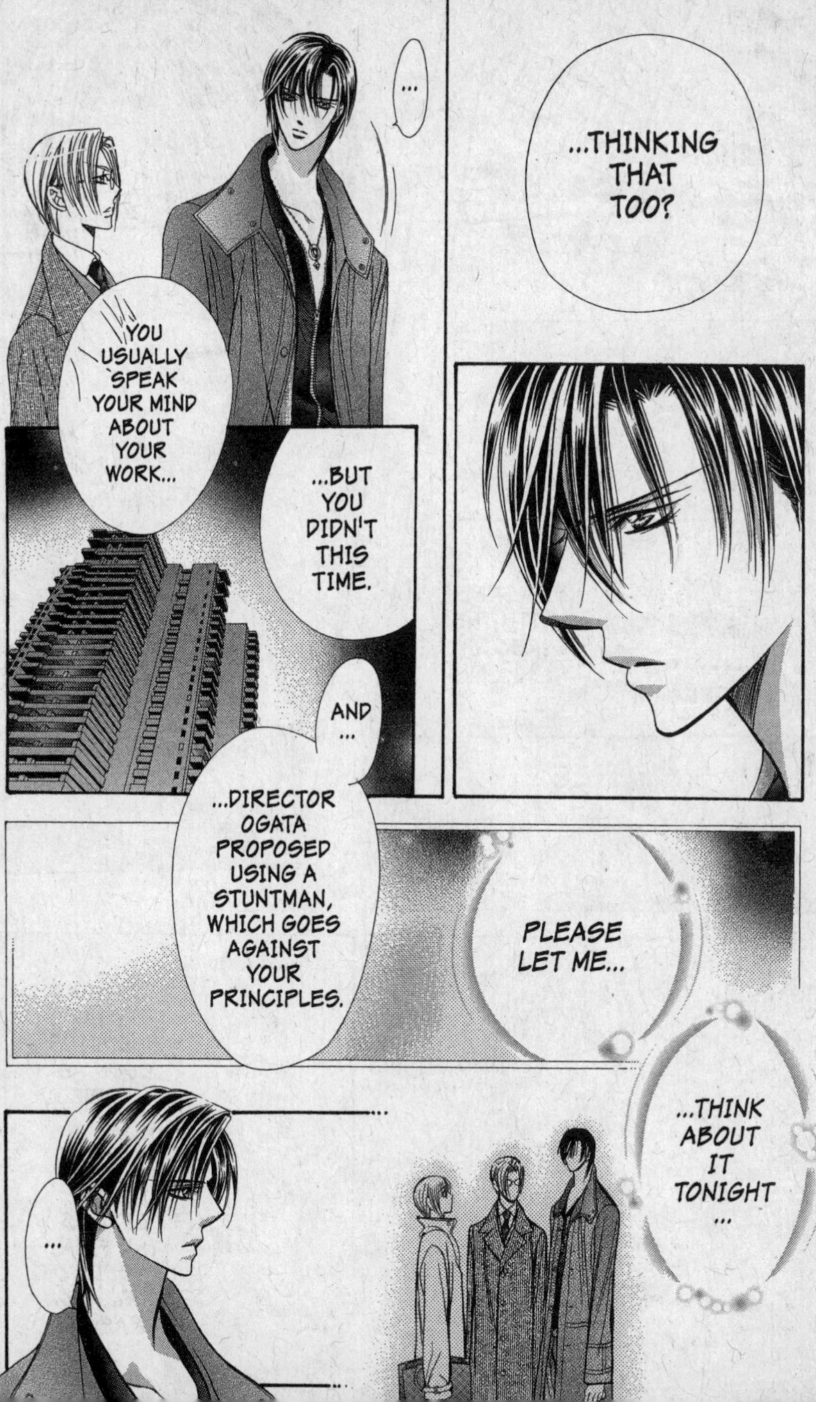
...THINKING THAT TOO?
...
YOU USUALLY SPEAK YOUR MIND ABOUT YOUR WORK...
...BUT YOU DIDN'T THIS TIME.
AND...
...DIRECTOR OGATA PROPOSED USING A STUNTMAN, WHICH GOES AGAINST YOUR PRINCIPLES.
PLEASE LET ME...
...THINK ABOUT IT TONIGHT...
...

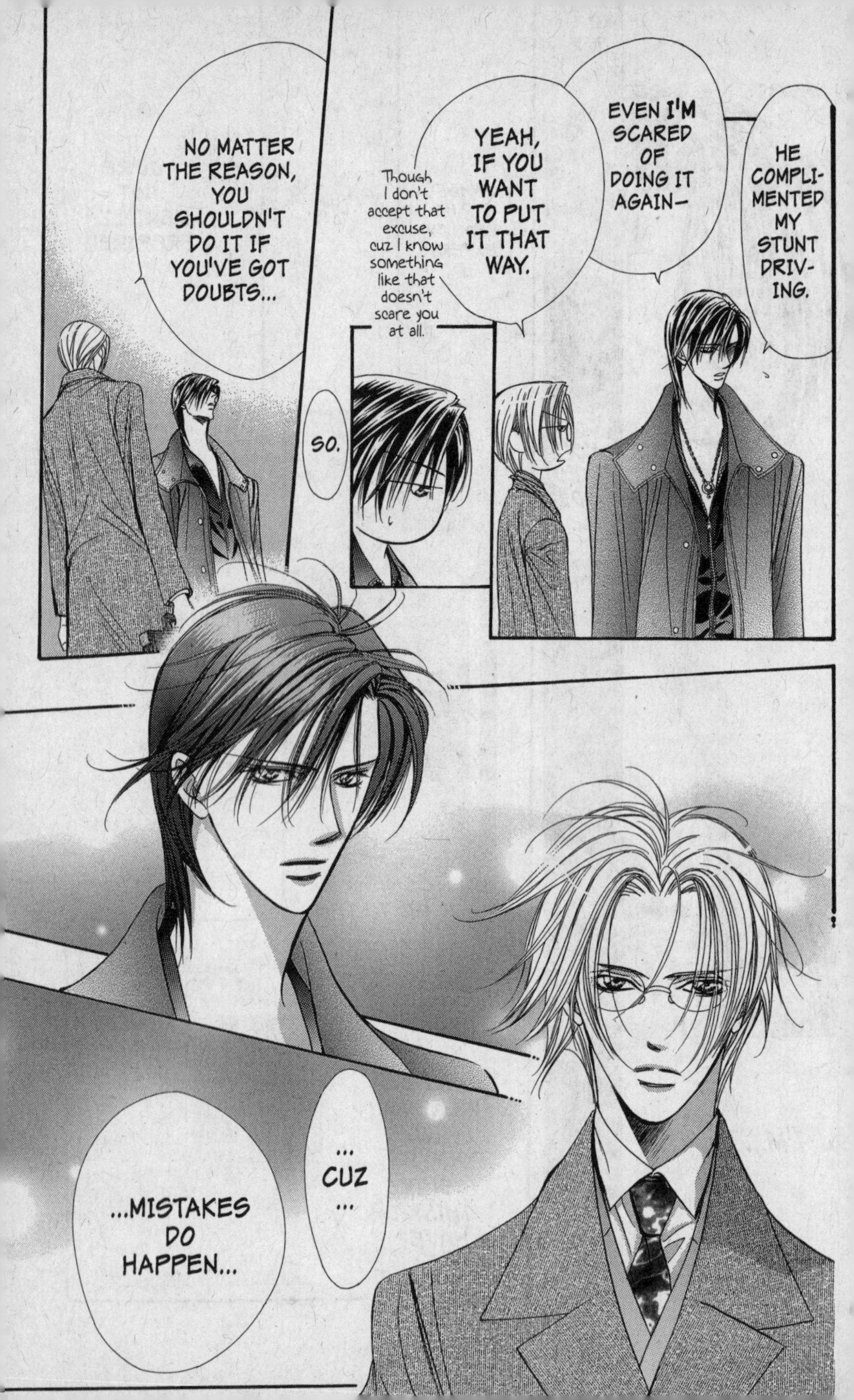
HE COMPLIMENTED MY STUNT DRIVING.
EVEN I'M SCARED OF DOING IT AGAIN—
YEAH, IF YOU WANT TO PUT IT THAT WAY.
Though I don't accept that excuse, cuz I know something like that doesn't scare you at all.
SO.
NO MATTER THE REASON, YOU SHOULDN'T DO IT IF YOU'VE GOT DOUBTS...
...CUZ...
...MISTAKES DO HAPPEN...

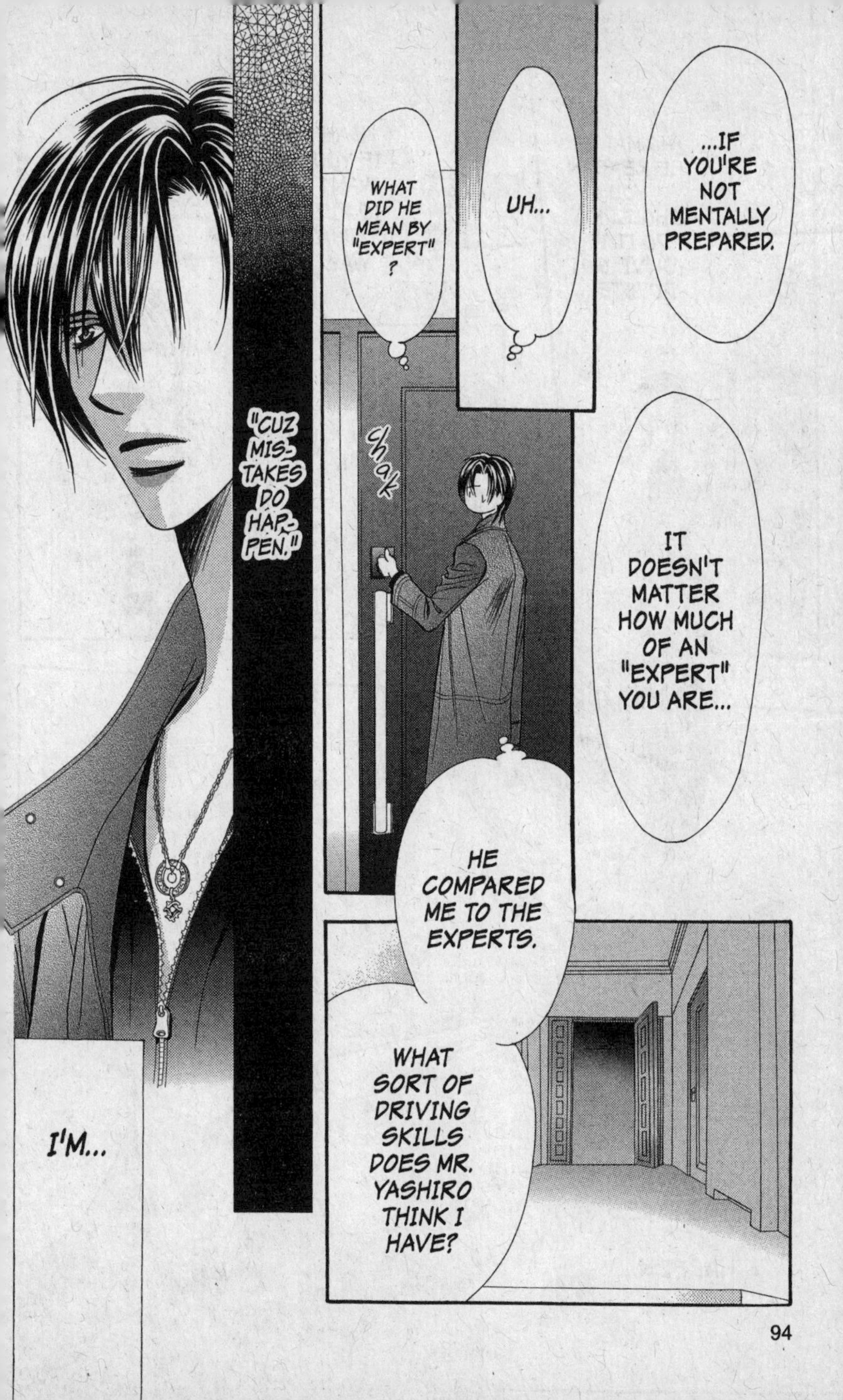
...IF YOU'RE NOT MENTALLY PREPARED.
UH...
WHAT DID HE MEAN BY "EXPERT" ?
shak
IT DOESN'T MATTER HOW MUCH OF AN "EXPERT" YOU ARE...
HE COMPARED ME TO THE EXPERTS.
WHAT SORT OF DRIVING SKILLS DOES MR. YASHIRO THINK I HAVE?
"CUZ MIS-TAKES DO HAP-PEN."
I'M...

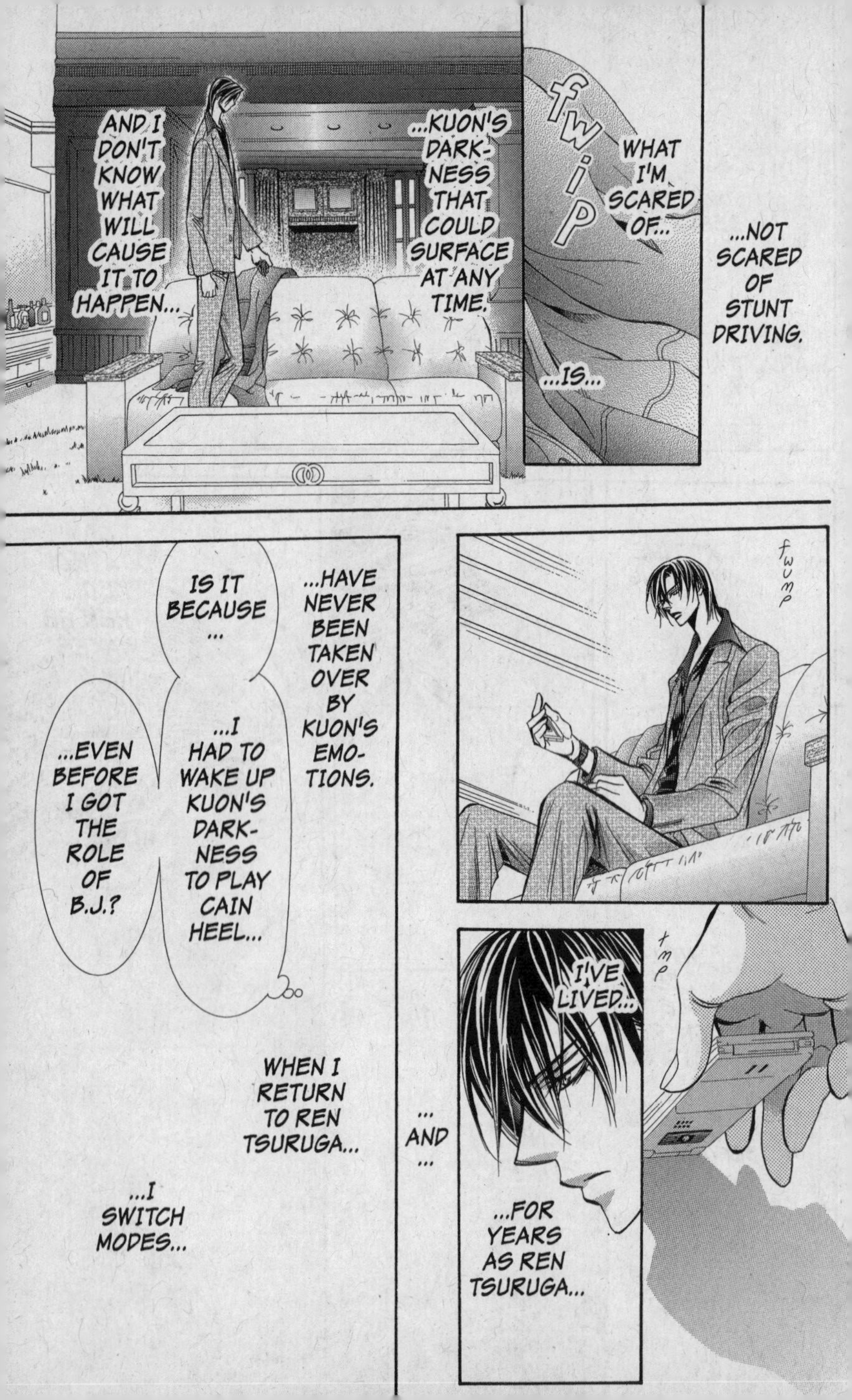
...NOT SCARED OF STUNT DRIVING.
fwip
WHAT I'M SCARED OF...
...IS...
...KUON'S DARKNESS THAT COULD SURFACE AT ANY TIME.
AND I DON'T KNOW WHAT WILL CAUSE IT TO HAPPEN...
fwump
tmp
I'VE LIVED...
...FOR YEARS AS REN TSURUGA...
...AND...
WHEN I RETURN TO REN TSURUGA...
...I SWITCH MODES...
...HAVE NEVER BEEN TAKEN OVER BY KUON'S EMOTIONS.
IS IT BECAUSE...
...I HAD TO WAKE UP KUON'S DARKNESS TO PLAY CAIN HEEL...
...EVEN BEFORE I GOT THE ROLE OF B.J.?

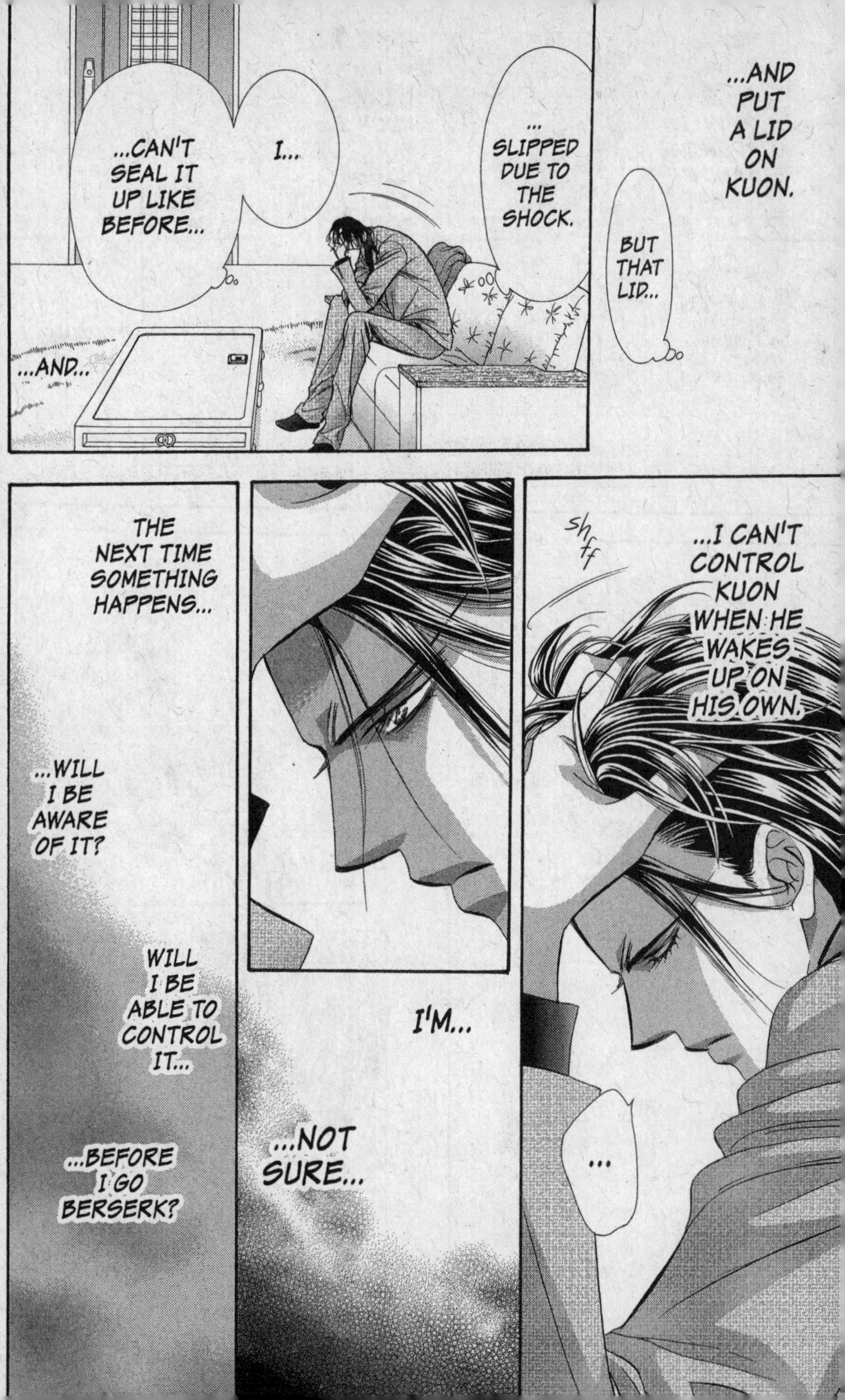
...AND PUT A LID ON KUON.
BUT THAT LID...
... SLIPPED DUE TO THE SHOCK.
I...
...CAN'T SEAL IT UP LIKE BEFORE...
...AND...
shff
...I CAN'T CONTROL KUON WHEN HE WAKES UP ON HIS OWN.
...
THE NEXT TIME SOMETHING HAPPENS...
...WILL I BE AWARE OF IT?
WILL I BE ABLE TO CONTROL IT...
...BEFORE I GO BERSERK?
I'M...
...NOT SURE...

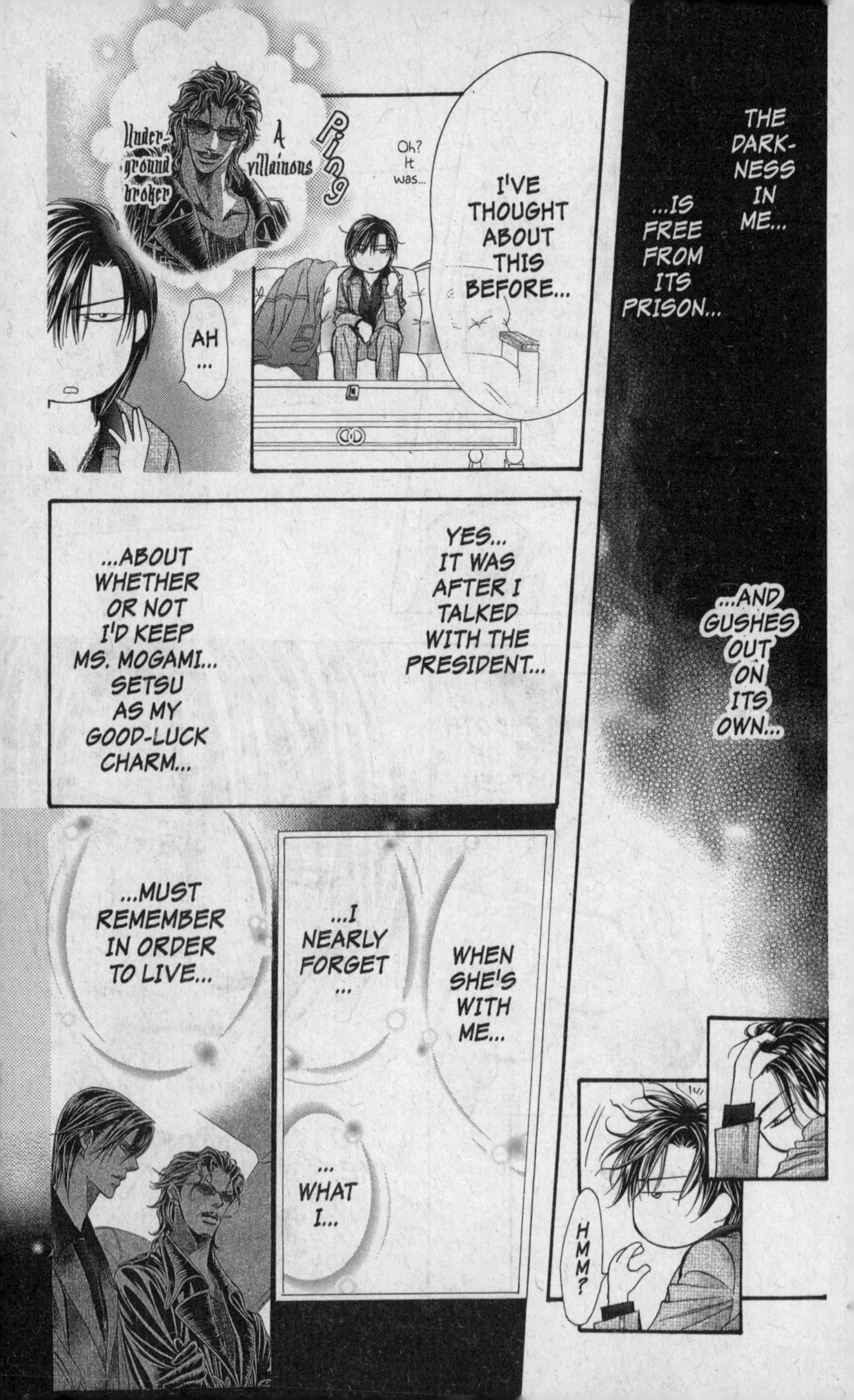
THE DARKNESS IN ME...
...IS FREE FROM ITS PRISON...
...AND GUSHES OUT ON ITS OWN...
HMM?
Ping
I'VE THOUGHT ABOUT THIS BEFORE...
Oh? It was...
A villainous
Underground broker
AH...
YES... IT WAS AFTER I TALKED WITH THE PRESIDENT...
...ABOUT WHETHER OR NOT I'D KEEP MS. MOGAMI... SETSU AS MY GOOD-LUCK CHARM...
WHEN SHE'S WITH ME...
...I NEARLY FORGET...
...WHAT I...
...MUST REMEMBER IN ORDER TO LIVE...

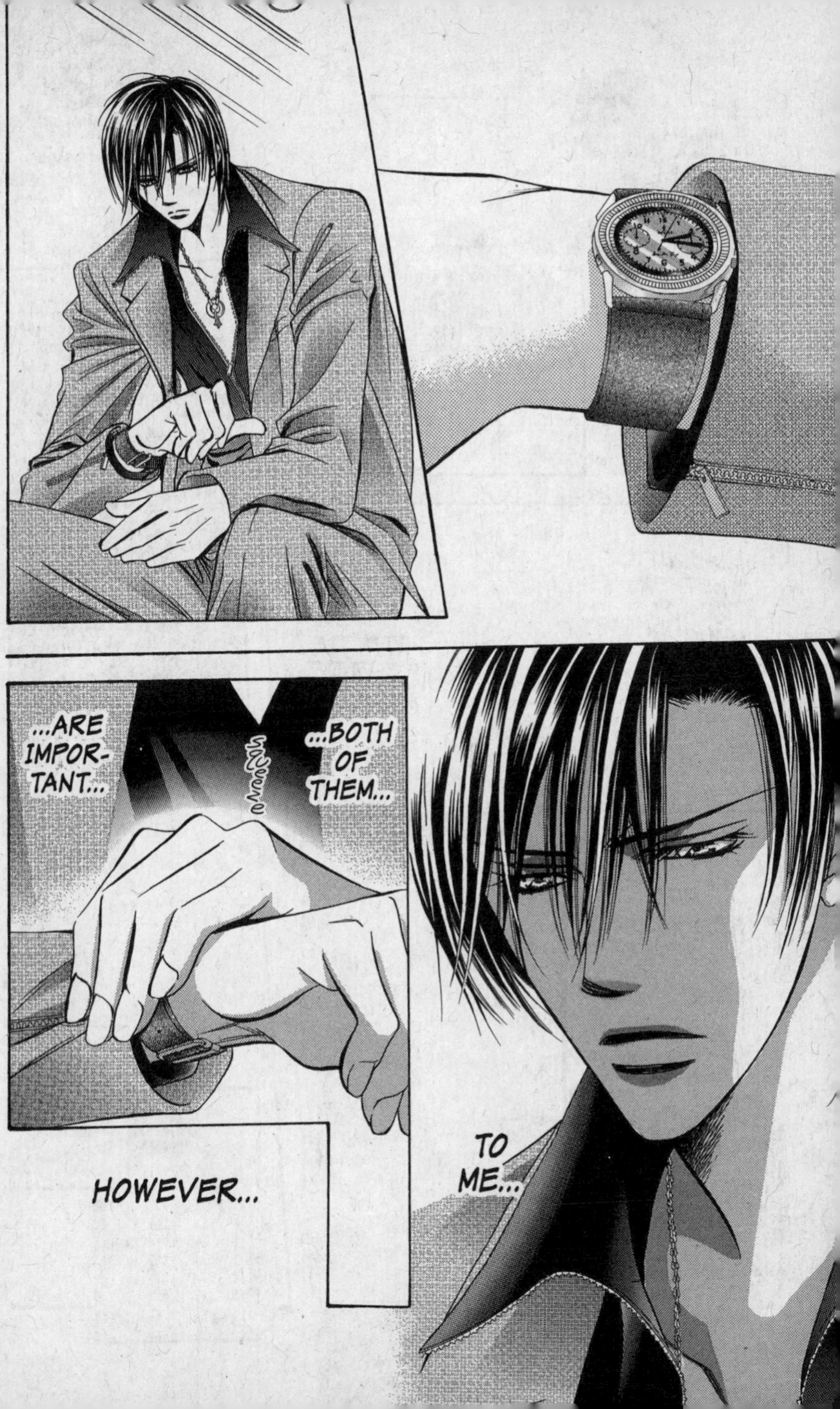
...BOTH OF THEM...
squeeze
...ARE IMPORTANT...
TO ME...
HOWEVER...

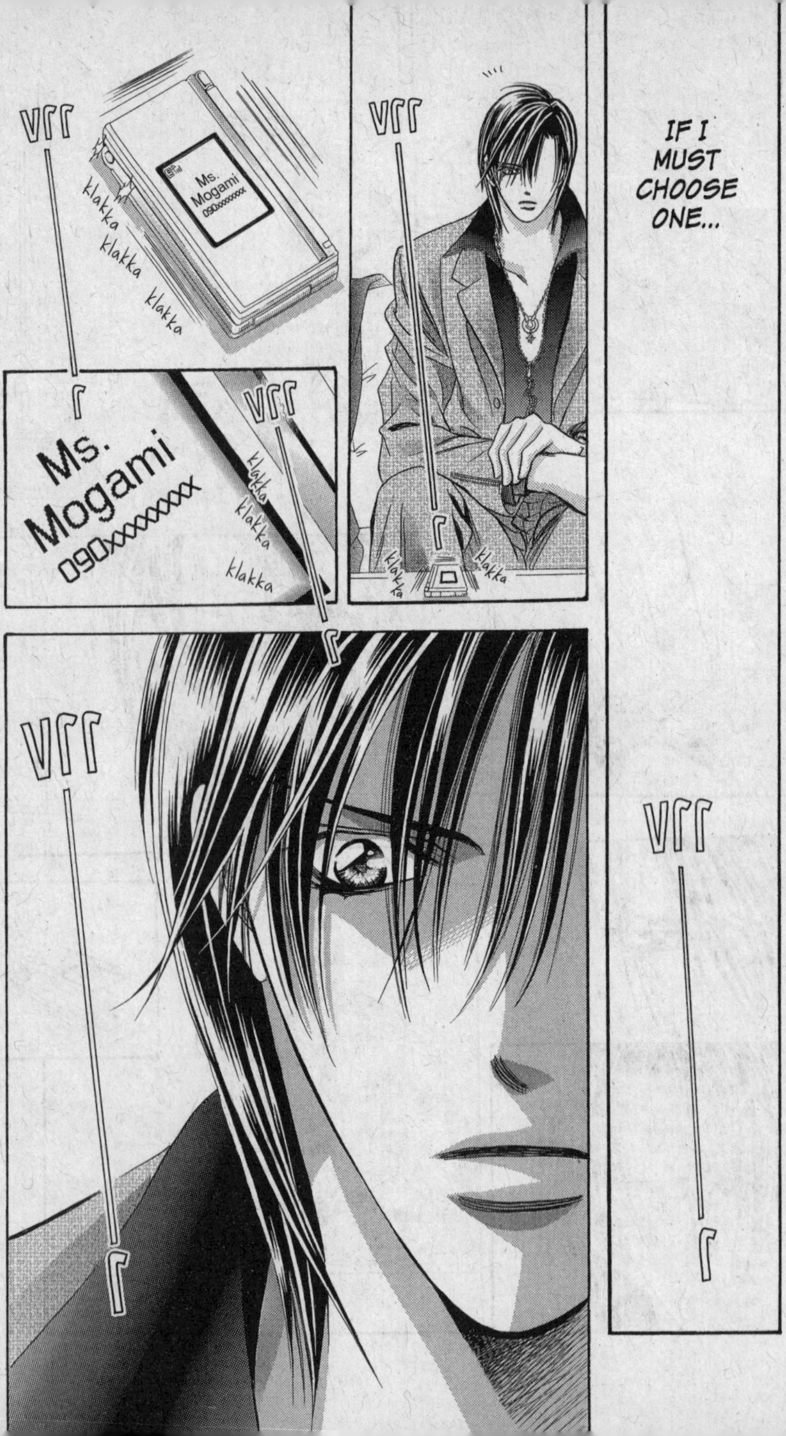
IF I MUST CHOOSE ONE...
Vrr
Vrr
klakka
klakka
Vrr
Ms. Mogami
090xxxxxxx
klakka
klakka
klakka
Vrr
Ms. Mogami
090xxxxxxx
klakka
klakka
klakka
Vrr

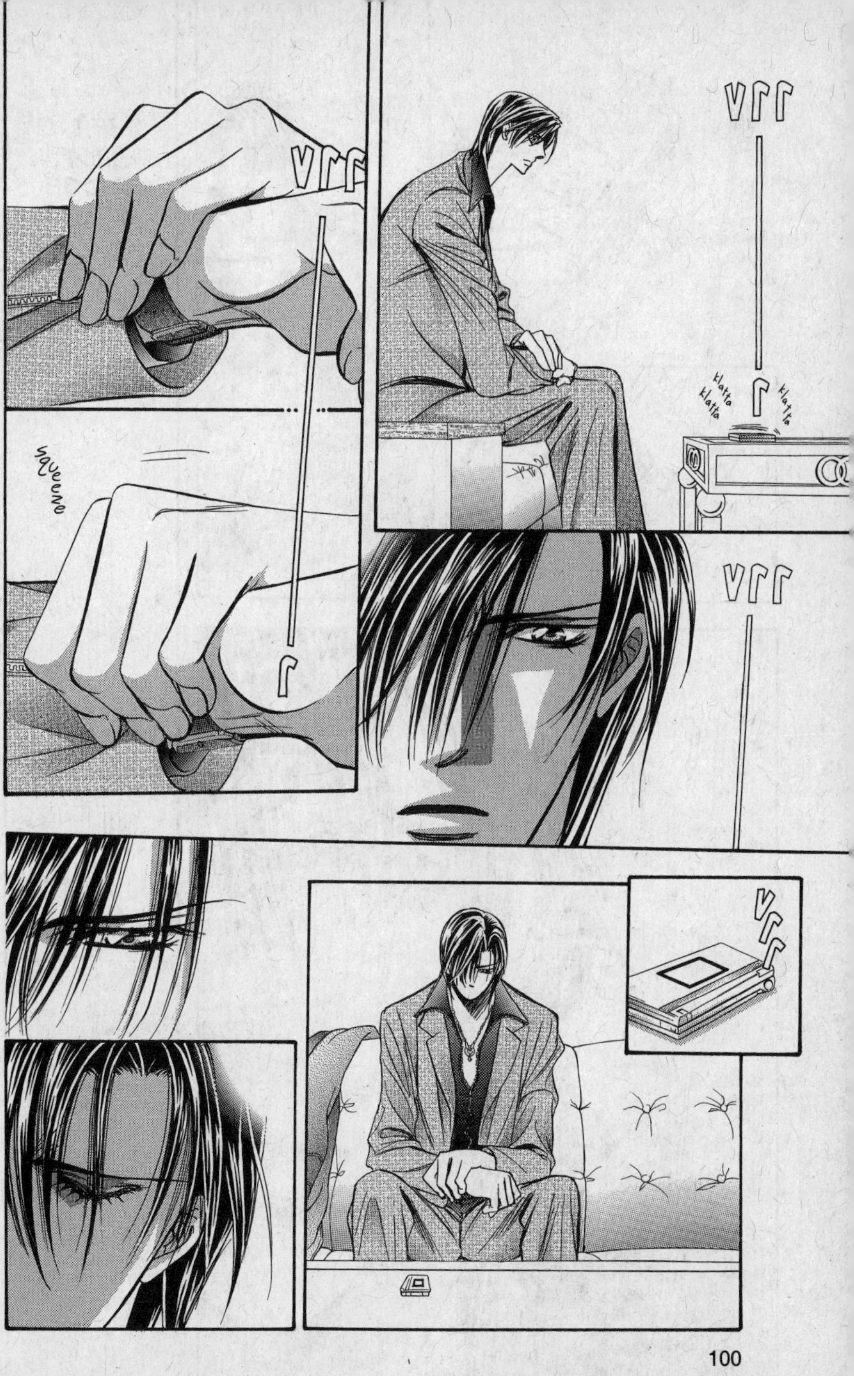
Vrr
klatta klatta klatta
Vrr
squeeeze
Vrr
Vrr

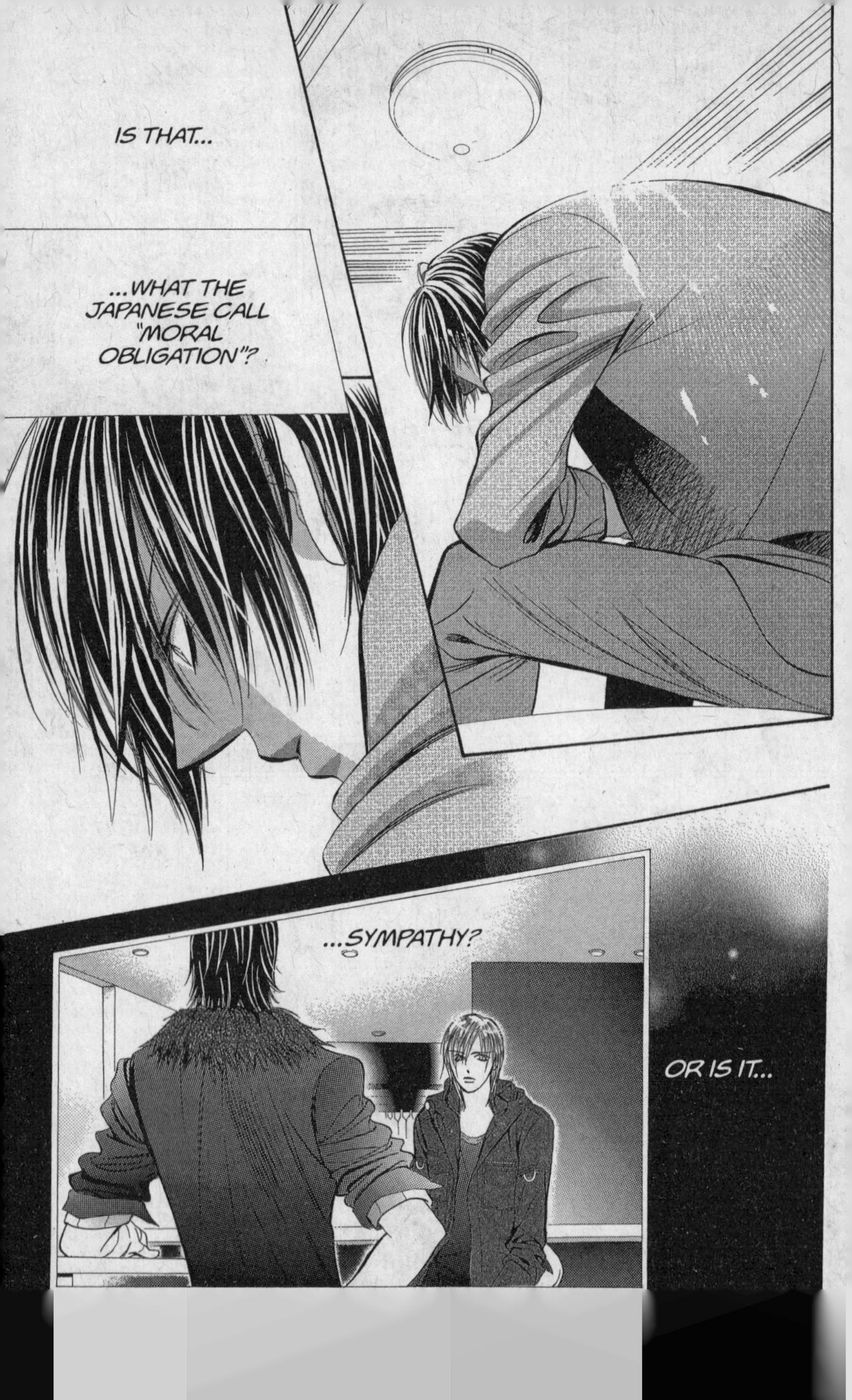
IS THAT...
...WHAT THE JAPANESE CALL "MORAL OBLIGATION"?
OR IS IT...
...SYMPATHY?

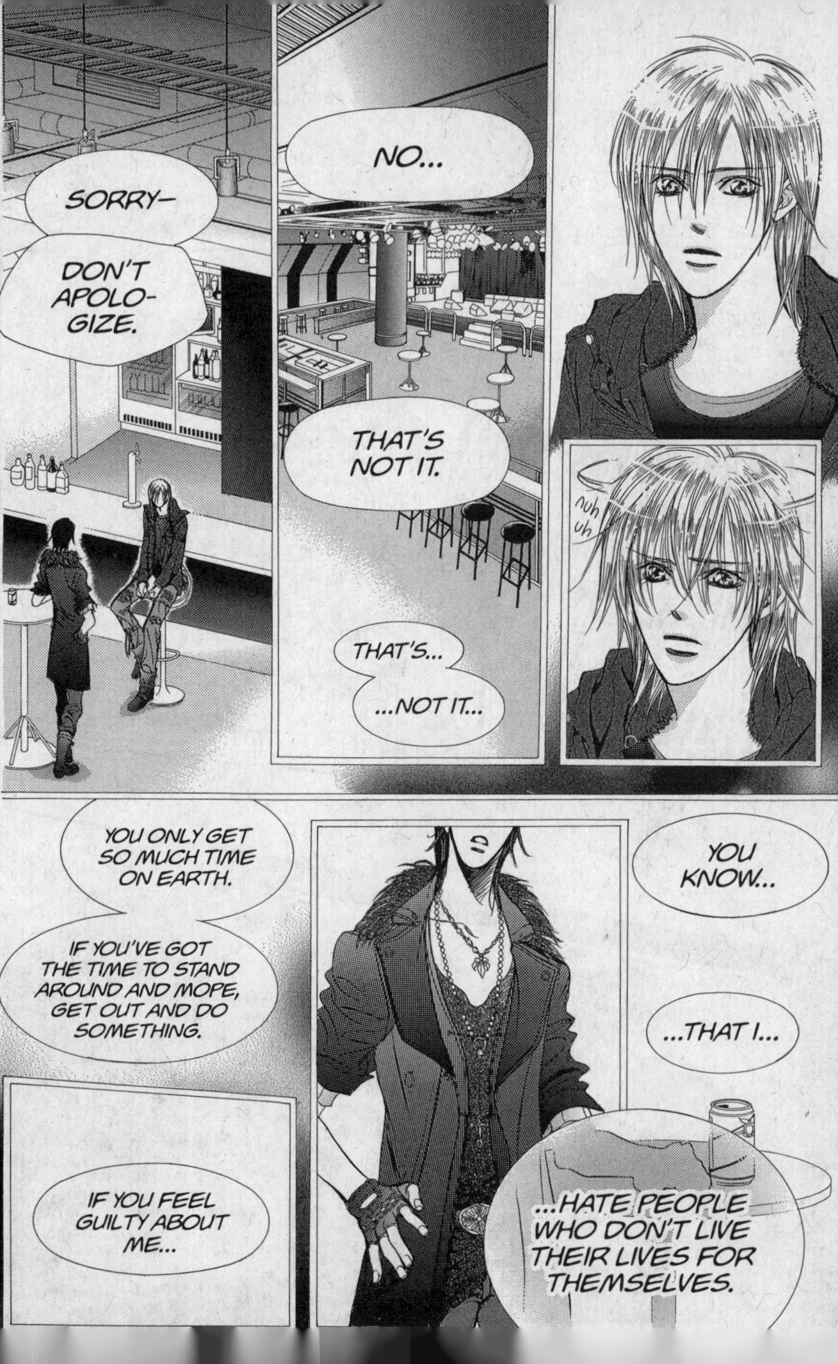
nuh uh
NO...
THAT'S NOT IT.
THAT'S...
...NOT IT...
SORRY—
DON'T APOLO-GIZE.
YOU KNOW...
...THAT I...
...HATE PEOPLE WHO DON'T LIVE THEIR LIVES FOR THEMSELVES.
YOU ONLY GET SO MUCH TIME ON EARTH.
IF YOU'VE GOT THE TIME TO STAND AROUND AND MOPE, GET OUT AND DO SOMETHING.
IF YOU FEEL GUILTY ABOUT ME...

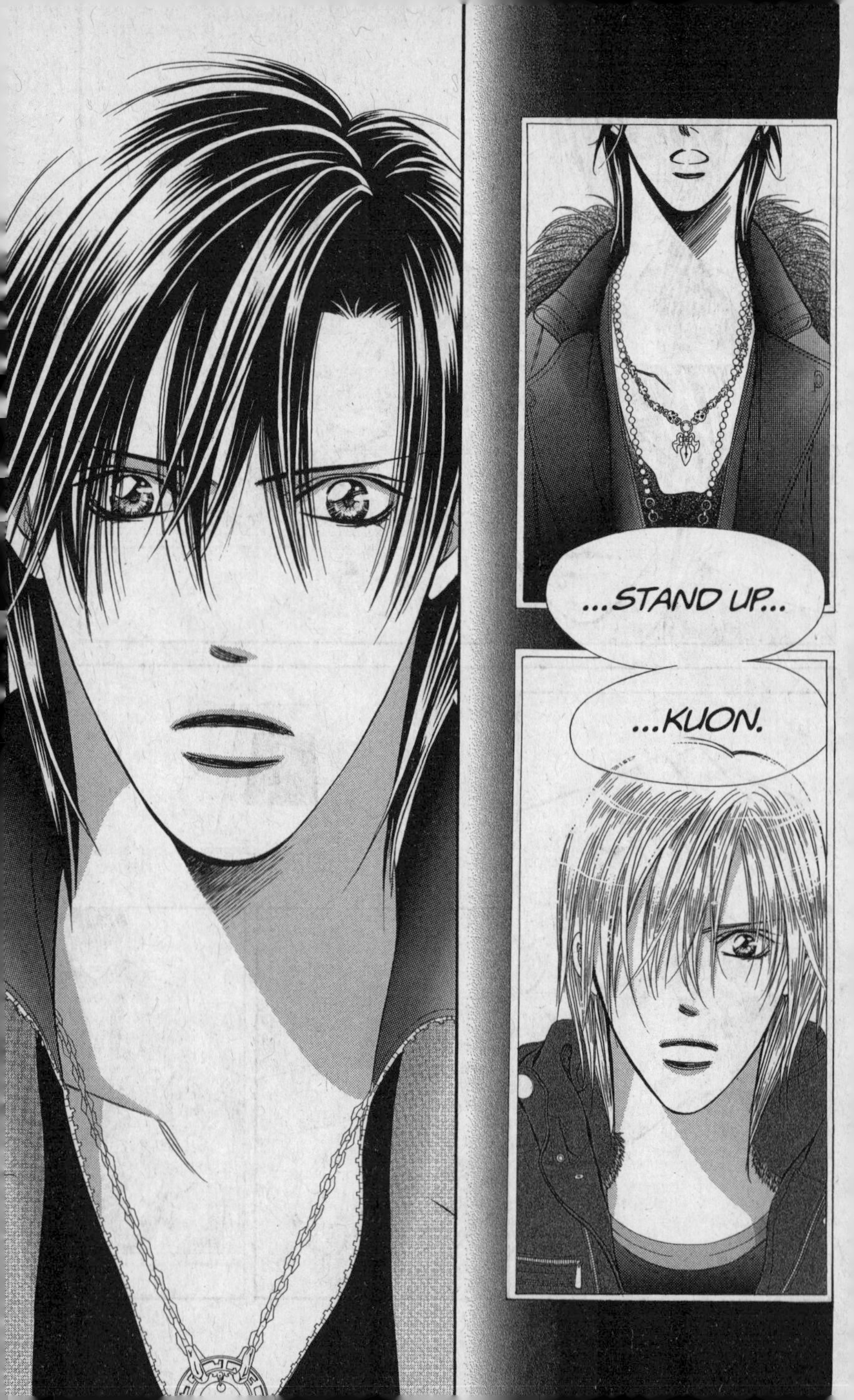
...STAND UP...
...KUON.

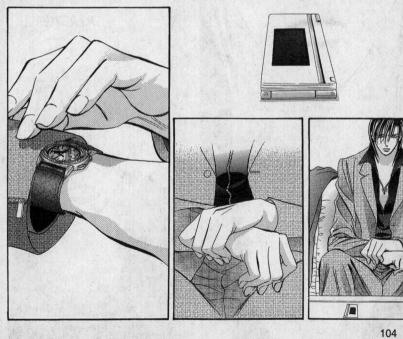

104

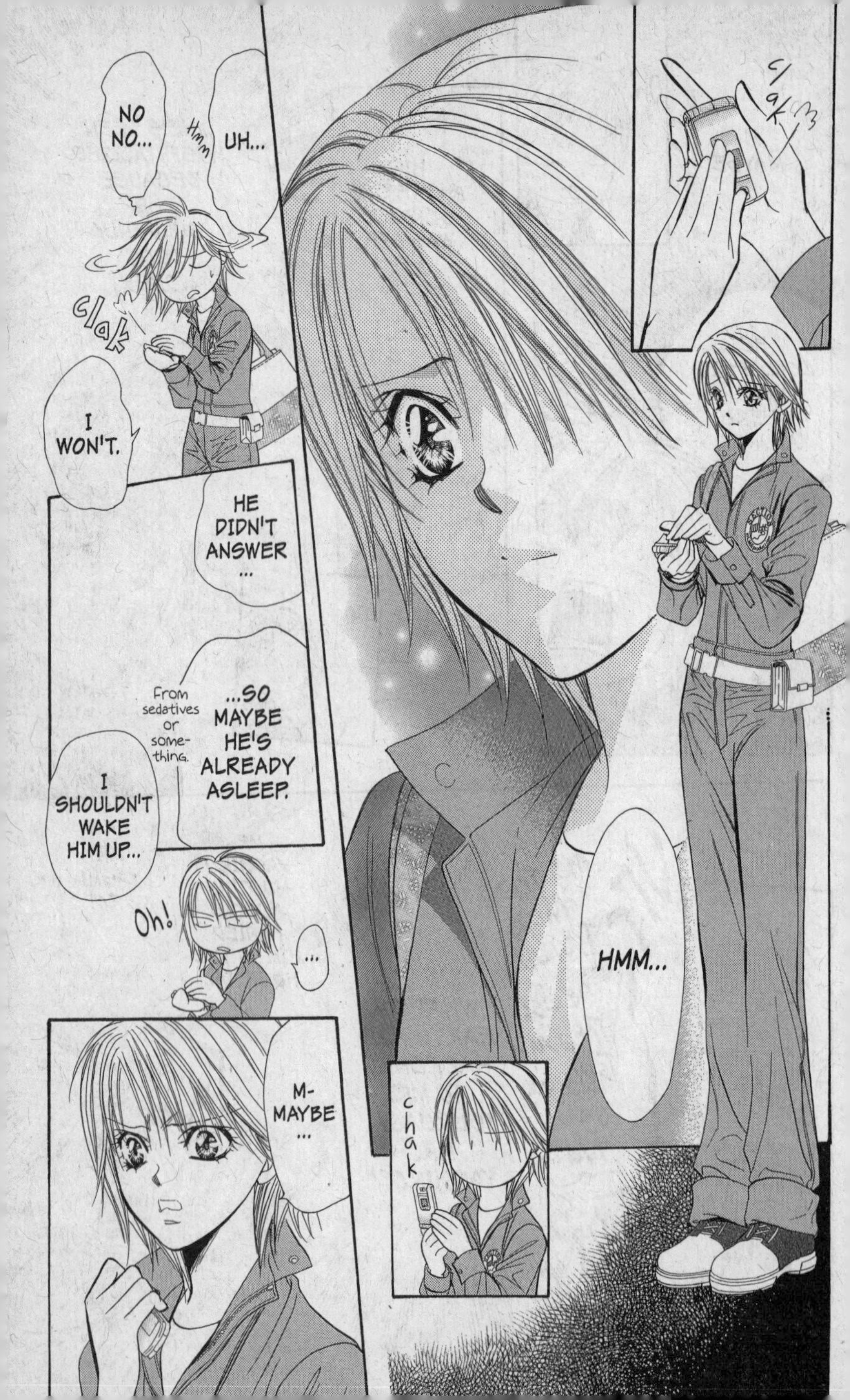

clak
HMM...
UH...
Hmm
NO NO...
clak
I WON'T.
HE DIDN'T ANSWER...
...SO MAYBE HE'S ALREADY ASLEEP.
From sedatives or something.
I SHOULDN'T WAKE HIM UP...
Oh!
...
chak
M-MAYBE...

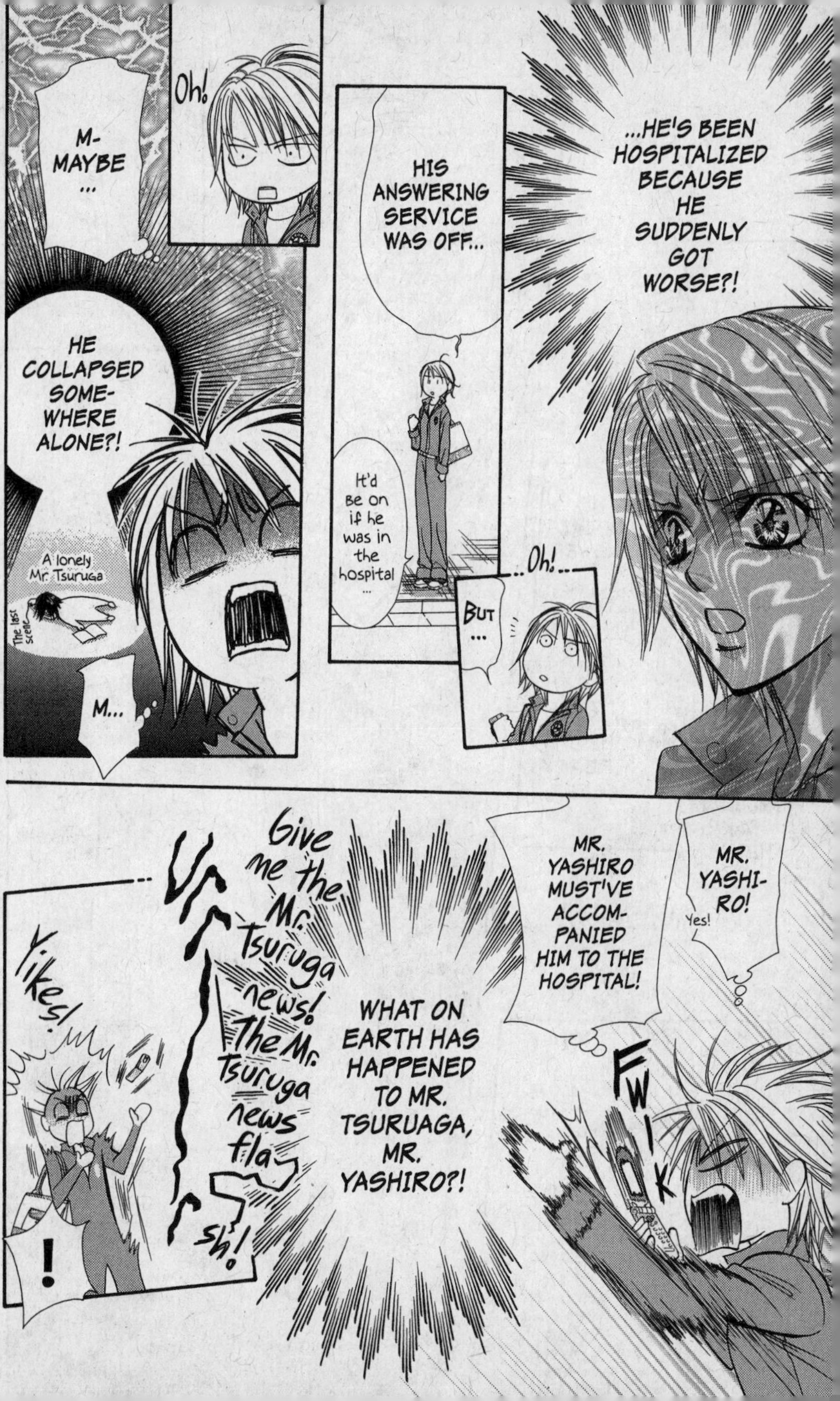
...HE'S BEEN HOSPITALIZED BECAUSE HE SUDDENLY GOT WORSE?!
HIS ANSWERING SERVICE WAS OFF...
It'd be on if he was in the hospital...
...Oh!...
BUT...
Oh!
M-MAYBE...
HE COLLAPSED SOMEWHERE ALONE?!
A lonely Mr. Tsuruga
The last scene
M...
MR. YASHIRO!
Yes!
MR. YASHIRO MUST'VE ACCOMPANIED HIM TO THE HOSPITAL!
FWIK
WHAT ON EARTH HAS HAPPENED TO MR. TSURUAGA, MR. YASHIRO?!
Give me the Mr. Tsuruga news! The Mr. Tsuruga news flash!
Yikes!
!

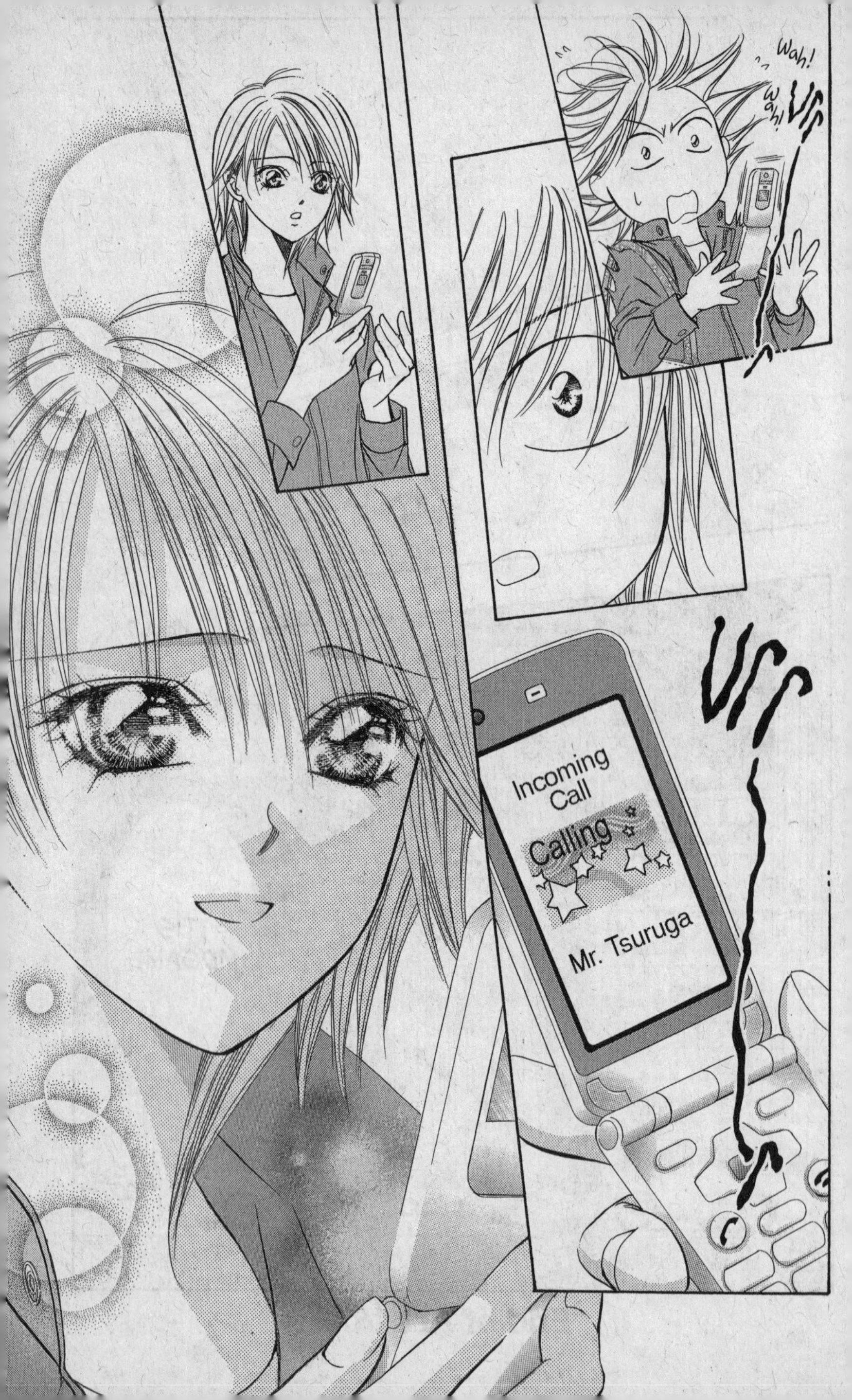
Wah! Wah!
Vrr
Incoming Call
Calling
Mr. Tsuruga
Vrr

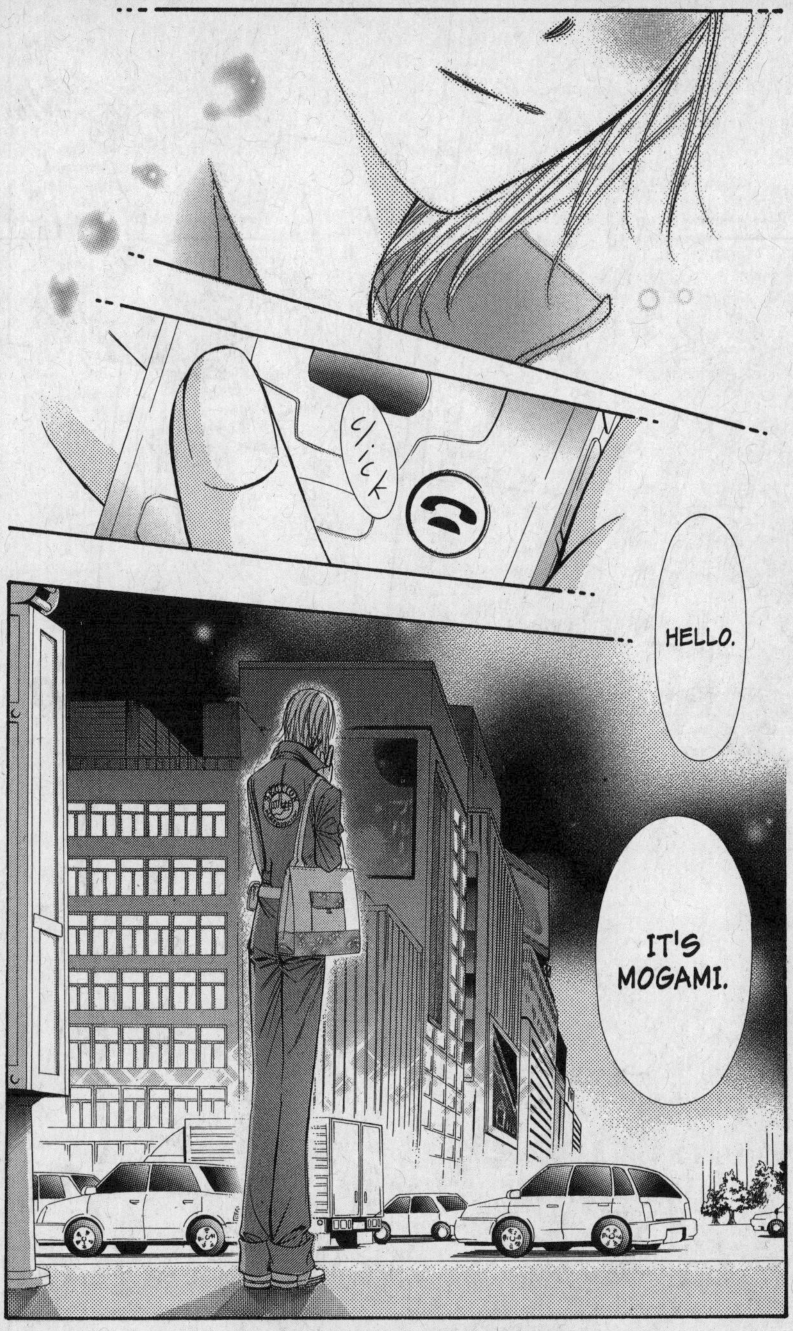
click
HELLO.
IT'S MOGAMI.

End of Act 167

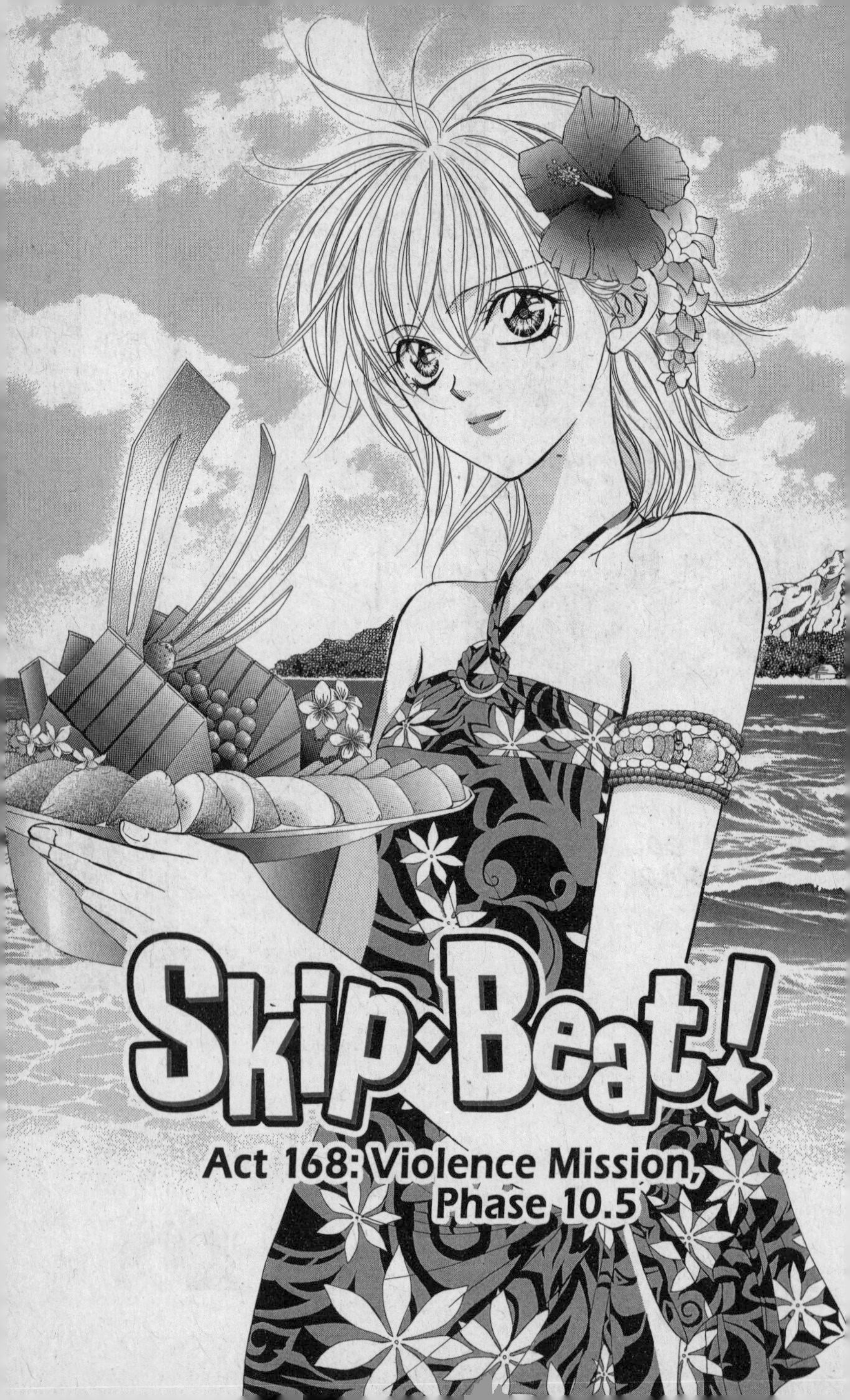
Skip·Beat!
Act 168: Violence Mission, Phase 10.5

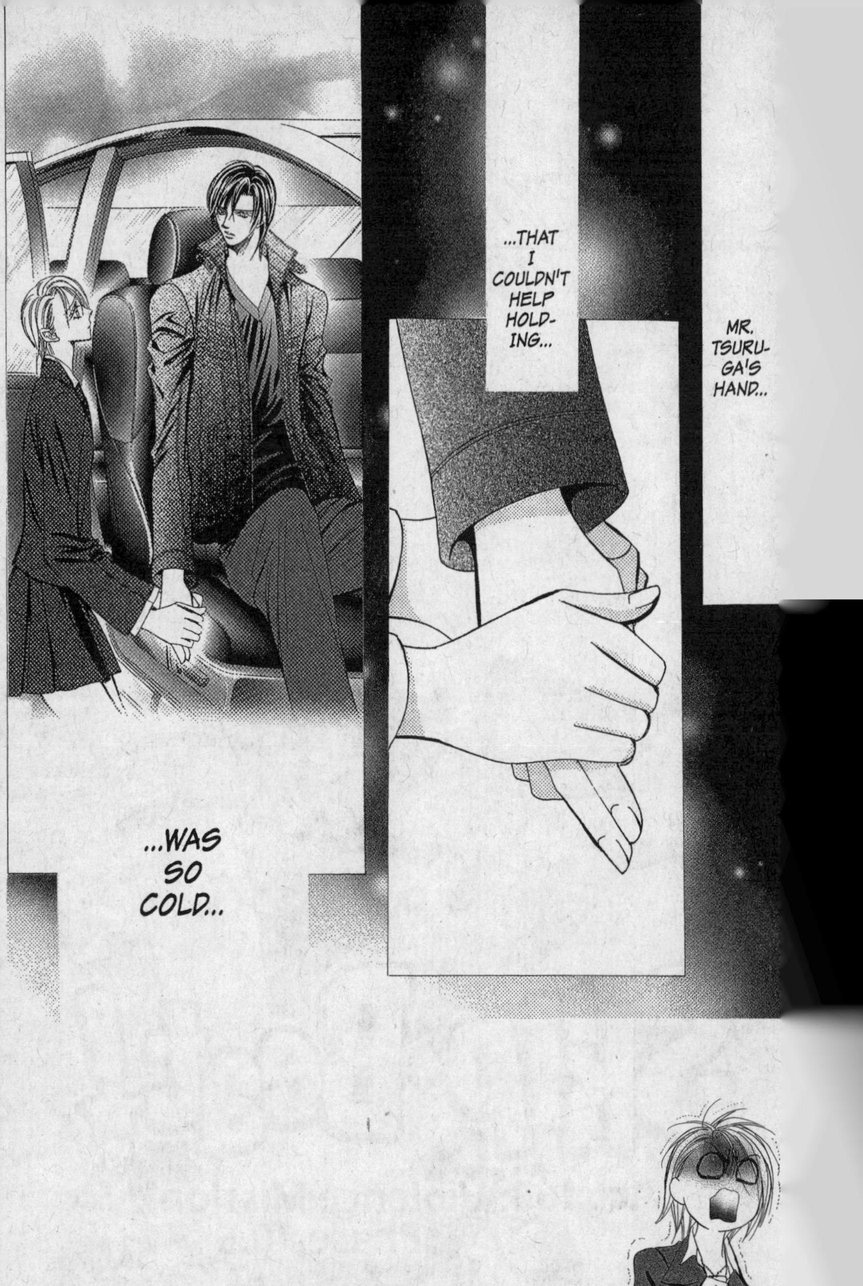
MR. TSURUGA'S HAND...
...THAT I COULDN'T HELP HOLDING...
...WAS SO COLD...

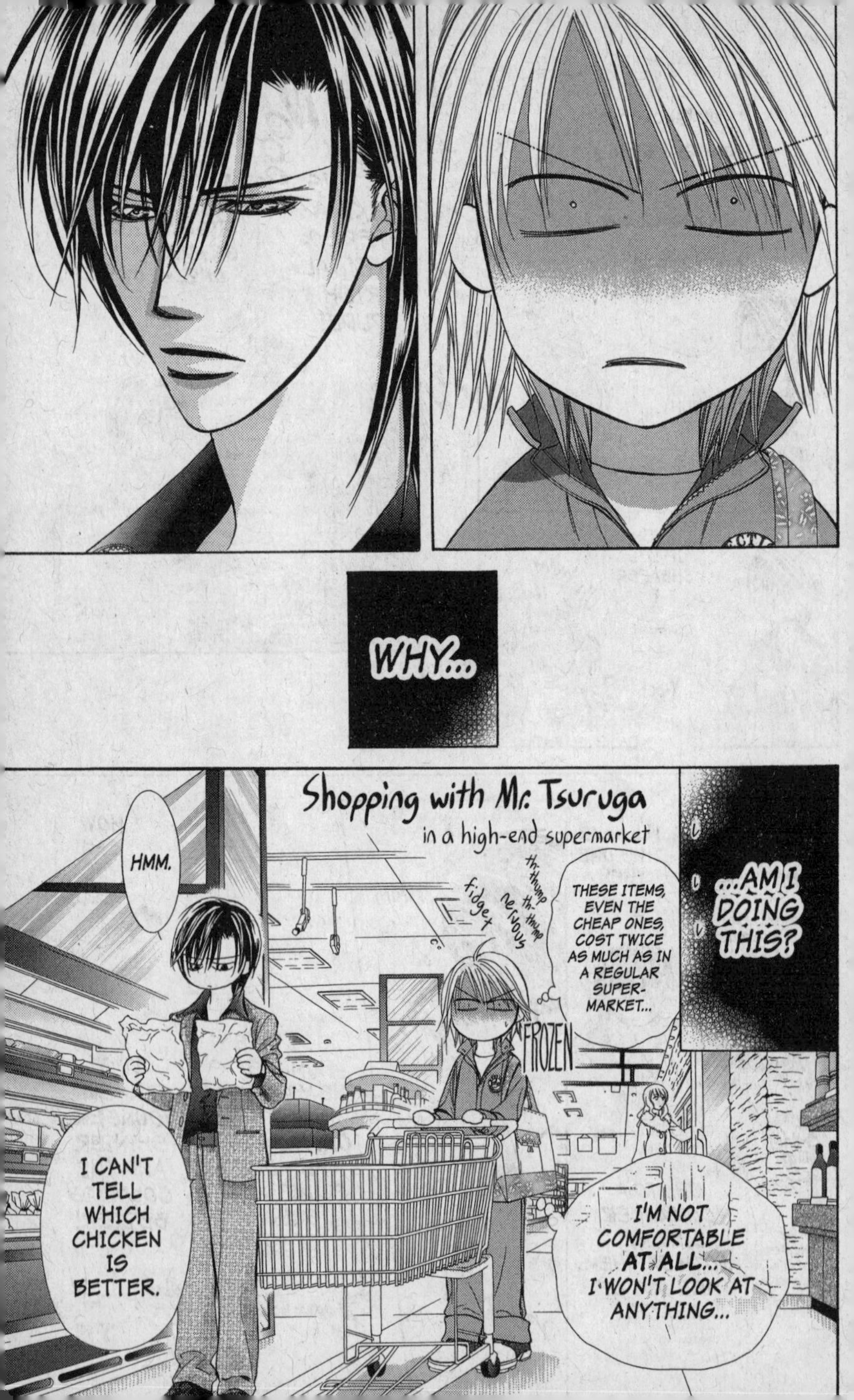
WHY...
...AM I DOING THIS?
Shopping with Mr. Tsuruga
in a high-end supermarket
THESE ITEMS, EVEN THE CHEAP ONES, COST TWICE AS MUCH AS IN A REGULAR SUPER-MARKET...
th-thump th-thump
nervous
fidget
HMM.
FROZEN
I'M NOT COMFORTABLE AT ALL... I WON'T LOOK AT ANYTHING...
I CAN'T TELL WHICH CHICKEN IS BETTER.

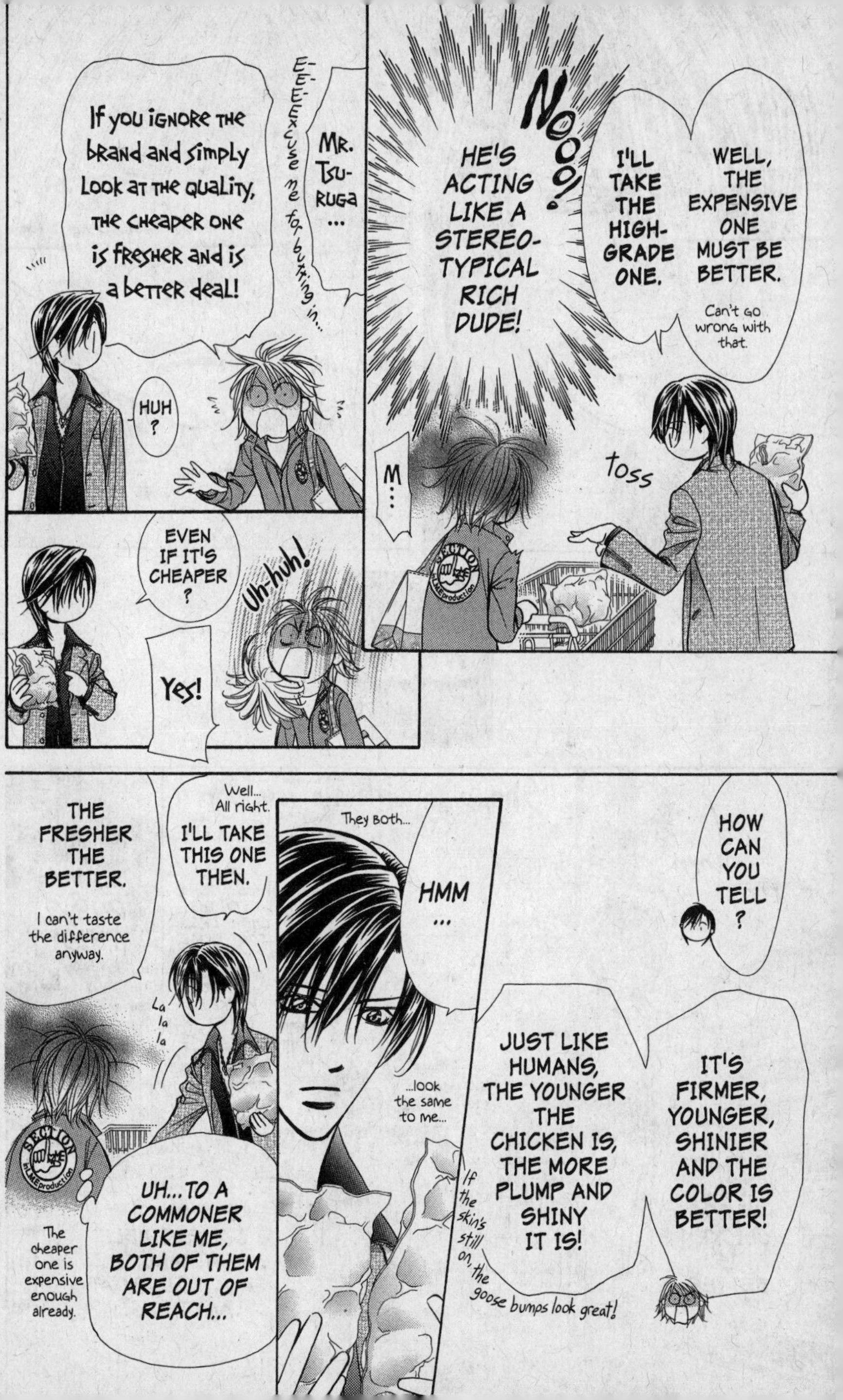
WELL, THE EXPENSIVE ONE MUST BE BETTER.
Can't go wrong with that.
I'LL TAKE THE HIGH-GRADE ONE.
NOOOO!
HE'S ACTING LIKE A STEREOTYPICAL RICH DUDE!
toss
M...
MR. TSURUGA...
E-E-E-Excuse me for butting in...
If you ignore the brand and simply look at the quality, the cheaper one is fresher and is a better deal!
HUH?
EVEN IF IT'S CHEAPER?
Uh-huh!
Yes!
HOW CAN YOU TELL?
IT'S FIRMER, YOUNGER, SHINIER AND THE COLOR IS BETTER!
JUST LIKE HUMANS, THE YOUNGER THE CHICKEN IS, THE MORE PLUMP AND SHINY IT IS!
If the skin's still on, the goose bumps look great!
They both...
HMM...
...look the same to me...
Well... All right.
I'LL TAKE THIS ONE THEN.
THE FRESHER THE BETTER.
I can't taste the difference anyway.
La la la
UH...TO A COMMONER LIKE ME, BOTH OF THEM ARE OUT OF REACH...
The cheaper one is expensive enough already.

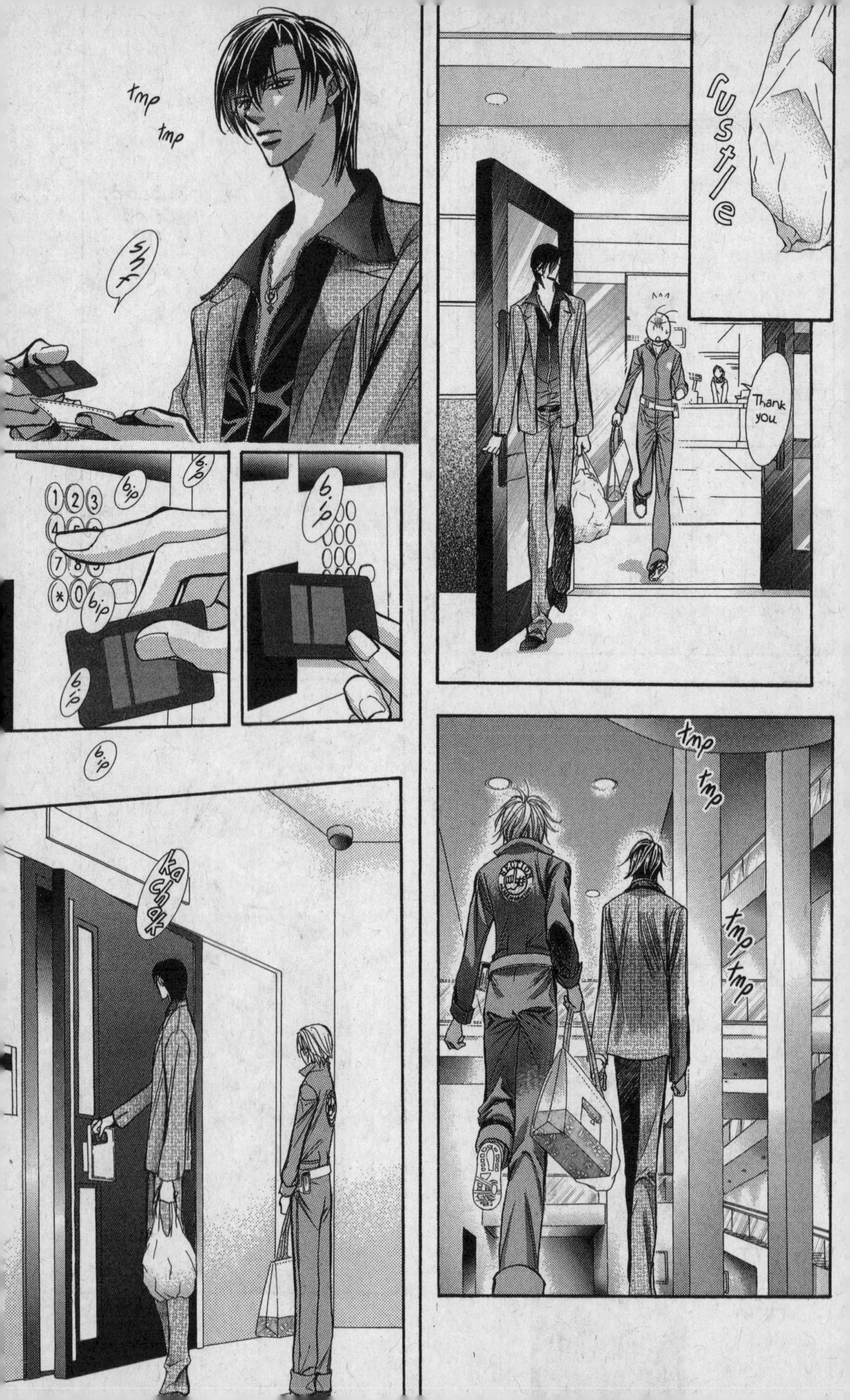
rustle
Thank you.
tmp tmp
tmp tmp
tmp tmp
shf
bip
bip
bip
bip
bip
bip
kachak

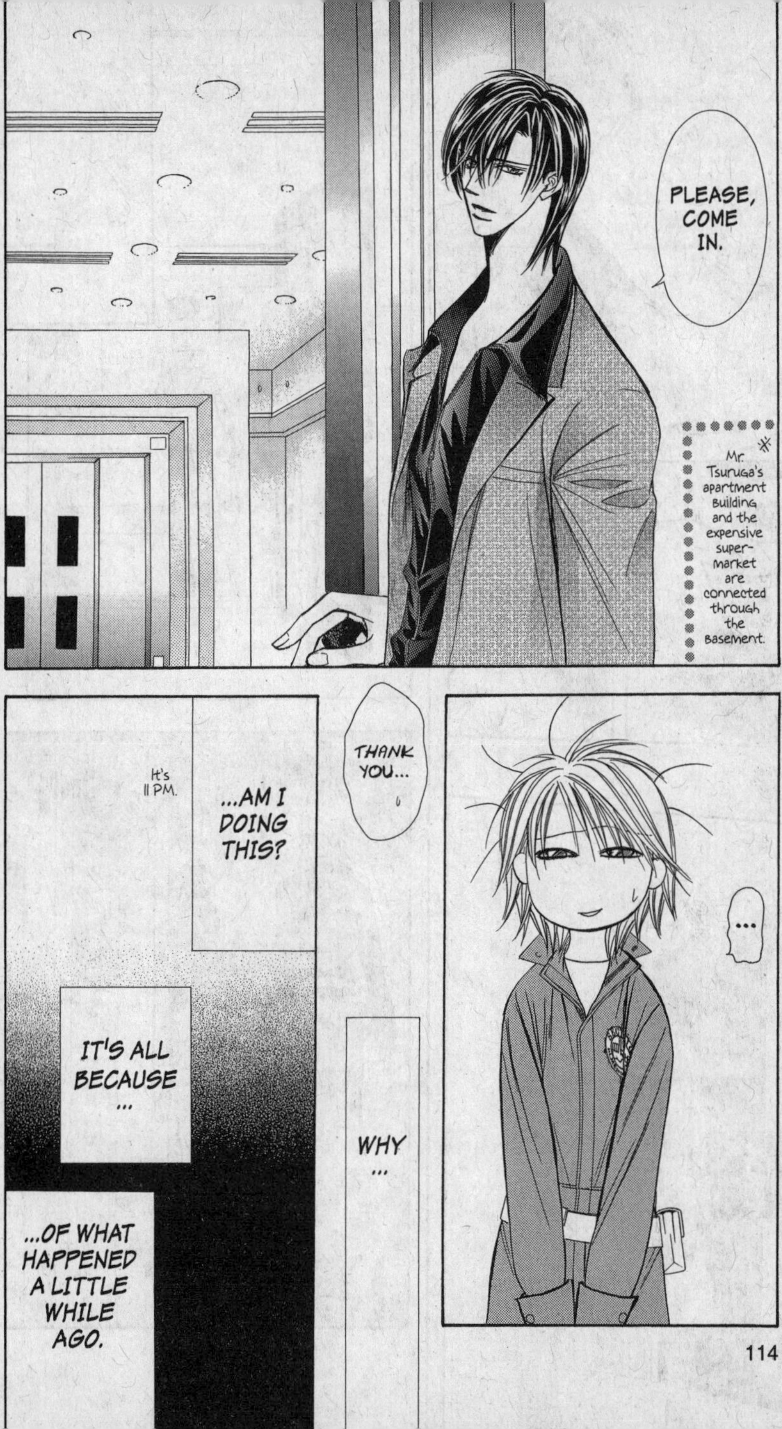

PLEASE, COME IN.
※ Mr. Tsuruga's apartment building and the expensive super-market are connected through the basement.
THANK YOU...
...
WHY...
...AM I DOING THIS?
It's 11 PM.
IT'S ALL BECAUSE...
...OF WHAT HAPPENED A LITTLE WHILE AGO.

Incoming
Call
Calling

Mr. Tsuruga

Mr. Tsuruga

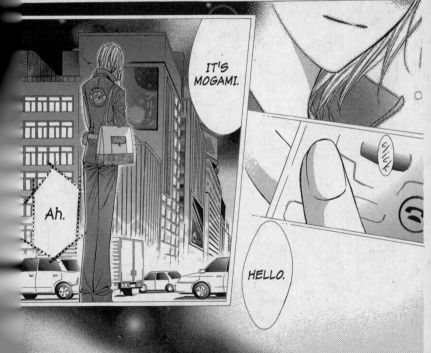

IT'S MOGAMI.

Ah.

HELLO.

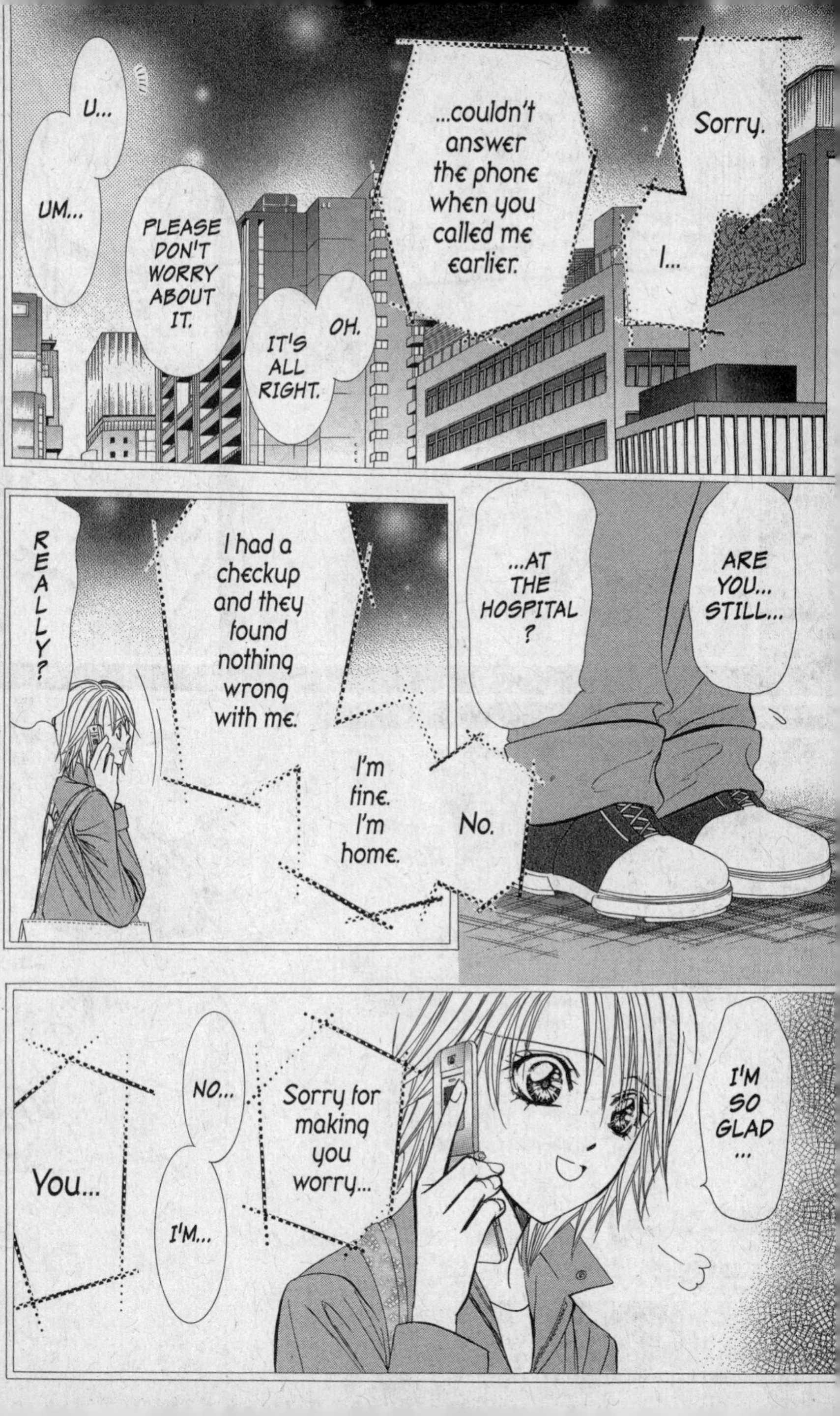
Sorry.
I...
...couldn't answer the phone when you called me earlier.
OH. IT'S ALL RIGHT.
PLEASE DON'T WORRY ABOUT IT.
U... UM...
ARE YOU... STILL...
...AT THE HOSPITAL?
No.
I'm fine. I'm home.
I had a checkup and they found nothing wrong with me.
REALLY?
I'M SO GLAD...
Sorry for making you worry...
NO... I'M...
You...

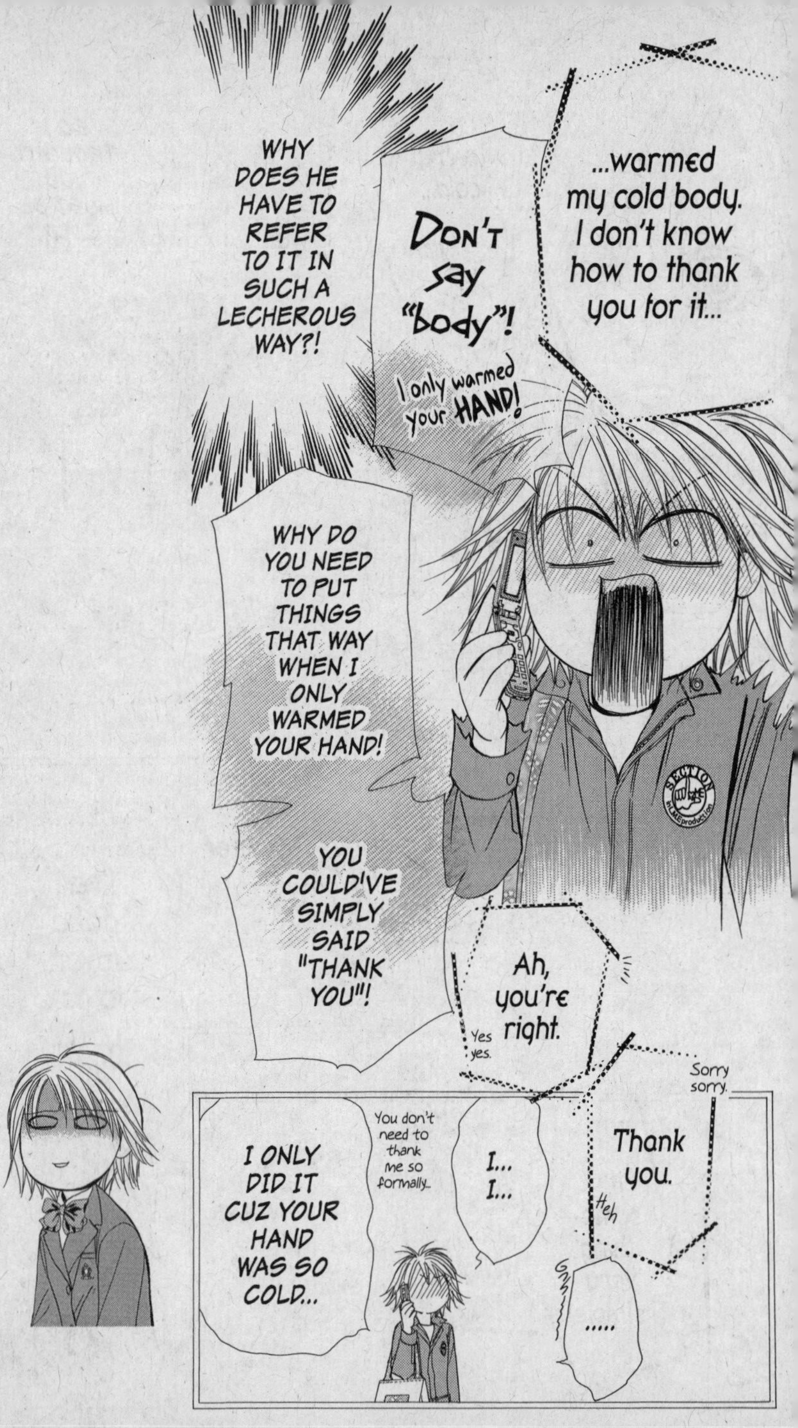
...warmed my cold body. I don't know how to thank you for it...
Don't say "body"!
I only warmed your HAND!
WHY DOES HE HAVE TO REFER TO IT IN SUCH A LECHEROUS WAY?!
WHY DO YOU NEED TO PUT THINGS THAT WAY WHEN I ONLY WARMED YOUR HAND!
YOU COULD'VE SIMPLY SAID "THANK YOU"!
Ah, you're right.
Yes yes.
Sorry sorry.
Thank you.
Heh
.....
I... I...
You don't need to thank me so formally...
I ONLY DID IT CUZ YOUR HAND WAS SO COLD...

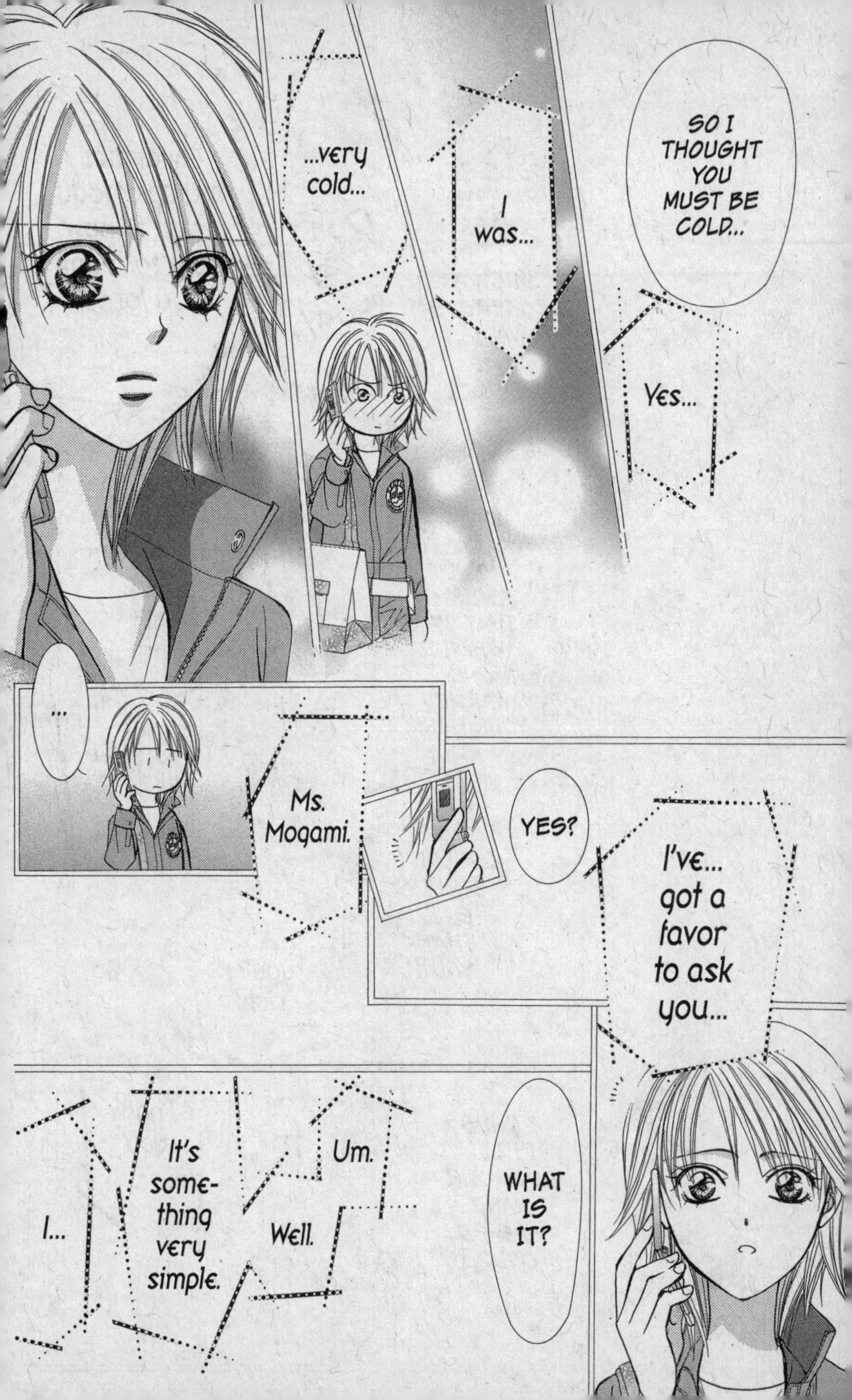
SO I THOUGHT YOU MUST BE COLD...
Yes...
I was...
...very cold...
...
Ms. Mogami.
YES?
I've... got a favor to ask you...
WHAT IS IT?
Um.
Well.
It's some-thing very simple.
I...

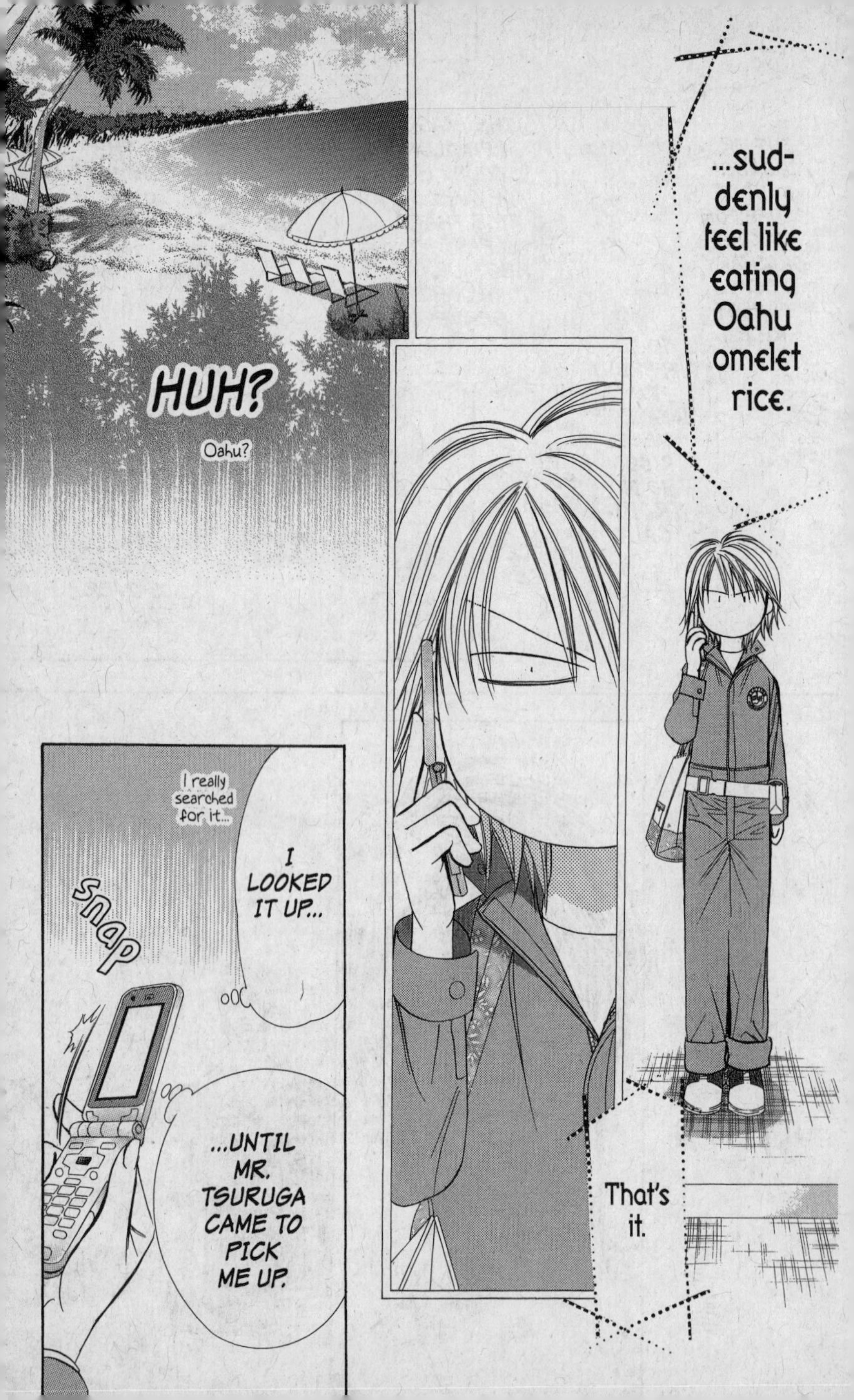
...sud-
denly
feel like
eating
Oahu
omelet
rice.
That's
it.
HUH?
Oahu?
I really
searched
for it...
I
LOOKED
IT UP...
Snap
...UNTIL
MR.
TSURUGA
CAME TO
PICK
ME UP.

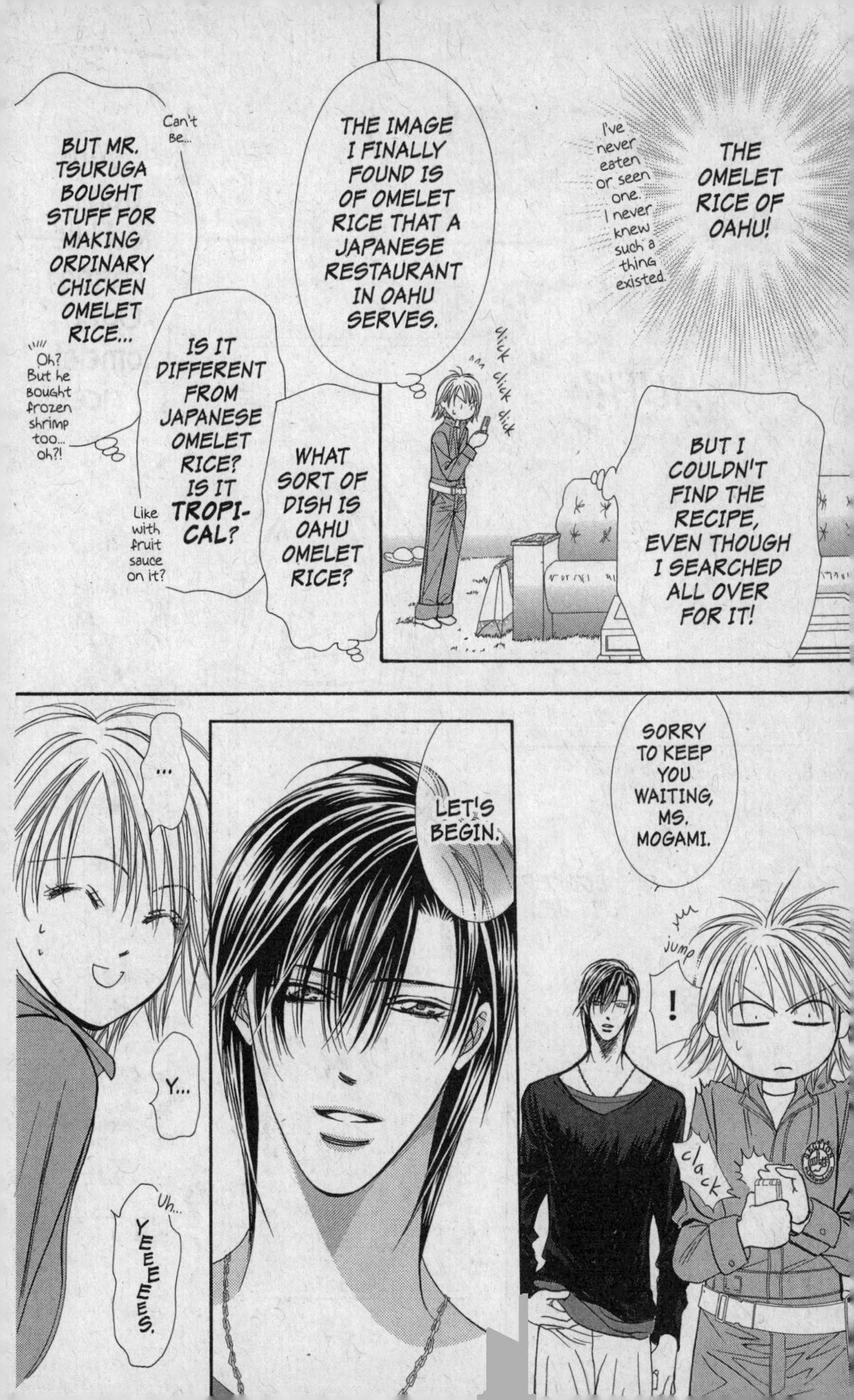
THE OMELET RICE OF OAHU!
I've never eaten or seen one. I never knew such a thing existed.
click click click
BUT I COULDN'T FIND THE RECIPE, EVEN THOUGH I SEARCHED ALL OVER FOR IT!
THE IMAGE I FINALLY FOUND IS OF OMELET RICE THAT A JAPANESE RESTAURANT IN OAHU SERVES.
WHAT SORT OF DISH IS OAHU OMELET RICE?
IS IT DIFFERENT FROM JAPANESE OMELET RICE? IS IT TROPICAL?
Like with fruit sauce on it?
BUT MR. TSURUGA BOUGHT STUFF FOR MAKING ORDINARY CHICKEN OMELET RICE...
Can't be...
Oh? But he bought frozen shrimp too... oh?!
SORRY TO KEEP YOU WAITING, MS. MOGAMI.
jump
!
clack
LET'S BEGIN.
...
Y...
Uh...
YEEEEES.

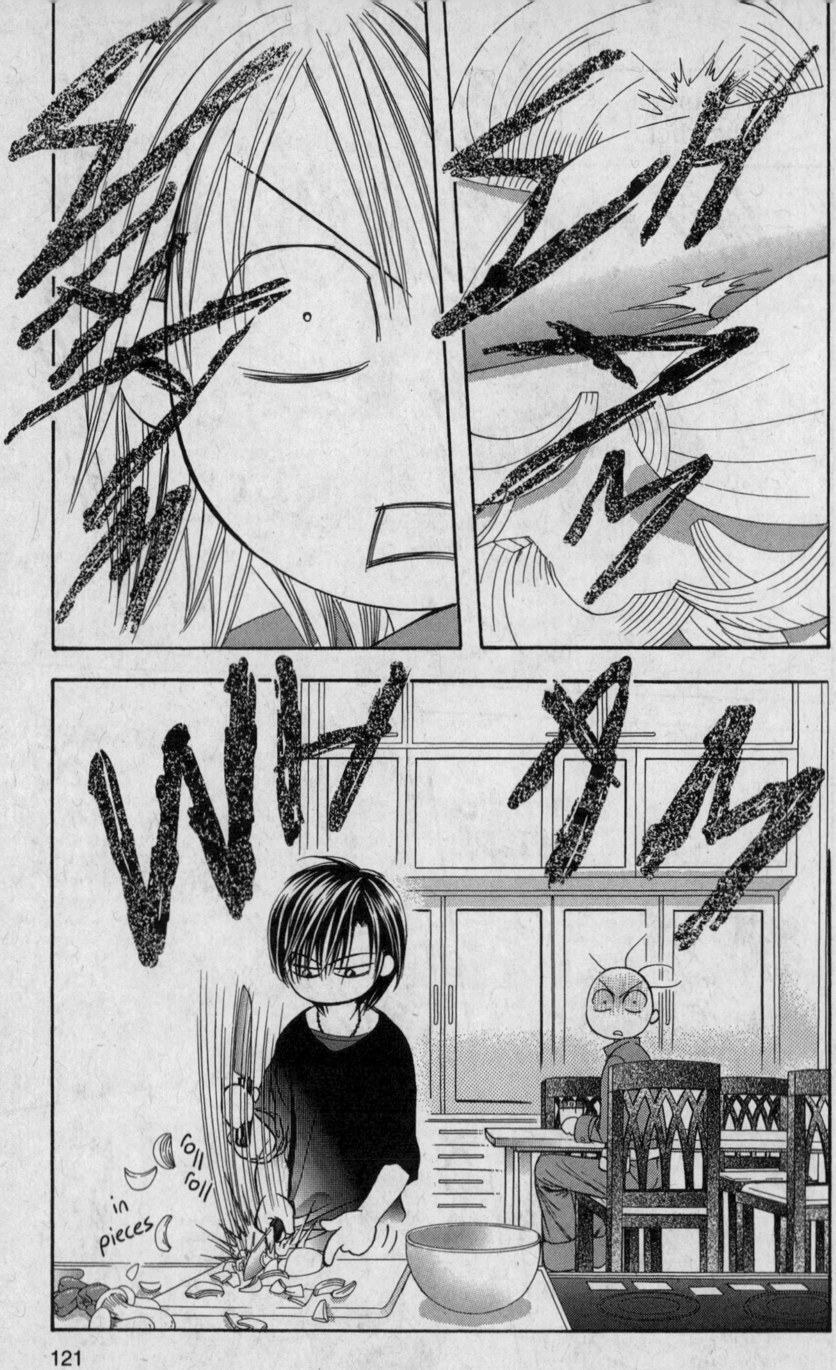
WHAM
roll roll
in pieces

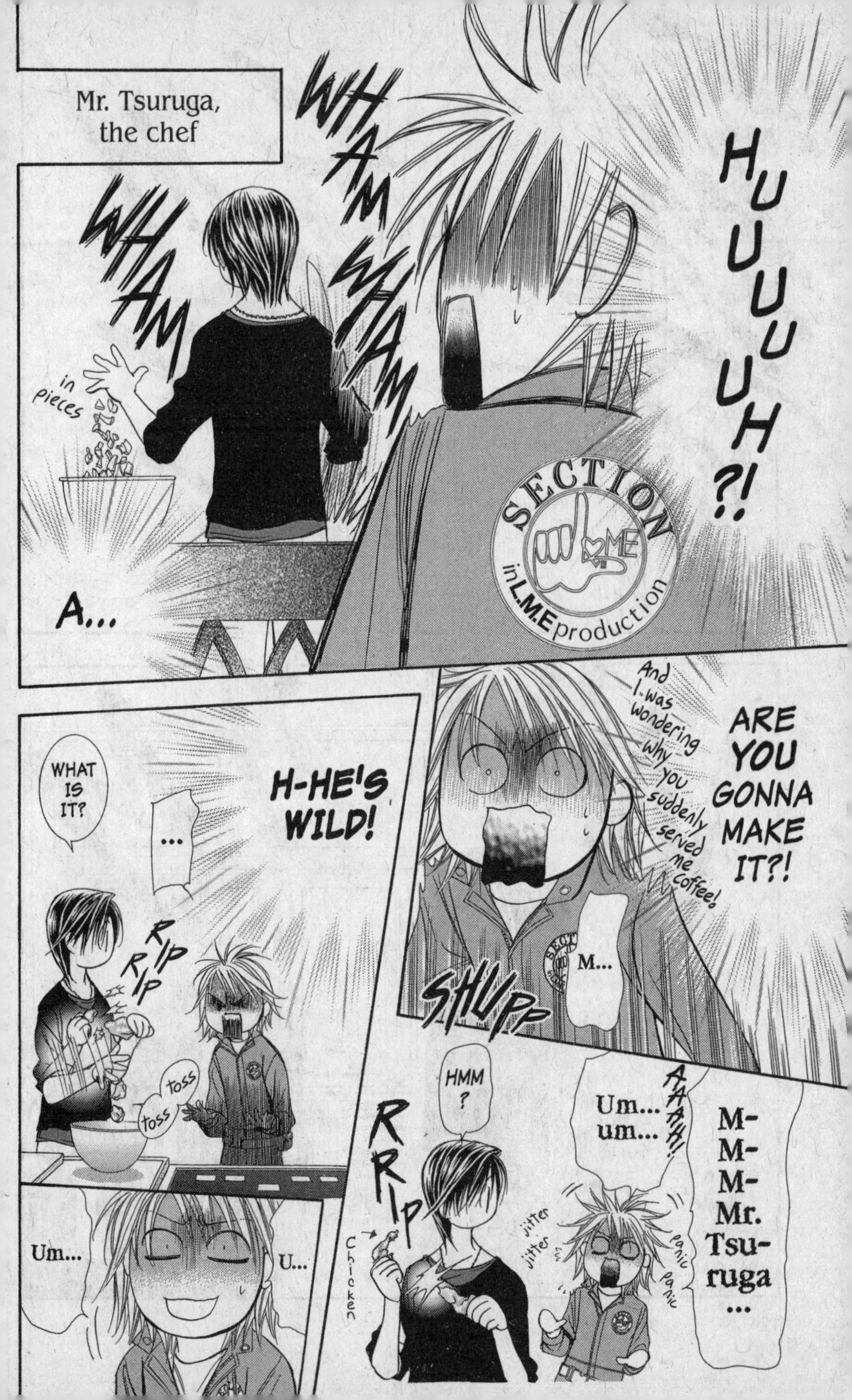
HUUUUUH?!
WHAM WHAM WHAM
Mr. Tsuruga, the chef
WHAM WHAM
in pieces
A...
SECTION
LME
in L.M.E production
ARE YOU GONNA MAKE IT?!
And I was wondering why you suddenly served me coffee!
M...
SHUPP
H-HE'S WILD!
...
WHAT IS IT?
RIP RIP
toss toss
M-M-M-Mr. Tsuru-ga...
AAAHH!
Um... um...
panic panic
jitter jitter
HMM?
RRIP
Chicken
U...
Um...

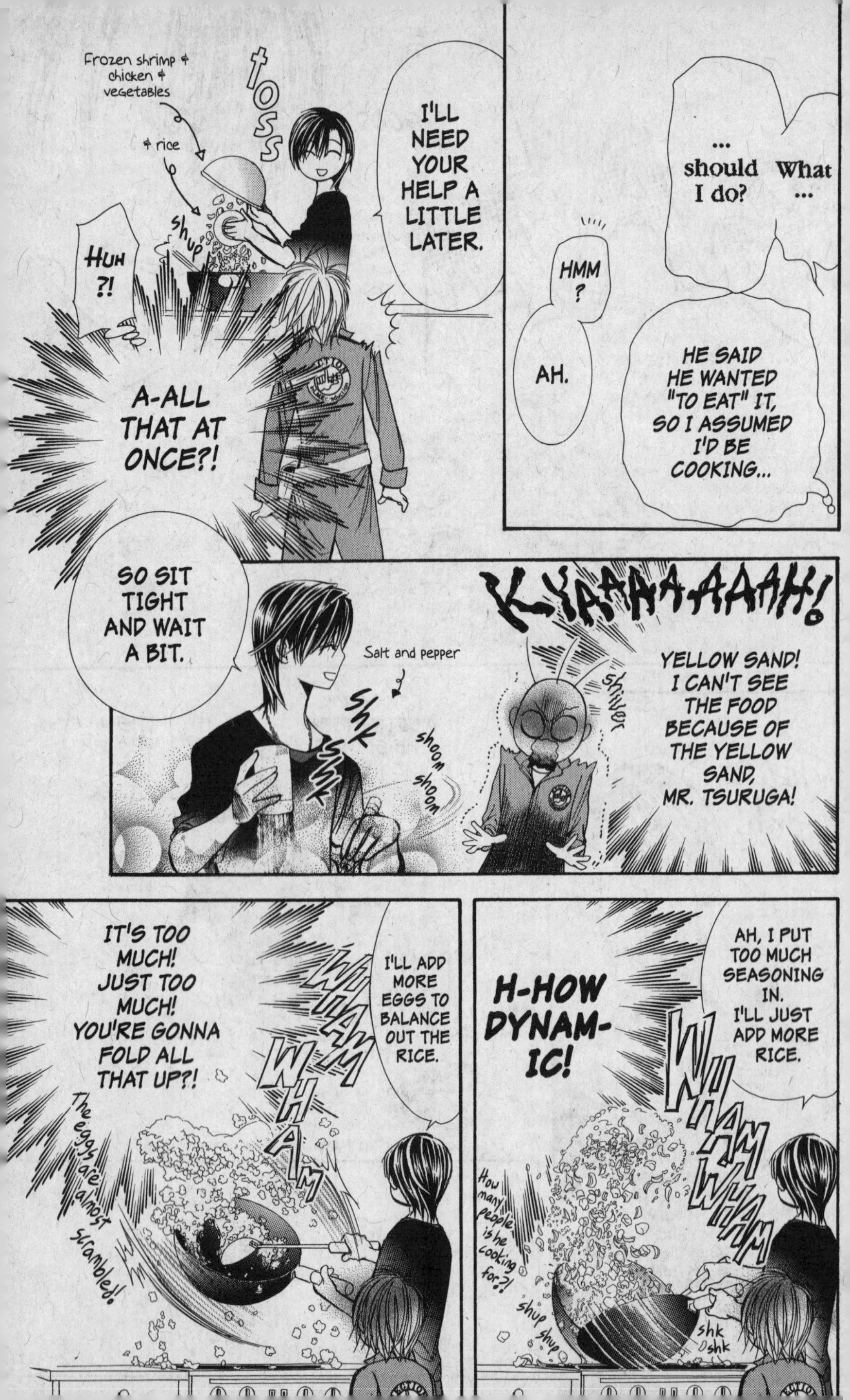
What ...
... should I do?
HMM?
AH.
HE SAID HE WANTED "TO EAT" IT, SO I ASSUMED I'D BE COOKING...
I'LL NEED YOUR HELP A LITTLE LATER.
TOSS
Frozen shrimp & chicken & vegetables
& rice
shup
HUH?!
A-ALL THAT AT ONCE?!
KYAAAAAAH!
YELLOW SAND! I CAN'T SEE THE FOOD BECAUSE OF THE YELLOW SAND, MR. TSURUGA!
shiver
SO SIT TIGHT AND WAIT A BIT.
Salt and pepper
SHK SHK
shoom shoom
AH, I PUT TOO MUCH SEASONING IN. I'LL JUST ADD MORE RICE.
WHAM WHAM
H-HOW DYNAMIC!
How many people is he cooking for?!
shup shup
shk shk
I'LL ADD MORE EGGS TO BALANCE OUT THE RICE.
WHAM WHAM
IT'S TOO MUCH! JUST TOO MUCH! YOU'RE GONNA FOLD ALL THAT UP?!
The eggs are almost scrambled!

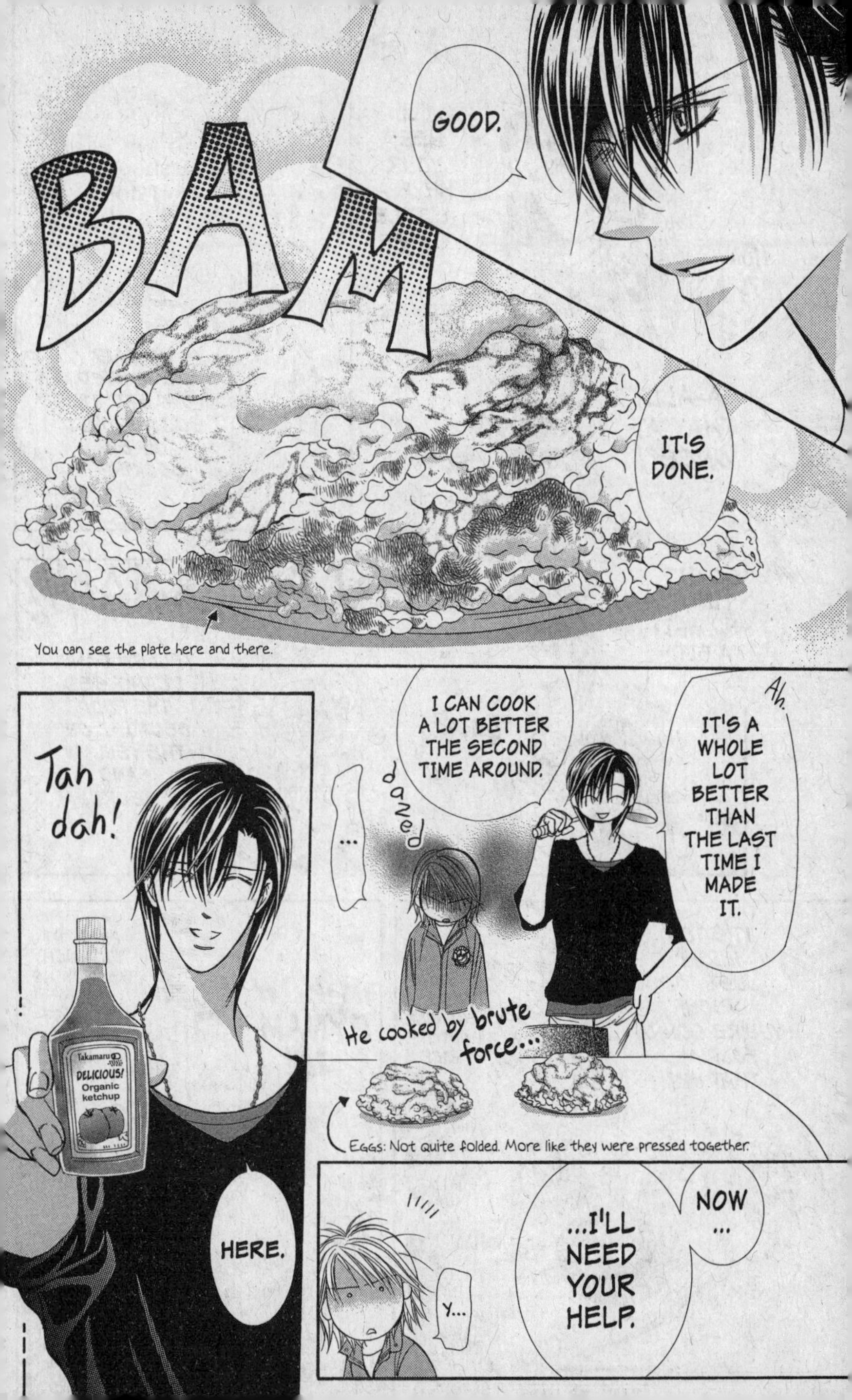
GOOD.
BAM
IT'S DONE.
You can see the plate here and there.
Ah.
IT'S A WHOLE LOT BETTER THAN THE LAST TIME I MADE IT.
I CAN COOK A LOT BETTER THE SECOND TIME AROUND.
dazed
...
He cooked by brute force...
Eggs: Not quite folded. More like they were pressed together.
NOW...
...I'LL NEED YOUR HELP.
Y...
Tah dah!
Takamaru
DELICIOUS!
Organic ketchup
HERE.

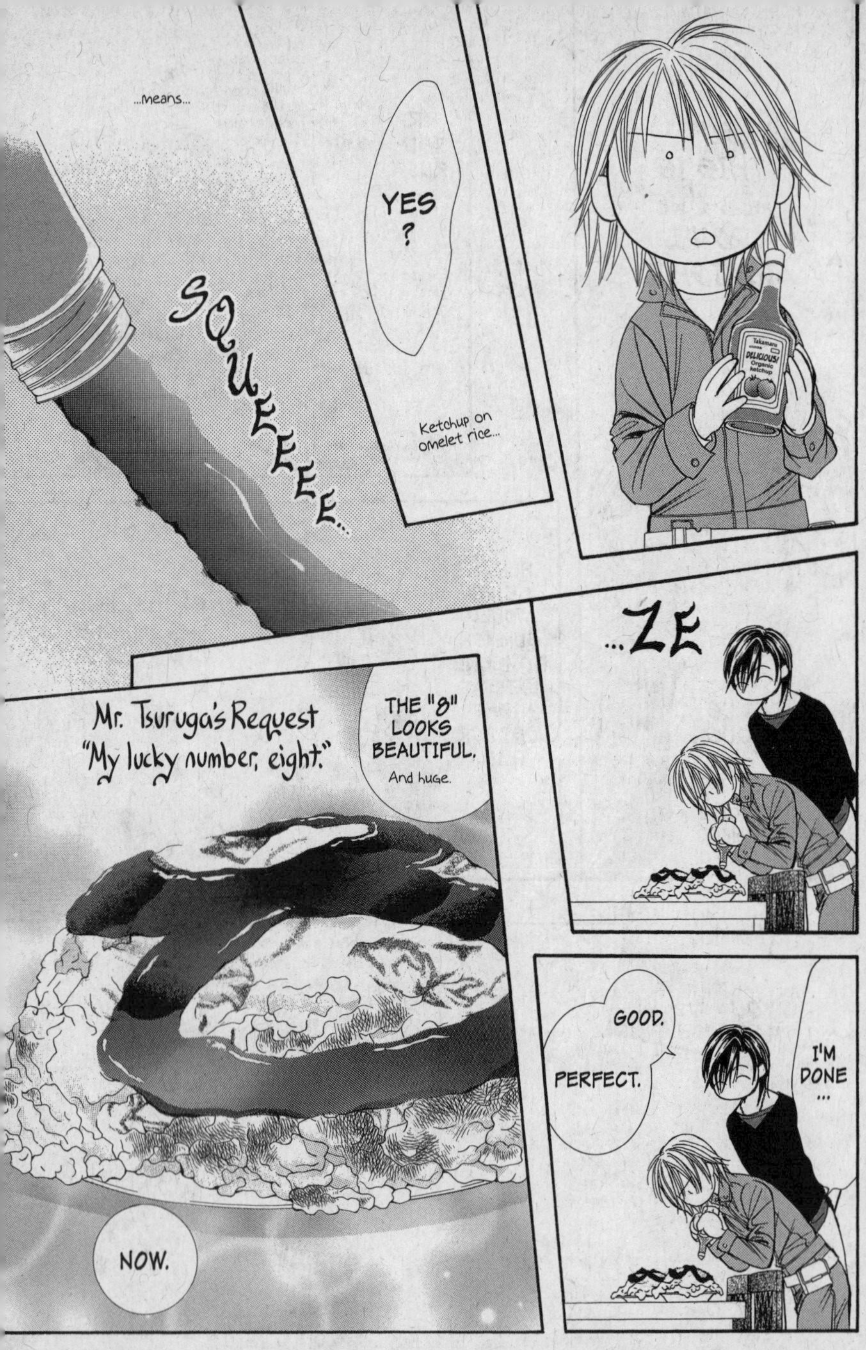

Takamaru
DELICIOUS!
Organic ketchup
YES ?
Ketchup on omelet rice...
...means...
SQUEEEEE...
...ZE
I'M DONE ...
GOOD.
PERFECT.
Mr. Tsuruga's Request
"My lucky number, eight."
THE "8" LOOKS BEAUTIFUL.
And huge.
NOW.

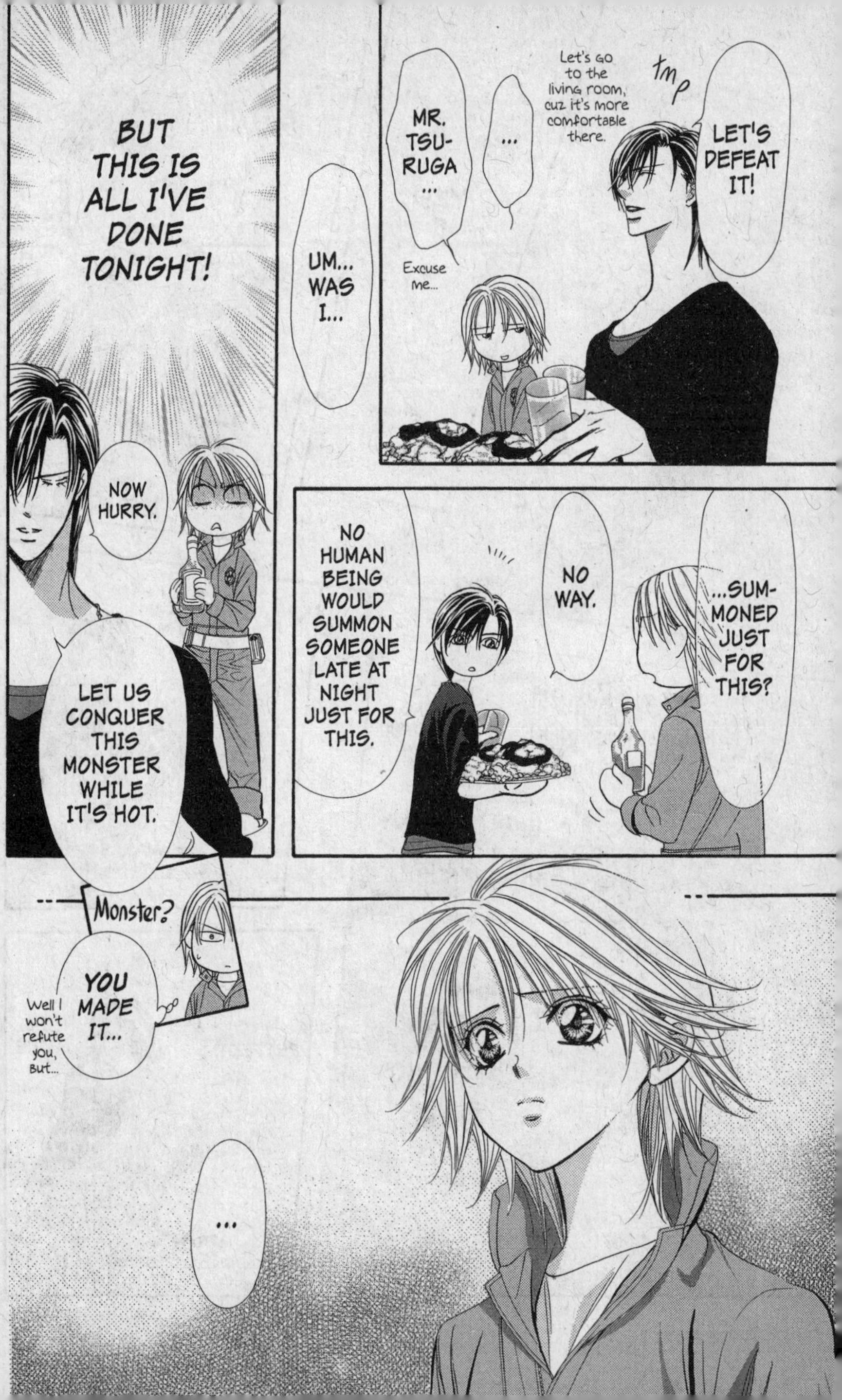

tmp
LET'S DEFEAT IT!
Let's go to the living room, cuz it's more comfortable there.
...
MR. TSURUGA ...
Excuse me...
UM... WAS I...
...SUMMONED JUST FOR THIS?
NO WAY.
NO HUMAN BEING WOULD SUMMON SOMEONE LATE AT NIGHT JUST FOR THIS.
BUT THIS IS ALL I'VE DONE TONIGHT!
NOW HURRY.
LET US CONQUER THIS MONSTER WHILE IT'S HOT.
...
Monster?
YOU MADE IT...
Well I won't refute you, but...

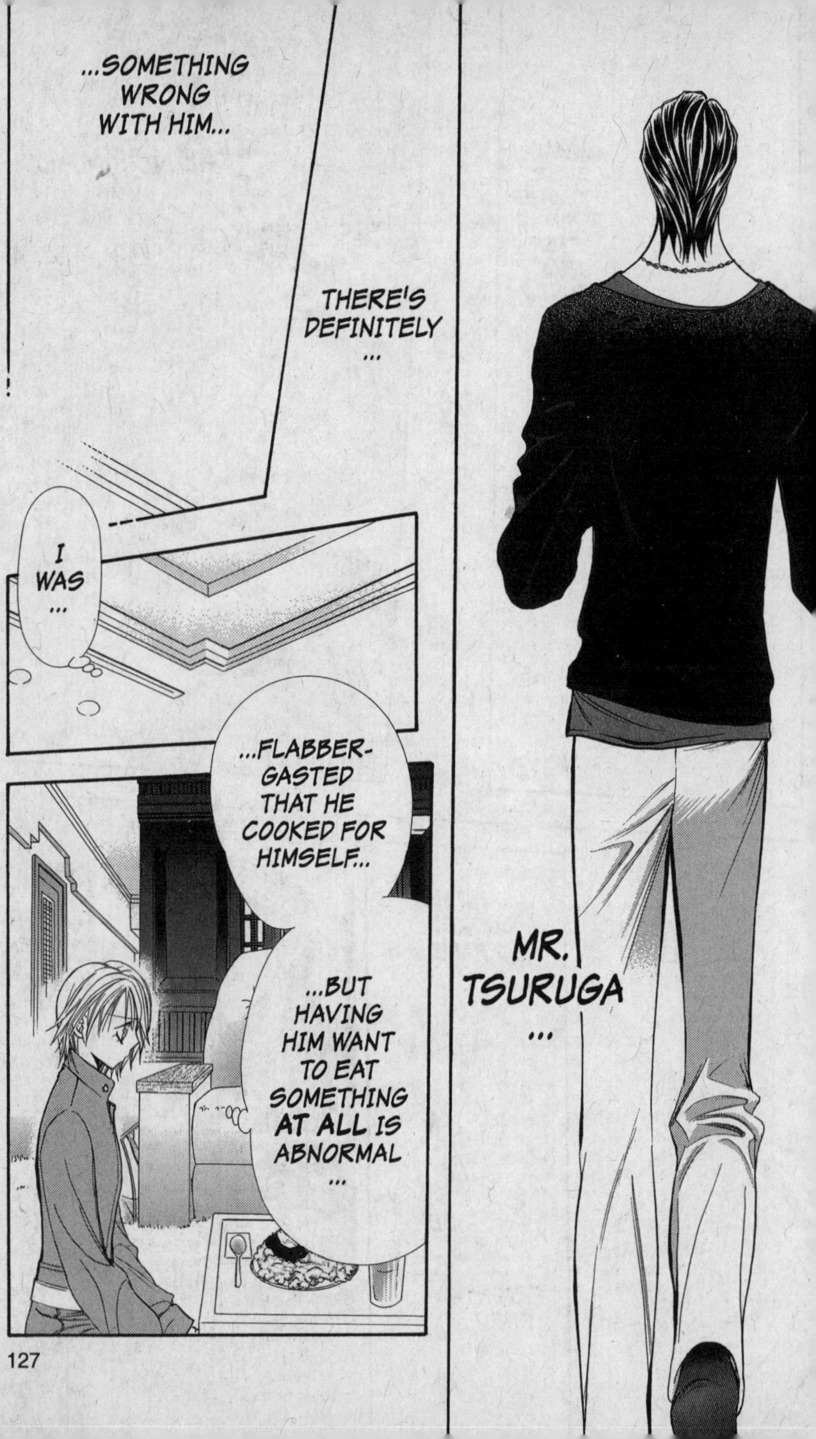
MR. TSURUGA ...
THERE'S DEFINITELY ...
...SOMETHING WRONG WITH HIM...
I WAS ...
...FLABBERGASTED THAT HE COOKED FOR HIMSELF...
...BUT HAVING HIM WANT TO EAT SOMETHING AT ALL IS ABNORMAL ...

"ABNORMAL"...

...WHATEVER AFFECTED HIM AFTER THAT STUNT...

...IS...

...STILL AFFECTING HIM...

MAYBE...

I CAN'T DENY IT...

CUZ...

...HE...

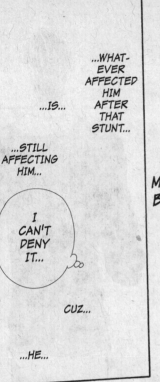

FRIGHTENED...

...AND...

...AND HE LOOKED SO PALE...

I'D BE...

...FRIGHTENED...

Peek

ALL...

...MUST'VE BEEN...

...FROZE UP...

...HIS SENSES...

...TERRIFIED.

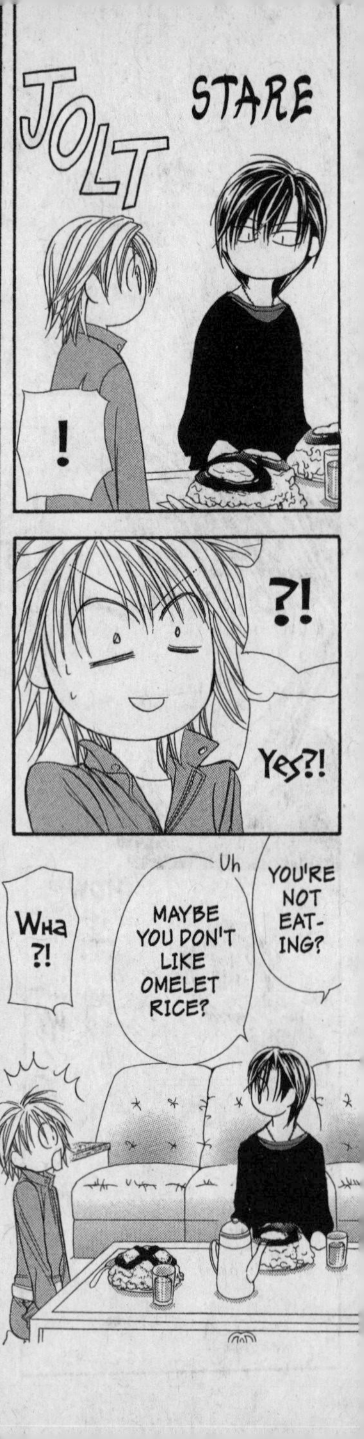
JOLT
STARE
!
?!
Yes?!
YOU'RE NOT EAT-ING?
Uh
MAYBE YOU DON'T LIKE OMELET RICE?
Wha ?!
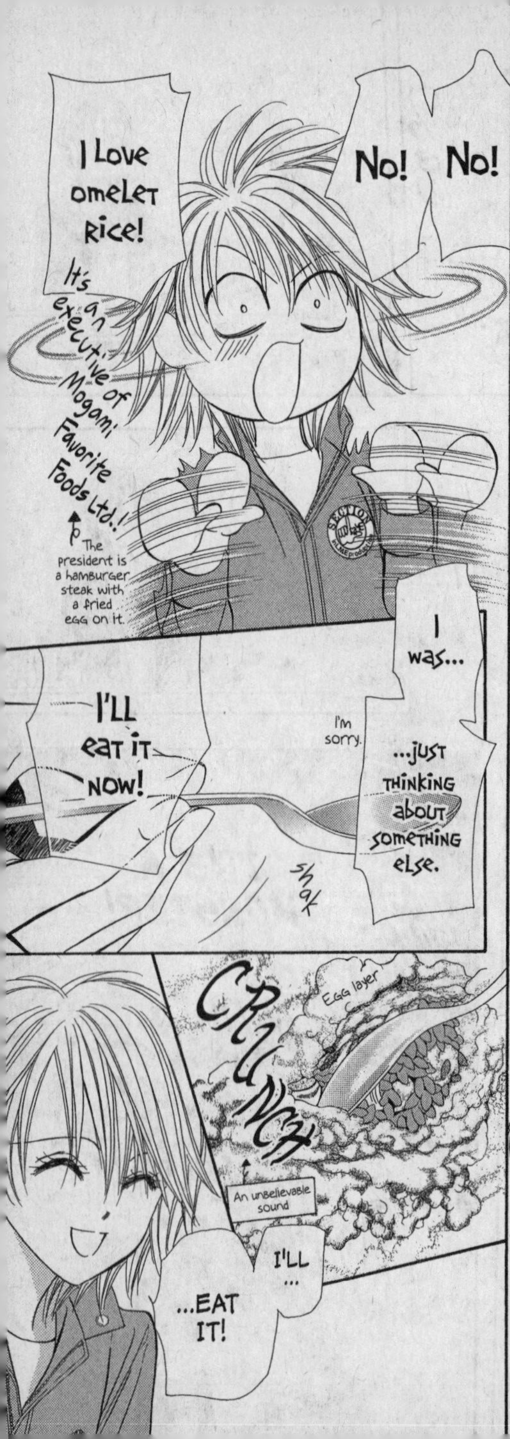
No! No!
I Love omelet rice!
It's an executive of Mogami Favorite Foods Ltd.!
The president is a hamburger steak with a fried egg on it.
I was...
...just thinking about something else.
I'm sorry.
I'LL eat it now!
shak
CRUNCH
Egg layer
An unbelievable sound
I'LL ...
...EAT IT!

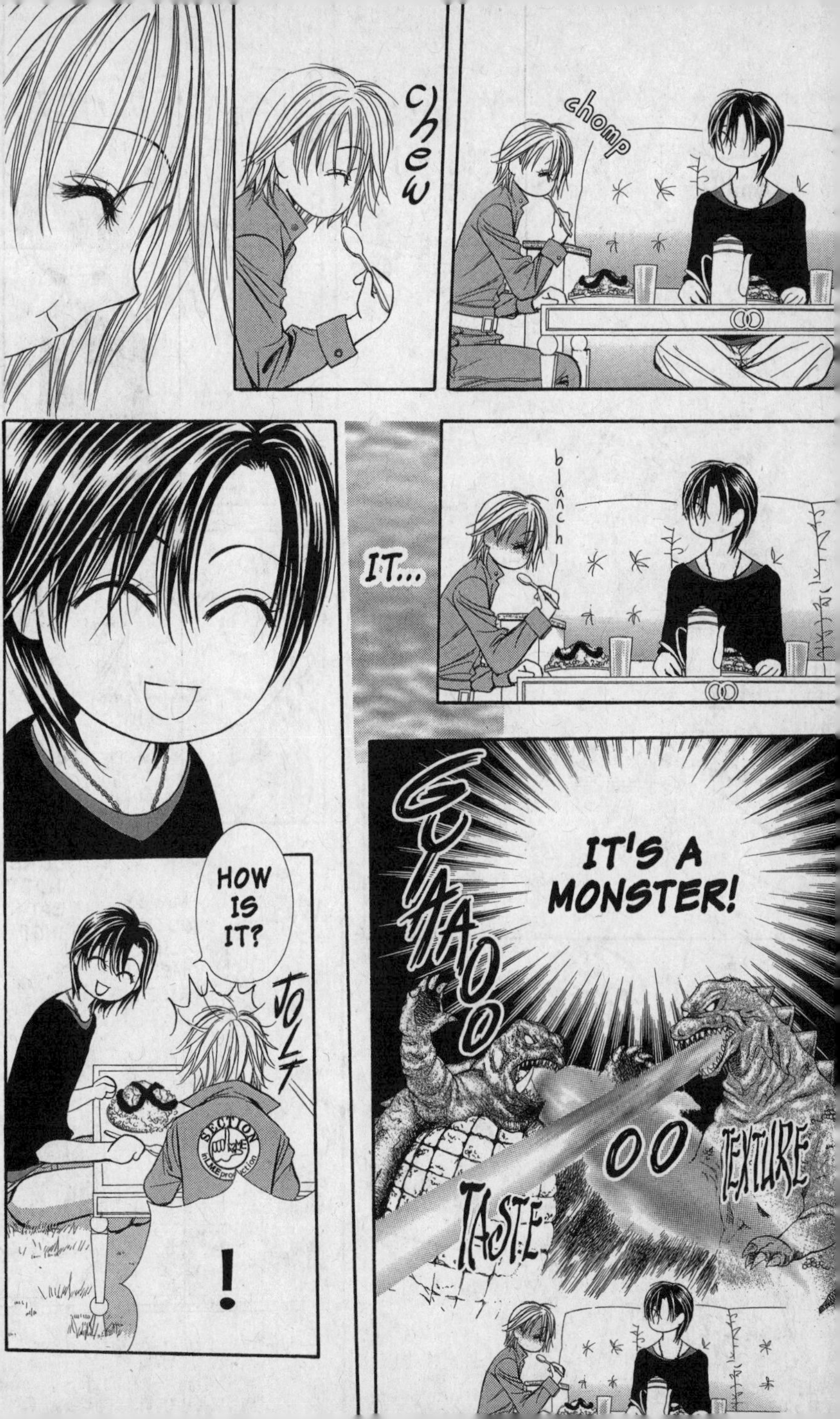
chomp
chew
blanch
IT...
GYAAOO
IT'S A MONSTER!
TEXTURE
OO
TASTE
HOW IS IT?
JOLT
!

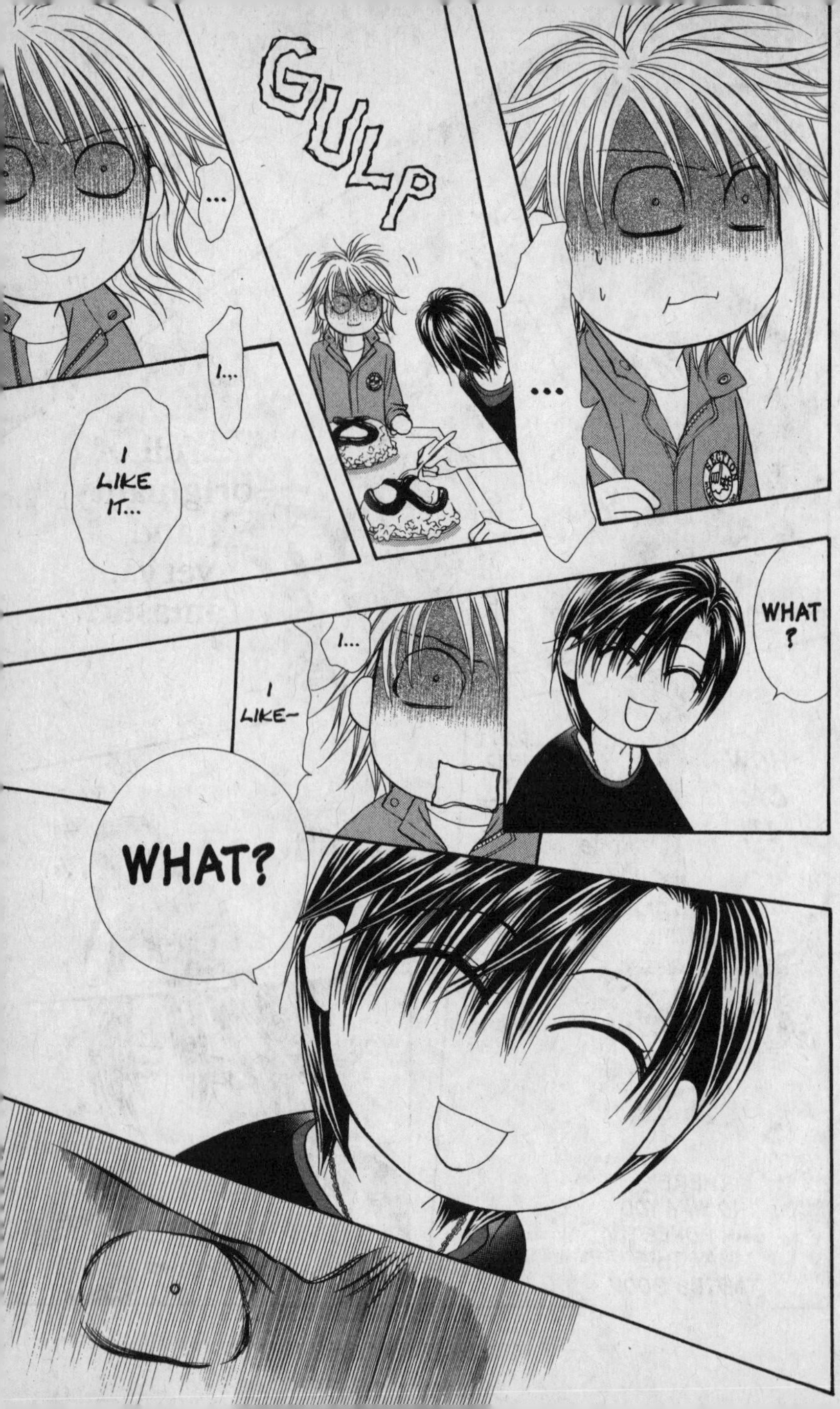
...
GULP
...
I...
I LIKE IT...
WHAT ?
I...
I LIKE-
WHAT?

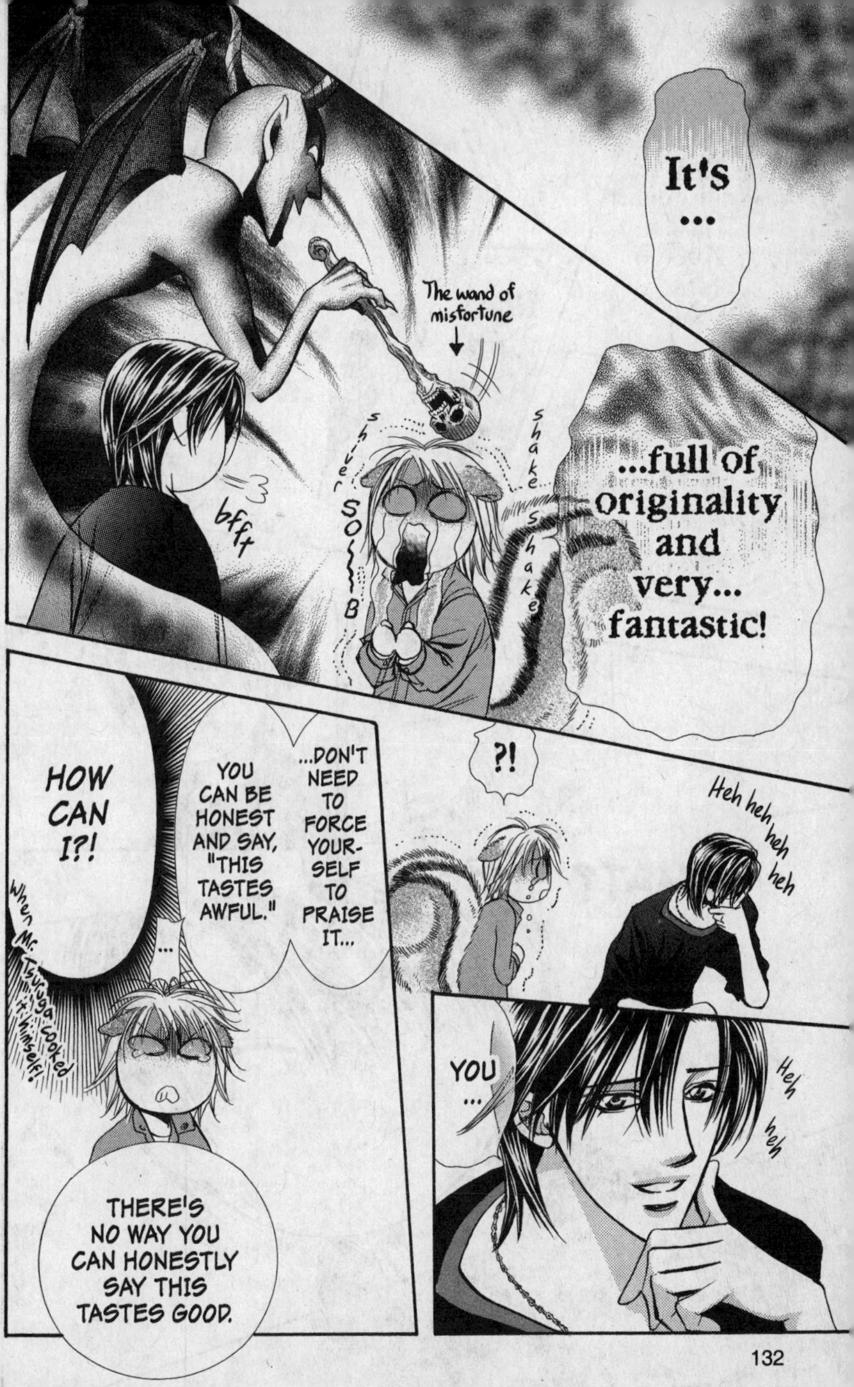

It's ...
...full of originality and very... fantastic!
The wand of misfortune
shake shake
shiver
SOB
bfft
?!
Heh heh heh heh
YOU ...
Heh heh
...DON'T NEED TO FORCE YOUR-SELF TO PRAISE IT...
YOU CAN BE HONEST AND SAY, "THIS TASTES AWFUL."
HOW CAN I?!
...
When Mr. Tsuruga cooked it himself!
THERE'S NO WAY YOU CAN HONESTLY SAY THIS TASTES GOOD.

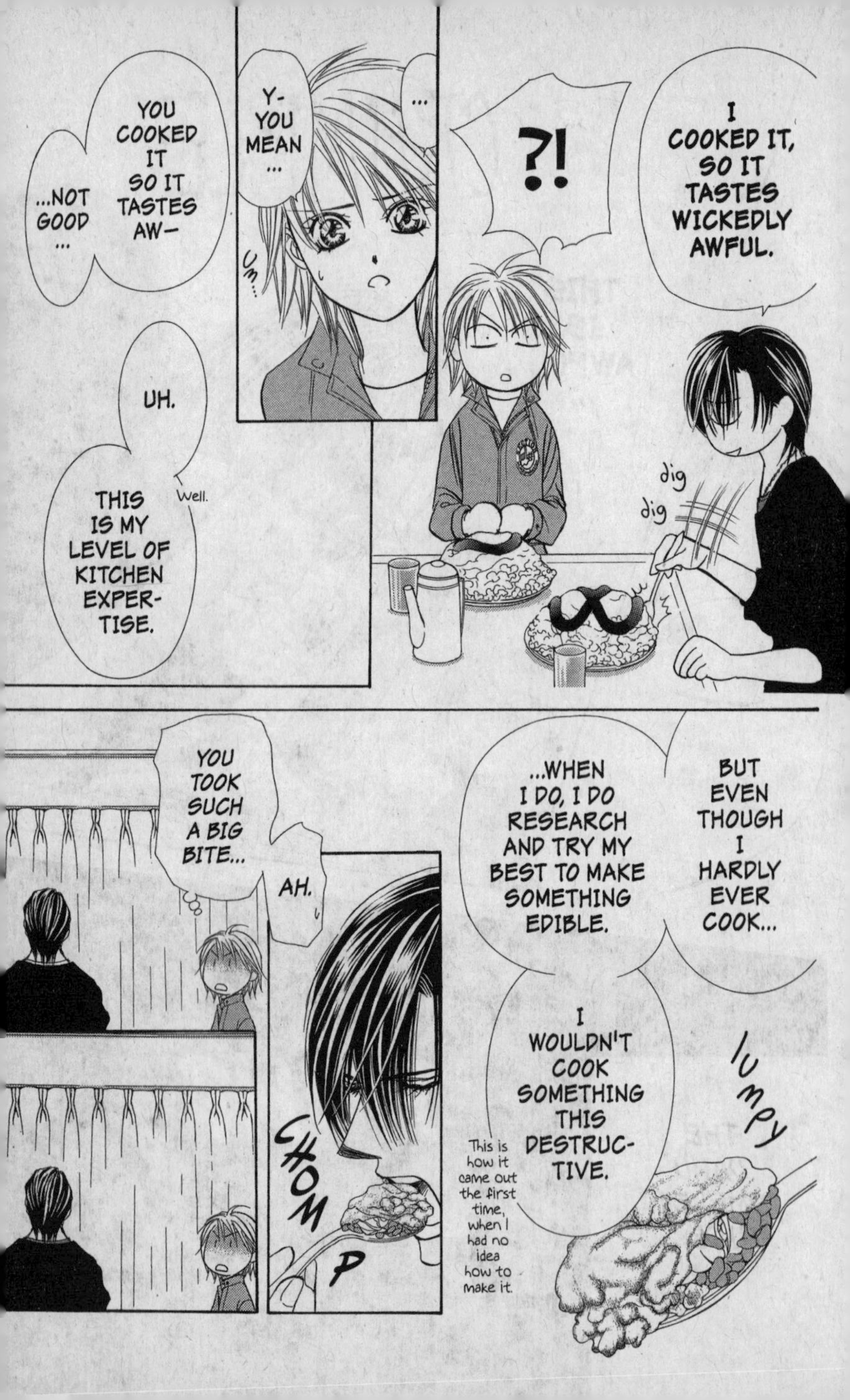
I COOKED IT, SO IT TASTES WICKEDLY AWFUL.
?!
dig dig
...
Y-YOU MEAN...
Um...
YOU COOKED IT SO IT TASTES AW—
...NOT GOOD...
UH.
Well.
THIS IS MY LEVEL OF KITCHEN EXPERTISE.
BUT EVEN THOUGH I HARDLY EVER COOK...
...WHEN I DO, I DO RESEARCH AND TRY MY BEST TO MAKE SOMETHING EDIBLE.
I WOULDN'T COOK SOMETHING THIS DESTRUCTIVE.
This is how it came out the first time, when I had no idea how to make it.
lumpy
AH.
CHOMP
YOU TOOK SUCH A BIG BITE...

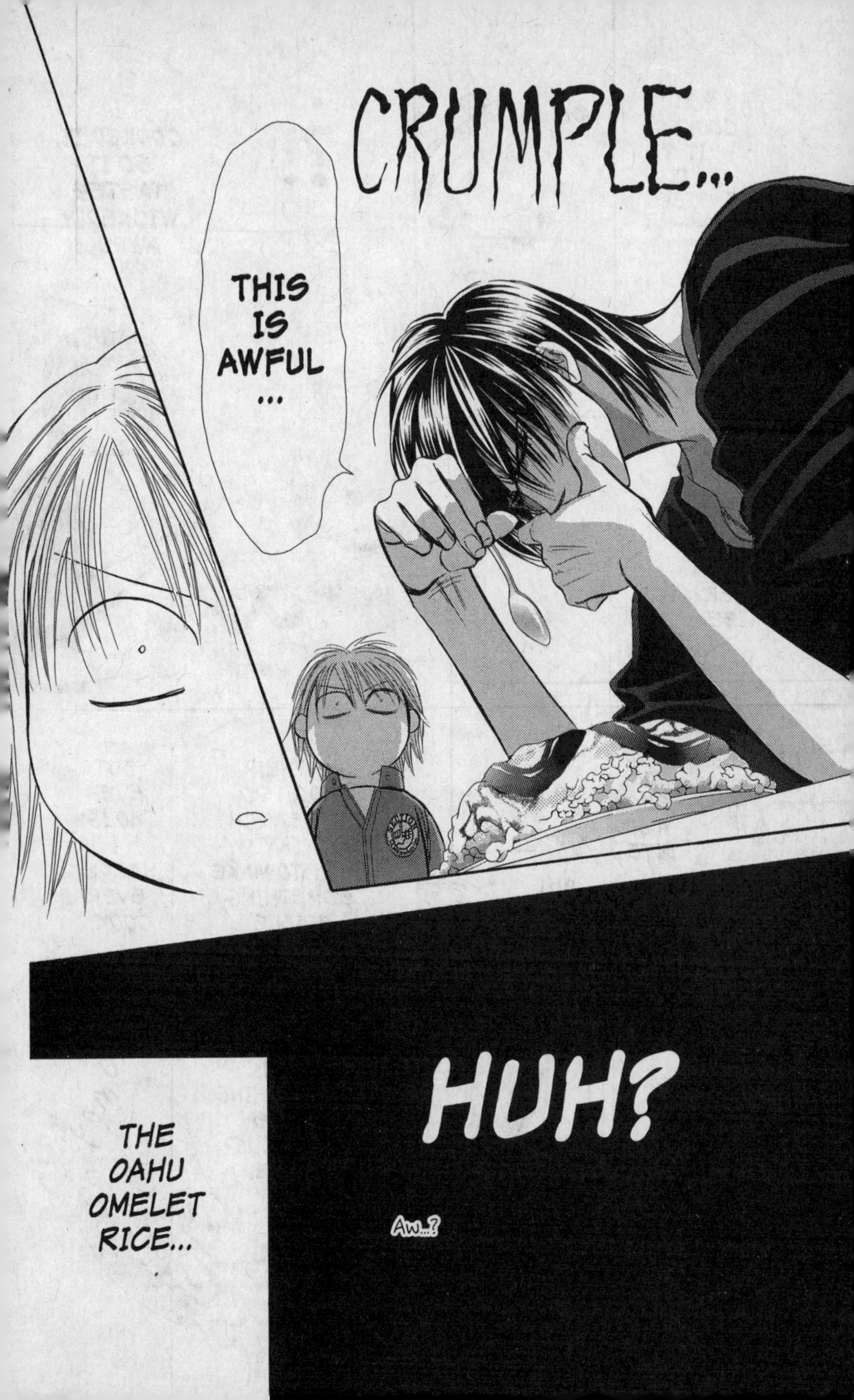
CRUMPLE...
THIS IS AWFUL...
HUH?
Aw...?
THE OAHU OMELET RICE...

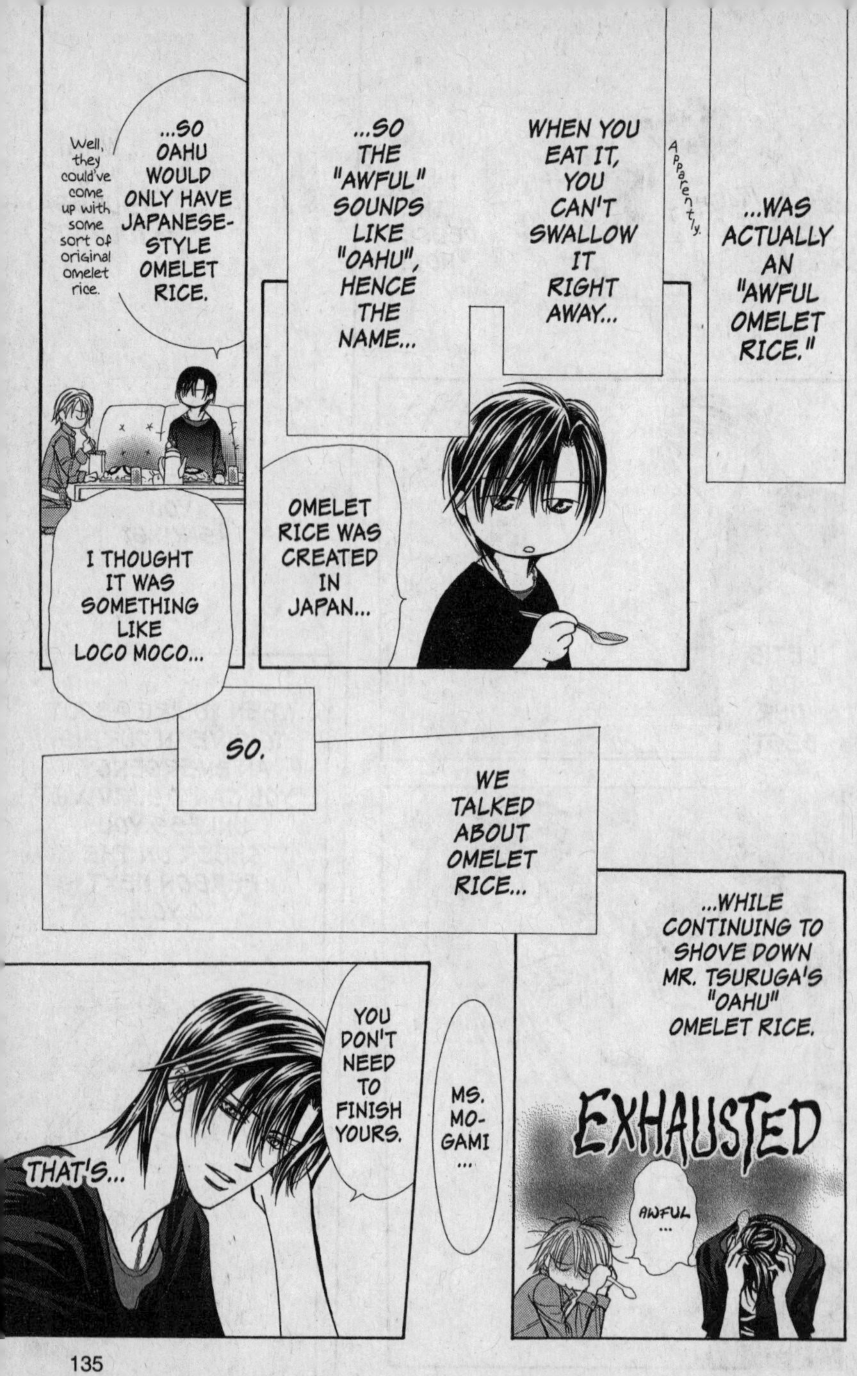
...WAS ACTUALLY AN "AWFUL OMELET RICE."
Apparently.
WHEN YOU EAT IT, YOU CAN'T SWALLOW IT RIGHT AWAY...
...SO THE "AWFUL" SOUNDS LIKE "OAHU", HENCE THE NAME...
OMELET RICE WAS CREATED IN JAPAN...
...SO OAHU WOULD ONLY HAVE JAPANESE-STYLE OMELET RICE.
Well, they could've come up with some sort of original omelet rice.
I THOUGHT IT WAS SOMETHING LIKE LOCO MOCO...
SO.
WE TALKED ABOUT OMELET RICE...
...WHILE CONTINUING TO SHOVE DOWN MR. TSURUGA'S "OAHU" OMELET RICE.
EXHAUSTED
AWFUL...
MS. MOGAMI...
YOU DON'T NEED TO FINISH YOURS.
THAT'S...

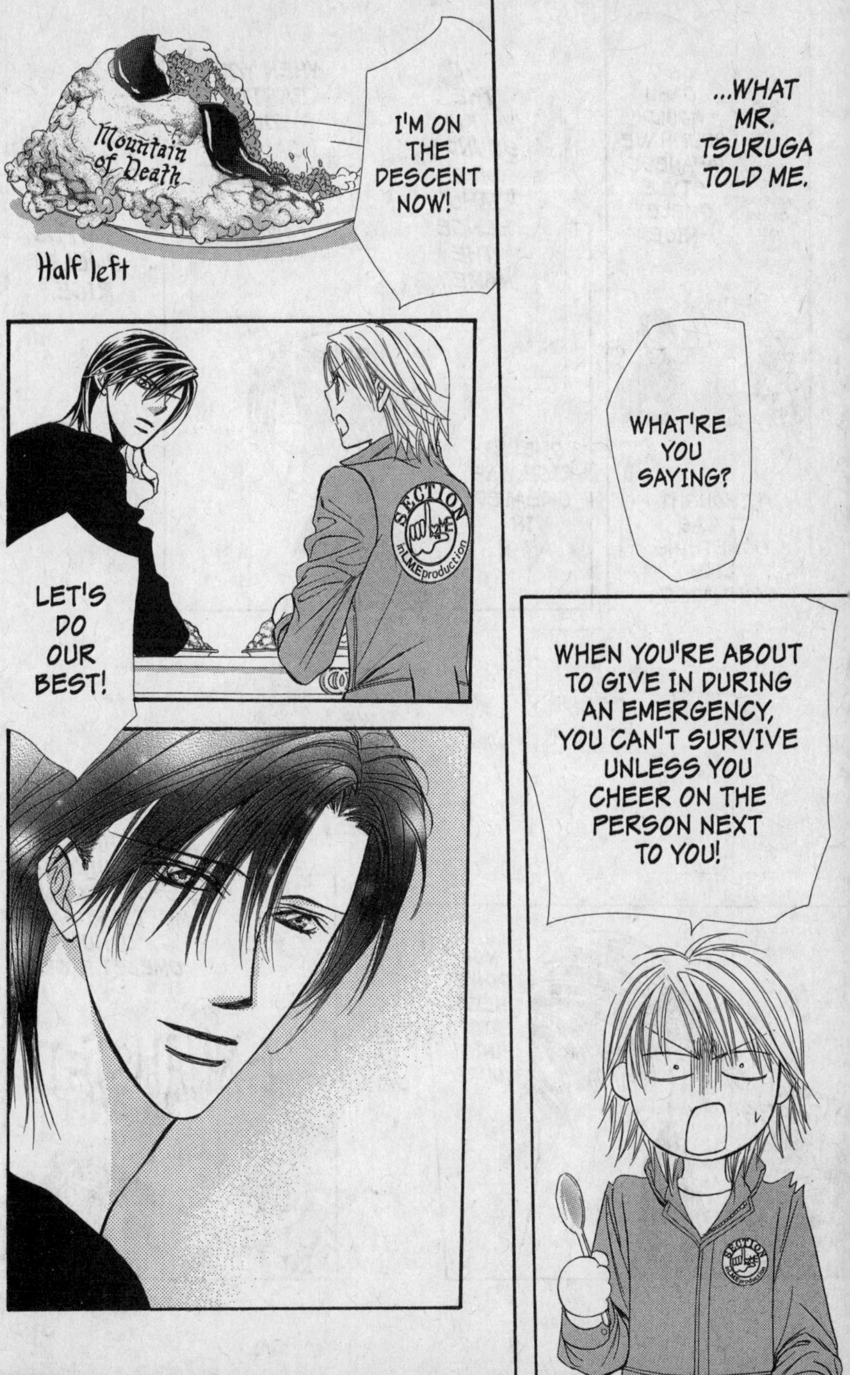
...WHAT MR. TSURUGA TOLD ME.
WHAT'RE YOU SAYING?
WHEN YOU'RE ABOUT TO GIVE IN DURING AN EMERGENCY, YOU CAN'T SURVIVE UNLESS YOU CHEER ON THE PERSON NEXT TO YOU!
I'M ON THE DESCENT NOW!
Mountain of Death
Half left
SECTION
inLMEproduction
LET'S DO OUR BEST!

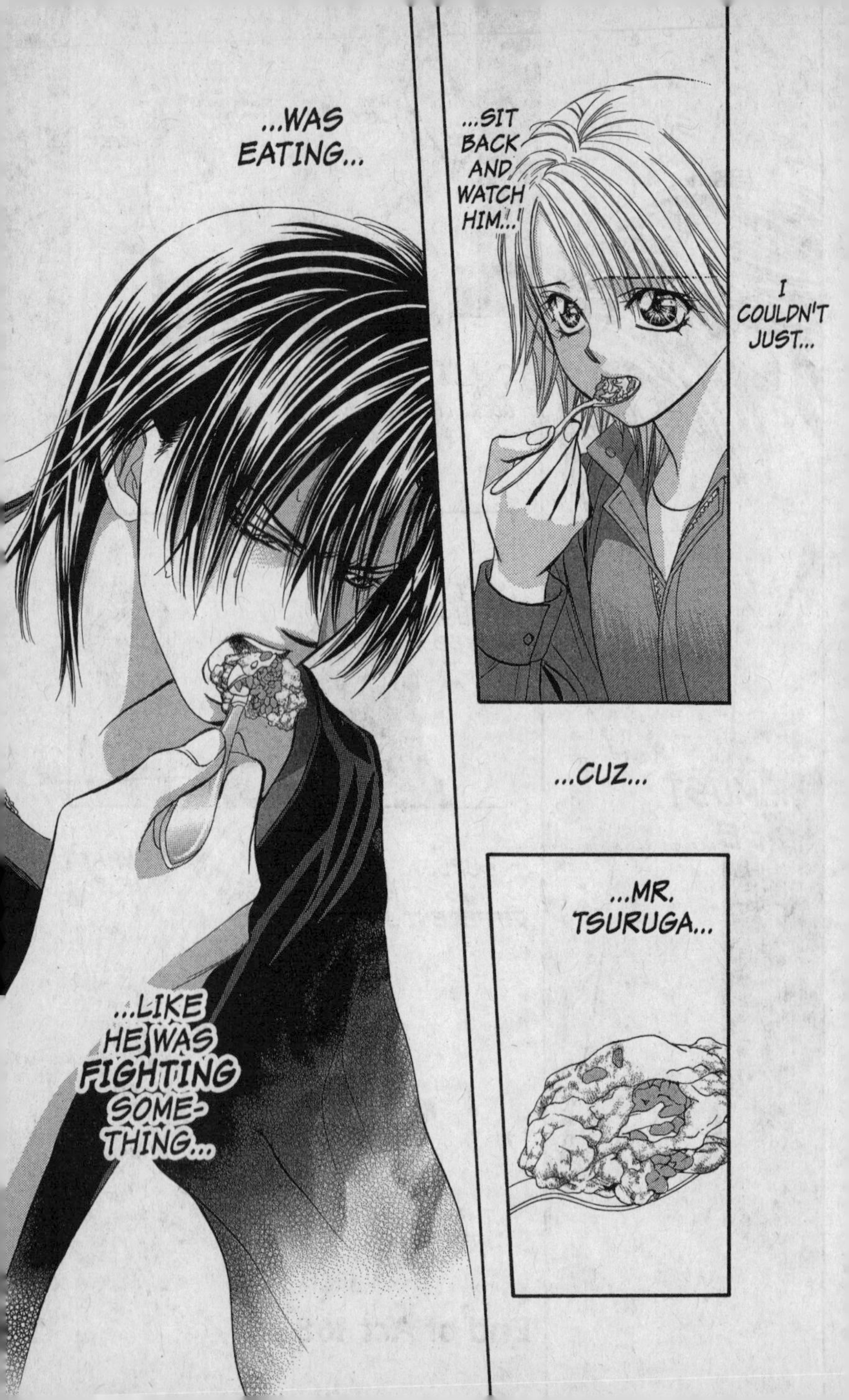
I COULDN'T JUST...
...SIT BACK AND WATCH HIM...
...CUZ...
...MR. TSURUGA...
...WAS EATING...
...LIKE HE WAS FIGHTING SOME-THING...

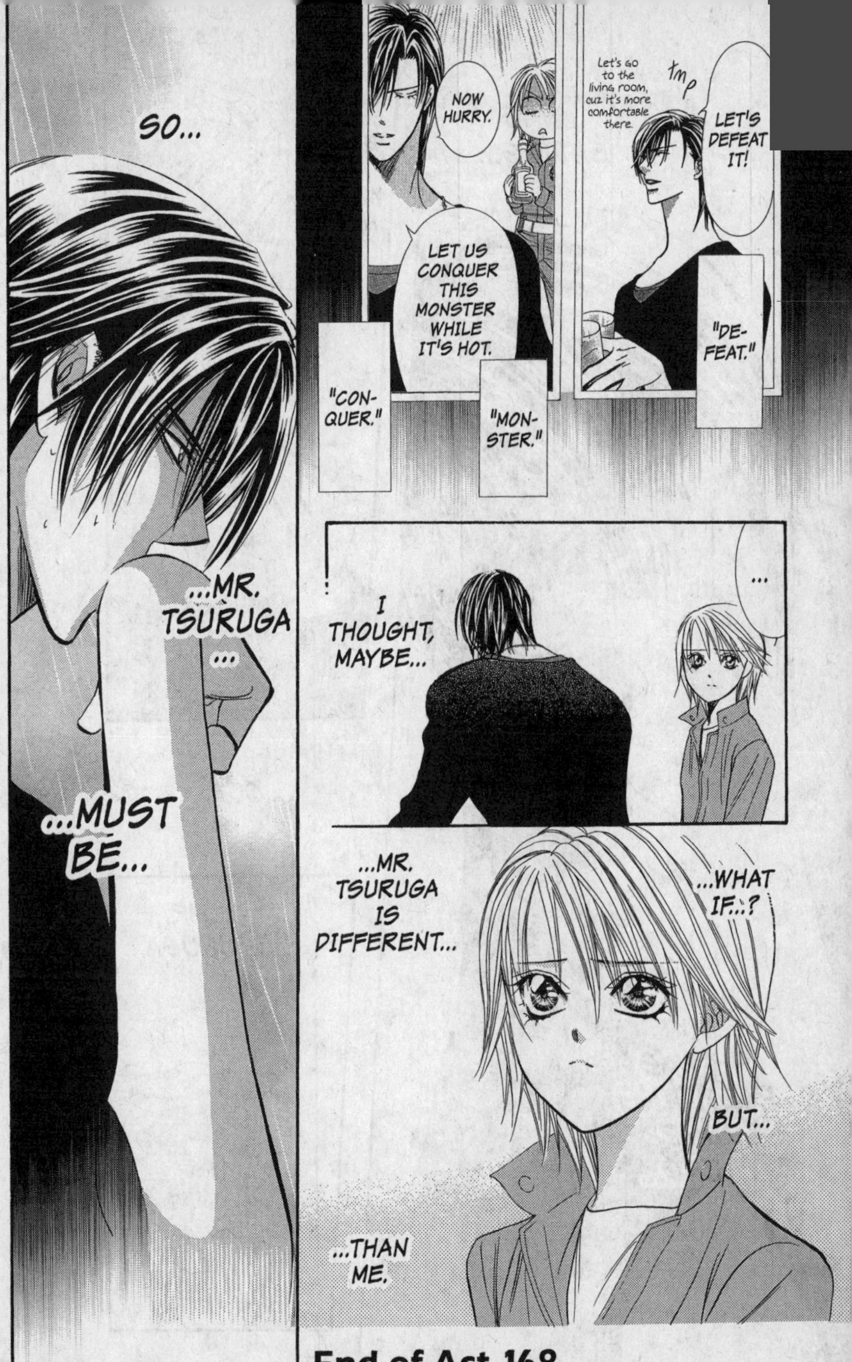
Let's go to the living room, cuz it's more comfortable there.
tmp
LET'S DEFEAT IT!
"DE-FEAT."
NOW HURRY.
LET US CONQUER THIS MONSTER WHILE IT'S HOT.
"MON-STER."
"CON-QUER."
...
I THOUGHT, MAYBE...
...WHAT IF...?
...MR. TSURUGA IS DIFFERENT...
BUT...
...THAN ME.
SO...
...MR. TSURUGA ...
...MUST BE...

End of Act 168

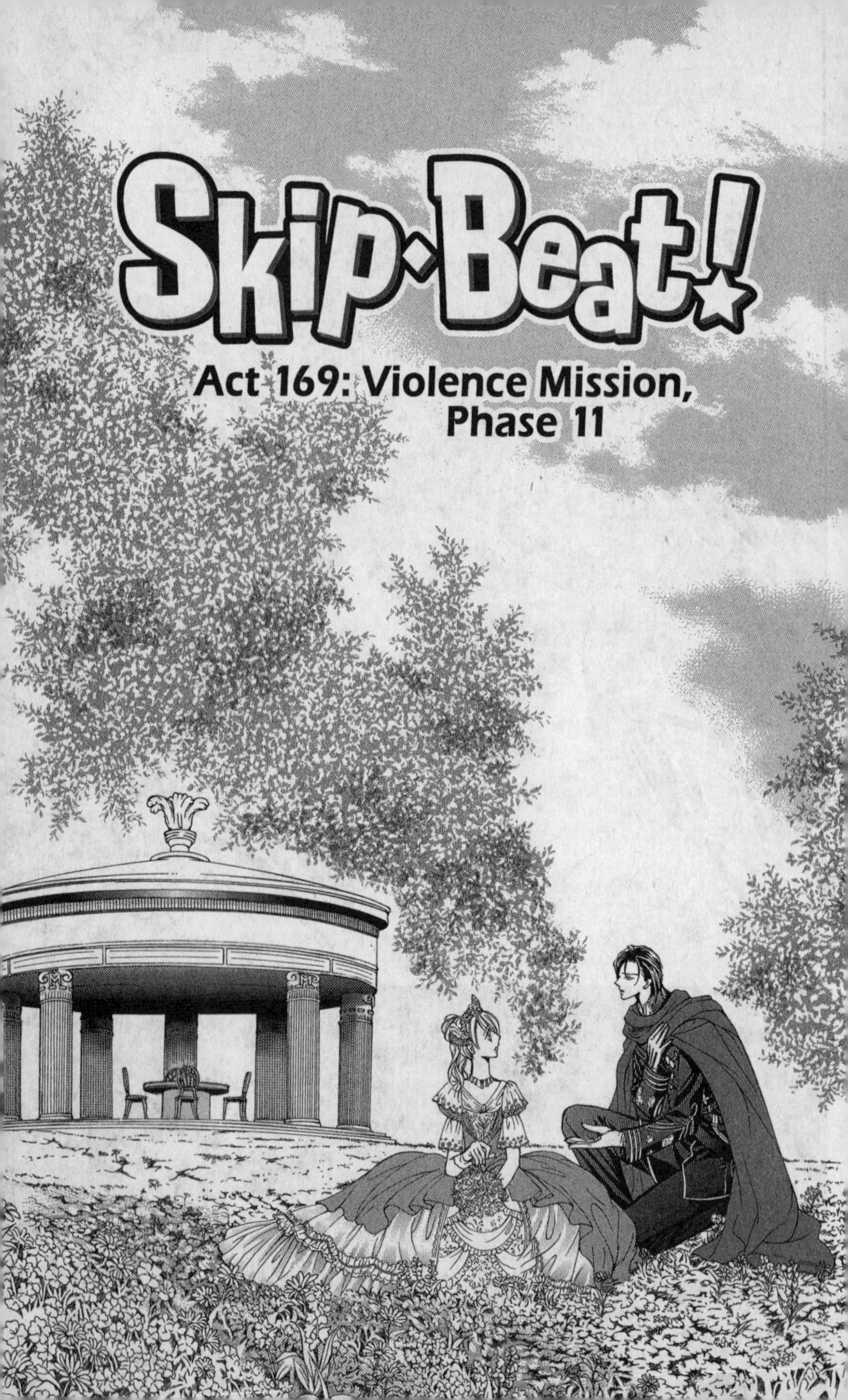
Skip·Beat!
Act 169: Violence Mission, Phase 11

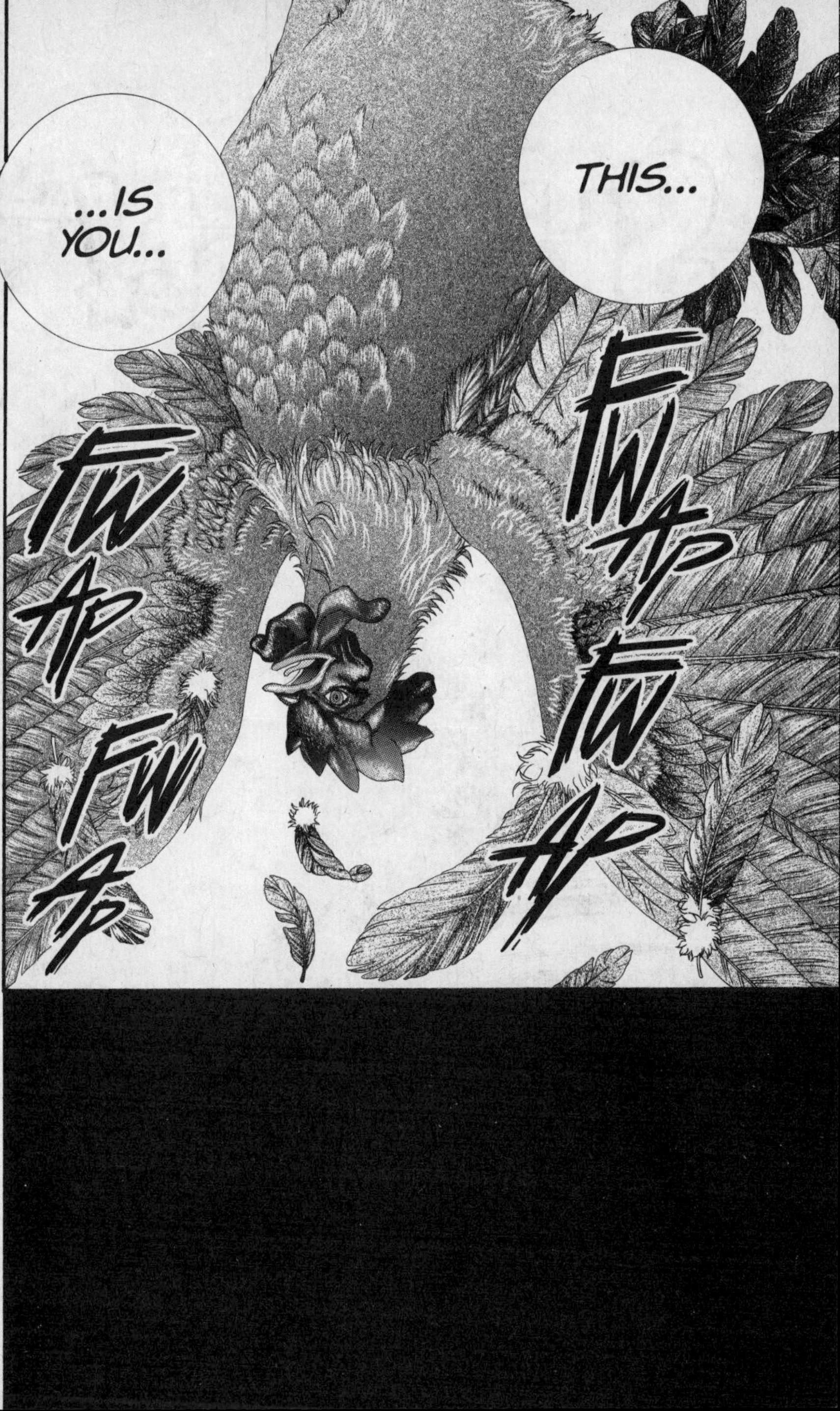
THIS...
FWAP FWAP
...IS YOU...
FWAP FWAP

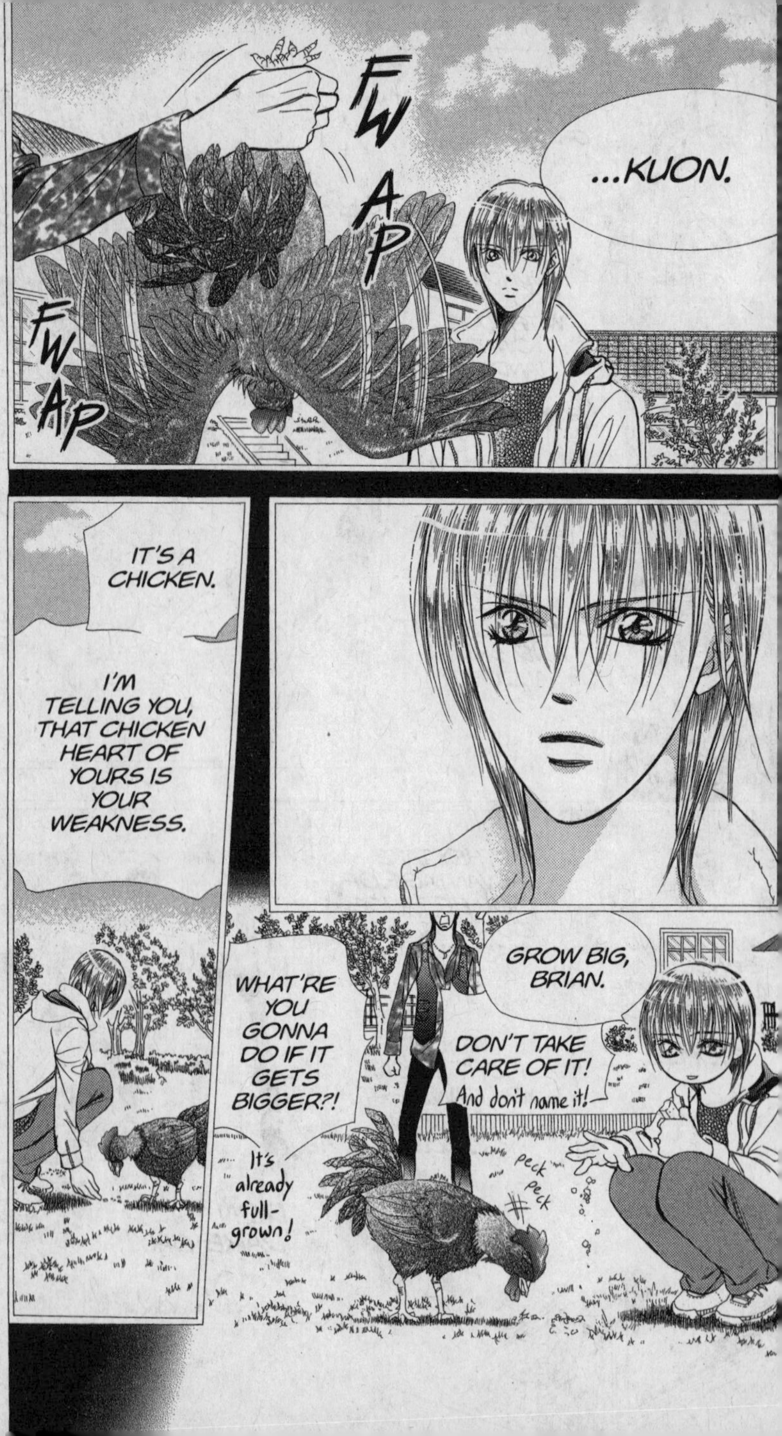
...KUON.
FWAP
FWAP
GROW BIG, BRIAN.
DON'T TAKE CARE OF IT!
And don't name it!
WHAT'RE YOU GONNA DO IF IT GETS BIGGER?!
peck peck
It's already full-grown!
IT'S A CHICKEN.
I'M TELLING YOU, THAT CHICKEN HEART OF YOURS IS YOUR WEAKNESS.

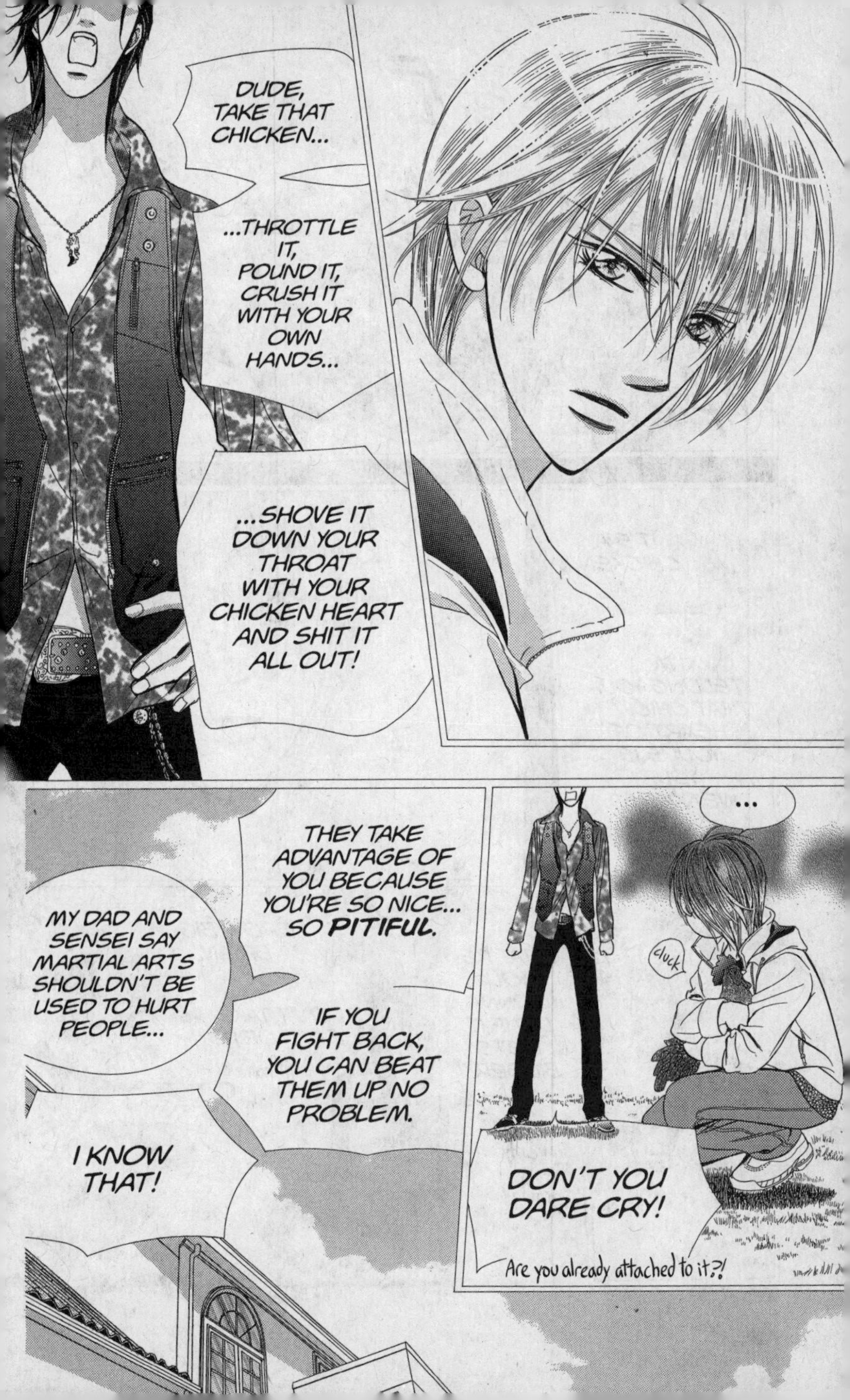

DUDE, TAKE THAT CHICKEN...
...THROTTLE IT, POUND IT, CRUSH IT WITH YOUR OWN HANDS...
...SHOVE IT DOWN YOUR THROAT WITH YOUR CHICKEN HEART AND SHIT IT ALL OUT!
...
cluck
DON'T YOU DARE CRY!
Are you already attached to it?!
THEY TAKE ADVANTAGE OF YOU BECAUSE YOU'RE SO NICE... SO **PITIFUL.**
IF YOU FIGHT BACK, YOU CAN BEAT THEM UP NO PROBLEM.
MY DAD AND SENSEI SAY MARTIAL ARTS SHOULDN'T BE USED TO HURT PEOPLE...
I KNOW THAT!

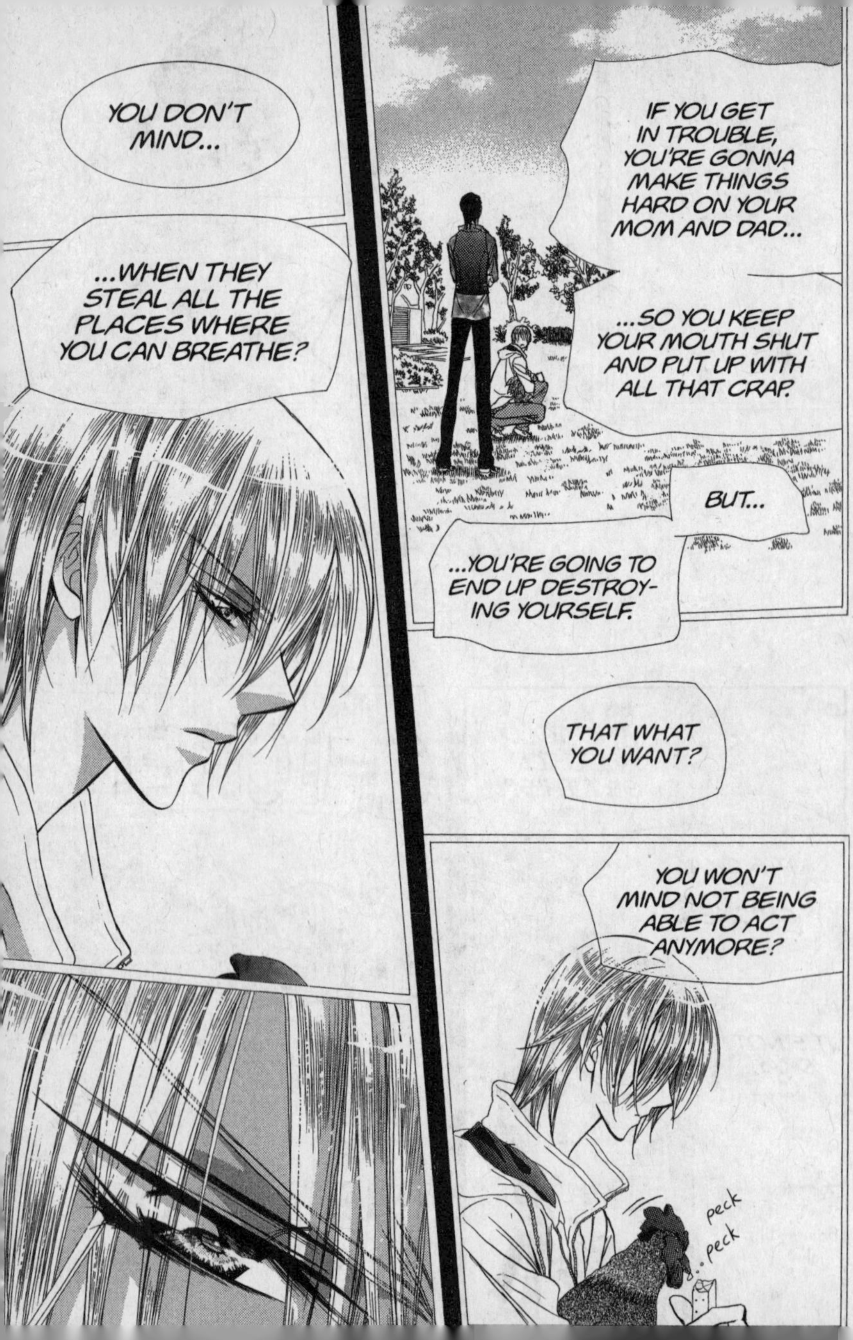
IF YOU GET IN TROUBLE, YOU'RE GONNA MAKE THINGS HARD ON YOUR MOM AND DAD...
...SO YOU KEEP YOUR MOUTH SHUT AND PUT UP WITH ALL THAT CRAP.
BUT...
...YOU'RE GOING TO END UP DESTROY-ING YOURSELF.
THAT WHAT YOU WANT?
YOU WON'T MIND NOT BEING ABLE TO ACT ANYMORE?
peck
peck
YOU DON'T MIND...
...WHEN THEY STEAL ALL THE PLACES WHERE YOU CAN BREATHE?

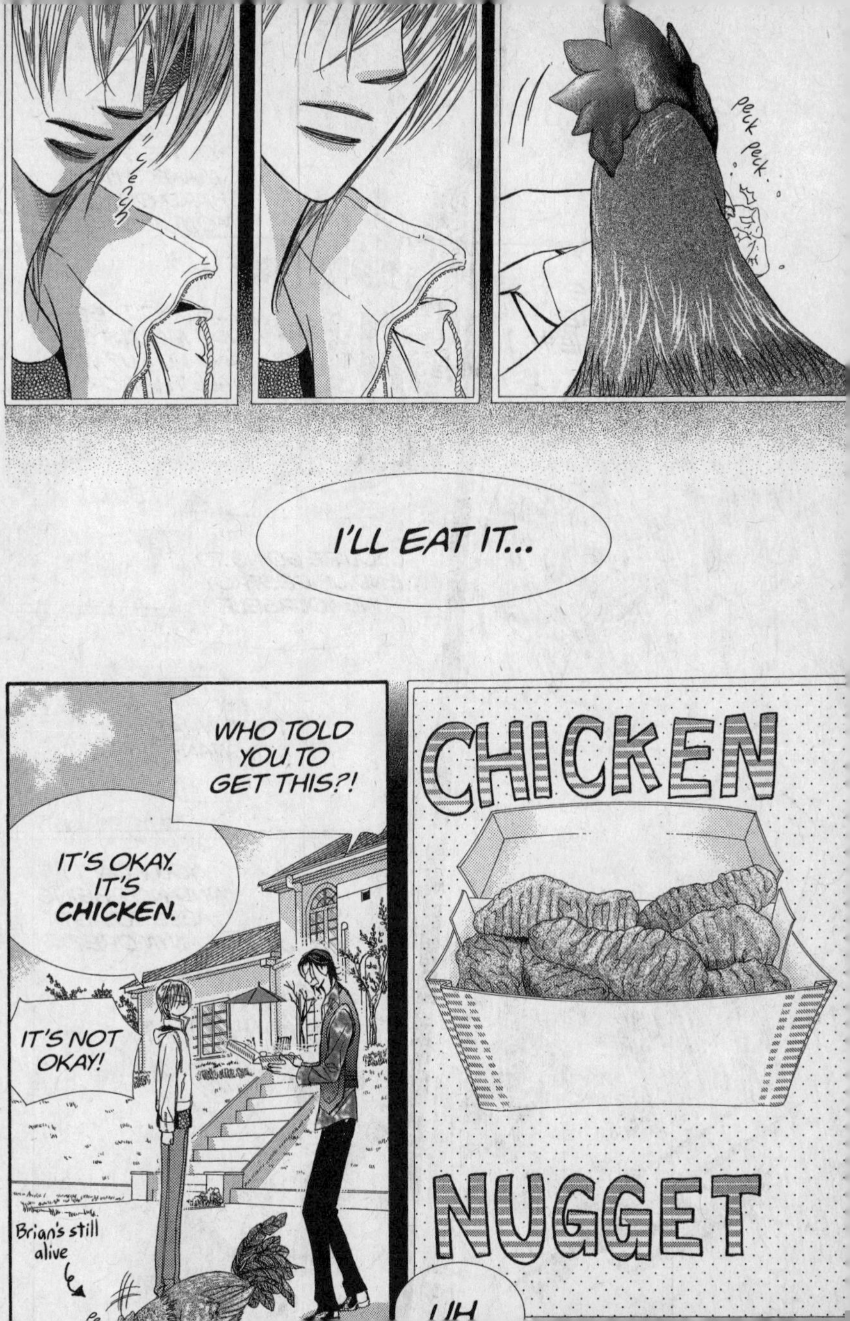
peck peck
clench
I'LL EAT IT...
CHICKEN
NUGGET
UH
WHO TOLD YOU TO GET THIS?!
IT'S OKAY. IT'S CHICKEN.
IT'S NOT OKAY!
Brian's still alive

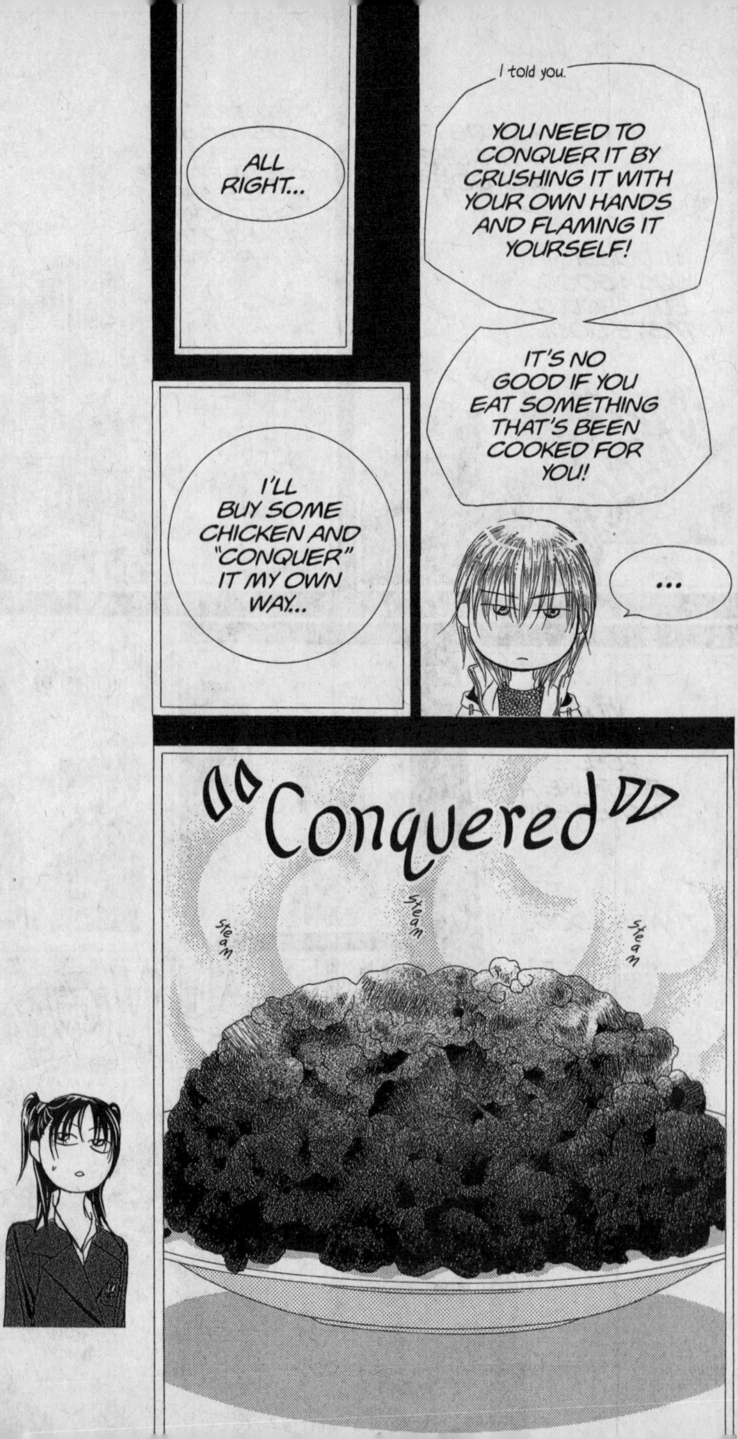
I told you.
YOU NEED TO CONQUER IT BY CRUSHING IT WITH YOUR OWN HANDS AND FLAMING IT YOURSELF!
IT'S NO GOOD IF YOU EAT SOMETHING THAT'S BEEN COOKED FOR YOU!
...
ALL RIGHT...
I'LL BUY SOME CHICKEN AND "CONQUER" IT MY OWN WAY...
"Conquered"
Steam
Steam
Steam

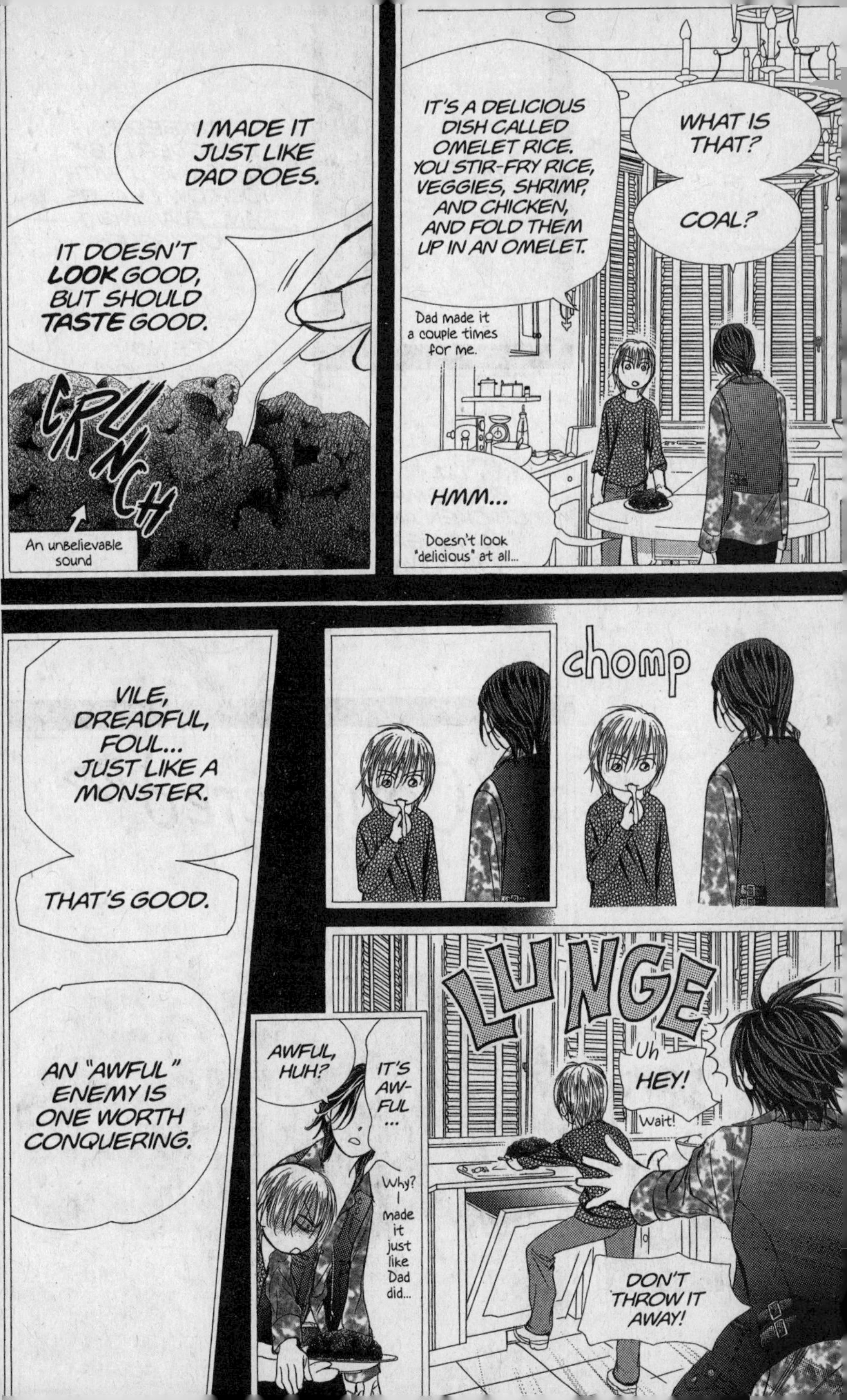
WHAT IS THAT?
COAL?
IT'S A DELICIOUS DISH CALLED OMELET RICE. YOU STIR-FRY RICE, VEGGIES, SHRIMP, AND CHICKEN, AND FOLD THEM UP IN AN OMELET.
Dad made it a couple times for me.
HMM...
Doesn't look "delicious" at all...
I MADE IT JUST LIKE DAD DOES.
IT DOESN'T **LOOK** GOOD, BUT SHOULD **TASTE** GOOD.
CRUNCH
An unbelievable sound
chomp
LUNGE
Uh
HEY!
Wait!
DON'T THROW IT AWAY!
IT'S AWFUL...
AWFUL, HUH?
Why? I made it just like Dad did...
VILE, DREADFUL, FOUL... JUST LIKE A MONSTER.
THAT'S GOOD.
AN "AWFUL" ENEMY IS ONE WORTH CONQUERING.

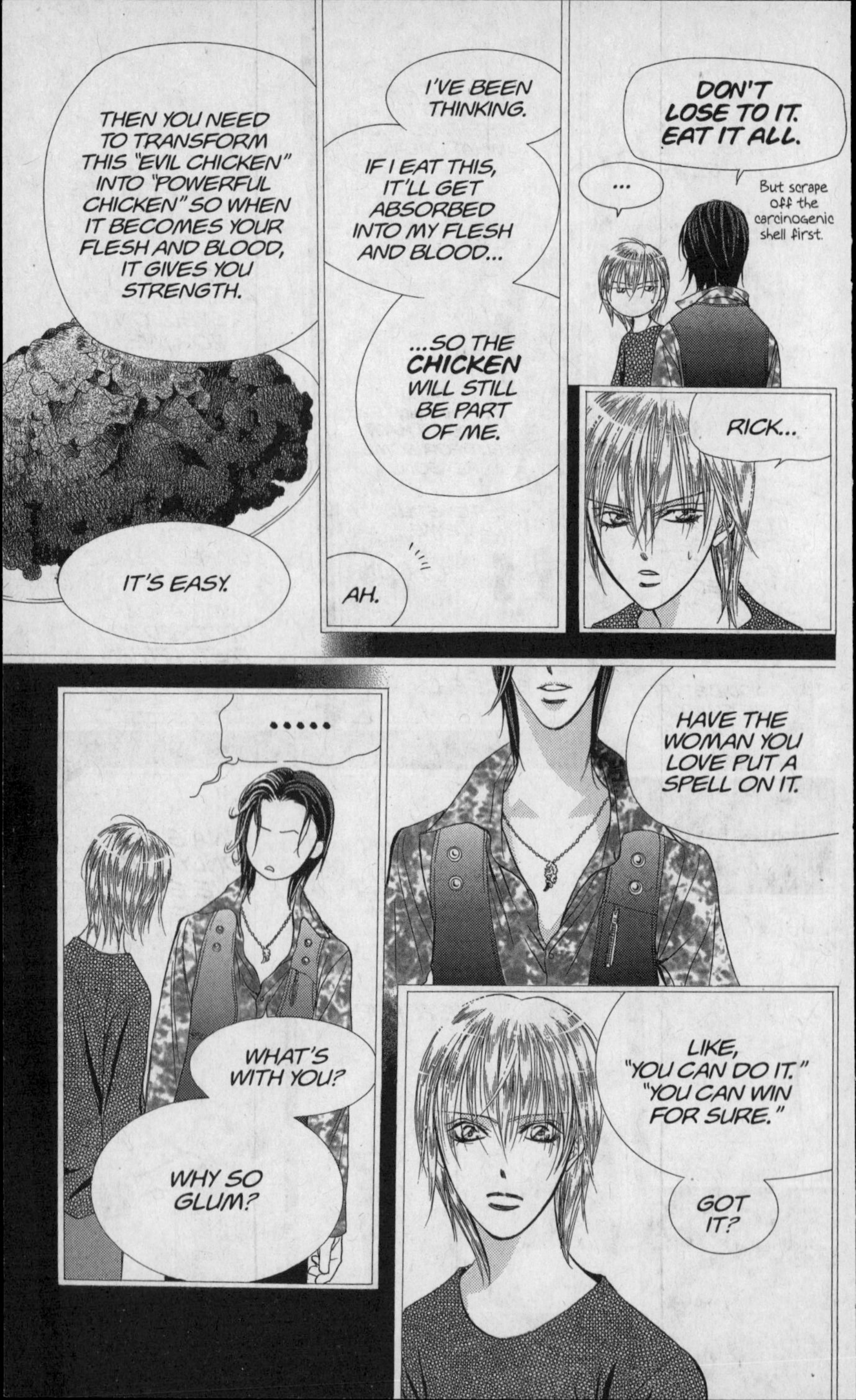
DON'T LOSE TO IT. EAT IT ALL.
...
But scrape off the carcinogenic shell first.
RICK...
I'VE BEEN THINKING.
IF I EAT THIS, IT'LL GET ABSORBED INTO MY FLESH AND BLOOD...
...SO THE CHICKEN WILL STILL BE PART OF ME.
AH.
THEN YOU NEED TO TRANSFORM THIS "EVIL CHICKEN" INTO "POWERFUL CHICKEN" SO WHEN IT BECOMES YOUR FLESH AND BLOOD, IT GIVES YOU STRENGTH.
IT'S EASY.
HAVE THE WOMAN YOU LOVE PUT A SPELL ON IT.
LIKE, "YOU CAN DO IT." "YOU CAN WIN FOR SURE."
GOT IT?
.....
WHAT'S WITH YOU?
WHY SO GLUM?

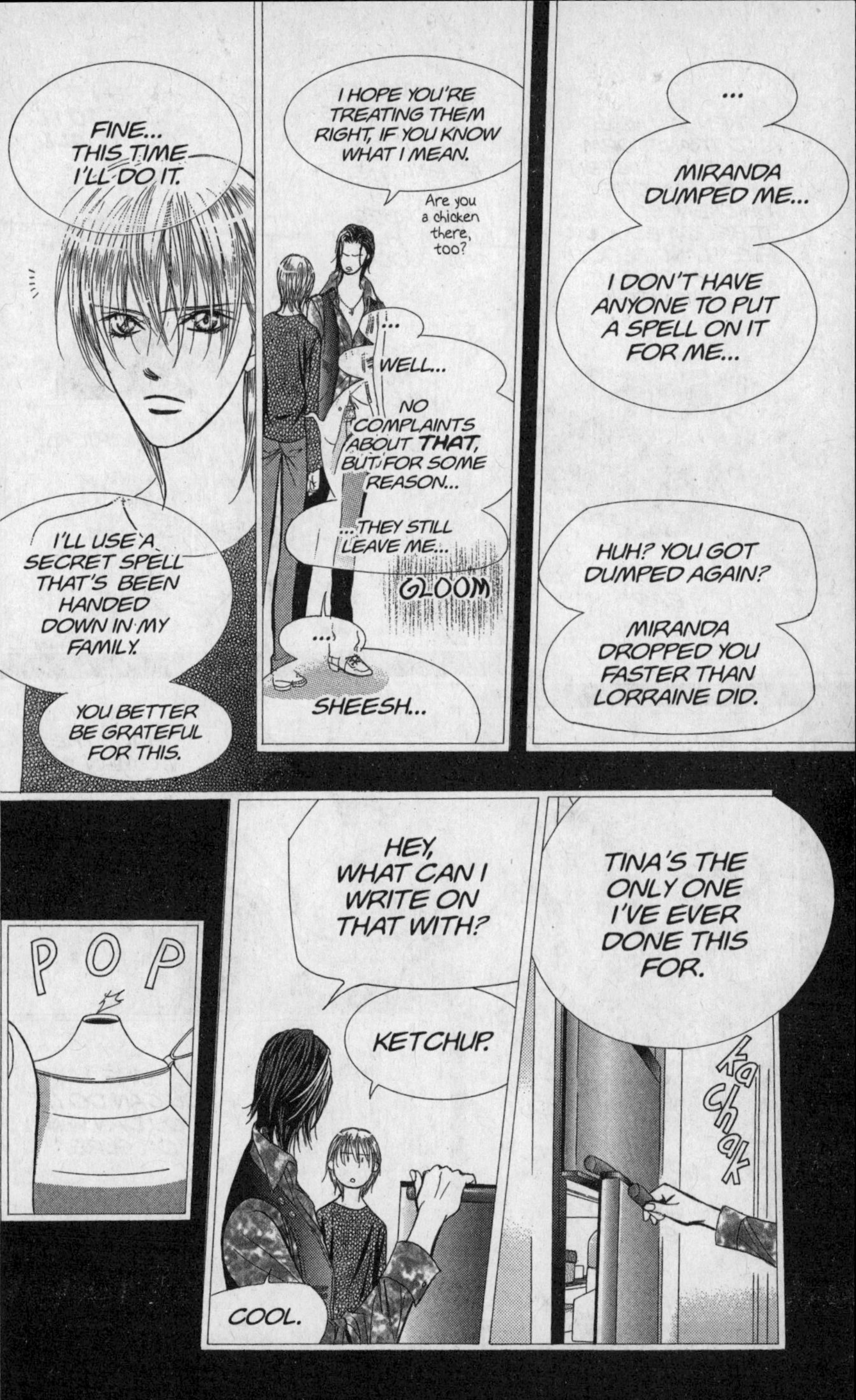
...
MIRANDA DUMPED ME...
I DON'T HAVE ANYONE TO PUT A SPELL ON IT FOR ME...
HUH? YOU GOT DUMPED AGAIN?
MIRANDA DROPPED YOU FASTER THAN LORRAINE DID.
I HOPE YOU'RE TREATING THEM RIGHT, IF YOU KNOW WHAT I MEAN.
Are you a chicken there, too?
...
WELL...
NO COMPLAINTS ABOUT THAT, BUT FOR SOME REASON...
...THEY STILL LEAVE ME...
GLOOM
...
SHEESH...
FINE... THIS TIME I'LL DO IT.
I'LL USE A SECRET SPELL THAT'S BEEN HANDED DOWN IN MY FAMILY.
YOU BETTER BE GRATEFUL FOR THIS.
TINA'S THE ONLY ONE I'VE EVER DONE THIS FOR.
ka chak
HEY, WHAT CAN I WRITE ON THAT WITH?
KETCHUP.
COOL.
POP

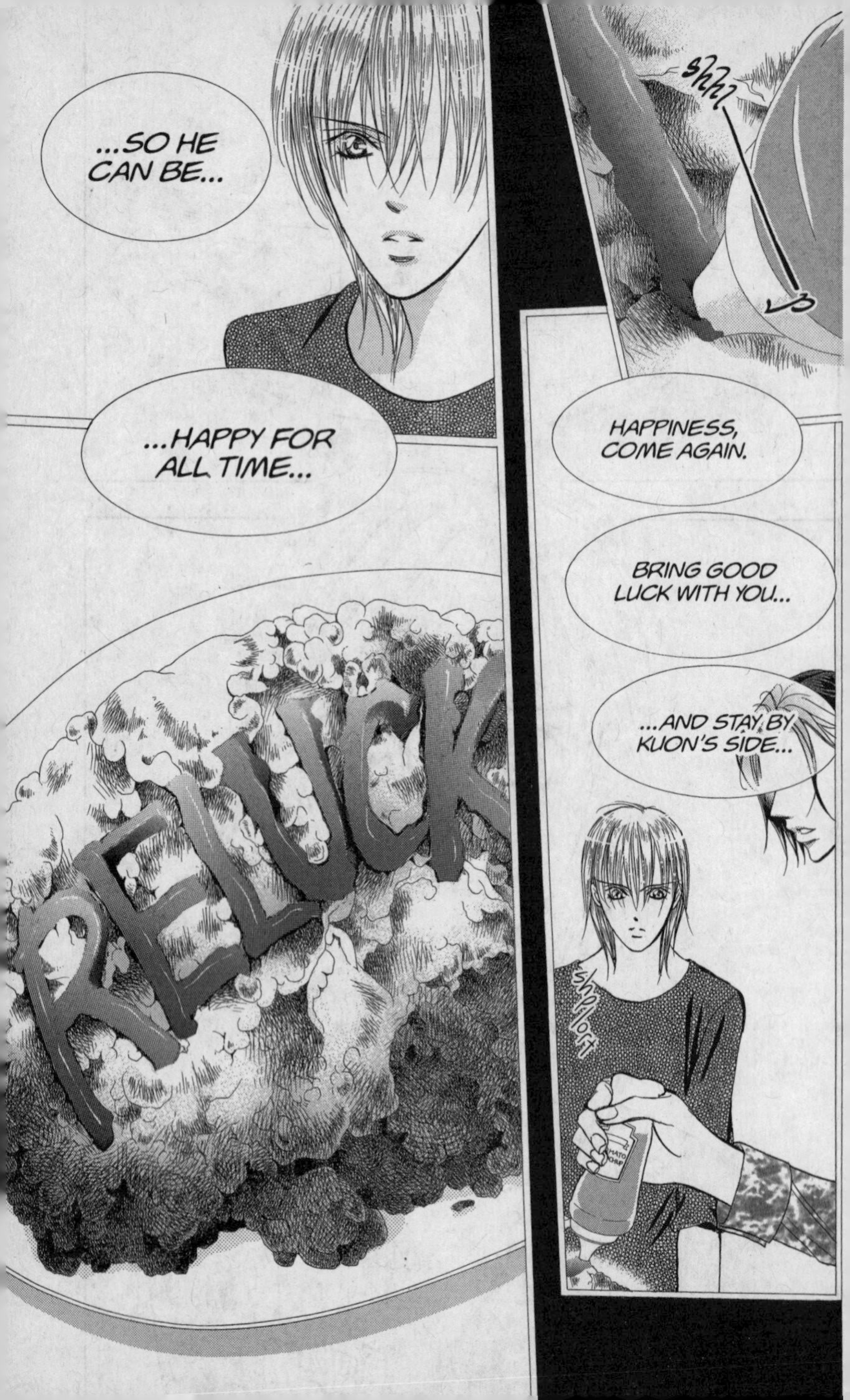
shhh
HAPPINESS, COME AGAIN.
BRING GOOD LUCK WITH YOU...
...AND STAY BY KUON'S SIDE...
shpllort
...SO HE CAN BE...
...HAPPY FOR ALL TIME...

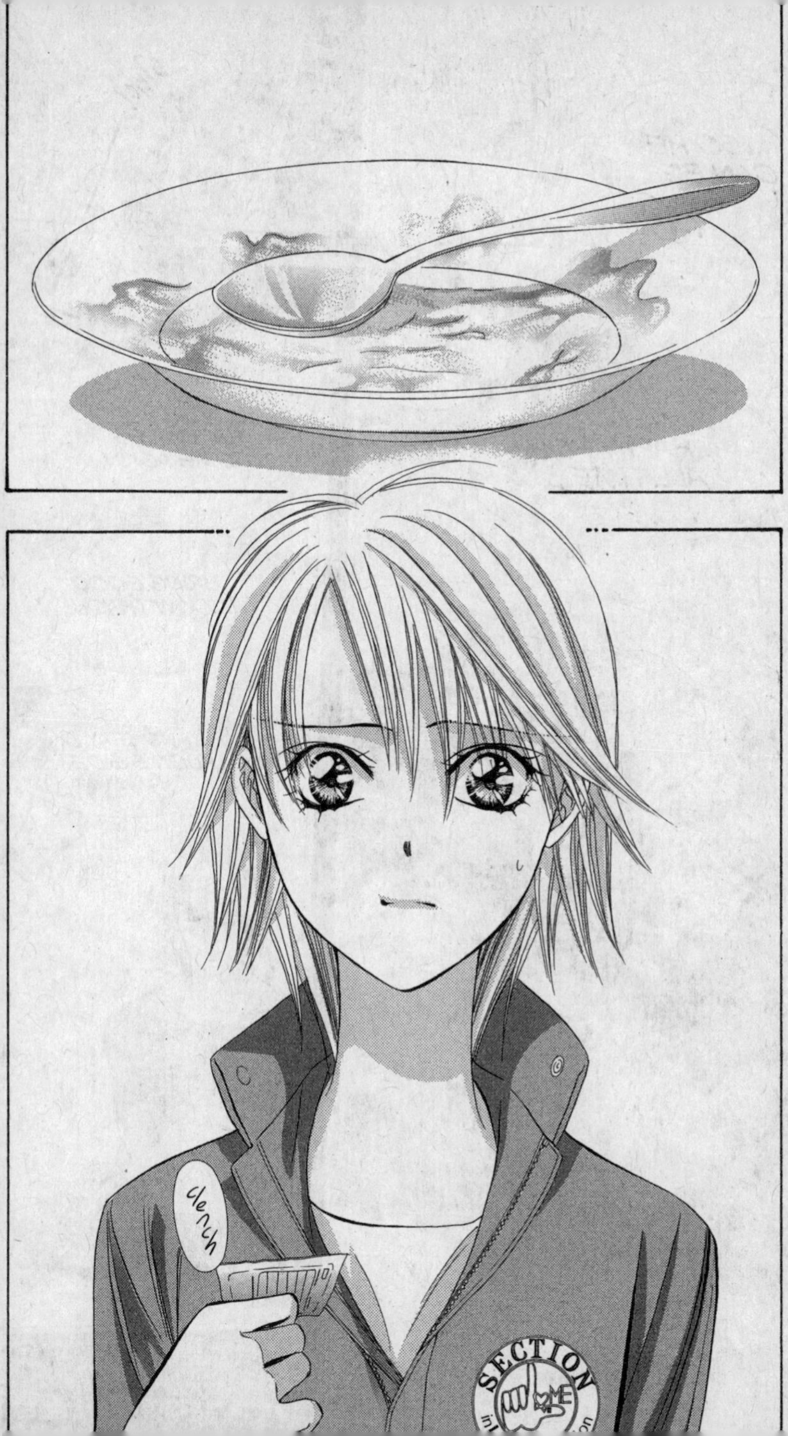
clench
SECTION

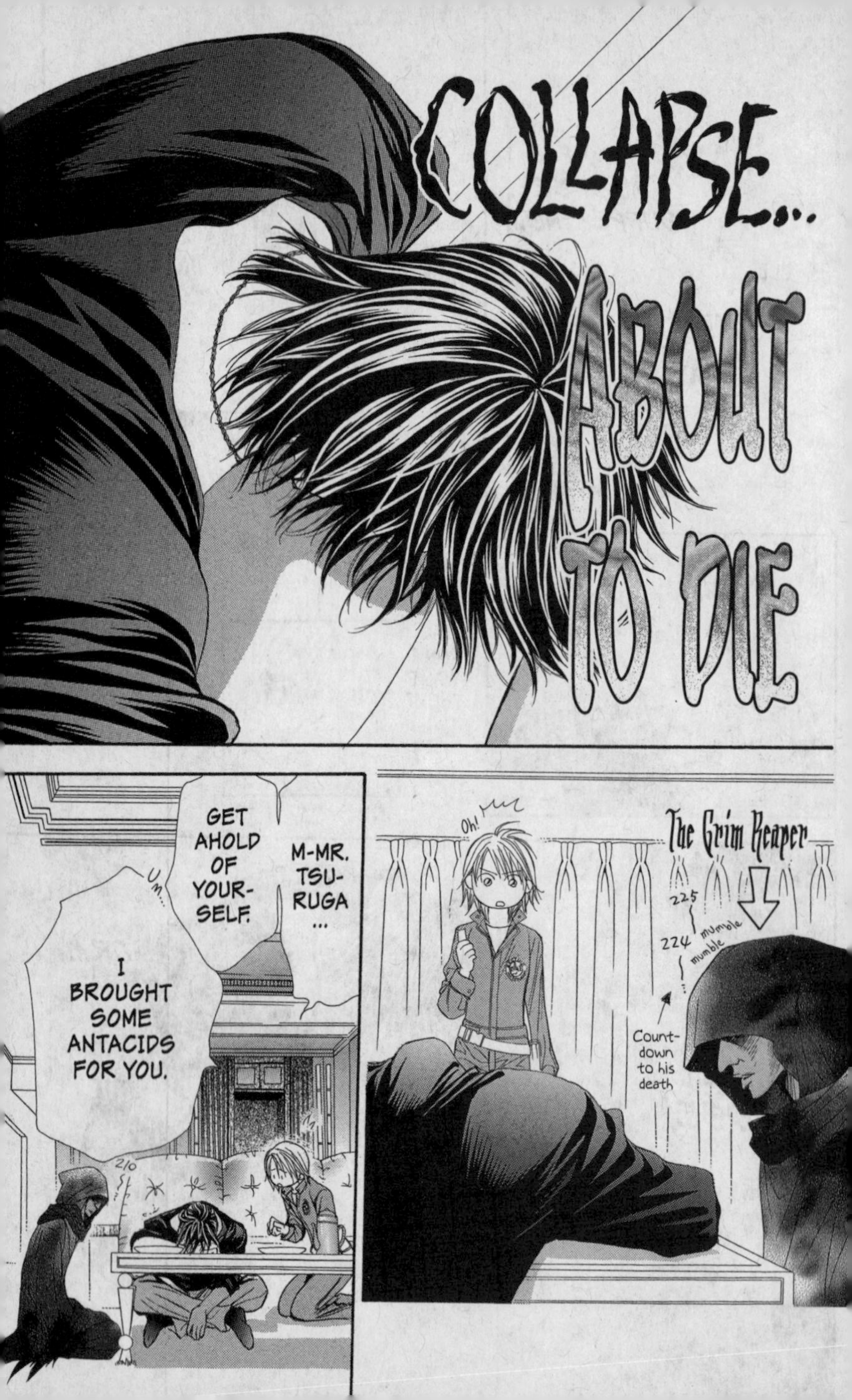
COLLAPSE...
ABOUT TO DIE
Oh!
The Grim Reaper
225
224
mumble mumble
Count-down to his death
M-MR. TSURUGA...
GET AHOLD OF YOURSELF.
Um...
I BROUGHT SOME ANTACIDS FOR YOU.
210

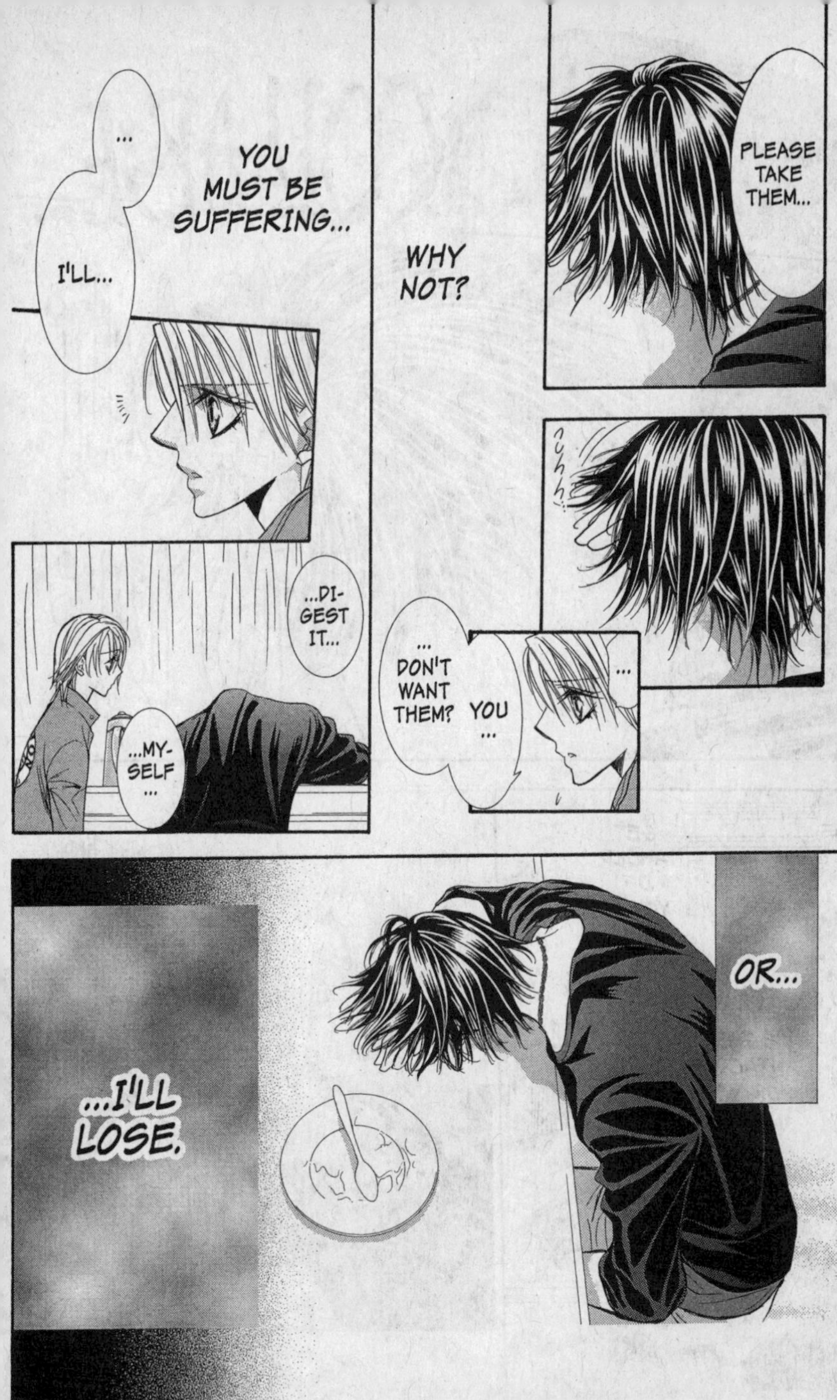
PLEASE TAKE THEM...
...
YOU ...
... DON'T WANT THEM?
WHY NOT?
YOU MUST BE SUFFERING...
...
I'LL...
...DI-GEST IT...
...MY-SELF ...
OR...
...I'LL LOSE.

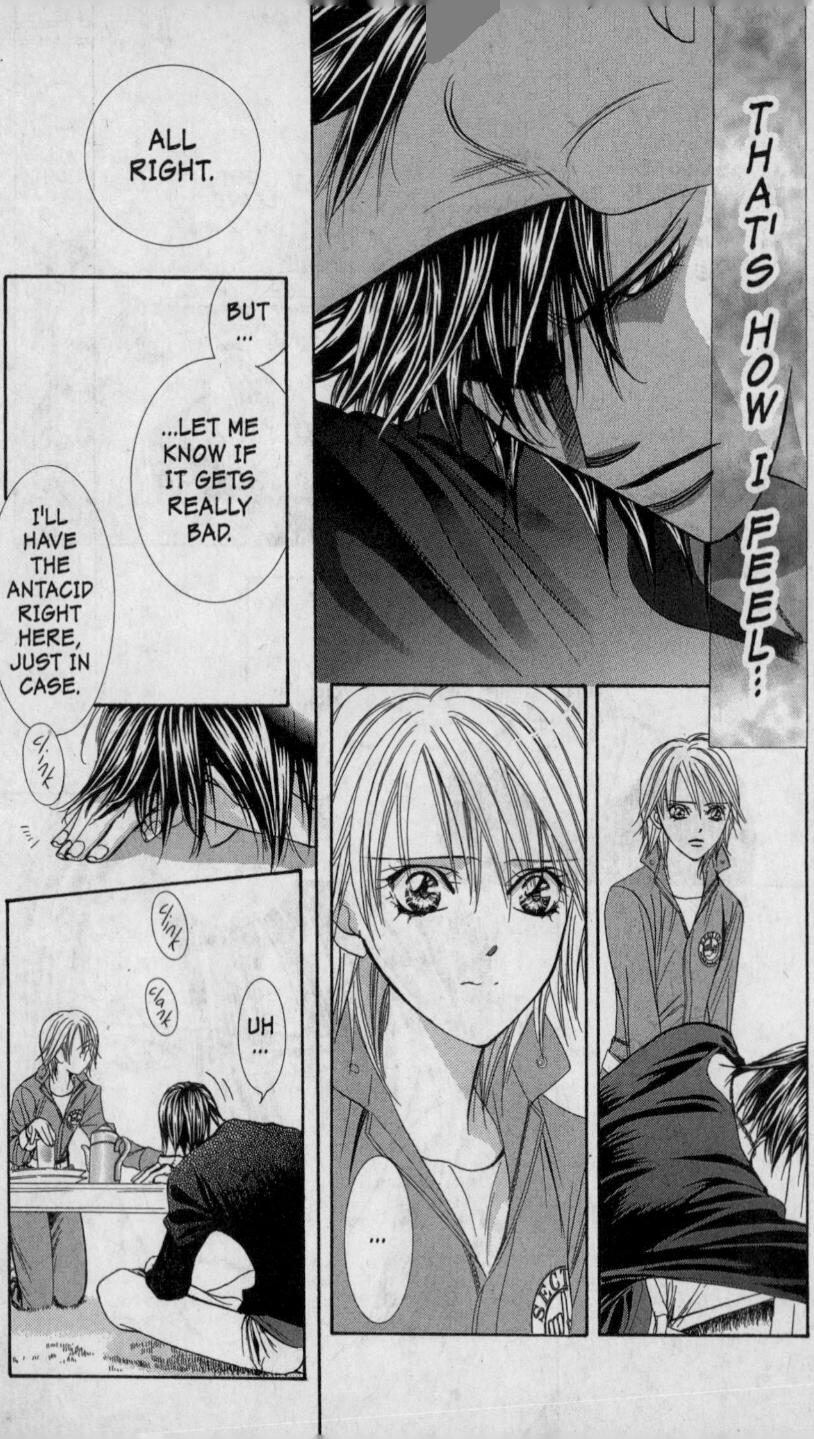
THAT'S HOW I FEEL...
...
ALL RIGHT.
BUT ...
...LET ME KNOW IF IT GETS REALLY BAD.
I'LL HAVE THE ANTACID RIGHT HERE, JUST IN CASE.
clink
UH ...
clink
clank

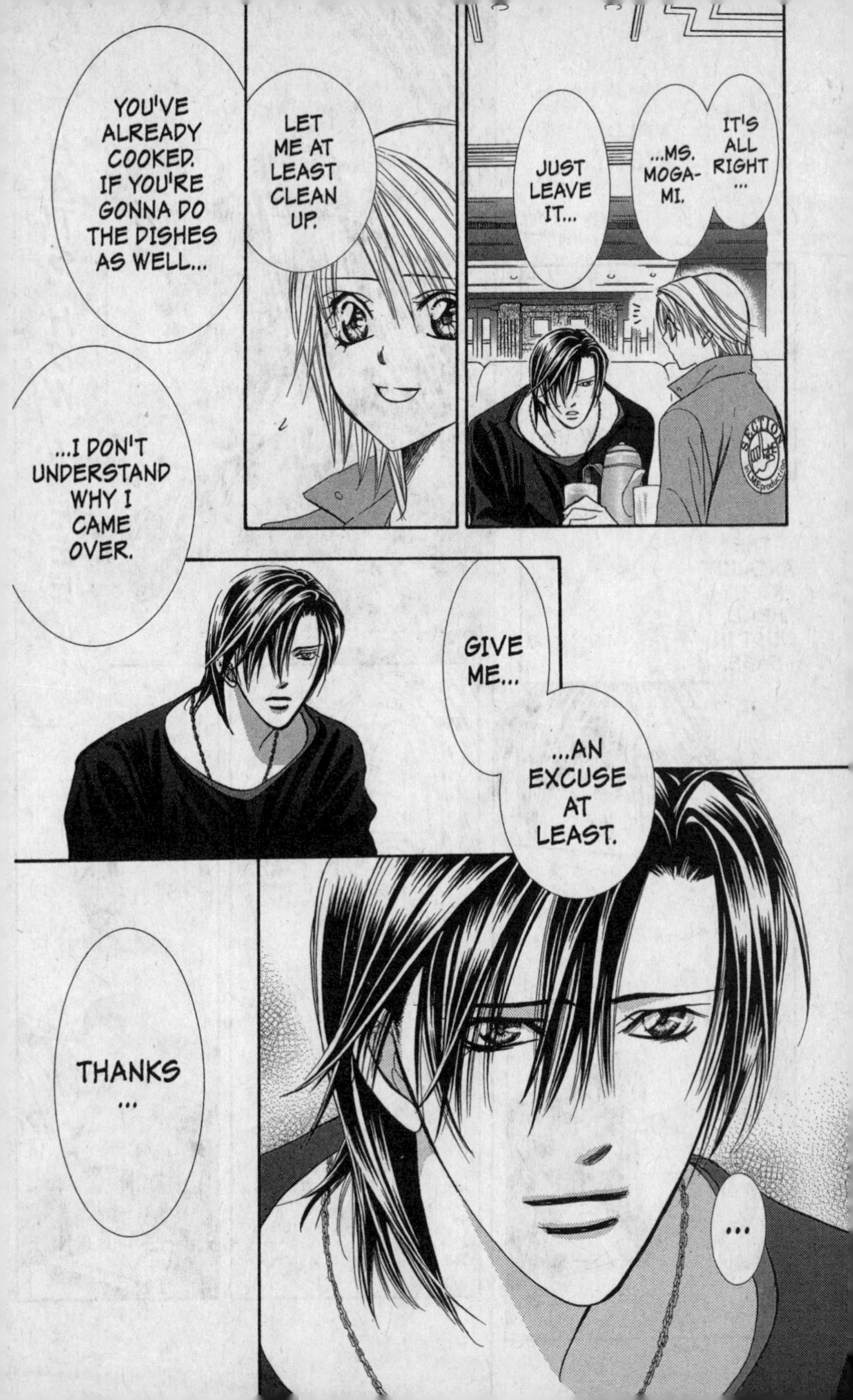
IT'S ALL RIGHT...
...MS. MOGA-MI.
JUST LEAVE IT...
LET ME AT LEAST CLEAN UP.
YOU'VE ALREADY COOKED. IF YOU'RE GONNA DO THE DISHES AS WELL...
...I DON'T UNDERSTAND WHY I CAME OVER.
GIVE ME...
...AN EXCUSE AT LEAST.
...
THANKS...

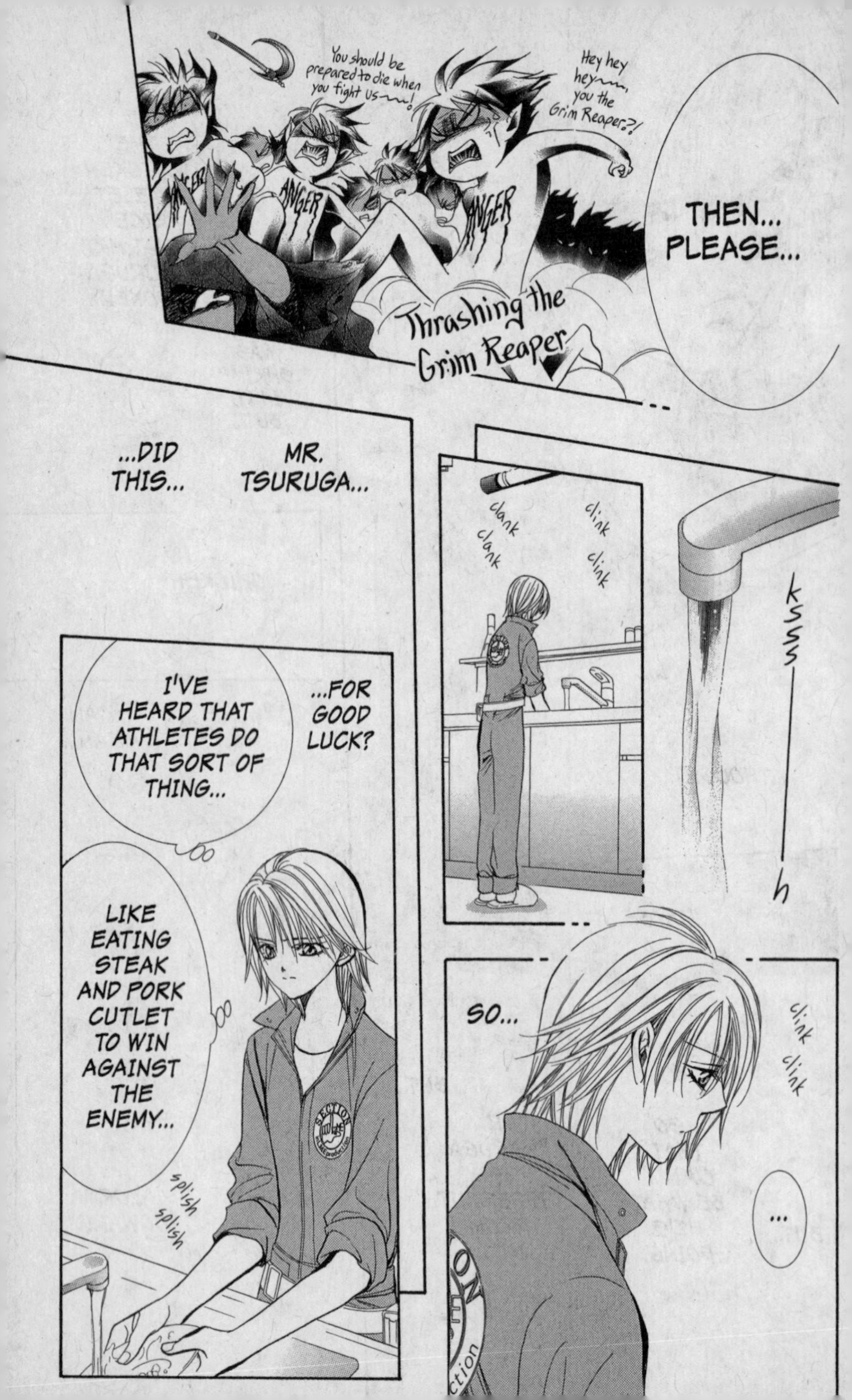
THEN... PLEASE...
Hey hey hey~, you the Grim Reaper?!
You should be prepared to die when you fight us~!
ANGER
ANGER
ANGER
Thrashing the Grim Reaper
ksss—h
clink clink
clank clank
MR. TSURUGA...
...DID THIS...
SO...
clink clink
...
...FOR GOOD LUCK?
I'VE HEARD THAT ATHLETES DO THAT SORT OF THING...
LIKE EATING STEAK AND PORK CUTLET TO WIN AGAINST THE ENEMY...
splish splish

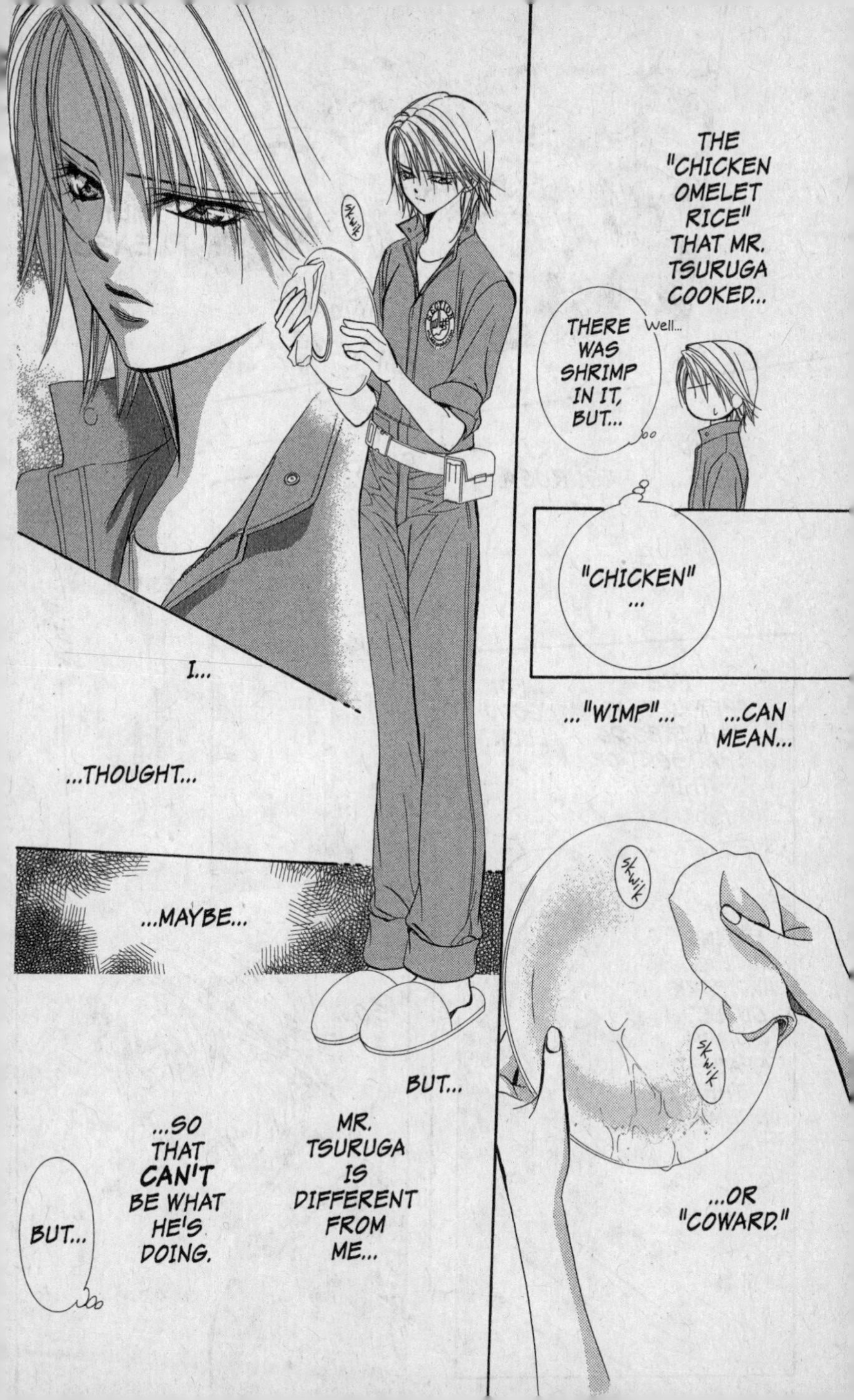
THE "CHICKEN OMELET RICE" THAT MR. TSURUGA COOKED...
Well...
THERE WAS SHRIMP IN IT, BUT...
"CHICKEN" ...
...CAN MEAN...
..."WIMP"...
SKWIK
SKWIK
...OR "COWARD."
SKWIK
I...
...THOUGHT...
...MAYBE...
BUT...
MR. TSURUGA IS DIFFERENT FROM ME...
...SO THAT CAN'T BE WHAT HE'S DOING.
BUT...

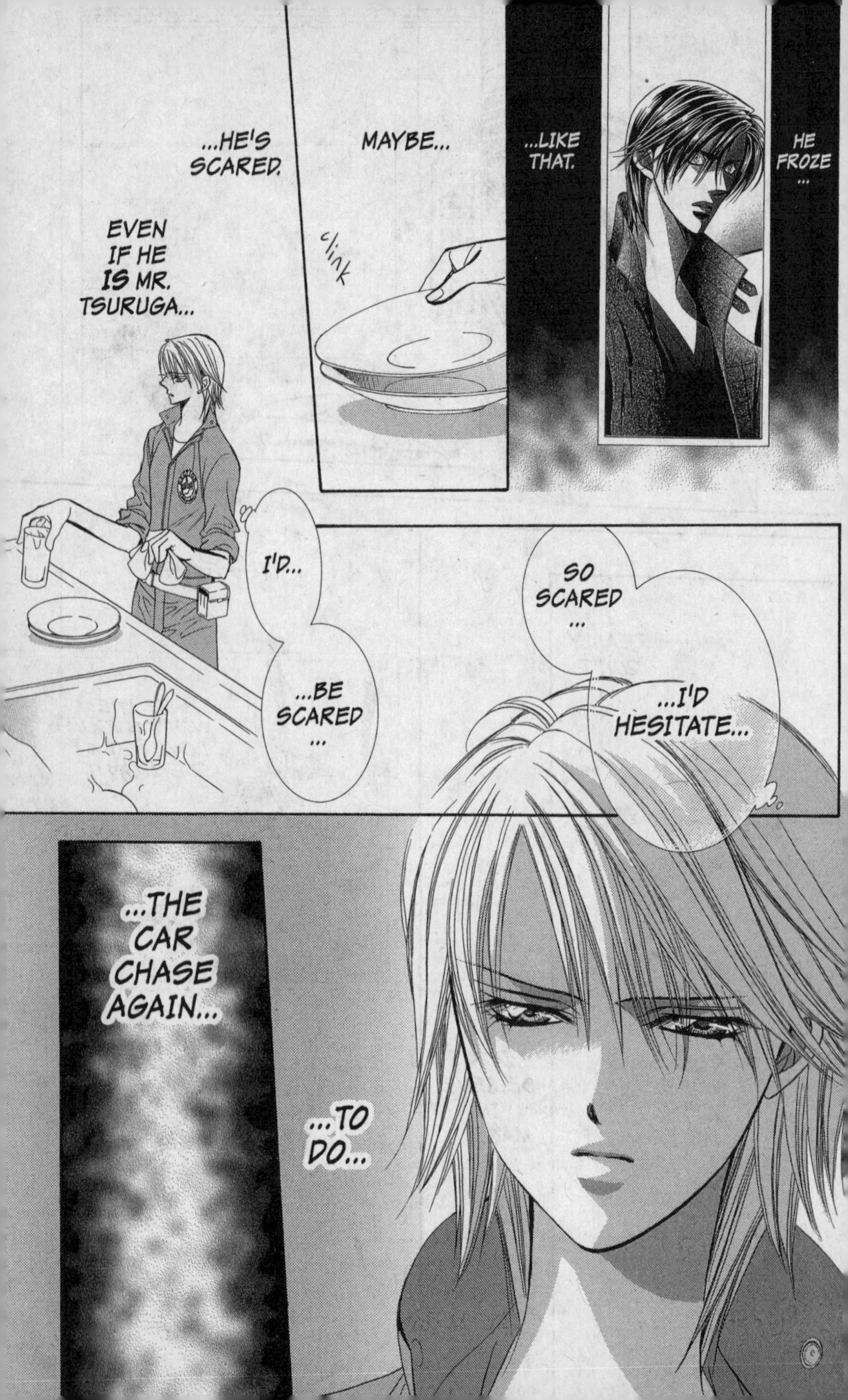
HE FROZE ...
...LIKE THAT.
MAYBE...
clink
...HE'S SCARED.
EVEN IF HE IS MR. TSURUGA...
I'D...
...BE SCARED ...
SO SCARED ...
...I'D HESITATE...
...TO DO...
...THE CAR CHASE AGAIN...

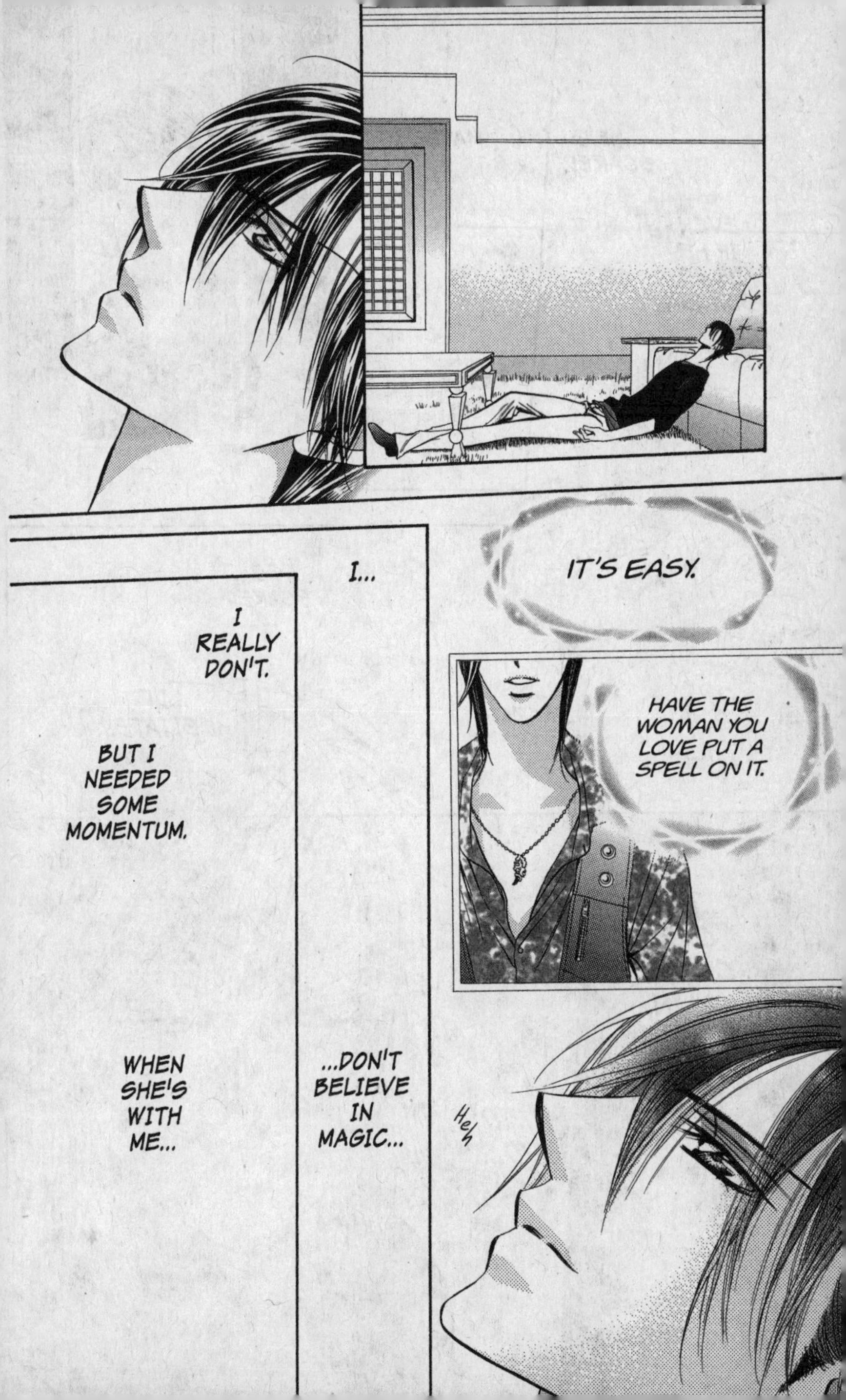
IT'S EASY.
HAVE THE WOMAN YOU LOVE PUT A SPELL ON IT.
I...
Heh
...DON'T BELIEVE IN MAGIC...
I REALLY DON'T.
BUT I NEEDED SOME MOMENTUM.
WHEN SHE'S WITH ME...

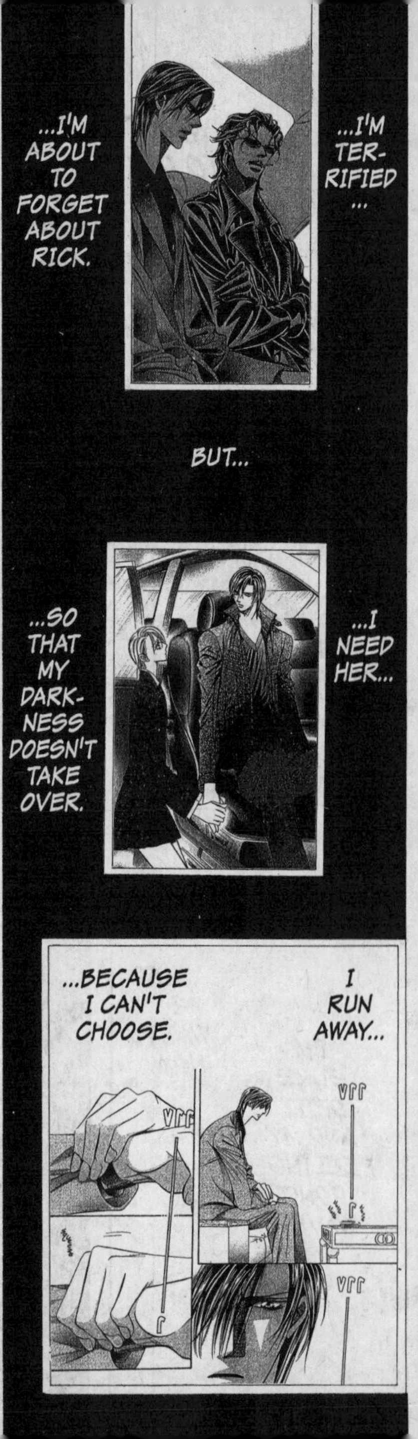
...I'M TERRIFIED...
...I'M ABOUT TO FORGET ABOUT RICK.
BUT...
...I NEED HER...
...SO THAT MY DARKNESS DOESN'T TAKE OVER.
I RUN AWAY...
...BECAUSE I CAN'T CHOOSE.
VRR
VRR
VRR

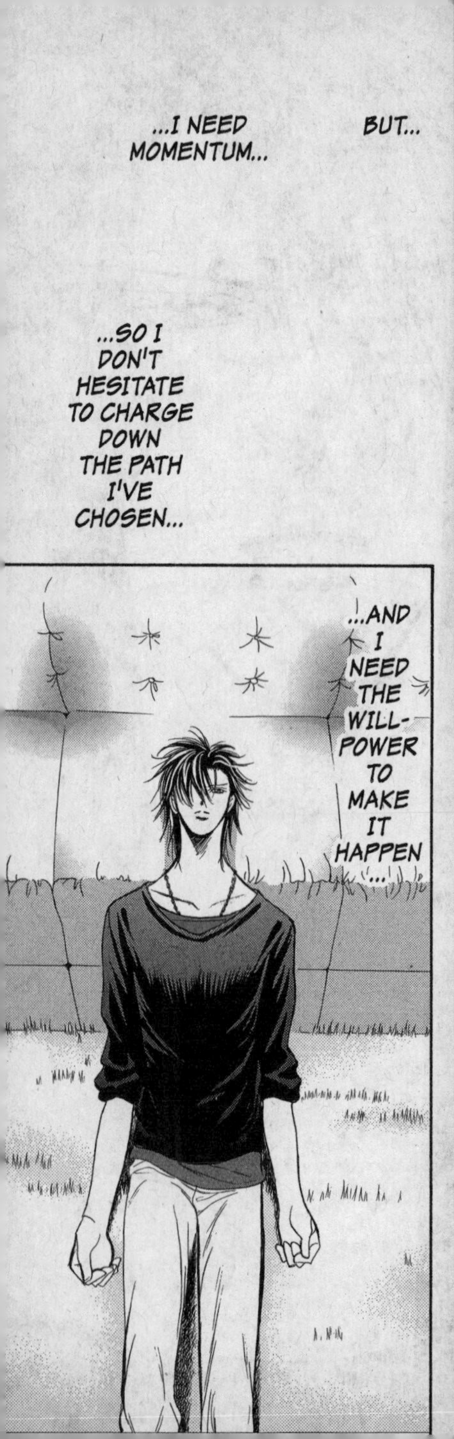
BUT...
...I NEED MOMENTUM...
...SO I DON'T HESITATE TO CHARGE DOWN THE PATH I'VE CHOSEN...
...AND I NEED THE WILL-POWER TO MAKE IT HAPPEN...

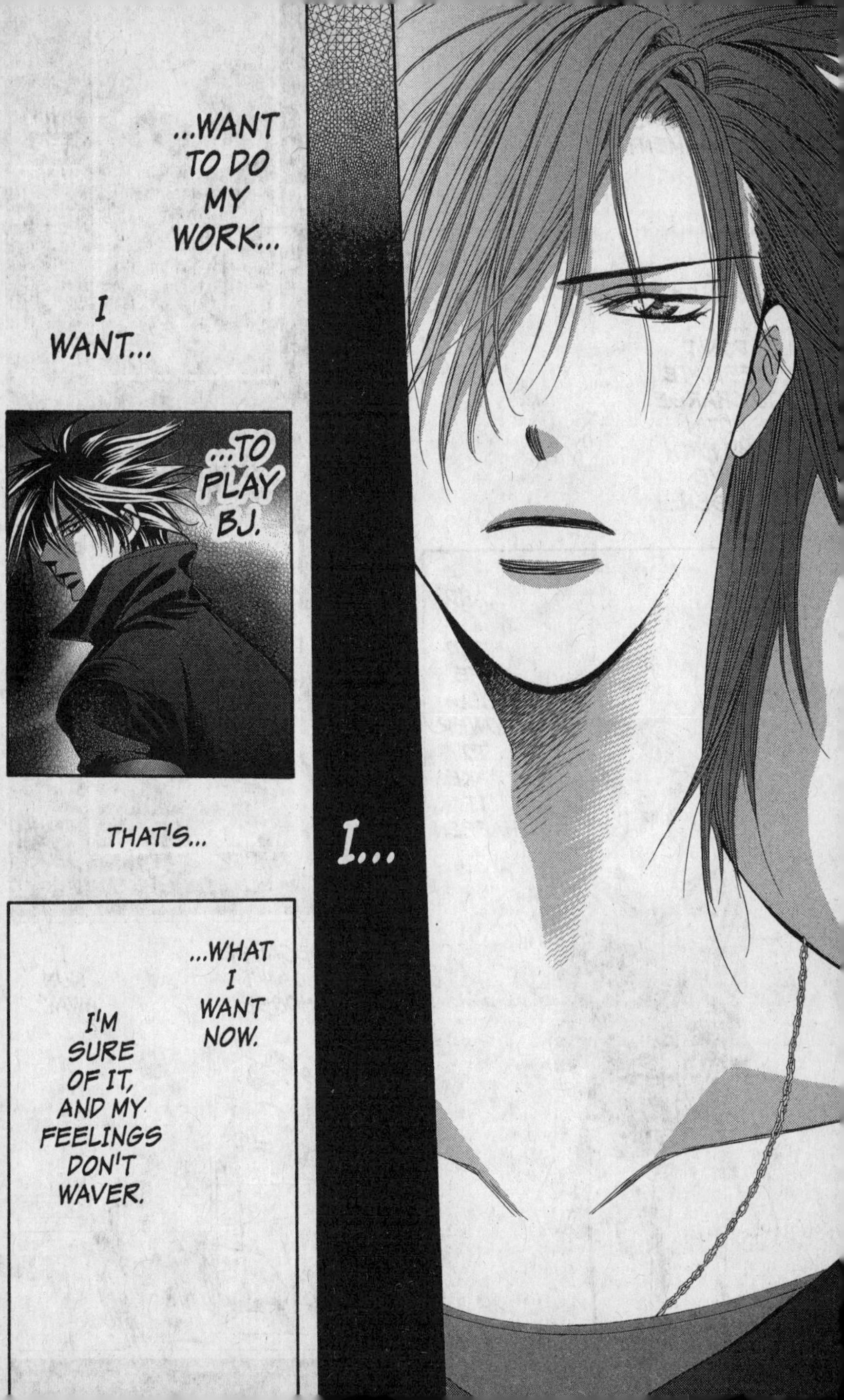
I...
...WANT TO DO MY WORK...
I WANT...
...TO PLAY BJ.
THAT'S...
...WHAT I WANT NOW.
I'M SURE OF IT, AND MY FEELINGS DON'T WAVER.

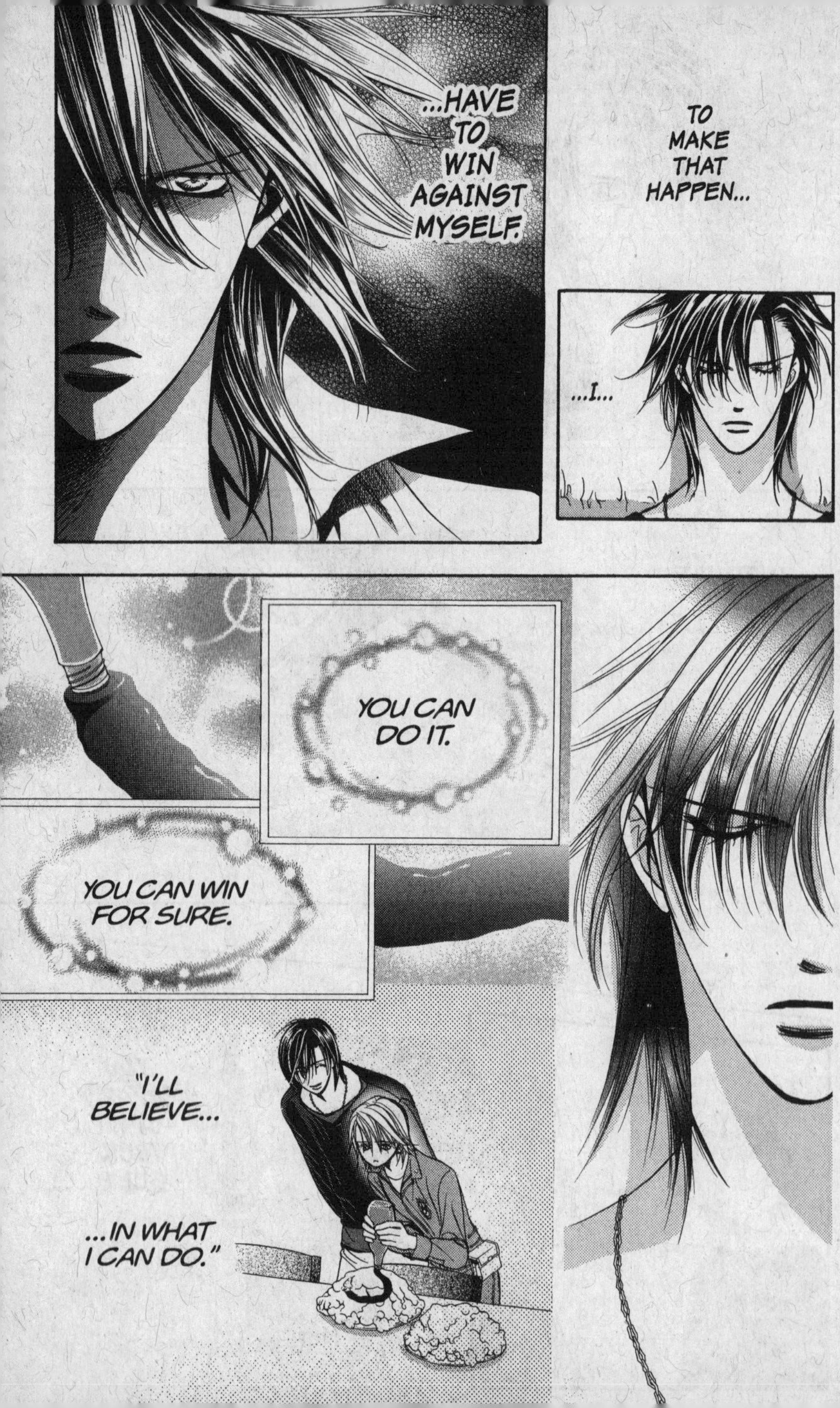
TO MAKE THAT HAPPEN...
...I...
...HAVE TO WIN AGAINST MYSELF.
YOU CAN DO IT.
YOU CAN WIN FOR SURE.
"I'LL BELIEVE...
...IN WHAT I CAN DO."

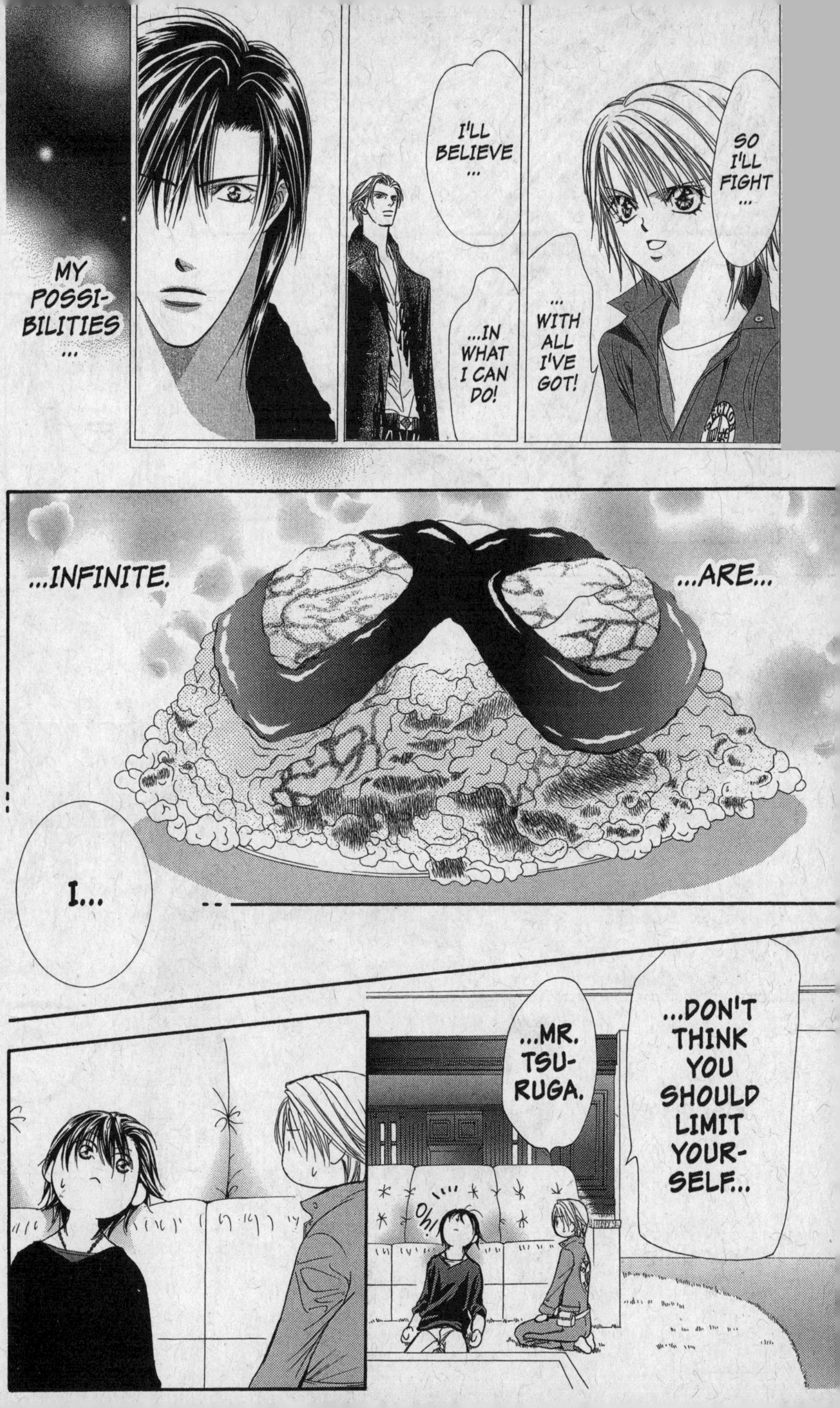
SO I'LL FIGHT ...
... WITH ALL I'VE GOT!
I'LL BELIEVE ...
...IN WHAT I CAN DO!
MY POSSI-BILITIES ...
...ARE...
...INFINITE.
I...
...DON'T THINK YOU SHOULD LIMIT YOUR-SELF...
...MR. TSU-RUGA.
Oh!?

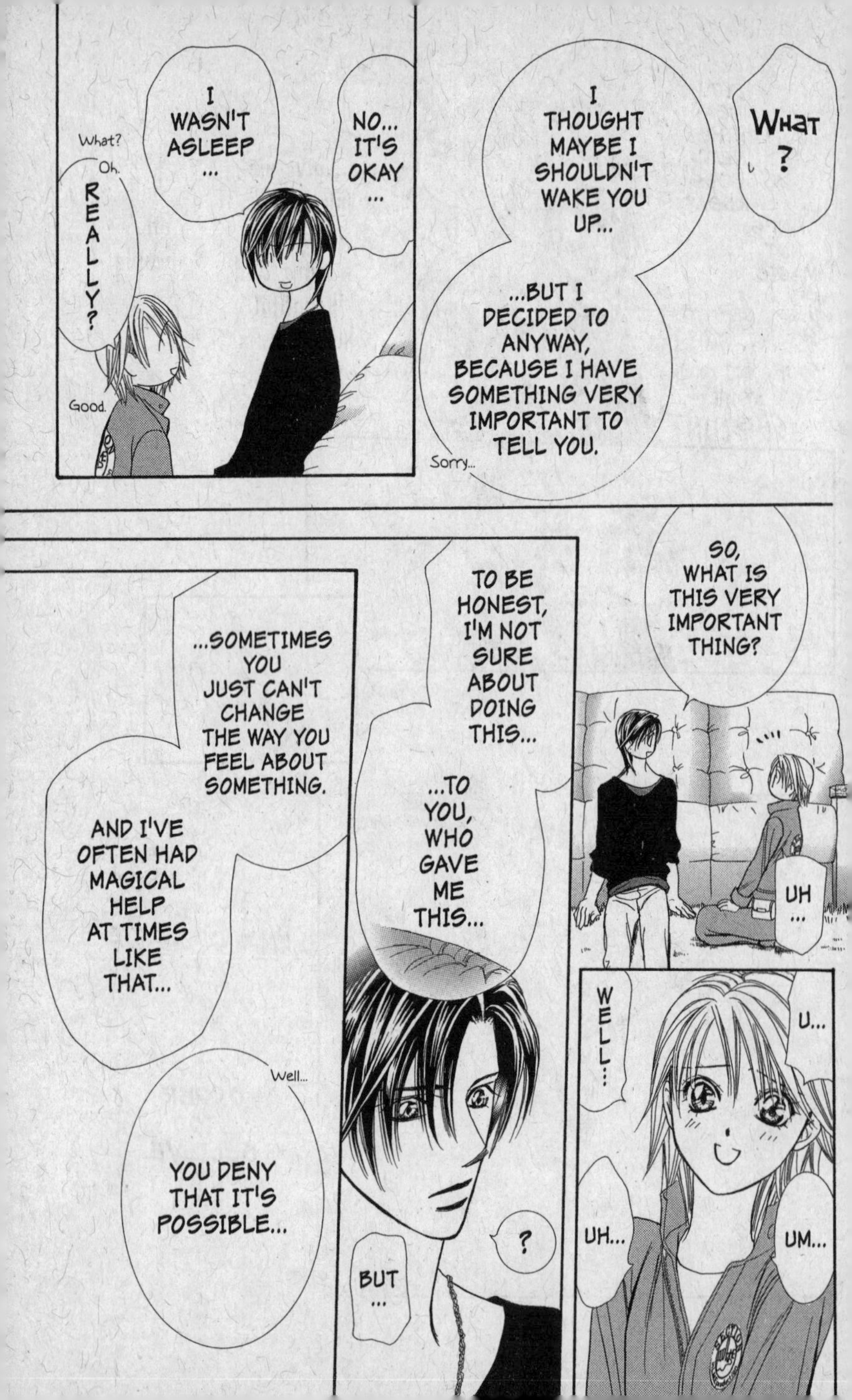
WHAT?
I THOUGHT MAYBE I SHOULDN'T WAKE YOU UP...
...BUT I DECIDED TO ANYWAY, BECAUSE I HAVE SOMETHING VERY IMPORTANT TO TELL YOU.
Sorry...
NO... IT'S OKAY...
I WASN'T ASLEEP...
What?
Oh.
REALLY?
Good.
SO, WHAT IS THIS VERY IMPORTANT THING?
...
UH...
U...
WELL...
UM...
UH...
TO BE HONEST, I'M NOT SURE ABOUT DOING THIS...
...TO YOU, WHO GAVE ME THIS...
?
BUT...
...SOMETIMES YOU JUST CAN'T CHANGE THE WAY YOU FEEL ABOUT SOMETHING.
AND I'VE OFTEN HAD MAGICAL HELP AT TIMES LIKE THAT...
Well...
YOU DENY THAT IT'S POSSIBLE...

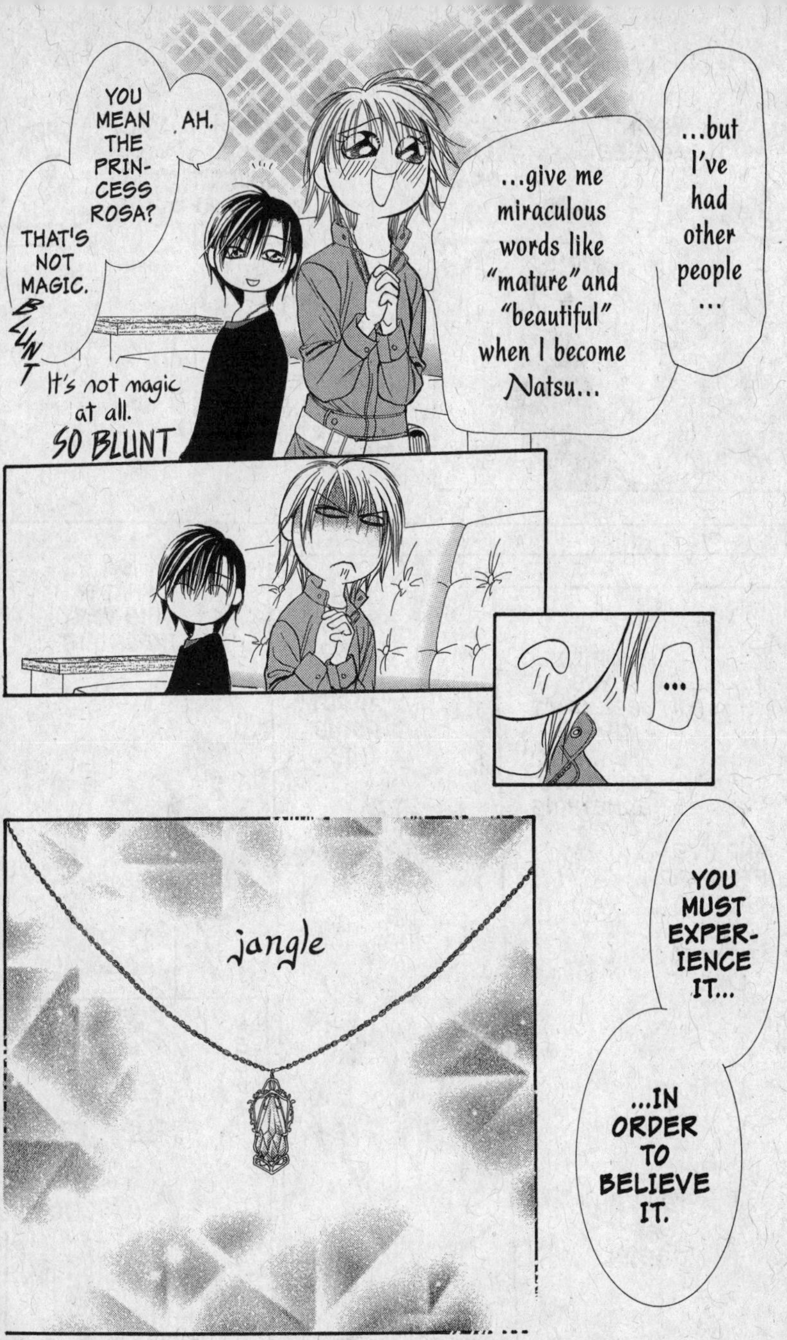
...but I've had other people...
...give me miraculous words like "mature" and "beautiful" when I become Natsu...
AH.
YOU MEAN THE PRINCESS ROSA?
THAT'S NOT MAGIC.
BLUNT
It's not magic at all.
SO BLUNT
...
YOU MUST EXPERIENCE IT...
...IN ORDER TO BELIEVE IT.
jangle

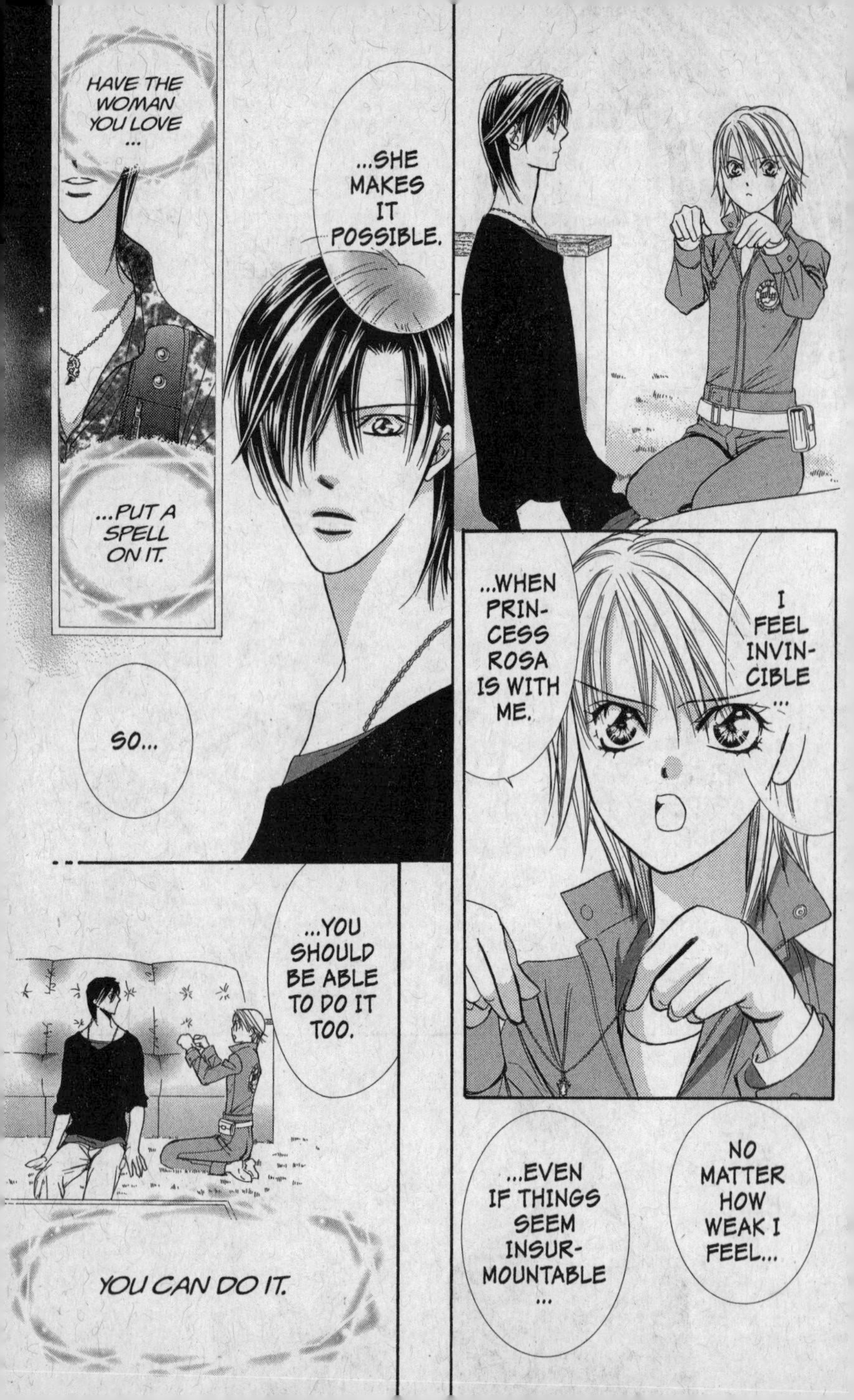
I FEEL INVINCIBLE...
...WHEN PRINCESS ROSA IS WITH ME.
NO MATTER HOW WEAK I FEEL...
...EVEN IF THINGS SEEM INSURMOUNTABLE...
...SHE MAKES IT POSSIBLE.
HAVE THE WOMAN YOU LOVE...
...PUT A SPELL ON IT.
SO...
...YOU SHOULD BE ABLE TO DO IT TOO.
YOU CAN DO IT.

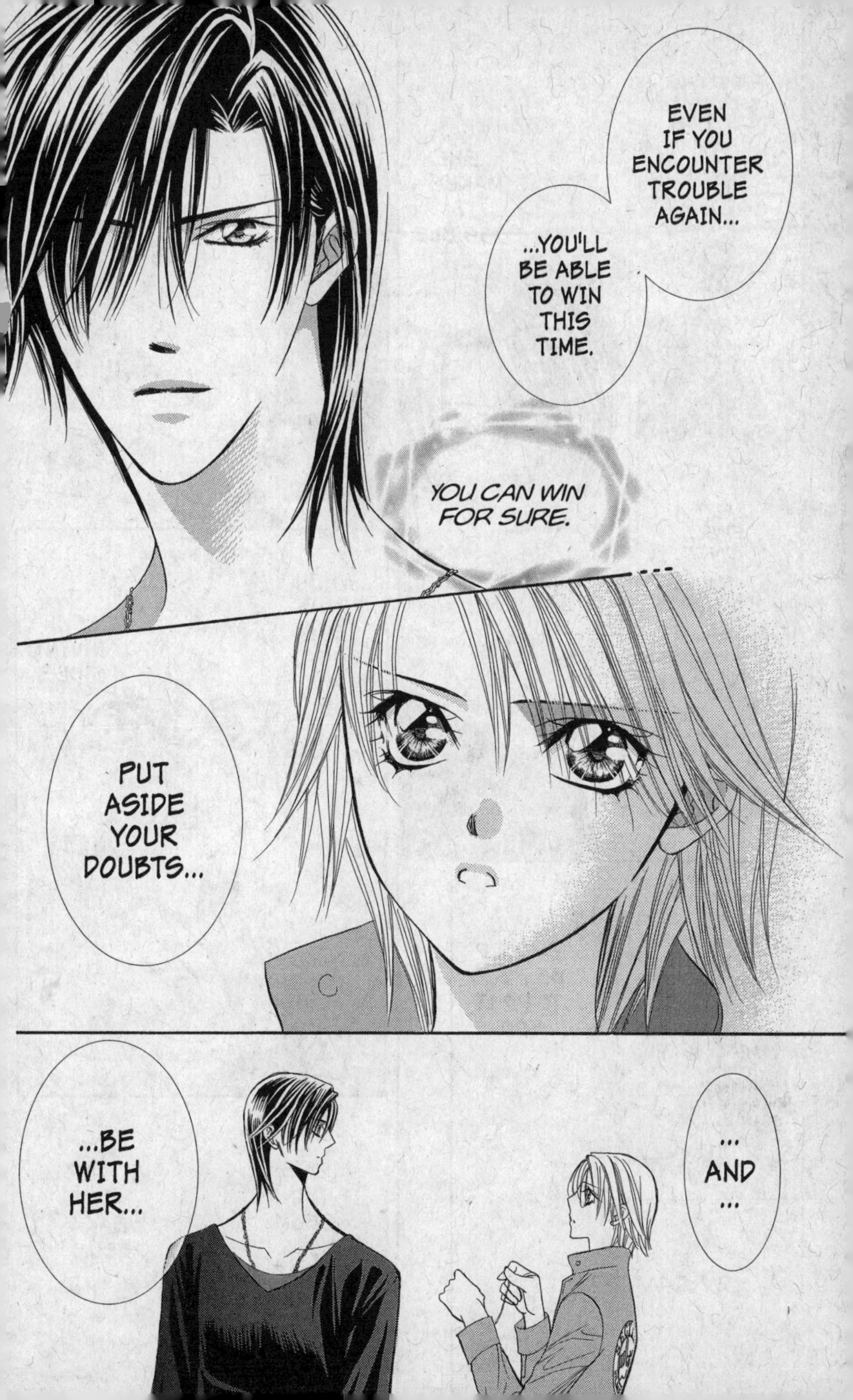
EVEN IF YOU ENCOUNTER TROUBLE AGAIN...
...YOU'LL BE ABLE TO WIN THIS TIME.
YOU CAN WIN FOR SURE.
PUT ASIDE YOUR DOUBTS...
... AND ...
...BE WITH HER...

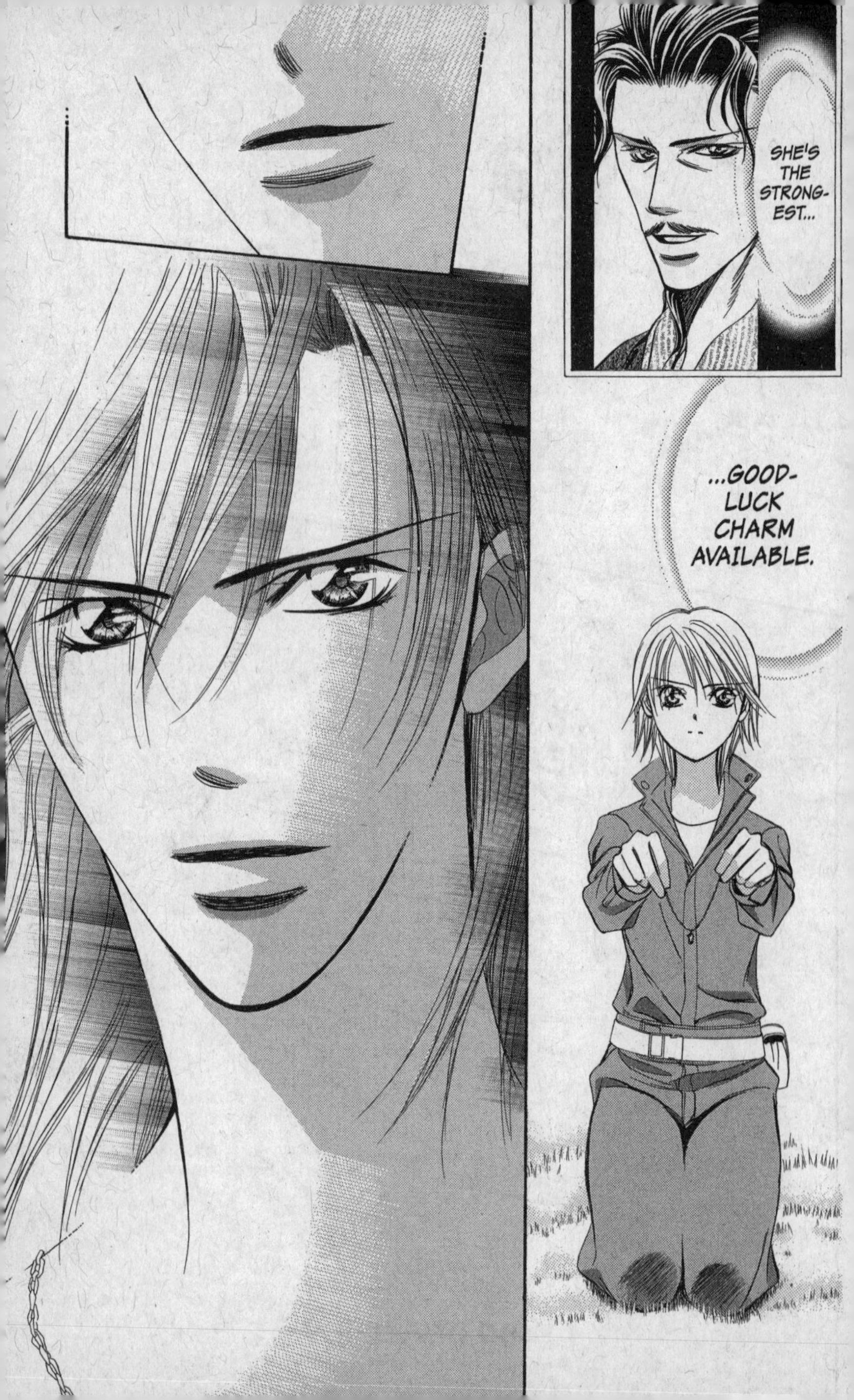
SHE'S THE STRONG-EST...
...GOOD-LUCK CHARM AVAILABLE.

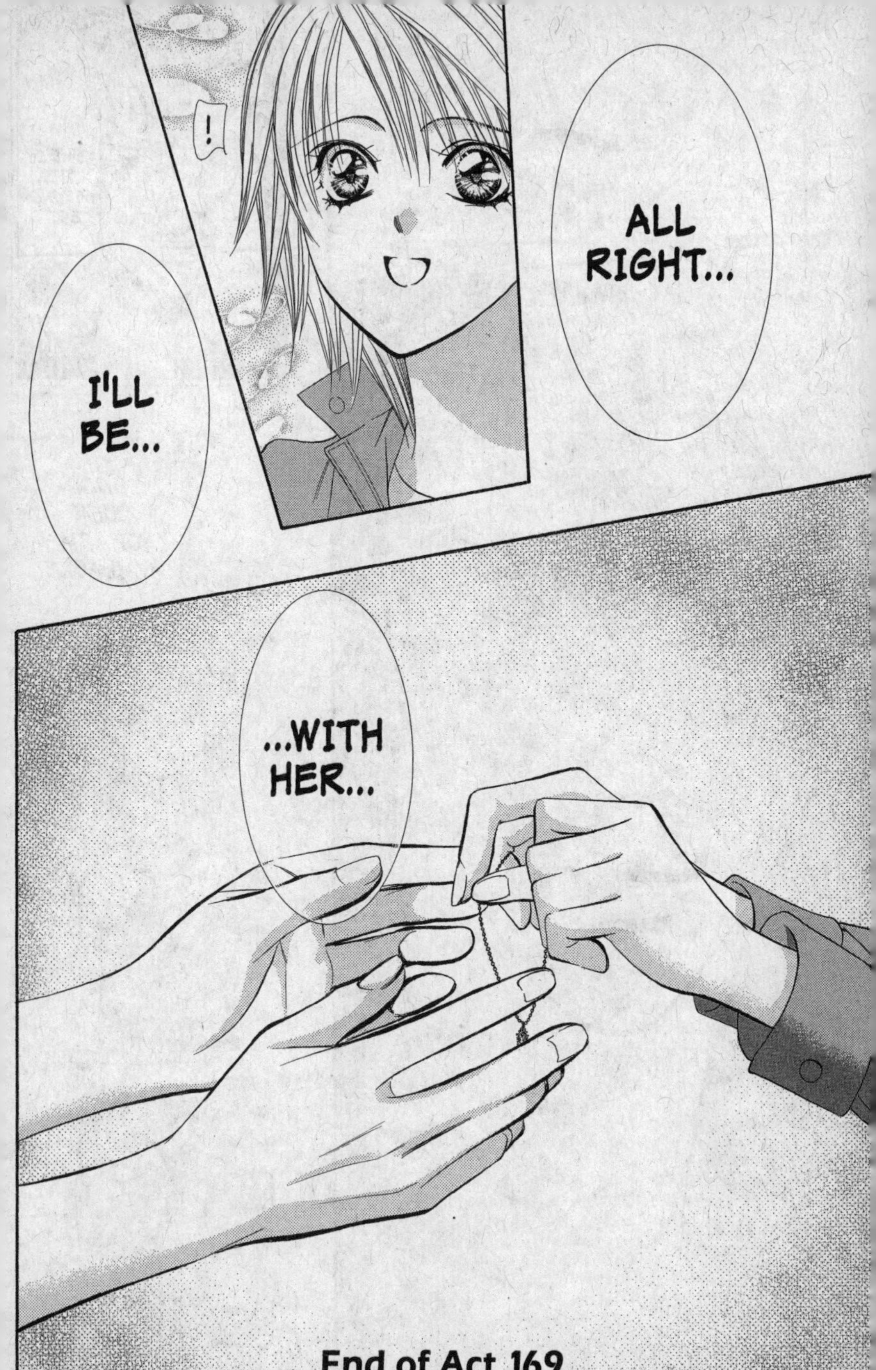
!
ALL RIGHT...
I'LL BE...
...WITH HER...

End of Act 169

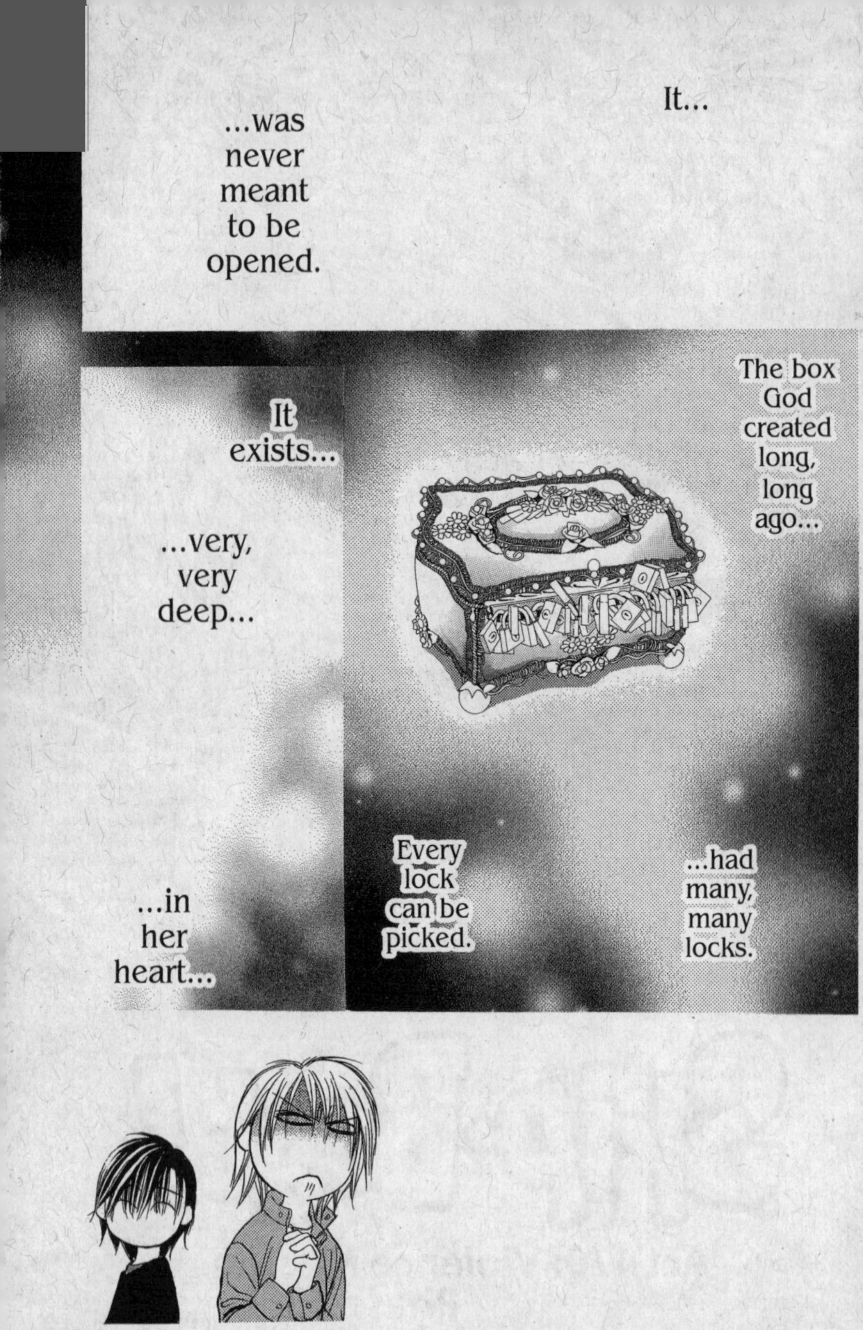
It...
...was never meant to be opened.
The box God created long, long ago...
...had many, many locks.
Every lock can be picked.
It exists...
...very, very deep...
...in her heart...

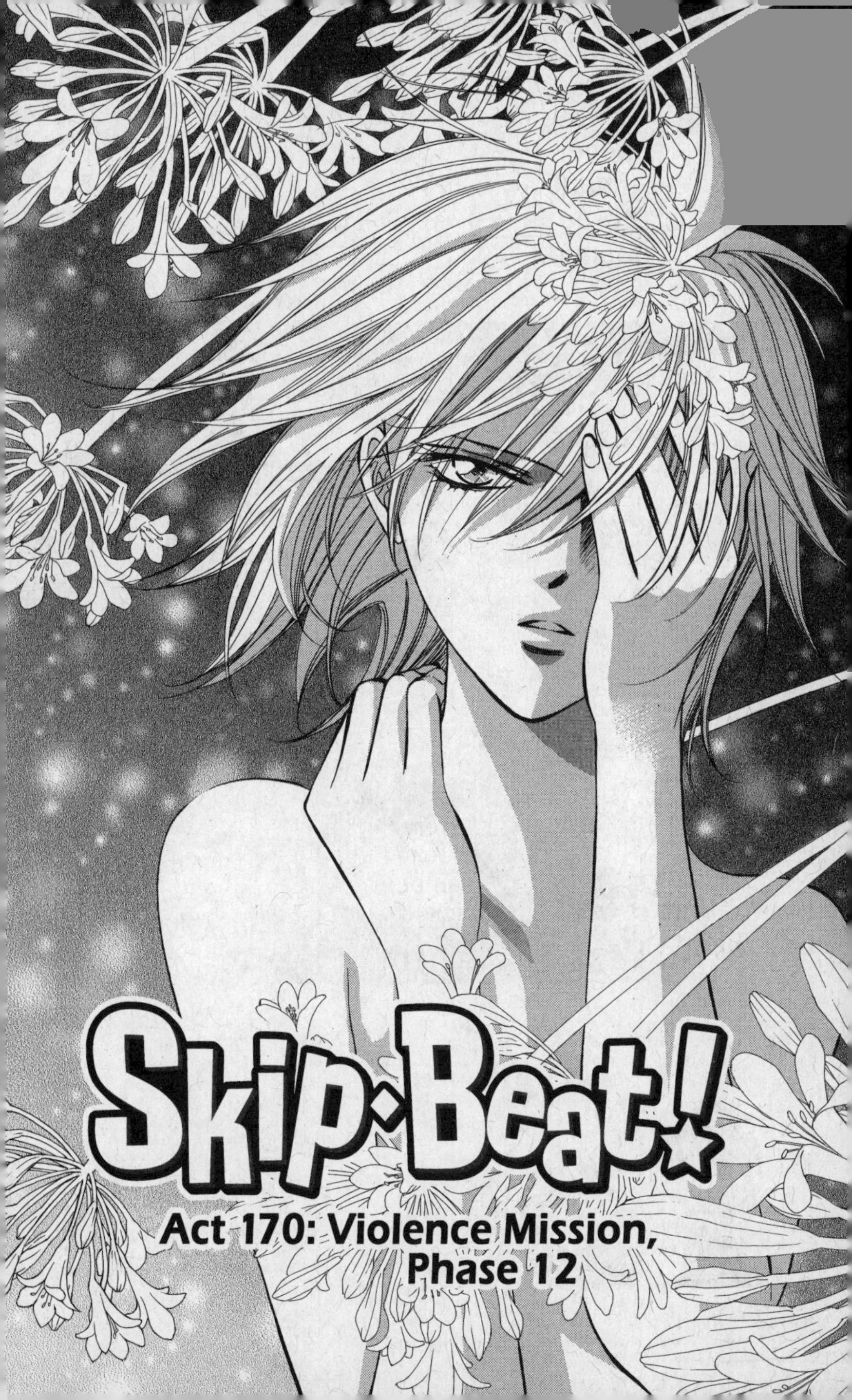
Skip·Beat!
Act 170: Violence Mission, Phase 12

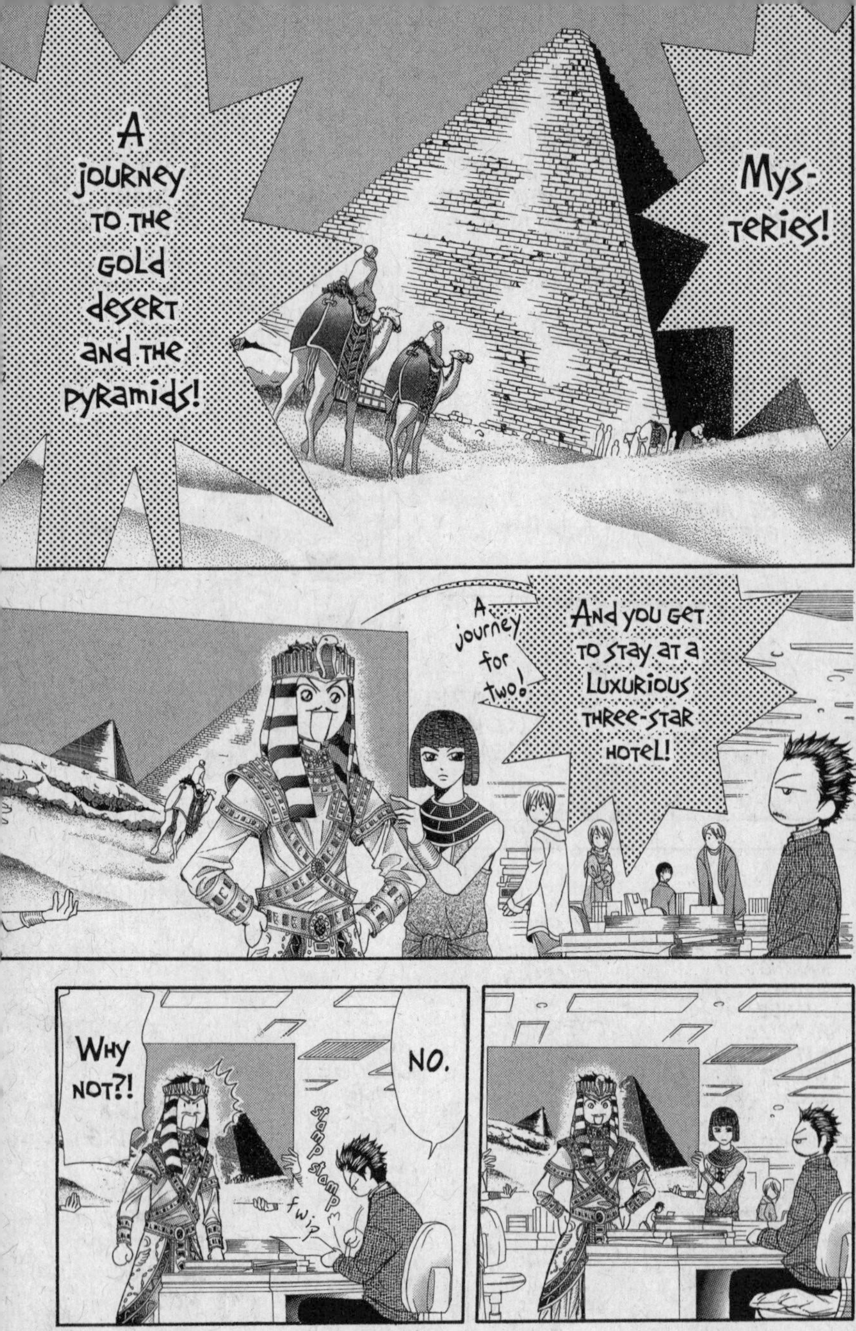
A journey to the gold desert and the pyramids!
Mys-teries!
A journey for two!
And you get to stay at a luxurious three-star hotel!
NO.
stamp stamp
fwip
WHY NOT?!

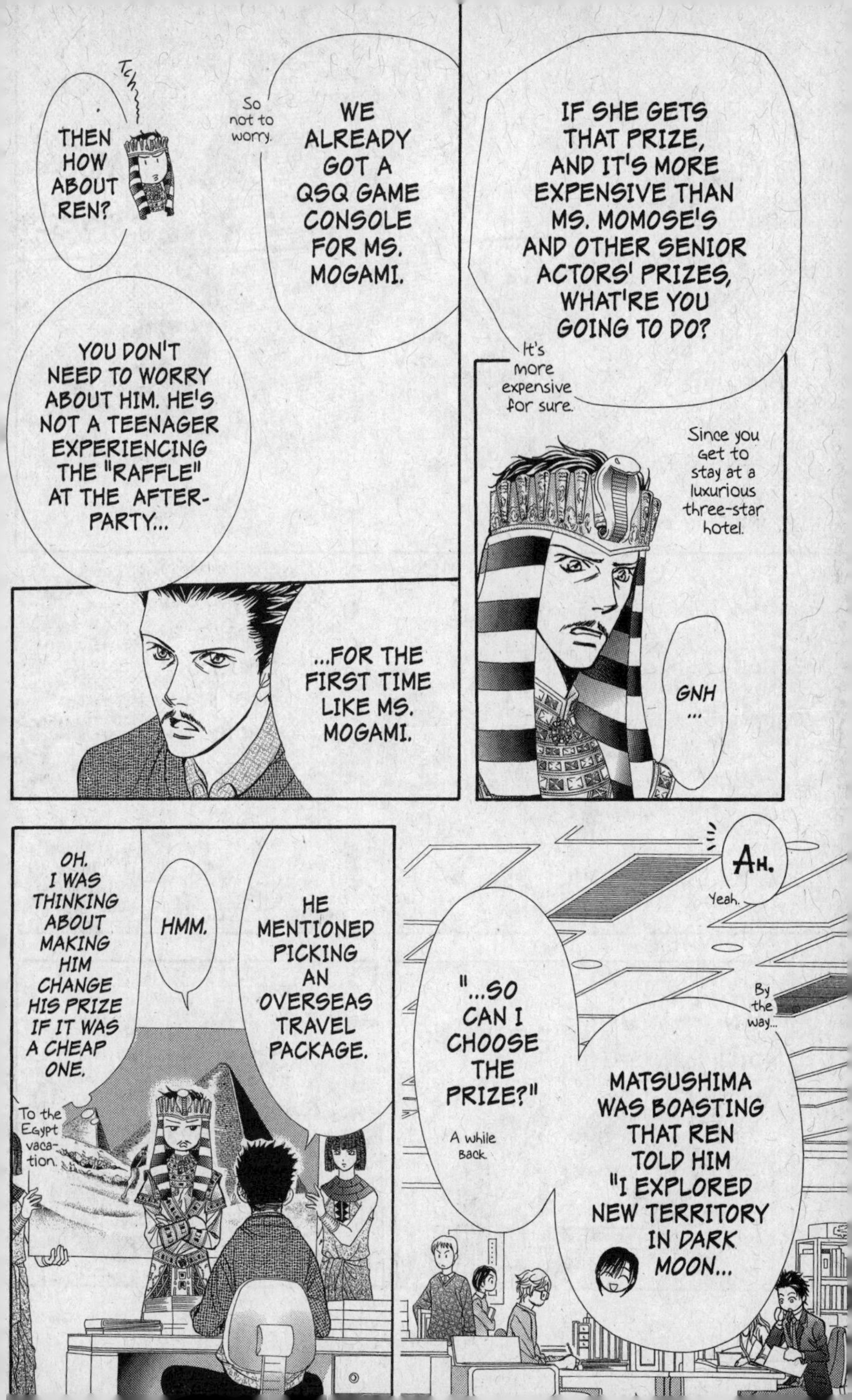

IF SHE GETS THAT PRIZE, AND IT'S MORE EXPENSIVE THAN MS. MOMOSE'S AND OTHER SENIOR ACTORS' PRIZES, WHAT'RE YOU GOING TO DO?
It's more expensive for sure.
Since you get to stay at a luxurious three-star hotel.
GNH...
WE ALREADY GOT A QSQ GAME CONSOLE FOR MS. MOGAMI.
So not to worry.
THEN HOW ABOUT REN?
Tch
YOU DON'T NEED TO WORRY ABOUT HIM. HE'S NOT A TEENAGER EXPERIENCING THE "RAFFLE" AT THE AFTER-PARTY...
...FOR THE FIRST TIME LIKE MS. MOGAMI.
AH.
Yeah.
By the way...
MATSUSHIMA WAS BOASTING THAT REN TOLD HIM "I EXPLORED NEW TERRITORY IN DARK MOON...
"...SO CAN I CHOOSE THE PRIZE?"
A while back.
HE MENTIONED PICKING AN OVERSEAS TRAVEL PACKAGE.
HMM.
OH. I WAS THINKING ABOUT MAKING HIM CHANGE HIS PRIZE IF IT WAS A CHEAP ONE.
To the Egypt vacation.

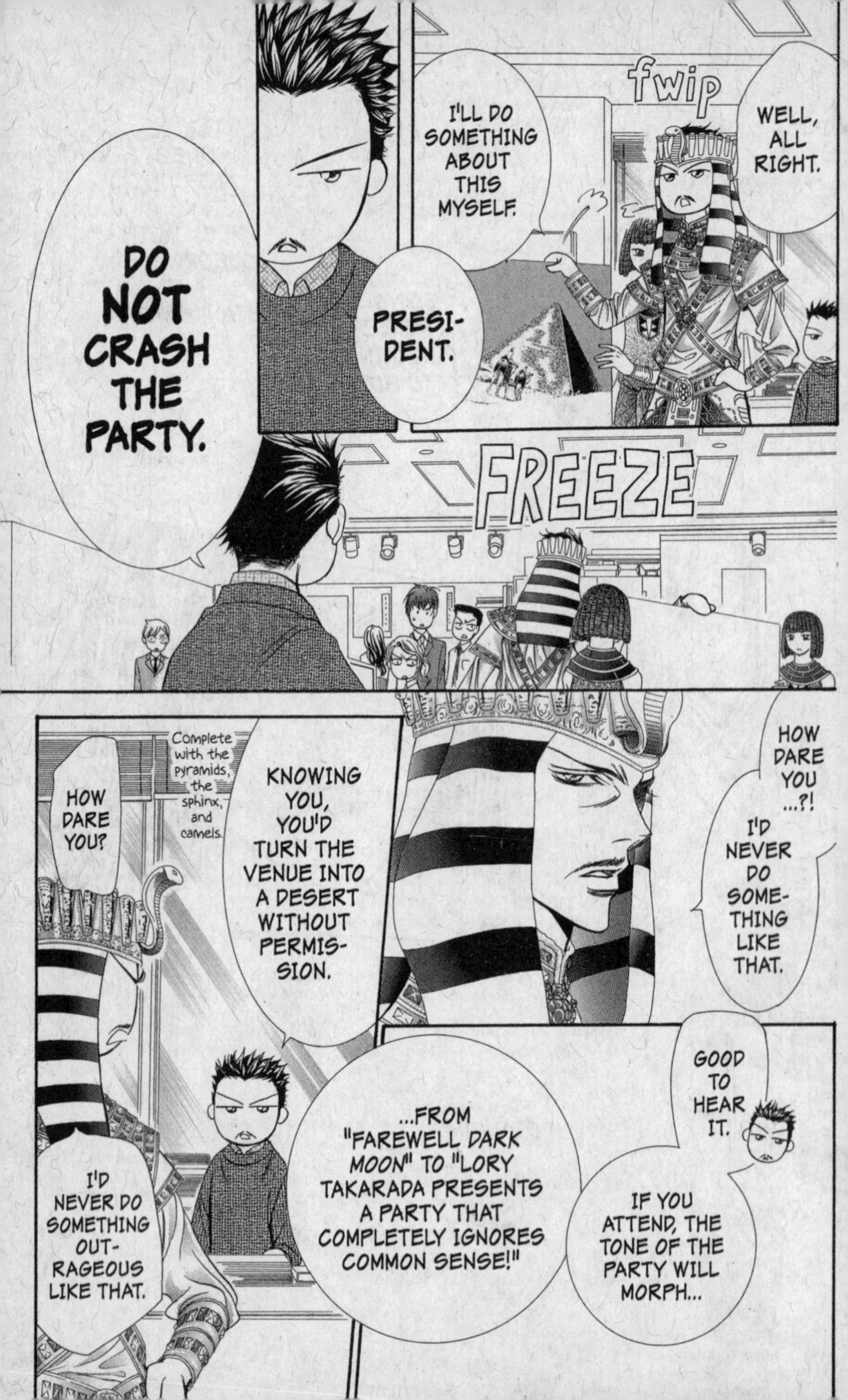
fwip
WELL, ALL RIGHT.
I'LL DO SOMETHING ABOUT THIS MYSELF.
PRESIDENT.
DO NOT CRASH THE PARTY.
FREEZE
HOW DARE YOU ...?!
I'D NEVER DO SOMETHING LIKE THAT.
HOW DARE YOU?
KNOWING YOU, YOU'D TURN THE VENUE INTO A DESERT WITHOUT PERMISSION.
Complete with the pyramids, the sphinx, and camels.
GOOD TO HEAR IT.
IF YOU ATTEND, THE TONE OF THE PARTY WILL MORPH...
...FROM "FAREWELL DARK MOON" TO "LORY TAKARADA PRESENTS A PARTY THAT COMPLETELY IGNORES COMMON SENSE!"
I'D NEVER DO SOMETHING OUTRAGEOUS LIKE THAT.

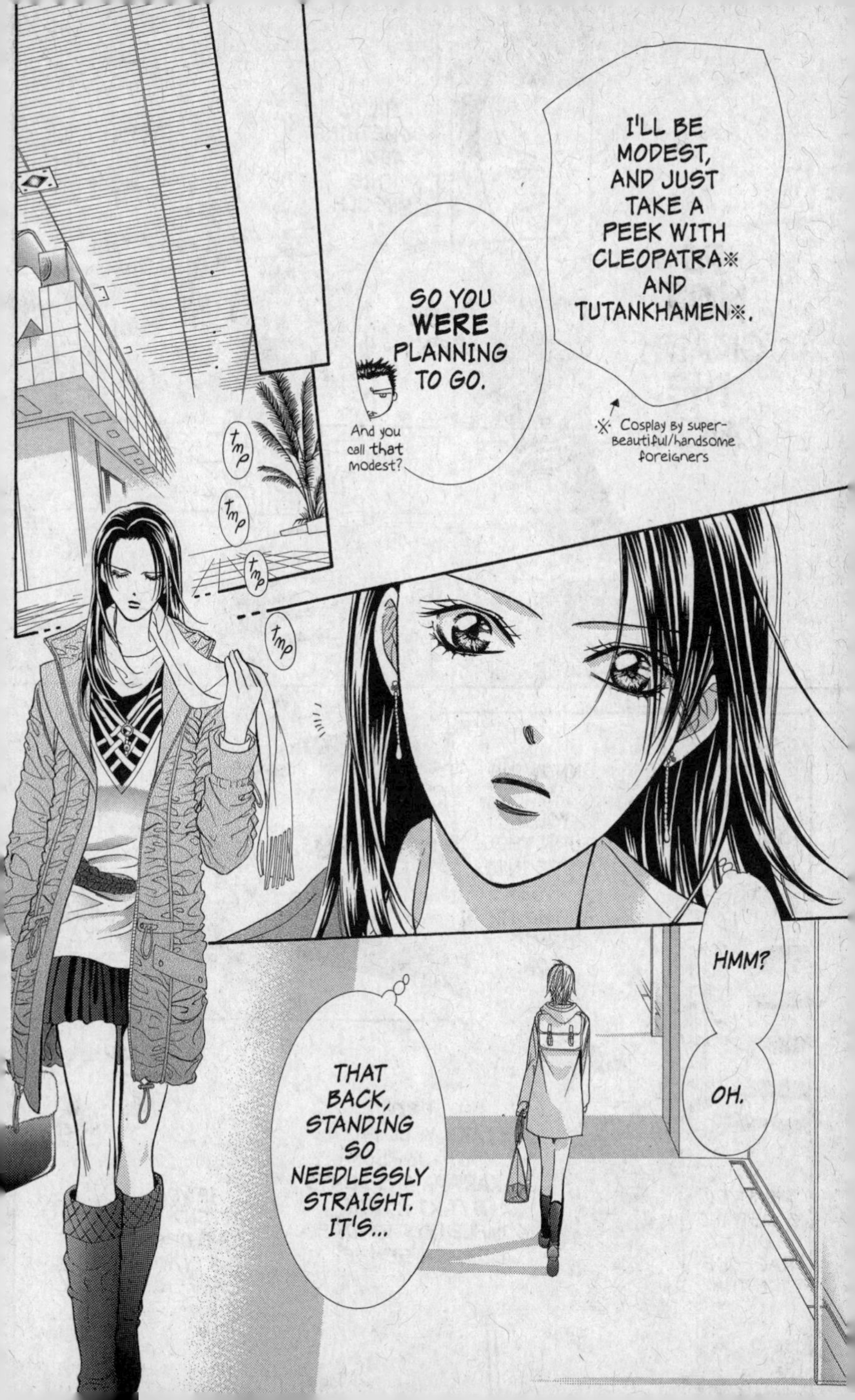
I'LL BE MODEST, AND JUST TAKE A PEEK WITH CLEOPATRA※ AND TUTANKHAMEN※.
※ Cosplay by super-beautiful/handsome foreigners
SO YOU WERE PLANNING TO GO.
And you call that modest?
tmp
tmp
tmp
tmp
HMM?
OH.
THAT BACK, STANDING SO NEEDLESSLY STRAIGHT. IT'S...

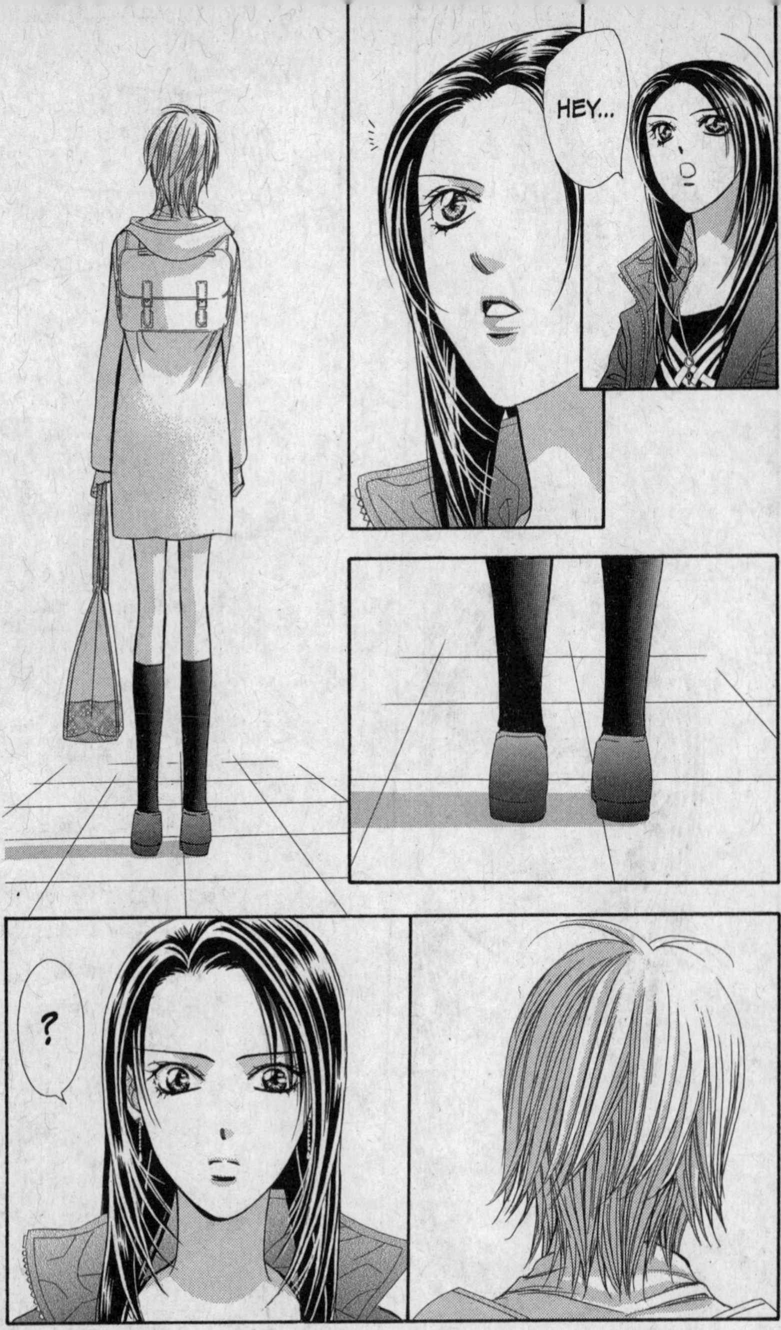
HEY...
?

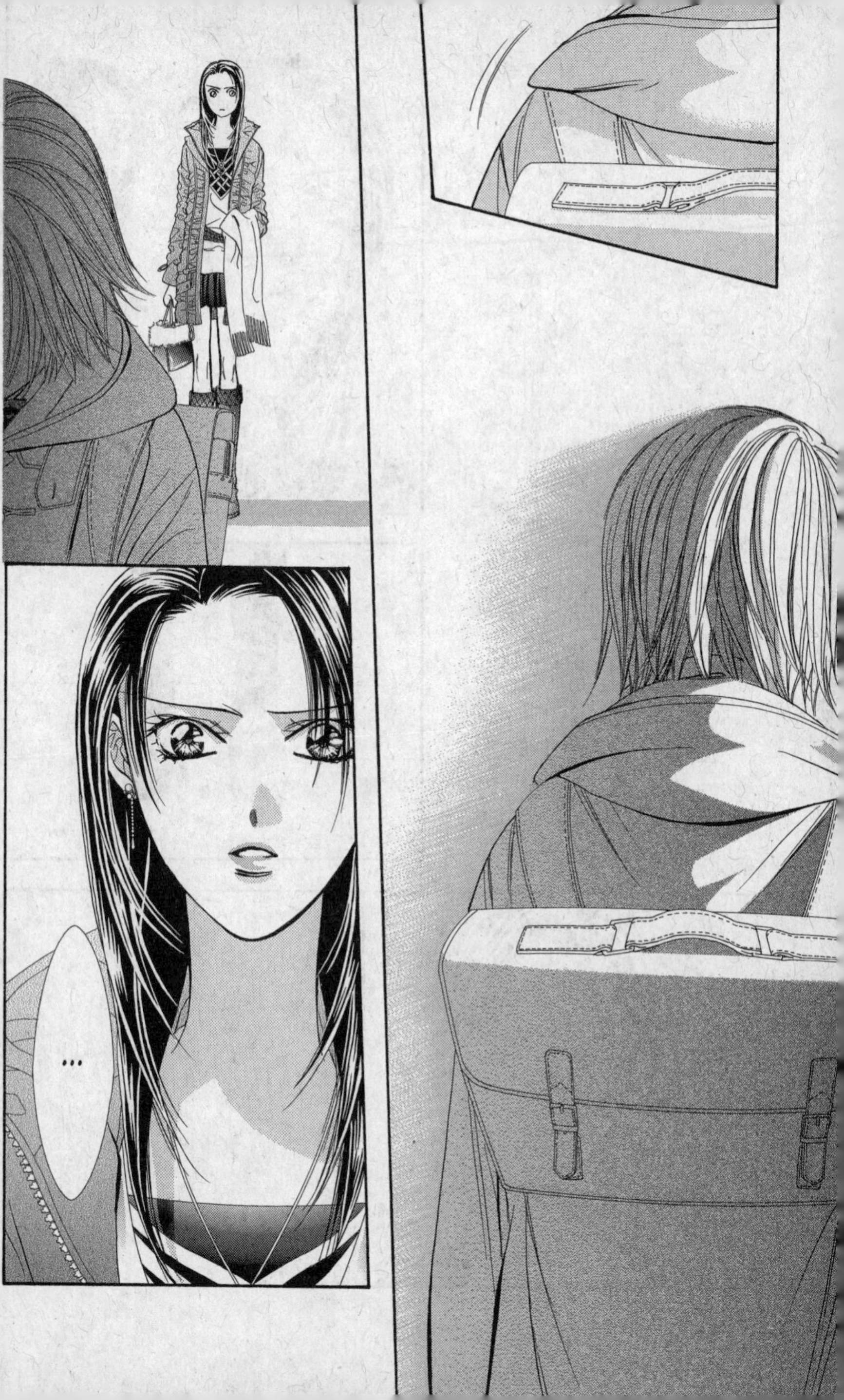
...

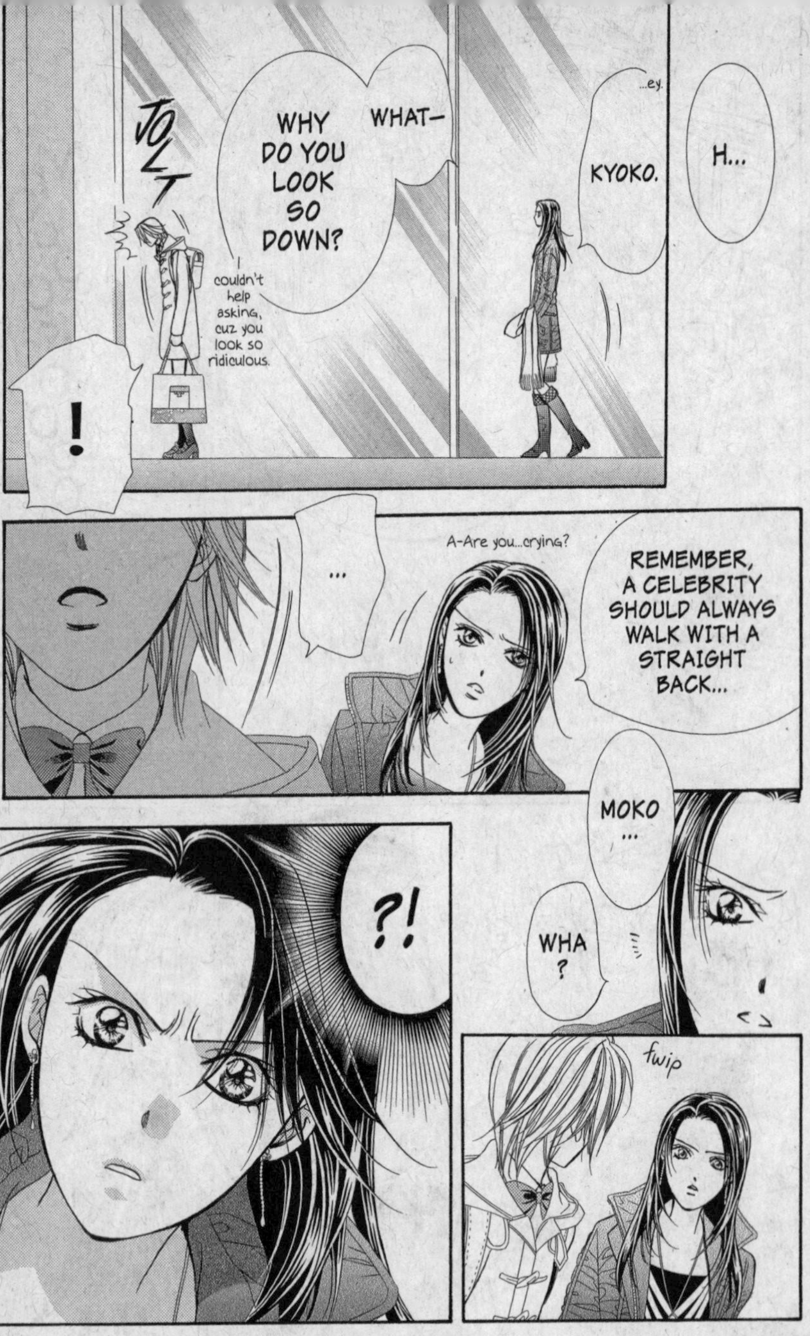
H...
...ey.
KYOKO.
WHAT—
WHY DO YOU LOOK SO DOWN?
I couldn't help asking, cuz you look so ridiculous.
JOLT
!
REMEMBER, A CELEBRITY SHOULD ALWAYS WALK WITH A STRAIGHT BACK...
A-Are you...crying?
...
MOKO ...
WHA ?
fwip
?!

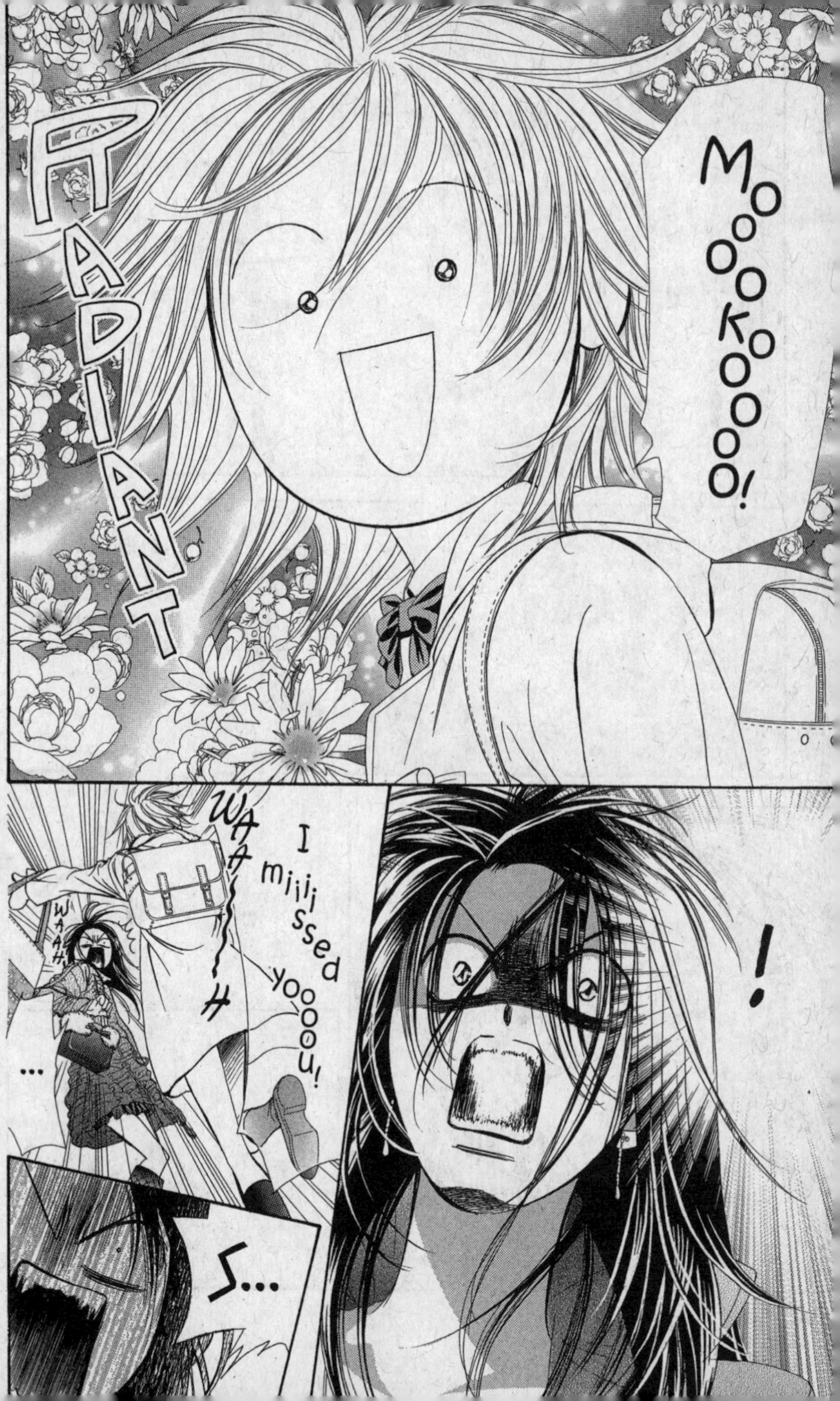
MOOOOKOOOOOOO!
RADIANT
!
I miiiissed yooooou!
WAAAH
WAAAH
...
S...

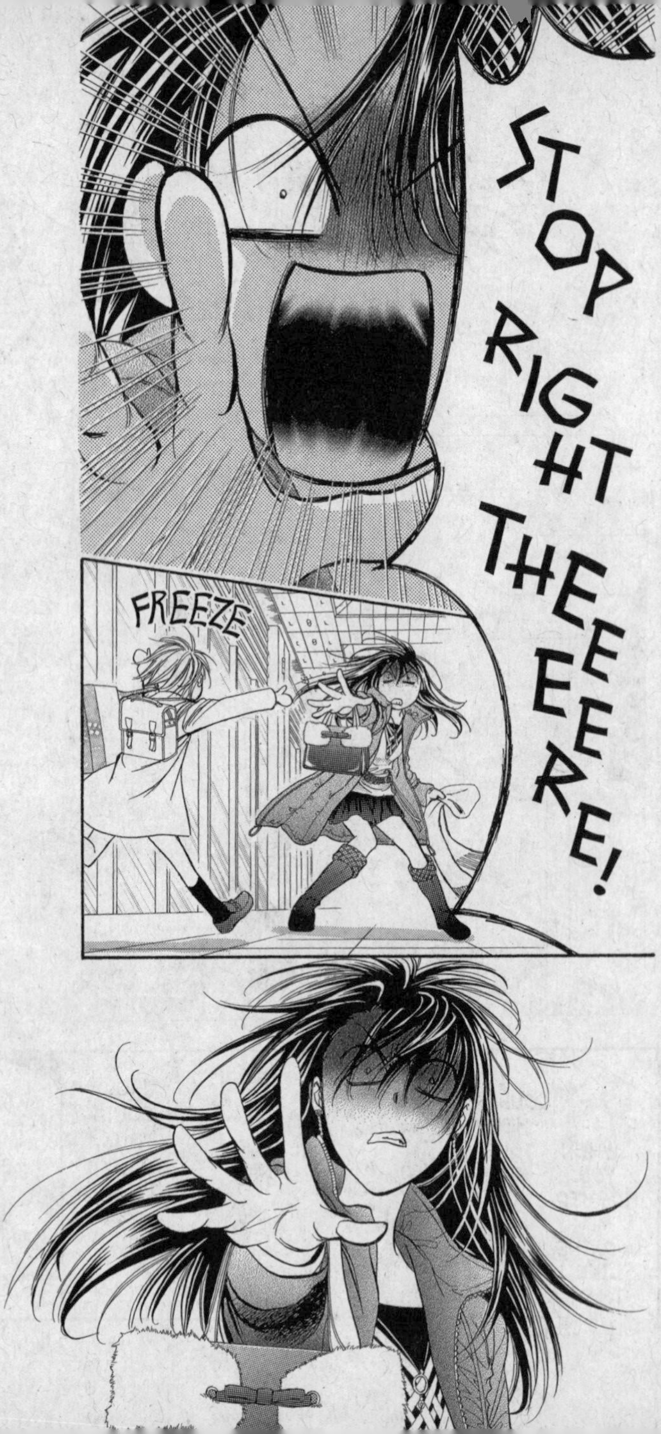
STOP RIGHT THEEEERE!
FREEZE

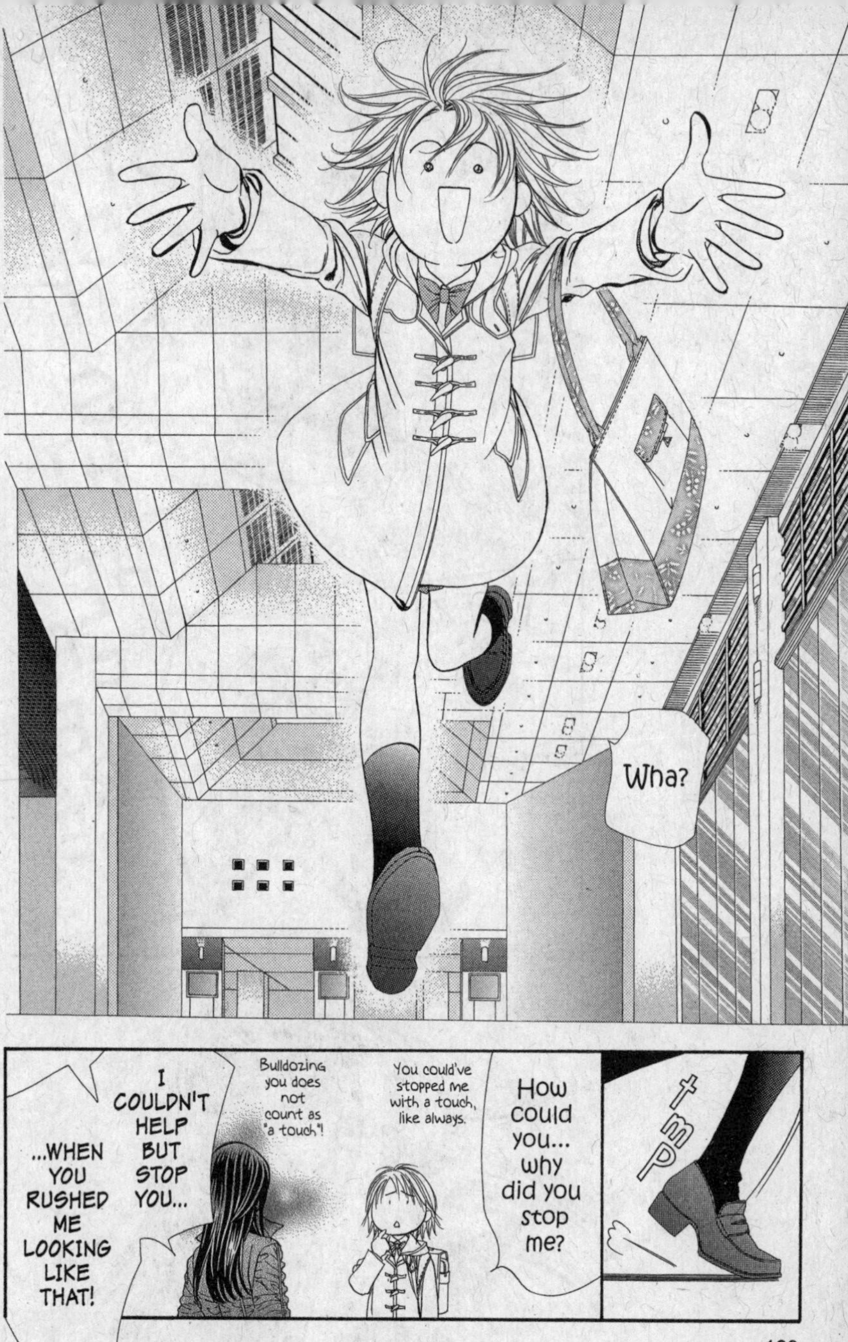
Wha?
tmp
How could you... why did you stop me?
You could've stopped me with a touch, like always.
Bulldozing you does not count as "a touch"!
I COULDN'T HELP BUT STOP YOU...
...WHEN YOU RUSHED ME LOOKING LIKE THAT!

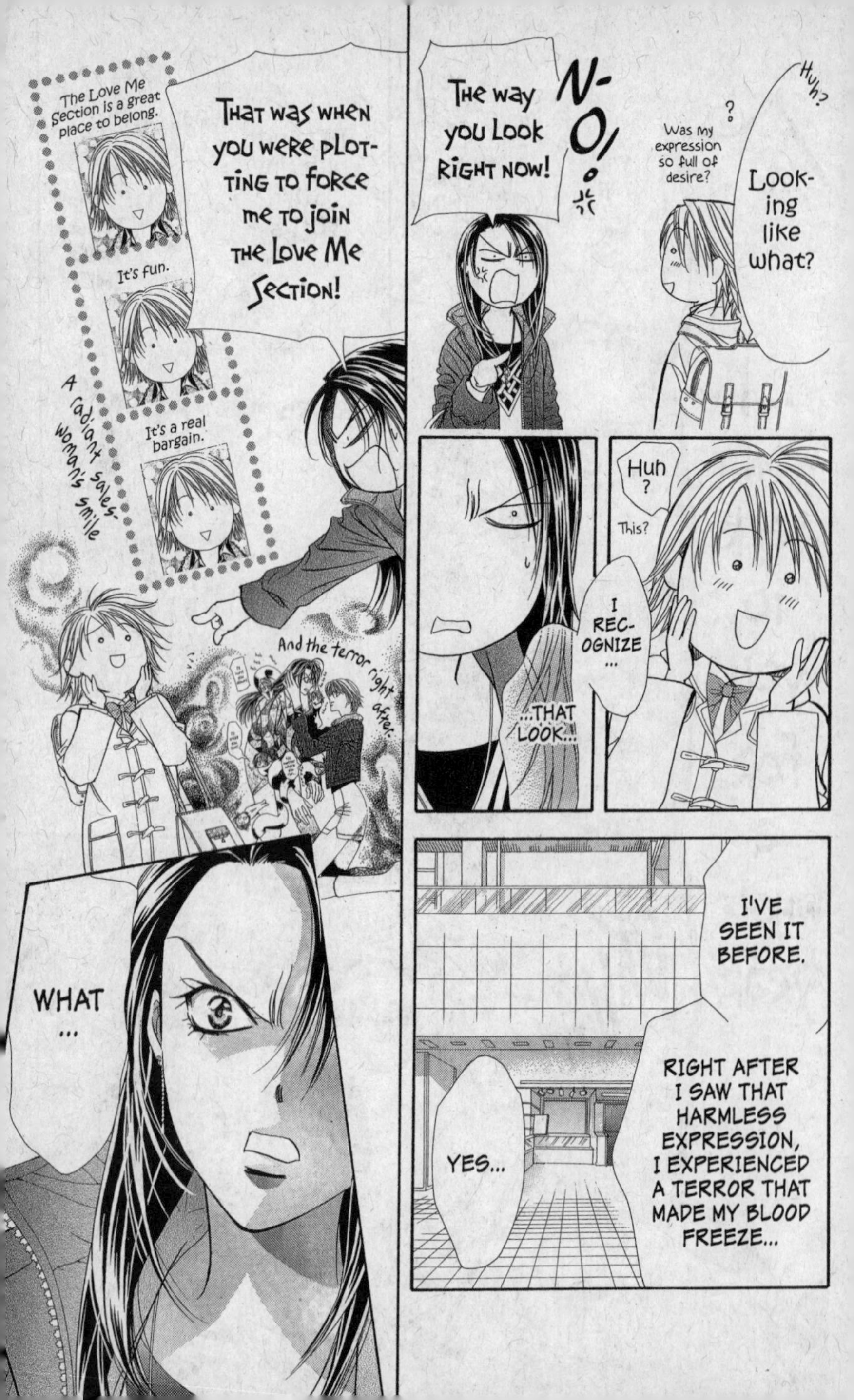
Huh?
Was my expression so full of desire?
?
Looking like what?
The way you look right now!
N-O!
Huh?
This?
I RECOGNIZE...
...THAT LOOK...
I'VE SEEN IT BEFORE.
RIGHT AFTER I SAW THAT HARMLESS EXPRESSION, I EXPERIENCED A TERROR THAT MADE MY BLOOD FREEZE...
YES...
That was when you were plotting to force me to join the Love Me Section!
The Love Me Section is a great place to belong.
It's fun.
It's a real bargain.
A radiant woman's sales-smile
And the terror right after.
WHAT...

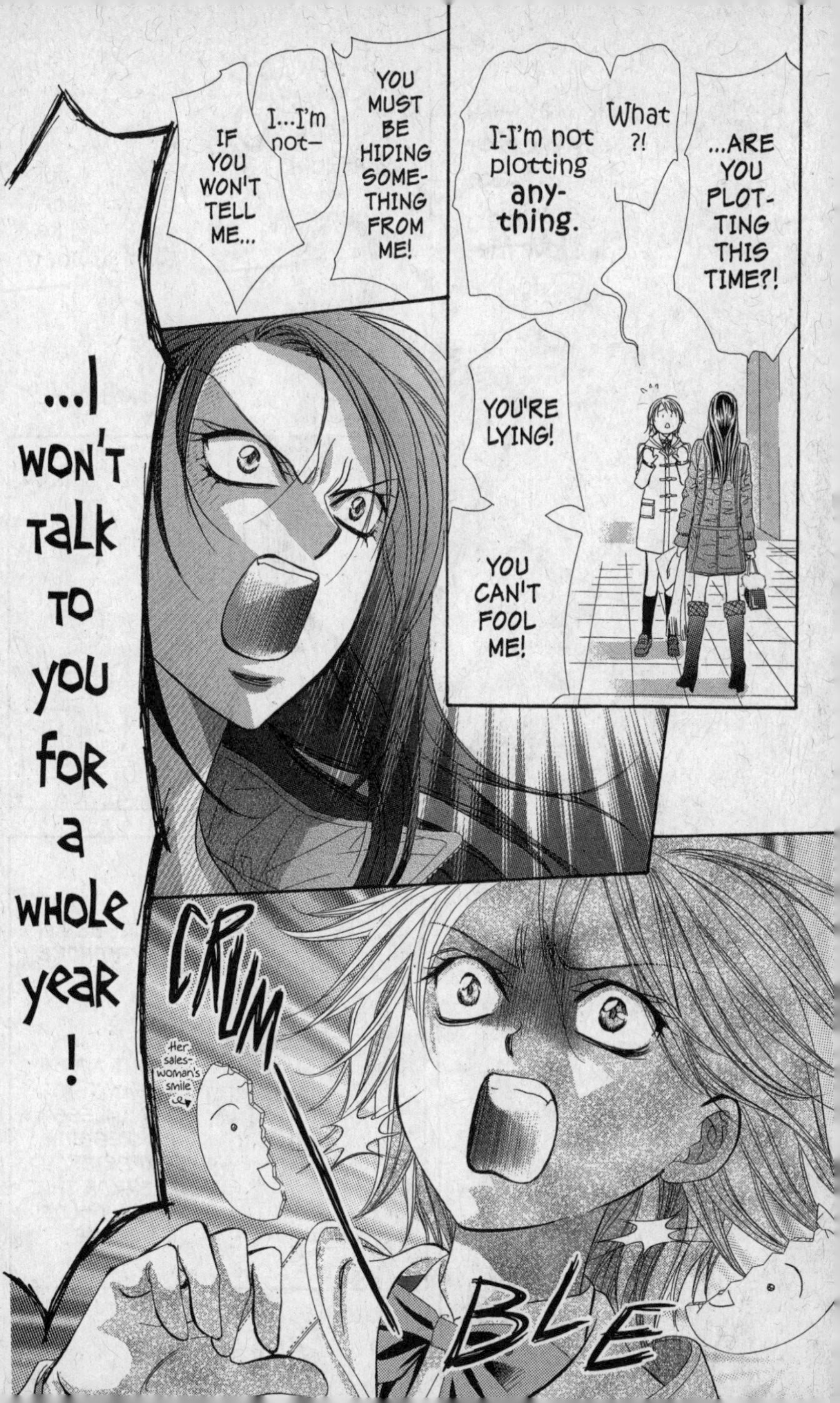
...ARE YOU PLOTTING THIS TIME?!
What ?!
I-I'm not plotting anything.
YOU'RE LYING!
YOU CAN'T FOOL ME!
YOU MUST BE HIDING SOMETHING FROM ME!
I...I'm not–
IF YOU WON'T TELL ME...
...I WON'T TALK TO YOU FOR A WHOLE YEAR!
CRUMBLE
Her saleswoman's smile

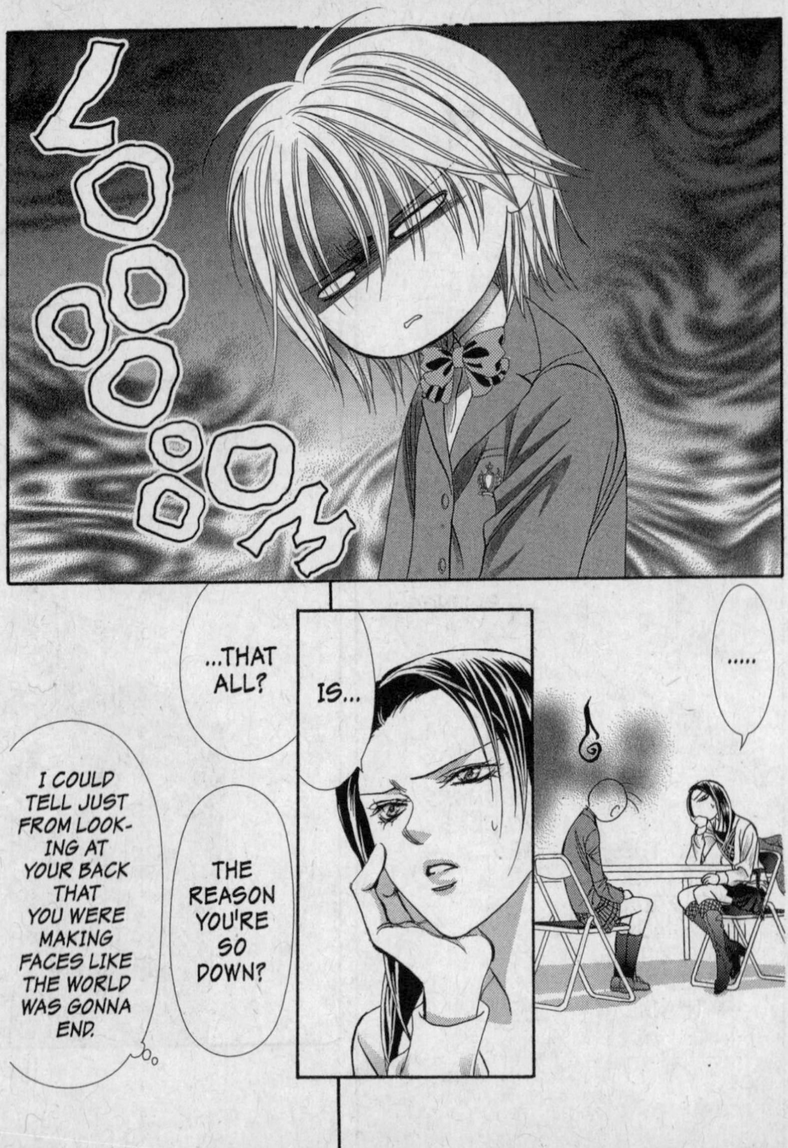
LOOOOOOOM
.....
IS...
...THAT ALL?
THE REASON YOU'RE SO DOWN?
I COULD TELL JUST FROM LOOK-ING AT YOUR BACK THAT YOU WERE MAKING FACES LIKE THE WORLD WAS GONNA END.

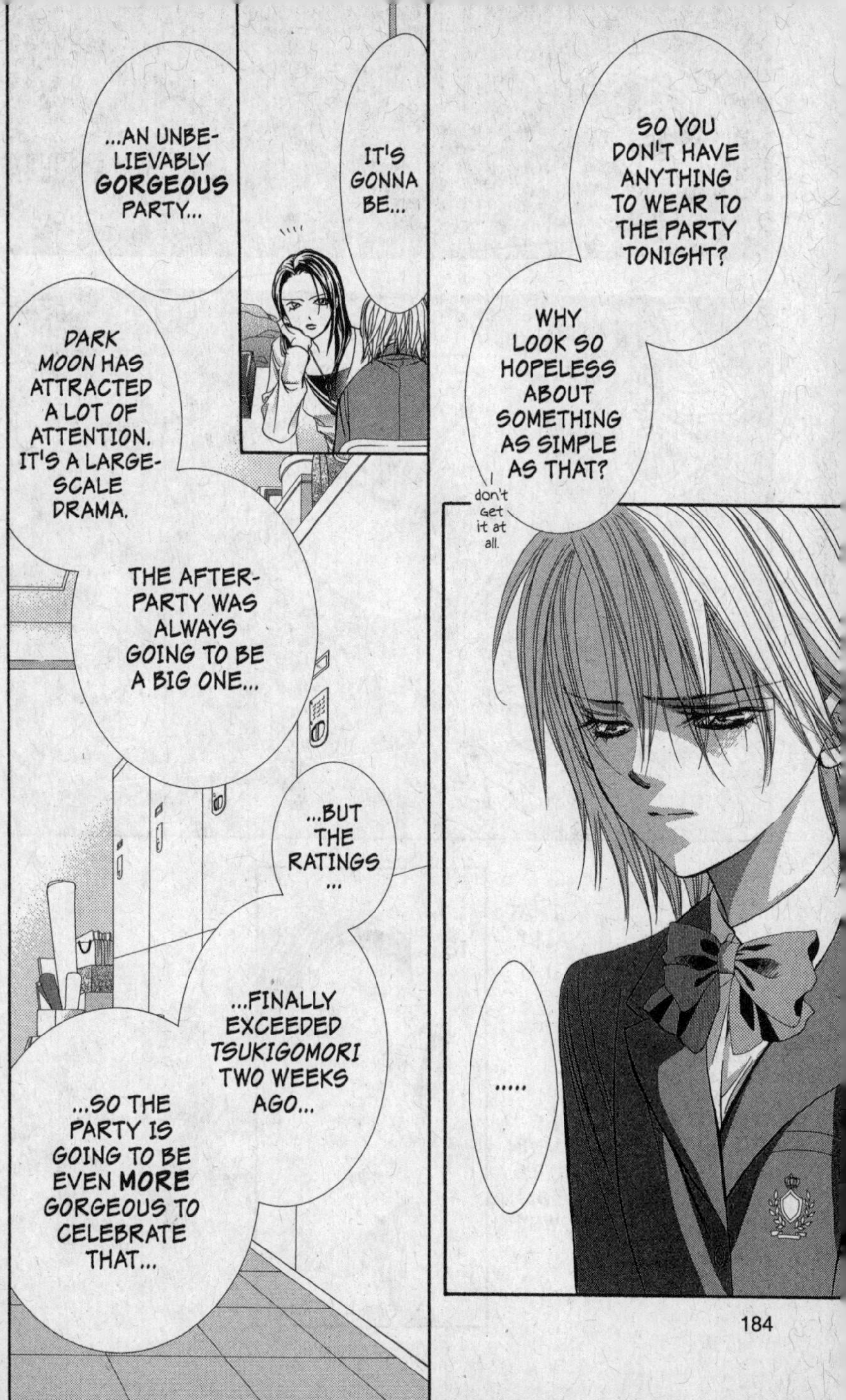
SO YOU DON'T HAVE ANYTHING TO WEAR TO THE PARTY TONIGHT?
WHY LOOK SO HOPELESS ABOUT SOMETHING AS SIMPLE AS THAT?
I don't get it at all.
.....
IT'S GONNA BE...
...AN UNBE-LIEVABLY **GORGEOUS** PARTY...
DARK MOON HAS ATTRACTED A LOT OF ATTENTION. IT'S A LARGE-SCALE DRAMA.
THE AFTER-PARTY WAS ALWAYS GOING TO BE A BIG ONE...
...BUT THE RATINGS...
...FINALLY EXCEEDED TSUKIGOMORI TWO WEEKS AGO...
...SO THE PARTY IS GOING TO BE EVEN **MORE** GORGEOUS TO CELEBRATE THAT...

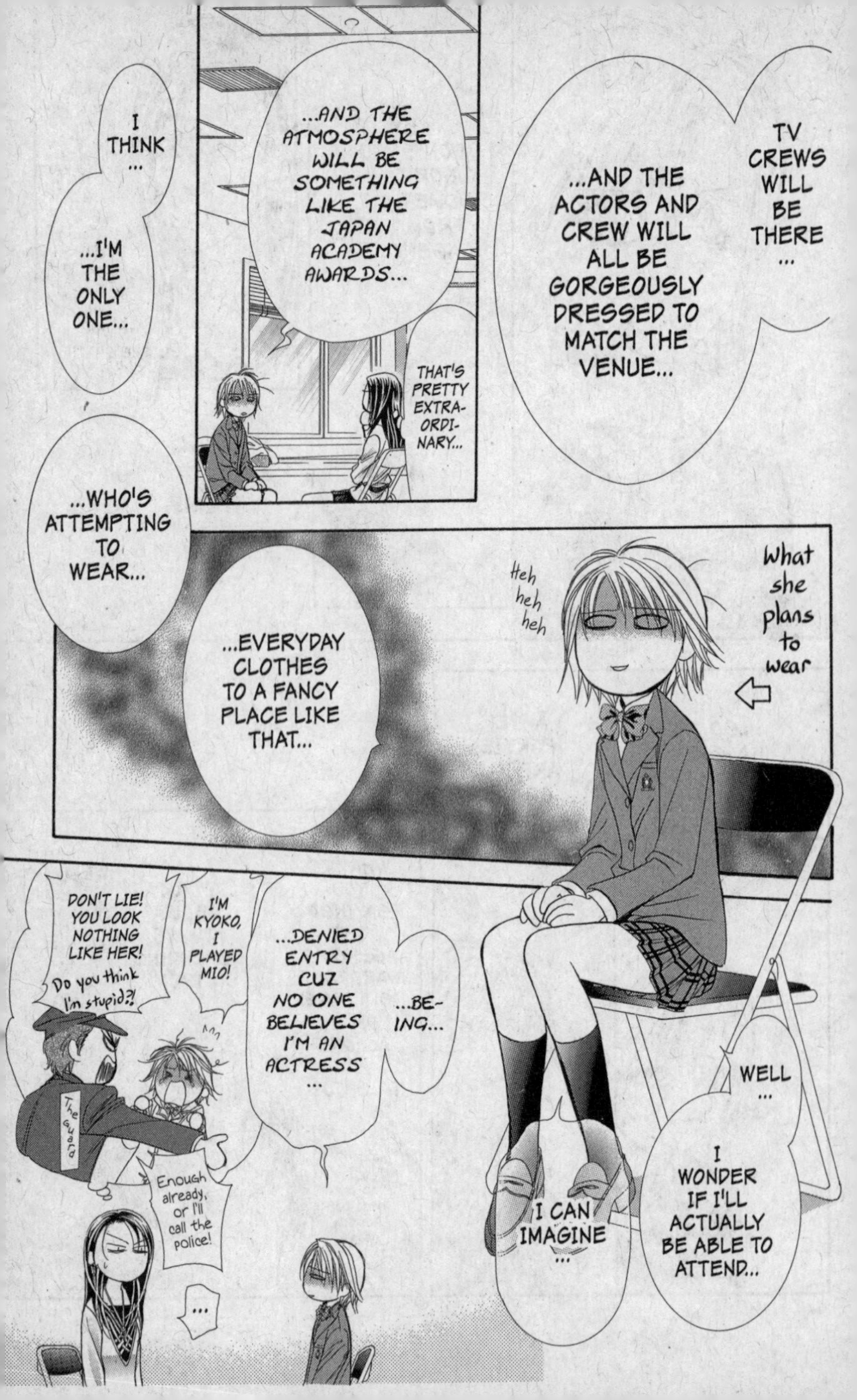
TV CREWS WILL BE THERE...
...AND THE ACTORS AND CREW WILL ALL BE GORGEOUSLY DRESSED TO MATCH THE VENUE...
...AND THE ATMOSPHERE WILL BE SOMETHING LIKE THE JAPAN ACADEMY AWARDS...
THAT'S PRETTY EXTRA-ORDINARY...
I THINK...
...I'M THE ONLY ONE...
...WHO'S ATTEMPTING TO WEAR...
What she plans to wear
Heh heh heh
...EVERYDAY CLOTHES TO A FANCY PLACE LIKE THAT...
WELL...
I WONDER IF I'LL ACTUALLY BE ABLE TO ATTEND...
I CAN IMAGINE...
...BE-ING...
...DENIED ENTRY CUZ NO ONE BELIEVES I'M AN ACTRESS...
I'M KYOKO, I PLAYED MIO!
DON'T LIE! YOU LOOK NOTHING LIKE HER!
Do you think I'm stupid?!
The Guard
Enough already, or I'll call the police!
...

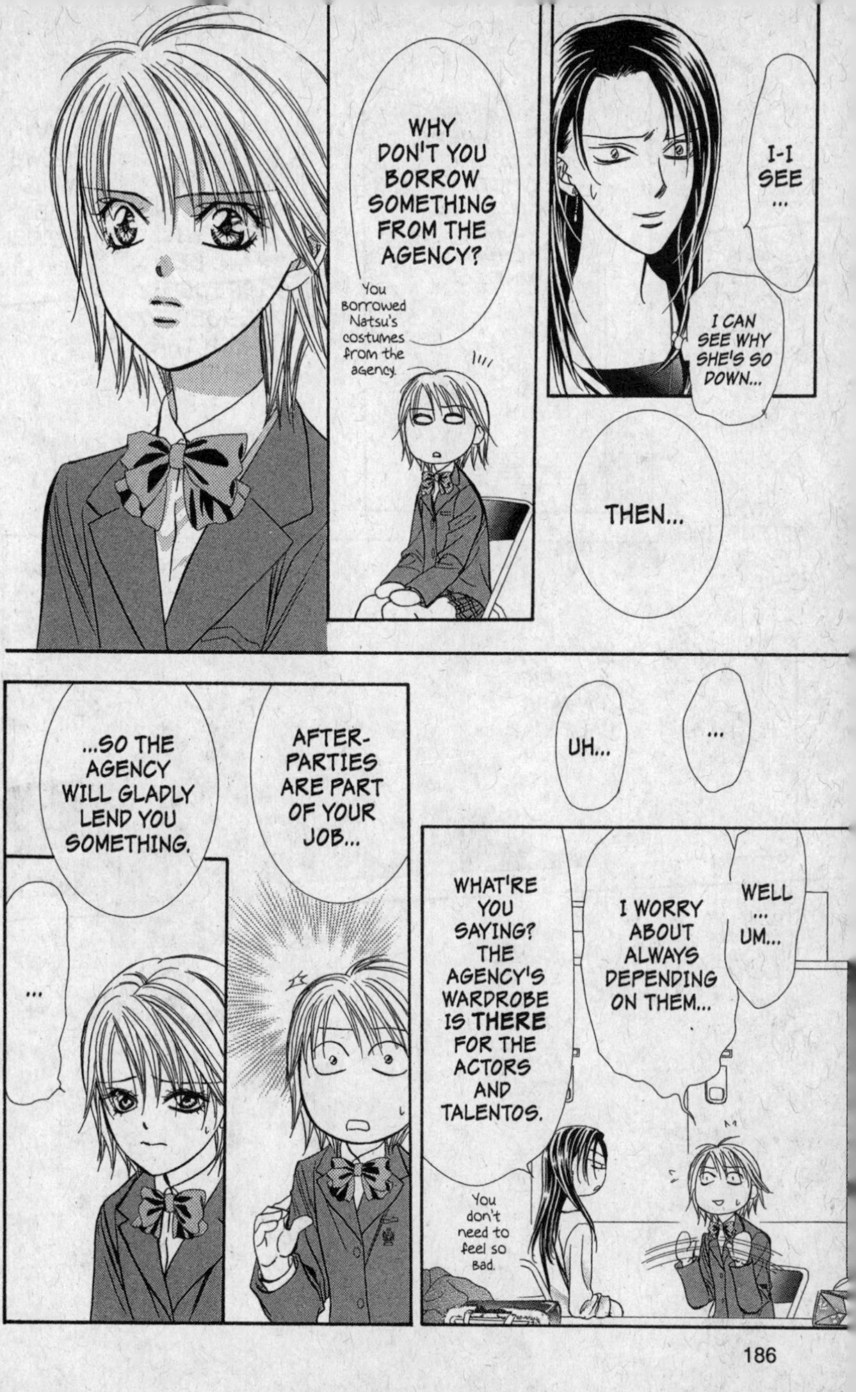
I-I SEE ...
I CAN SEE WHY SHE'S SO DOWN...
THEN...
WHY DON'T YOU BORROW SOMETHING FROM THE AGENCY?
You borrowed Natsu's costumes from the agency.
...
UH...
WELL ... UM...
I WORRY ABOUT ALWAYS DEPENDING ON THEM...
WHAT'RE YOU SAYING? THE AGENCY'S WARDROBE IS THERE FOR THE ACTORS AND TALENTOS.
You don't need to feel so bad.
AFTER-PARTIES ARE PART OF YOUR JOB...
...SO THE AGENCY WILL GLADLY LEND YOU SOMETHING.
...

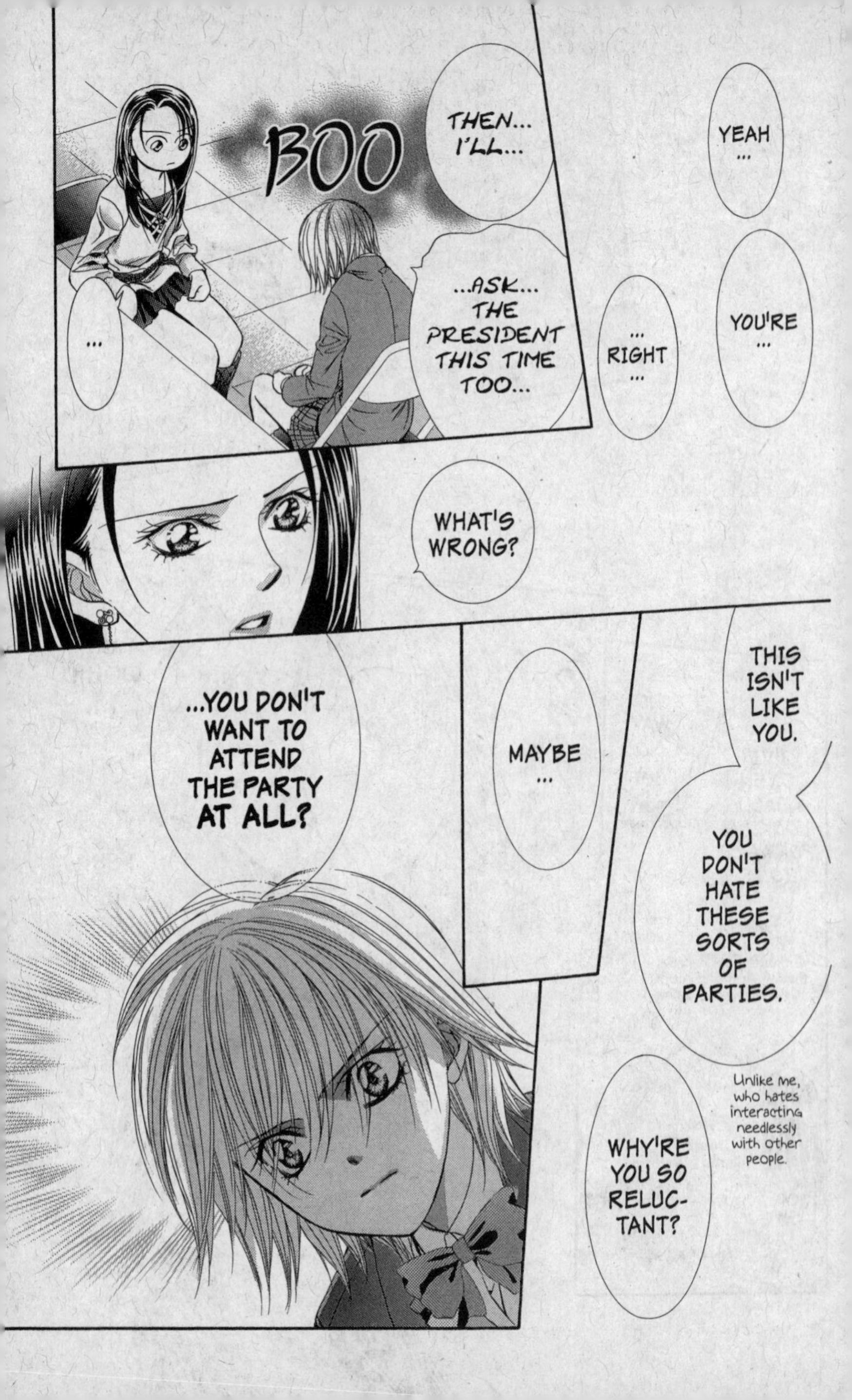
YEAH...
YOU'RE...
...RIGHT...
THEN... I'LL...
BOO
...ASK... THE PRESIDENT THIS TIME TOO...
...
WHAT'S WRONG?
THIS ISN'T LIKE YOU.
YOU DON'T HATE THESE SORTS OF PARTIES.
Unlike me, who hates interacting needlessly with other people.
WHY'RE YOU SO RELUCTANT?
MAYBE...
...YOU DON'T WANT TO ATTEND THE PARTY AT ALL?

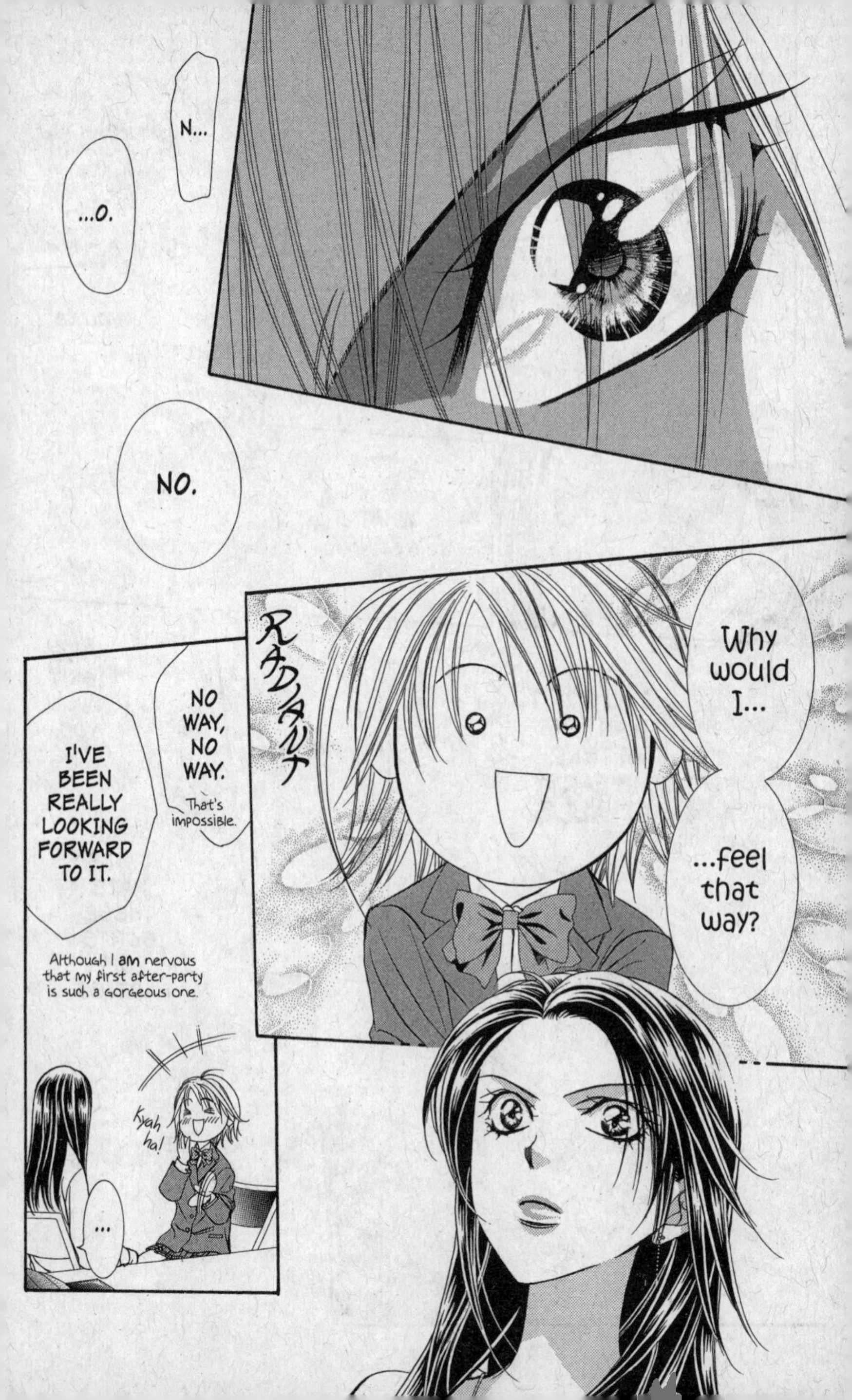

N...
...O.
NO.
RADIANT
Why would I...
...feel that way?
NO WAY, NO WAY.
That's impossible.
I'VE BEEN REALLY LOOKING FORWARD TO IT.
Although I am nervous that my first after-party is such a gorgeous one.
Kyah ha!
...

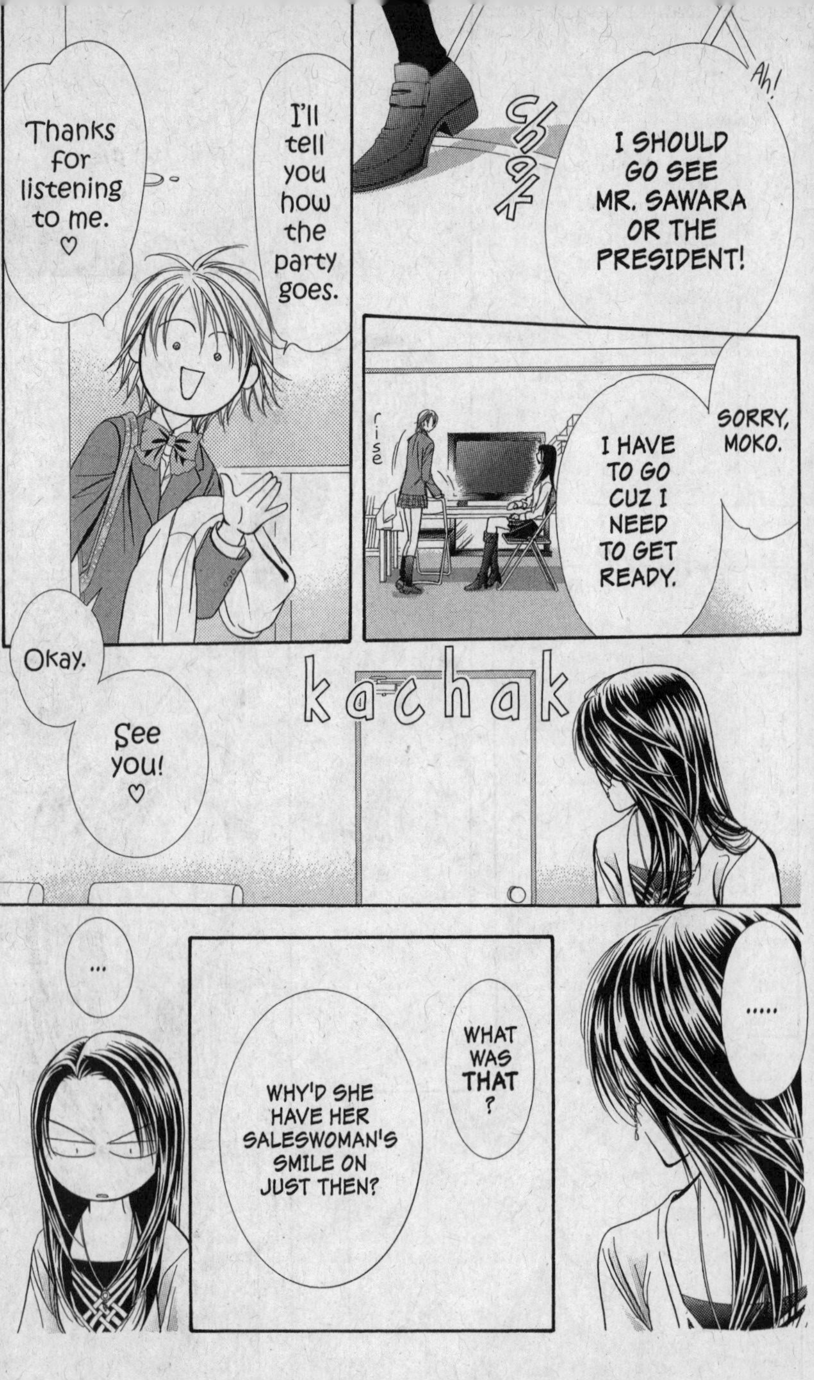
Ah!
I SHOULD GO SEE MR. SAWARA OR THE PRESIDENT!
chak
SORRY, MOKO.
I HAVE TO GO CUZ I NEED TO GET READY.
rise
I'll tell you how the party goes.
Thanks for listening to me. ♡
kachak
Okay.
See you! ♡
.....
WHAT WAS THAT?
WHY'D SHE HAVE HER SALESWOMAN'S SMILE ON JUST THEN?
...

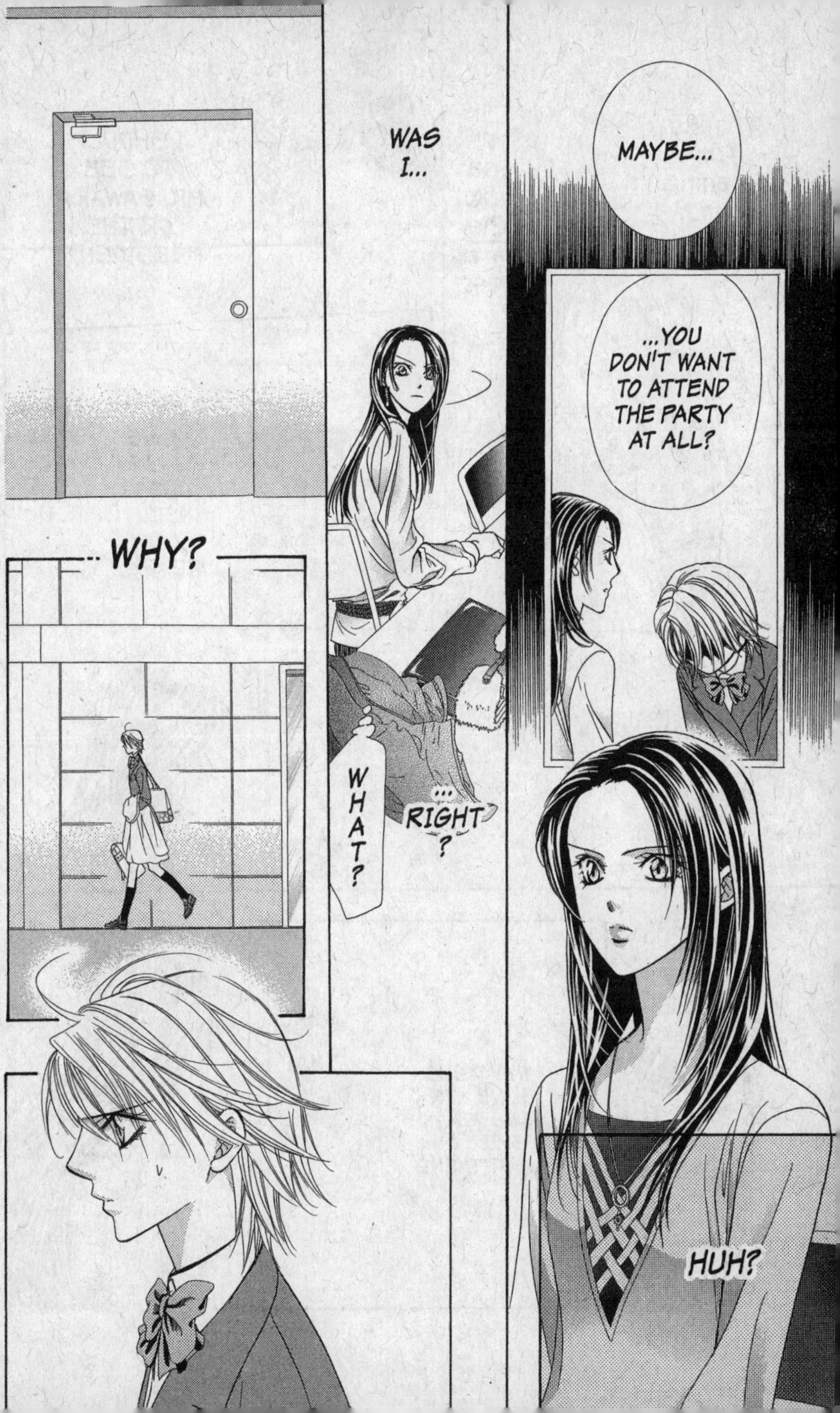
MAYBE...
...YOU DON'T WANT TO ATTEND THE PARTY AT ALL?
HUH?
WAS I...
...RIGHT?
WHAT?
WHY?

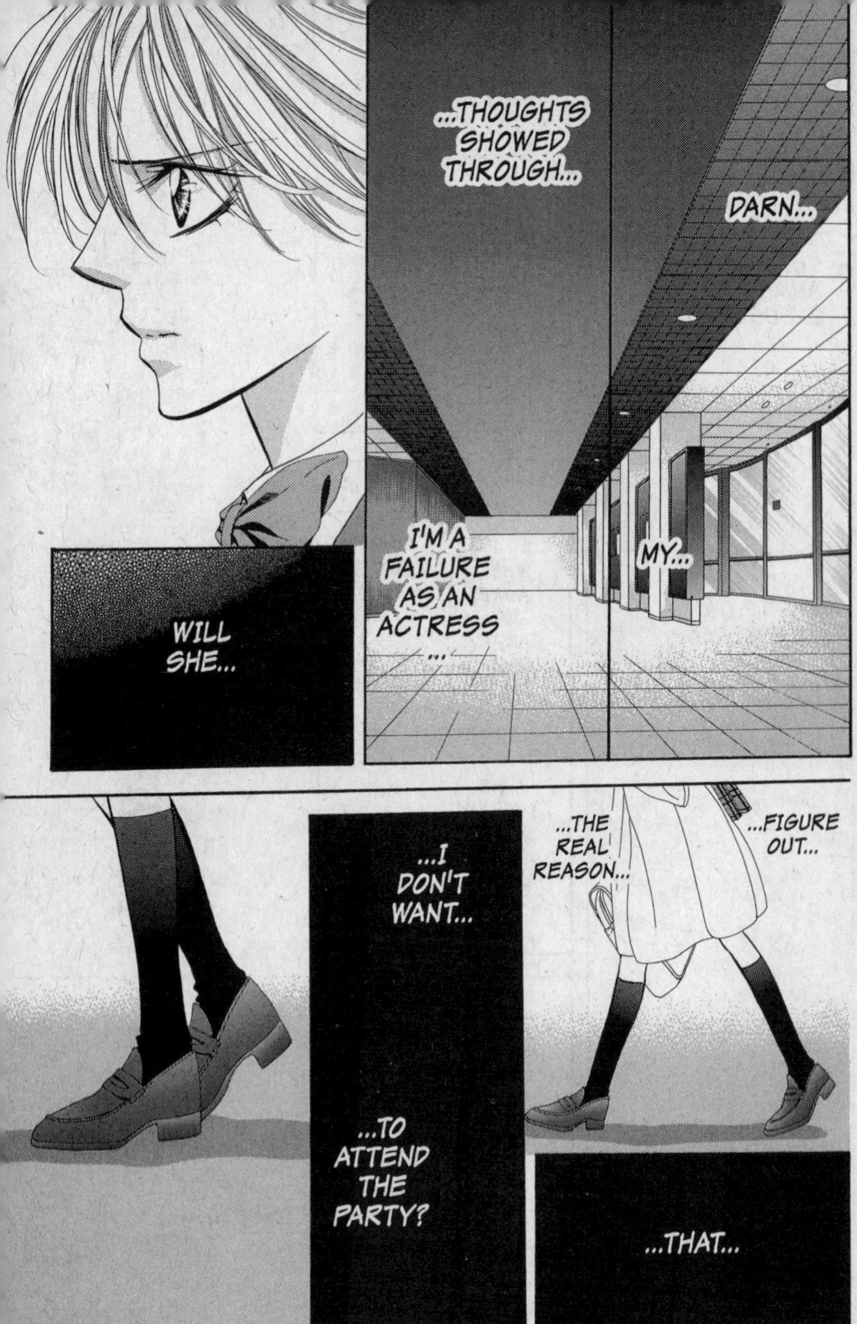
DARN...
MY...
...THOUGHTS SHOWED THROUGH...
I'M A FAILURE AS AN ACTRESS...
WILL SHE...
...FIGURE OUT...
...THE REAL REASON...
...THAT...
...I DON'T WANT...
...TO ATTEND THE PARTY?

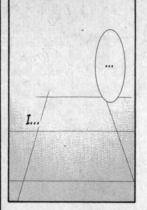

...
I...
...WASN'T WORRIED ABOUT WHAT TO WEAR...
WHEN I ASKED MR. SAWARA ABOUT IT...
...HE SAID MY SCHOOL UNIFORM WOULD BE ACCEPTABLE.
I CONSIDER MY UNIFORM...
...APPROPRIATE TO MY STATUS ANYWAY...
...SO I WAS RELIEVED...
...INSTEAD OF EMBARRASSED.
BUT...
I...
...COULDN'T THINK OF ANOTHER EXCUSE...
"I DON'T HAVE ANYTHING TO WEAR TO THE PARTY."
SO...
...I MADE THAT MY EXCUSE.

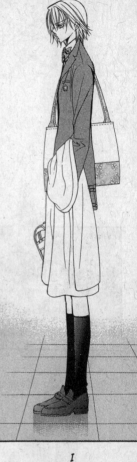

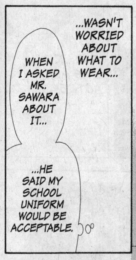

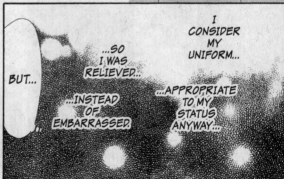

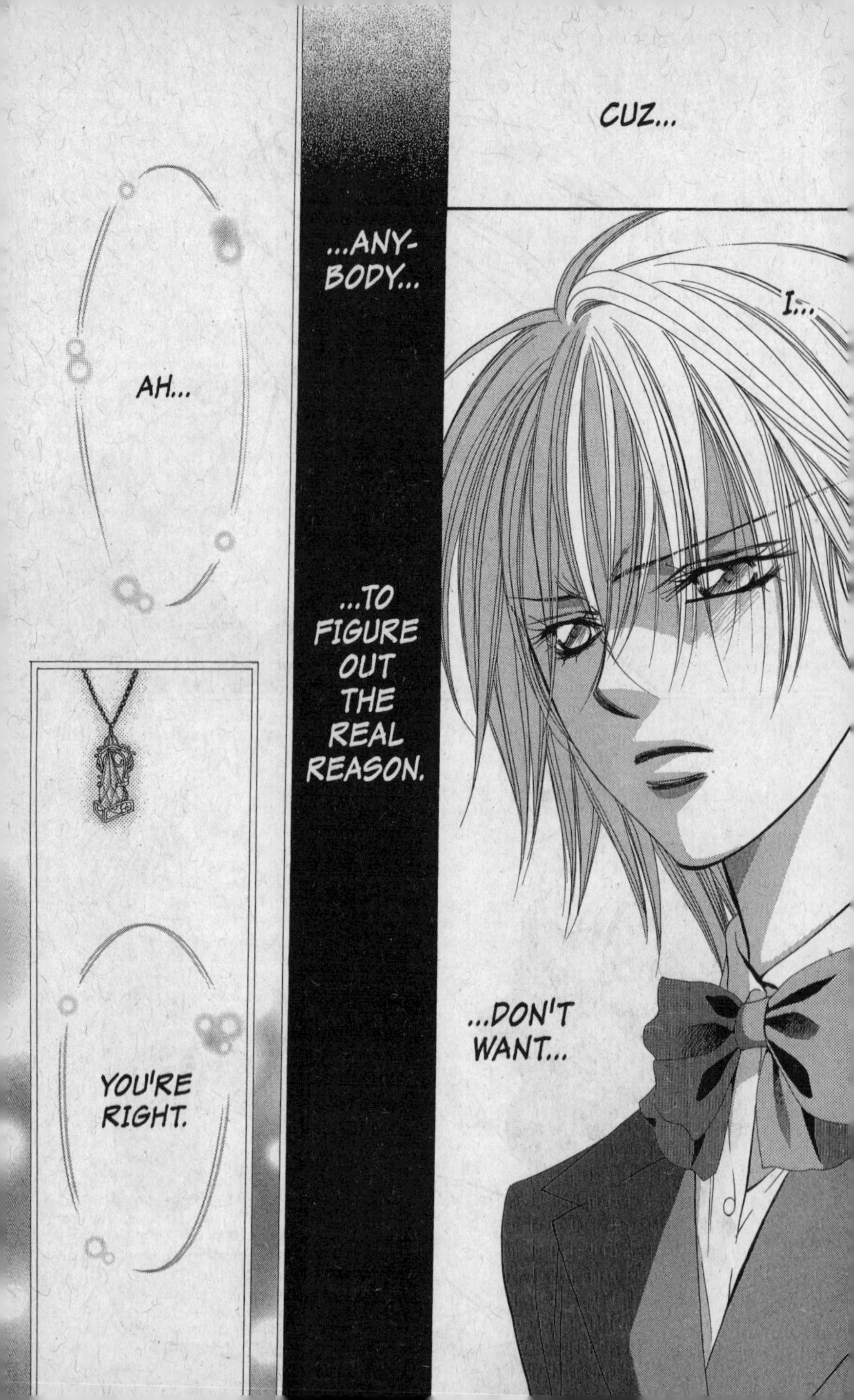
CUZ...
I...
...DON'T WANT...
...ANY-BODY...
...TO FIGURE OUT THE REAL REASON.
AH...
YOU'RE RIGHT.

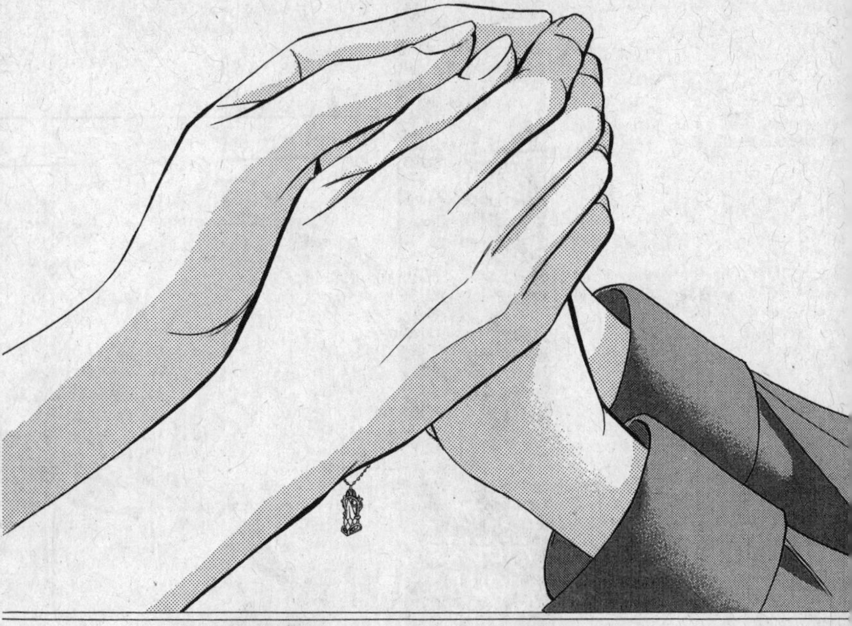
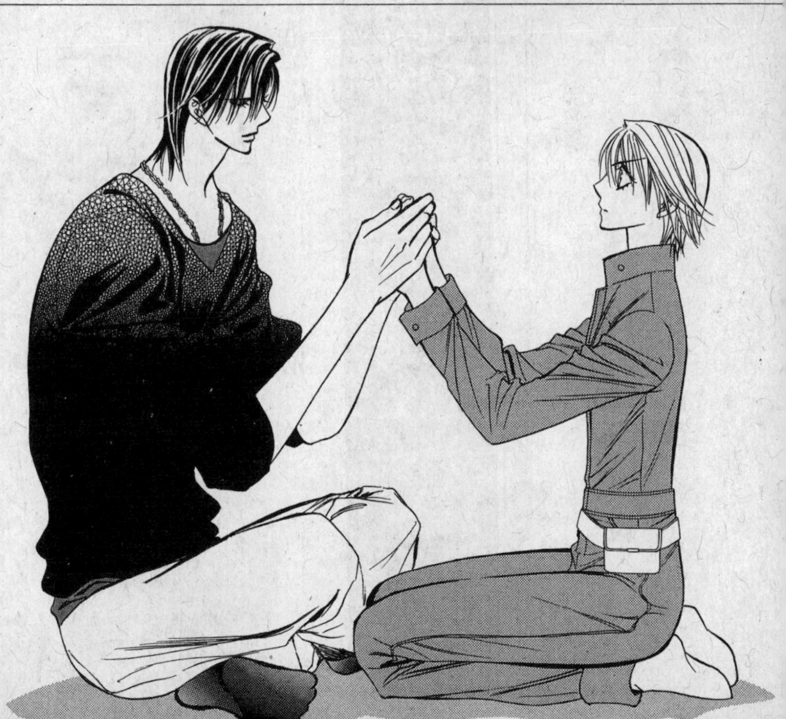

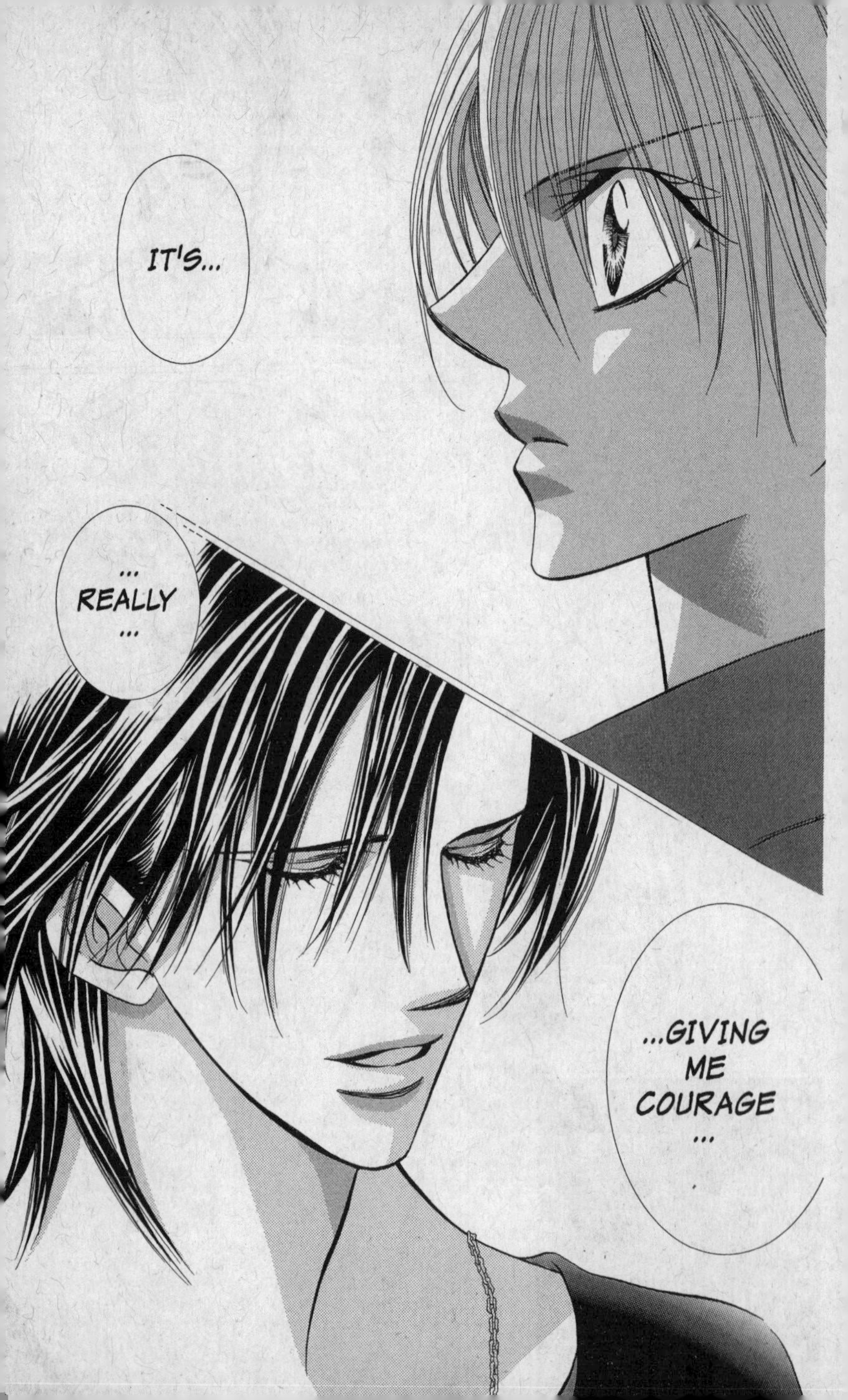
IT'S...
...REALLY...
...GIVING ME COURAGE...

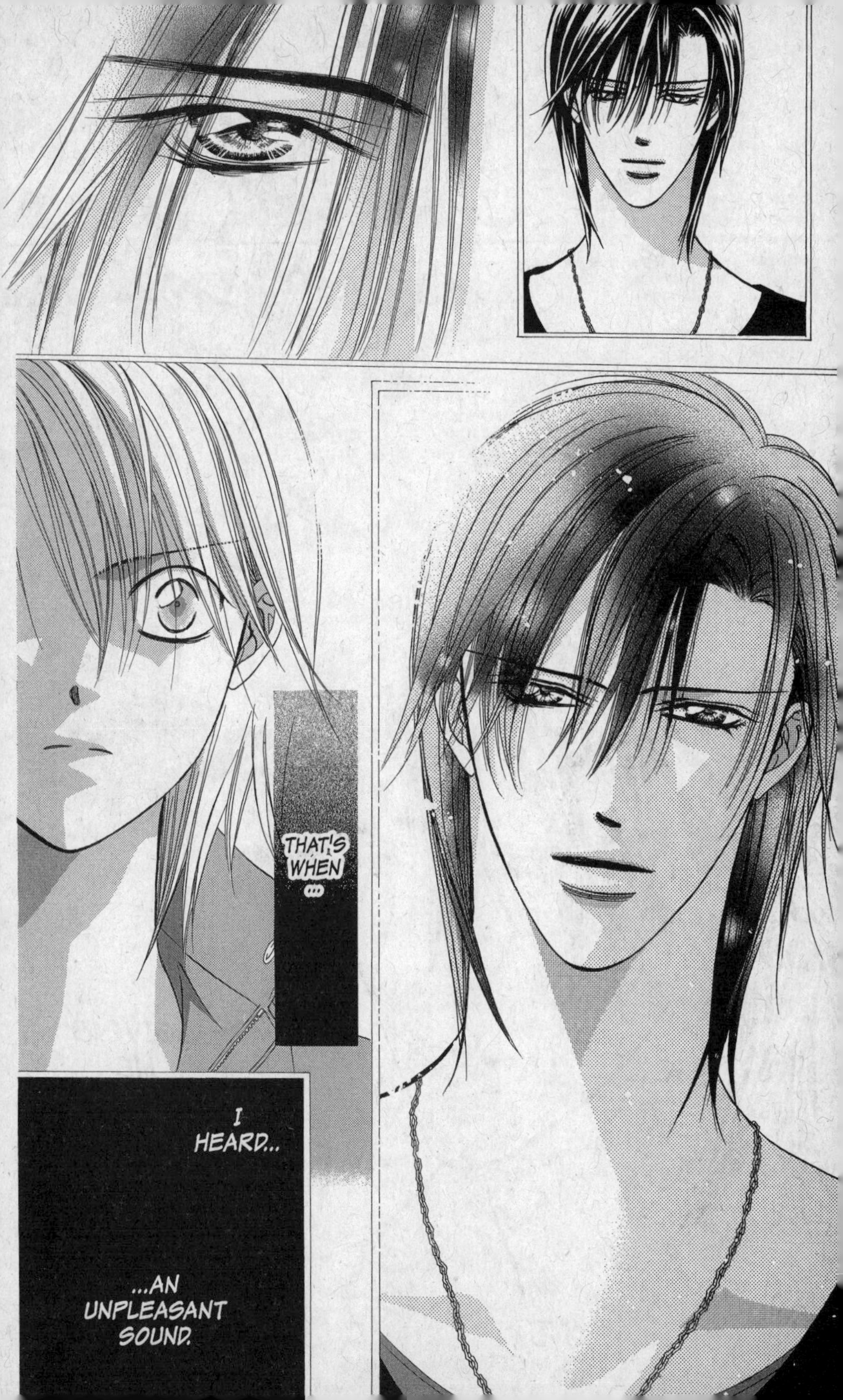
THAT'S WHEN ...
I HEARD...
...AN UNPLEASANT SOUND.

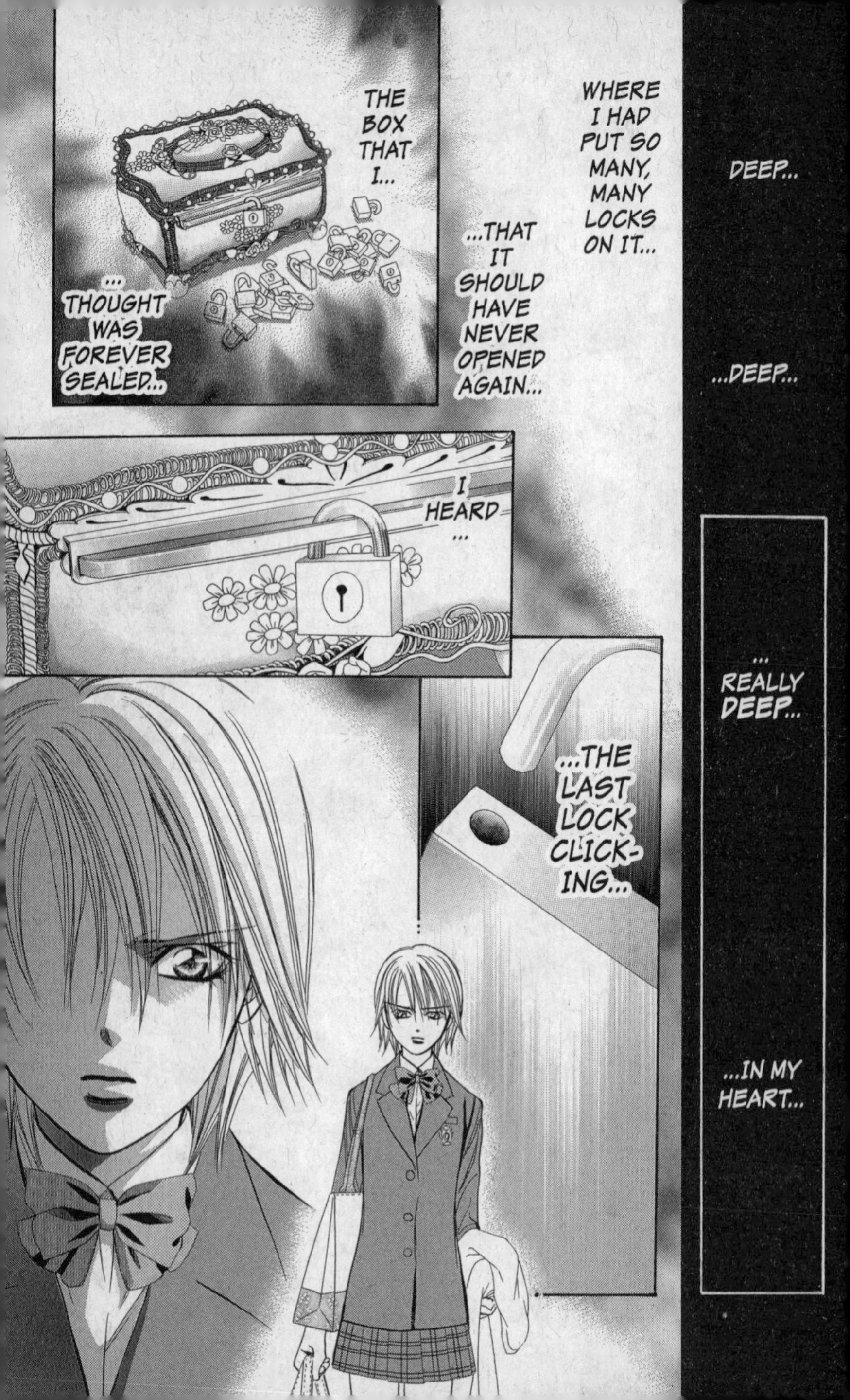
DEEP...
...DEEP...
...REALLY DEEP...
...IN MY HEART...
WHERE I HAD PUT SO MANY, MANY LOCKS ON IT...
THE BOX THAT I...
...THOUGHT WAS FOREVER SEALED...
...THAT IT SHOULD HAVE NEVER OPENED AGAIN...
I HEARD...
...THE LAST LOCK CLICKING...

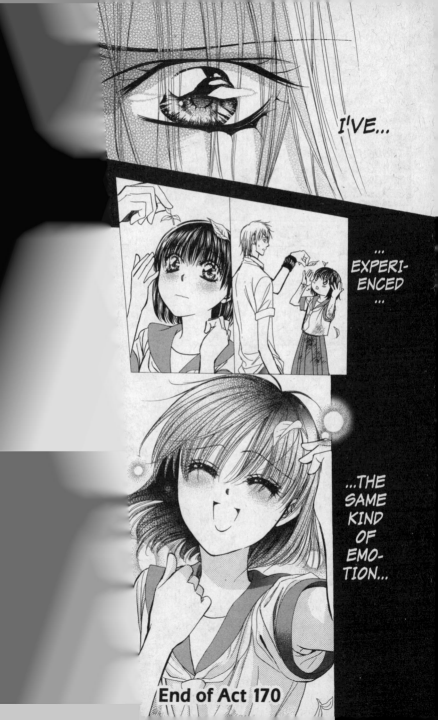

I'VE...

...
EXPERI-
ENCED
...

...THE
SAME
KIND
OF
EMO-
TION...

End of Act 170

Skip-Beat! End Notes

Everyone knows how to be a fan, but sometimes cool things from other cultures need a little help crossing the language barrier.

Page 5, panel 1: Yorozuya
Yorozuya means "a dealer in all sorts of articles," and tends to refer to a general store, but here it is the name of the store.

**Page 13, panel 1: Initial **
Refers to *Initial D,* a manga about street racing.

Page 125, panel 2: Ketchup on omelet rice
Writing things on omelet rice in ketchup is a common way to serve the dish. Some maid cafés even offer a service where the maid will draw or write things on your omelet rice.

Page 155, panel 6: "Win against the enemy"
The *teki* from *steki* (steak) can be read as "enemy" and the *katsu* (pork cutlet) can be read as "to win."

Shojo Beat

Skip·Beat!

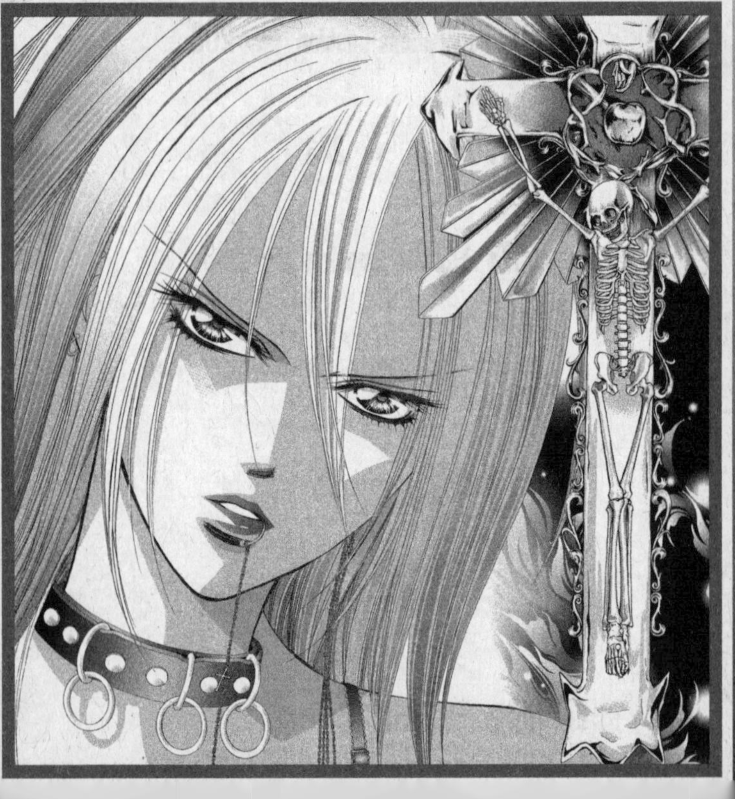

Skip·Beat!

Volume 29

CONTENTS

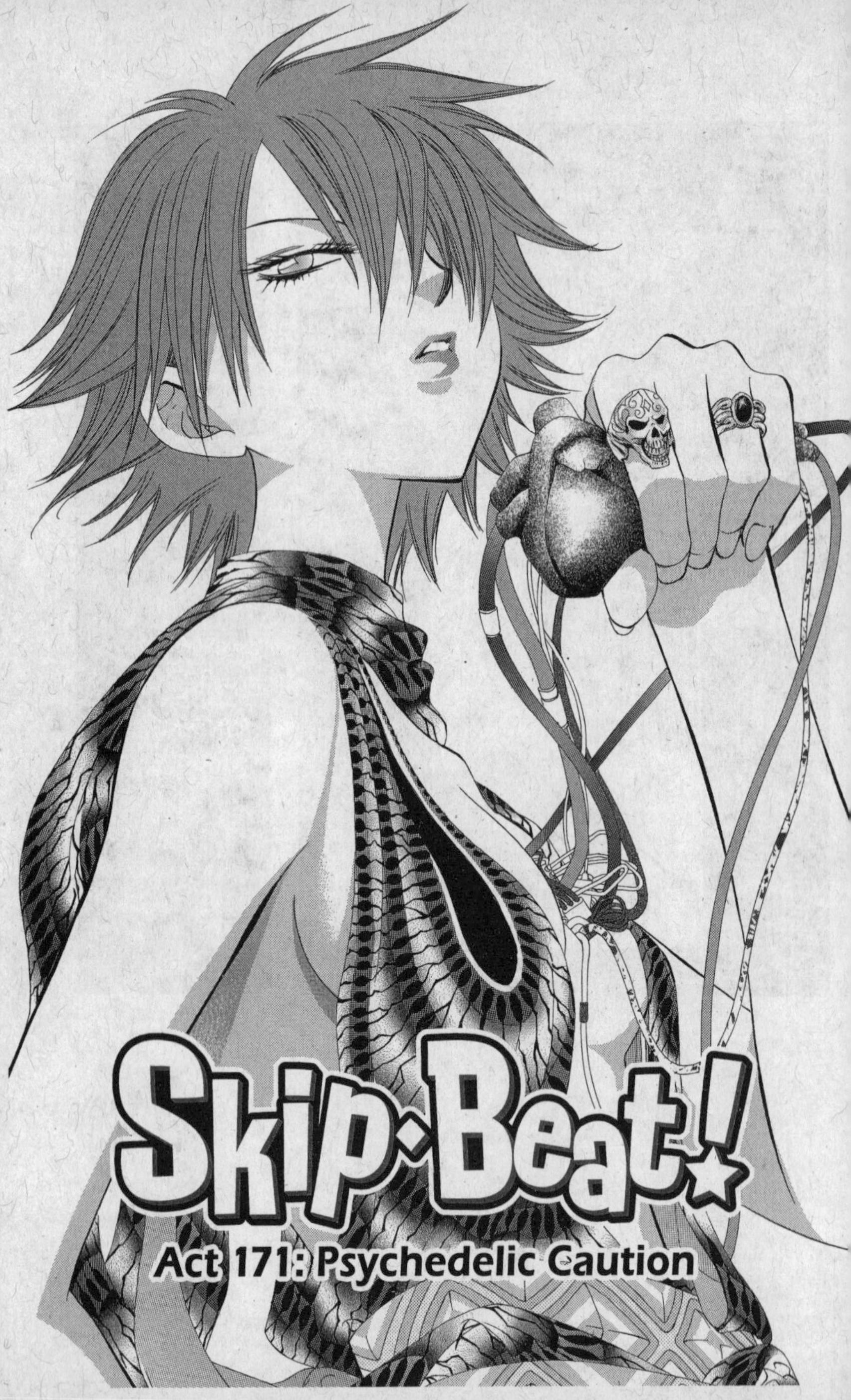
Skip·Beat!
Act 171: Psychedelic Caution

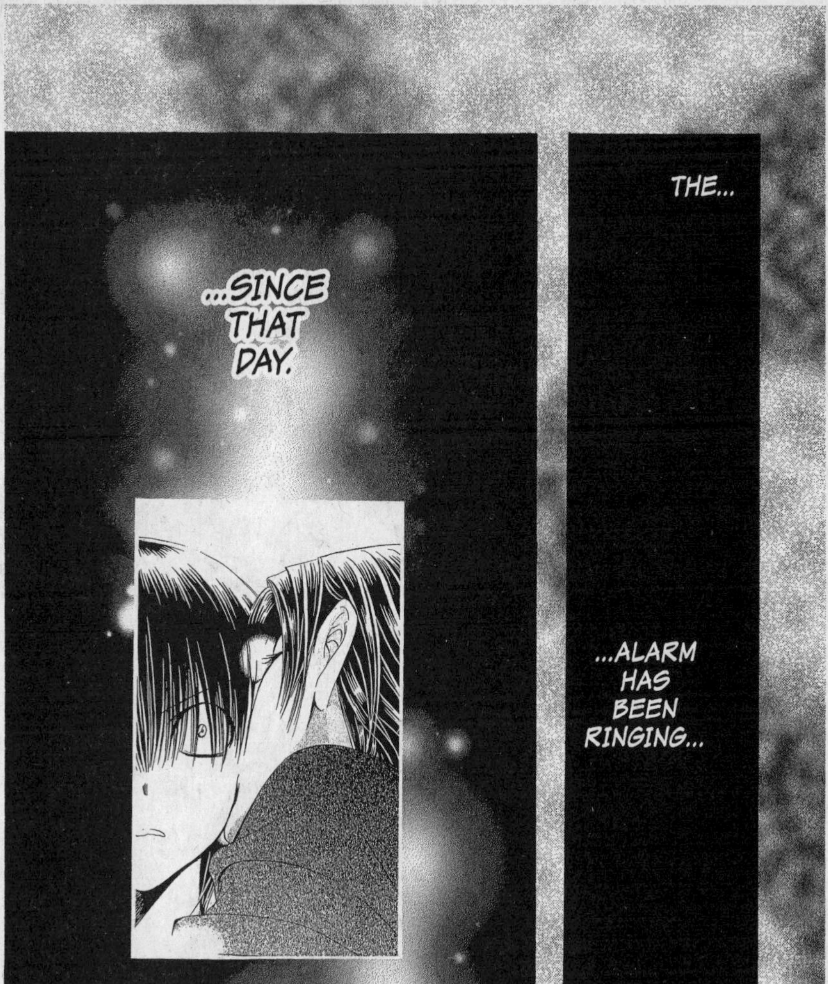
THE...
...ALARM HAS BEEN RINGING...
...SINCE THAT DAY.

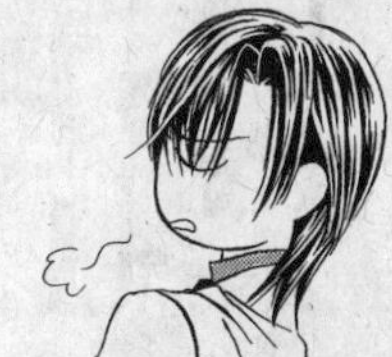

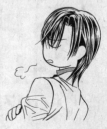

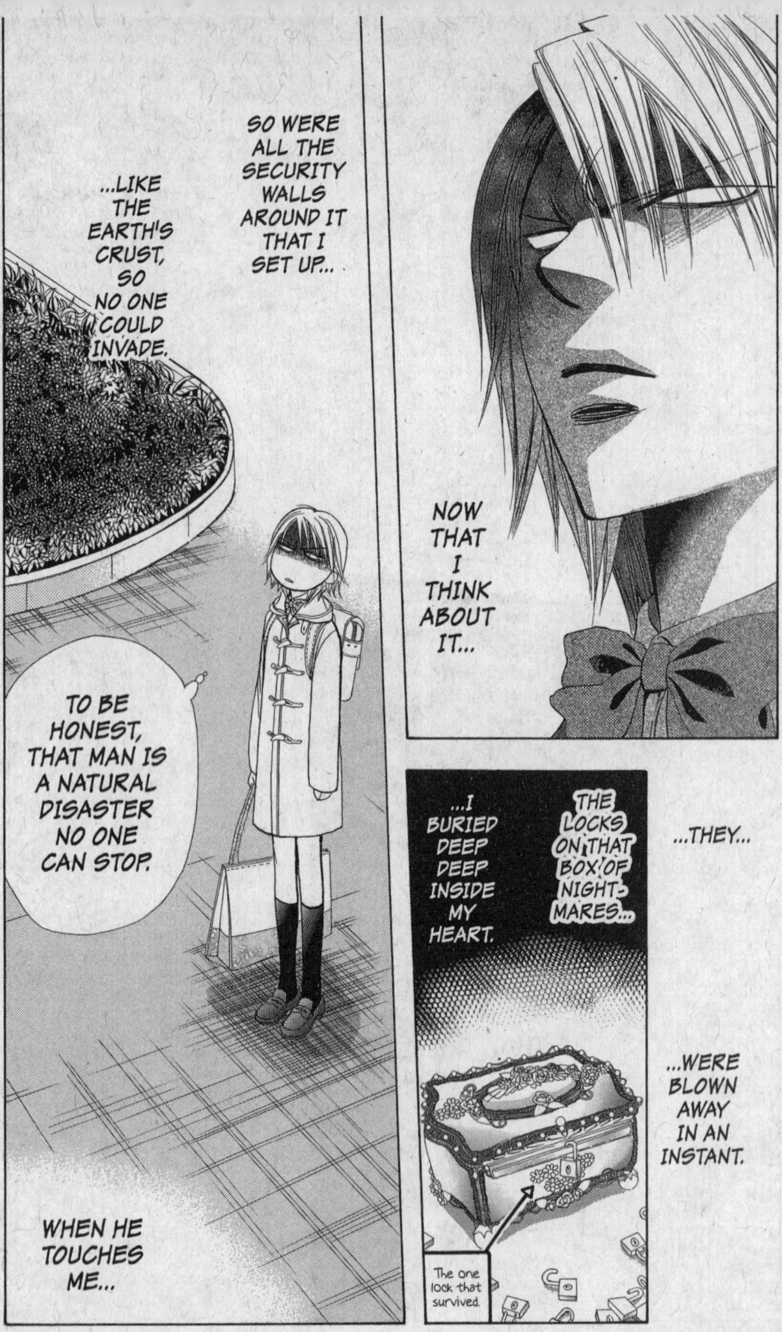
NOW THAT I THINK ABOUT IT...
...THEY...
THE LOCKS ON THAT BOX OF NIGHT-MARES...
...I BURIED DEEP DEEP INSIDE MY HEART.
...WERE BLOWN AWAY IN AN INSTANT.
The one lock that survived.
SO WERE ALL THE SECURITY WALLS AROUND IT THAT I SET UP...
...LIKE THE EARTH'S CRUST, SO NO ONE COULD INVADE.
TO BE HONEST, THAT MAN IS A NATURAL DISASTER NO ONE CAN STOP.
WHEN HE TOUCHES ME...

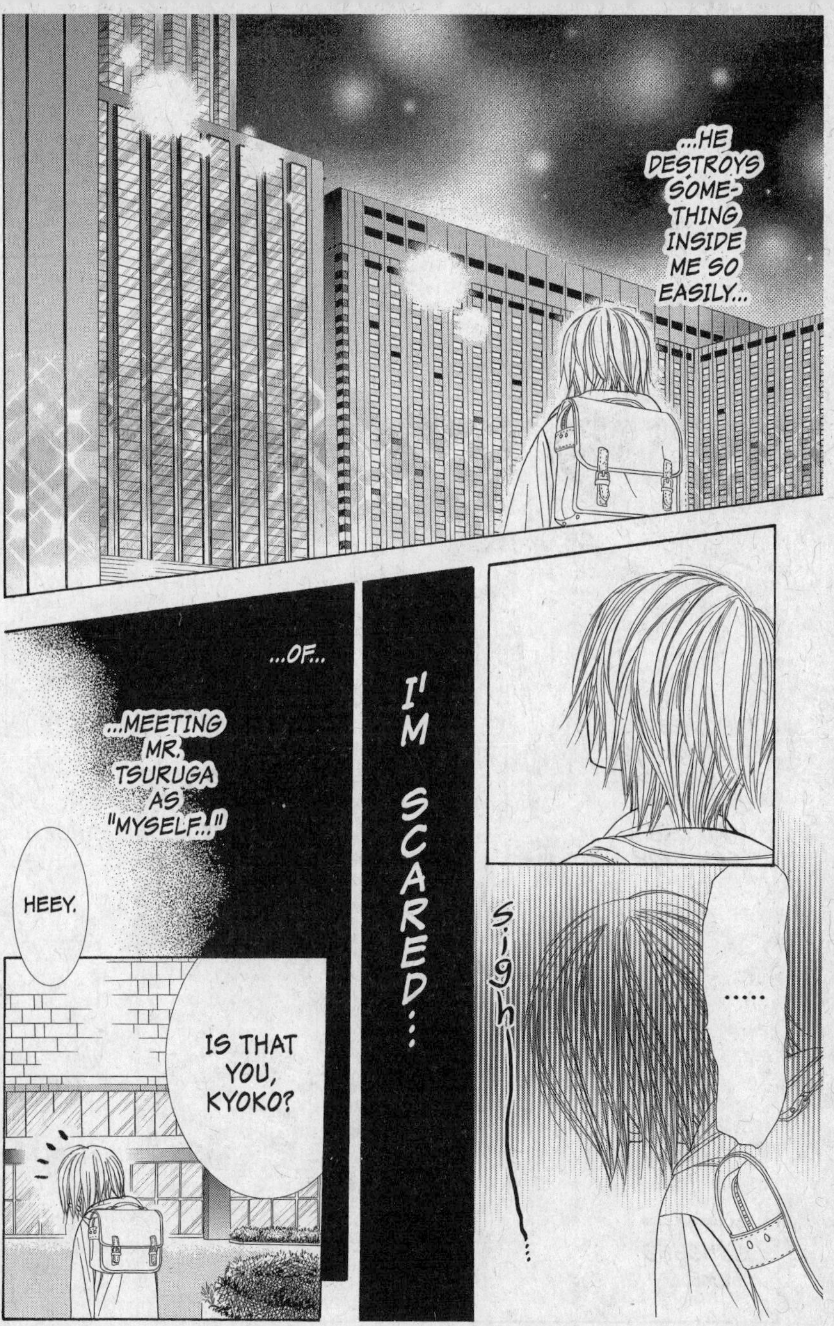
...HE DESTROYS SOME-THING INSIDE ME SO EASILY...
Sigh...
.....
I'M SCARED...
...OF...
...MEETING MR. TSURUGA AS "MYSELF..."
HEEY.
IS THAT YOU, KYOKO?

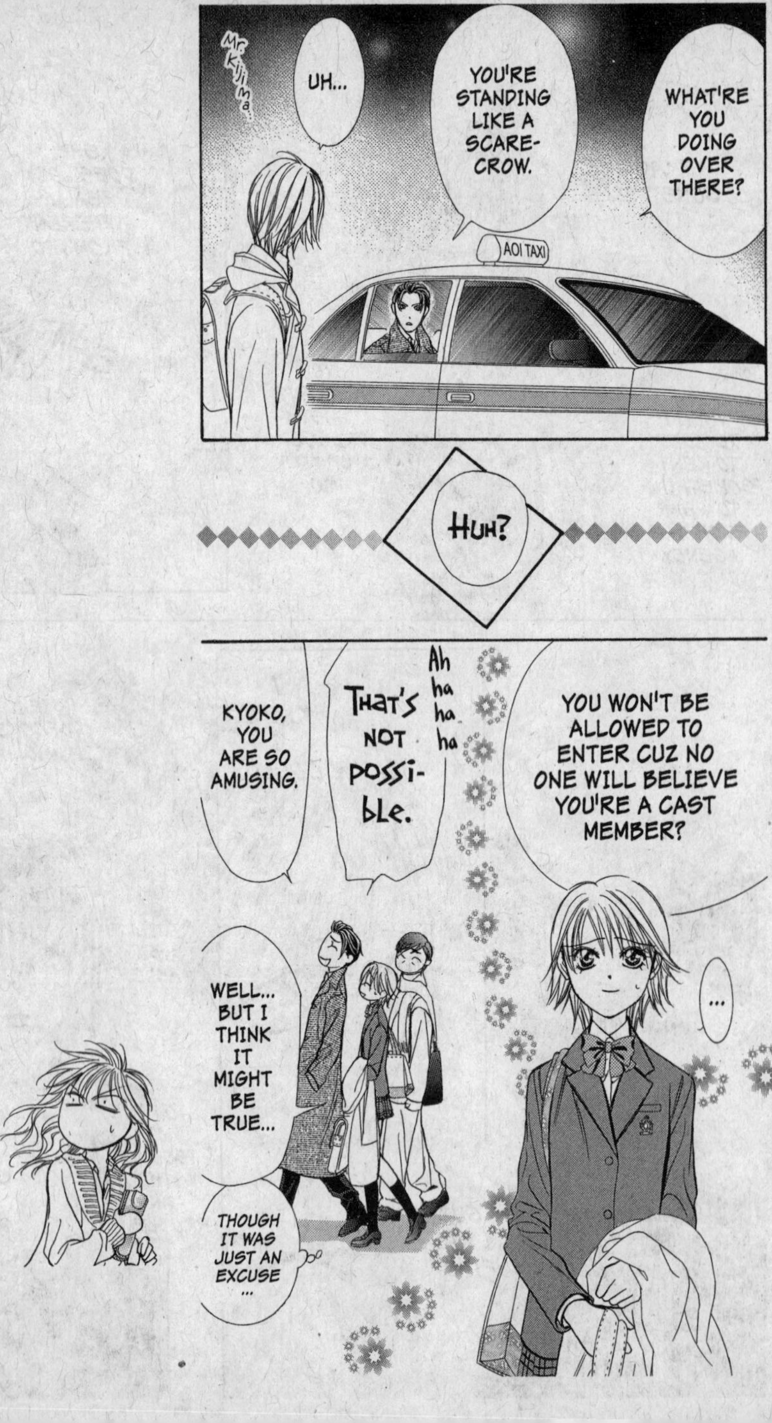
AOI TAXI
WHAT'RE YOU DOING OVER THERE?
YOU'RE STANDING LIKE A SCARE-CROW.
UH...
Mr. Kijima..
HUH?
YOU WON'T BE ALLOWED TO ENTER CUZ NO ONE WILL BELIEVE YOU'RE A CAST MEMBER?
Ah ha ha ha
THAT'S NOT POSSI-BLE.
KYOKO, YOU ARE SO AMUSING.
...
WELL... BUT I THINK IT MIGHT BE TRUE...
THOUGH IT WAS JUST AN EXCUSE ...

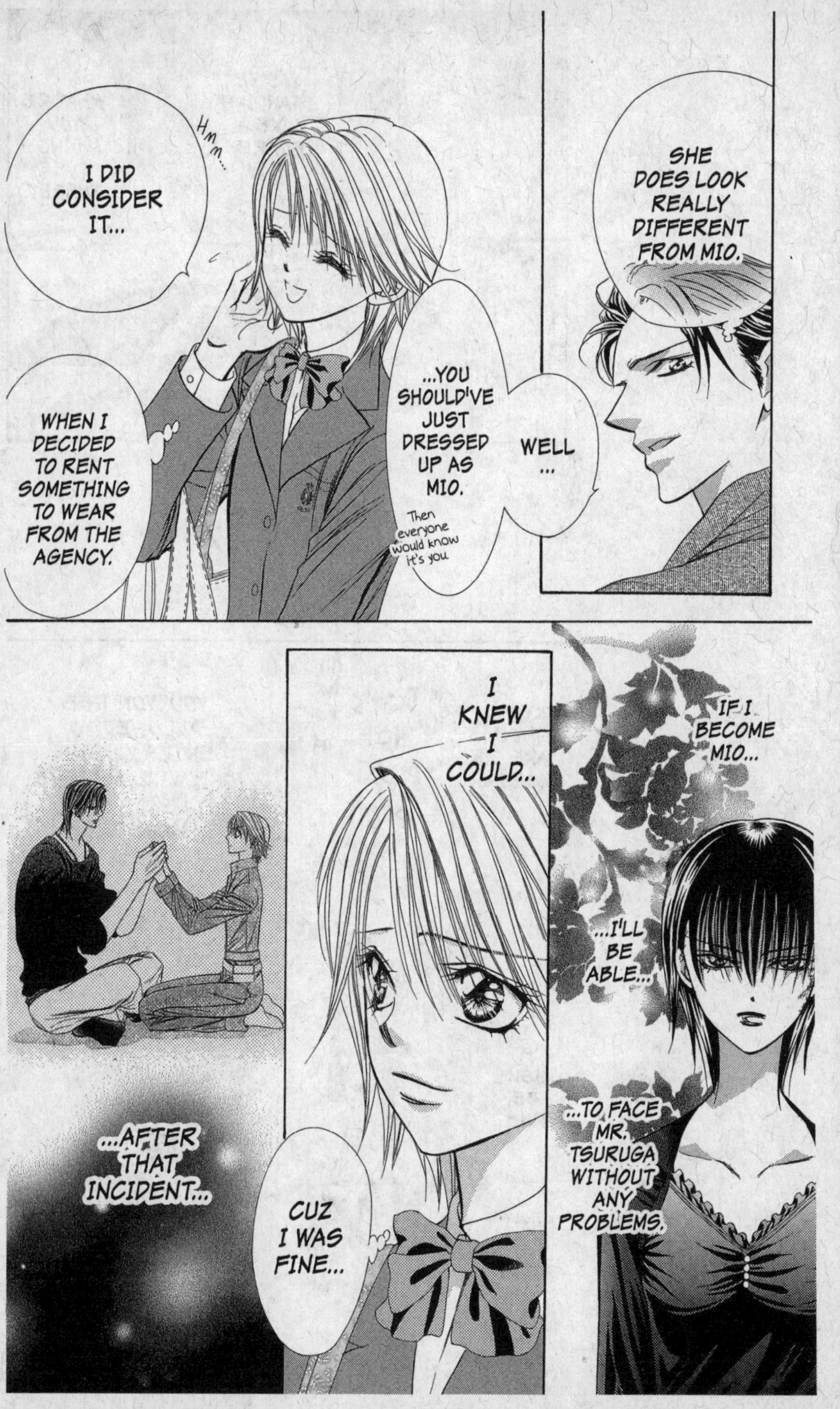
SHE DOES LOOK REALLY DIFFERENT FROM MIO.
WELL ...
...YOU SHOULD'VE JUST DRESSED UP AS MIO.
Then everyone would know it's you.
Hmm...
I DID CONSIDER IT...
WHEN I DECIDED TO RENT SOMETHING TO WEAR FROM THE AGENCY.
IF I BECOME MIO...
...I'LL BE ABLE...
...TO FACE MR. TSURUGA WITHOUT ANY PROBLEMS.
I KNEW I COULD...
CUZ I WAS FINE...
...AFTER THAT INCIDENT...

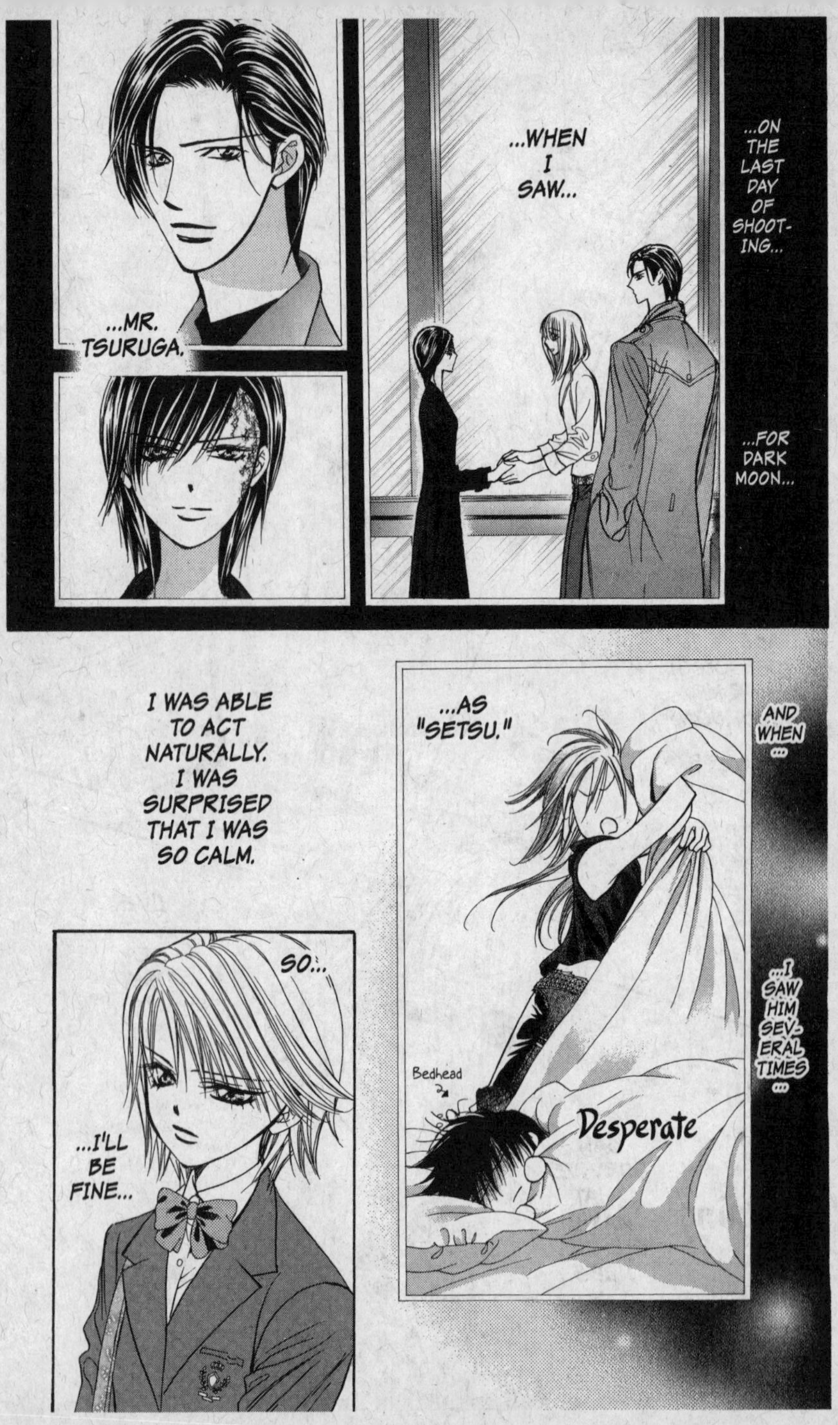
...ON THE LAST DAY OF SHOOTING...
...FOR DARK MOON...
...WHEN I SAW...
...MR. TSURUGA.
AND WHEN...
...I SAW HIM SEVERAL TIMES...
...AS "SETSU."
Bedhead
Desperate
I WAS ABLE TO ACT NATURALLY. I WAS SURPRISED THAT I WAS SO CALM.
SO...
...I'LL BE FINE...

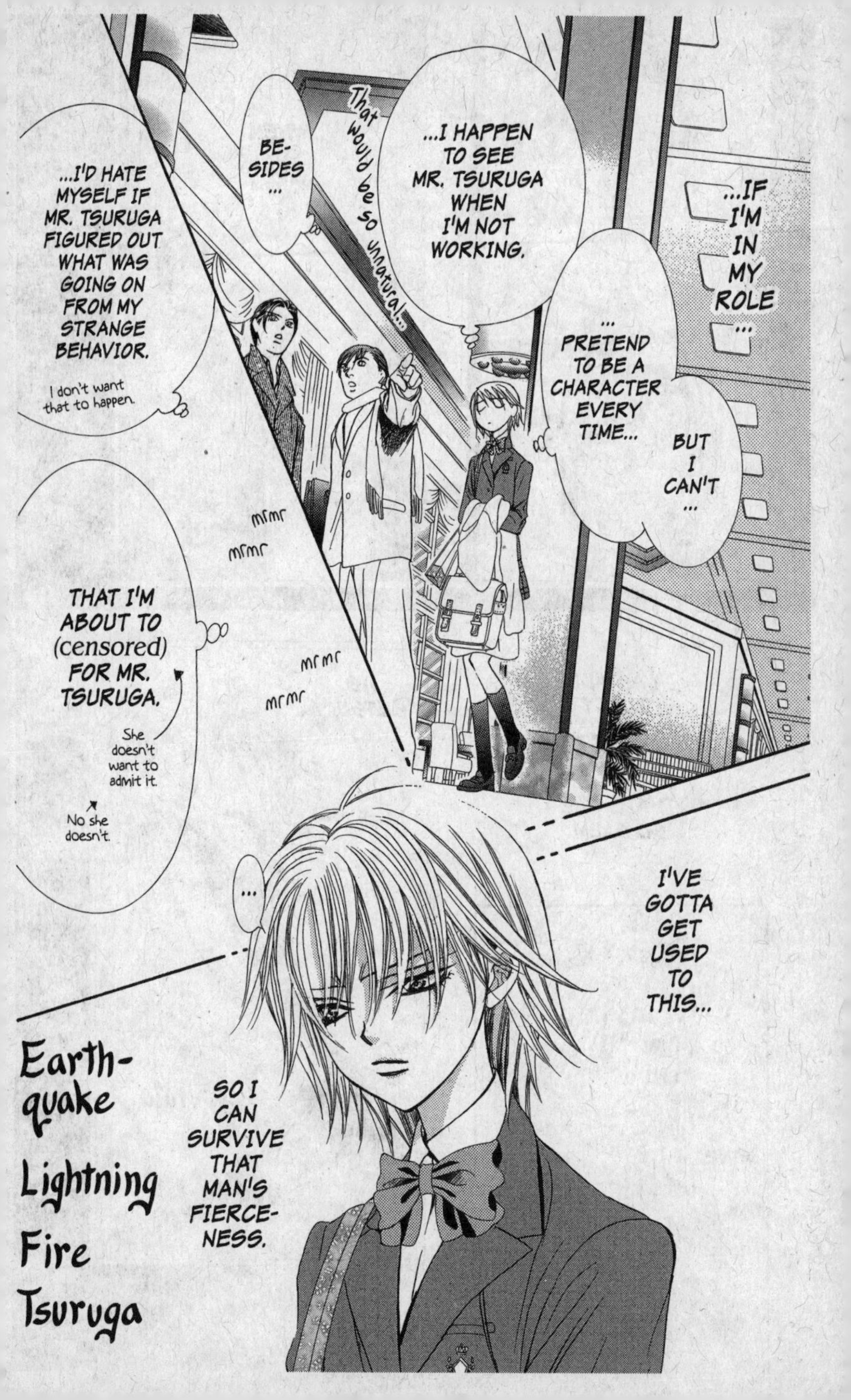

...IF I'M IN MY ROLE...
BUT I CAN'T...
...PRETEND TO BE A CHARACTER EVERY TIME...
...I HAPPEN TO SEE MR. TSURUGA WHEN I'M NOT WORKING.
That would be so unnatural...
BE-SIDES...
...I'D HATE MYSELF IF MR. TSURUGA FIGURED OUT WHAT WAS GOING ON FROM MY STRANGE BEHAVIOR.
I don't want that to happen.
mrmr
mrmr
mrmr
mrmr
THAT I'M ABOUT TO (censored) FOR MR. TSURUGA.
She doesn't want to admit it.
No she doesn't.
I'VE GOTTA GET USED TO THIS...
...
SO I CAN SURVIVE THAT MAN'S FIERCE-NESS.
Earth-quake Lightning Fire Tsuruga

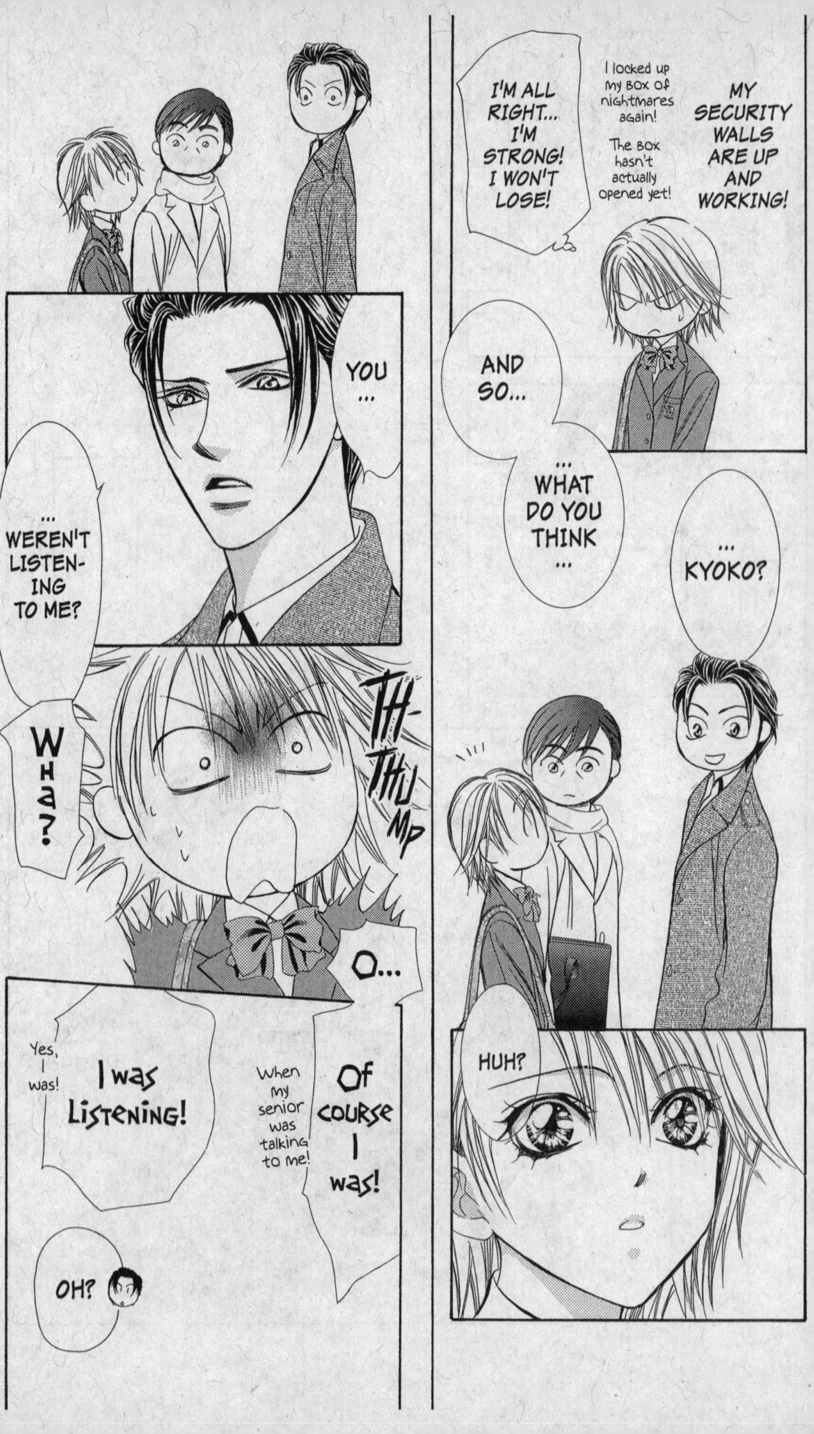
MY SECURITY WALLS ARE UP AND WORKING!
I locked up my box of nightmares again!
The box hasn't actually opened yet!
I'M ALL RIGHT... I'M STRONG! I WON'T LOSE!
AND SO...
... WHAT DO YOU THINK ...
... KYOKO?
HUH?
YOU ...
... WEREN'T LISTEN-ING TO ME?
TH-THUMP
Wha?
O...
Of course I was!
When my senior was talking to me!
I was listening!
Yes, I was!
OH?

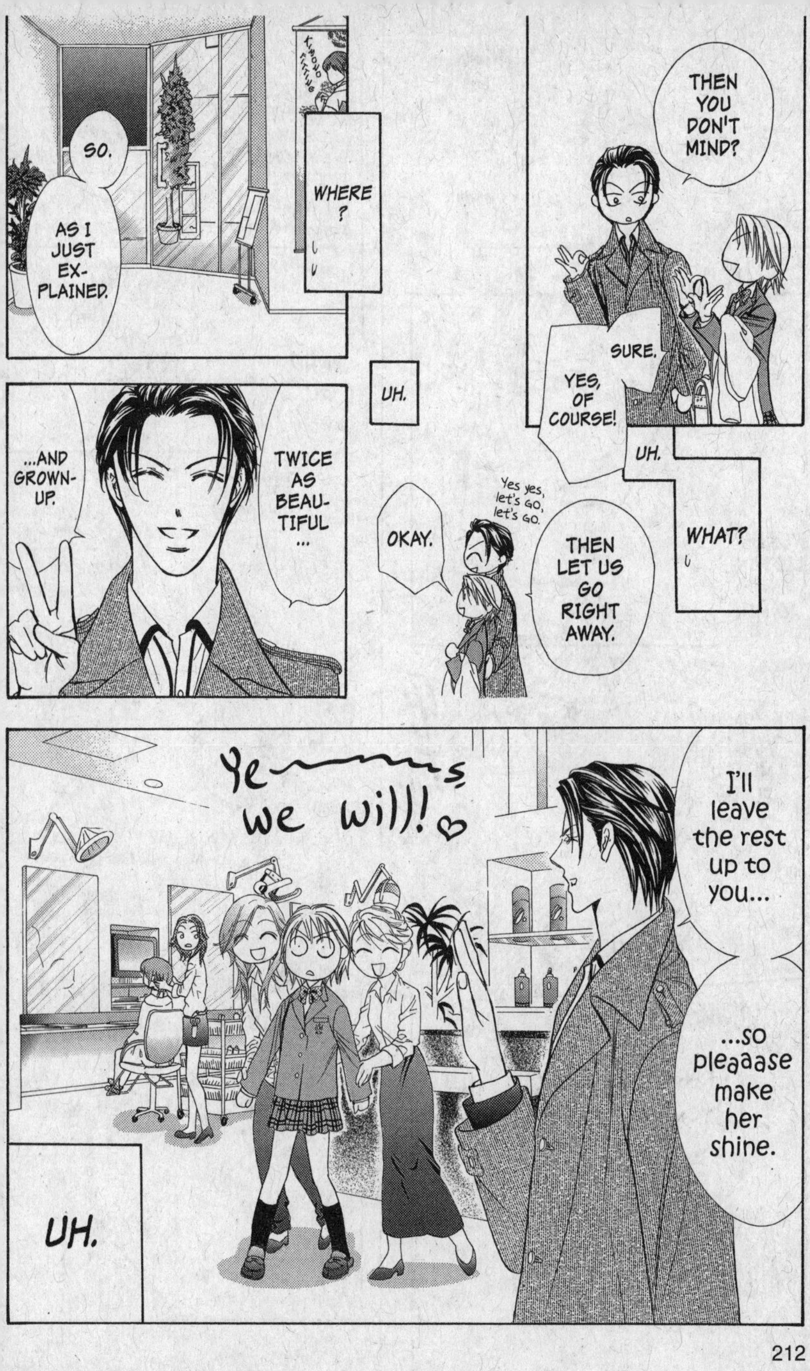
THEN YOU DON'T MIND?
SURE.
YES, OF COURSE!
UH.
WHAT?
WHERE?
SO.
AS I JUST EX-PLAINED.
UH.
THEN LET US GO RIGHT AWAY.
Yes yes, let's GO, let's GO.
OKAY.
TWICE AS BEAU-TIFUL...
...AND GROWN-UP.
I'll leave the rest up to you...
...so pleaaase make her shine.
Ye~s, we will!
UH.

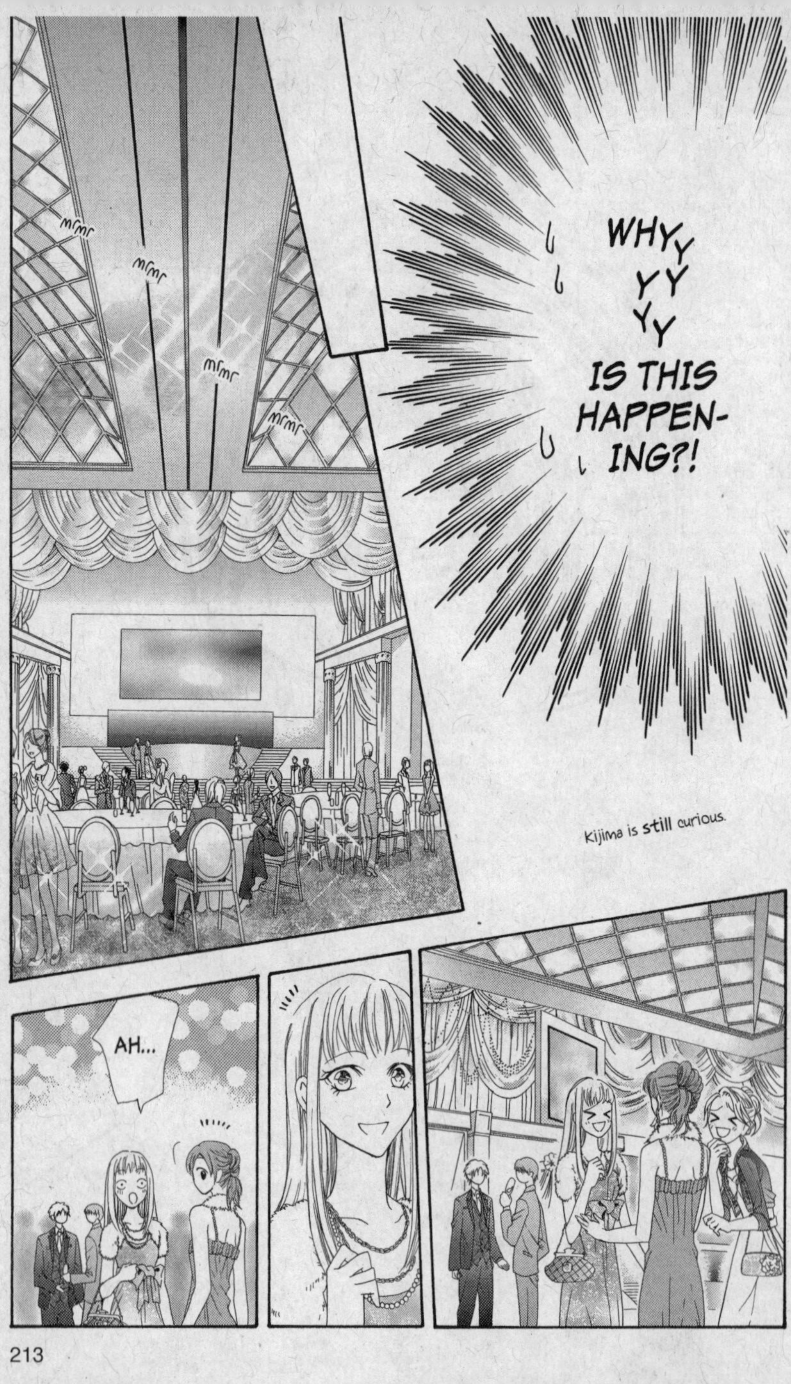
WHYYYYYY IS THIS HAPPEN-ING?!
Kijima is still curious.
mrmr
mrmr
mrmr
mrmr
AH...

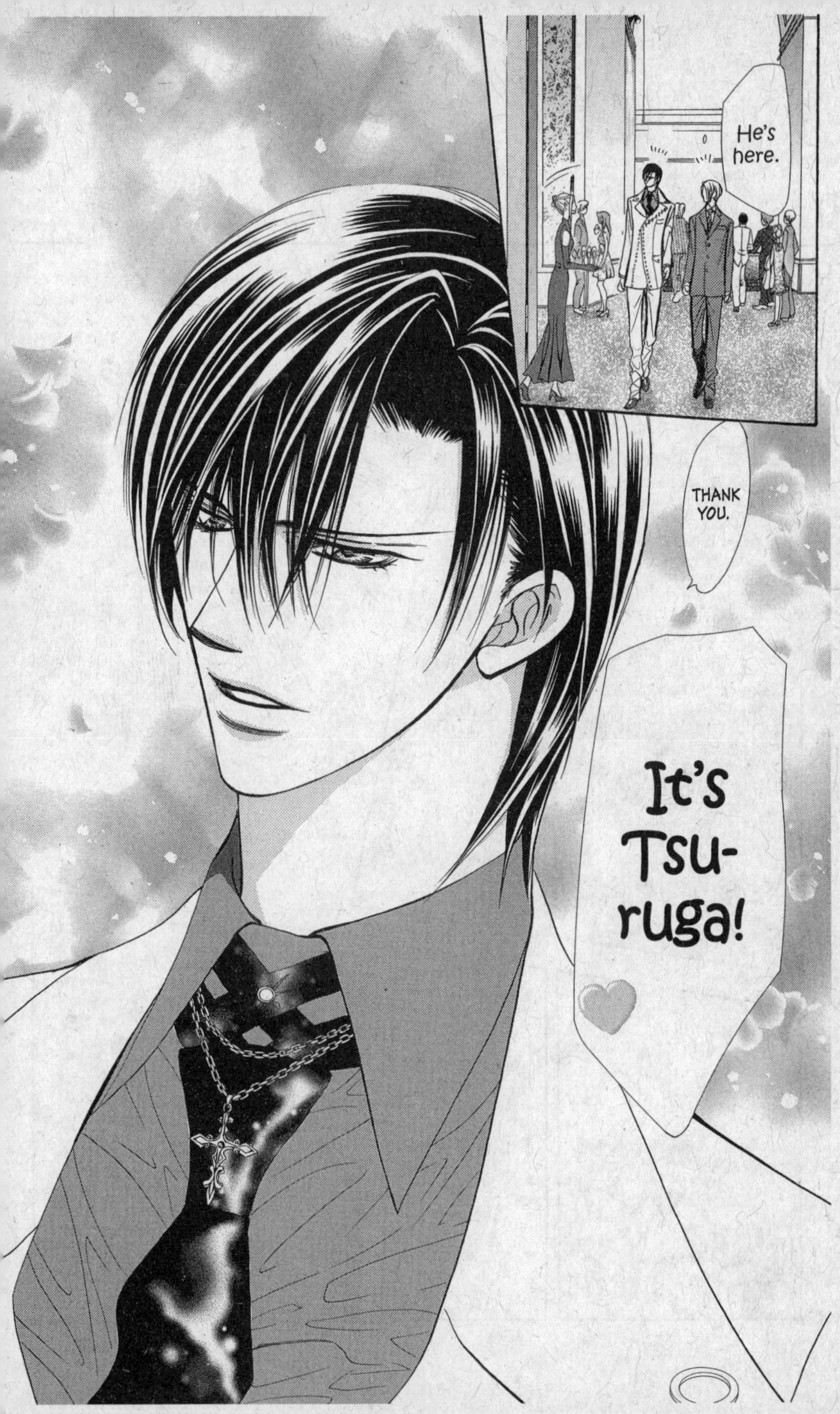
He's here.
THANK YOU.
It's Tsu-ruga!

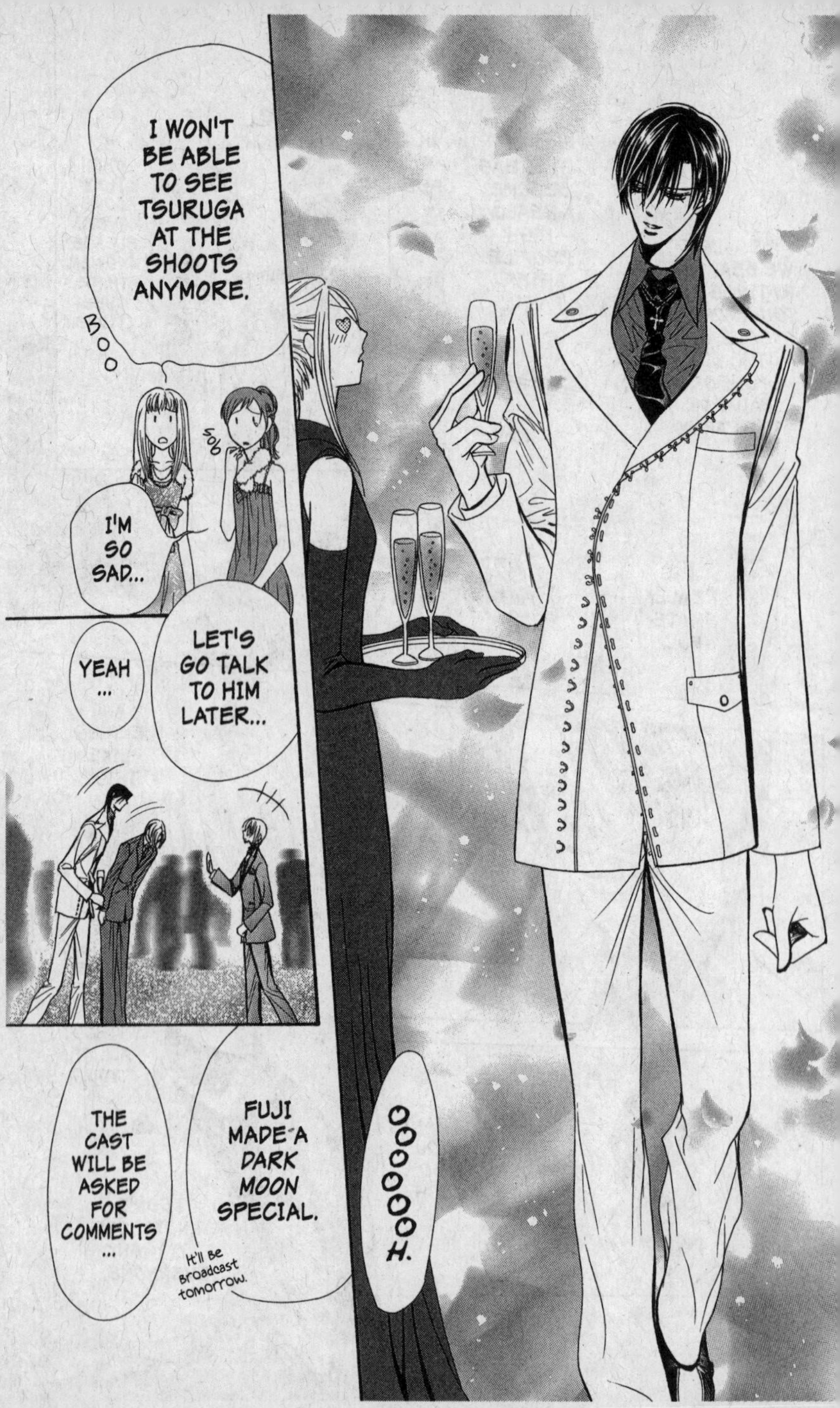

OOOOOOH.
I WON'T BE ABLE TO SEE TSURUGA AT THE SHOOTS ANYMORE.
BOO
I'M SO SAD...
sob
LET'S GO TALK TO HIM LATER...
YEAH...
FUJI MADE A DARK MOON SPECIAL.
It'll be broadcast tomorrow.
THE CAST WILL BE ASKED FOR COMMENTS...

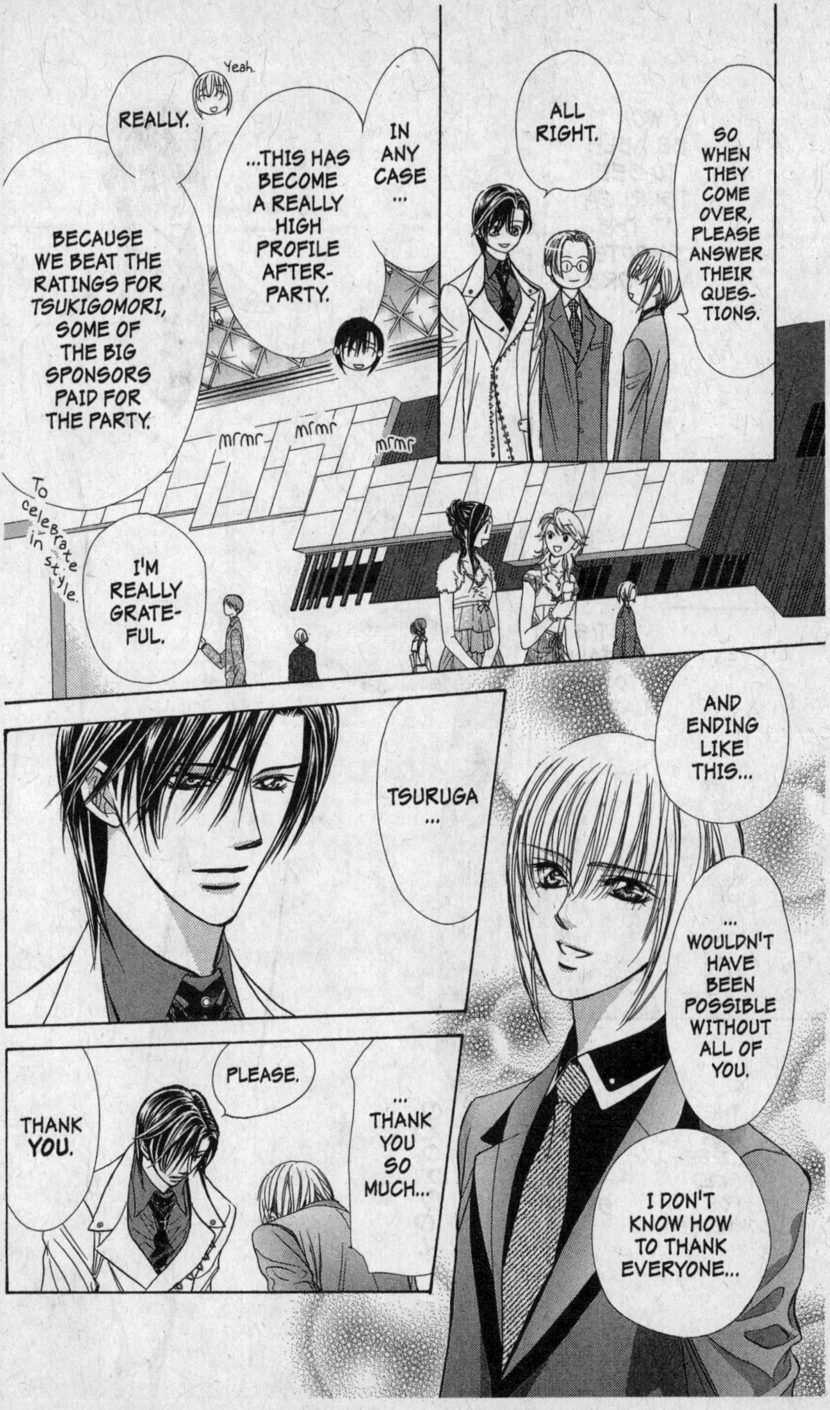
SO WHEN THEY COME OVER, PLEASE ANSWER THEIR QUES-TIONS.
ALL RIGHT.
IN ANY CASE...
...THIS HAS BECOME A REALLY HIGH PROFILE AFTER-PARTY.
REALLY.
Yeah.
BECAUSE WE BEAT THE RATINGS FOR TSUKIGOMORI, SOME OF THE BIG SPONSORS PAID FOR THE PARTY.
mrmr
mrmr
mrmr
To celebrate in style.
I'M REALLY GRATE-FUL.
AND ENDING LIKE THIS...
...WOULDN'T HAVE BEEN POSSIBLE WITHOUT ALL OF YOU.
I DON'T KNOW HOW TO THANK EVERYONE...
TSURUGA...
...THANK YOU SO MUCH...
PLEASE.
THANK YOU.

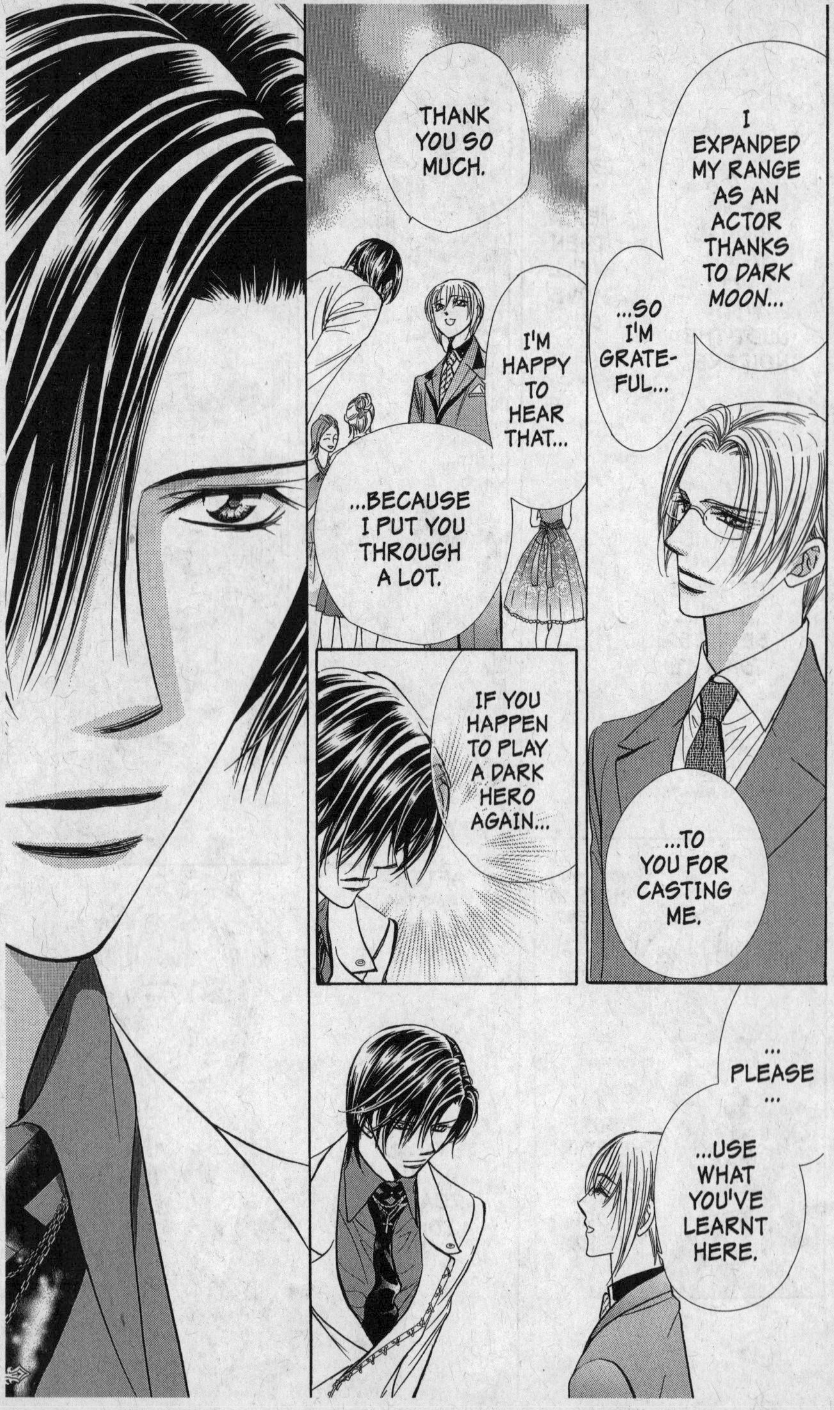
I EXPANDED MY RANGE AS AN ACTOR THANKS TO DARK MOON...
...SO I'M GRATE-FUL...
...TO YOU FOR CASTING ME.
THANK YOU SO MUCH.
I'M HAPPY TO HEAR THAT...
...BECAUSE I PUT YOU THROUGH A LOT.
IF YOU HAPPEN TO PLAY A DARK HERO AGAIN...
...PLEASE...
...USE WHAT YOU'VE LEARNT HERE.

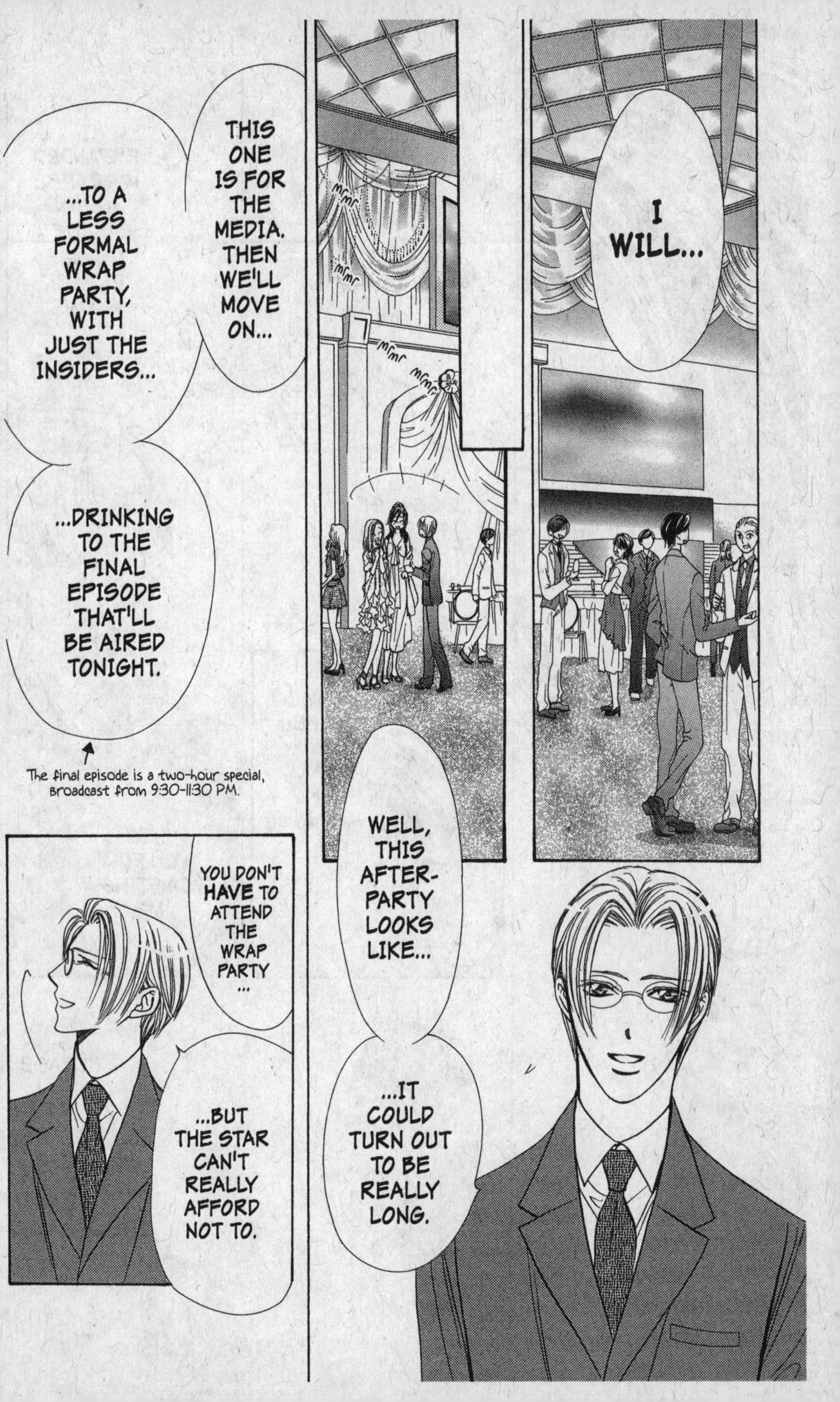
I WILL...
THIS ONE IS FOR THE MEDIA. THEN WE'LL MOVE ON...
...TO A LESS FORMAL WRAP PARTY, WITH JUST THE INSIDERS...
...DRINKING TO THE FINAL EPISODE THAT'LL BE AIRED TONIGHT.
The final episode is a two-hour special, broadcast from 9:30-11:30 PM.
WELL, THIS AFTER-PARTY LOOKS LIKE...
...IT COULD TURN OUT TO BE REALLY LONG.
YOU DON'T HAVE TO ATTEND THE WRAP PARTY...
...BUT THE STAR CAN'T REALLY AFFORD NOT TO.

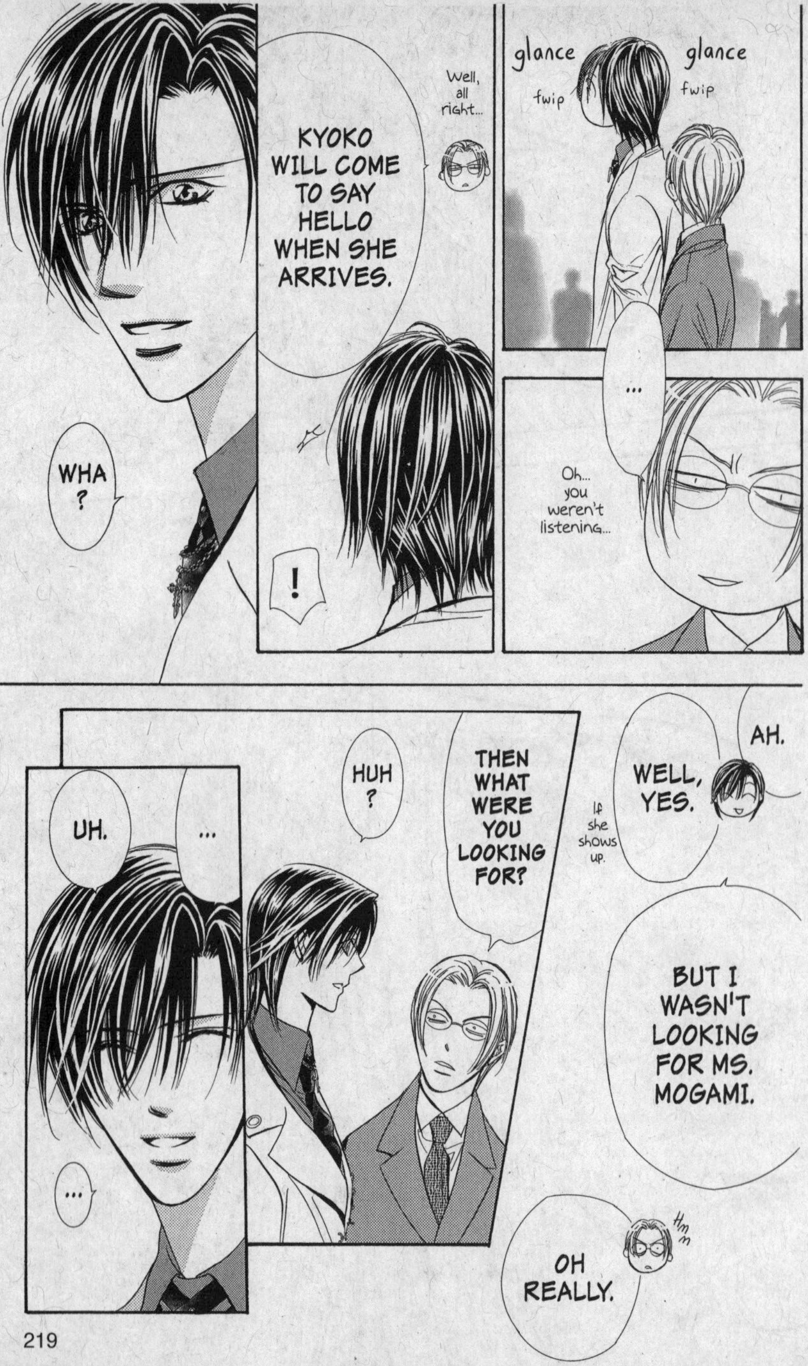
glance
glance
fwip
fwip
...
Oh... you weren't listening...
Well, all right...
KYOKO WILL COME TO SAY HELLO WHEN SHE ARRIVES.
!
WHA?
AH.
WELL, YES.
If she shows up.
BUT I WASN'T LOOKING FOR MS. MOGAMI.
Hmm
OH REALLY.
THEN WHAT WERE YOU LOOKING FOR?
HUH?
...
UH.
...

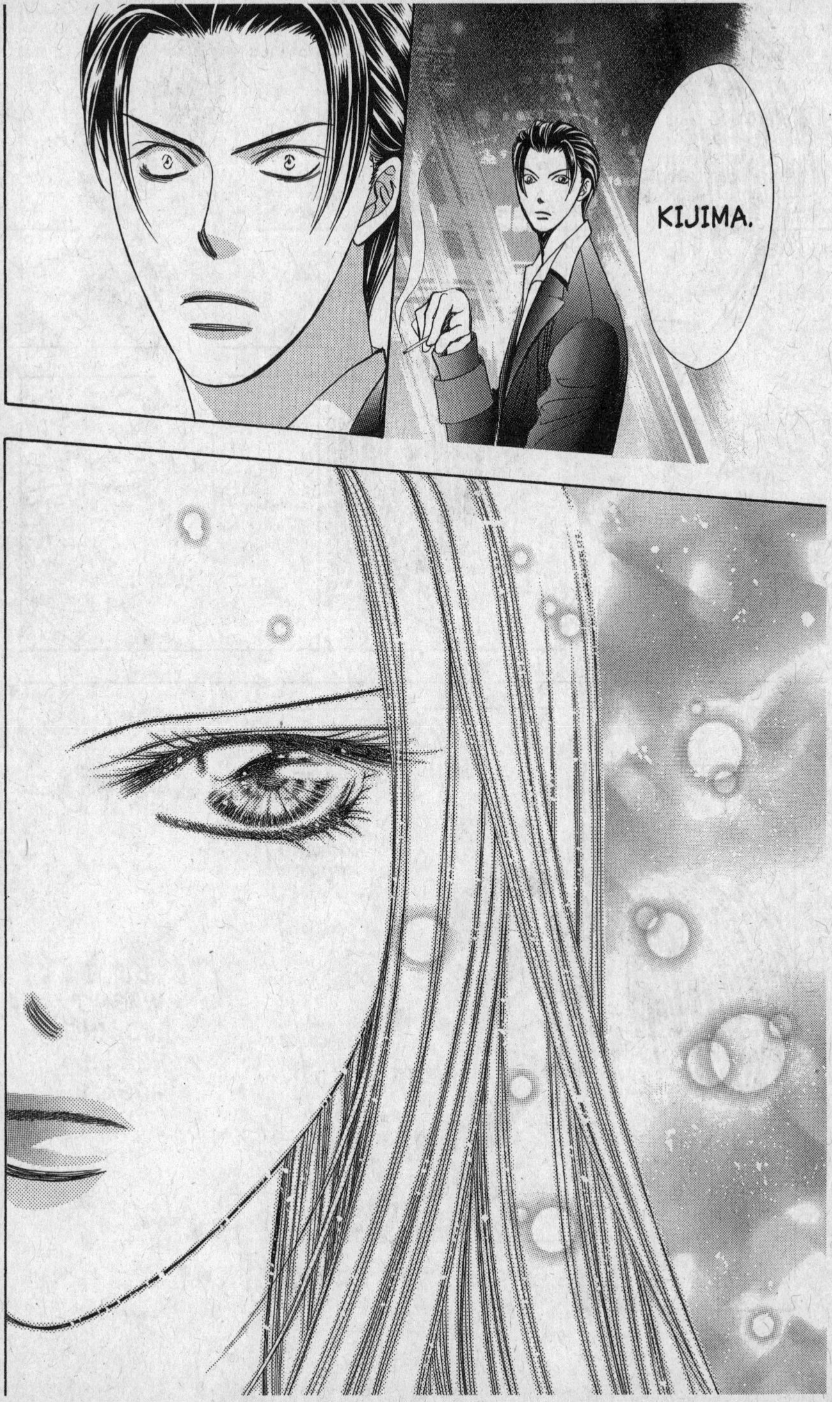
KIJIMA.

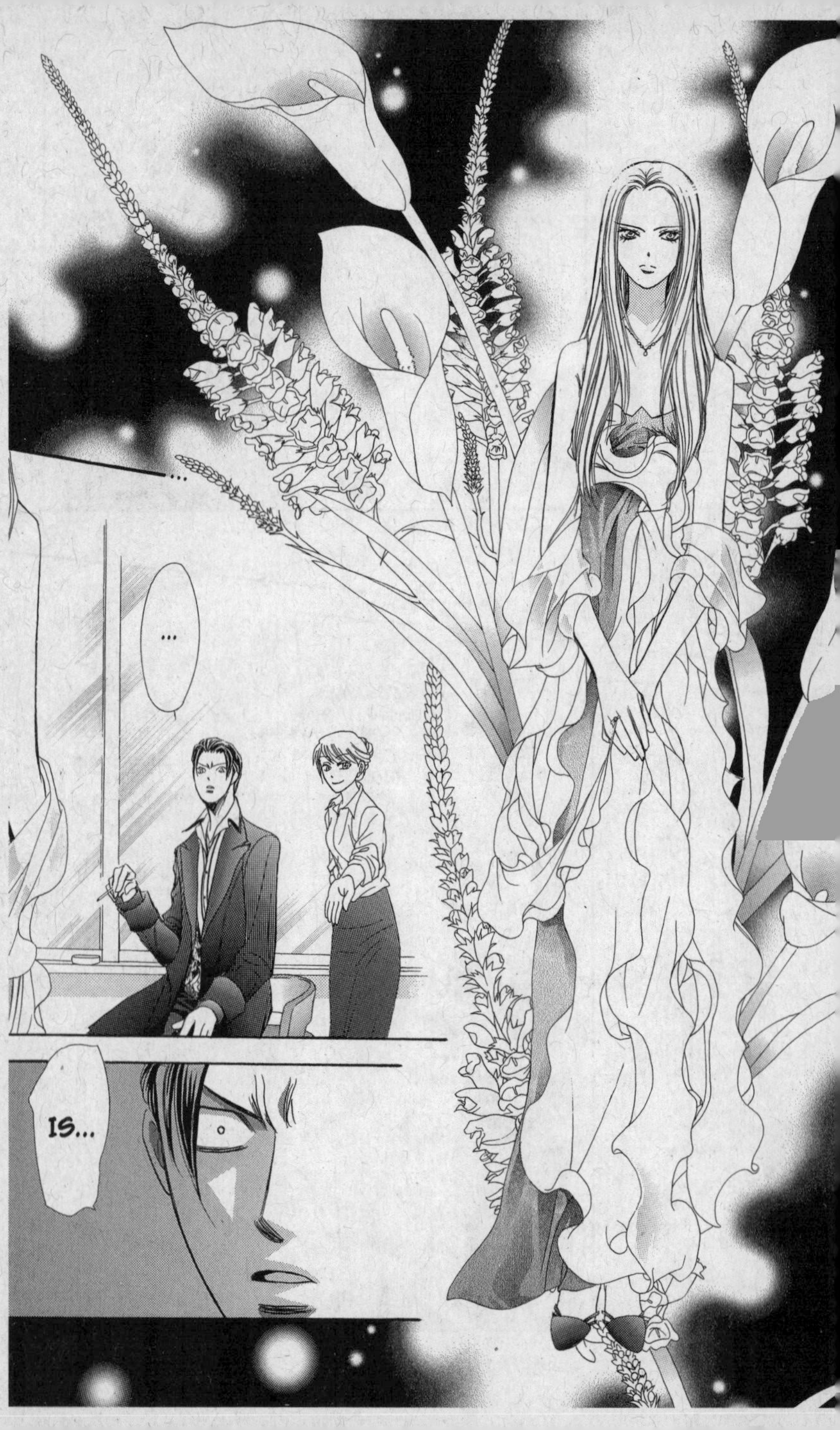
...
...
IS...

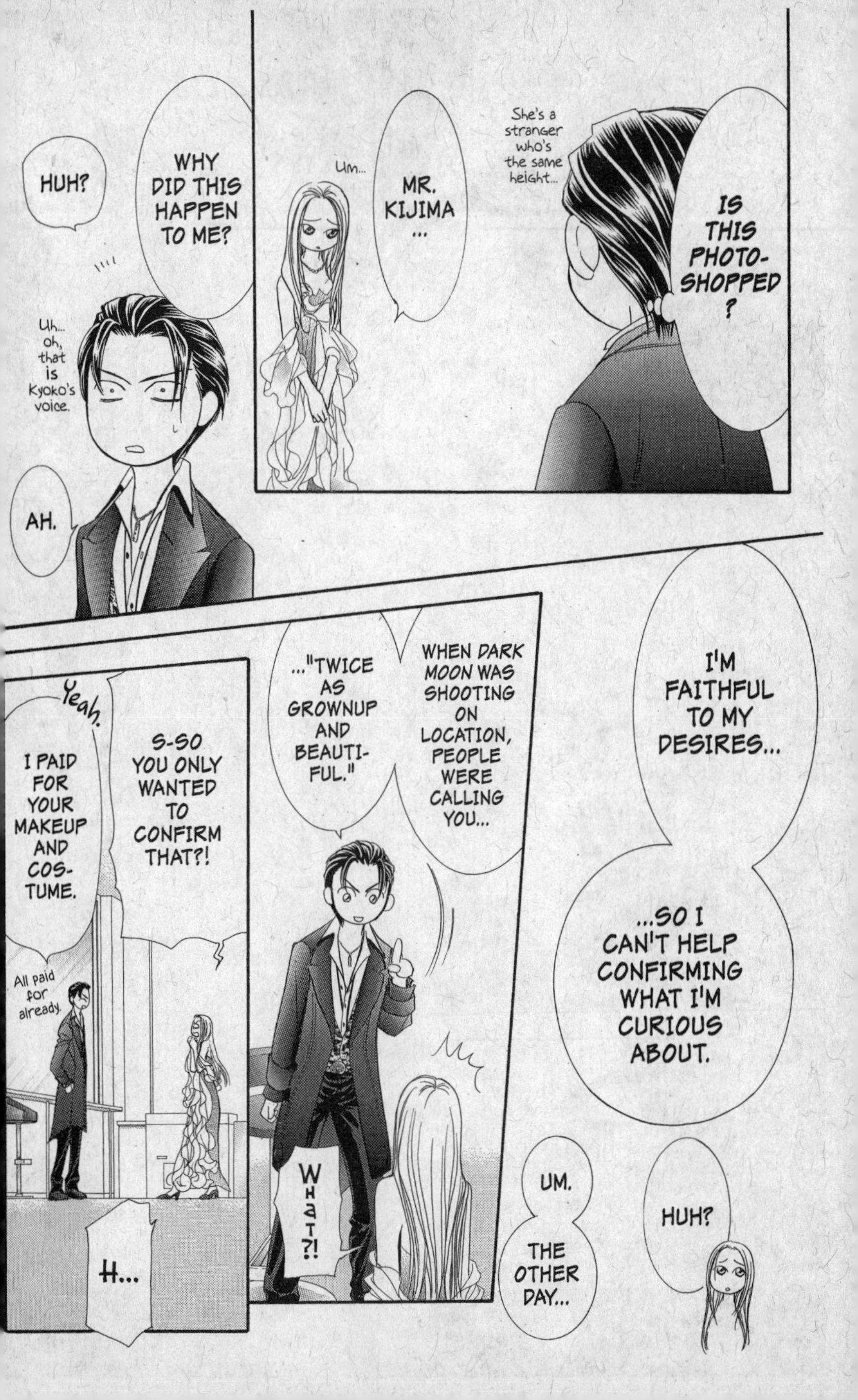
IS THIS PHOTO-SHOPPED?
She's a stranger who's the same height...
MR. KIJIMA ...
Um...
WHY DID THIS HAPPEN TO ME?
HUH?
Uh... oh, that is Kyoko's voice.
AH.
I'M FAITHFUL TO MY DESIRES...
...SO I CAN'T HELP CONFIRMING WHAT I'M CURIOUS ABOUT.
HUH?
UM. THE OTHER DAY...
WHEN DARK MOON WAS SHOOTING ON LOCATION, PEOPLE WERE CALLING YOU...
..."TWICE AS GROWNUP AND BEAUTI-FUL."
WHAT?!
S-SO YOU ONLY WANTED TO CONFIRM THAT?!
Yeah.
I PAID FOR YOUR MAKEUP AND COS-TUME.
All paid for already.
H...

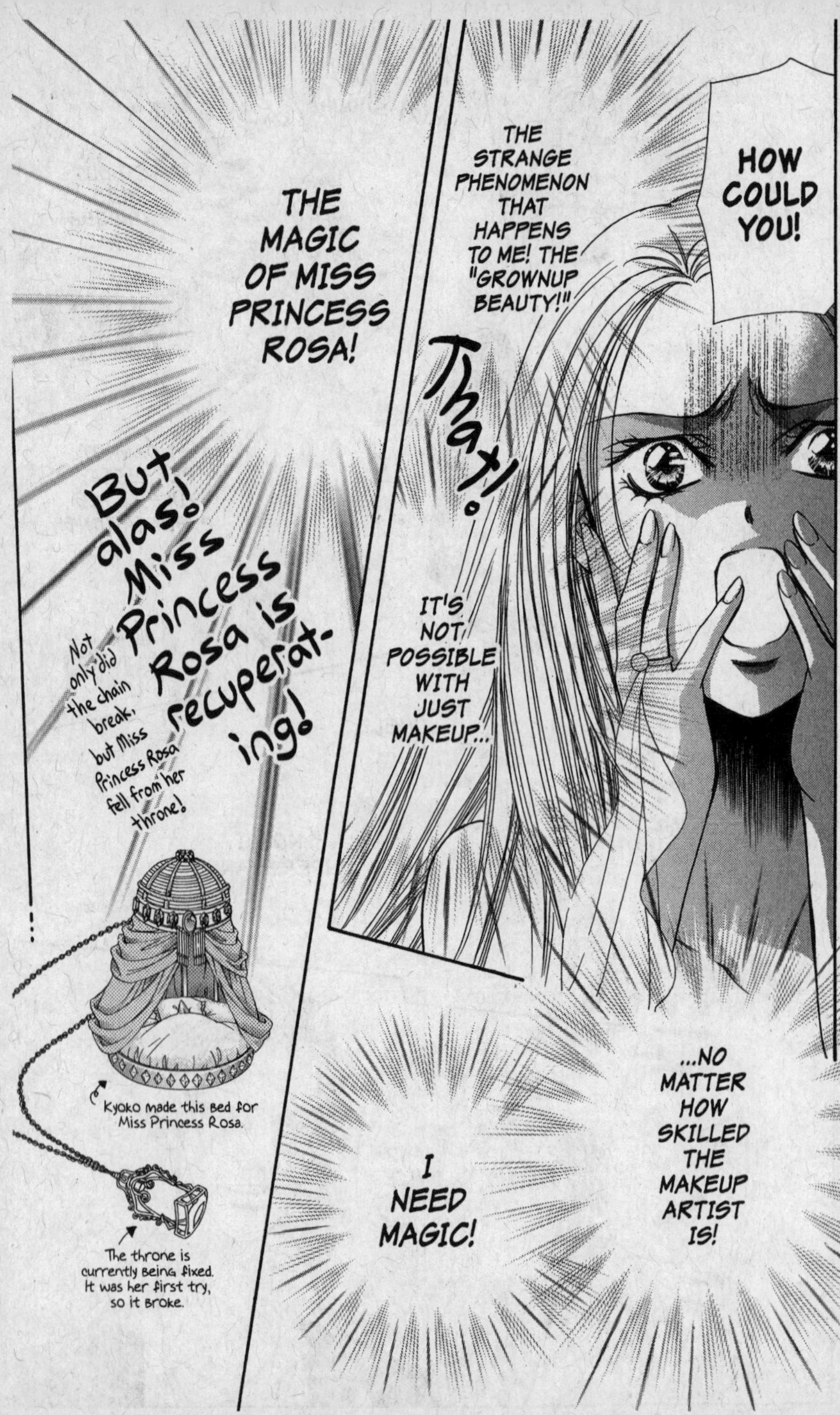

HOW COULD YOU!
THE STRANGE PHENOMENON THAT HAPPENS TO ME! THE "GROWNUP BEAUTY!"
That!
IT'S NOT POSSIBLE WITH JUST MAKEUP...
...NO MATTER HOW SKILLED THE MAKEUP ARTIST IS!
I NEED MAGIC!
THE MAGIC OF MISS PRINCESS ROSA!
But alas! Miss Princess Rosa is recuperating!
Not only did the chain break, but Miss Princess Rosa fell from her throne!
...
Kyoko made this bed for Miss Princess Rosa.
The throne is currently being fixed. It was her first try, so it broke.

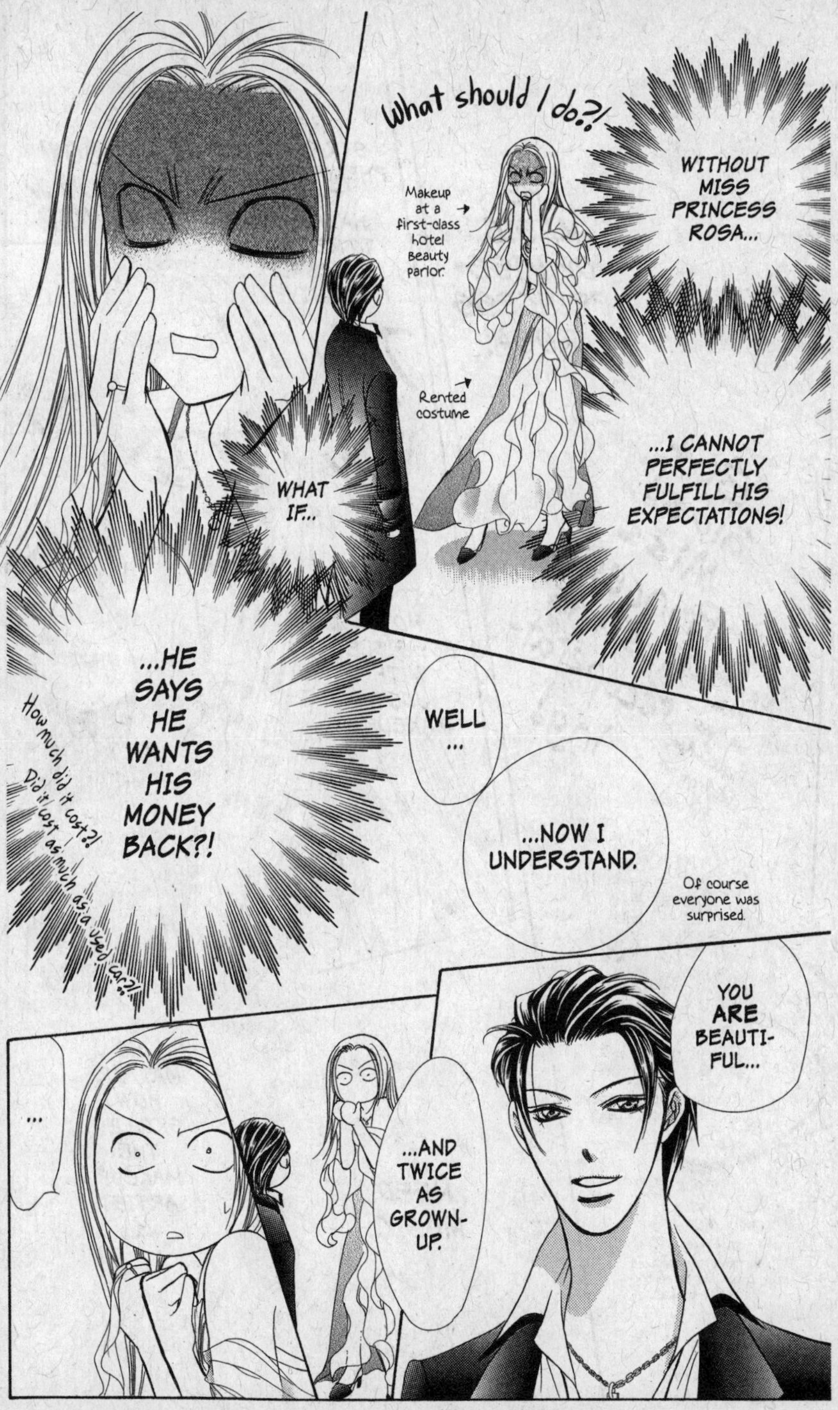
What should I do?!
WITHOUT MISS PRINCESS ROSA...
Makeup at a first-class hotel beauty parlor.
Rented costume
...I CANNOT PERFECTLY FULFILL HIS EXPECTATIONS!
WHAT IF...
...HE SAYS HE WANTS HIS MONEY BACK?!
How much did it cost?! Did it cost as much as a used car?!
WELL ...
...NOW I UNDERSTAND.
Of course everyone was surprised.
YOU ARE BEAUTIFUL...
...AND TWICE AS GROWN-UP.
...

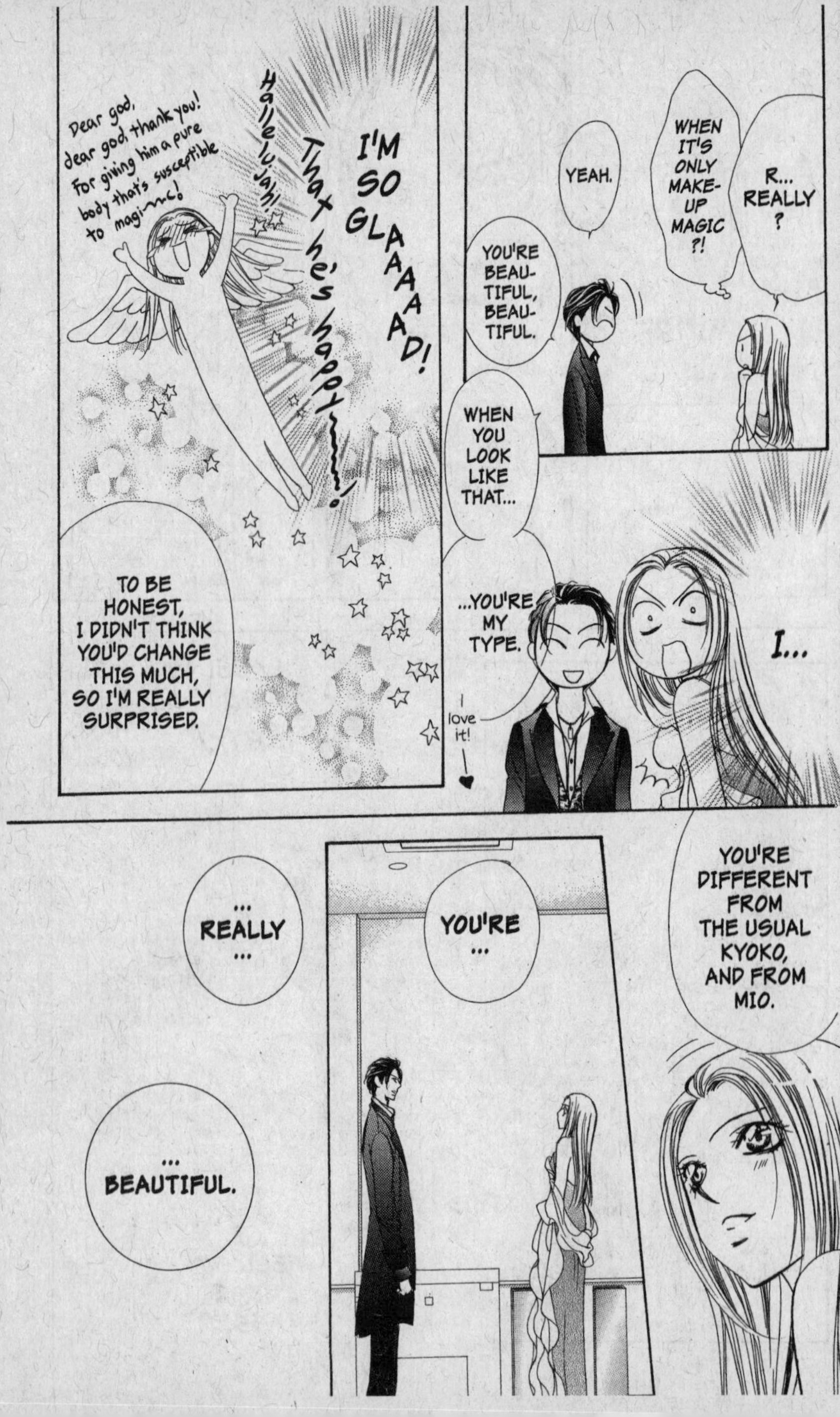
R... REALLY?
WHEN IT'S ONLY MAKE-UP MAGIC?!
YEAH.
YOU'RE BEAUTIFUL, BEAUTIFUL.
I...
WHEN YOU LOOK LIKE THAT...
...YOU'RE MY TYPE.
I love it!
I'M SO GLAAAAAD!
That he's happy~~!
Hallelujah!
Dear god, dear god thank you! For giving him a pure body that's susceptible to magi~c!
TO BE HONEST, I DIDN'T THINK YOU'D CHANGE THIS MUCH, SO I'M REALLY SURPRISED.
YOU'RE DIFFERENT FROM THE USUAL KYOKO, AND FROM MIO.
YOU'RE...
...REALLY...
...BEAUTIFUL.

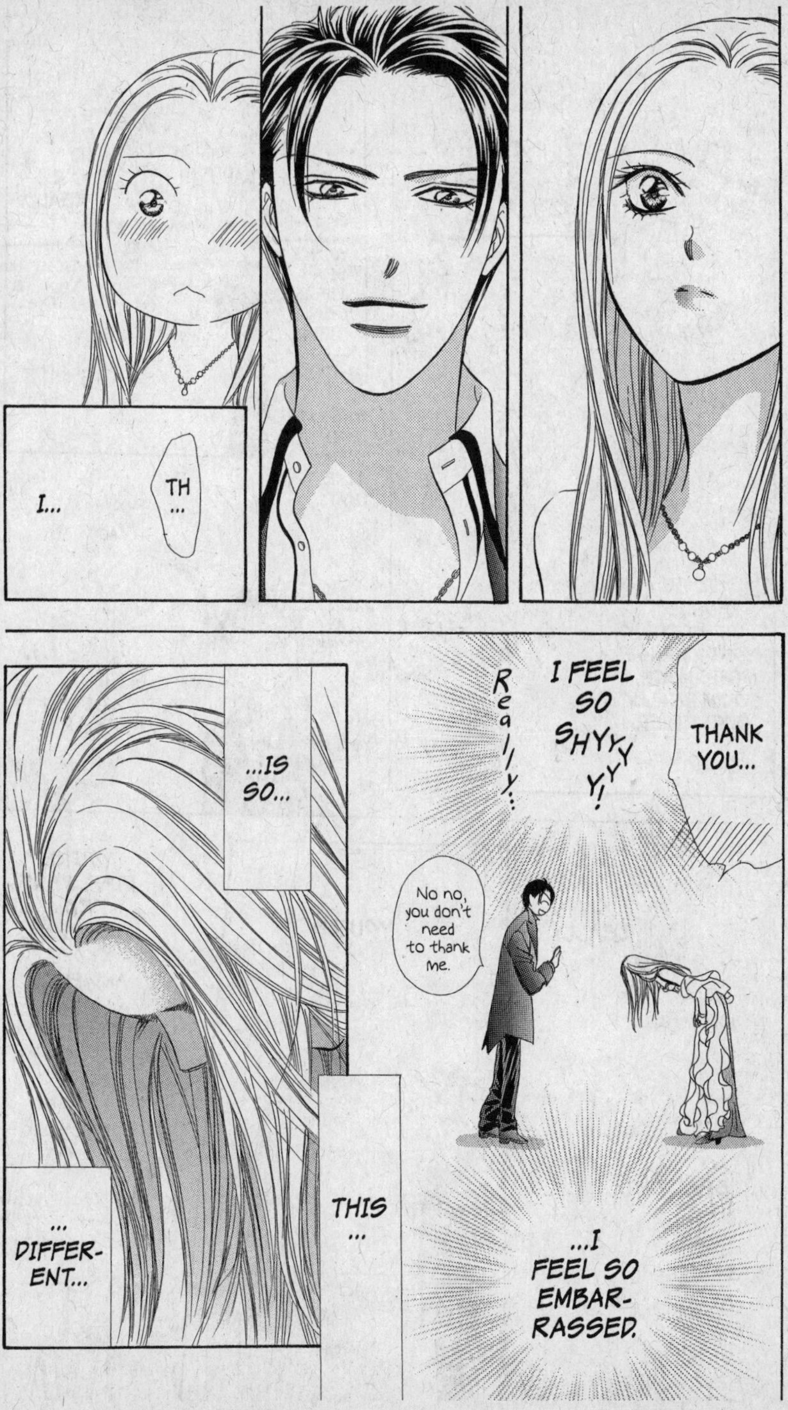
TH
...
I...
THANK YOU...
I FEEL SO SHYYYYY!
Really...
No no, you don't need to thank me.
...I FEEL SO EMBARRASSED.
...IS SO...
THIS ...
... DIFFER-ENT...

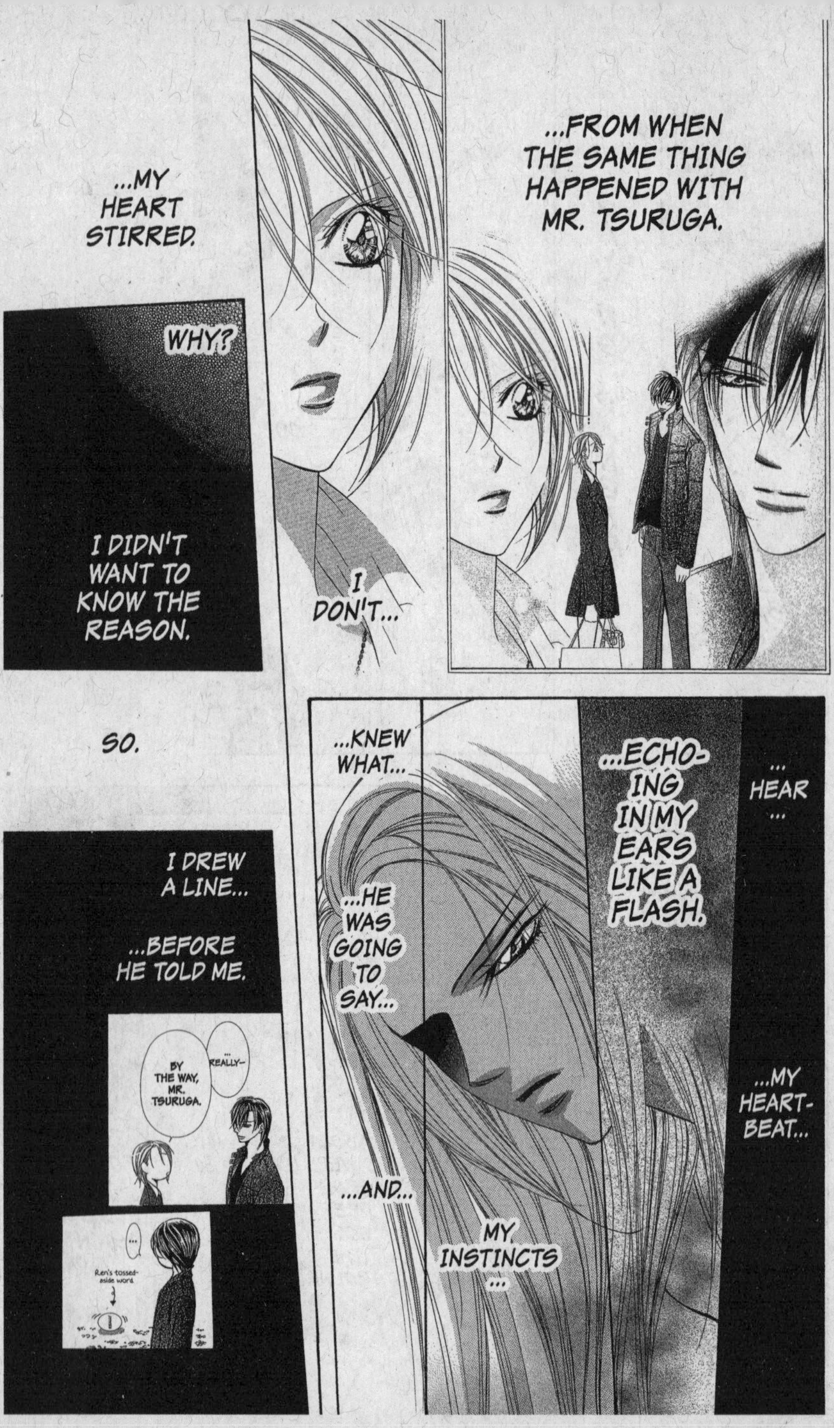
...FROM WHEN THE SAME THING HAPPENED WITH MR. TSURUGA.
I DON'T...
...MY HEART STIRRED.
WHY?
I DIDN'T WANT TO KNOW THE REASON.
... HEAR ...
...MY HEART-BEAT...
...ECHO-ING IN MY EARS LIKE A FLASH.
...KNEW WHAT...
...HE WAS GOING TO SAY...
...AND...
MY INSTINCTS ...
SO.
I DREW A LINE...
...BEFORE HE TOLD ME.
...REALLY—
BY THE WAY, MR. TSURUGA.
...
Ren's tossed-aside word

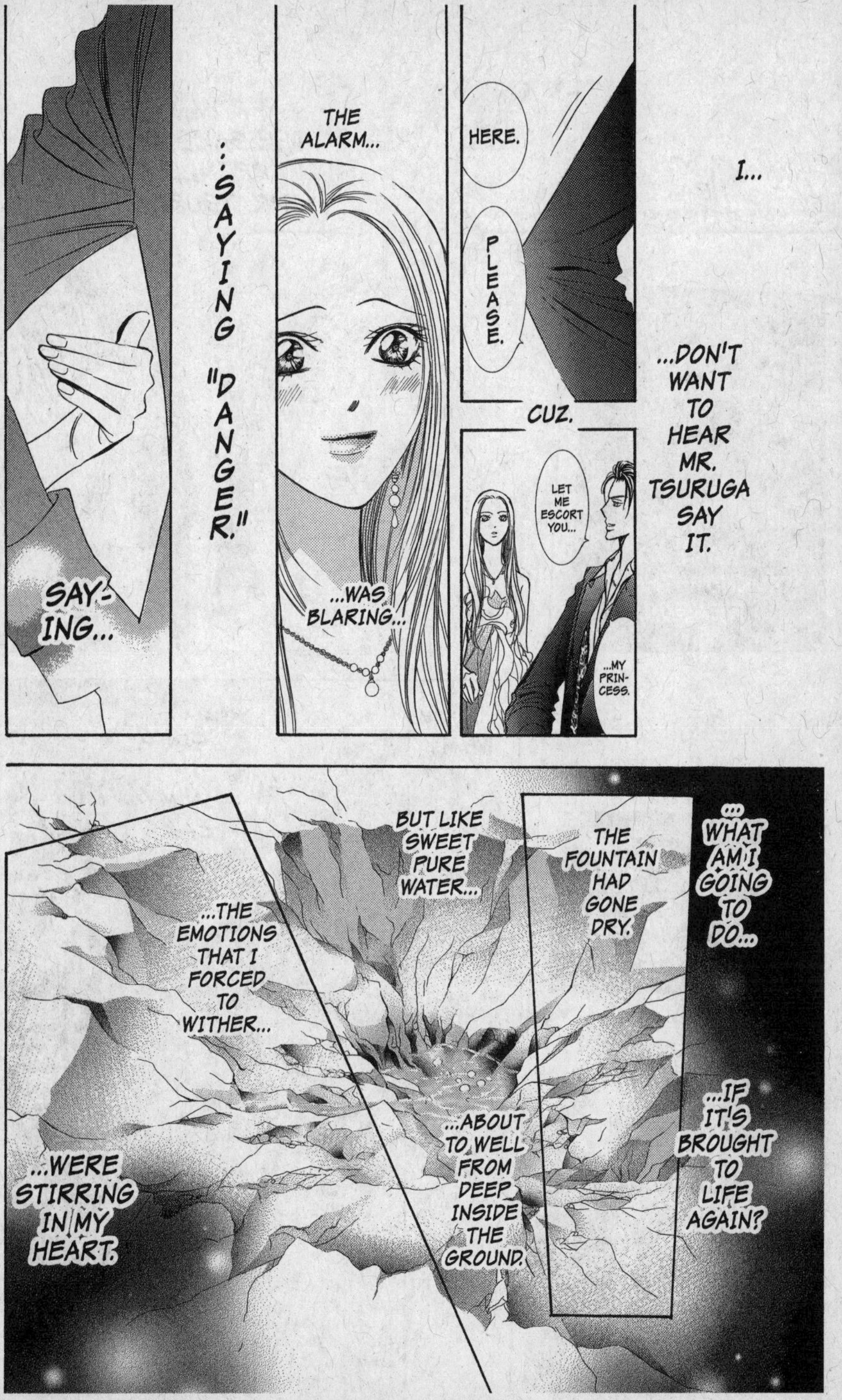
I...
...DON'T WANT TO HEAR MR. TSURUGA SAY IT.
HERE.
PLEASE.
CUZ.
LET ME ESCORT YOU...
...MY PRINCESS.
THE ALARM...
...WAS BLARING...
...SAYING "DANGER."
SAY-ING...
...WHAT AM I GOING TO DO...
...IF IT'S BROUGHT TO LIFE AGAIN?
THE FOUNTAIN HAD GONE DRY.
BUT LIKE SWEET PURE WATER...
...ABOUT TO WELL FROM DEEP INSIDE THE GROUND.
...THE EMOTIONS THAT I FORCED TO WITHER...
...WERE STIRRING IN MY HEART.

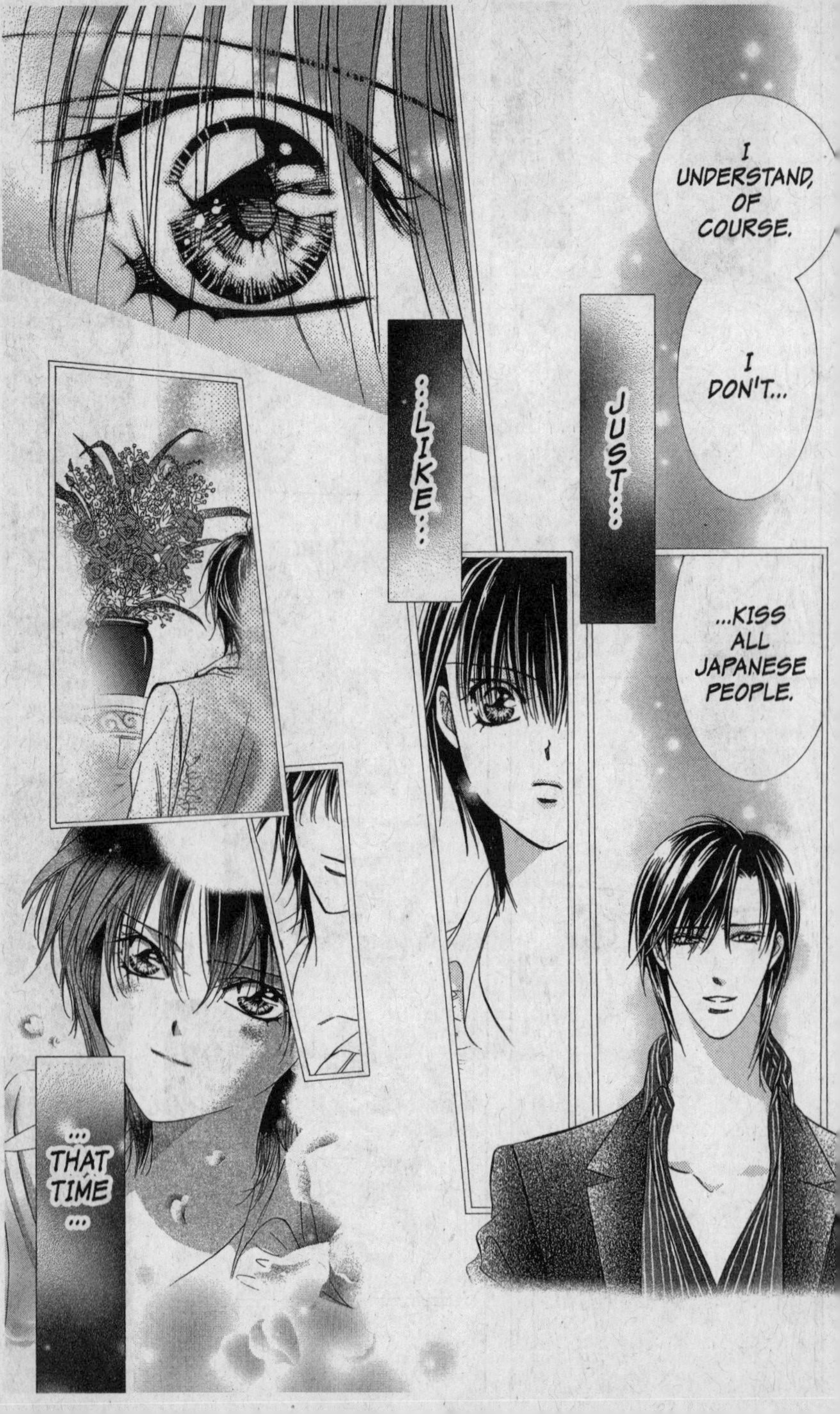
I UNDERSTAND, OF COURSE.
I DON'T...
JUST...
...KISS ALL JAPANESE PEOPLE.
...LIKE...
...THAT TIME...

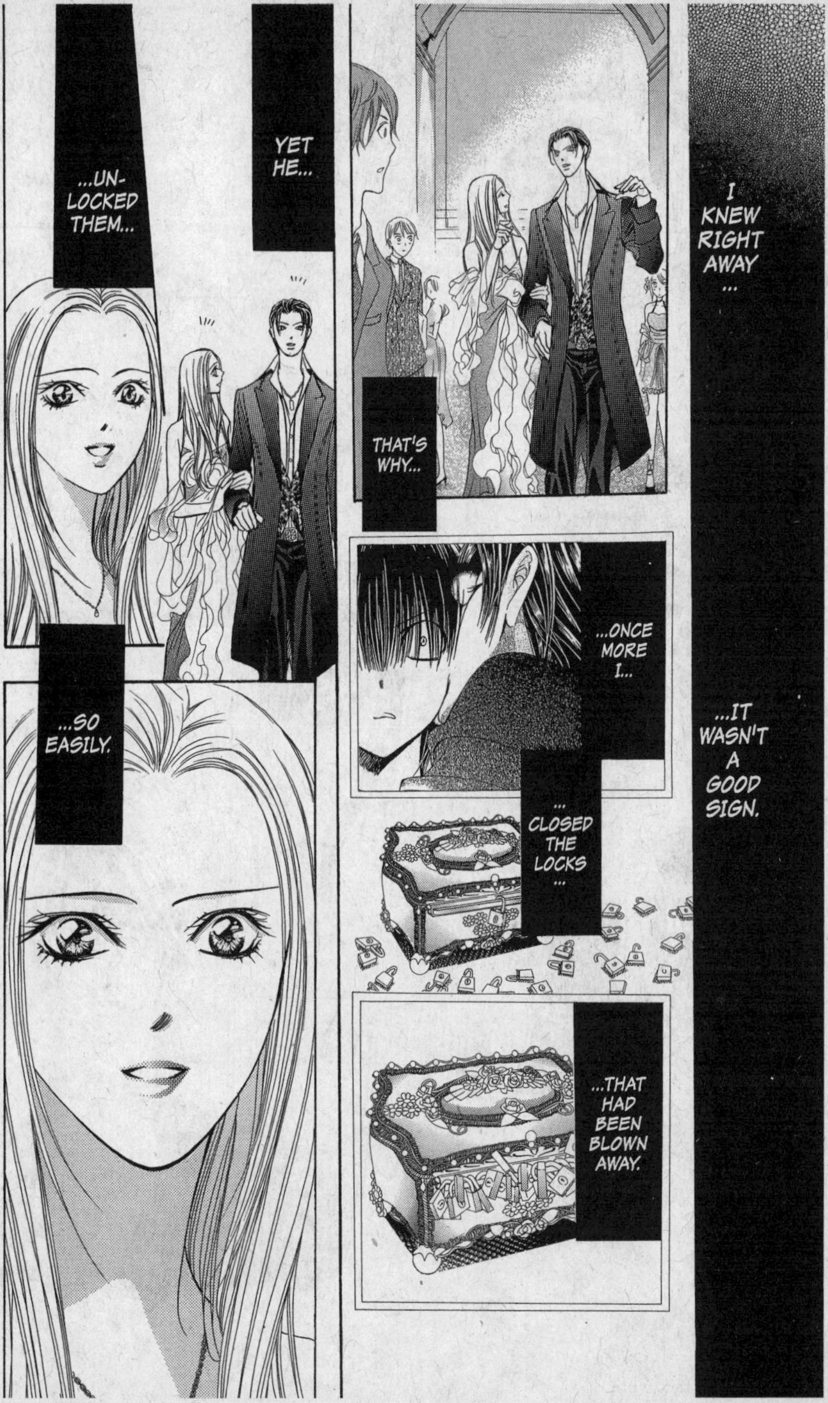
I KNEW RIGHT AWAY ...
...IT WASN'T A GOOD SIGN.
THAT'S WHY...
...ONCE MORE I...
... CLOSED THE LOCKS ...
...THAT HAD BEEN BLOWN AWAY.
YET HE...
...UN-LOCKED THEM...
...SO EASILY.

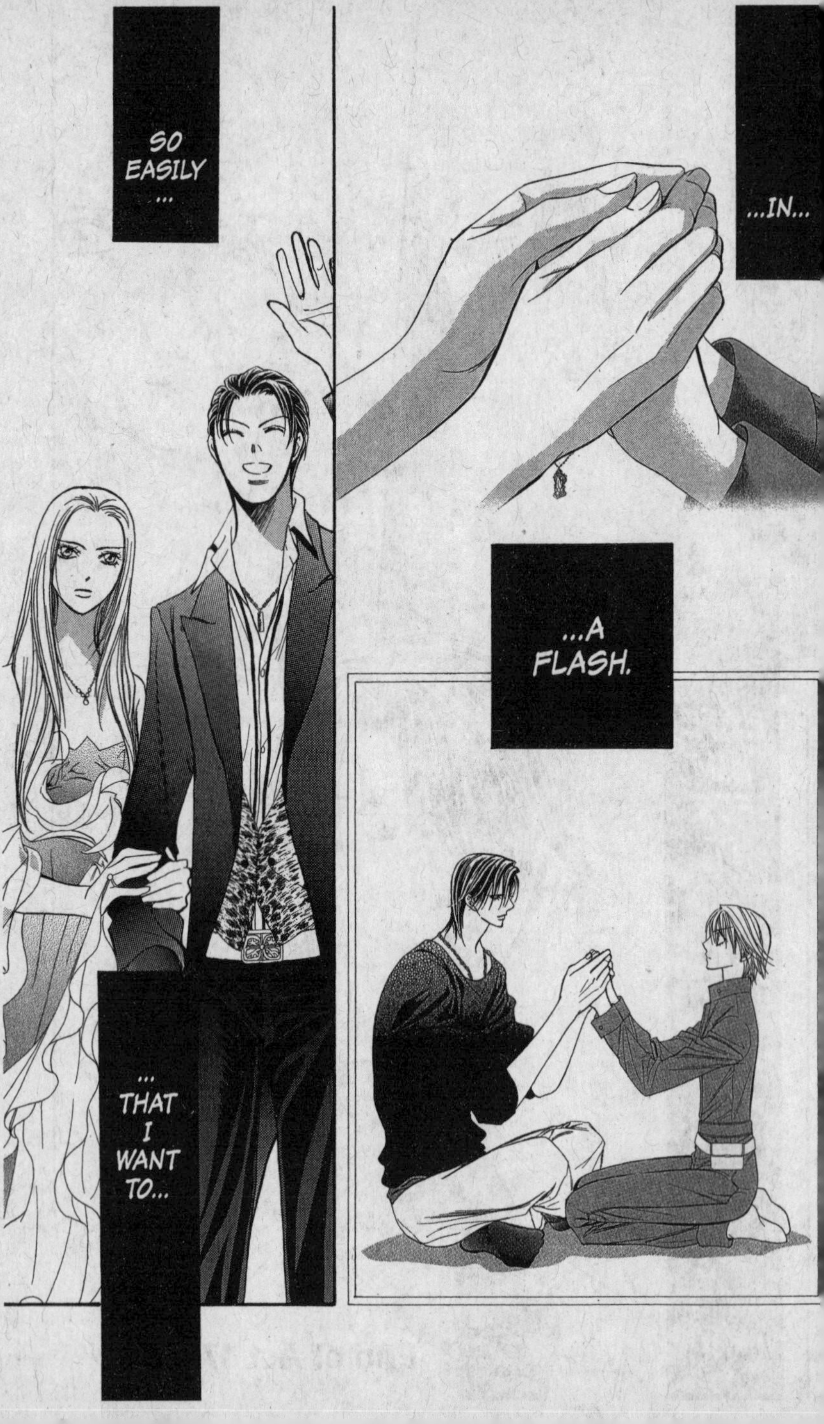
...IN...
...A FLASH.
SO EASILY ...
... THAT I WANT TO...

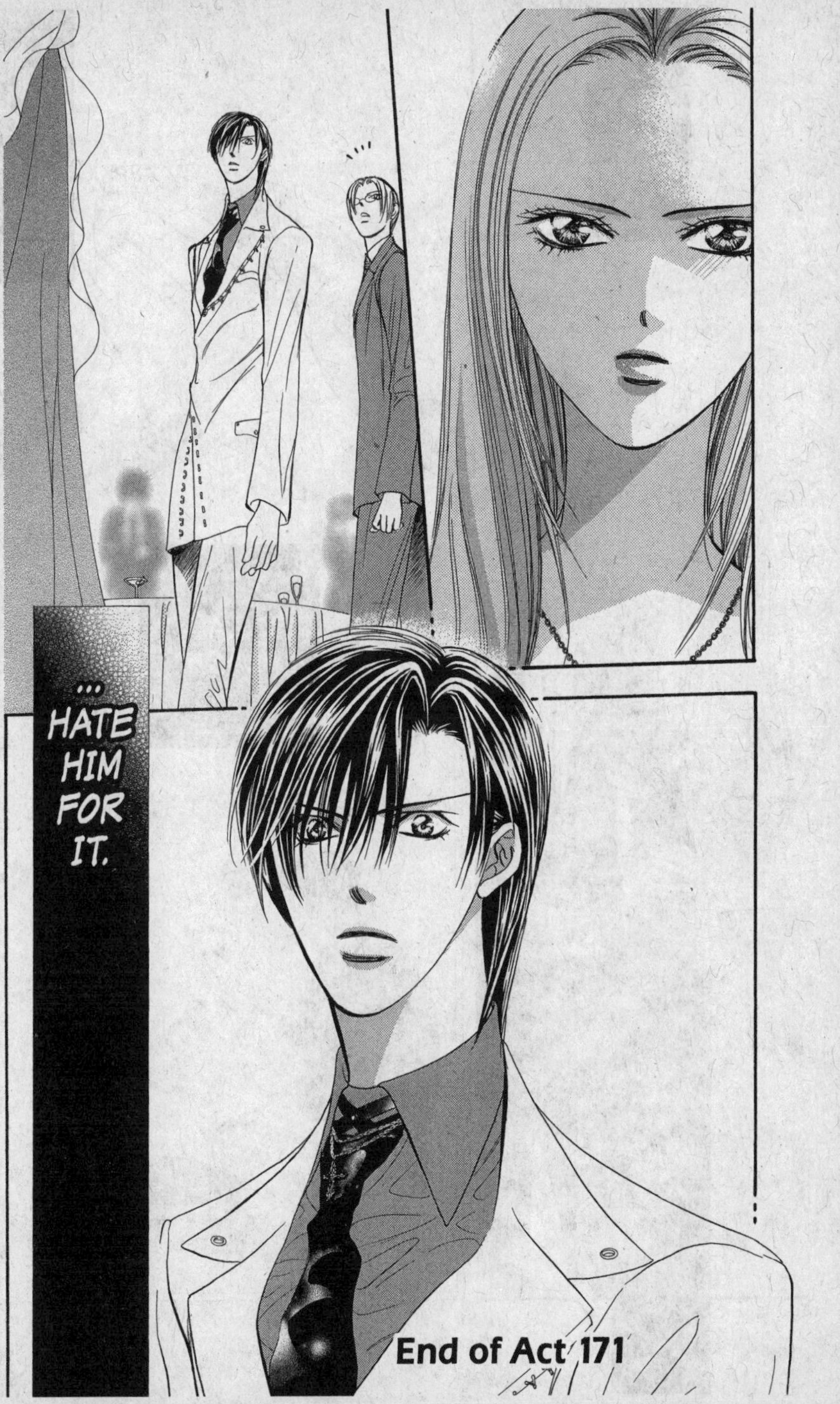
...HATE HIM FOR IT.
End of Act 171

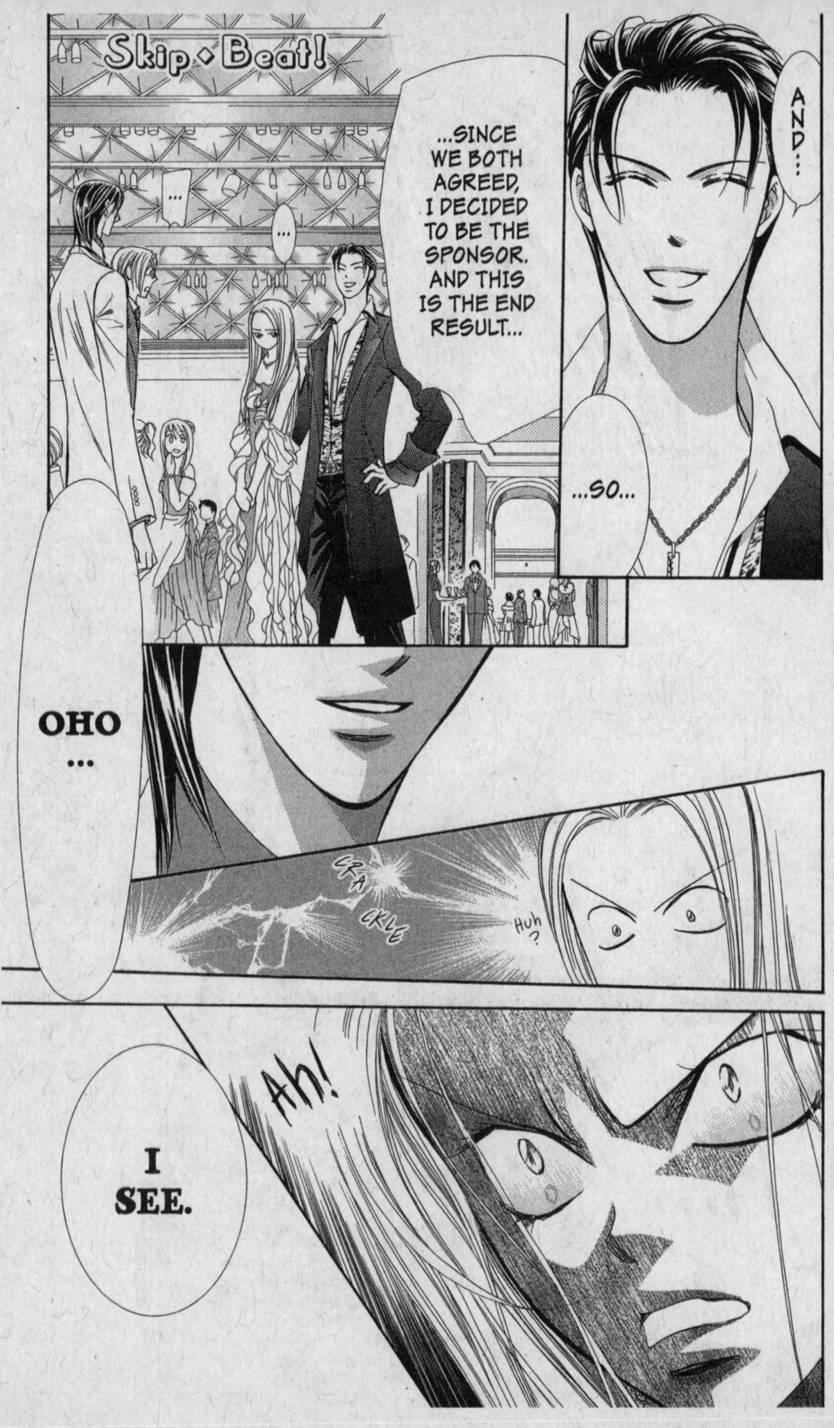

Skip・Beat!
AND...
...SO...
...SINCE WE BOTH AGREED, I DECIDED TO BE THE SPONSOR. AND THIS IS THE END RESULT...
...
...
OHO...
CRACKLE
Huh?
Ah!
I SEE.

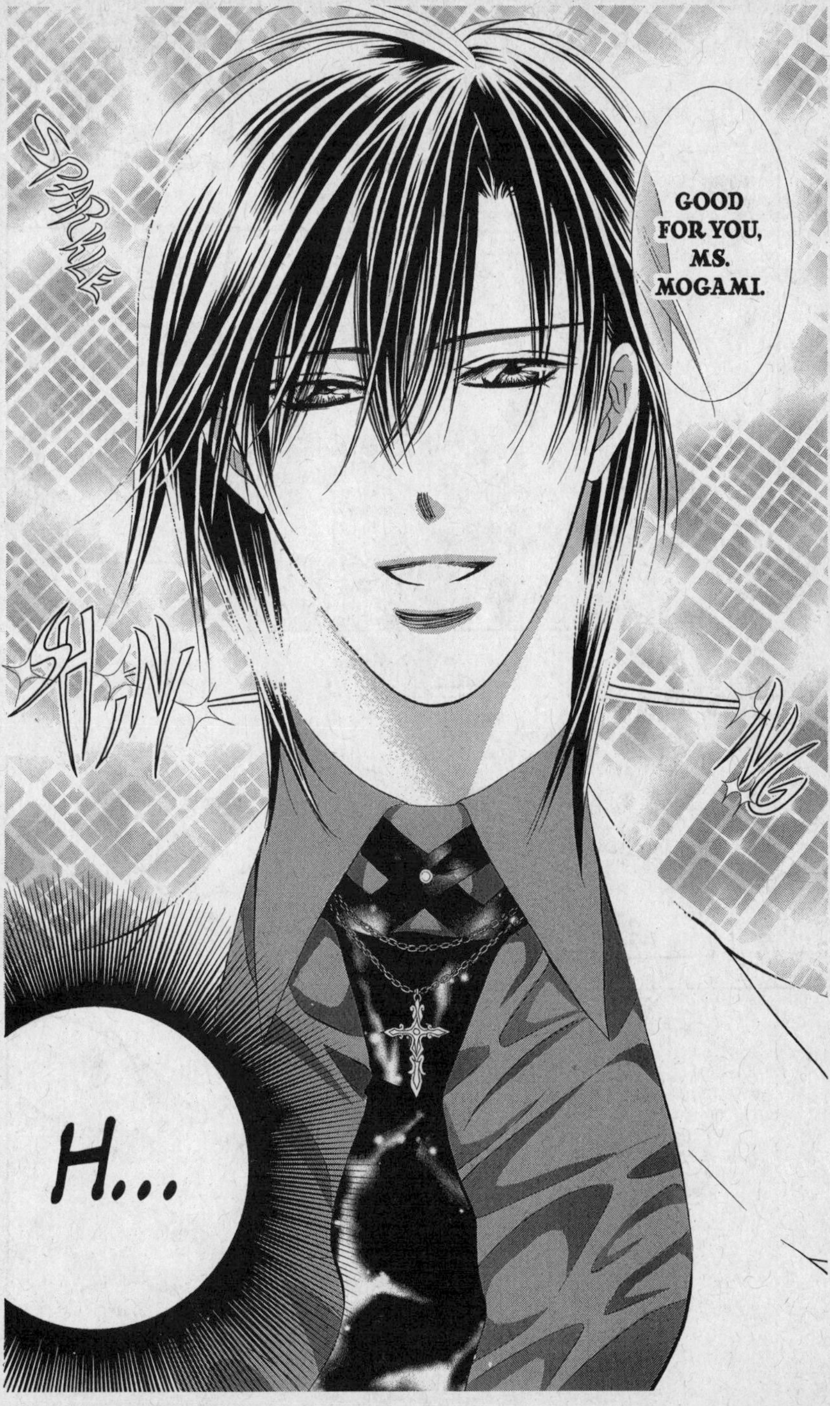
GOOD FOR YOU, MS. MOGAMI.
SPARKLE
SHINNNG
H...

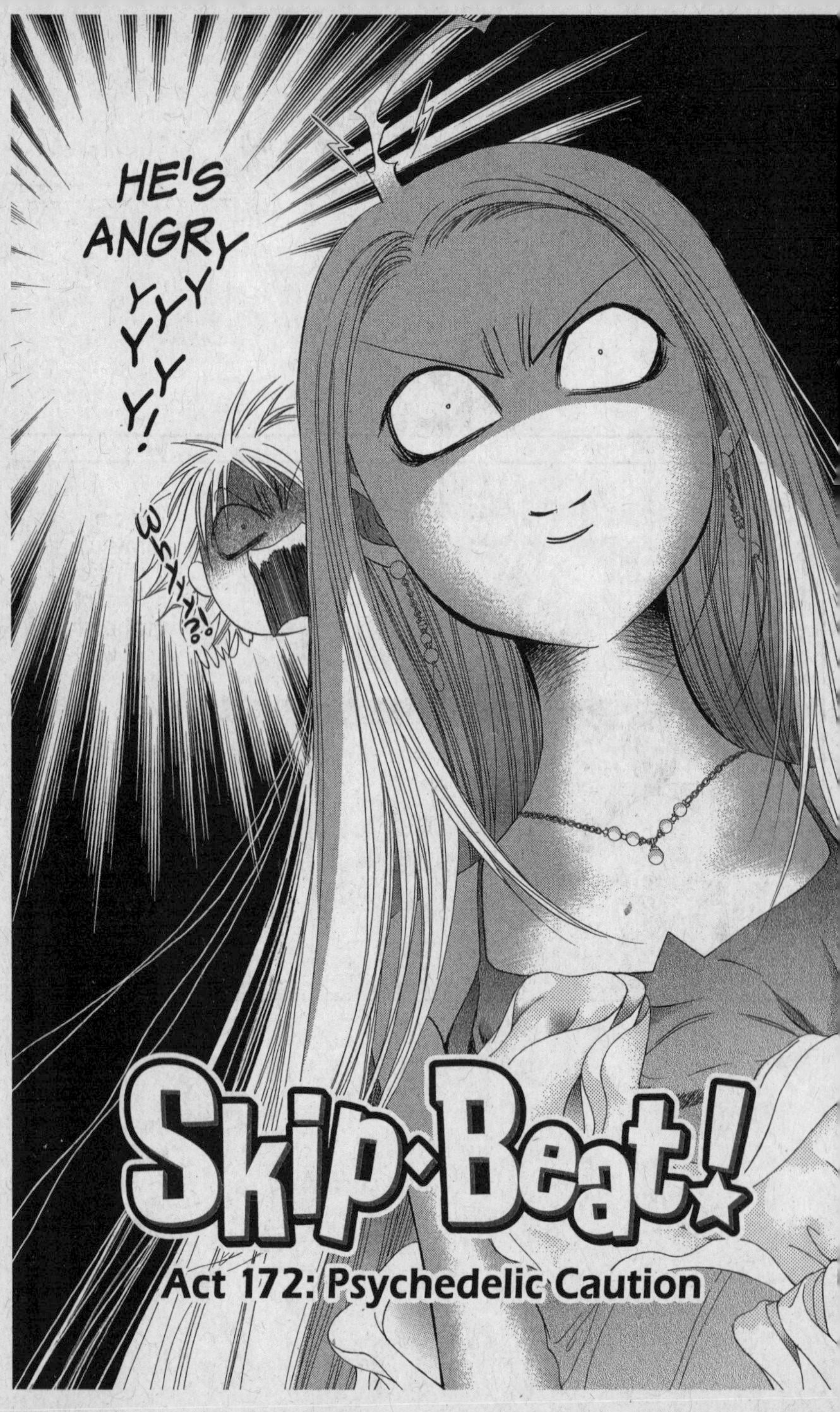
HE'S ANGRYYYYYYY!
Skip·Beat!
Act 172: Psychedelic Caution

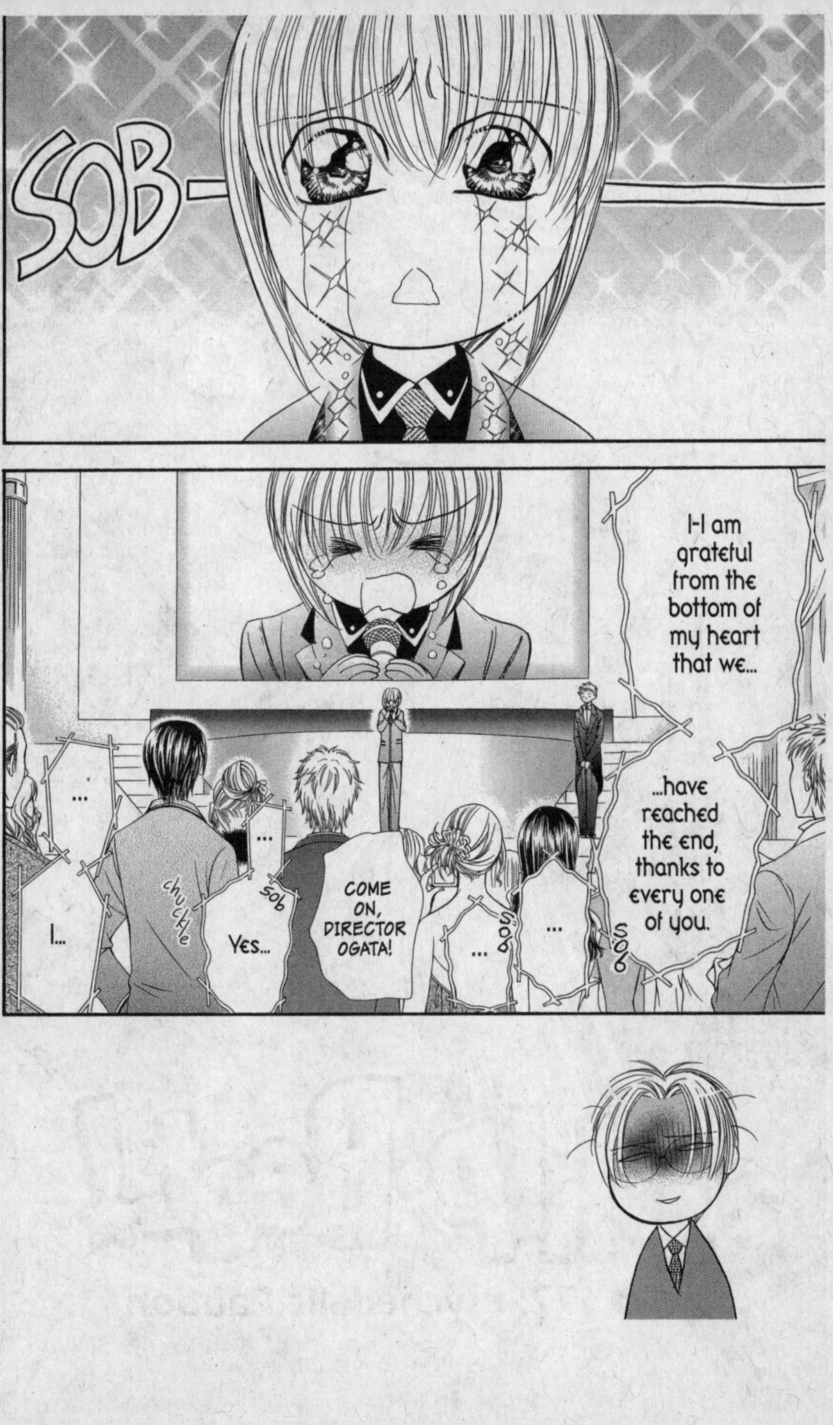
SOB-
I-I am grateful from the bottom of my heart that we...
...have reached the end, thanks to every one of you.
SOB
sob
...
...
COME ON, DIRECTOR OGATA!
sob
Yes...
...
chuckle
I...
...

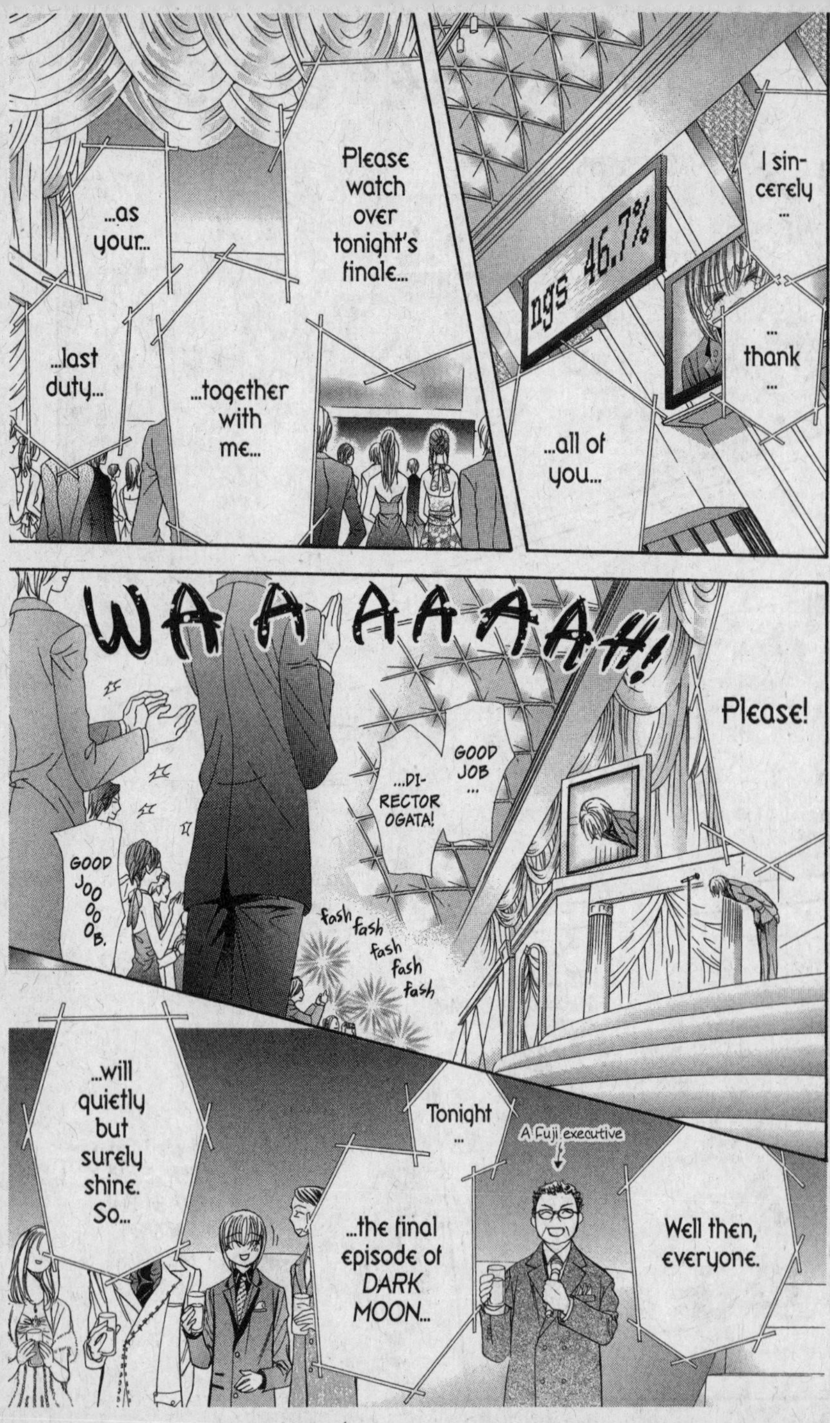
I sincerely ...
... thank ...
...all of you...
ngs 46.7%
Please watch over tonight's finale...
...as your...
...together with me...
...last duty...
Please!
WAAAAAAH!
GOOD JOB ...
...DIRECTOR OGATA!
fash fash fash fash fash
GOOD JOOOOOOB.
Well then, everyone.
A Fuji executive
Tonight ...
...the final episode of DARK MOON...
...will quietly but surely shine. So...

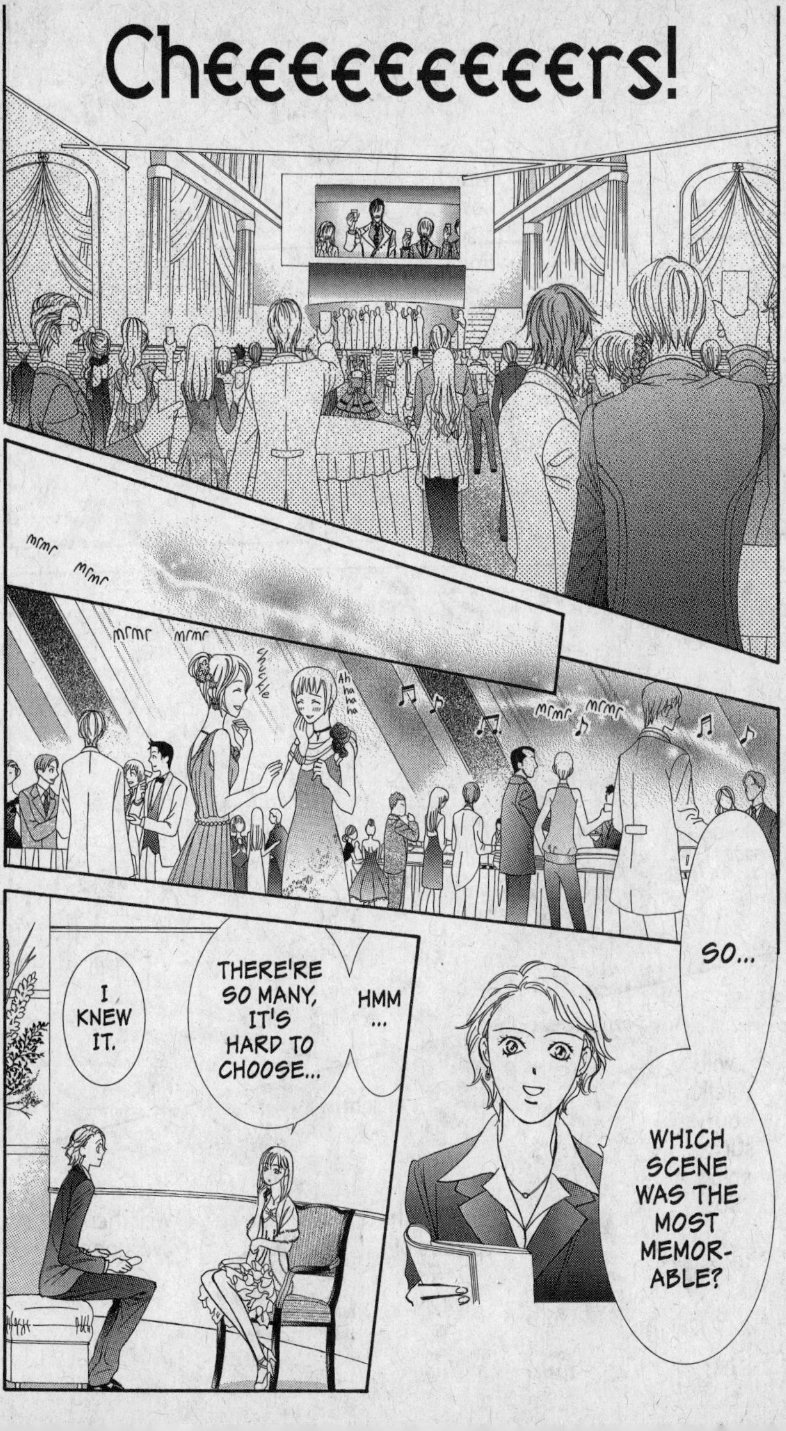
Cheeeeeeeeeers!
mrmr
mrmr
mrmr
mrmr
chuckle
Ah ha ha ha
mrmr
mrmr
SO...
WHICH SCENE WAS THE MOST MEMORABLE?
HMM ...
THERE'RE SO MANY, IT'S HARD TO CHOOSE...
I KNEW IT.

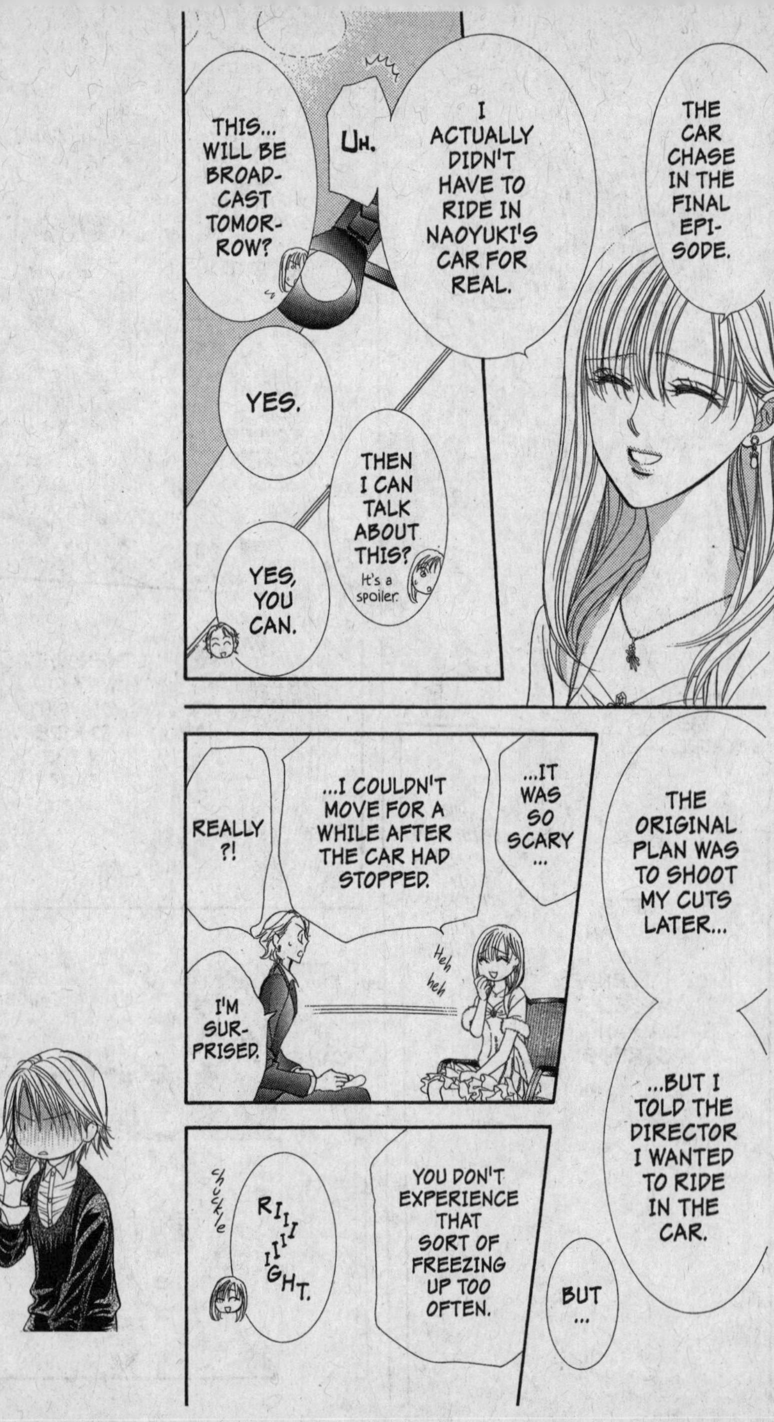
THE CAR CHASE IN THE FINAL EPISODE.
I ACTUALLY DIDN'T HAVE TO RIDE IN NAOYUKI'S CAR FOR REAL.
UH.
THIS... WILL BE BROADCAST TOMORROW?
YES.
THEN I CAN TALK ABOUT THIS?
It's a spoiler.
YES, YOU CAN.
THE ORIGINAL PLAN WAS TO SHOOT MY CUTS LATER...
...BUT I TOLD THE DIRECTOR I WANTED TO RIDE IN THE CAR.
...IT WAS SO SCARY...
...I COULDN'T MOVE FOR A WHILE AFTER THE CAR HAD STOPPED.
REALLY?!
Heh heh
I'M SURPRISED.
BUT...
YOU DON'T EXPERIENCE THAT SORT OF FREEZING UP TOO OFTEN.
RIIIIIIIGHT.
chuckle

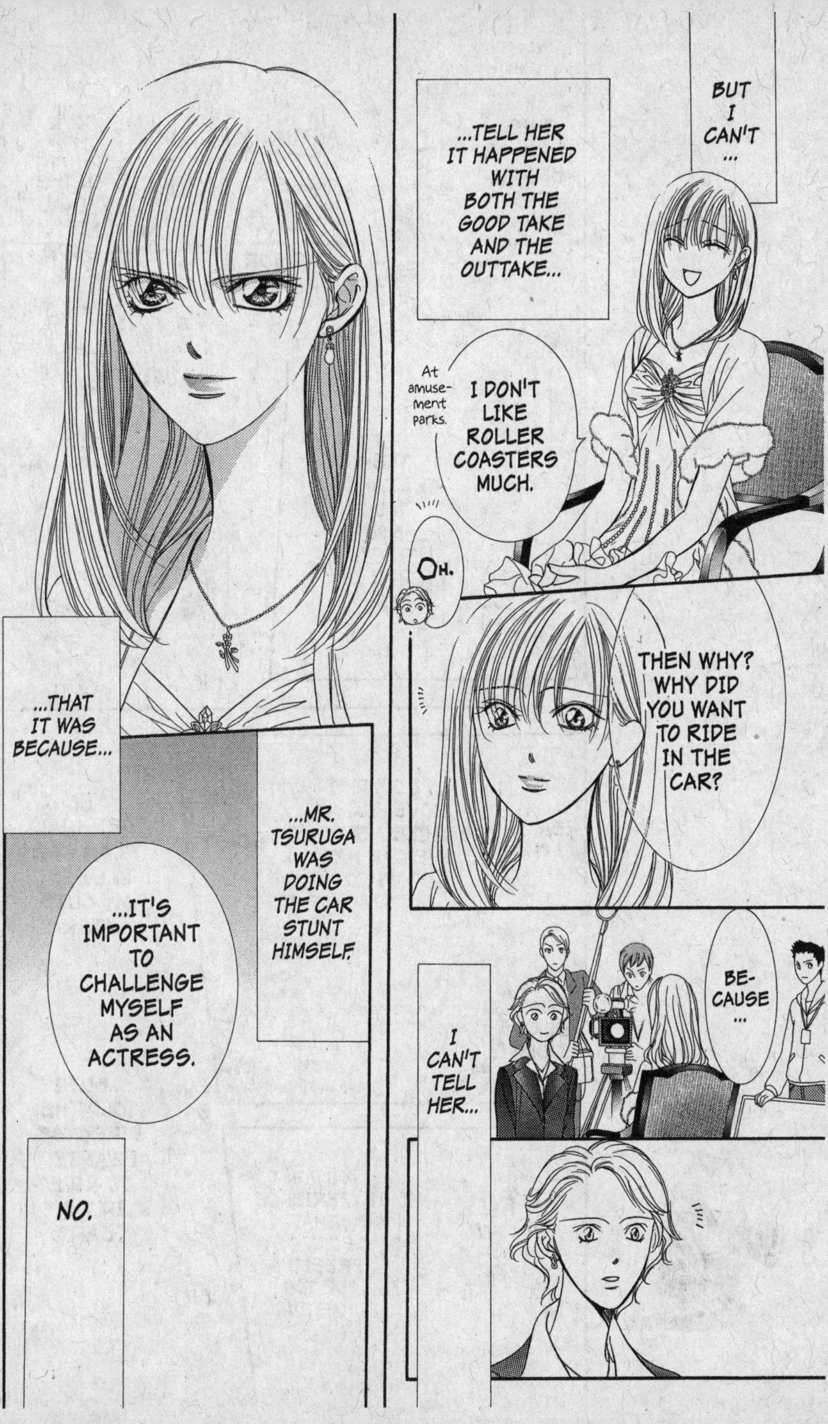
BUT I CAN'T...
...TELL HER IT HAPPENED WITH BOTH THE GOOD TAKE AND THE OUTTAKE...
At amusement parks.
I DON'T LIKE ROLLER COASTERS MUCH.
OH.
THEN WHY? WHY DID YOU WANT TO RIDE IN THE CAR?
BECAUSE...
I CAN'T TELL HER...
...THAT IT WAS BECAUSE...
...MR. TSURUGA WAS DOING THE CAR STUNT HIMSELF.
...IT'S IMPORTANT TO CHALLENGE MYSELF AS AN ACTRESS.
NO.

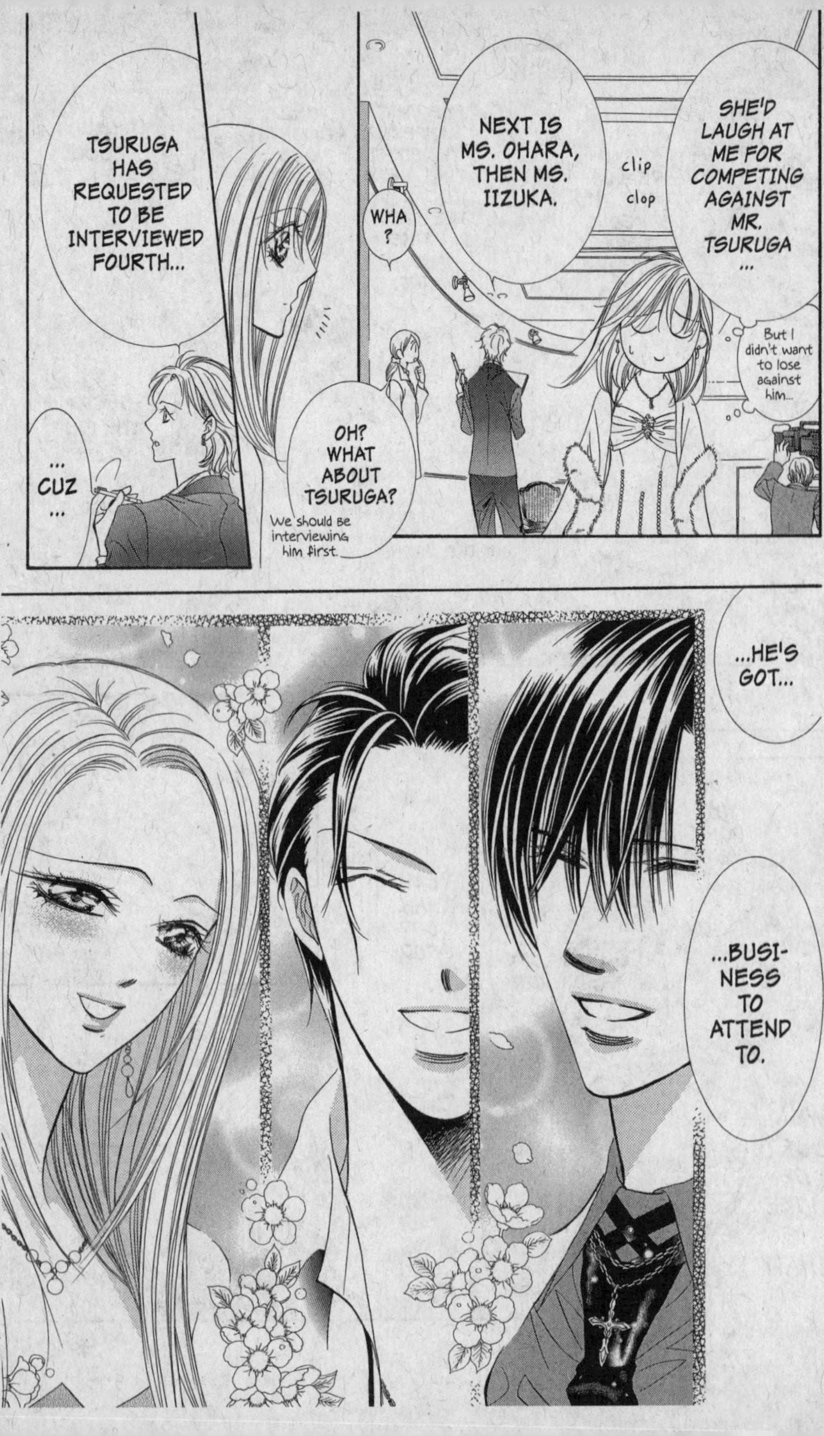
SHE'D LAUGH AT ME FOR COMPETING AGAINST MR. TSURUGA...
But I didn't want to lose against him...
clip clop
NEXT IS MS. OHARA, THEN MS. IIZUKA.
WHA?
OH? WHAT ABOUT TSURUGA?
We should be interviewing him first.
TSURUGA HAS REQUESTED TO BE INTERVIEWED FOURTH...
...CUZ...
...HE'S GOT...
...BUSI-NESS TO ATTEND TO.

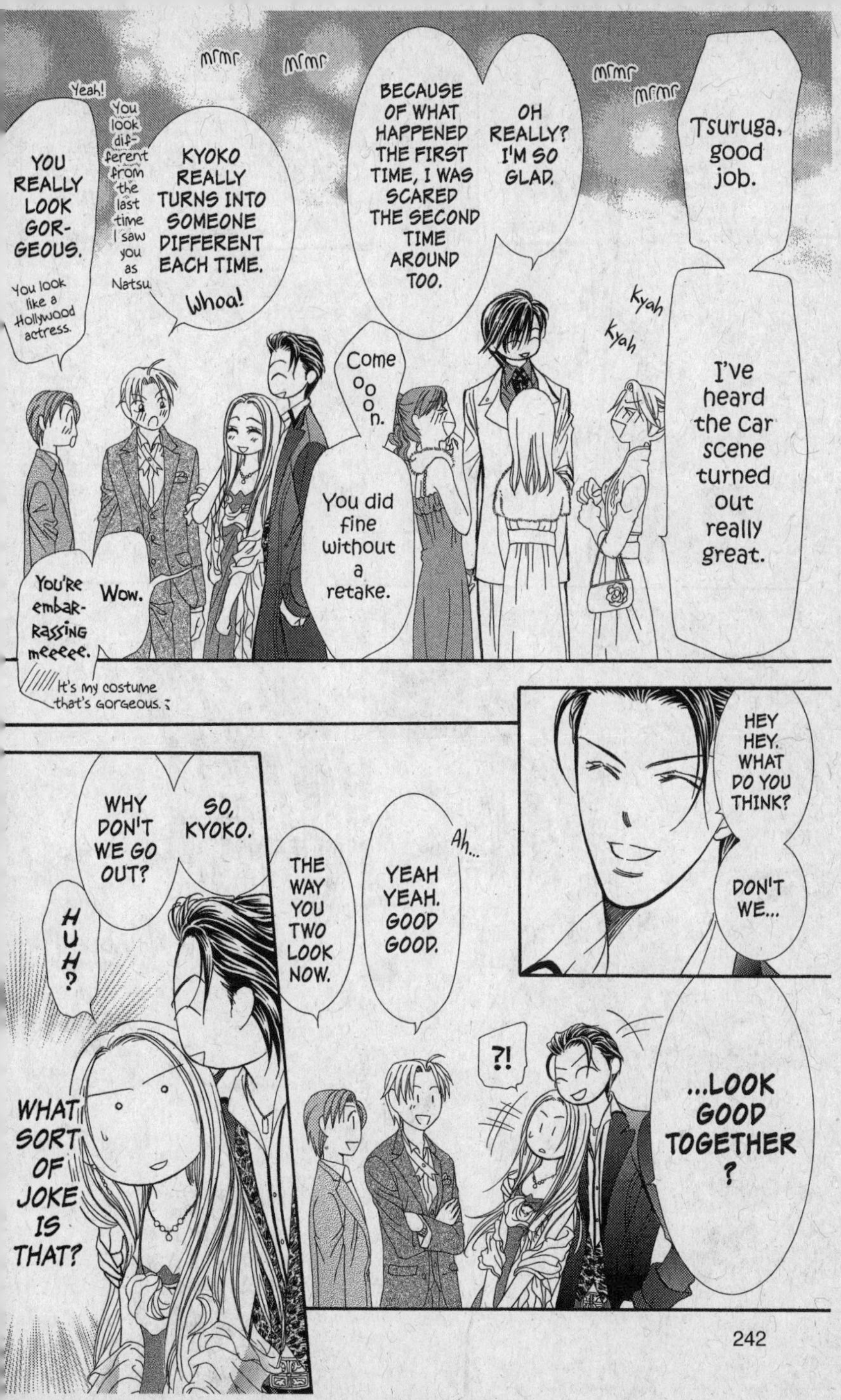
Tsuruga, good job.
I've heard the car scene turned out really great.
Kyah Kyah
mrmr mrmr
OH REALLY? I'M SO GLAD.
BECAUSE OF WHAT HAPPENED THE FIRST TIME, I WAS SCARED THE SECOND TIME AROUND TOO.
mrmr mrmr
Come ooon.
You did fine without a retake.
KYOKO REALLY TURNS INTO SOMEONE DIFFERENT EACH TIME.
Whoa!
You look different from the last time I saw you as Natsu.
Yeah!
YOU REALLY LOOK GORGEOUS.
You look like a Hollywood actress.
Wow.
You're embarrassing meeeee.
It's my costume that's gorgeous.
HEY HEY. WHAT DO YOU THINK? DON'T WE...
...LOOK GOOD TOGETHER?
?!
Ah...
YEAH YEAH. GOOD GOOD.
THE WAY YOU TWO LOOK NOW.
SO, KYOKO. WHY DON'T WE GO OUT?
HUH?
WHAT SORT OF JOKE IS THAT?

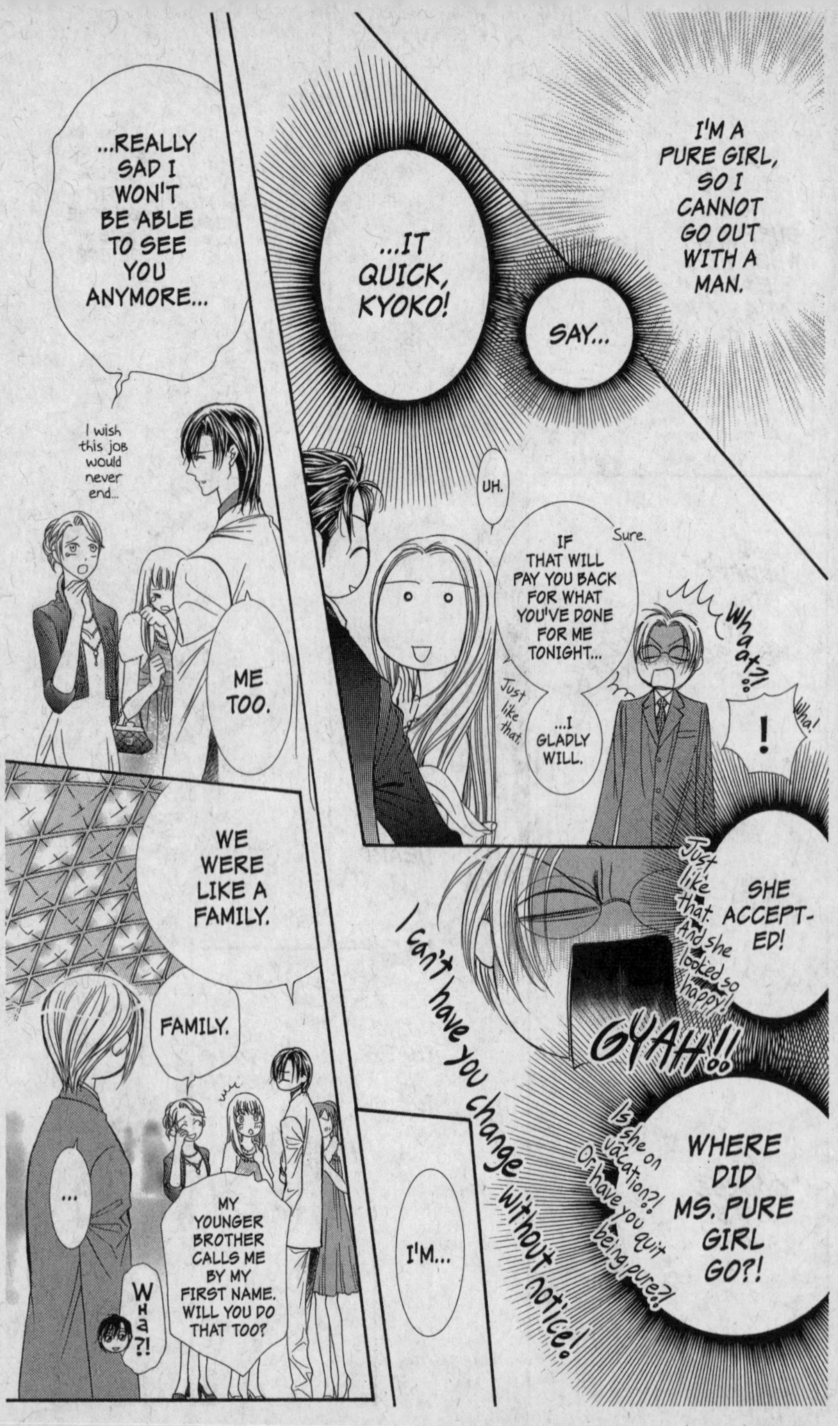

I'M A PURE GIRL, SO I CANNOT GO OUT WITH A MAN.
SAY...
...IT QUICK, KYOKO!
UH.
Sure.
IF THAT WILL PAY YOU BACK FOR WHAT YOU'VE DONE FOR ME TONIGHT...
Just like that.
...I GLADLY WILL.
What?!
!
Wha!
SHE ACCEPTED!
Just like that. And she looked so happy!
GYAH!!
WHERE DID MS. PURE GIRL GO?!
Is she on vacation?! Or have you quit being pure?!
I can't have you change without notice!
...REALLY SAD I WON'T BE ABLE TO SEE YOU ANYMORE...
I wish this job would never end...
ME TOO.
WE WERE LIKE A FAMILY.
FAMILY.
...
MY YOUNGER BROTHER CALLS ME BY MY FIRST NAME. WILL YOU DO THAT TOO?
Wha?!
I'M...

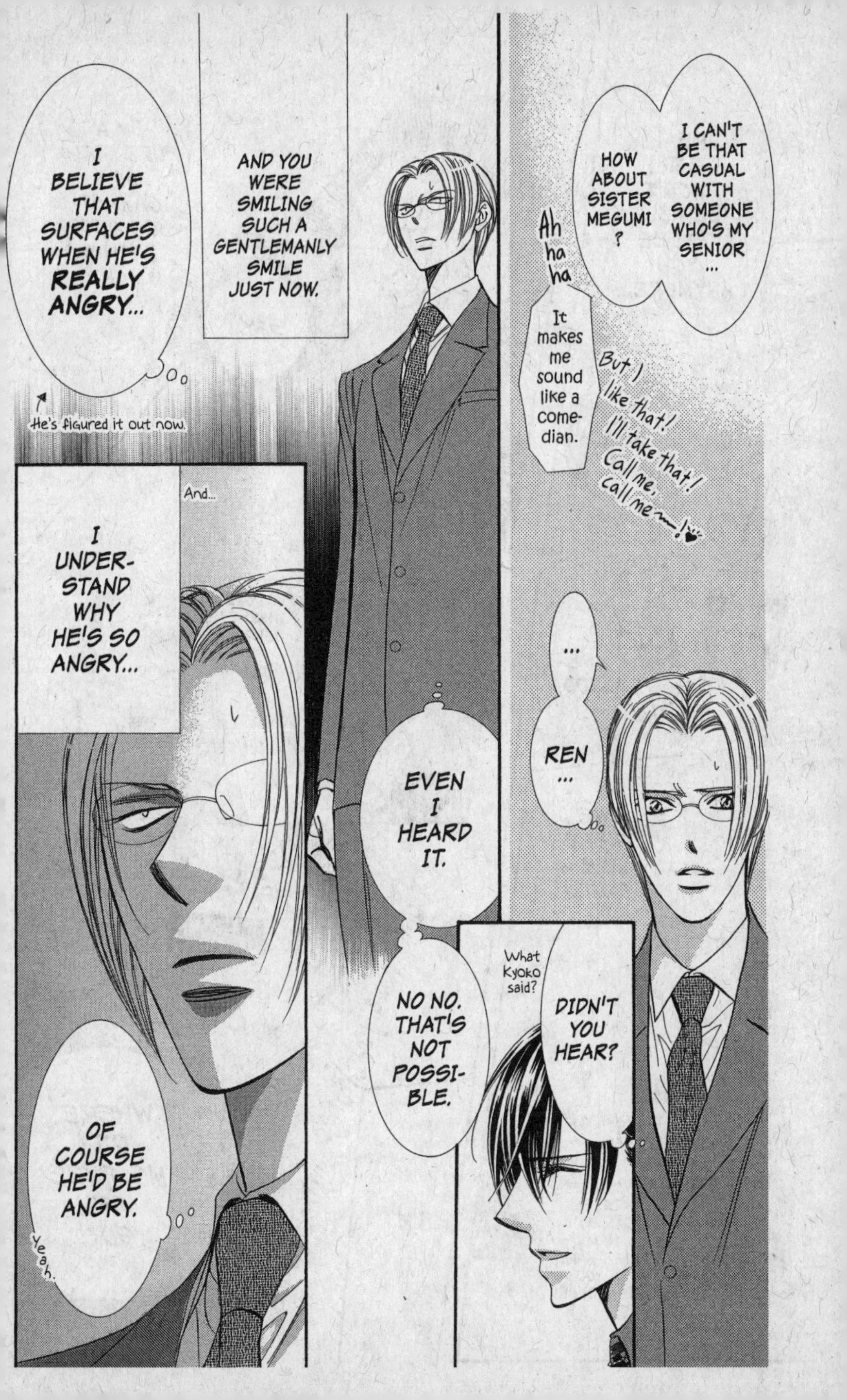
I CAN'T BE THAT CASUAL WITH SOMEONE WHO'S MY SENIOR...
HOW ABOUT SISTER MEGUMI?
Ah ha ha
It makes me sound like a comedian.
But I like that! I'll take that! Call me, call me~!
...
REN...
What Kyoko said?
DIDN'T YOU HEAR?
AND YOU WERE SMILING SUCH A GENTLEMANLY SMILE JUST NOW.
EVEN I HEARD IT.
NO NO. THAT'S NOT POSSIBLE.
I BELIEVE THAT SURFACES WHEN HE'S REALLY ANGRY...
He's figured it out now.
And...
I UNDERSTAND WHY HE'S SO ANGRY...
OF COURSE HE'D BE ANGRY.
Yeah.

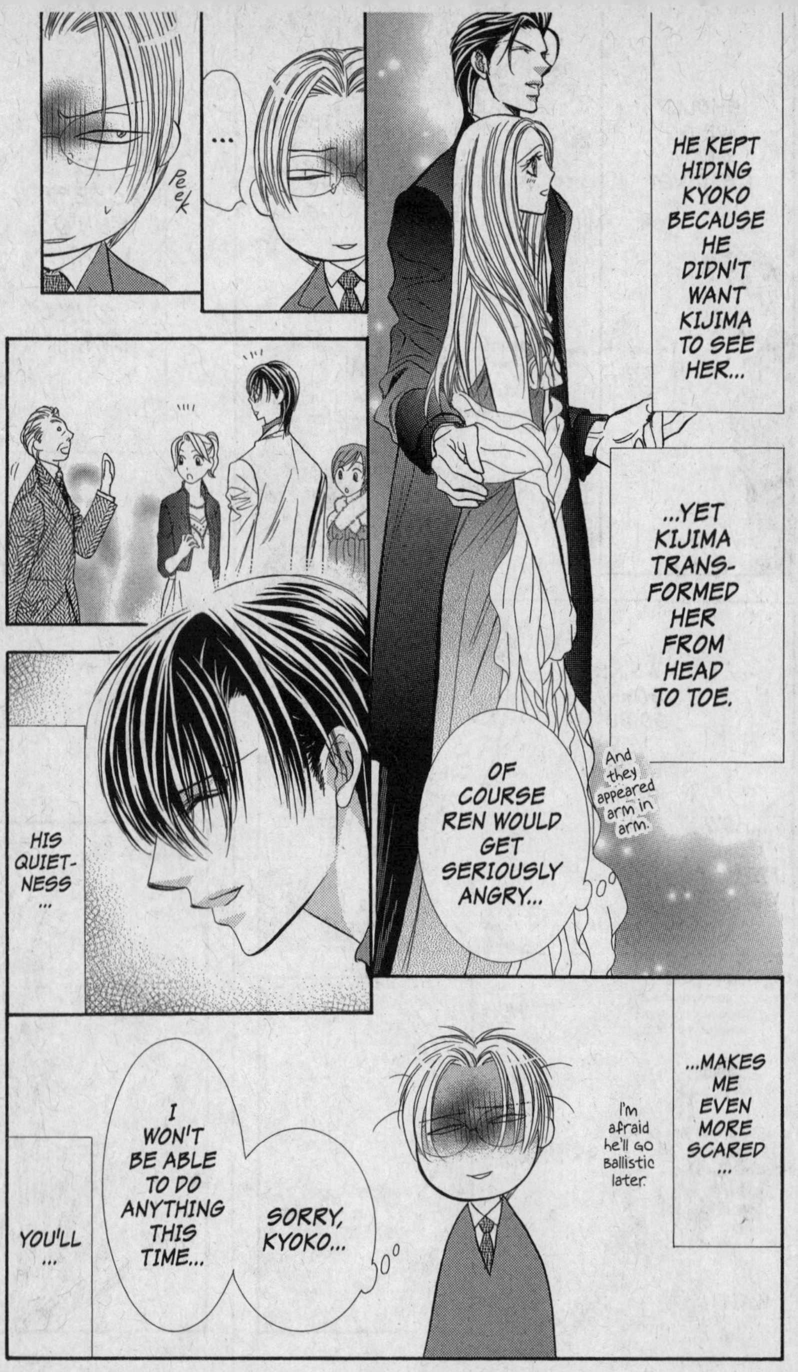
HE KEPT HIDING KYOKO BECAUSE HE DIDN'T WANT KIJIMA TO SEE HER...
...YET KIJIMA TRANSFORMED HER FROM HEAD TO TOE.
And they appeared arm in arm.
OF COURSE REN WOULD GET SERIOUSLY ANGRY...
...
Peek
HIS QUIET-NESS...
...MAKES ME EVEN MORE SCARED...
I'm afraid he'll GO Ballistic later.
SORRY, KYOKO...
I WON'T BE ABLE TO DO ANYTHING THIS TIME...
YOU'LL...

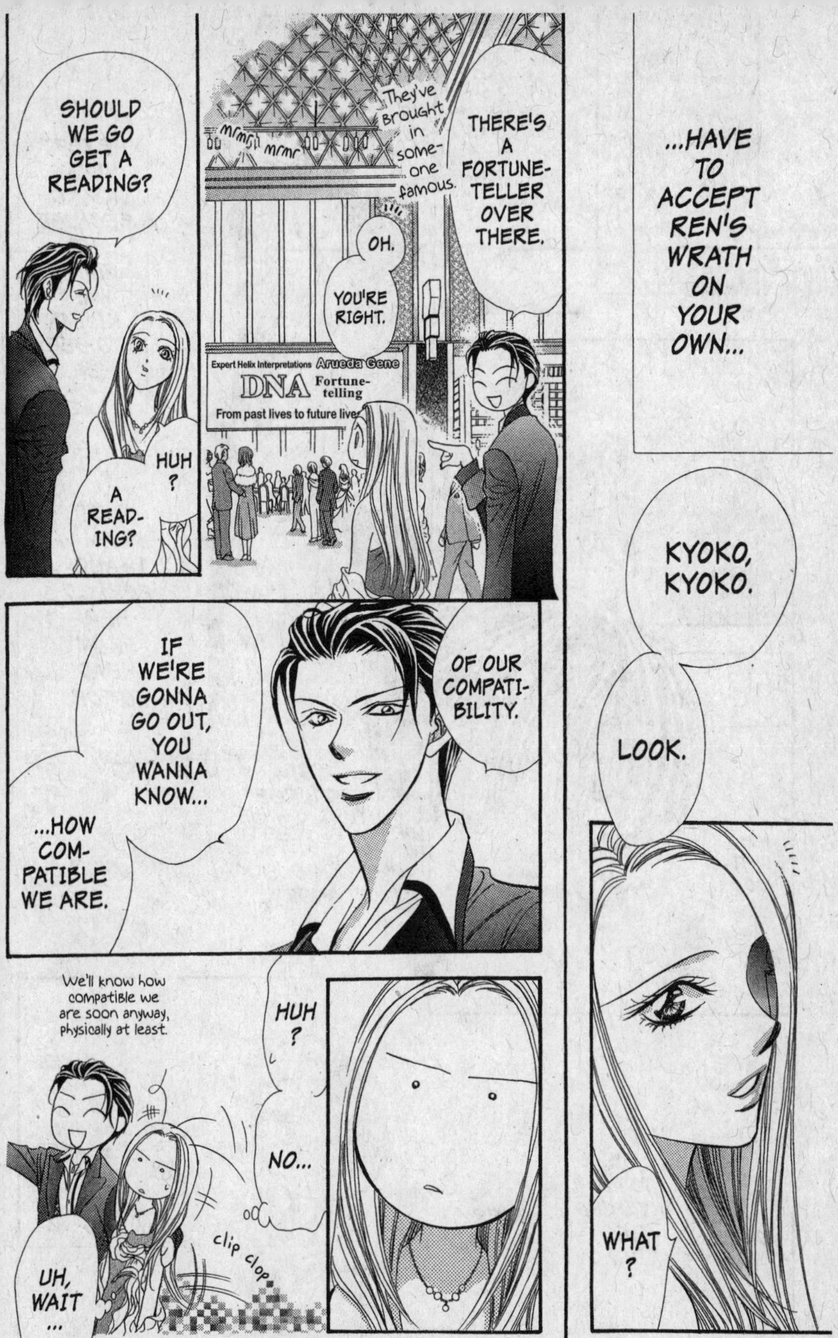
...HAVE TO ACCEPT REN'S WRATH ON YOUR OWN...
KYOKO, KYOKO.
LOOK.
WHAT?
THERE'S A FORTUNE-TELLER OVER THERE.
They've brought in someone famous.
mrmr mrmr
OH.
YOU'RE RIGHT.
Expert Helix Interpretations Arueda Gene
DNA Fortune-telling
From past lives to future lives
SHOULD WE GO GET A READING?
HUH?
A READING?
OF OUR COMPATIBILITY.
IF WE'RE GONNA GO OUT, YOU WANNA KNOW...
...HOW COMPATIBLE WE ARE.
HUH?
NO...
We'll know how compatible we are soon anyway, physically at least.
clip clop
UH, WAIT...

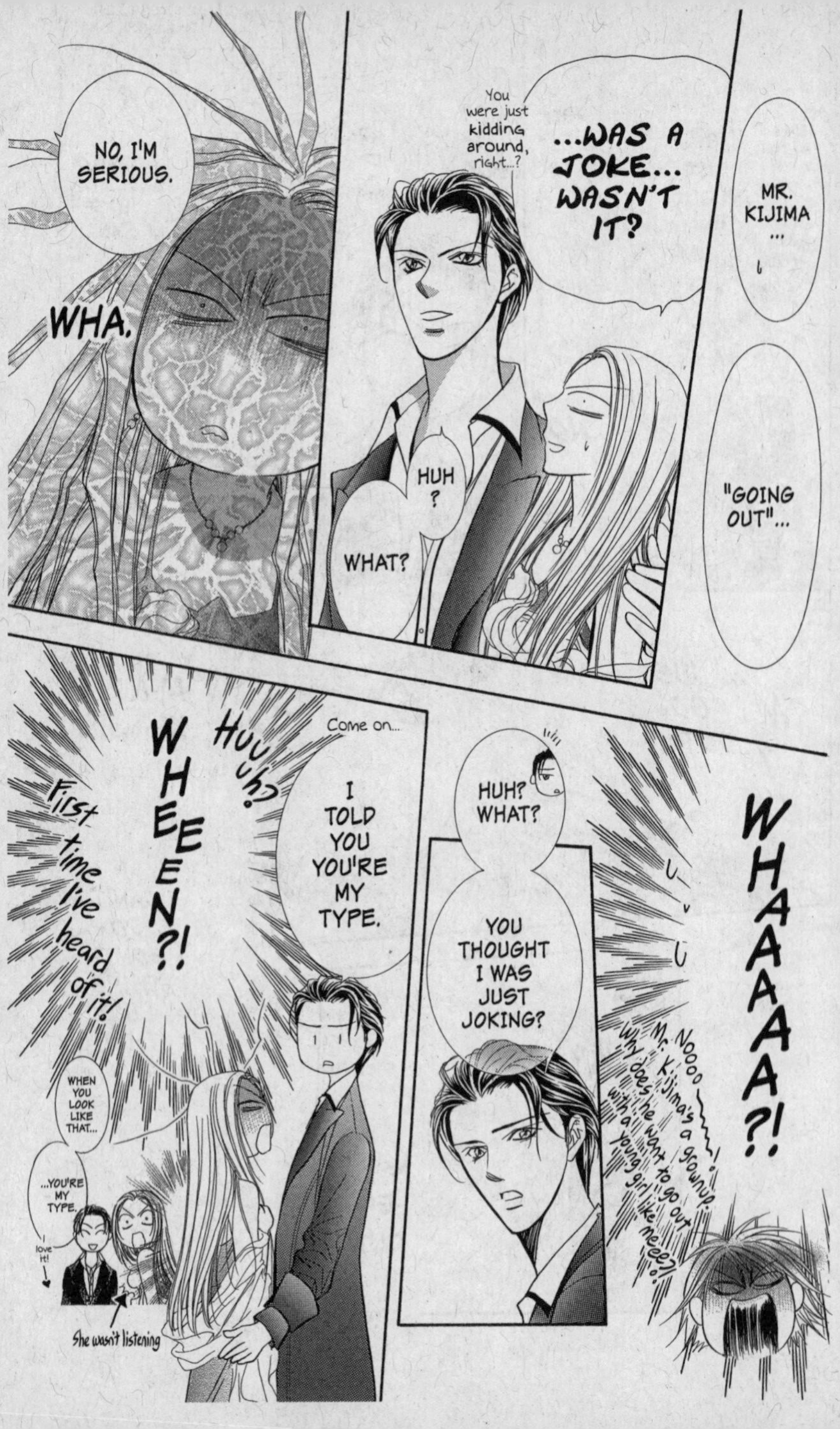
MR. KIJIMA...
"GOING OUT"...
...WAS A JOKE... WASN'T IT?
You were just kidding around, right...?
HUH?
WHAT?
NO, I'M SERIOUS.
WHA.
WHAAAAA?!
Noooo~! Mr. Kijima's a grownup. Why does he want to go out with a young girl like meee?!
HUH? WHAT?
YOU THOUGHT I WAS JUST JOKING?
Come on...
I TOLD YOU YOU'RE MY TYPE.
Huuuh?
WHEEEN?!
First time I've heard of it!
WHEN YOU LOOK LIKE THAT...
...YOU'RE MY TYPE.
I love it!
She wasn't listening

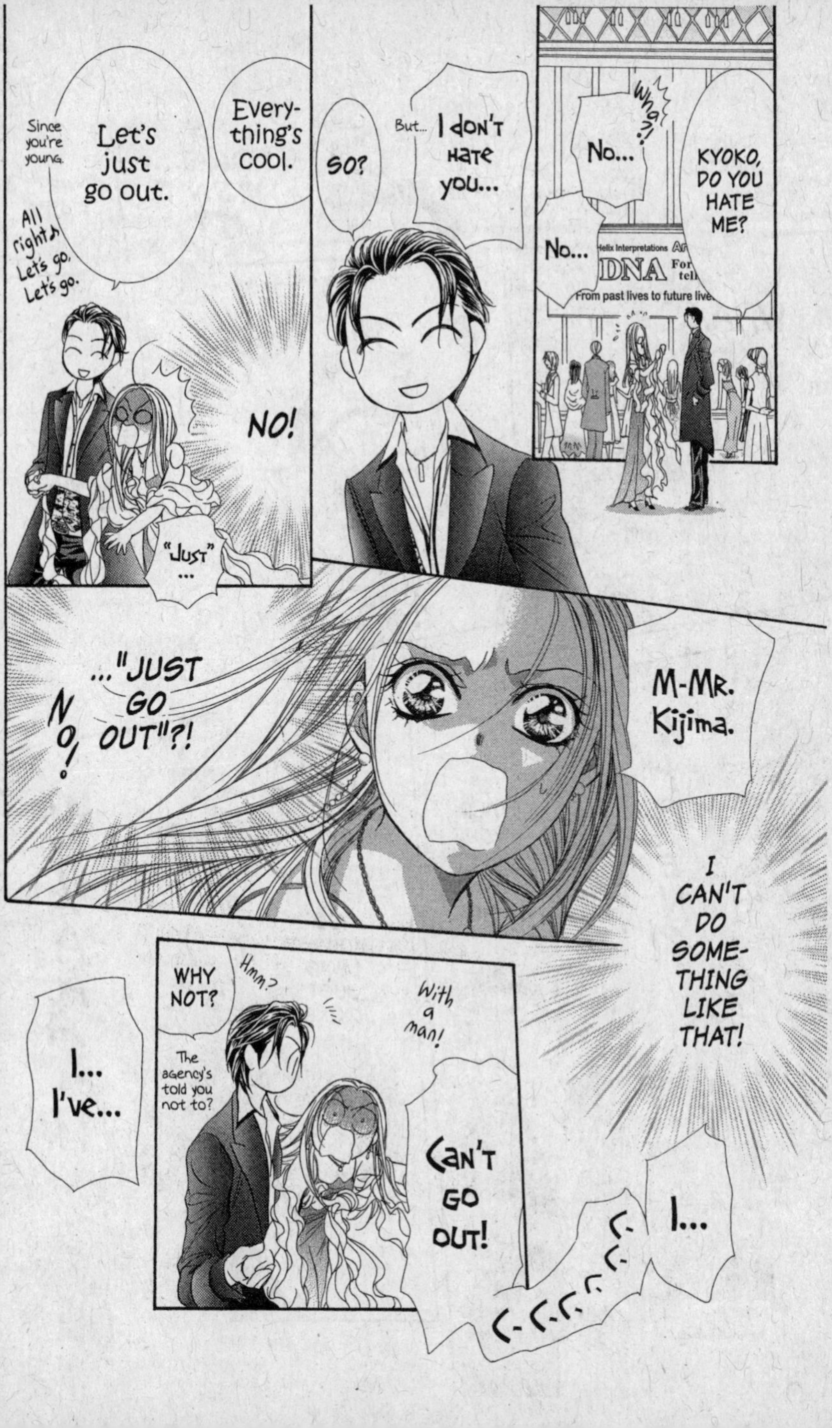
Wha?!
KYOKO, DO YOU HATE ME?
No...
No...
Helix Interpretations
DNA
But... I don't hate you...
So?
Every-thing's cool.
Since you're young. Let's just go out.
All right♪ Let's go, Let's go.
NO!
"Just" ...
M-Mr. Kijima.
..."JUST GO OUT"?!
NO!
I CAN'T DO SOME-THING LIKE THAT!
I...
Can't go out!
With a man!
Hmm?
WHY NOT?
The agency's told you not to?
I... I've...

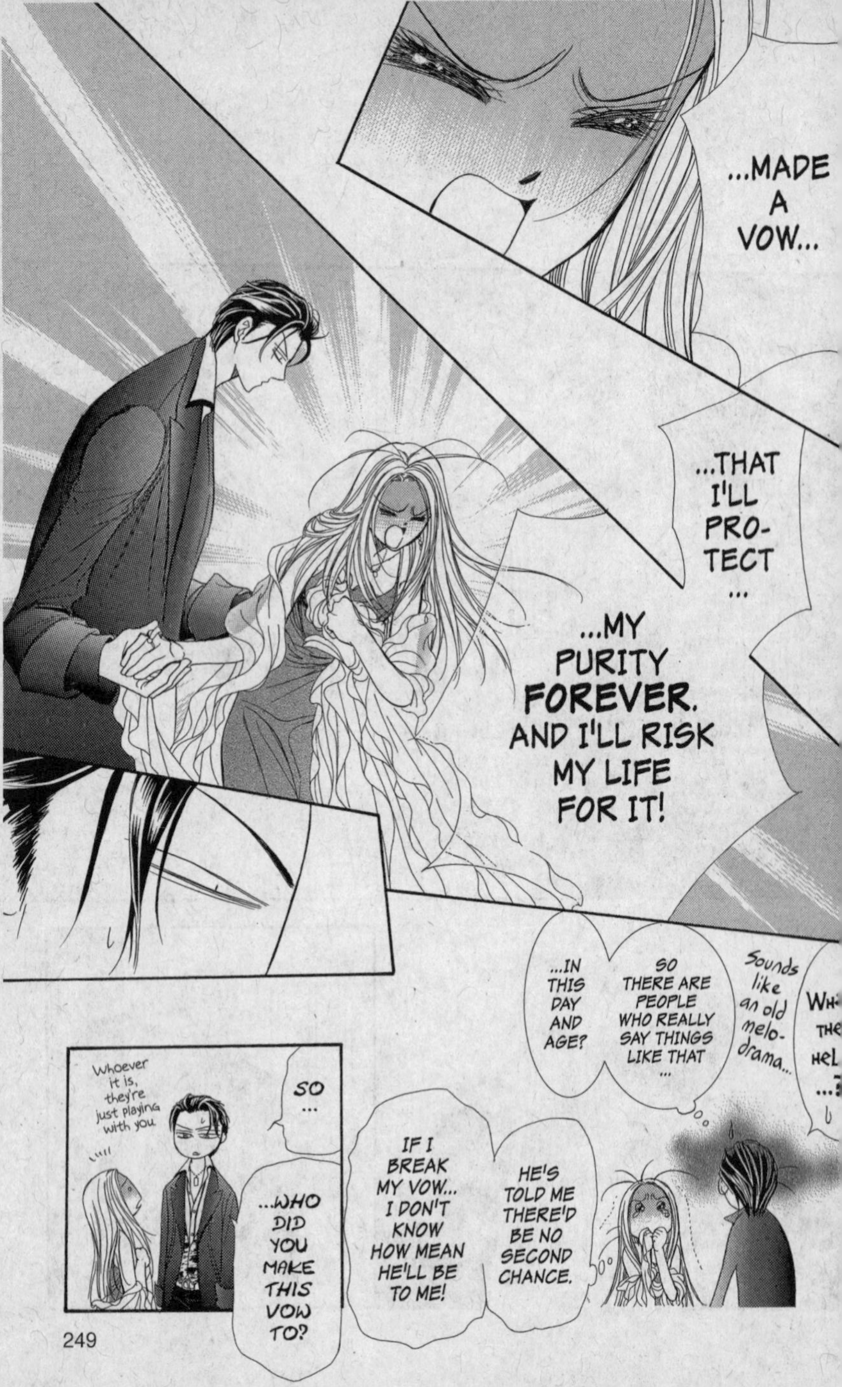
...MADE A VOW...
...THAT I'LL PROTECT...
...MY PURITY FOREVER. AND I'LL RISK MY LIFE FOR IT!
WHA THE HEL...?
Sounds like an old melodrama...
SO THERE ARE PEOPLE WHO REALLY SAY THINGS LIKE THAT...
...IN THIS DAY AND AGE?
HE'S TOLD ME THERE'D BE NO SECOND CHANCE.
IF I BREAK MY VOW... I DON'T KNOW HOW MEAN HE'LL BE TO ME!
SO...
...WHO DID YOU MAKE THIS VOW TO?
Whoever it is, they're just playing with you.

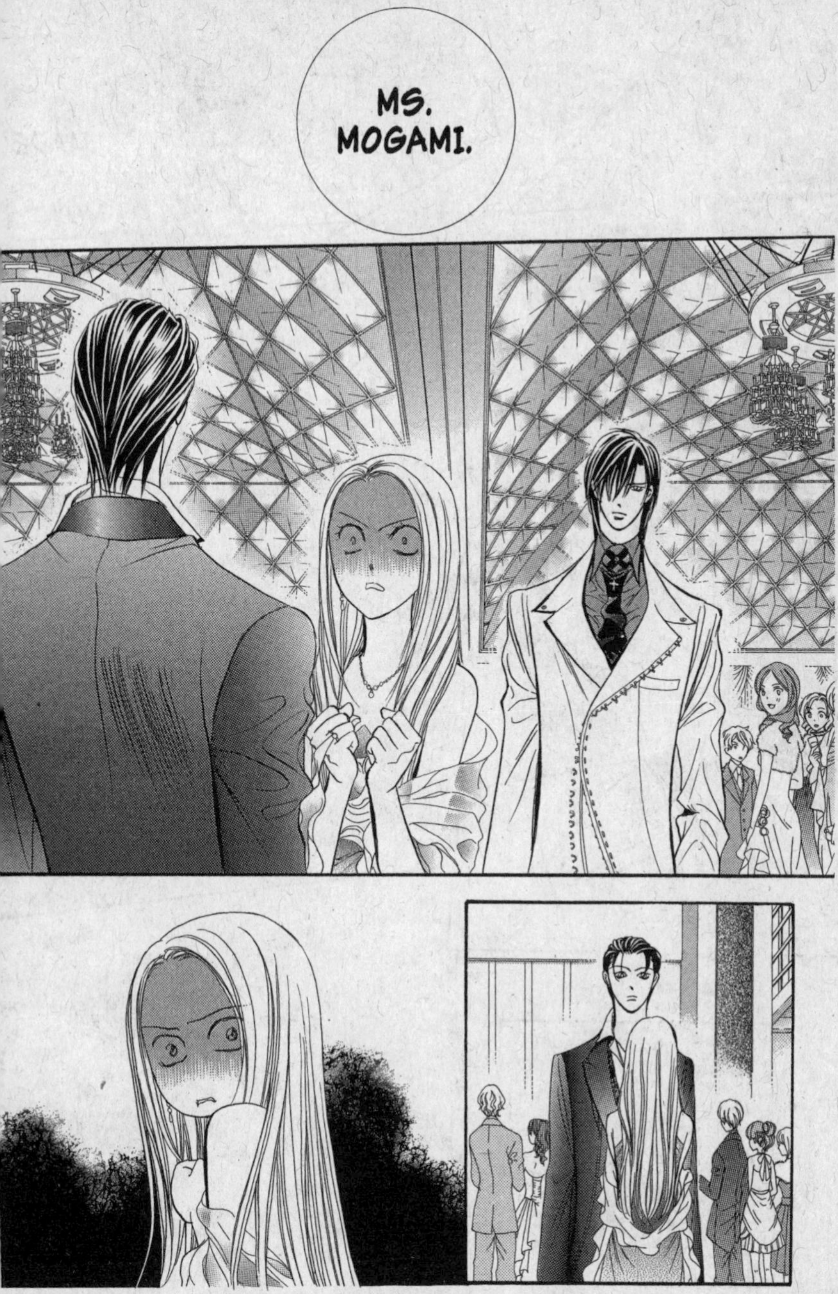
MS.
MOGAMI.

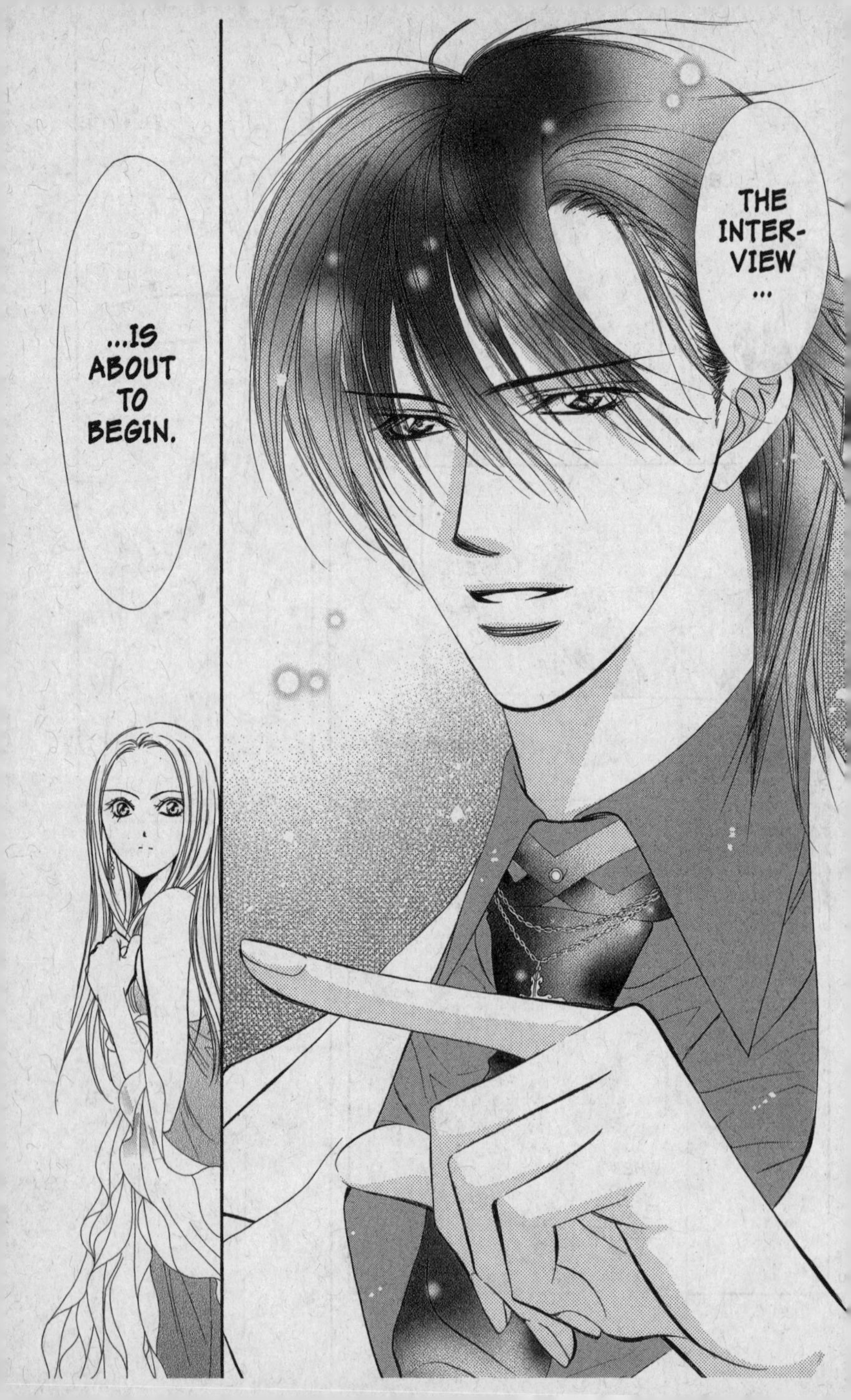
THE INTER-VIEW ...
...IS ABOUT TO BEGIN.

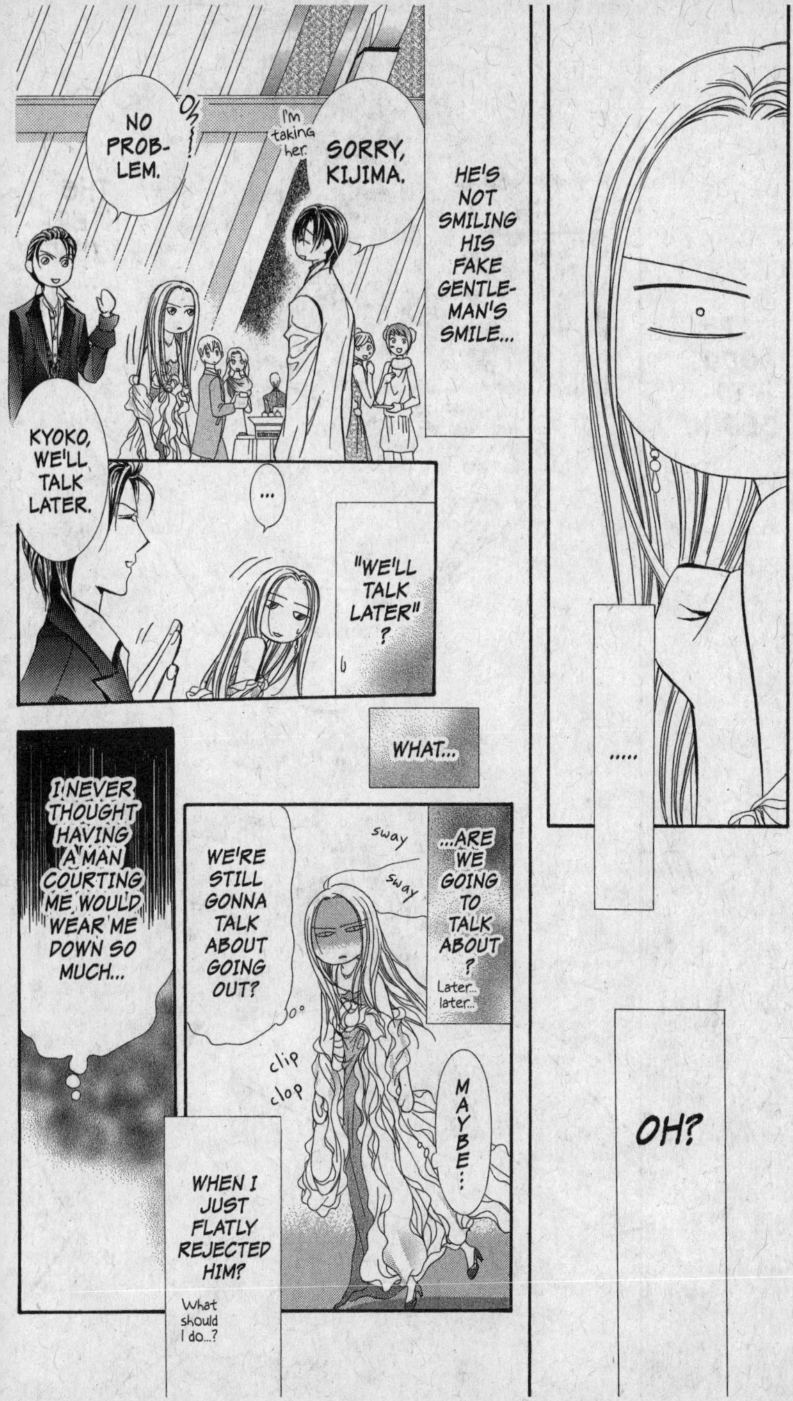
.....
OH?
HE'S NOT SMILING HIS FAKE GENTLE-MAN'S SMILE...
SORRY, KIJIMA.
I'm taking her.
Oh~!
NO PROB-LEM.
KYOKO, WE'LL TALK LATER.
"WE'LL TALK LATER"?
...
WHAT...
...ARE WE GOING TO TALK ABOUT?
Later... later...
sway
sway
WE'RE STILL GONNA TALK ABOUT GOING OUT?
MAYBE...
clip
clop
WHEN I JUST FLATLY REJECTED HIM?
What should I do...?
I NEVER THOUGHT HAVING A MAN COURTING ME WOULD WEAR ME DOWN SO MUCH...

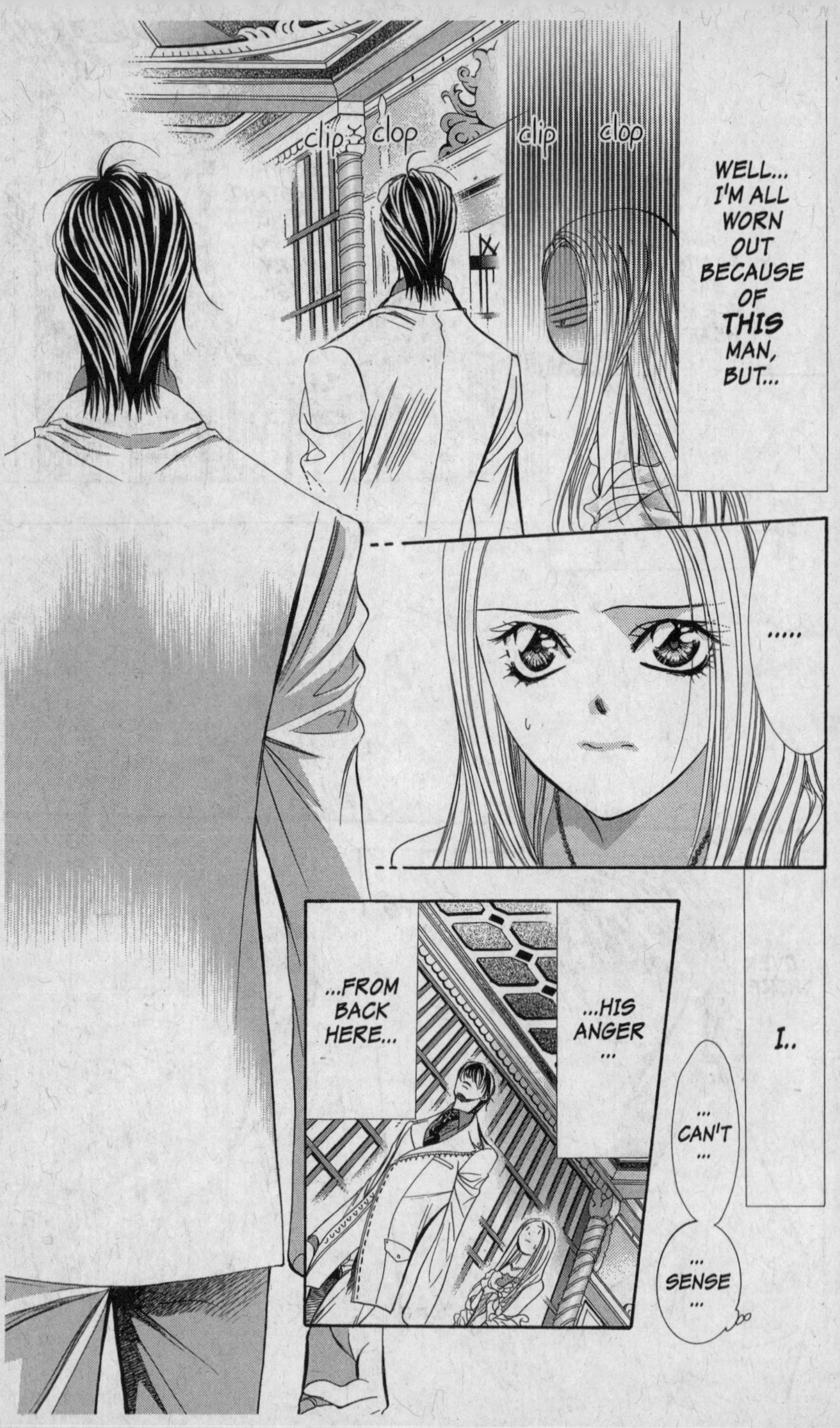
WELL... I'M ALL WORN OUT BECAUSE OF THIS MAN, BUT...
clip clop
clip clop
.....
I..
...CAN'T...
...SENSE...
...HIS ANGER...
...FROM BACK HERE...

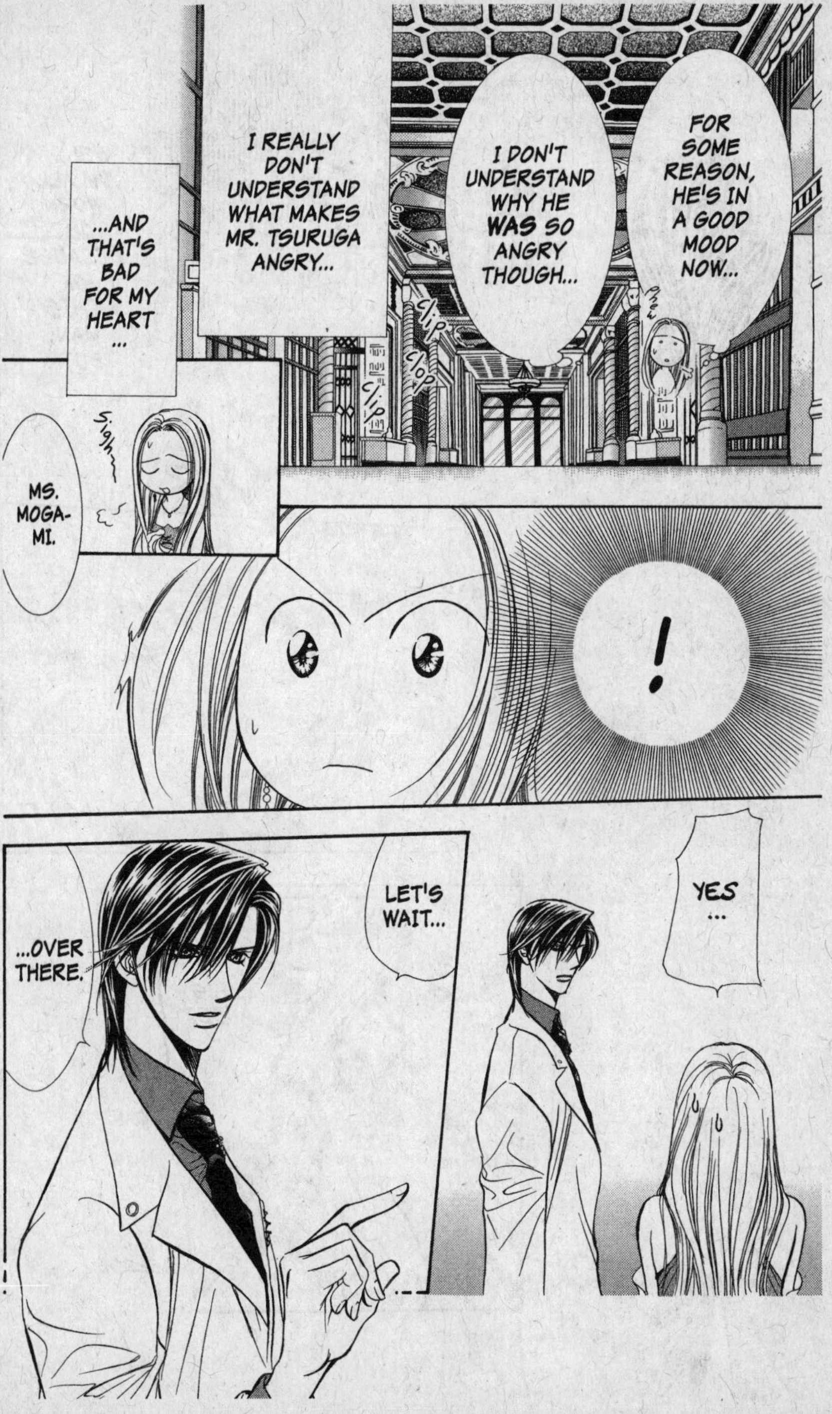
FOR SOME REASON, HE'S IN A GOOD MOOD NOW...
I DON'T UNDERSTAND WHY HE WAS SO ANGRY THOUGH...
phew
clip clop clip
I REALLY DON'T UNDERSTAND WHAT MAKES MR. TSURUGA ANGRY...
...AND THAT'S BAD FOR MY HEART ...
Sigh
MS. MOGA-MI.
!
YES ...
LET'S WAIT...
...OVER THERE.

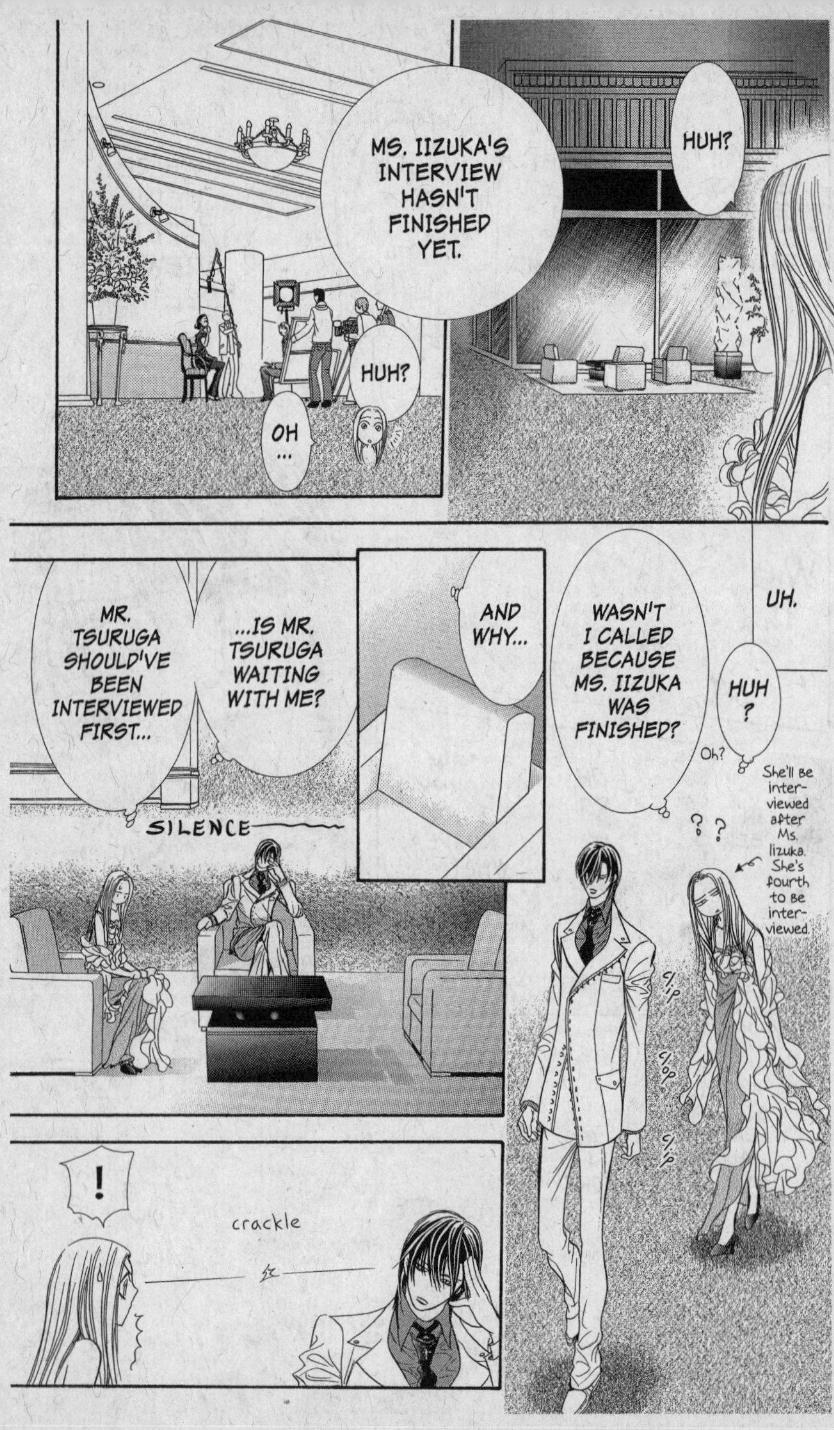
HUH?
MS. IIZUKA'S INTERVIEW HASN'T FINISHED YET.
HUH?
OH ...
UH.
HUH?
Oh?
WASN'T I CALLED BECAUSE MS. IIZUKA WAS FINISHED?
? ?
She'll be interviewed after Ms. Iizuka. She's fourth to be interviewed.
clip
clop
clip
AND WHY...
...IS MR. TSURUGA WAITING WITH ME?
MR. TSURUGA SHOULD'VE BEEN INTERVIEWED FIRST...
SILENCE
!
crackle

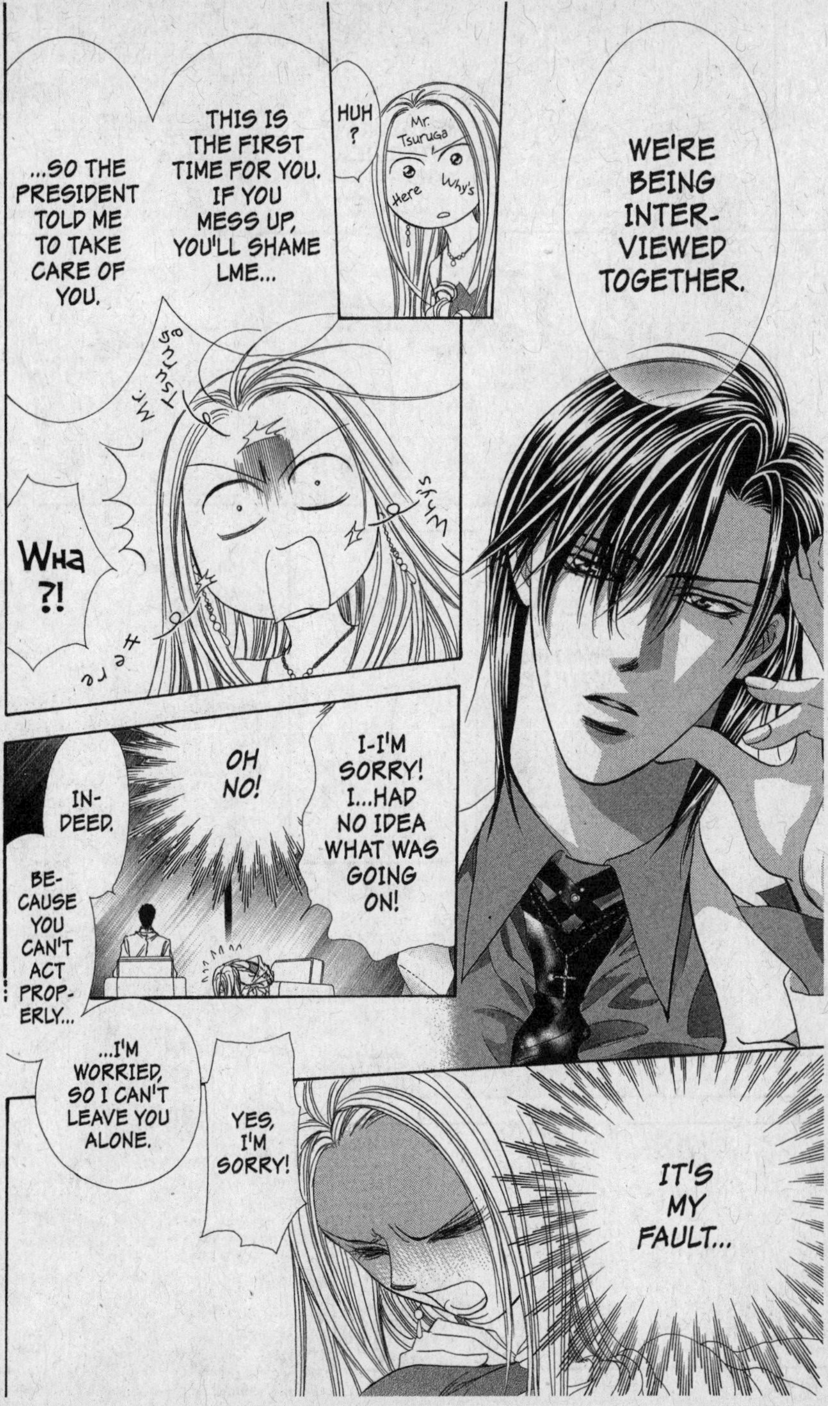
WE'RE BEING INTER-VIEWED TOGETHER.
HUH ?
Mr. Tsuruga Why's Here
THIS IS THE FIRST TIME FOR YOU. IF YOU MESS UP, YOU'LL SHAME LME...
...SO THE PRESIDENT TOLD ME TO TAKE CARE OF YOU.
Mr. Tsuruga Why's Here
WHA ?!
I-I'M SORRY! I...HAD NO IDEA WHAT WAS GOING ON!
OH NO!
IN-DEED.
BE-CAUSE YOU CAN'T ACT PROP-ERLY...
...I'M WORRIED, SO I CAN'T LEAVE YOU ALONE.
IT'S MY FAULT...
YES, I'M SORRY!

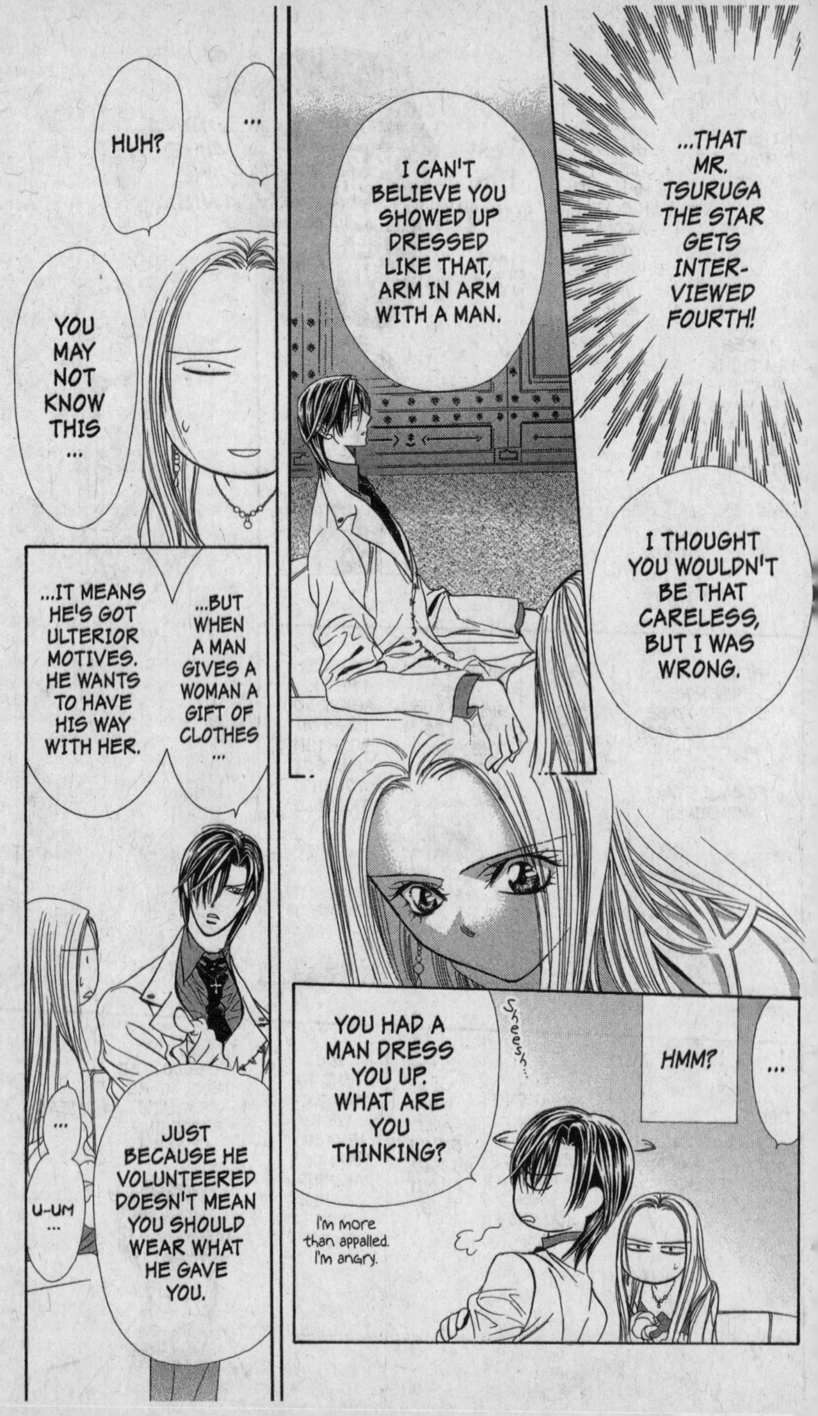
...THAT MR. TSURUGA THE STAR GETS INTER-VIEWED FOURTH!
I CAN'T BELIEVE YOU SHOWED UP DRESSED LIKE THAT, ARM IN ARM WITH A MAN.
I THOUGHT YOU WOULDN'T BE THAT CARELESS, BUT I WAS WRONG.
...
HMM?
Sheesh...
YOU HAD A MAN DRESS YOU UP. WHAT ARE YOU THINKING?
I'm more than appalled. I'm angry.
...
HUH?
YOU MAY NOT KNOW THIS...
...BUT WHEN A MAN GIVES A WOMAN A GIFT OF CLOTHES...
...IT MEANS HE'S GOT ULTERIOR MOTIVES. HE WANTS TO HAVE HIS WAY WITH HER.
JUST BECAUSE HE VOLUNTEERED DOESN'T MEAN YOU SHOULD WEAR WHAT HE GAVE YOU.
...
U-UM...

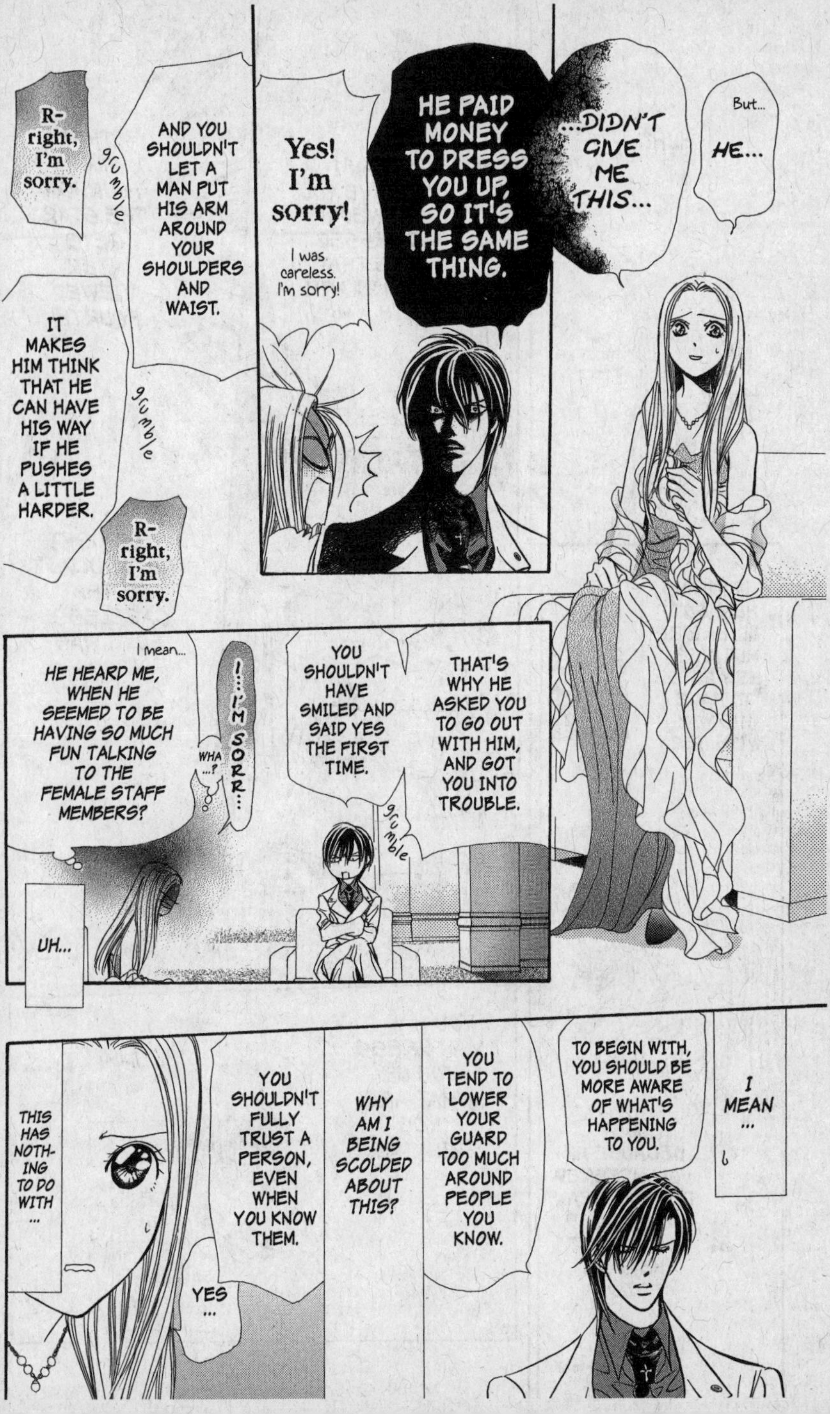
But...
HE...
...DIDN'T GIVE ME THIS...
HE PAID MONEY TO DRESS YOU UP, SO IT'S THE SAME THING.
Yes! I'm sorry!
I was careless. I'm sorry!
AND YOU SHOULDN'T LET A MAN PUT HIS ARM AROUND YOUR SHOULDERS AND WAIST.
grumble
R-right, I'm sorry.
IT MAKES HIM THINK THAT HE CAN HAVE HIS WAY IF HE PUSHES A LITTLE HARDER.
grumble
R-right, I'm sorry.
THAT'S WHY HE ASKED YOU TO GO OUT WITH HIM, AND GOT YOU INTO TROUBLE.
grumble
YOU SHOULDN'T HAVE SMILED AND SAID YES THE FIRST TIME.
I... I'M SORR...
WHA ...?
I mean...
HE HEARD ME, WHEN HE SEEMED TO BE HAVING SO MUCH FUN TALKING TO THE FEMALE STAFF MEMBERS?
UH...
I MEAN ...
TO BEGIN WITH, YOU SHOULD BE MORE AWARE OF WHAT'S HAPPENING TO YOU.
YOU TEND TO LOWER YOUR GUARD TOO MUCH AROUND PEOPLE YOU KNOW.
WHY AM I BEING SCOLDED ABOUT THIS?
YOU SHOULDN'T FULLY TRUST A PERSON, EVEN WHEN YOU KNOW THEM.
YES ...
THIS HAS NOTHING TO DO WITH ...

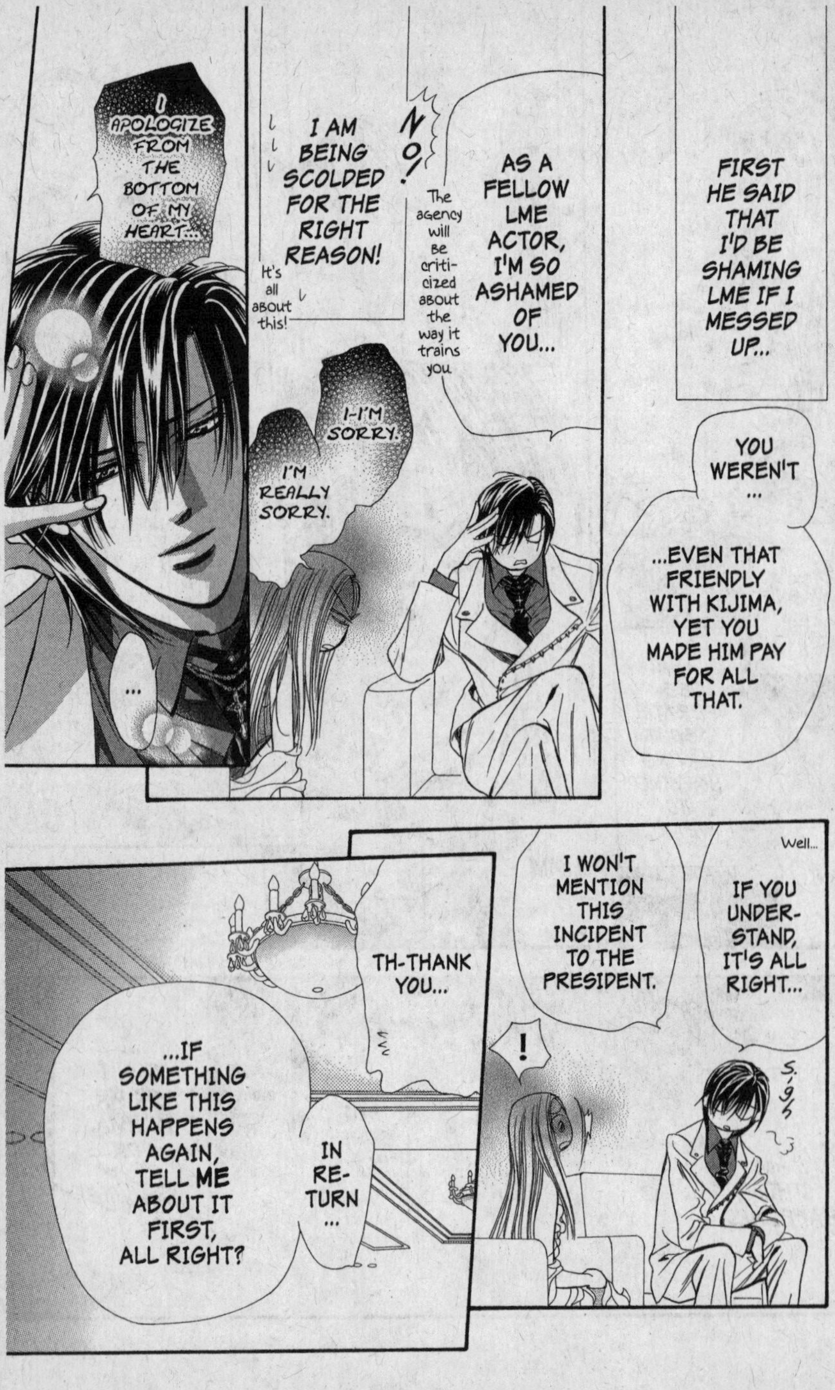

FIRST HE SAID THAT I'D BE SHAMING LME IF I MESSED UP...
YOU WEREN'T ...
...EVEN THAT FRIENDLY WITH KIJIMA, YET YOU MADE HIM PAY FOR ALL THAT.
AS A FELLOW LME ACTOR, I'M SO ASHAMED OF YOU...
The agency will be criticized about the way it trains you
NO!
I AM BEING SCOLDED FOR THE RIGHT REASON!
It's all about this!
I-I'M SORRY.
I'M REALLY SORRY.
I APOLOGIZE FROM THE BOTTOM OF MY HEART...
...
Well...
IF YOU UNDERSTAND, IT'S ALL RIGHT...
I WON'T MENTION THIS INCIDENT TO THE PRESIDENT.
!
TH-THANK YOU...
IN RETURN...
...IF SOMETHING LIKE THIS HAPPENS AGAIN, TELL ME ABOUT IT FIRST, ALL RIGHT?

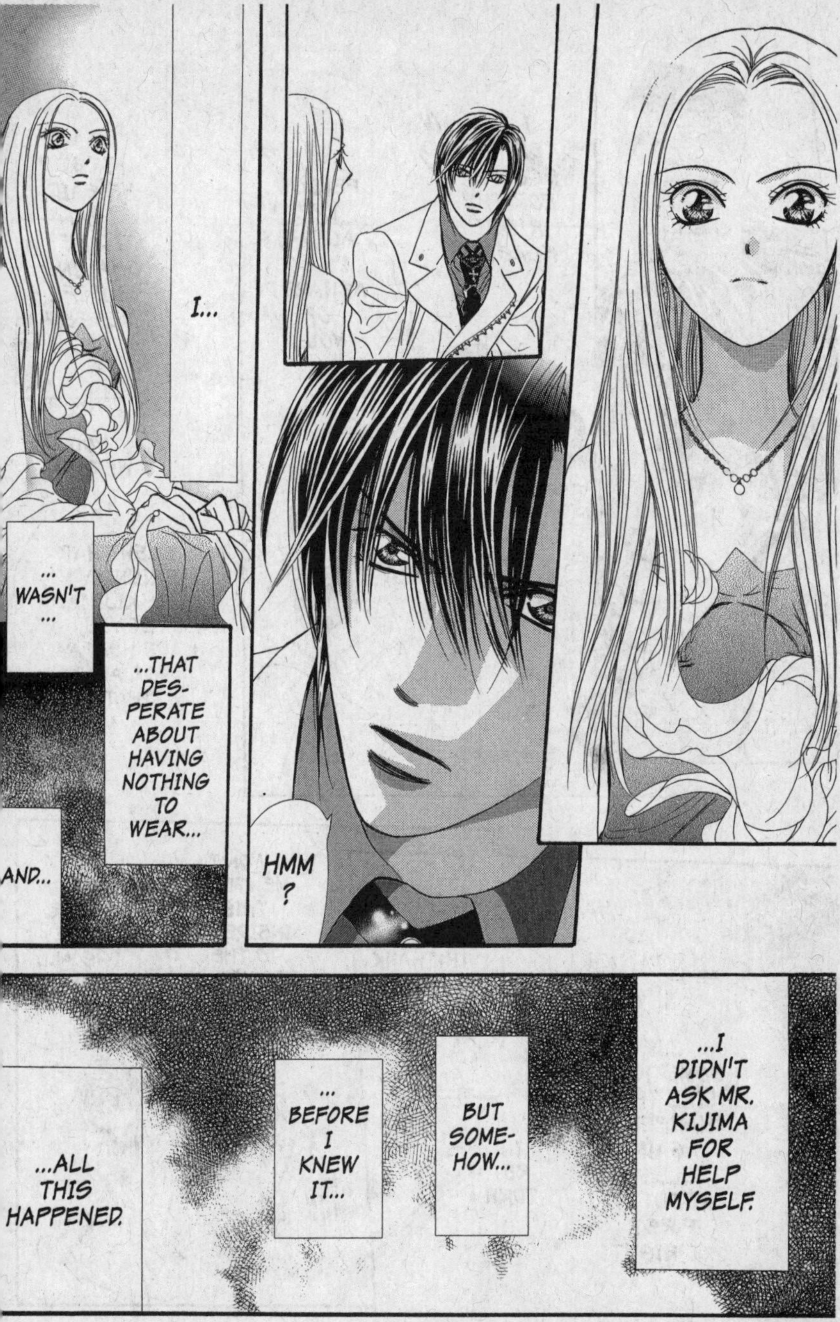
HMM?
I...
...WASN'T...
...THAT DESPERATE ABOUT HAVING NOTHING TO WEAR...
AND...
...I DIDN'T ASK MR. KIJIMA FOR HELP MYSELF.
BUT SOMEHOW...
...BEFORE I KNEW IT...
...ALL THIS HAPPENED.

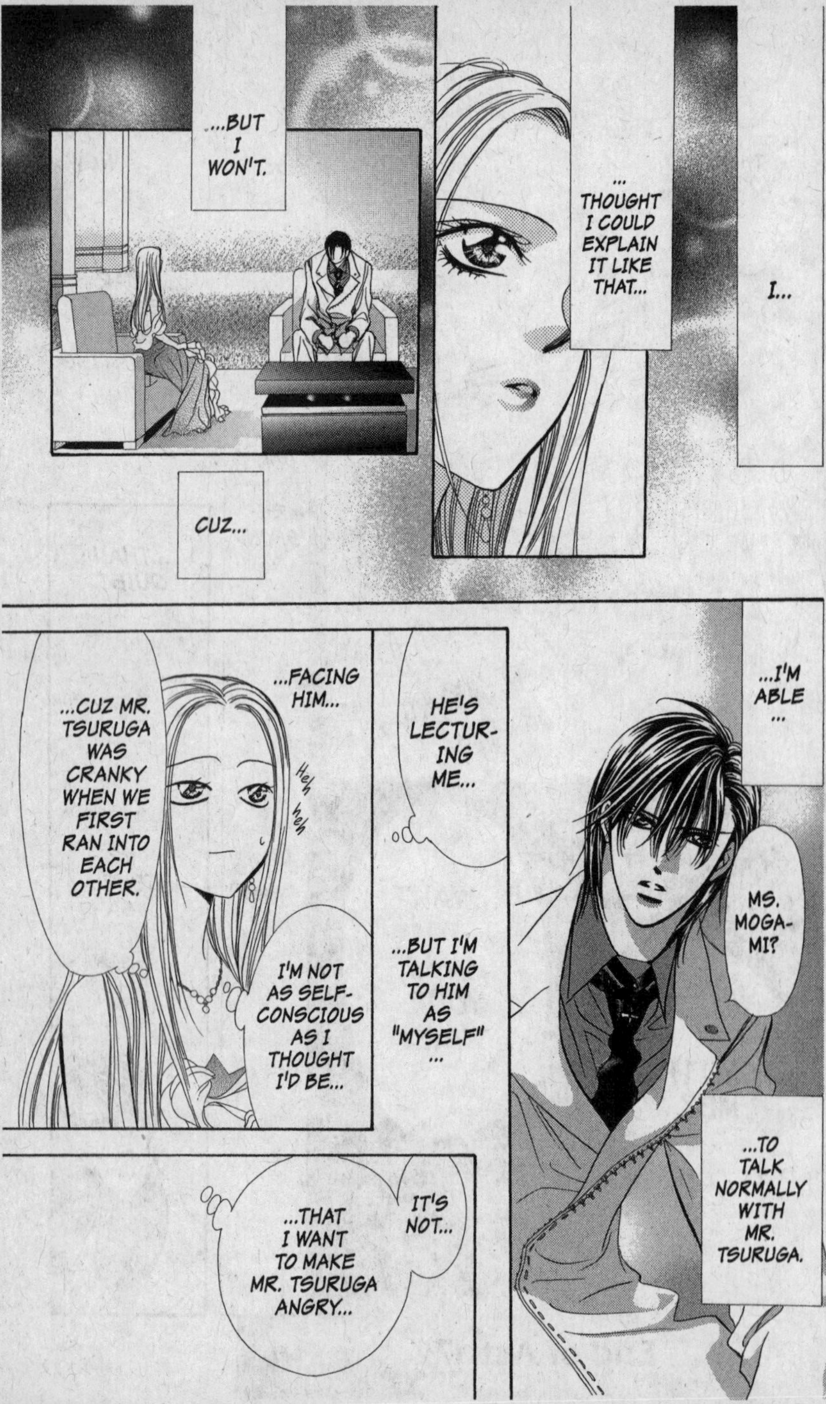
I...
... THOUGHT I COULD EXPLAIN IT LIKE THAT...
...BUT I WON'T.
CUZ...
...I'M ABLE ...
MS. MOGA-MI?
...TO TALK NORMALLY WITH MR. TSURUGA.
HE'S LECTUR-ING ME...
...BUT I'M TALKING TO HIM AS "MYSELF" ...
...FACING HIM...
I'M NOT AS SELF-CONSCIOUS AS I THOUGHT I'D BE...
...CUZ MR. TSURUGA WAS CRANKY WHEN WE FIRST RAN INTO EACH OTHER.
Heh heh
IT'S NOT...
...THAT I WANT TO MAKE MR. TSURUGA ANGRY...

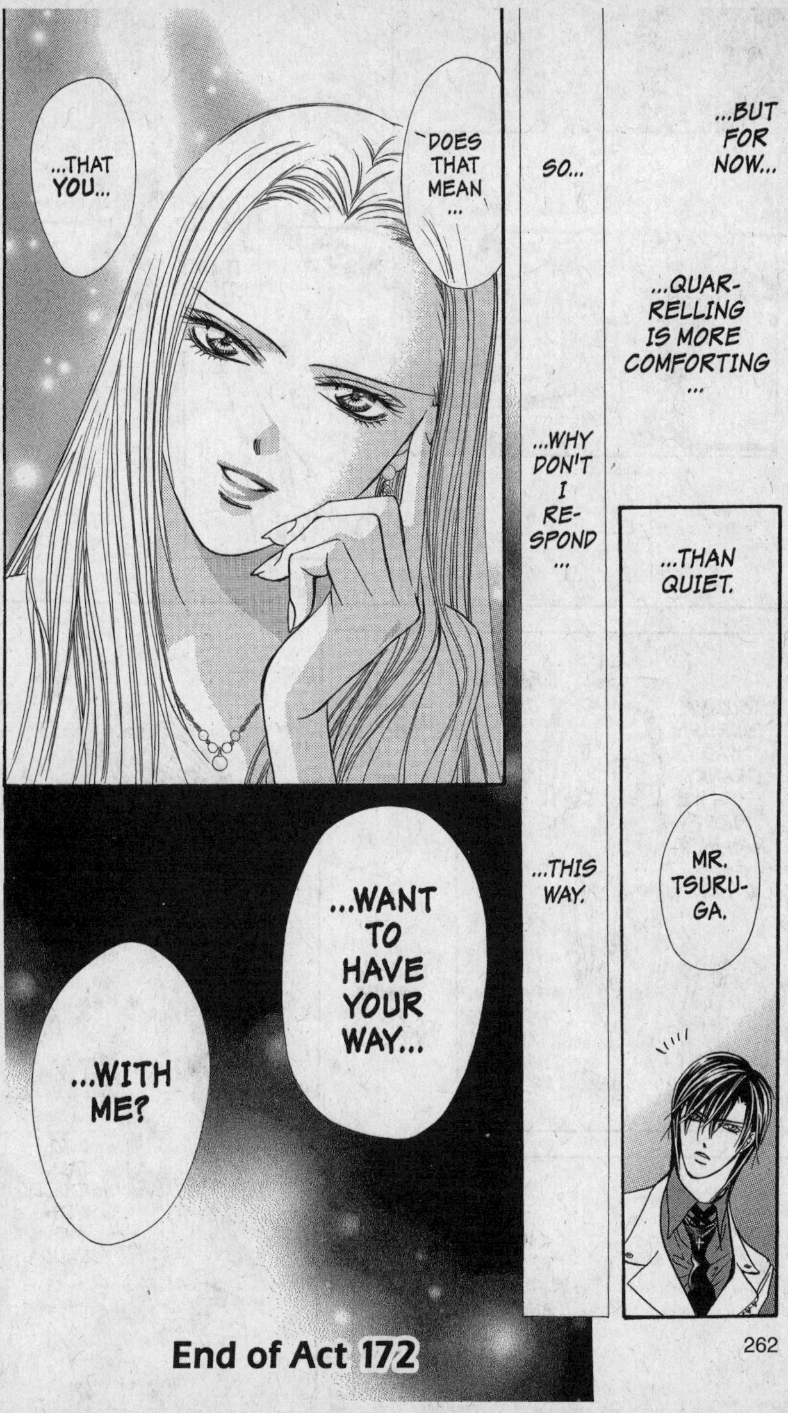
...BUT FOR NOW...
...QUARRELLING IS MORE COMFORTING...
...THAN QUIET.
MR. TSURUGA.
SO...
...WHY DON'T I RESPOND...
...THIS WAY.
DOES THAT MEAN...
...THAT YOU...
...WANT TO HAVE YOUR WAY...
...WITH ME?

End of Act 172

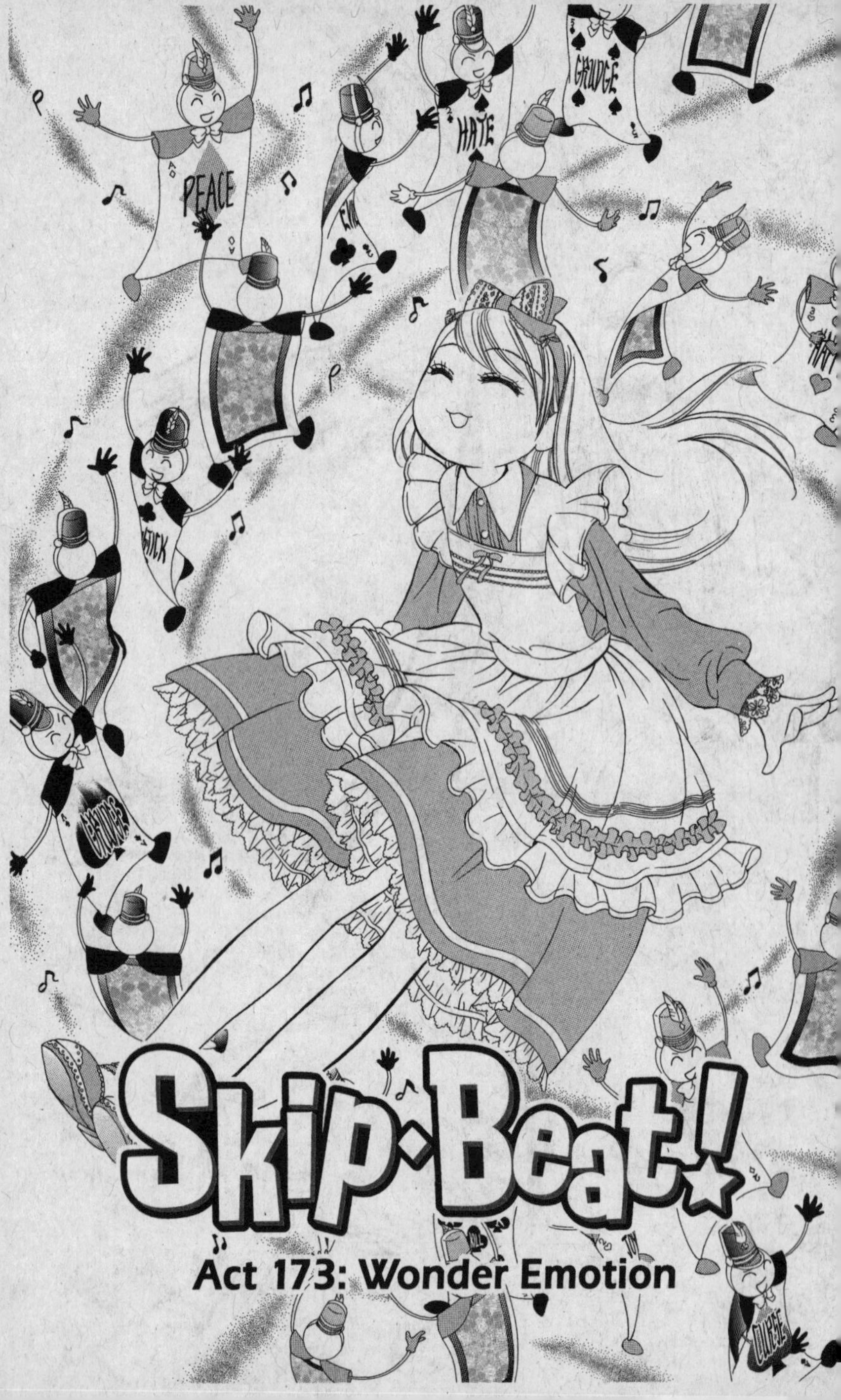
PEACE
HATE
GRUDGE
Skip·Beat!
Act 173: Wonder Emotion

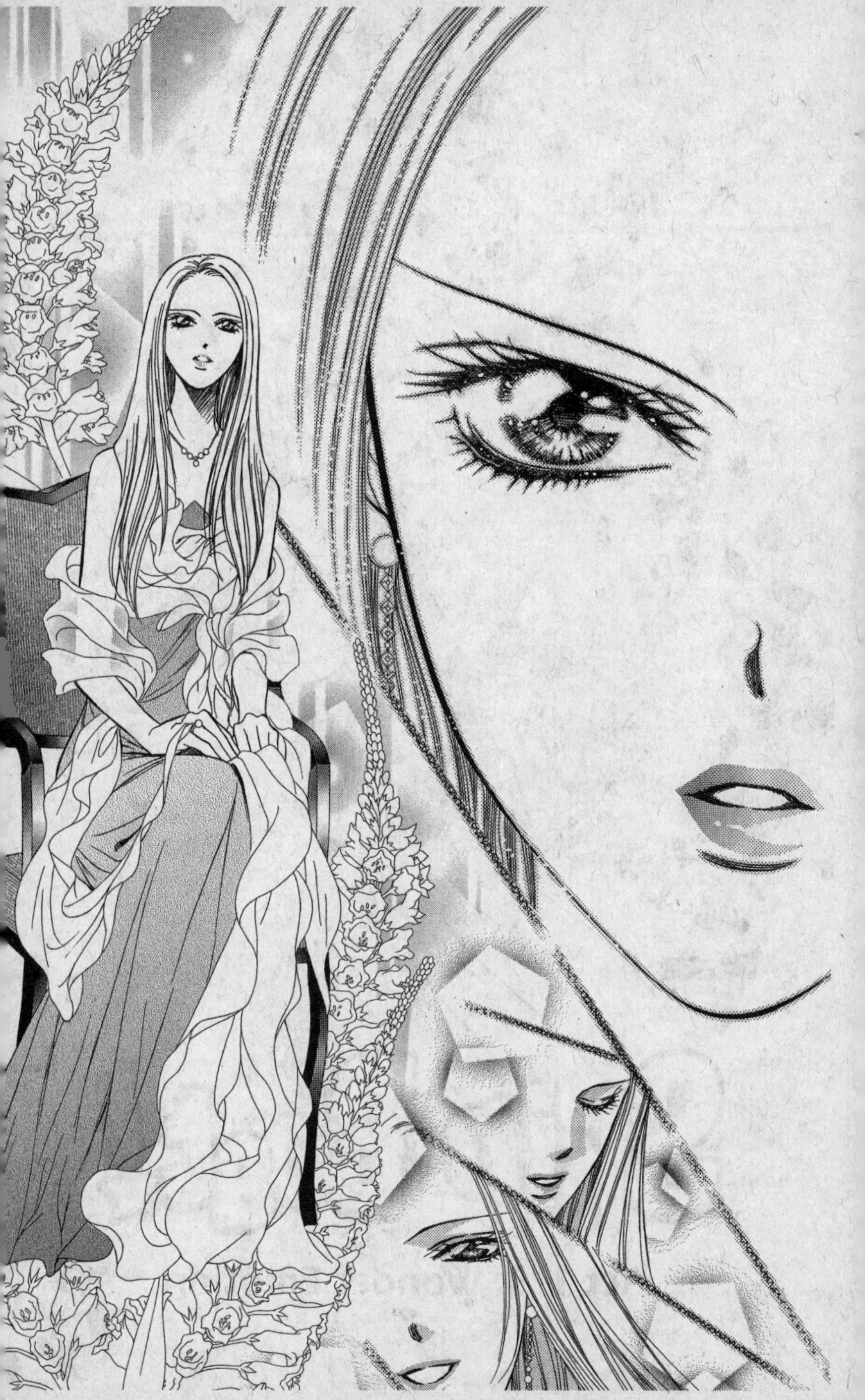

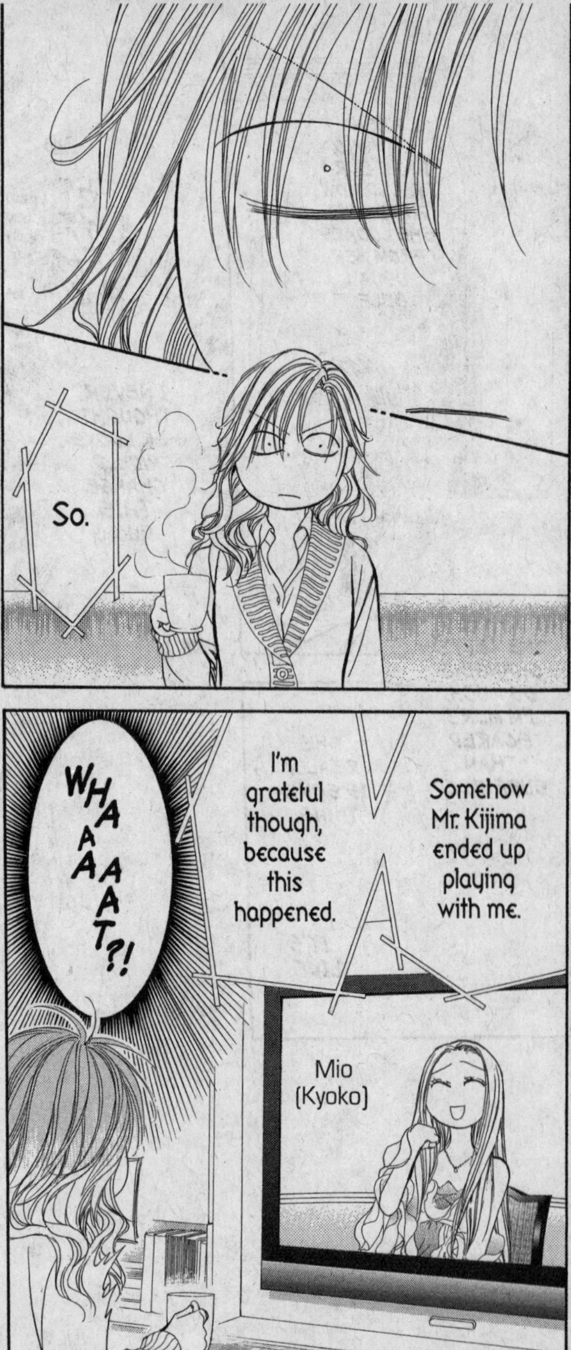
So.
Somehow Mr. Kijima ended up playing with me.
I'm grateful though, because this happened.
WHAAAAAT?!
Mio (Kyoko)

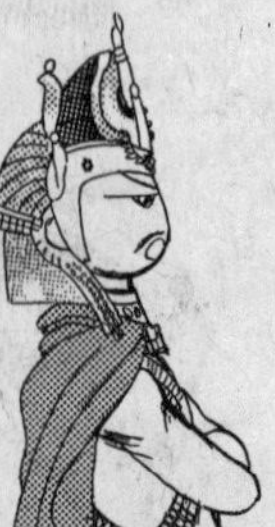

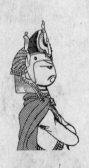

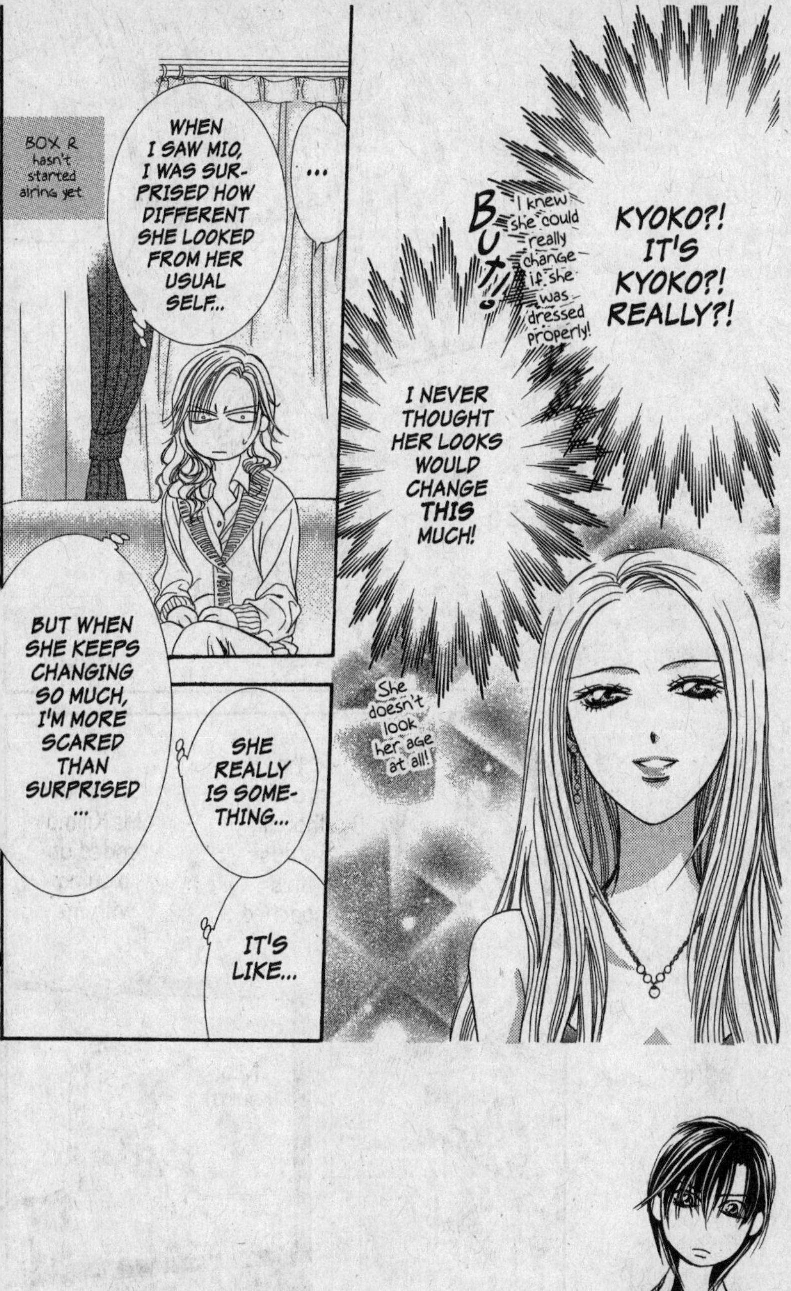
KYOKO?! IT'S KYOKO?! REALLY?!
BUT!
I knew she could really change if she was dressed properly!
I NEVER THOUGHT HER LOOKS WOULD CHANGE THIS MUCH!
She doesn't look her age at all!
...
WHEN I SAW MIO, I WAS SURPRISED HOW DIFFERENT SHE LOOKED FROM HER USUAL SELF...
BOX R hasn't started airing yet
BUT WHEN SHE KEEPS CHANGING SO MUCH, I'M MORE SCARED THAN SURPRISED...
SHE REALLY IS SOMETHING...
IT'S LIKE...

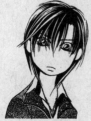

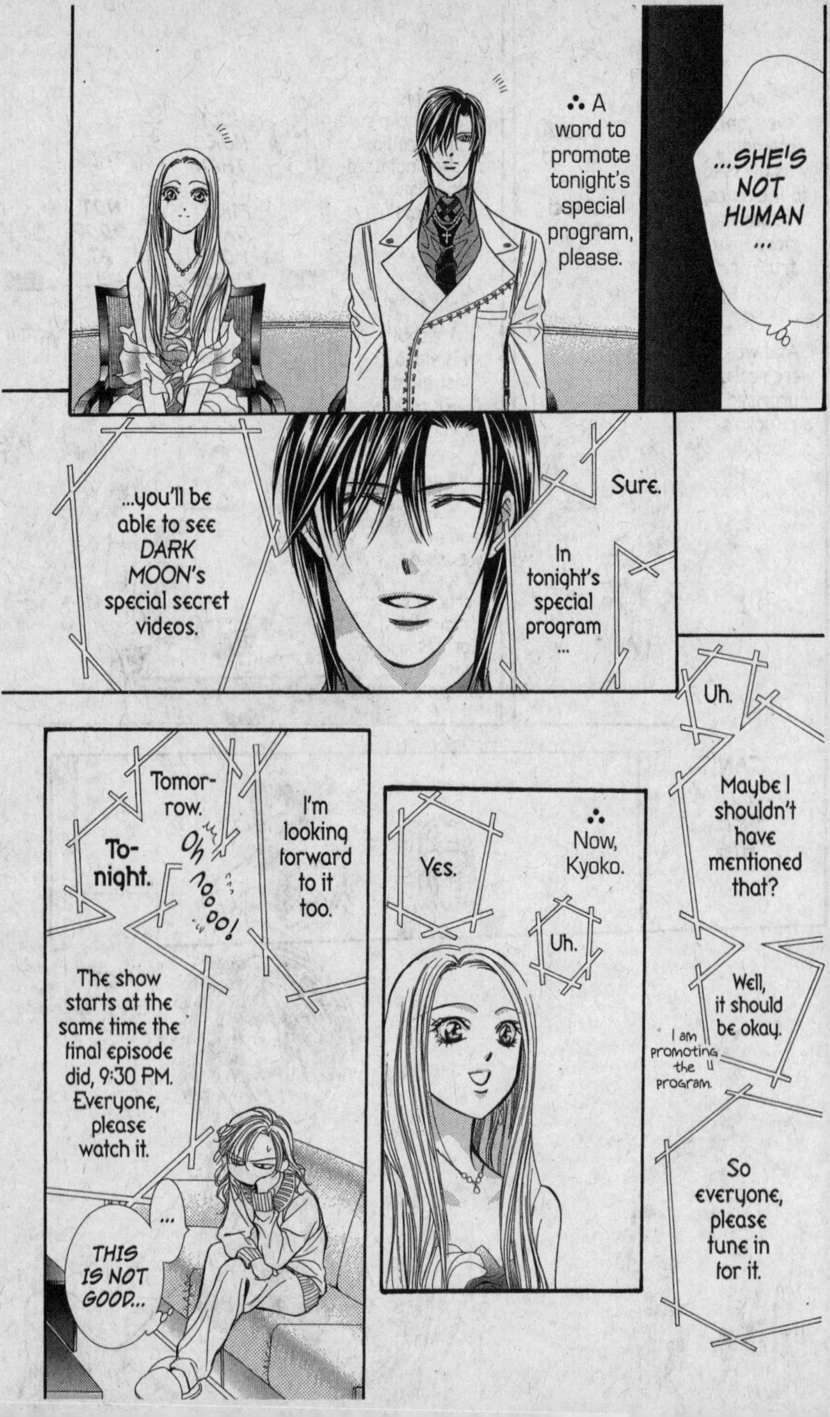
...SHE'S NOT HUMAN...
A word to promote tonight's special program, please.
Sure.
In tonight's special program...
...you'll be able to see DARK MOON's special secret videos.
Uh.
Maybe I shouldn't have mentioned that?
Well, it should be okay.
I am promoting the program.
So everyone, please tune in for it.
Now, Kyoko.
Yes.
Uh.
I'm looking forward to it too.
Tomorrow.
To-night.
Oh nooo!
The show starts at the same time the final episode did, 9:30 PM. Everyone, please watch it.
...
THIS IS NOT GOOD...

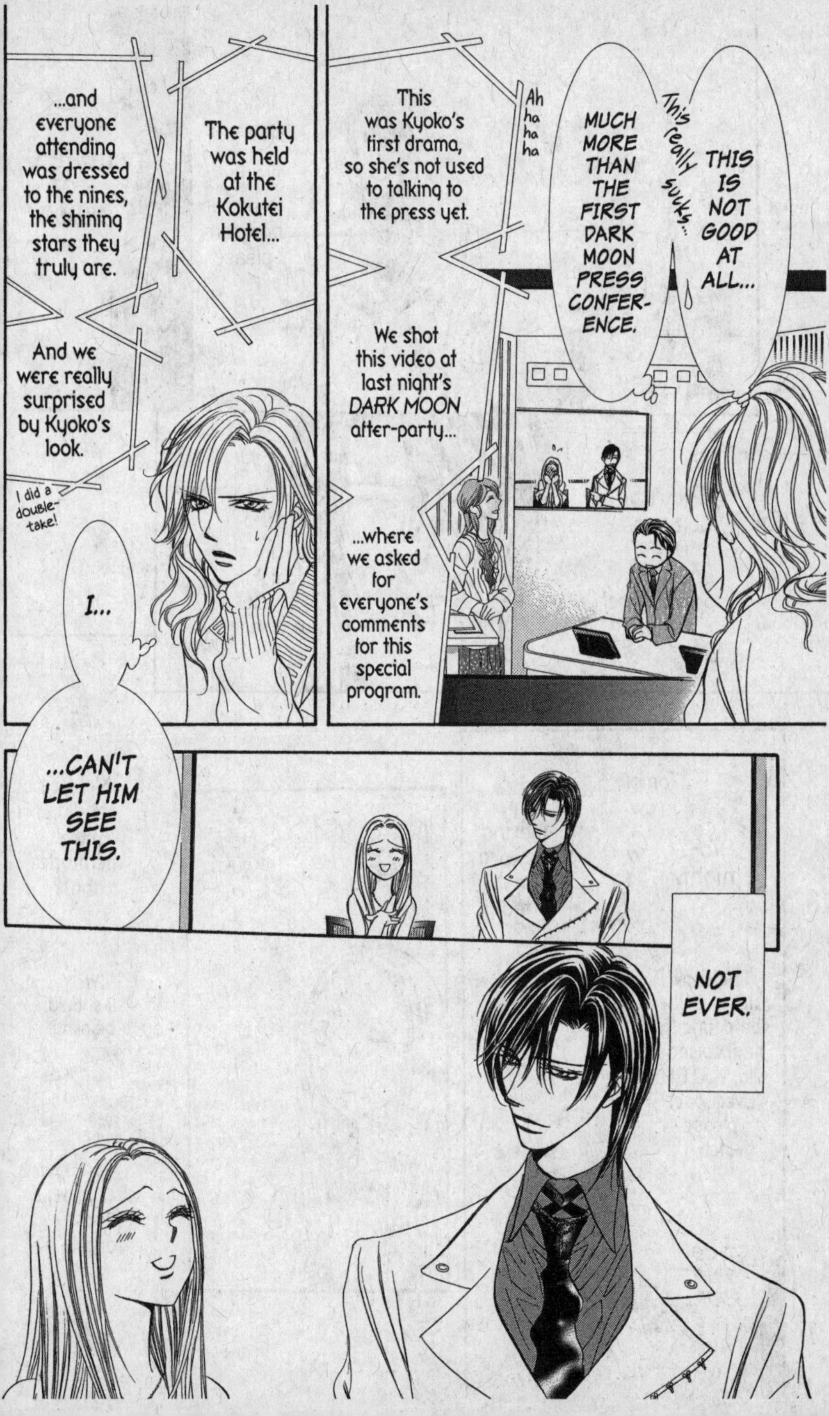
THIS IS NOT GOOD AT ALL...
This really sucks...
MUCH MORE THAN THE FIRST DARK MOON PRESS CONFERENCE.
Ah ha ha ha
This was Kyoko's first drama, so she's not used to talking to the press yet.
We shot this video at last night's *DARK MOON* after-party...
...where we asked for everyone's comments for this special program.
The party was held at the Kokutei Hotel...
...and everyone attending was dressed to the nines, the shining stars they truly are.
And we were really surprised by Kyoko's look.
I did a double-take!
I...
...CAN'T LET HIM SEE THIS.
NOT EVER.

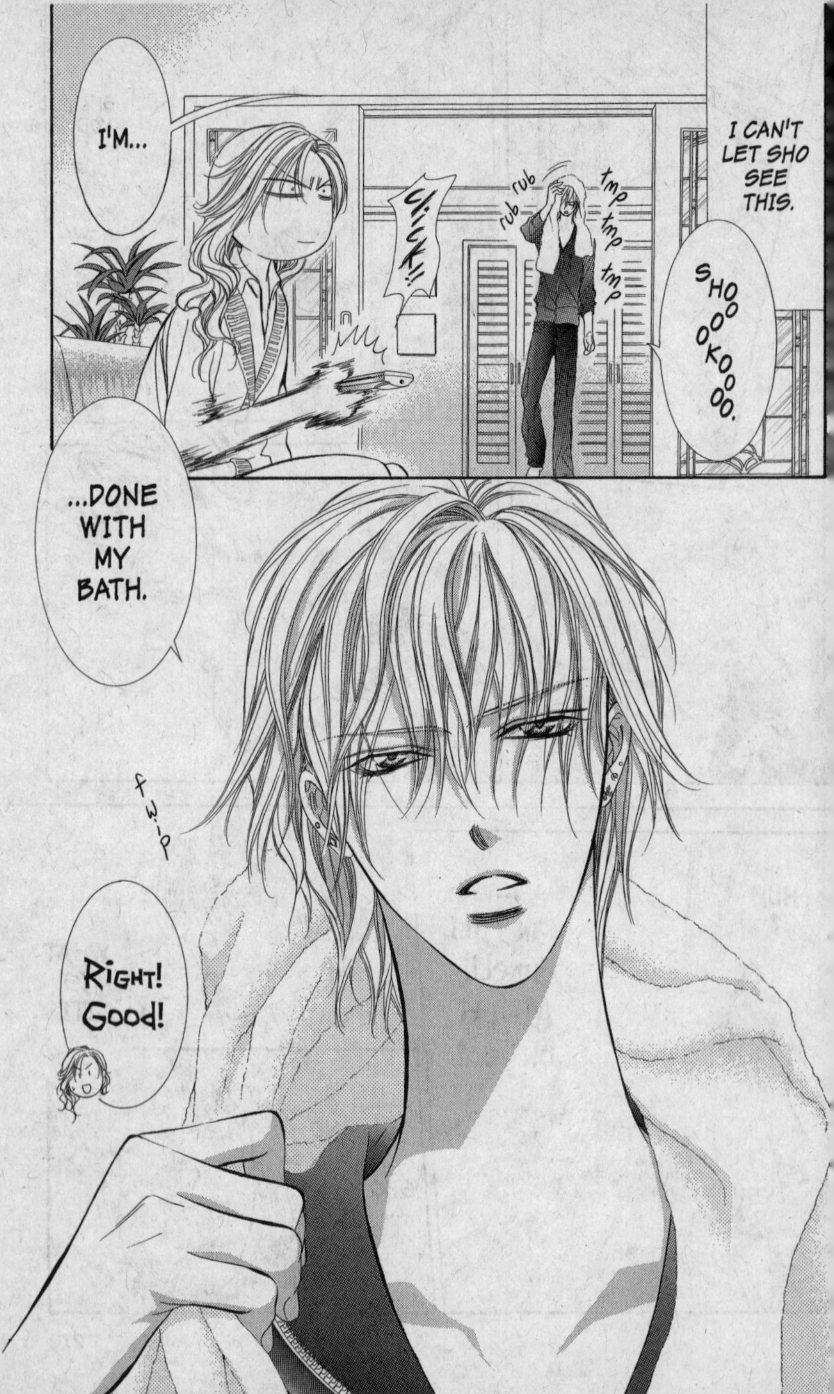
I CAN'T LET SHO SEE THIS.
SHOOOOOKOOOOO.
tmp tmp tmp tmp
rub rub
CLICK!!
I'M...
...DONE WITH MY BATH.
fwip
Right! Good!

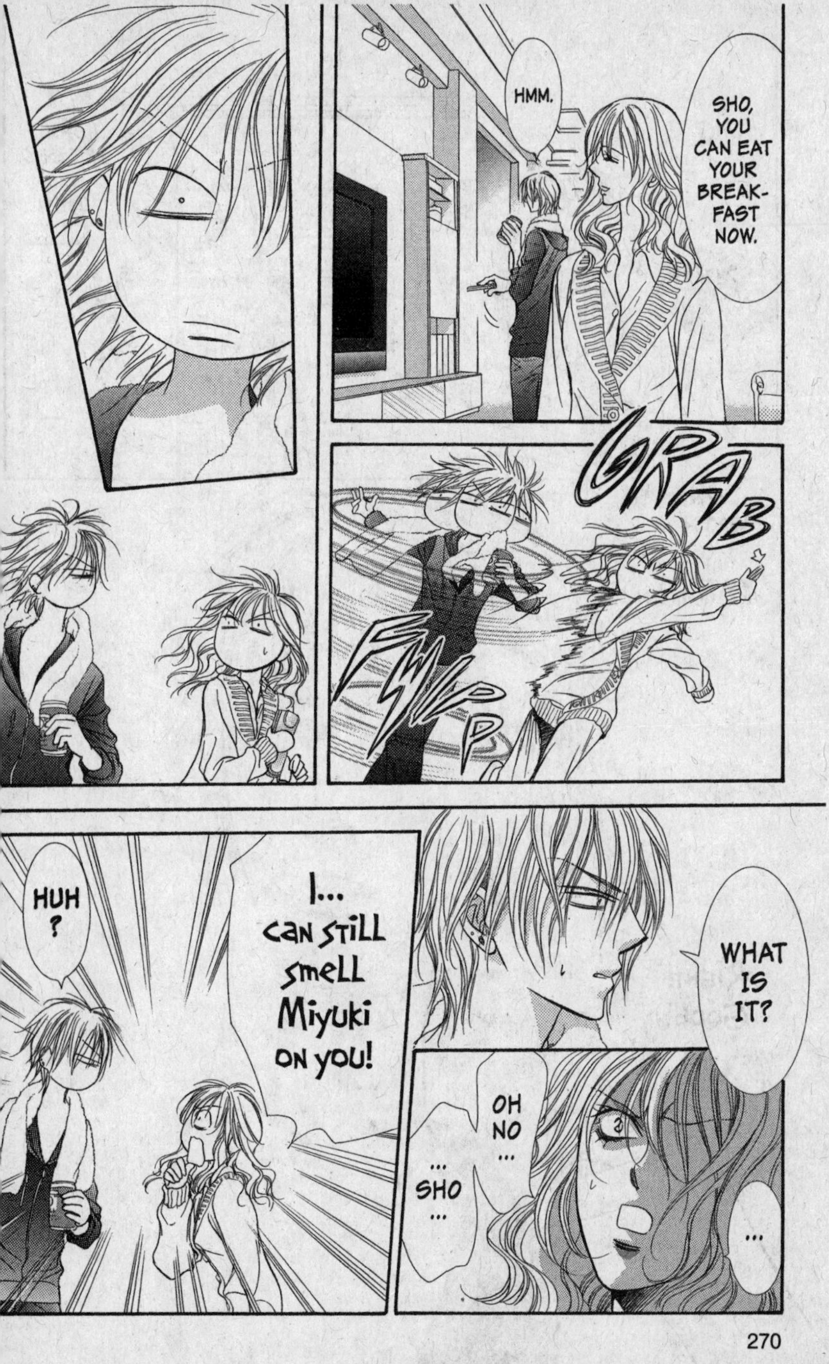
SHO, YOU CAN EAT YOUR BREAK-FAST NOW.
HMM.
GRAB
FWIP
WHAT IS IT?
...
OH NO ...
... SHO ...
I... can still smell Miyuki on you!
HUH?

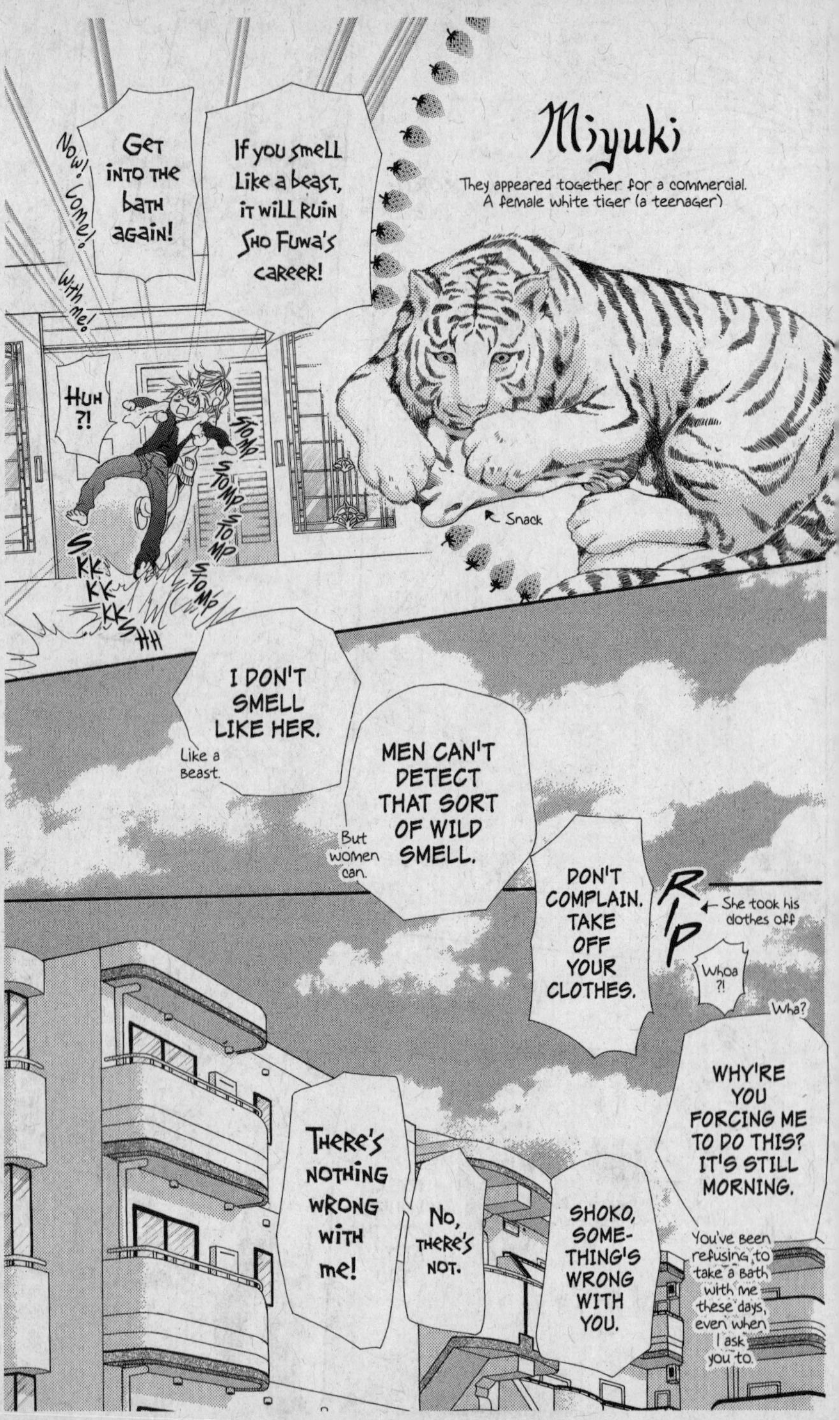
Miyuki
They appeared together for a commercial.
A female white tiger (a teenager)
If you smell like a beast, it will ruin Sho Fuwa's career!
Get into the bath again!
Now! Come! With me!
Snack
Huh?!
STOMP STOMP STOMP STOMP
SKKKKKKSHH
I DON'T SMELL LIKE HER.
Like a beast.
MEN CAN'T DETECT THAT SORT OF WILD SMELL.
But women can.
RIP
She took his clothes off
DON'T COMPLAIN. TAKE OFF YOUR CLOTHES.
Whoa?!
Wha?
WHY'RE YOU FORCING ME TO DO THIS? IT'S STILL MORNING.
You've been refusing to take a bath with me these days, even when I ask you to.
SHOKO, SOMETHING'S WRONG WITH YOU.
No, there's not.
There's nothing wrong with me!

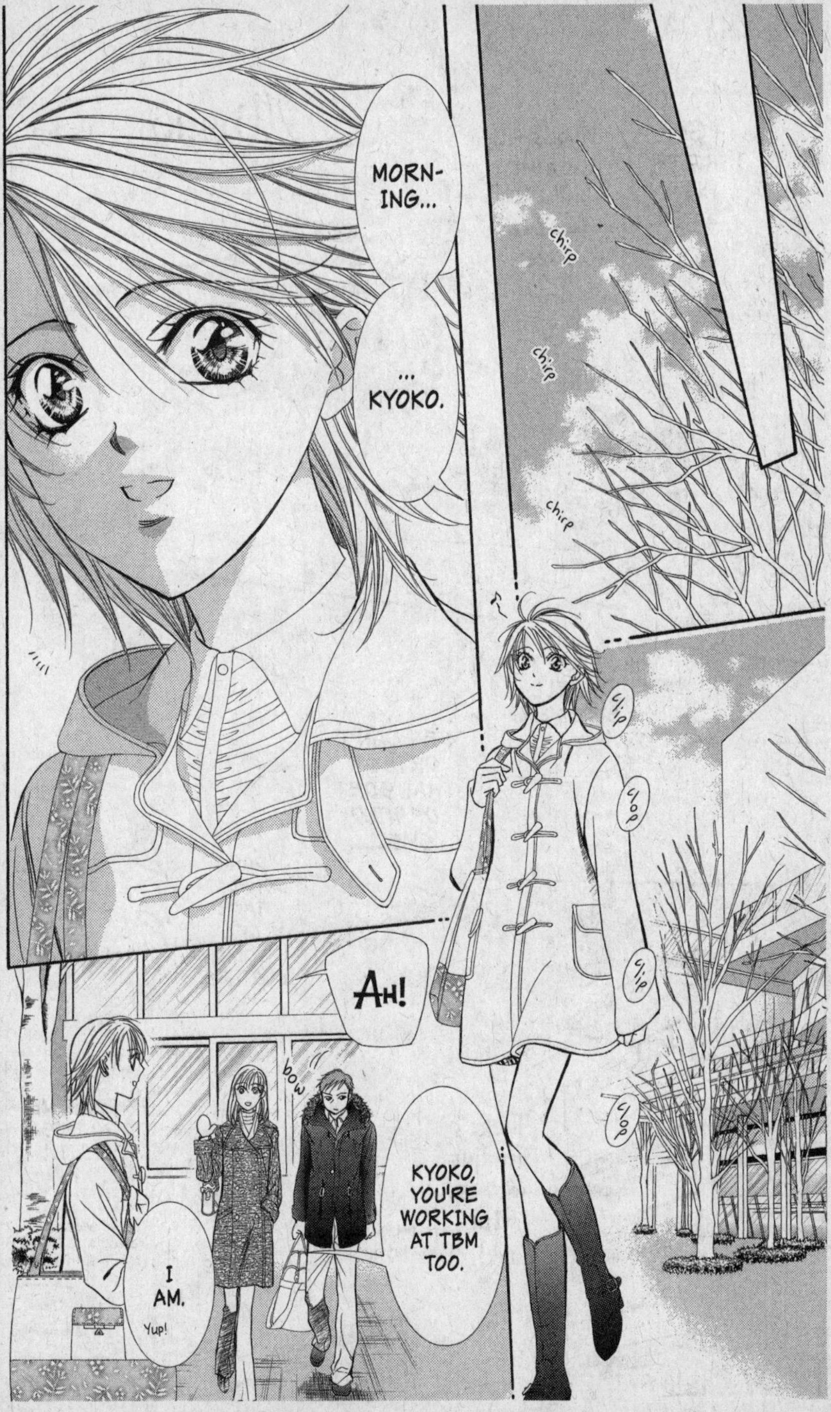
chirp
chirp
chirp
MORNING...
...KYOKO.
clip
clop
clip
clop
AH!
KYOKO, YOU'RE WORKING AT TBM TOO.
I AM.
Yup!
bow

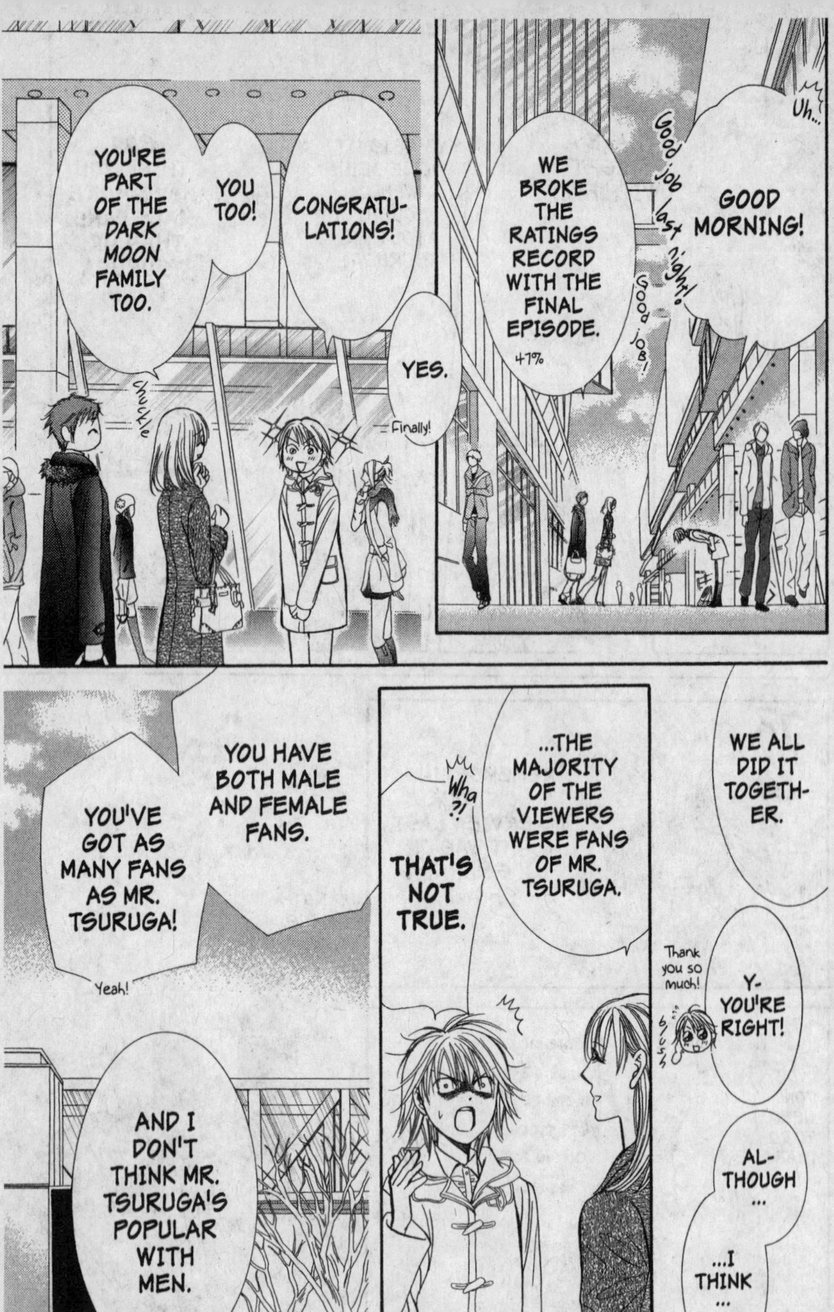
Uh...
GOOD MORNING!
Good job last night!
Good job!
WE BROKE THE RATINGS RECORD WITH THE FINAL EPISODE.
47%
YES.
Finally!
CONGRATULATIONS!
YOU TOO!
YOU'RE PART OF THE DARK MOON FAMILY TOO.
chuckle
WE ALL DID IT TOGETHER.
Y-YOU'RE RIGHT!
Thank you so much!
blush
ALTHOUGH...
...I THINK...
...THE MAJORITY OF THE VIEWERS WERE FANS OF MR. TSURUGA.
Wha?!
THAT'S NOT TRUE.
YOU HAVE BOTH MALE AND FEMALE FANS.
YOU'VE GOT AS MANY FANS AS MR. TSURUGA!
Yeah!
AND I DON'T THINK MR. TSURUGA'S POPULAR WITH MEN.

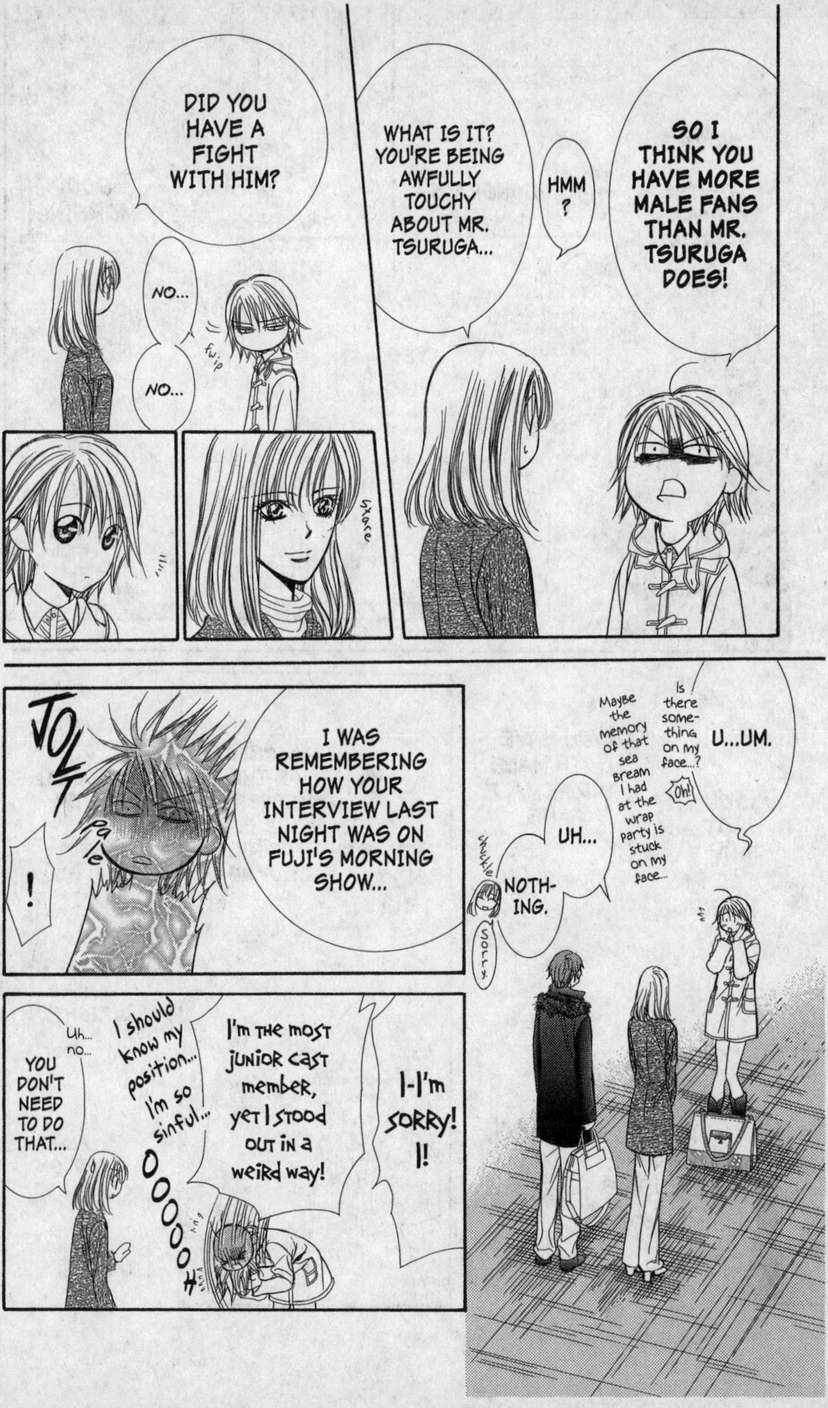
SO I THINK YOU HAVE MORE MALE FANS THAN MR. TSURUGA DOES!
HMM?
WHAT IS IT? YOU'RE BEING AWFULLY TOUCHY ABOUT MR. TSURUGA...
DID YOU HAVE A FIGHT WITH HIM?
NO...
NO...
fwip
stare
U...UM.
Is there something on my face...?
Oh!
Maybe the memory of that sea Bream I had at the wrap party is stuck on my face...
UH...
NOTHING.
chuckle
Sorry.
I WAS REMEMBERING HOW YOUR INTERVIEW LAST NIGHT WAS ON FUJI'S MORNING SHOW...
JOLT
pale
!
I-I'm SORRY!!
I'm THE most junior cast member, yet I stood out in a weird way!
I should know my position... I'm so sinful...
OOOOOH
Uh... no...
YOU DON'T NEED TO DO THAT...

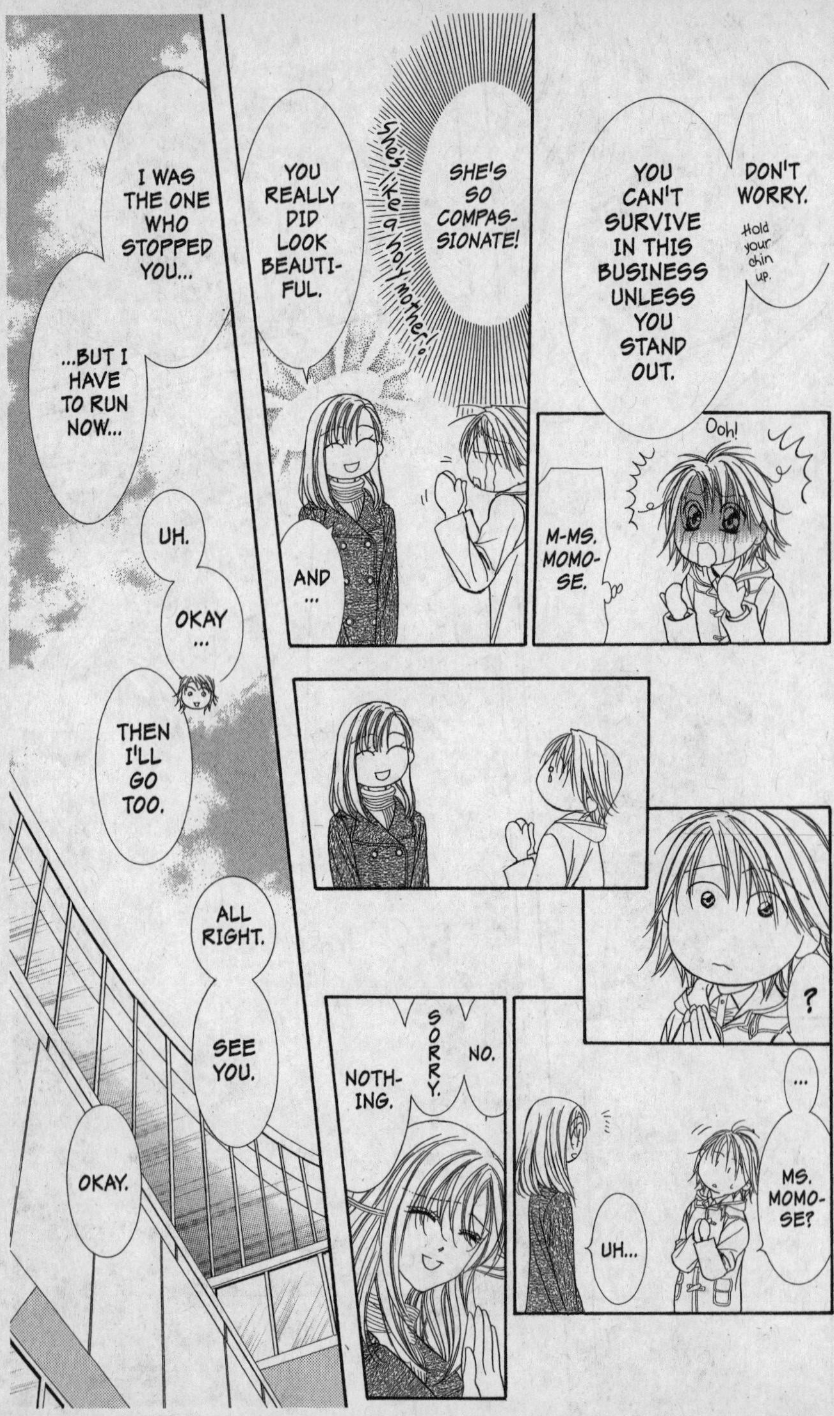

DON'T WORRY.
YOU CAN'T SURVIVE IN THIS BUSINESS UNLESS YOU STAND OUT.
Hold your chin up.
Ooh!
M-MS. MOMOSE.
SHE'S SO COMPASSIONATE!
She's like a holy mother!
YOU REALLY DID LOOK BEAUTIFUL.
AND...
?
...
MS. MOMOSE?
UH...
NO.
SORRY.
NOTHING.
I WAS THE ONE WHO STOPPED YOU...
...BUT I HAVE TO RUN NOW...
UH.
OKAY...
THEN I'LL GO TOO.
ALL RIGHT.
SEE YOU.
OKAY.

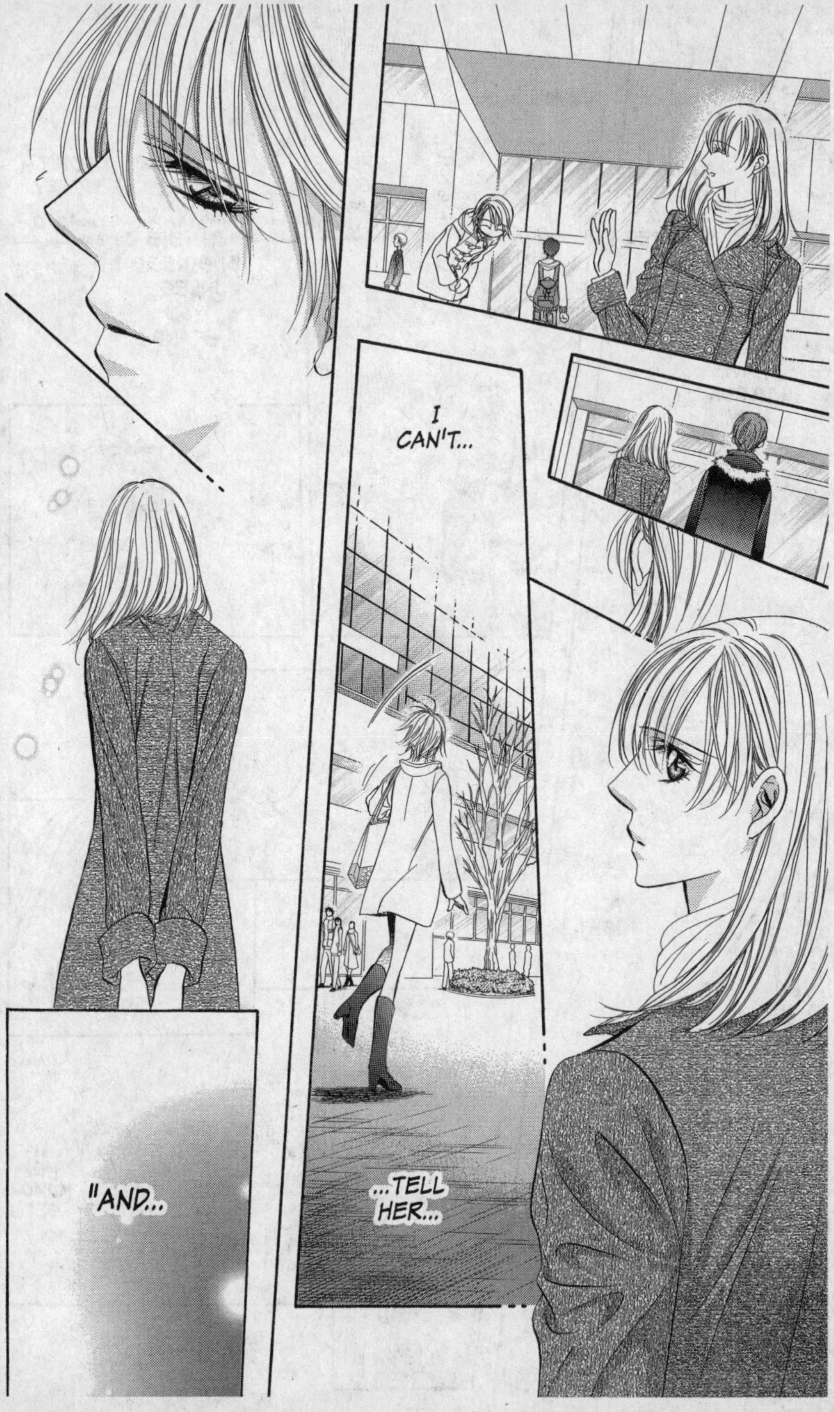
I CAN'T...
...TELL HER...
"AND...

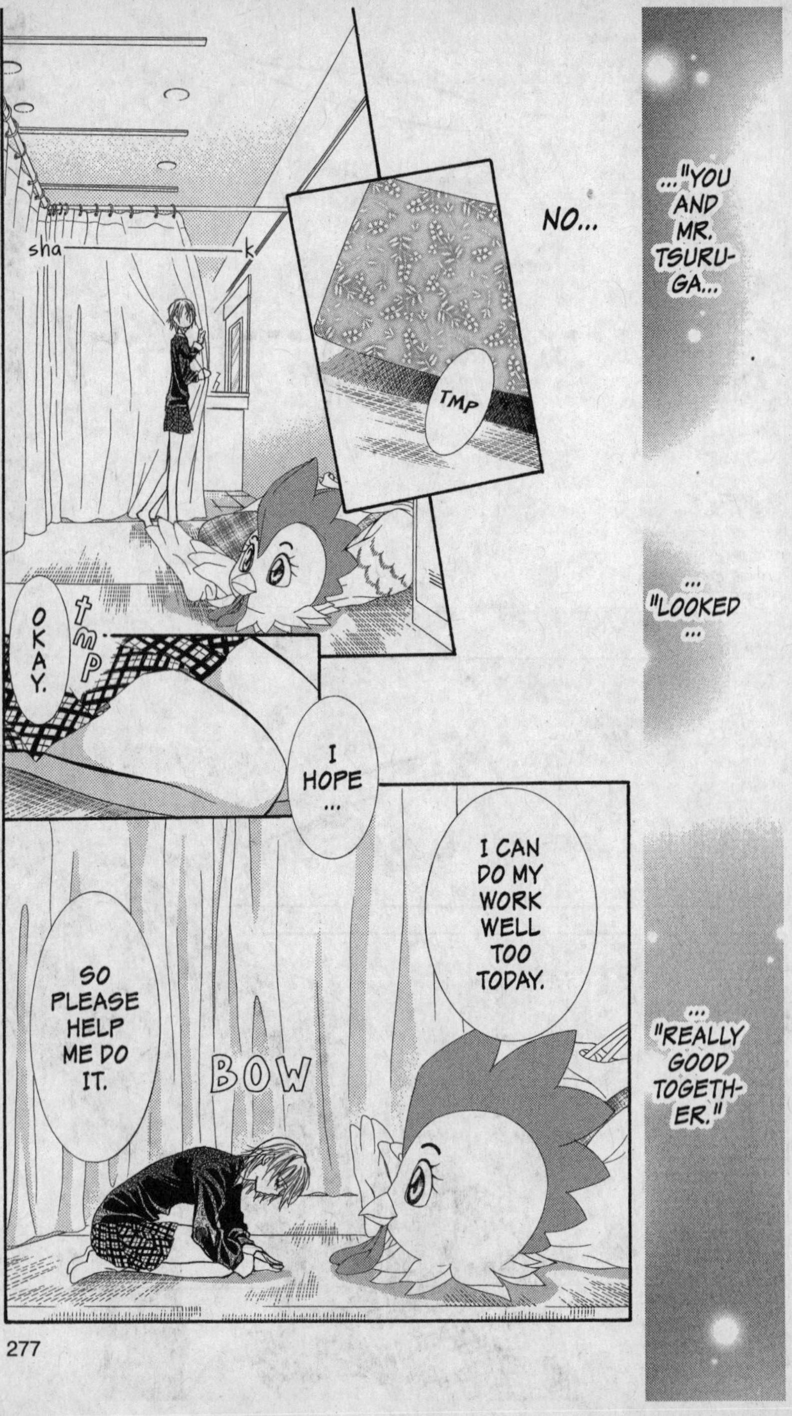

..."YOU AND MR. TSURUGA...
... "LOOKED ...
... "REALLY GOOD TOGETHER."
NO...
TMP
sha—k
OKAY.
tmp
I HOPE ...
I CAN DO MY WORK WELL TOO TODAY.
SO PLEASE HELP ME DO IT.
BOW

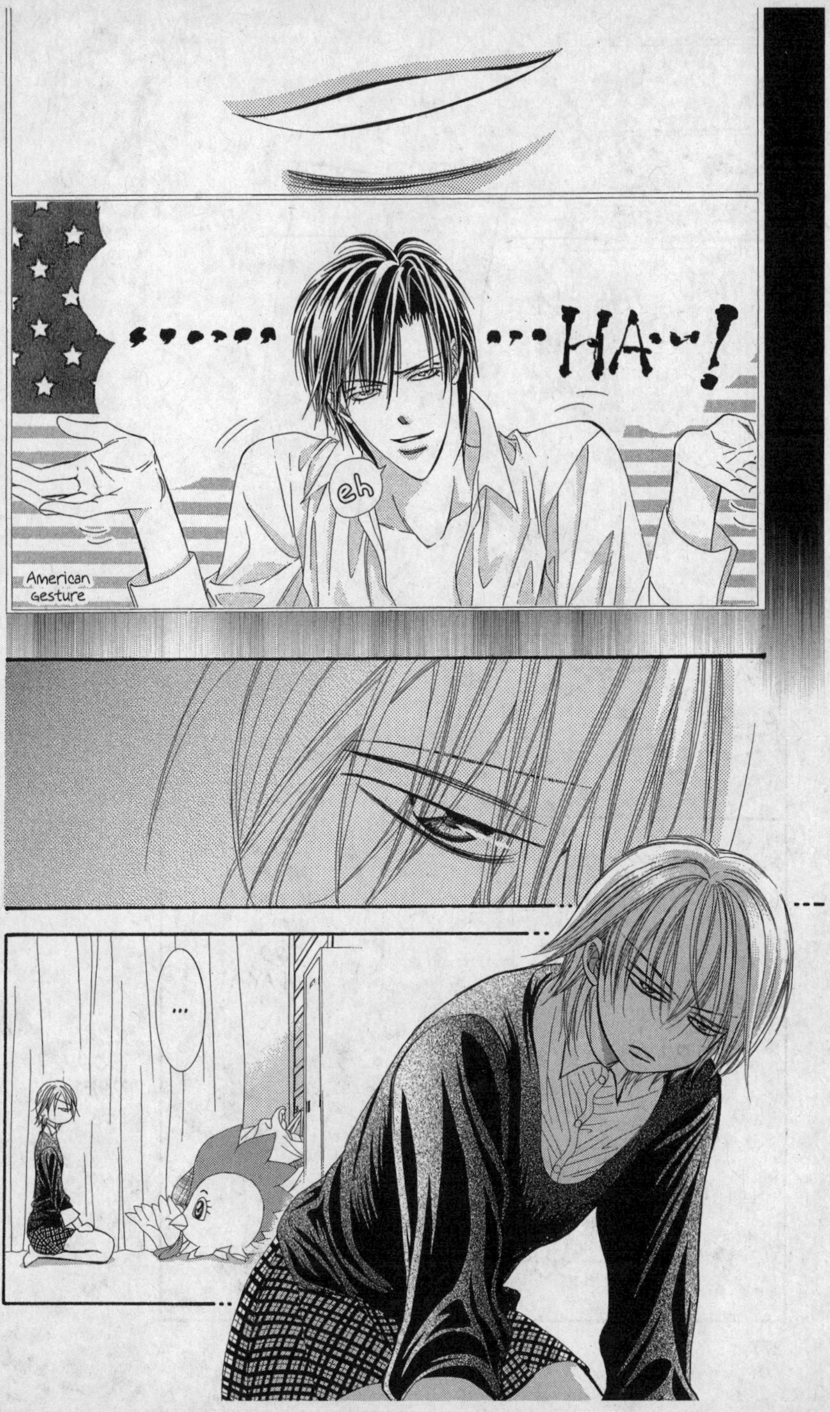

"..."...HA--!
eh
American Gesture
...

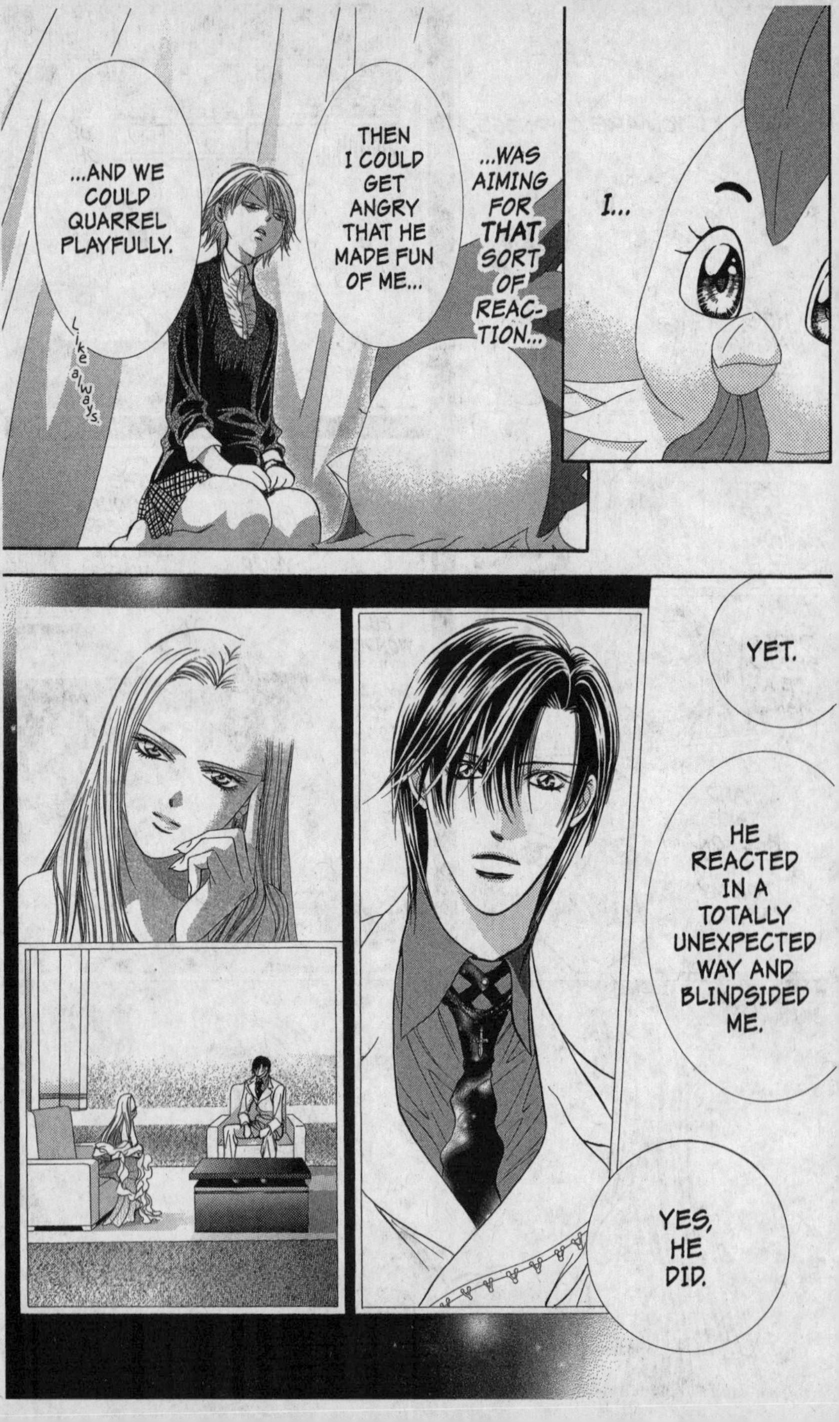
I...
...WAS AIMING FOR THAT SORT OF REACTION...
THEN I COULD GET ANGRY THAT HE MADE FUN OF ME...
...AND WE COULD QUARREL PLAYFULLY.
Like always.
YET.
HE REACTED IN A TOTALLY UNEXPECTED WAY AND BLINDSIDED ME.
YES, HE DID.

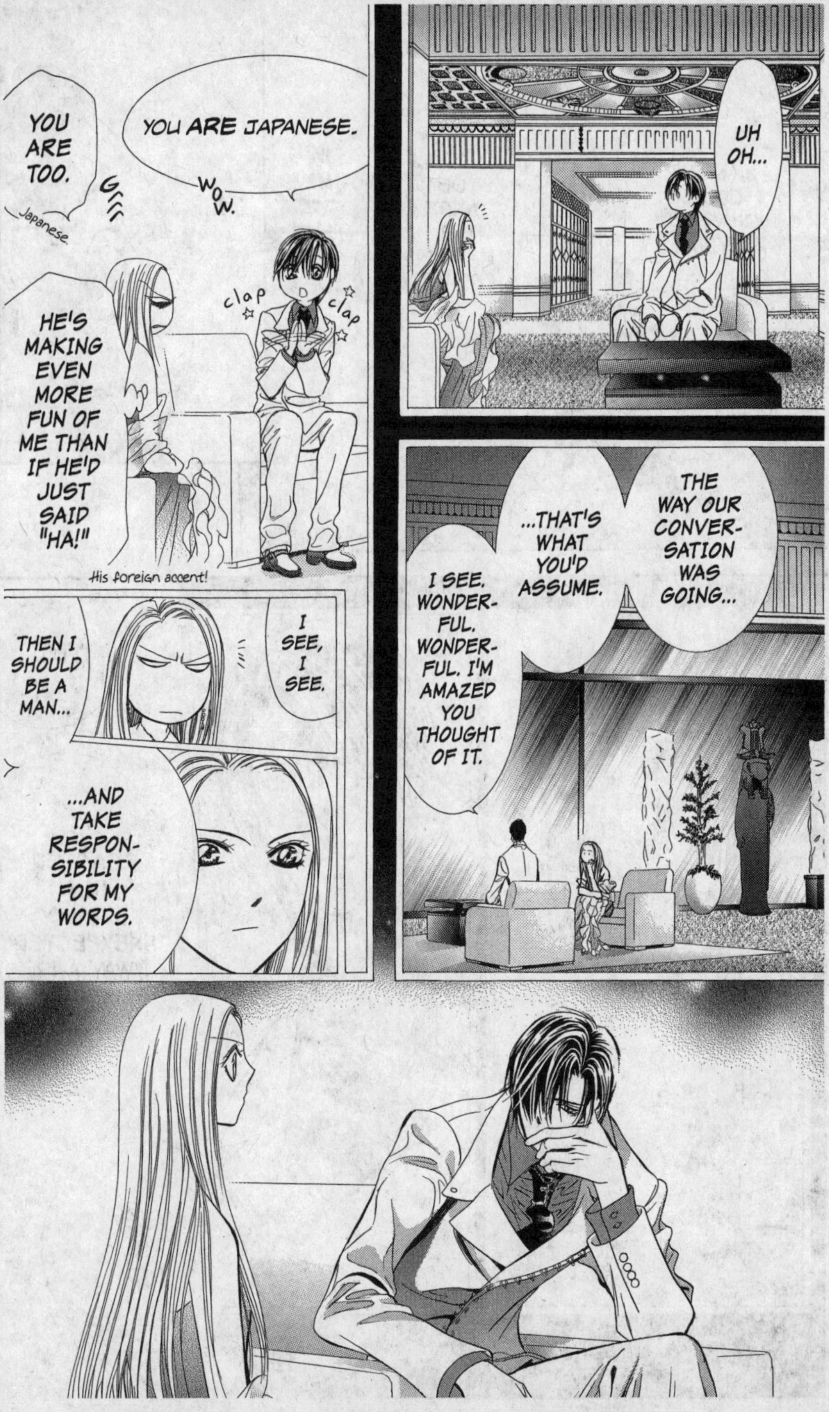
UH OH...
YOU ARE JAPANESE.
WOW.
CLAP CLAP
YOU ARE TOO.
Japanese.
GRRR
HE'S MAKING EVEN MORE FUN OF ME THAN IF HE'D JUST SAID "HA!"
His foreign accent!
THE WAY OUR CONVERSATION WAS GOING...
...THAT'S WHAT YOU'D ASSUME.
I SEE. WONDERFUL. WONDERFUL. I'M AMAZED YOU THOUGHT OF IT.
I SEE, I SEE.
THEN I SHOULD BE A MAN...
...AND TAKE RESPONSIBILITY FOR MY WORDS.

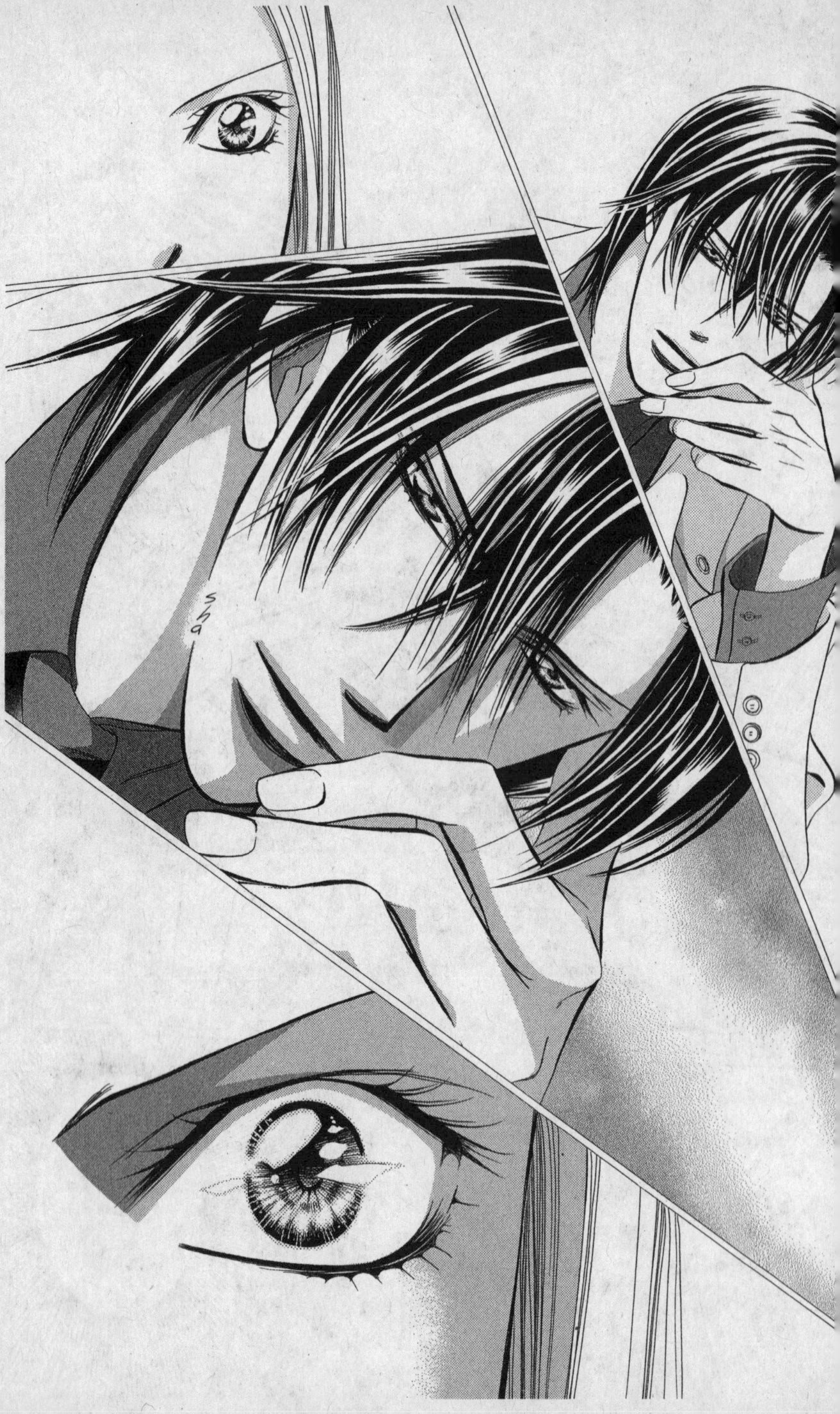
sha

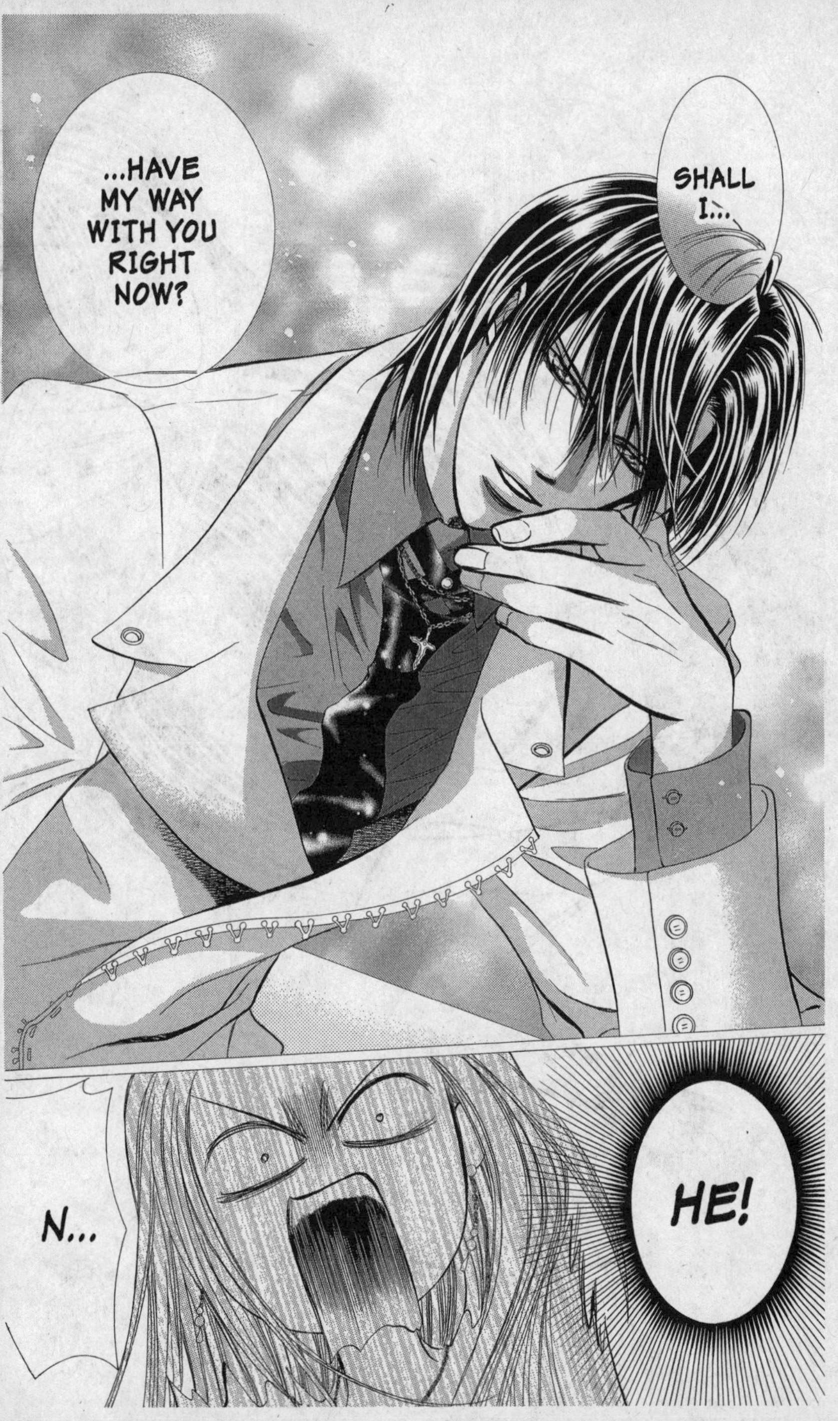
SHALL I...
...HAVE MY WAY WITH YOU RIGHT NOW?
HE!
N...

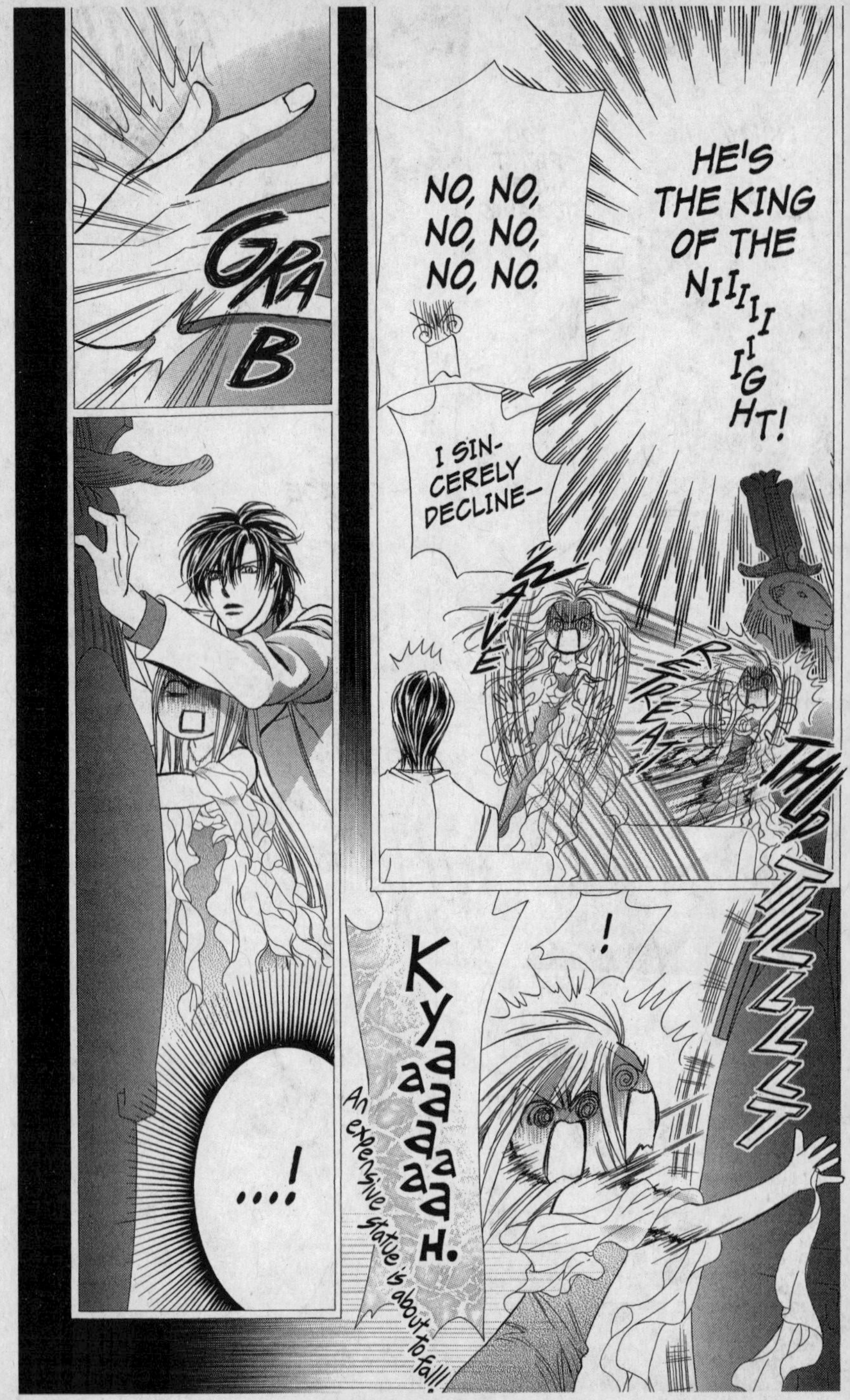
HE'S THE KING OF THE NIIIIIIGHT!
NO, NO, NO, NO, NO, NO.
I SIN-CERELY DECLINE-
WAVE
RETREAT
THUD
!
TILLLLT
Kyaaaaaah.
An expensive statue is about to fall!!
GRAB
...!

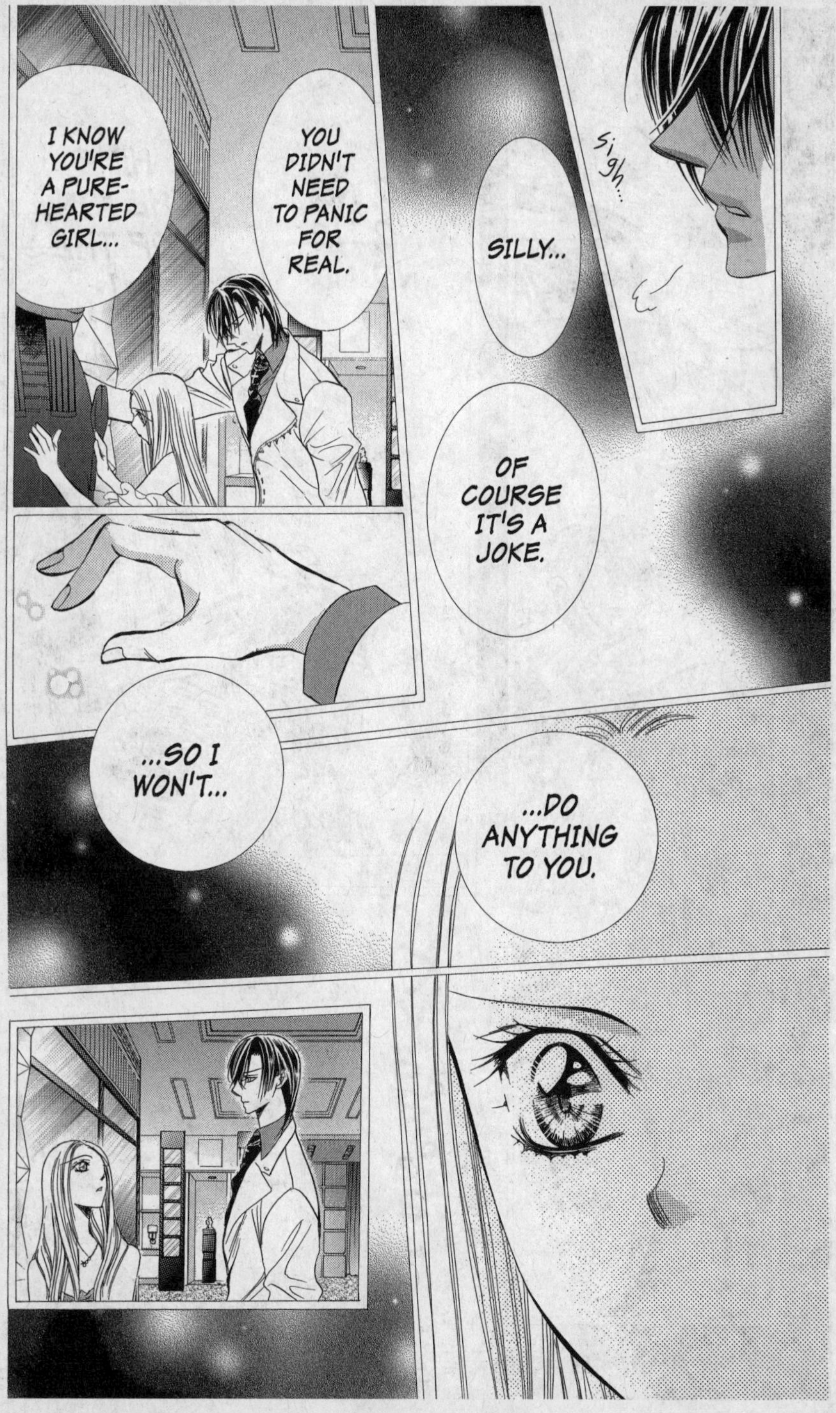
Sigh...
SILLY...
OF COURSE IT'S A JOKE.
YOU DIDN'T NEED TO PANIC FOR REAL.
I KNOW YOU'RE A PURE-HEARTED GIRL...
...SO I WON'T...
...DO ANYTHING TO YOU.

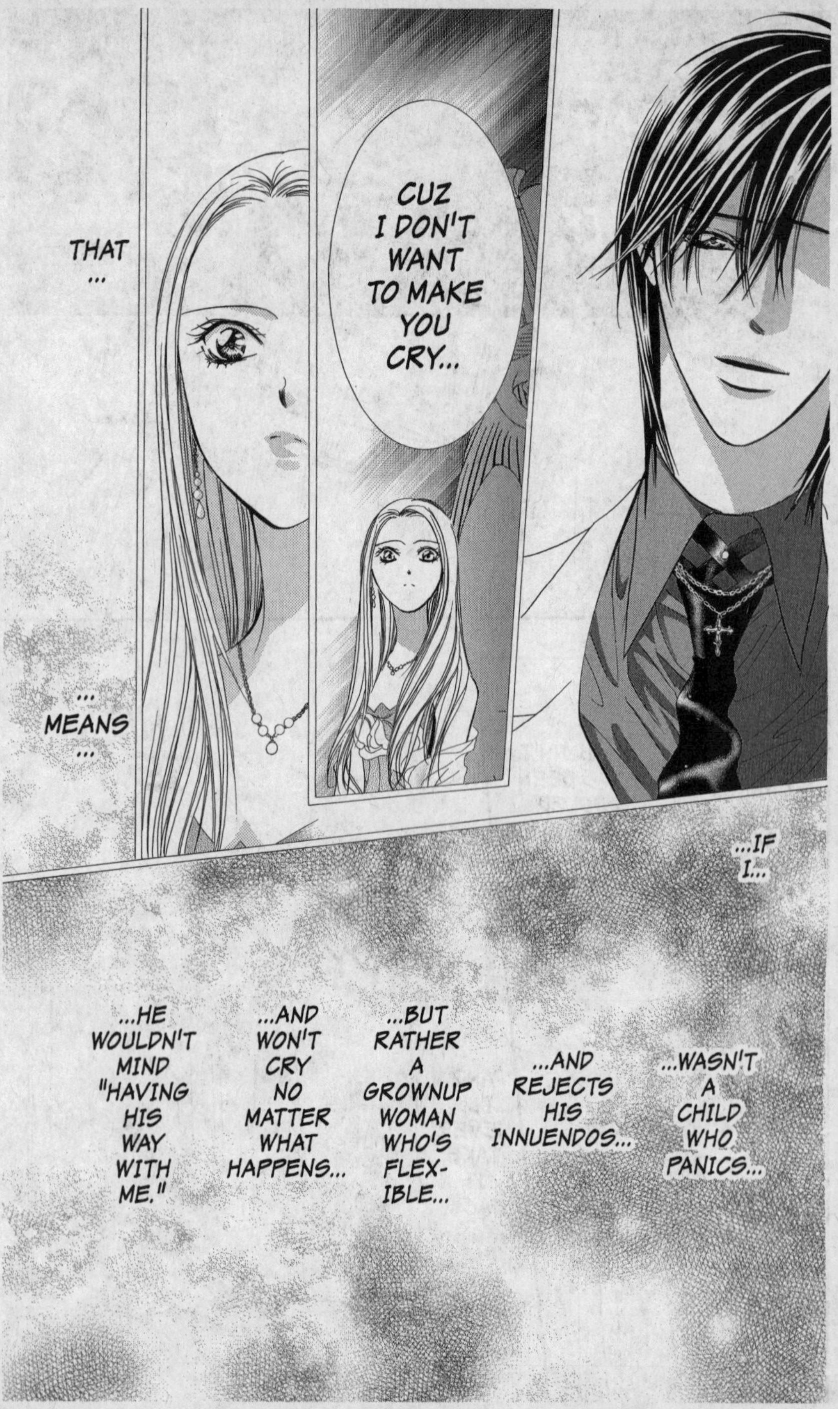
CUZ I DON'T WANT TO MAKE YOU CRY...
THAT ...
... MEANS ...
...IF I...
...WASN'T A CHILD WHO PANICS...
...AND REJECTS HIS INNUENDOS...
...BUT RATHER A GROWNUP WOMAN WHO'S FLEX- IBLE...
...AND WON'T CRY NO MATTER WHAT HAPPENS...
...HE WOULDN'T MIND "HAVING HIS WAY WITH ME."

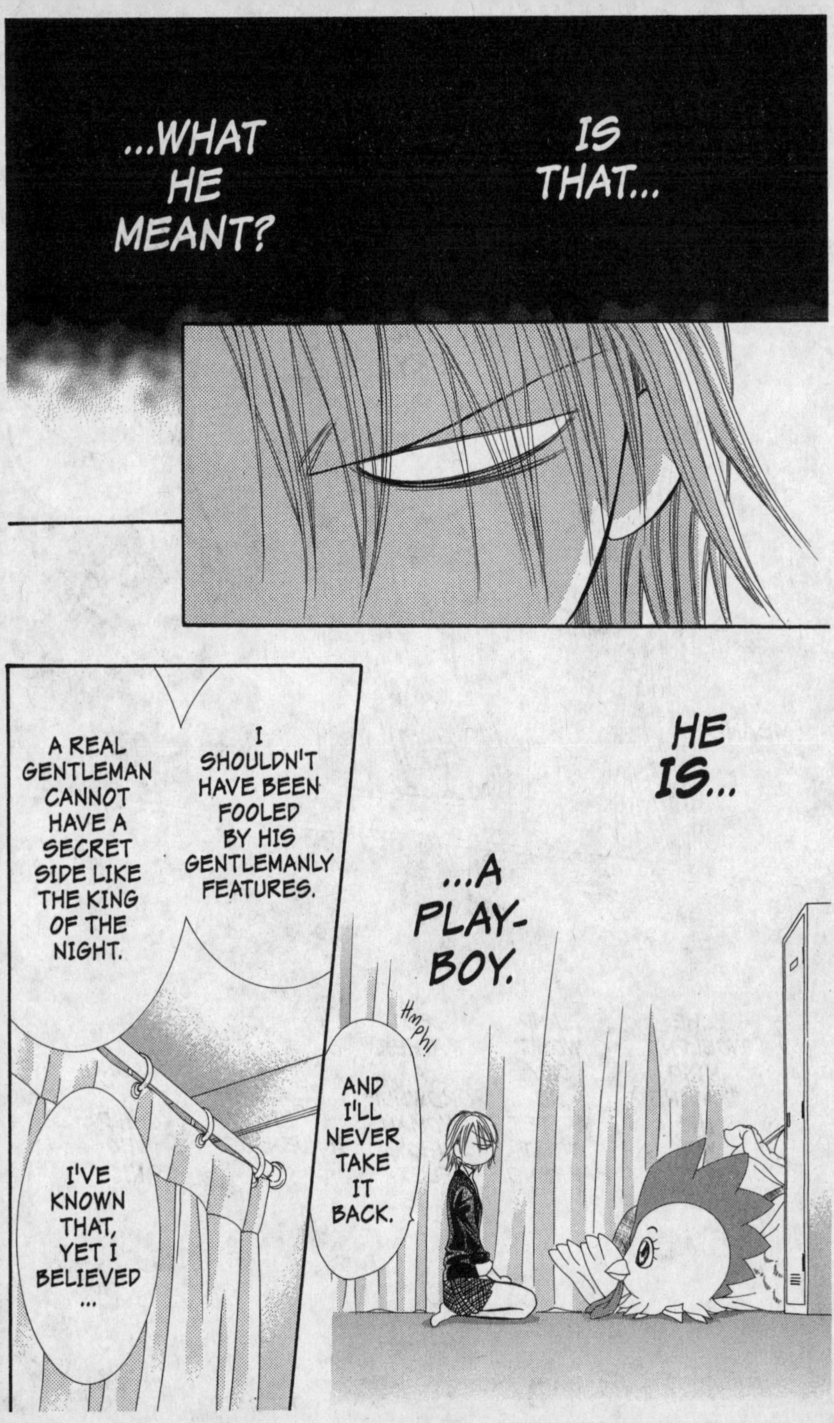
IS THAT...
...WHAT HE MEANT?
HE IS...
...A PLAY-BOY.
Hmph!
AND I'LL NEVER TAKE IT BACK.
I SHOULDN'T HAVE BEEN FOOLED BY HIS GENTLEMANLY FEATURES.
A REAL GENTLEMAN CANNOT HAVE A SECRET SIDE LIKE THE KING OF THE NIGHT.
I'VE KNOWN THAT, YET I BELIEVED ...

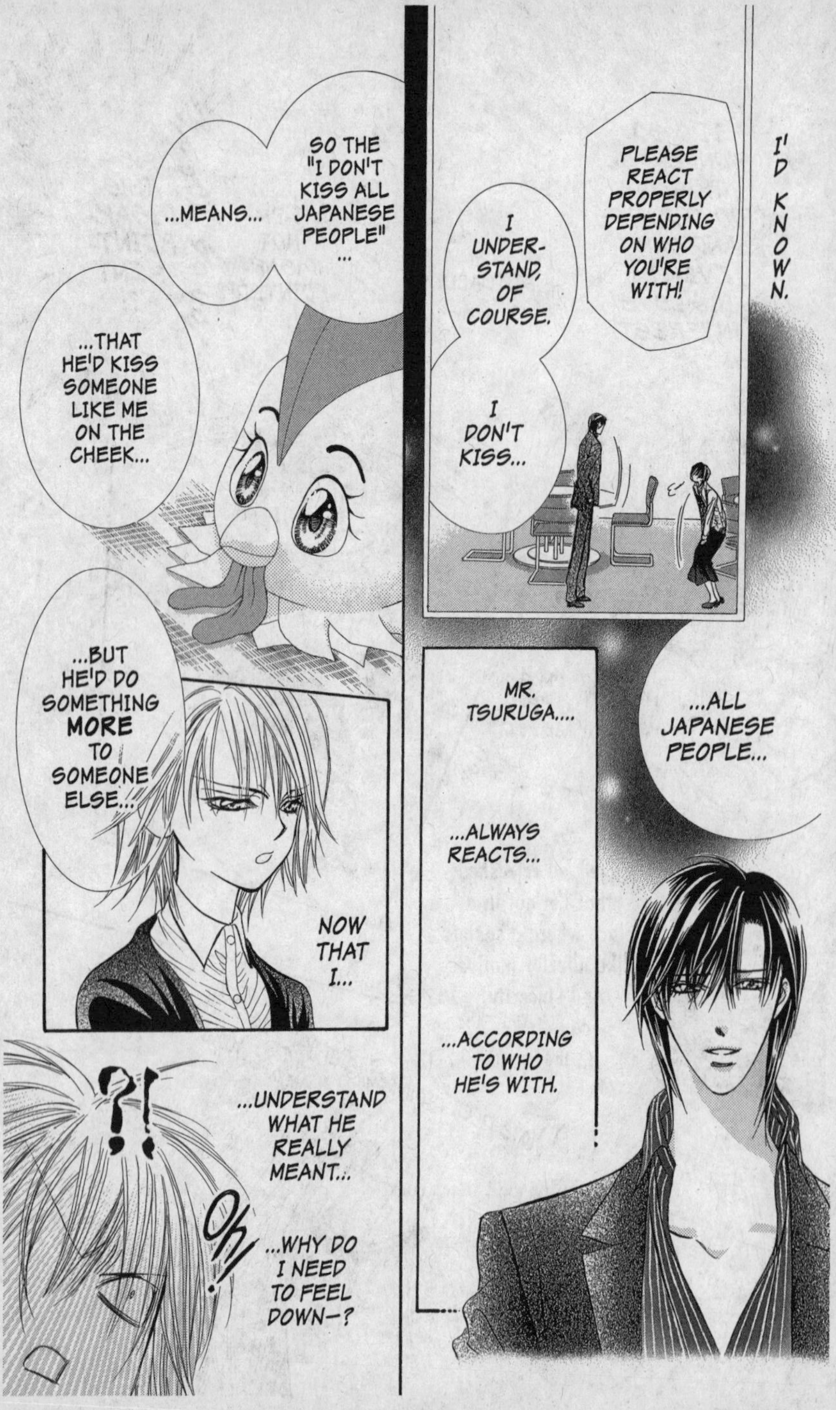
I'D KNOWN.
PLEASE REACT PROPERLY DEPENDING ON WHO YOU'RE WITH!
I UNDERSTAND, OF COURSE.
I DON'T KISS...
...ALL JAPANESE PEOPLE...
MR. TSURUGA....
...ALWAYS REACTS...
...ACCORDING TO WHO HE'S WITH.
SO THE "I DON'T KISS ALL JAPANESE PEOPLE" ...
...MEANS...
...THAT HE'D KISS SOMEONE LIKE ME ON THE CHEEK...
...BUT HE'D DO SOMETHING MORE TO SOMEONE ELSE...
NOW THAT I...
?!
...UNDERSTAND WHAT HE REALLY MEANT...
OH!
...WHY DO I NEED TO FEEL DOWN—?

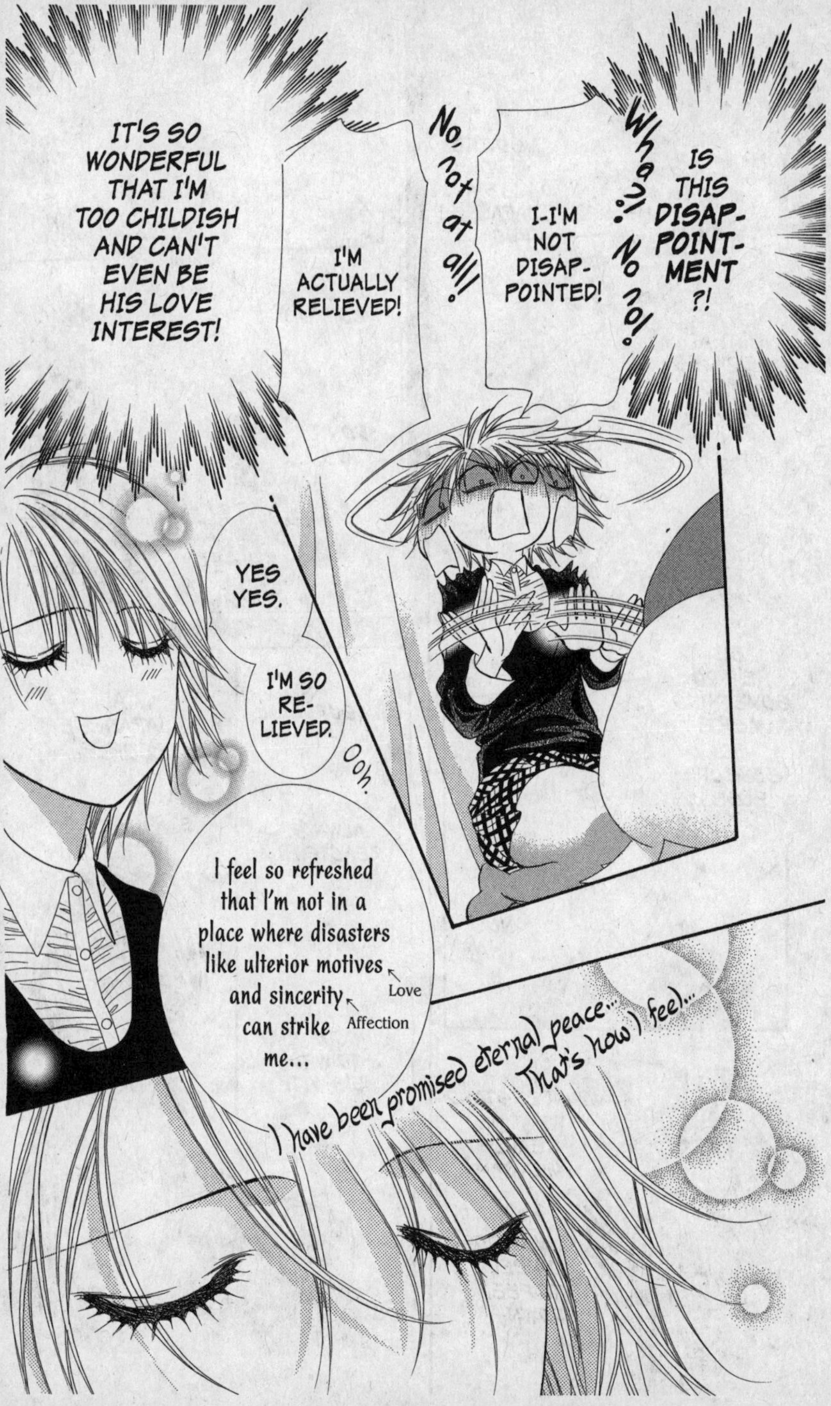
IS THIS DISAPPOINTMENT?!
Wha?! No no!
I-I'M NOT DISAPPOINTED!
No, not at all!
I'M ACTUALLY RELIEVED!
IT'S SO WONDERFUL THAT I'M TOO CHILDISH AND CAN'T EVEN BE HIS LOVE INTEREST!
Ooh.
YES YES.
I'M SO RELIEVED.
I feel so refreshed that I'm not in a place where disasters like ulterior motives and sincerity can strike me...
Love
Affection
I have been promised eternal peace... That's how I feel...

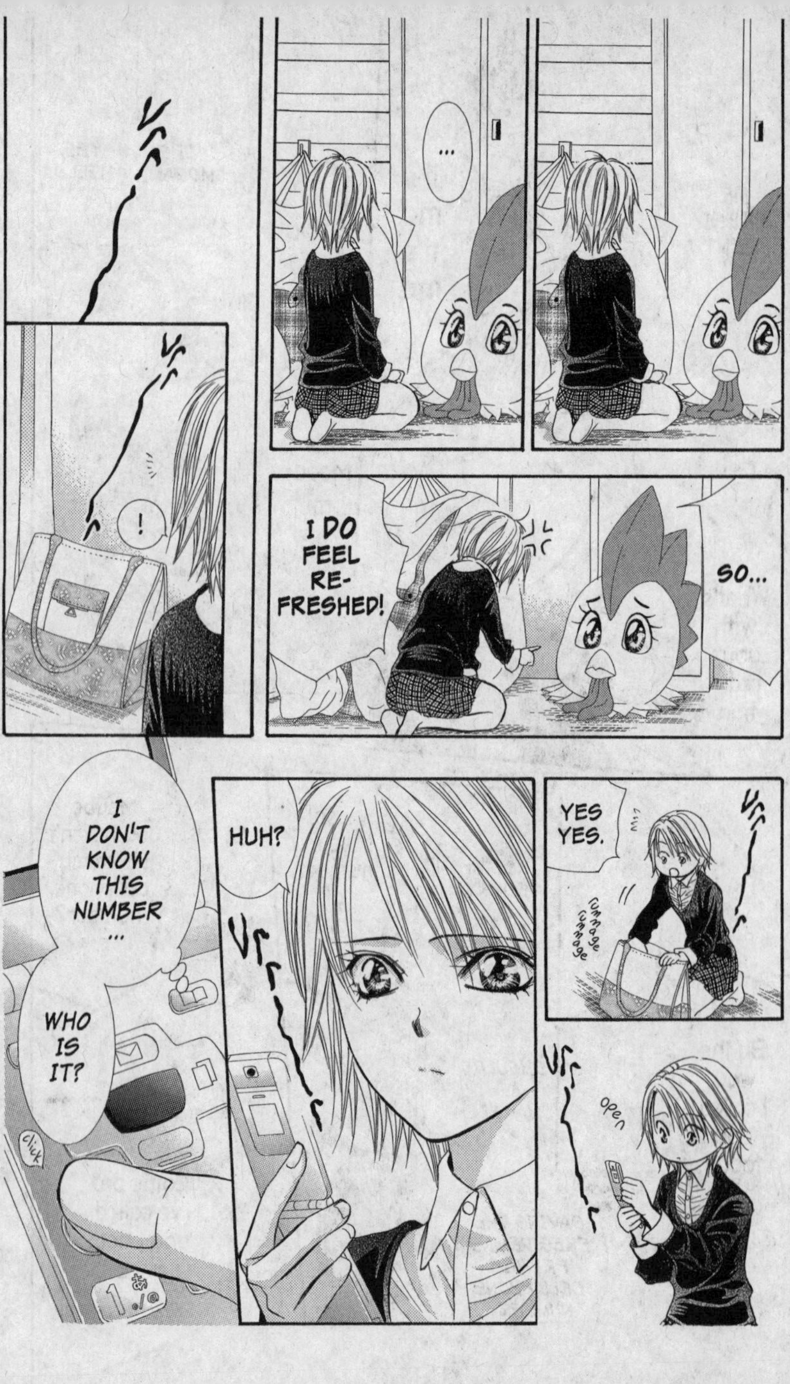
...
SO...
I DO FEEL RE-FRESHED!
!
YES YES.
rummage rummage rummage
open
HUH?
I DON'T KNOW THIS NUMBER...
WHO IS IT?
click

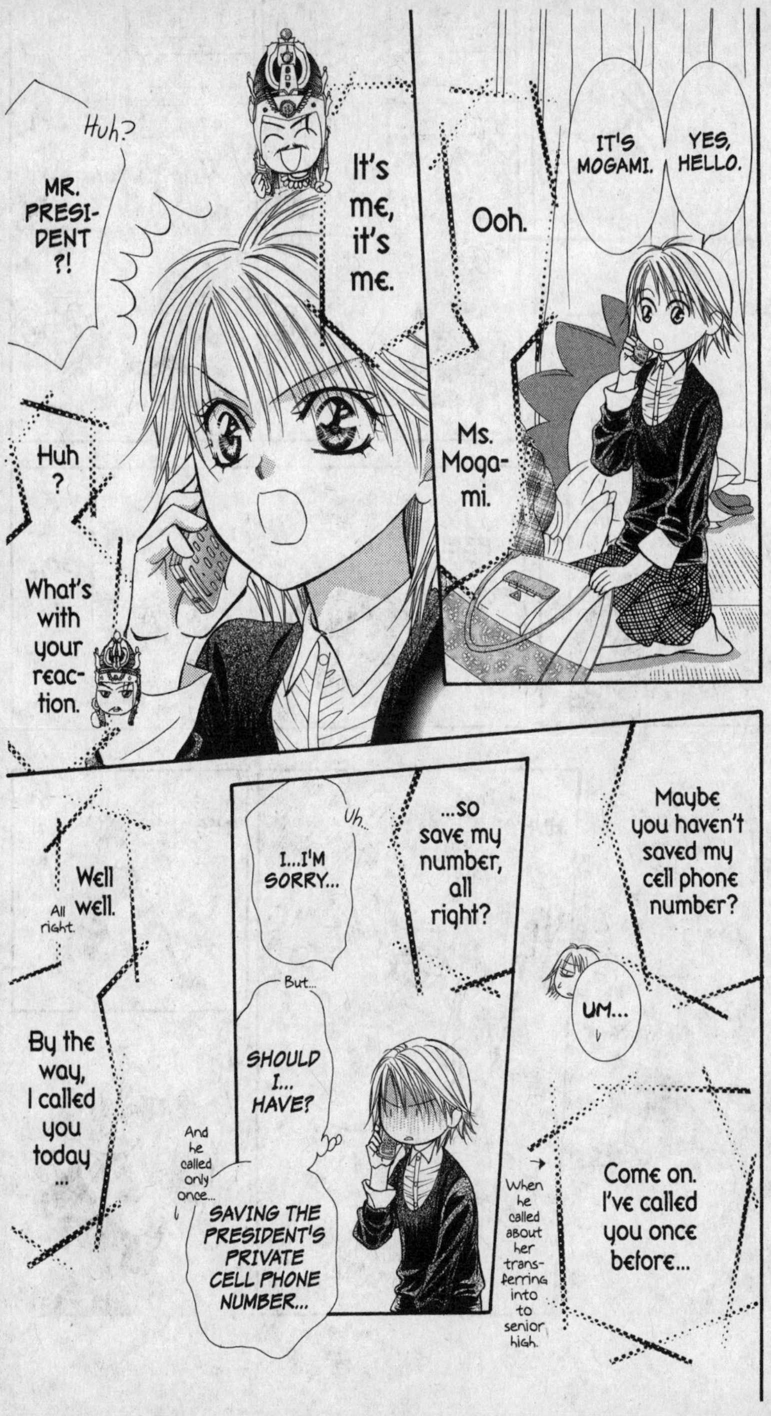
YES, HELLO.
IT'S MOGAMI.
Ooh.
Ms. Moga-mi.
It's me, it's me.
Huh?
MR. PRESI-DENT?!
Huh?
What's with your reac-tion.
Maybe you haven't saved my cell phone number?
UM...
Come on. I've called you once before...
When he called about her trans-ferring into to senior high.
...so save my number, all right?
Uh..
I...I'M SORRY...
But...
SHOULD I... HAVE?
SAVING THE PRESIDENT'S PRIVATE CELL PHONE NUMBER...
And he called only once...
Well well.
All right.
By the way, I called you today...

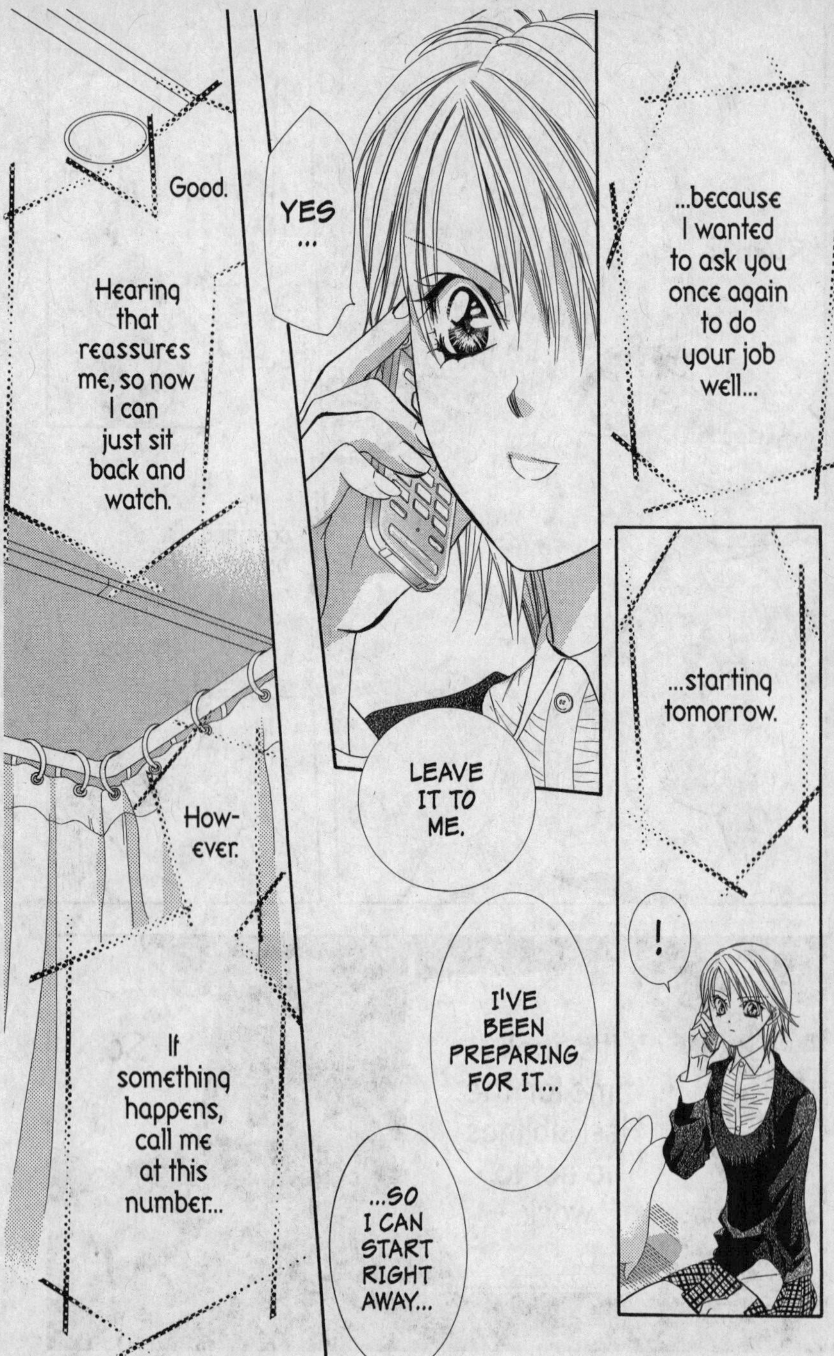

...because I wanted to ask you once again to do your job well...
...starting tomorrow.
!
YES ...
LEAVE IT TO ME.
I'VE BEEN PREPARING FOR IT...
...SO I CAN START RIGHT AWAY...
Good.
Hearing that reassures me, so now I can just sit back and watch.
How-ever.
If something happens, call me at this number...

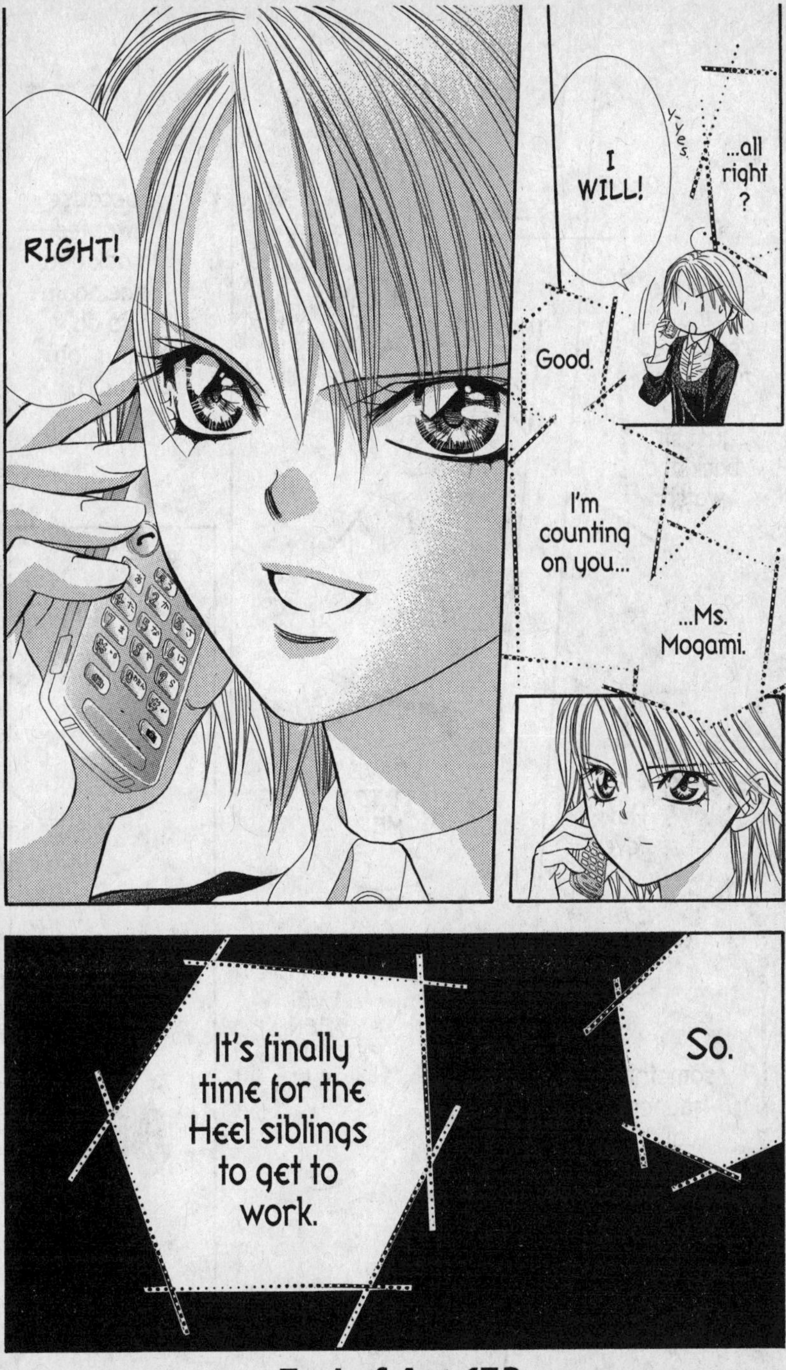
...all right?
Y-yes.
I WILL!
Good.
I'm counting on you...
...Ms. Mogami.
RIGHT!
So.
It's finally time for the Heel siblings to get to work.

End of Act 173

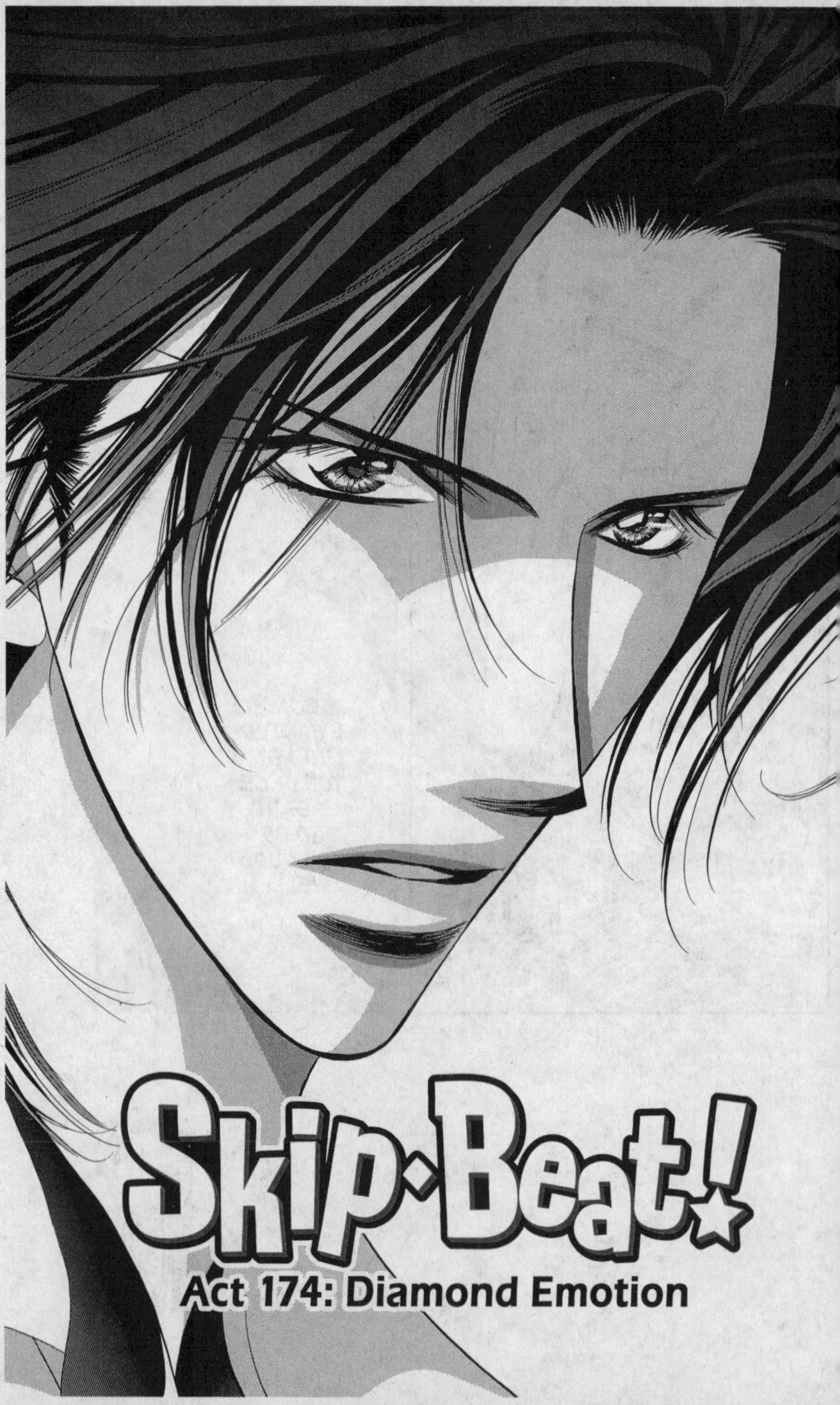
Skip·Beat!
Act 174: Diamond Emotion

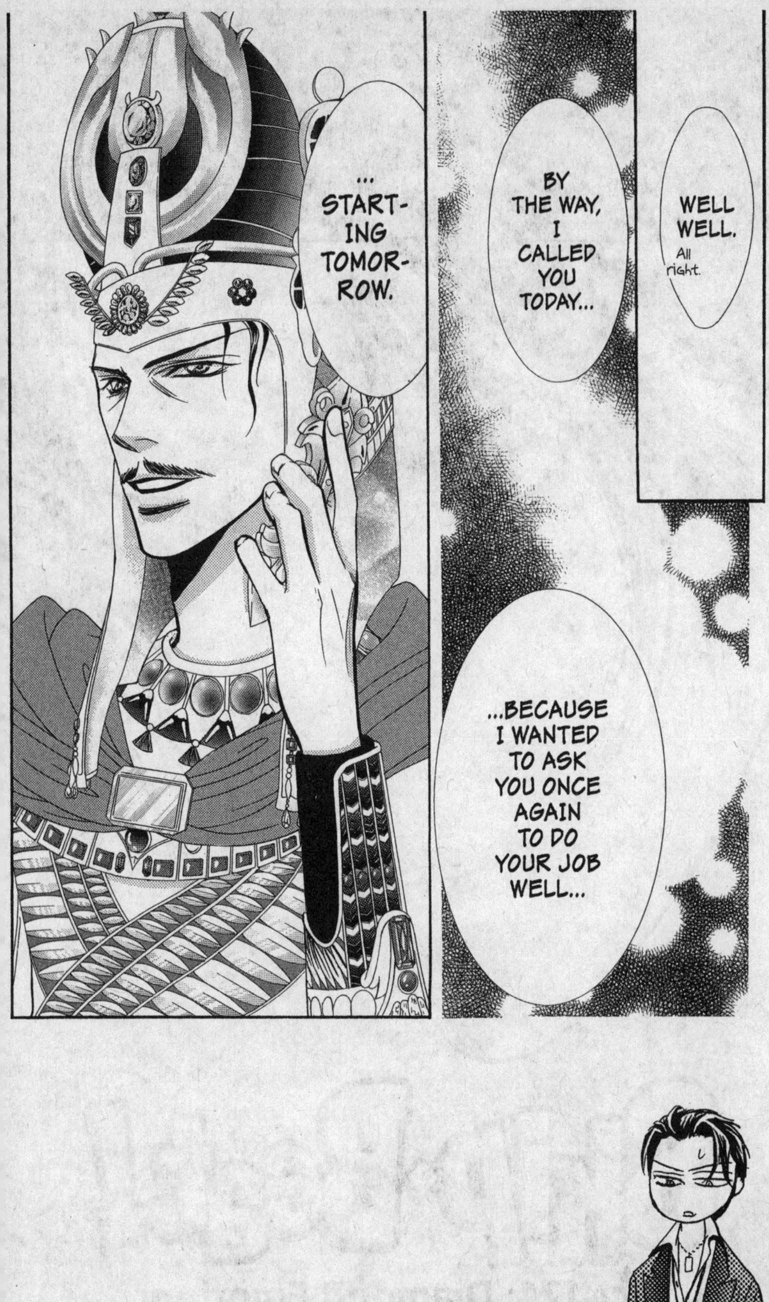
WELL WELL.
All right.
BY THE WAY, I CALLED YOU TODAY...
...BECAUSE I WANTED TO ASK YOU ONCE AGAIN TO DO YOUR JOB WELL...
... START-ING TOMOR-ROW.

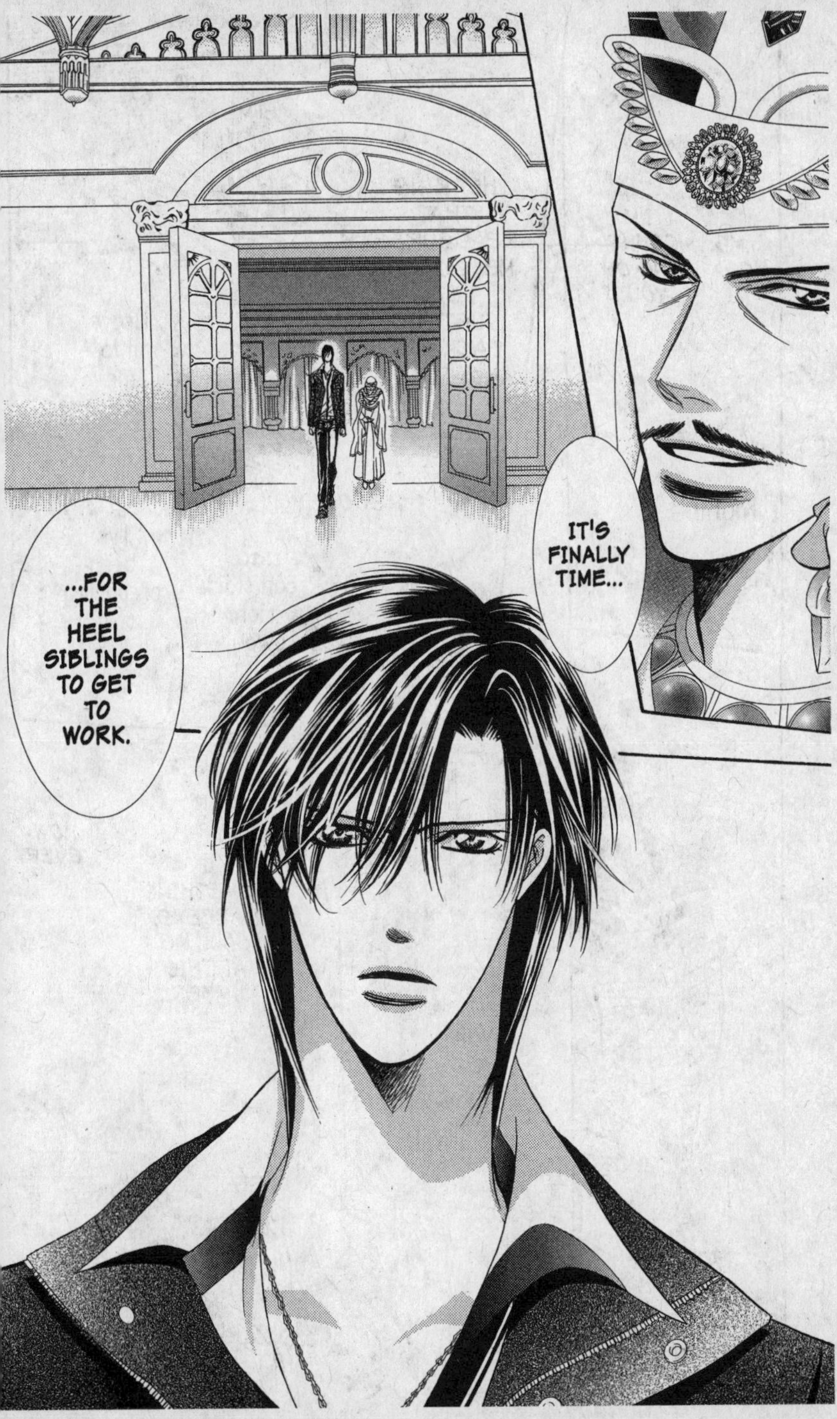
IT'S FINALLY TIME...
...FOR THE HEEL SIBLINGS TO GET TO WORK.

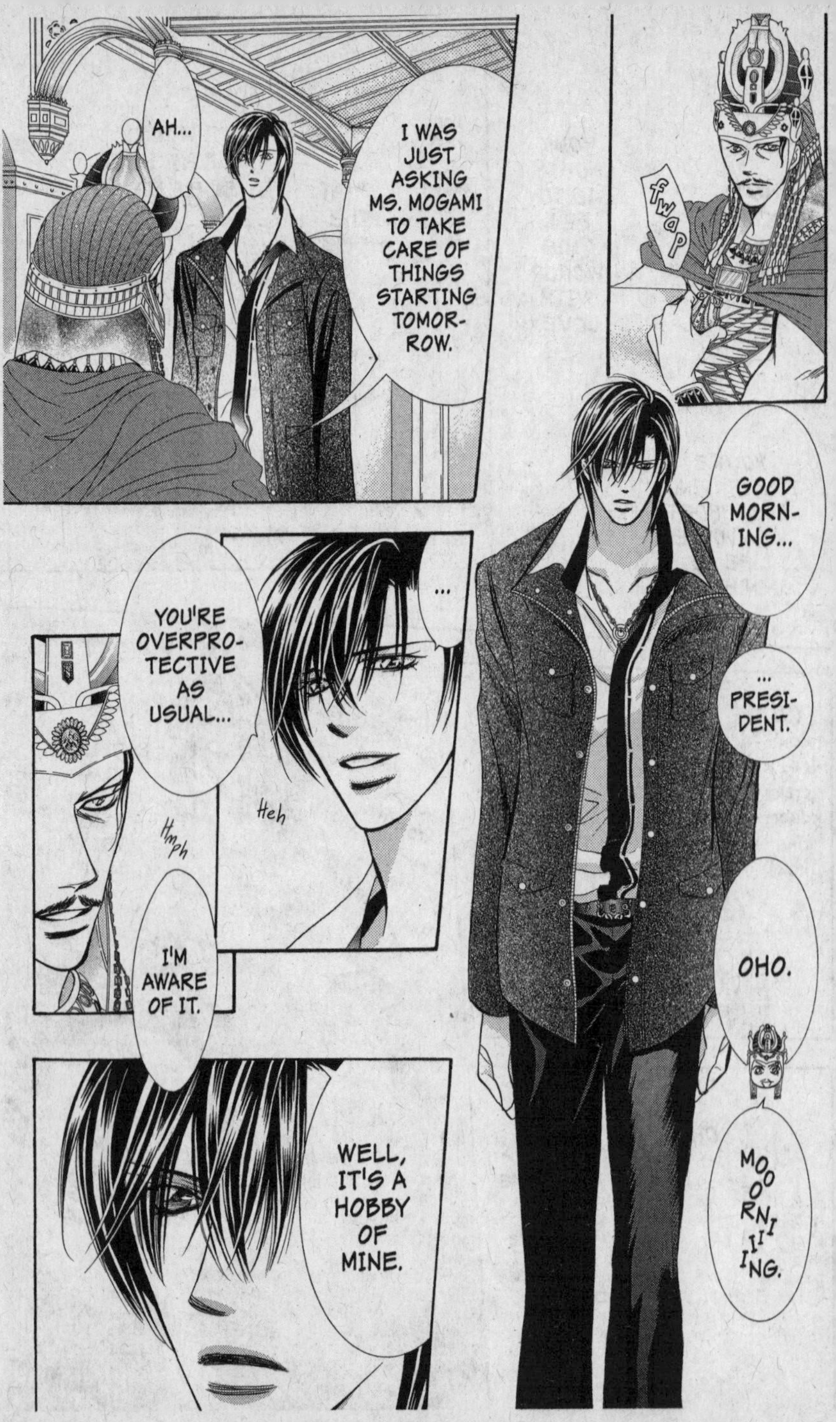
fwap
AH...
I WAS JUST ASKING MS. MOGAMI TO TAKE CARE OF THINGS STARTING TOMOR-ROW.
GOOD MORN-ING...
... PRESI-DENT.
OHO.
MOOORNIIIING.
...
YOU'RE OVERPRO-TECTIVE AS USUAL...
Heh
Hmph
I'M AWARE OF IT.
WELL, IT'S A HOBBY OF MINE.

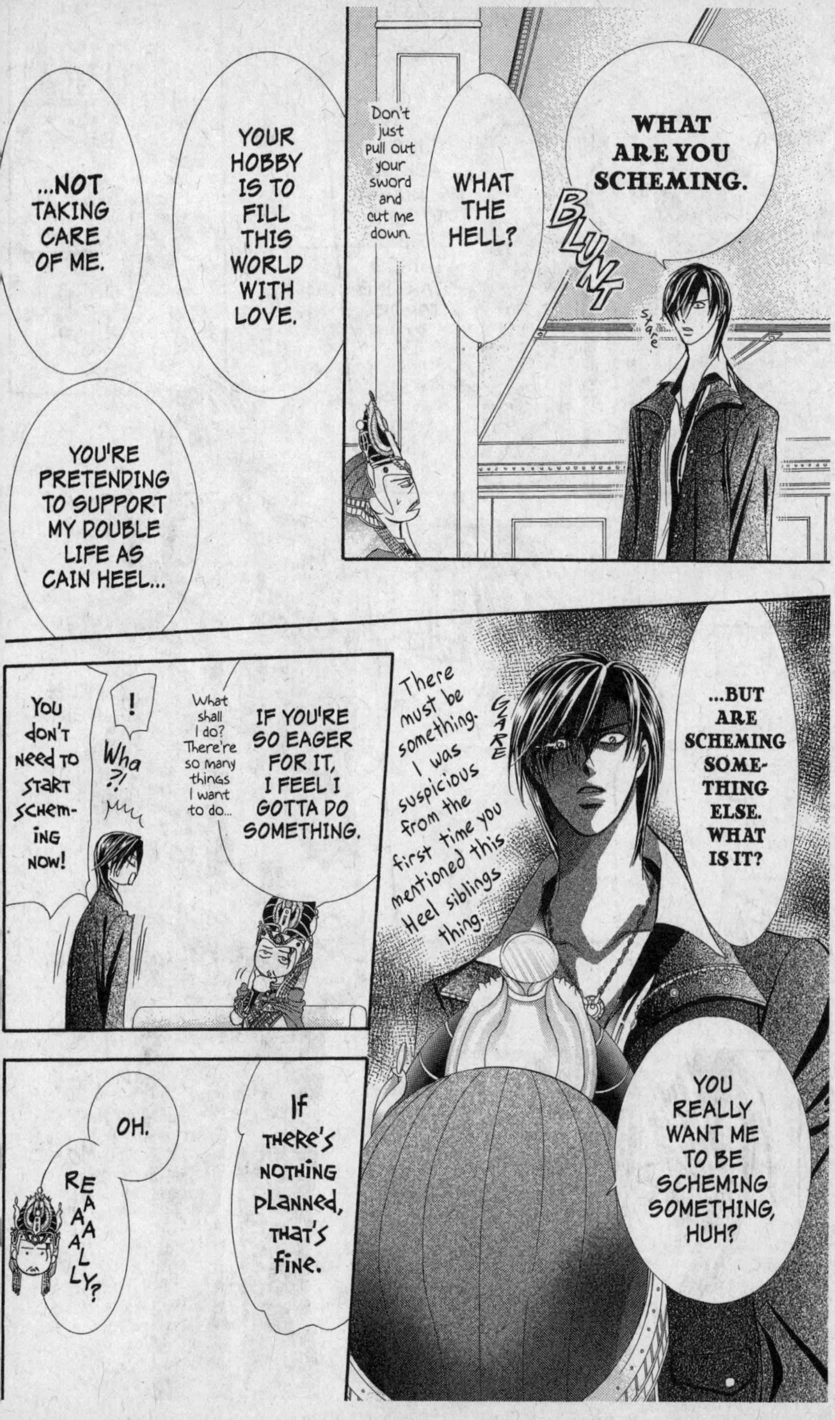
WHAT ARE YOU SCHEMING.
BLUNT
stare
WHAT THE HELL?
Don't just pull out your sword and cut me down.
YOUR HOBBY IS TO FILL THIS WORLD WITH LOVE.
...NOT TAKING CARE OF ME.
YOU'RE PRETENDING TO SUPPORT MY DOUBLE LIFE AS CAIN HEEL...
...BUT ARE SCHEMING SOMETHING ELSE. WHAT IS IT?
GLARE
There must be something. I was suspicious from the first time you mentioned this Heel siblings thing.
YOU REALLY WANT ME TO BE SCHEMING SOMETHING, HUH?
IF YOU'RE SO EAGER FOR IT, I FEEL I GOTTA DO SOMETHING.
What shall I do? There're so many things I want to do...
!
Wha ?!
You don't need to start scheming now!
If there's nothing planned, that's fine.
OH.
REAAAALLY?

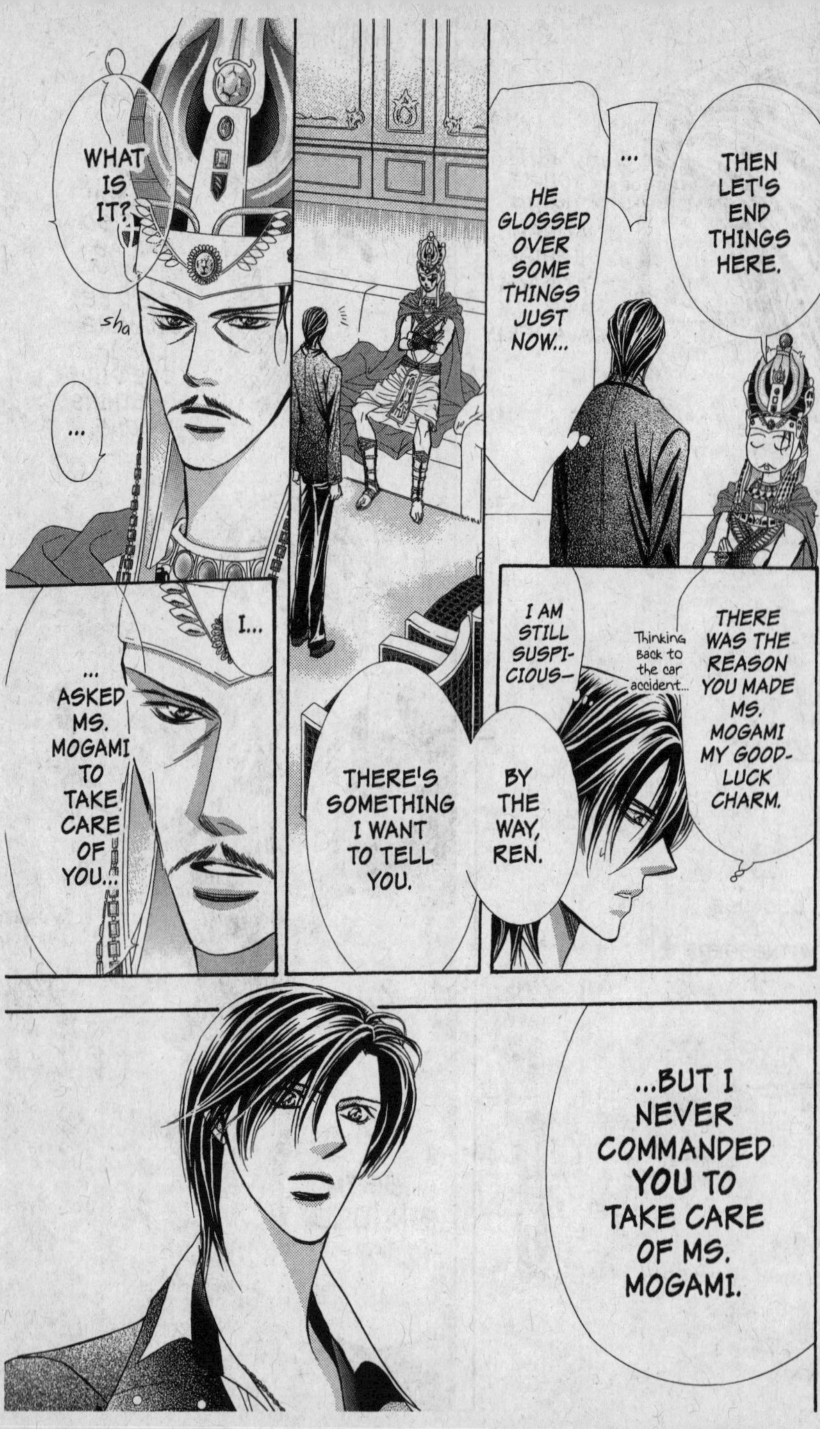
THEN LET'S END THINGS HERE.
...
HE GLOSSED OVER SOME THINGS JUST NOW...
THERE WAS THE REASON YOU MADE MS. MOGAMI MY GOOD-LUCK CHARM.
Thinking back to the car accident...
I AM STILL SUSPICIOUS-
BY THE WAY, REN.
THERE'S SOMETHING I WANT TO TELL YOU.
WHAT IS IT?
sha
...
I...
...ASKED MS. MOGAMI TO TAKE CARE OF YOU...
...BUT I NEVER COMMANDED YOU TO TAKE CARE OF MS. MOGAMI.

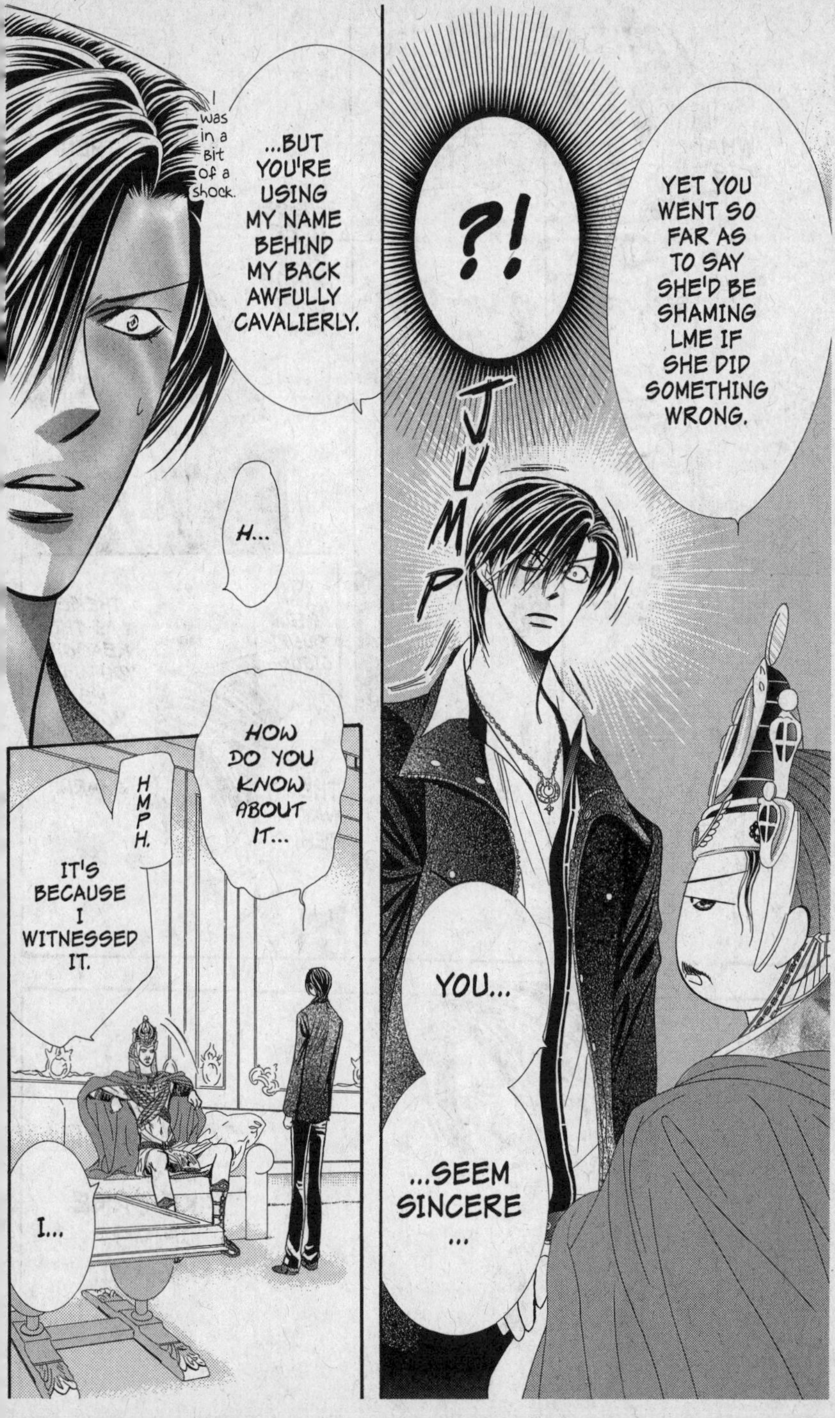
YET YOU WENT SO FAR AS TO SAY SHE'D BE SHAMING LME IF SHE DID SOMETHING WRONG.
?!
JUMP
YOU...
...SEEM SINCERE ...
...BUT YOU'RE USING MY NAME BEHIND MY BACK AWFULLY CAVALIERLY.
I was in a Bit of a shock.
H...
HOW DO YOU KNOW ABOUT IT...
HMPH.
IT'S BECAUSE I WITNESSED IT.
I...

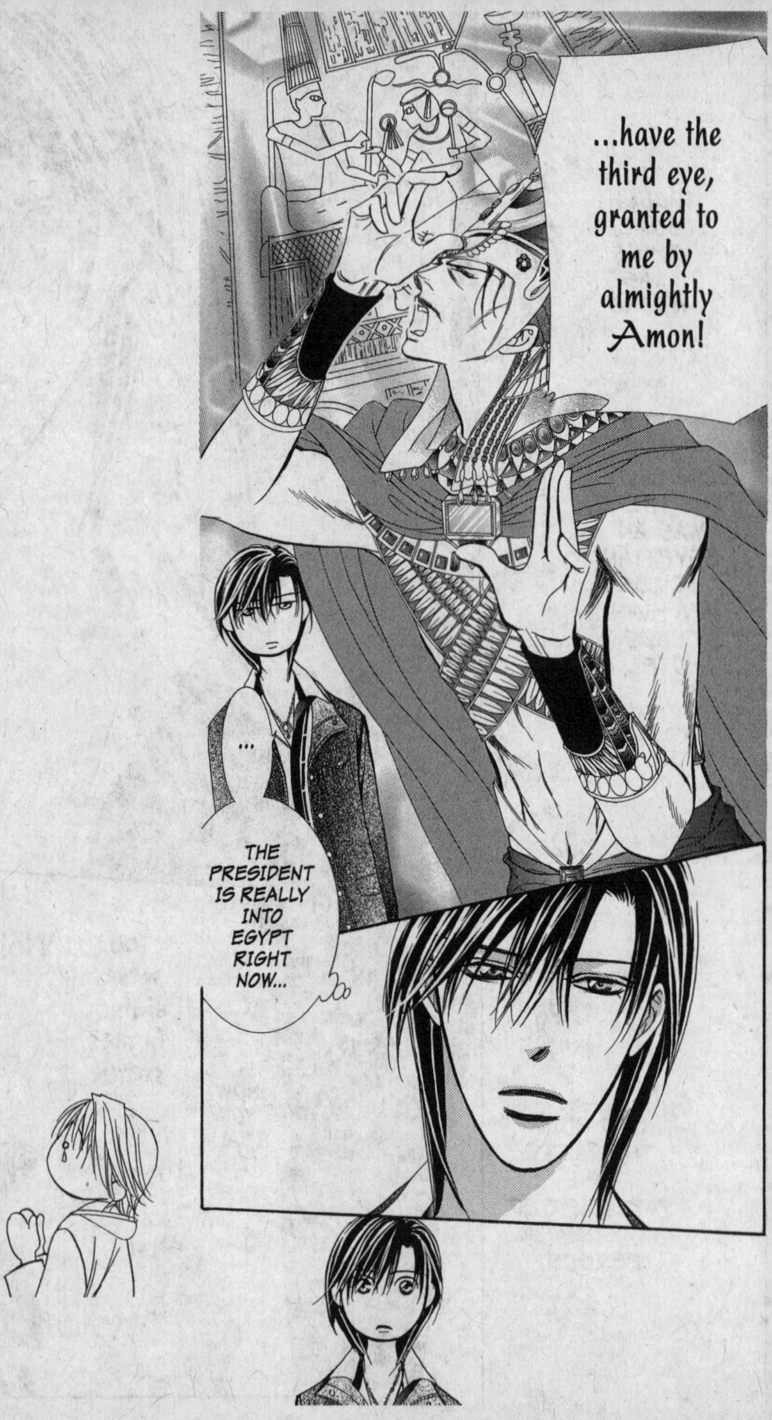
...have the third eye, granted to me by almightly Amon!
...
THE PRESIDENT IS REALLY INTO EGYPT RIGHT NOW...

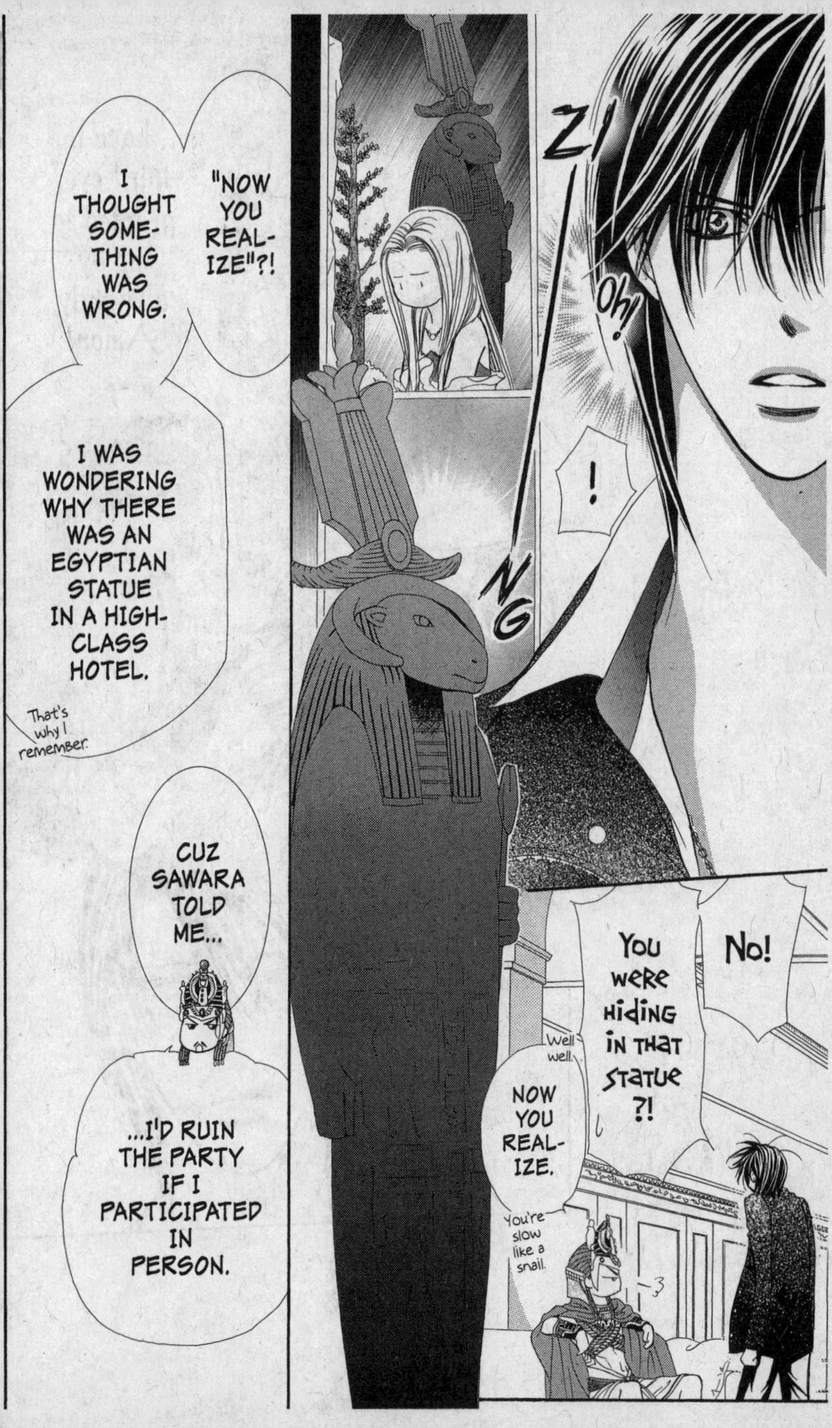
ZING
Oh!
!
No!
You were hiding in that statue?!
Well well.
NOW YOU REALIZE.
You're slow like a snail.
"NOW YOU REALIZE"?!
I THOUGHT SOMETHING WAS WRONG.
I WAS WONDERING WHY THERE WAS AN EGYPTIAN STATUE IN A HIGH-CLASS HOTEL.
That's why I remember.
CUZ SAWARA TOLD ME...
...I'D RUIN THE PARTY IF I PARTICIPATED IN PERSON.

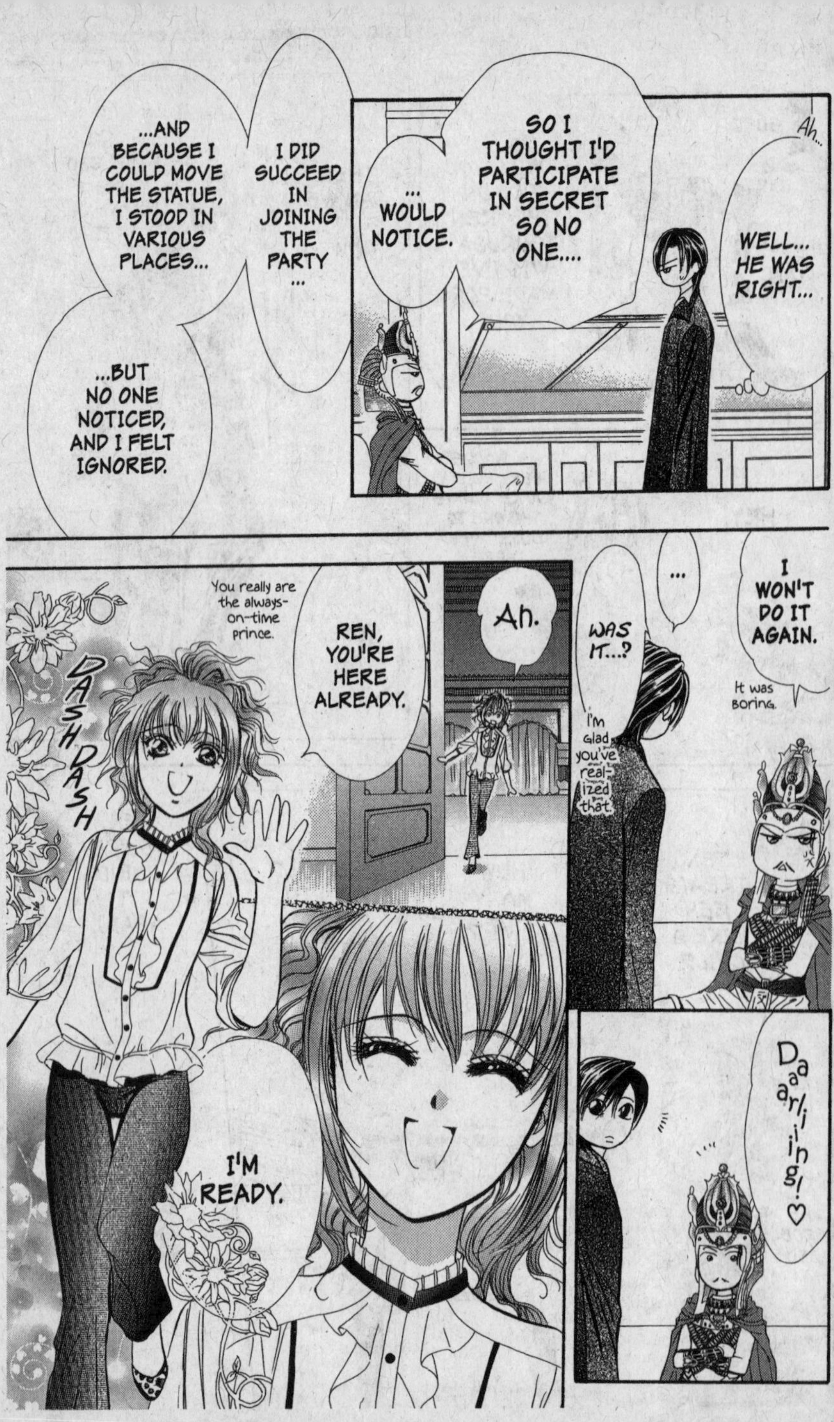
Ah...
WELL... HE WAS RIGHT...
SO I THOUGHT I'D PARTICIPATE IN SECRET SO NO ONE....
... WOULD NOTICE.
I DID SUCCEED IN JOINING THE PARTY ...
...AND BECAUSE I COULD MOVE THE STATUE, I STOOD IN VARIOUS PLACES...
...BUT NO ONE NOTICED, AND I FELT IGNORED.
I WON'T DO IT AGAIN.
It was boring.
...
WAS IT...?
I'm glad you've real-ized that.
Daaarliiing!♡
Ah.
REN, YOU'RE HERE ALREADY.
You really are the always-on-time prince.
DASH DASH
I'M READY.

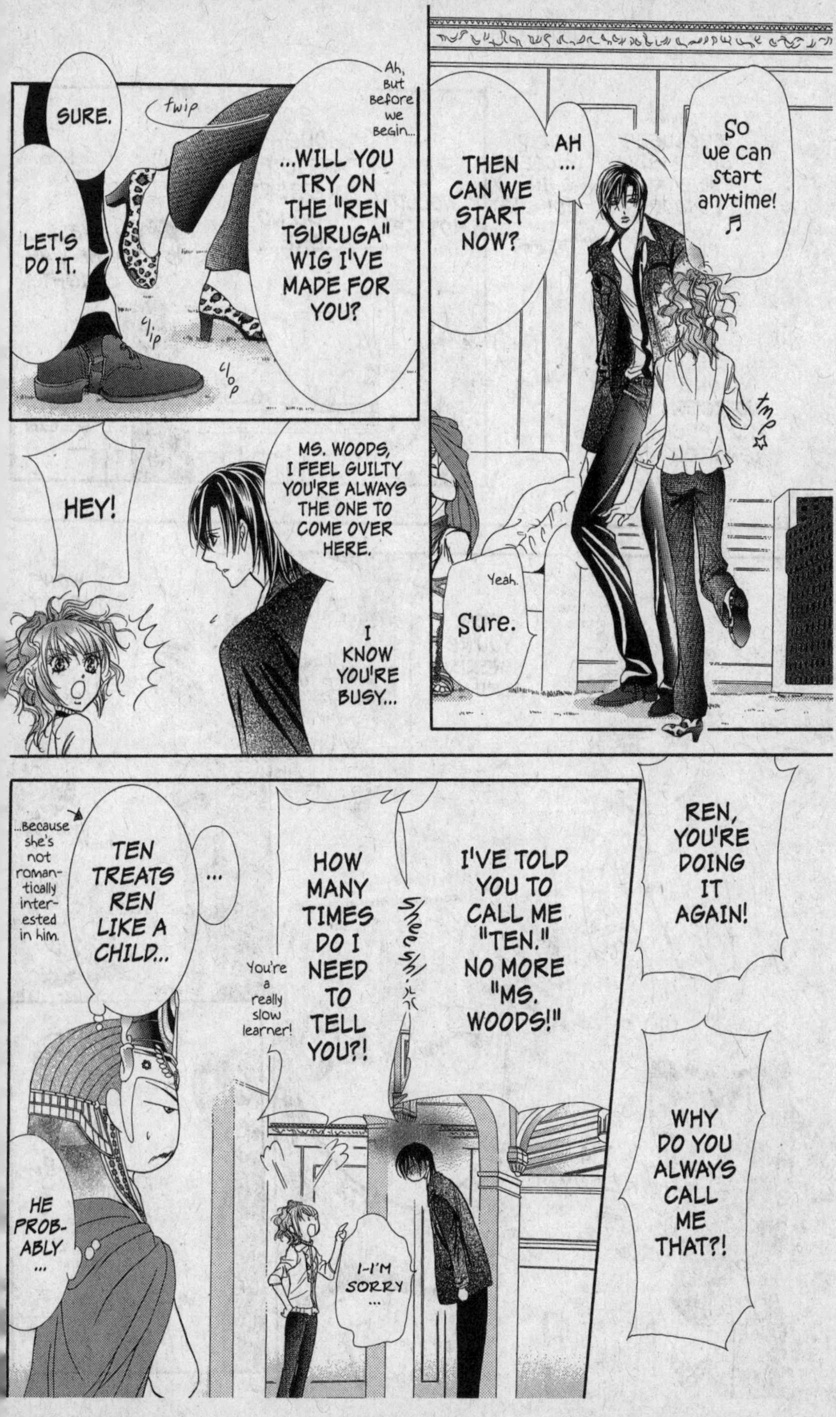
So we can start anytime! ♫
tmp
AH ...
THEN CAN WE START NOW?
Yeah.
Sure.
Ah, But Before we Begin...
...WILL YOU TRY ON THE "REN TSURUGA" WIG I'VE MADE FOR YOU?
fwip
SURE.
LET'S DO IT.
clip
clop
MS. WOODS, I FEEL GUILTY YOU'RE ALWAYS THE ONE TO COME OVER HERE.
I KNOW YOU'RE BUSY...
HEY!
REN, YOU'RE DOING IT AGAIN!
WHY DO YOU ALWAYS CALL ME THAT?!
I'VE TOLD YOU TO CALL ME "TEN." NO MORE "MS. WOODS!"
HOW MANY TIMES DO I NEED TO TELL YOU?!
Sheesh!
You're a really slow learner!
I-I'M SORRY ...
...
TEN TREATS REN LIKE A CHILD...
...Because she's not romantically interested in him.
HE PROBABLY ...

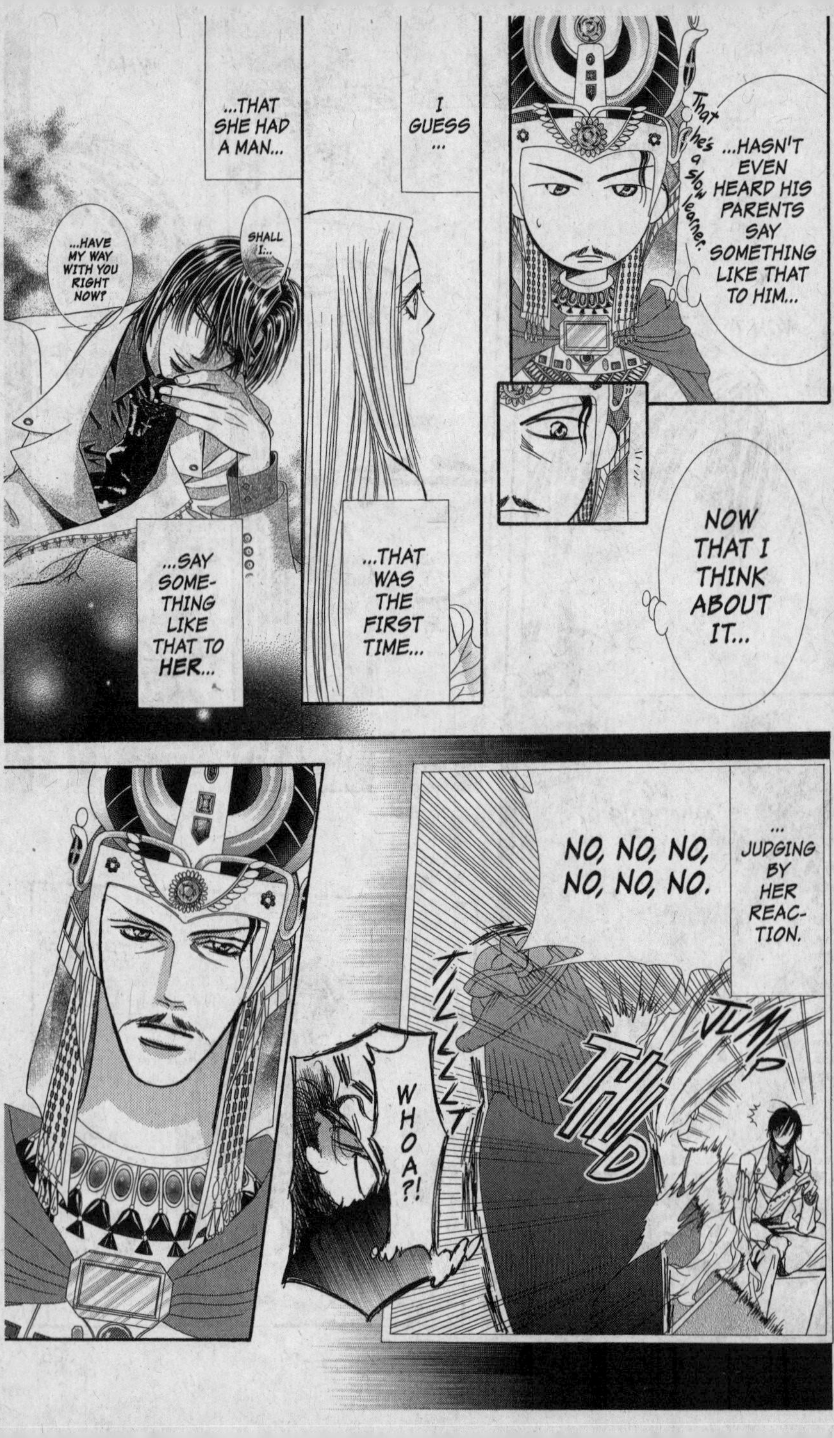
...HASN'T EVEN HEARD HIS PARENTS SAY SOMETHING LIKE THAT TO HIM...
That he's a slow learner.
NOW THAT I THINK ABOUT IT...
I GUESS...
...THAT WAS THE FIRST TIME...
...THAT SHE HAD A MAN...
SHALL I...
...HAVE MY WAY WITH YOU RIGHT NOW?
...SAY SOMETHING LIKE THAT TO HER...
...JUDGING BY HER REACTION.
NO, NO, NO, NO, NO, NO.
JUMP
THUD
TILT
WHOA?!

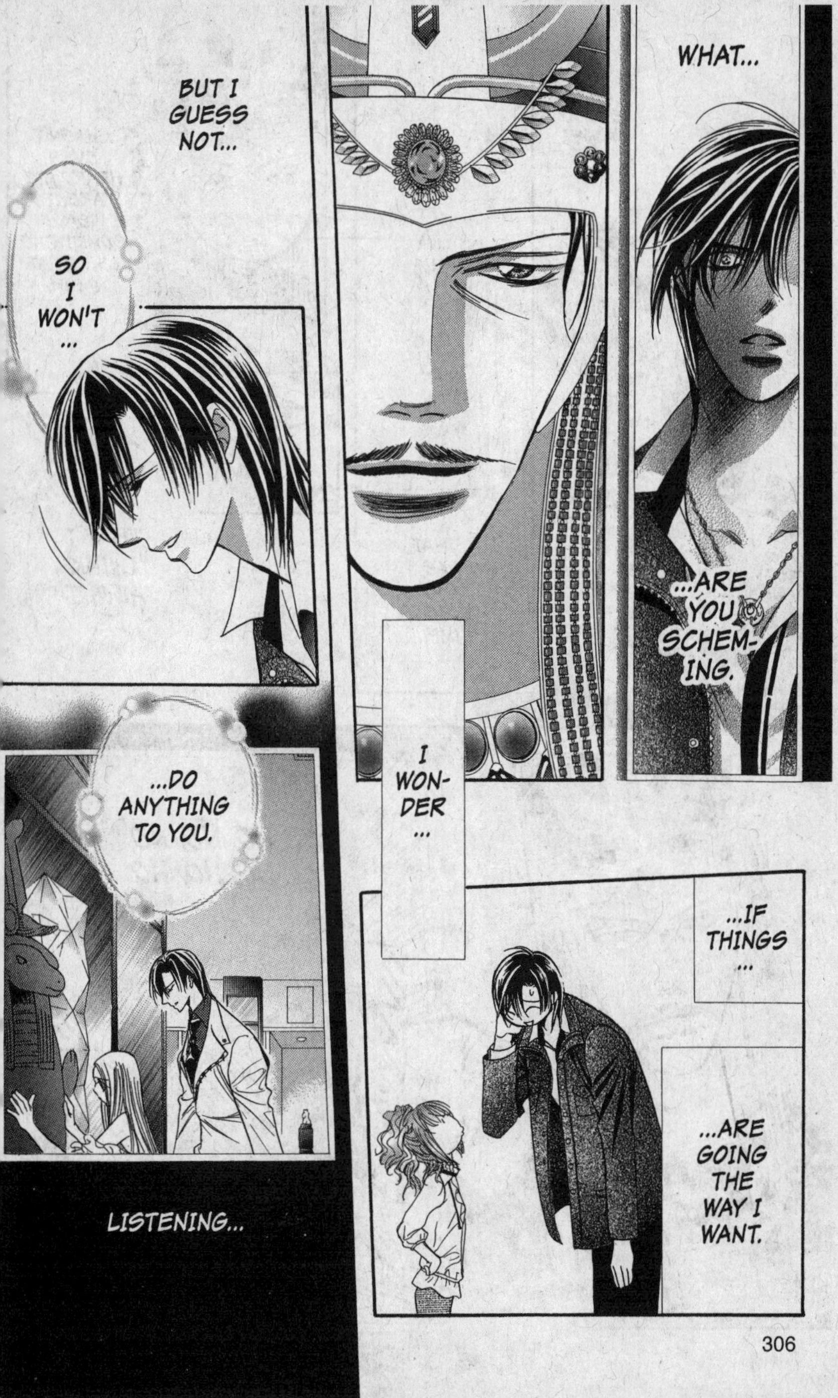
WHAT...
...ARE YOU SCHEMING.
I WONDER...
BUT I GUESS NOT...
SO I WON'T...
...DO ANYTHING TO YOU.
LISTENING...
...IF THINGS...
...ARE GOING THE WAY I WANT.

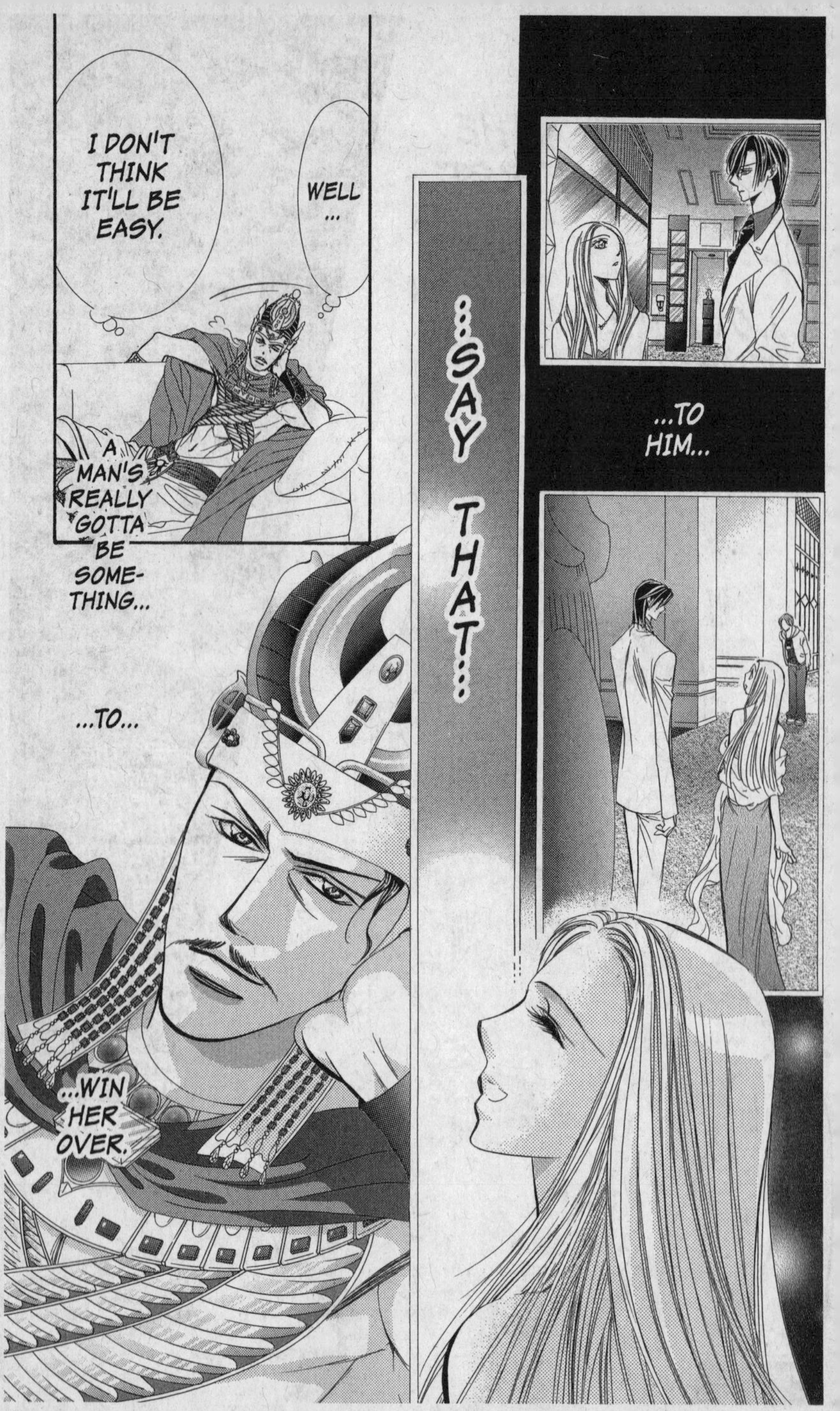
...TO HIM...
...SAY THAT...
WELL...
I DON'T THINK IT'LL BE EASY.
A MAN'S REALLY GOTTA BE SOME-THING...
...TO...
...WIN HER OVER.

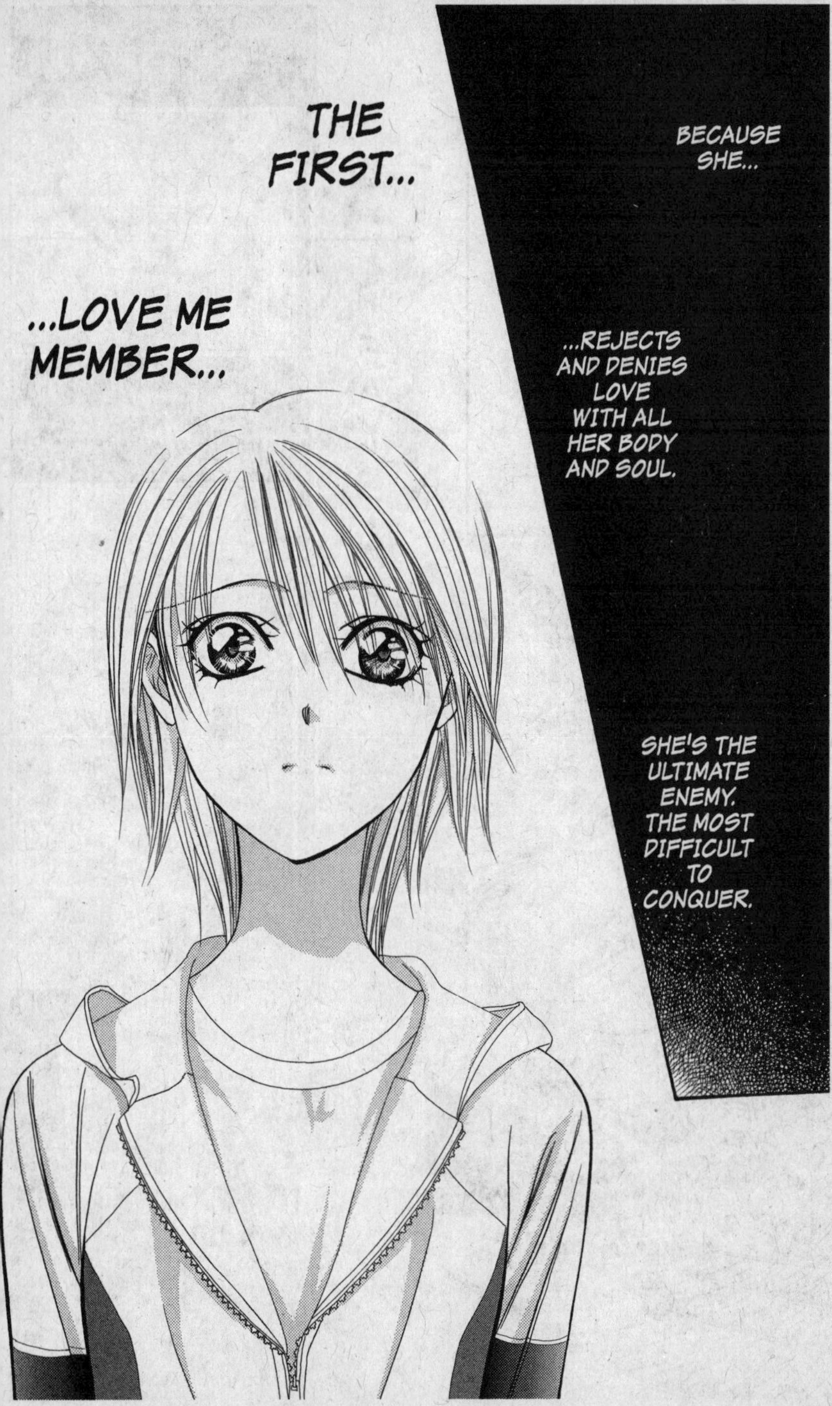
BECAUSE SHE...
...REJECTS AND DENIES LOVE WITH ALL HER BODY AND SOUL.
SHE'S THE ULTIMATE ENEMY. THE MOST DIFFICULT TO CONQUER.
THE FIRST...
...LOVE ME MEMBER...

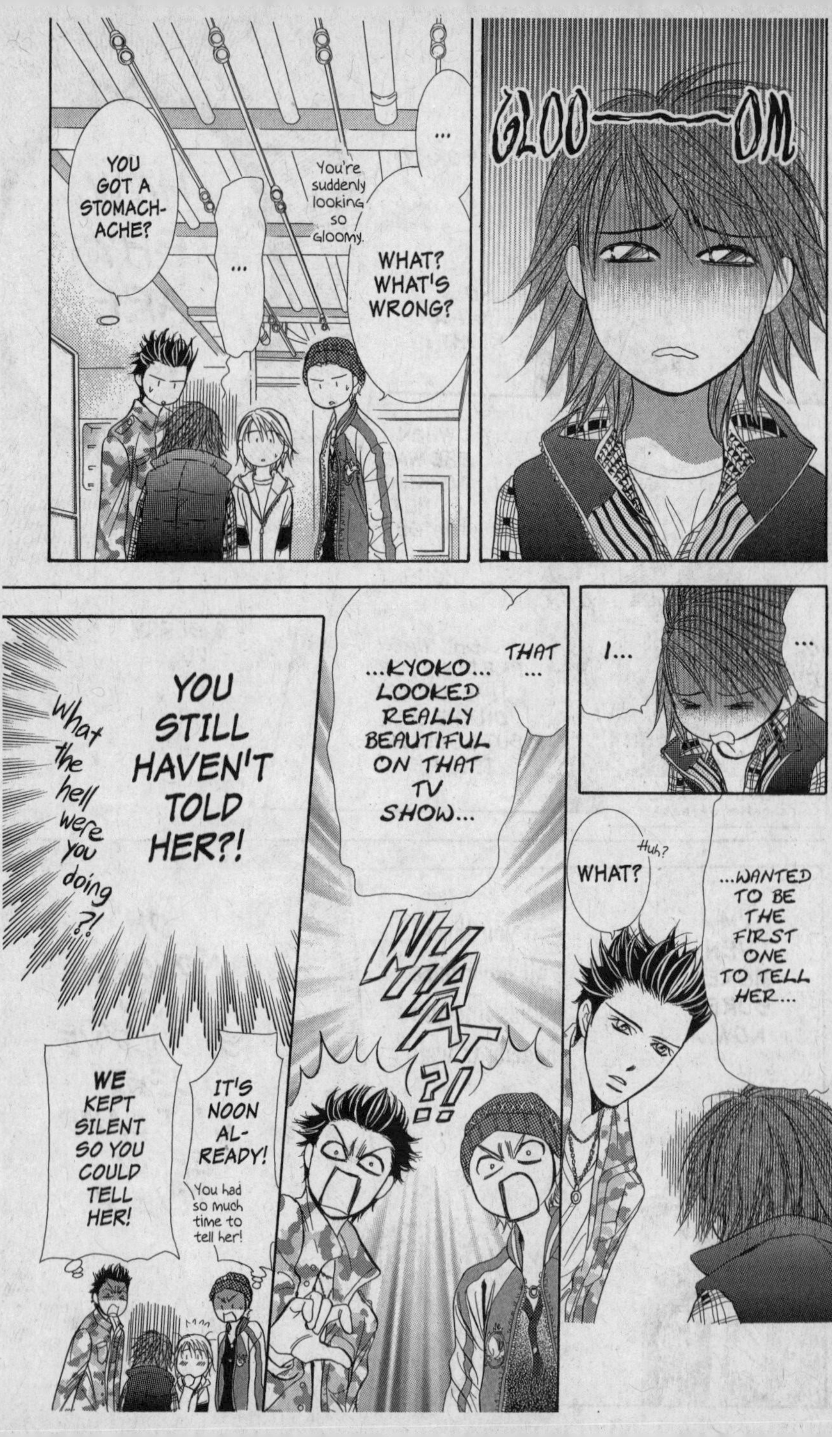
GLOO———OM
...
You're suddenly looking so gloomy.
WHAT? WHAT'S WRONG?
...
YOU GOT A STOMACHACHE?
...
I...
...WANTED TO BE THE FIRST ONE TO TELL HER...
Huh?
WHAT?
THAT ...
...KYOKO... LOOKED REALLY BEAUTIFUL ON THAT TV SHOW...
WHAT ?!
YOU STILL HAVEN'T TOLD HER?!
What the hell were you doing ?!
IT'S NOON AL-READY!
You had so much time to tell her!
WE KEPT SILENT SO YOU COULD TELL HER!

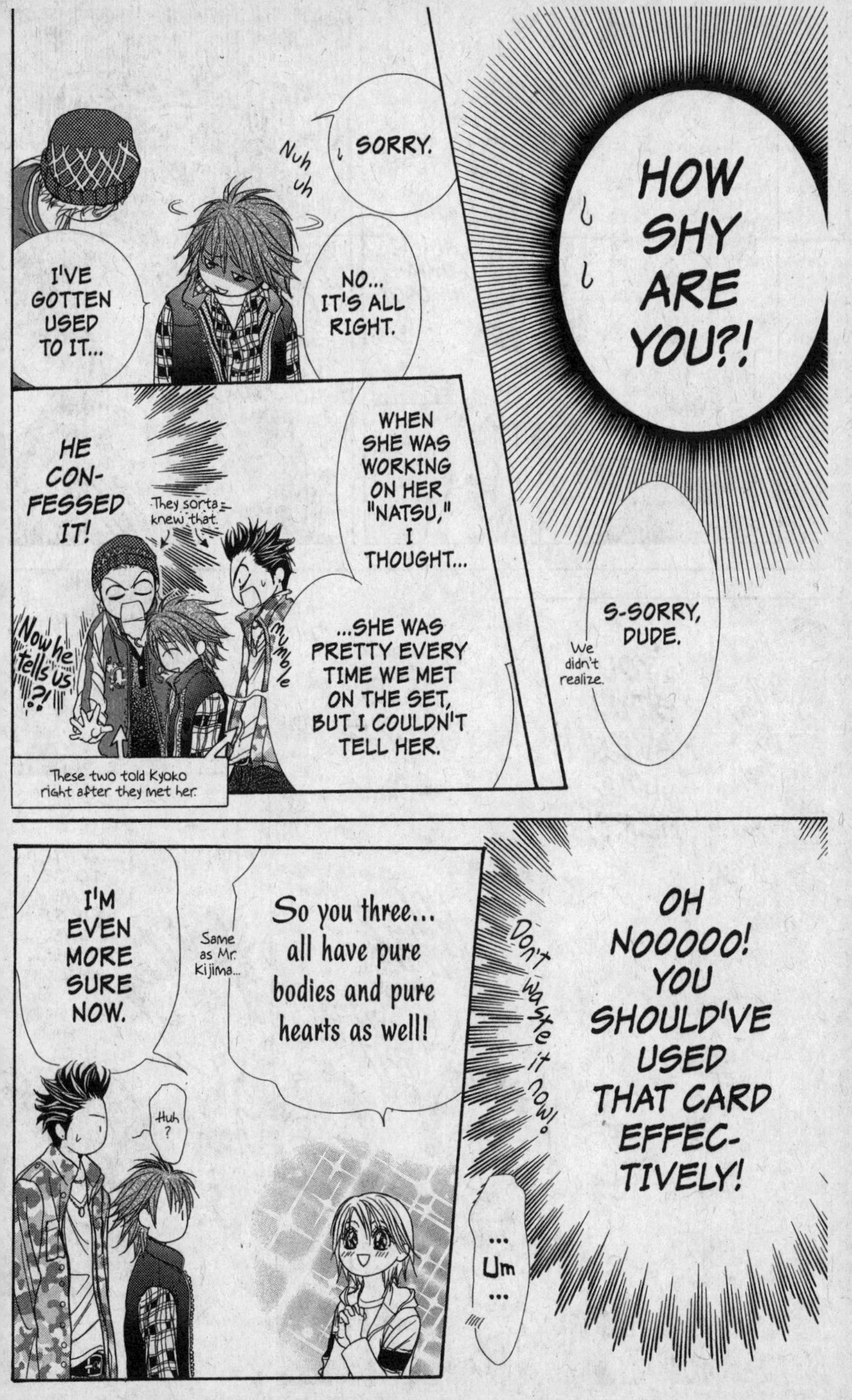
HOW SHY ARE YOU?!
S-SORRY, DUDE.
We didn't realize.
SORRY.
Nuh uh
NO... IT'S ALL RIGHT.
I'VE GOTTEN USED TO IT...
WHEN SHE WAS WORKING ON HER "NATSU," I THOUGHT...
...SHE WAS PRETTY EVERY TIME WE MET ON THE SET, BUT I COULDN'T TELL HER.
mumble
HE CON-FESSED IT!
They sorta knew that.
Now he tells us?!
These two told Kyoko right after they met her.
OH NOOOOO! YOU SHOULD'VE USED THAT CARD EFFEC-TIVELY!
Don't waste it now!
... Um ...
So you three... all have pure bodies and pure hearts as well!
Same as Mr. Kijima...
I'M EVEN MORE SURE NOW.
Huh ?

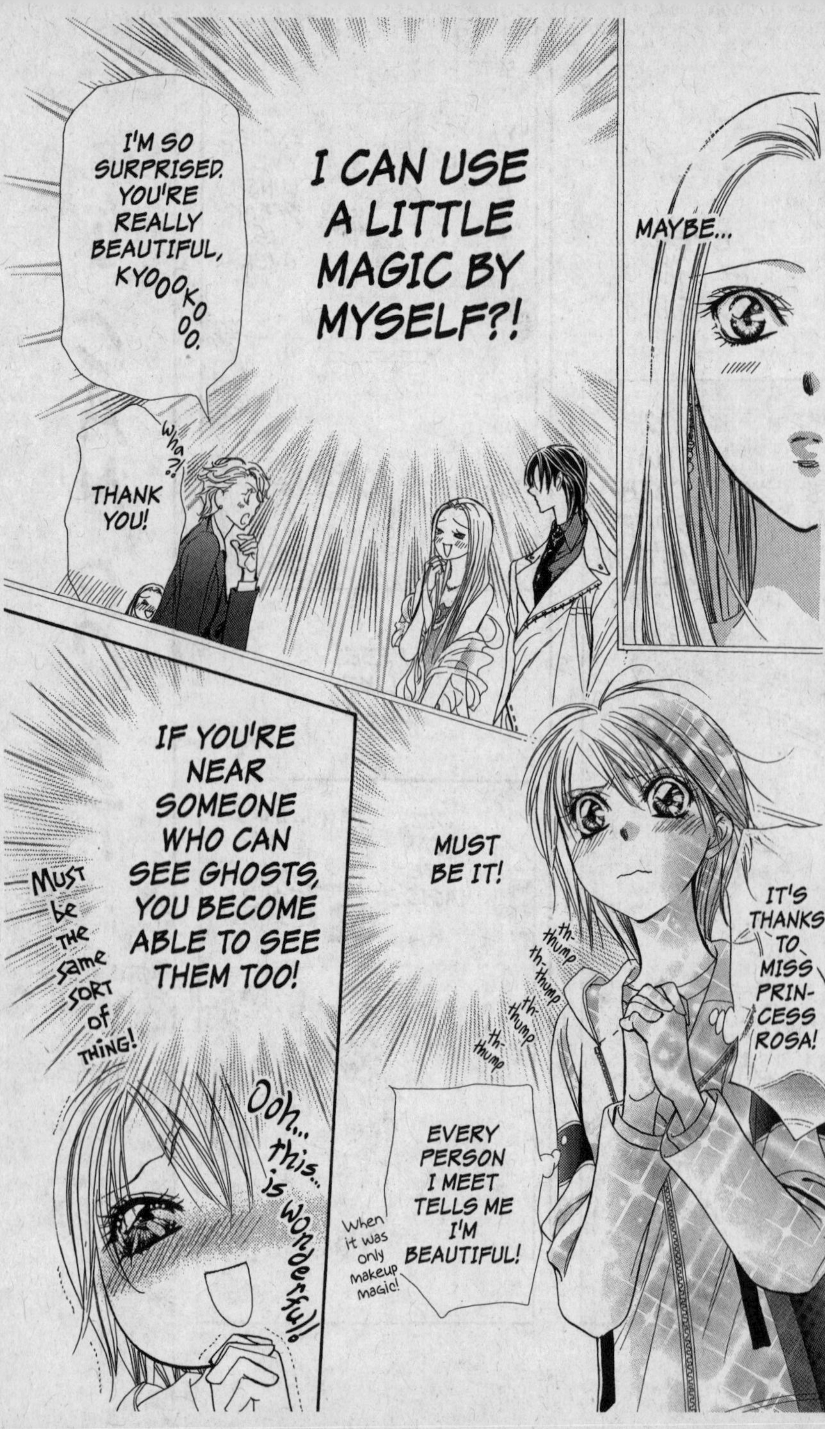
MAYBE...
I CAN USE A LITTLE MAGIC BY MYSELF?!
I'M SO SURPRISED. YOU'RE REALLY BEAUTIFUL, KYOOOKOOOO.
wha?!
THANK YOU!
IT'S THANKS TO MISS PRINCESS ROSA!
MUST BE IT!
th-thump th-thump th-thump th-thump
EVERY PERSON I MEET TELLS ME I'M BEAUTIFUL!
When it was only makeup magic!
IF YOU'RE NEAR SOMEONE WHO CAN SEE GHOSTS, YOU BECOME ABLE TO SEE THEM TOO!
MUST be THE same SORT of THING!
Ooh... this... is wonderful!

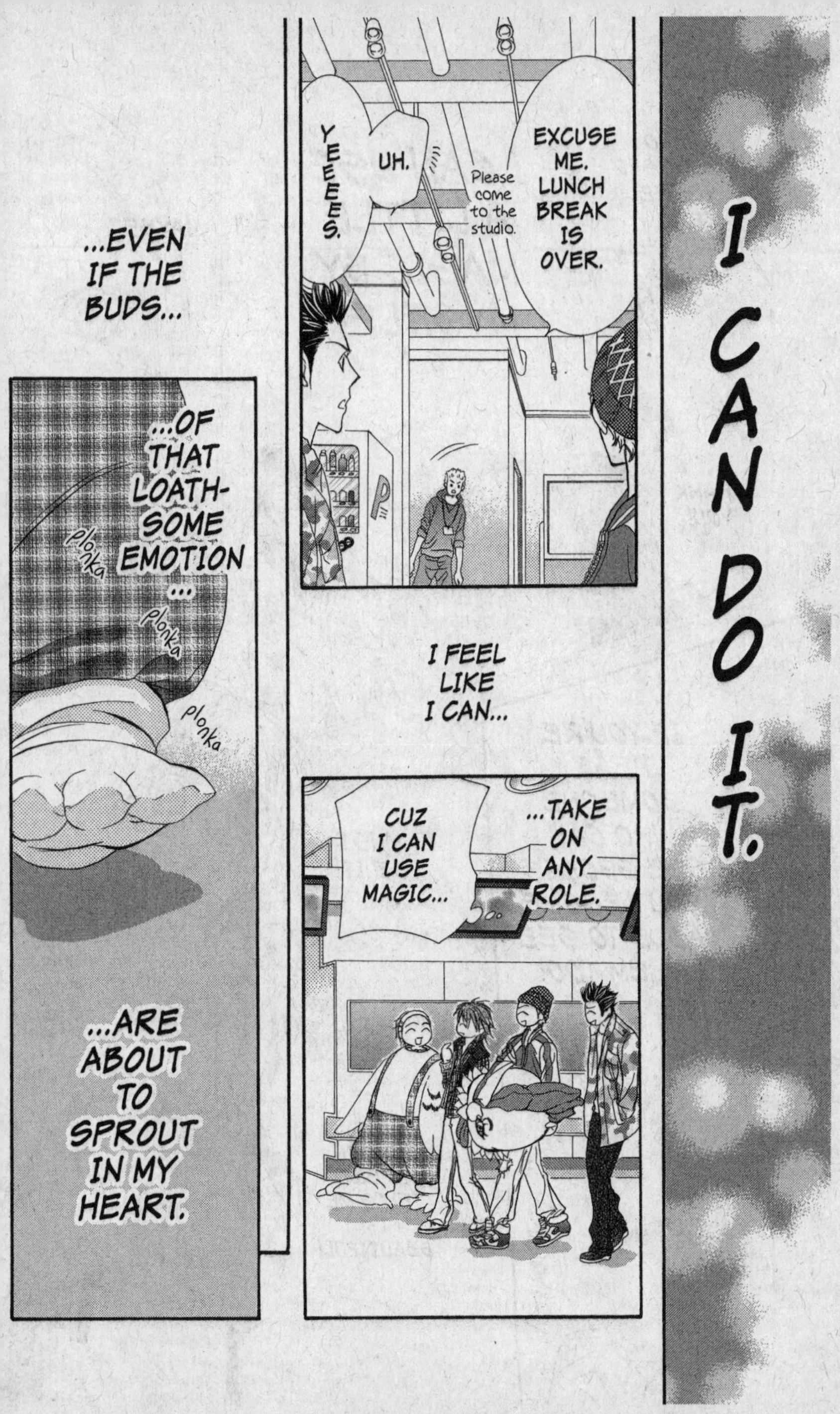
I CAN DO IT.
EXCUSE ME. LUNCH BREAK IS OVER.
Please come to the studio.
UH.
YEEEEES.
I FEEL LIKE I CAN...
...TAKE ON ANY ROLE.
CUZ I CAN USE MAGIC...
...EVEN IF THE BUDS...
...OF THAT LOATH-SOME EMOTION...
plonka
plonka
plonka
...ARE ABOUT TO SPROUT IN MY HEART.

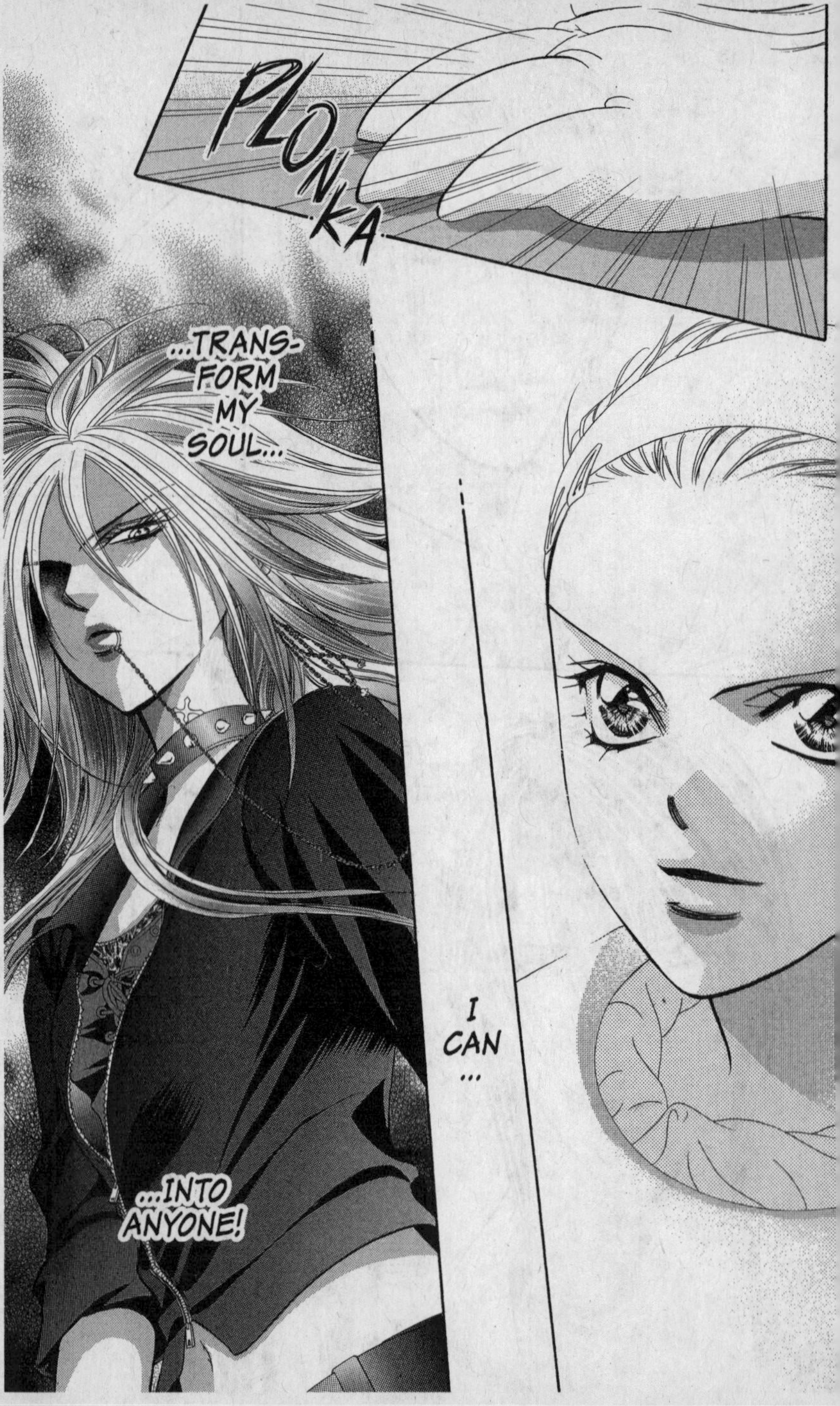
PLONKA
I CAN ...
...TRANS-FORM MY SOUL...
...INTO ANYONE!

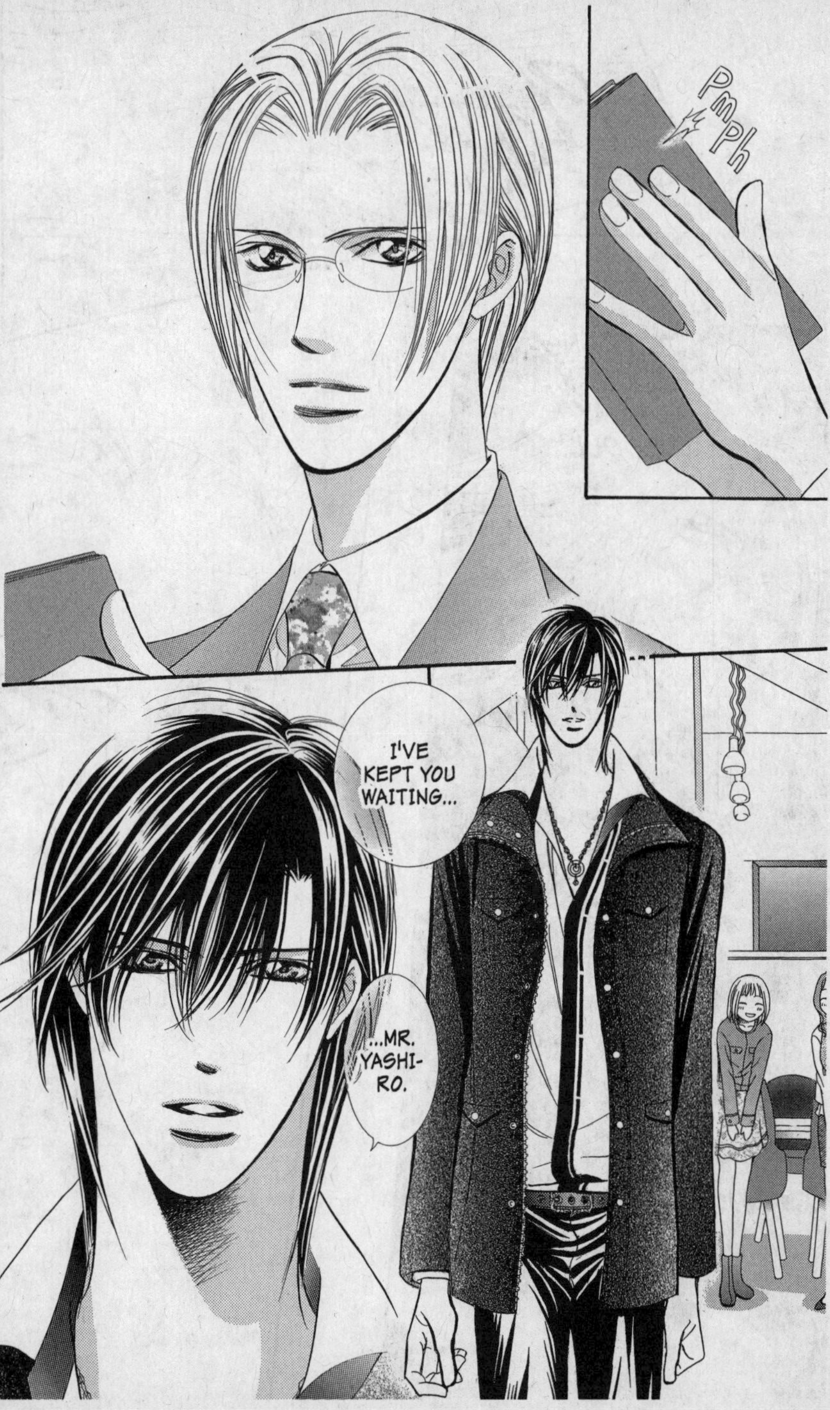
PmPh
I'VE KEPT YOU WAITING...
...MR. YASHIRO.

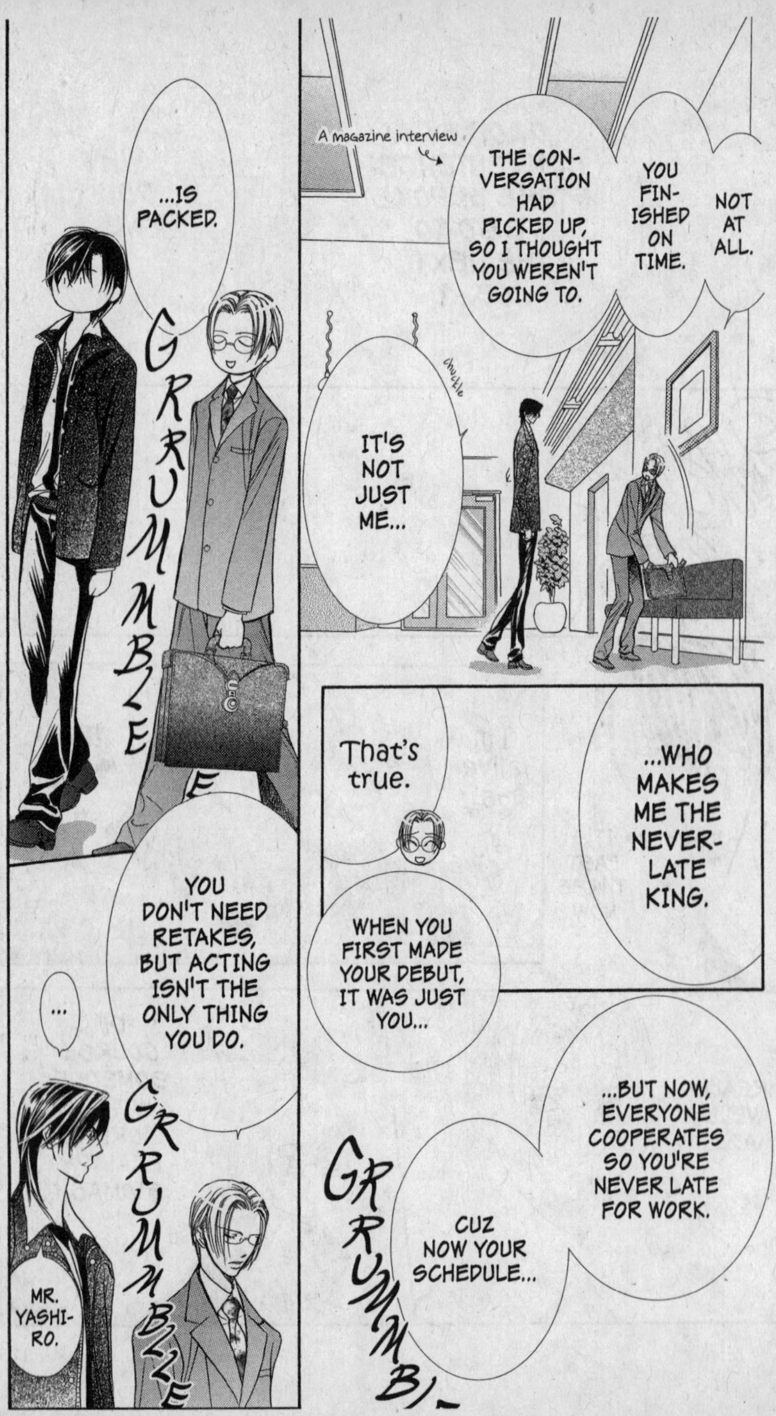
A magazine interview
NOT AT ALL.
YOU FIN-ISHED ON TIME.
THE CON-VERSATION HAD PICKED UP, SO I THOUGHT YOU WEREN'T GOING TO.
chuckle
IT'S NOT JUST ME...
...WHO MAKES ME THE NEVER-LATE KING.
That's true.
WHEN YOU FIRST MADE YOUR DEBUT, IT WAS JUST YOU...
...BUT NOW, EVERYONE COOPERATES SO YOU'RE NEVER LATE FOR WORK.
CUZ NOW YOUR SCHEDULE...
GRRUMMBL-
...IS PACKED.
GRRUMMBLE
YOU DON'T NEED RETAKES, BUT ACTING ISN'T THE ONLY THING YOU DO.
...
GRRUMMBLE
MR. YASHI-RO.

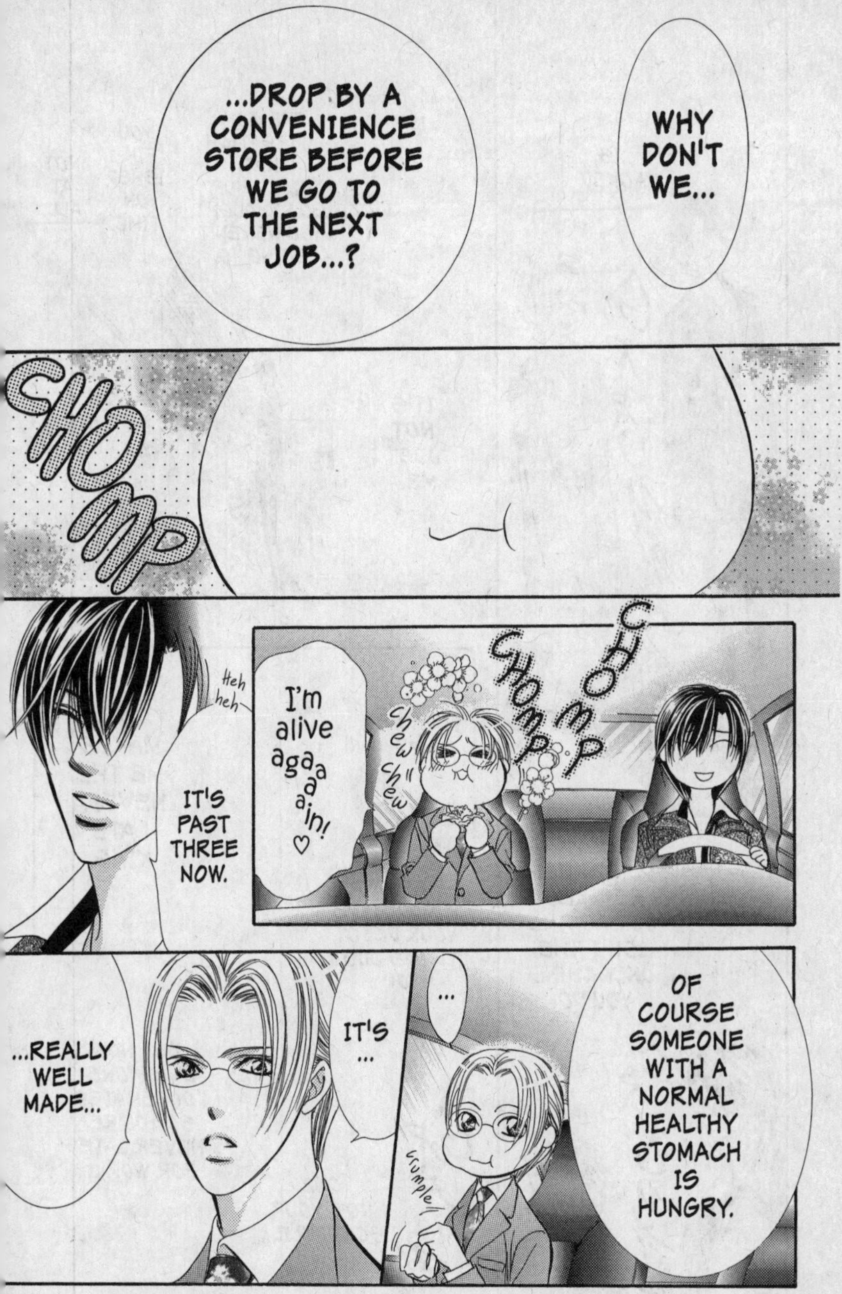
WHY DON'T WE...
...DROP BY A CONVENIENCE STORE BEFORE WE GO TO THE NEXT JOB...?
CHOMP
CHOMP CHOMP
I'm alive agaaaain! ♡
chew chew
Heh heh
IT'S PAST THREE NOW.
OF COURSE SOMEONE WITH A NORMAL HEALTHY STOMACH IS HUNGRY.
...
crumple
IT'S ...
...REALLY WELL MADE...

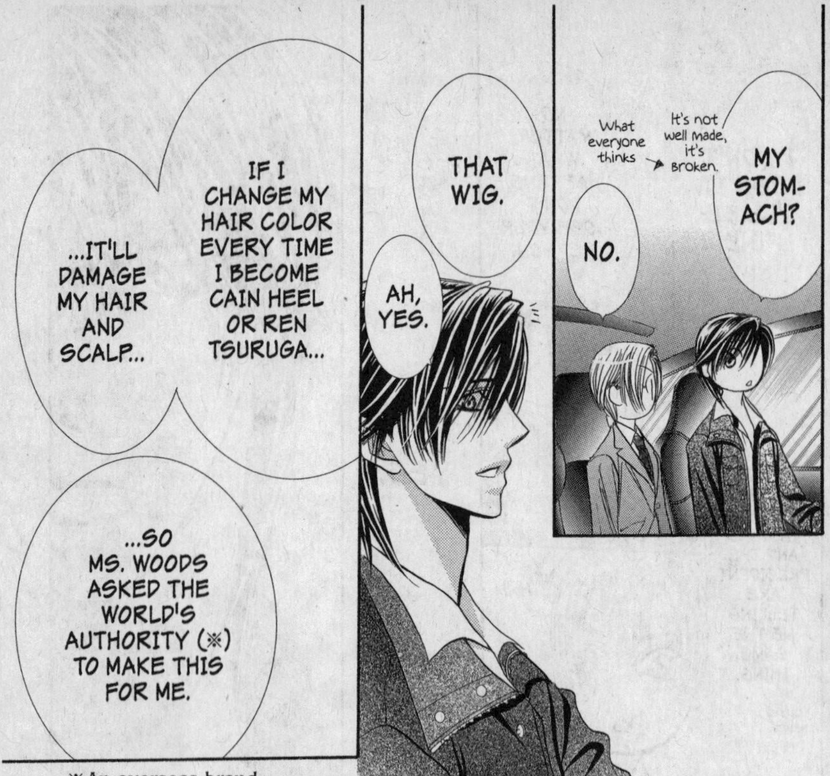
MY STOMACH?
NO.
What everyone thinks → It's not well made, it's broken.
THAT WIG.
AH, YES.
IF I CHANGE MY HAIR COLOR EVERY TIME I BECOME CAIN HEEL OR REN TSURUGA...
...IT'LL DAMAGE MY HAIR AND SCALP...
...SO MS. WOODS ASKED THE WORLD'S AUTHORITY (※) TO MAKE THIS FOR ME.

※An overseas brand

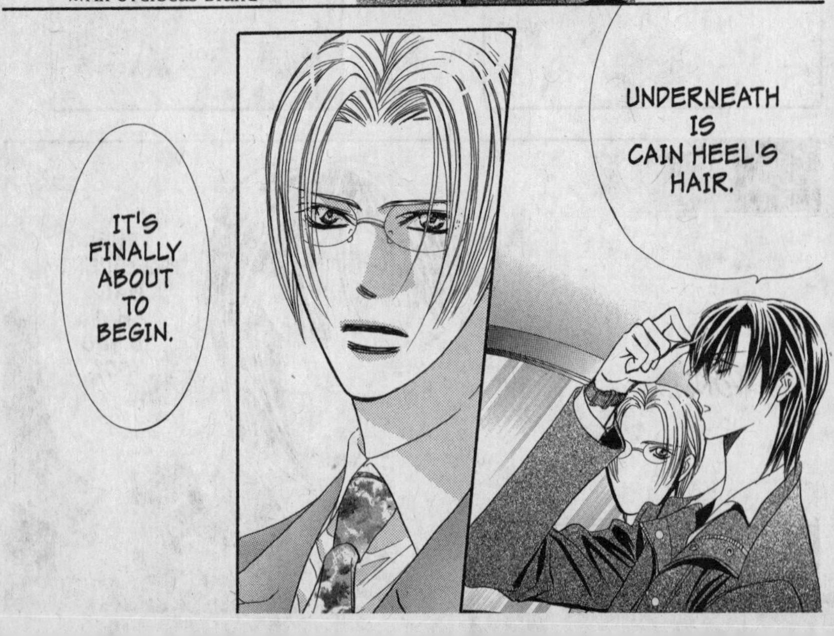
UNDERNEATH IS CAIN HEEL'S HAIR.
IT'S FINALLY ABOUT TO BEGIN.

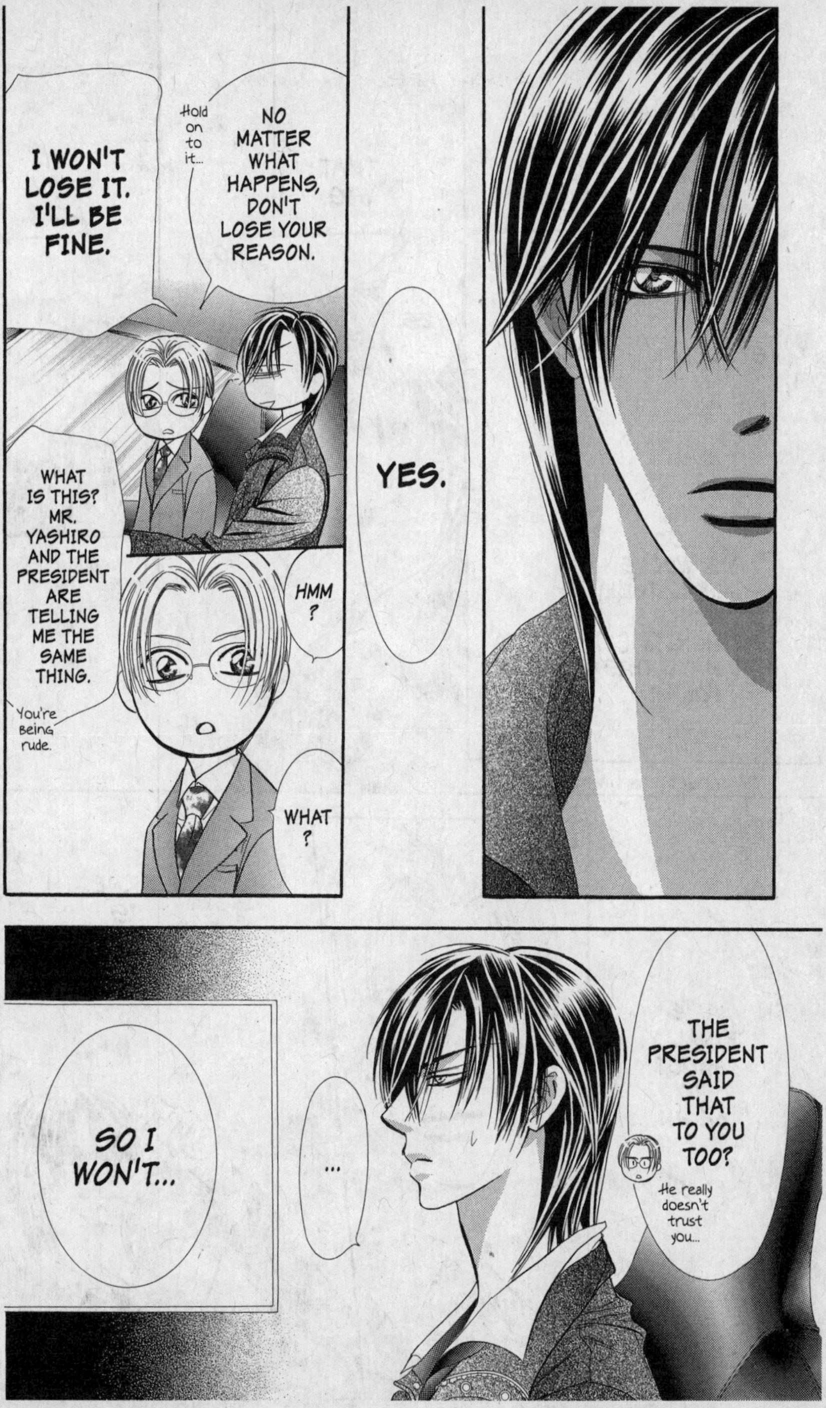
YES.
NO MATTER WHAT HAPPENS, DON'T LOSE YOUR REASON.
Hold on to it...
I WON'T LOSE IT. I'LL BE FINE.
WHAT IS THIS? MR. YASHIRO AND THE PRESIDENT ARE TELLING ME THE SAME THING.
HMM?
You're being rude.
WHAT?
THE PRESIDENT SAID THAT TO YOU TOO?
He really doesn't trust you...
...
SO I WON'T...

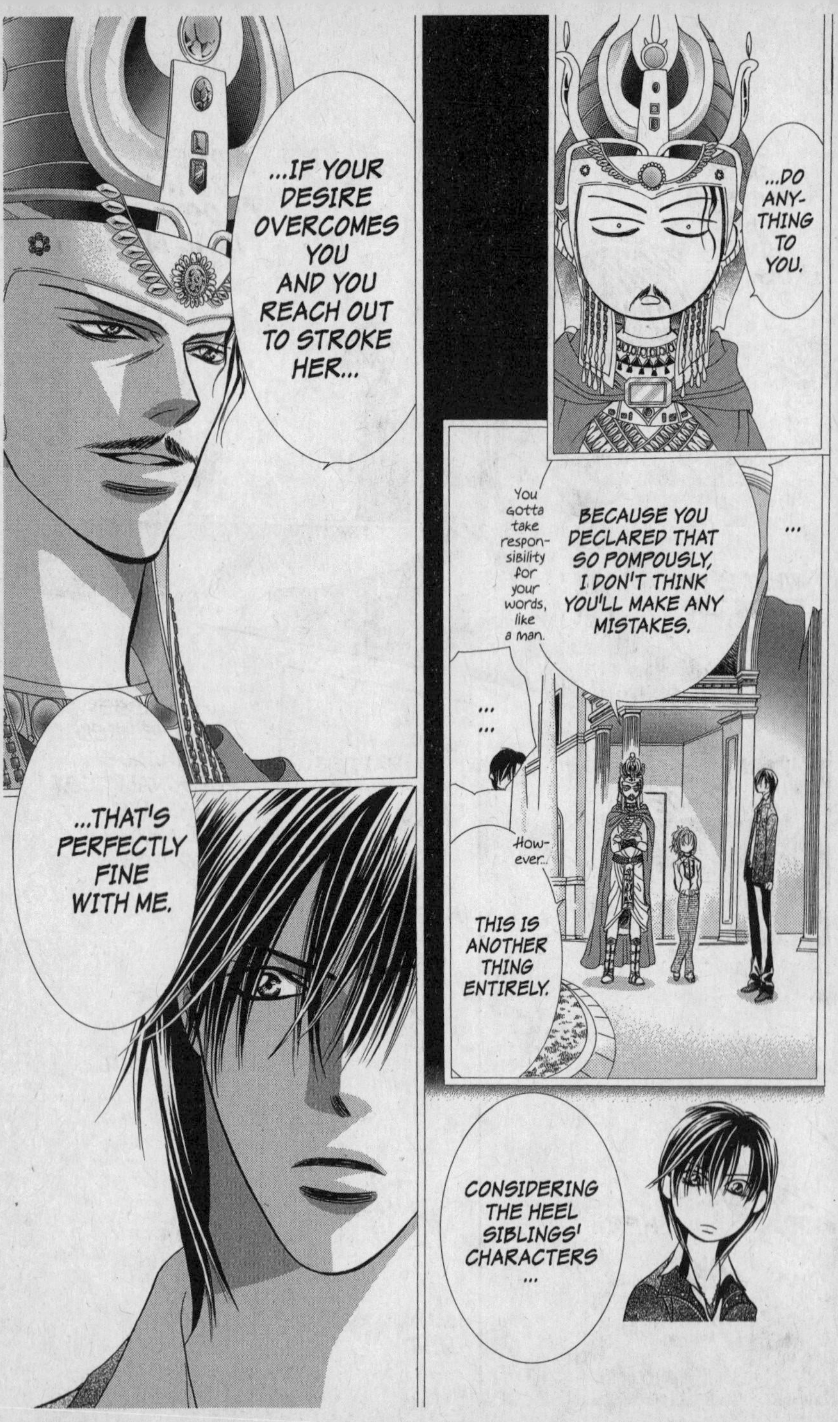
...DO ANY-THING TO YOU.
...
BECAUSE YOU DECLARED THAT SO POMPOUSLY, I DON'T THINK YOU'LL MAKE ANY MISTAKES.
You gotta take respon-sibility for your words, like a man.
... ...
How-ever...
THIS IS ANOTHER THING ENTIRELY.
CONSIDERING THE HEEL SIBLINGS' CHARACTERS ...
...IF YOUR DESIRE OVERCOMES YOU AND YOU REACH OUT TO STROKE HER...
...THAT'S PERFECTLY FINE WITH ME.

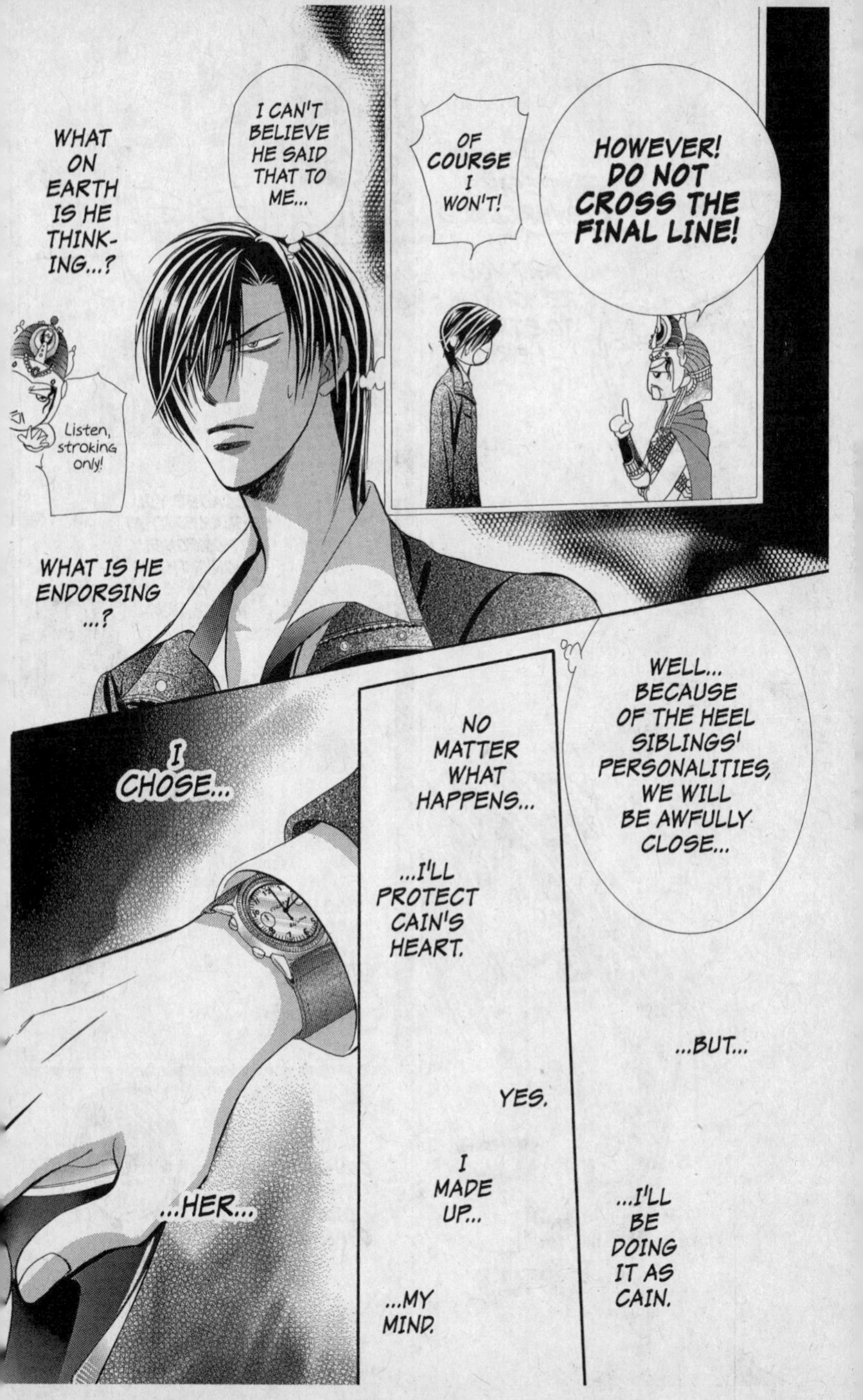
HOWEVER! DO NOT CROSS THE FINAL LINE!
OF COURSE I WON'T!
I CAN'T BELIEVE HE SAID THAT TO ME...
WHAT ON EARTH IS HE THINKING...?
Listen, stroking only!
WHAT IS HE ENDORSING...?
WELL... BECAUSE OF THE HEEL SIBLINGS' PERSONALITIES, WE WILL BE AWFULLY CLOSE...
...BUT...
...I'LL BE DOING IT AS CAIN.
NO MATTER WHAT HAPPENS...
...I'LL PROTECT CAIN'S HEART.
YES.
I MADE UP...
...MY MIND.
I CHOSE...
...HER...

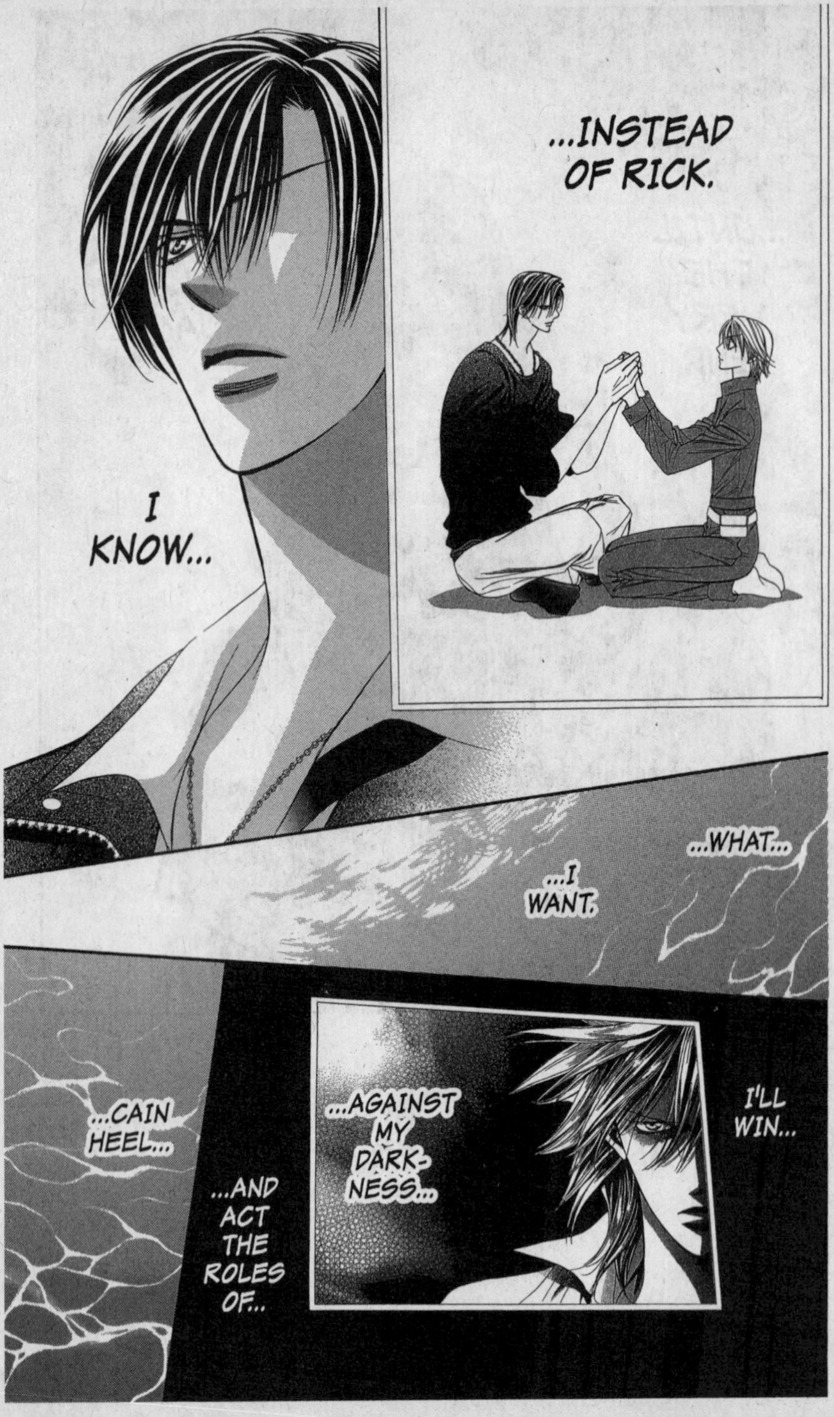
...INSTEAD OF RICK.
I KNOW...
...WHAT...
...I WANT.
I'LL WIN...
...AGAINST MY DARKNESS...
...AND ACT THE ROLES OF...
...CAIN HEEL...

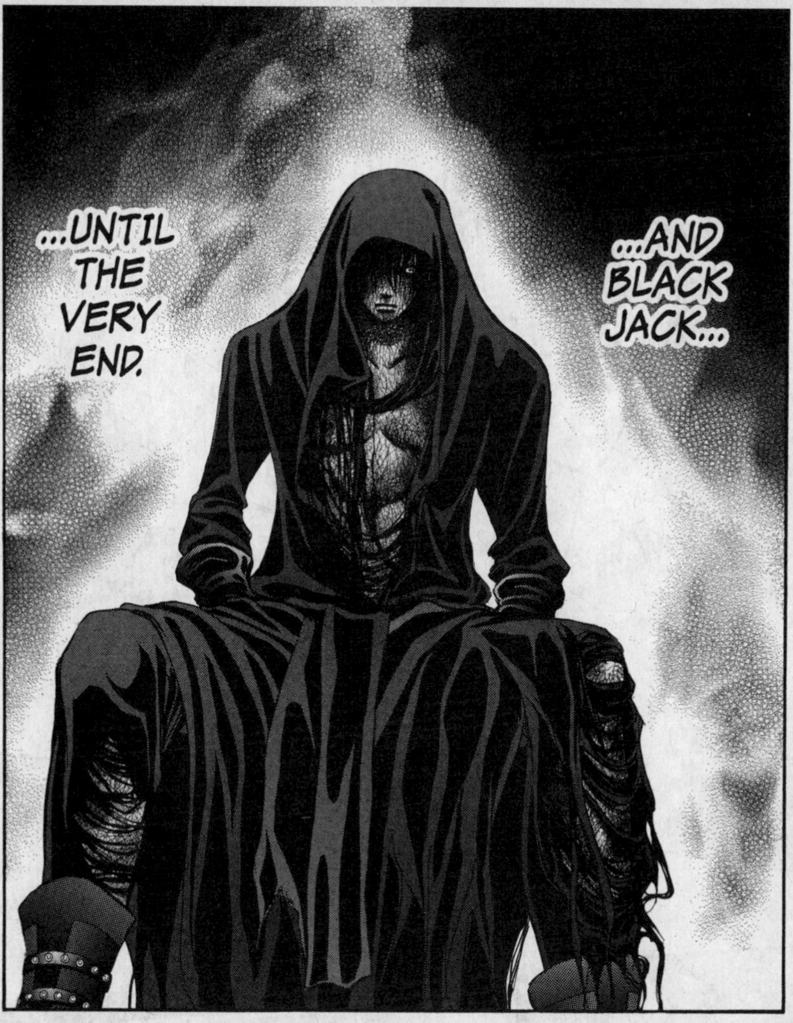
...AND BLACK JACK...
...UNTIL THE VERY END.

AND I'LL DO IT PERFECTLY.

End of Act 174

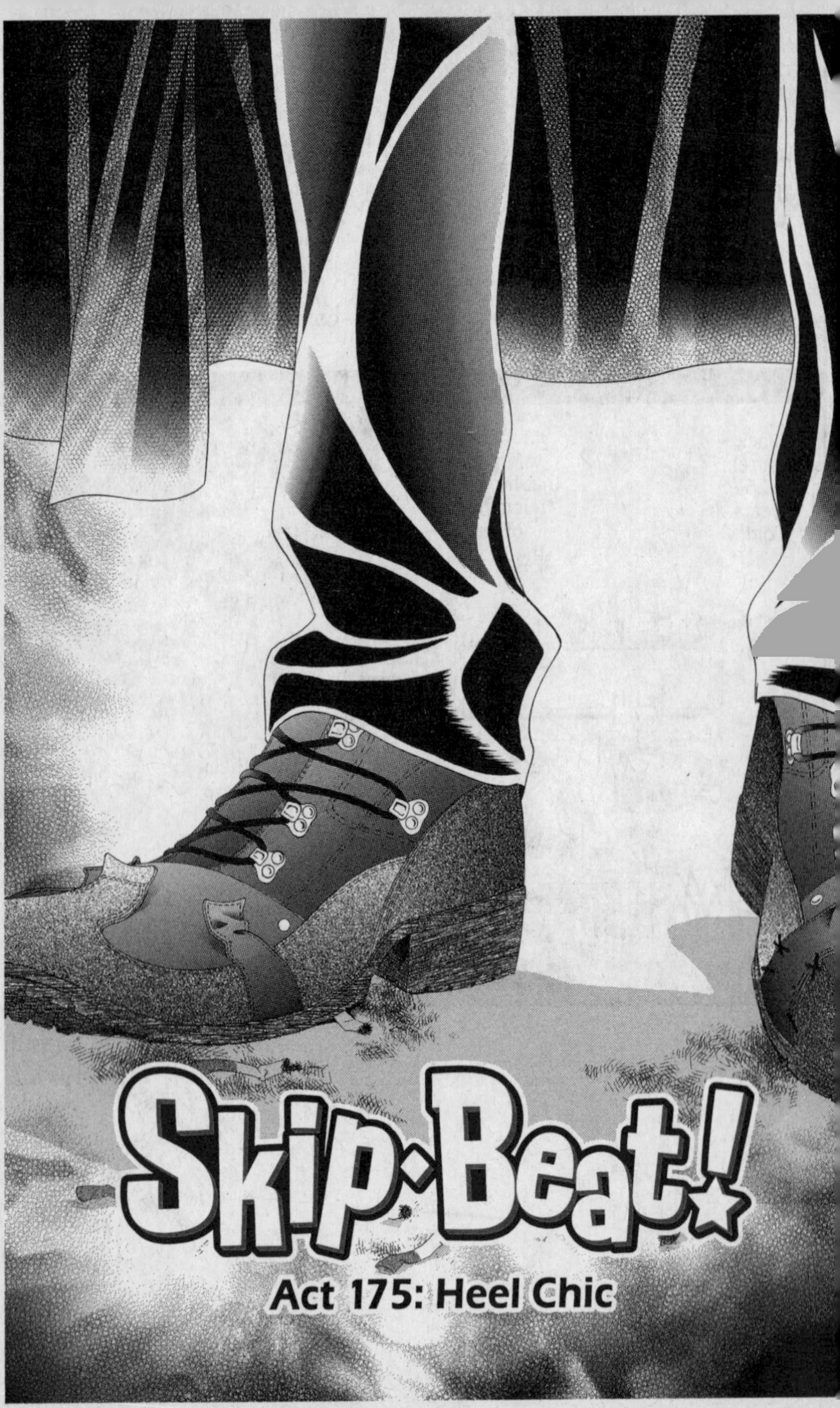
Skip·Beat!
Act 175: Heel Chic

1986.
In Great Britain, a series of grisly murders were committed.
The victims, five in total, were young and old, male and female.
At each crime scene, a message was left scrawled in the victim's blood...
...and their hearts were missing. The perpetrator of these bizarre and lust-fueled murders...
Jack Darrel. 25 years old.
...repeatedly told people that he was the "reincarnation of Jack the Ripper."

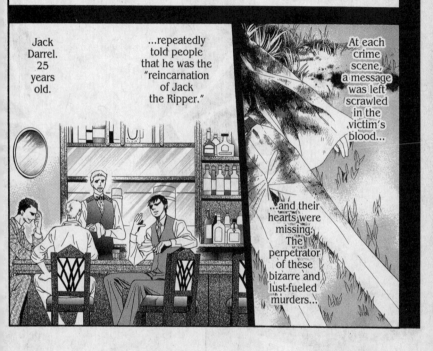

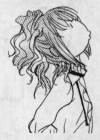

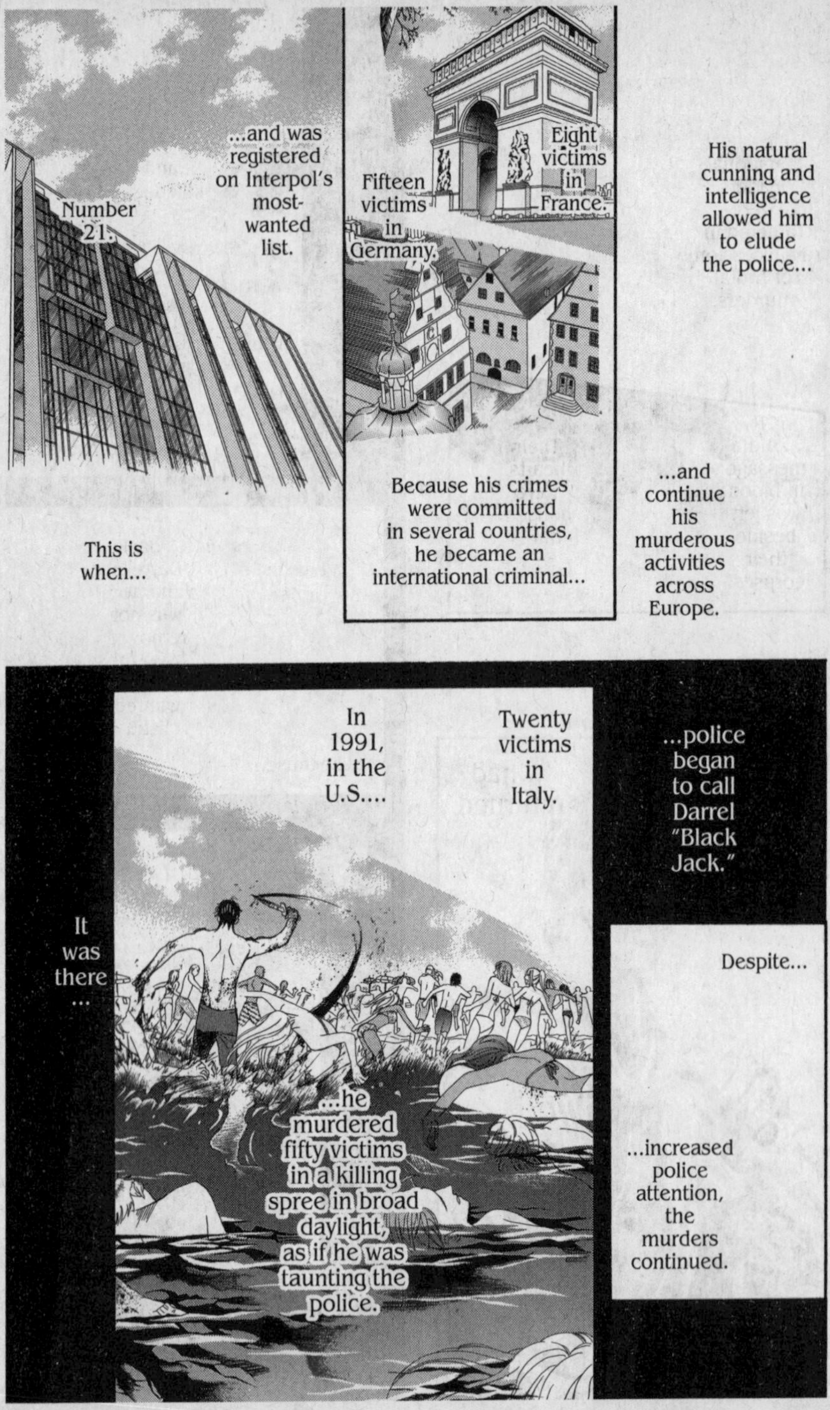
His natural cunning and intelligence allowed him to elude the police...
...and continue his murderous activities across Europe.
Eight victims in France.
Fifteen victims in Germany.
Because his crimes were committed in several countries, he became an international criminal...
...and was registered on Interpol's most-wanted list.
Number 21.
This is when...
...police began to call Darrel "Black Jack."
Despite...
...increased police attention, the murders continued.
Twenty victims in Italy.
In 1991, in the U.S....
It was there...
...he murdered fifty victims in a killing spree in broad daylight, as if he was taunting the police.

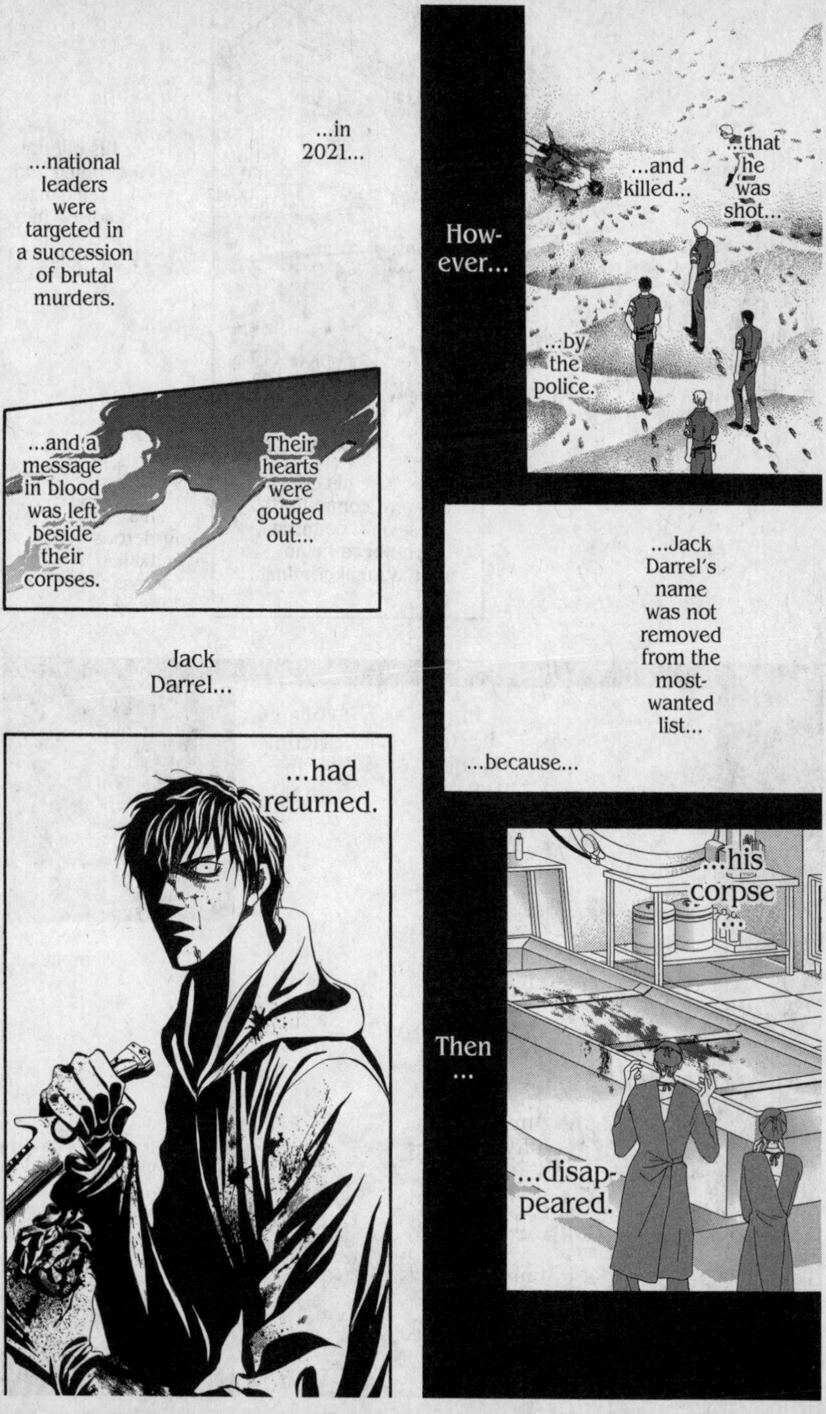
However...
...that he was shot...
...and killed...
...by the police.
...Jack Darrel's name was not removed from the most-wanted list...
...because...
Then...
...his corpse...
...disappeared.
...in 2021...
...national leaders were targeted in a succession of brutal murders.
Their hearts were gouged out...
...and a message in blood was left beside their corpses.
Jack Darrel...
...had returned.

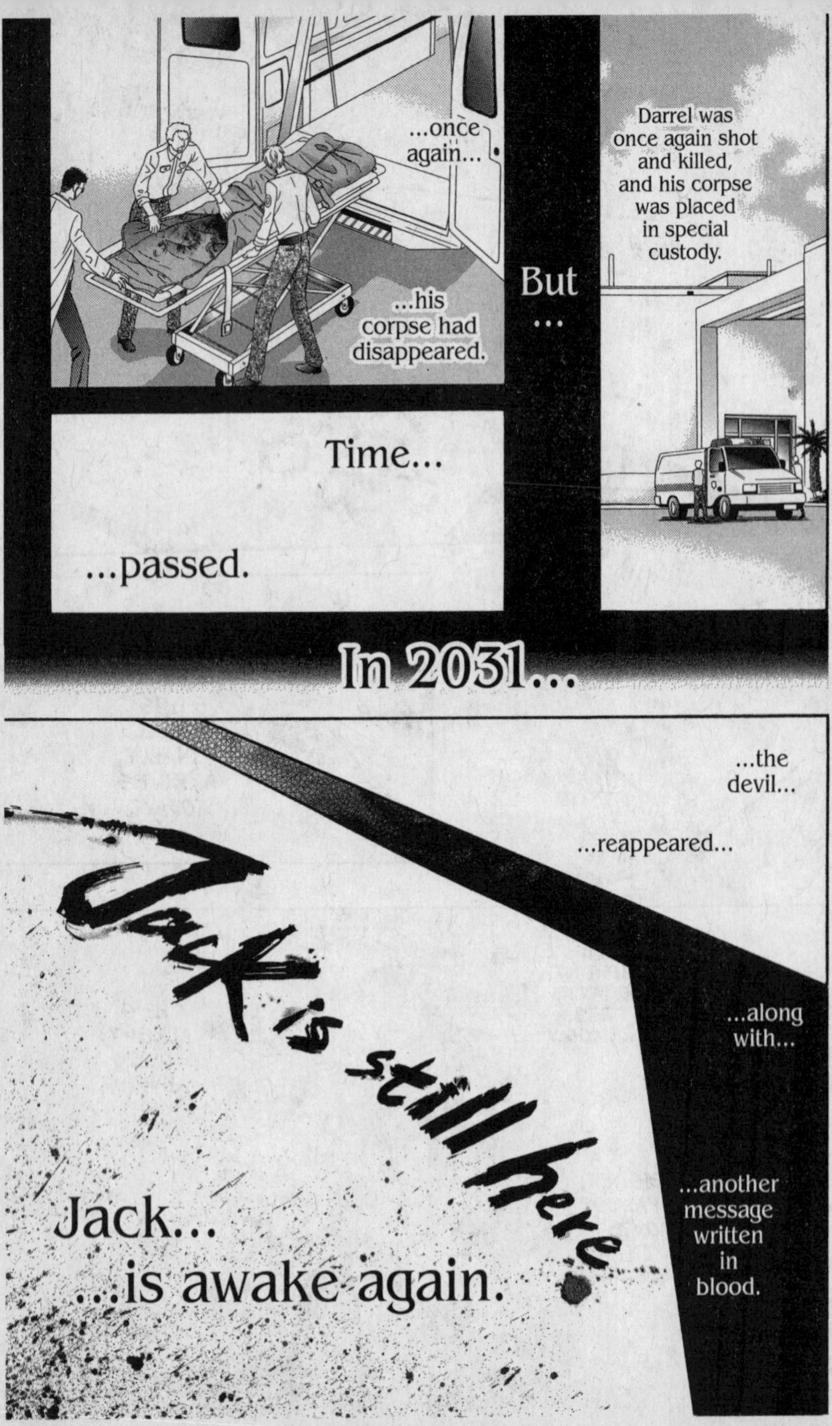
Darrel was once again shot and killed, and his corpse was placed in special custody.
But...
...once again...
...his corpse had disappeared.
Time...
...passed.
In 2031...
...the devil...
...reappeared...
...along with...
...another message written in blood.
Jack is still here.
Jack...
...is awake again.

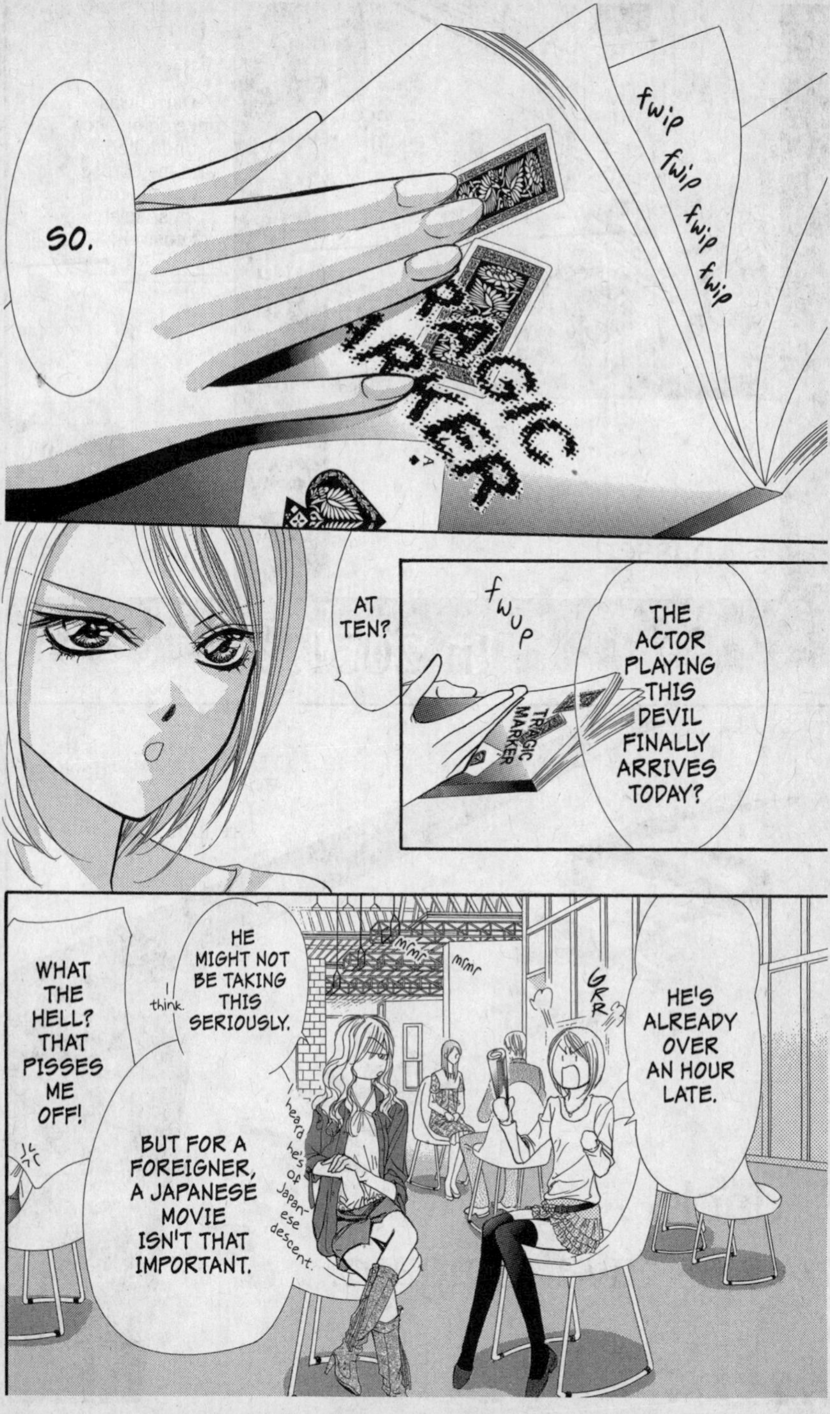
fwip fwip fwip fwip
SO.
fwup
TRAGIC MARKER
THE ACTOR PLAYING THIS DEVIL FINALLY ARRIVES TODAY?
AT TEN?
HE'S ALREADY OVER AN HOUR LATE.
GRR
mrmr
mrmr
HE MIGHT NOT BE TAKING THIS SERIOUSLY.
I think.
I heard he's of Japanese descent.
BUT FOR A FOREIGNER, A JAPANESE MOVIE ISN'T THAT IMPORTANT.
WHAT THE HELL? THAT PISSES ME OFF!

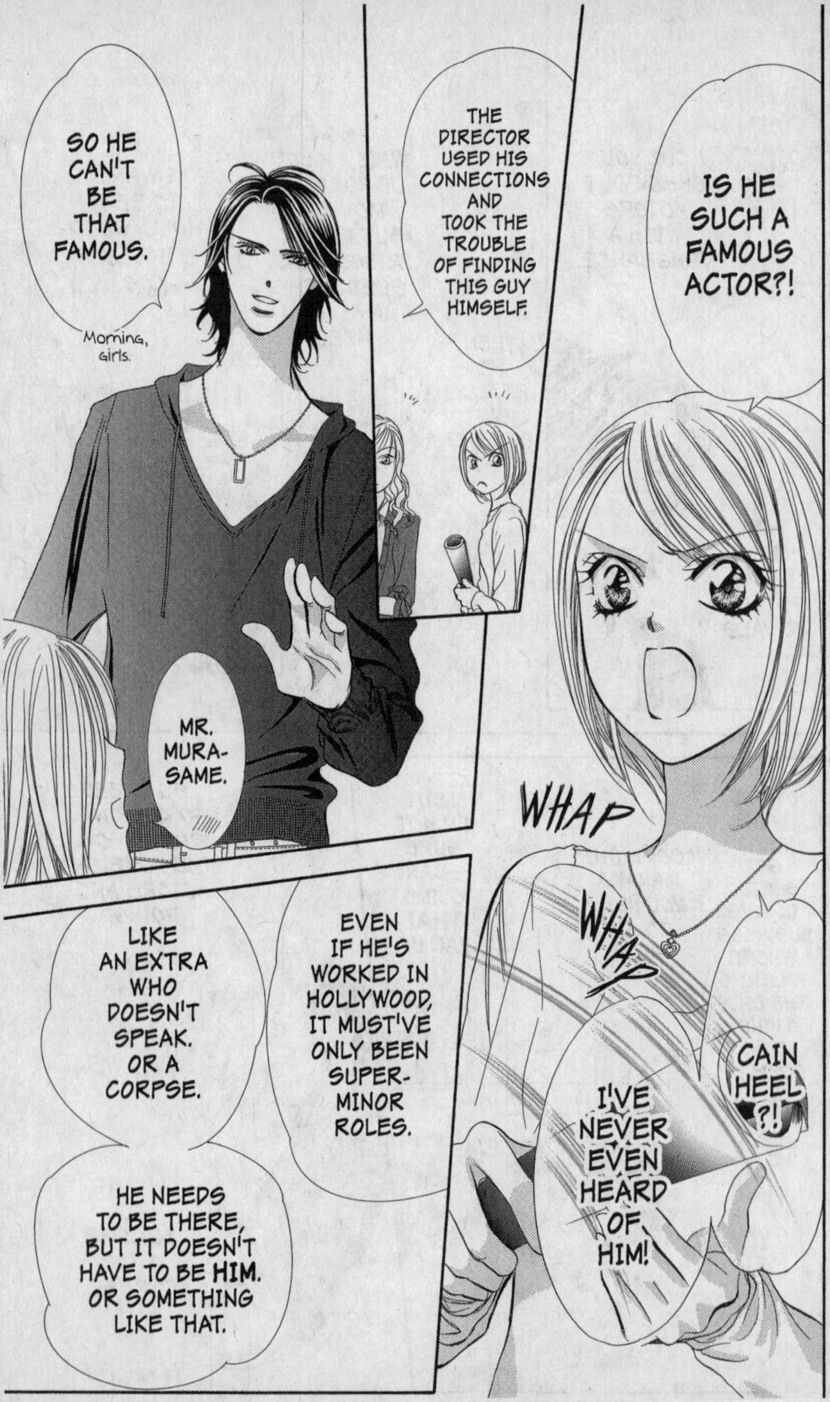

IS HE SUCH A FAMOUS ACTOR?!
THE DIRECTOR USED HIS CONNECTIONS AND TOOK THE TROUBLE OF FINDING THIS GUY HIMSELF.
SO HE CAN'T BE THAT FAMOUS.
Morning, Girls.
MR. MURA-SAME.
WHAP
WHAP
CAIN HEEL ?!
I'VE NEVER EVEN HEARD OF HIM!
EVEN IF HE'S WORKED IN HOLLYWOOD, IT MUST'VE ONLY BEEN SUPER-MINOR ROLES.
LIKE AN EXTRA WHO DOESN'T SPEAK. OR A CORPSE.
HE NEEDS TO BE THERE, BUT IT DOESN'T HAVE TO BE **HIM**. OR SOMETHING LIKE THAT.

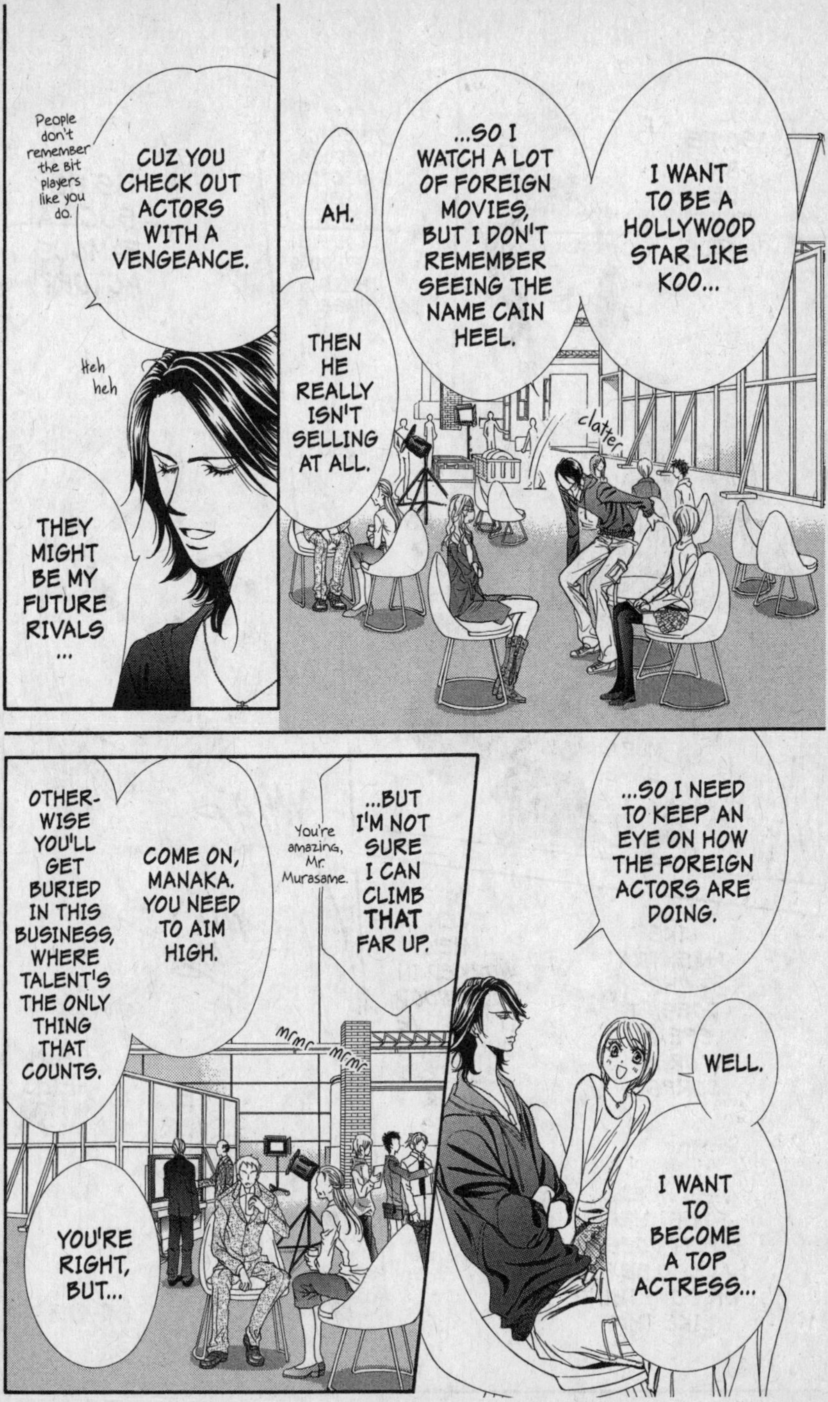
I WANT TO BE A HOLLYWOOD STAR LIKE KOO...
...SO I WATCH A LOT OF FOREIGN MOVIES, BUT I DON'T REMEMBER SEEING THE NAME CAIN HEEL.
clatter
AH.
THEN HE REALLY ISN'T SELLING AT ALL.
CUZ YOU CHECK OUT ACTORS WITH A VENGEANCE.
People don't remember the bit players like you do.
Heh heh
THEY MIGHT BE MY FUTURE RIVALS...
...SO I NEED TO KEEP AN EYE ON HOW THE FOREIGN ACTORS ARE DOING.
WELL.
I WANT TO BECOME A TOP ACTRESS...
...BUT I'M NOT SURE I CAN CLIMB THAT FAR UP.
You're amazing, Mr. Murasame.
COME ON, MANAKA. YOU NEED TO AIM HIGH.
OTHERWISE YOU'LL GET BURIED IN THIS BUSINESS, WHERE TALENT'S THE ONLY THING THAT COUNTS.
mrmr mrmr
YOU'RE RIGHT, BUT...

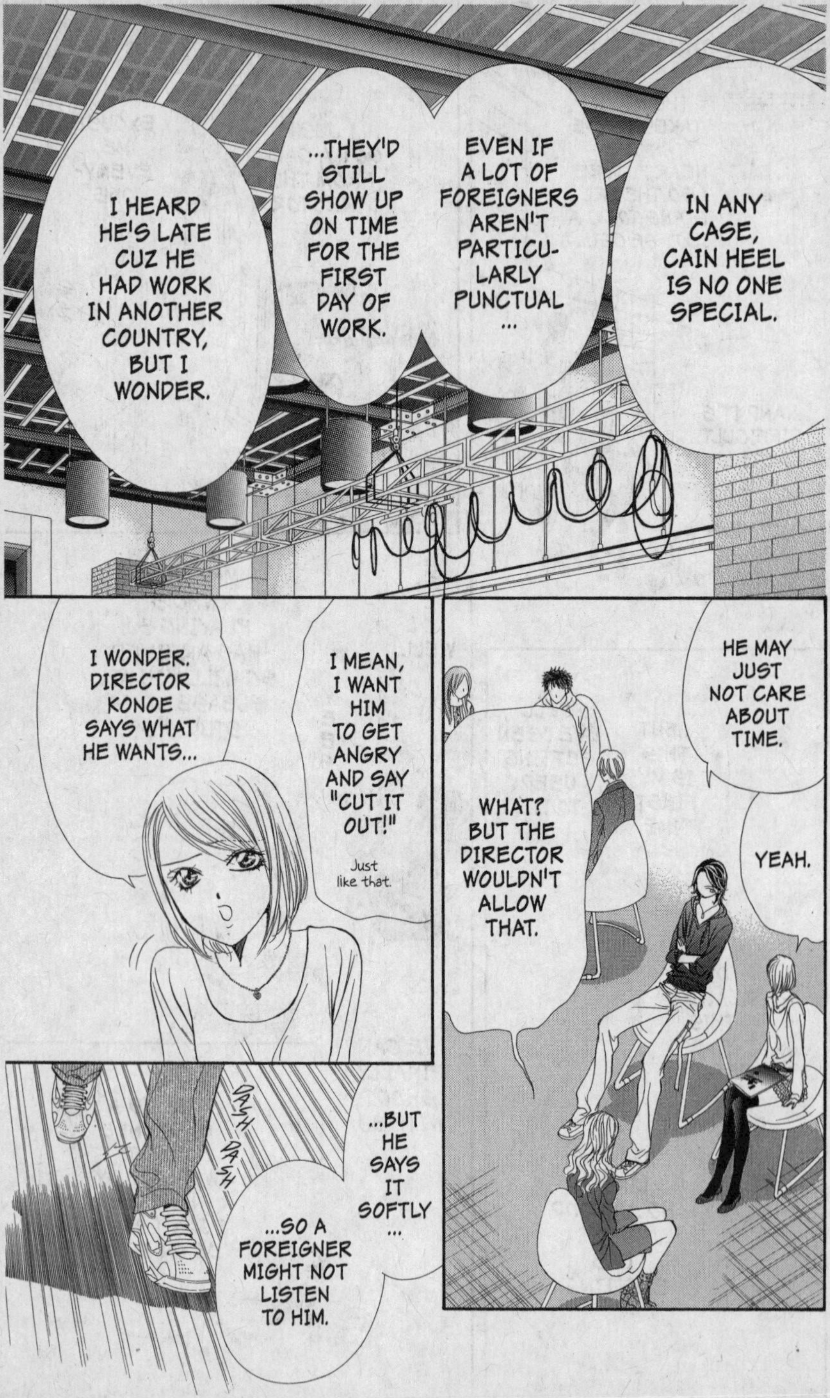
IN ANY CASE, CAIN HEEL IS NO ONE SPECIAL.
EVEN IF A LOT OF FOREIGNERS AREN'T PARTICULARLY PUNCTUAL...
...THEY'D STILL SHOW UP ON TIME FOR THE FIRST DAY OF WORK.
I HEARD HE'S LATE CUZ HE HAD WORK IN ANOTHER COUNTRY, BUT I WONDER.
HE MAY JUST NOT CARE ABOUT TIME.
YEAH.
WHAT? BUT THE DIRECTOR WOULDN'T ALLOW THAT.
I MEAN, I WANT HIM TO GET ANGRY AND SAY "CUT IT OUT!"
Just like that.
I WONDER. DIRECTOR KONOE SAYS WHAT HE WANTS...
...BUT HE SAYS IT SOFTLY...
...SO A FOREIGNER MIGHT NOT LISTEN TO HIM.
DASH
DASH

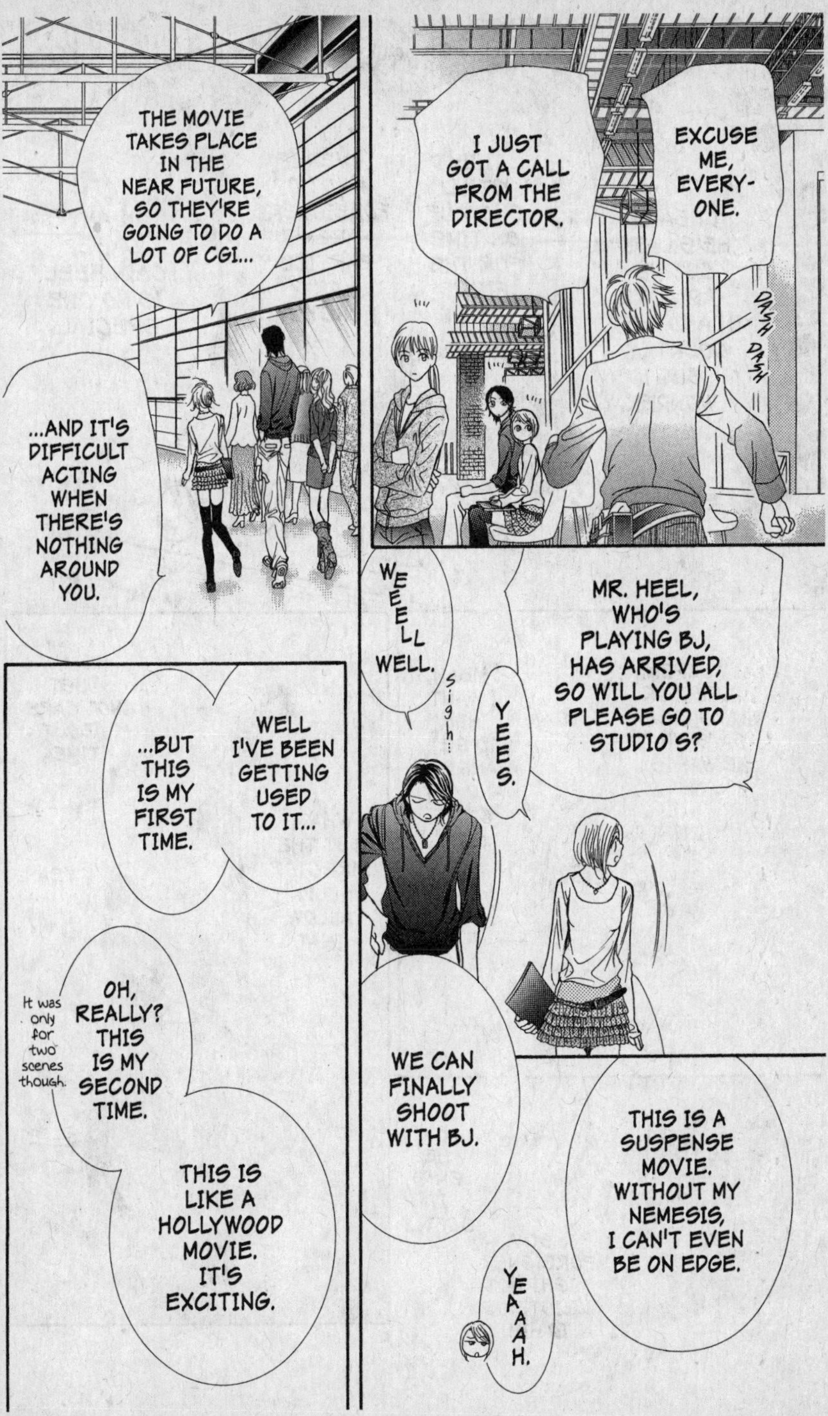
EXCUSE ME, EVERY-ONE.
I JUST GOT A CALL FROM THE DIRECTOR.
DASH DASH
MR. HEEL, WHO'S PLAYING BJ, HAS ARRIVED, SO WILL YOU ALL PLEASE GO TO STUDIO S?
WEEELL WELL.
Sigh...
YEES.
WE CAN FINALLY SHOOT WITH BJ.
THIS IS A SUSPENSE MOVIE. WITHOUT MY NEMESIS, I CAN'T EVEN BE ON EDGE.
YEAAAH.
THE MOVIE TAKES PLACE IN THE NEAR FUTURE, SO THEY'RE GOING TO DO A LOT OF CGI...
...AND IT'S DIFFICULT ACTING WHEN THERE'S NOTHING AROUND YOU.
WELL I'VE BEEN GETTING USED TO IT...
...BUT THIS IS MY FIRST TIME.
OH, REALLY? THIS IS MY SECOND TIME.
It was only for two scenes though.
THIS IS LIKE A HOLLYWOOD MOVIE. IT'S EXCITING.

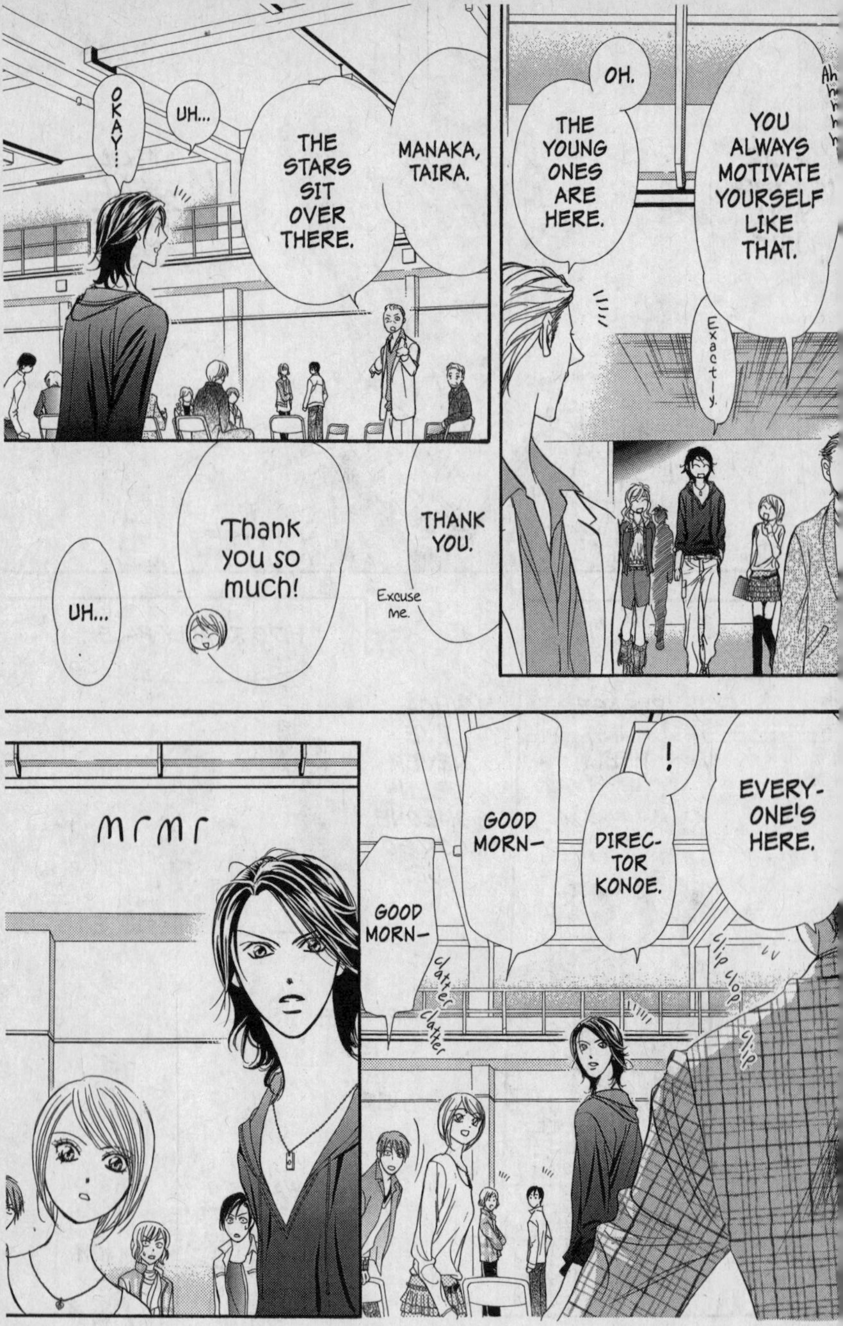

Ahhhhh
YOU ALWAYS MOTIVATE YOURSELF LIKE THAT.
Exactly.
OH.
THE YOUNG ONES ARE HERE.
MANAKA, TAIRA.
THE STARS SIT OVER THERE.
UH...
OKAY...
THANK YOU.
Excuse me.
Thank you so much!
UH...
EVERY-ONE'S HERE.
!
DIRECTOR KONOE.
GOOD MORN-
GOOD MORN-
clatter clatter
clip clop clip
mrmr

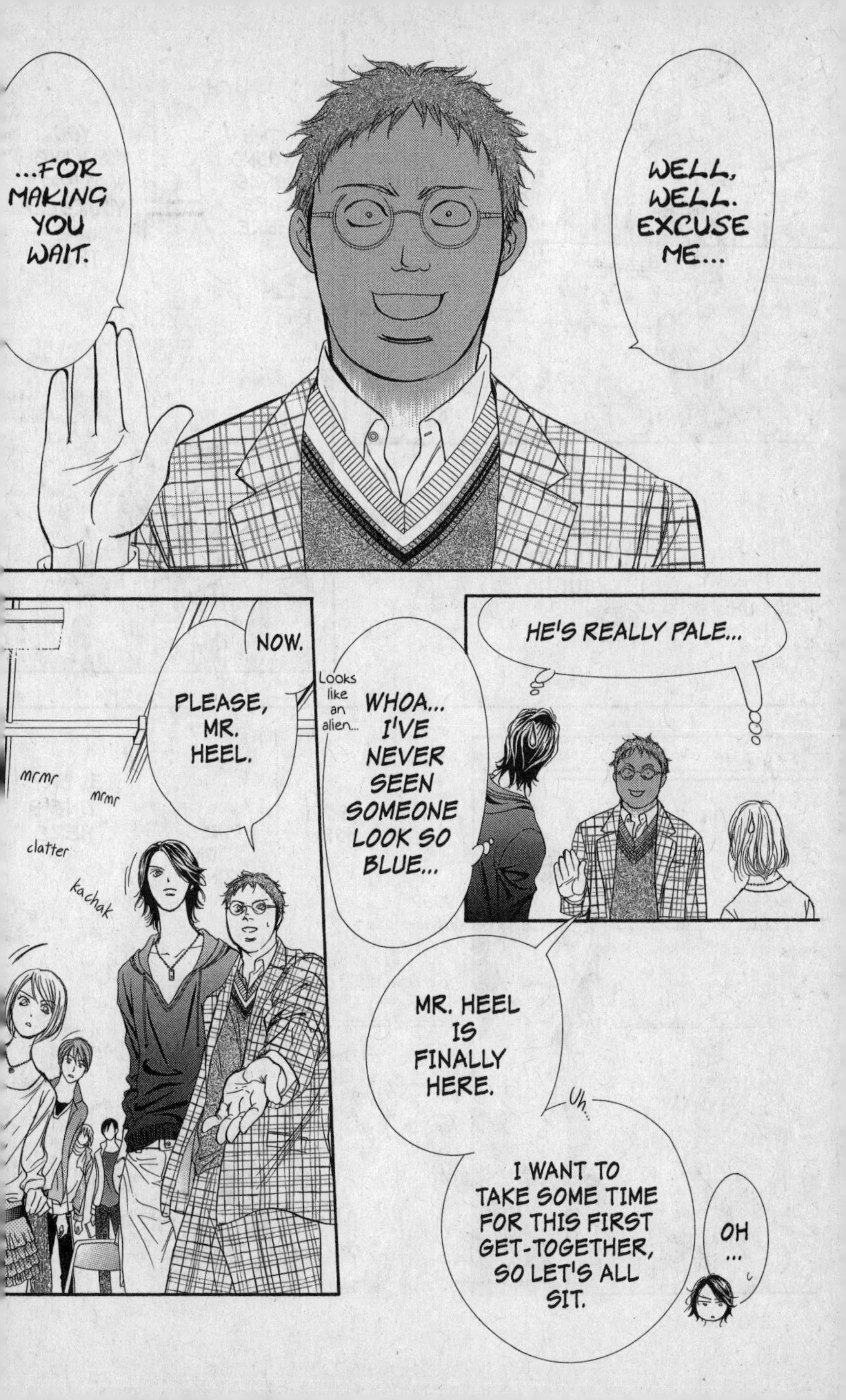
WELL, WELL. EXCUSE ME...
...FOR MAKING YOU WAIT.
HE'S REALLY PALE...
WHOA... I'VE NEVER SEEN SOMEONE LOOK SO BLUE...
Looks like an alien...
MR. HEEL IS FINALLY HERE.
Uh...
I WANT TO TAKE SOME TIME FOR THIS FIRST GET-TOGETHER, SO LET'S ALL SIT.
OH...
NOW.
PLEASE, MR. HEEL.
mrmr
mrmr
clatter
kachak

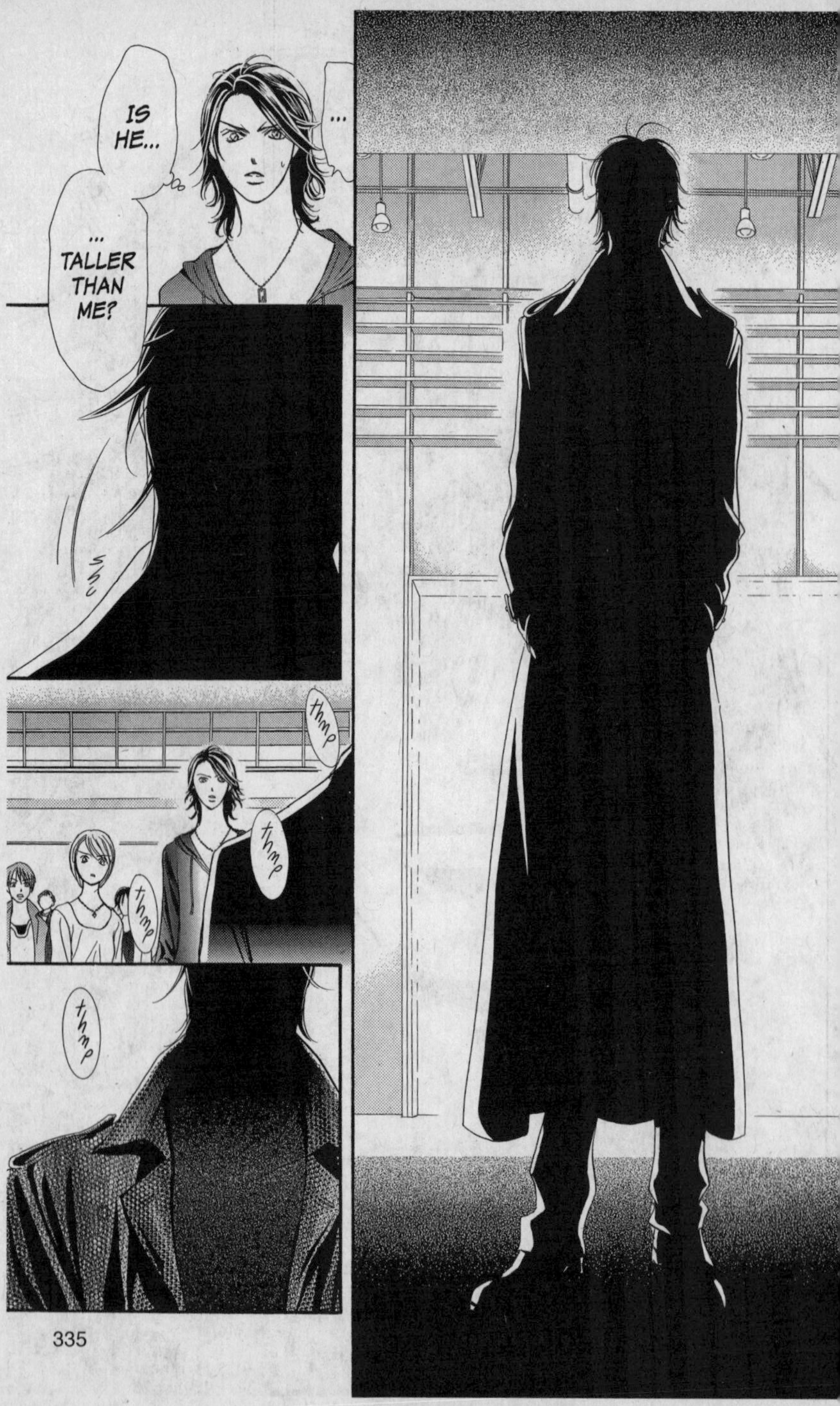
...
IS HE...
... TALLER THAN ME?
shu
thmp
thmp
thmp
thmp

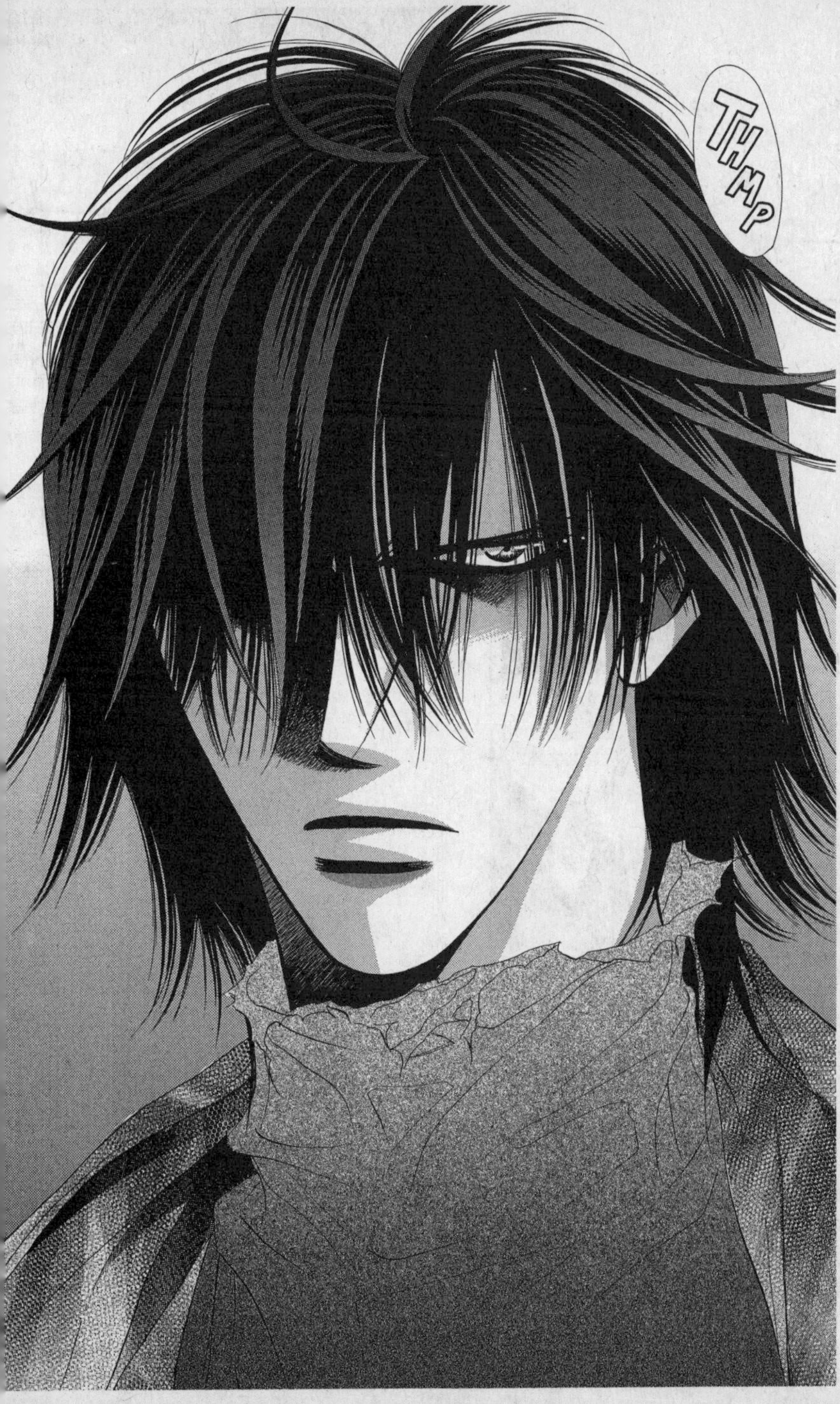
THMP

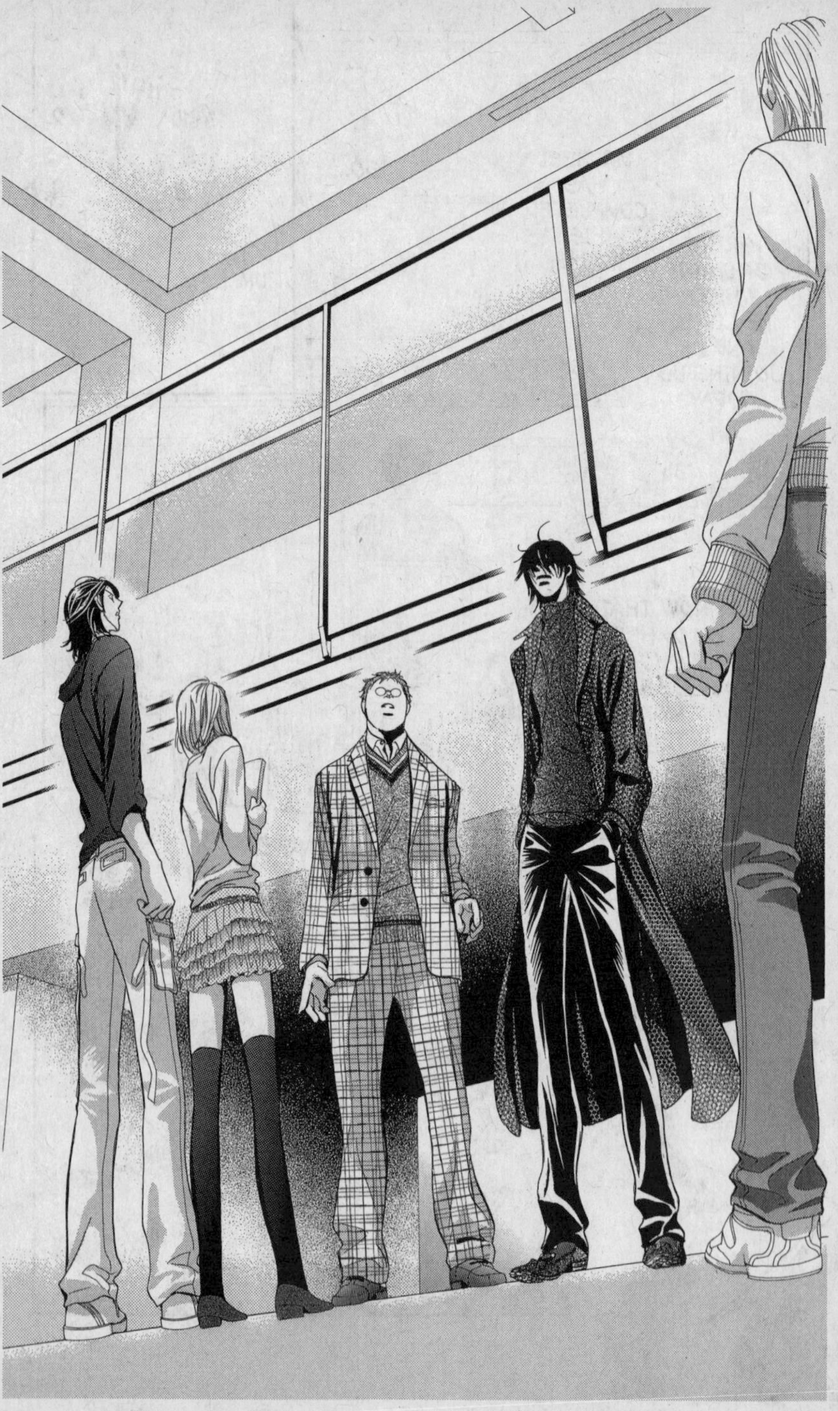

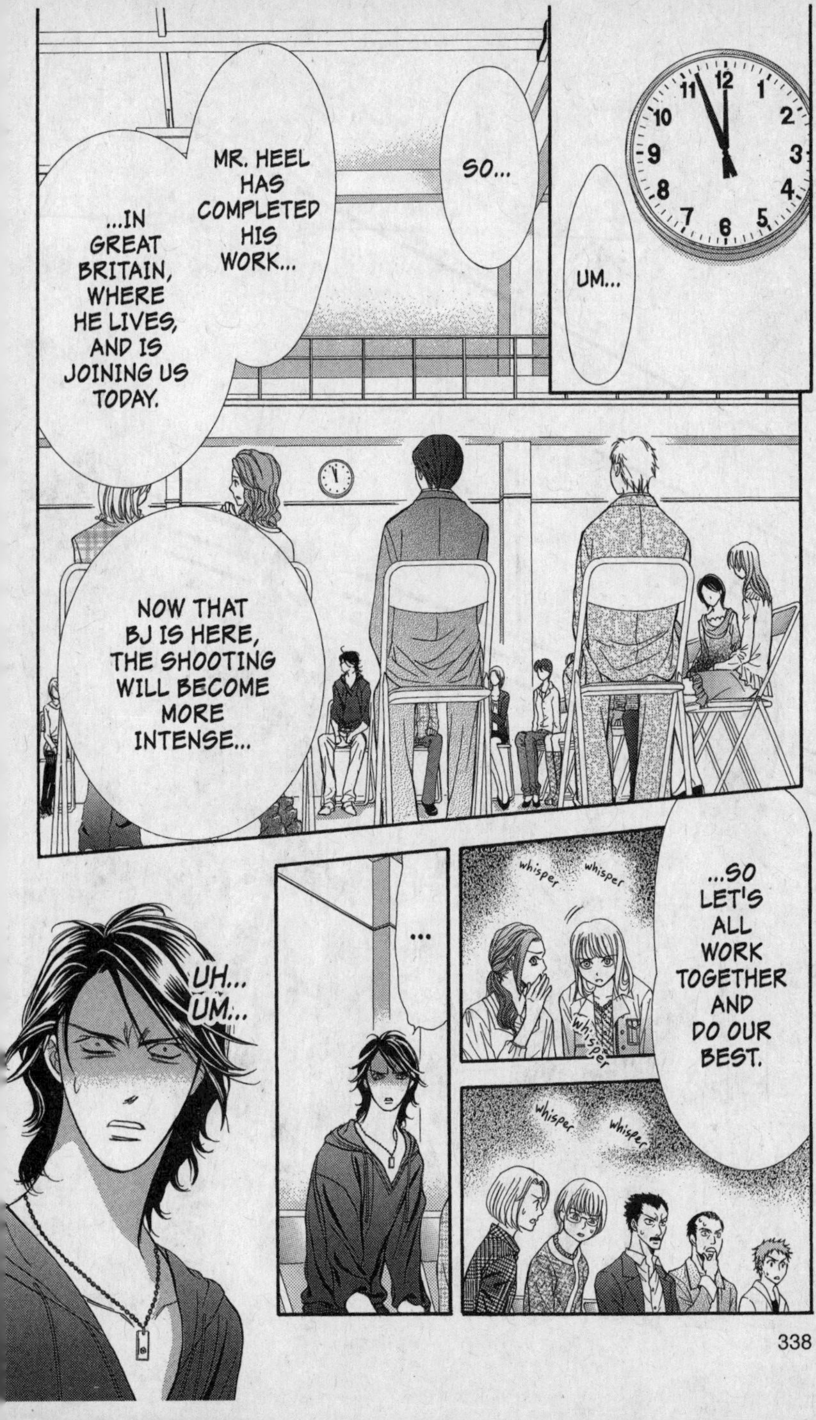
UM...
SO...
MR. HEEL HAS COMPLETED HIS WORK...
...IN GREAT BRITAIN, WHERE HE LIVES, AND IS JOINING US TODAY.
NOW THAT BJ IS HERE, THE SHOOTING WILL BECOME MORE INTENSE...
...SO LET'S ALL WORK TOGETHER AND DO OUR BEST.
whisper
whisper
whisper
whisper
whisper
...
UH... UM...

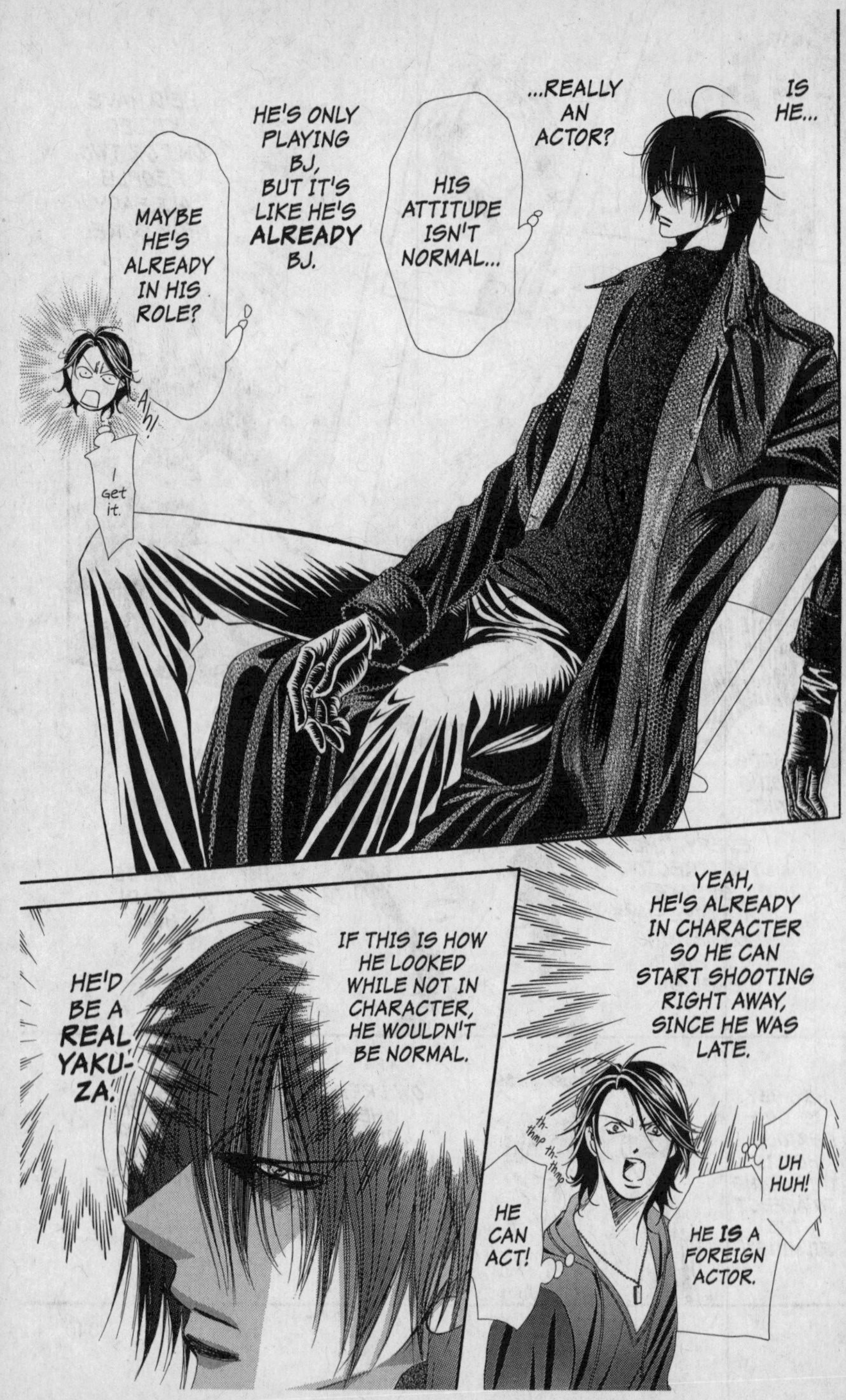
IS HE...
...REALLY AN ACTOR?
HIS ATTITUDE ISN'T NORMAL...
HE'S ONLY PLAYING BJ, BUT IT'S LIKE HE'S ALREADY BJ.
MAYBE HE'S ALREADY IN HIS ROLE?
Ah!
I Get it.
YEAH, HE'S ALREADY IN CHARACTER SO HE CAN START SHOOTING RIGHT AWAY, SINCE HE WAS LATE.
UH HUH!
HE IS A FOREIGN ACTOR.
HE CAN ACT!
th-thump th-thump
IF THIS IS HOW HE LOOKED WHILE NOT IN CHARACTER, HE WOULDN'T BE NORMAL.
HE'D BE A REAL YAKU-ZA!

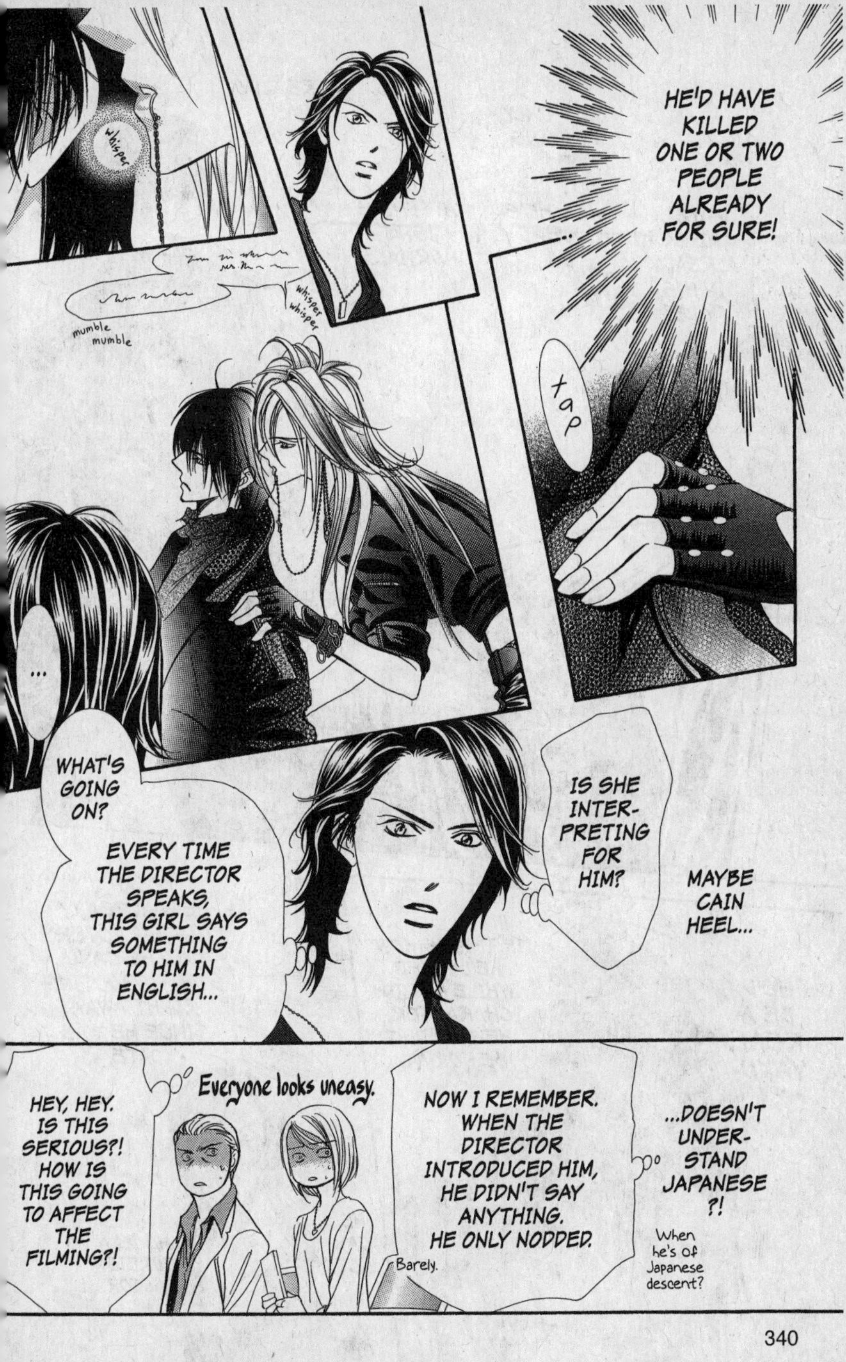

...
HE'D HAVE KILLED ONE OR TWO PEOPLE ALREADY FOR SURE!
tap
whisper whisper
whisper
mumble mumble
...
MAYBE CAIN HEEL...
IS SHE INTERPRETING FOR HIM?
WHAT'S GOING ON?
EVERY TIME THE DIRECTOR SPEAKS, THIS GIRL SAYS SOMETHING TO HIM IN ENGLISH...
...DOESN'T UNDERSTAND JAPANESE?!
When he's of Japanese descent?
NOW I REMEMBER. WHEN THE DIRECTOR INTRODUCED HIM, HE DIDN'T SAY ANYTHING. HE ONLY NODDED.
Barely.
Everyone looks uneasy.
HEY, HEY. IS THIS SERIOUS?! HOW IS THIS GOING TO AFFECT THE FILMING?!

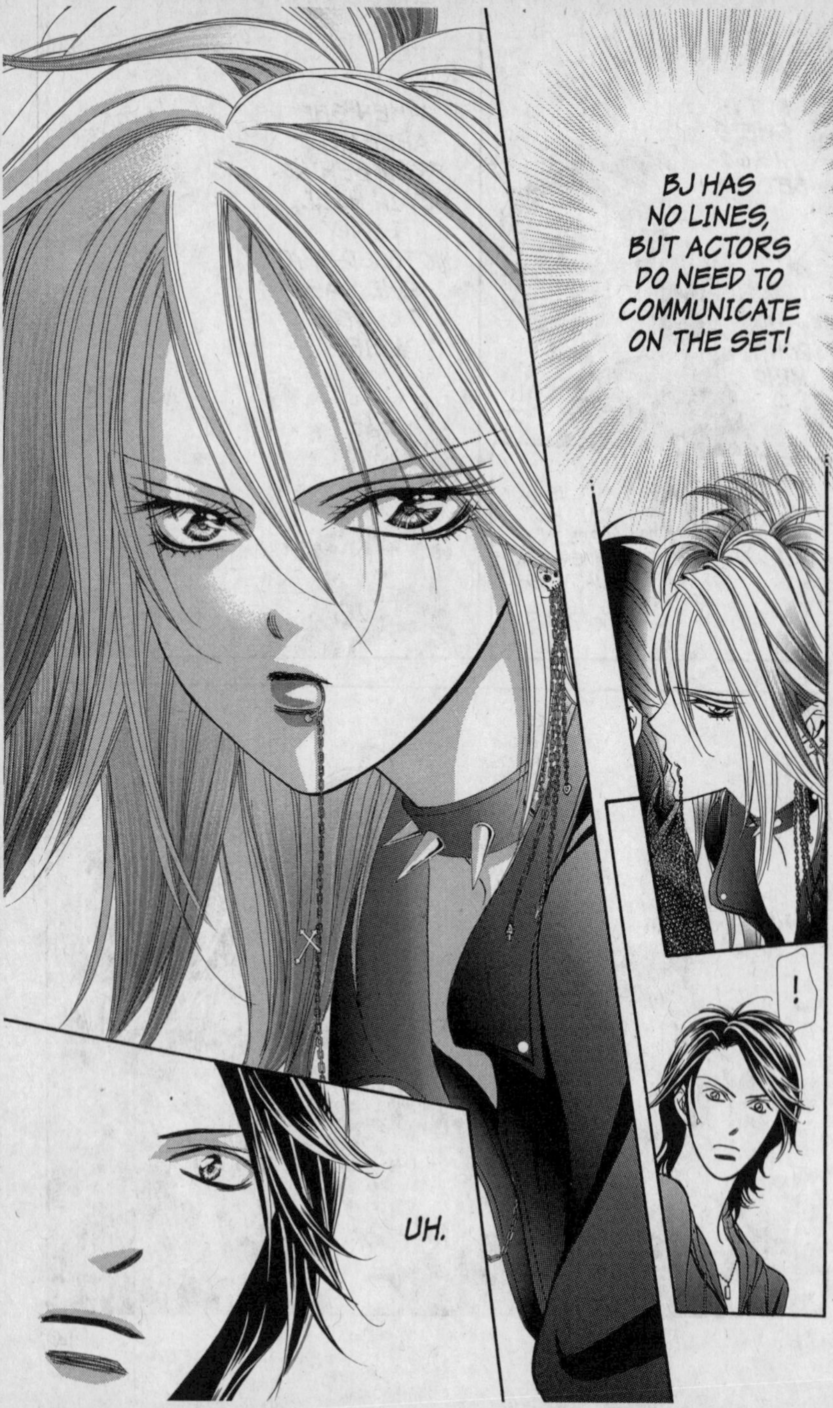
BJ HAS NO LINES, BUT ACTORS DO NEED TO COMMUNICATE ON THE SET!
!
UH.

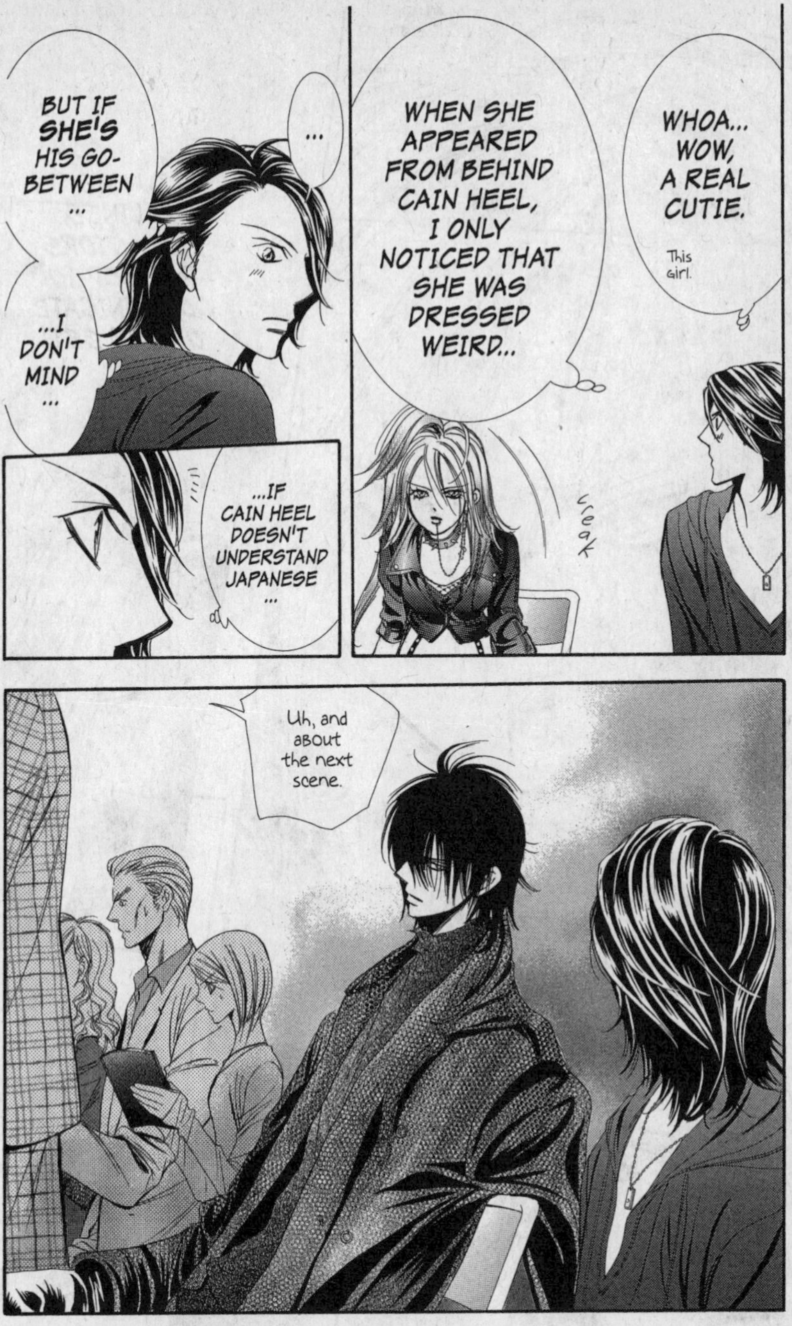
WHOA... WOW, A REAL CUTIE.
This girl.
WHEN SHE APPEARED FROM BEHIND CAIN HEEL, I ONLY NOTICED THAT SHE WAS DRESSED WEIRD...
creak
...
BUT IF SHE'S HIS GO-BETWEEN...
...I DON'T MIND...
...IF CAIN HEEL DOESN'T UNDERSTAND JAPANESE...
Uh, and about the next scene.

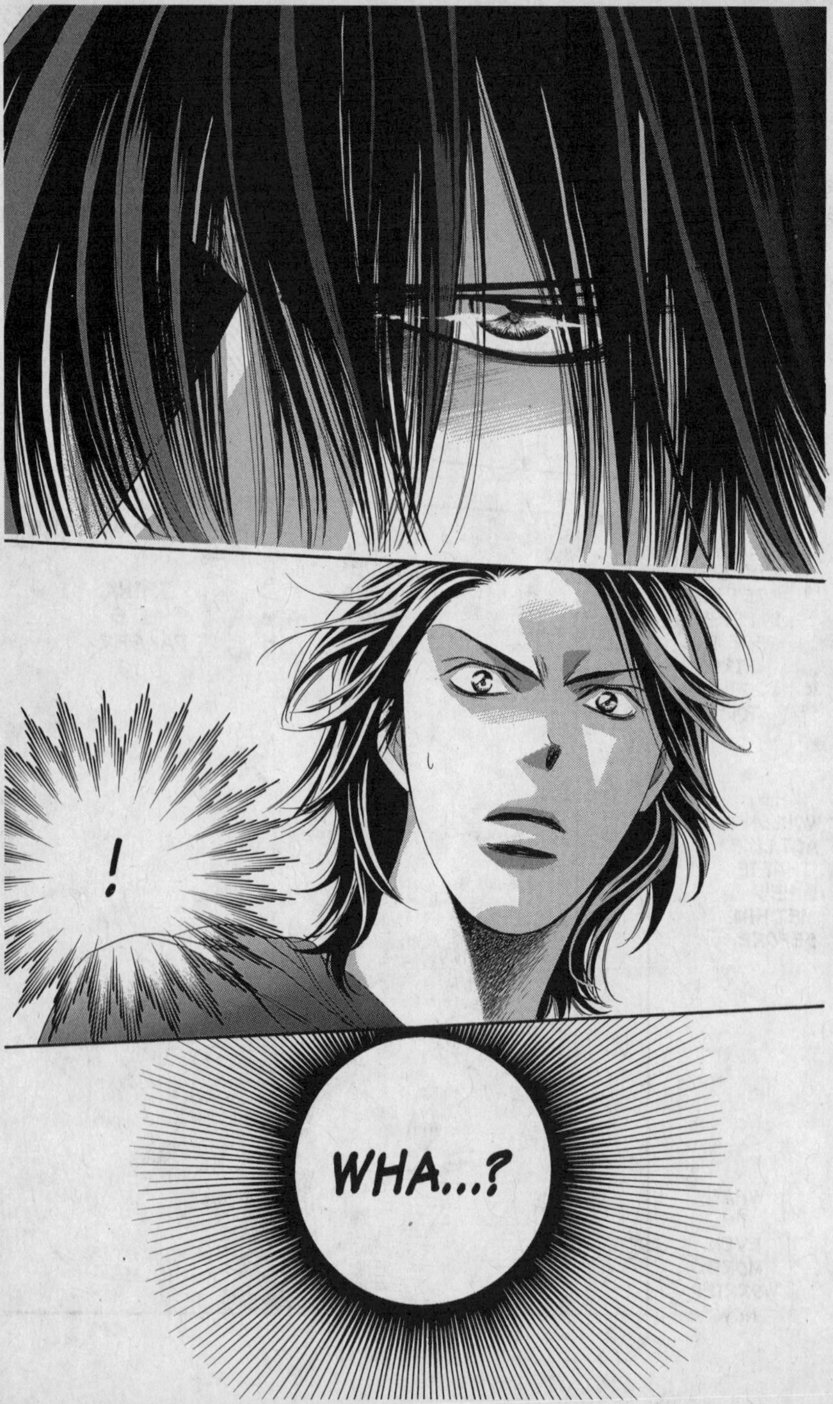
!
WHA...?

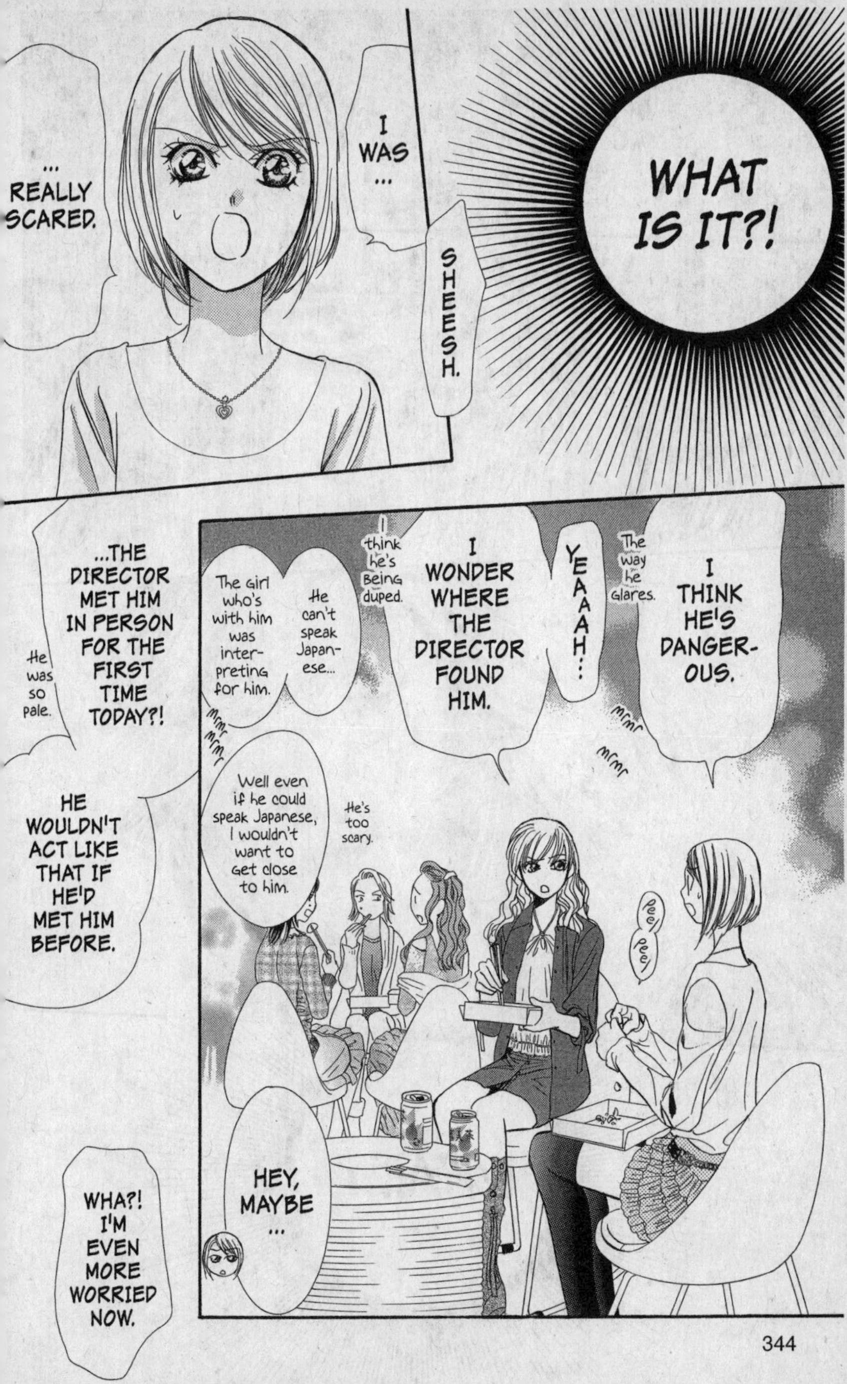
WHAT IS IT?!
SHEESH.
I WAS...
...REALLY SCARED.
I THINK HE'S DANGEROUS.
The way he glares.
YEAAAH...
I WONDER WHERE THE DIRECTOR FOUND HIM.
I think he's being duped.
mrmr
mrmr
He can't speak Japanese...
The girl who's with him was interpreting for him.
mrmr mrmr
He's too scary.
Well even if he could speak Japanese, I wouldn't want to get close to him.
Peel peel
...THE DIRECTOR MET HIM IN PERSON FOR THE FIRST TIME TODAY?!
He was so pale.
HE WOULDN'T ACT LIKE THAT IF HE'D MET HIM BEFORE.
HEY, MAYBE...
WHA?! I'M EVEN MORE WORRIED NOW.

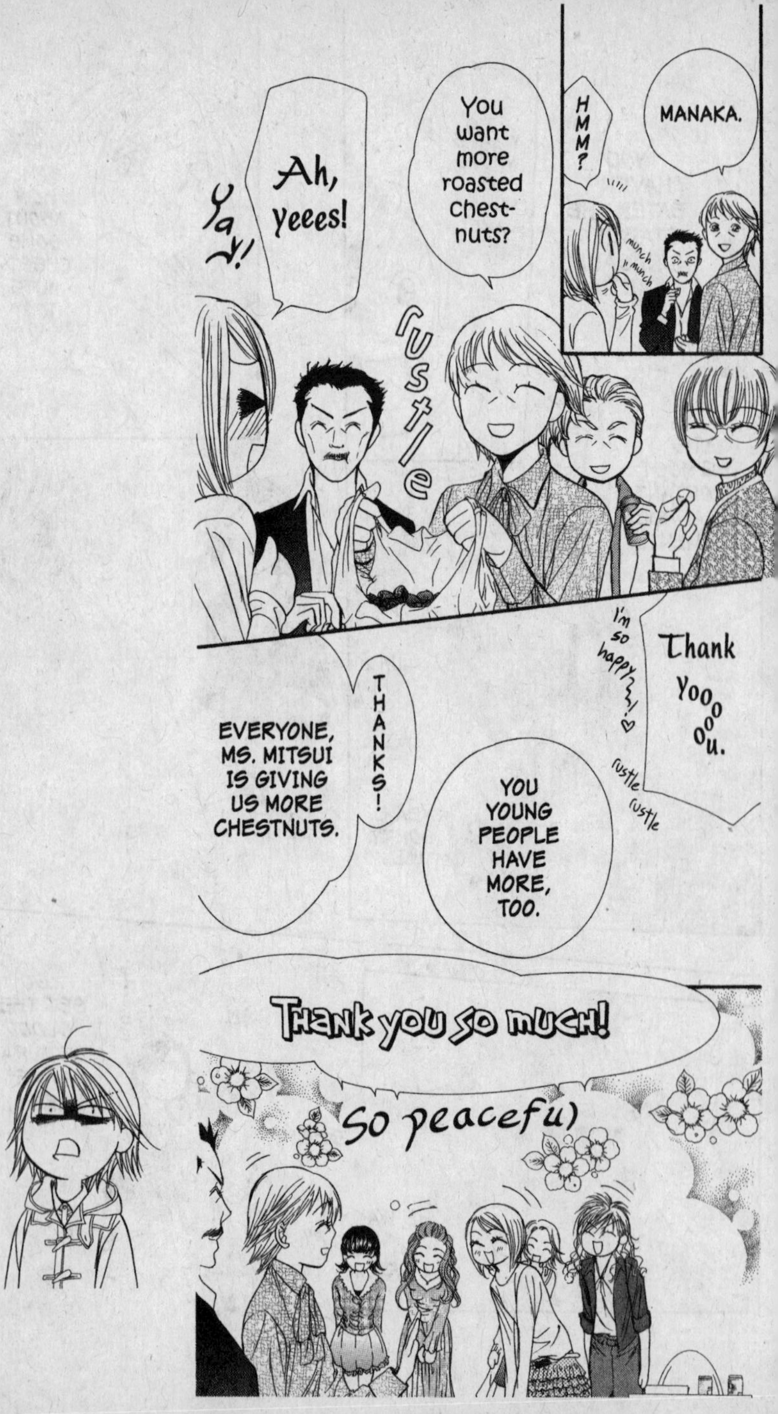
MANAKA.
HMM?
munch munch
You want more roasted chest-nuts?
Ah, yeees!
Yay!
rustle
Thank Yoooou.
I'm so happy~!♡
rustle rustle
You young people have more, too.
THANKS!
EVERYONE, MS. MITSUI IS GIVING US MORE CHESTNUTS.
THANK YOU SO MUCH!
So peaceful

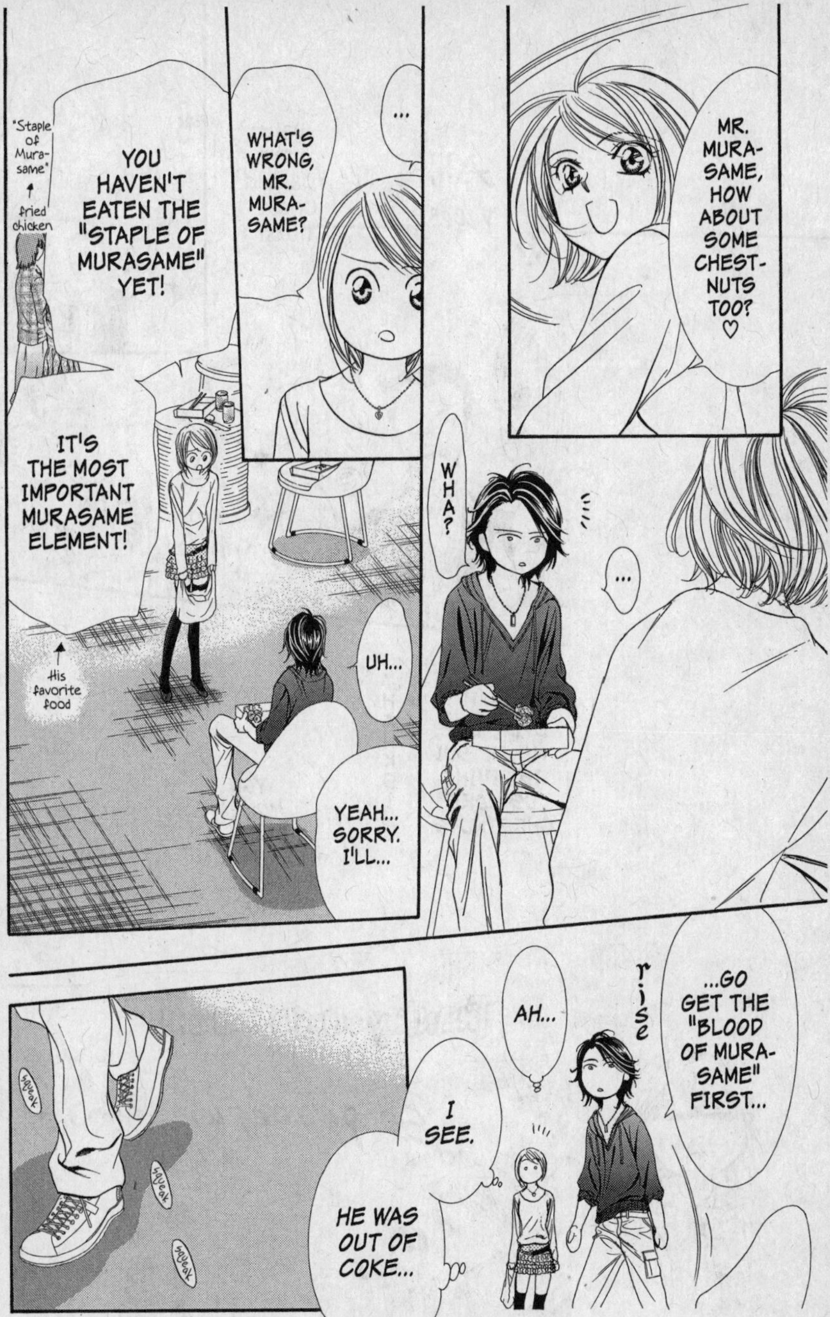
MR. MURA-SAME, HOW ABOUT SOME CHEST-NUTS TOO? ♡
...
WHAT'S WRONG, MR. MURA-SAME?
WHA?
...
YOU HAVEN'T EATEN THE "STAPLE OF MURASAME" YET!
"Staple of Mura-same"
↑ fried chicken
IT'S THE MOST IMPORTANT MURASAME ELEMENT!
↑ His favorite food
UH...
YEAH... SORRY. I'LL...
...GO GET THE "BLOOD OF MURA-SAME" FIRST...
rise
AH...
I SEE.
HE WAS OUT OF COKE...
squeak
squeak
squeak

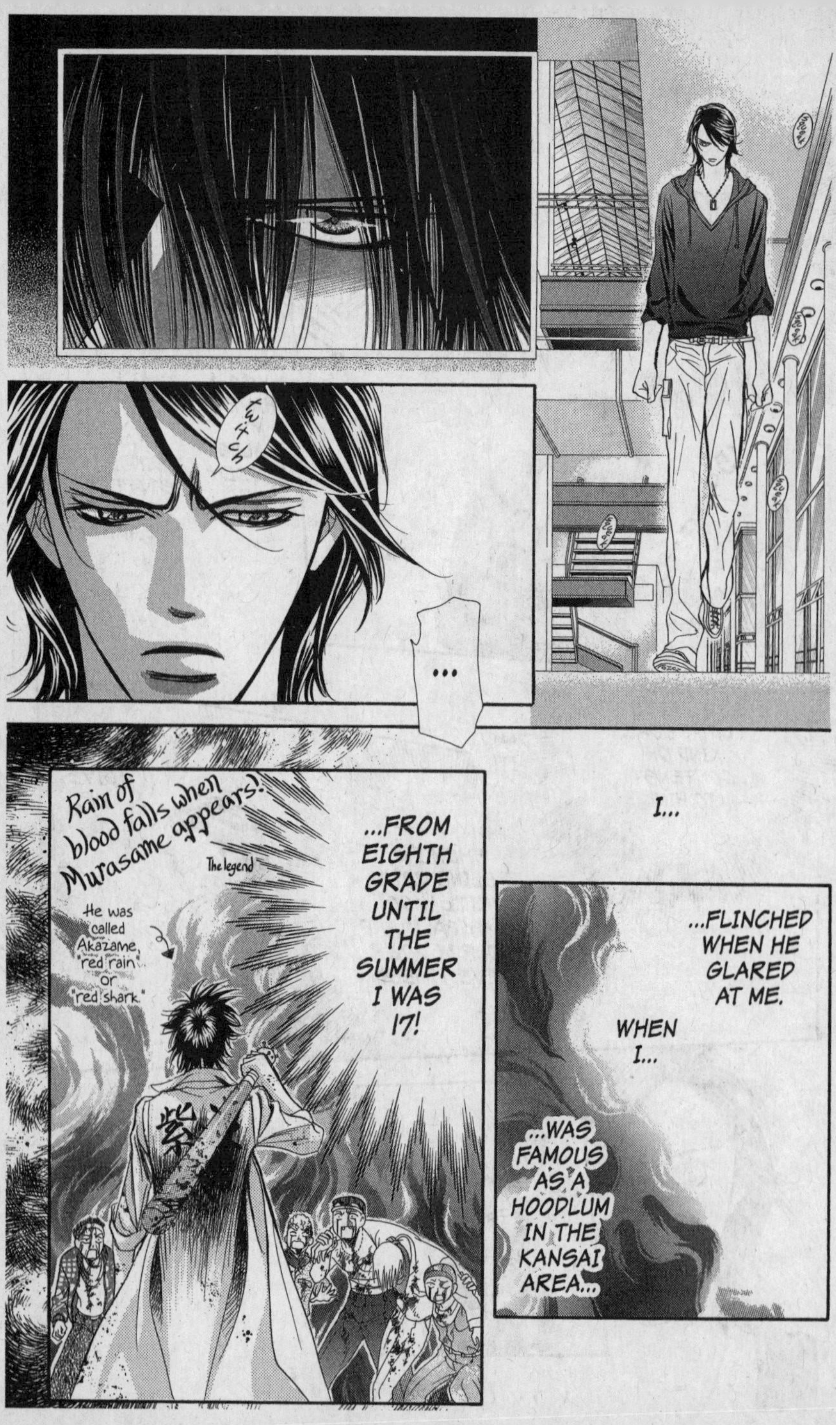
squeak
squeak
squeak
squeak
twitch
...
I...
...FLINCHED WHEN HE GLARED AT ME.
WHEN I...
...WAS FAMOUS AS A HOODLUM IN THE KANSAI AREA...
...FROM EIGHTH GRADE UNTIL THE SUMMER I WAS 17!
Rain of blood falls when Murasame appears!
The legend
He was called Akazame, "red rain" or "red shark."

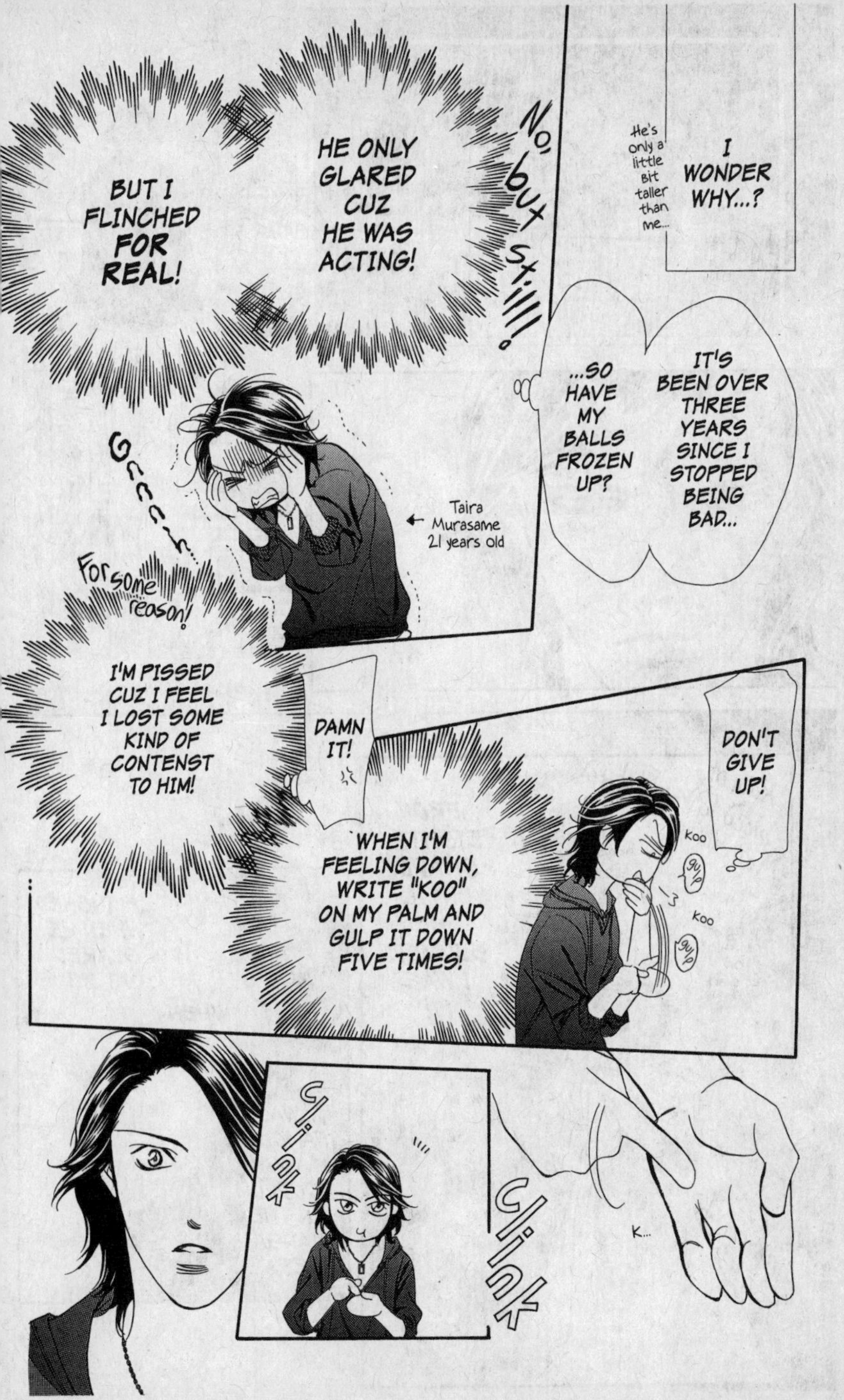
I WONDER WHY...?
He's only a little bit taller than me...
IT'S BEEN OVER THREE YEARS SINCE I STOPPED BEING BAD...
...SO HAVE MY BALLS FROZEN UP?
No, but still!!!
HE ONLY GLARED CUZ HE WAS ACTING!
BUT I FLINCHED FOR REAL!
Grrrr...
Taira Murasame 21 years old
For some reason!
I'M PISSED CUZ I FEEL I LOST SOME KIND OF CONTENST TO HIM!
DON'T GIVE UP!
Koo
gulp
Koo
gulp
WHEN I'M FEELING DOWN, WRITE "KOO" ON MY PALM AND GULP IT DOWN FIVE TIMES!
DAMN IT!
K...
Clink
Clink

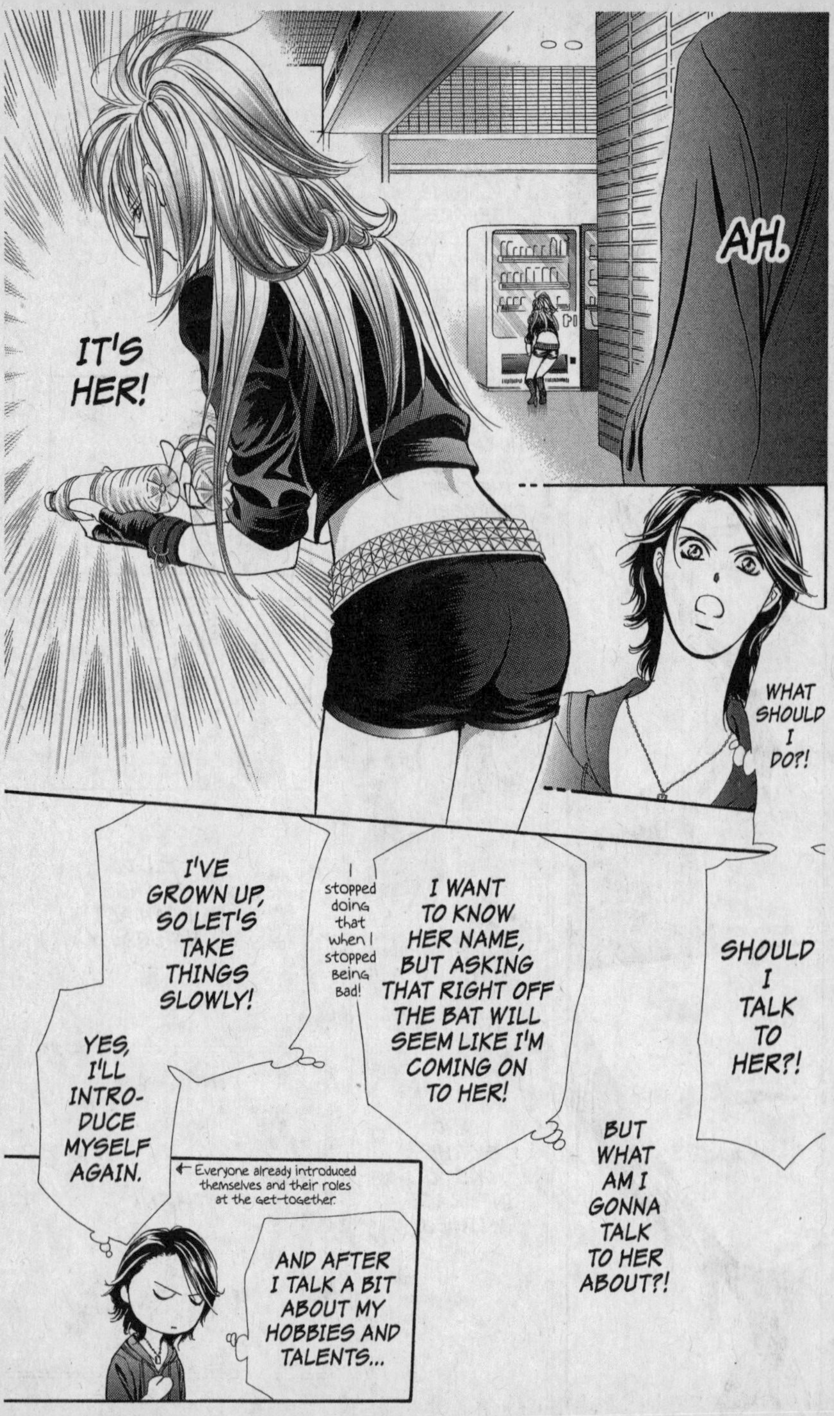
AH.
WHAT SHOULD I DO?!
IT'S HER!
SHOULD I TALK TO HER?!
BUT WHAT AM I GONNA TALK TO HER ABOUT?!
I WANT TO KNOW HER NAME, BUT ASKING THAT RIGHT OFF THE BAT WILL SEEM LIKE I'M COMING ON TO HER!
I stopped doing that when I stopped being bad!
I'VE GROWN UP, SO LET'S TAKE THINGS SLOWLY!
YES, I'LL INTRODUCE MYSELF AGAIN.
← Everyone already introduced themselves and their roles at the get-together.
AND AFTER I TALK A BIT ABOUT MY HOBBIES AND TALENTS...

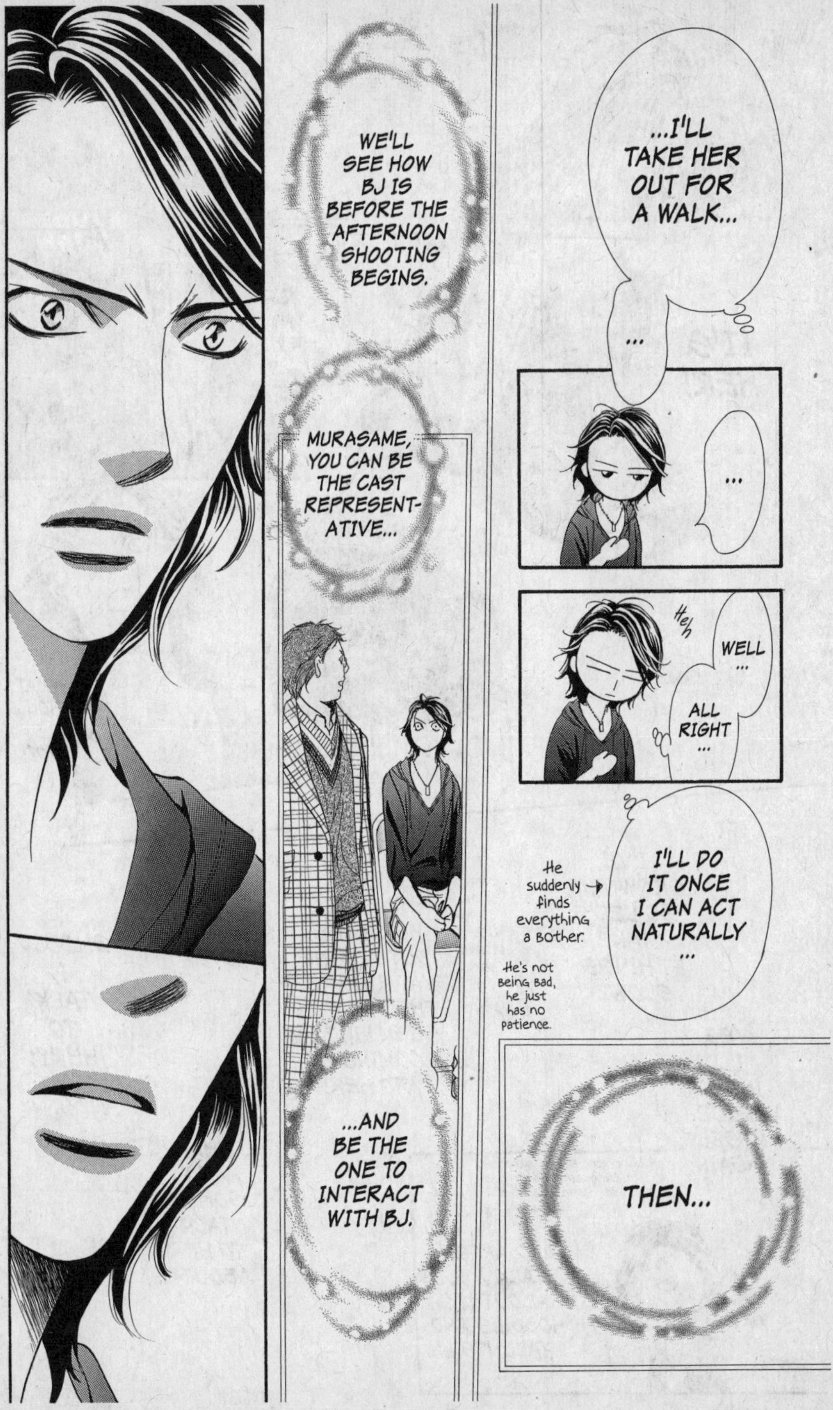
...I'LL TAKE HER OUT FOR A WALK...
...
...
Heh
WELL...
ALL RIGHT...
I'LL DO IT ONCE I CAN ACT NATURALLY...
He suddenly finds everything a bother.
He's not being bad, he just has no patience.
THEN...
WE'LL SEE HOW BJ IS BEFORE THE AFTERNOON SHOOTING BEGINS.
MURASAME, YOU CAN BE THE CAST REPRESENTATIVE...
...AND BE THE ONE TO INTERACT WITH BJ.

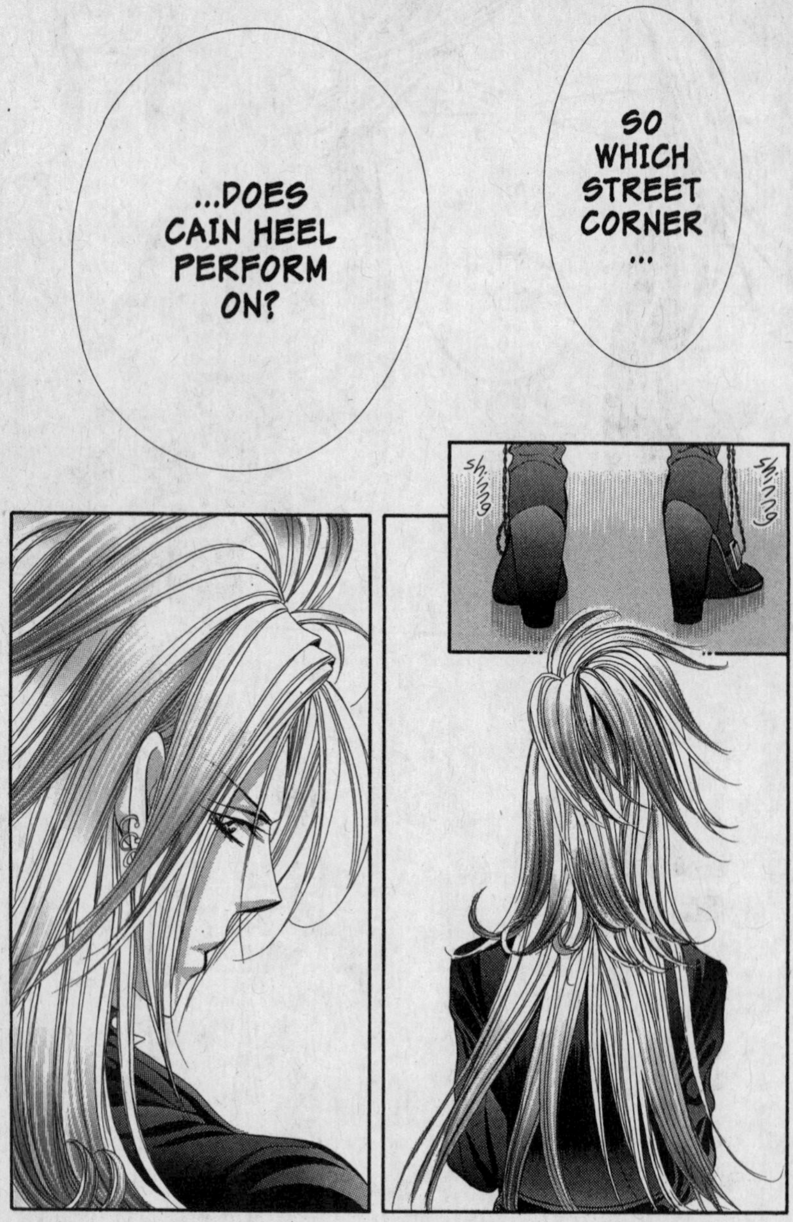
SO WHICH STREET CORNER ...
...DOES CAIN HEEL PERFORM ON?
shiing
shiing

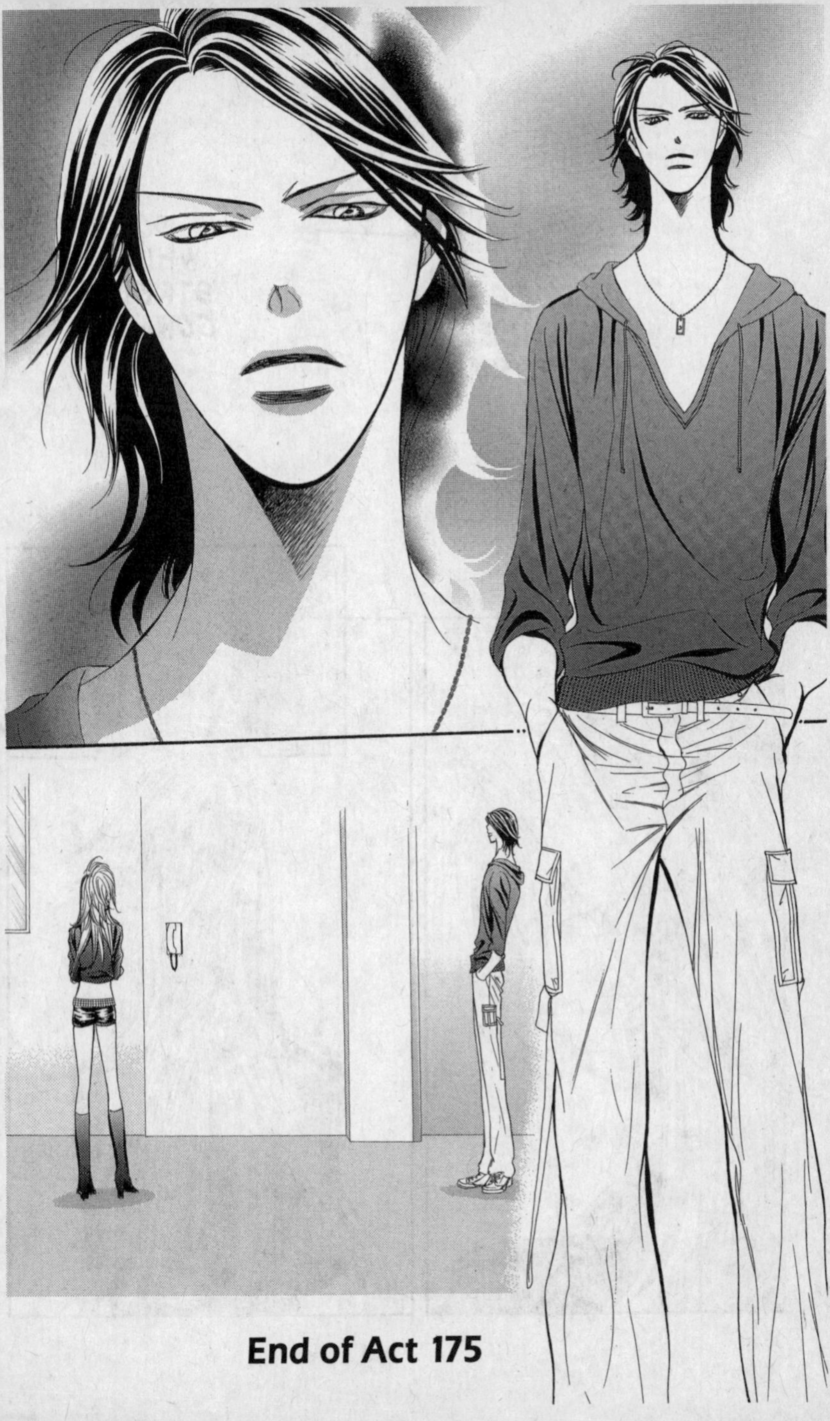

End of Act 175

Skip·Beat!

Act 176: Hero's High

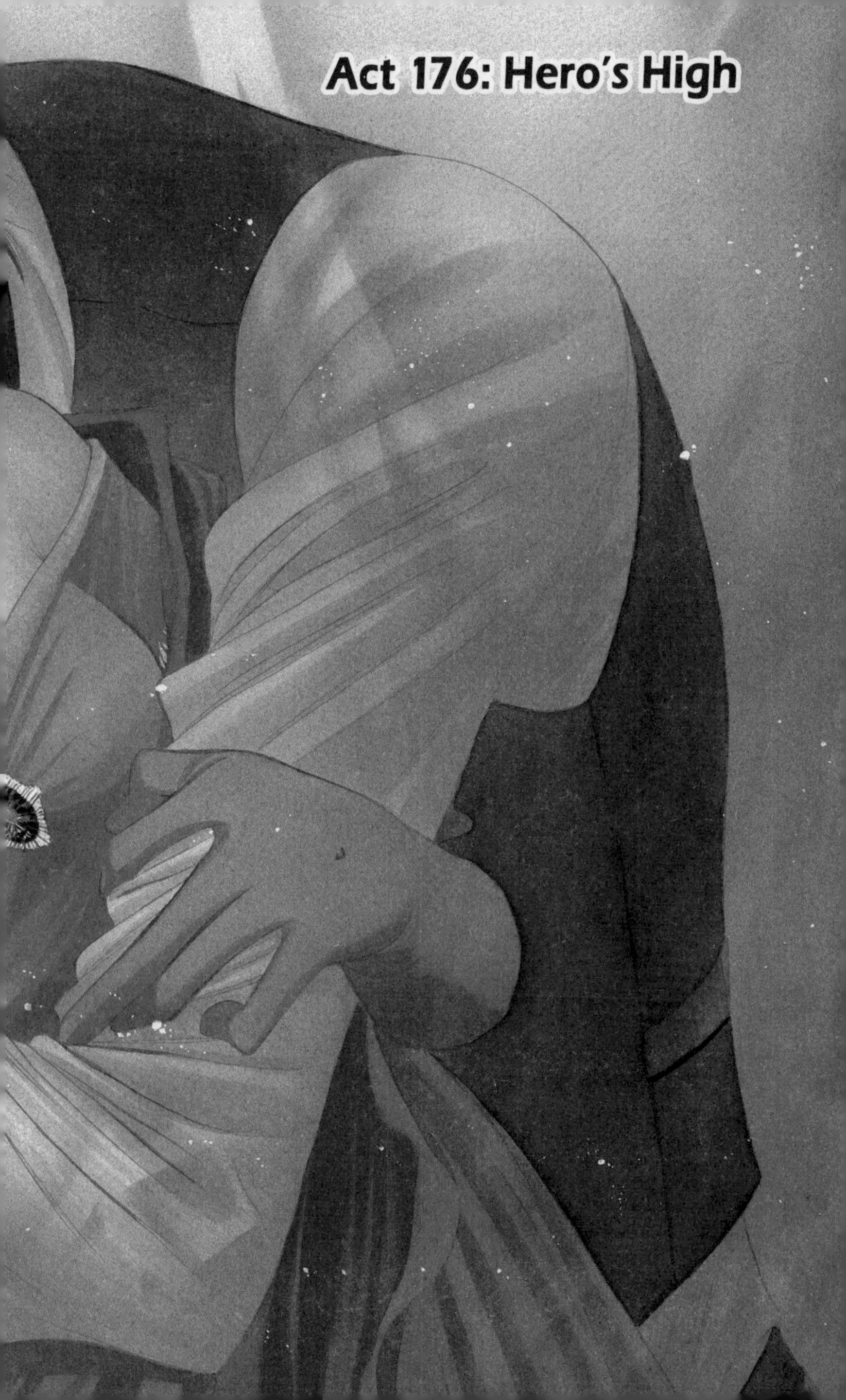

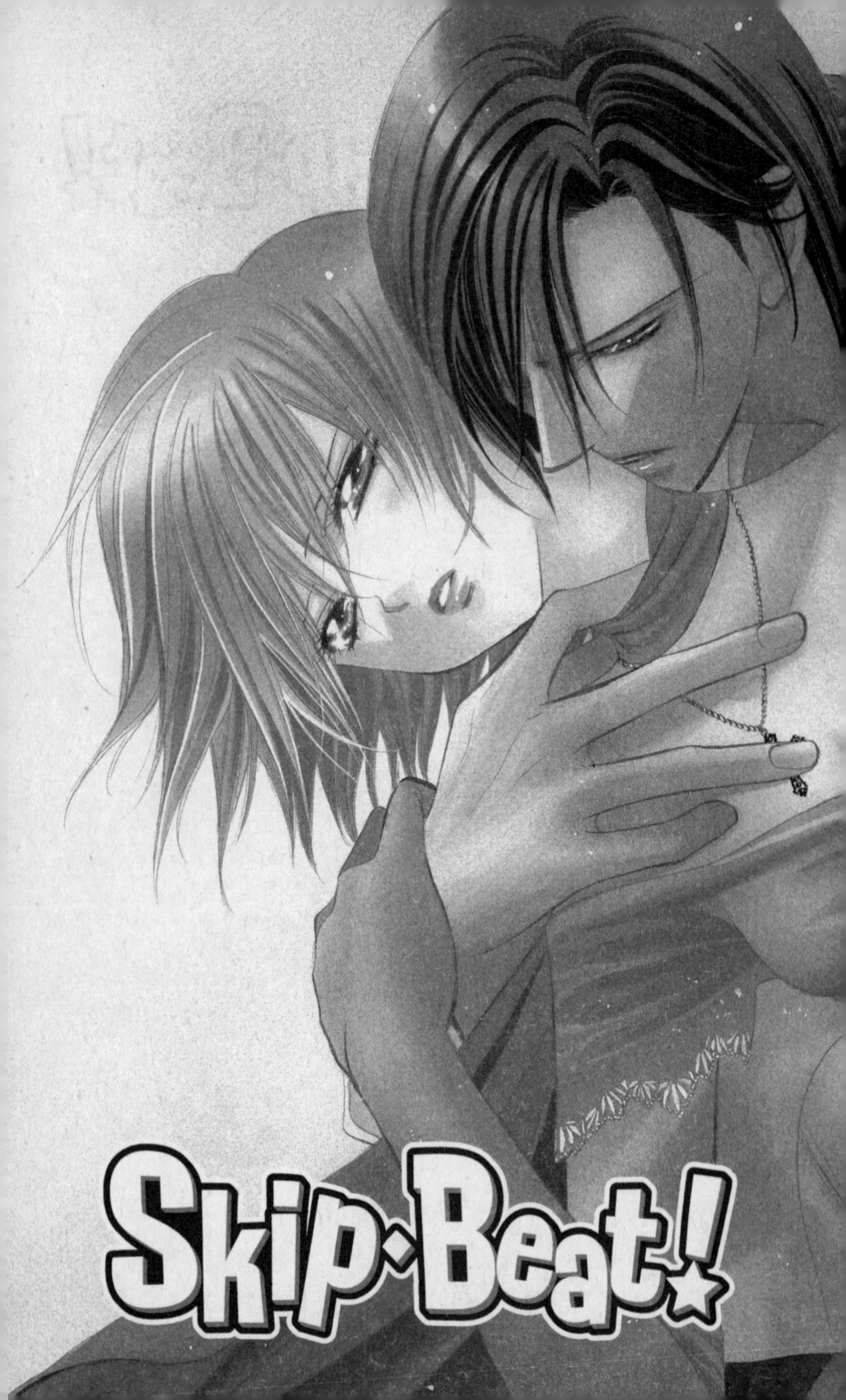
Skip·Beat!

Skip·Beat!

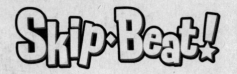

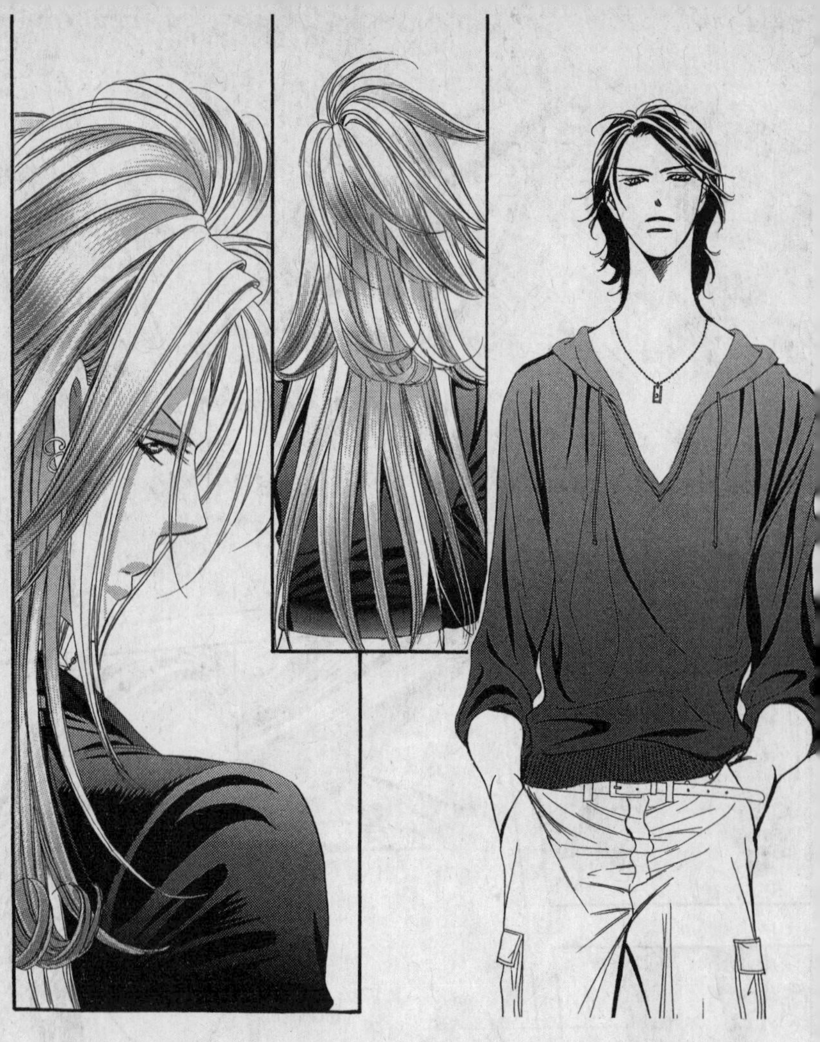
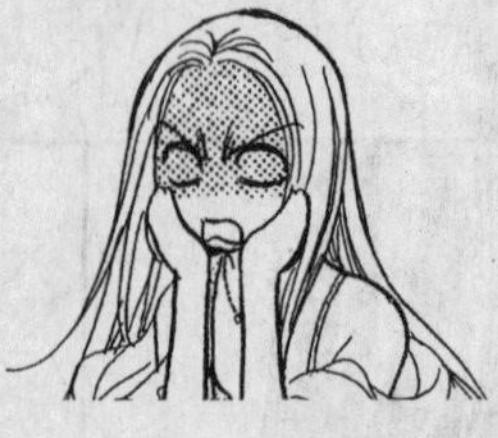

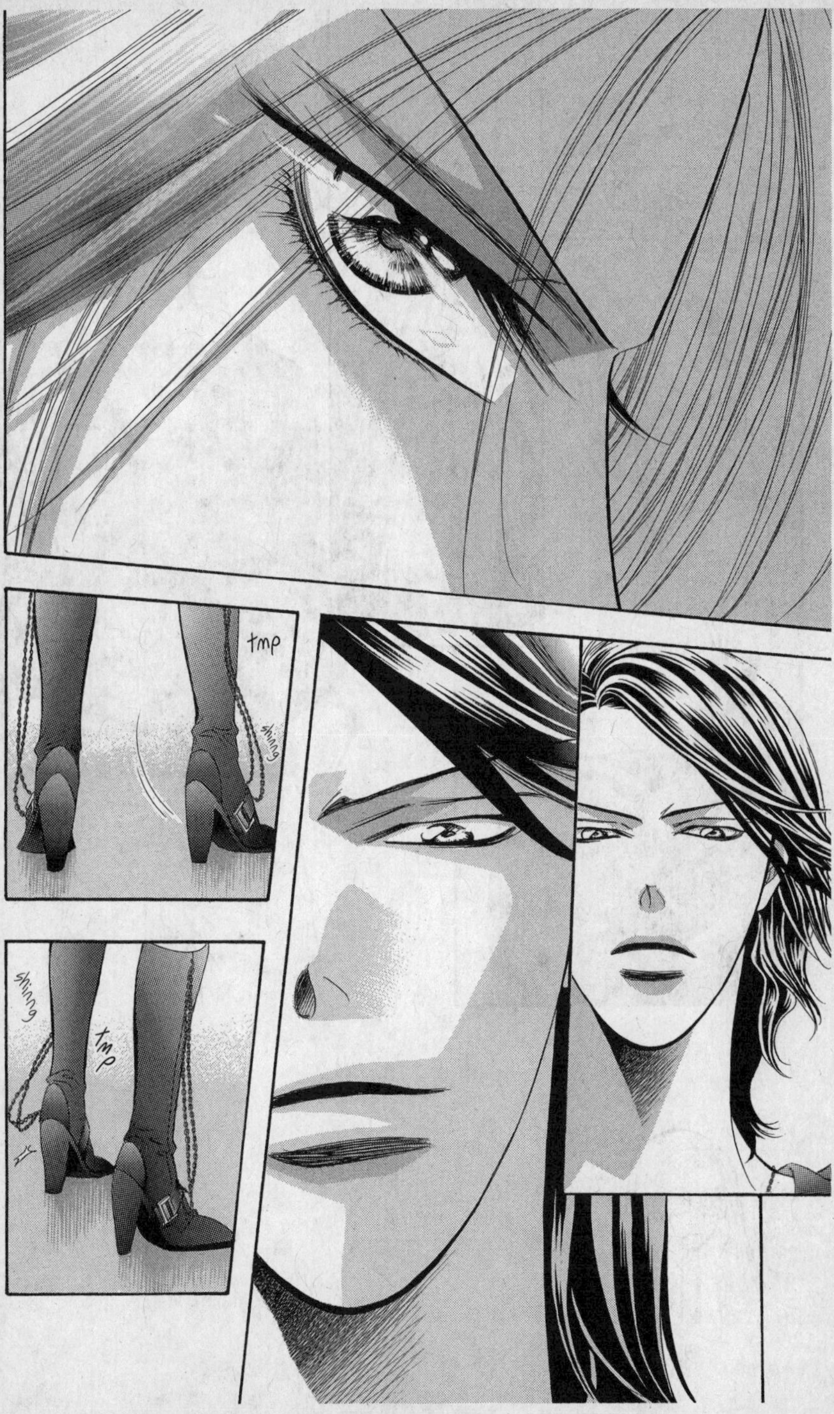
tmp
shinng
tmp
shinng

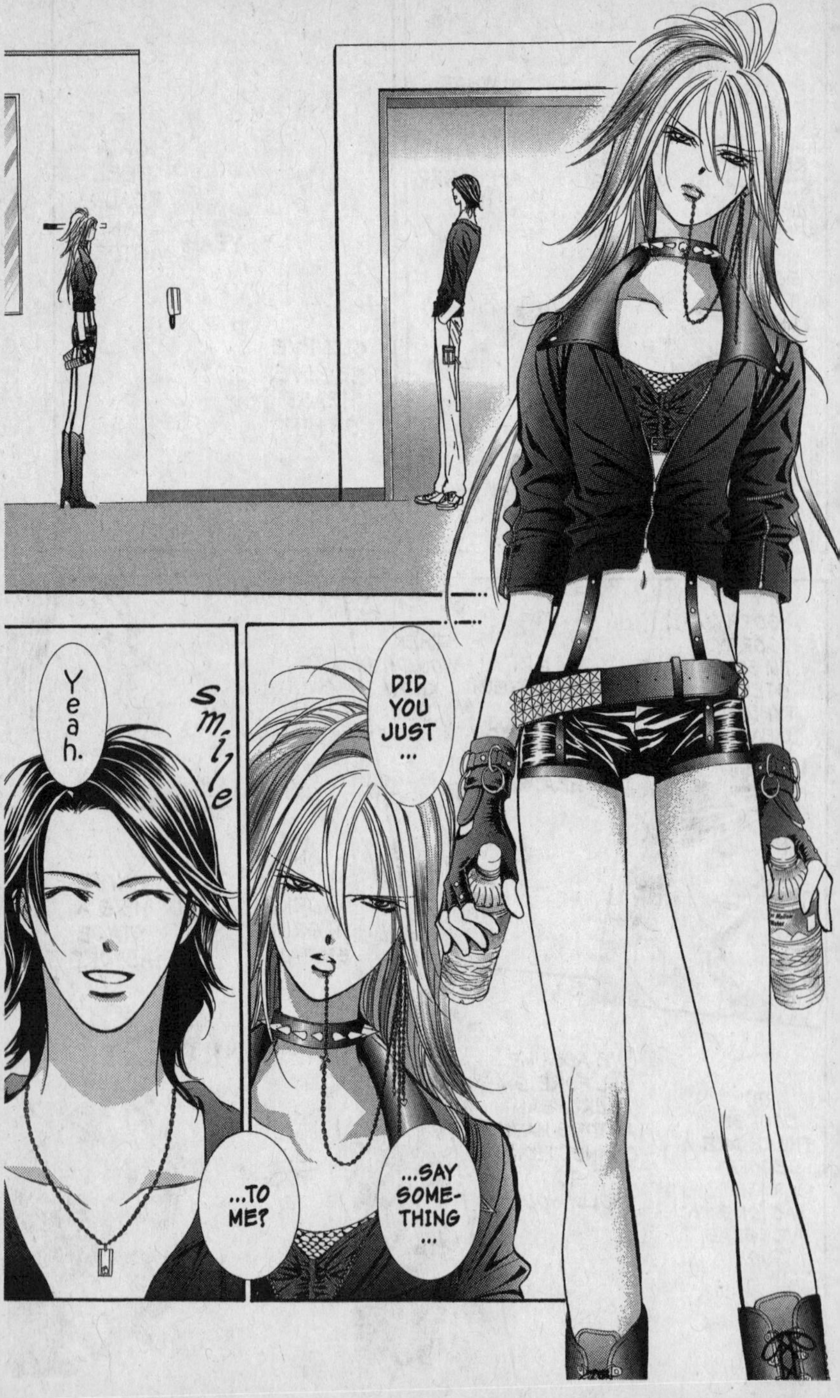
DID YOU JUST ...
...SAY SOME-THING ...
...TO ME?
Yeah.
smile

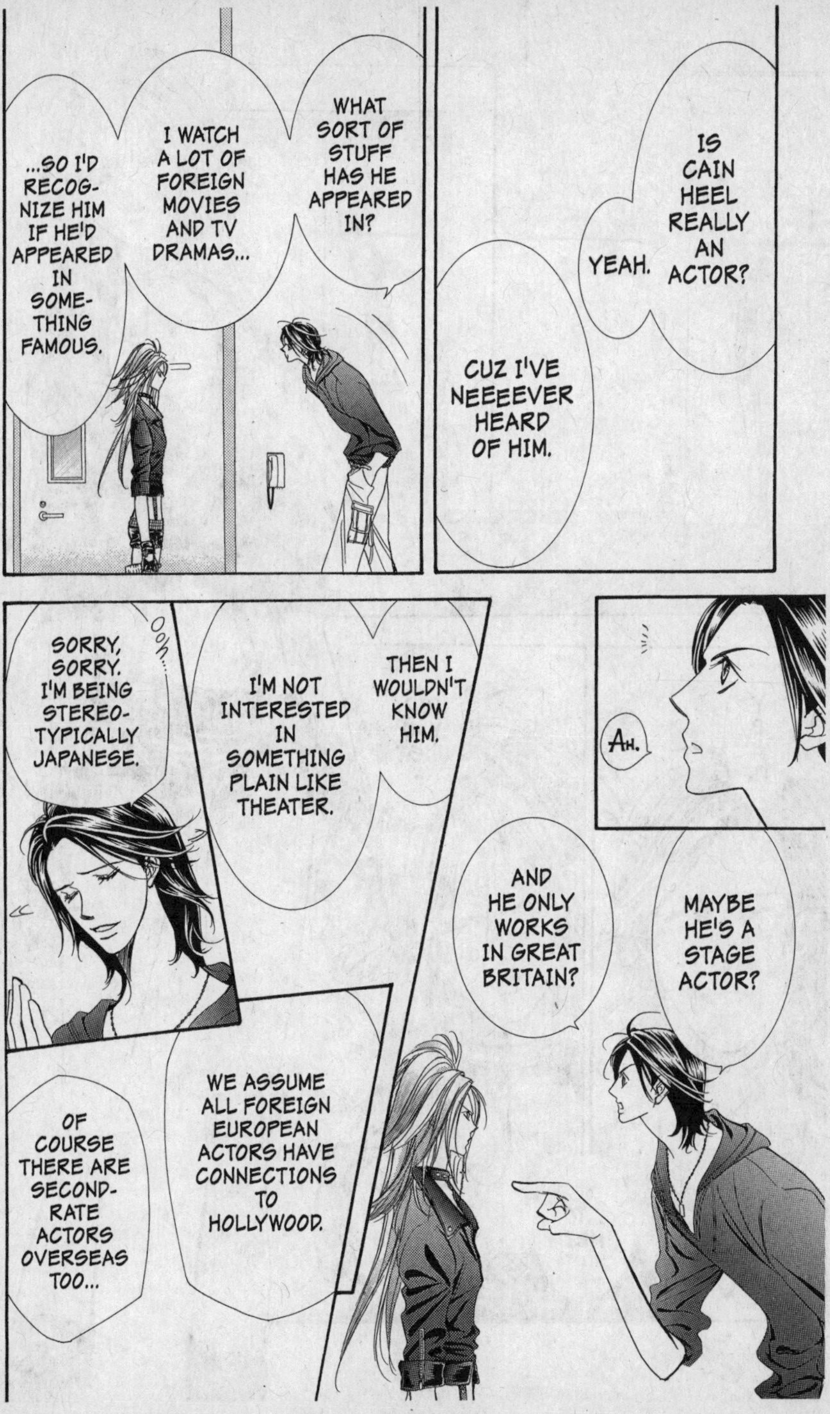
IS CAIN HEEL REALLY AN ACTOR?
YEAH.
CUZ I'VE NEEEEVER HEARD OF HIM.
WHAT SORT OF STUFF HAS HE APPEARED IN?
I WATCH A LOT OF FOREIGN MOVIES AND TV DRAMAS...
...SO I'D RECOG-NIZE HIM IF HE'D APPEARED IN SOME-THING FAMOUS.
AH.
MAYBE HE'S A STAGE ACTOR?
AND HE ONLY WORKS IN GREAT BRITAIN?
THEN I WOULDN'T KNOW HIM.
I'M NOT INTERESTED IN SOMETHING PLAIN LIKE THEATER.
SORRY, SORRY. I'M BEING STEREO-TYPICALLY JAPANESE.
Ooh...
WE ASSUME ALL FOREIGN EUROPEAN ACTORS HAVE CONNECTIONS TO HOLLYWOOD.
OF COURSE THERE ARE SECOND-RATE ACTORS OVERSEAS TOO...

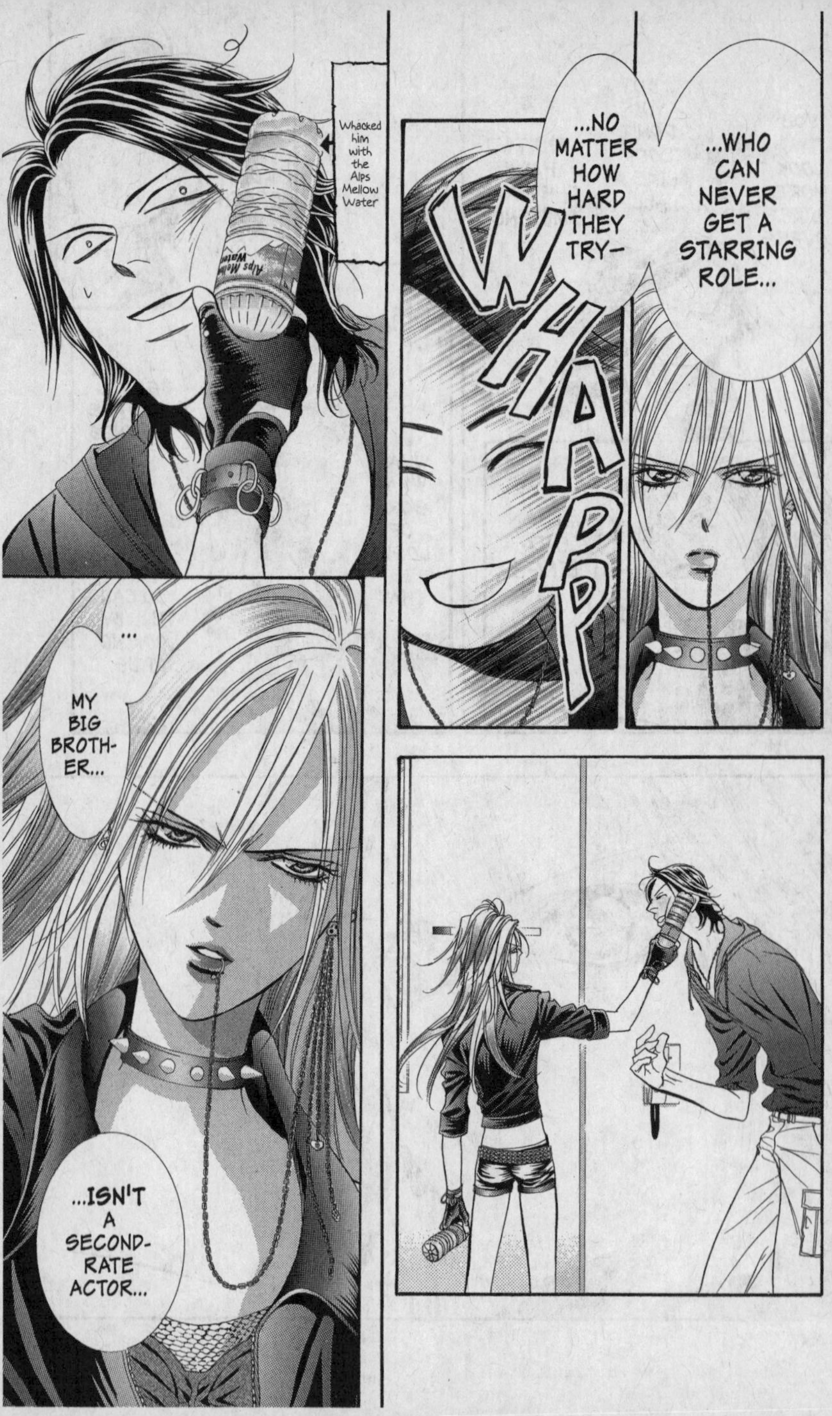
...WHO CAN NEVER GET A STARRING ROLE...
...NO MATTER HOW HARD THEY TRY-
WHAPP
Whacked him with the Alps Mellow Water
Alps Water
...
MY BIG BROTHER-ER...
...ISN'T A SECOND-RATE ACTOR...

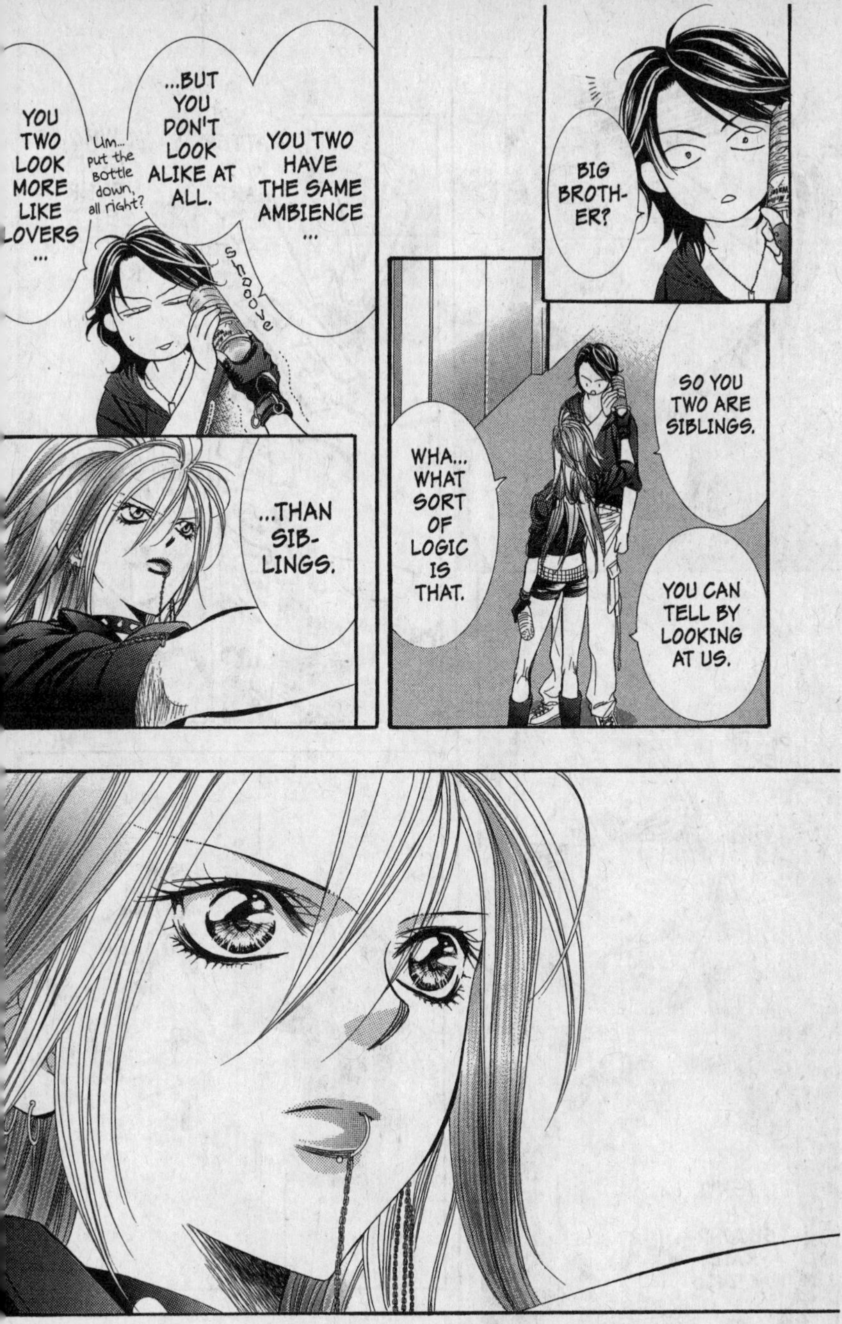
BIG BROTH-ER?
SO YOU TWO ARE SIBLINGS.
YOU CAN TELL BY LOOKING AT US.
WHA... WHAT SORT OF LOGIC IS THAT.
YOU TWO HAVE THE SAME AMBIENCE ...
...BUT YOU DON'T LOOK ALIKE AT ALL.
Shooove
Um... put the bottle down, all right?
YOU TWO LOOK MORE LIKE LOVERS ...
...THAN SIB-LINGS.

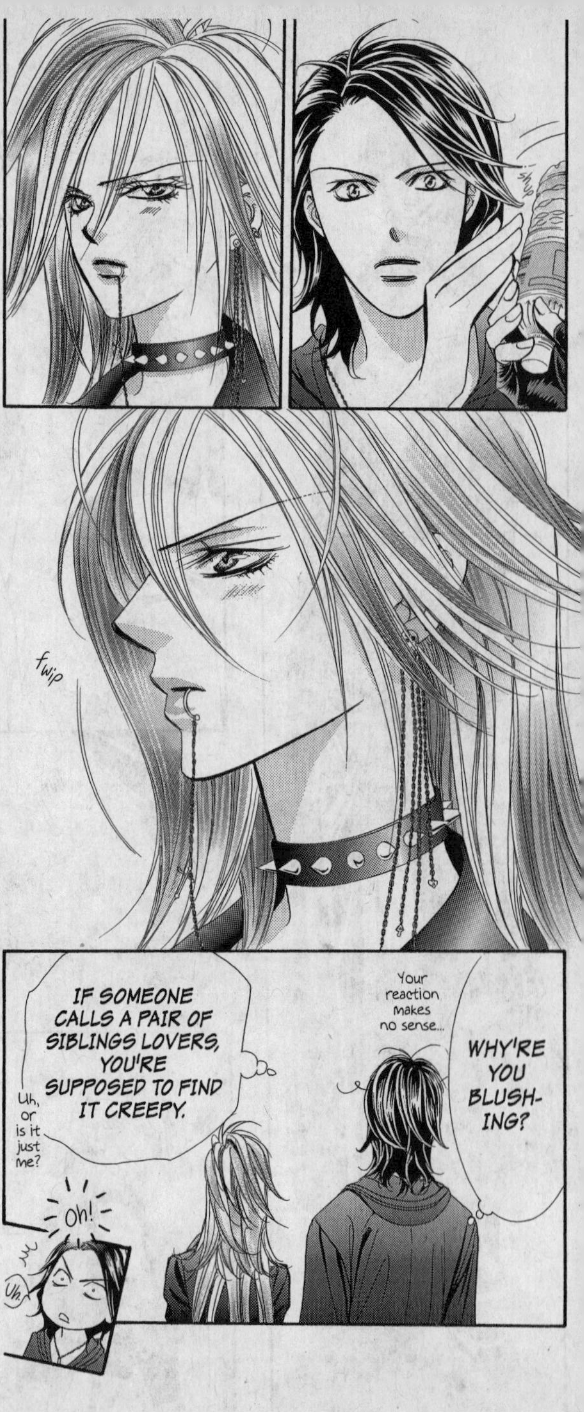
shup
fwip
Your reaction makes no sense...
WHY'RE YOU BLUSH-ING?
IF SOMEONE CALLS A PAIR OF SIBLINGS LOVERS, YOU'RE SUPPOSED TO FIND IT CREEPY.
Uh, or is it just me?
Oh!
Uh

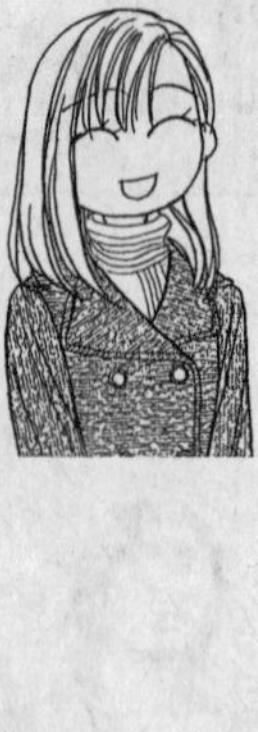

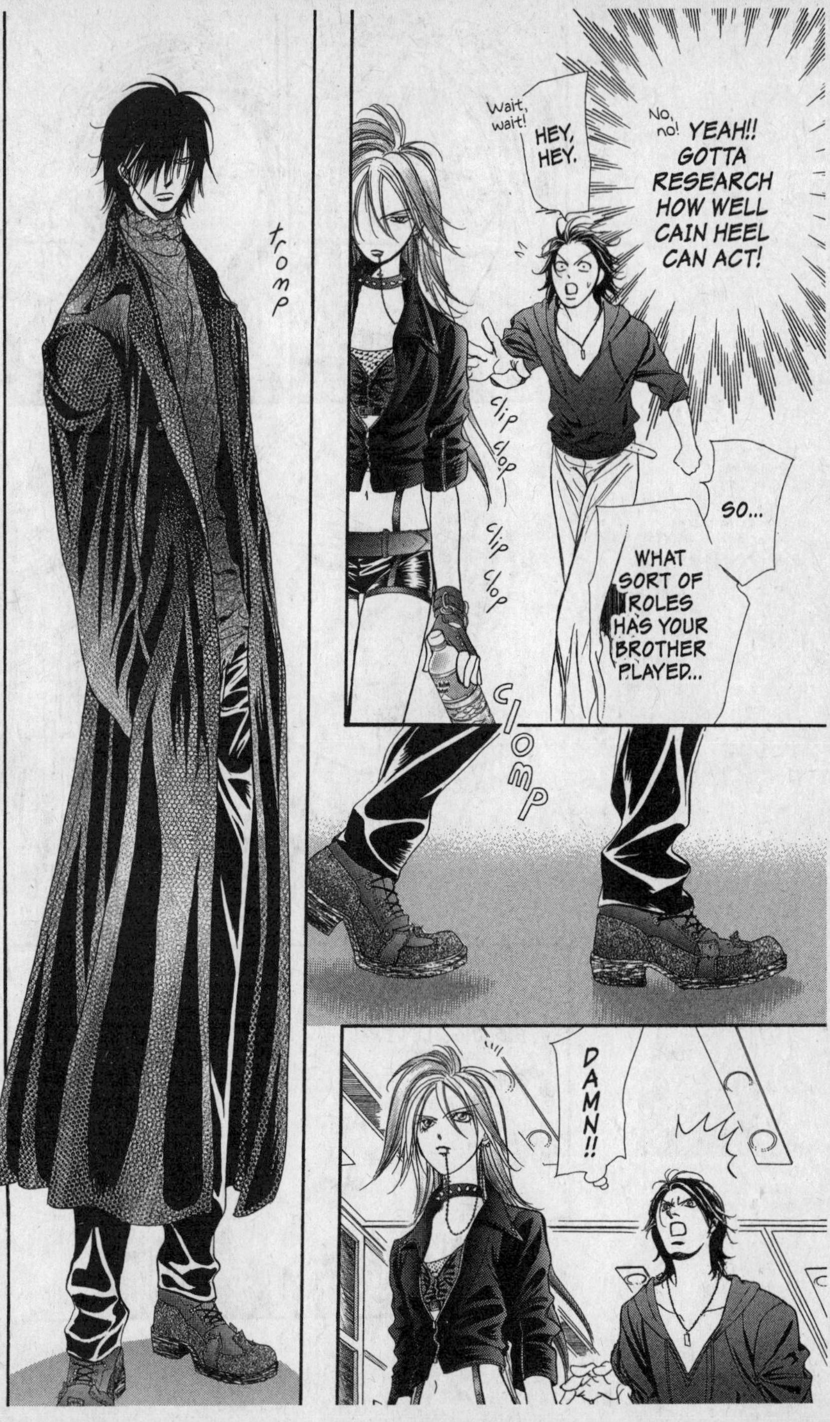
YEAH!! GOTTA RESEARCH HOW WELL CAIN HEEL CAN ACT!
No, no!
HEY, HEY.
Wait, wait!
SO...
WHAT SORT OF ROLES HAS YOUR BROTHER PLAYED...
clip clop
clip clop
CLOMP
DAMN!!
tromp

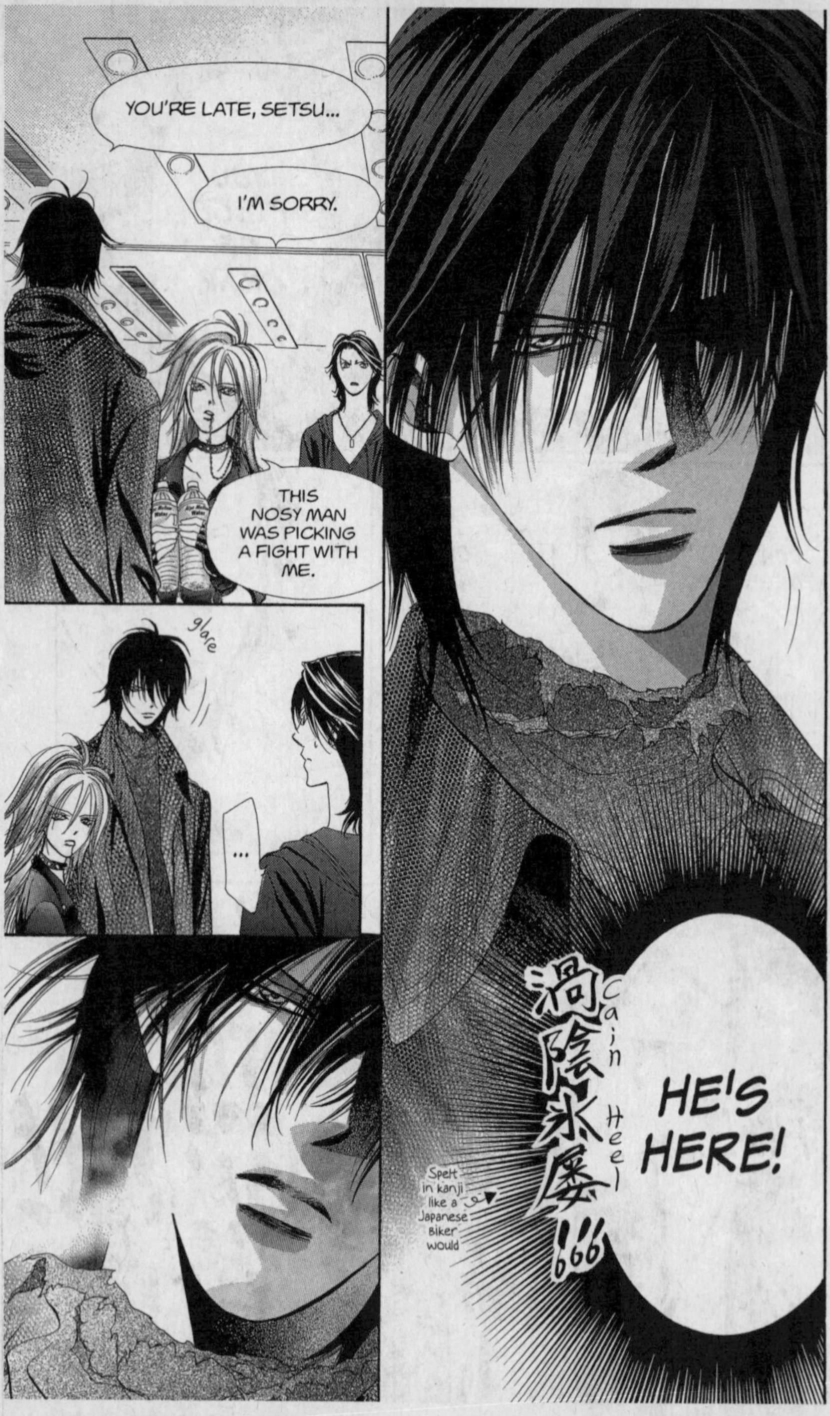
HE'S HERE!
Cain Heel
Spelt in kanji like a Japanese biker would
YOU'RE LATE, SETSU...
I'M SORRY.
THIS NOSY MAN WAS PICKING A FIGHT WITH ME.
glare
...

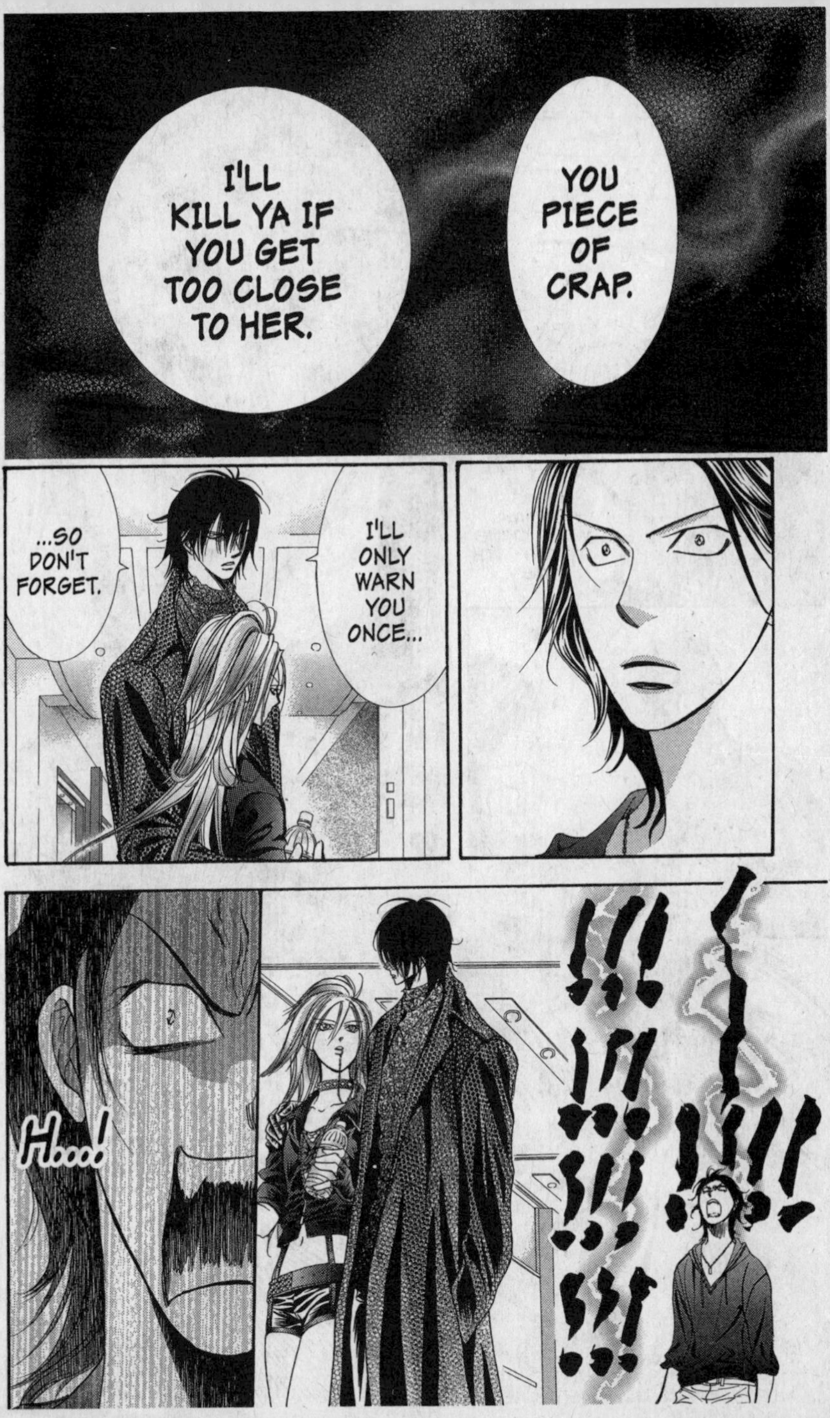
YOU PIECE OF CRAP.
I'LL KILL YA IF YOU GET TOO CLOSE TO HER.
I'LL ONLY WARN YOU ONCE...
...SO DON'T FORGET.

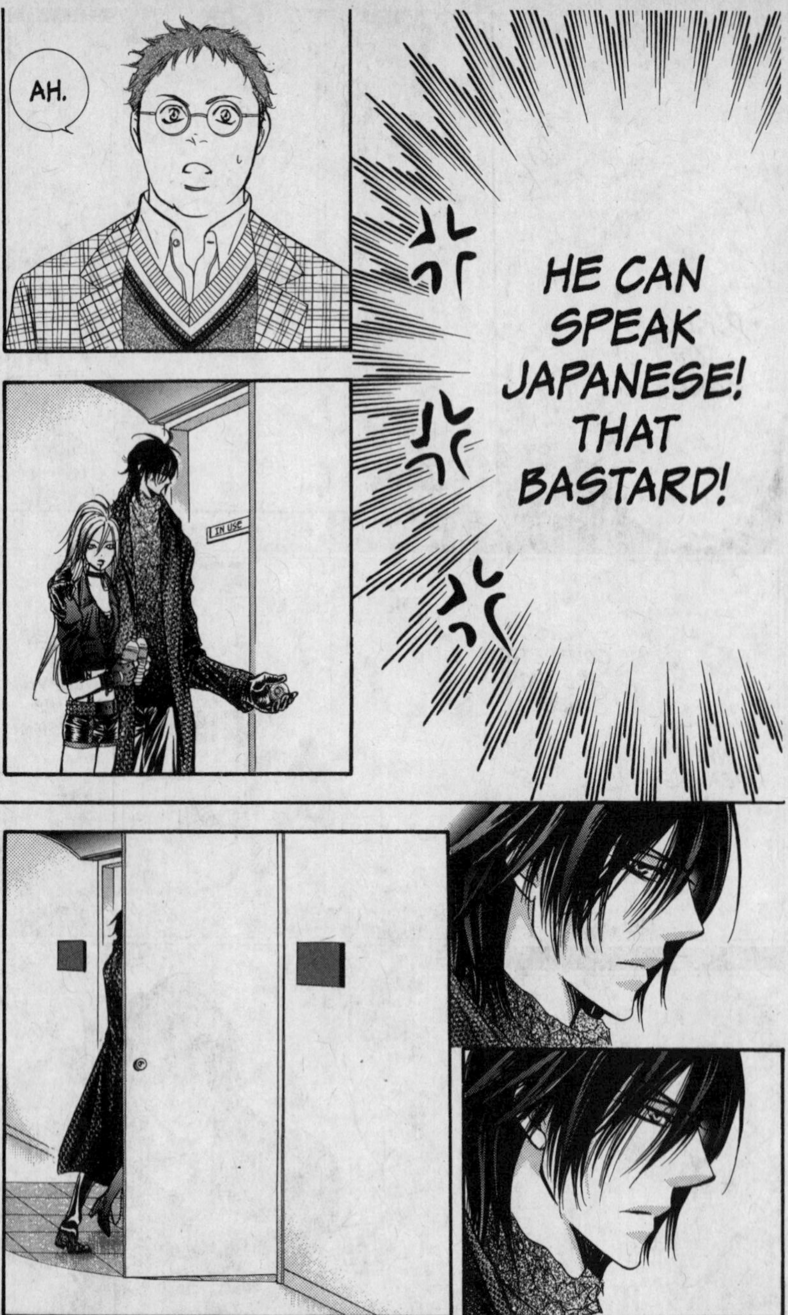
HE CAN SPEAK JAPANESE! THAT BASTARD!
AH.
IN USE

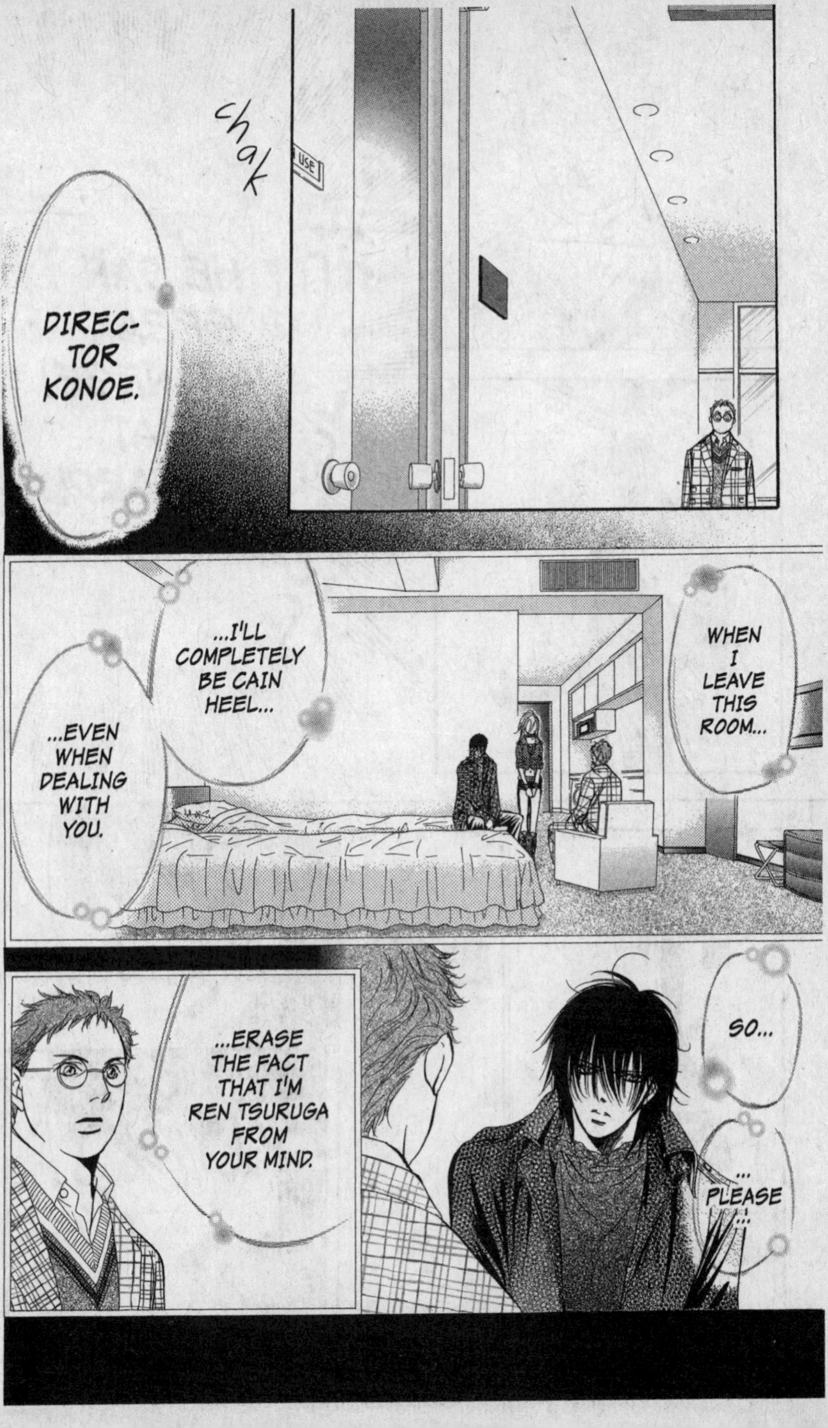
chak
DIREC-TOR KONOE.
WHEN I LEAVE THIS ROOM...
...I'LL COMPLETELY BE CAIN HEEL...
...EVEN WHEN DEALING WITH YOU.
SO...
...PLEASE...
...ERASE THE FACT THAT I'M REN TSURUGA FROM YOUR MIND.

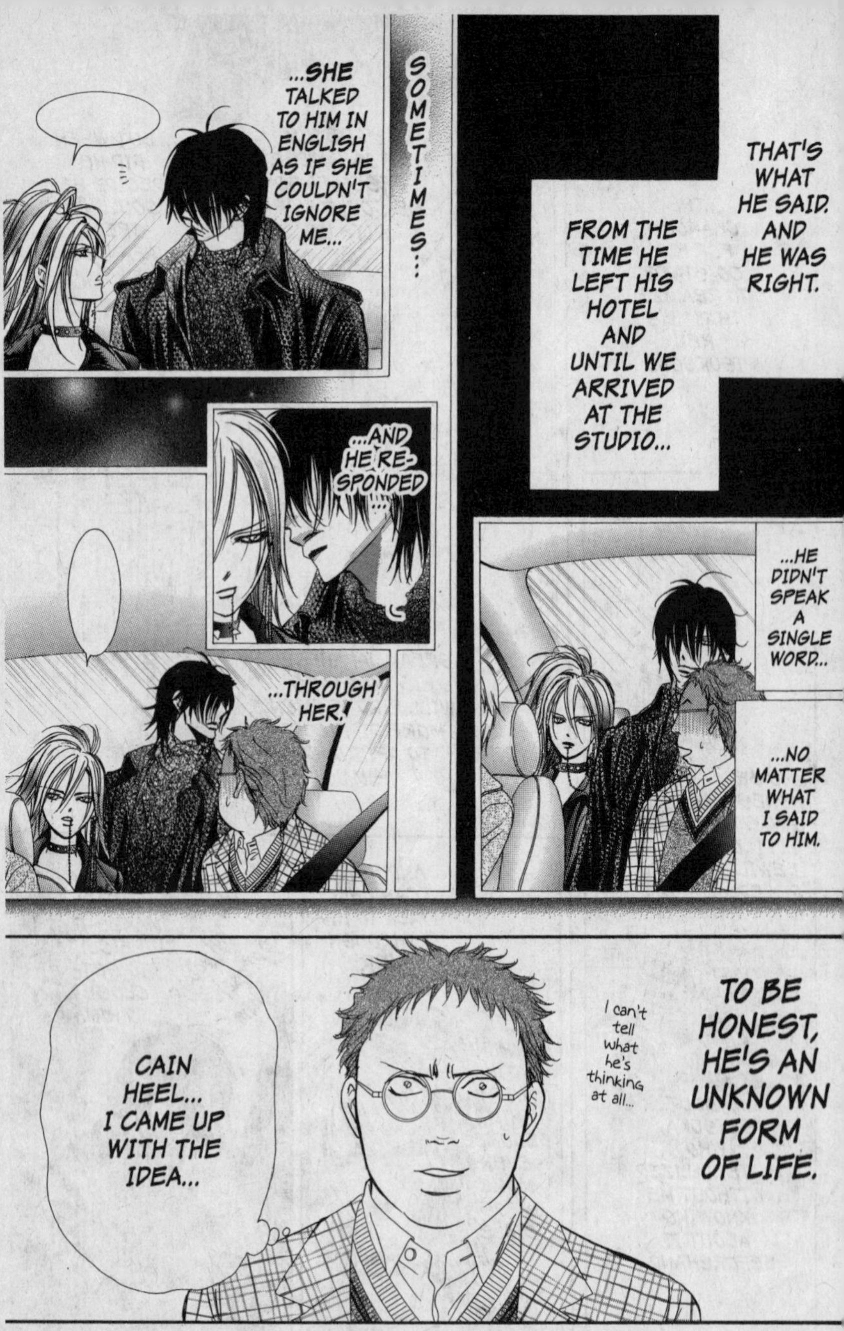
THAT'S WHAT HE SAID. AND HE WAS RIGHT.
FROM THE TIME HE LEFT HIS HOTEL AND UNTIL WE ARRIVED AT THE STUDIO...
...HE DIDN'T SPEAK A SINGLE WORD...
...NO MATTER WHAT I SAID TO HIM.
SOMETIMES...
...SHE TALKED TO HIM IN ENGLISH AS IF SHE COULDN'T IGNORE ME...
...AND HE RE-SPONDED...
...THROUGH HER.
TO BE HONEST, HE'S AN UNKNOWN FORM OF LIFE.
I can't tell what he's thinking at all...
CAIN HEEL... I CAME UP WITH THE IDEA...

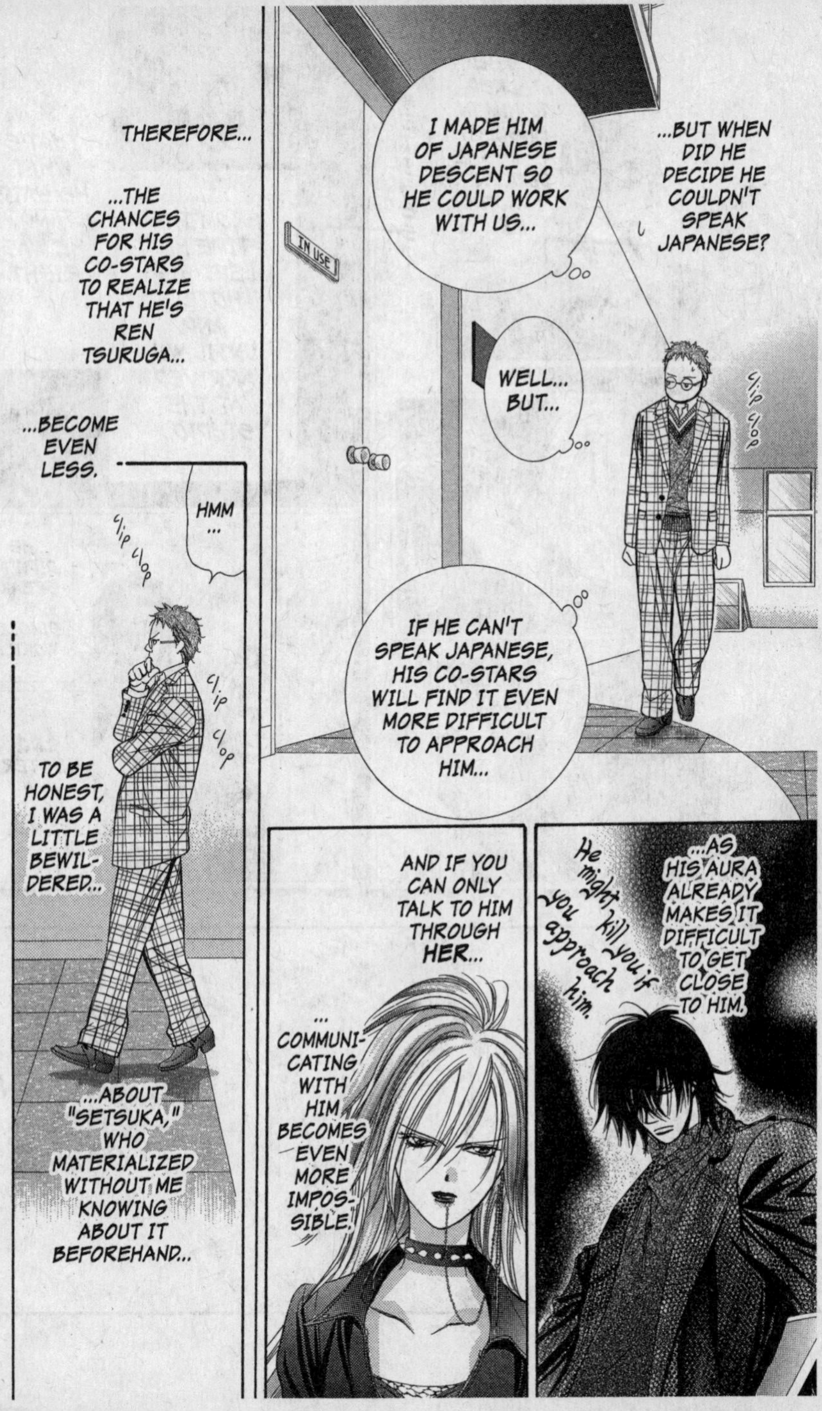
...BUT WHEN DID HE DECIDE HE COULDN'T SPEAK JAPANESE?
I MADE HIM OF JAPANESE DESCENT SO HE COULD WORK WITH US...
IN USE
WELL... BUT...
clip clop
IF HE CAN'T SPEAK JAPANESE, HIS CO-STARS WILL FIND IT EVEN MORE DIFFICULT TO APPROACH HIM...
...AS HIS AURA ALREADY MAKES IT DIFFICULT TO GET CLOSE TO HIM.
He might kill you if you approach him.
AND IF YOU CAN ONLY TALK TO HIM THROUGH HER...
...COMMUNICATING WITH HIM BECOMES EVEN MORE IMPOSSIBLE.
THEREFORE...
...THE CHANCES FOR HIS CO-STARS TO REALIZE THAT HE'S REN TSURUGA...
...BECOME EVEN LESS.
HMM...
clip clop
clip clop
TO BE HONEST, I WAS A LITTLE BEWILDERED...
...ABOUT "SETSUKA," WHO MATERIALIZED WITHOUT ME KNOWING ABOUT IT BEFOREHAND...

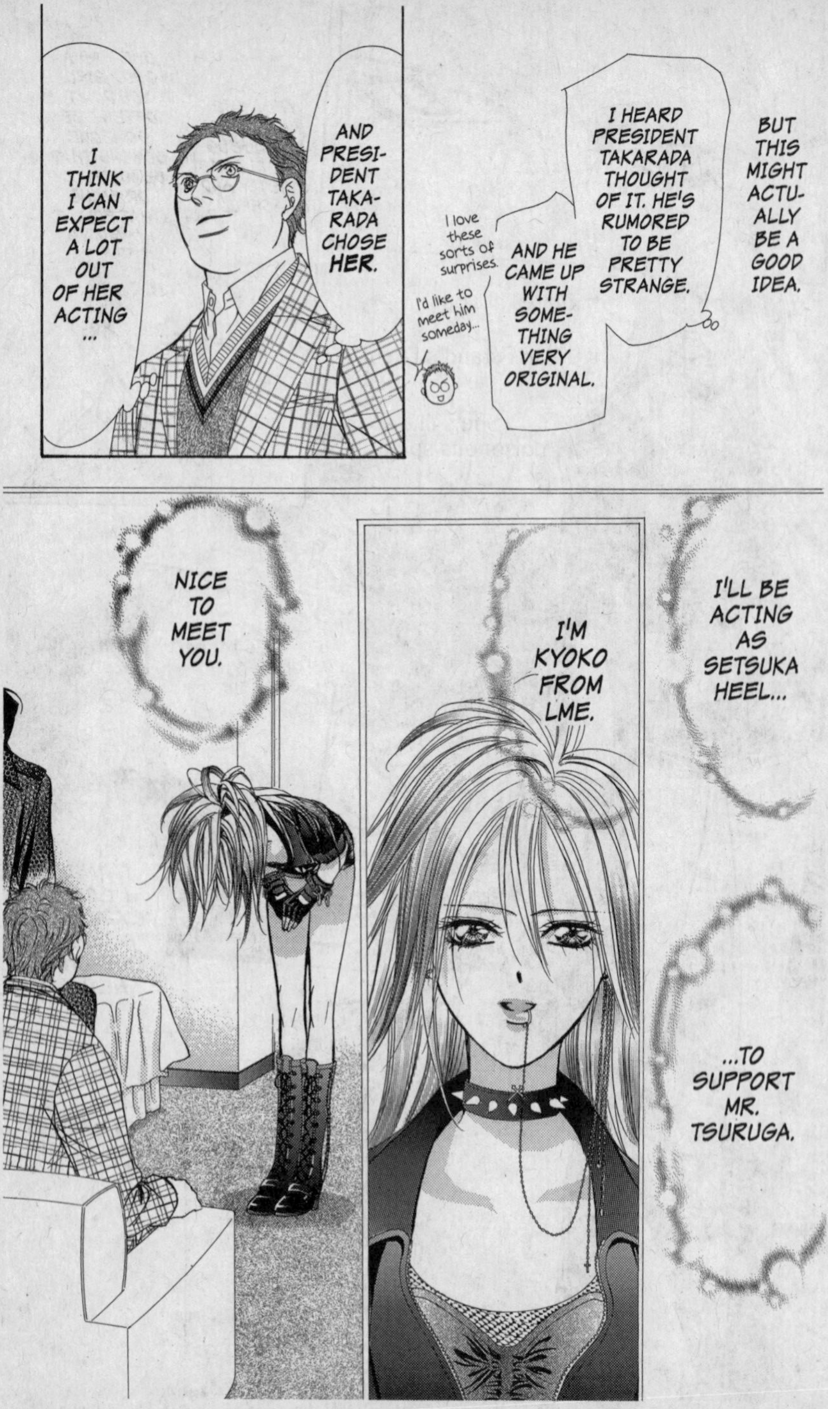
BUT THIS MIGHT ACTUALLY BE A GOOD IDEA.
I HEARD PRESIDENT TAKARADA THOUGHT OF IT. HE'S RUMORED TO BE PRETTY STRANGE.
AND HE CAME UP WITH SOMETHING VERY ORIGINAL.
I love these sorts of surprises.
I'd like to meet him someday...
AND PRESIDENT TAKARADA CHOSE HER.
I THINK I CAN EXPECT A LOT OUT OF HER ACTING...
I'LL BE ACTING AS SETSUKA HEEL...
...TO SUPPORT MR. TSURUGA.
I'M KYOKO FROM LME.
NICE TO MEET YOU.

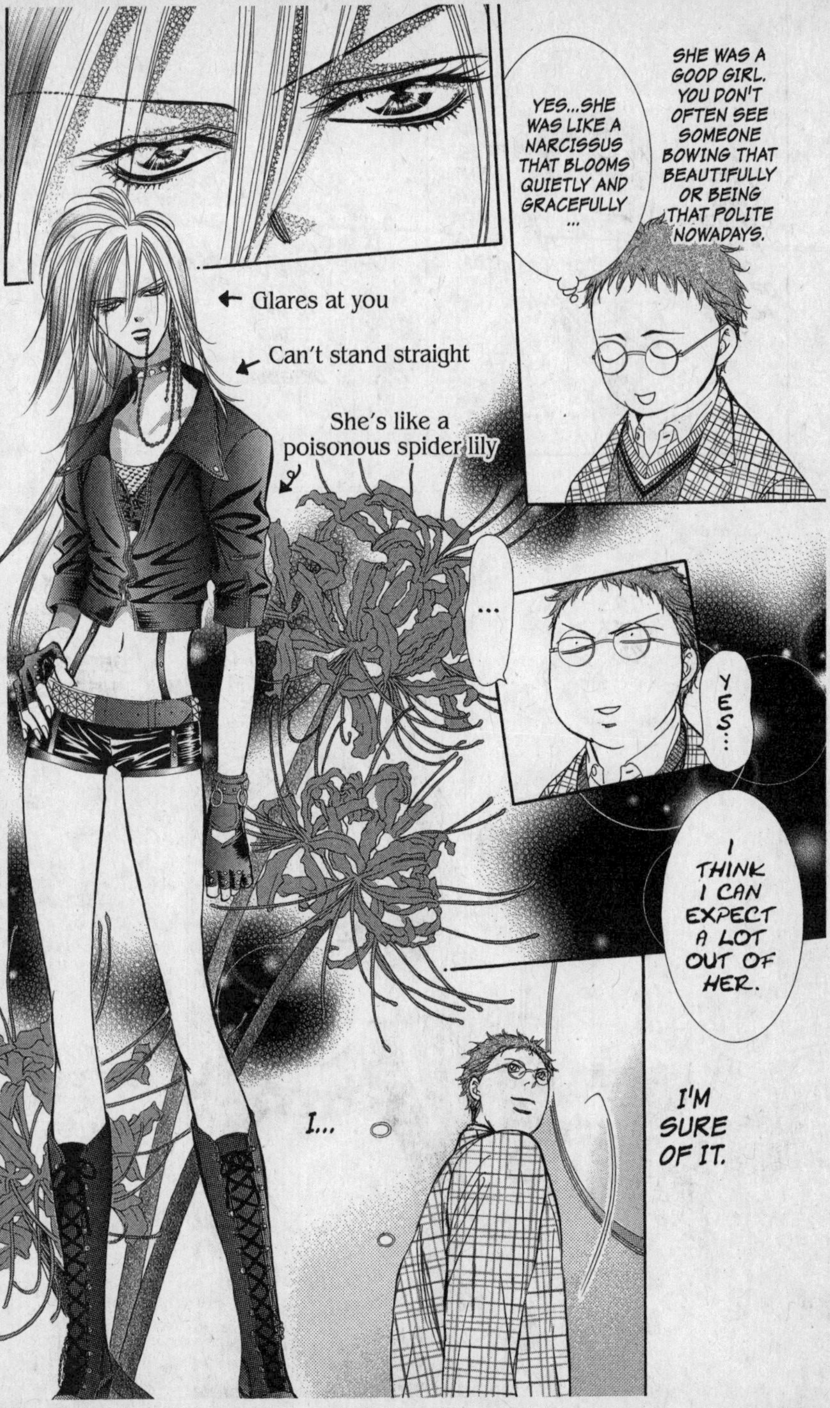
SHE WAS A GOOD GIRL. YOU DON'T OFTEN SEE SOMEONE BOWING THAT BEAUTIFULLY OR BEING THAT POLITE NOWADAYS.
YES...SHE WAS LIKE A NARCISSUS THAT BLOOMS QUIETLY AND GRACEFULLY ...
← Glares at you
Can't stand straight
She's like a poisonous spider lily
...
YES...
I THINK I CAN EXPECT A LOT OUT OF HER.
I'M SURE OF IT.
I...

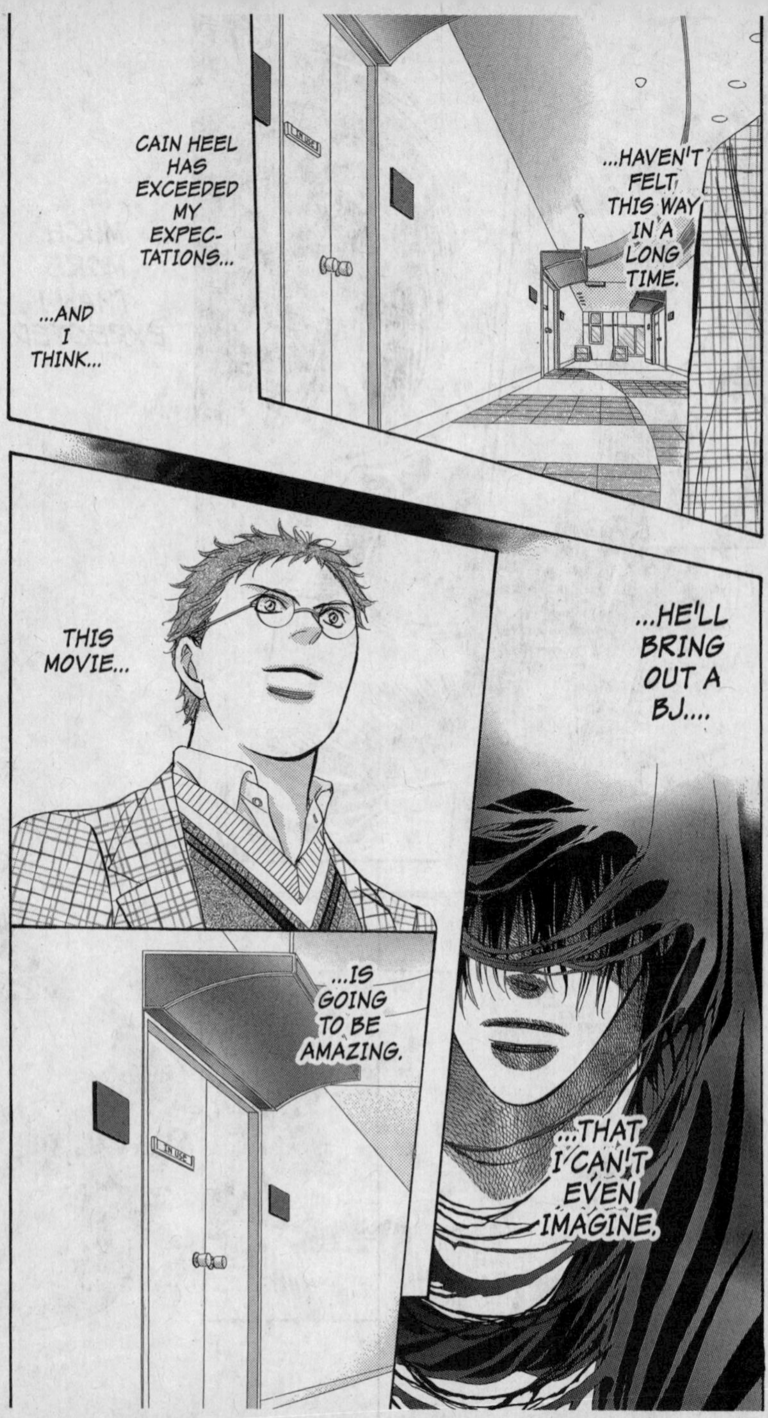
...HAVEN'T FELT THIS WAY IN A LONG TIME.
CAIN HEEL HAS EXCEEDED MY EXPECTATIONS...
...AND I THINK...
...HE'LL BRING OUT A BJ....
...THAT I CAN'T EVEN IMAGINE.
THIS MOVIE...
...IS GOING TO BE AMAZING.

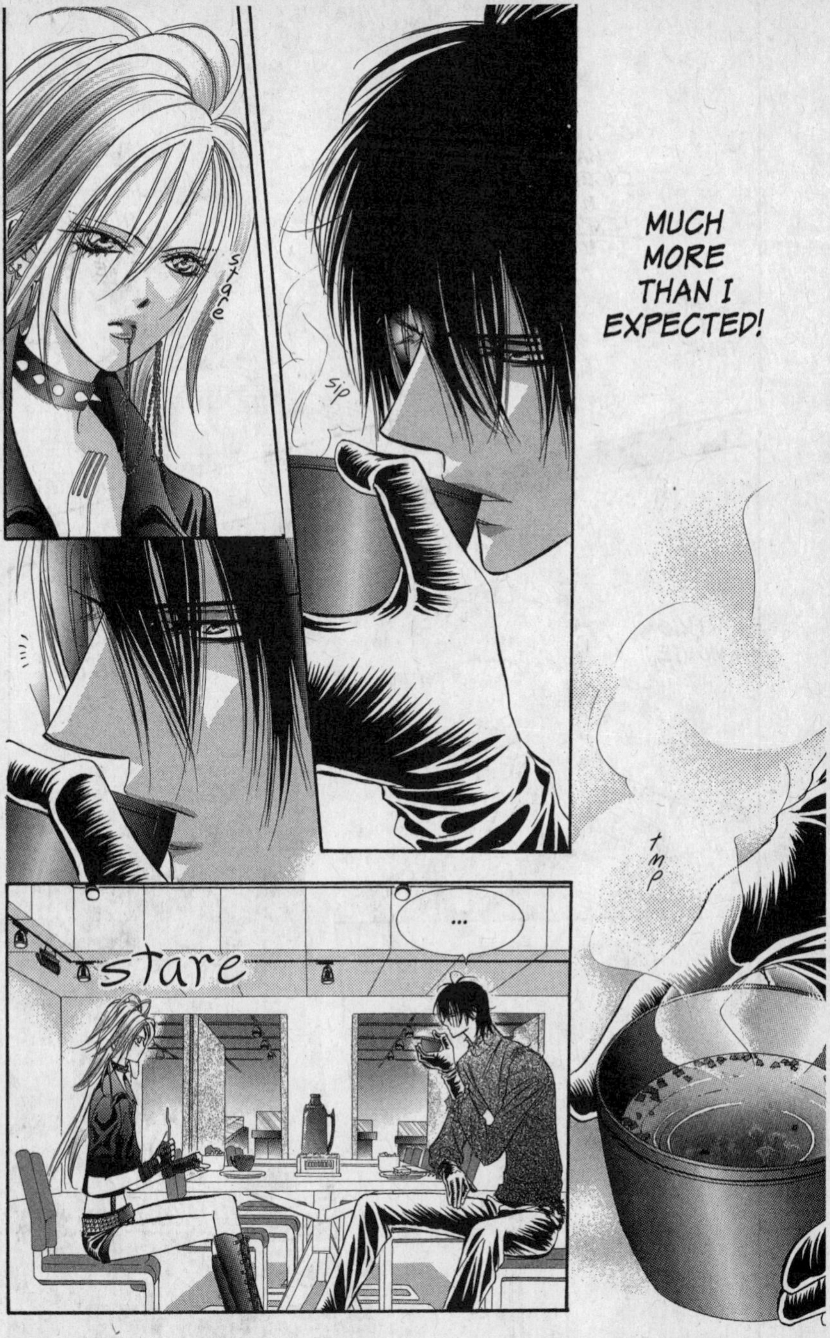
MUCH MORE THAN I EXPECTED!
tmp
sip
stare
...
stare

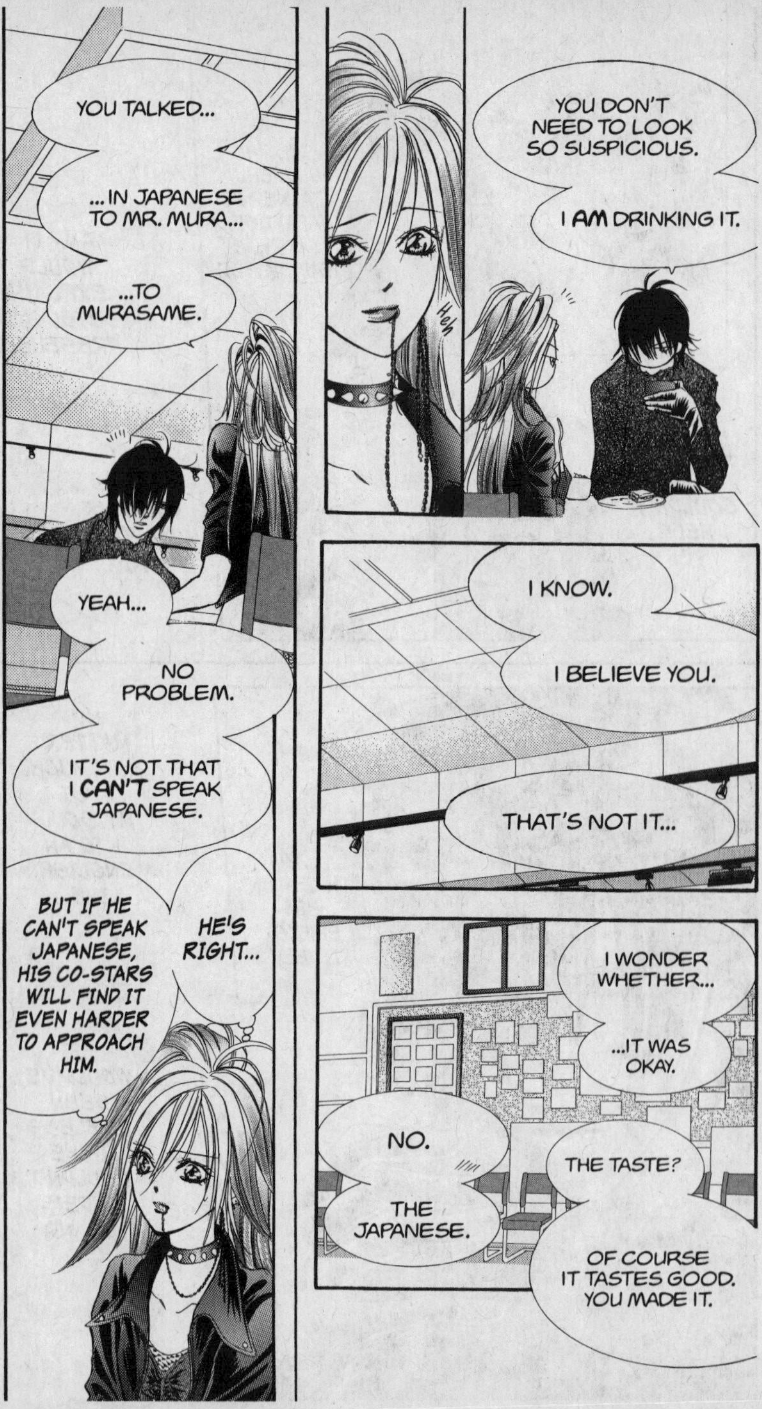
YOU DON'T NEED TO LOOK SO SUSPICIOUS.
I AM DRINKING IT.
Heh
I KNOW.
I BELIEVE YOU.
THAT'S NOT IT...
I WONDER WHETHER...
...IT WAS OKAY.
THE TASTE?
OF COURSE IT TASTES GOOD. YOU MADE IT.
NO.
THE JAPANESE.
YOU TALKED...
...IN JAPANESE TO MR. MURA...
...TO MURASAME.
YEAH...
NO PROBLEM.
IT'S NOT THAT I CAN'T SPEAK JAPANESE.
HE'S RIGHT...
BUT IF HE CAN'T SPEAK JAPANESE, HIS CO-STARS WILL FIND IT EVEN HARDER TO APPROACH HIM.

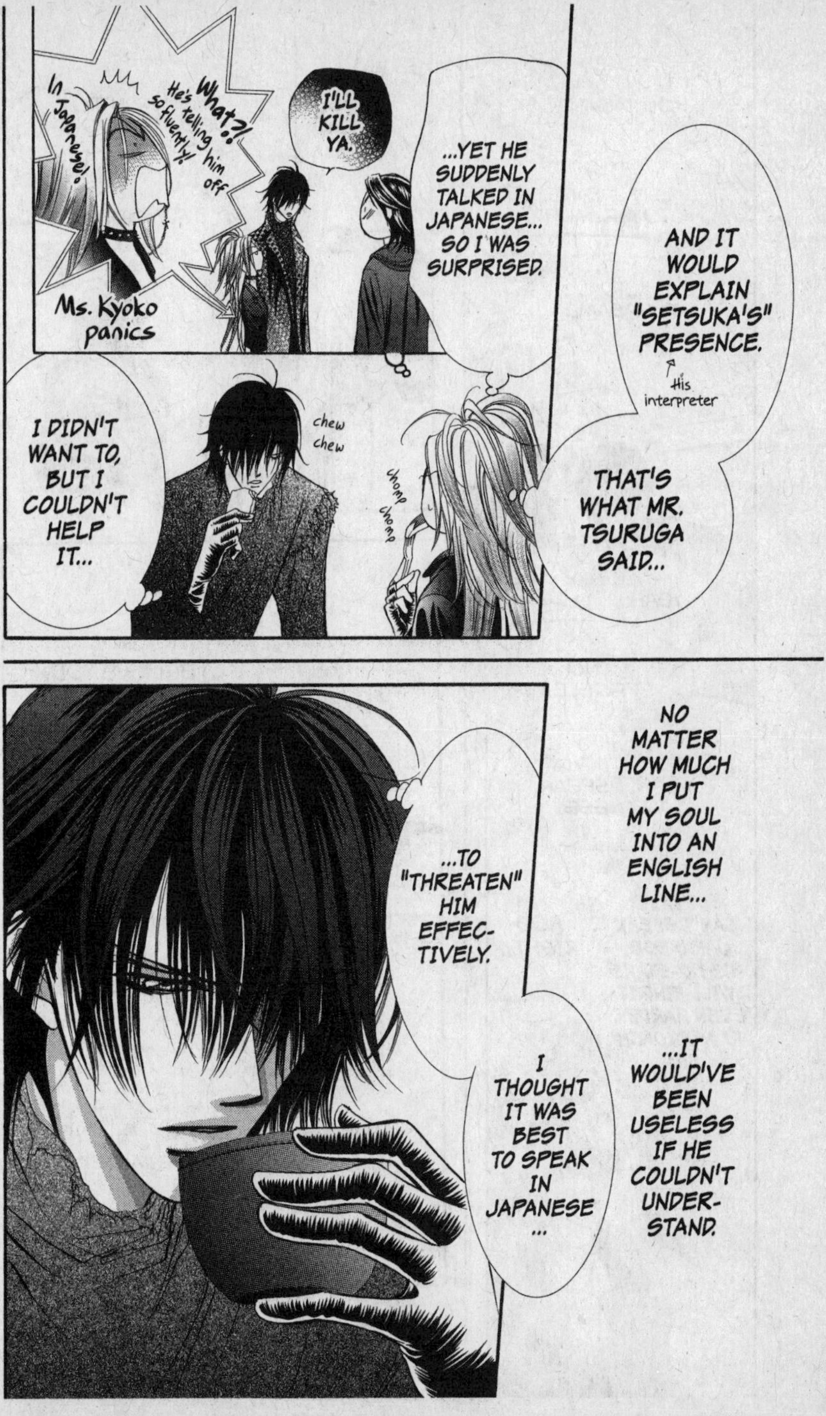
AND IT WOULD EXPLAIN "SETSUKA'S" PRESENCE.
His interpreter
THAT'S WHAT MR. TSURUGA SAID...
...YET HE SUDDENLY TALKED IN JAPANESE... SO I WAS SURPRISED.
I'LL KILL YA.
What?!
He's telling him off so fluently!
In Japanese!
Ms. Kyoko panics
chomp chomp
chew chew
I DIDN'T WANT TO, BUT I COULDN'T HELP IT...
NO MATTER HOW MUCH I PUT MY SOUL INTO AN ENGLISH LINE...
...IT WOULD'VE BEEN USELESS IF HE COULDN'T UNDERSTAND.
I THOUGHT IT WAS BEST TO SPEAK IN JAPANESE...
...TO "THREATEN" HIM EFFECTIVELY.

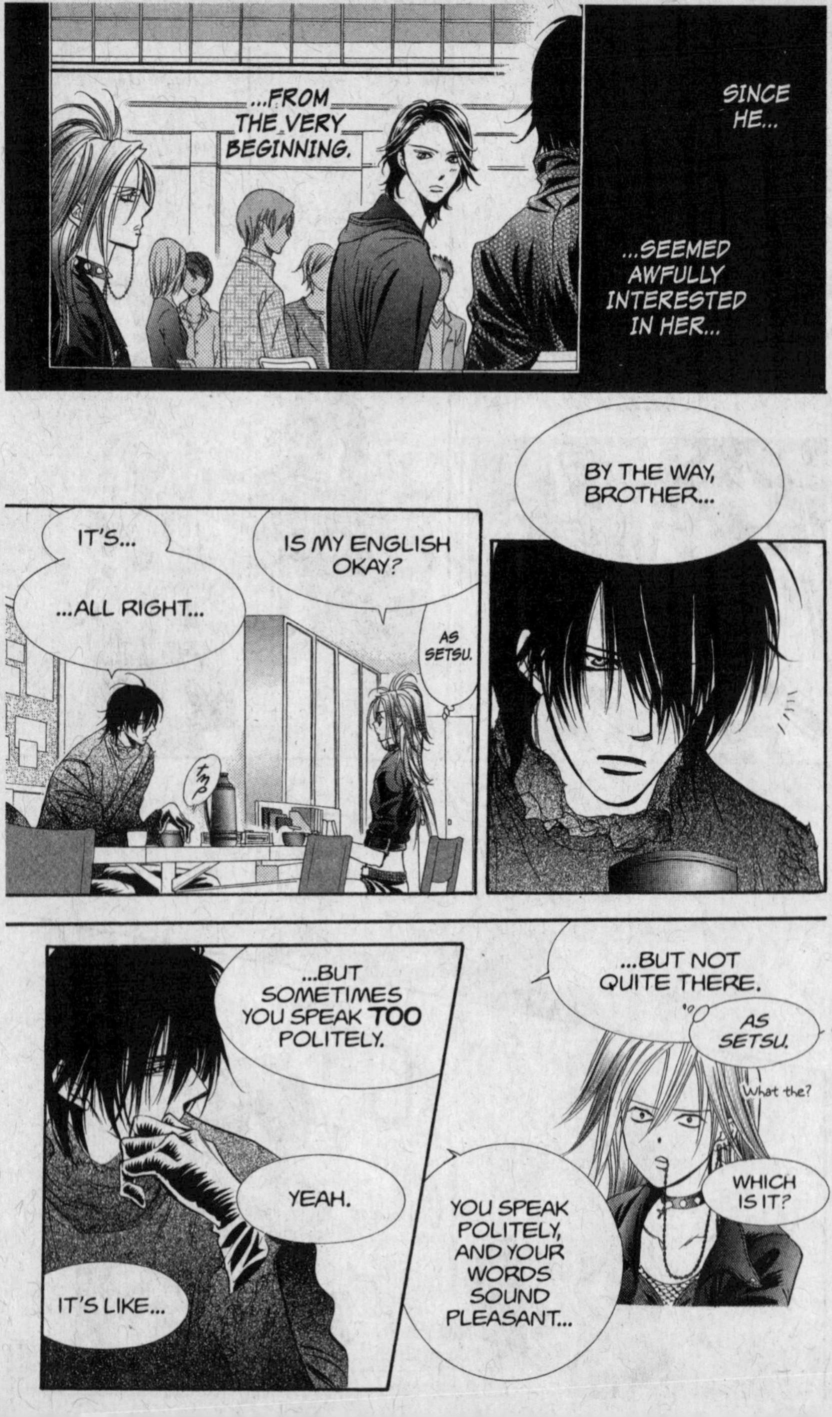
SINCE HE...
...SEEMED AWFULLY INTERESTED IN HER...
...FROM THE VERY BEGINNING.
BY THE WAY, BROTHER...
IS MY ENGLISH OKAY?
AS SETSU.
IT'S...
...ALL RIGHT...
tmp
...BUT NOT QUITE THERE.
AS SETSU.
What the?
WHICH IS IT?
YOU SPEAK POLITELY, AND YOUR WORDS SOUND PLEASANT...
YEAH.
...BUT SOMETIMES YOU SPEAK **TOO** POLITELY.
IT'S LIKE...

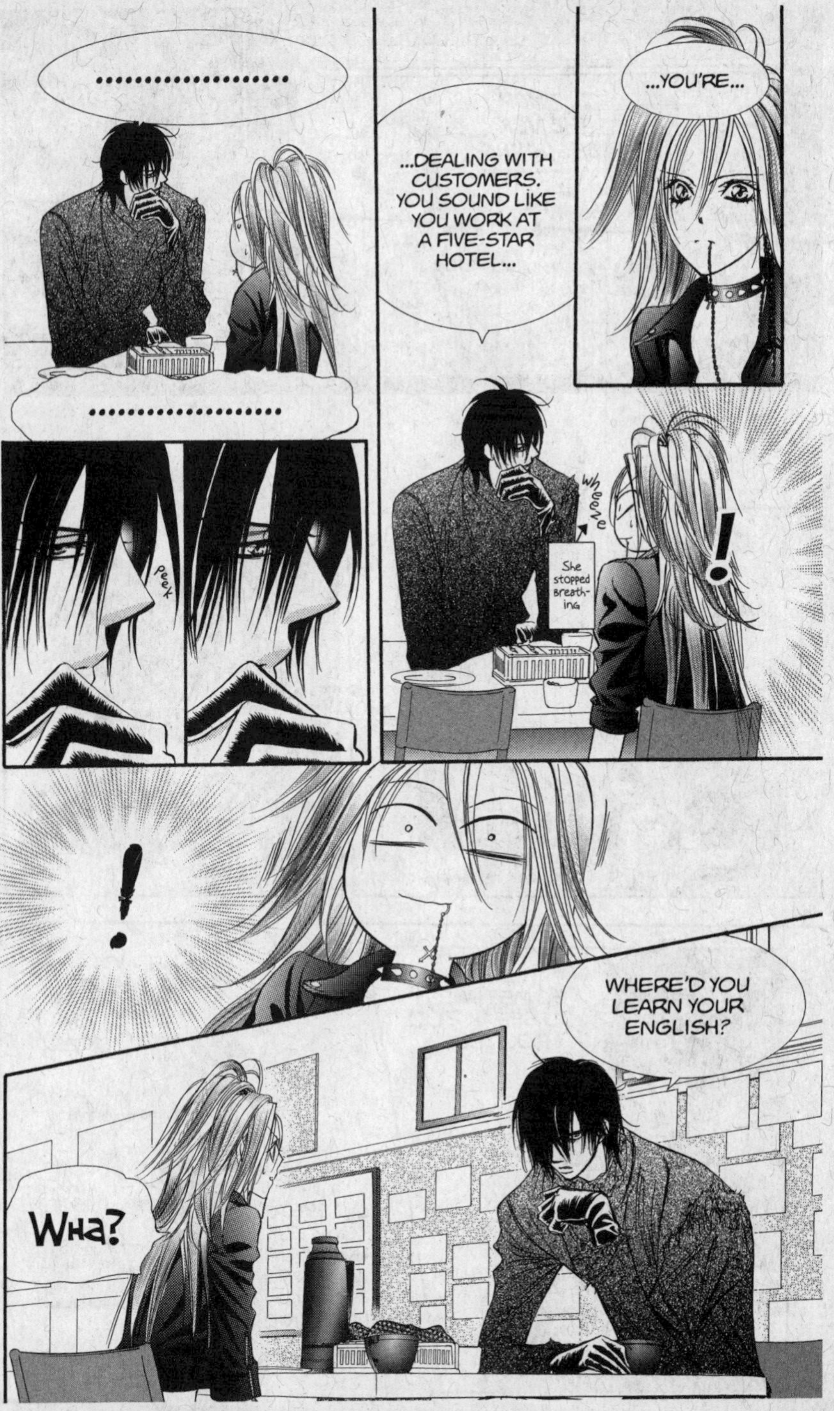
...YOU'RE...
...DEALING WITH CUSTOMERS. YOU SOUND LIKE YOU WORK AT A FIVE-STAR HOTEL...
....
....
wheeze
She stopped breathing
!
peek
!
WHERE'D YOU LEARN YOUR ENGLISH?
WHA?

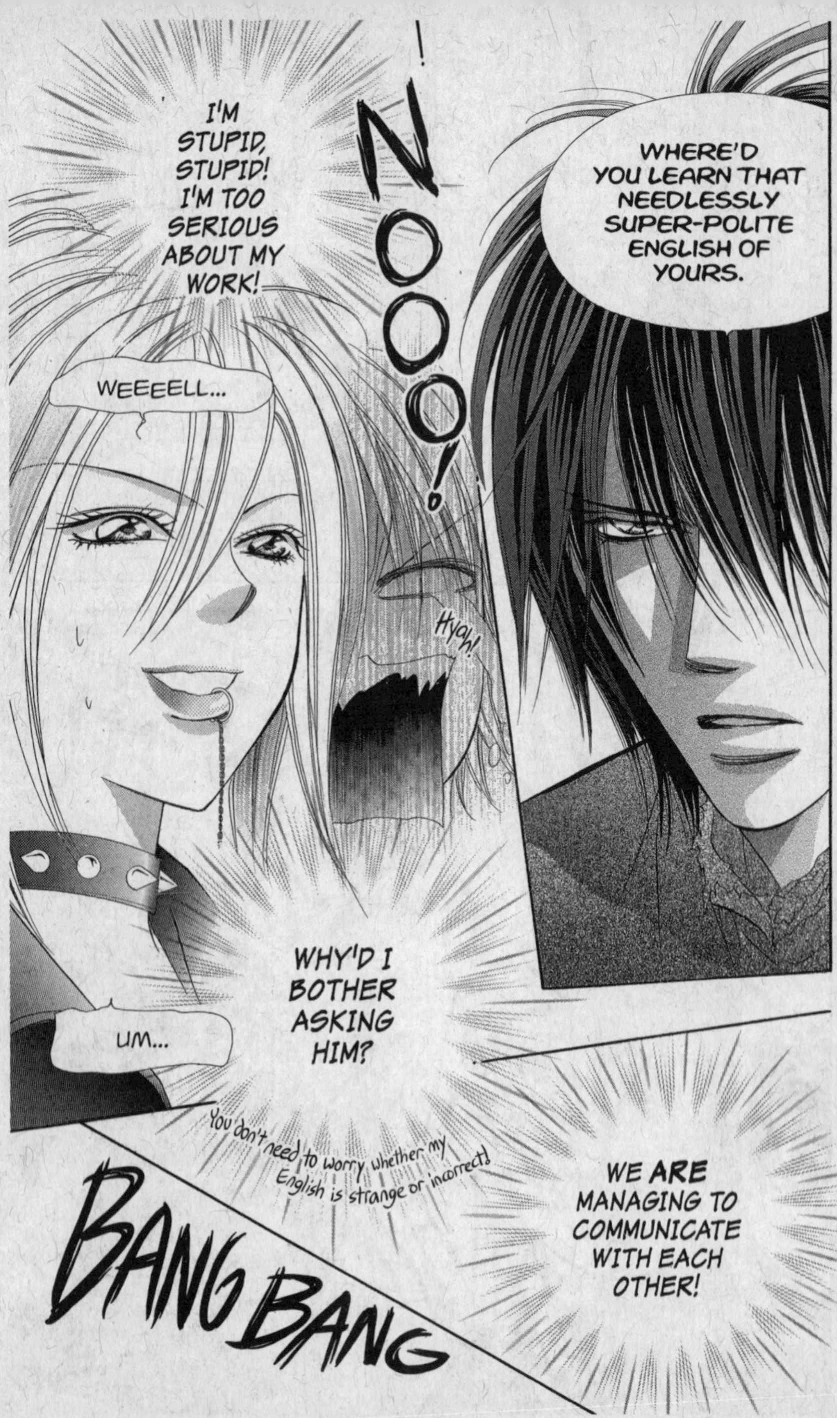
WHERE'D YOU LEARN THAT NEEDLESSLY SUPER-POLITE ENGLISH OF YOURS.
NOOOO!
I'M STUPID, STUPID! I'M TOO SERIOUS ABOUT MY WORK!
WEEEELL...
Hyah!
WHY'D I BOTHER ASKING HIM?
UM...
You don't need to worry whether my English is strange or incorrect!
WE ARE MANAGING TO COMMUNICATE WITH EACH OTHER!
BANG BANG

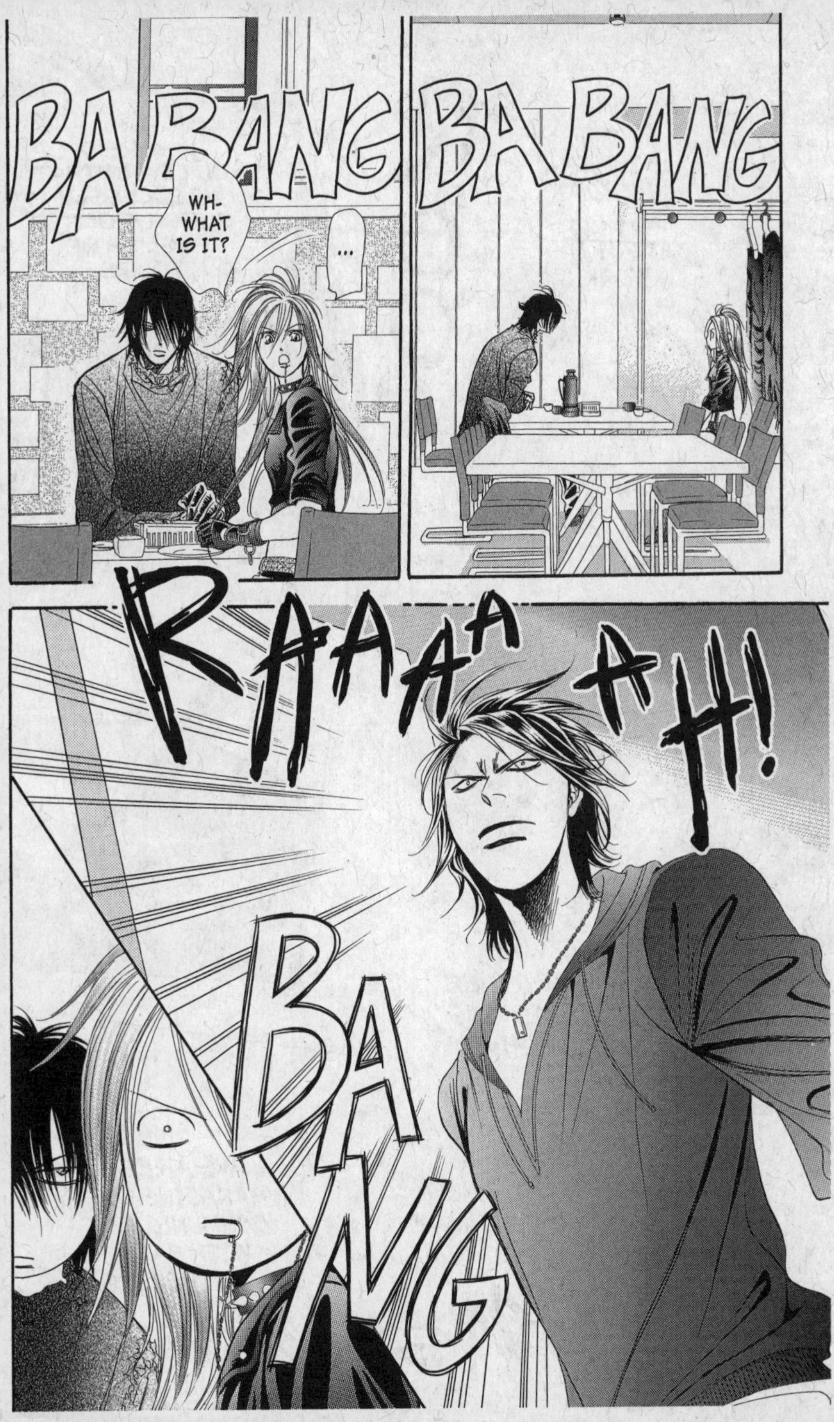
BA BANG
BA BANG
WH-WHAT IS IT?
...
RAAAAH!
BA BANG

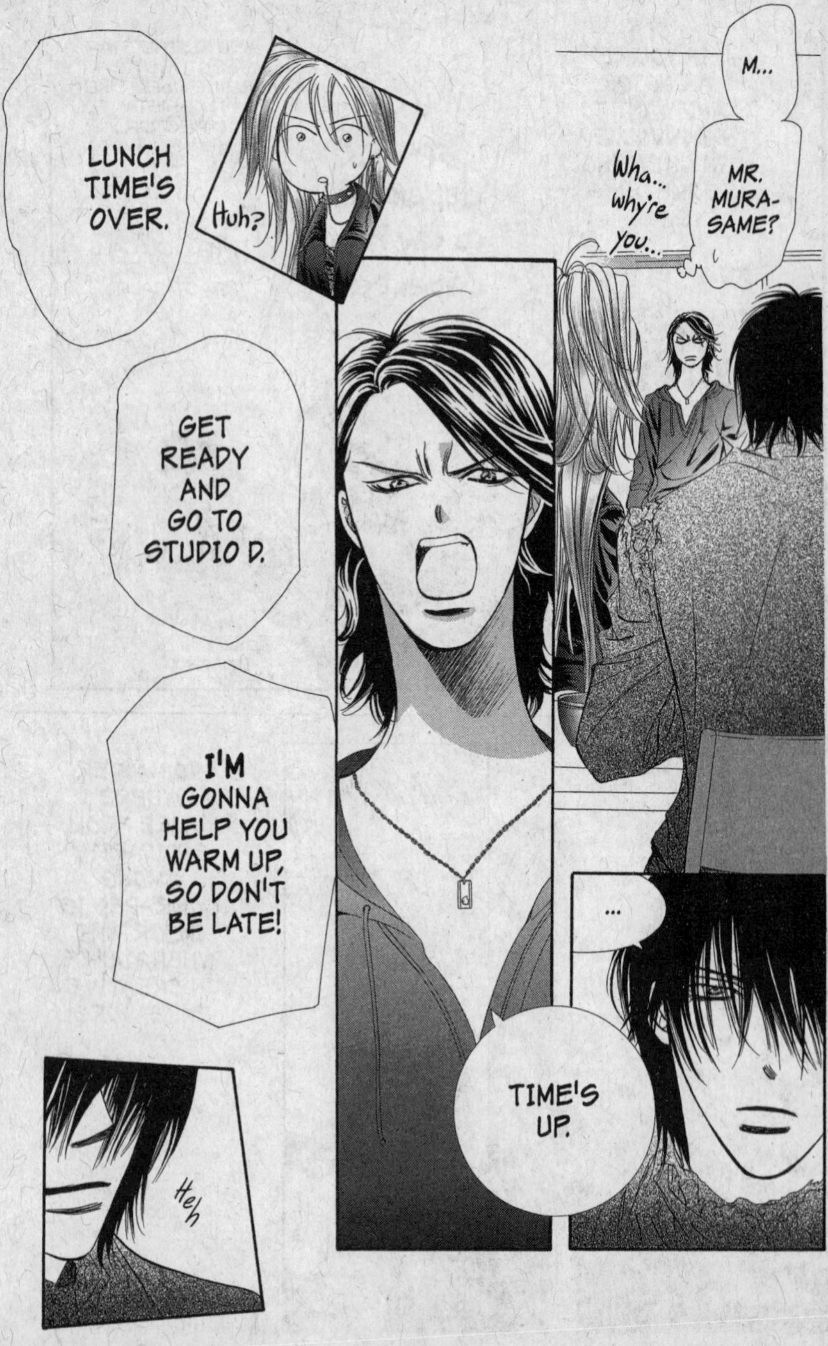
M...
MR. MURA-SAME?
Wha... why're you...
...
TIME'S UP.
Huh?
LUNCH TIME'S OVER.
GET READY AND GO TO STUDIO D.
I'M GONNA HELP YOU WARM UP, SO DON'T BE LATE!
Heh

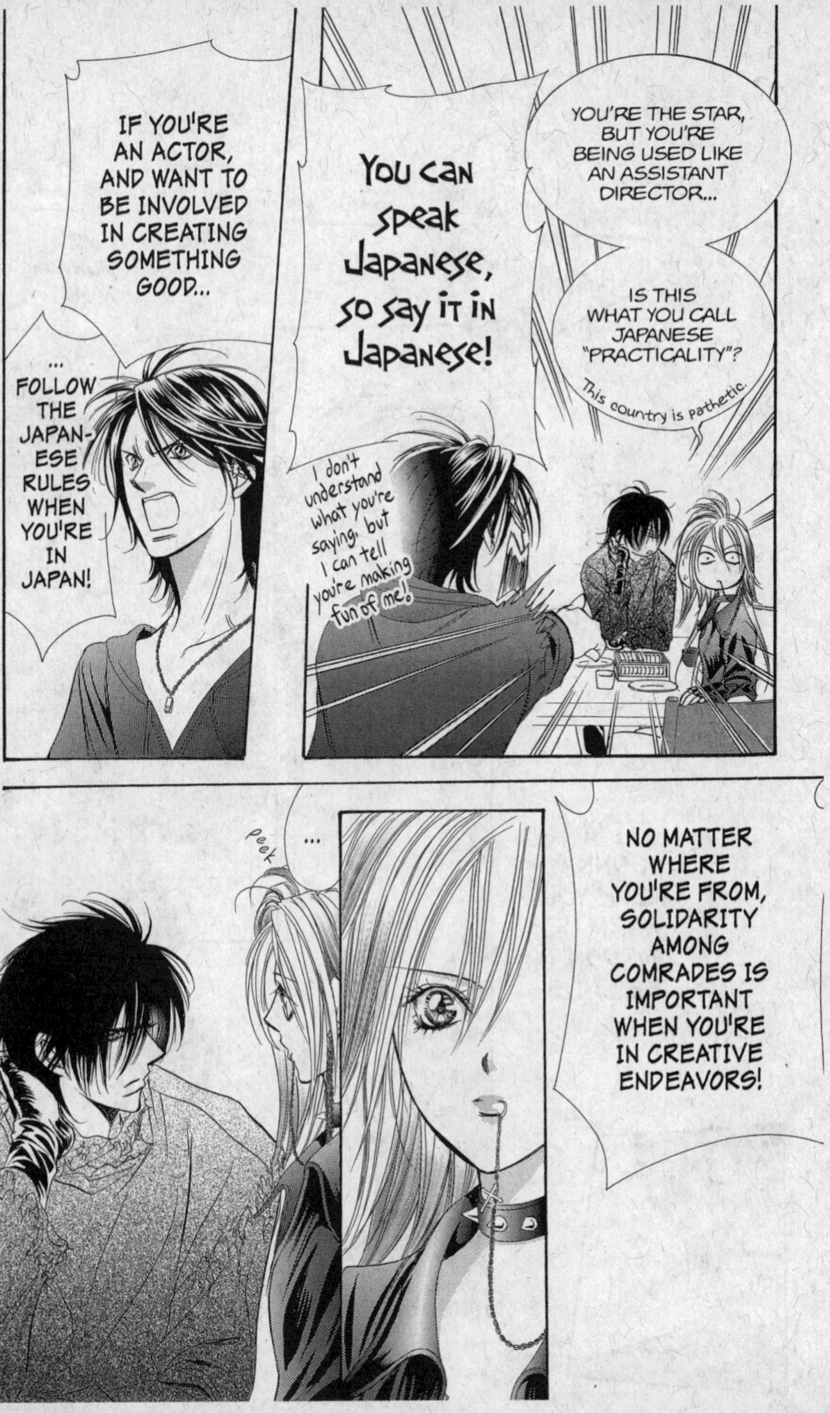

YOU'RE THE STAR, BUT YOU'RE BEING USED LIKE AN ASSISTANT DIRECTOR...
IS THIS WHAT YOU CALL JAPANESE "PRACTICALITY"?
This country is pathetic.
You can speak Japanese, so say it in Japanese!
I don't understand what you're saying, but I can tell you're making fun of me!
IF YOU'RE AN ACTOR, AND WANT TO BE INVOLVED IN CREATING SOMETHING GOOD...
...FOLLOW THE JAPAN-ESE RULES WHEN YOU'RE IN JAPAN!
NO MATTER WHERE YOU'RE FROM, SOLIDARITY AMONG COMRADES IS IMPORTANT WHEN YOU'RE IN CREATIVE ENDEAVORS!
Peek
...

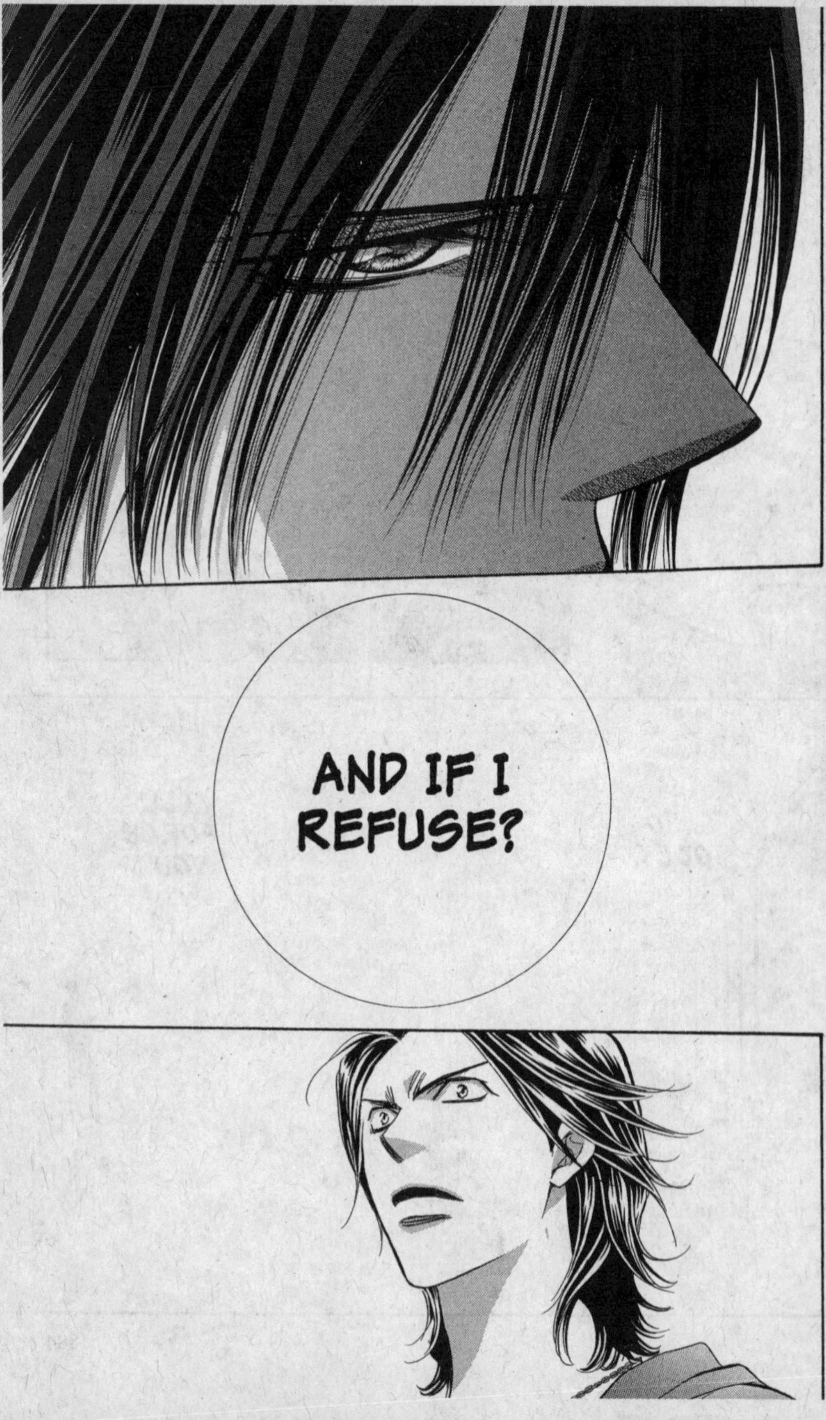
AND IF I REFUSE?

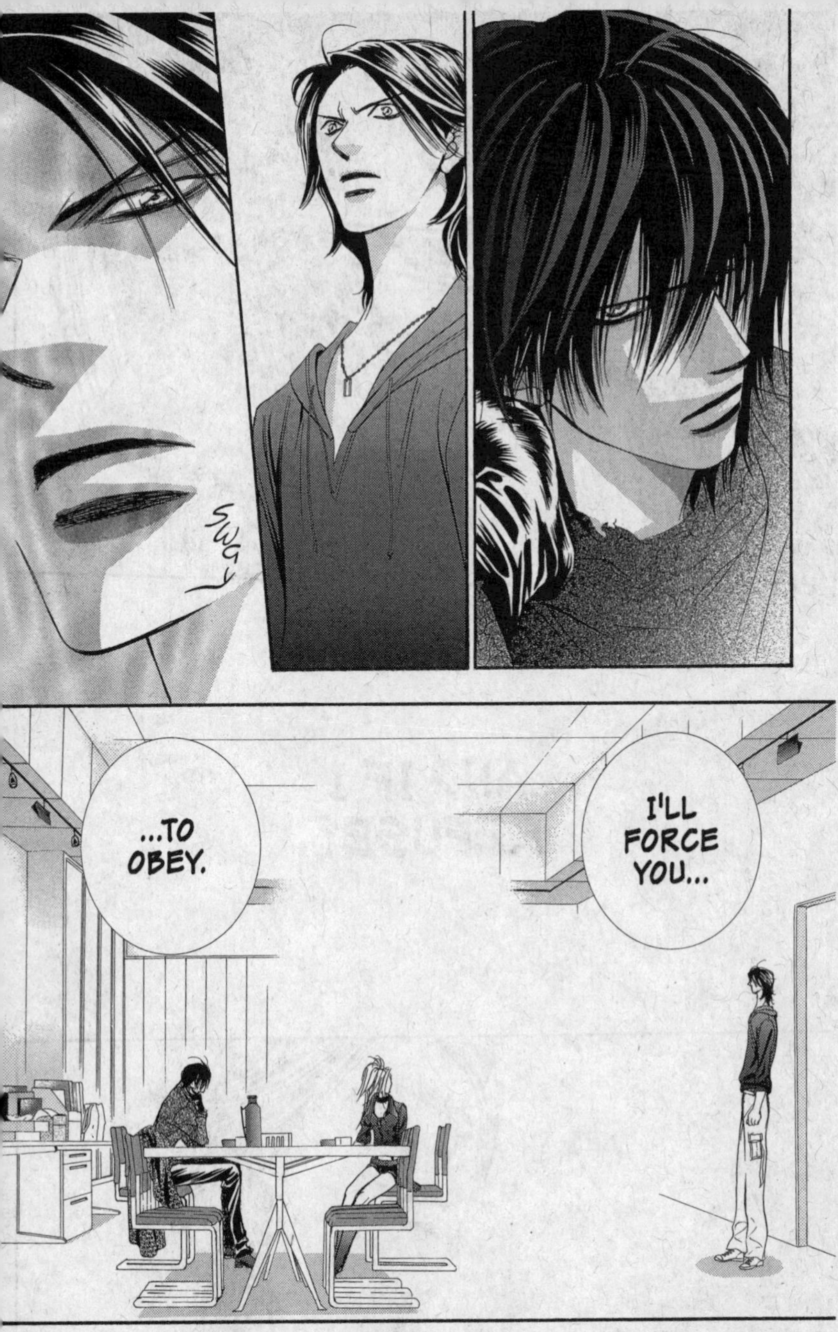
SWAY
I'LL FORCE YOU...
...TO OBEY.

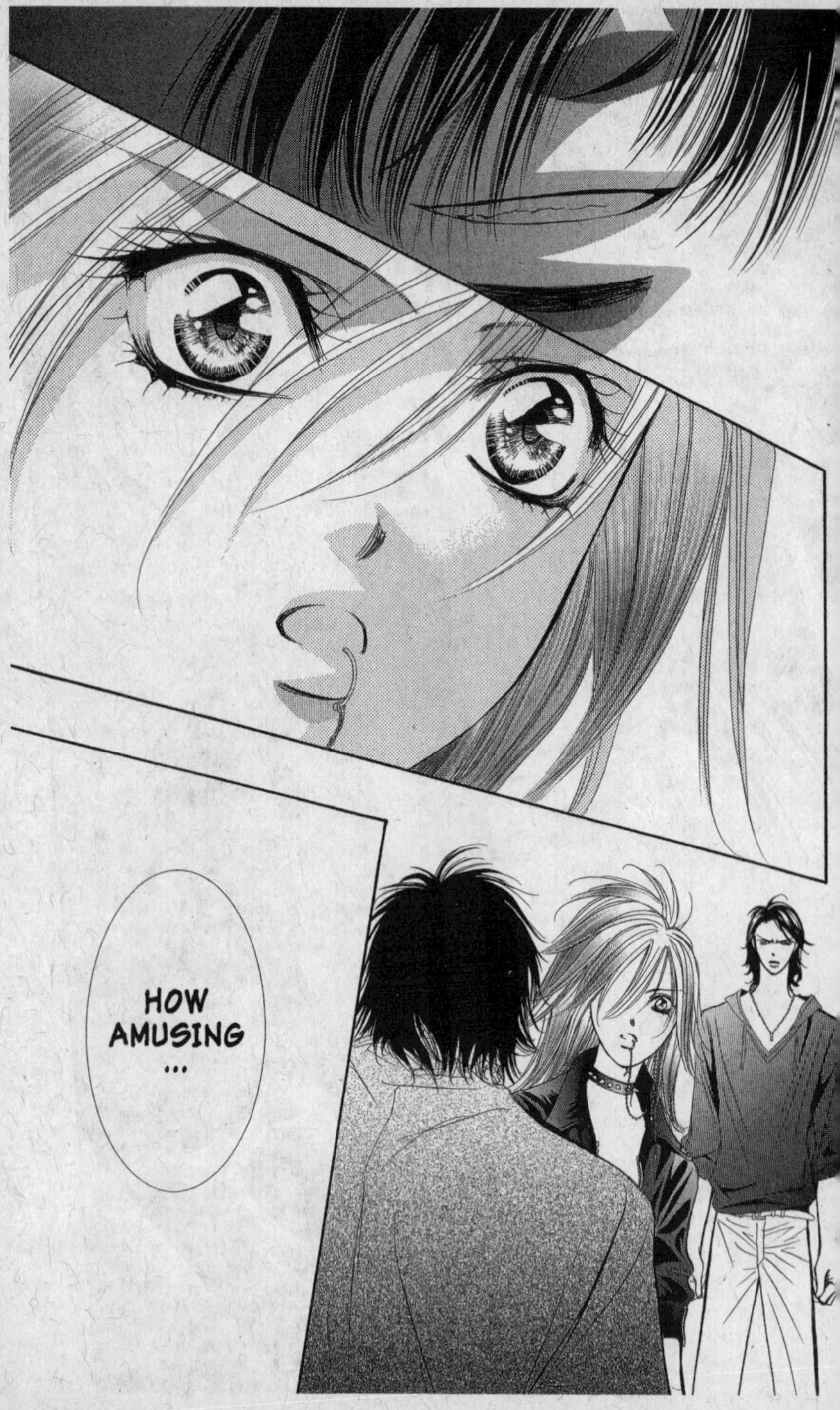
HOW AMUSING ...

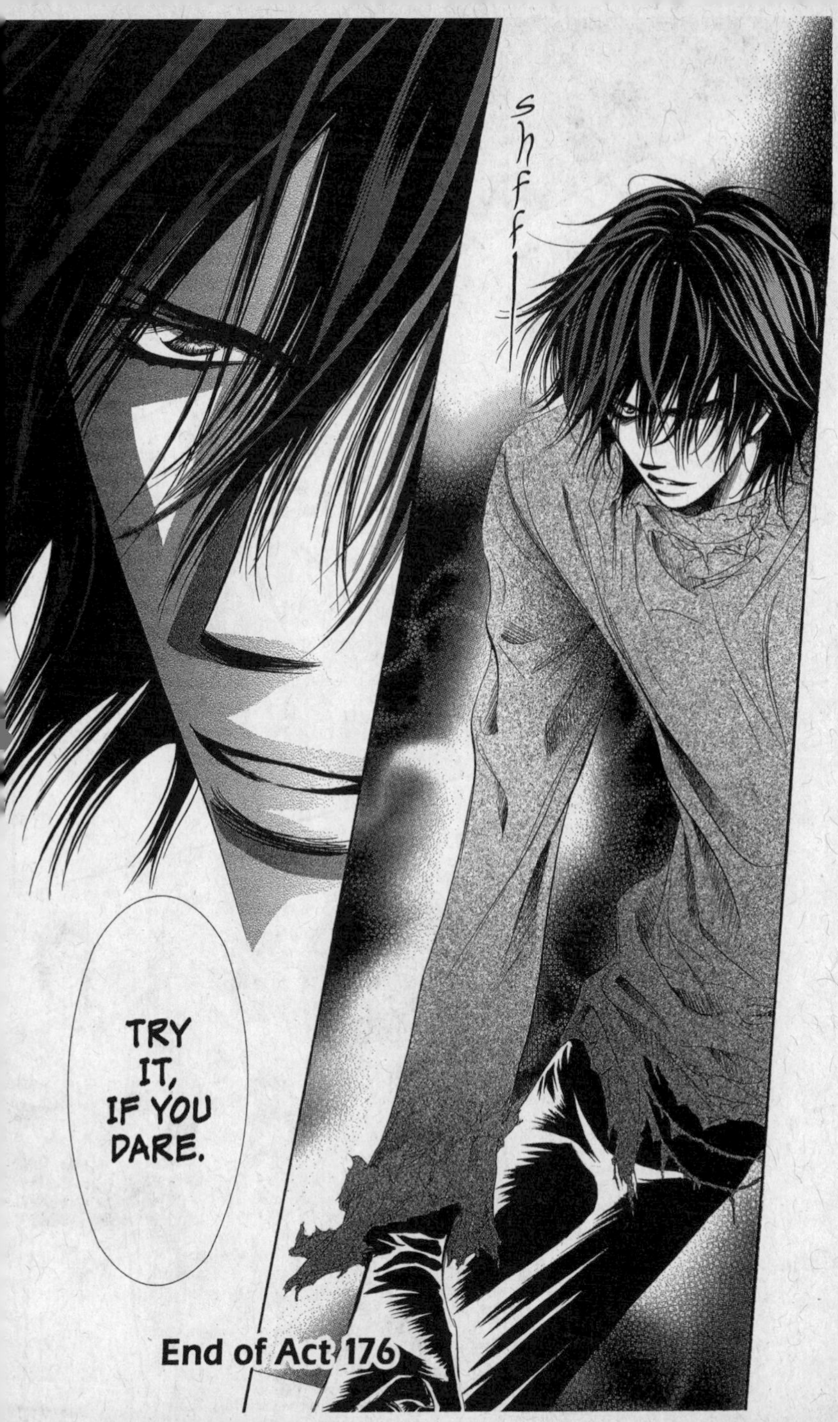
shff
TRY IT, IF YOU DARE.
End of Act 176

Skip·Beat! End Notes
Everyone knows how to be a fan, but sometimes cool things from other cultures need a little help crossing the language barrier.

Pg 365, panel 1: Like a Japanese biker
It is common for members of Japanese biker gangs to change the kanji spellings of their names, often picking more dangerous or tough sounding kanji than the originals.

Page 365, panel 1: Cain Heel kanji
The kanji Murasame imagines Cain Heel using are:
渦 (ka) means "whirlpool"
院 (in) means "shadow"
氷 (hi) means "ice"
屡 (ru) means "again and again"

Shojo Beat

Skip·Beat!

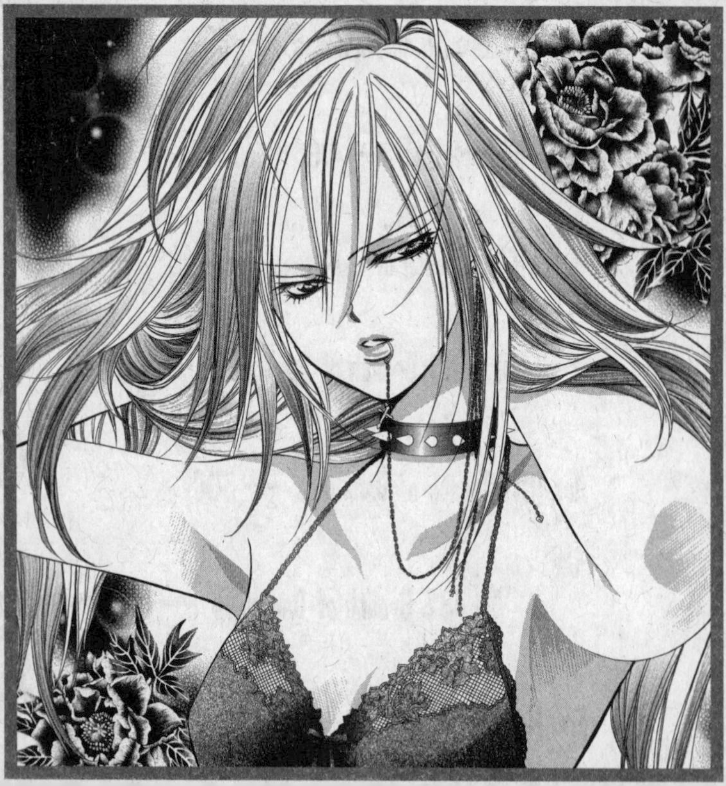

Skip·Beat!

Volume 30

CONTENTS

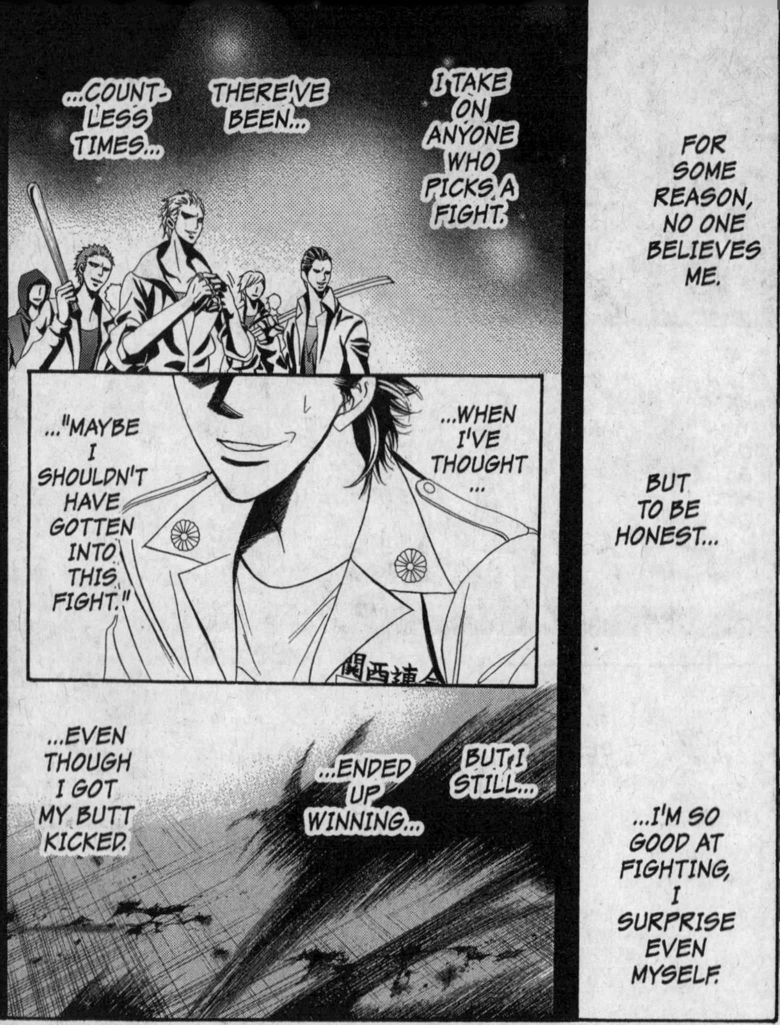
FOR SOME REASON, NO ONE BELIEVES ME.
BUT TO BE HONEST...
...I'M SO GOOD AT FIGHTING, I SURPRISE EVEN MYSELF.
I TAKE ON ANYONE WHO PICKS A FIGHT.
THERE'VE BEEN...
...COUNT-LESS TIMES...
...WHEN I'VE THOUGHT...
..."MAYBE I SHOULDN'T HAVE GOTTEN INTO THIS FIGHT."
関西連合
BUT I STILL...
...ENDED UP WINNING...
...EVEN THOUGH I GOT MY BUTT KICKED.

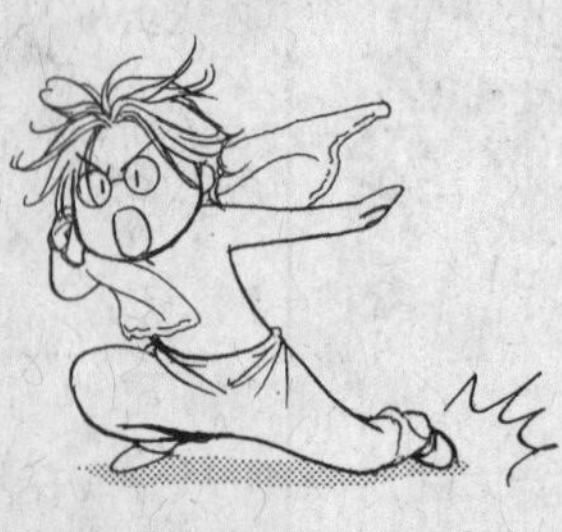

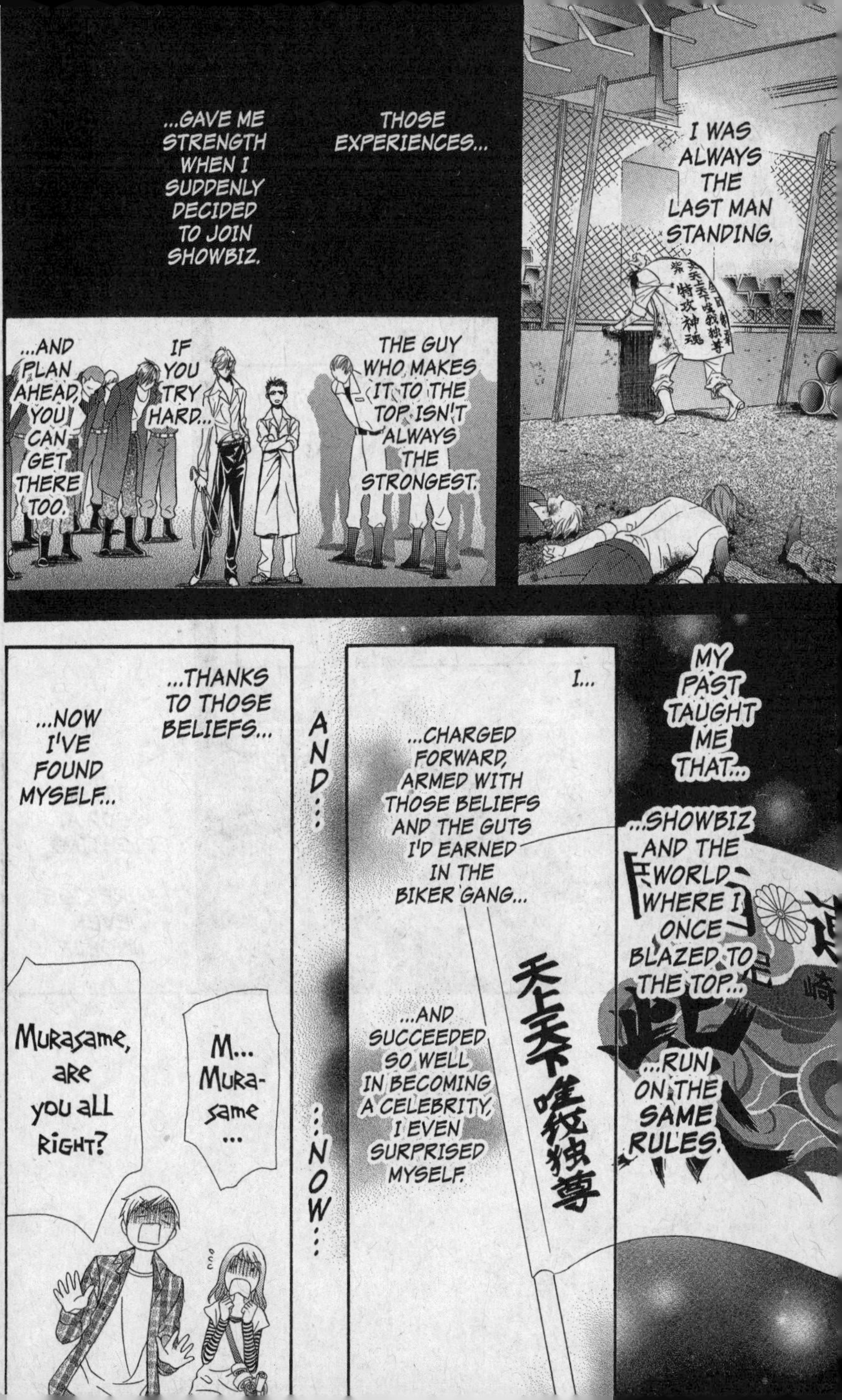
I WAS ALWAYS THE LAST MAN STANDING.
THOSE EXPERIENCES...
...GAVE ME STRENGTH WHEN I SUDDENLY DECIDED TO JOIN SHOWBIZ.
THE GUY WHO MAKES IT TO THE TOP ISN'T ALWAYS THE STRONGEST.
IF YOU TRY HARD...
...AND PLAN AHEAD, YOU CAN GET THERE TOO.
MY PAST TAUGHT ME THAT...
...SHOWBIZ AND THE WORLD WHERE I ONCE BLAZED TO THE TOP...
...RUN ON THE SAME RULES.
I...
...CHARGED FORWARD, ARMED WITH THOSE BELIEFS AND THE GUTS I'D EARNED IN THE BIKER GANG...
...AND SUCCEEDED SO WELL IN BECOMING A CELEBRITY, I EVEN SURPRISED MYSELF.
天上天下唯我独尊
AND...
...NOW...
...THANKS TO THOSE BELIEFS...
...NOW I'VE FOUND MYSELF...
M... Murasame...
Murasame, are you all right?

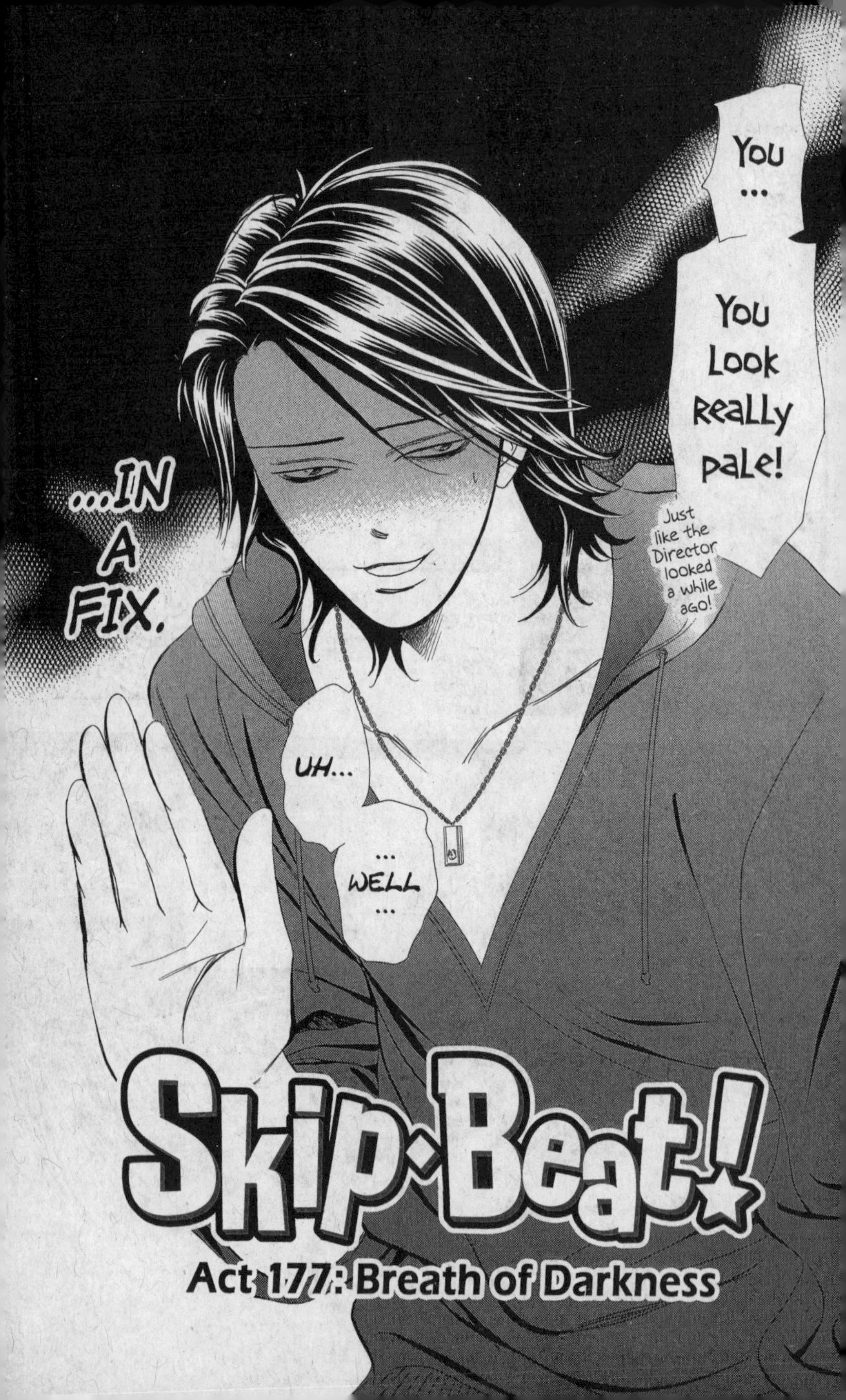
You ...
You look really pale!
Just like the Director looked a while ago!
...IN A FIX.
UH...
... WELL ...
Skip·Beat!
Act 177: Breath of Darkness

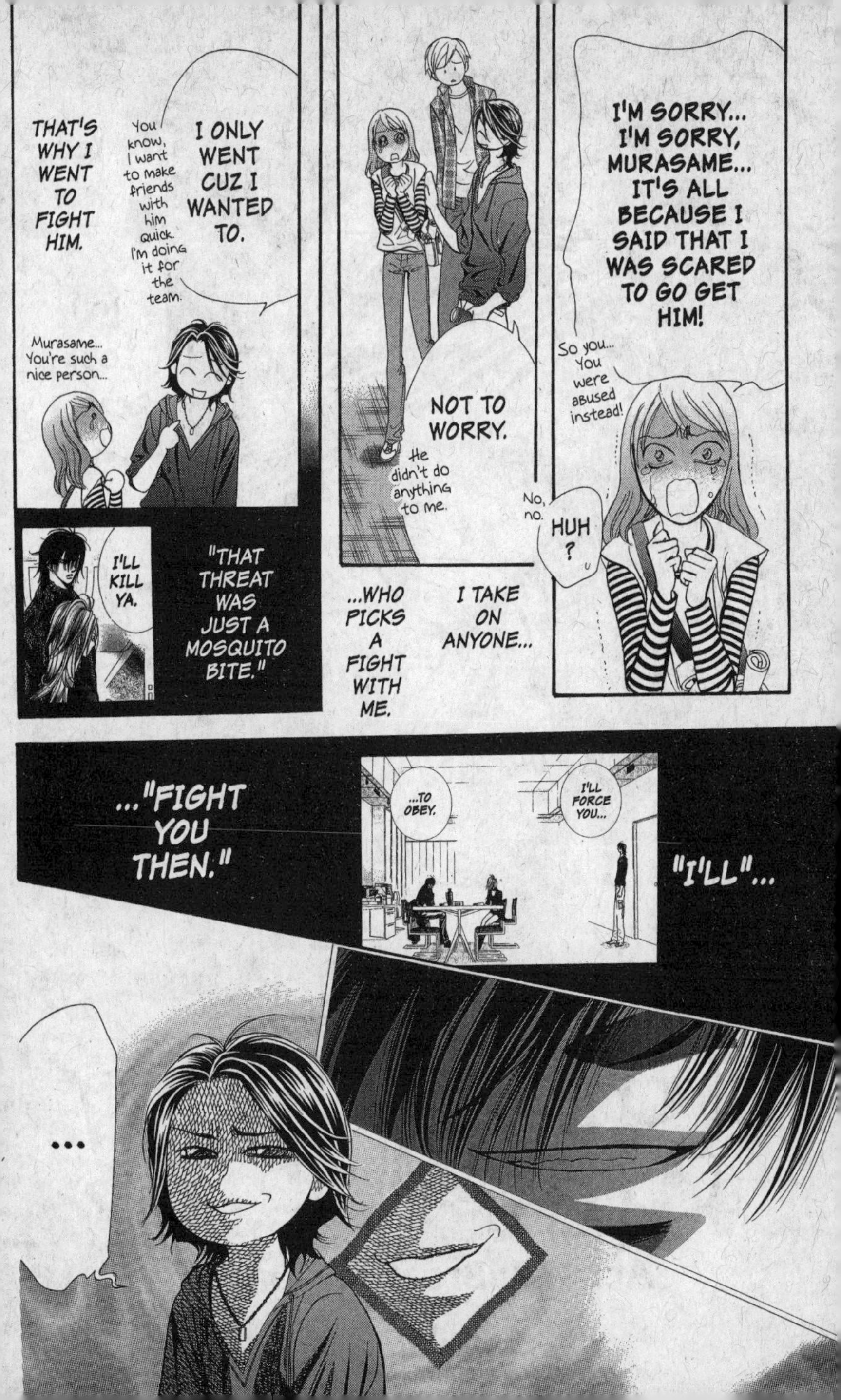
I'M SORRY... I'M SORRY, MURASAME... IT'S ALL BECAUSE I SAID THAT I WAS SCARED TO GO GET HIM!
So you... You were abused instead!
No, no.
HUH?
NOT TO WORRY.
He didn't do anything to me.
I TAKE ON ANYONE...
...WHO PICKS A FIGHT WITH ME.
I ONLY WENT CUZ I WANTED TO.
You know, I want to make friends with him quick. I'm doing it for the team.
THAT'S WHY I WENT TO FIGHT HIM.
Murasame... You're such a nice person...
"THAT THREAT WAS JUST A MOSQUITO BITE."
I'LL KILL YA.
"I'LL"...
I'LL FORCE YOU...
...TO OBEY.
..."FIGHT YOU THEN."
...

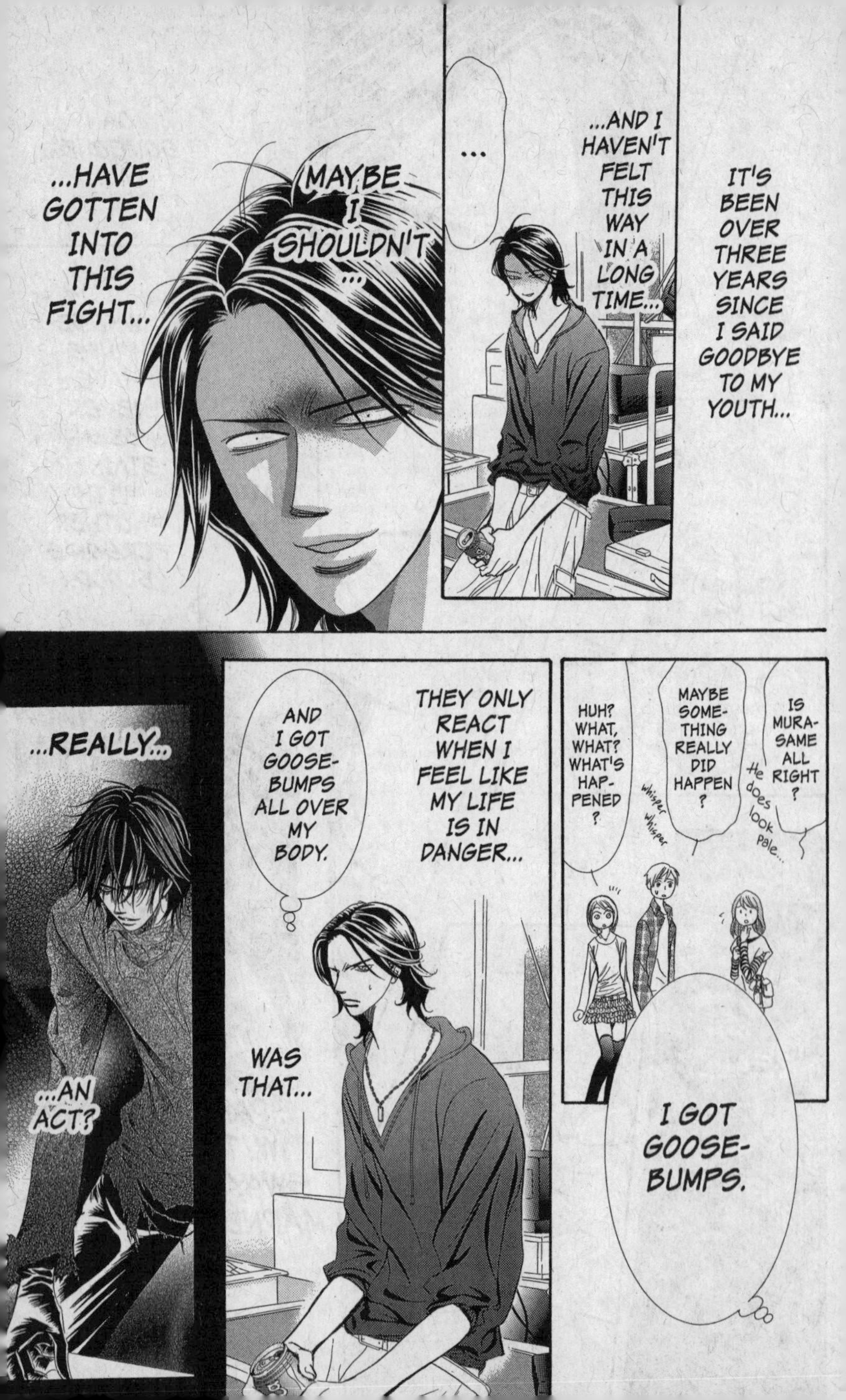
IT'S BEEN OVER THREE YEARS SINCE I SAID GOODBYE TO MY YOUTH...
...AND I HAVEN'T FELT THIS WAY IN A LONG TIME...
...
MAYBE I SHOULDN'T ...
...HAVE GOTTEN INTO THIS FIGHT...
IS MURASAME ALL RIGHT?
He does look pale...
MAYBE SOMETHING REALLY DID HAPPEN?
whisper whisper
HUH? WHAT, WHAT? WHAT'S HAPPENED?
I GOT GOOSEBUMPS.
THEY ONLY REACT WHEN I FEEL LIKE MY LIFE IS IN DANGER...
AND I GOT GOOSEBUMPS ALL OVER MY BODY.
WAS THAT...
...REALLY...
...AN ACT?

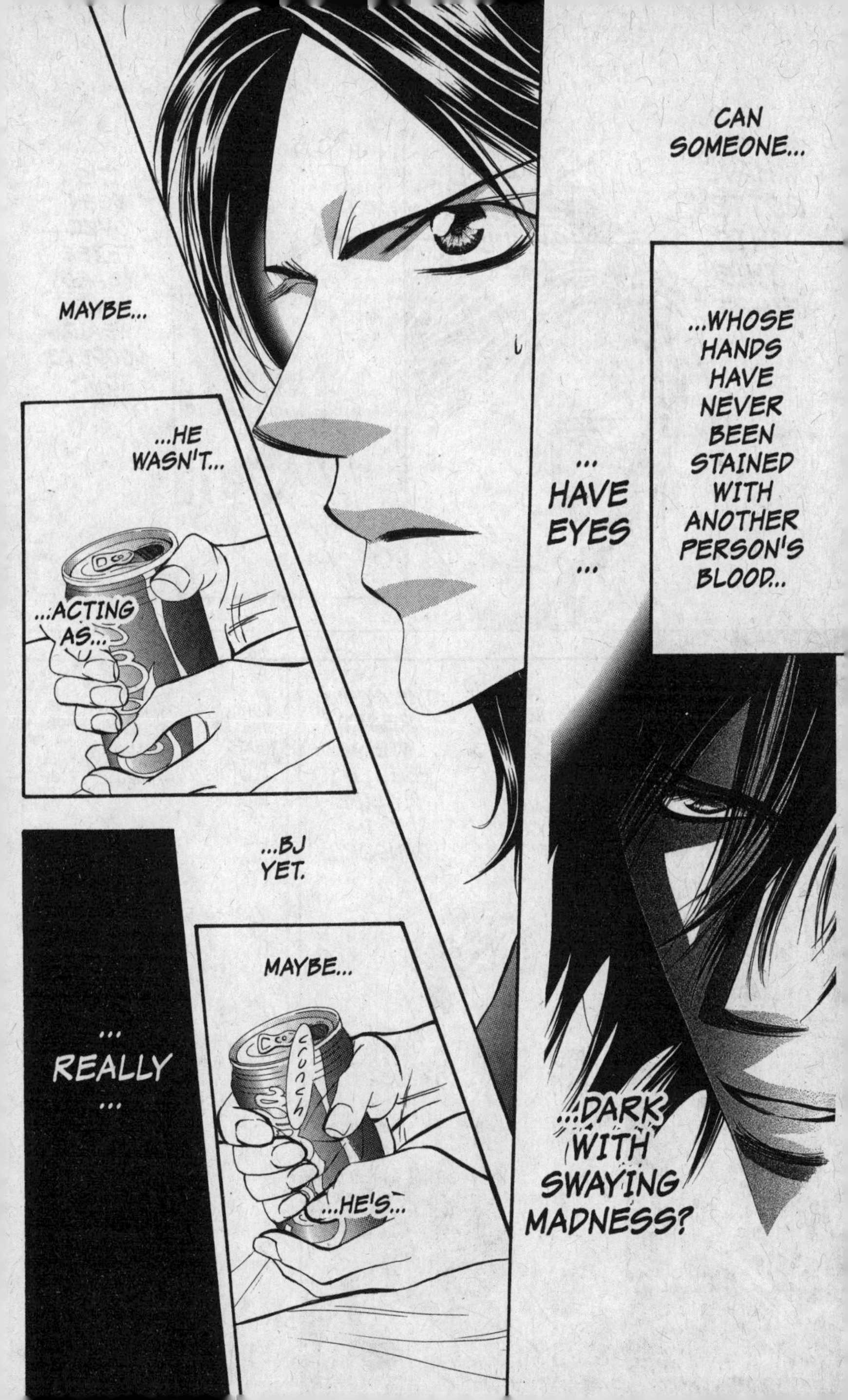
CAN SOMEONE...
...WHOSE HANDS HAVE NEVER BEEN STAINED WITH ANOTHER PERSON'S BLOOD...
...HAVE EYES...
...DARK WITH SWAYING MADNESS?
MAYBE...
...HE WASN'T...
...ACTING AS...
...BJ YET.
MAYBE...
crunch
...HE'S...
...REALLY...

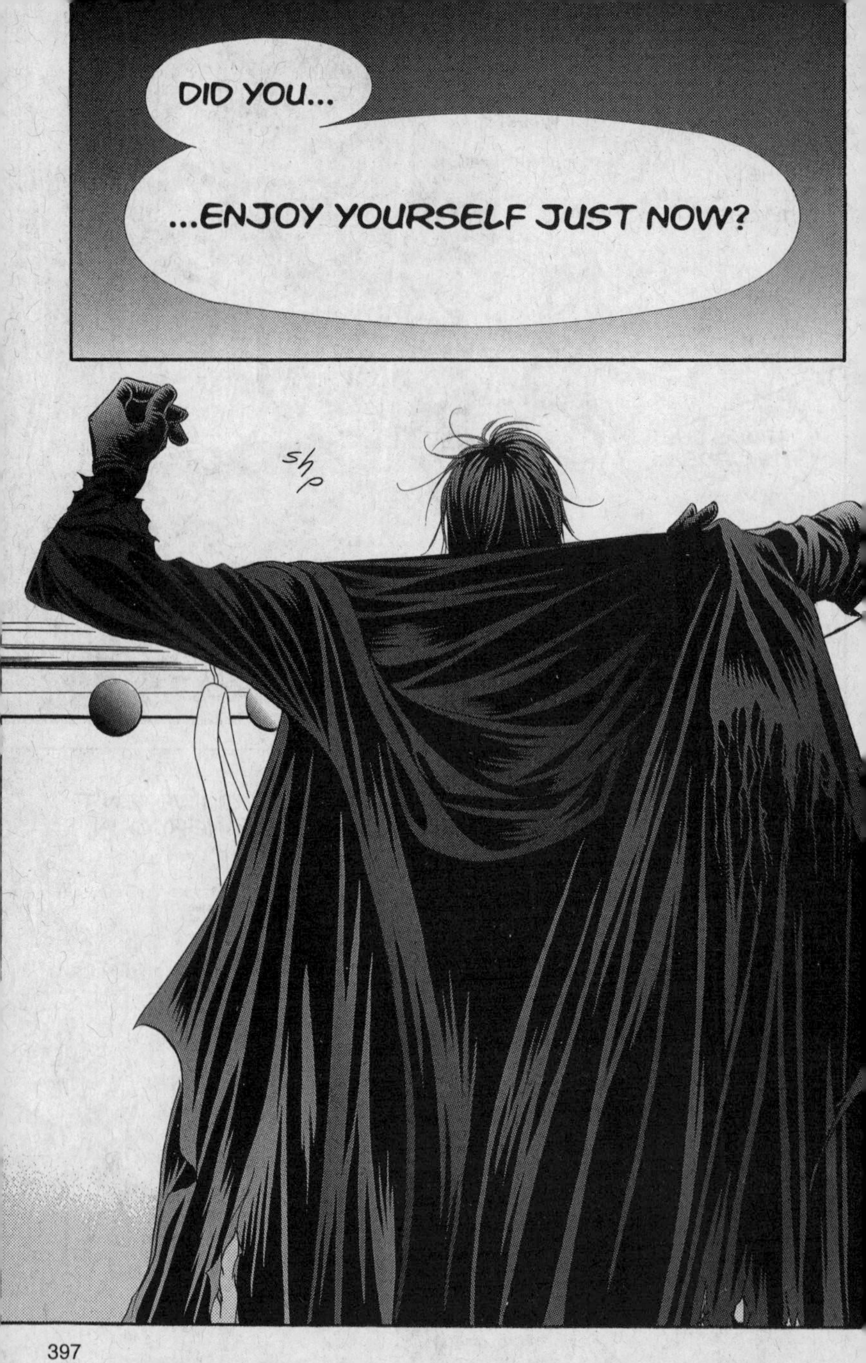
DID YOU...
...ENJOY YOURSELF JUST NOW?
shp

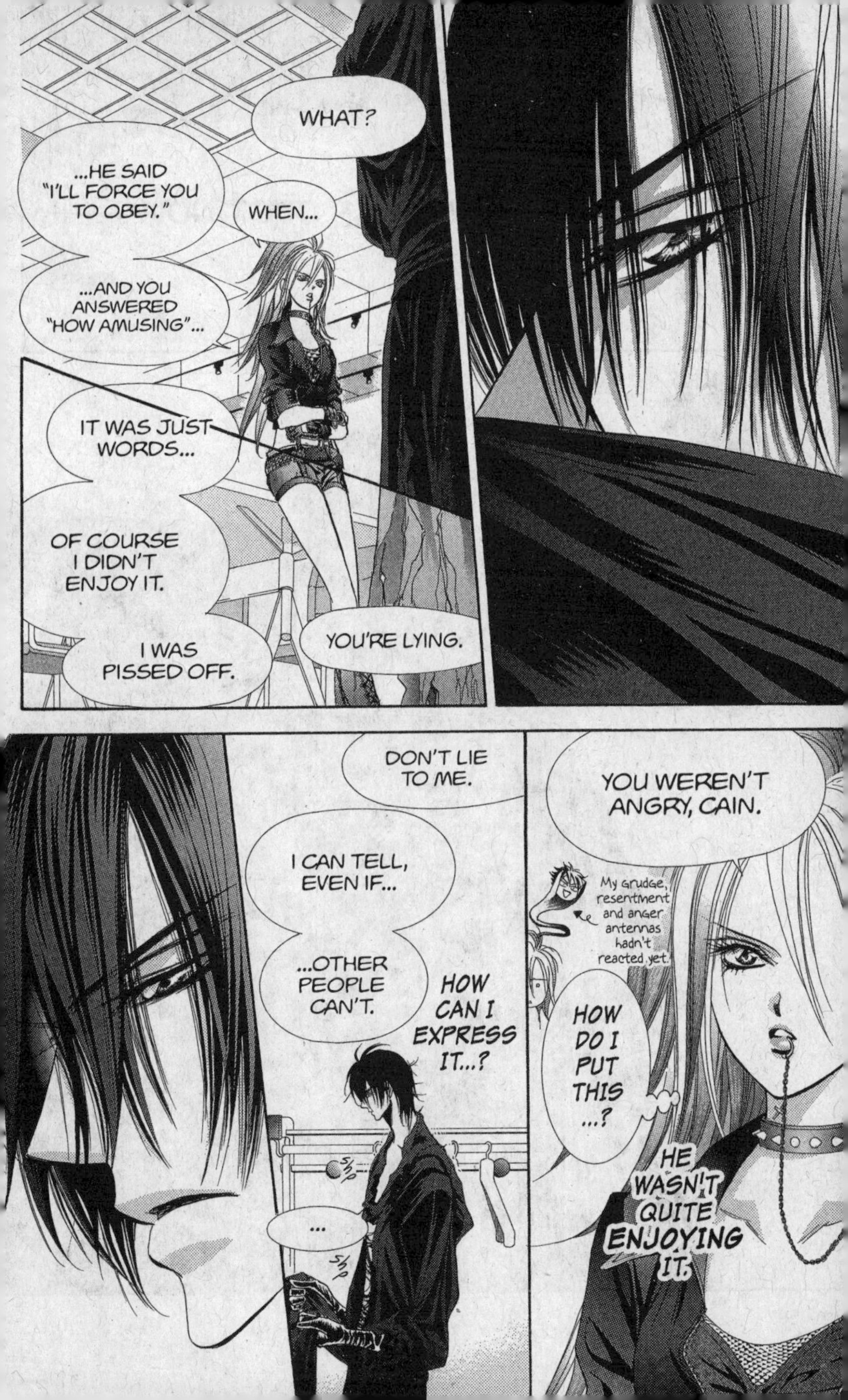
WHAT?
WHEN...
...HE SAID "I'LL FORCE YOU TO OBEY."
...AND YOU ANSWERED "HOW AMUSING"...
IT WAS JUST WORDS...
OF COURSE I DIDN'T ENJOY IT.
YOU'RE LYING.
I WAS PISSED OFF.
YOU WEREN'T ANGRY, CAIN.
My grudge, resentment and anger antennas hadn't reacted yet.
HOW DO I PUT THIS ...?
HE WASN'T QUITE ENJOYING IT.
DON'T LIE TO ME.
I CAN TELL, EVEN IF...
...OTHER PEOPLE CAN'T.
HOW CAN I EXPRESS IT...?
shp
...
shp

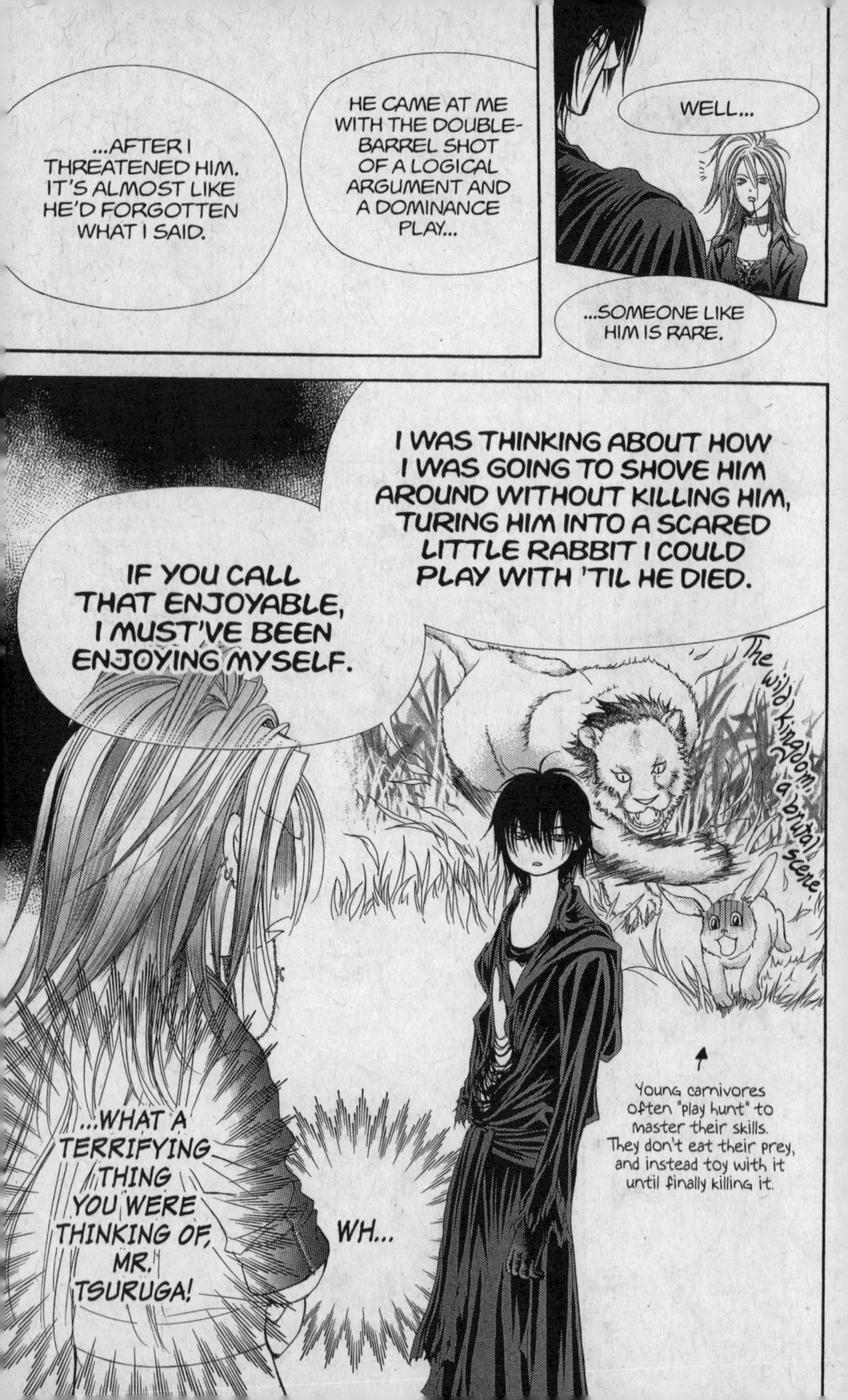
WELL...
...SOMEONE LIKE HIM IS RARE.
HE CAME AT ME WITH THE DOUBLE-BARREL SHOT OF A LOGICAL ARGUMENT AND A DOMINANCE PLAY...
...AFTER I THREATENED HIM. IT'S ALMOST LIKE HE'D FORGOTTEN WHAT I SAID.
I WAS THINKING ABOUT HOW I WAS GOING TO SHOVE HIM AROUND WITHOUT KILLING HIM, TURING HIM INTO A SCARED LITTLE RABBIT I COULD PLAY WITH 'TIL HE DIED.
IF YOU CALL THAT ENJOYABLE, I MUST'VE BEEN ENJOYING MYSELF.
The wild kingdom: a brutal scene.
Young carnivores often "play hunt" to master their skills. They don't eat their prey, and instead toy with it until finally killing it.
WH...
...WHAT A TERRIFYING THING YOU WERE THINKING OF, MR. TSURUGA!

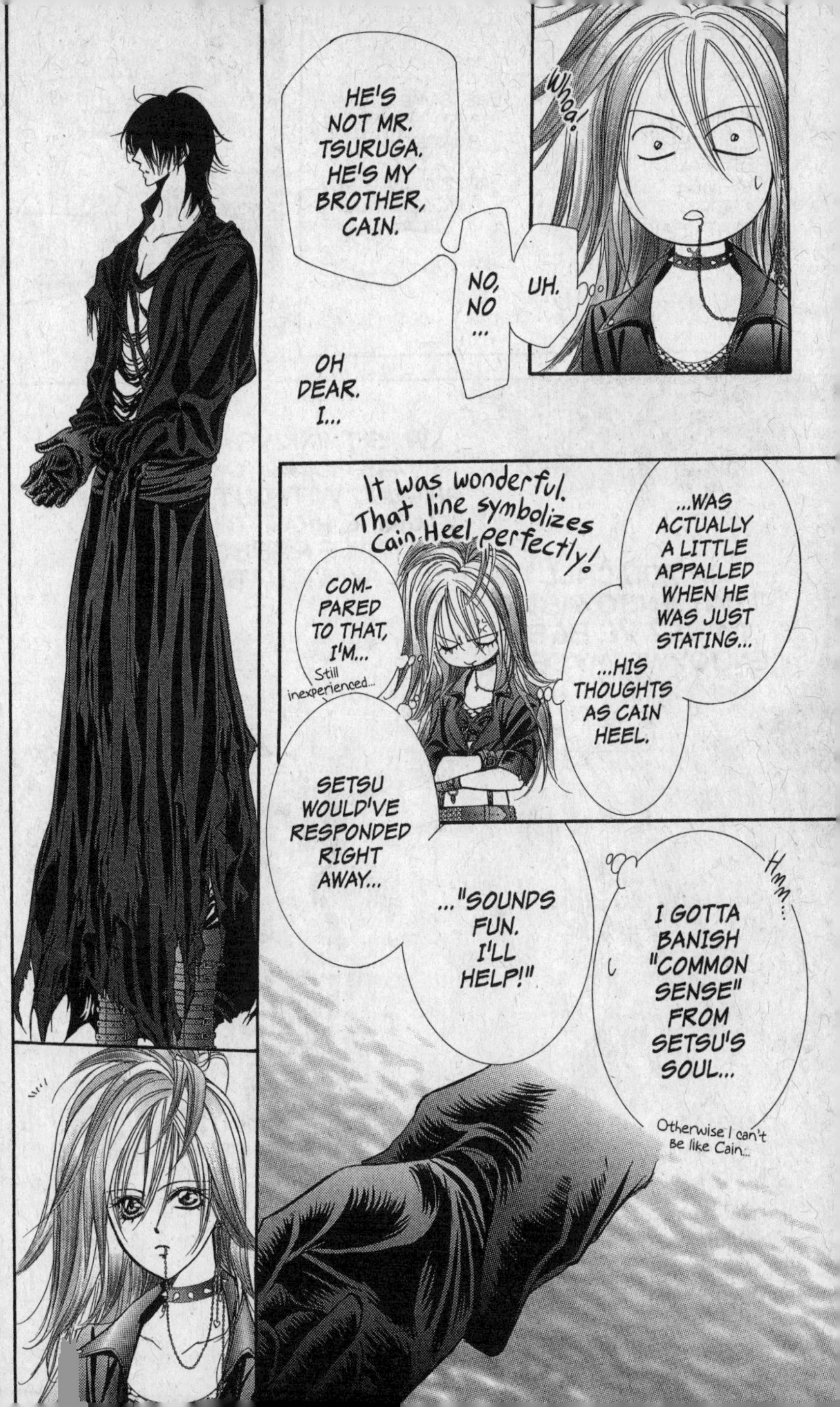
Whoa!
UH.
NO, NO ...
HE'S NOT MR. TSURUGA. HE'S MY BROTHER, CAIN.
OH DEAR. I...
...WAS ACTUALLY A LITTLE APPALLED WHEN HE WAS JUST STATING...
...HIS THOUGHTS AS CAIN HEEL.
It was wonderful. That line symbolizes Cain Heel perfectly!
COM-PARED TO THAT, I'M...
Still inexperienced...
Hmm...
I GOTTA BANISH "COMMON SENSE" FROM SETSU'S SOUL...
Otherwise I can't be like Cain...
..."SOUNDS FUN. I'LL HELP!"
SETSU WOULD'VE RESPONDED RIGHT AWAY...

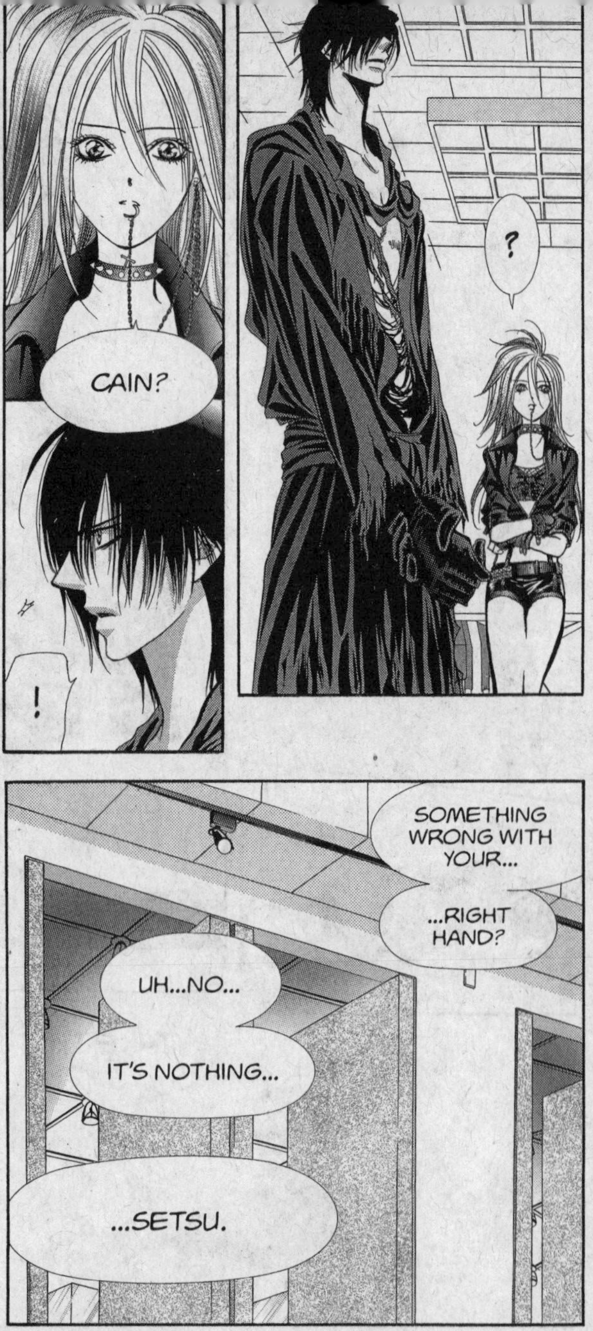
?
CAIN?
!
SOMETHING WRONG WITH YOUR...
...RIGHT HAND?
UH...NO...
IT'S NOTHING...
...SETSU.
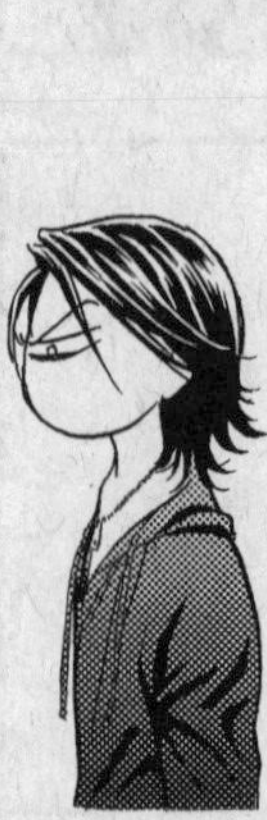

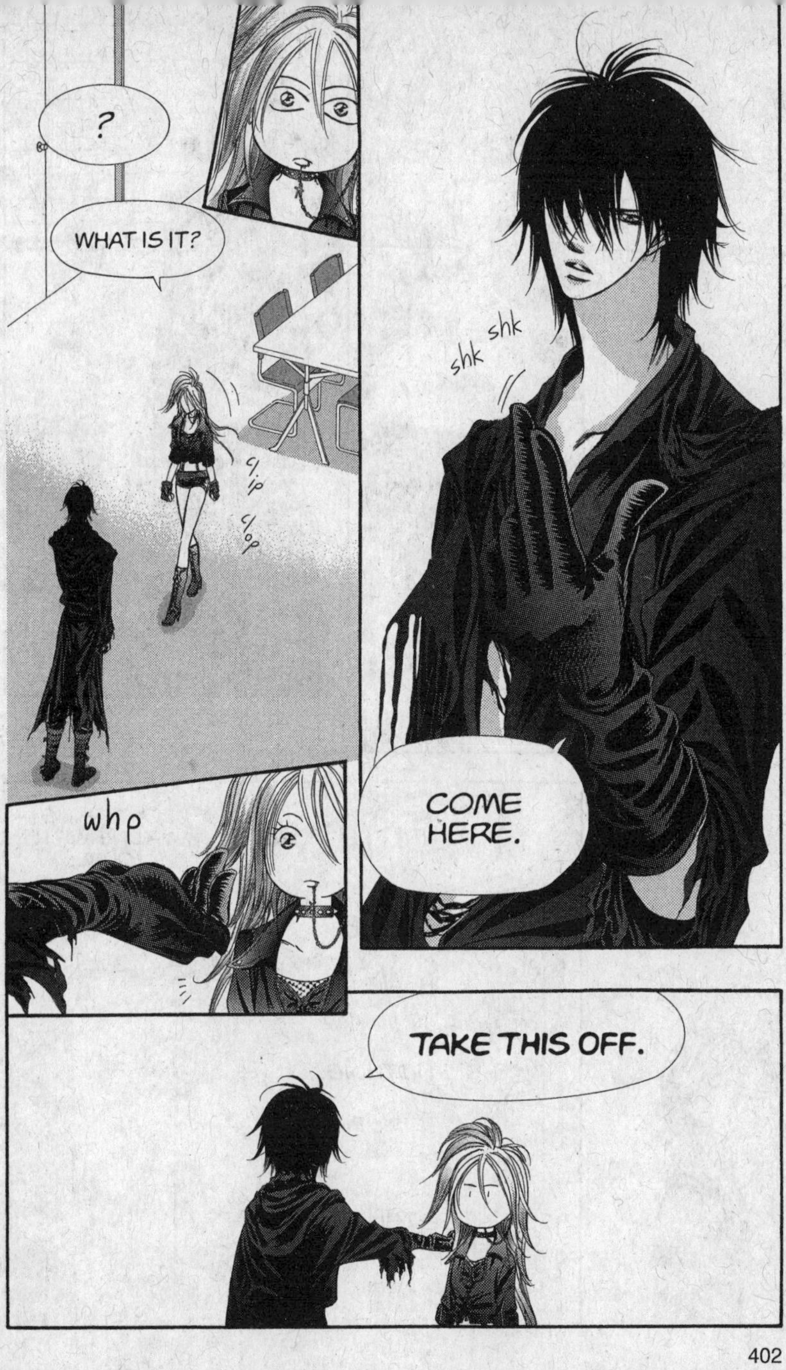
shk shk
COME HERE.
?
WHAT IS IT?
clip clop
whp
TAKE THIS OFF.

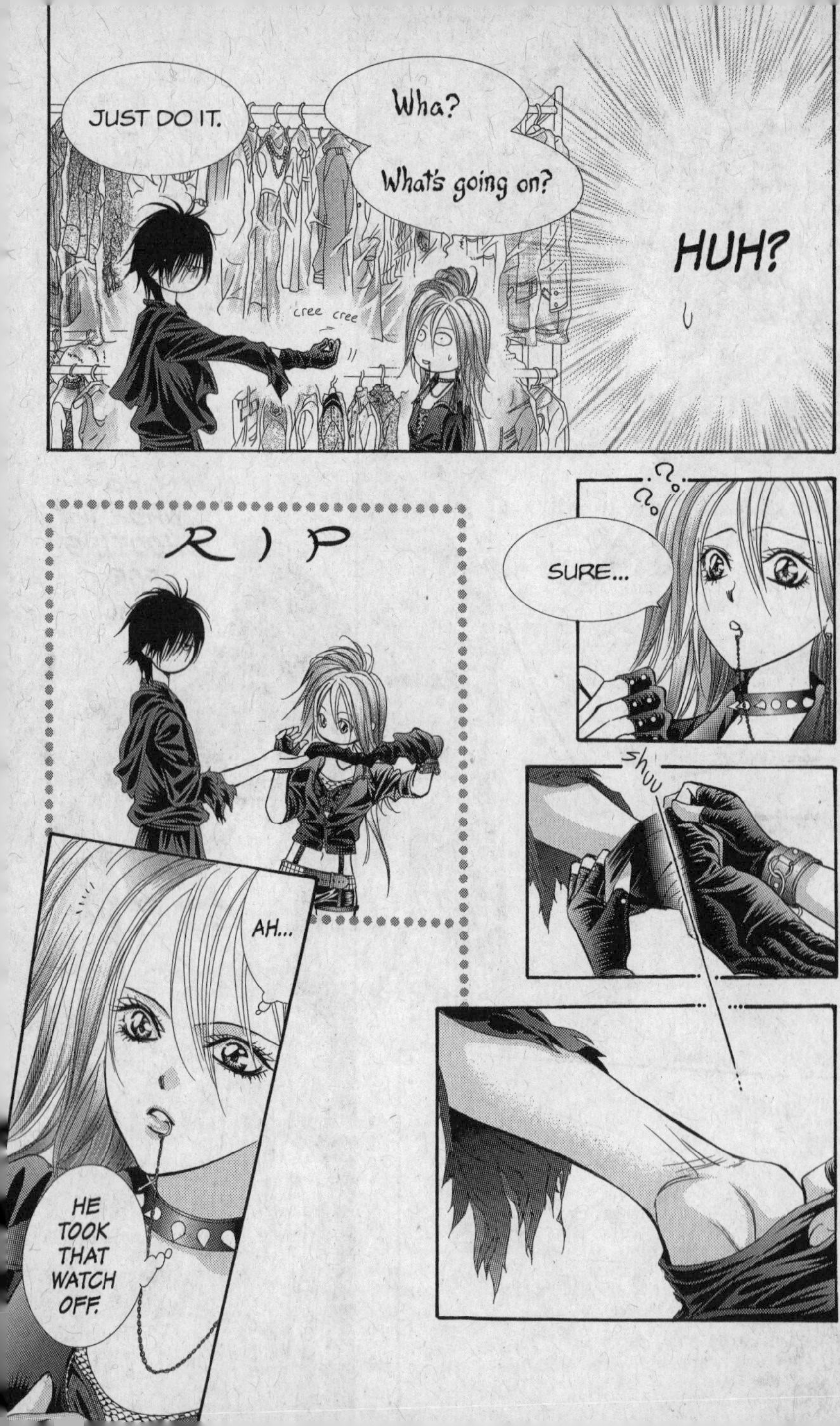
Wha?
What's going on?
JUST DO IT.
cree cree
HUH?
SURE...
shuu
RIP
AH...
HE TOOK THAT WATCH OFF.

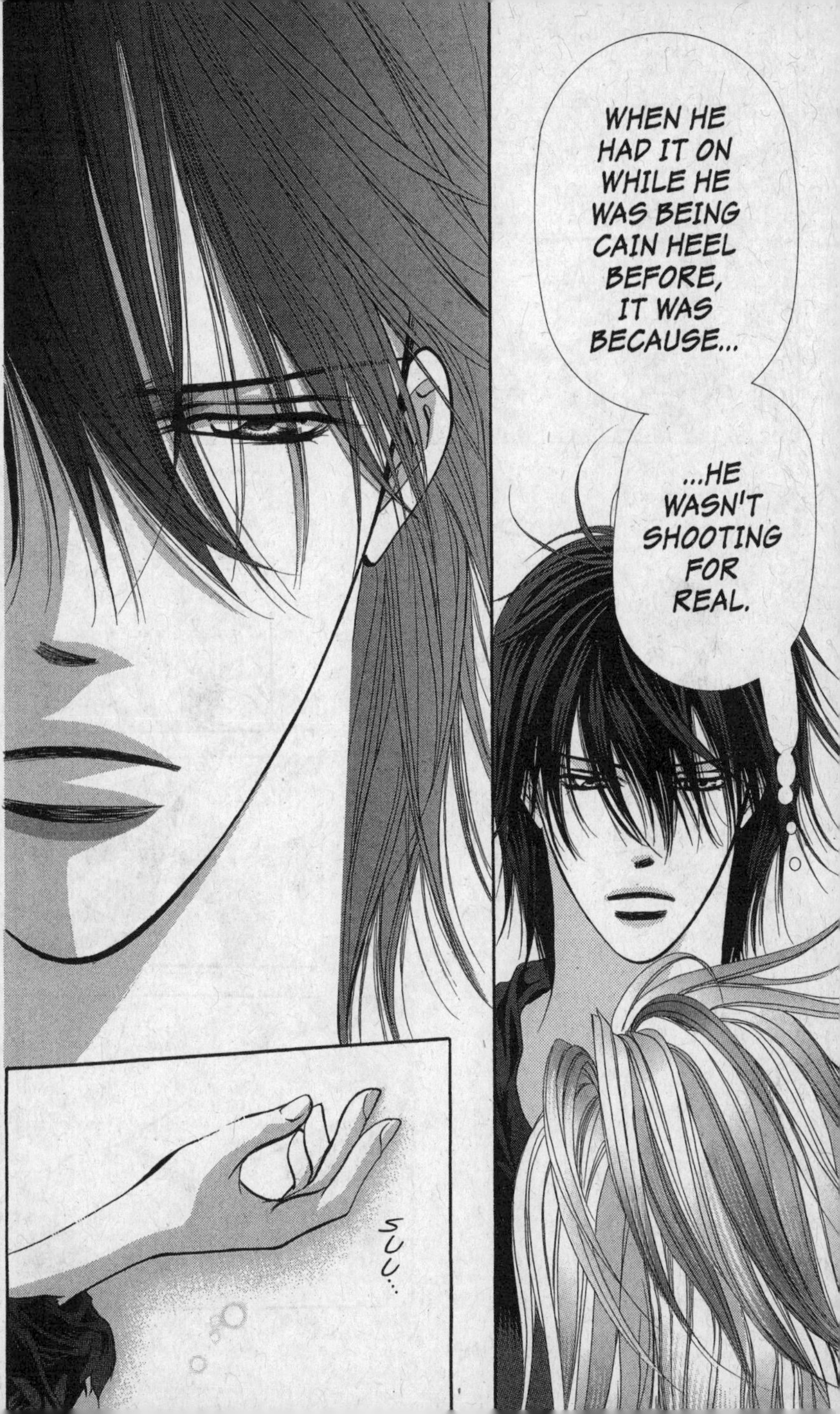
WHEN HE HAD IT ON WHILE HE WAS BEING CAIN HEEL BEFORE, IT WAS BECAUSE...
...HE WASN'T SHOOTING FOR REAL.
SUU...

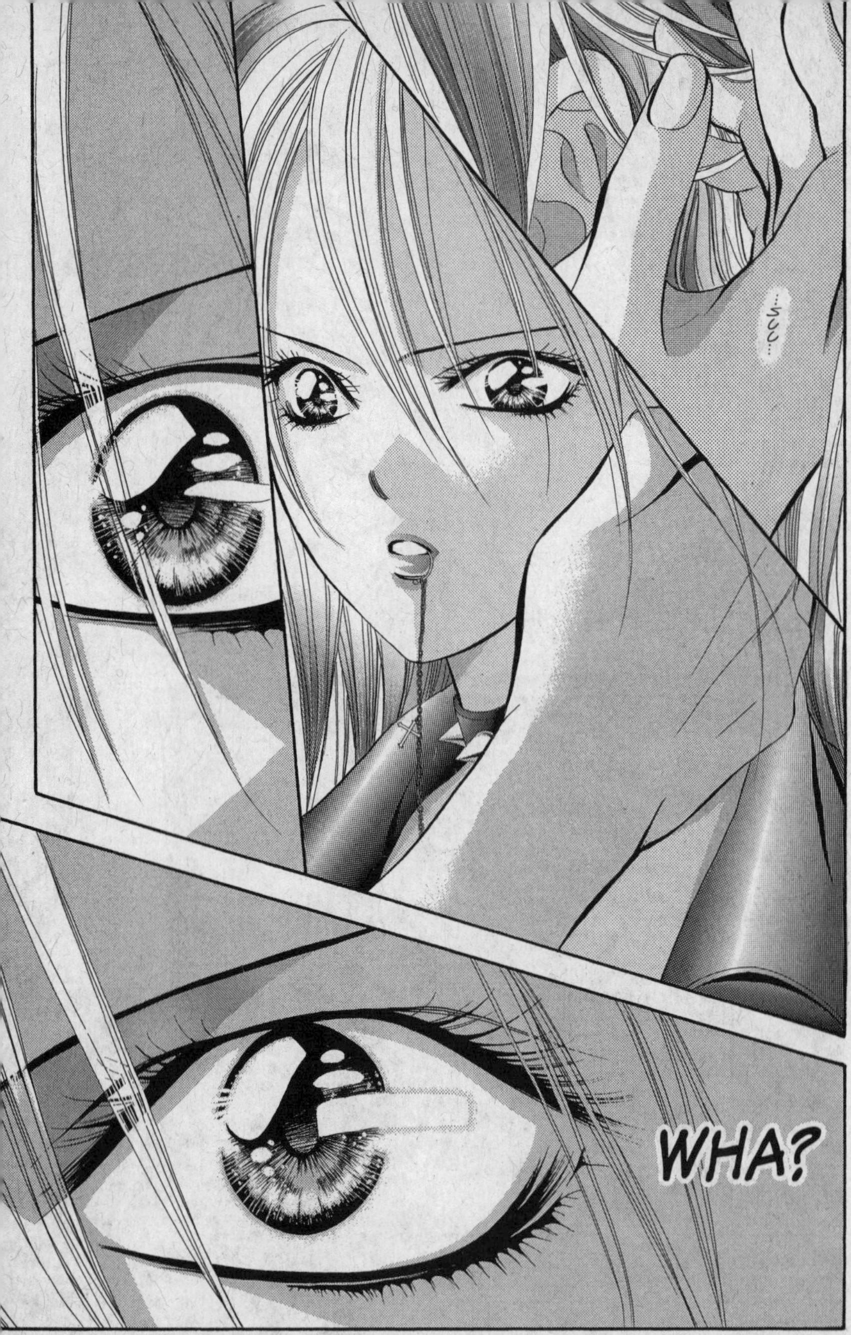
...SUU...
WHA?

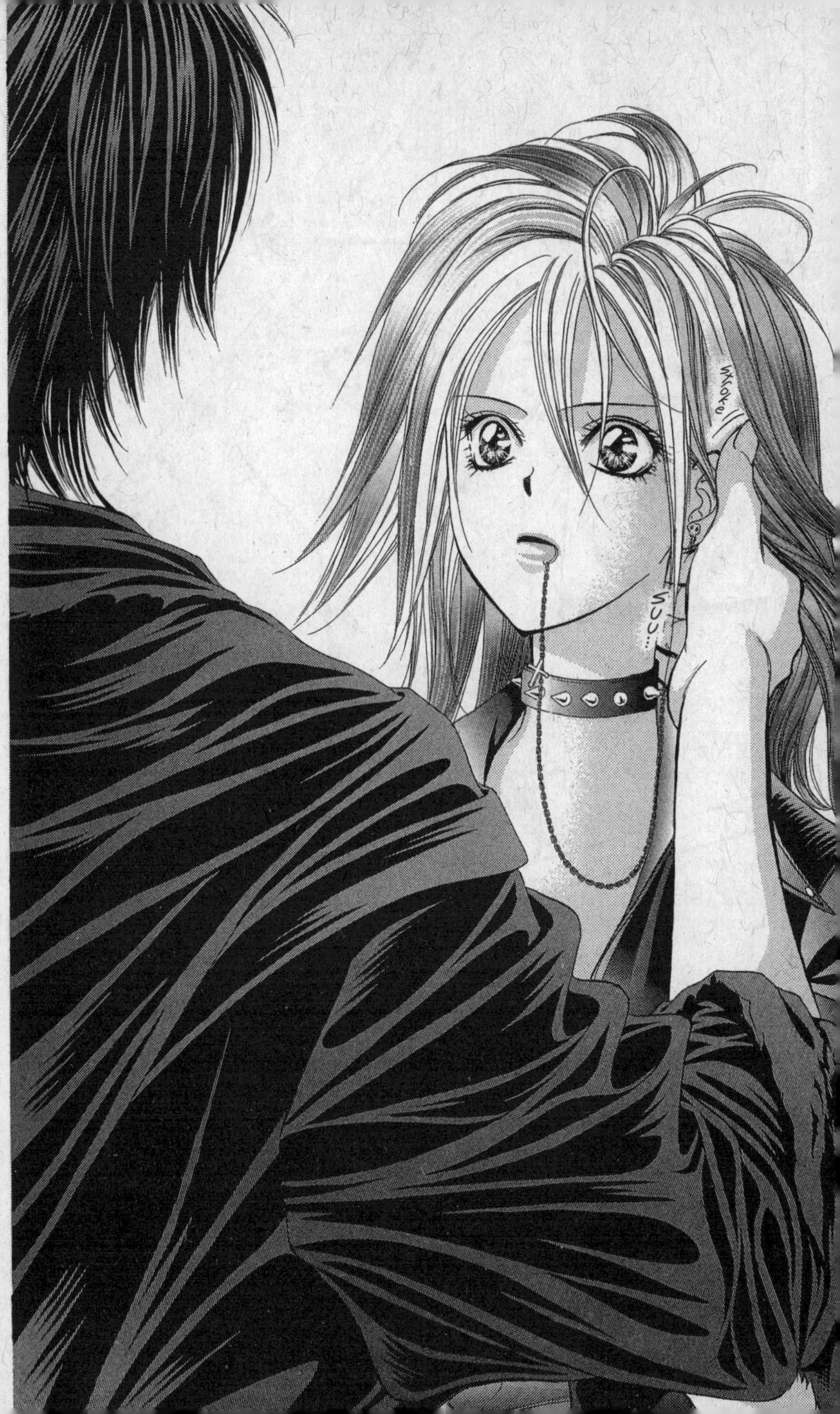
stroke
SUU...

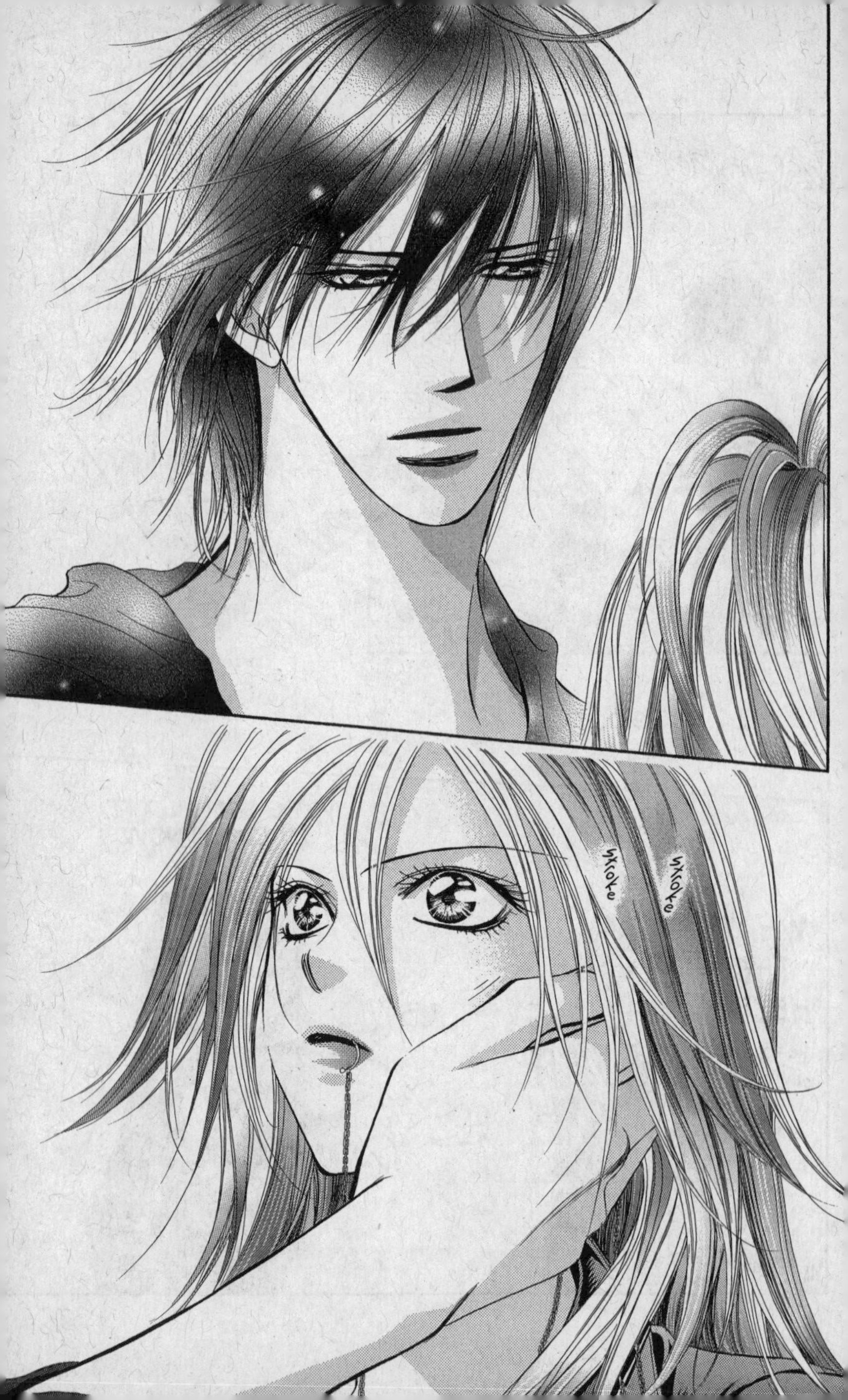
stroke
stroke

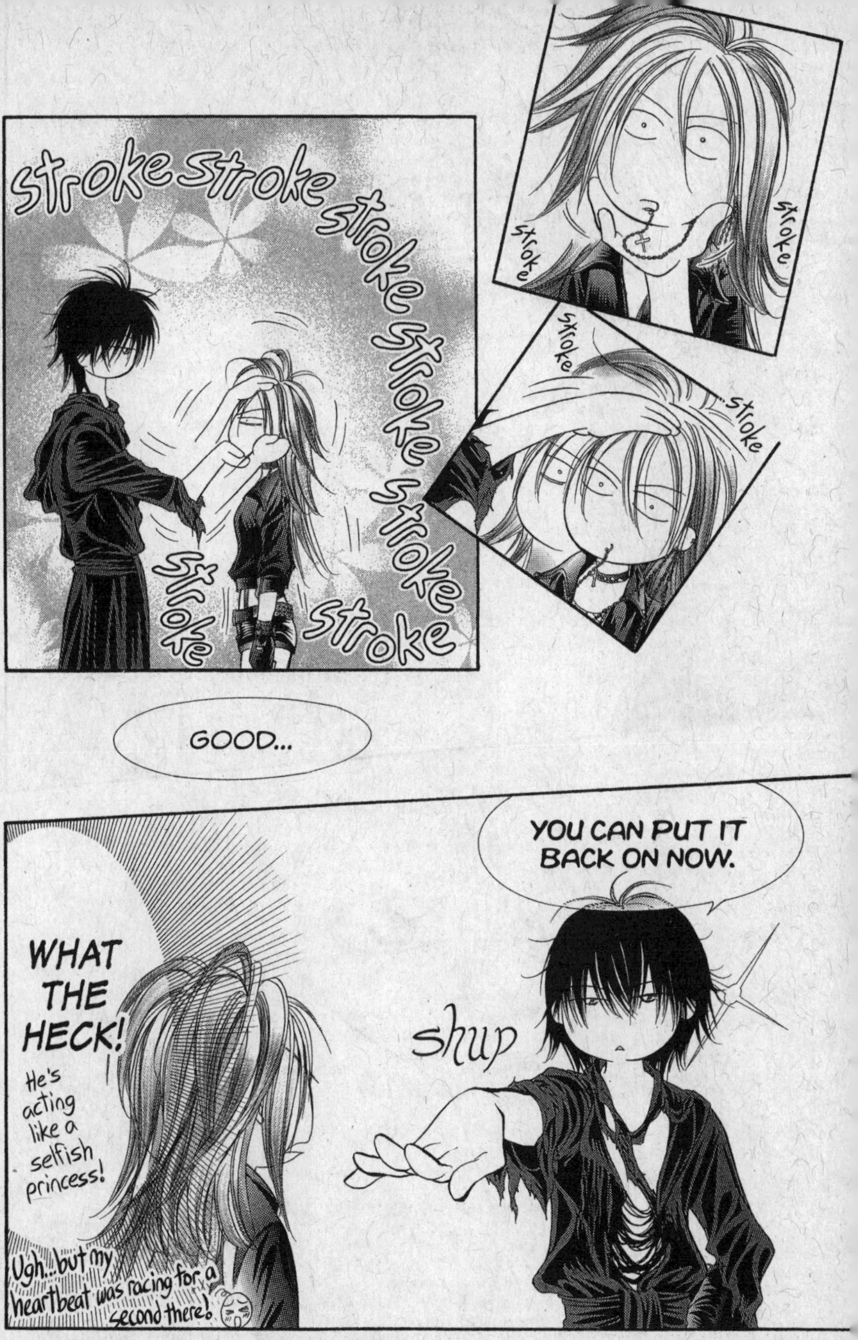
stroke
stroke
stroke
stroke
stroke stroke stroke stroke stroke stroke stroke stroke
GOOD...
YOU CAN PUT IT BACK ON NOW.
shup
WHAT THE HECK!
He's acting like a selfish princess!
Ugh...but my heartbeat was racing for a second there!

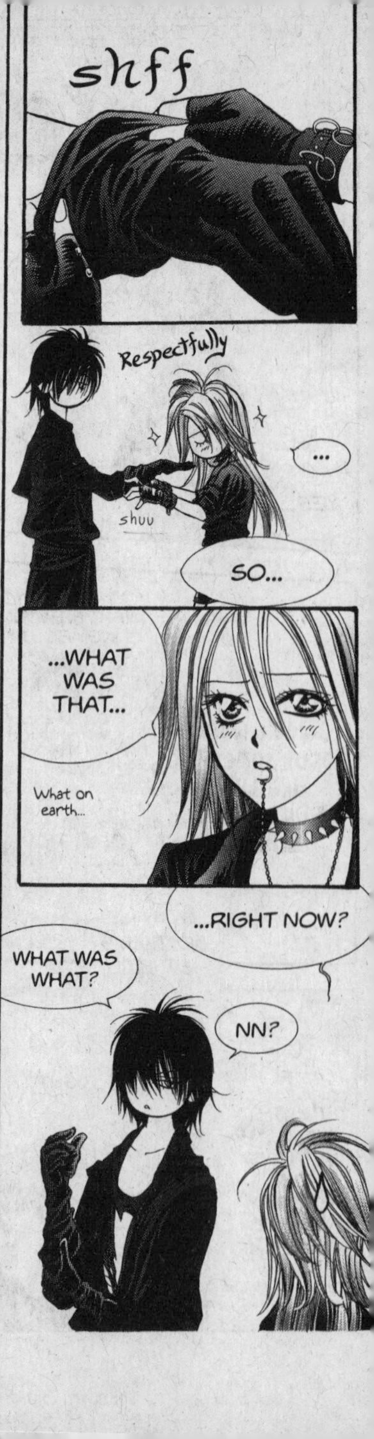
shff
Respectfully
...
shuu
SO...
...WHAT WAS THAT...
What on earth...
...RIGHT NOW?
NN?
WHAT WAS WHAT?
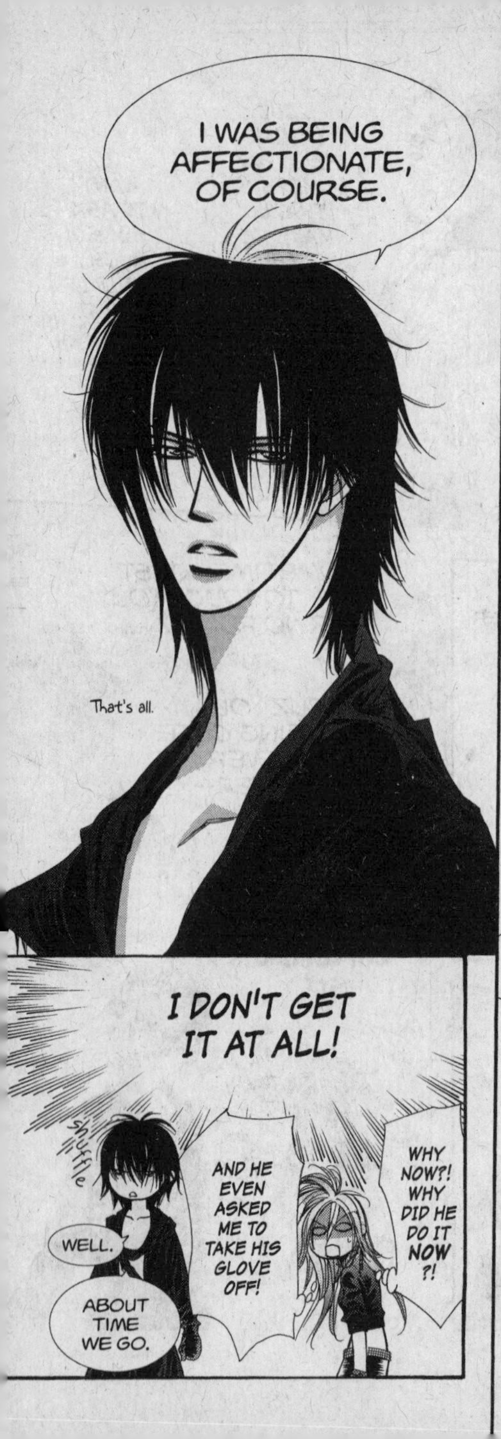
I WAS BEING AFFECTIONATE, OF COURSE.
That's all.
I DON'T GET IT AT ALL!
WHY NOW?! WHY DID HE DO IT NOW?!
AND HE EVEN ASKED ME TO TAKE HIS GLOVE OFF!
shuffle
WELL.
ABOUT TIME WE GO.

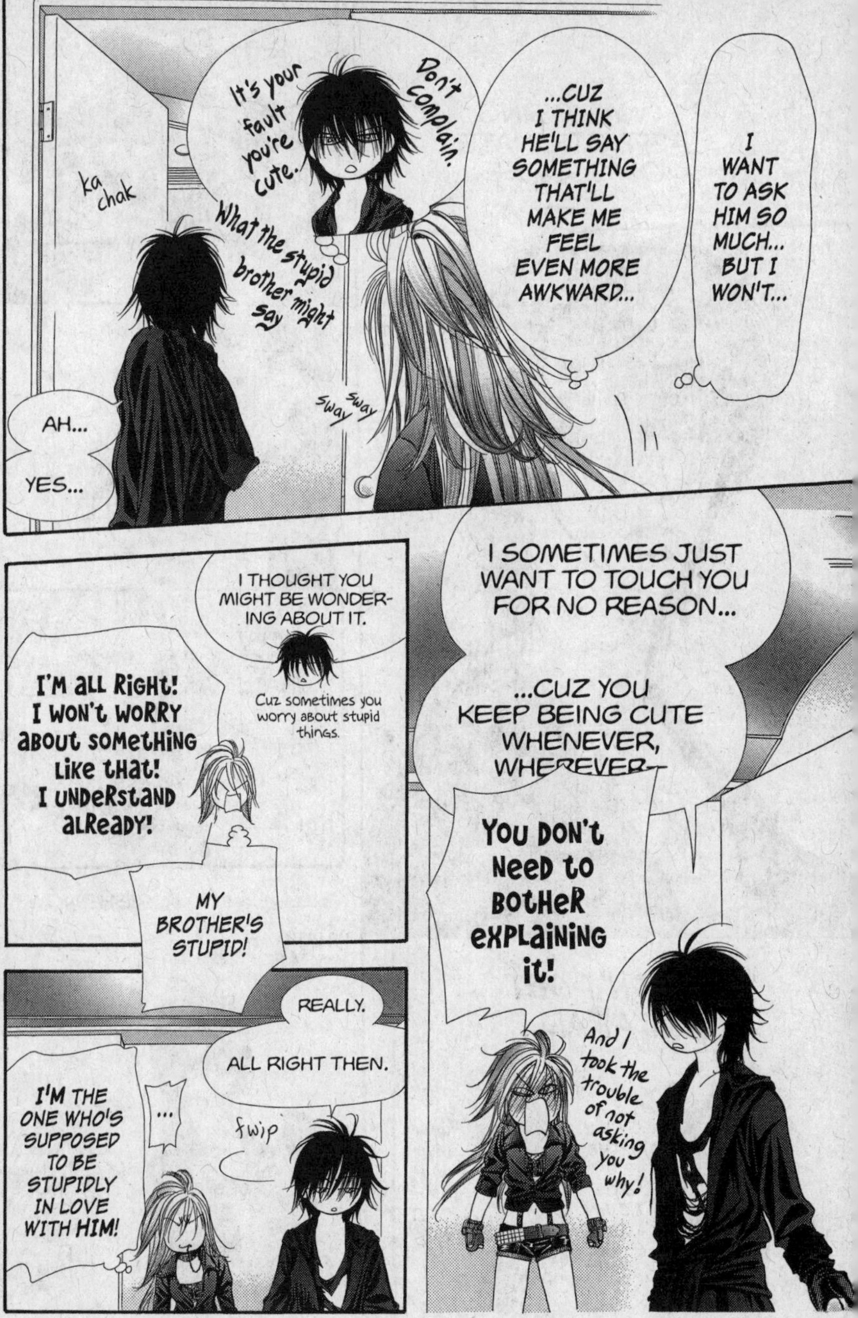
I WANT TO ASK HIM SO MUCH... BUT I WON'T...
...CUZ I THINK HE'LL SAY SOMETHING THAT'LL MAKE ME FEEL EVEN MORE AWKWARD...
Don't complain.
It's your fault you're cute.
What the stupid brother might say
ka chak
sway sway
AH...
YES...
I SOMETIMES JUST WANT TO TOUCH YOU FOR NO REASON...
...CUZ YOU KEEP BEING CUTE WHENEVER, WHEREVER–
YOU DON'T NEED TO BOTHER EXPLAINING IT!
And I took the trouble of not asking you why!
I THOUGHT YOU MIGHT BE WONDERING ABOUT IT.
Cuz sometimes you worry about stupid things.
I'M ALL RIGHT! I WON'T WORRY ABOUT SOMETHING LIKE THAT! I UNDERSTAND ALREADY!
MY BROTHER'S STUPID!
REALLY.
ALL RIGHT THEN.
fwip
...
I'M THE ONE WHO'S SUPPOSED TO BE STUPIDLY IN LOVE WITH HIM!

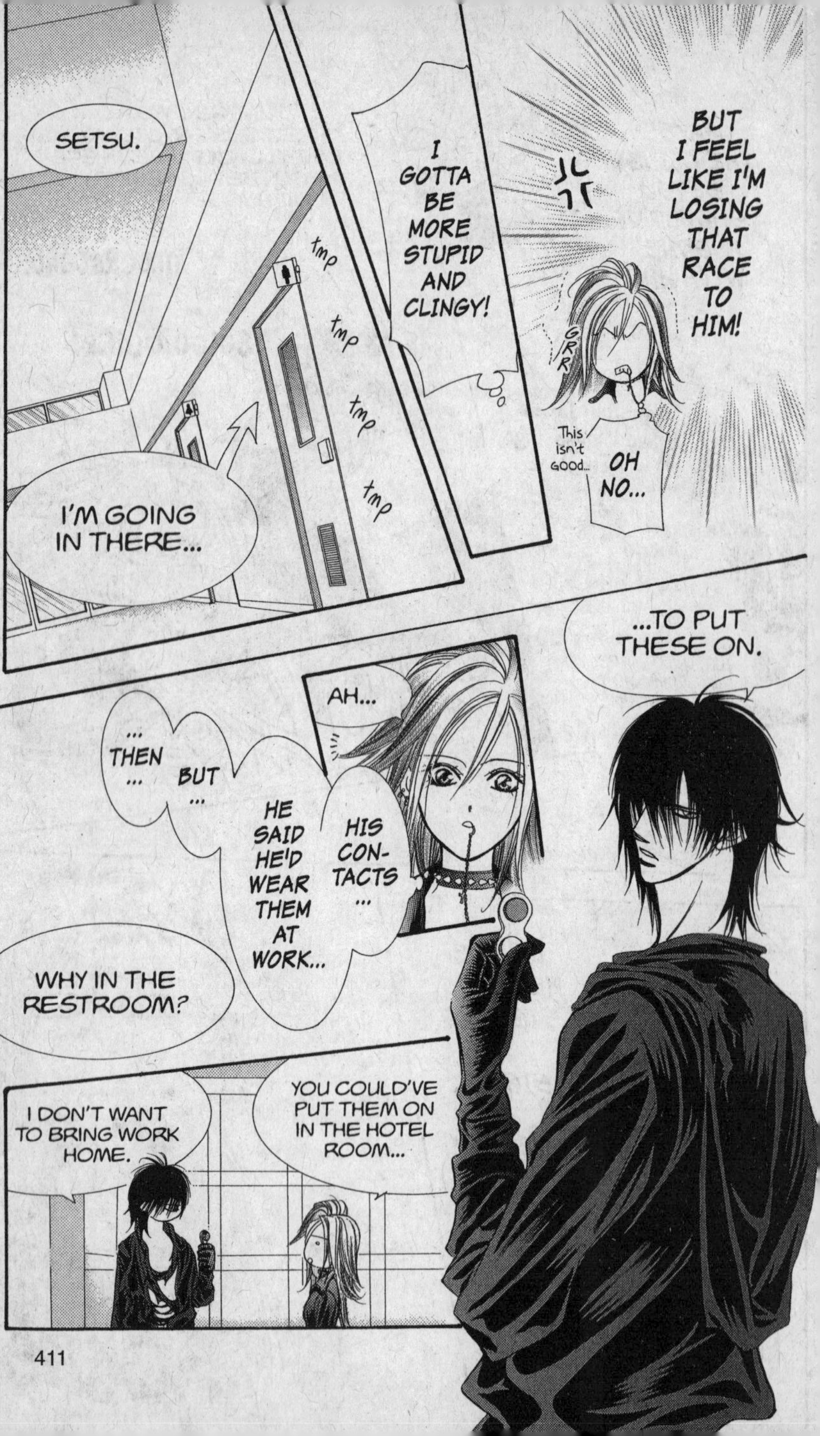
BUT I FEEL LIKE I'M LOSING THAT RACE TO HIM!
GRR
This isn't good...
OH NO...
I GOTTA BE MORE STUPID AND CLINGY!
SETSU.
tmp tmp tmp tmp
I'M GOING IN THERE...
...TO PUT THESE ON.
AH...
HIS CONTACTS...
HE SAID HE'D WEAR THEM AT WORK...
...THEN... BUT...
WHY IN THE RESTROOM?
YOU COULD'VE PUT THEM ON IN THE HOTEL ROOM...
I DON'T WANT TO BRING WORK HOME.

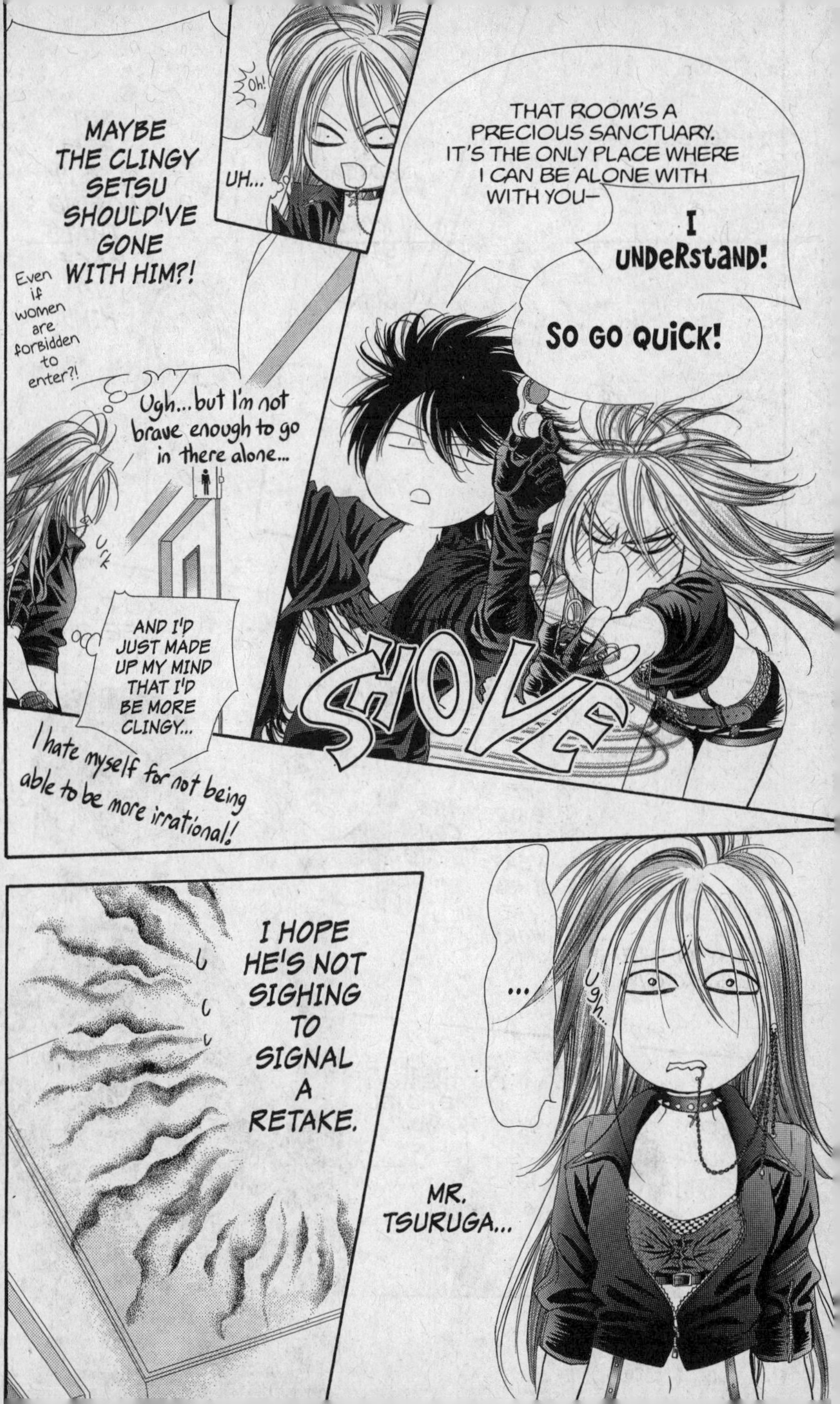
THAT ROOM'S A PRECIOUS SANCTUARY. IT'S THE ONLY PLACE WHERE I CAN BE ALONE WITH WITH YOU—
I UNDERSTAND!
SO GO QUICK!
SHOVE
Oh!
UH...
MAYBE THE CLINGY SETSU SHOULD'VE GONE WITH HIM?!
Even if women are forbidden to enter?!
Ugh...but I'm not brave enough to go in there alone...
Urk
AND I'D JUST MADE UP MY MIND THAT I'D BE MORE CLINGY...
I hate myself for not being able to be more irrational!
...
Ugh...
MR. TSURUGA...
I HOPE HE'S NOT SIGHING TO SIGNAL A RETAKE.

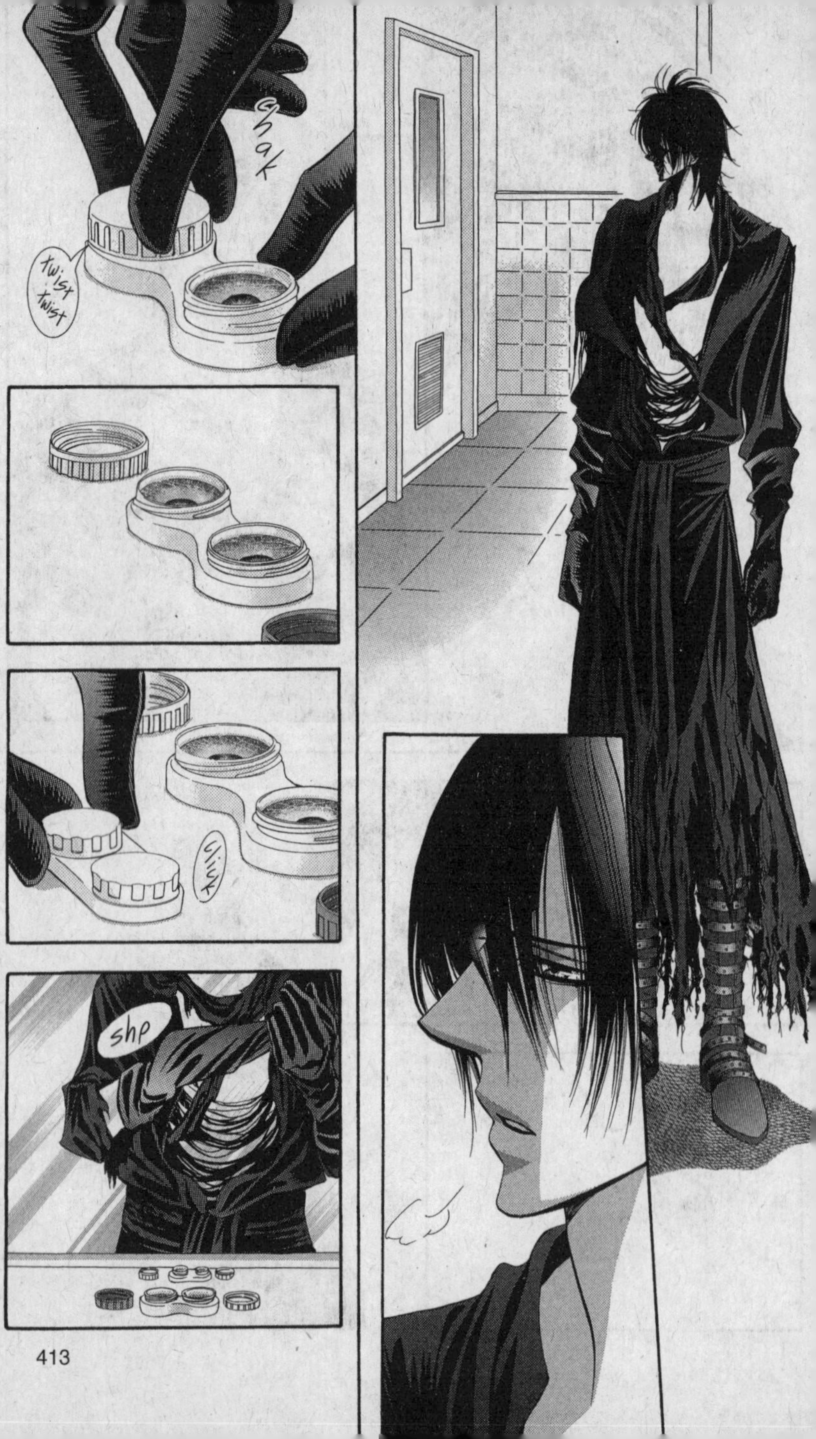
chak
twist twist
click
shp

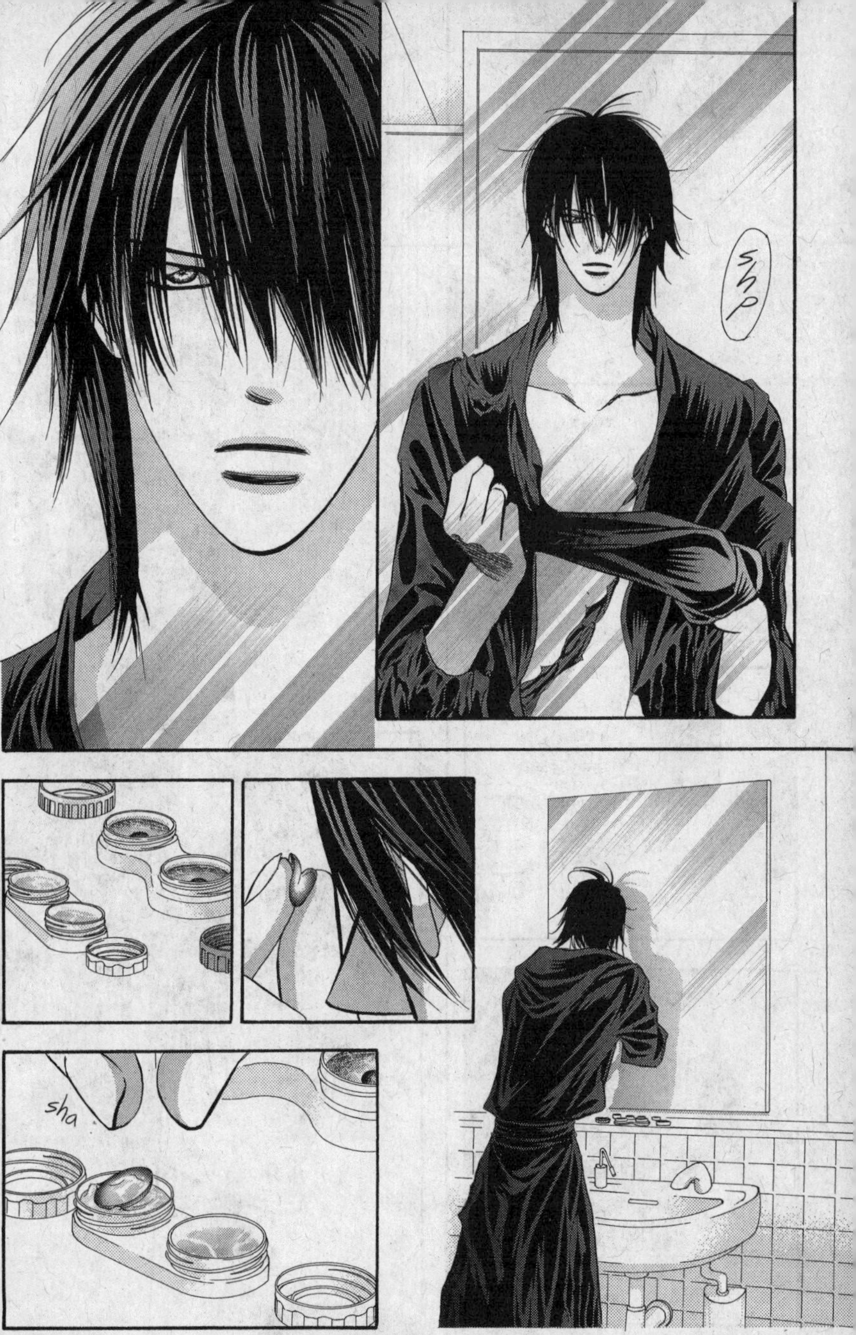
shp
sha

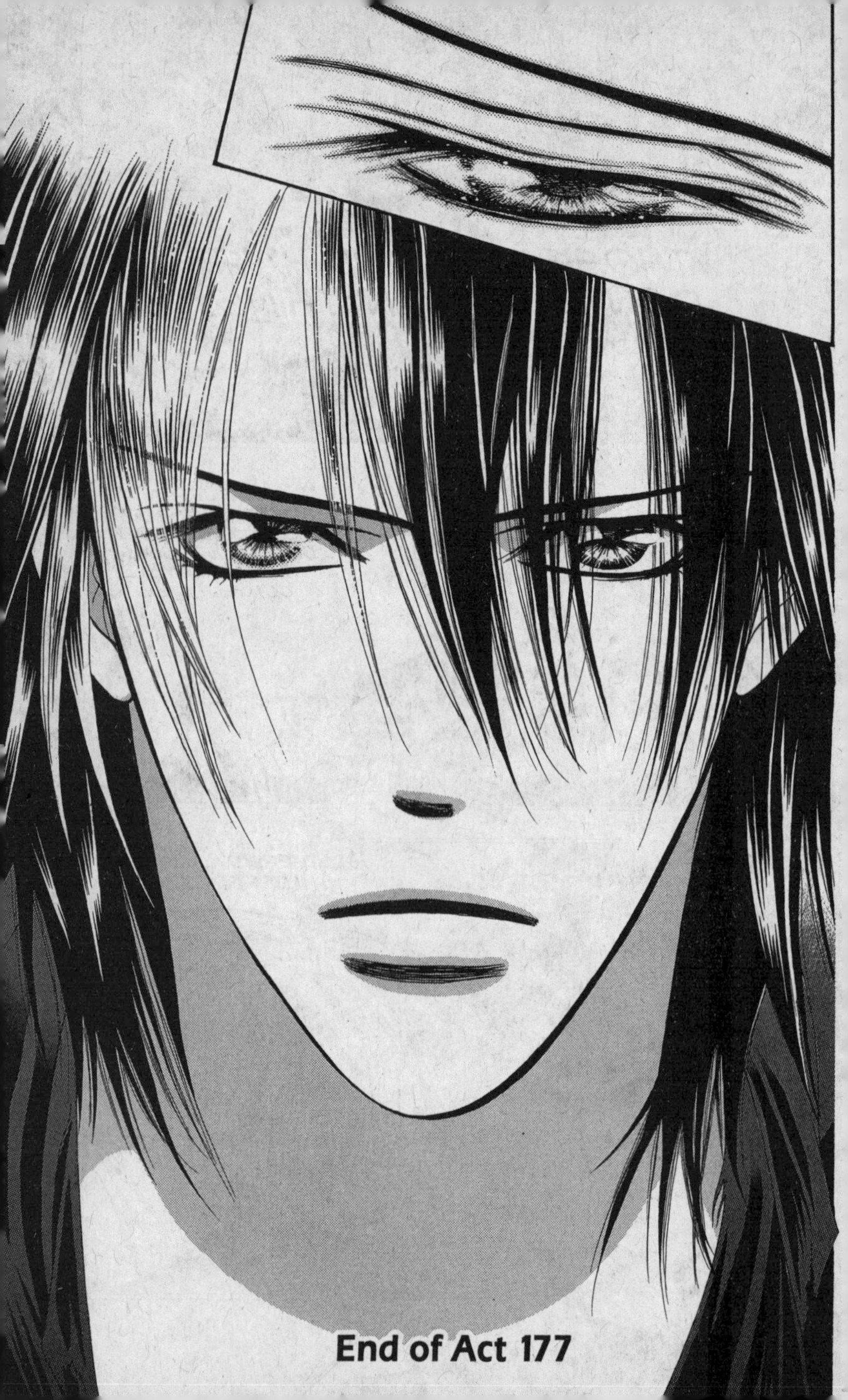
End of Act 177

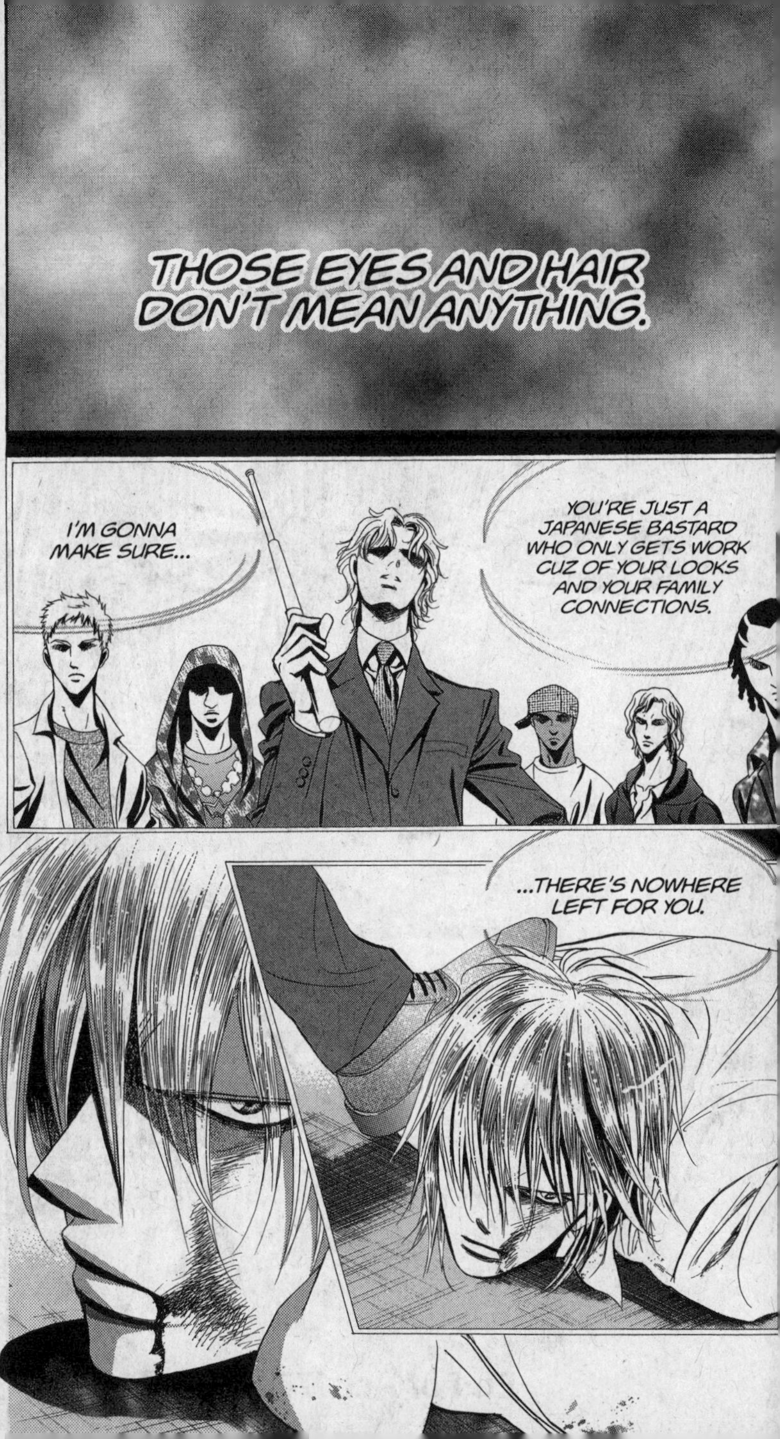
THOSE EYES AND HAIR DON'T MEAN ANYTHING.
YOU'RE JUST A JAPANESE BASTARD WHO ONLY GETS WORK CUZ OF YOUR LOOKS AND YOUR FAMILY CONNECTIONS.
I'M GONNA MAKE SURE...
...THERE'S NOWHERE LEFT FOR YOU.

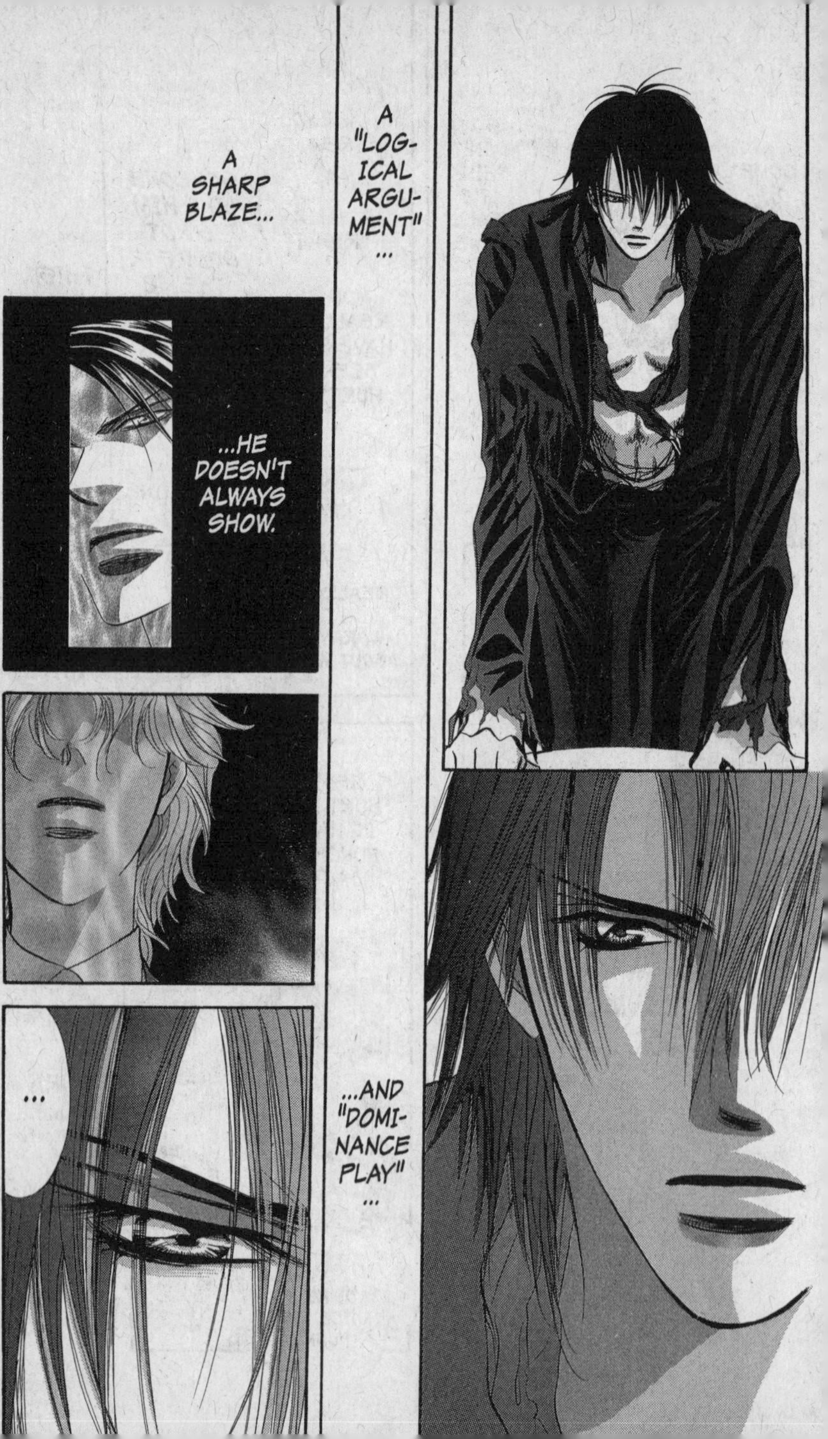
A "LOGICAL ARGUMENT"...
...AND "DOMINANCE PLAY"...
A SHARP BLAZE...
...HE DOESN'T ALWAYS SHOW.
...

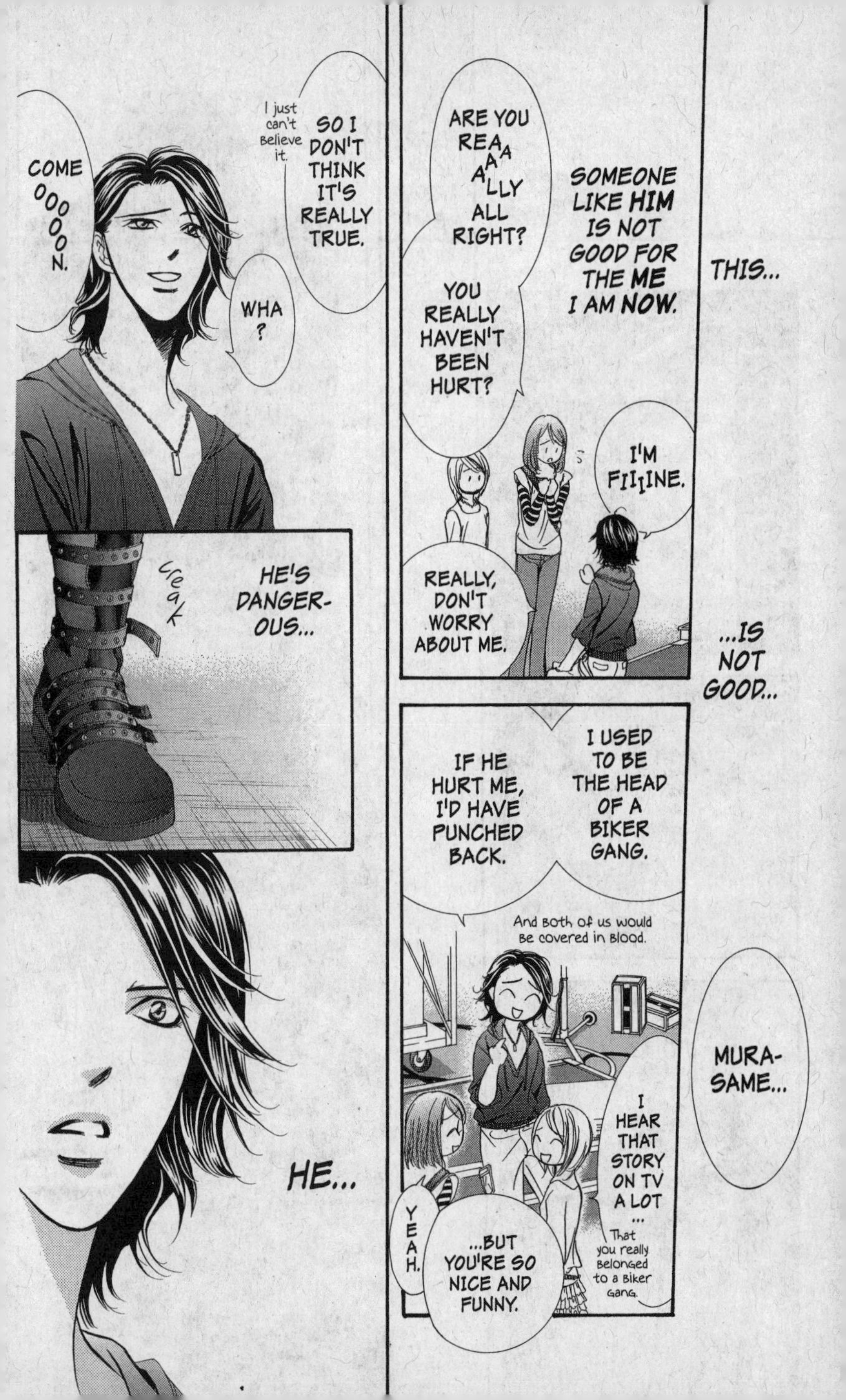
THIS...
SOMEONE LIKE HIM IS NOT GOOD FOR THE ME I AM NOW.
ARE YOU REAAAALLY ALL RIGHT?
YOU REALLY HAVEN'T BEEN HURT?
I'M FIIIINE.
REALLY, DON'T WORRY ABOUT ME.
...IS NOT GOOD...
I USED TO BE THE HEAD OF A BIKER GANG.
IF HE HURT ME, I'D HAVE PUNCHED BACK.
And both of us would be covered in blood.
MURA-SAME...
I HEAR THAT STORY ON TV A LOT...
That you really belonged to a biker gang.
...BUT YOU'RE SO NICE AND FUNNY.
YEAH.
SO I DON'T THINK IT'S REALLY TRUE.
I just can't believe it.
WHA?
COME OOOOOON.
HE'S DANGER-OUS...
creak
HE...

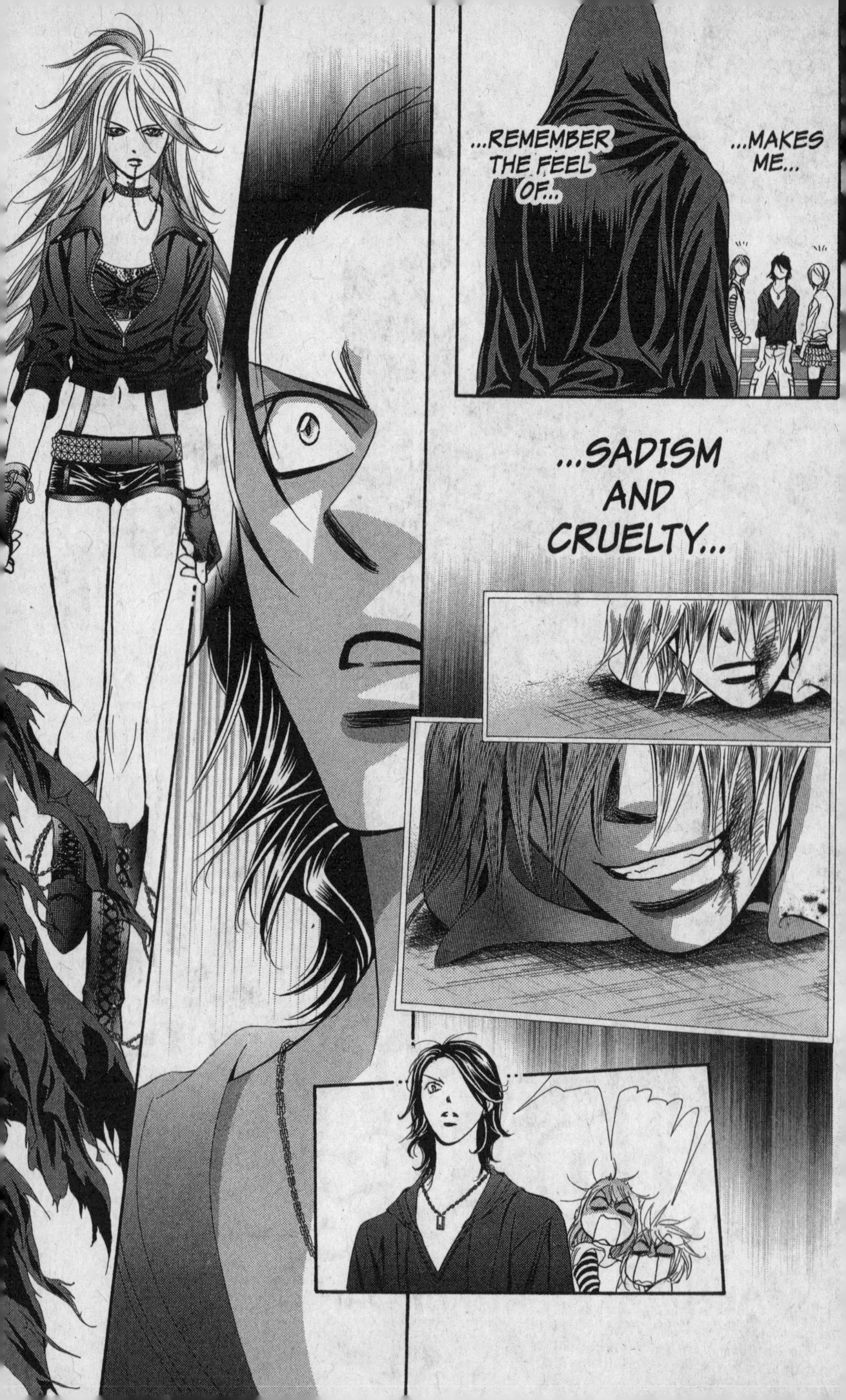
...MAKES ME...
...REMEMBER THE FEEL OF...
...SADISM AND CRUELTY...

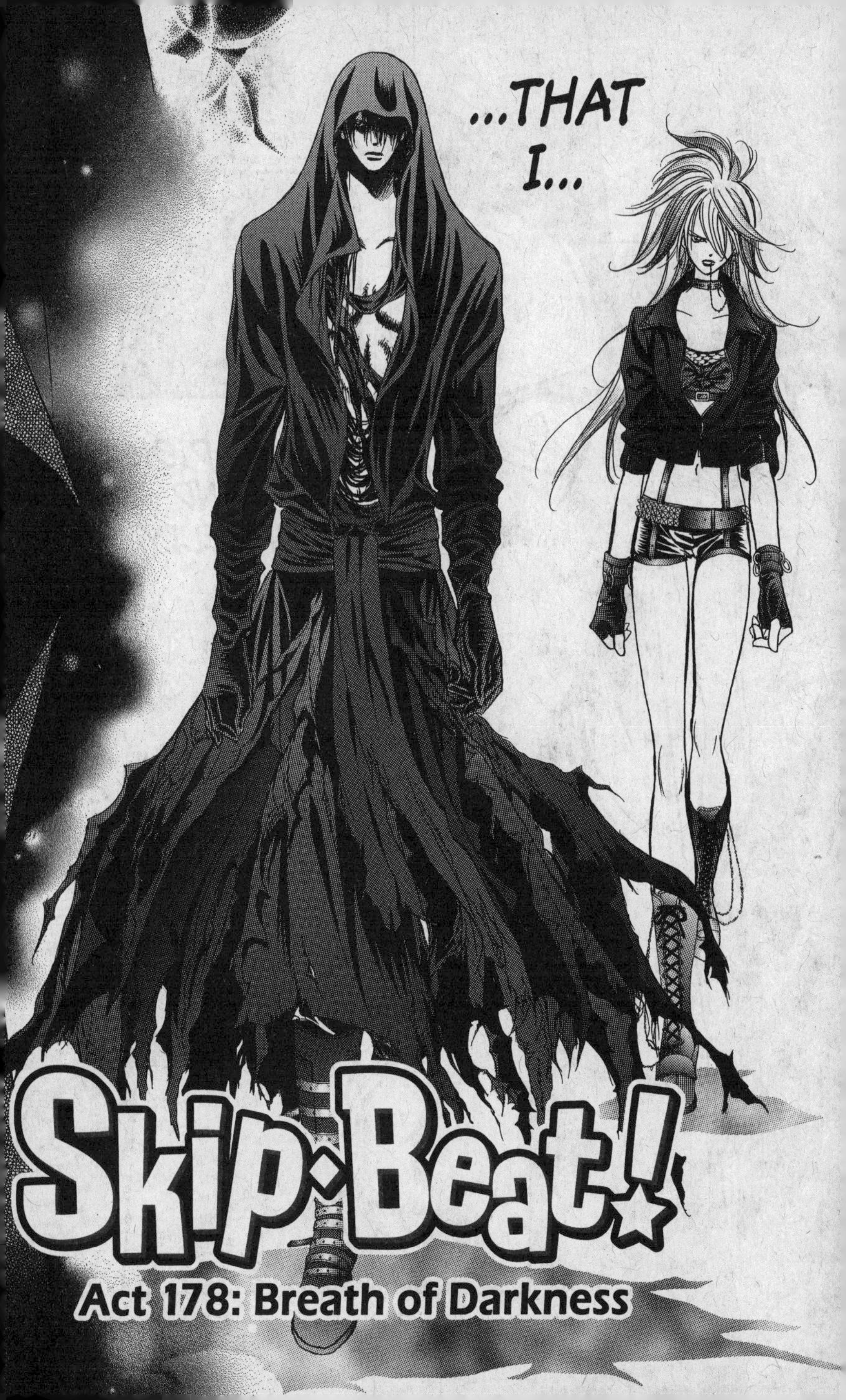
...THAT I...
Skip·Beat!
Act 178: Breath of Darkness

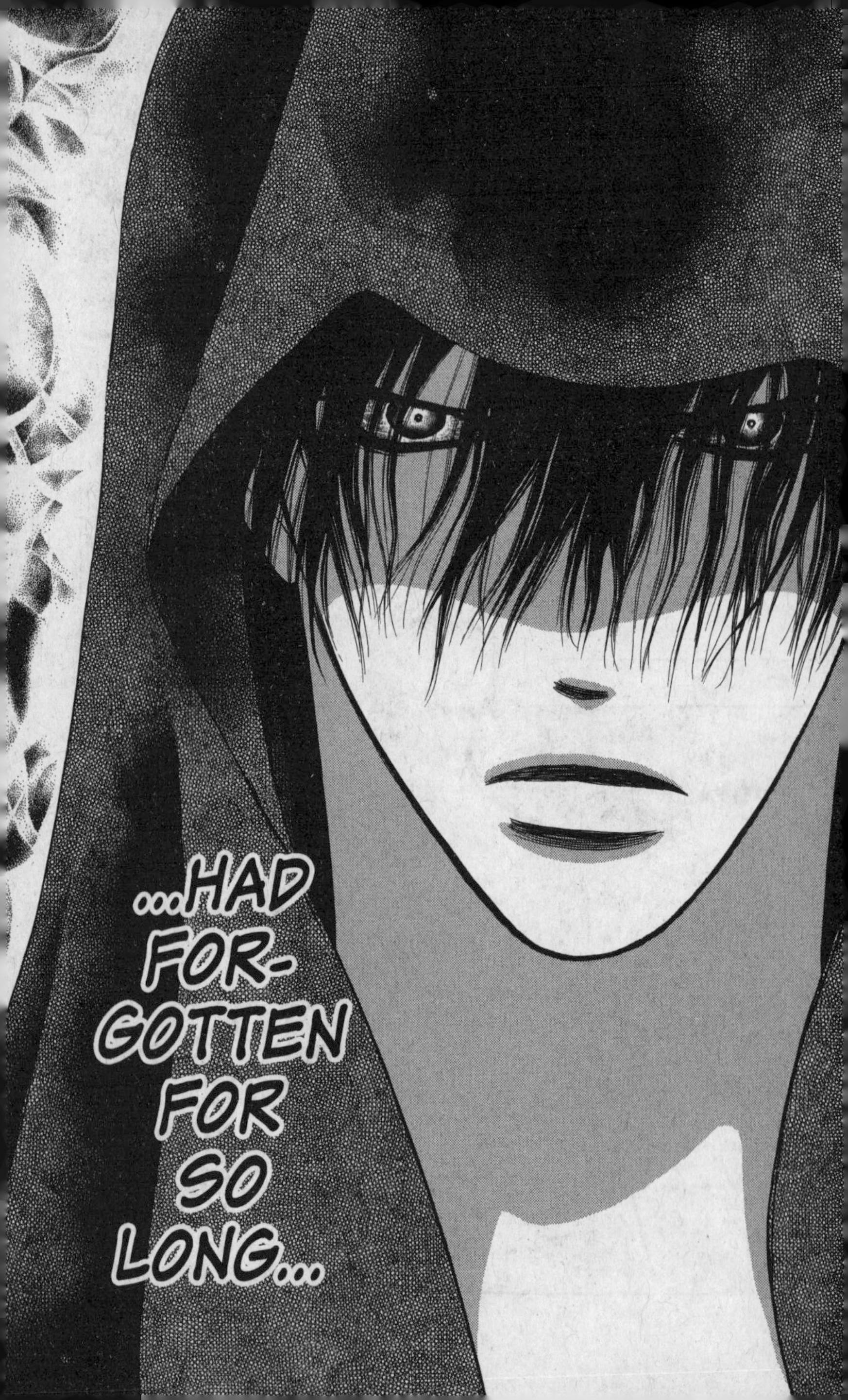
...HAD FOR-GOTTEN FOR SO LONG...

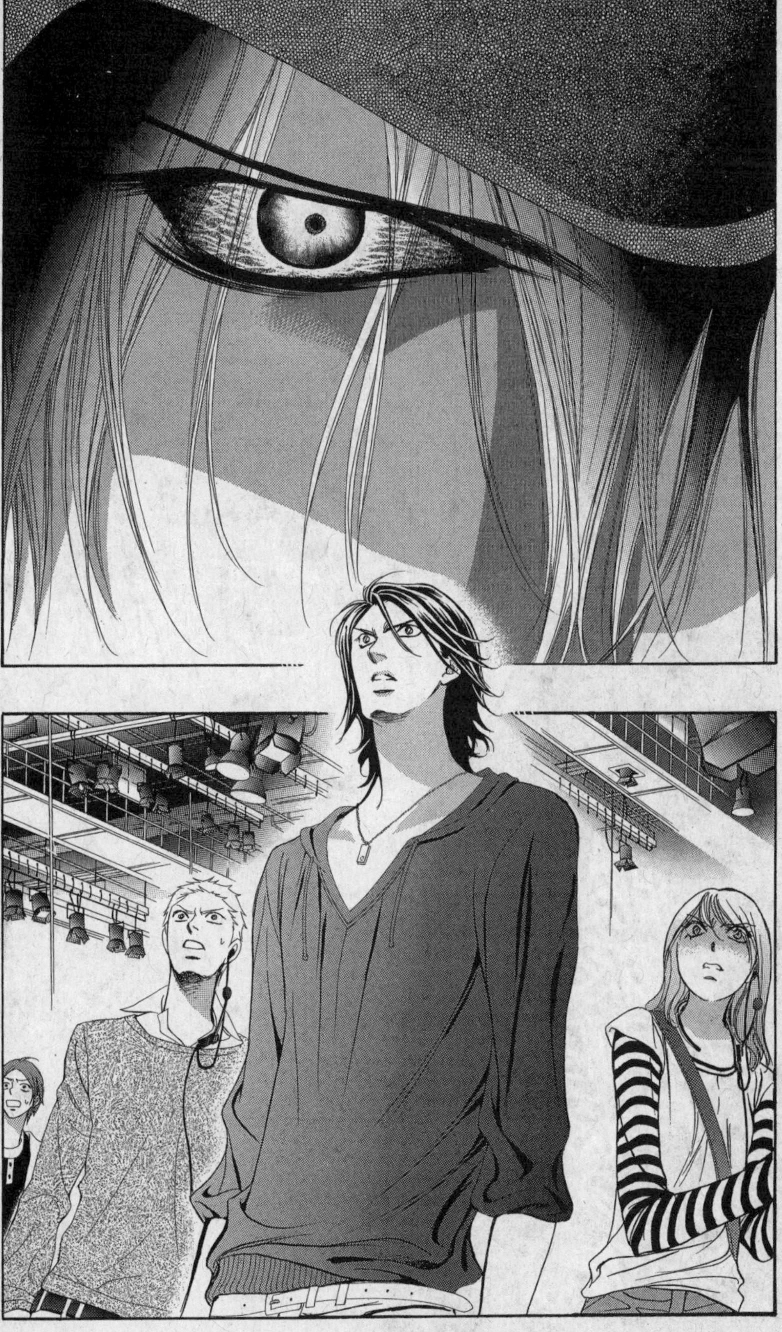

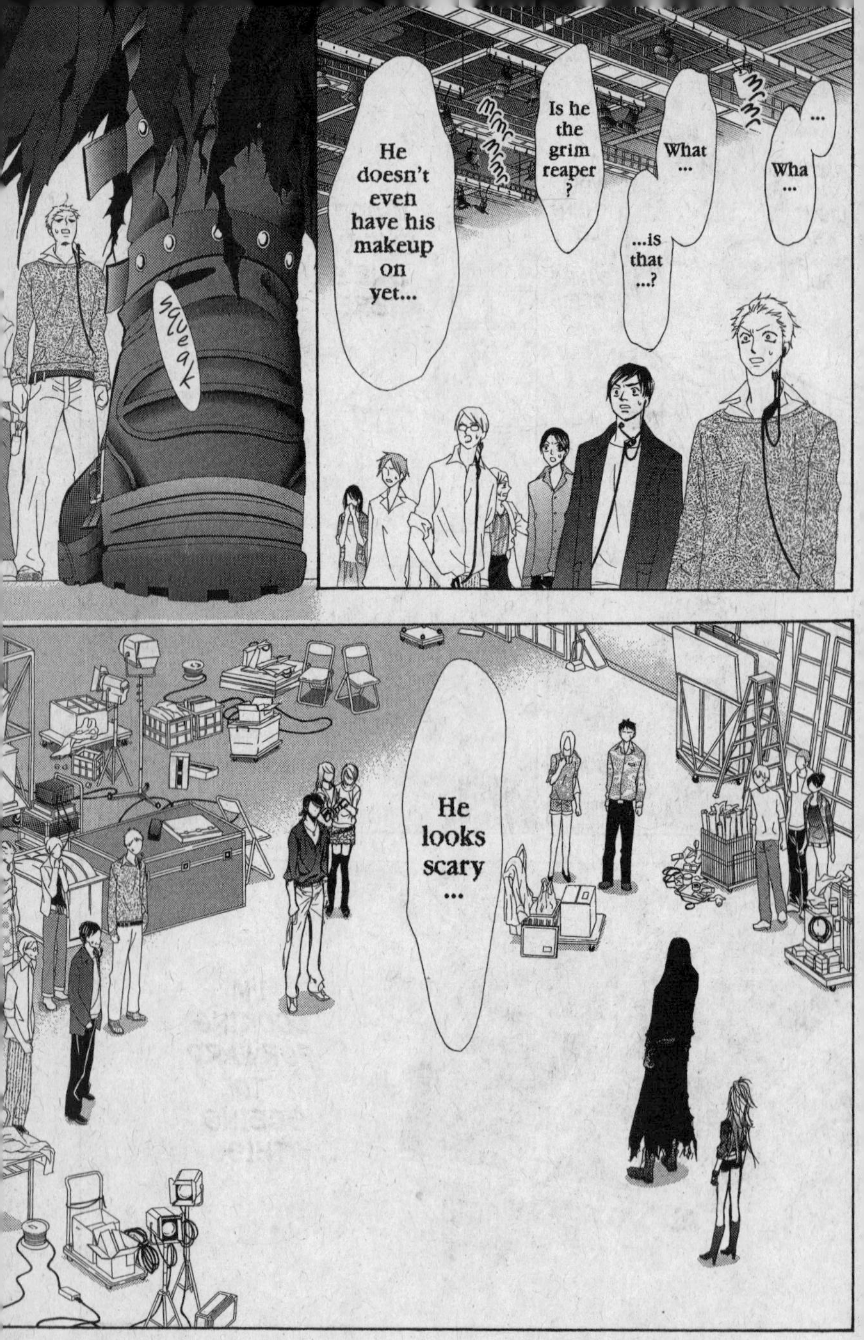
...
Wha ...
mrmr
What ...
...is that ...?
Is he the grim reaper?
mrmr
He doesn't even have his makeup on yet...
squeak
He looks scary ...

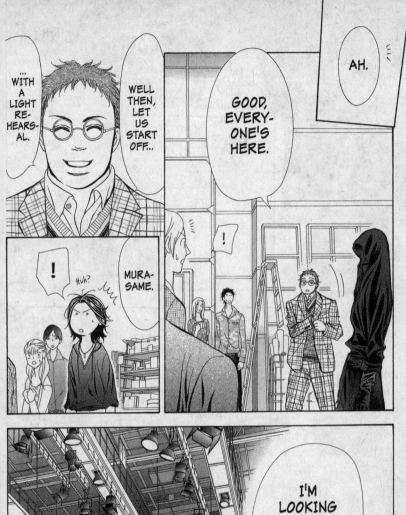

AH.
GOOD, EVERY-ONE'S HERE.
!
WELL THEN, LET US START OFF...
...WITH A LIGHT RE-HEARS-AL.
MURA-SAME.
!
Huh?
I'M LOOKING FORWARD TO SEEING THIS.

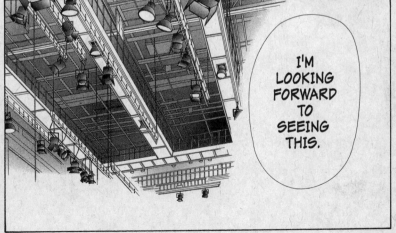

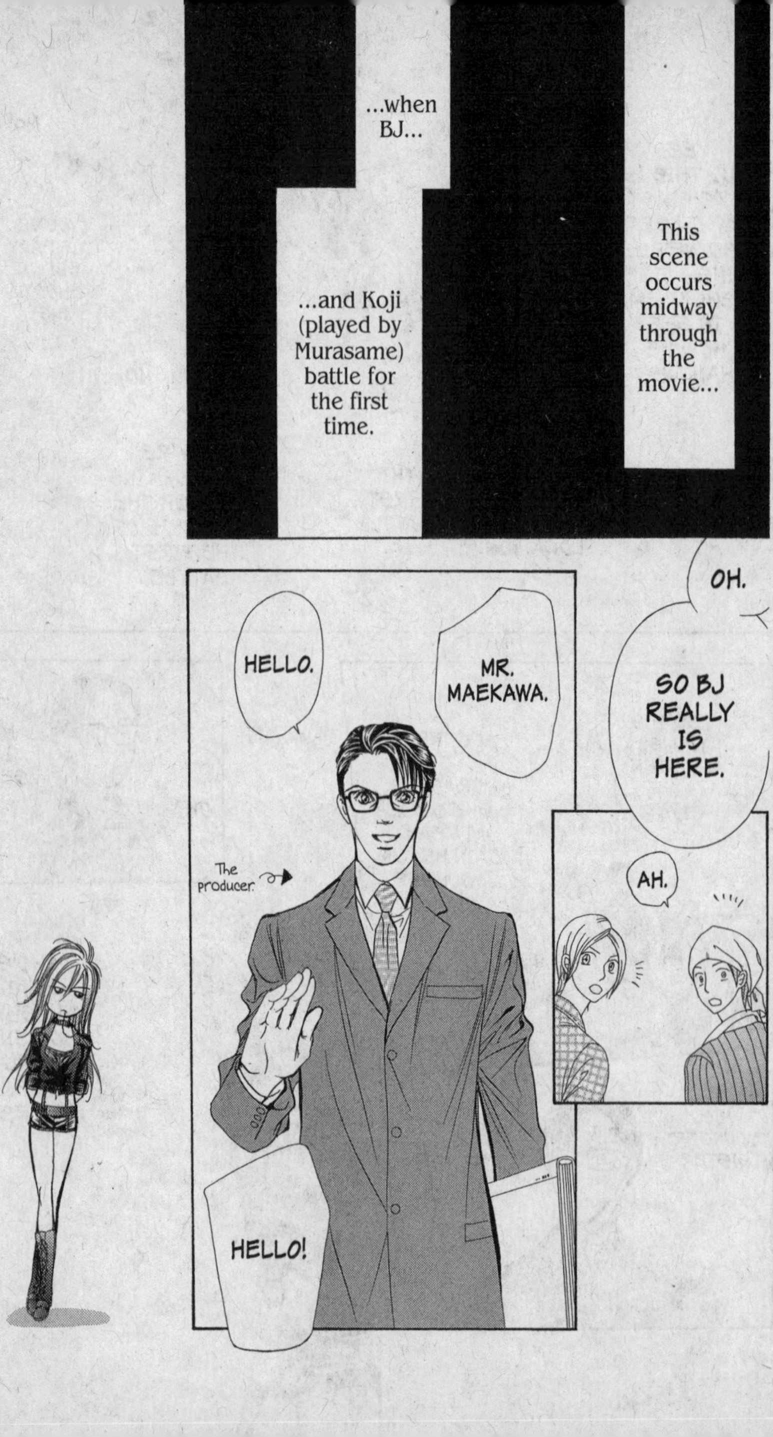
This scene occurs midway through the movie...
...when BJ...
...and Koji (played by Murasame) battle for the first time.
OH.
SO BJ REALLY IS HERE.
AH.
MR. MAEKAWA.
HELLO.
The producer.
HELLO!

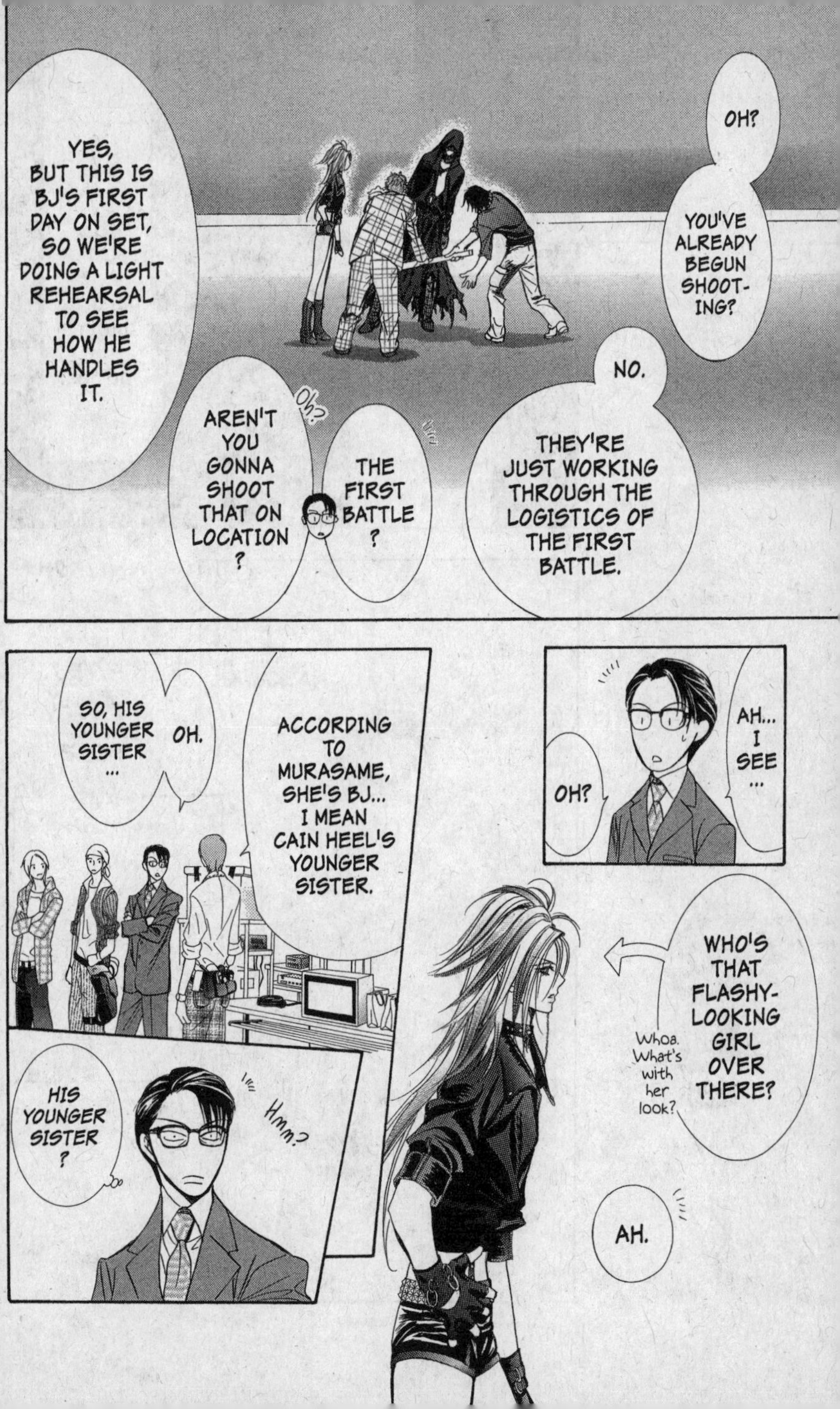
OH?
YOU'VE ALREADY BEGUN SHOOT-ING?
NO.
THEY'RE JUST WORKING THROUGH THE LOGISTICS OF THE FIRST BATTLE.
THE FIRST BATTLE?
Oh?
AREN'T YOU GONNA SHOOT THAT ON LOCATION?
YES, BUT THIS IS BJ'S FIRST DAY ON SET, SO WE'RE DOING A LIGHT REHEARSAL TO SEE HOW HE HANDLES IT.
AH... I SEE...
OH?
ACCORDING TO MURASAME, SHE'S BJ... I MEAN CAIN HEEL'S YOUNGER SISTER.
OH.
SO, HIS YOUNGER SISTER...
WHO'S THAT FLASHY-LOOKING GIRL OVER THERE?
Whoa. What's with her look?
AH.
HIS YOUNGER SISTER?
Hmm?

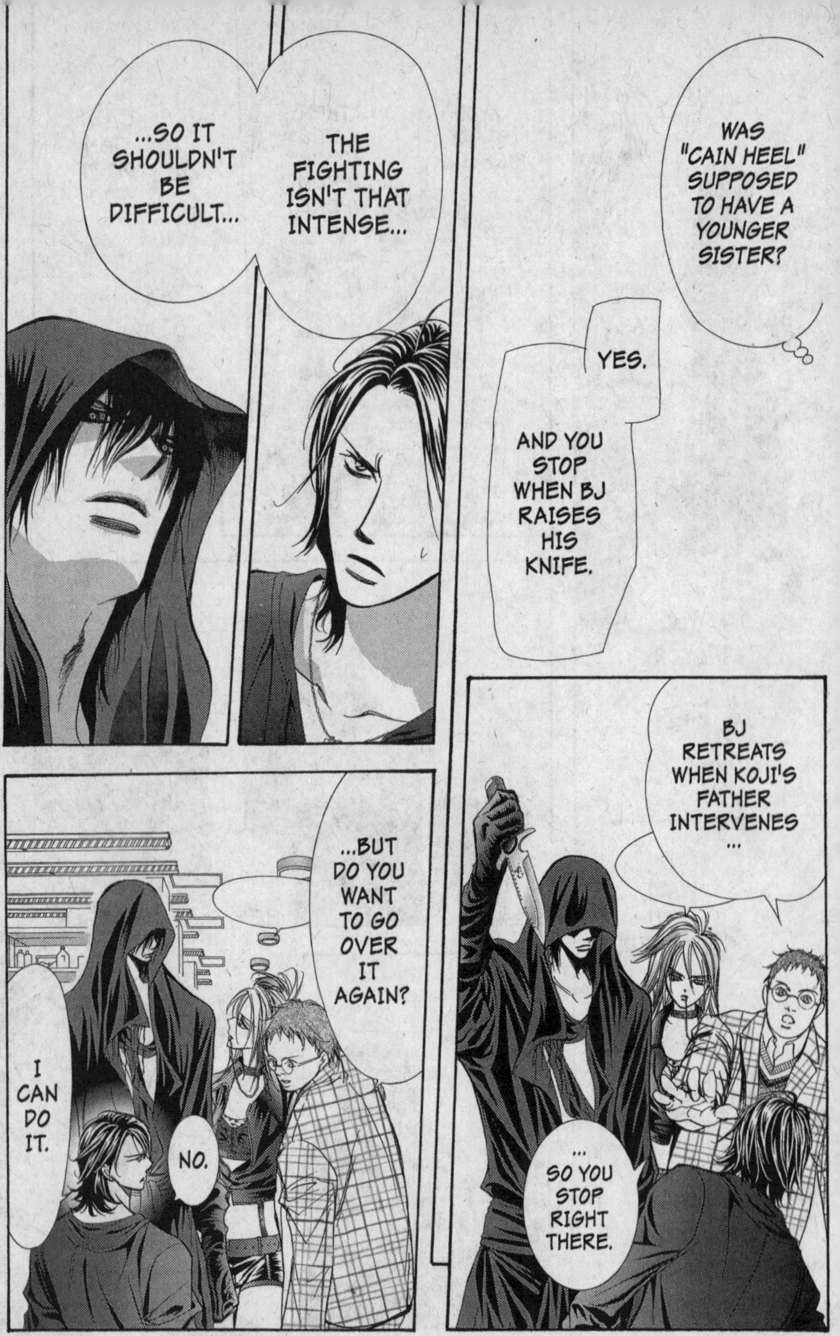
WAS "CAIN HEEL" SUPPOSED TO HAVE A YOUNGER SISTER?
YES.
AND YOU STOP WHEN BJ RAISES HIS KNIFE.
THE FIGHTING ISN'T THAT INTENSE...
...SO IT SHOULDN'T BE DIFFICULT...
BJ RETREATS WHEN KOJI'S FATHER INTERVENES ...
... SO YOU STOP RIGHT THERE.
...BUT DO YOU WANT TO GO OVER IT AGAIN?
NO.
I CAN DO IT.

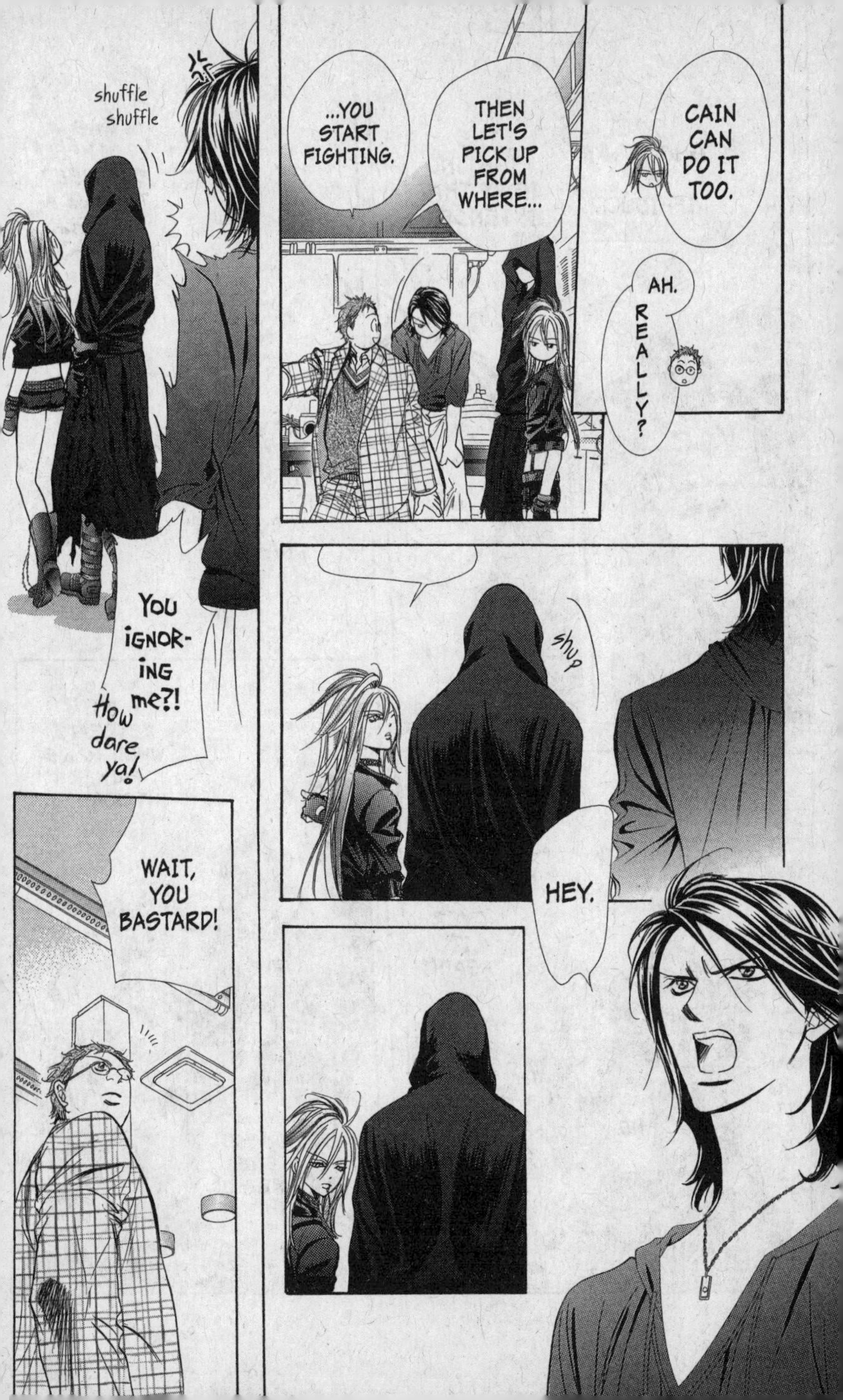

CAIN CAN DO IT TOO.
AH. REALLY?
THEN LET'S PICK UP FROM WHERE...
...YOU START FIGHTING.
shup
HEY.
shuffle shuffle
YOU IGNORING ME?!
How dare ya!
WAIT, YOU BASTARD!

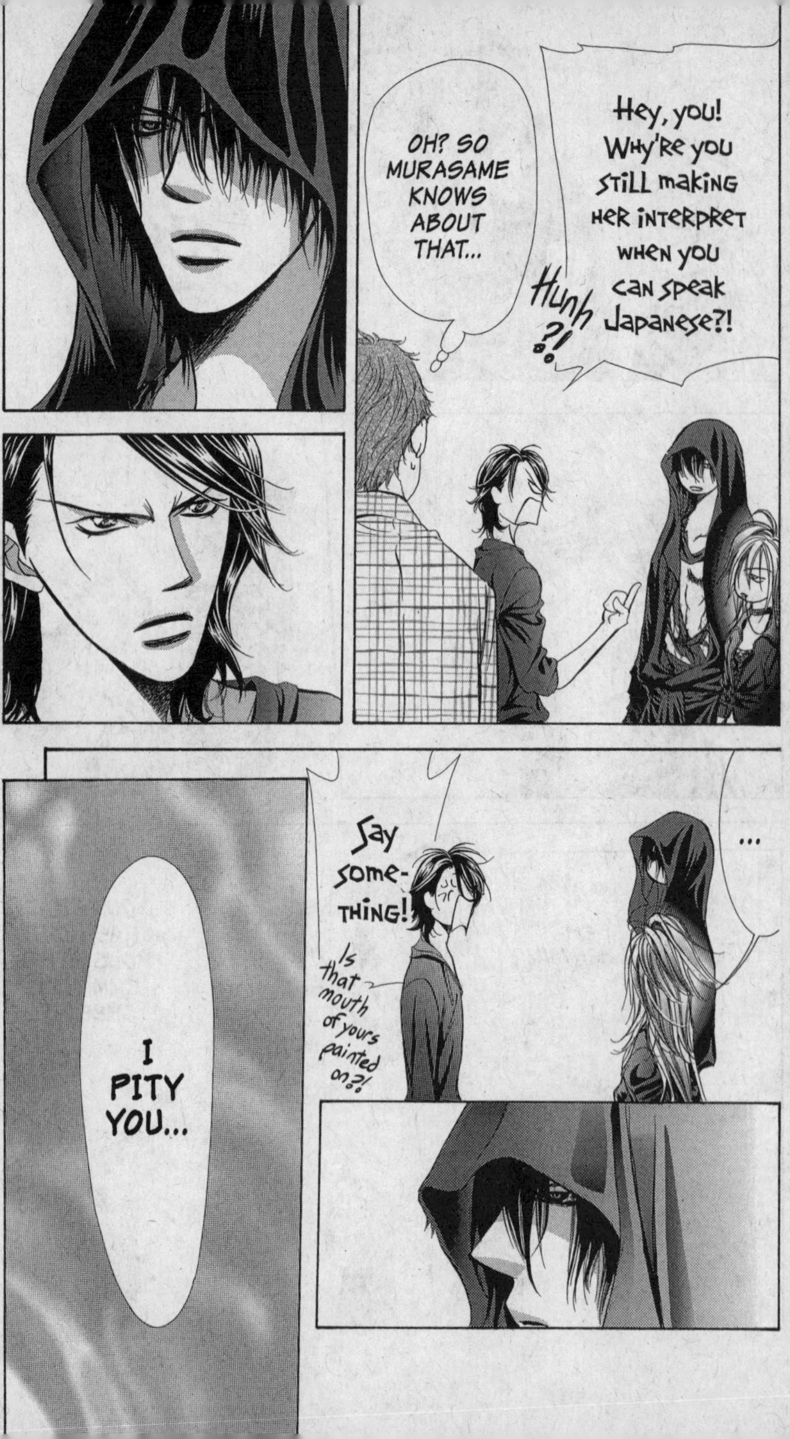
Hey, you! Why're you still making her interpret when you can speak Japanese?!
OH? SO MURASAME KNOWS ABOUT THAT...
Hunh ?!
...
Say some-THING!
Is that mouth of yours painted on?!
I PITY YOU...

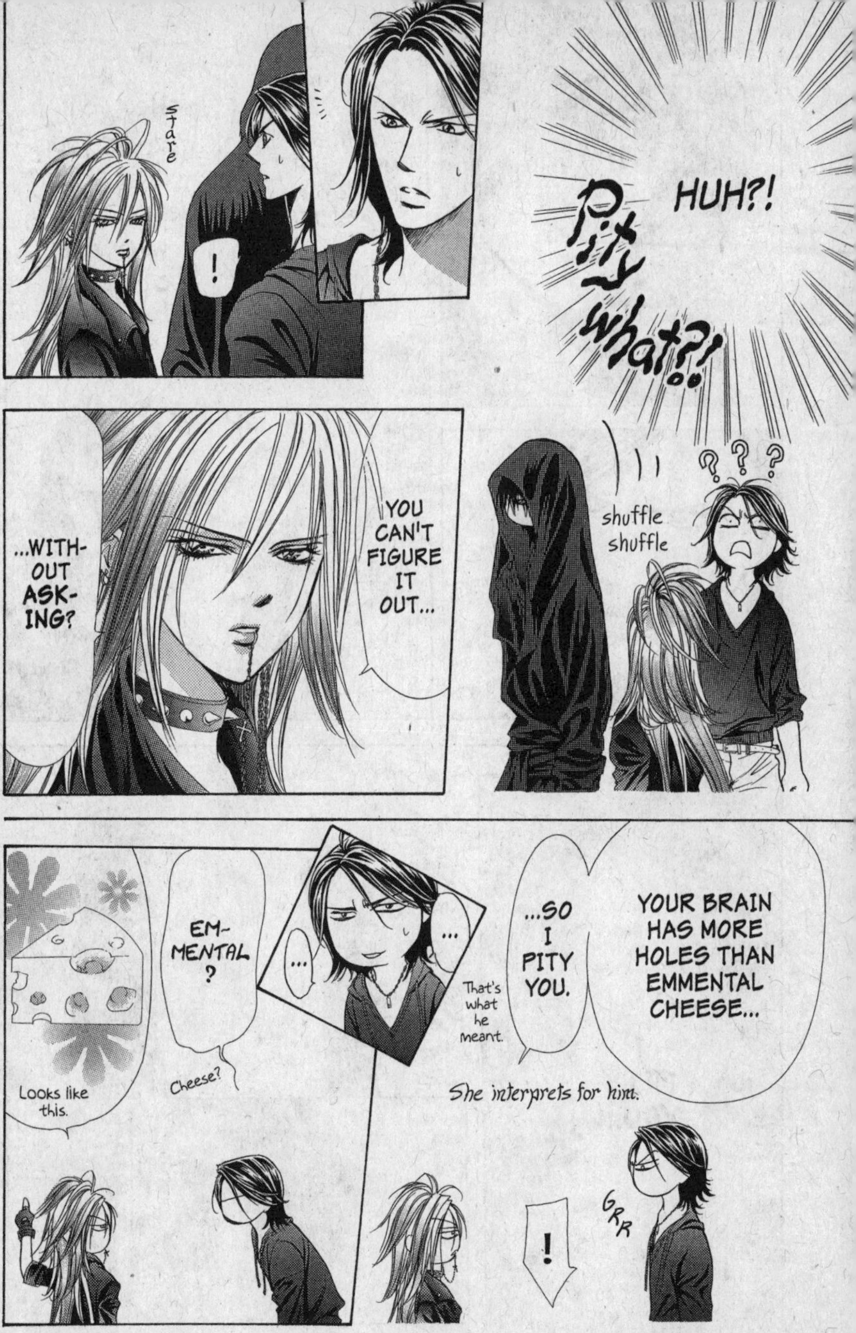
HUH?!
Pity what?!
stare
!
shuffle shuffle
YOU CAN'T FIGURE IT OUT...
...WITH-OUT ASK-ING?
YOUR BRAIN HAS MORE HOLES THAN EMMENTAL CHEESE...
...SO I PITY YOU.
That's what he meant.
She interprets for him.
...
...
EM-MENTAL?
Cheese?
Looks like this.
GRR
!

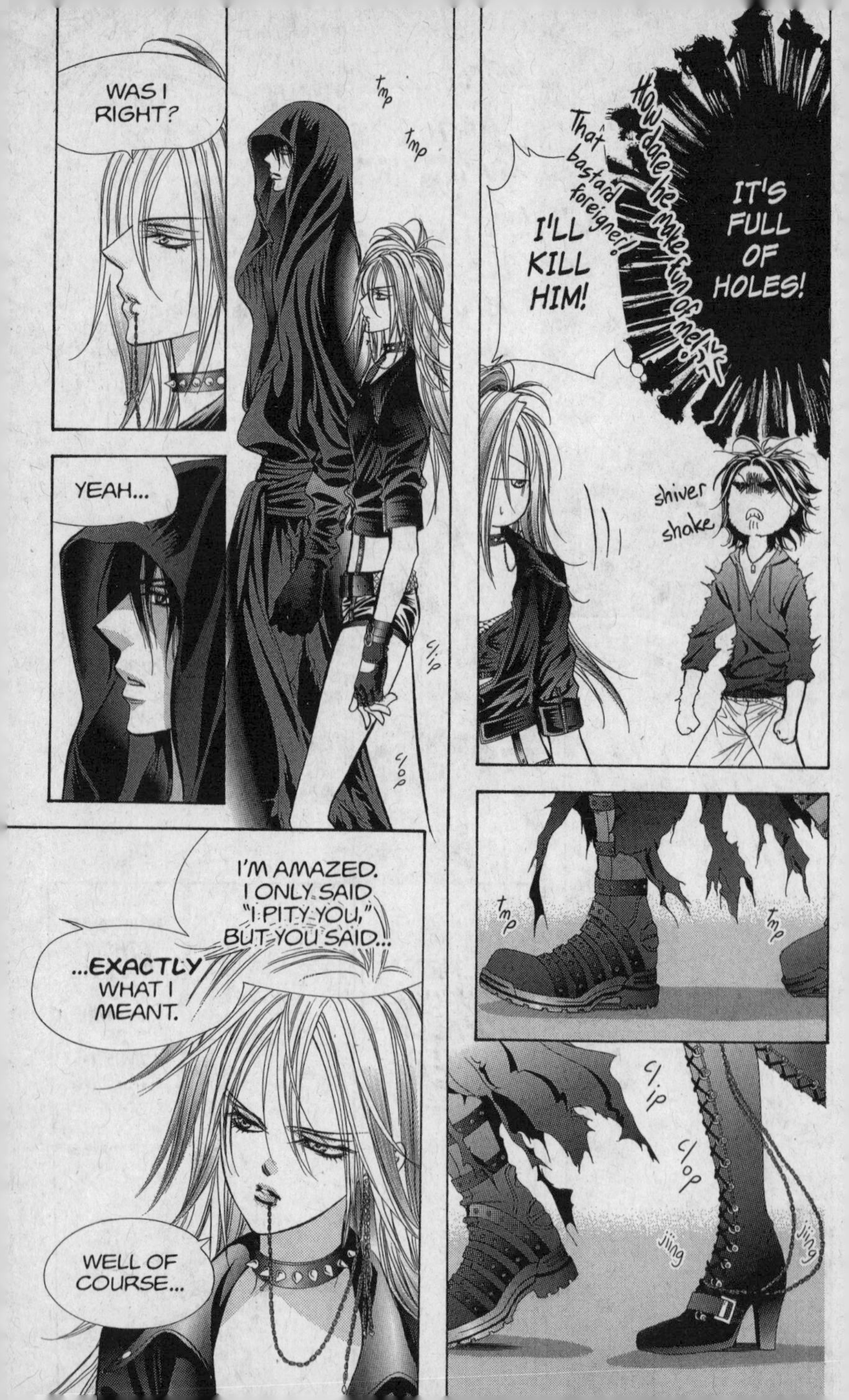
IT'S FULL OF HOLES!
How dare he make fun of me!!
That bastard foreigner!
I'LL KILL HIM!
shiver
shake
tmp
tmp
clip
clop
jiing
jiing
WAS I RIGHT?
tmp
tmp
YEAH...
clip
clop
I'M AMAZED. I ONLY SAID "I PITY YOU," BUT YOU SAID...
...EXACTLY WHAT I MEANT.
WELL OF COURSE...

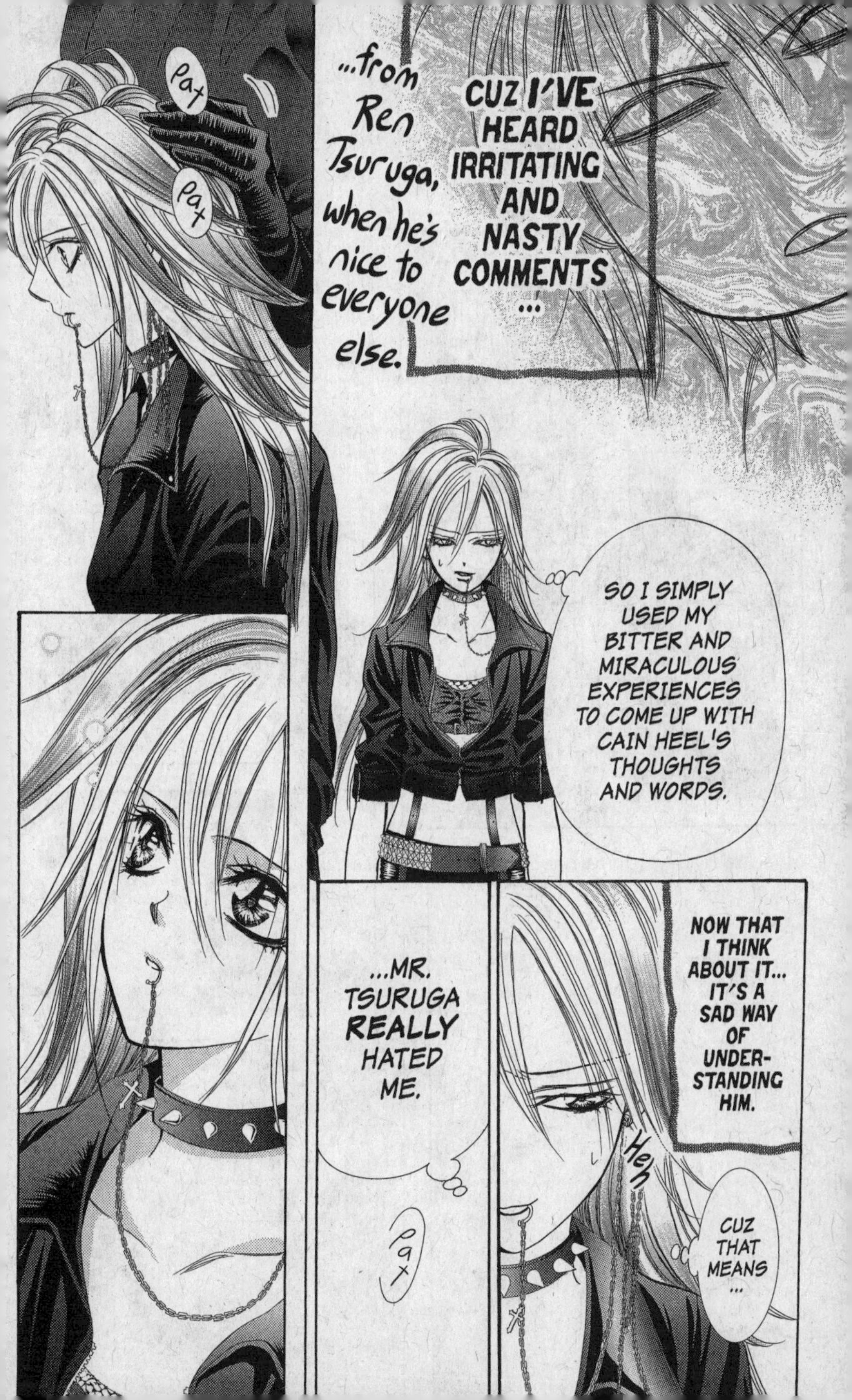

CUZ I'VE HEARD IRRITATING AND NASTY COMMENTS...
...from Ren Tsuruga, when he's nice to everyone else.
SO I SIMPLY USED MY BITTER AND MIRACULOUS EXPERIENCES TO COME UP WITH CAIN HEEL'S THOUGHTS AND WORDS.
Pat
Pat
NOW THAT I THINK ABOUT IT... IT'S A SAD WAY OF UNDER-STANDING HIM.
Heh
CUZ THAT MEANS...
...MR. TSURUGA REALLY HATED ME.
Pat

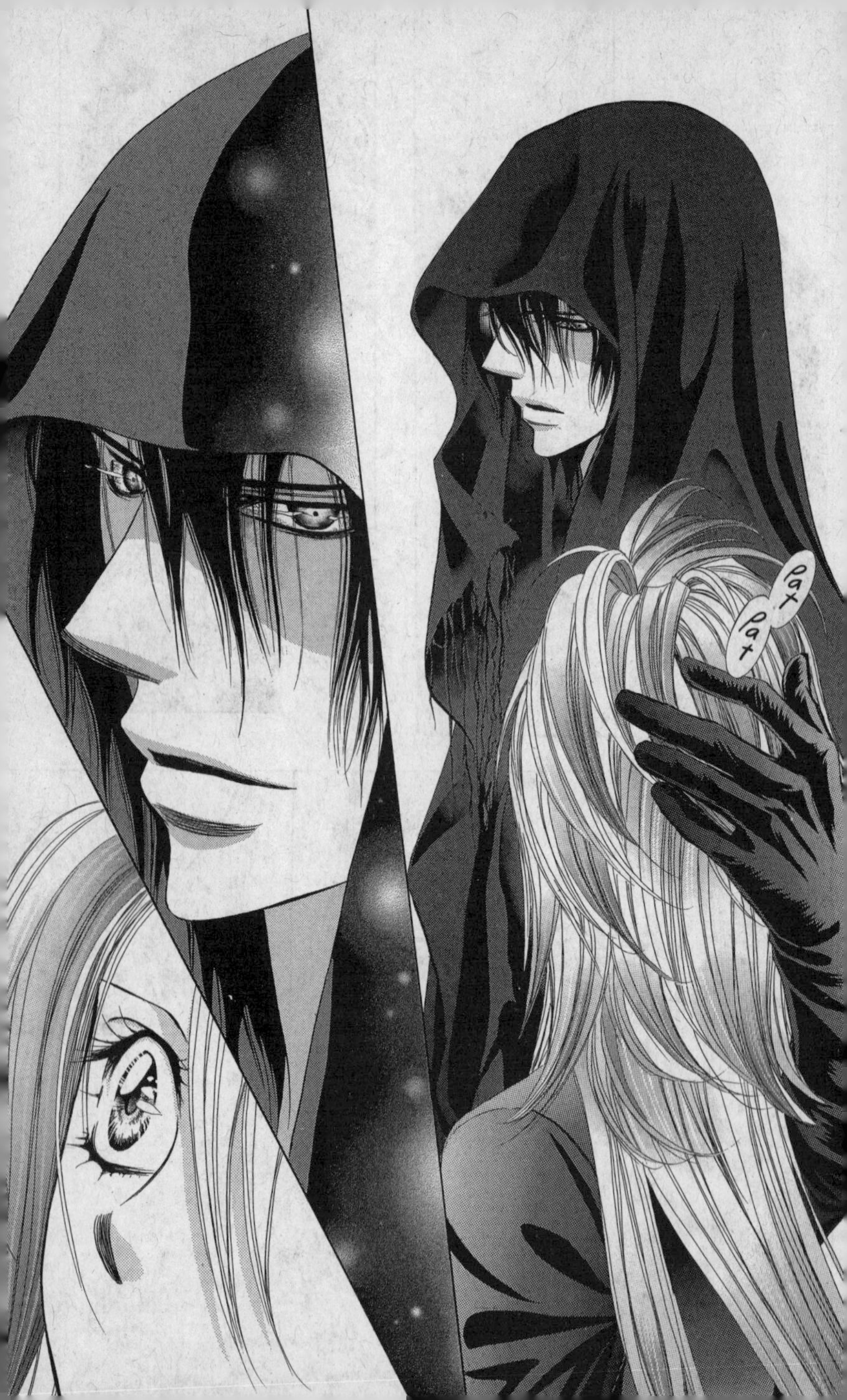
pat pat

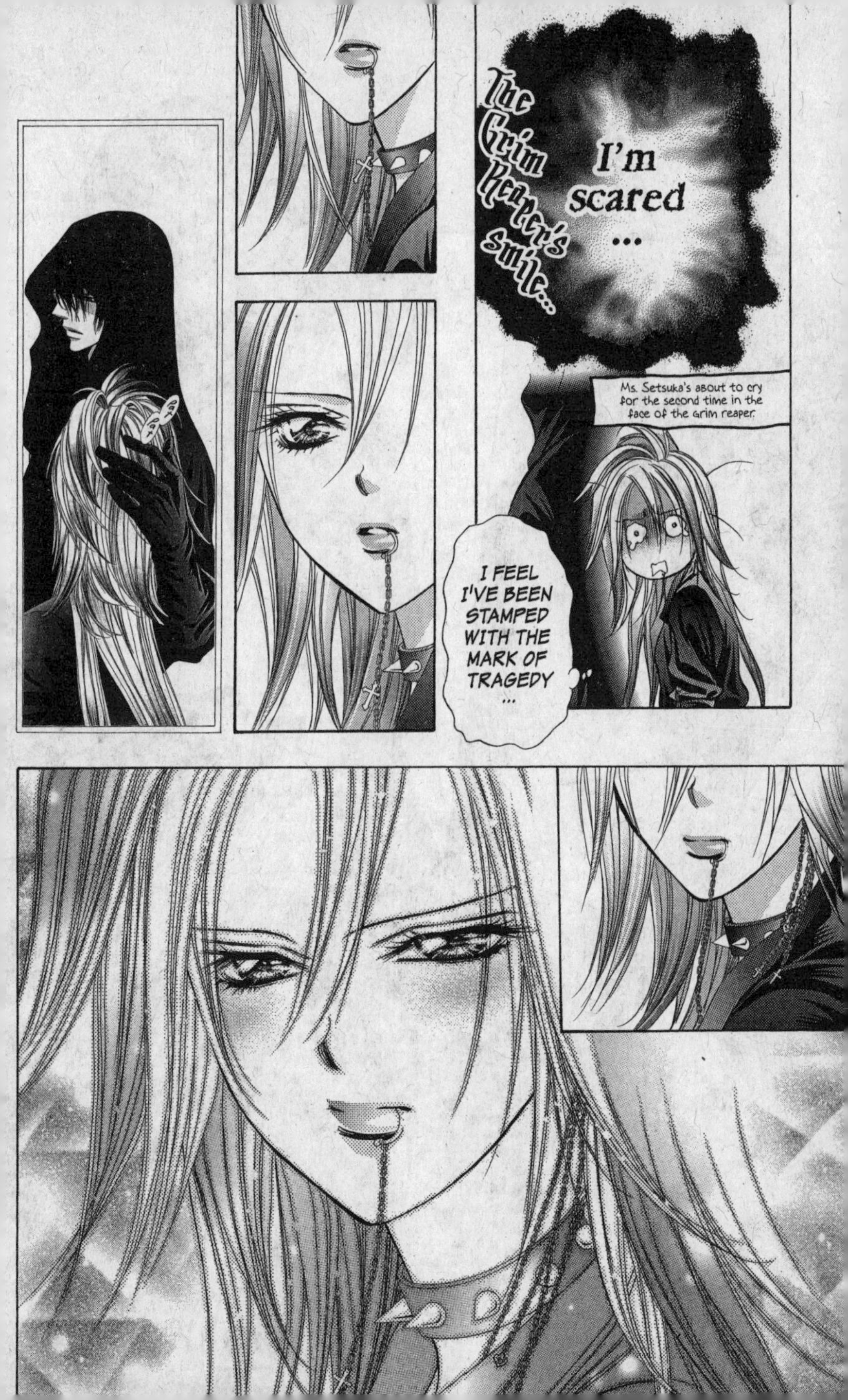
I'm scared ...
The Grim Reaper's smile...
Ms. Setsuka's about to cry for the second time in the face of the Grim reaper.
I FEEL I'VE BEEN STAMPED WITH THE MARK OF TRAGEDY ...

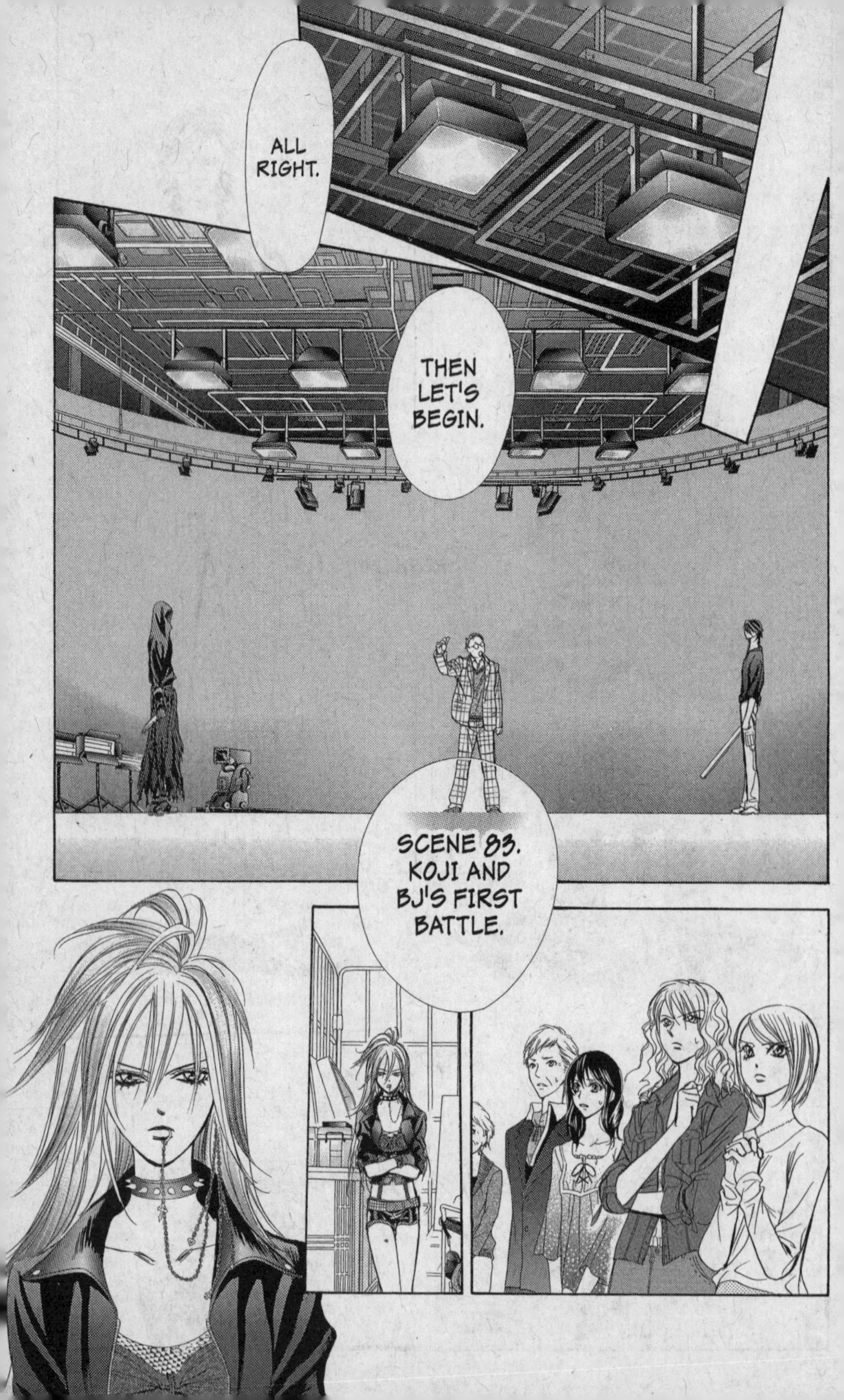
ALL RIGHT.
THEN LET'S BEGIN.
SCENE 83. KOJI AND BJ'S FIRST BATTLE.

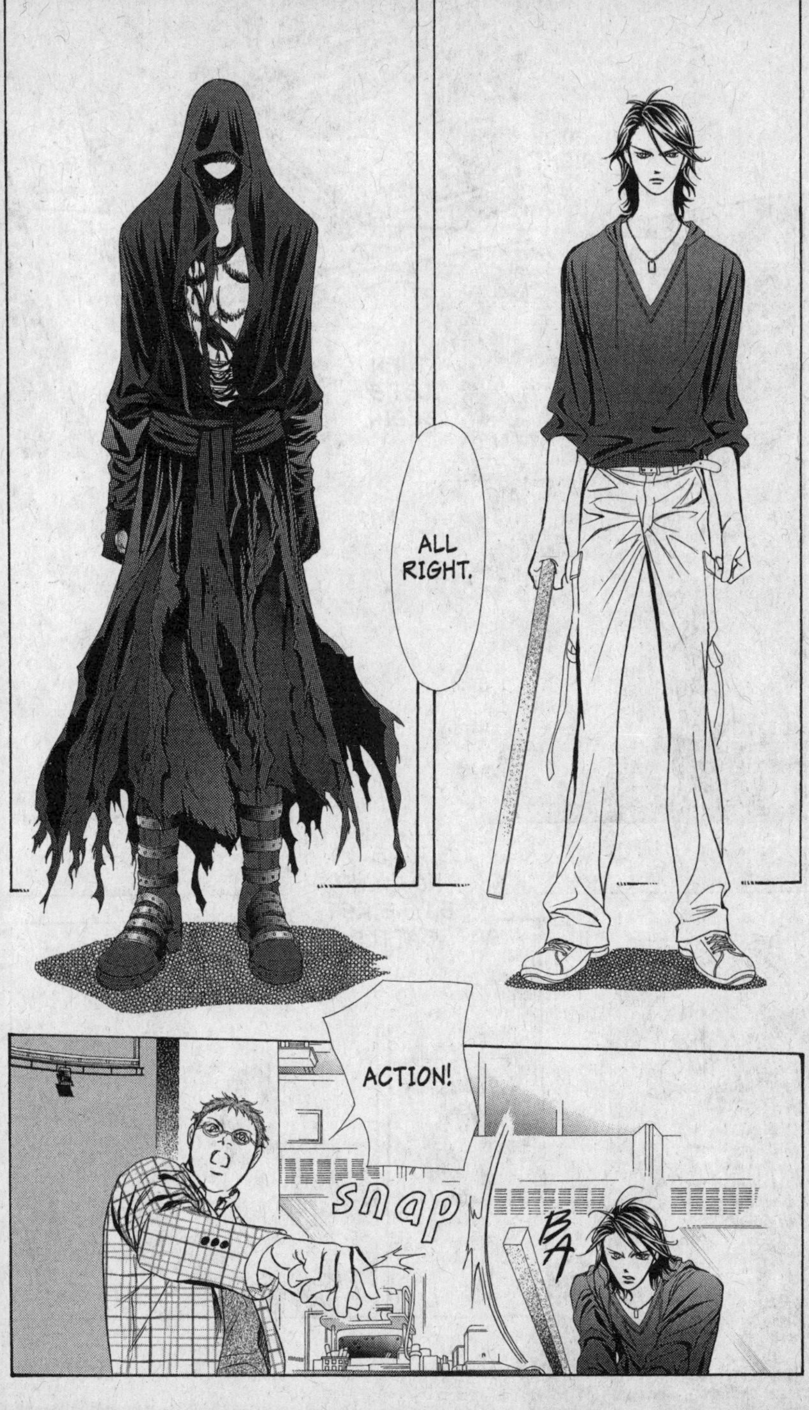
ALL RIGHT.
ACTION!
snap
BA

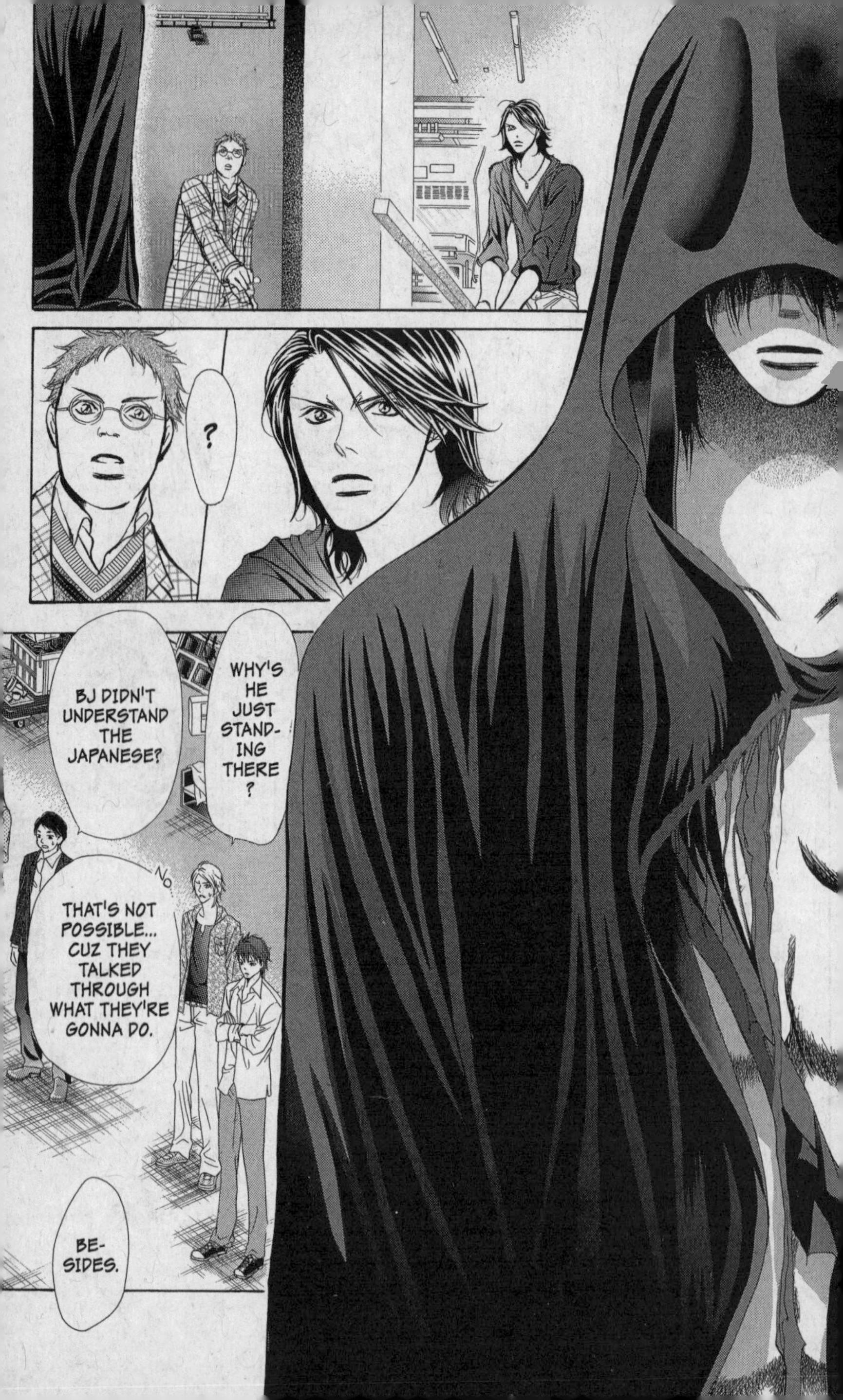
?
WHY'S HE JUST STAND-ING THERE?
BJ DIDN'T UNDERSTAND THE JAPANESE?
NO...
THAT'S NOT POSSIBLE... CUZ THEY TALKED THROUGH WHAT THEY'RE GONNA DO.
BE-SIDES.

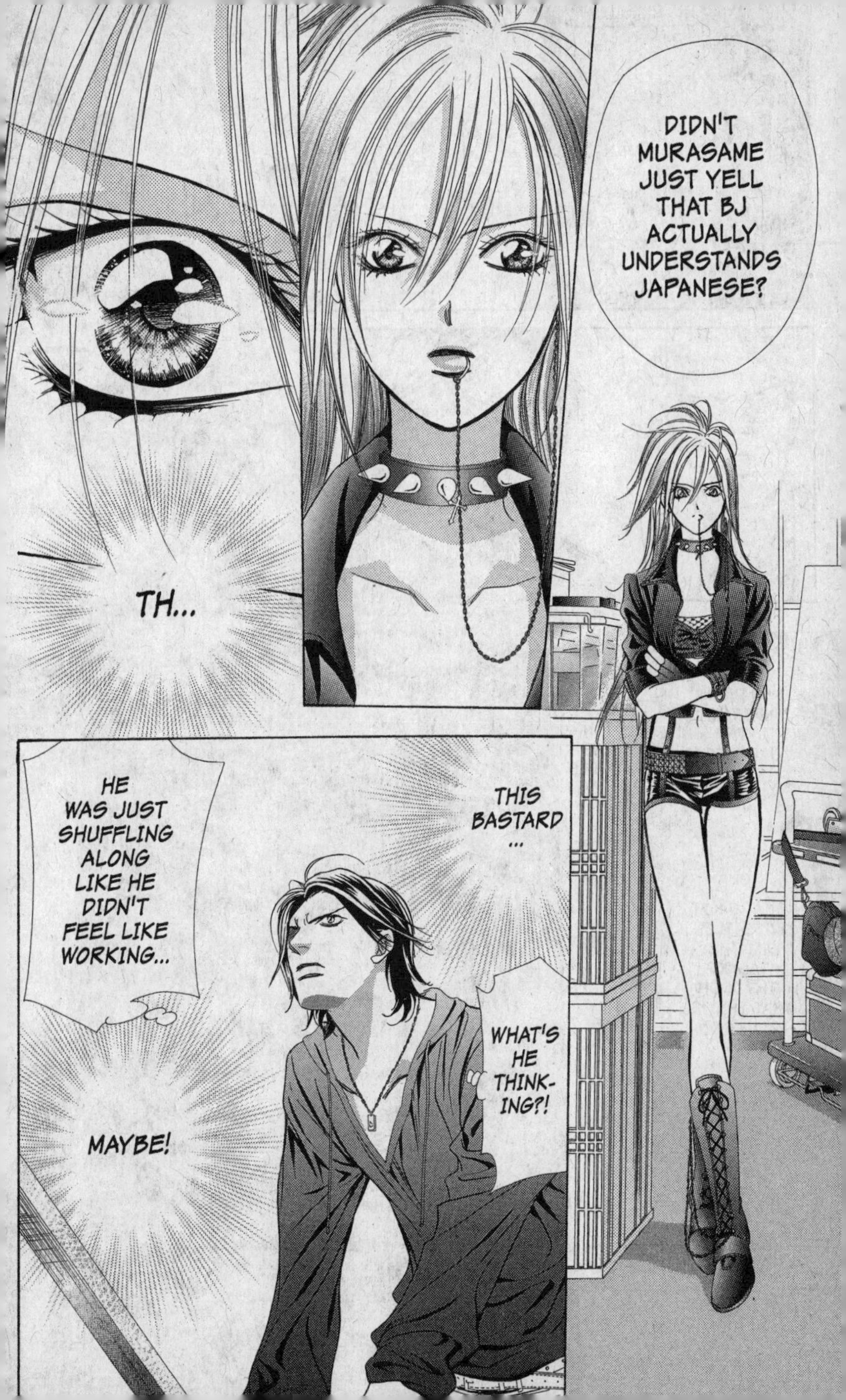
DIDN'T MURASAME JUST YELL THAT BJ ACTUALLY UNDERSTANDS JAPANESE?
TH...
THIS BASTARD ...
WHAT'S HE THINKING?!
HE WAS JUST SHUFFLING ALONG LIKE HE DIDN'T FEEL LIKE WORKING...
MAYBE!

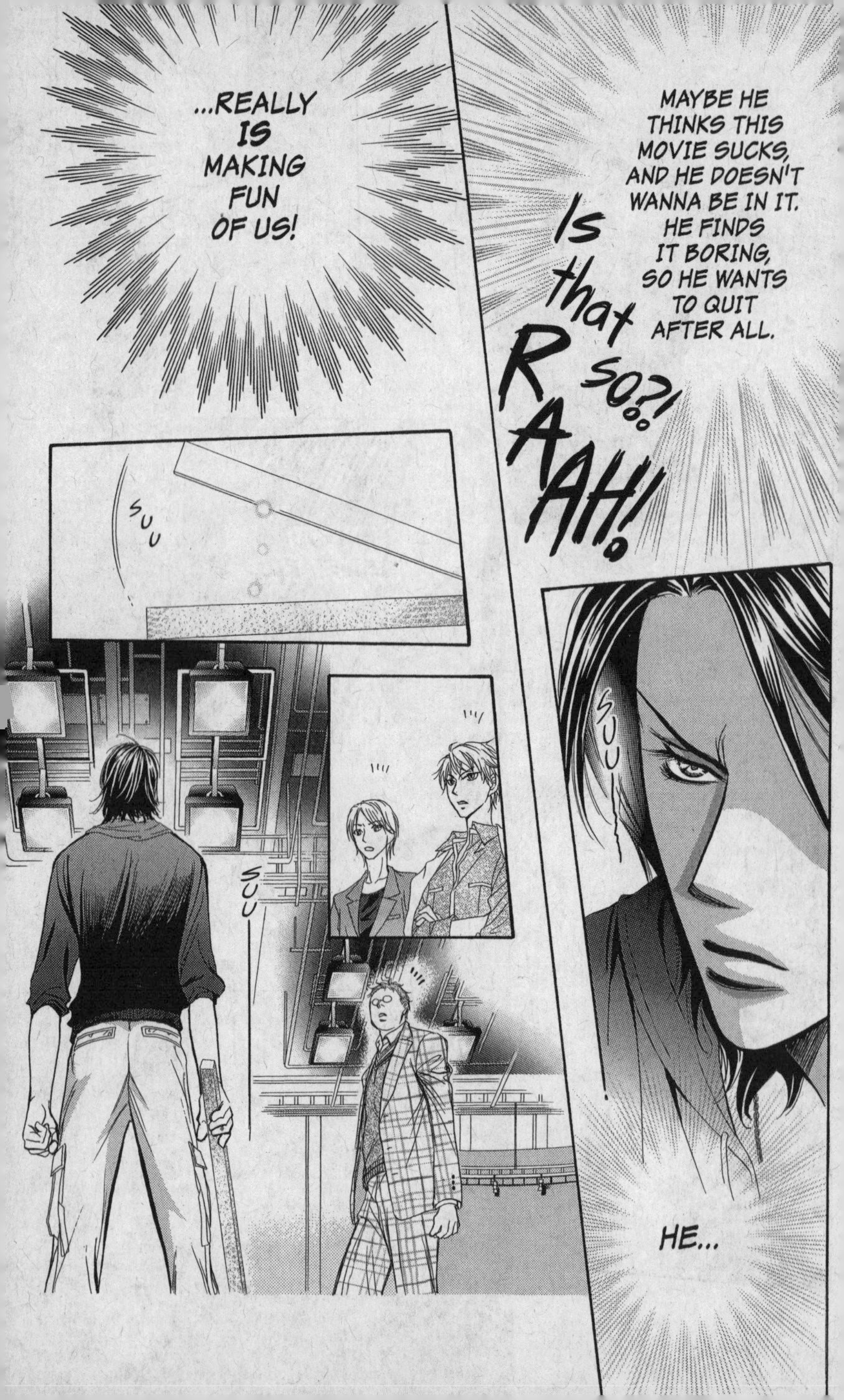
MAYBE HE THINKS THIS MOVIE SUCKS, AND HE DOESN'T WANNA BE IN IT. HE FINDS IT BORING, SO HE WANTS TO QUIT AFTER ALL.
Is that so?!
RAAH!
SUU
HE...
...REALLY IS MAKING FUN OF US!
SUU
SUU

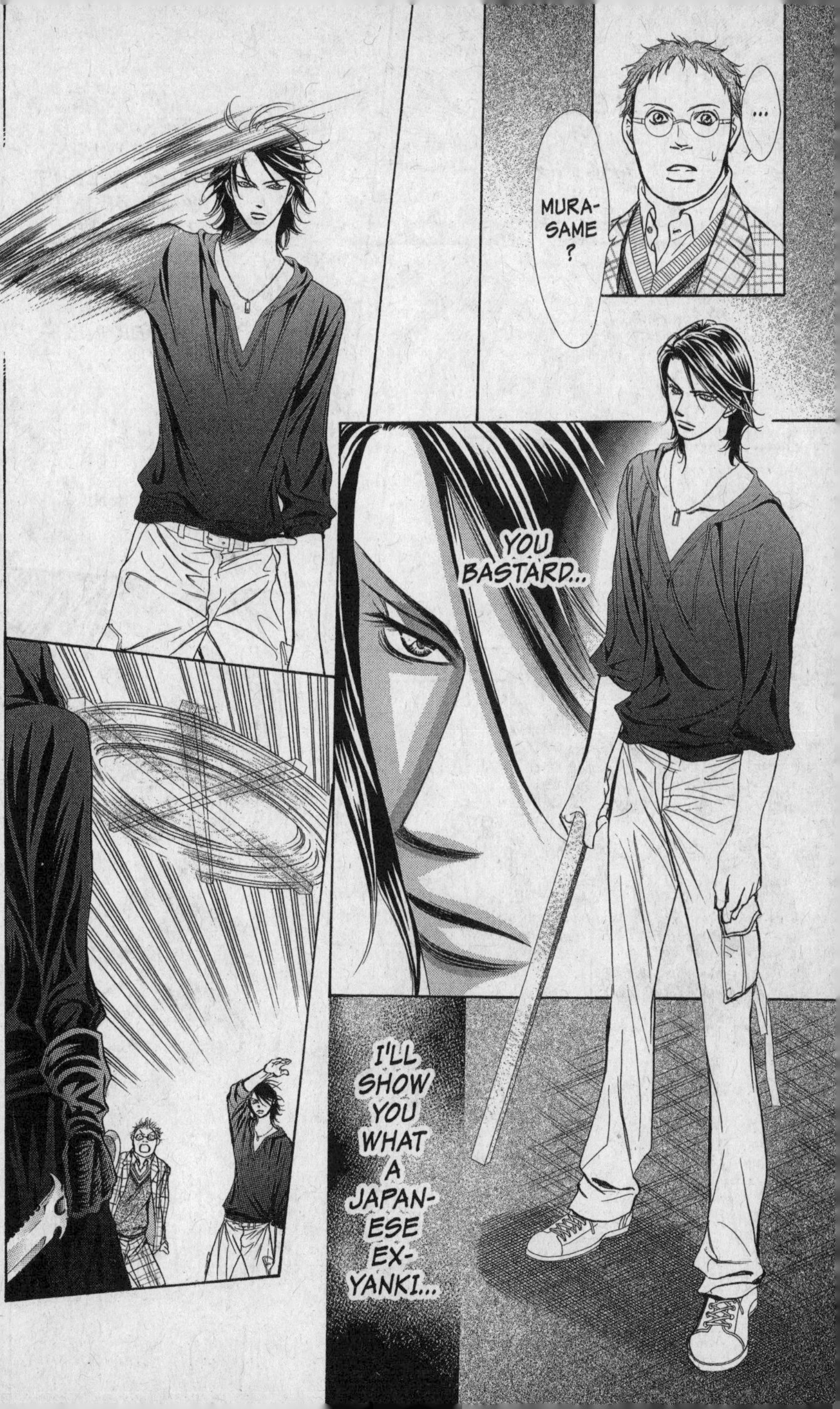
...
MURA-SAME ?
YOU BASTARD...
I'LL SHOW YOU WHAT A JAPAN-ESE EX-YANKI...

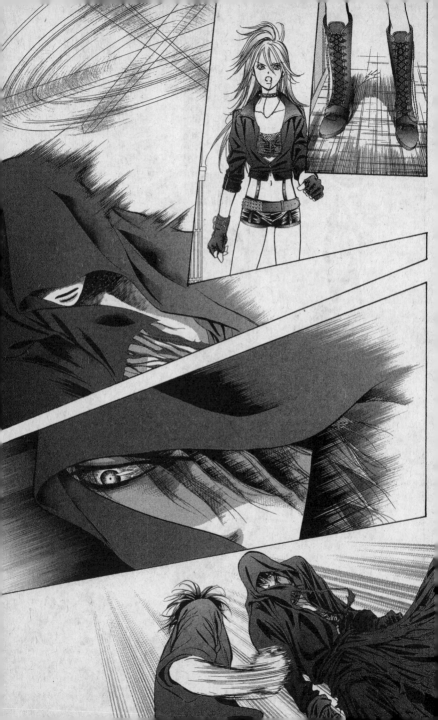

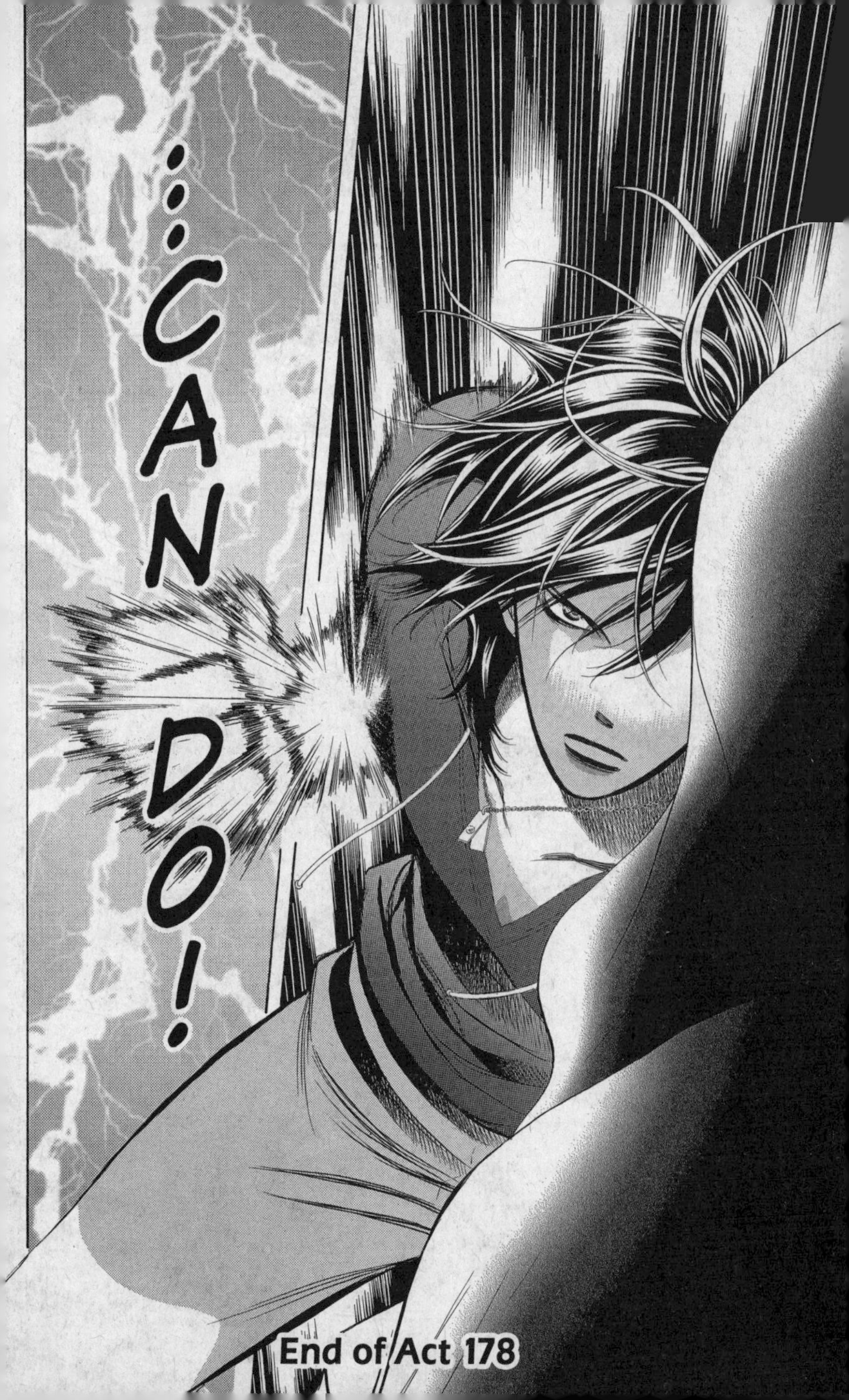
...CAN DO!
End of Act 178

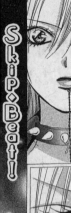

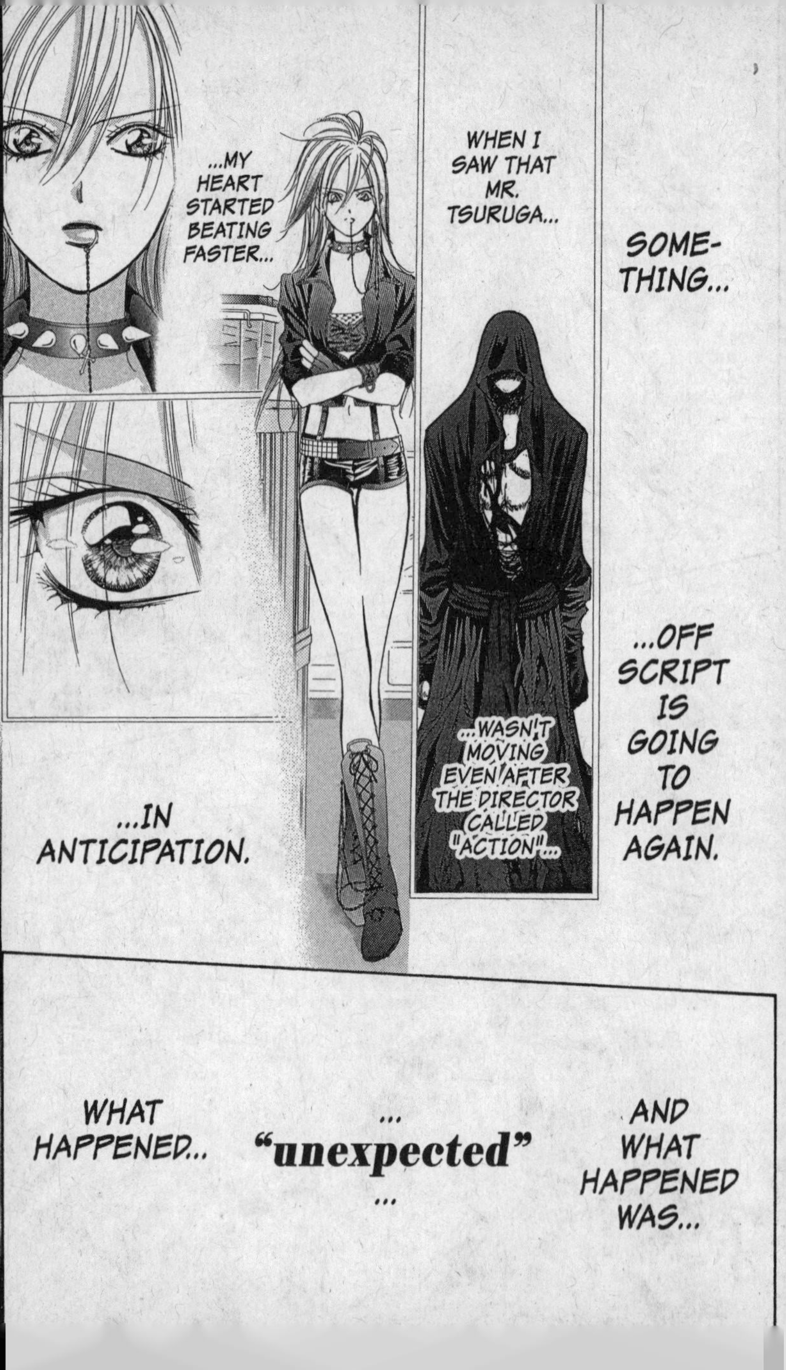
SOME-THING...
...OFF SCRIPT IS GOING TO HAPPEN AGAIN.
WHEN I SAW THAT MR. TSURUGA...
...WASN'T MOVING EVEN AFTER THE DIRECTOR CALLED "ACTION"...
...MY HEART STARTED BEATING FASTER...
...IN ANTICIPATION.
AND WHAT HAPPENED WAS...
... "unexpected" ...
WHAT HAPPENED...
Skip•Beat!

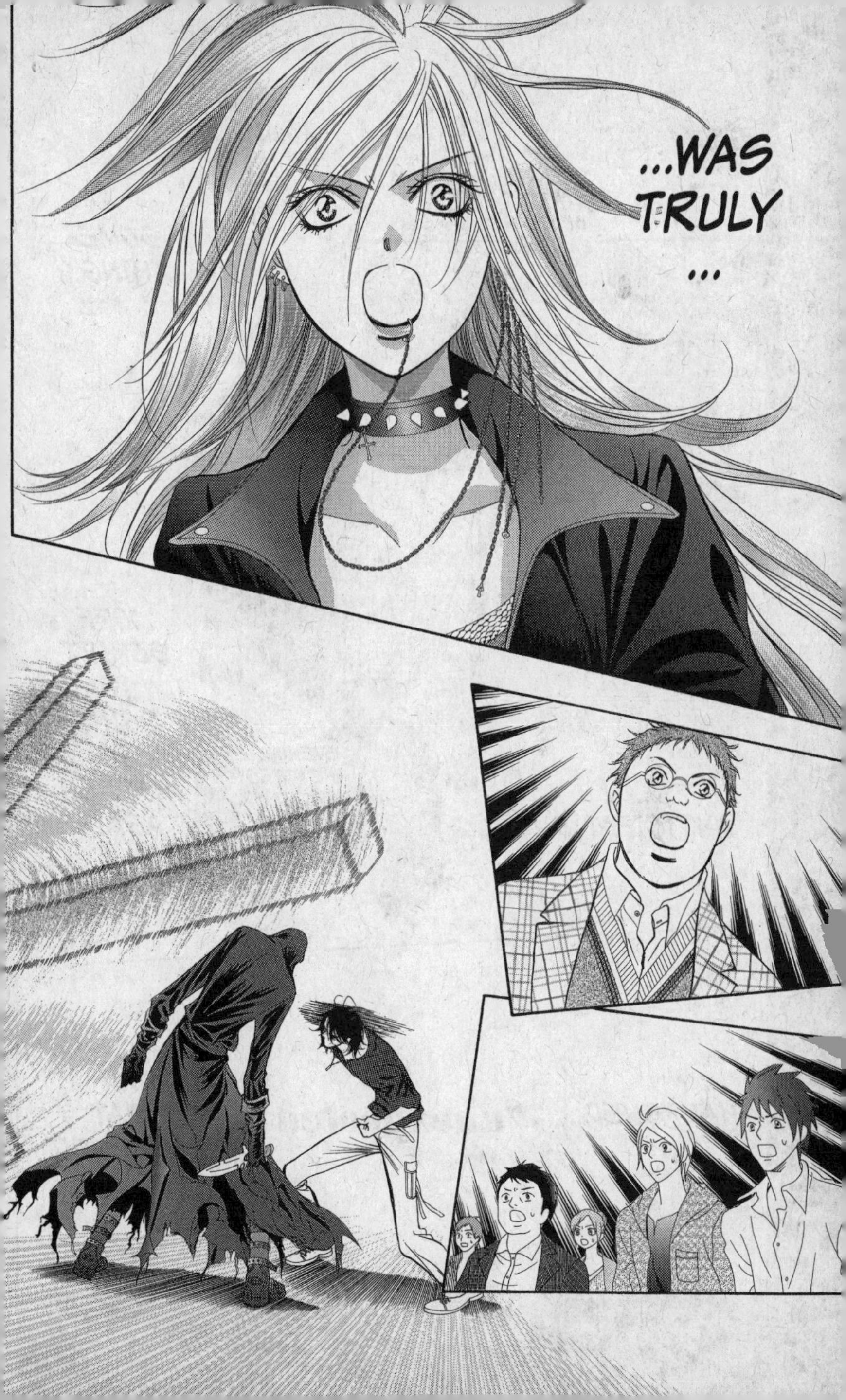
...WAS TRULY ...

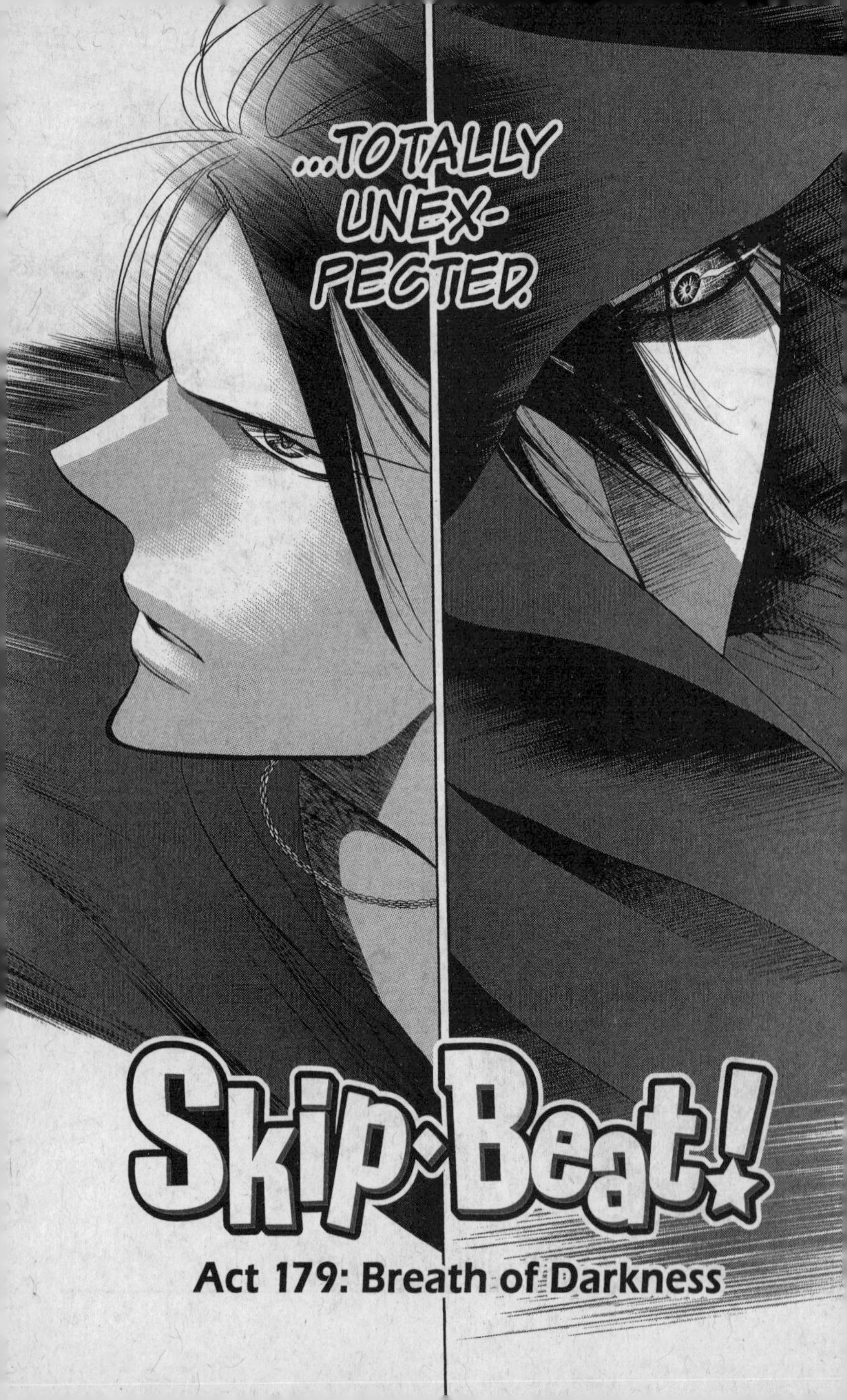
...TOTALLY UNEX-PECTED.
Skip·Beat!
Act 179: Breath of Darkness

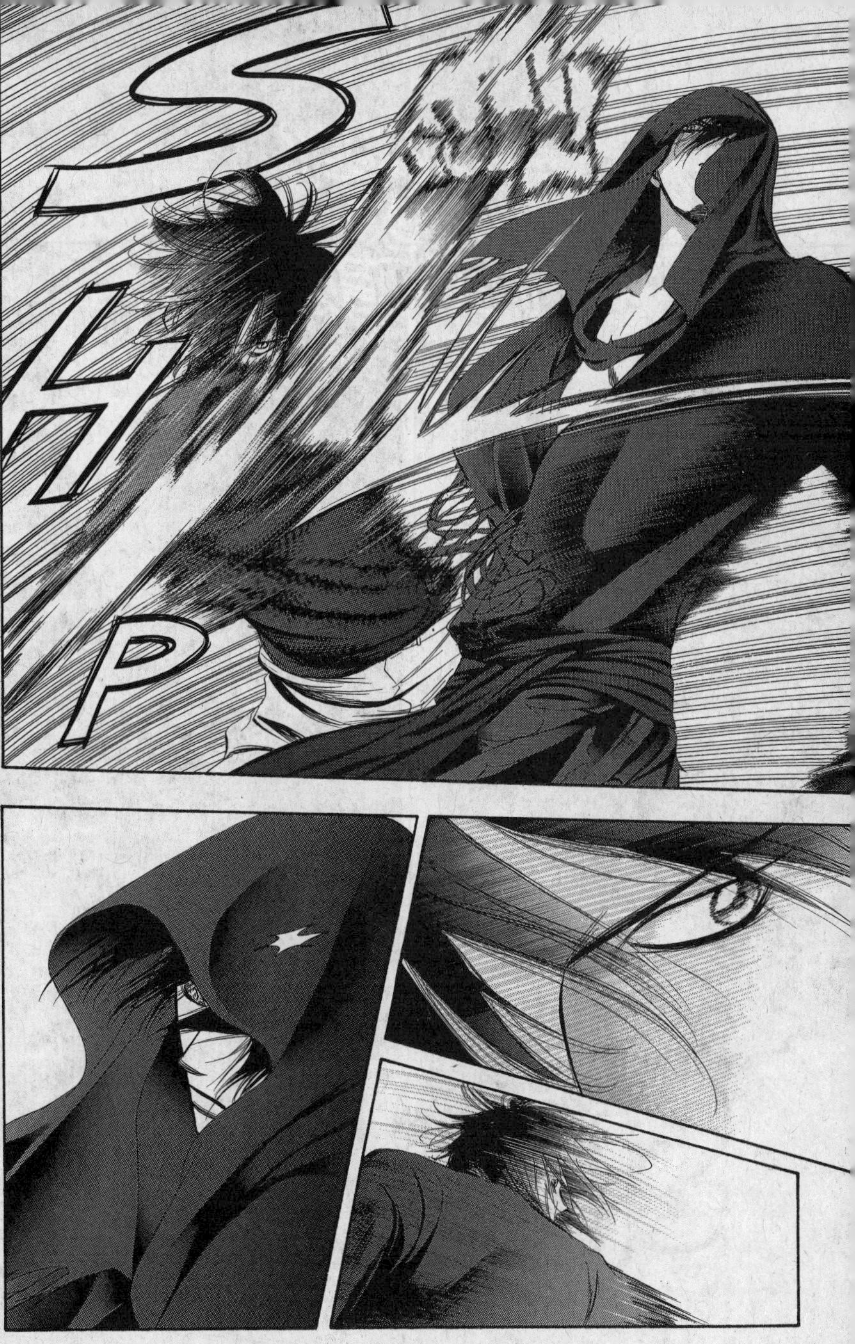
SHP

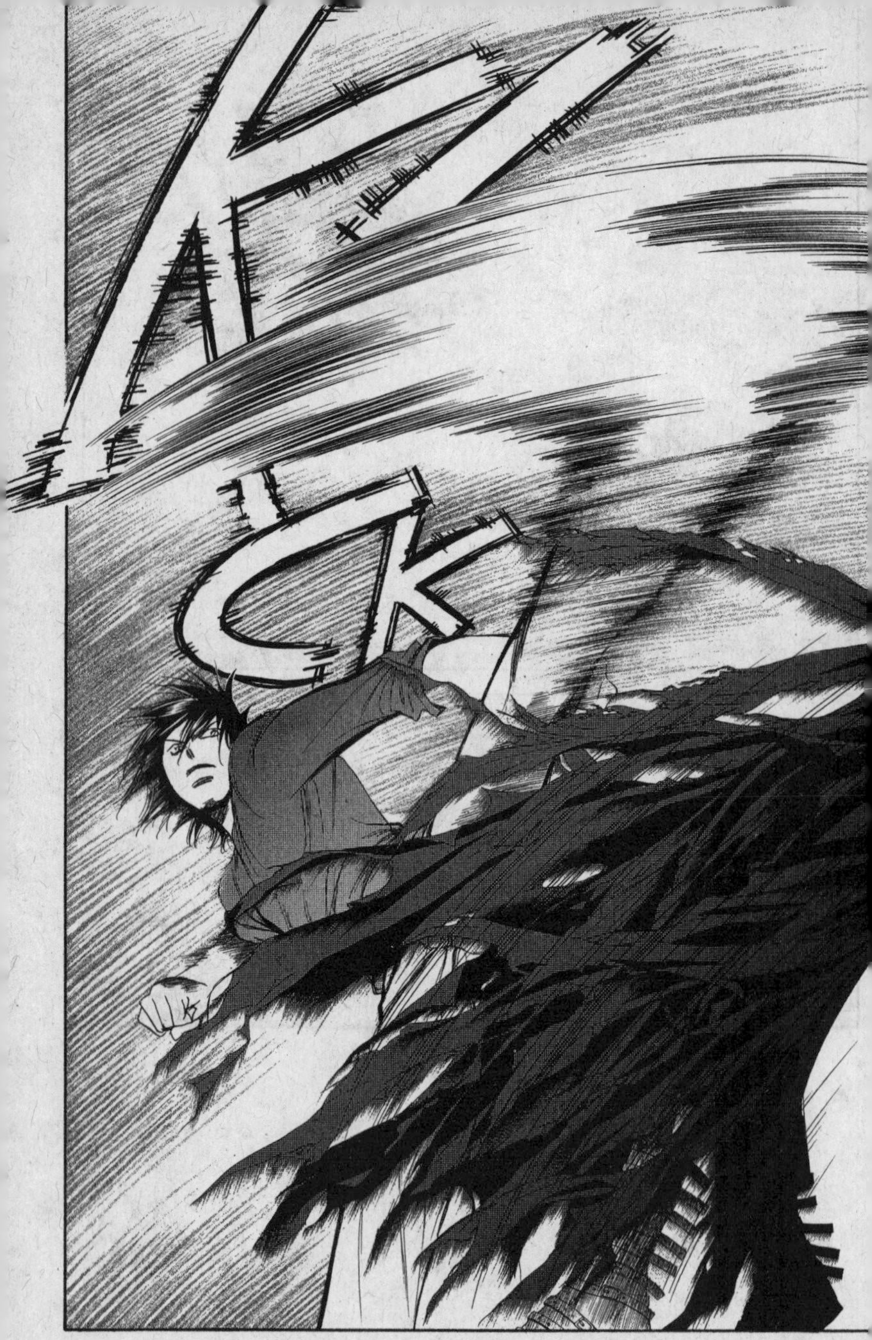

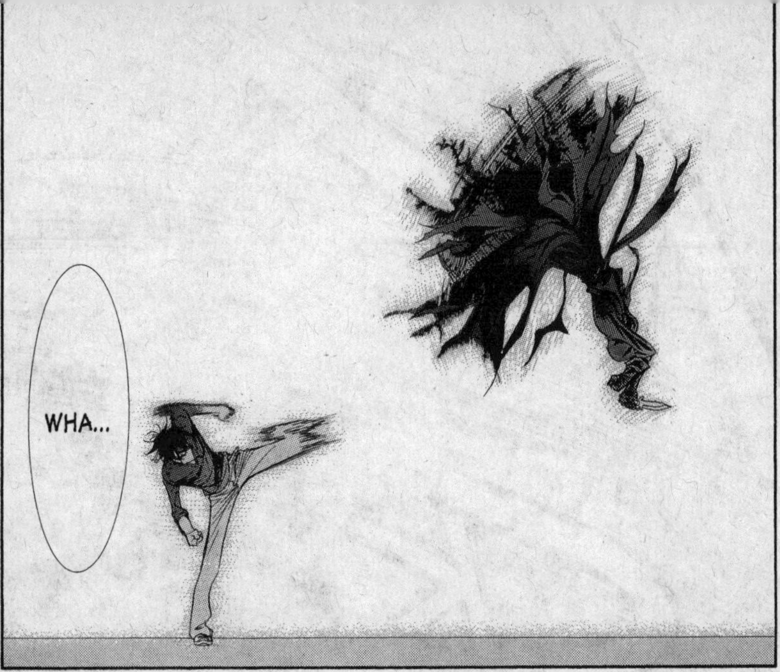
WHA...

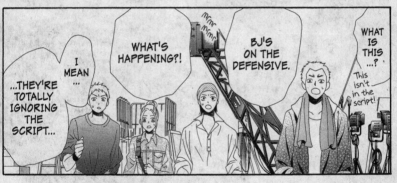

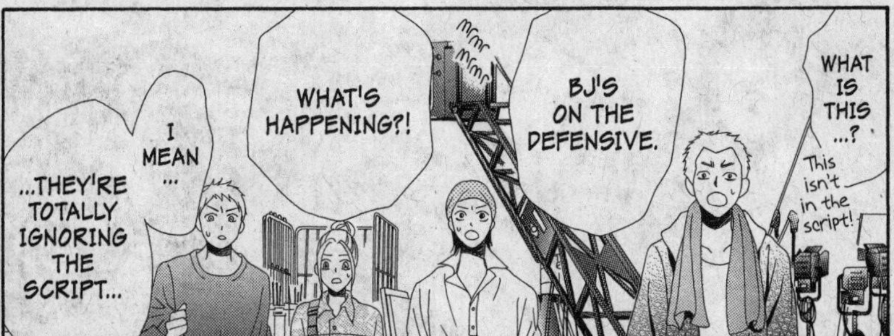
WHAT IS THIS ...?
This isn't in the script!
BJ'S ON THE DEFENSIVE.
mrmr mrmr
WHAT'S HAPPENING?!
I MEAN ...
...THEY'RE TOTALLY IGNORING THE SCRIPT...

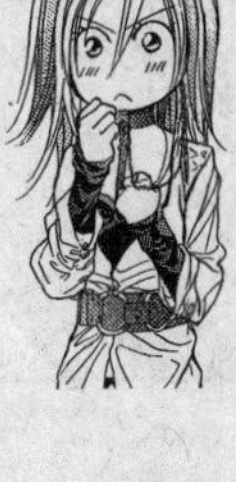

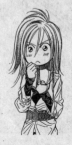

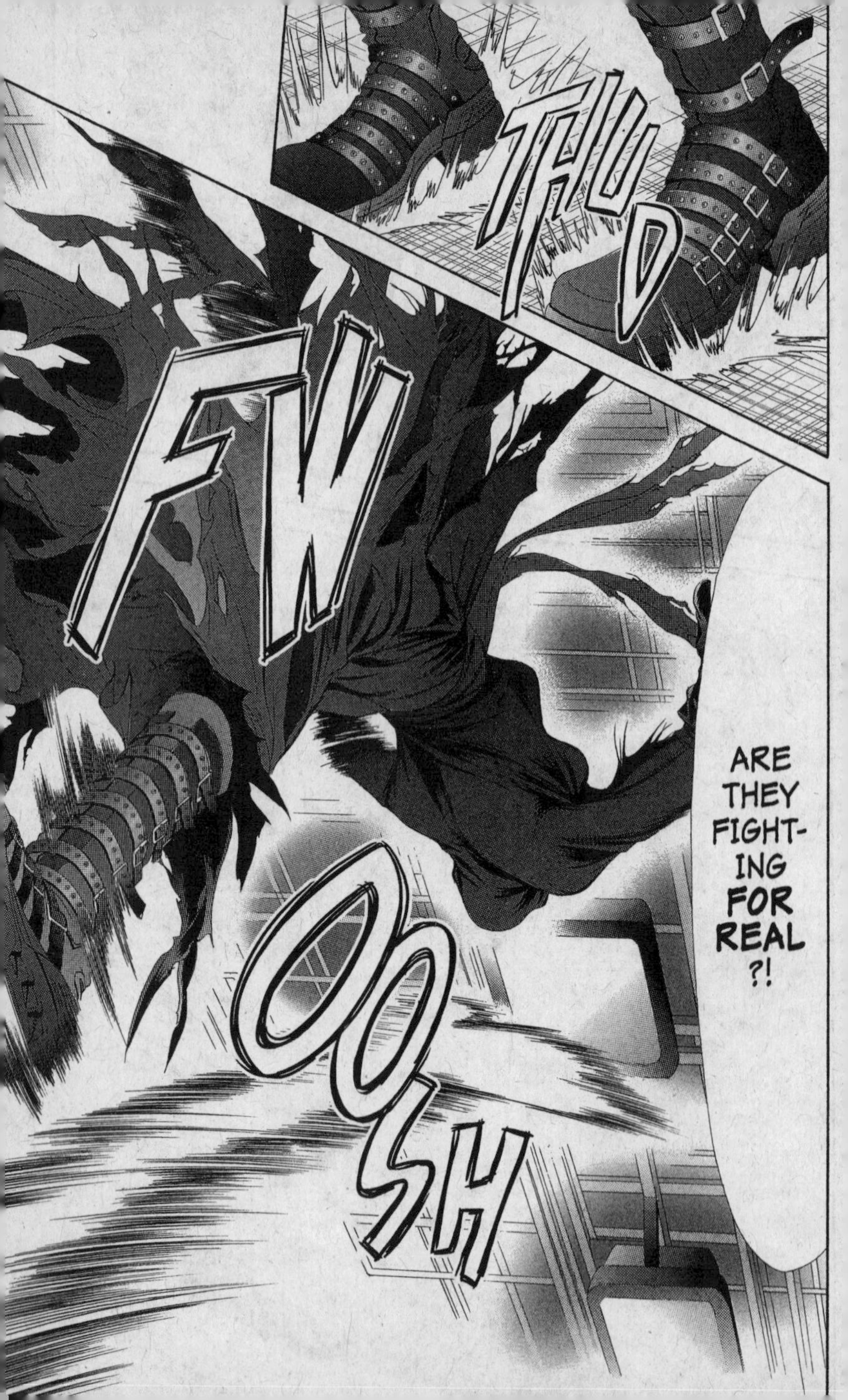
THUD
ARE THEY FIGHT-ING FOR REAL ?!
FWOOSH

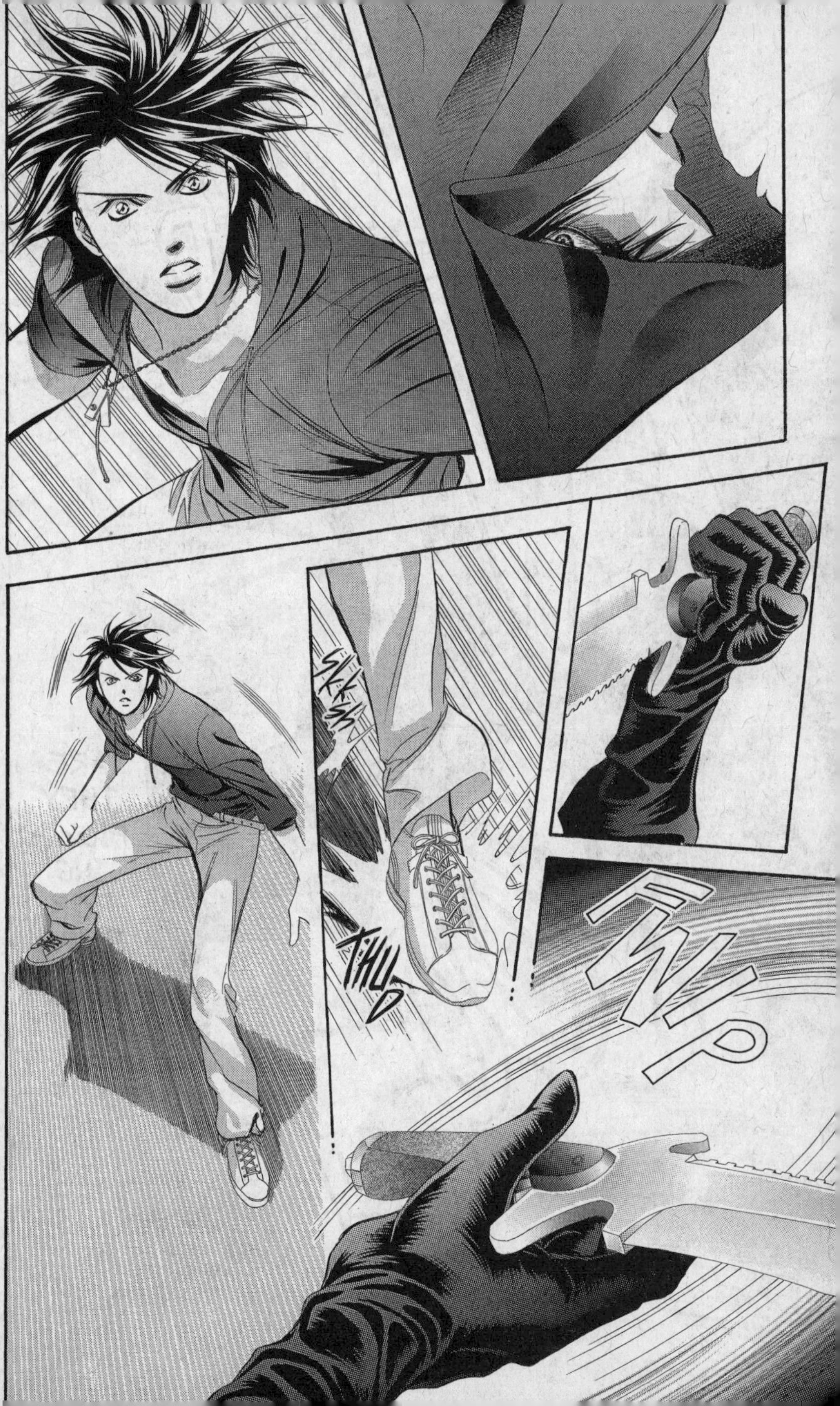
FWIP
SHKSH
THUD

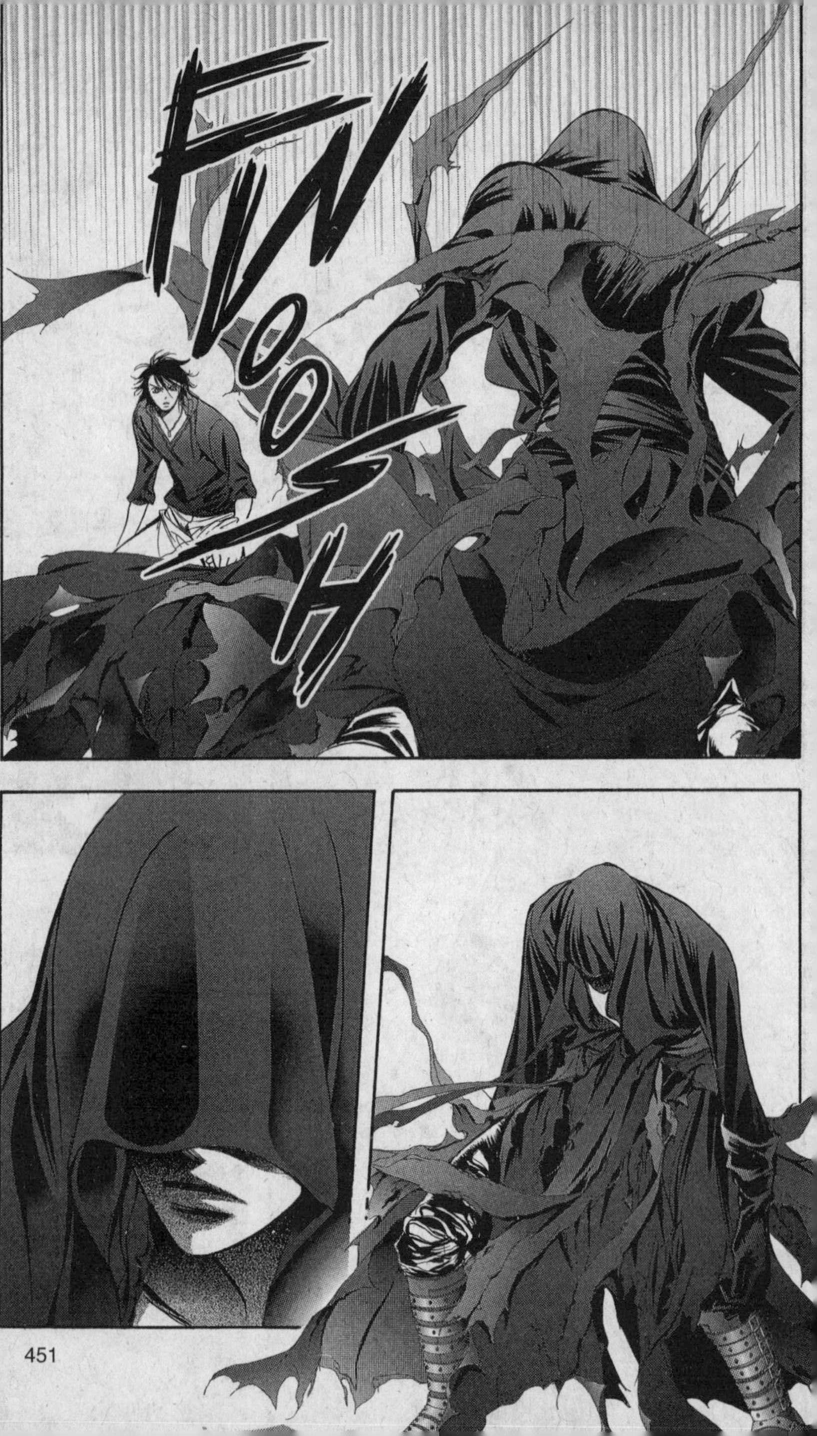
FWOOSH

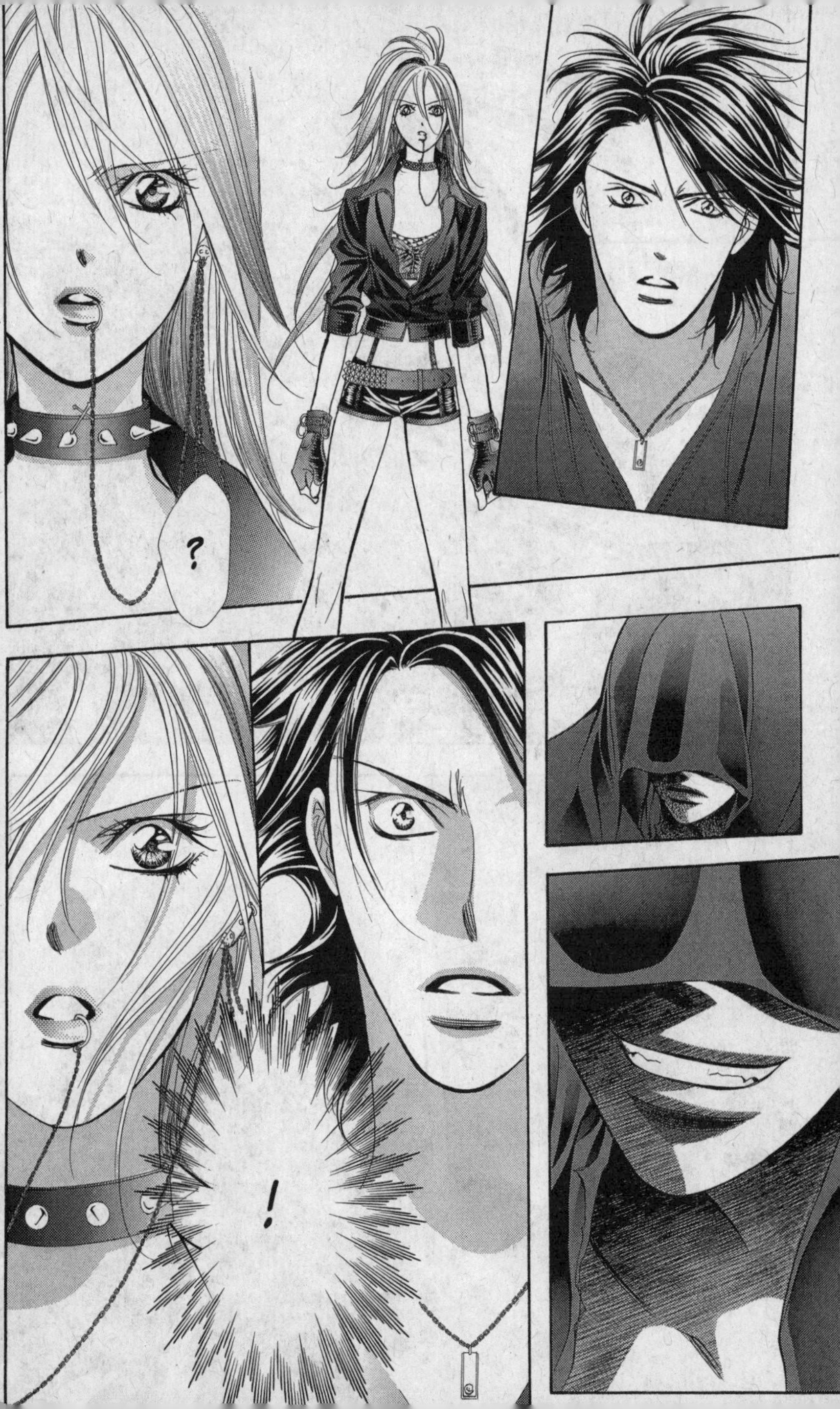
?
!

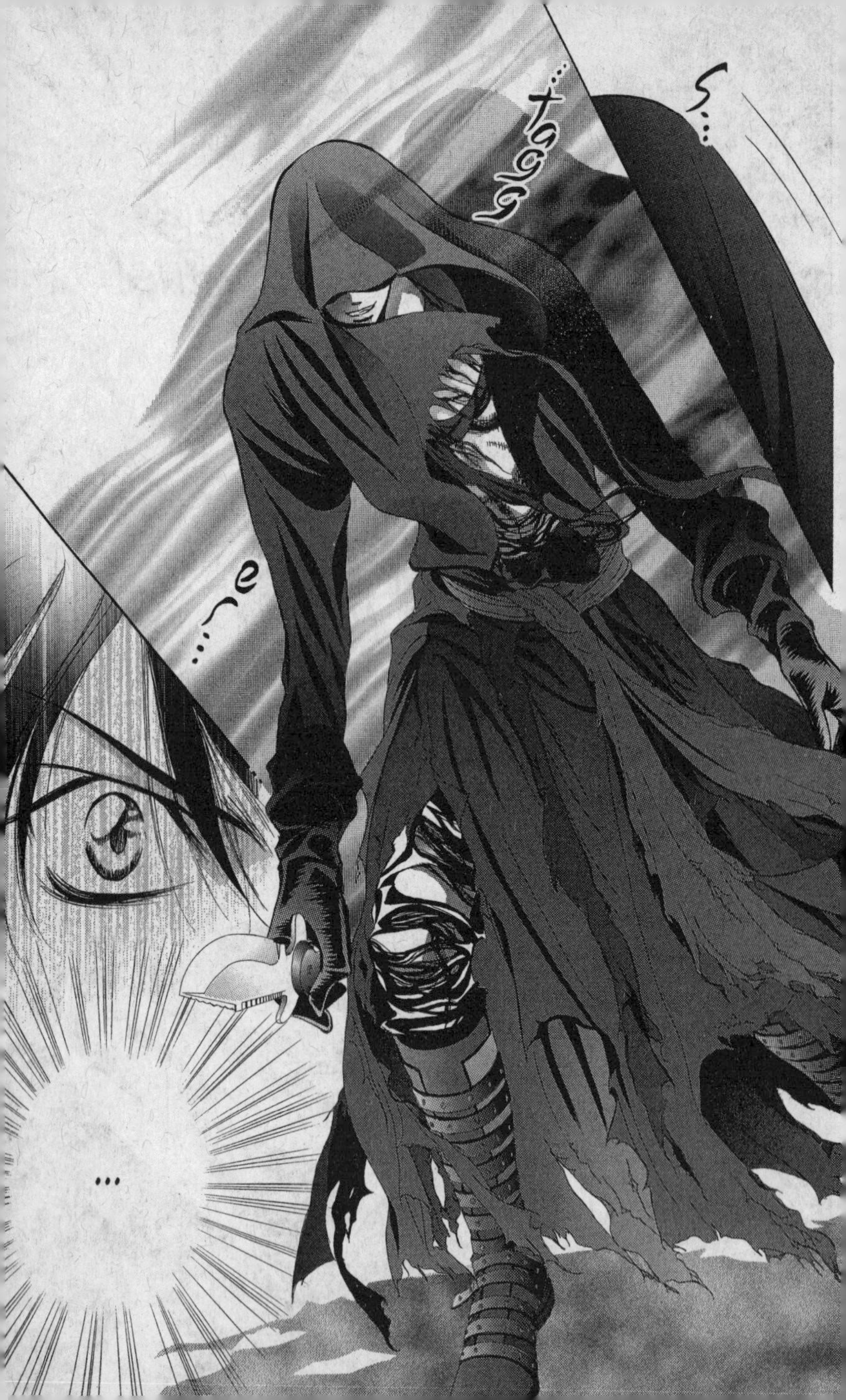
s...
...tagg
er...
...

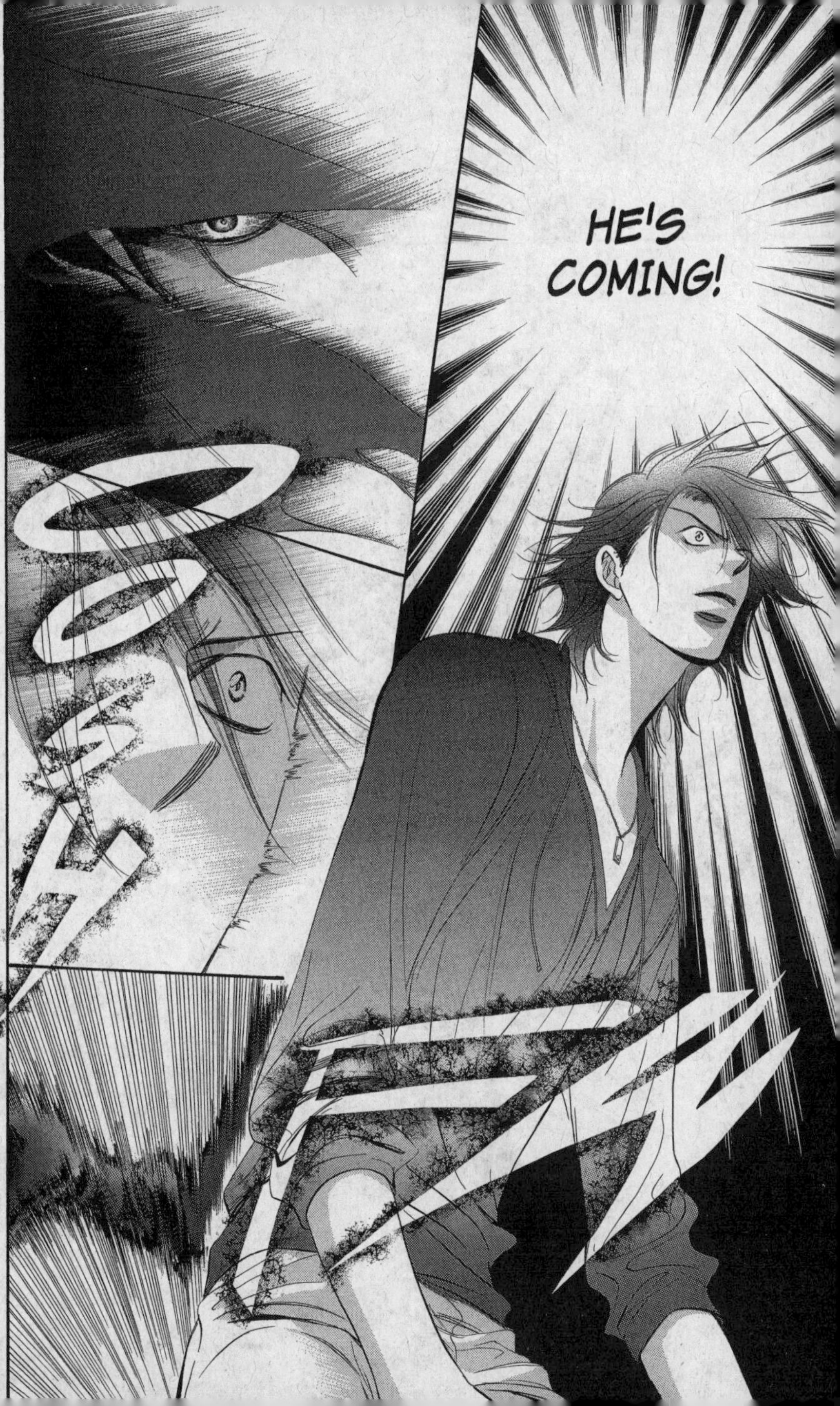
HE'S COMING!

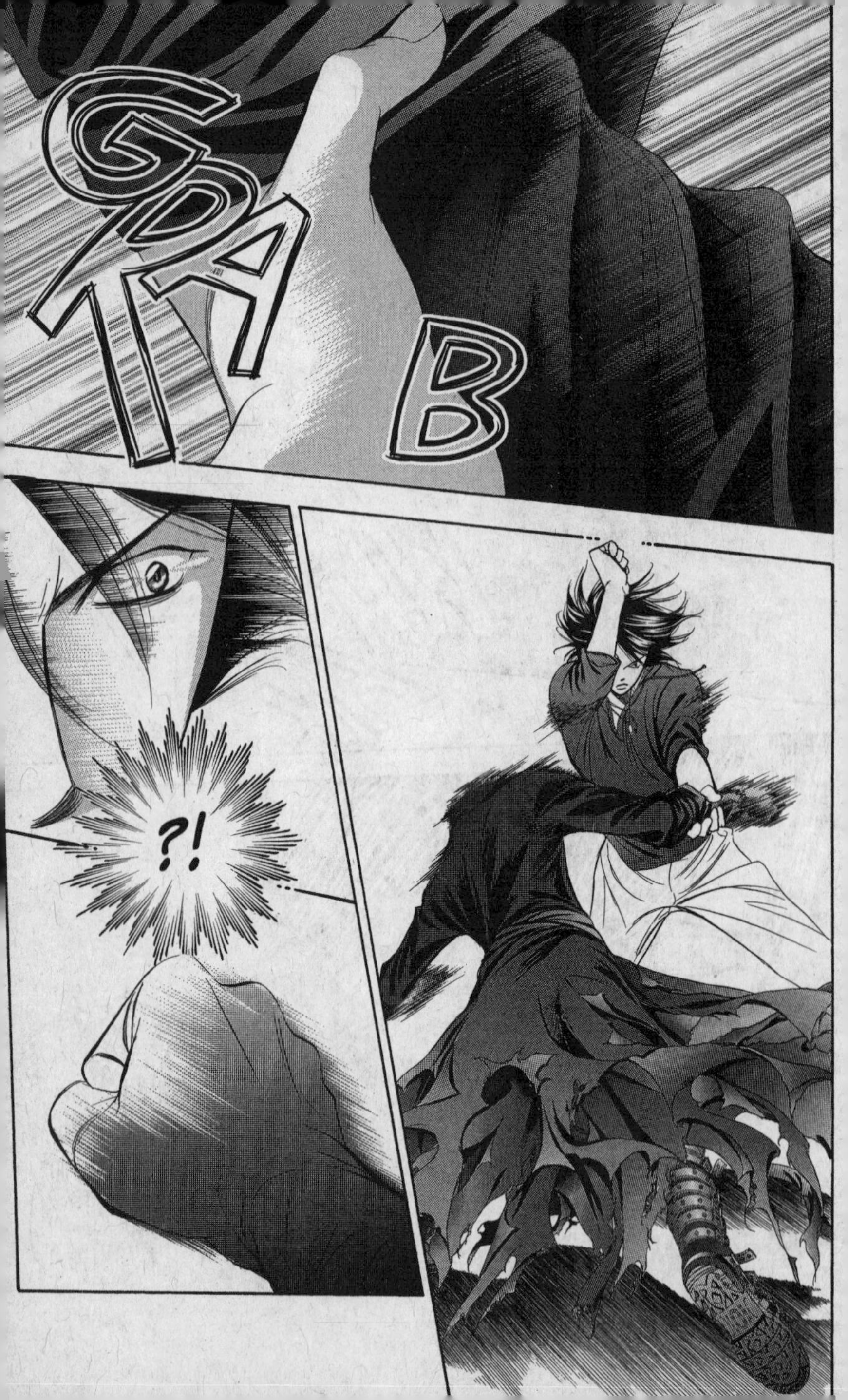
GRAB
?!

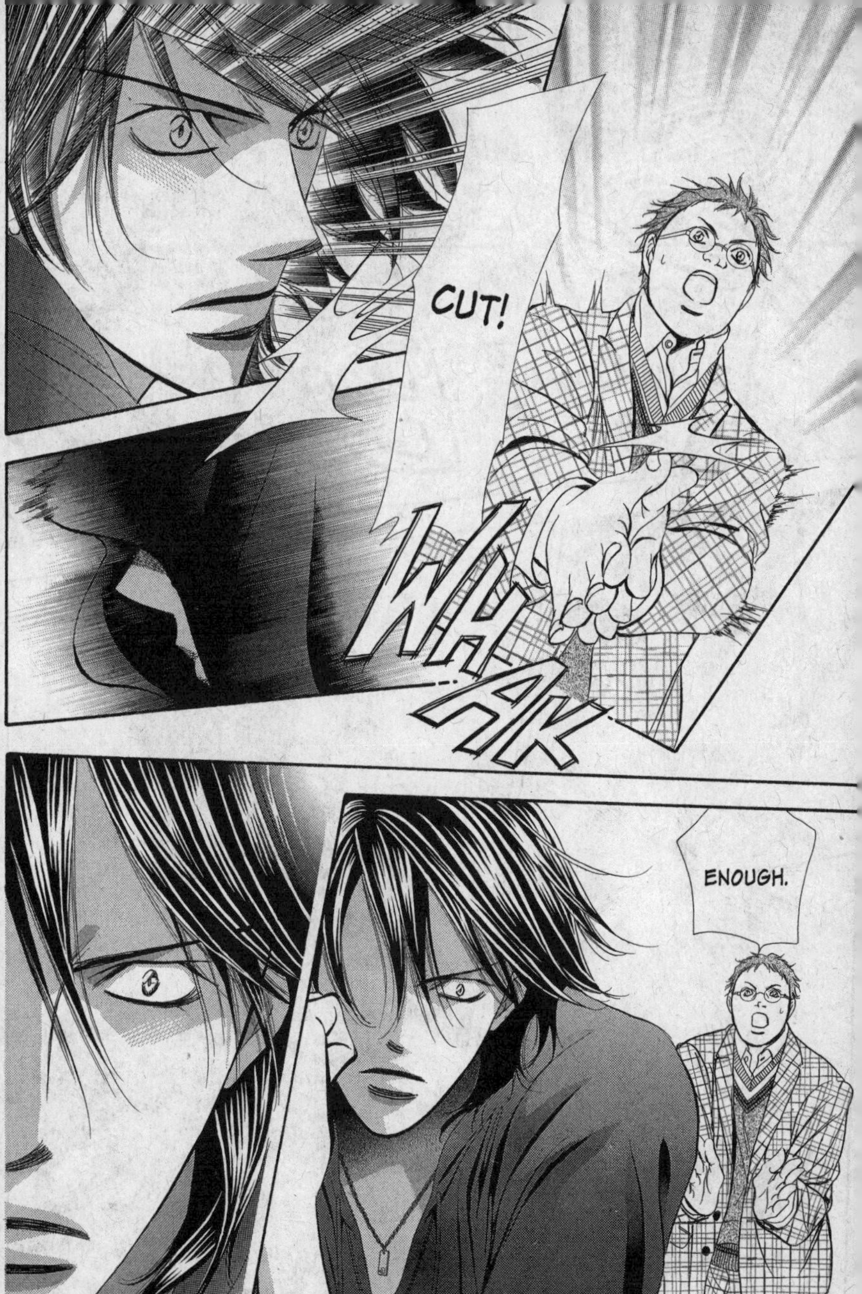
CUT!
WHAAK
ENOUGH.

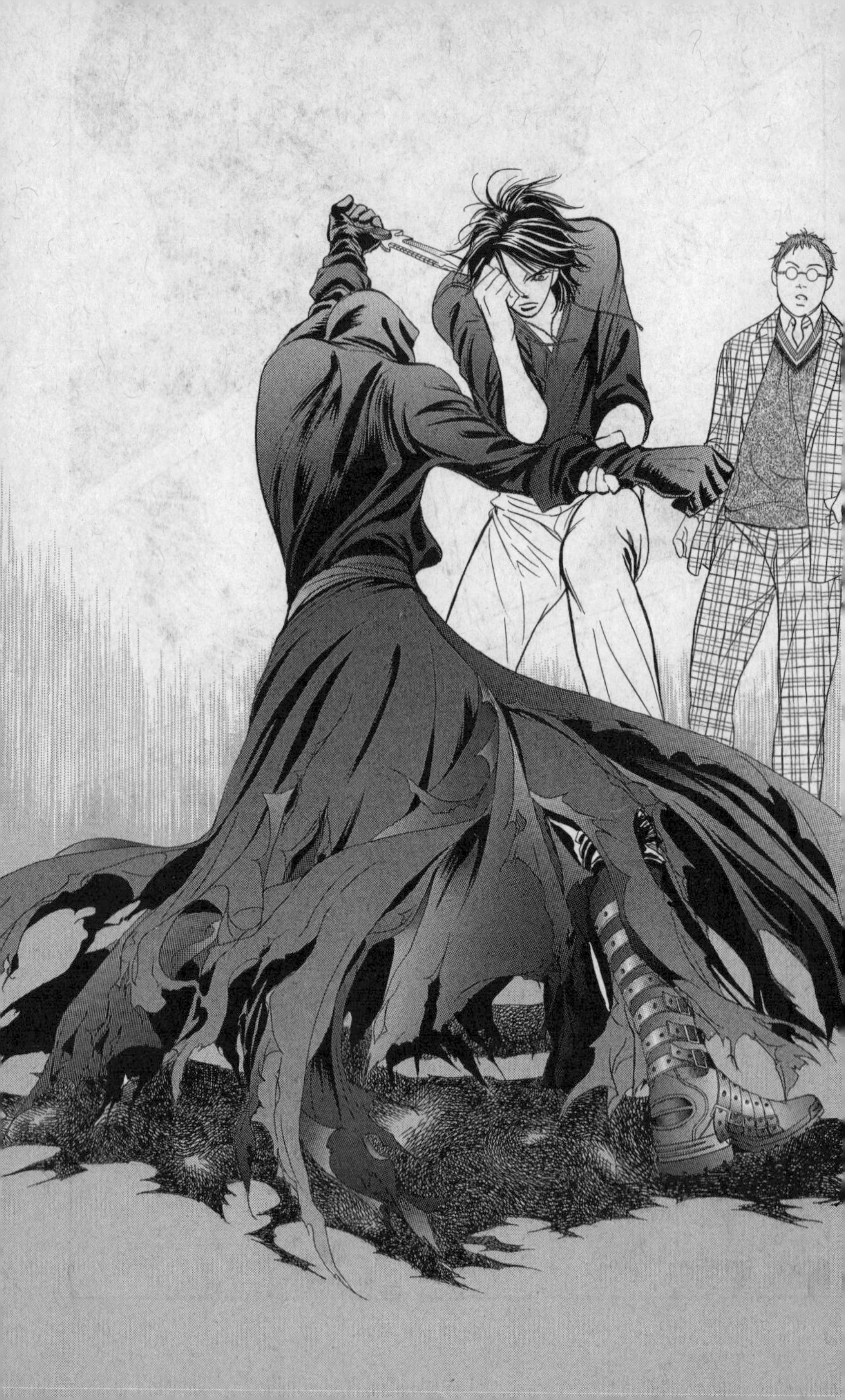

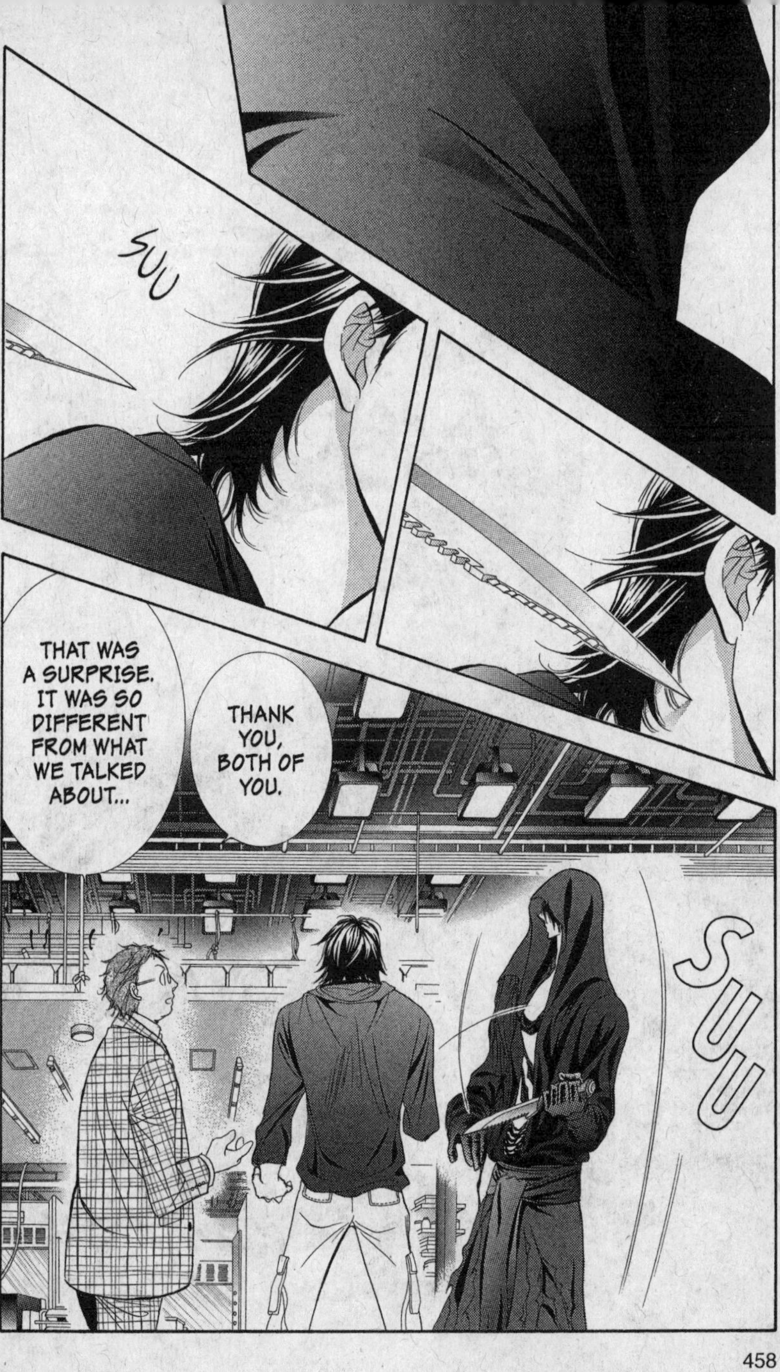
SUU
SUU
THANK YOU, BOTH OF YOU.
THAT WAS A SURPRISE. IT WAS SO DIFFERENT FROM WHAT WE TALKED ABOUT...

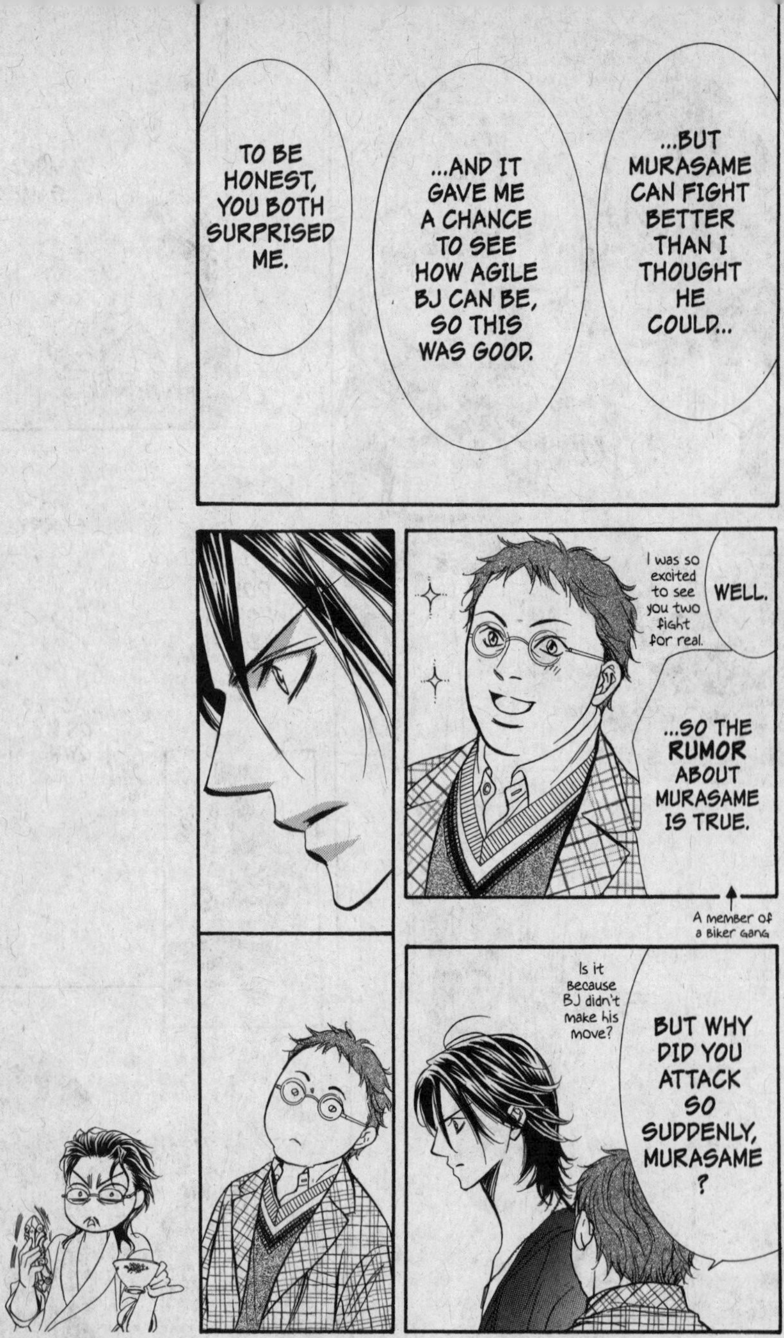
...BUT MURASAME CAN FIGHT BETTER THAN I THOUGHT HE COULD...
...AND IT GAVE ME A CHANCE TO SEE HOW AGILE BJ CAN BE, SO THIS WAS GOOD.
TO BE HONEST, YOU BOTH SURPRISED ME.
WELL.
I was so excited to see you two fight for real.
...SO THE RUMOR ABOUT MURASAME IS TRUE.
A member of a Biker Gang
BUT WHY DID YOU ATTACK SO SUDDENLY, MURASAME?
Is it because BJ didn't make his move?

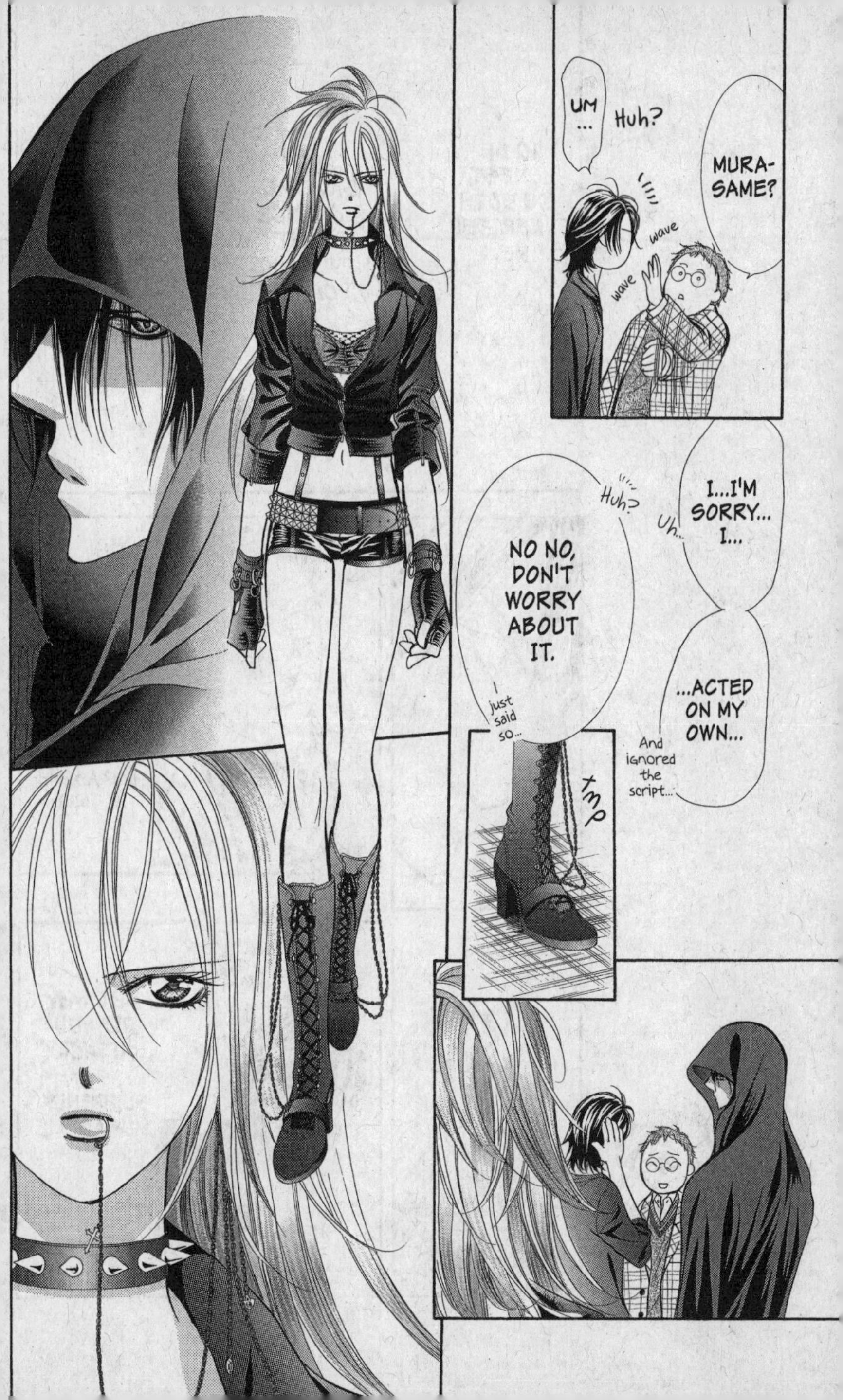
MURA-SAME?
wave
wave
Huh?
UM ...
I...I'M SORRY... I...
Uh...
...ACTED ON MY OWN...
And ignored the script...
Huh?
NO NO, DON'T WORRY ABOUT IT.
I just said so...
tmp

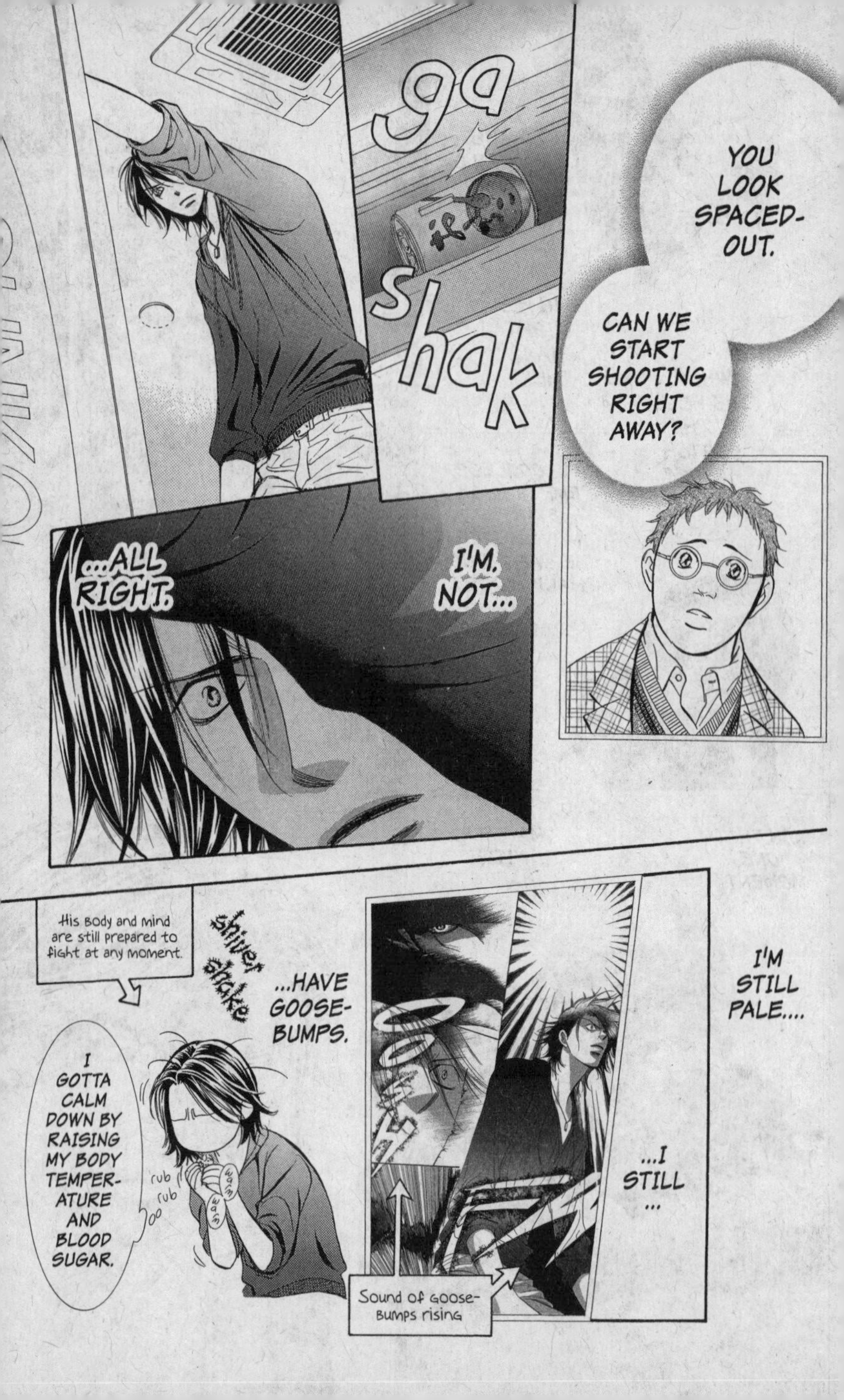
YOU LOOK SPACED-OUT.
CAN WE START SHOOTING RIGHT AWAY?
ga
shak
I'M. NOT...
...ALL RIGHT.
I'M STILL PALE....
...I STILL ...
Sound of goose-bumps rising
...HAVE GOOSE-BUMPS.
shiver shake
His body and mind are still prepared to fight at any moment.
I GOTTA CALM DOWN BY RAISING MY BODY TEMPER-ATURE AND BLOOD SUGAR.
rub rub
warm
warm

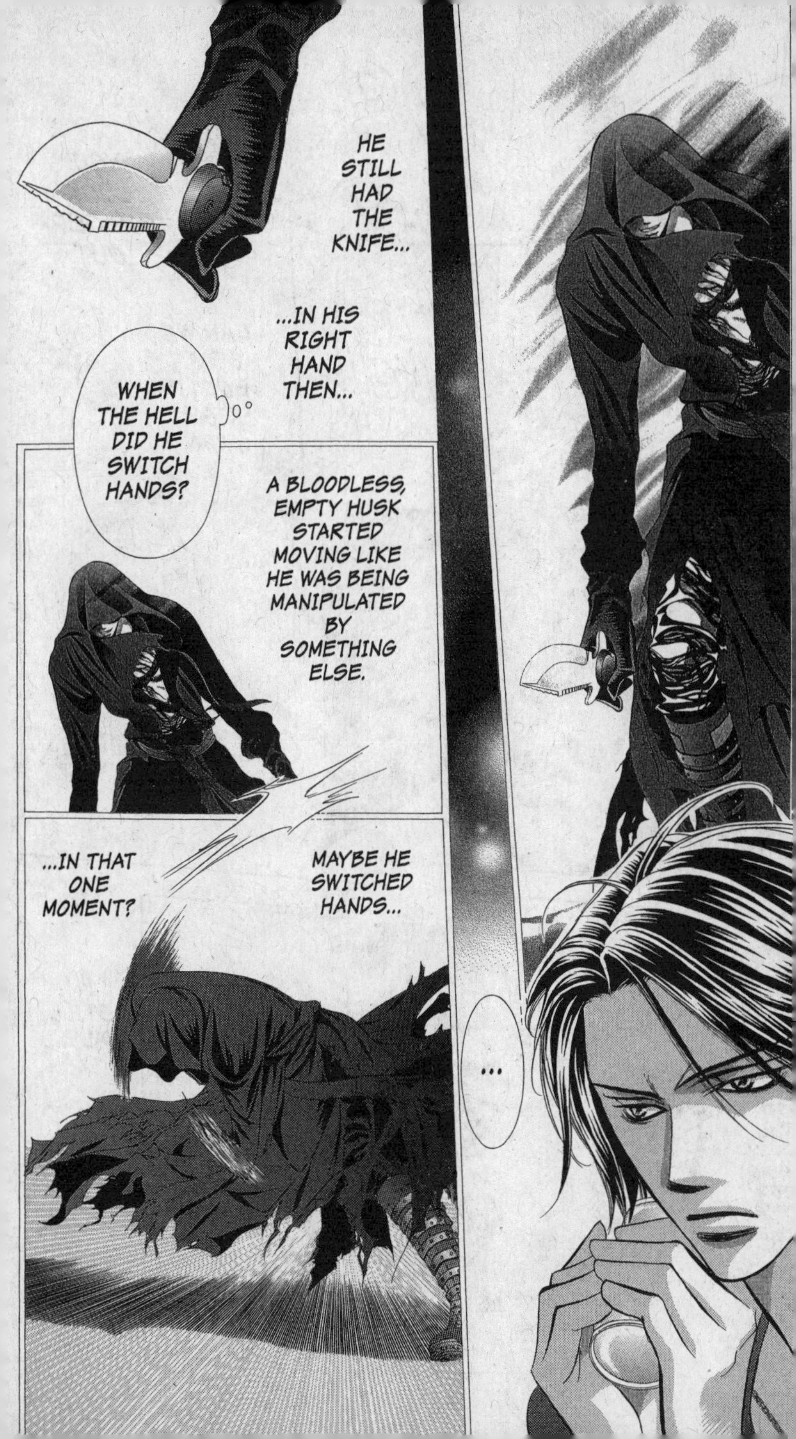
...
HE STILL HAD THE KNIFE...
...IN HIS RIGHT HAND THEN...
WHEN THE HELL DID HE SWITCH HANDS?
A BLOODLESS, EMPTY HUSK STARTED MOVING LIKE HE WAS BEING MANIPULATED BY SOMETHING ELSE.
MAYBE HE SWITCHED HANDS...
...IN THAT ONE MOMENT?

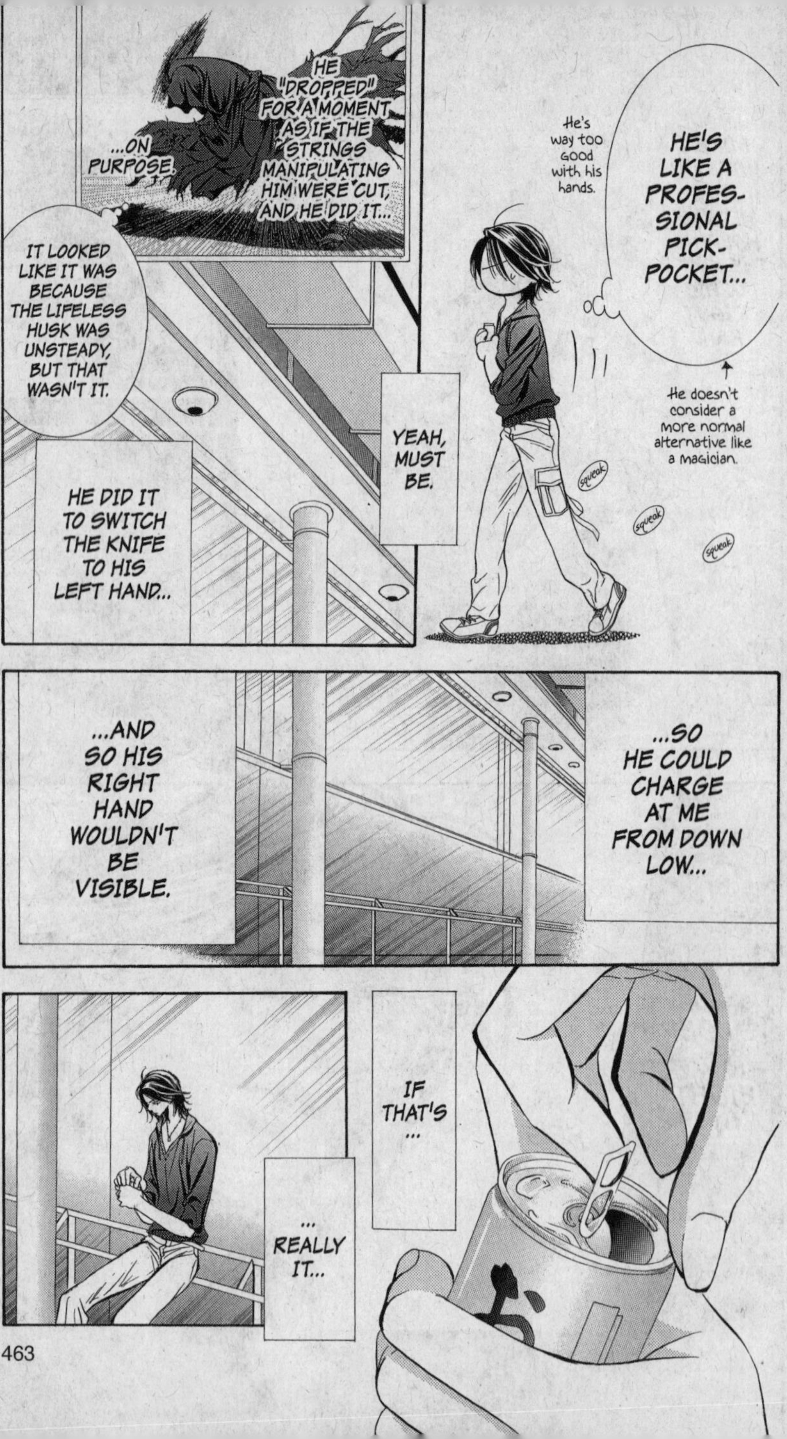
HE'S LIKE A PROFES-SIONAL PICK-POCKET...
He's way too good with his hands.
He doesn't consider a more normal alternative like a magician.
squeak
squeak
squeak
YEAH, MUST BE.
HE "DROPPED" FOR A MOMENT AS IF THE STRINGS MANIPULATING HIM WERE CUT, AND HE DID IT...
...ON PURPOSE.
IT LOOKED LIKE IT WAS BECAUSE THE LIFELESS HUSK WAS UNSTEADY, BUT THAT WASN'T IT.
HE DID IT TO SWITCH THE KNIFE TO HIS LEFT HAND...
...SO HE COULD CHARGE AT ME FROM DOWN LOW...
...AND SO HIS RIGHT HAND WOULDN'T BE VISIBLE.
IF THAT'S ...
... REALLY IT...

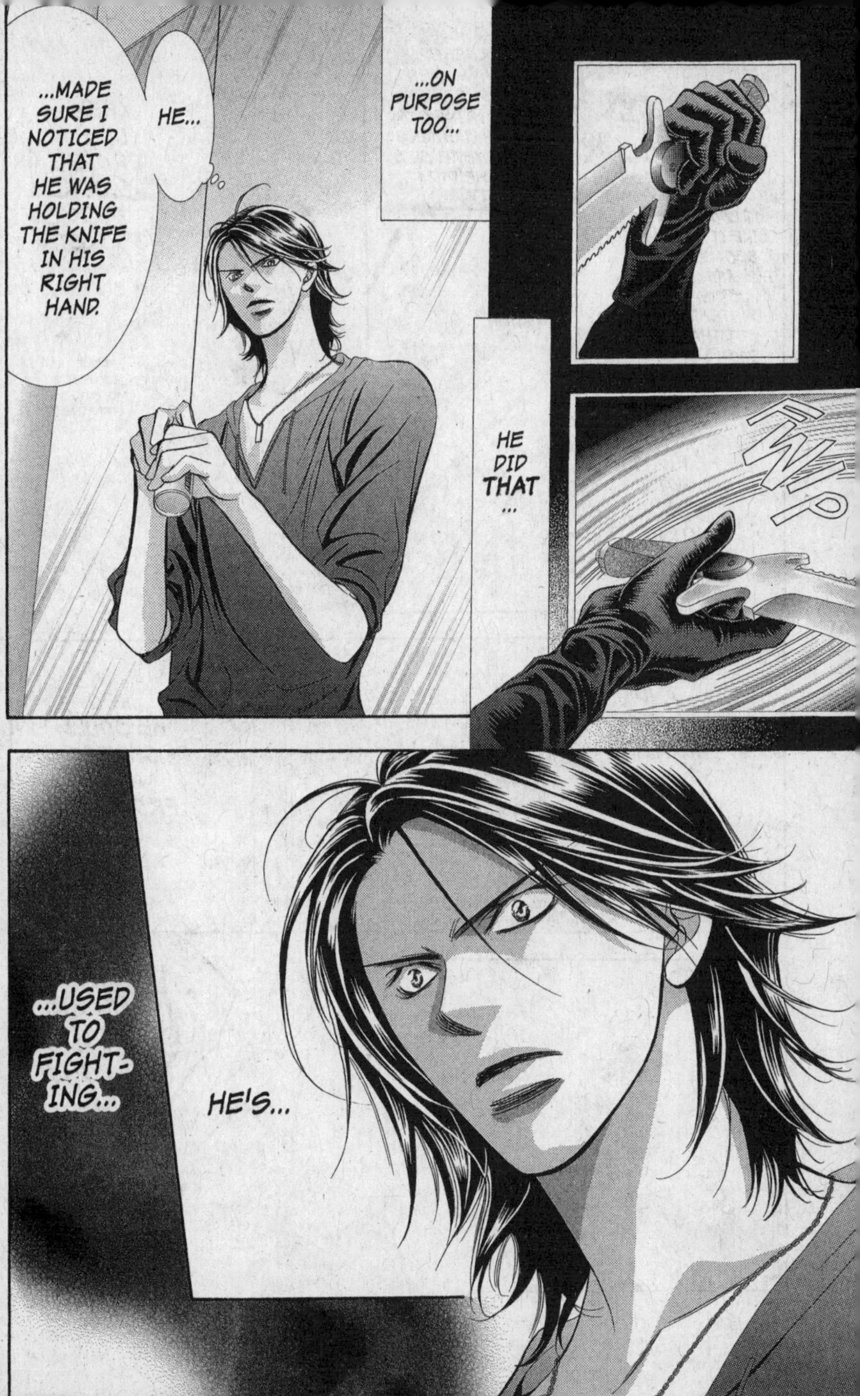
FWIP
HE DID THAT...
...ON PURPOSE TOO...
HE...
...MADE SURE I NOTICED THAT HE WAS HOLDING THE KNIFE IN HIS RIGHT HAND.
HE'S...
...USED TO FIGHTING...

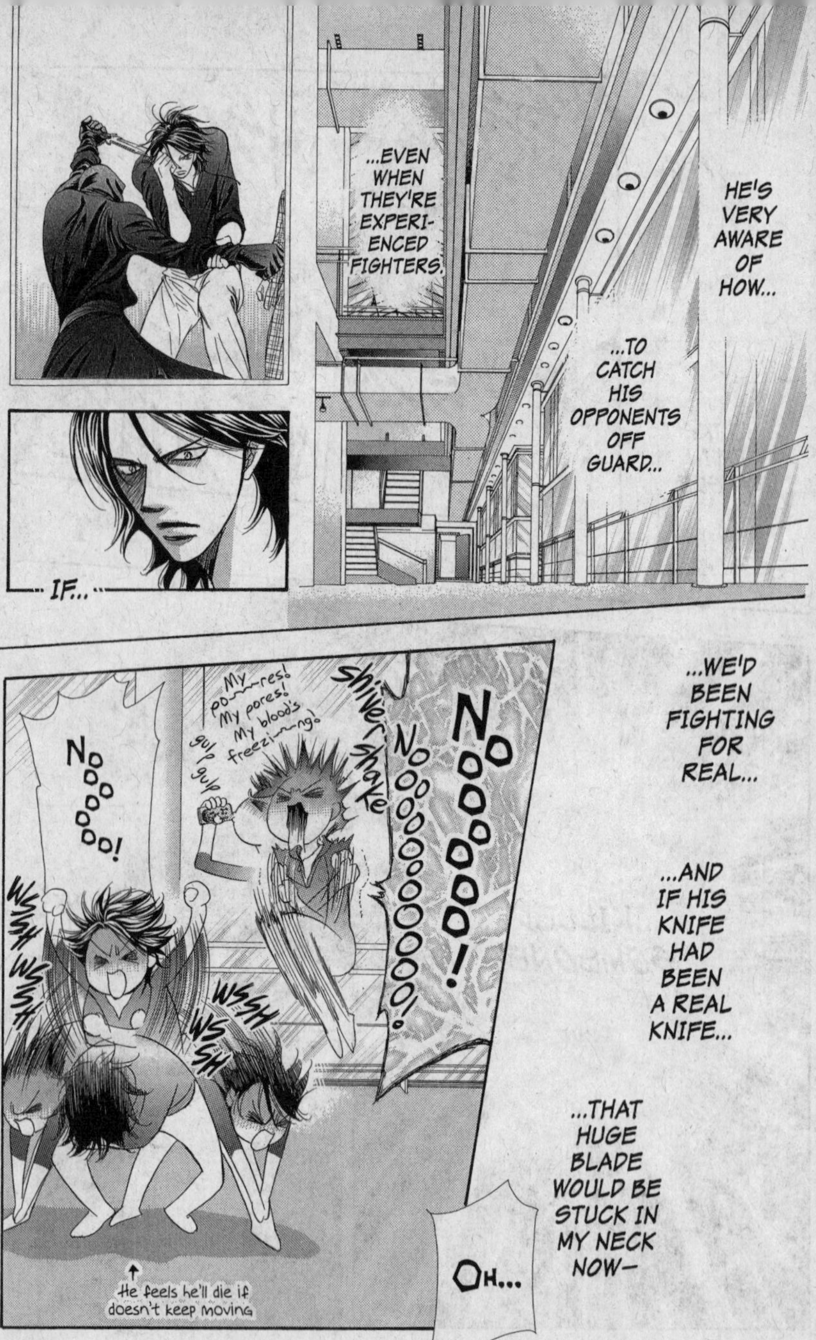
HE'S VERY AWARE OF HOW...
...TO CATCH HIS OPPONENTS OFF GUARD...
...EVEN WHEN THEY'RE EXPERI-ENCED FIGHTERS.
IF...
...WE'D BEEN FIGHTING FOR REAL...
...AND IF HIS KNIFE HAD BEEN A REAL KNIFE...
...THAT HUGE BLADE WOULD BE STUCK IN MY NECK NOW—
OH...
NOOOOOOOO!
NOOOOOOOOOOOOOOOO!
shiver shake
My po~~res! My pores! My blood's freezi~~ng!
gulp gulp
NOOOOOOO!
WSSH WSSH
WSSH WSSH
He feels he'll die if doesn't keep moving

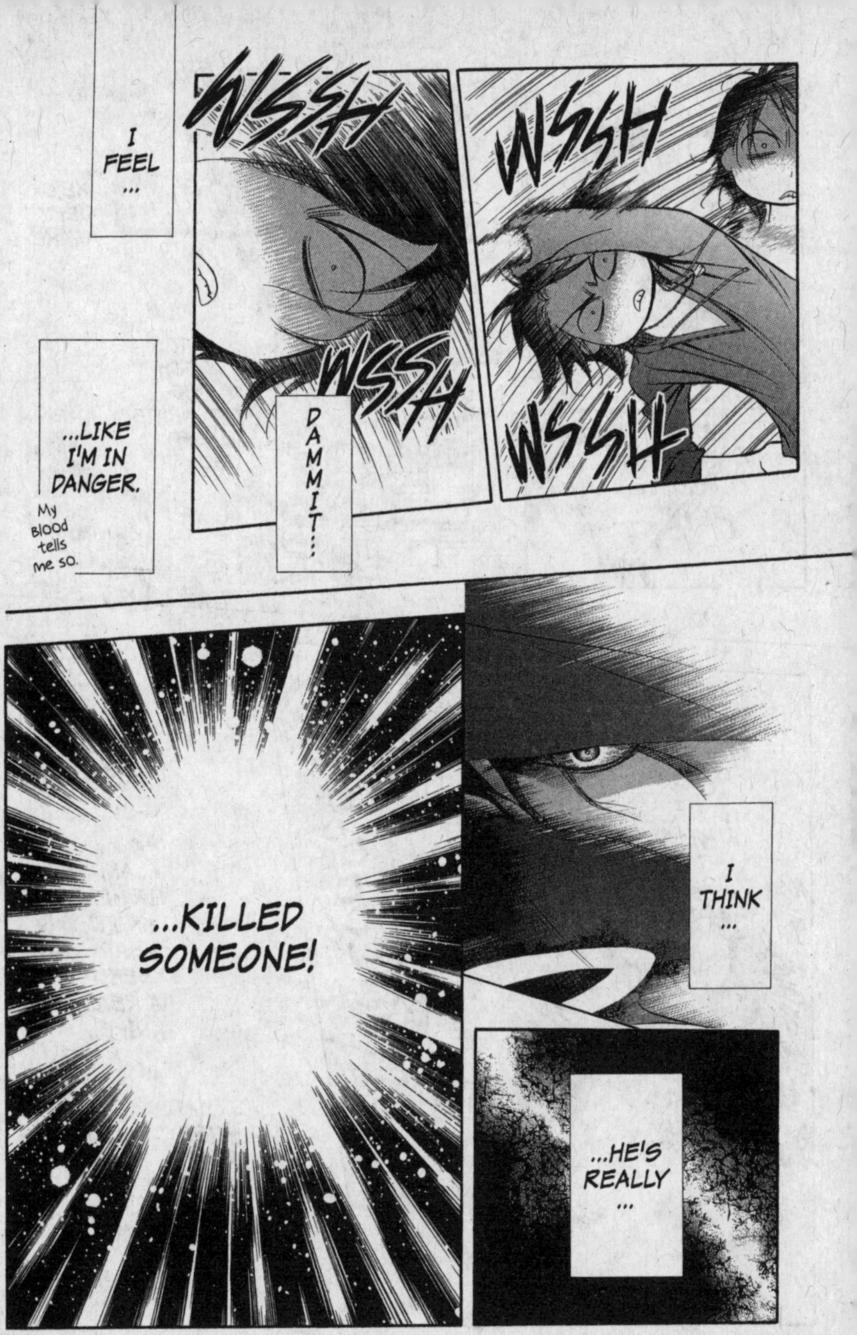
WSSH
WSSH
WSSH
WSSH
DAMMIT...
I FEEL...
...LIKE I'M IN DANGER.
My blood tells me so.
I THINK...
...HE'S REALLY...
...KILLED SOMEONE!

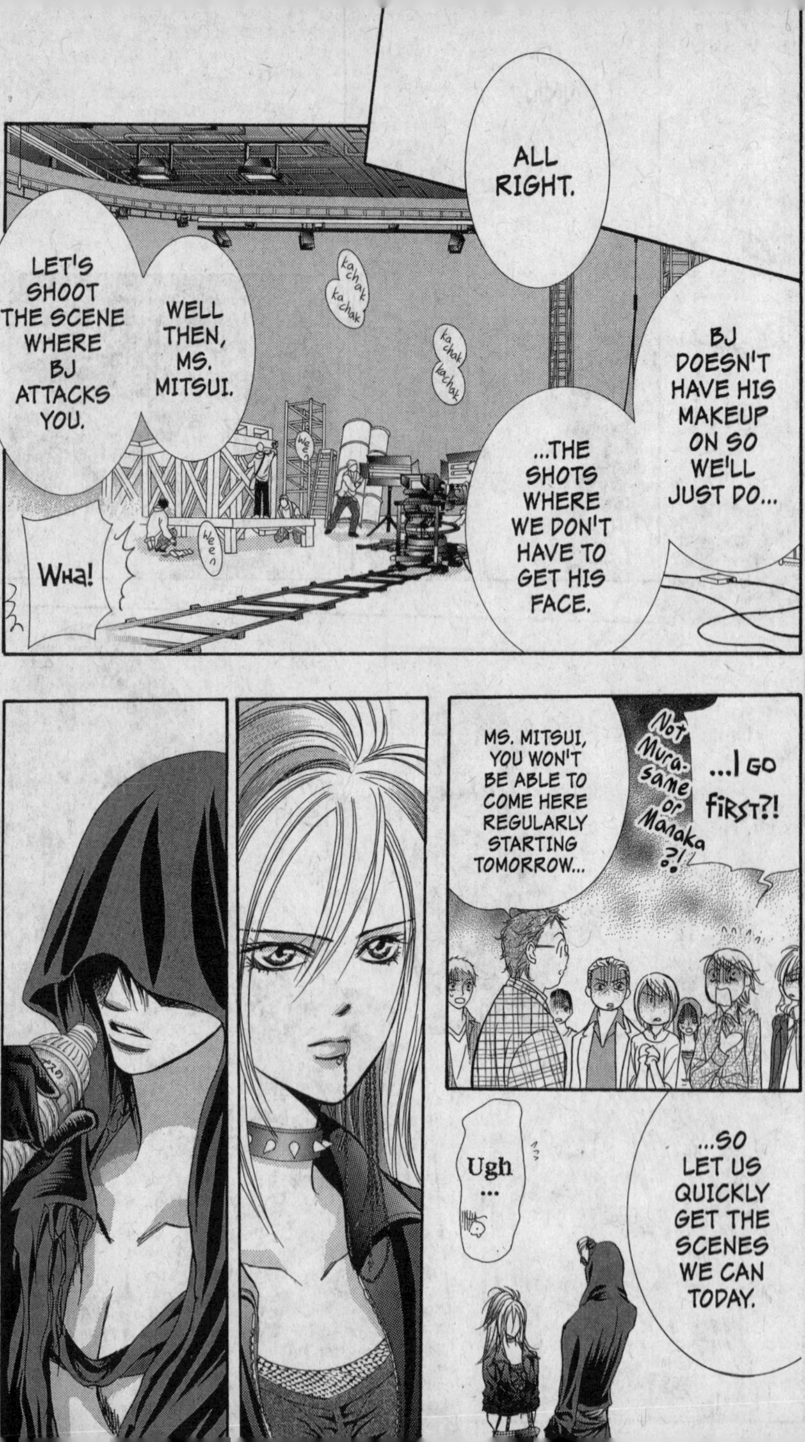
ALL RIGHT.
BJ DOESN'T HAVE HIS MAKEUP ON SO WE'LL JUST DO...
...THE SHOTS WHERE WE DON'T HAVE TO GET HIS FACE.
ka chak kachak
ka chak ka chak
WELL THEN, MS. MITSUI.
LET'S SHOOT THE SCENE WHERE BJ ATTACKS YOU.
Wha!
...I GO FIRST?!
Not Mura-same or Manaka?!
MS. MITSUI, YOU WON'T BE ABLE TO COME HERE REGULARLY STARTING TOMORROW...
...SO LET US QUICKLY GET THE SCENES WE CAN TODAY.
Ugh ...

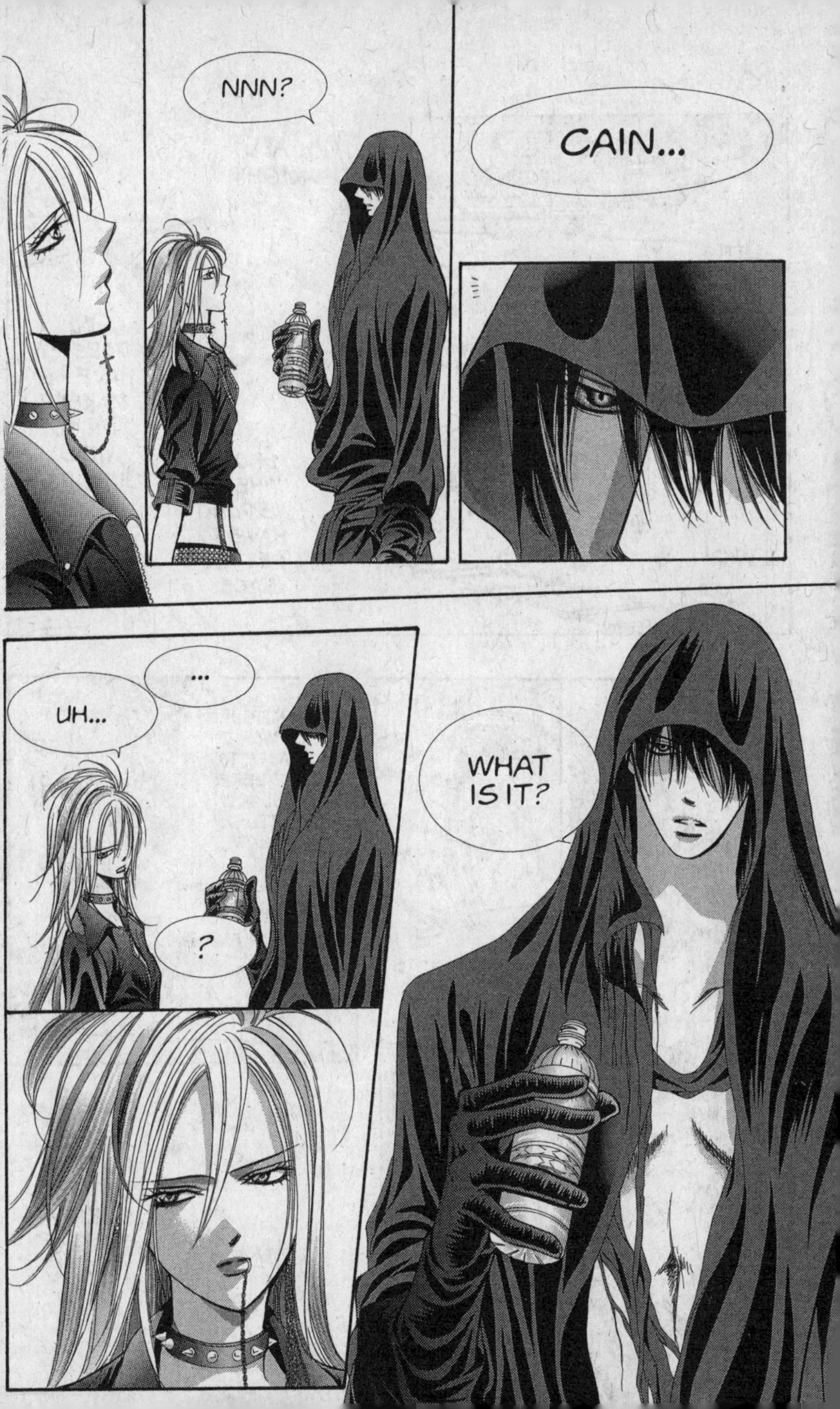
CAIN...
NNN?
WHAT IS IT?
...
UH...
?

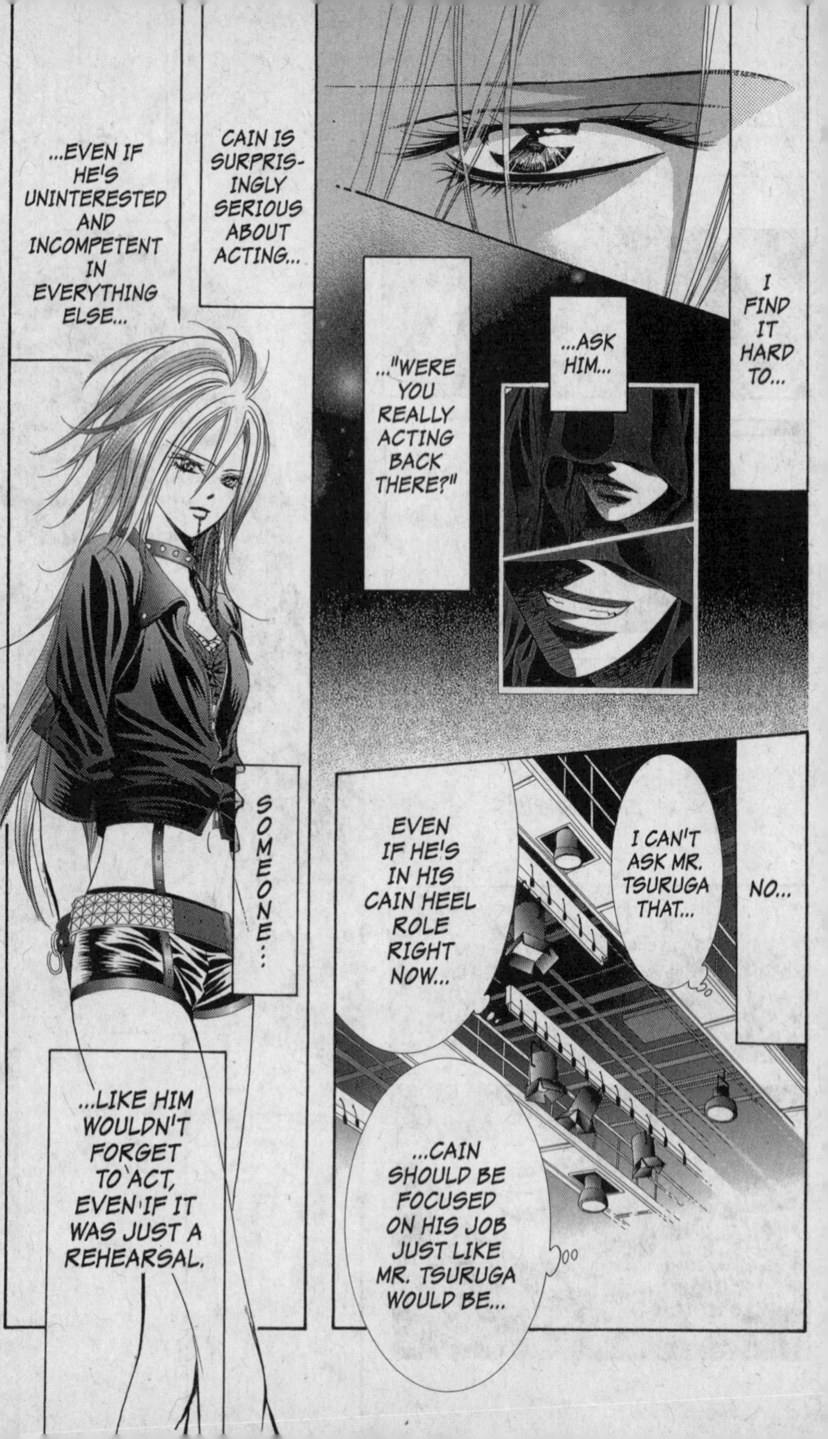

I FIND IT HARD TO...
...ASK HIM...
..."WERE YOU REALLY ACTING BACK THERE?"
NO...
I CAN'T ASK MR. TSURUGA THAT...
EVEN IF HE'S IN HIS CAIN HEEL ROLE RIGHT NOW...
...CAIN SHOULD BE FOCUSED ON HIS JOB JUST LIKE MR. TSURUGA WOULD BE...
CAIN IS SURPRISINGLY SERIOUS ABOUT ACTING...
...EVEN IF HE'S UNINTERESTED AND INCOMPETENT IN EVERYTHING ELSE...
SOMEONE...
...LIKE HIM WOULDN'T FORGET TO ACT, EVEN IF IT WAS JUST A REHEARSAL.

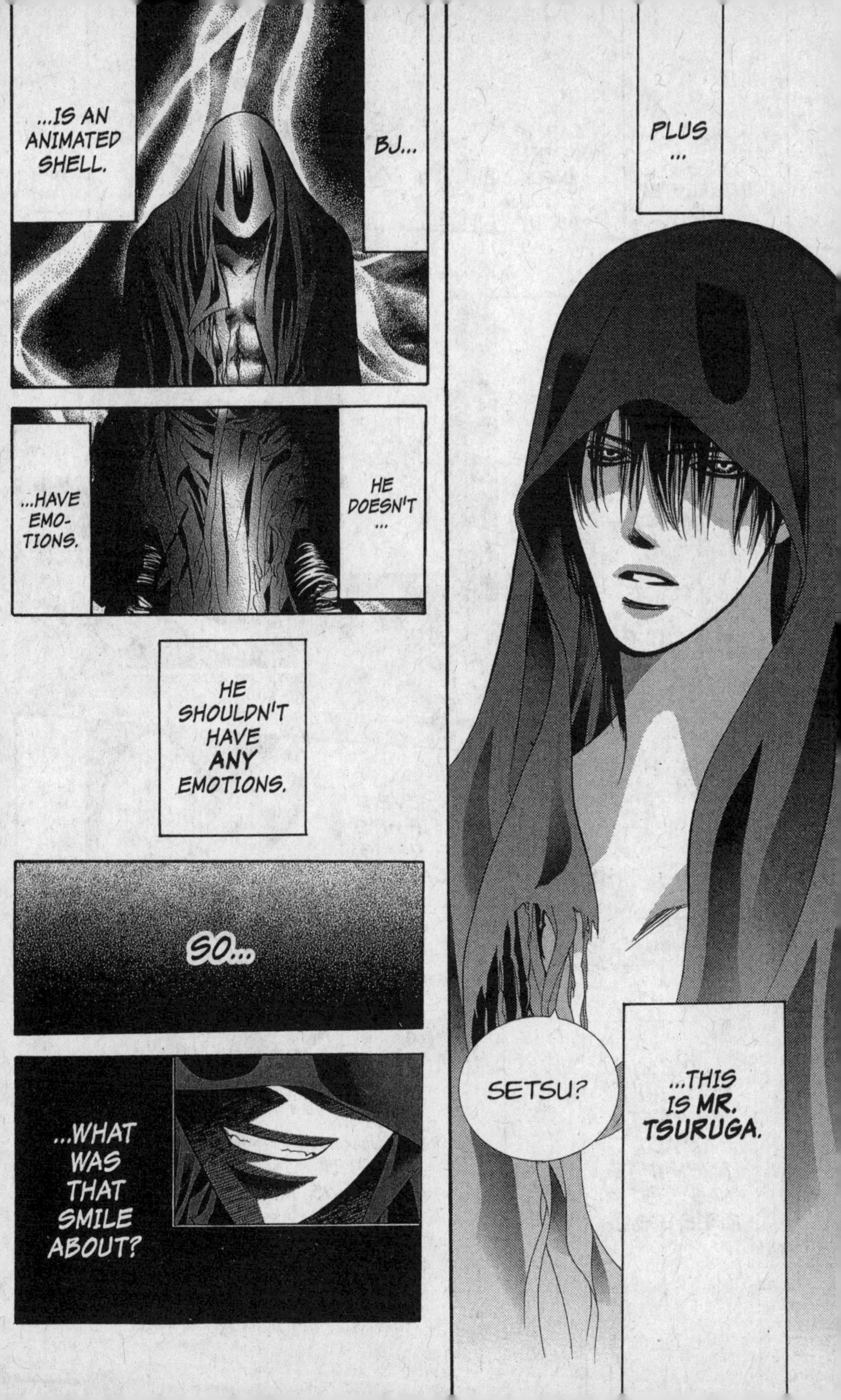
PLUS...
...THIS IS MR. TSURUGA.
SETSU?
BJ...
...IS AN ANIMATED SHELL.
HE DOESN'T...
...HAVE EMOTIONS.
HE SHOULDN'T HAVE ANY EMOTIONS.
SO...
...WHAT WAS THAT SMILE ABOUT?

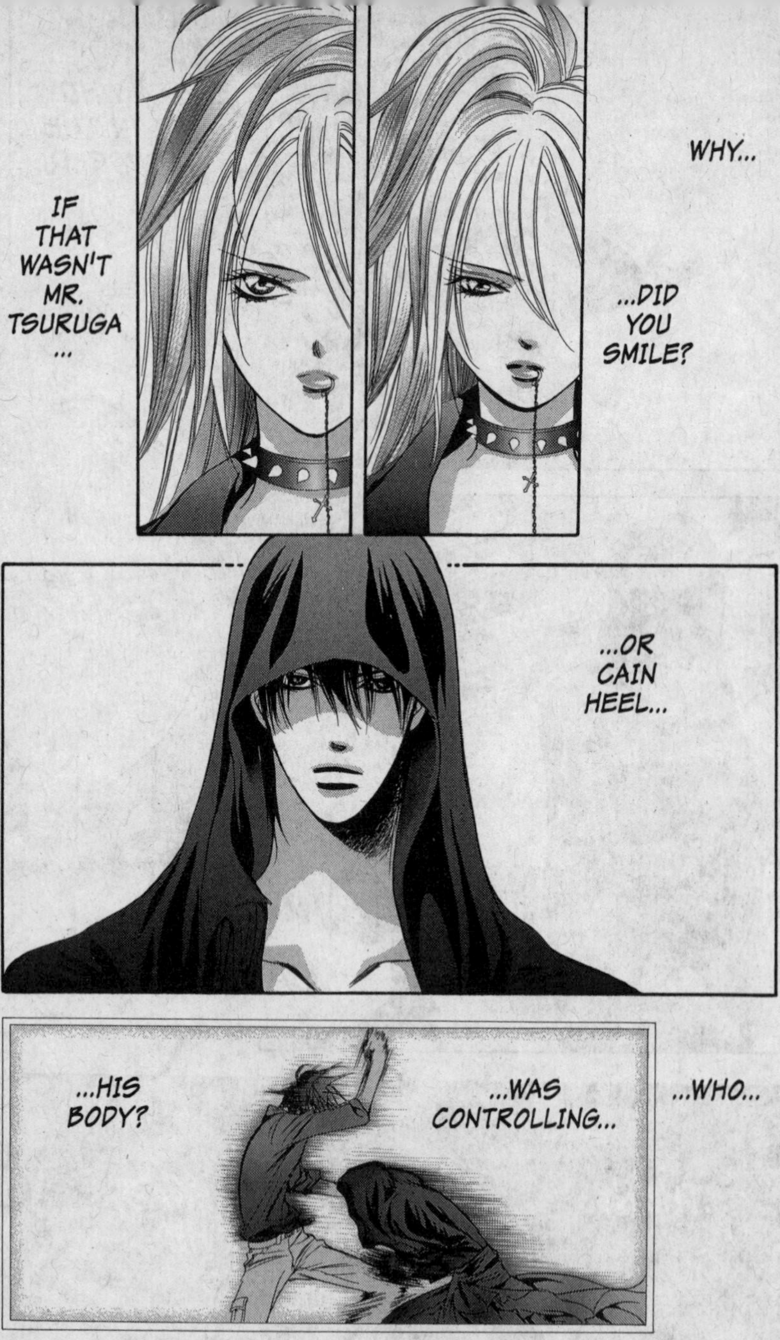
WHY...
...DID YOU SMILE?
IF THAT WASN'T MR. TSURUGA ...
...OR CAIN HEEL...
...WHO...
...WAS CONTROLLING...
...HIS BODY?

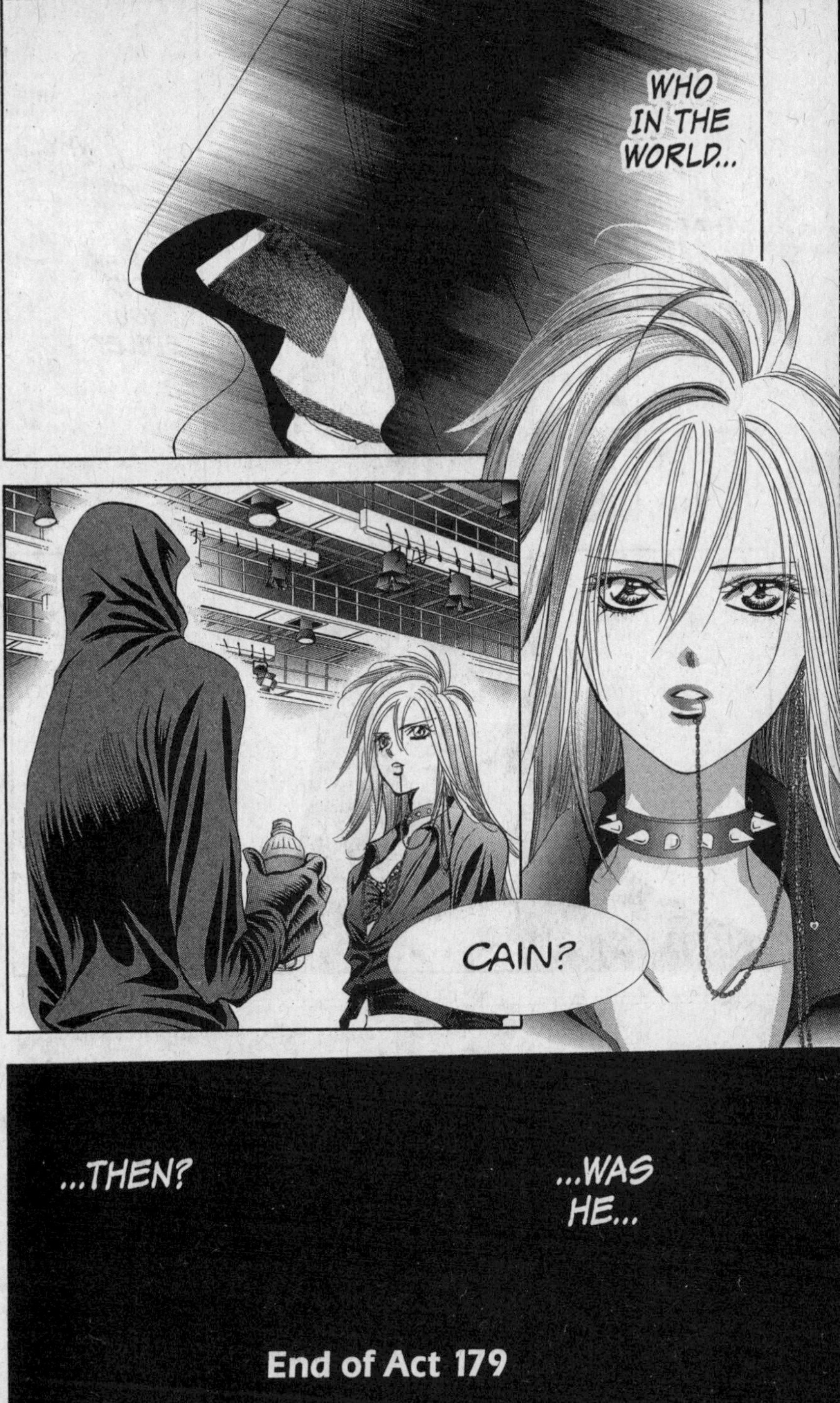
WHO IN THE WORLD...
CAIN?
...WAS HE...
...THEN?
End of Act 179

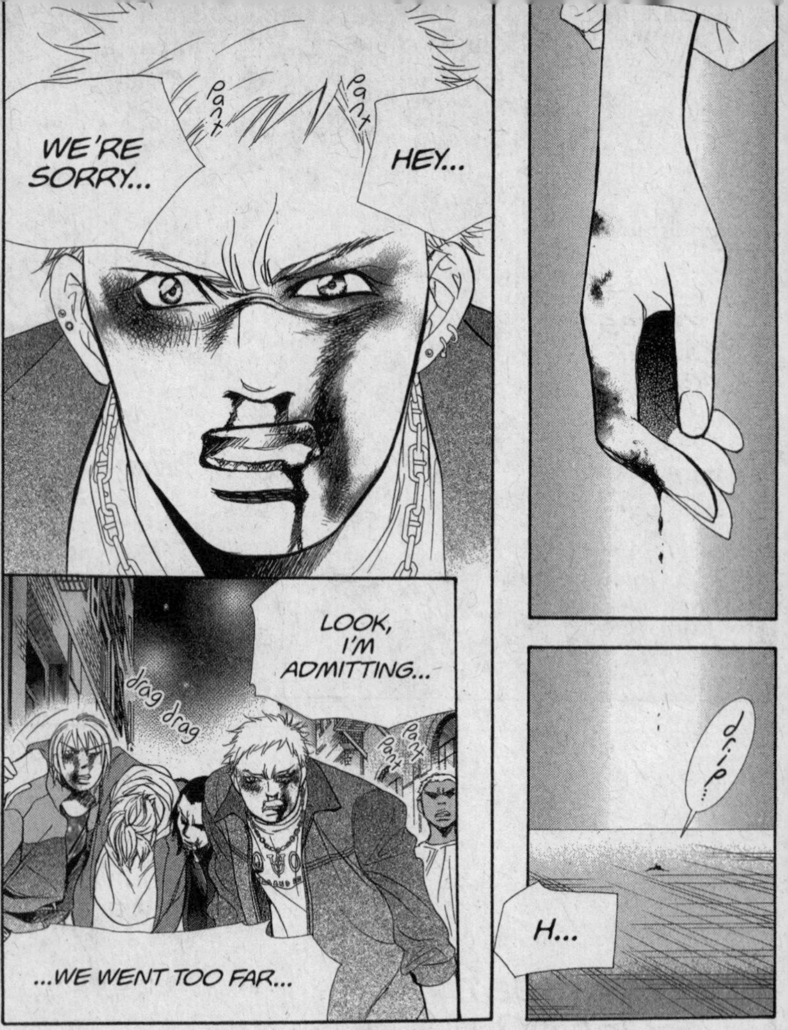
Pant
Pant
HEY...
WE'RE SORRY...
dr.i.p...
H...
LOOK, I'M ADMITTING...
Pant
Pant
drag drag
...WE WENT TOO FAR...

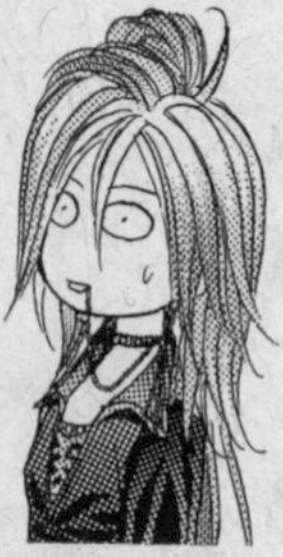

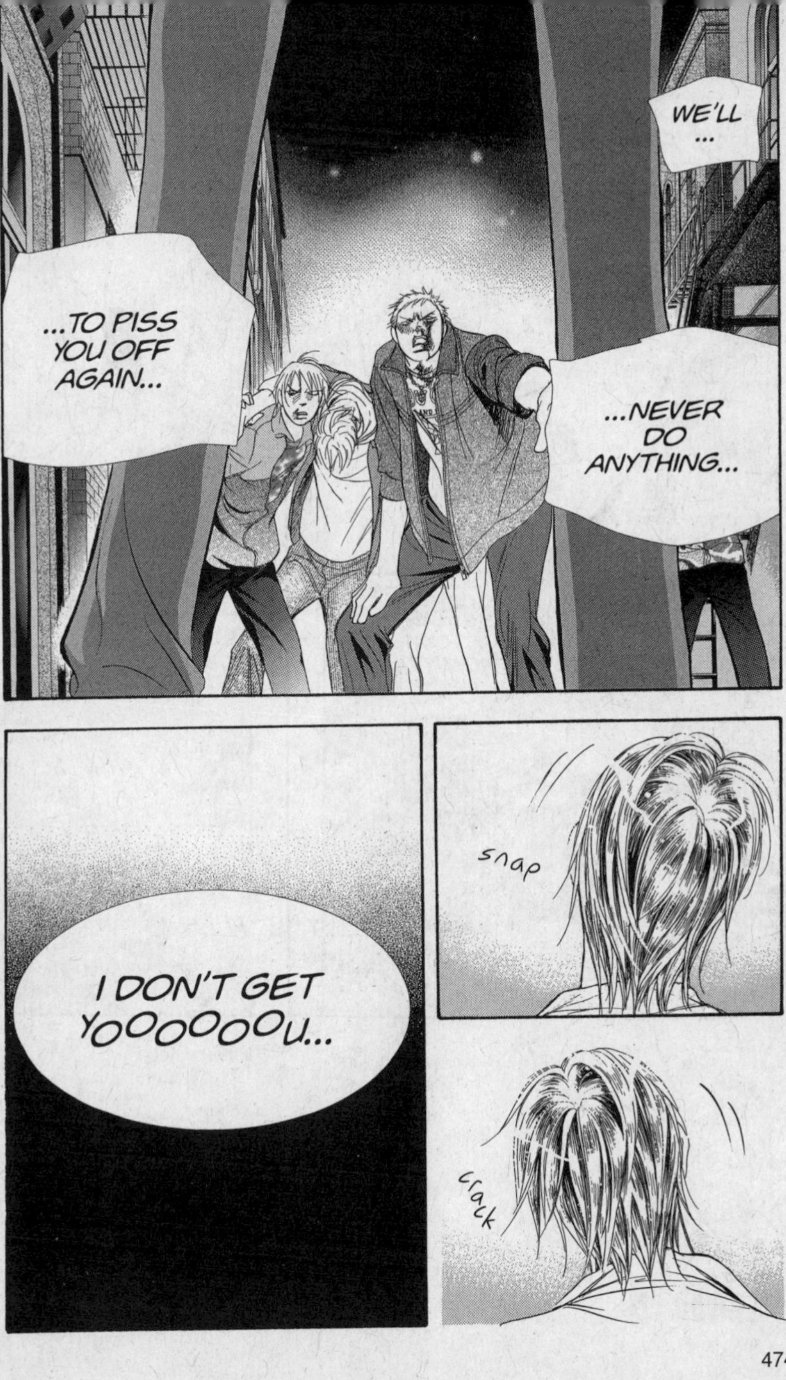
WE'LL ...
...NEVER DO ANYTHING...
...TO PISS YOU OFF AGAIN...
snap
crack
I DON'T GET YOOOOOOU...

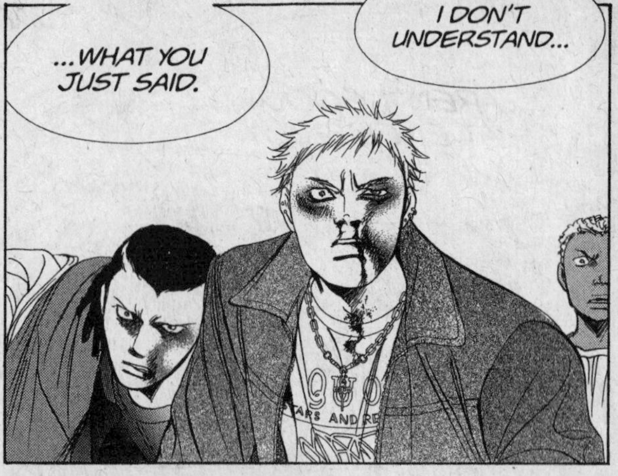
I DON'T UNDERSTAND...
...WHAT YOU JUST SAID.

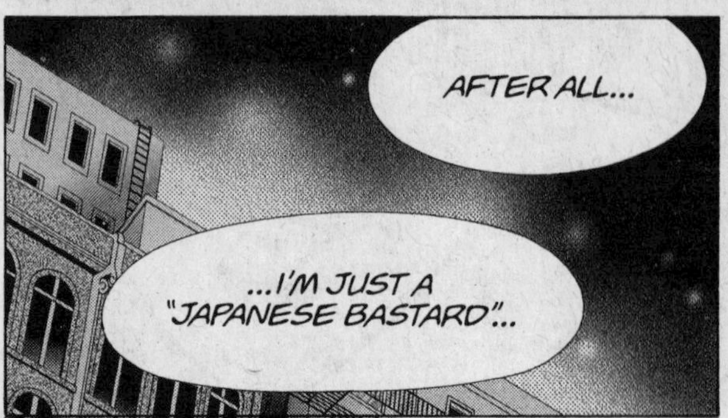
AFTER ALL...
...I'M JUST A "JAPANESE BASTARD"...

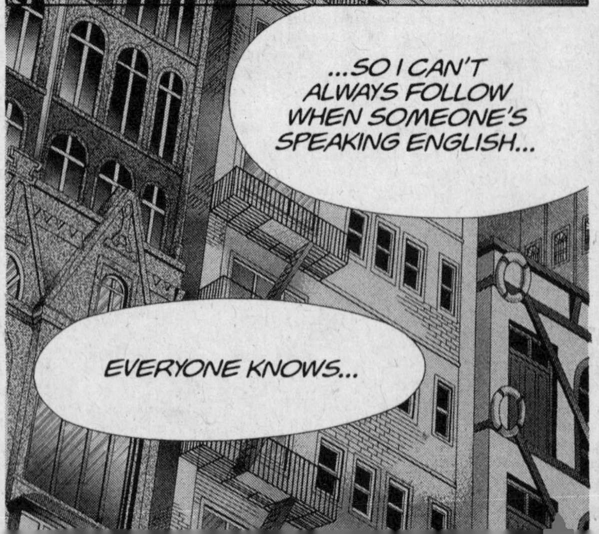
...SO I CAN'T ALWAYS FOLLOW WHEN SOMEONE'S SPEAKING ENGLISH...
EVERYONE KNOWS...

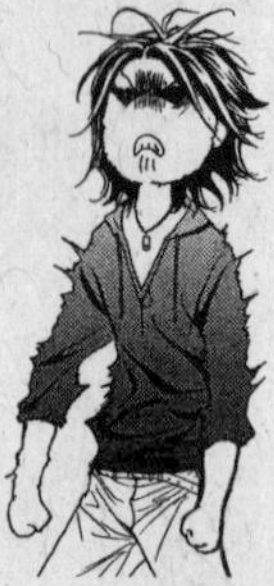

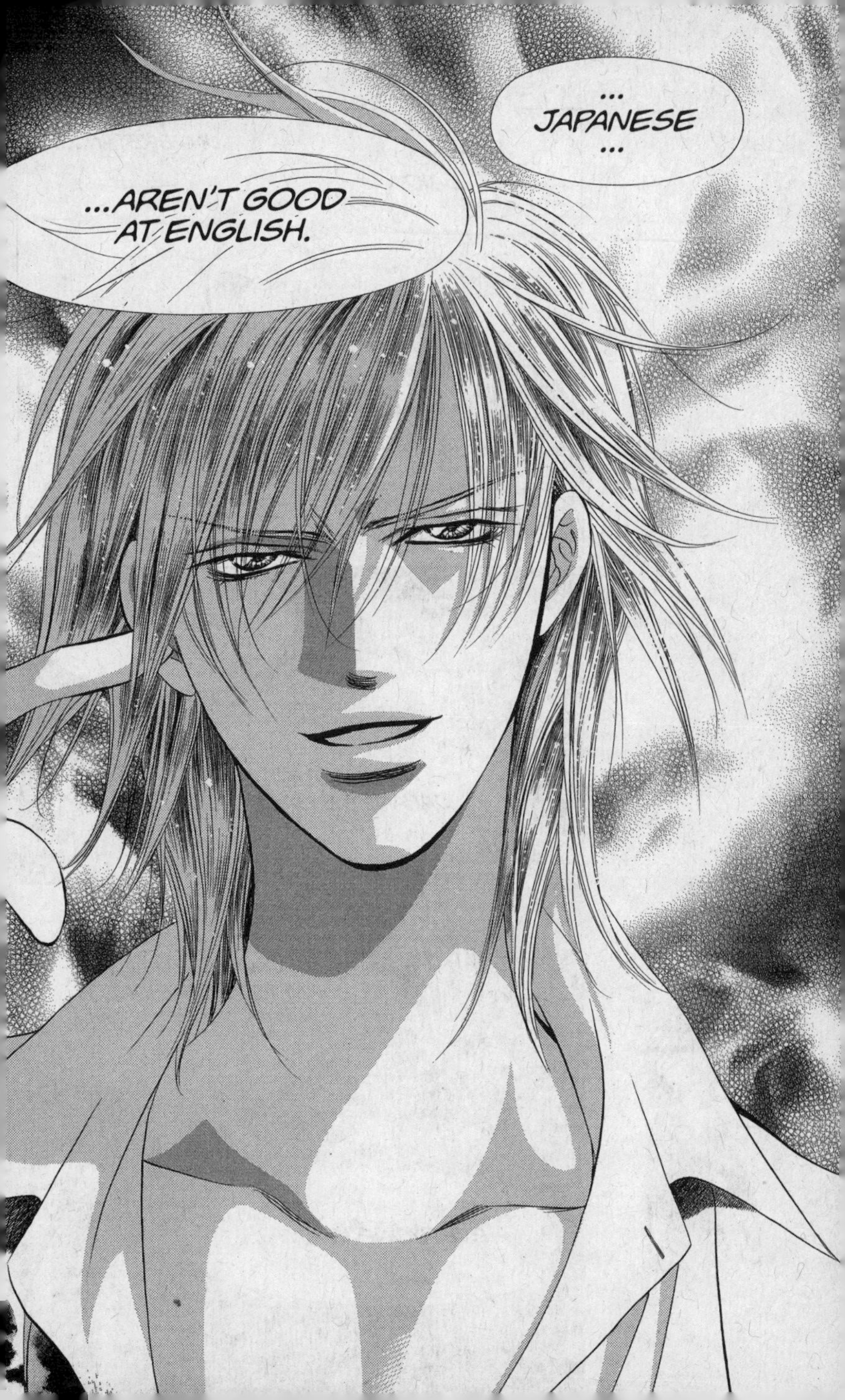
... JAPANESE ...
...AREN'T GOOD AT ENGLISH.

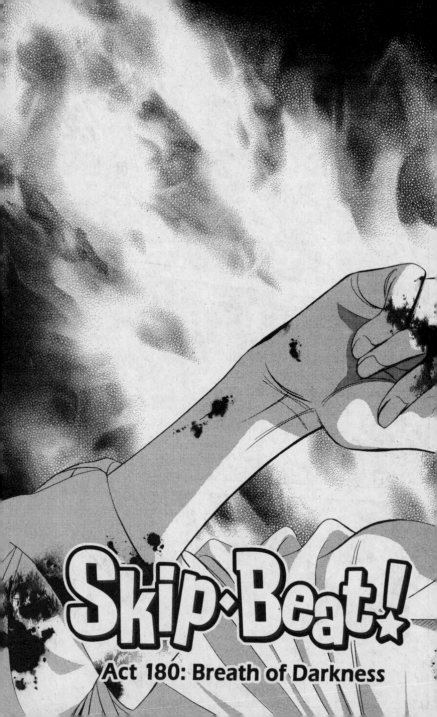

Skip·Beat!

Act 180: Breath of Darkness

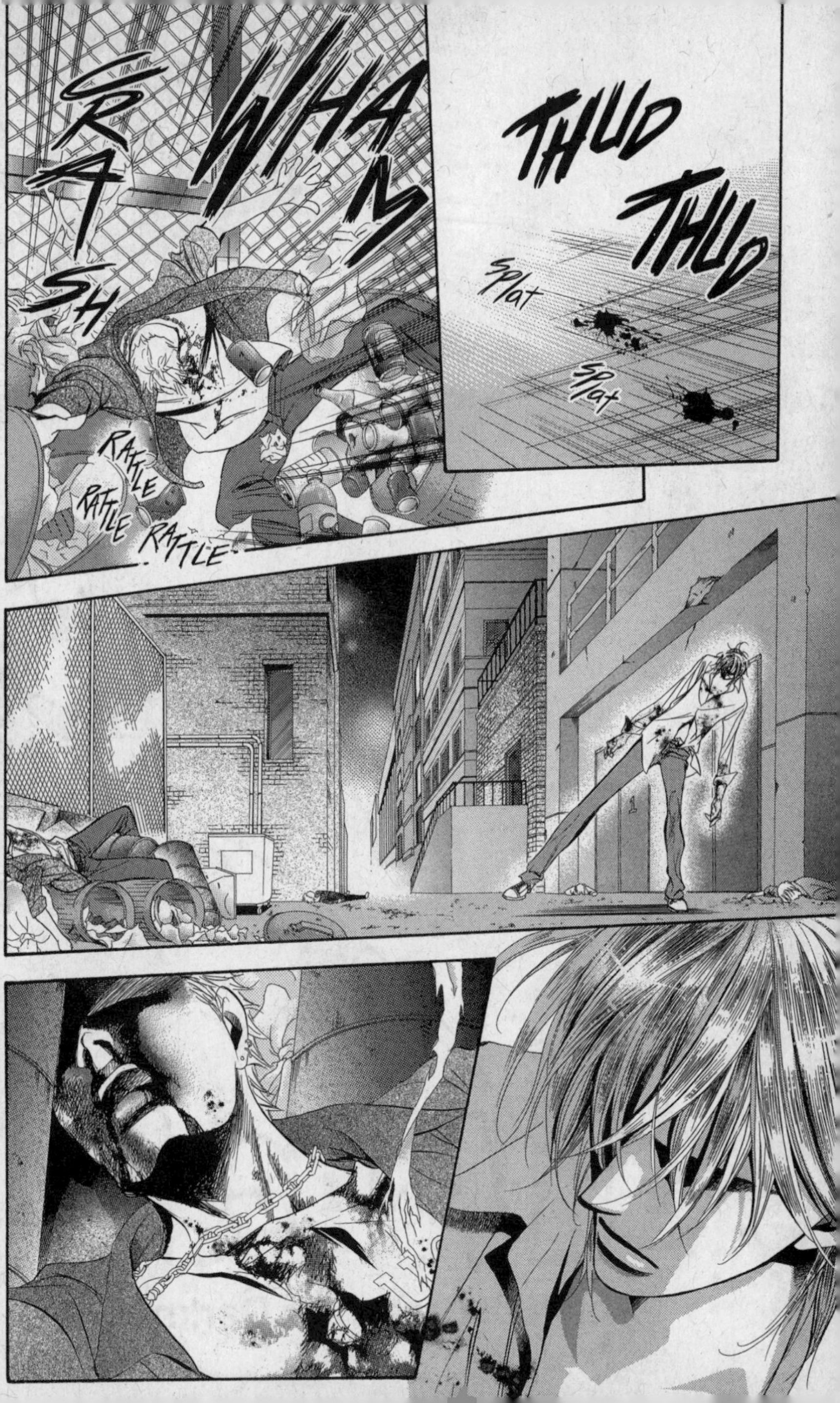
THUD
THUD
Splat
Splat
WHAM
CRASH
RATTLE
RATTLE
RATTLE

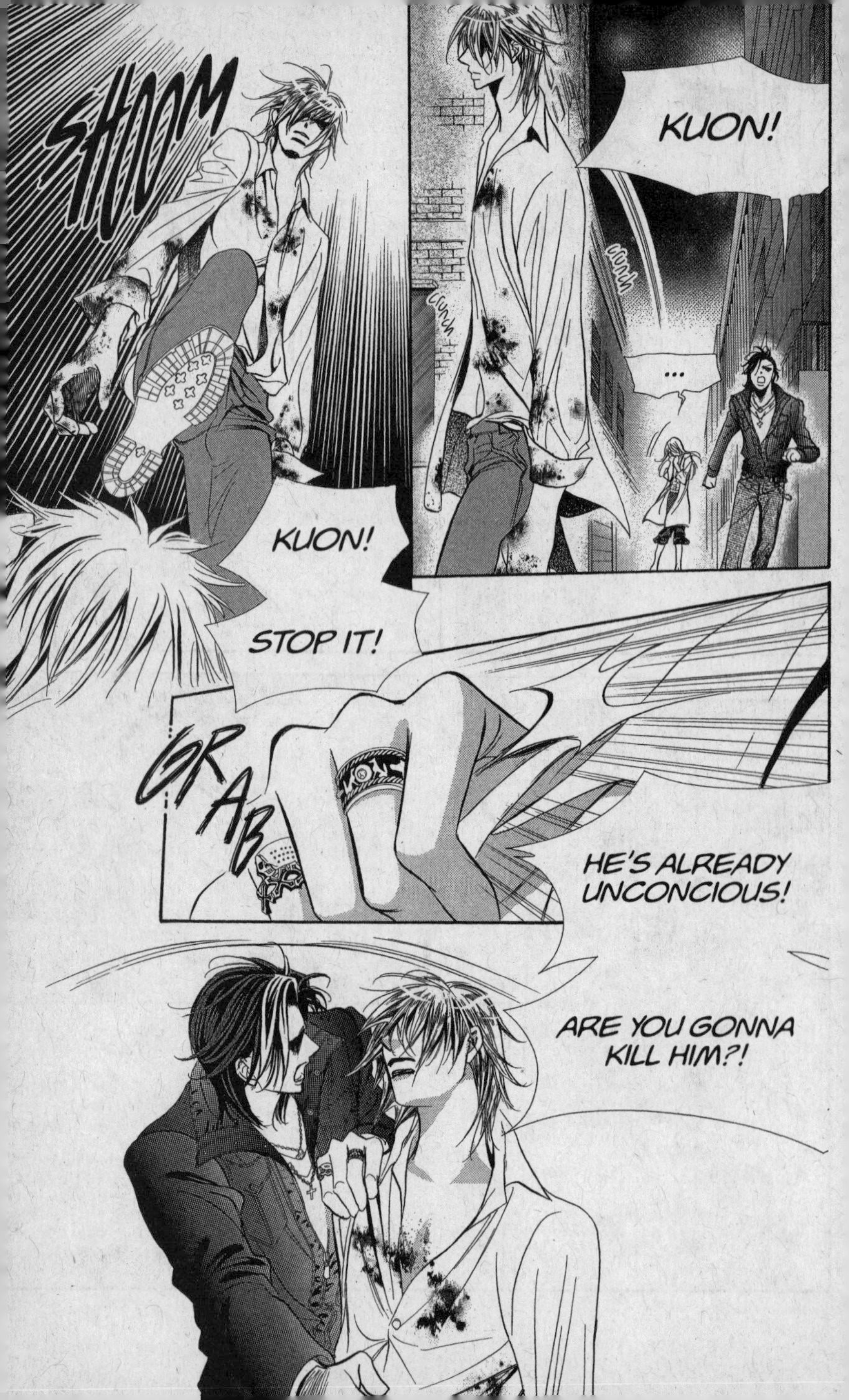
KUON!
crunch
crunch
...
SHOOM
KUON!
STOP IT!
GRAB
HE'S ALREADY UNCONCIOUS!
ARE YOU GONNA KILL HIM?!

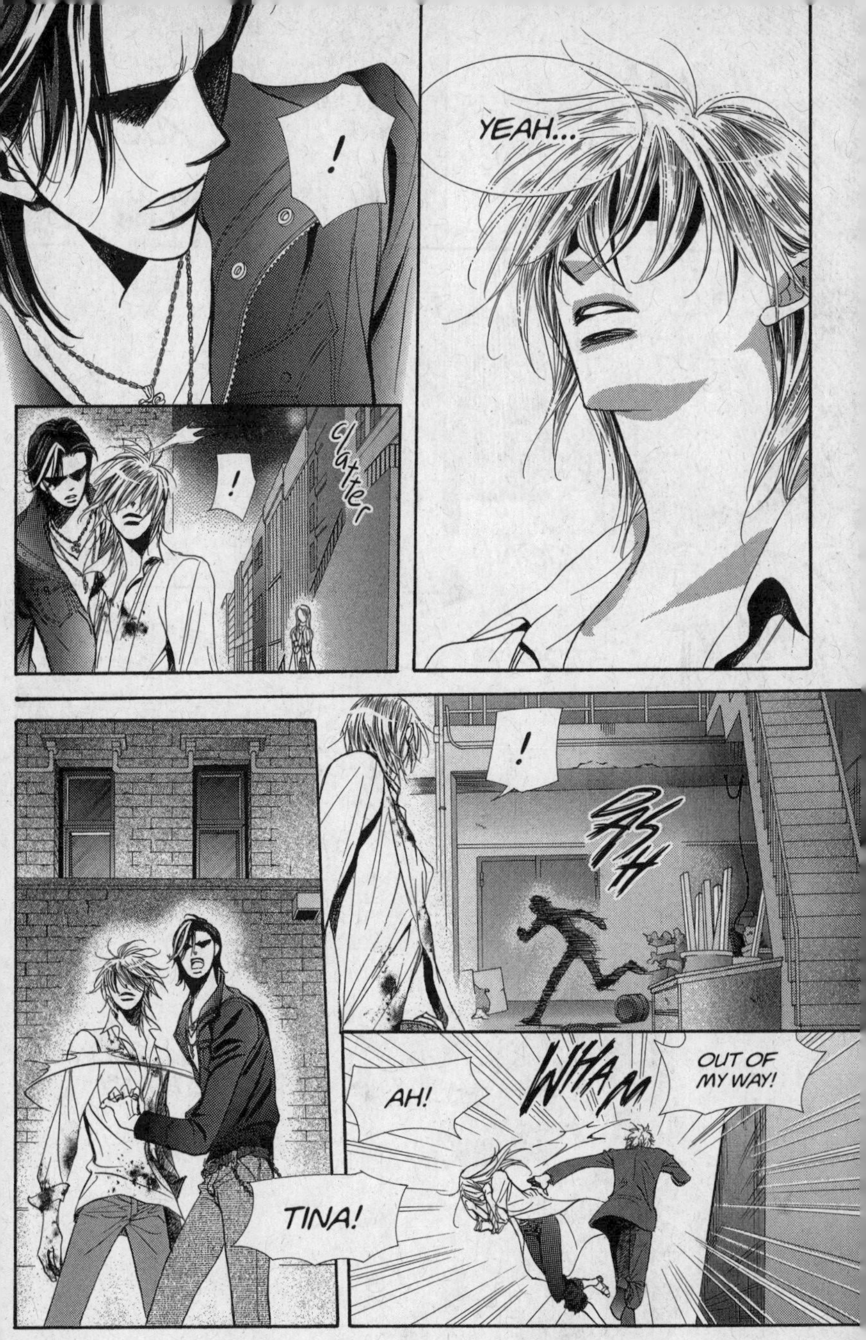
YEAH...
!
!
clatter
!
GASH
OUT OF MY WAY!
WHAM
AH!
TINA!

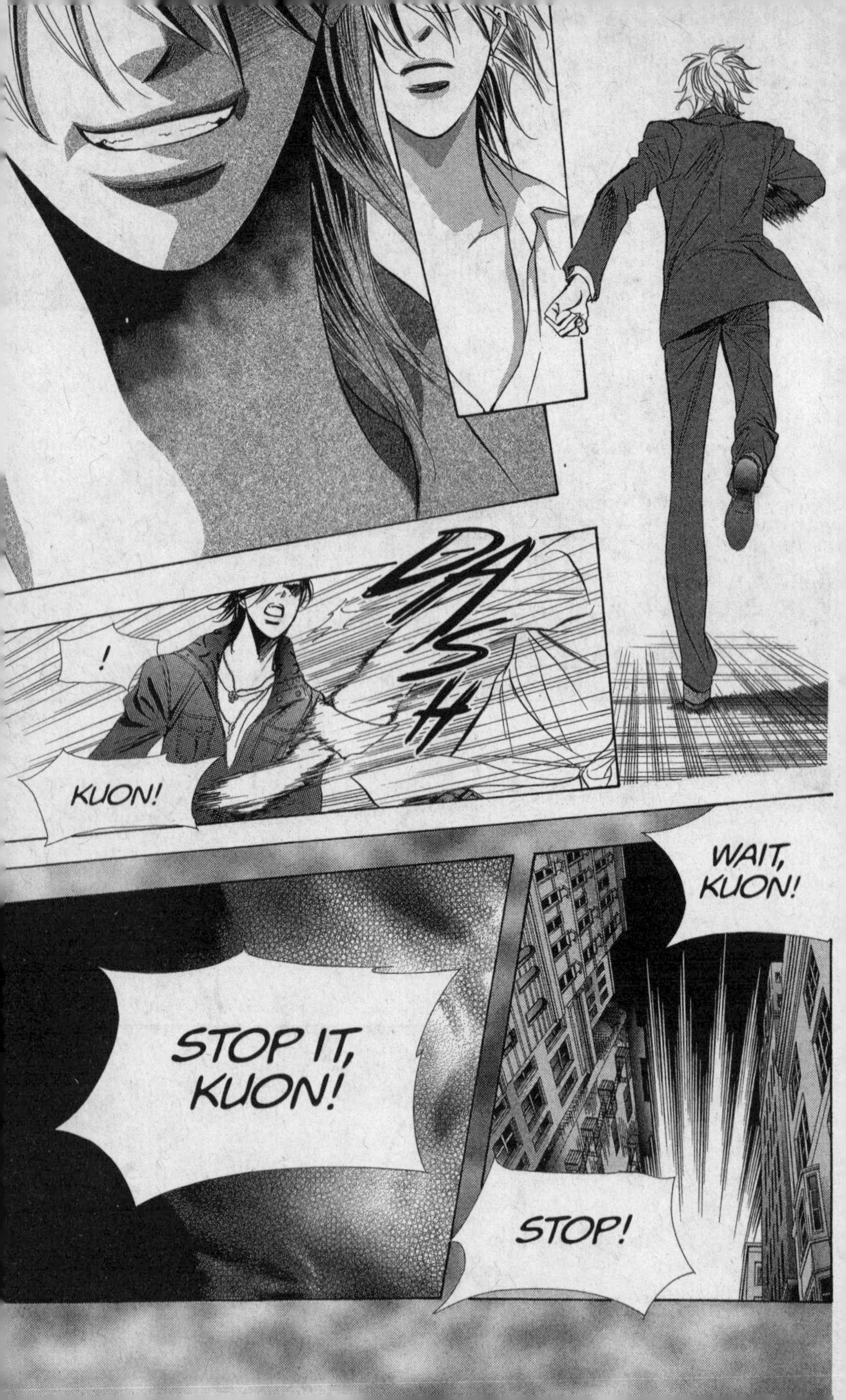
DASH
!
KUON!
WAIT, KUON!
STOP!
STOP IT, KUON!

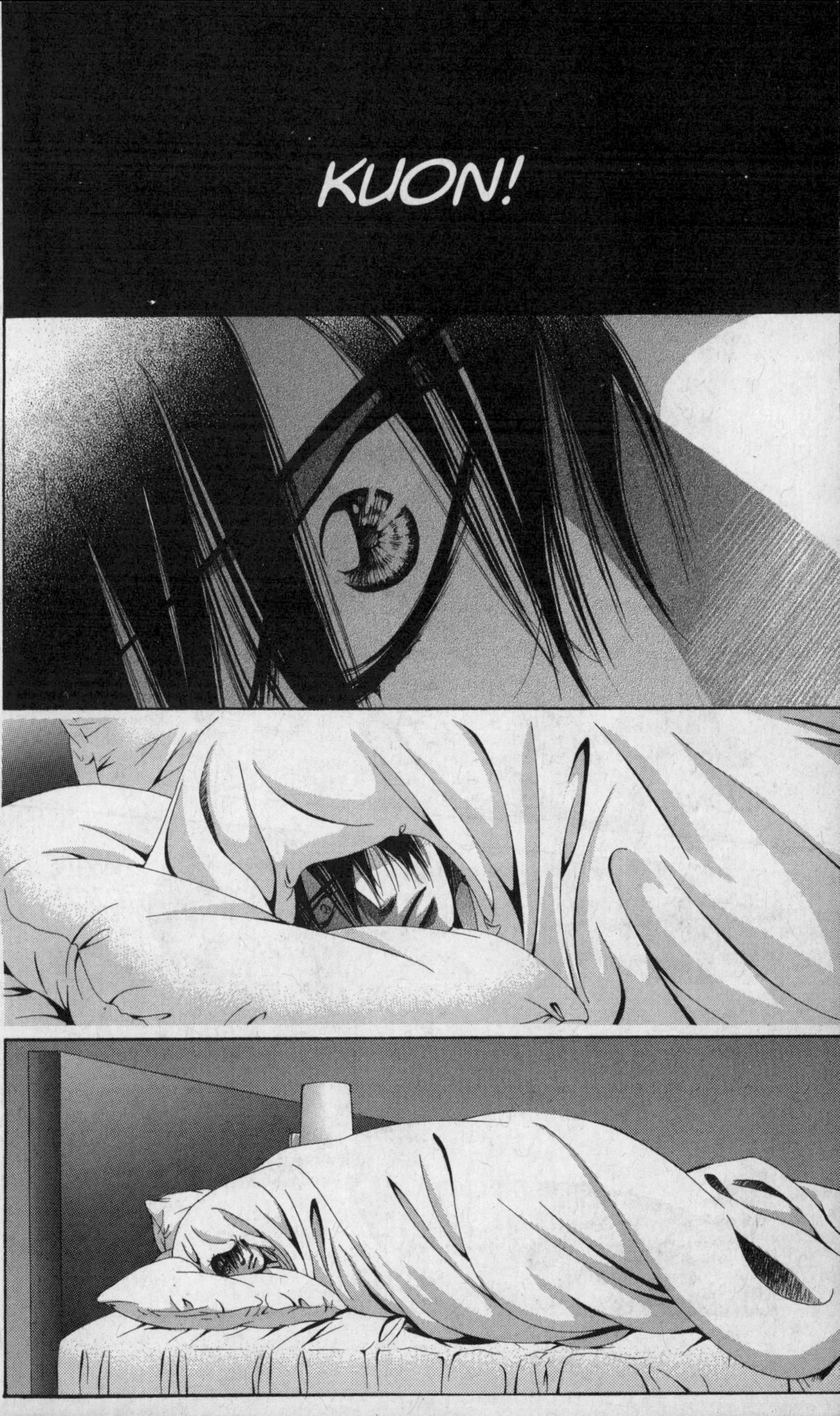
KUON!

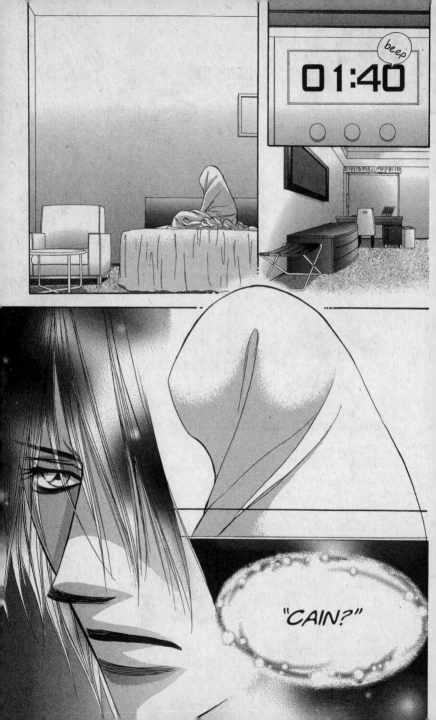

beep

01:40

"CAIN?"

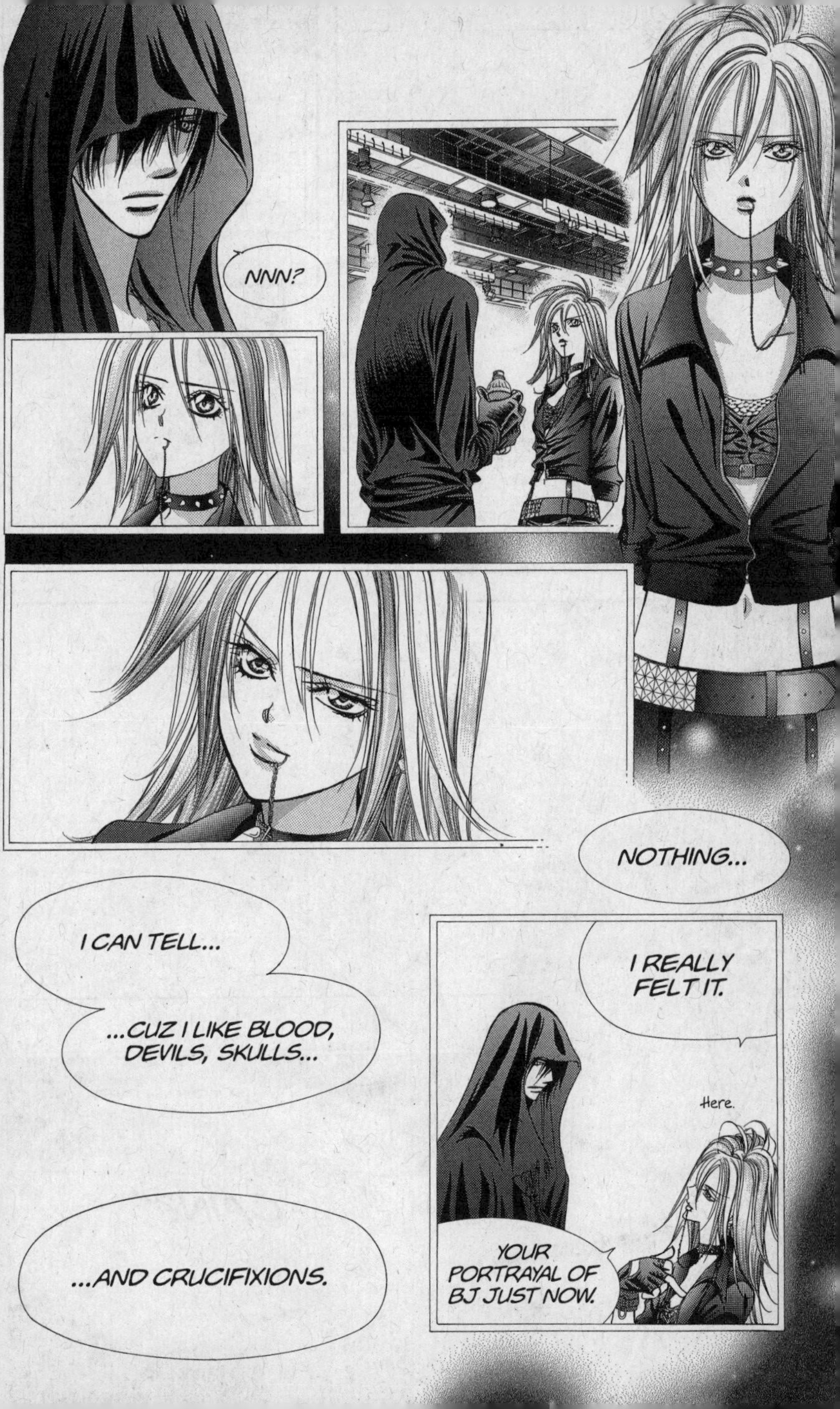
NNN?
NOTHING...
I REALLY FELT IT.
Here.
YOUR PORTRAYAL OF BJ JUST NOW.
I CAN TELL...
...CUZ I LIKE BLOOD, DEVILS, SKULLS...
...AND CRUCIFIXIONS.

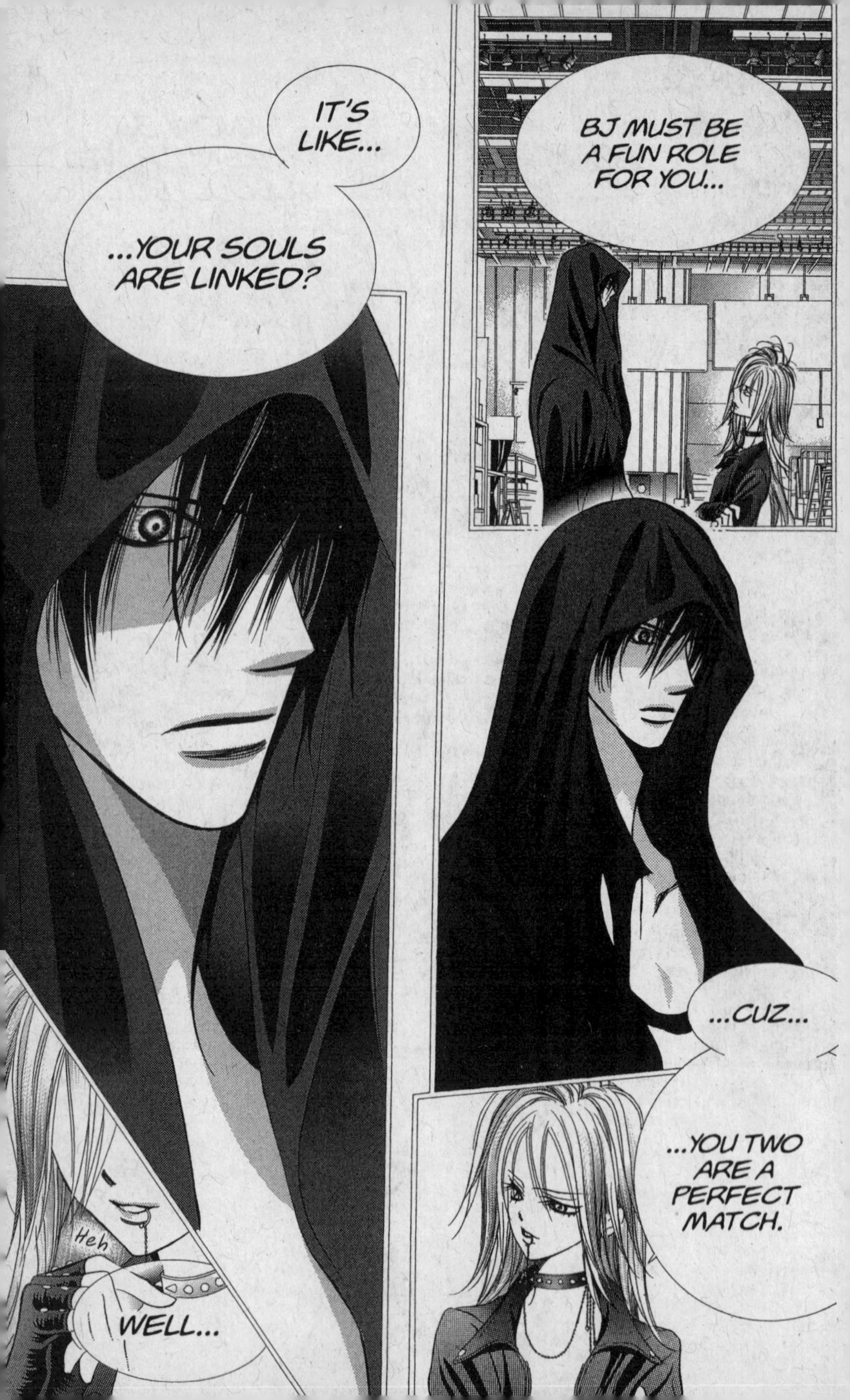
BJ MUST BE A FUN ROLE FOR YOU...
...CUZ...
...YOU TWO ARE A PERFECT MATCH.
IT'S LIKE...
...YOUR SOULS ARE LINKED?
Heh
WELL...

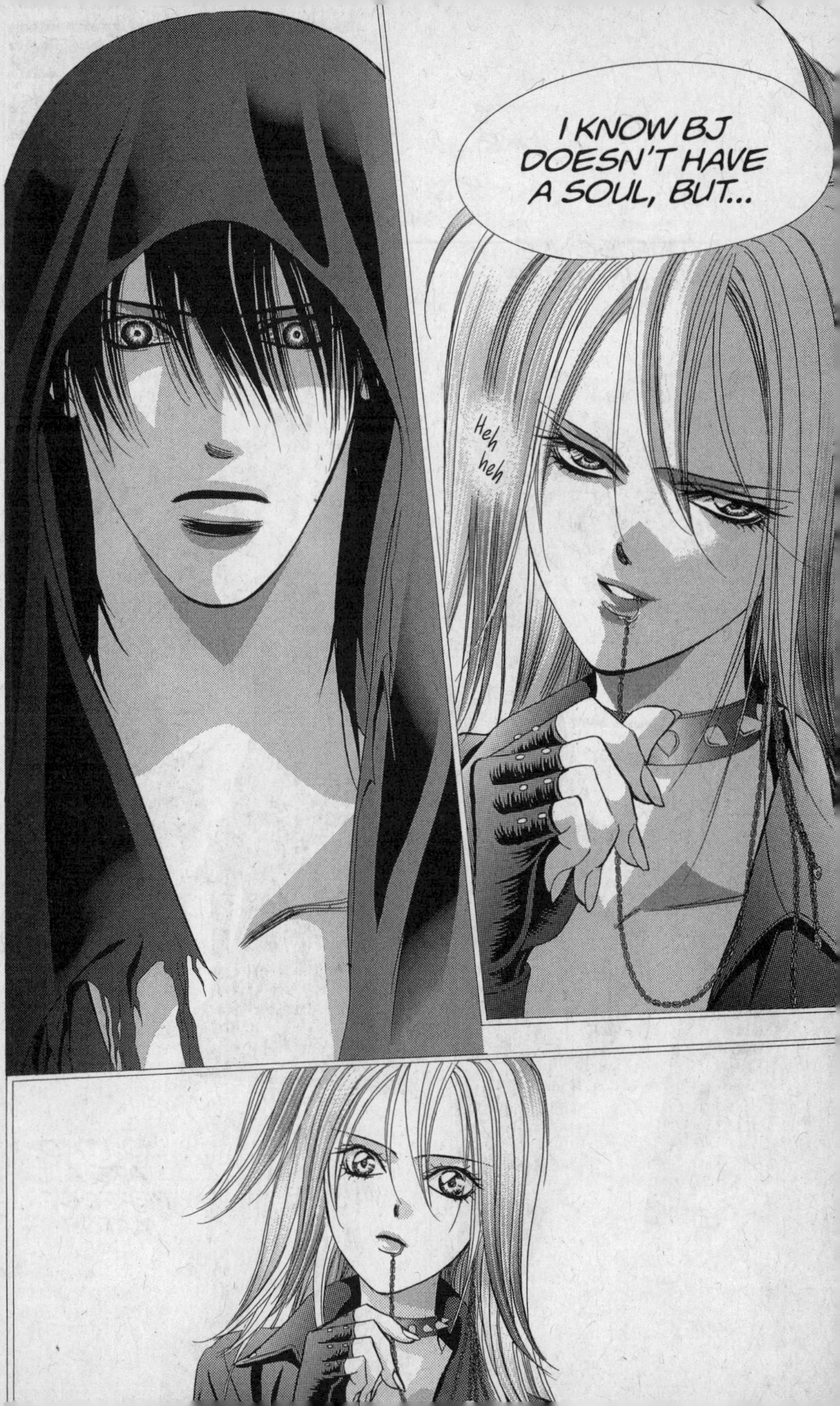
I KNOW BJ DOESN'T HAVE A SOUL, BUT...
Heh heh

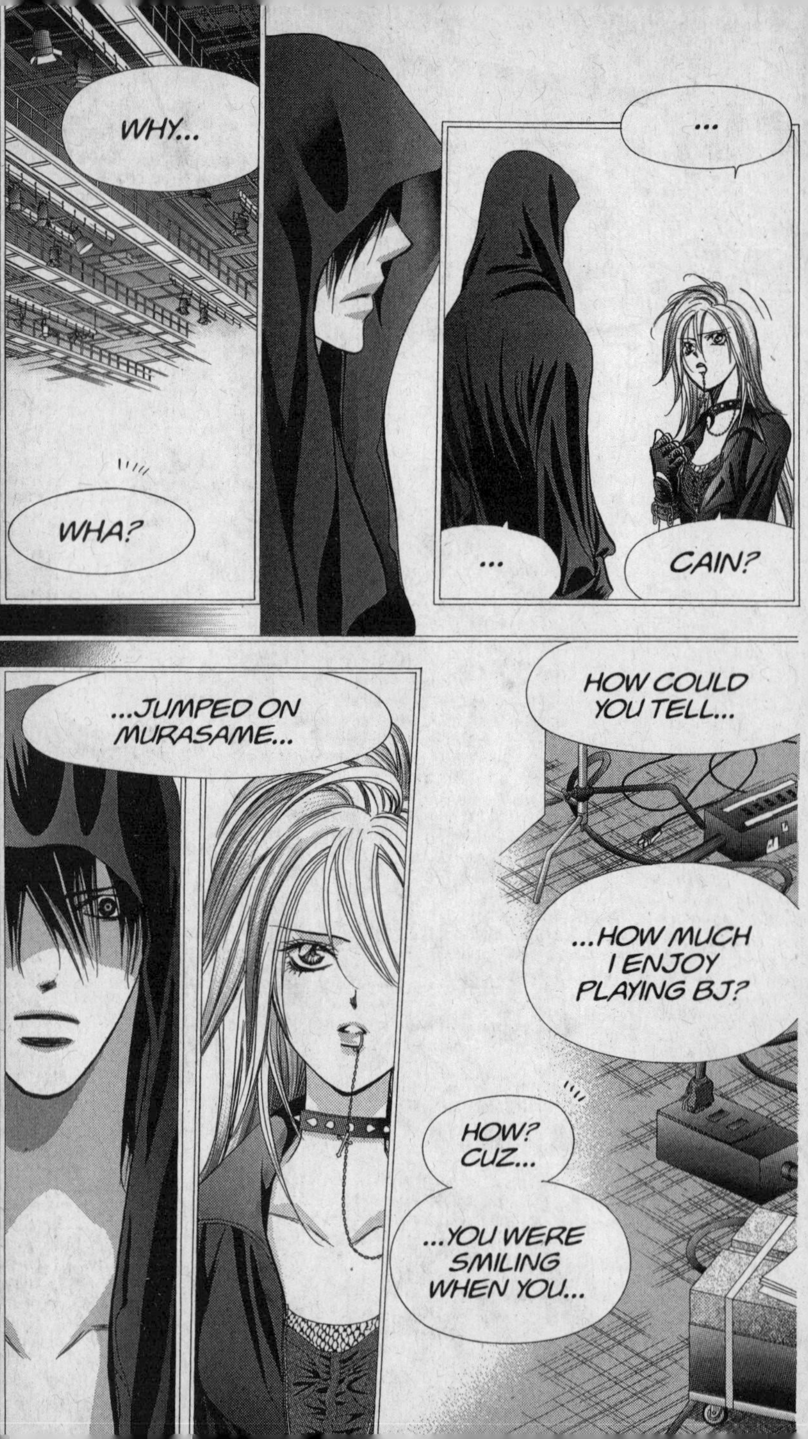
...
CAIN?
...
WHY...
WHA?
HOW COULD YOU TELL...
...HOW MUCH I ENJOY PLAYING BJ?
HOW? CUZ...
...YOU WERE SMILING WHEN YOU...
...JUMPED ON MURASAME...

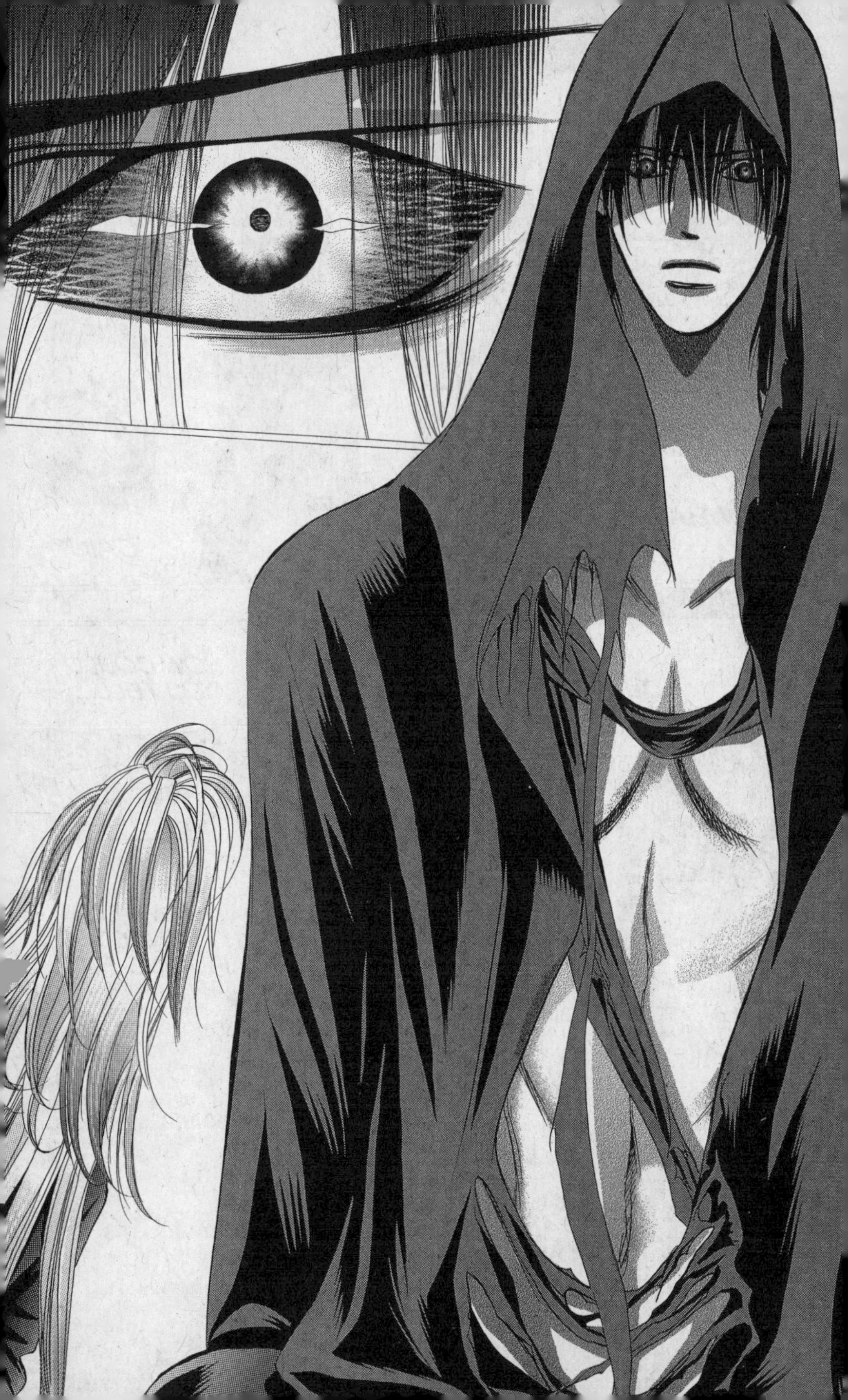

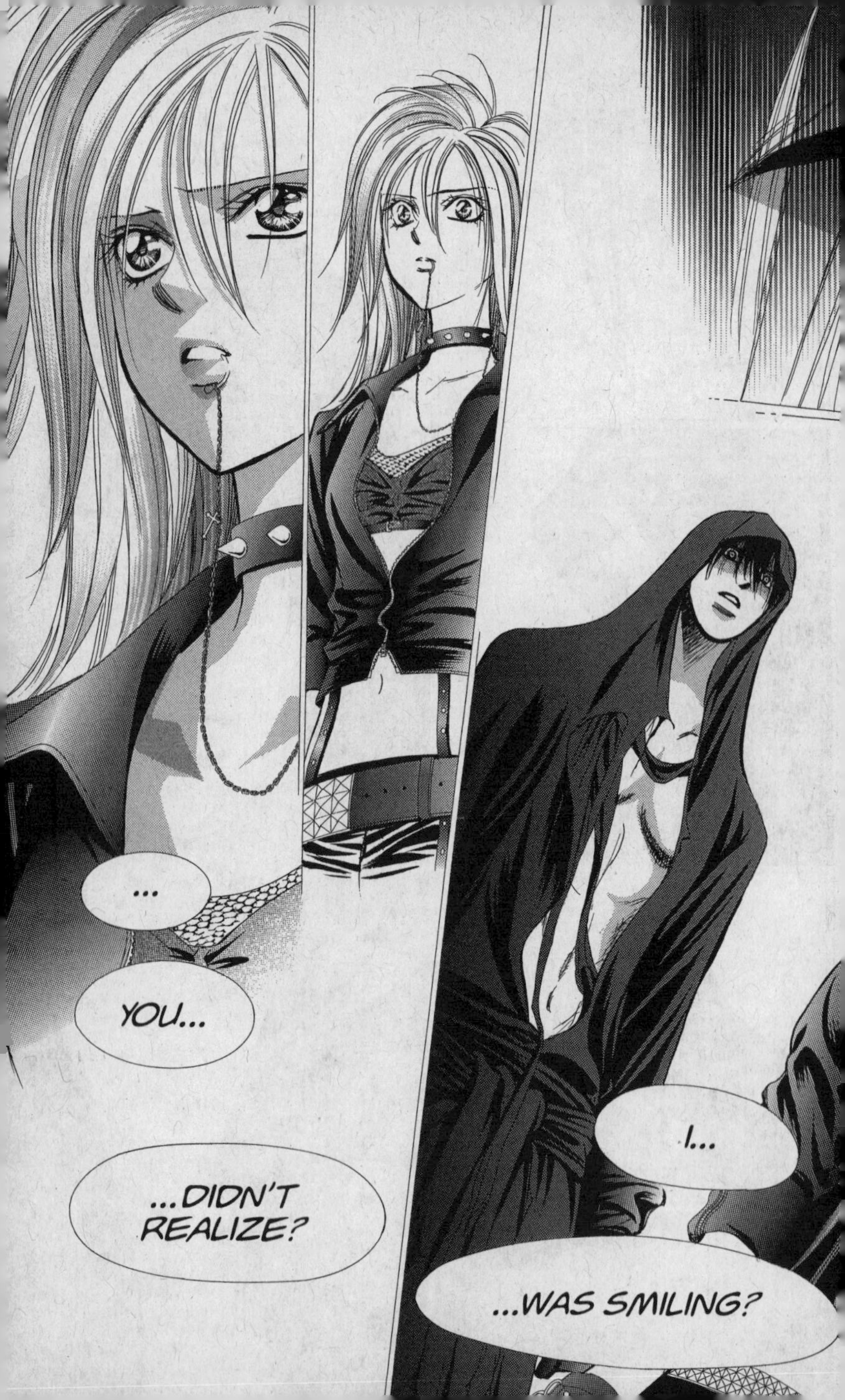
I...
...WAS SMILING?
...
YOU...
...DIDN'T REALIZE?

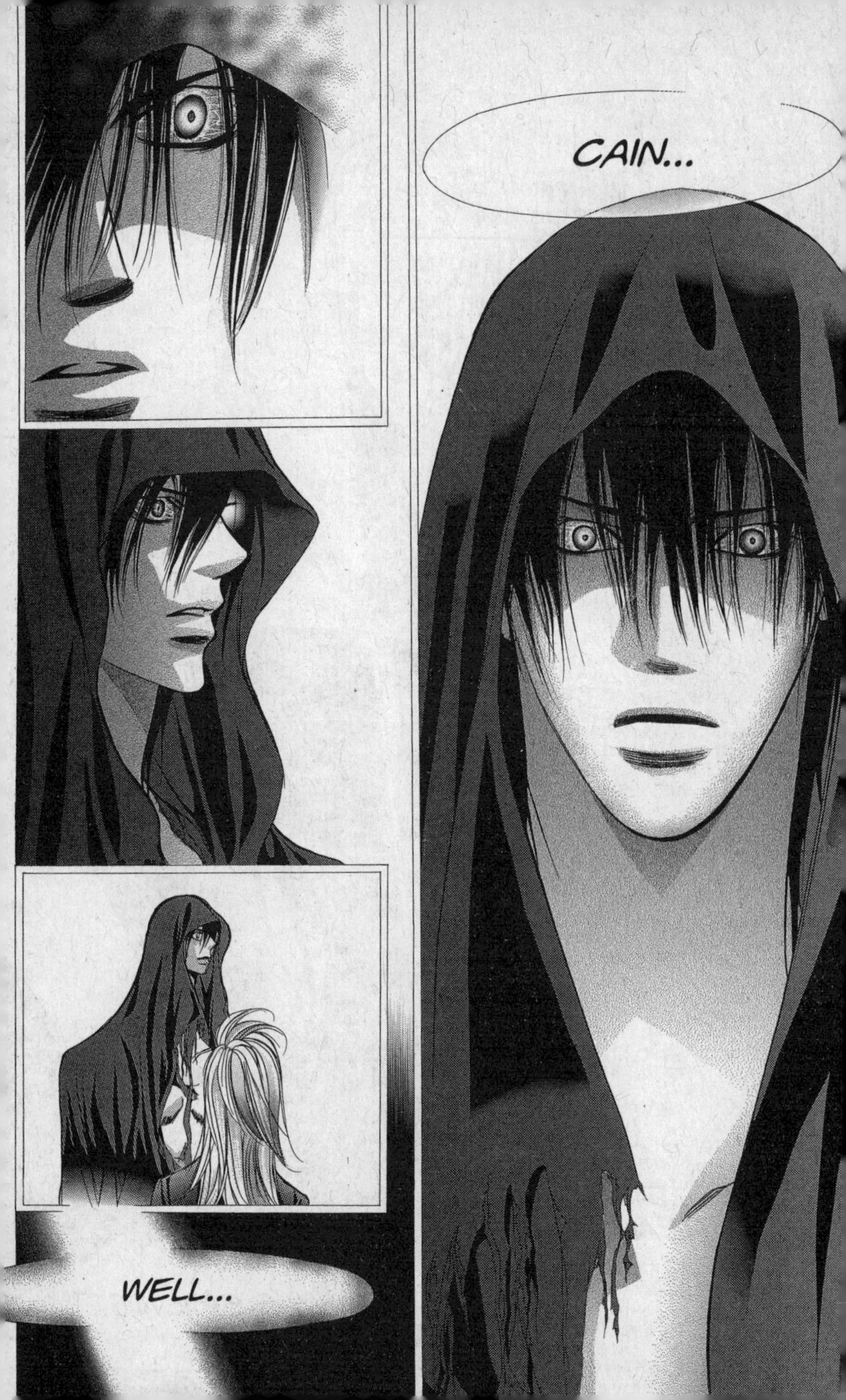
CAIN...
WELL...

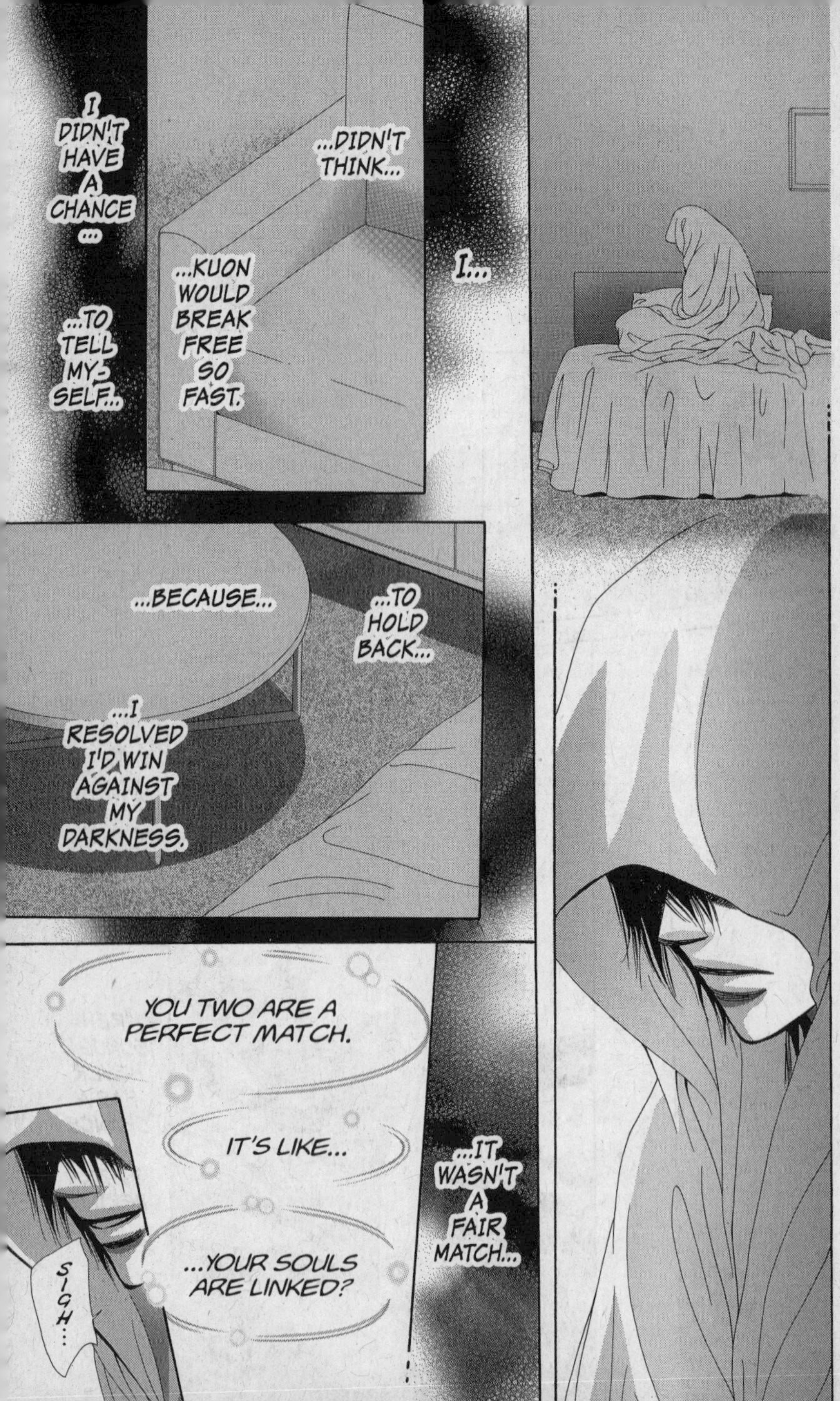
I...
...DIDN'T THINK...
...KUON WOULD BREAK FREE SO FAST.
I DIDN'T HAVE A CHANCE...
...TO TELL MYSELF...
...TO HOLD BACK...
...BECAUSE...
...I RESOLVED I'D WIN AGAINST MY DARKNESS.
...IT WASN'T A FAIR MATCH...
YOU TWO ARE A PERFECT MATCH.
IT'S LIKE...
...YOUR SOULS ARE LINKED?
SIGH...

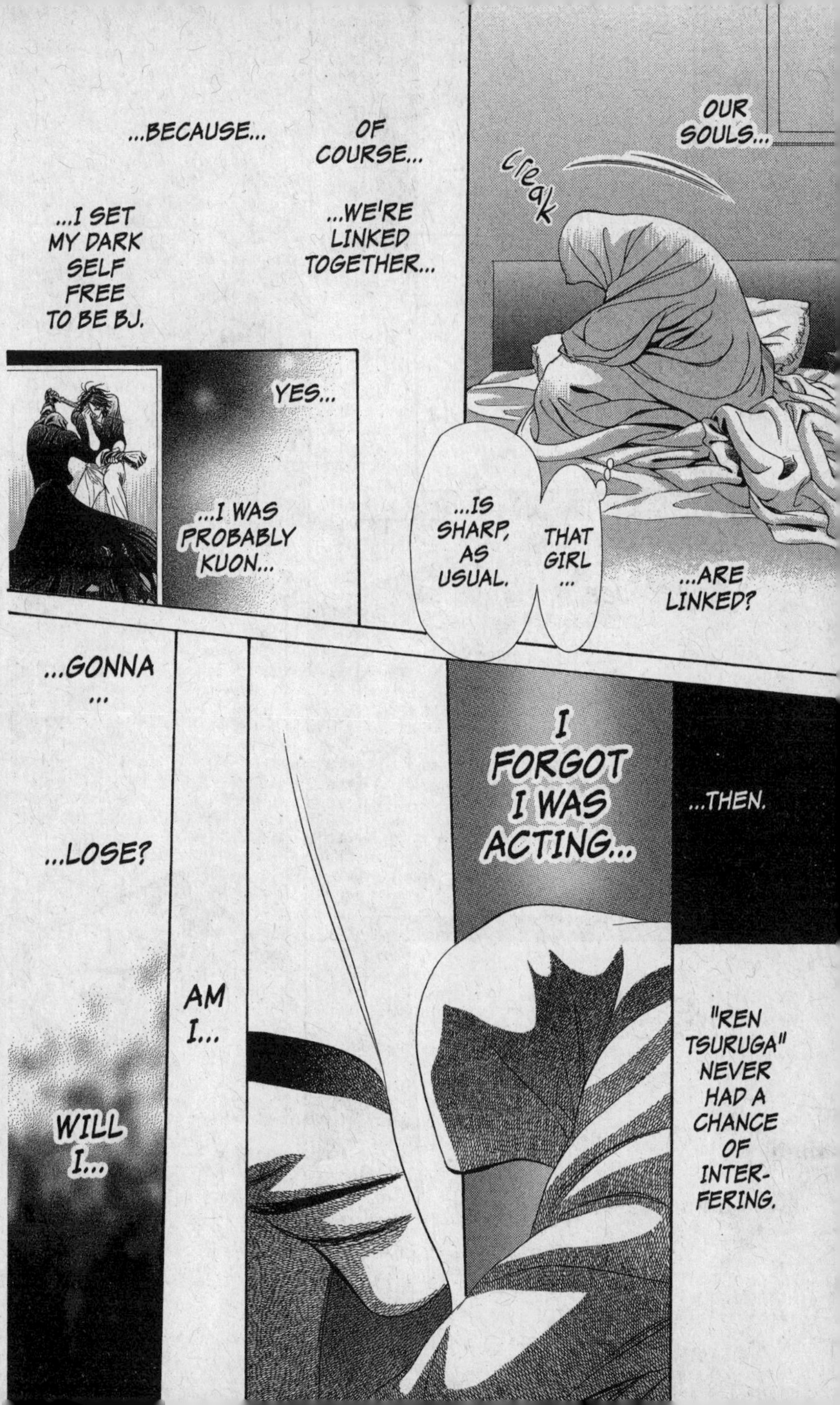
OUR SOULS...
creak
...ARE LINKED?
THAT GIRL...
...IS SHARP, AS USUAL.
OF COURSE...
...WE'RE LINKED TOGETHER...
...BECAUSE...
...I SET MY DARK SELF FREE TO BE BJ.
YES...
...I WAS PROBABLY KUON...
I FORGOT I WAS ACTING...
...THEN.
"REN TSURUGA" NEVER HAD A CHANCE OF INTER-FERING.
AM I...
...GONNA...
...LOSE?
WILL I...

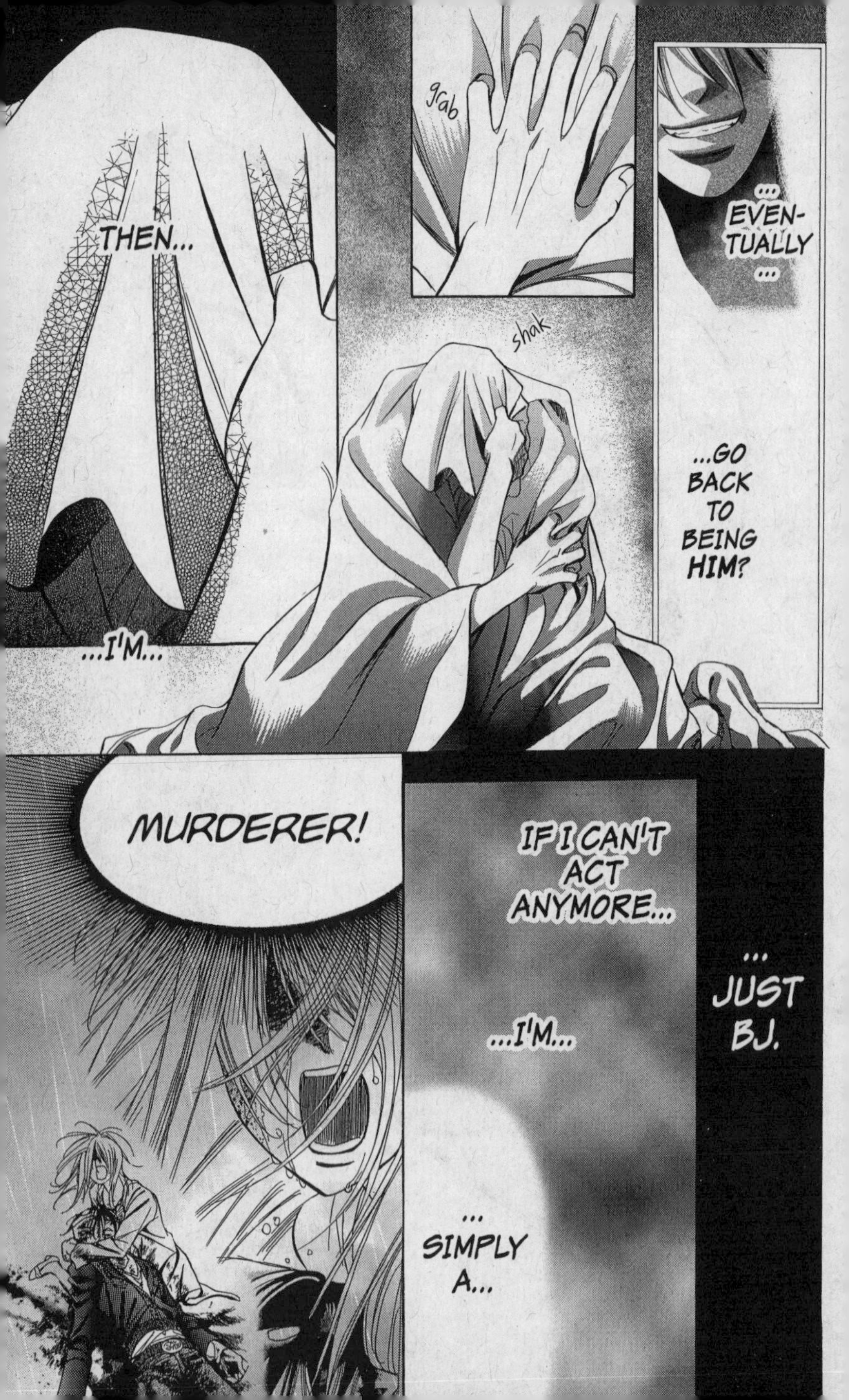

... EVEN- TUALLY ...
...GO BACK TO BEING HIM?
grab
shak
THEN...
...I'M...
IF I CAN'T ACT ANYMORE...
... JUST BJ.
...I'M...
... SIMPLY A...
MURDERER!

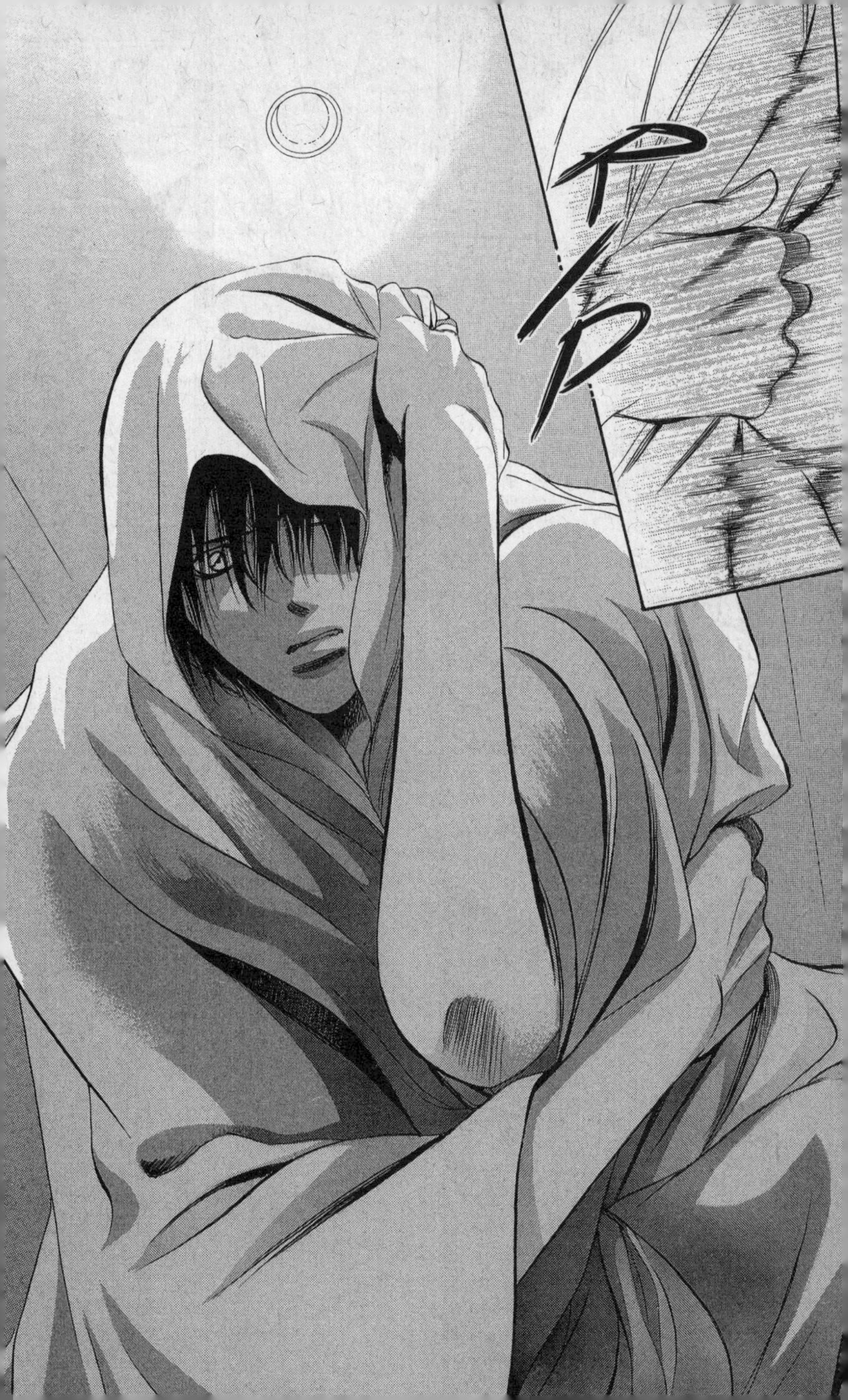
RIP

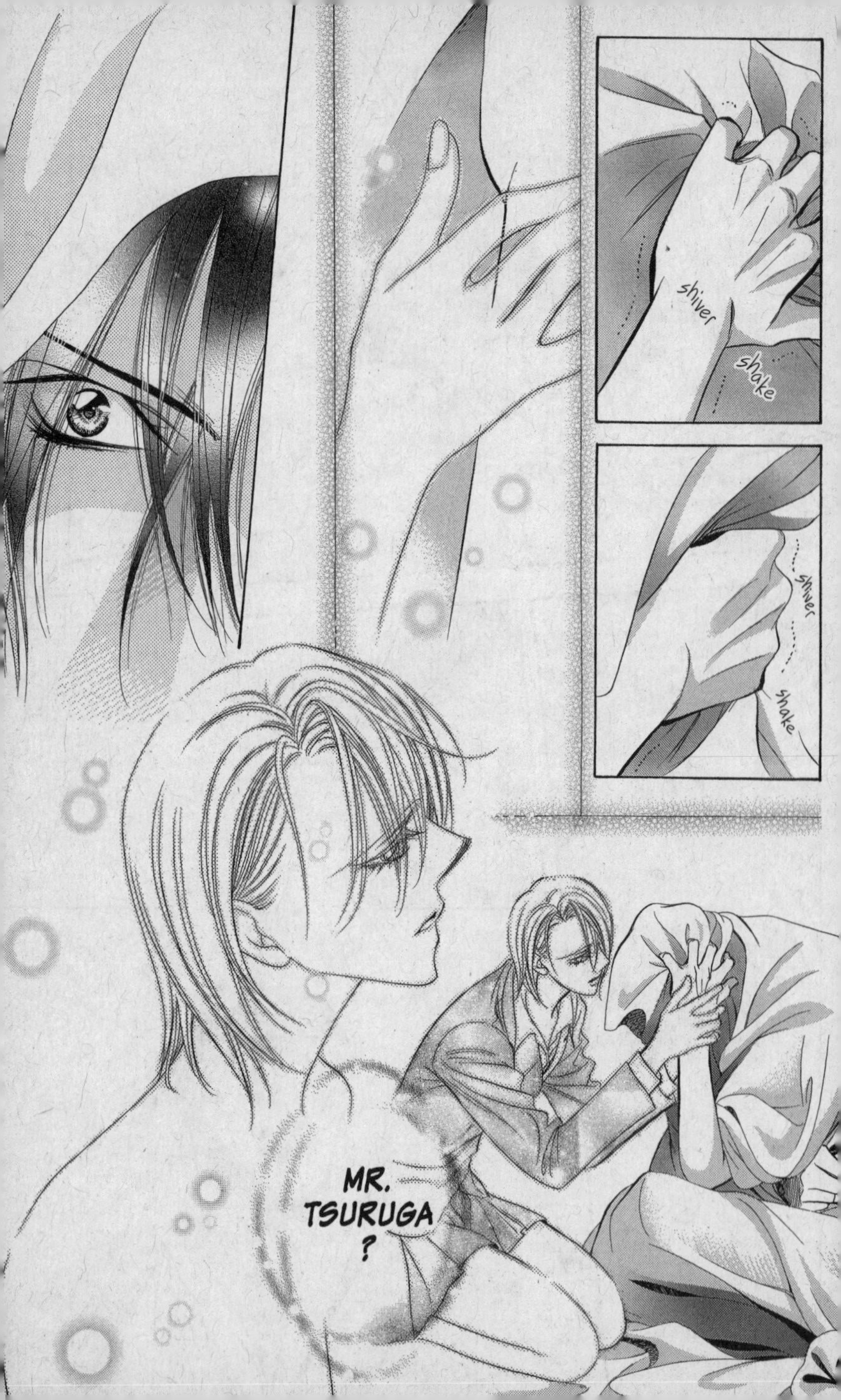
shiver
shake
shiver
shake
MR. TSURUGA?

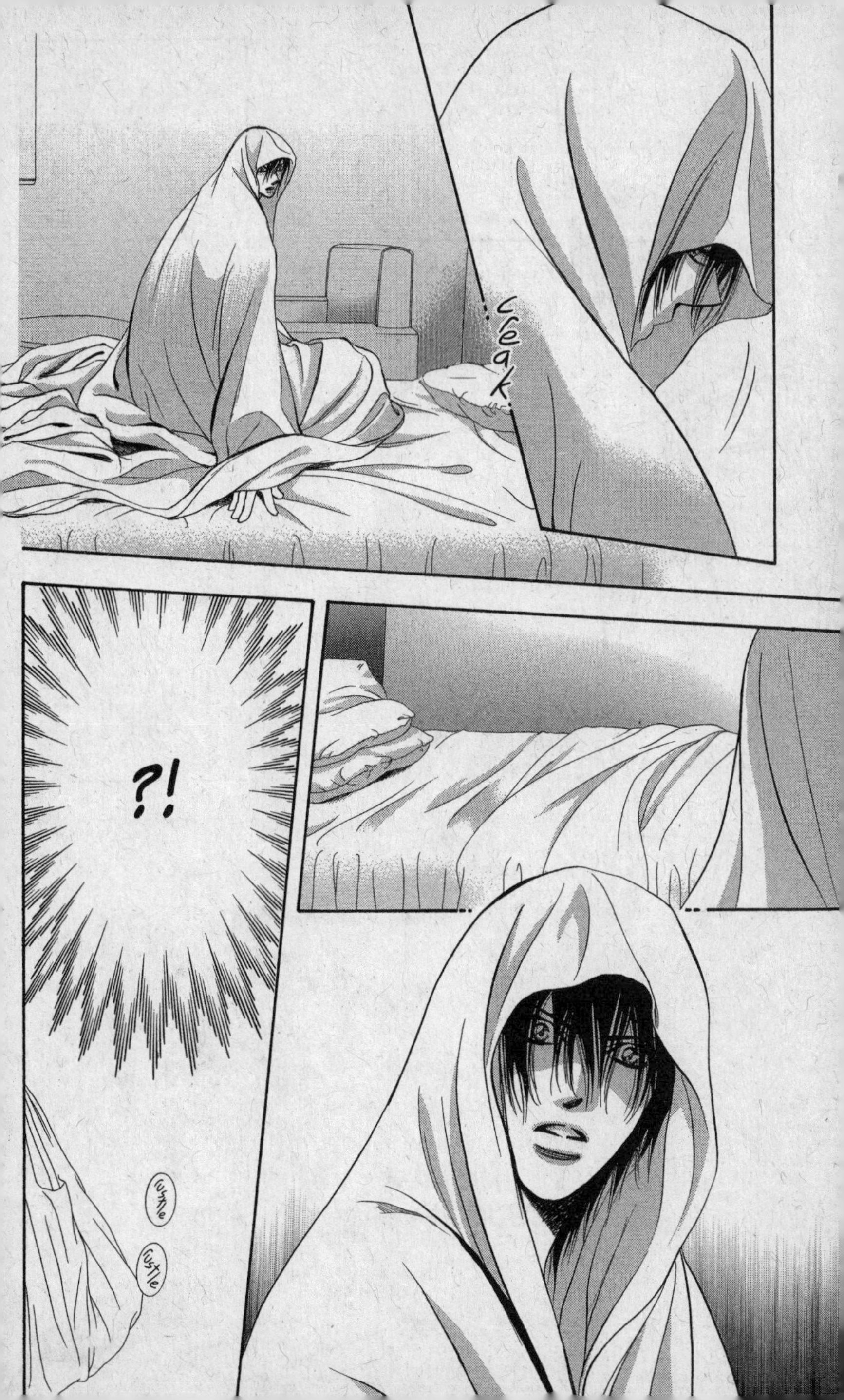
...creak...
?!
rustle
rustle

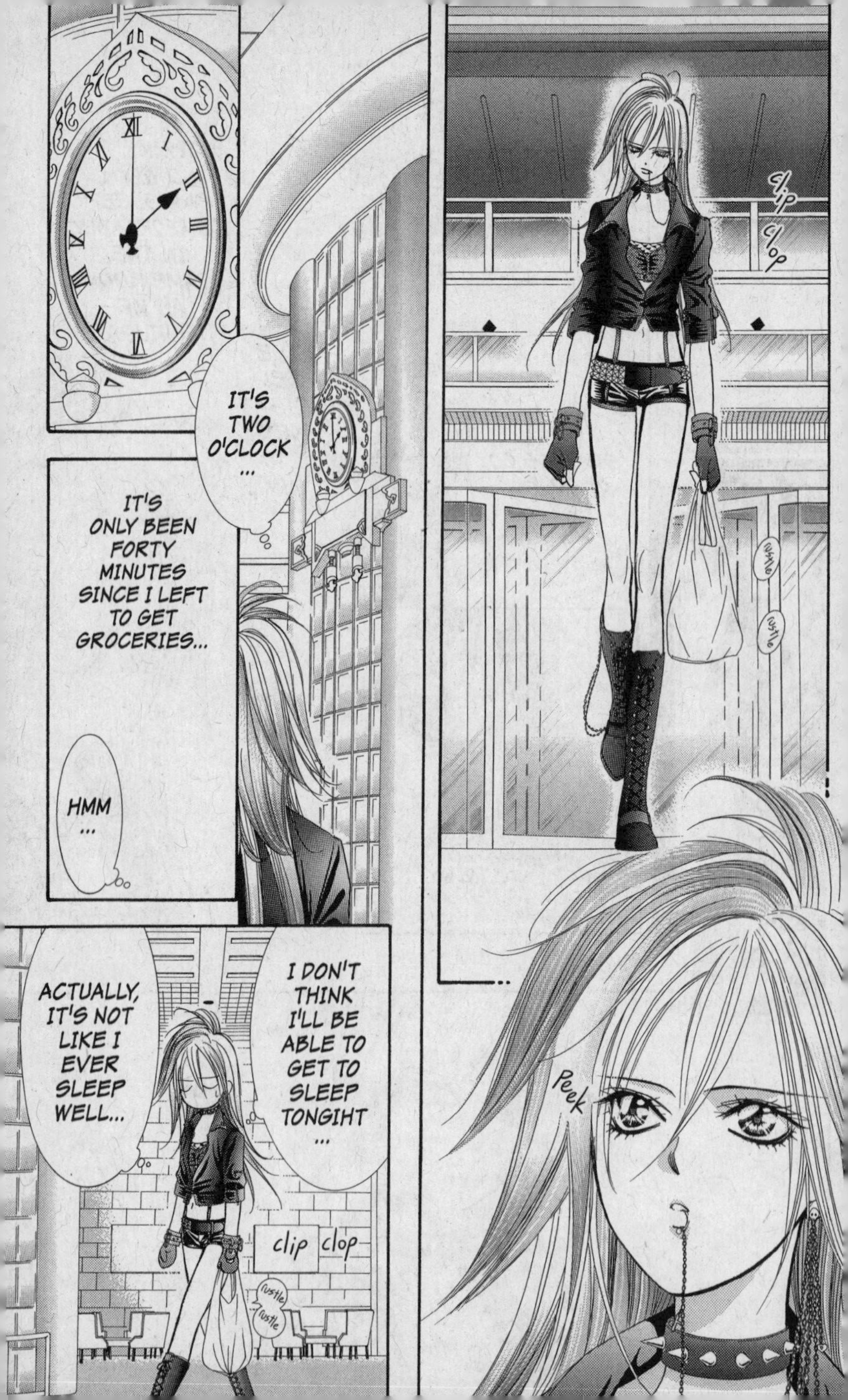
clip clop
rustle
rustle
IT'S TWO O'CLOCK...
IT'S ONLY BEEN FORTY MINUTES SINCE I LEFT TO GET GROCERIES...
HMM...
Peek
I DON'T THINK I'LL BE ABLE TO GET TO SLEEP TONGIHT...
ACTUALLY, IT'S NOT LIKE I EVER SLEEP WELL...
clip clop
rustle
rustle

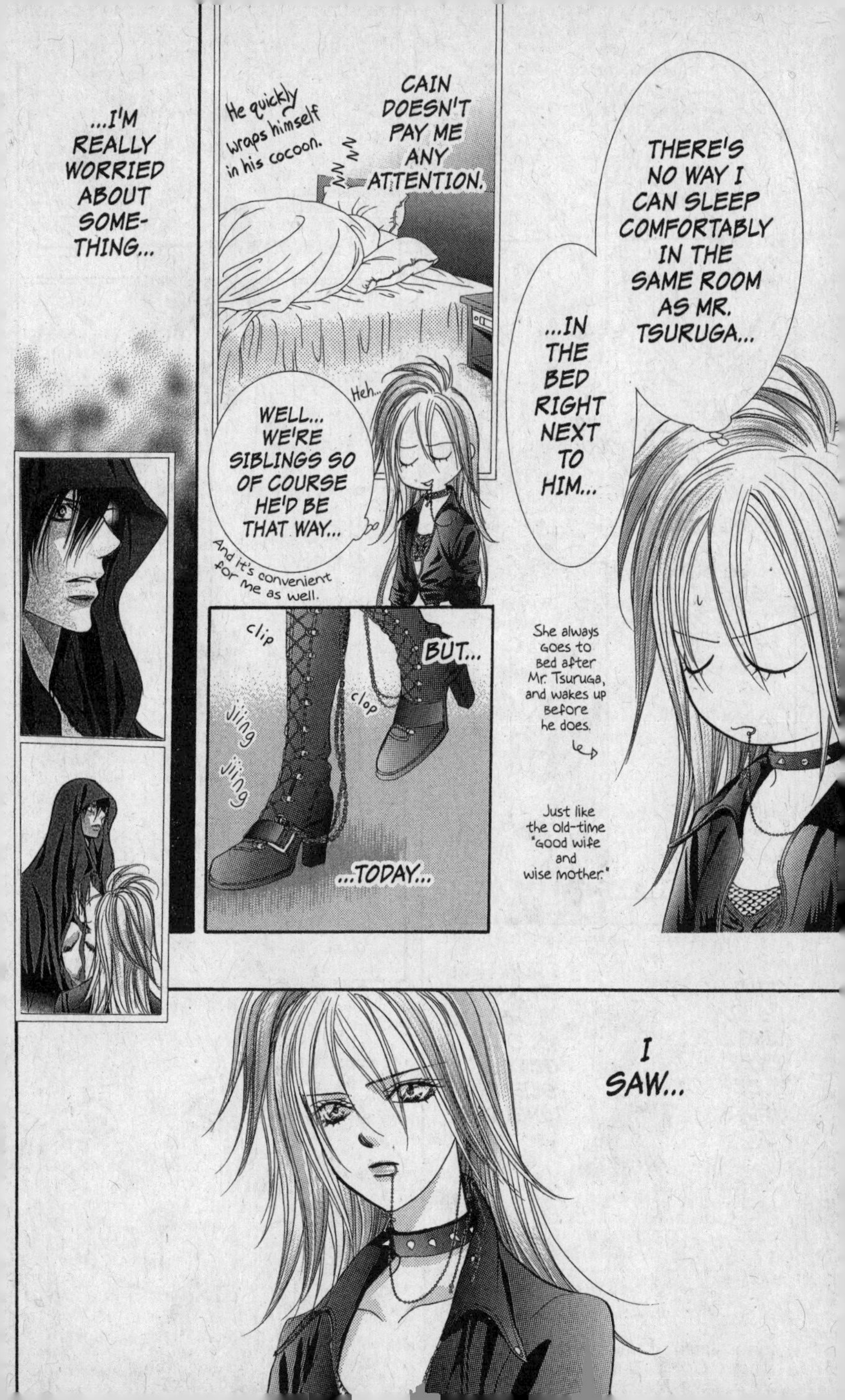
THERE'S NO WAY I CAN SLEEP COMFORTABLY IN THE SAME ROOM AS MR. TSURUGA...
...IN THE BED RIGHT NEXT TO HIM...
She always goes to bed after Mr. Tsuruga, and wakes up before he does.
Just like the old-time "good wife and wise mother."
CAIN DOESN'T PAY ME ANY ATTENTION.
He quickly wraps himself in his cocoon.
ZZZ
Heh...
WELL... WE'RE SIBLINGS SO OF COURSE HE'D BE THAT WAY...
And it's convenient for me as well.
BUT...
clip
clop
jiing
jiing
...TODAY...
...I'M REALLY WORRIED ABOUT SOME-THING...
I SAW...

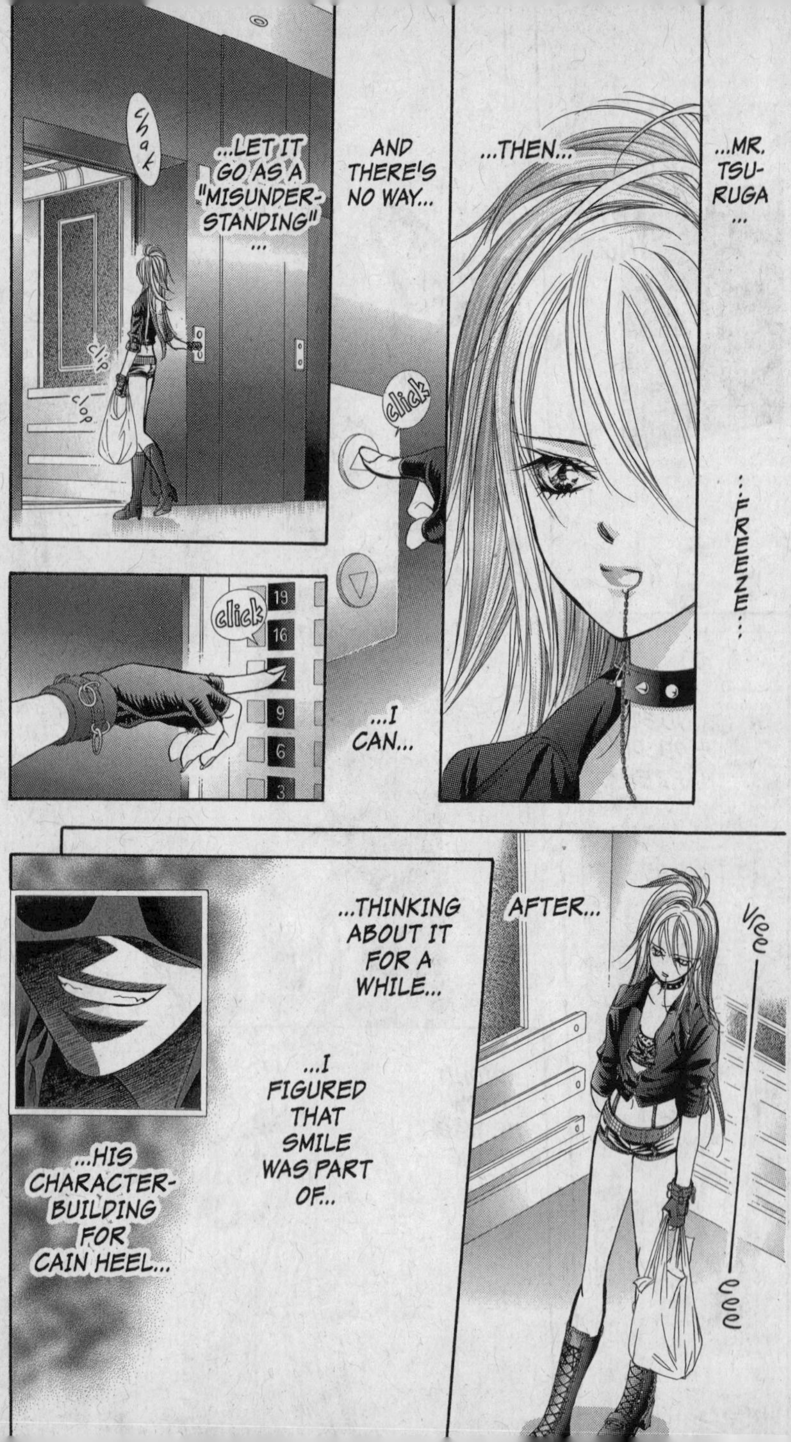
...MR. TSURUGA...
...FREEZE...
...THEN...
click
AND THERE'S NO WAY...
...LET IT GO AS A "MISUNDERSTANDING"...
chak
clip clop
click
...I CAN...
vree—eee
AFTER...
...THINKING ABOUT IT FOR A WHILE...
...I FIGURED THAT SMILE WAS PART OF...
...HIS CHARACTER-BUILDING FOR CAIN HEEL...

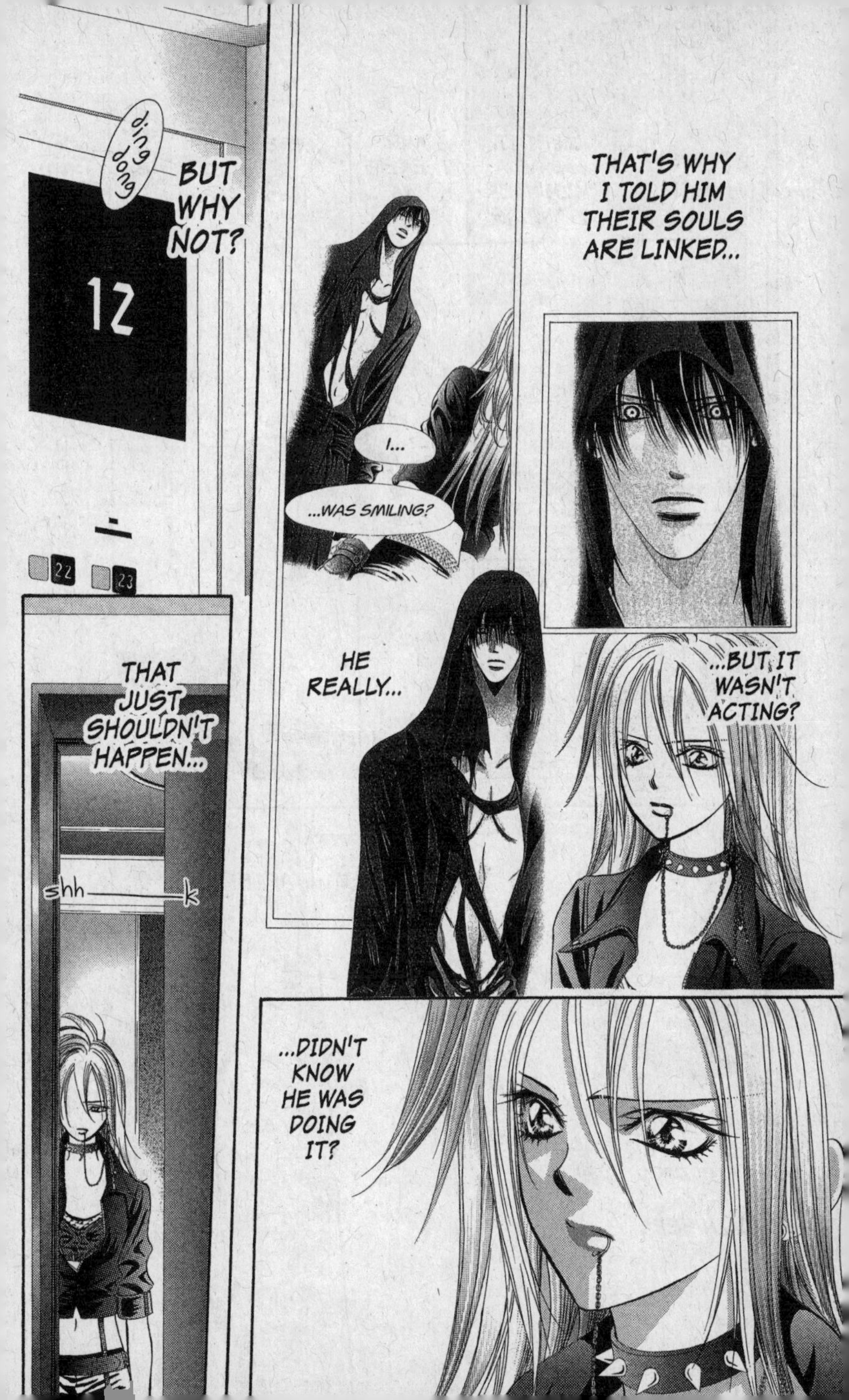
THAT'S WHY I TOLD HIM THEIR SOULS ARE LINKED...
I...
...WAS SMILING?
ding dong
BUT WHY NOT?
12
...BUT IT WASN'T ACTING?
HE REALLY...
...DIDN'T KNOW HE WAS DOING IT?
THAT JUST SHOULDN'T HAPPEN...
shh——k

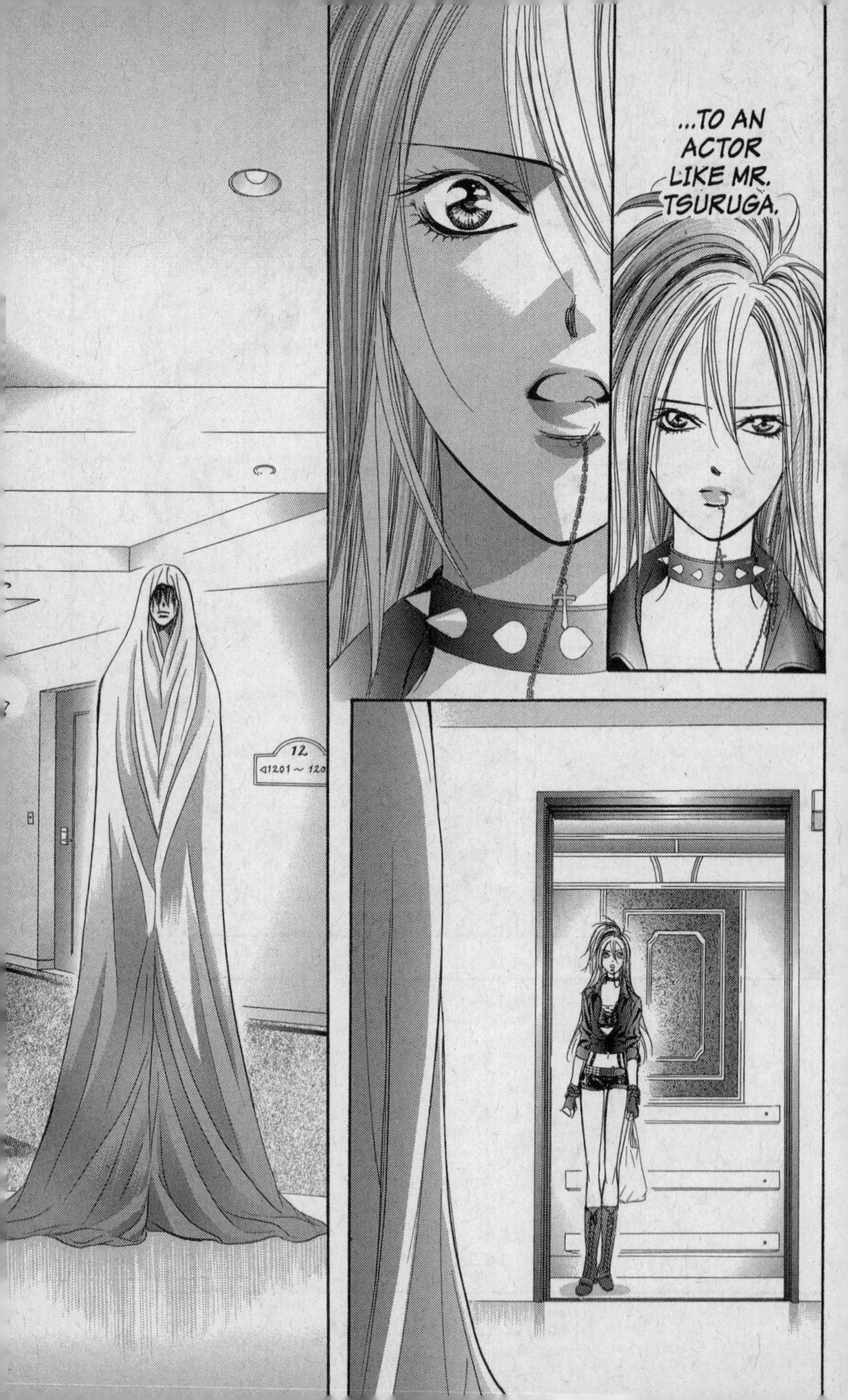
...TO AN ACTOR LIKE MR. TSURUGA.
12
◁1201 ~ 120

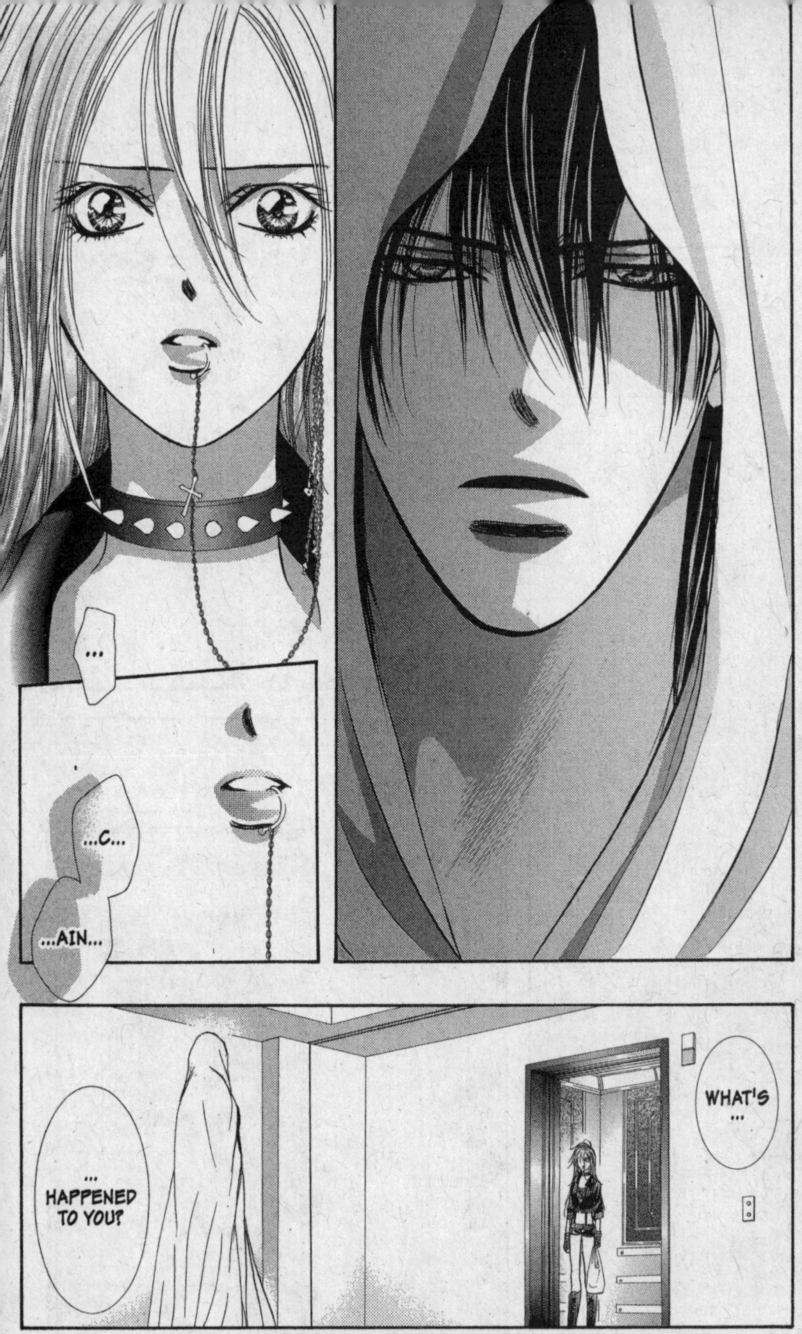
...
...C...
...AIN...
WHAT'S ...
... HAPPENED TO YOU?

End of Act 180

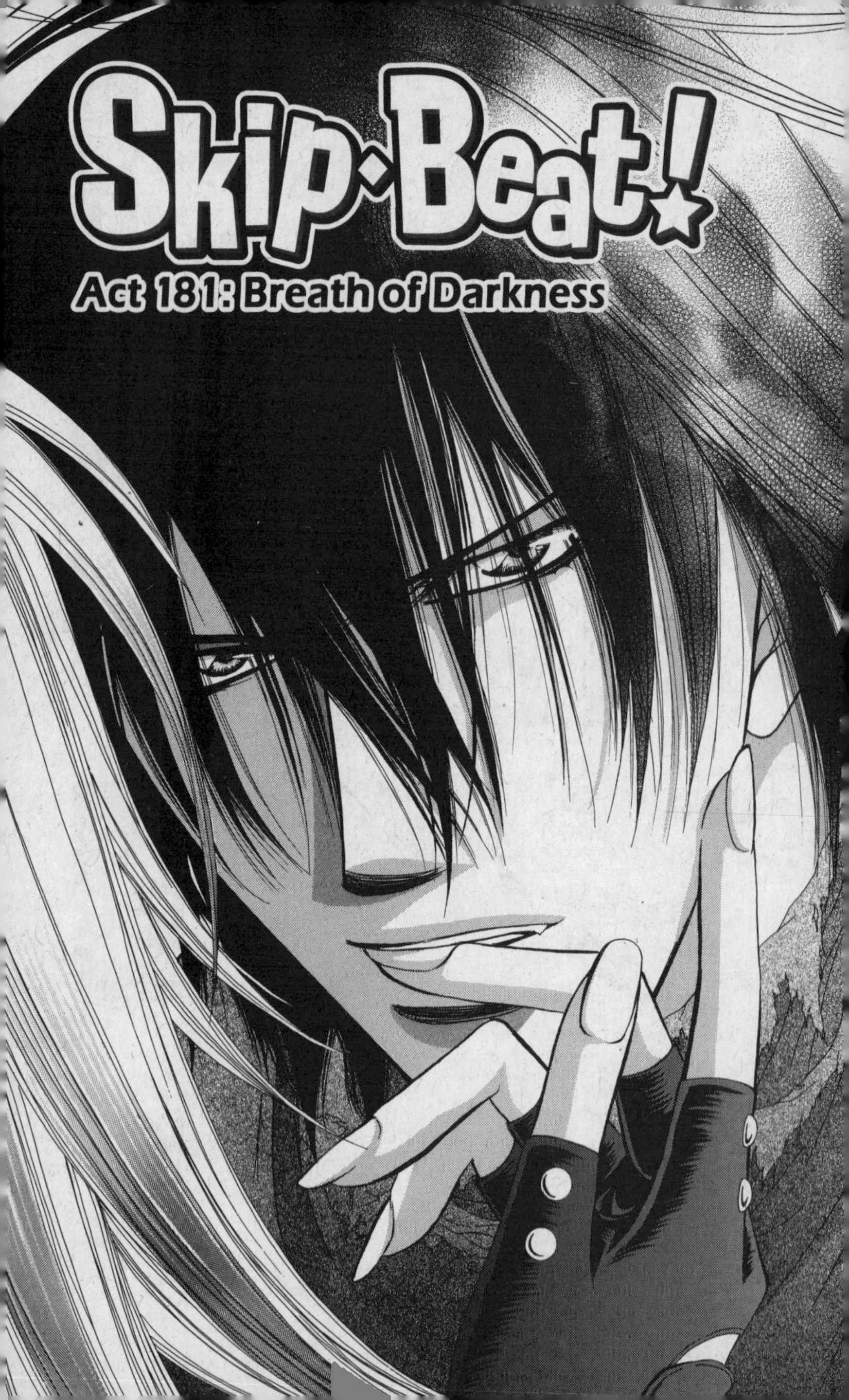
Skip·Beat!
Act 181: Breath of Darkness

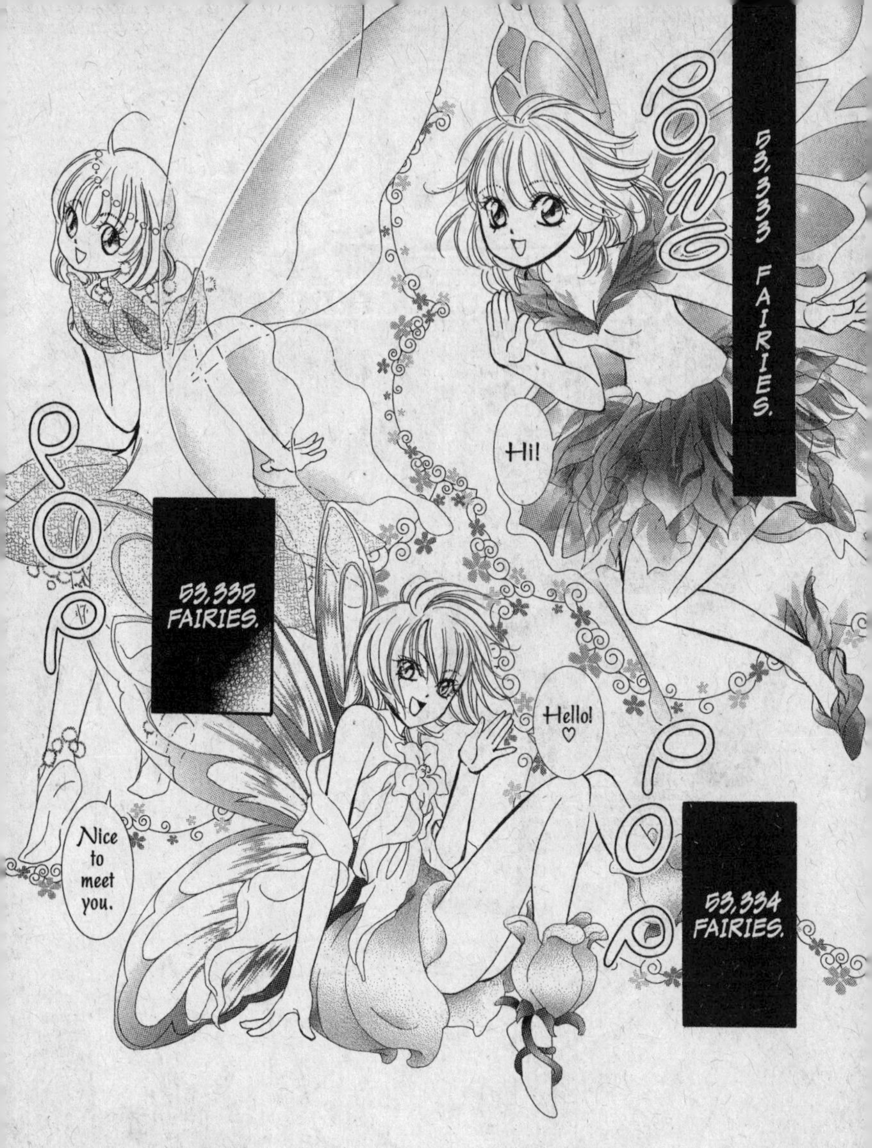
53,333 FAIRIES.
POING
Hi!
53,334 FAIRIES.
POP
Hello! ♡
53,335 FAIRIES.
POP
Nice to meet you.

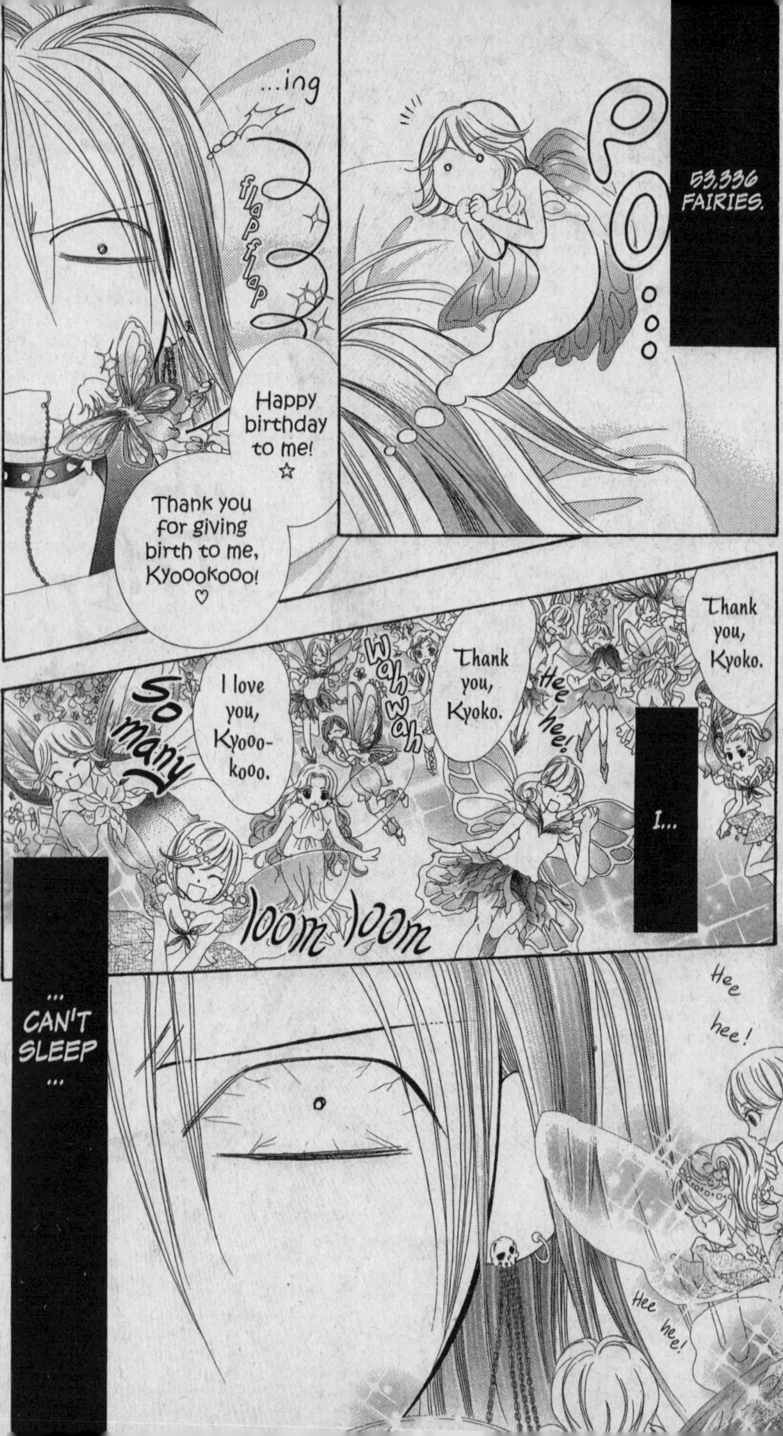
53,336 FAIRIES.
Pooo...
...ing
flapflap
Happy birthday to me! ☆
Thank you for giving birth to me, Kyoookooo! ♡
I...
Thank you, Kyoko.
Hee hee!
Thank you, Kyoko.
Wahwah
I love you, Kyooo-kooo.
So many
loom loom
Hee hee!
Hee hee!
... CAN'T SLEEP ...

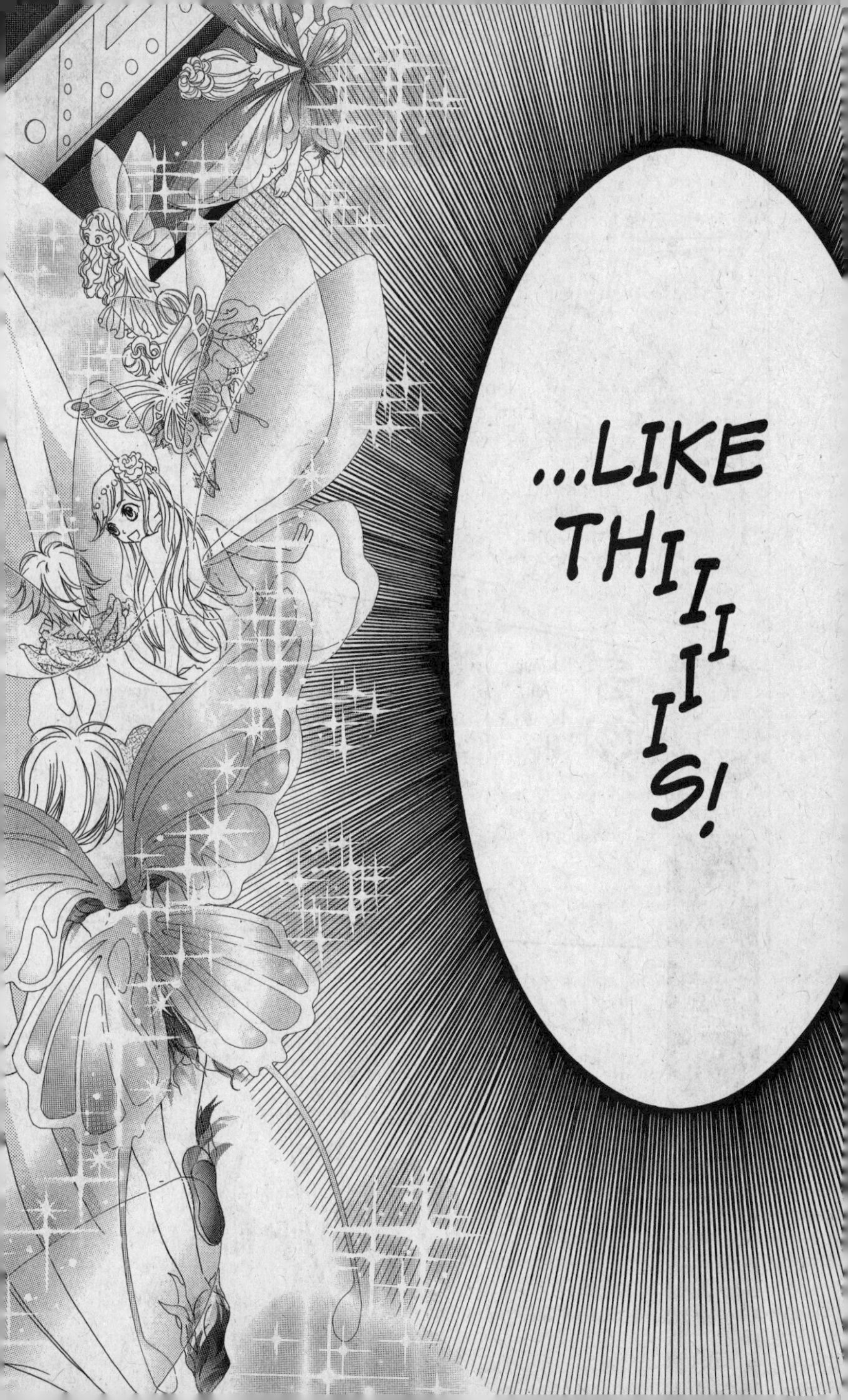
...LIKE THIIIIS!

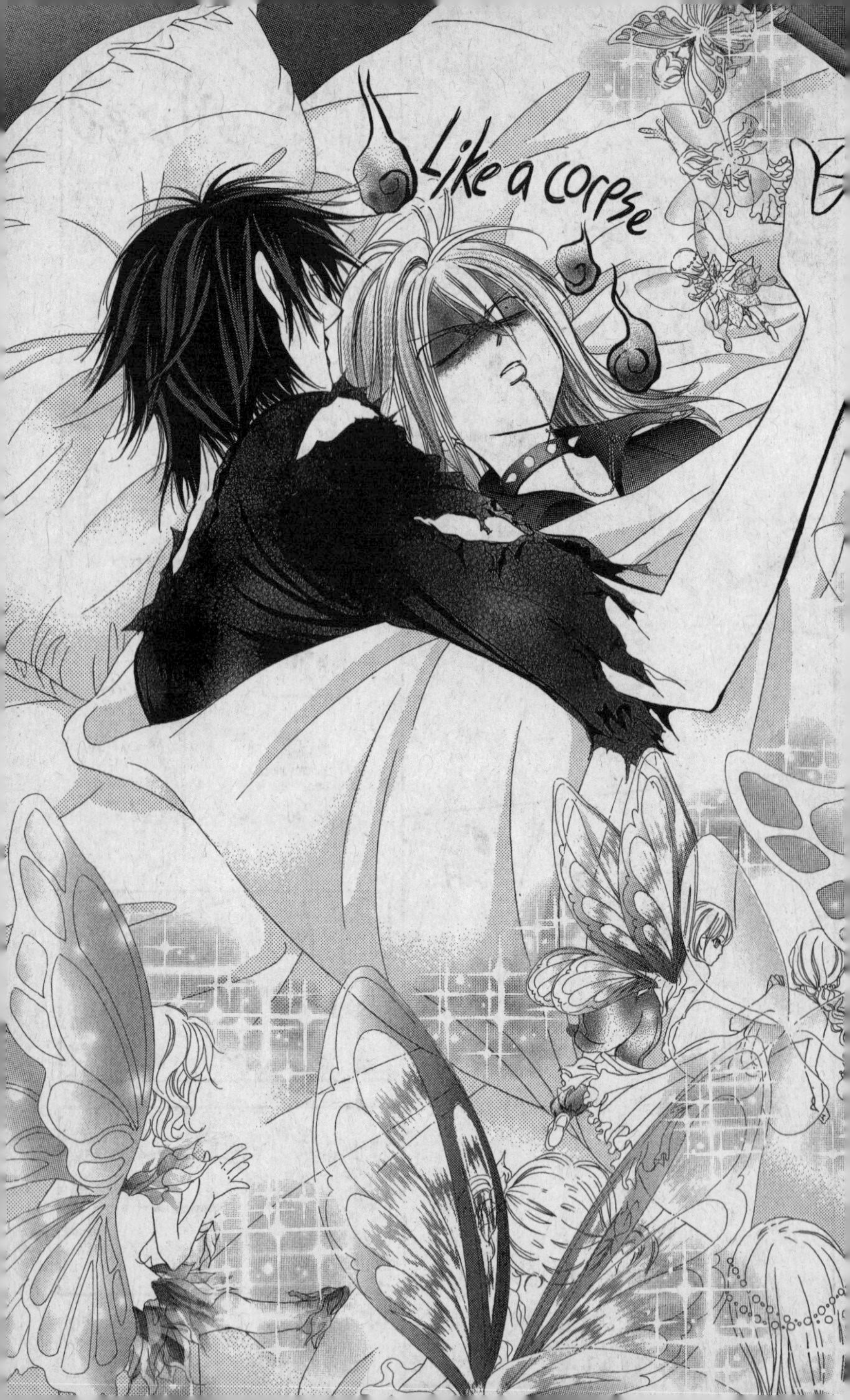
Like a corpse

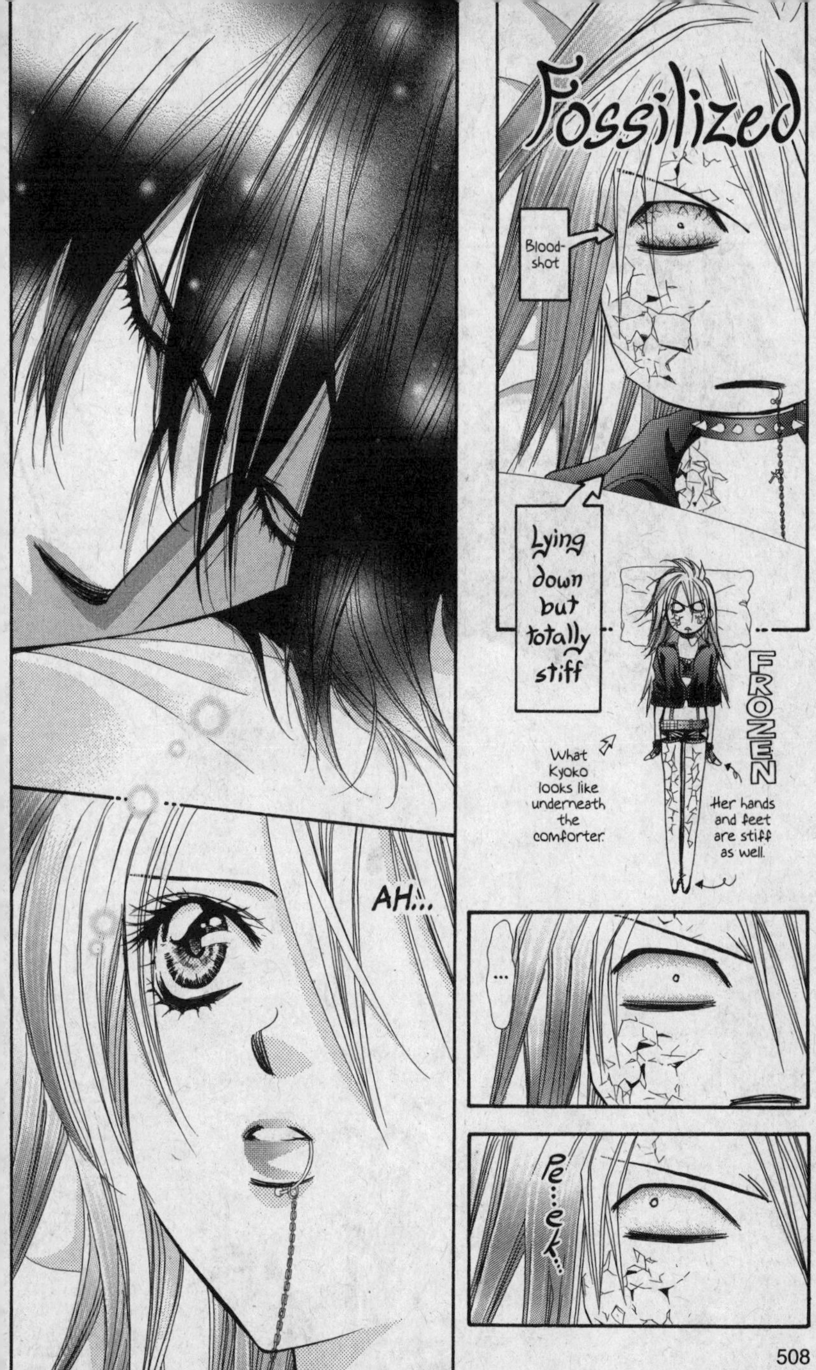
Fossilized
Blood-shot
Lying down but totally stiff
FROZEN
What Kyoko looks like underneath the comforter.
Her hands and feet are stiff as well.
...
Pe...ek...
AH...

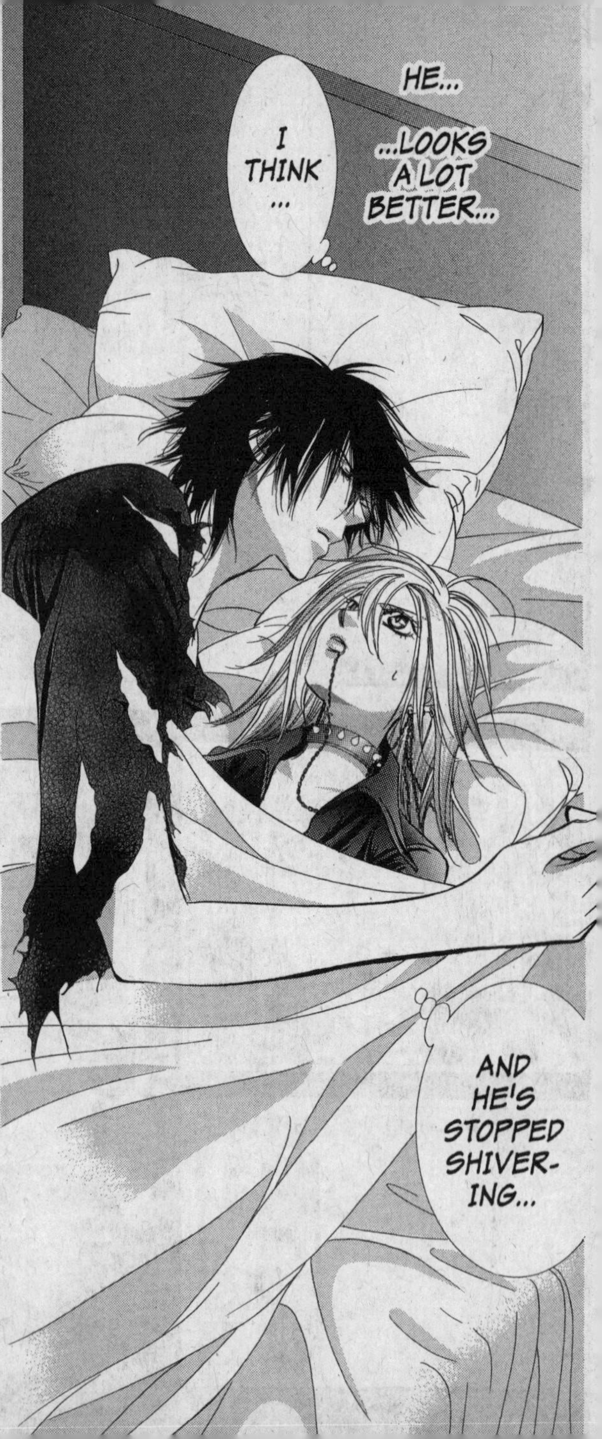
HE...
...LOOKS A LOT BETTER...
I THINK...
AND HE'S STOPPED SHIVER-ING...

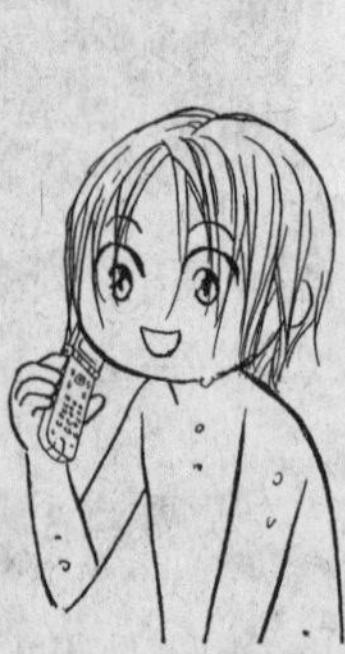

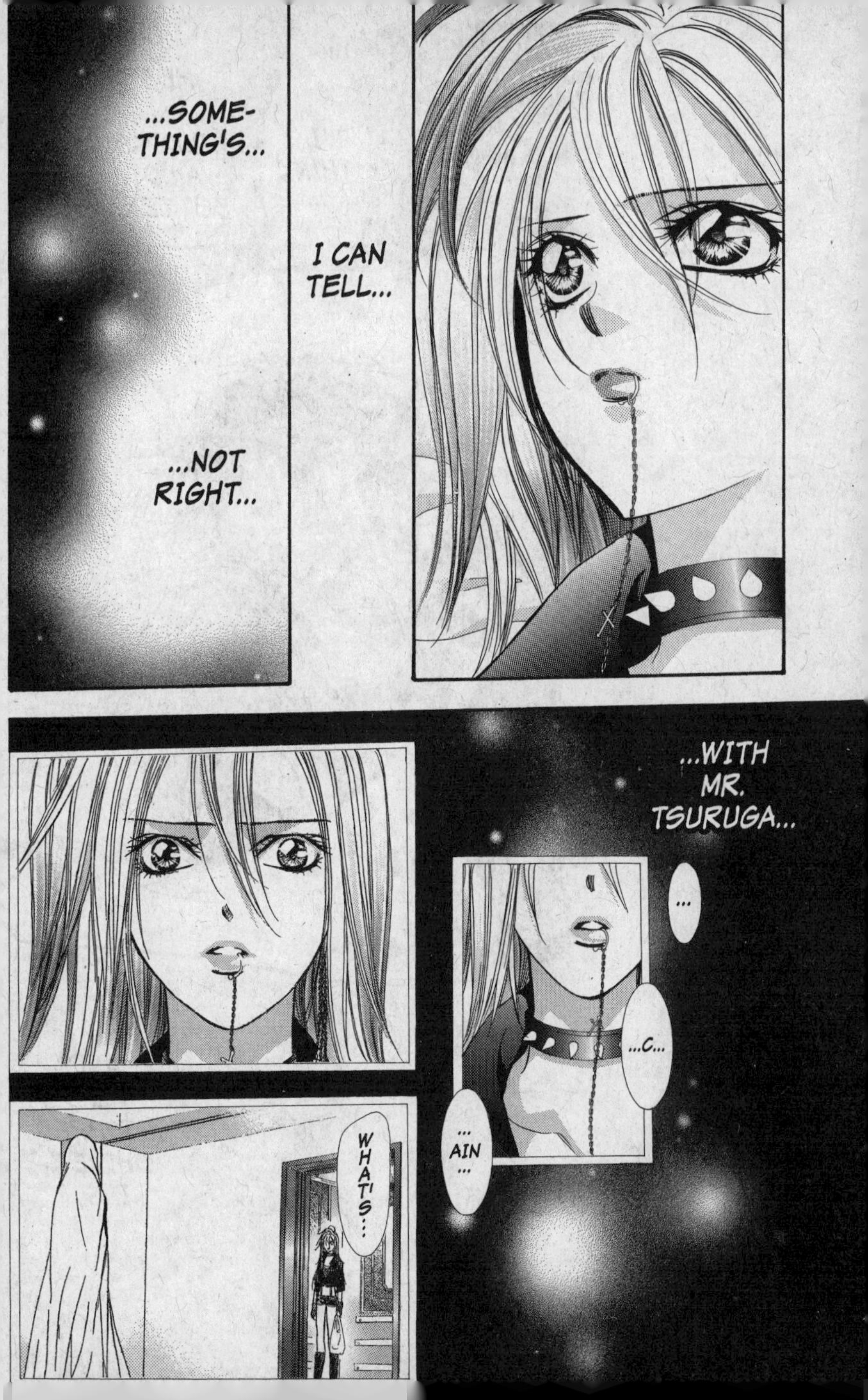
I CAN TELL...
...SOME-THING'S...
...NOT RIGHT...
...WITH MR. TSURUGA...
...
...C...
...AIN...
WHAT'S...

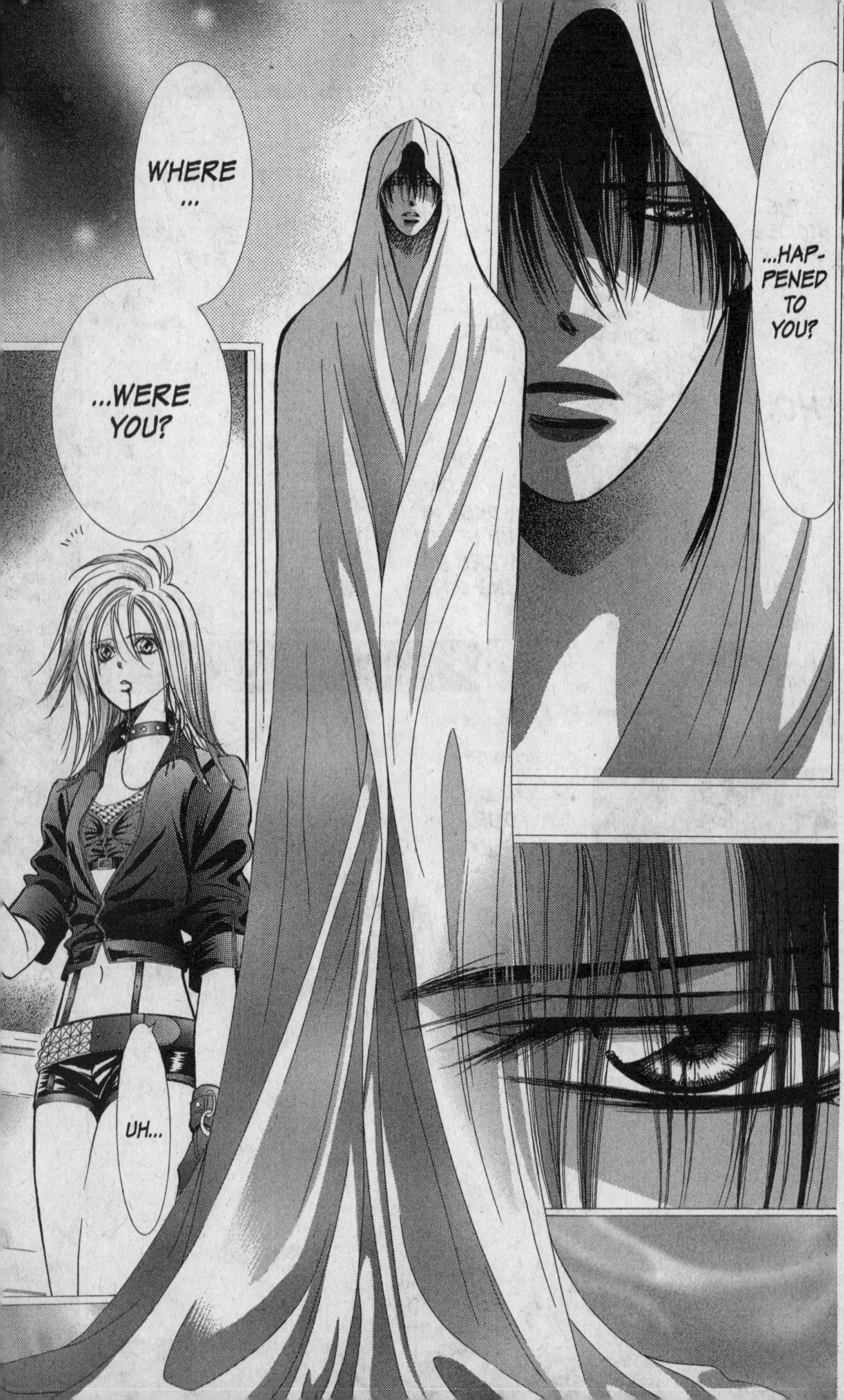
...HAP-PENED TO YOU?
WHERE ...
...WERE YOU?
UH...

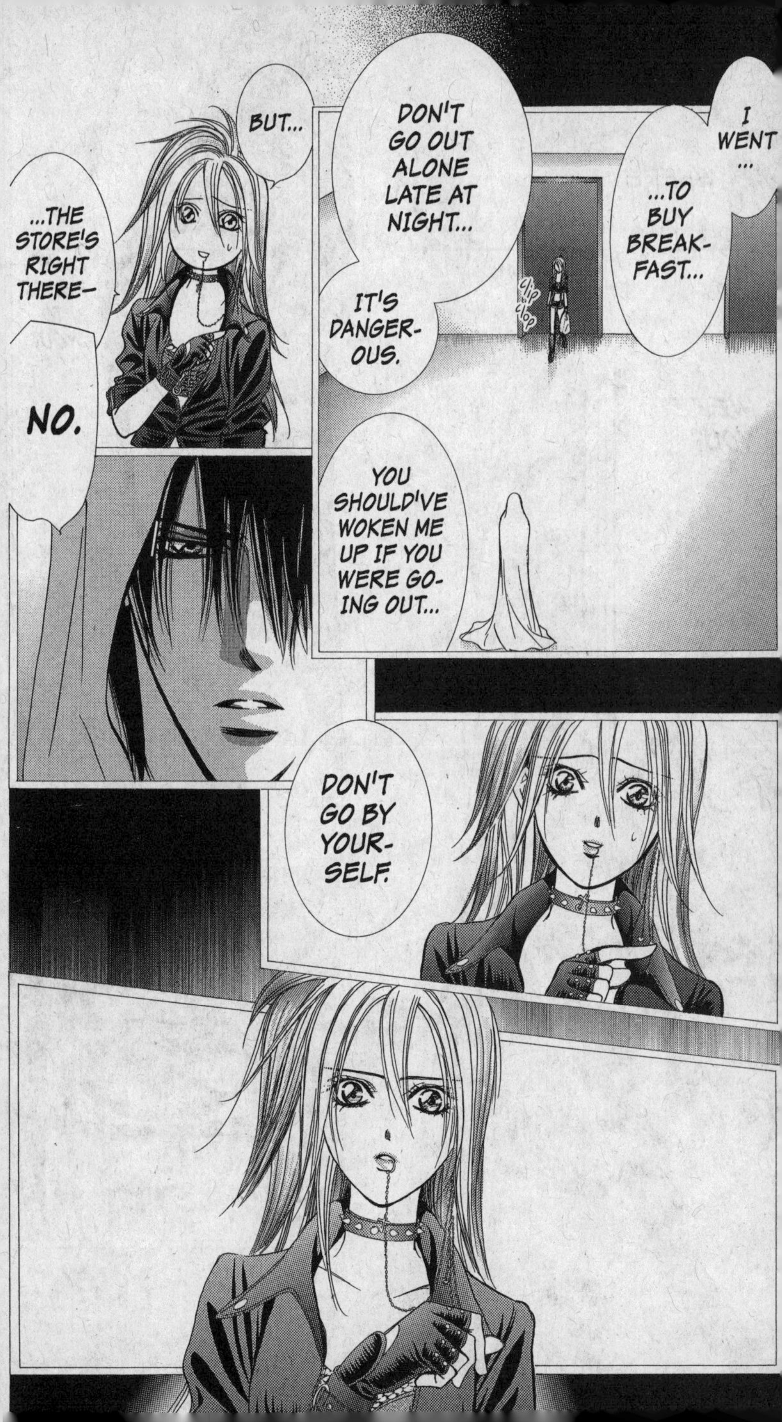
I WENT...
...TO BUY BREAKFAST...
DON'T GO OUT ALONE LATE AT NIGHT...
IT'S DANGEROUS.
YOU SHOULD'VE WOKEN ME UP IF YOU WERE GOING OUT...
BUT...
...THE STORE'S RIGHT THERE—
NO.
DON'T GO BY YOURSELF.

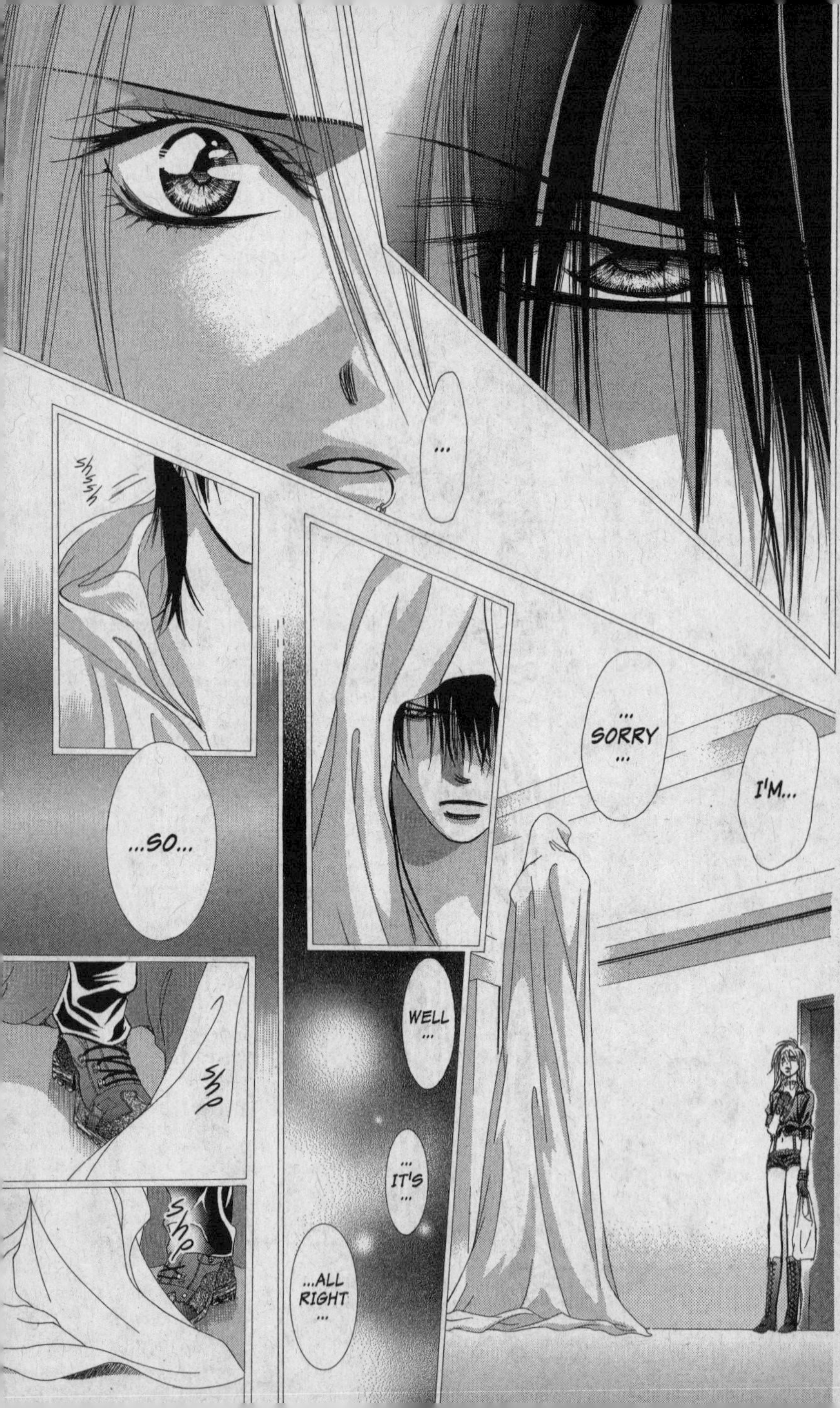
...
I'M...
...SORRY...
shssh
...SO...
WELL...
...IT'S...
...ALL RIGHT...
shp
shp

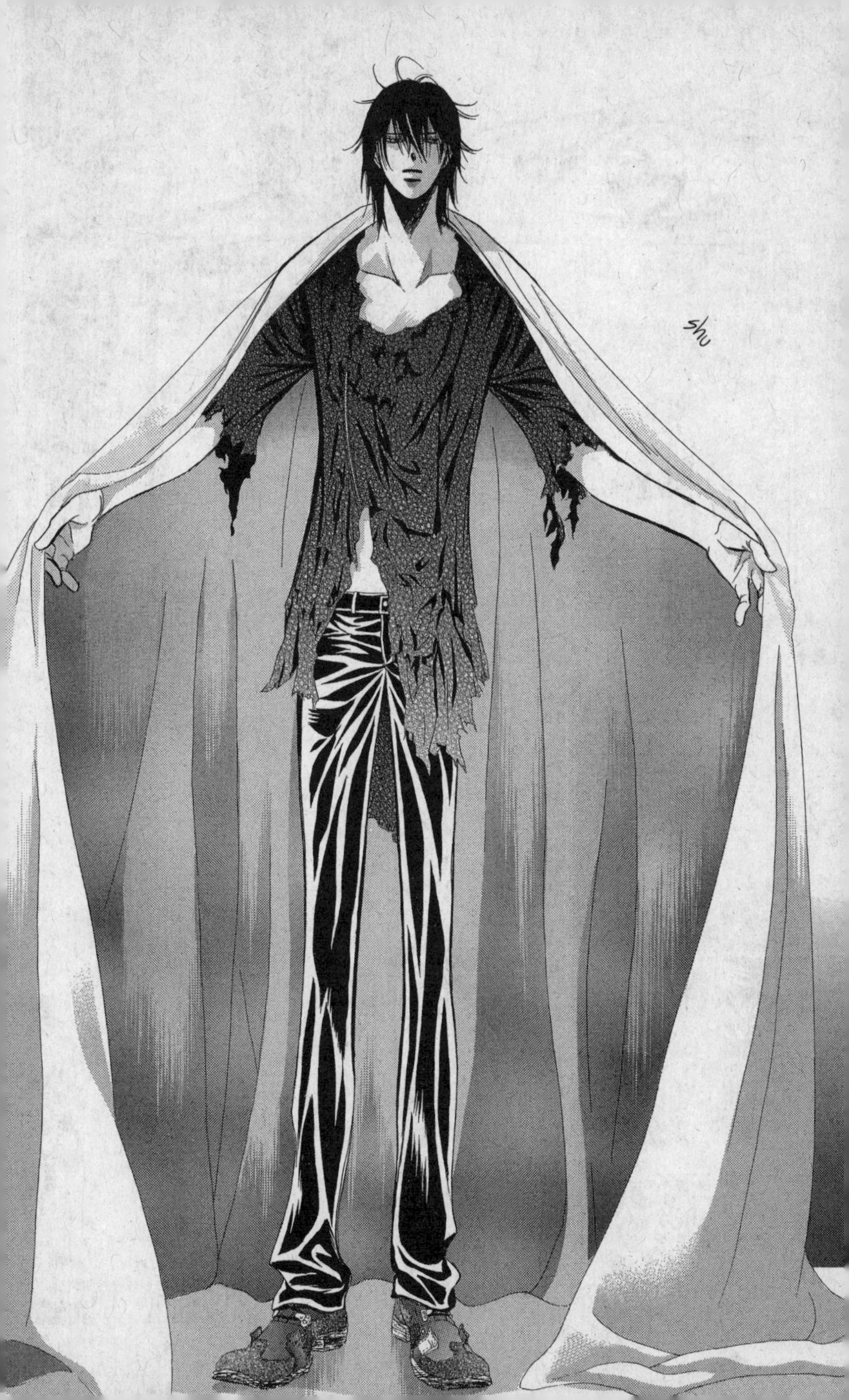
shu

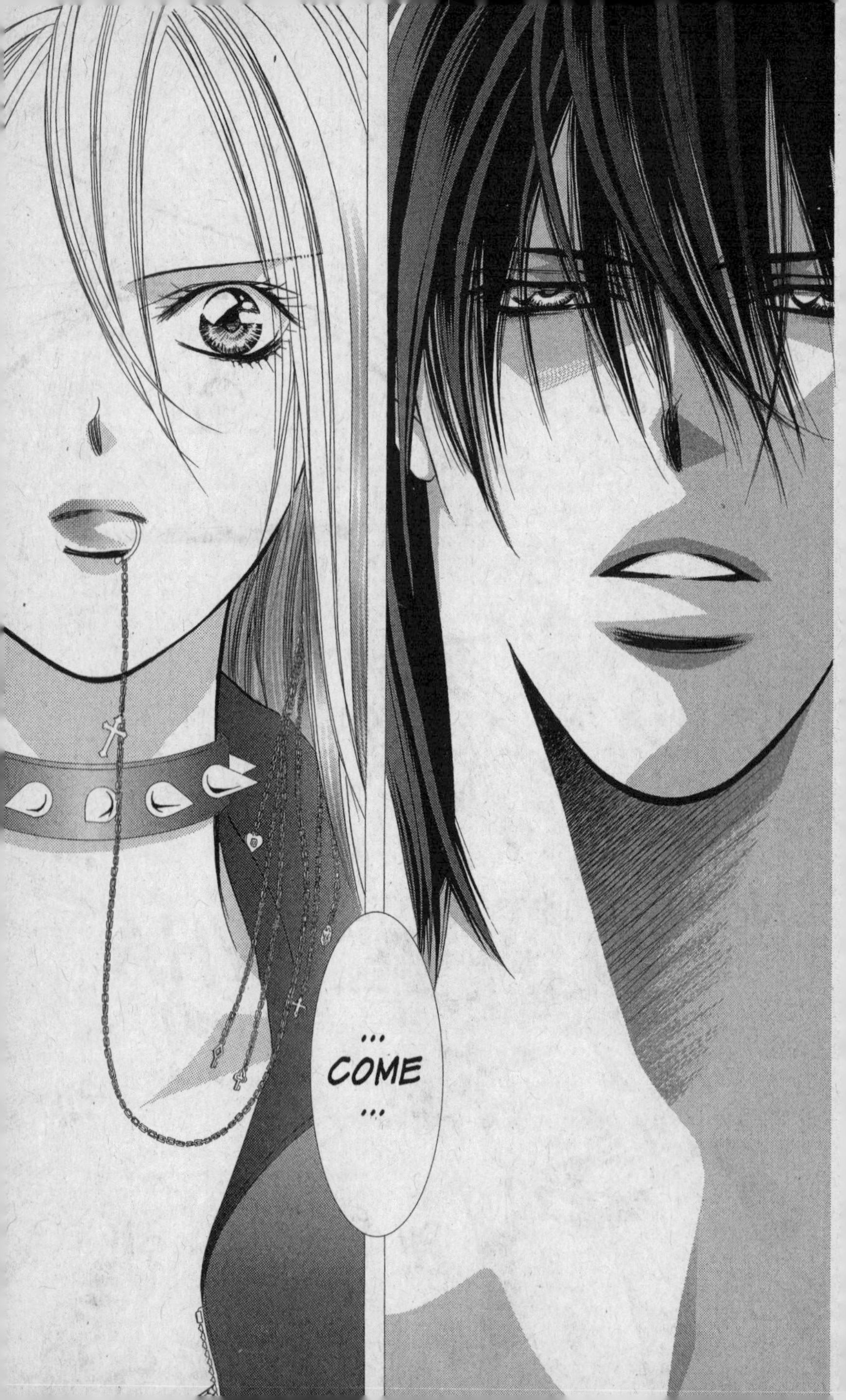
... COME ...

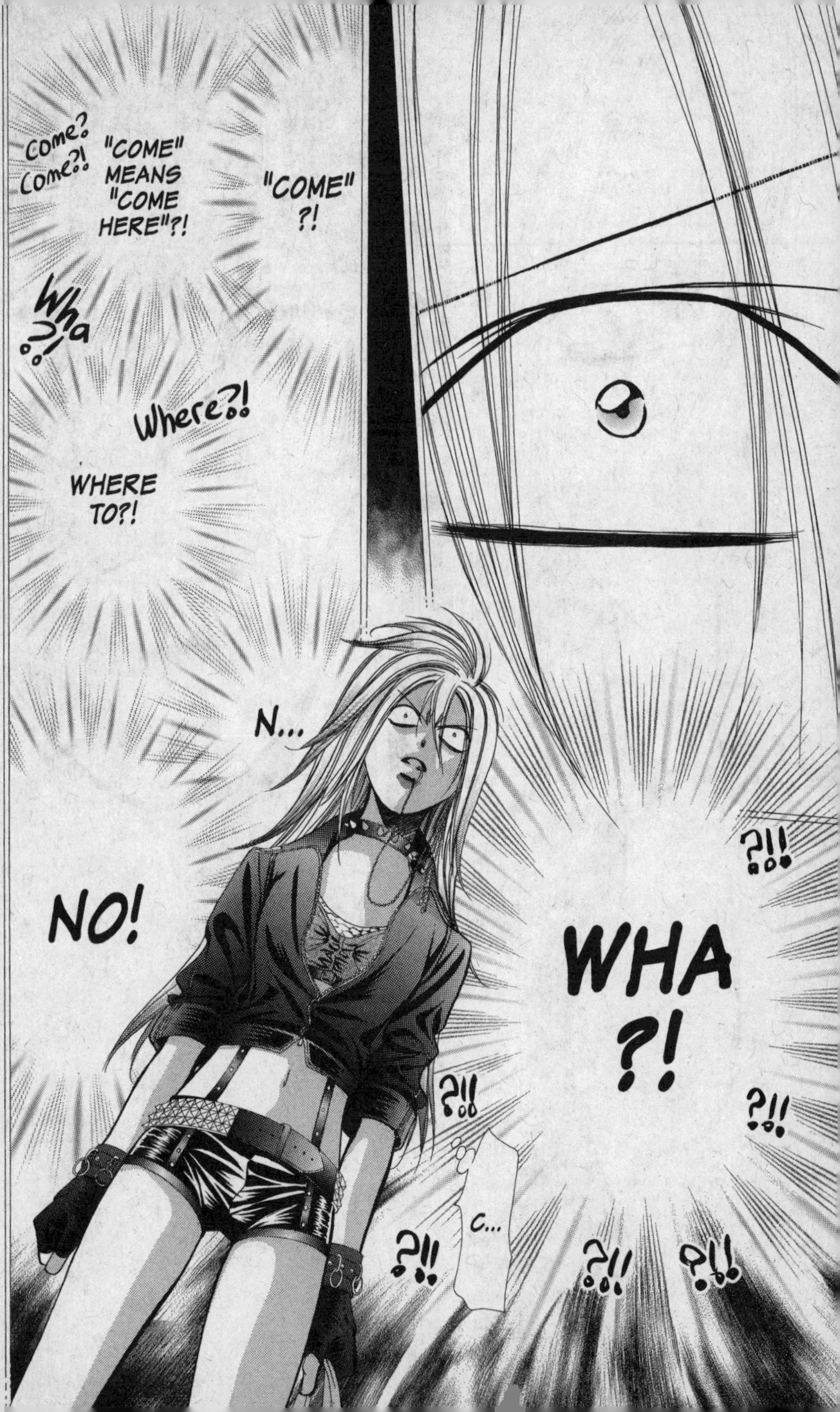
?!!
WHA ?!
?!!
C...
?!!
?!!
?!!
?!!
"COME" ?!
"COME" MEANS "COME HERE"?!
Come? Come?!
Wha ?!
Where?!
WHERE TO?!
N...
NO!

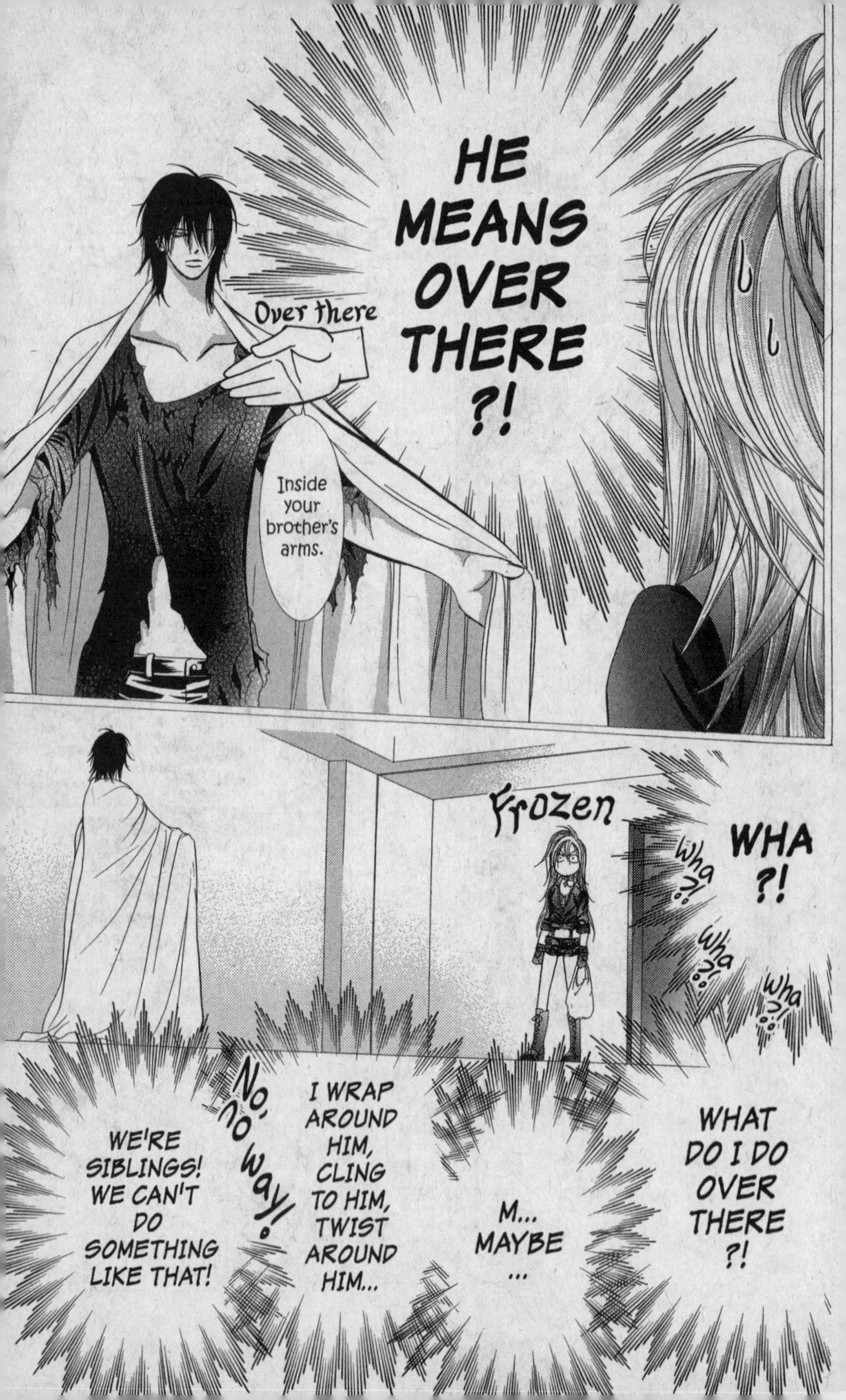
Over there
Inside your brother's arms.
HE MEANS OVER THERE ?!
Frozen
WHA ?!
Wha ?!
Wha ?!
Wha ?!
WHAT DO I DO OVER THERE ?!
M... MAYBE ...
I WRAP AROUND HIM, CLING TO HIM, TWIST AROUND HIM...
No, no way!
WE'RE SIBLINGS! WE CAN'T DO SOMETHING LIKE THAT!

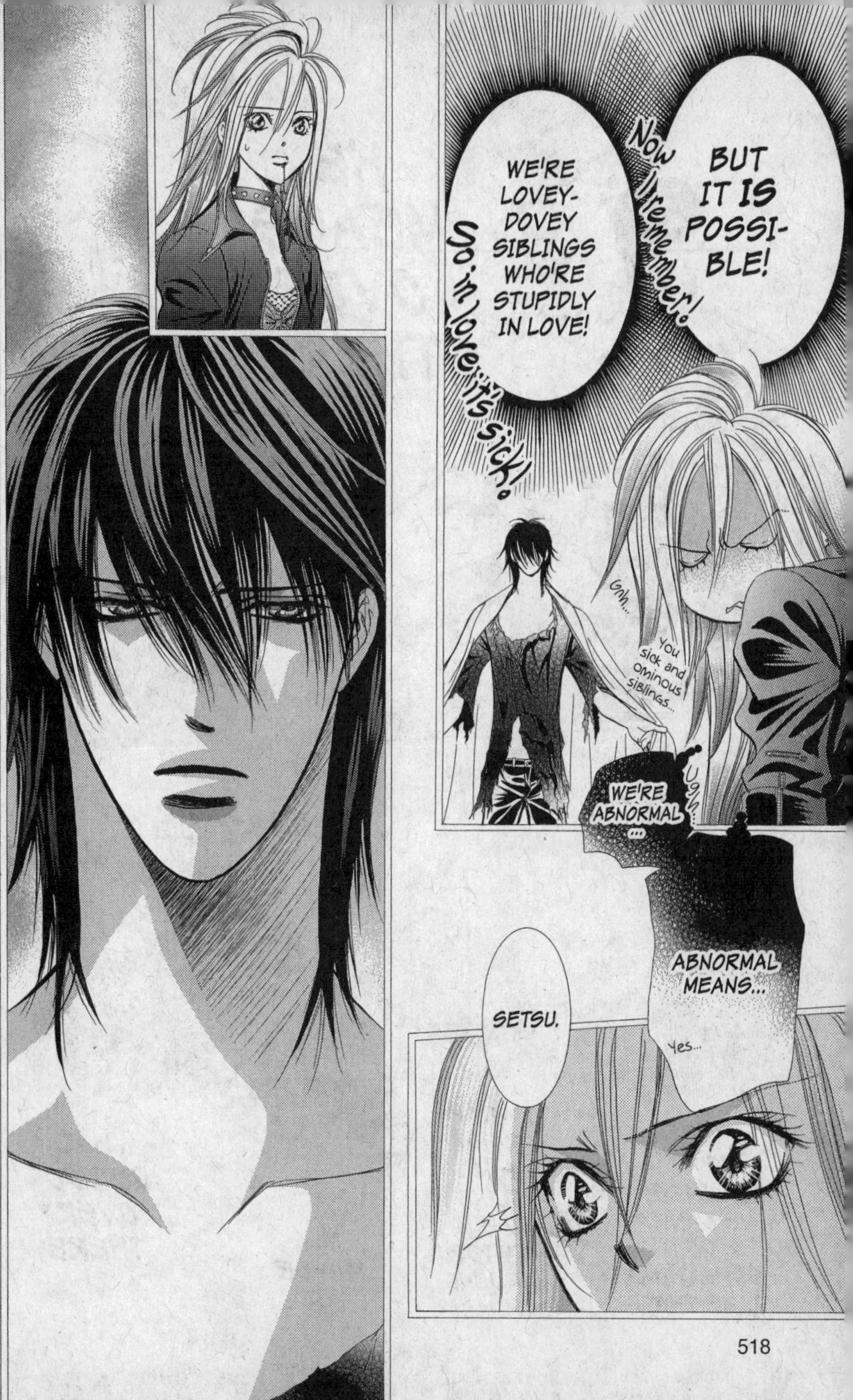
BUT IT IS POSSIBLE!
Now I remember!
WE'RE LOVEY-DOVEY SIBLINGS WHO'RE STUPIDLY IN LOVE!
So in love it's sick!
Gnh...
You sick and ominous siblings...
Ugh...
WE'RE ABNORMAL...
ABNORMAL MEANS...
Yes...
SETSU.

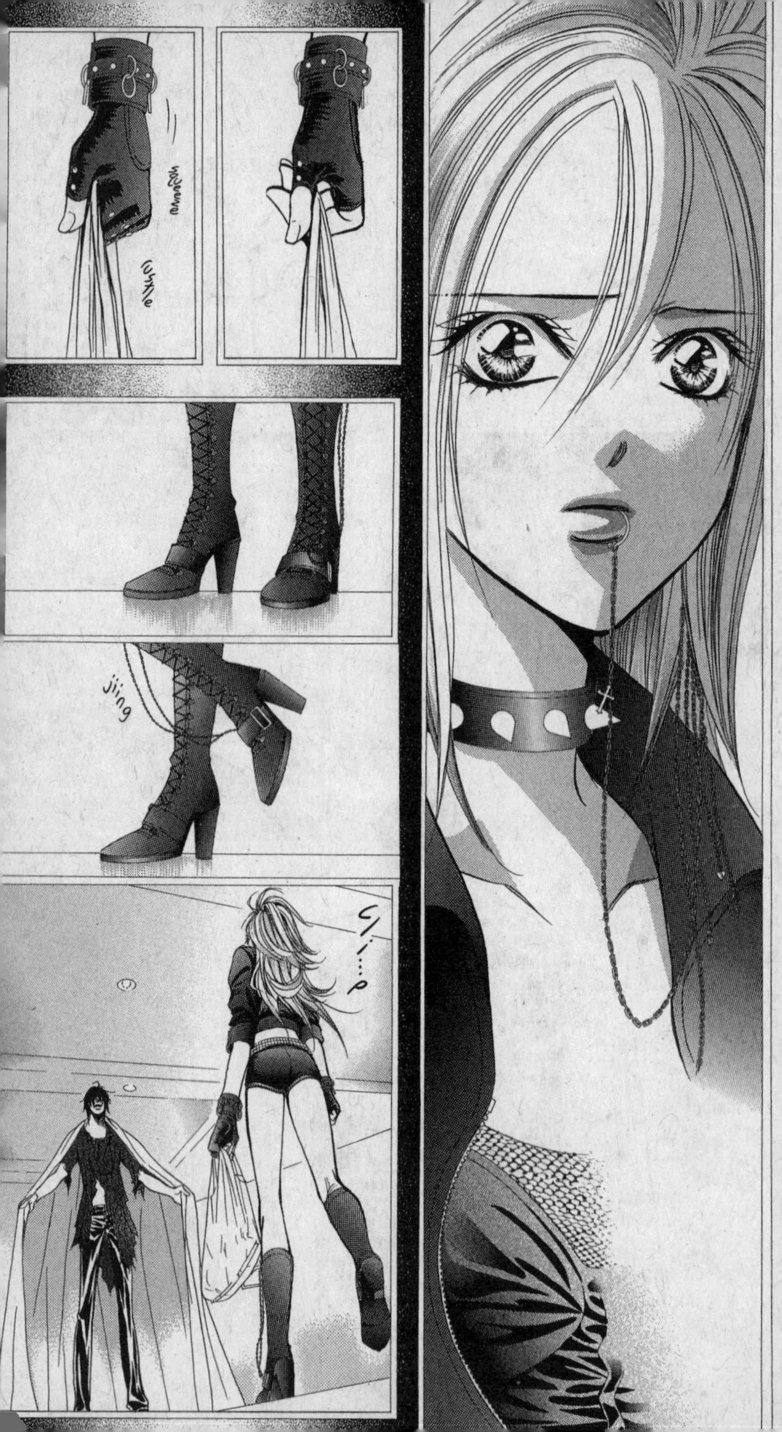
squeeze
rustle
jiiing
Cli...p

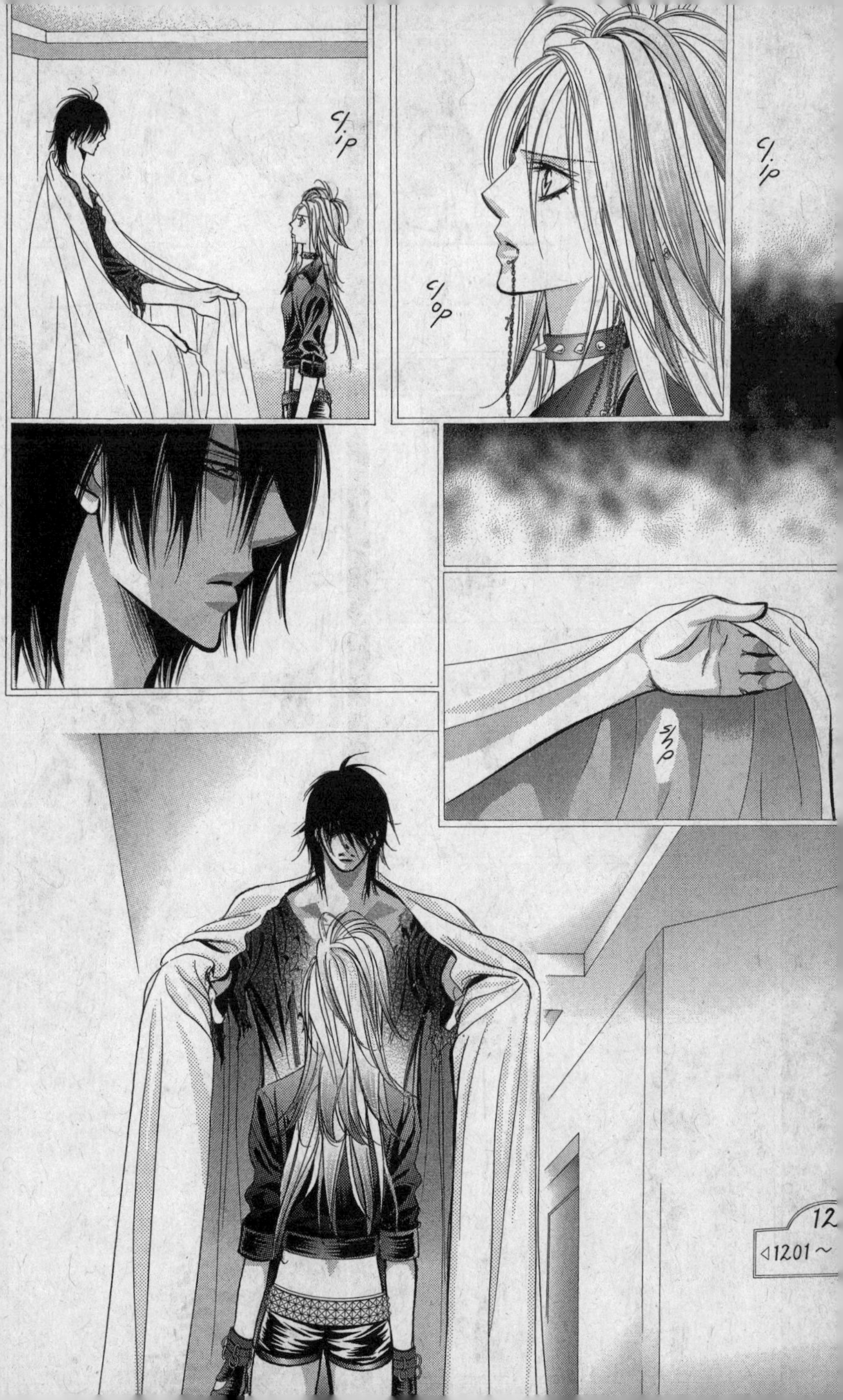
clip
clop
clip
slip
12
◁1201~

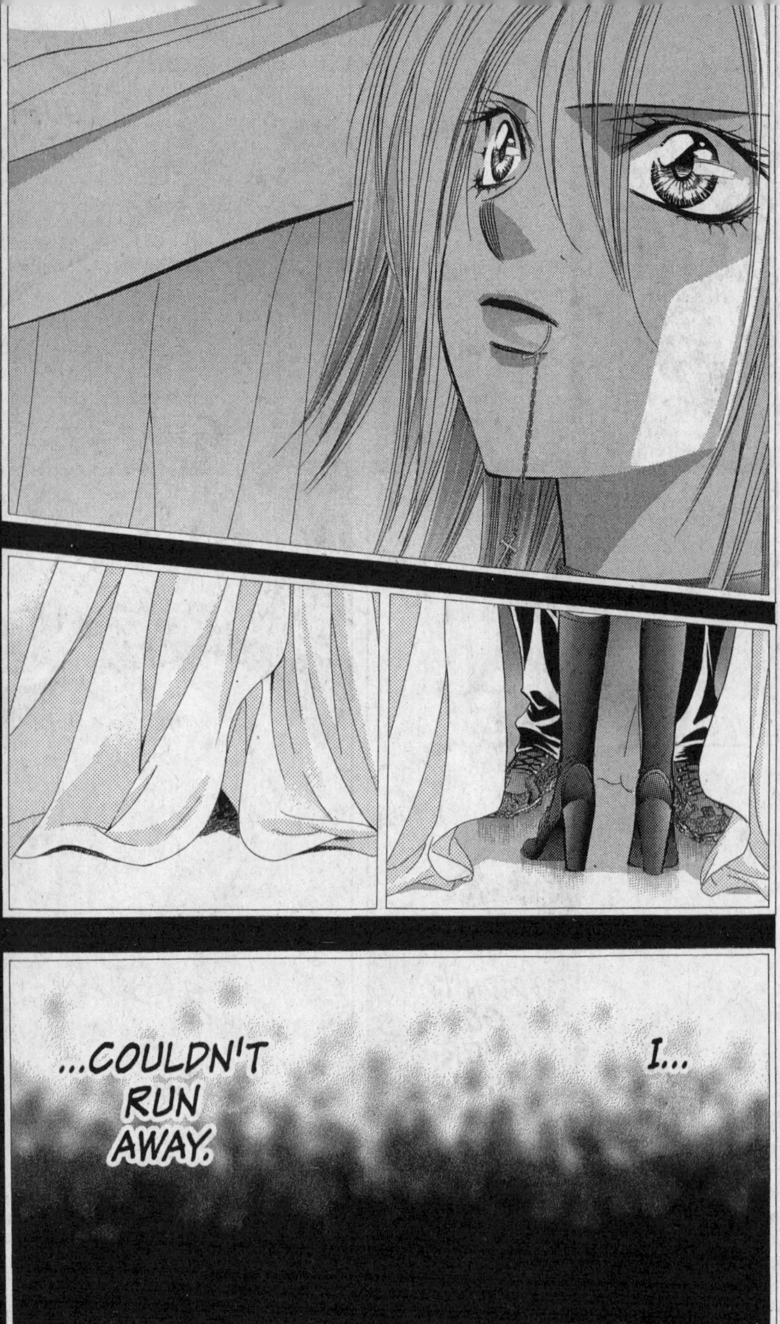
I...
...COULDN'T RUN AWAY.

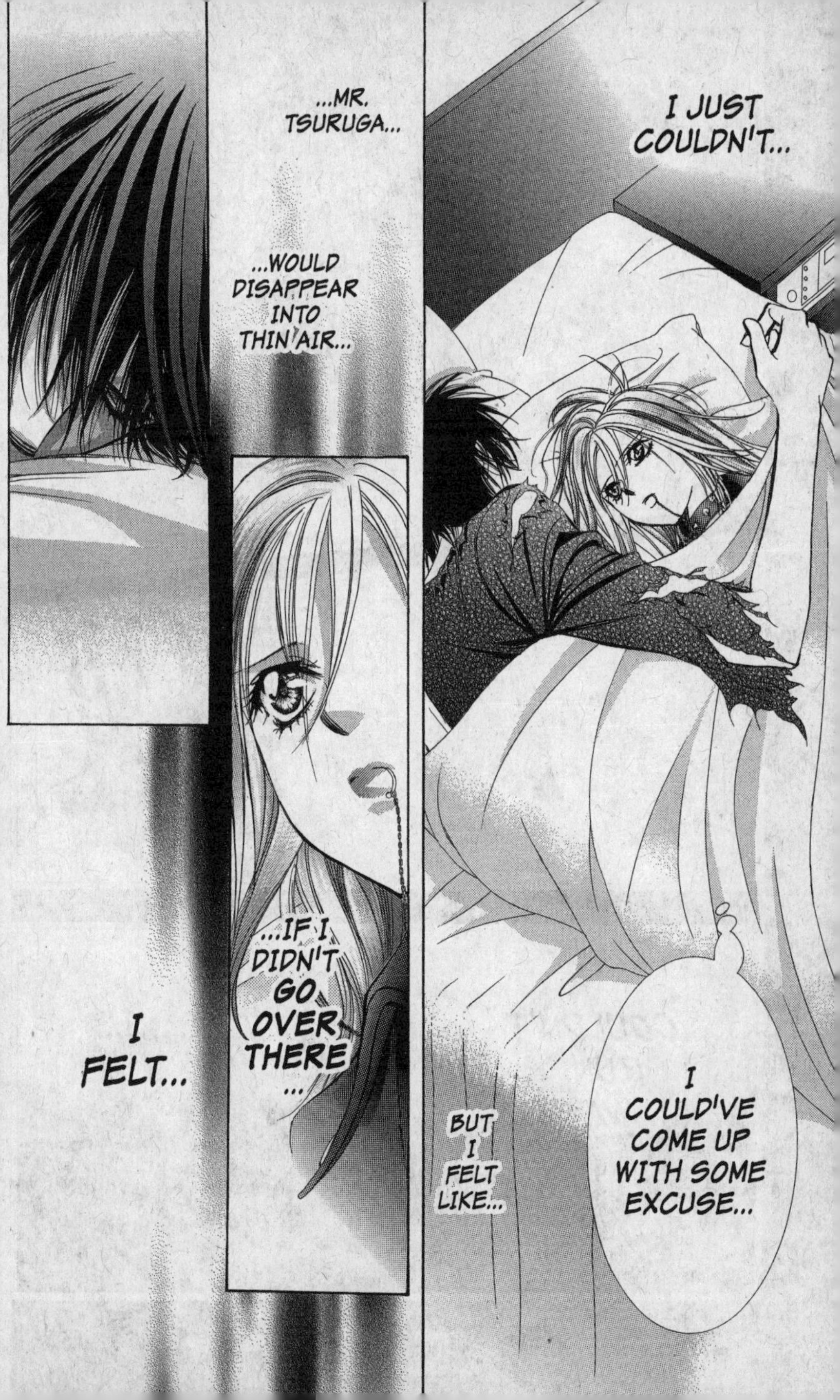
I JUST COULDN'T...
I COULD'VE COME UP WITH SOME EXCUSE...
BUT I FELT LIKE...
...MR. TSURUGA...
...WOULD DISAPPEAR INTO THIN AIR...
...IF I DIDN'T GO OVER THERE...
I FELT...

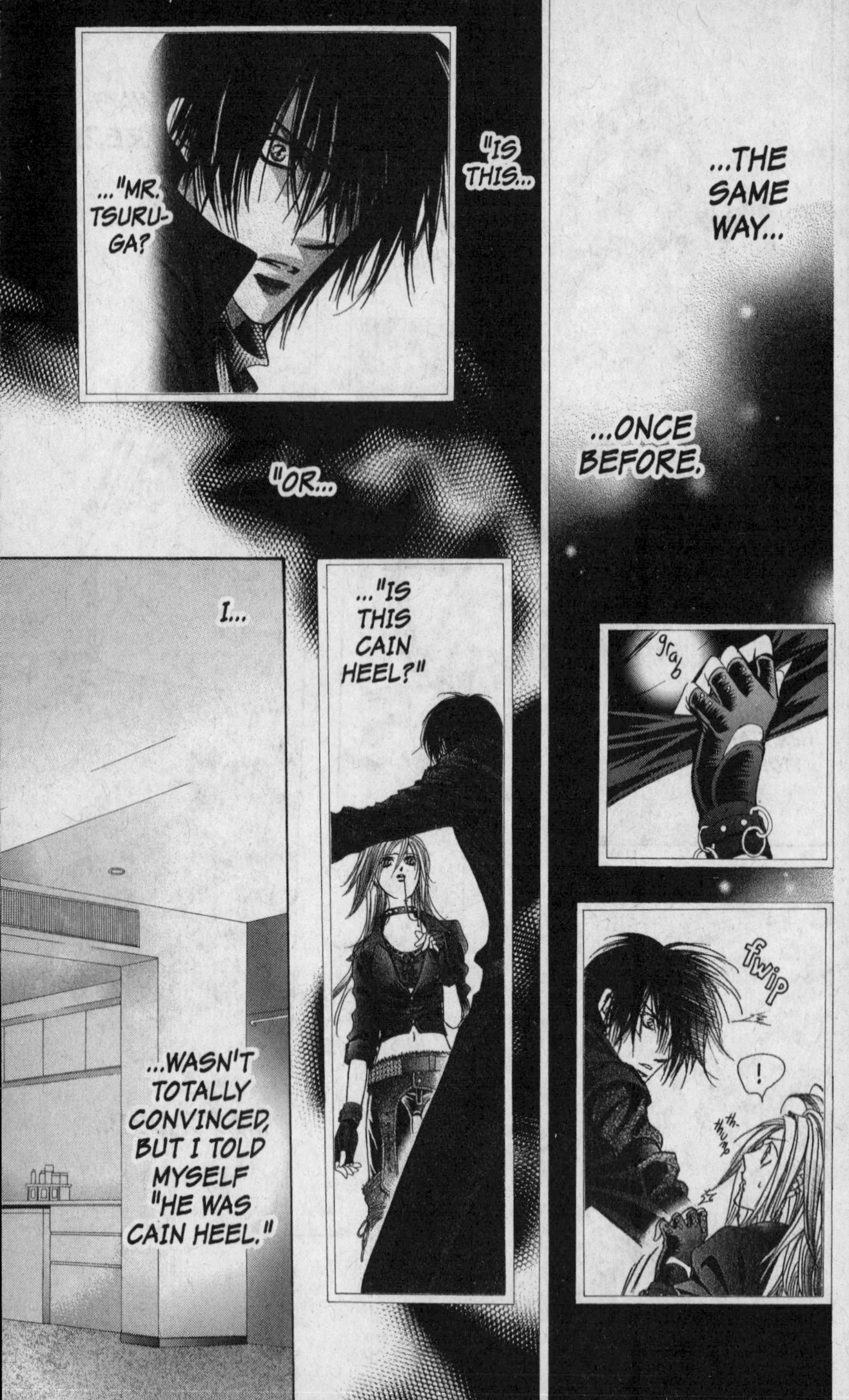
...THE SAME WAY...
...ONCE BEFORE.
grab
fwip
!
th-thump
"IS THIS...
..."MR. TSURUGA?
"OR...
..."IS THIS CAIN HEEL?"
I...
...WASN'T TOTALLY CONVINCED, BUT I TOLD MYSELF "HE WAS CAIN HEEL."

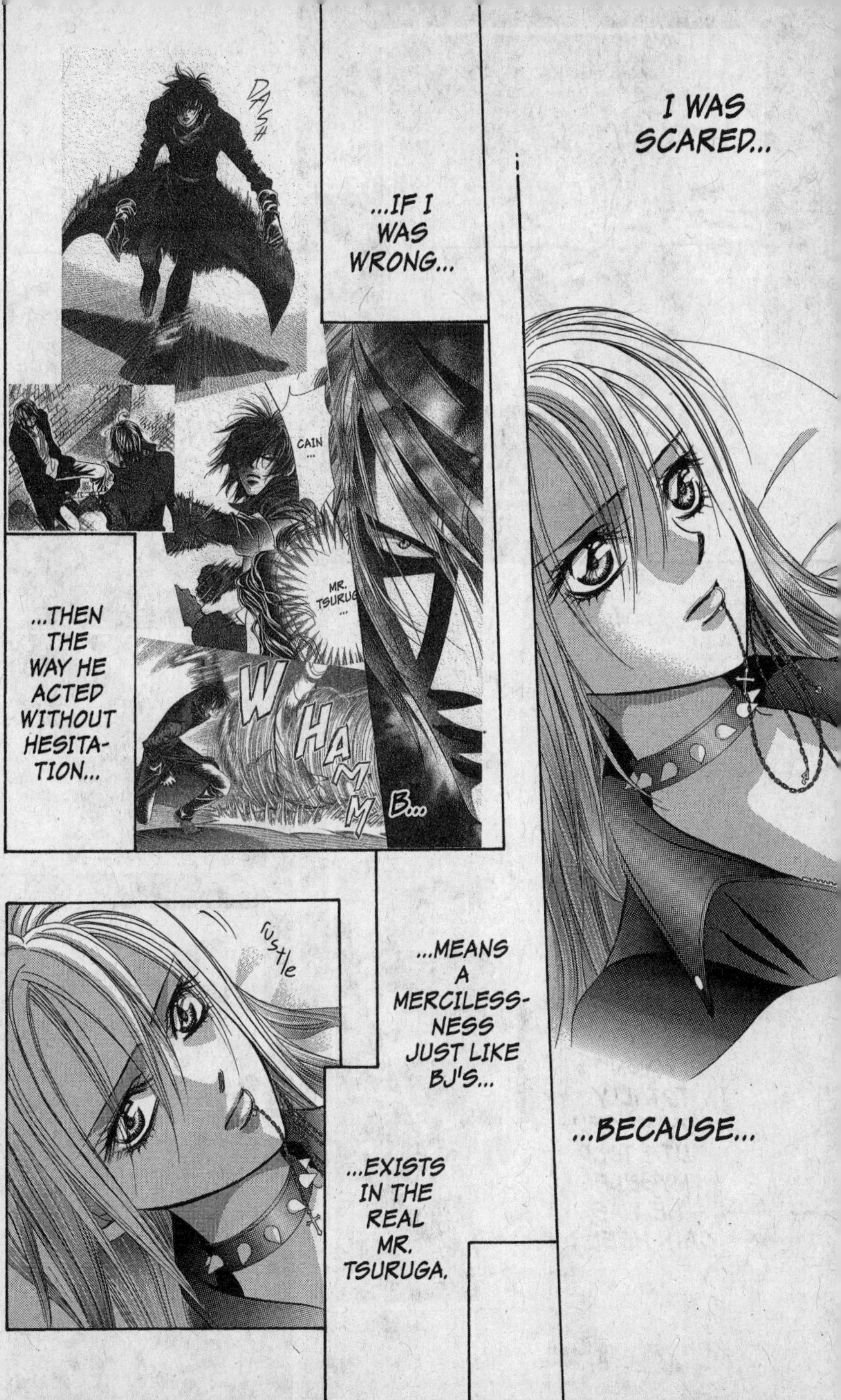
I WAS SCARED...
...BECAUSE...
...IF I WAS WRONG...
DASH
CAIN...
MR. TSURUGA...
WHAMM
B...
...THEN THE WAY HE ACTED WITHOUT HESITATION...
...MEANS A MERCILESSNESS JUST LIKE BJ'S...
rustle
...EXISTS IN THE REAL MR. TSURUGA.

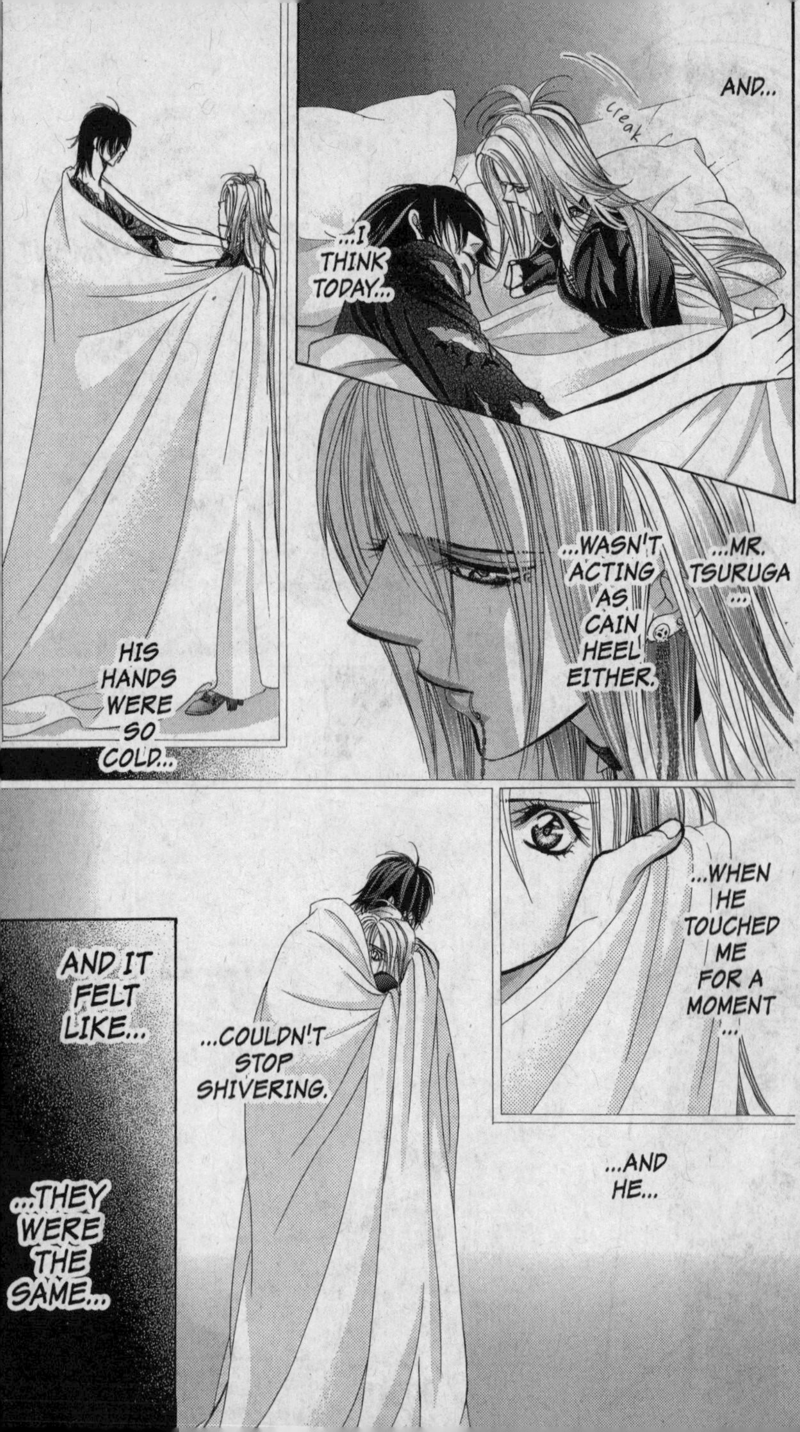
AND...
creak
...I THINK TODAY...
...MR. TSURUGA...
...WASN'T ACTING AS CAIN HEEL EITHER.
HIS HANDS WERE SO COLD...
...WHEN HE TOUCHED ME FOR A MOMENT...
...AND HE...
...COULDN'T STOP SHIVERING.
AND IT FELT LIKE...
...THEY WERE THE SAME...

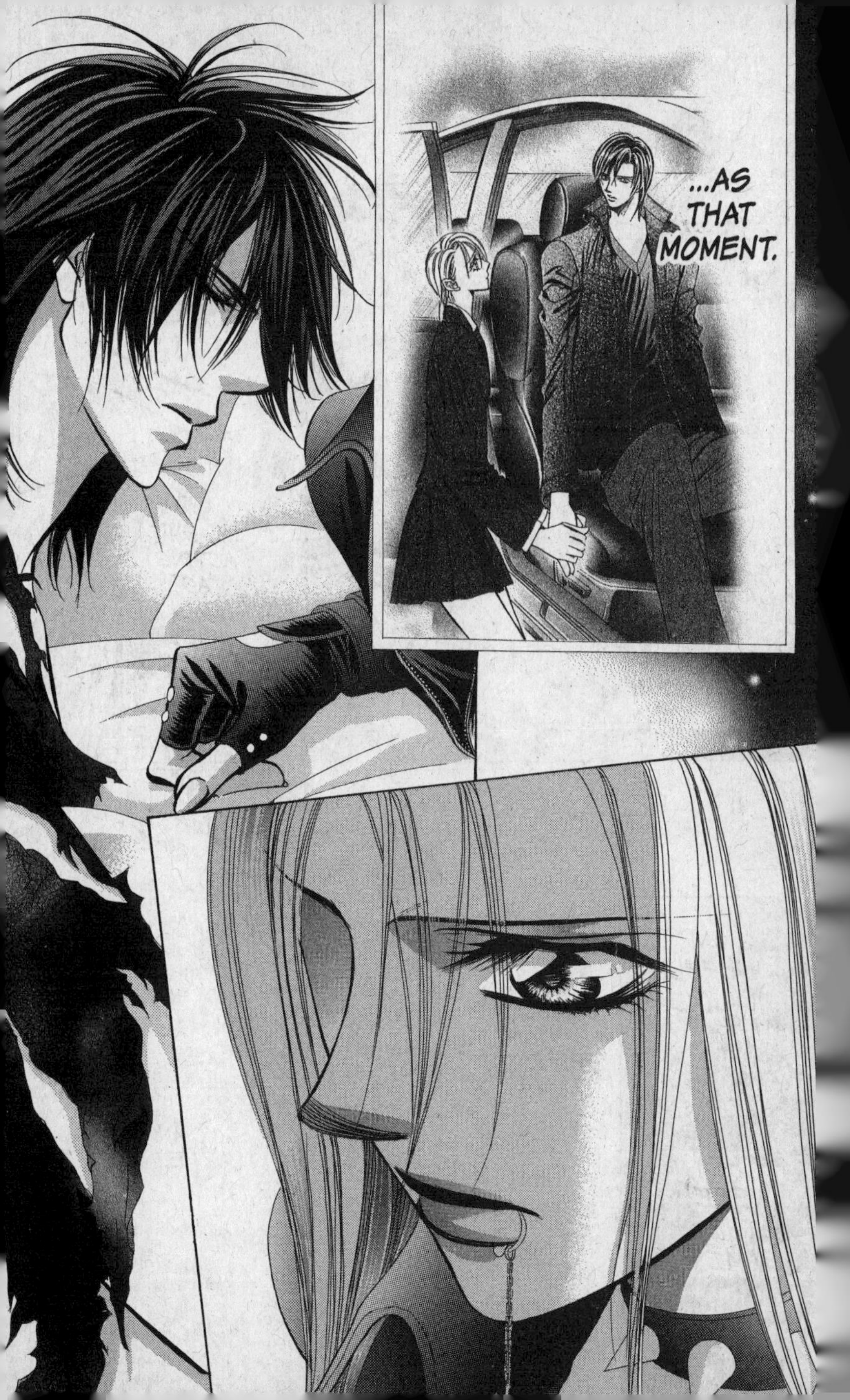
...AS THAT MOMENT.

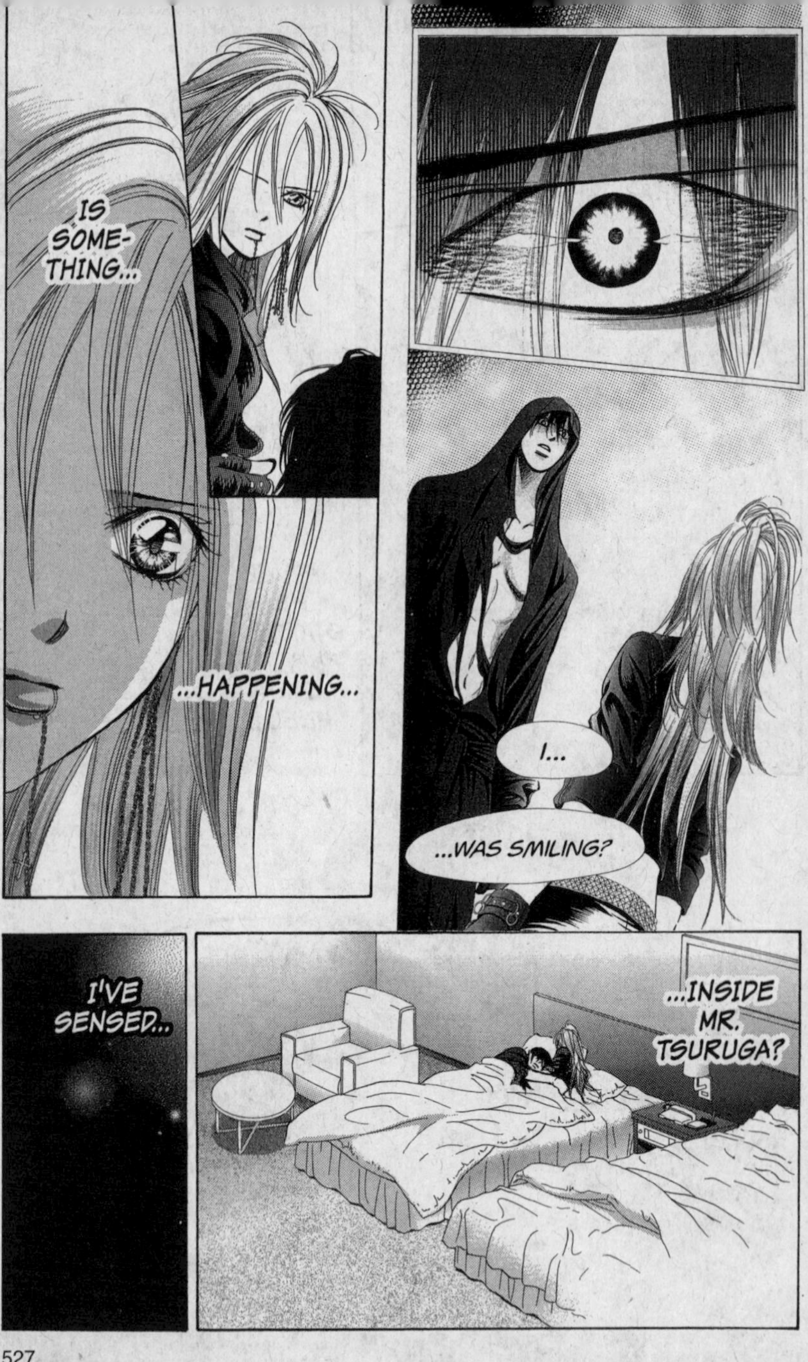
I...
...WAS SMILING?
IS SOMETHING...
...HAPPENING...
...INSIDE MR. TSURUGA?
I'VE SENSED...

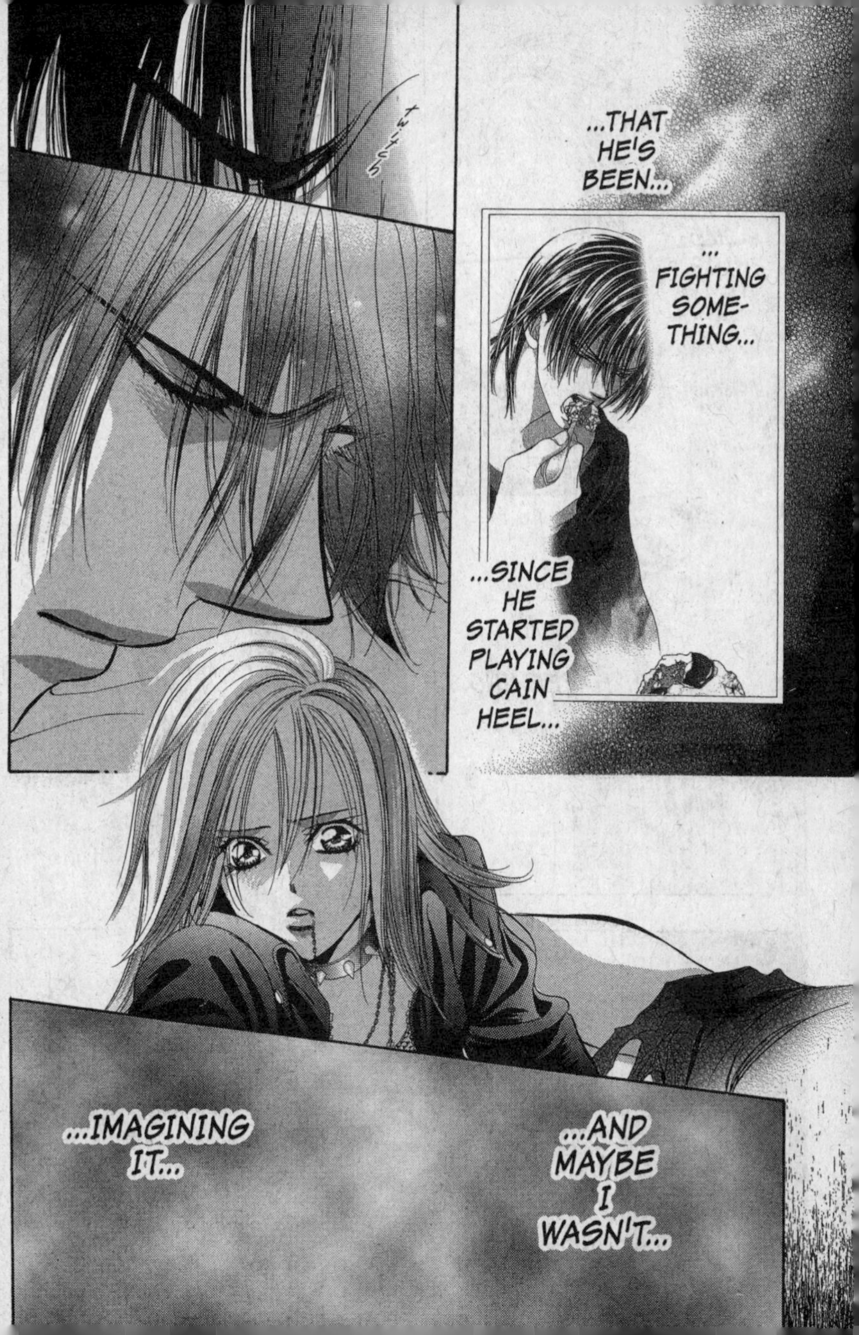

...THAT HE'S BEEN...
...FIGHTING SOMETHING...
...SINCE HE STARTED PLAYING CAIN HEEL...
twitch
...AND MAYBE I WASN'T...
...IMAGINING IT...

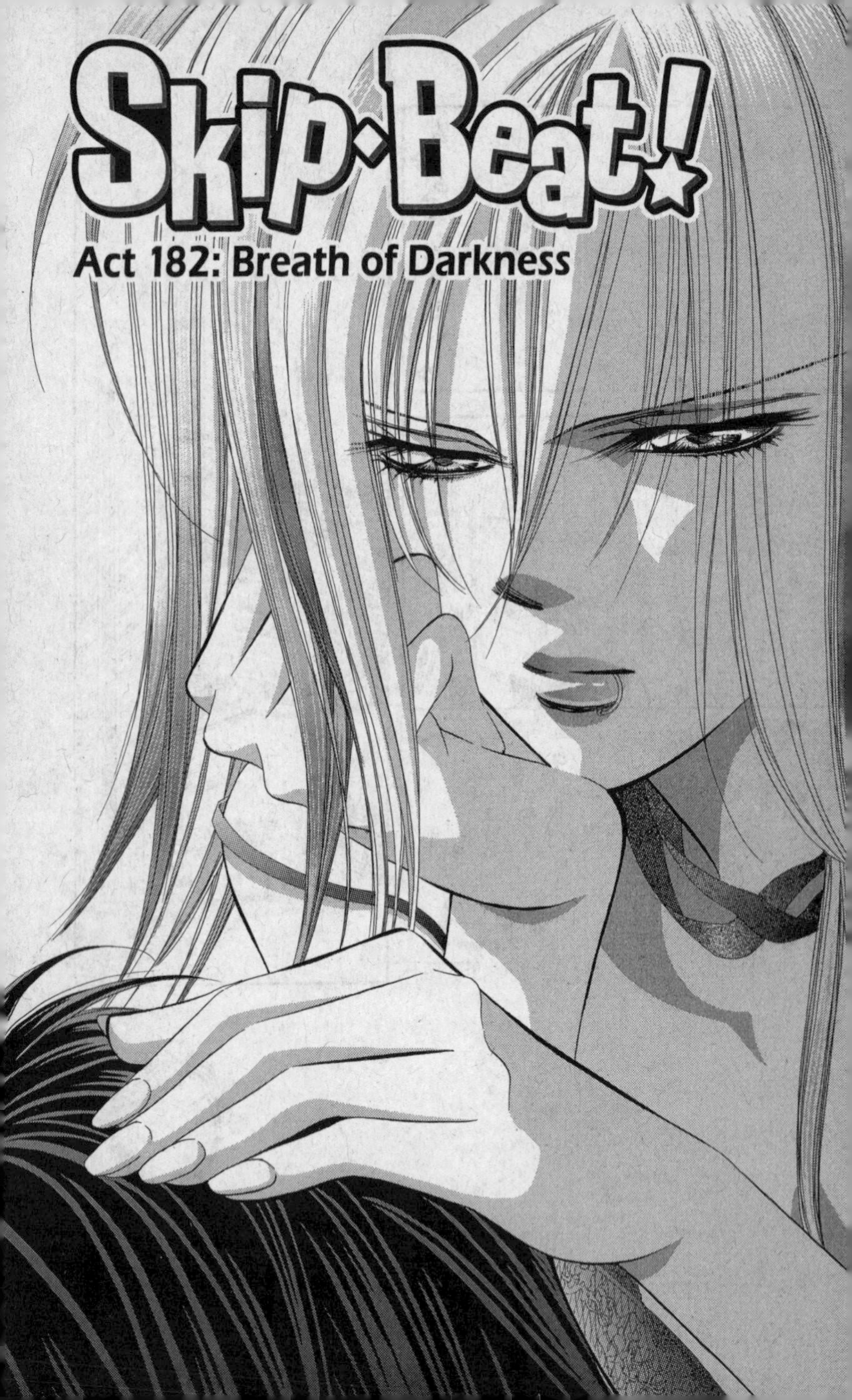
Skip·Beat!
Act 182: Breath of Darkness

bzz
bzz
bzz
bzz
bzz

nnn
nnn
nnn
nnn
nnn

chirp
chirp

bee——p!
bee——p!
bee——p!

Oh!

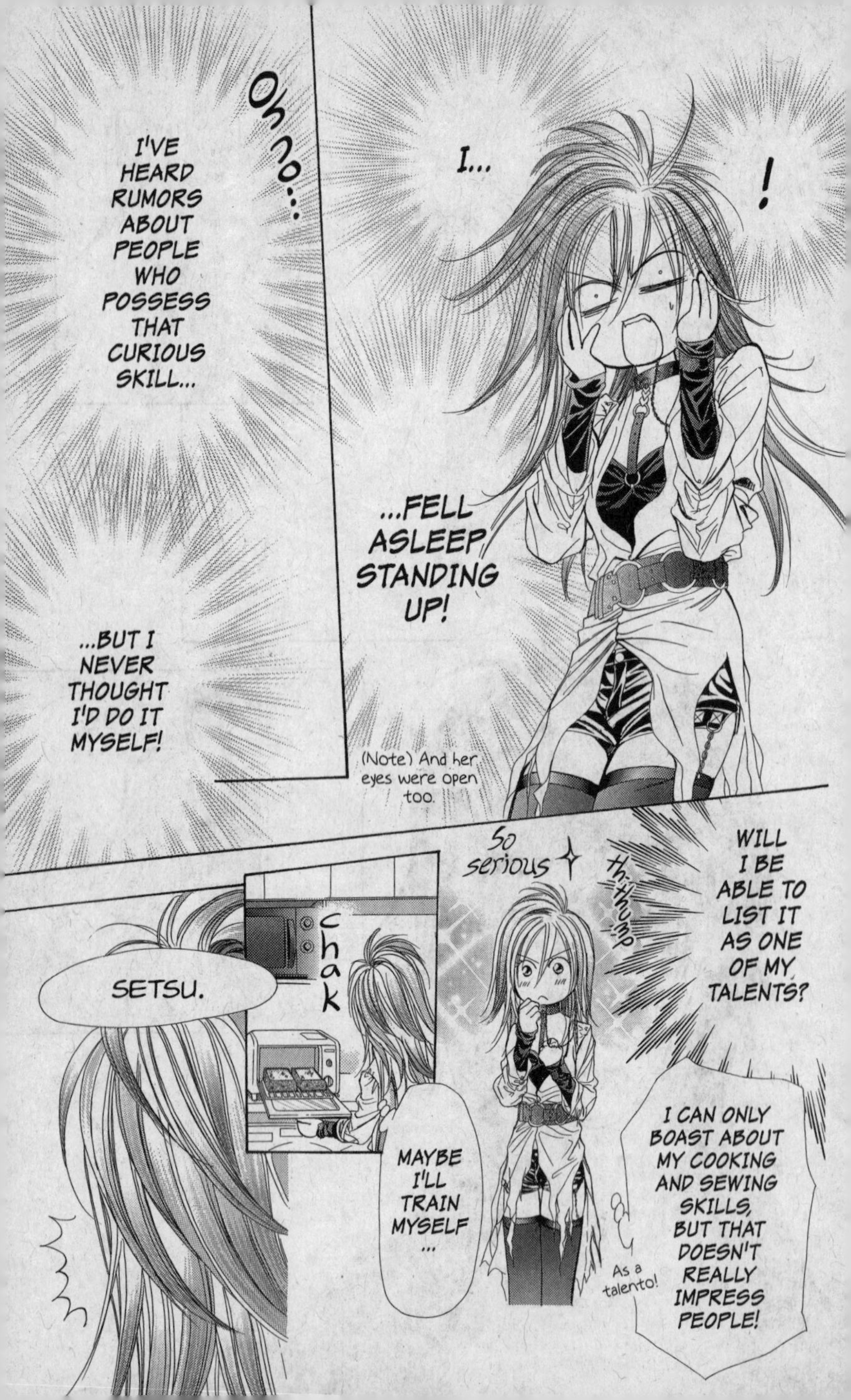
I...
!
...FELL ASLEEP STANDING UP!
(Note) And her eyes were open too.
Oh no...
I'VE HEARD RUMORS ABOUT PEOPLE WHO POSSESS THAT CURIOUS SKILL...
...BUT I NEVER THOUGHT I'D DO IT MYSELF!
So serious
th-thump
WILL I BE ABLE TO LIST IT AS ONE OF MY TALENTS?
I CAN ONLY BOAST ABOUT MY COOKING AND SEWING SKILLS, BUT THAT DOESN'T REALLY IMPRESS PEOPLE!
As a talento!
MAYBE I'LL TRAIN MYSELF ...
chak
SETSU.

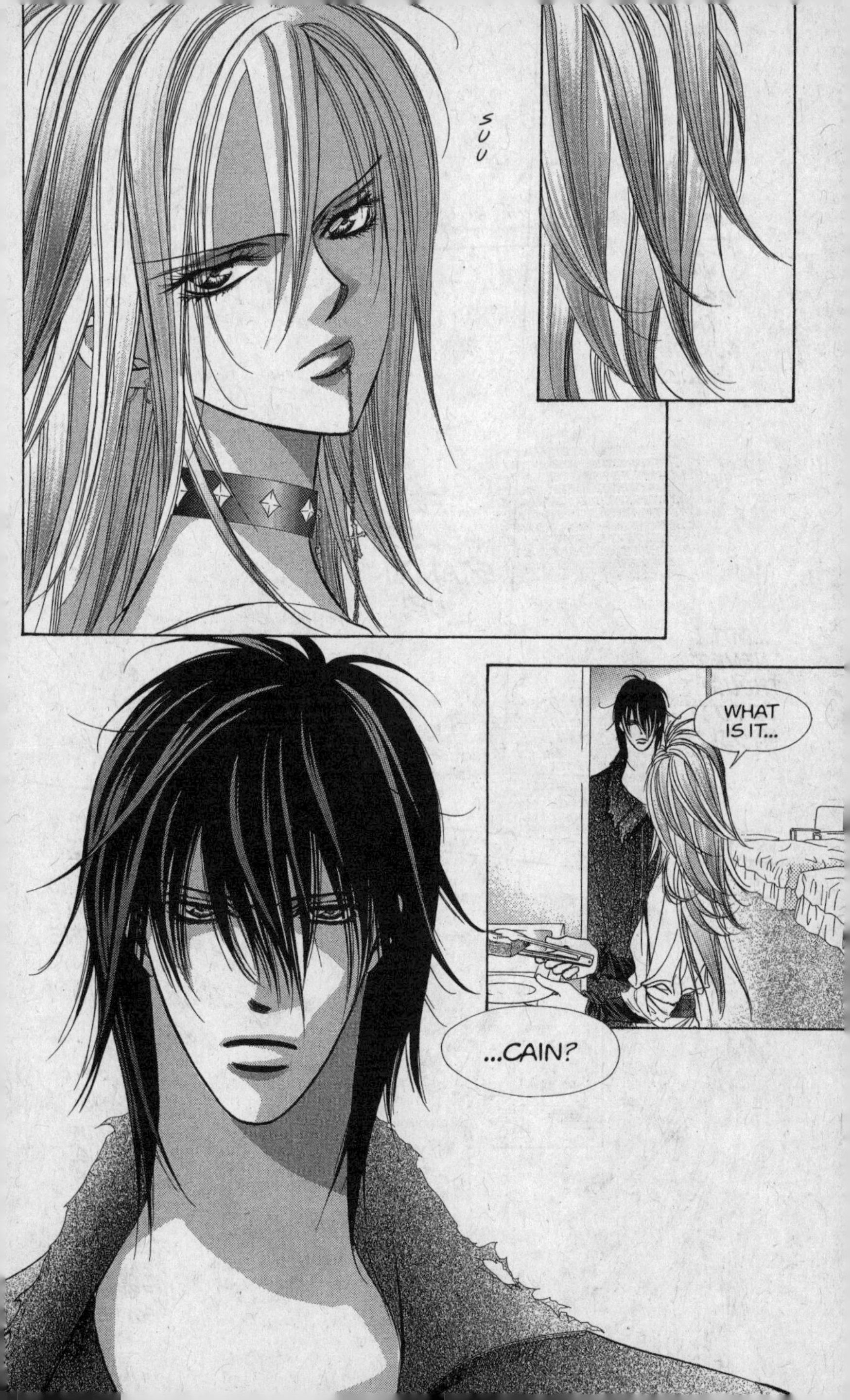
SUU
WHAT IS IT...
...CAIN?

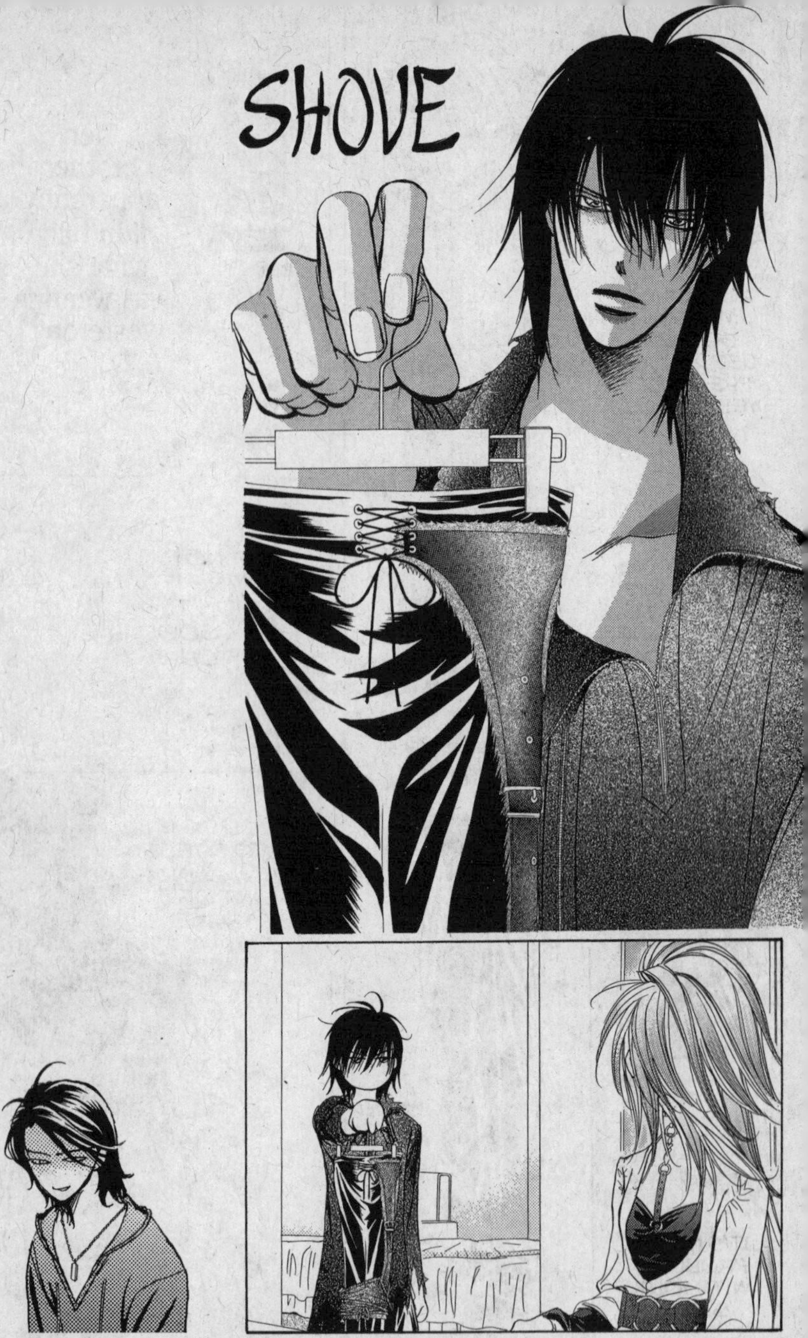
SHOVE

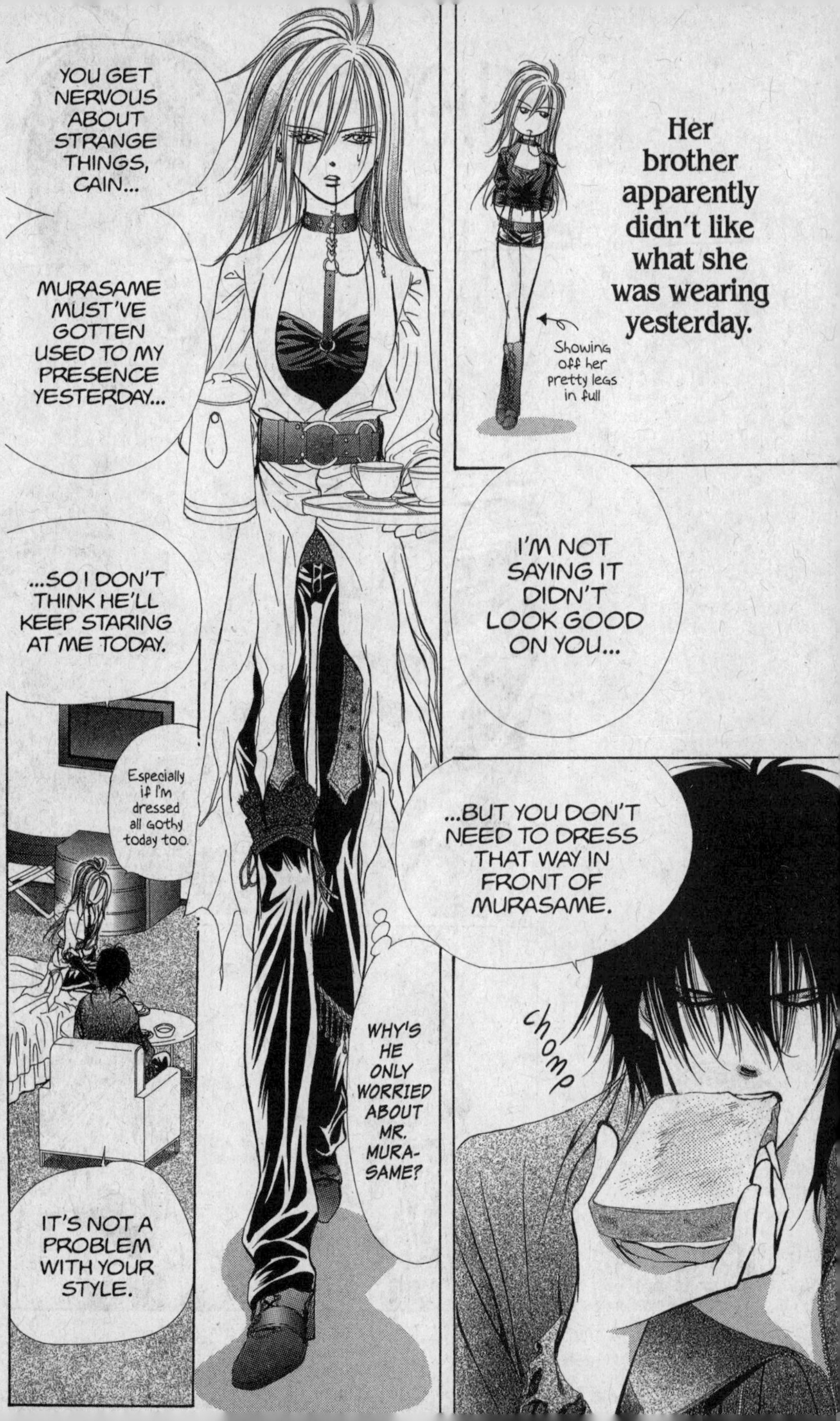

Her brother apparently didn't like what she was wearing yesterday.
Showing off her pretty legs in full
I'M NOT SAYING IT DIDN'T LOOK GOOD ON YOU...
...BUT YOU DON'T NEED TO DRESS THAT WAY IN FRONT OF MURASAME.
chomp
YOU GET NERVOUS ABOUT STRANGE THINGS, CAIN...
MURASAME MUST'VE GOTTEN USED TO MY PRESENCE YESTERDAY...
...SO I DON'T THINK HE'LL KEEP STARING AT ME TODAY.
Especially if I'm dressed all gothy today too.
IT'S NOT A PROBLEM WITH YOUR STYLE.
WHY'S HE ONLY WORRIED ABOUT MR. MURA-SAME?

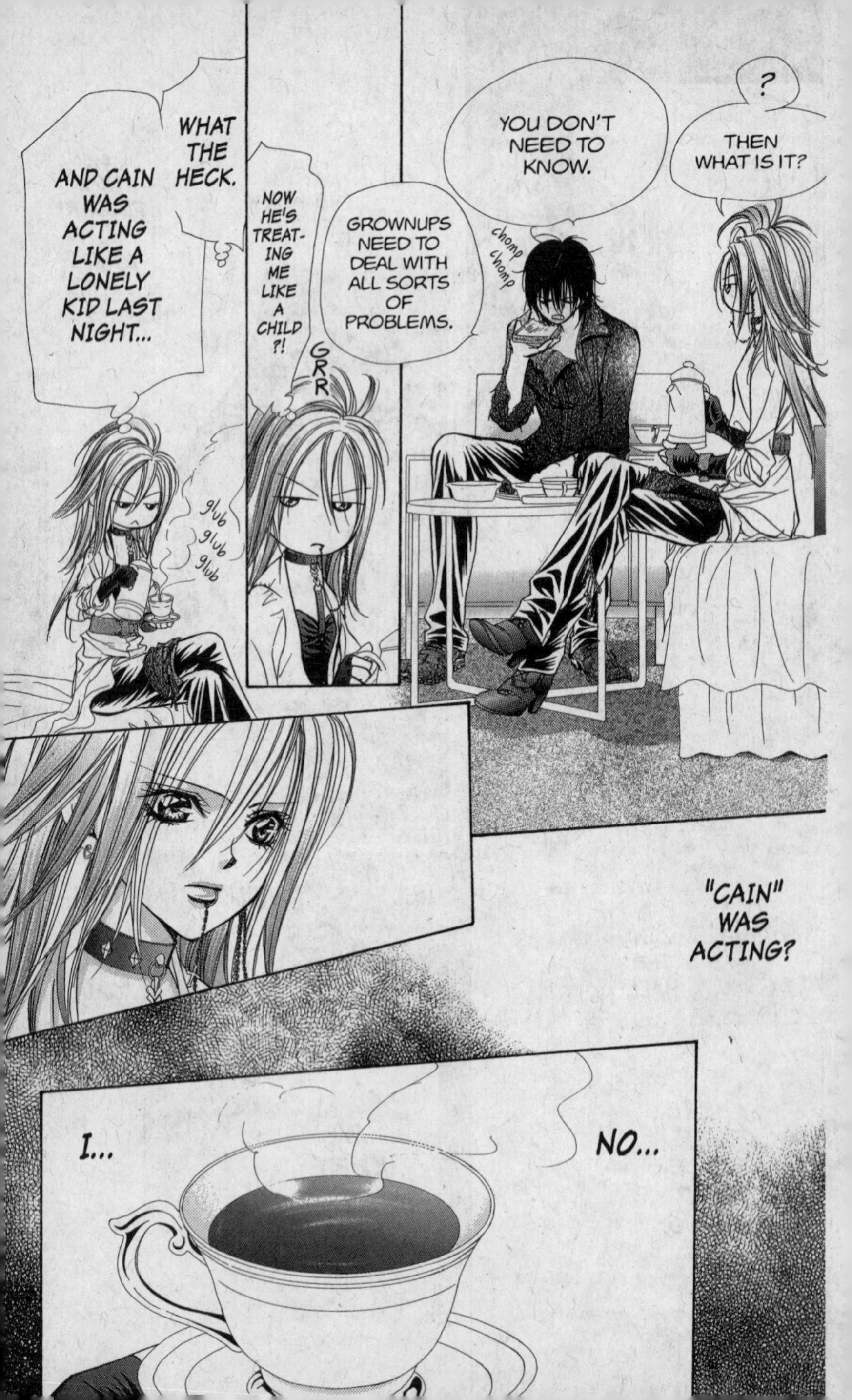
?
THEN WHAT IS IT?
YOU DON'T NEED TO KNOW.
chomp chomp
GROWNUPS NEED TO DEAL WITH ALL SORTS OF PROBLEMS.
NOW HE'S TREATING ME LIKE A CHILD?!
GRR
WHAT THE HECK.
AND CAIN WAS ACTING LIKE A LONELY KID LAST NIGHT...
glub glub glub
"CAIN" WAS ACTING?
NO...
I...

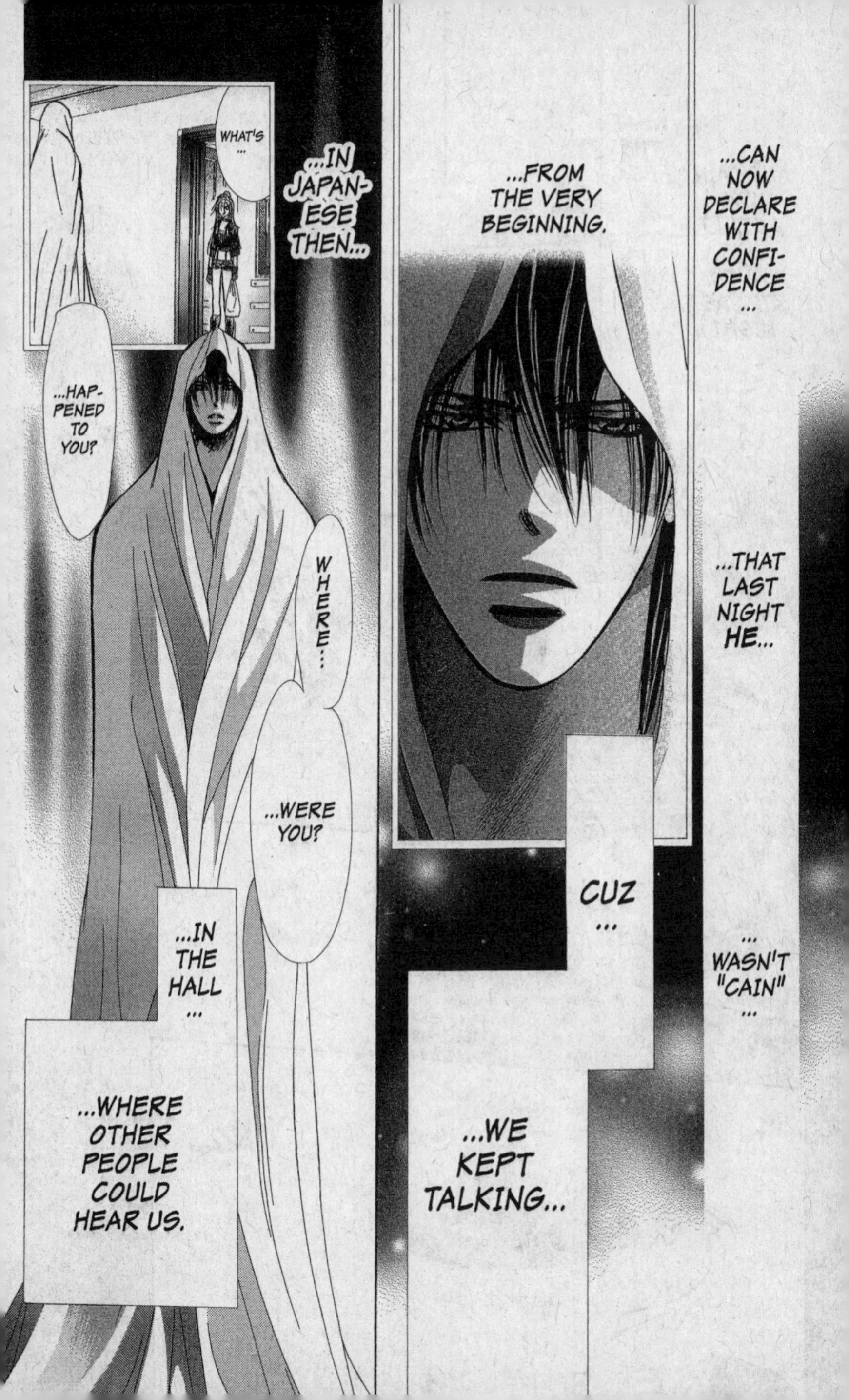
...CAN NOW DECLARE WITH CONFIDENCE...
...THAT LAST NIGHT HE...
...WASN'T "CAIN"...
...FROM THE VERY BEGINNING.
CUZ...
...WE KEPT TALKING...
...IN JAPANESE THEN...
WHAT'S...
...HAPPENED TO YOU?
WHERE...
...WERE YOU?
...IN THE HALL...
...WHERE OTHER PEOPLE COULD HEAR US.

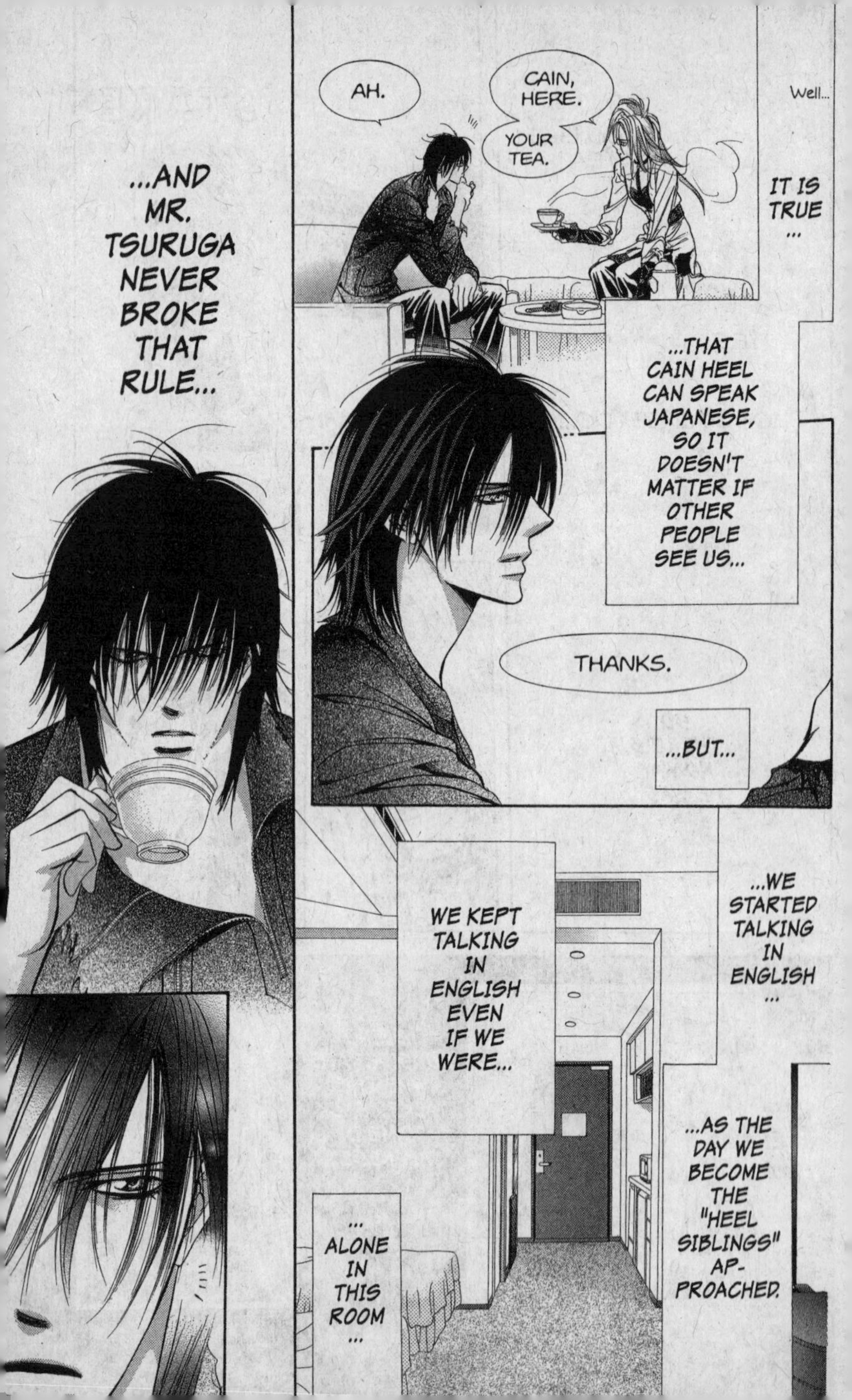
Well...
IT IS TRUE...
CAIN, HERE.
YOUR TEA.
AH.
...THAT CAIN HEEL CAN SPEAK JAPANESE, SO IT DOESN'T MATTER IF OTHER PEOPLE SEE US...
THANKS.
...BUT...
...WE STARTED TALKING IN ENGLISH...
...AS THE DAY WE BECOME THE "HEEL SIBLINGS" AP-PROACHED.
WE KEPT TALKING IN ENGLISH EVEN IF WE WERE...
...ALONE IN THIS ROOM...
...AND MR. TSURUGA NEVER BROKE THAT RULE...

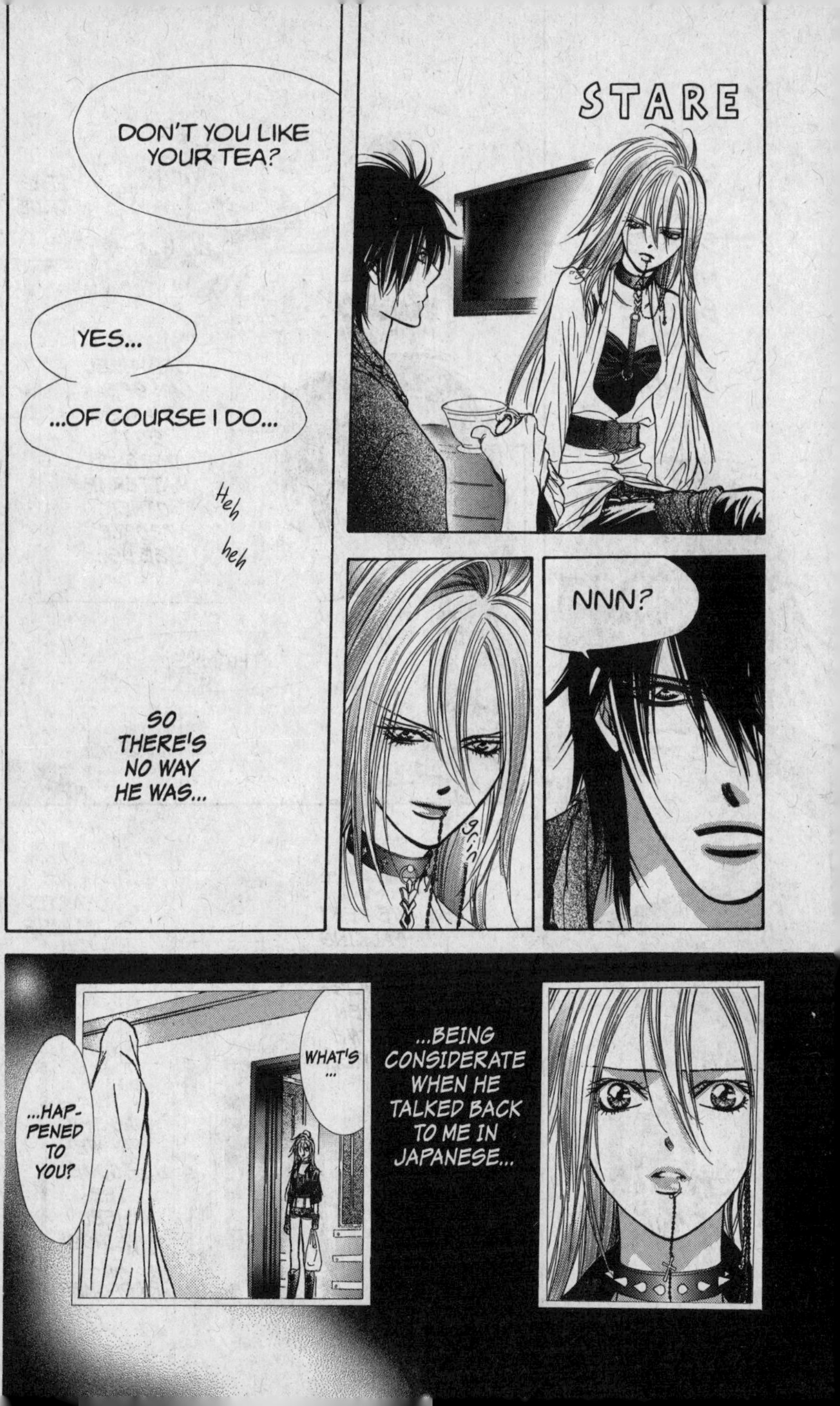
STARE
NNN?
grin
DON'T YOU LIKE YOUR TEA?
YES...
...OF COURSE I DO...
Heh heh
SO THERE'S NO WAY HE WAS...
...BEING CONSIDERATE WHEN HE TALKED BACK TO ME IN JAPANESE...
WHAT'S...
...HAP-PENED TO YOU?

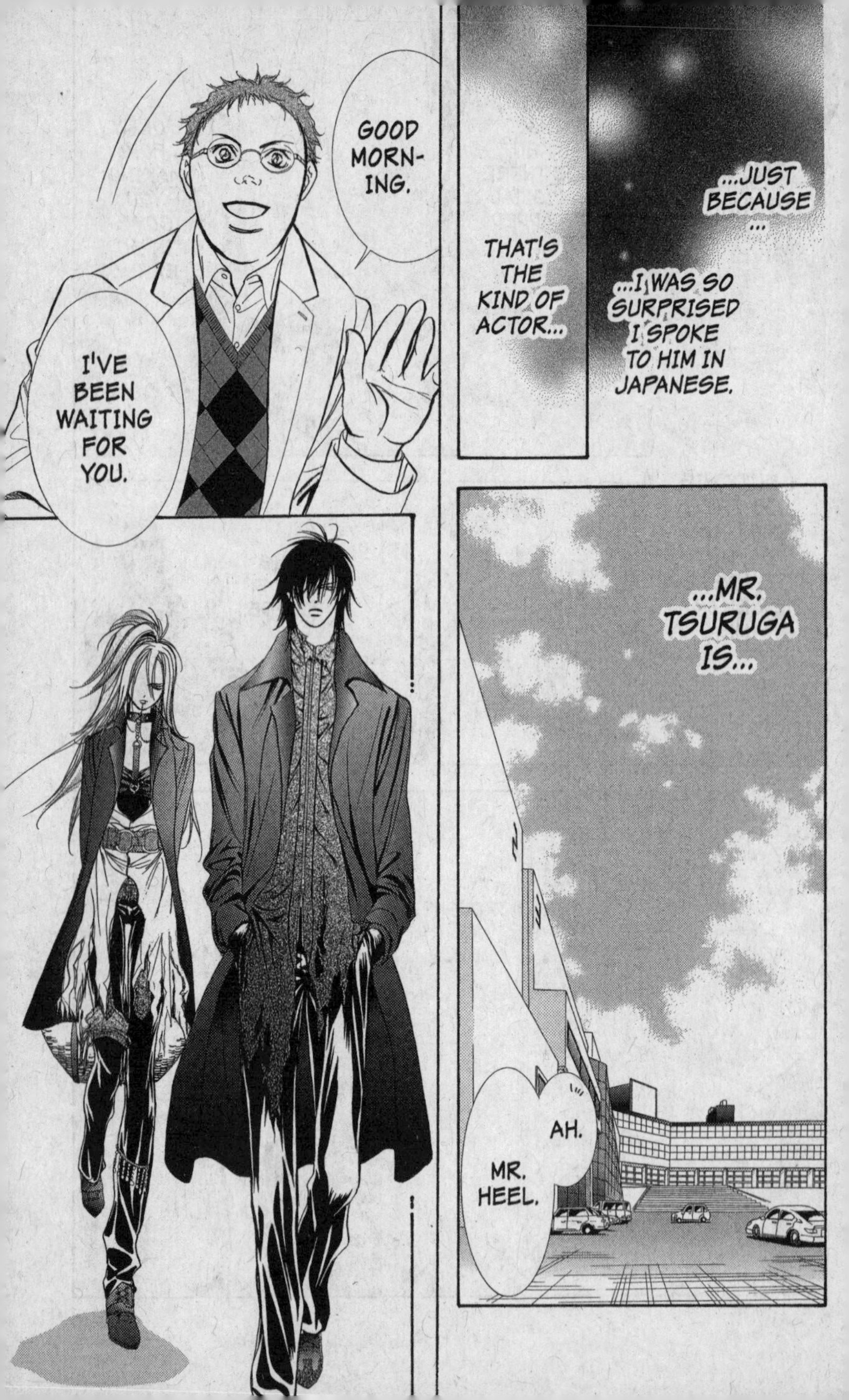
...JUST BECAUSE...
...I WAS SO SURPRISED I SPOKE TO HIM IN JAPANESE.
THAT'S THE KIND OF ACTOR...
...MR. TSURUGA IS...
AH.
MR. HEEL.
GOOD MORNING.
I'VE BEEN WAITING FOR YOU.

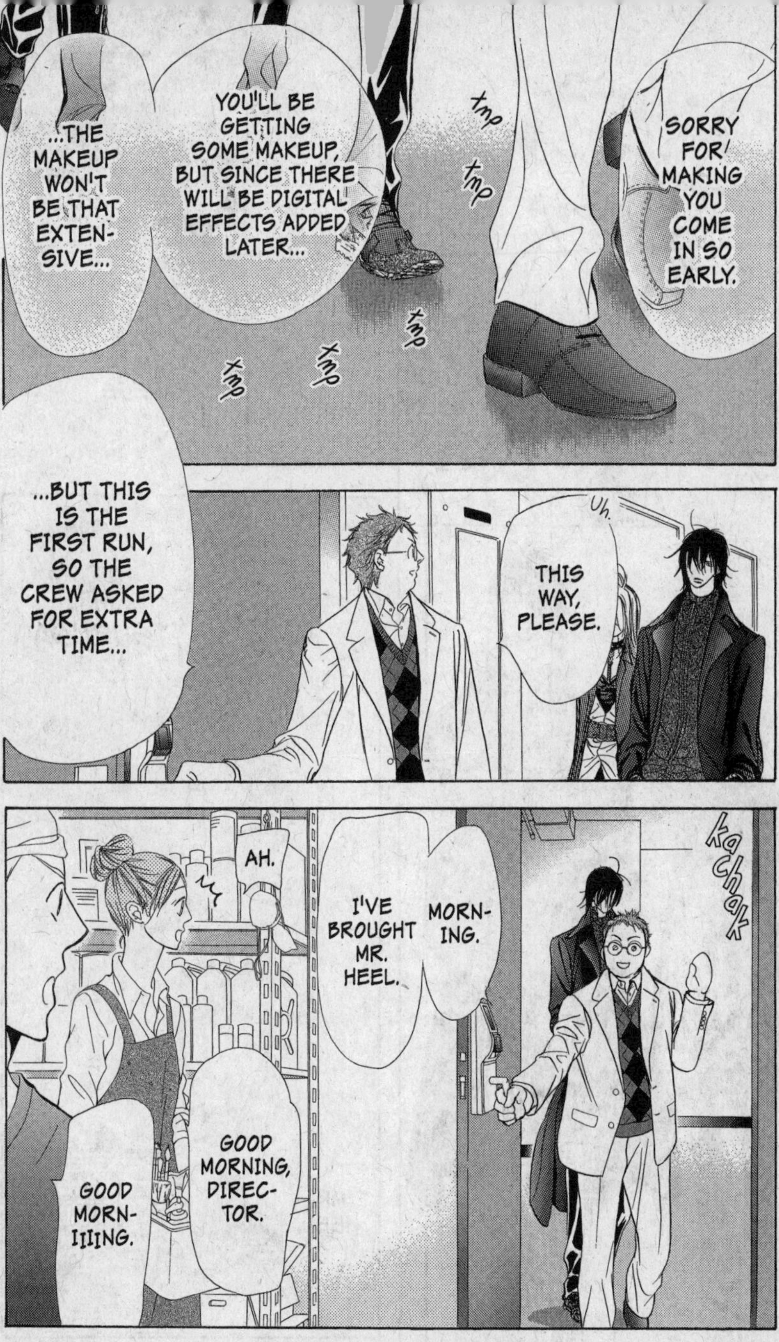
SORRY FOR MAKING YOU COME IN SO EARLY.
tmp
tmp
YOU'LL BE GETTING SOME MAKEUP, BUT SINCE THERE WILL BE DIGITAL EFFECTS ADDED LATER...
...THE MAKEUP WON'T BE THAT EXTEN-SIVE...
tmp
tmp
tmp
...BUT THIS IS THE FIRST RUN, SO THE CREW ASKED FOR EXTRA TIME...
Uh.
THIS WAY, PLEASE.
kachak
MORN-ING.
I'VE BROUGHT MR. HEEL.
AH.
GOOD MORNING, DIREC-TOR.
GOOD MORN-IIIING.

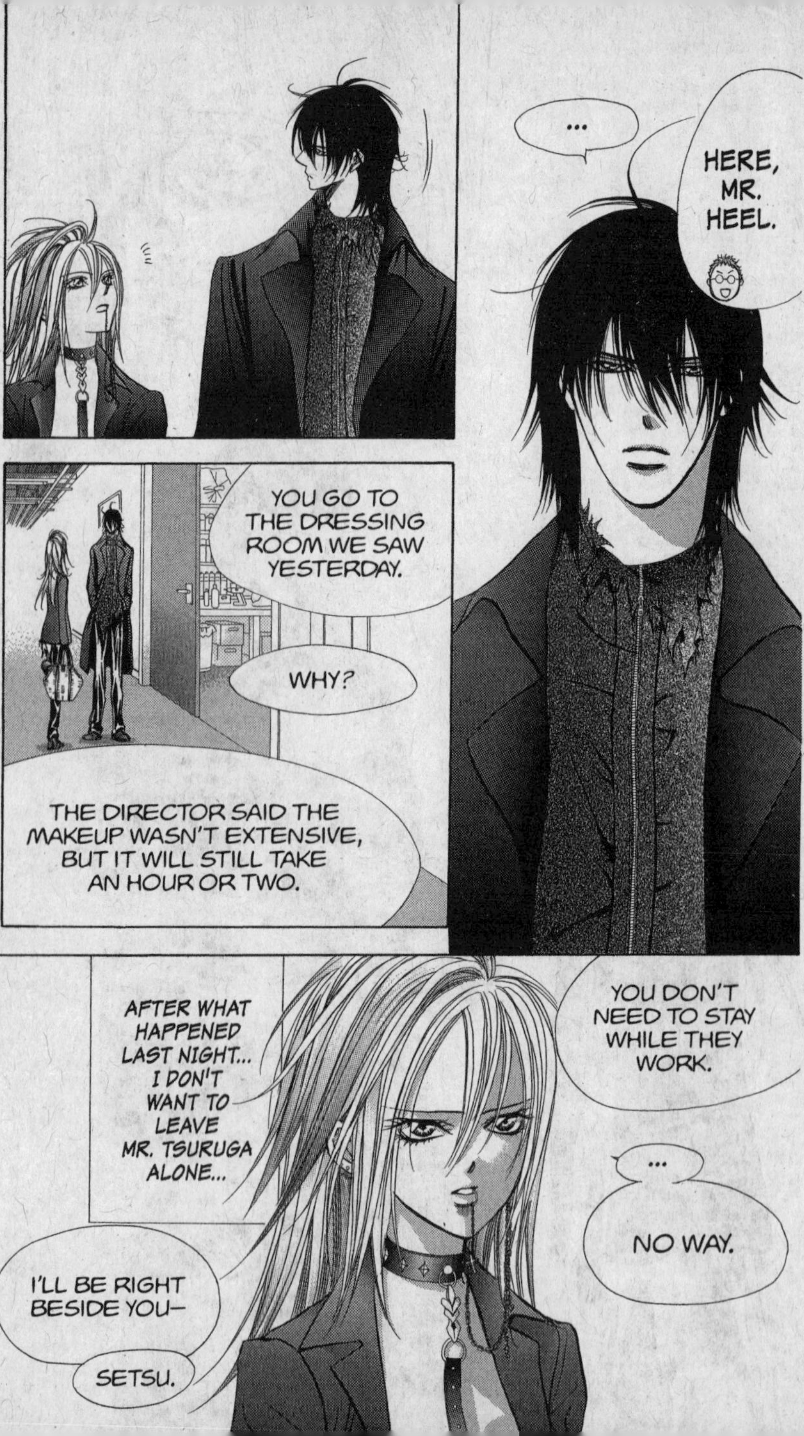
HERE, MR. HEEL.
...
YOU GO TO THE DRESSING ROOM WE SAW YESTERDAY.
WHY?
THE DIRECTOR SAID THE MAKEUP WASN'T EXTENSIVE, BUT IT WILL STILL TAKE AN HOUR OR TWO.
YOU DON'T NEED TO STAY WHILE THEY WORK.
...
NO WAY.
AFTER WHAT HAPPENED LAST NIGHT... I DON'T WANT TO LEAVE MR. TSURUGA ALONE...
I'LL BE RIGHT BESIDE YOU—
SETSU.

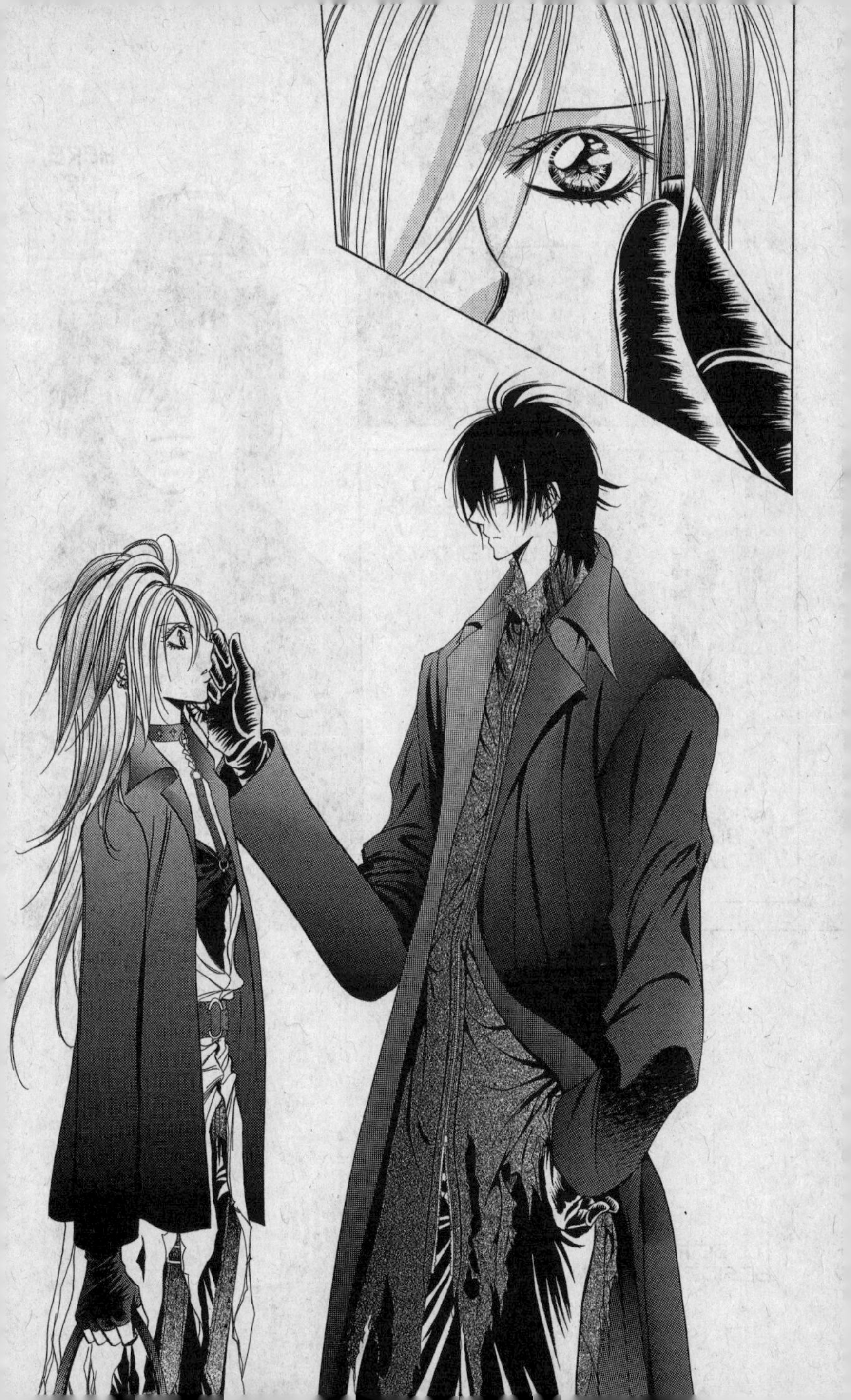

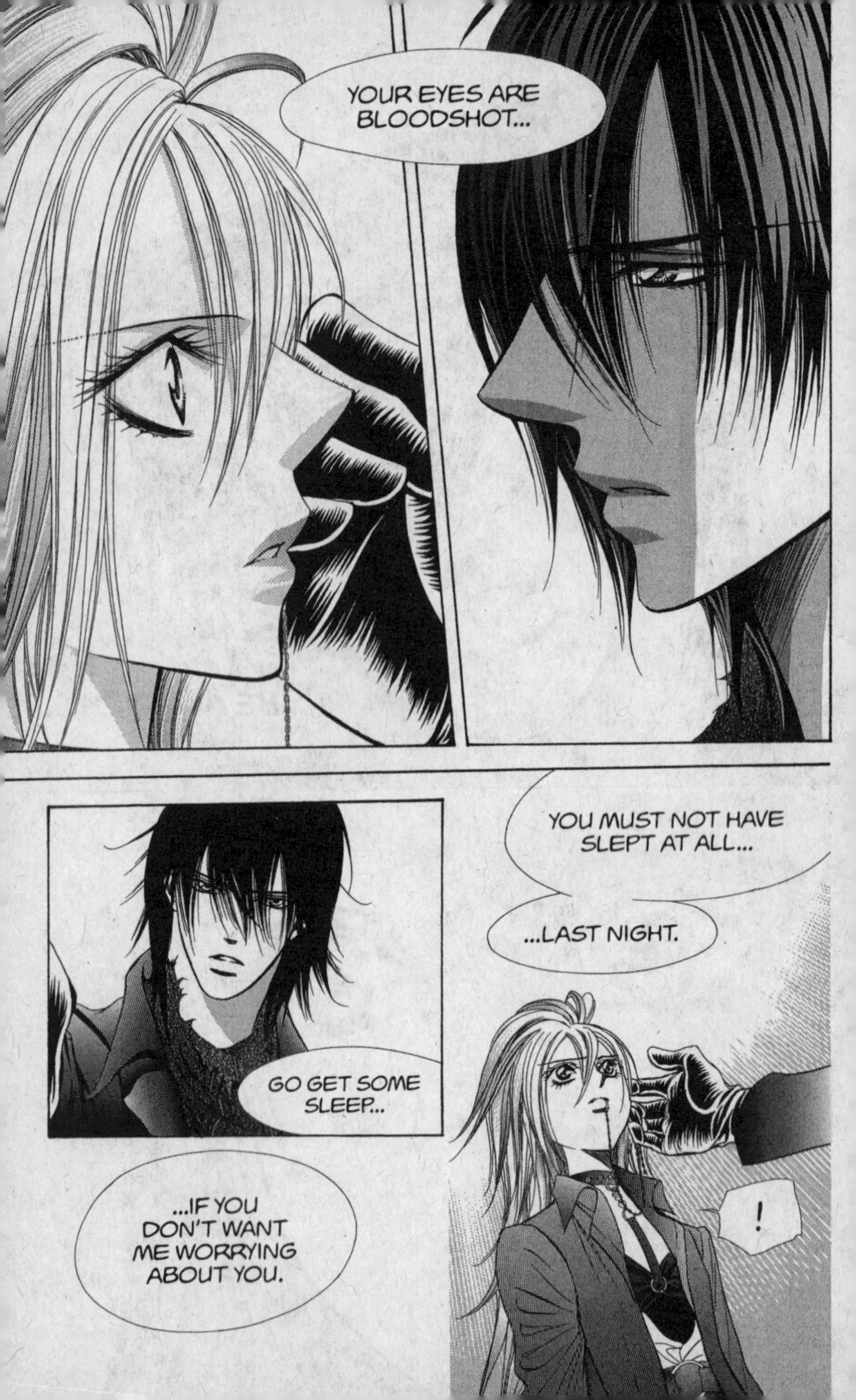
YOUR EYES ARE BLOODSHOT...
YOU MUST NOT HAVE SLEPT AT ALL...
...LAST NIGHT.
GO GET SOME SLEEP...
...IF YOU DON'T WANT ME WORRYING ABOUT YOU.
!

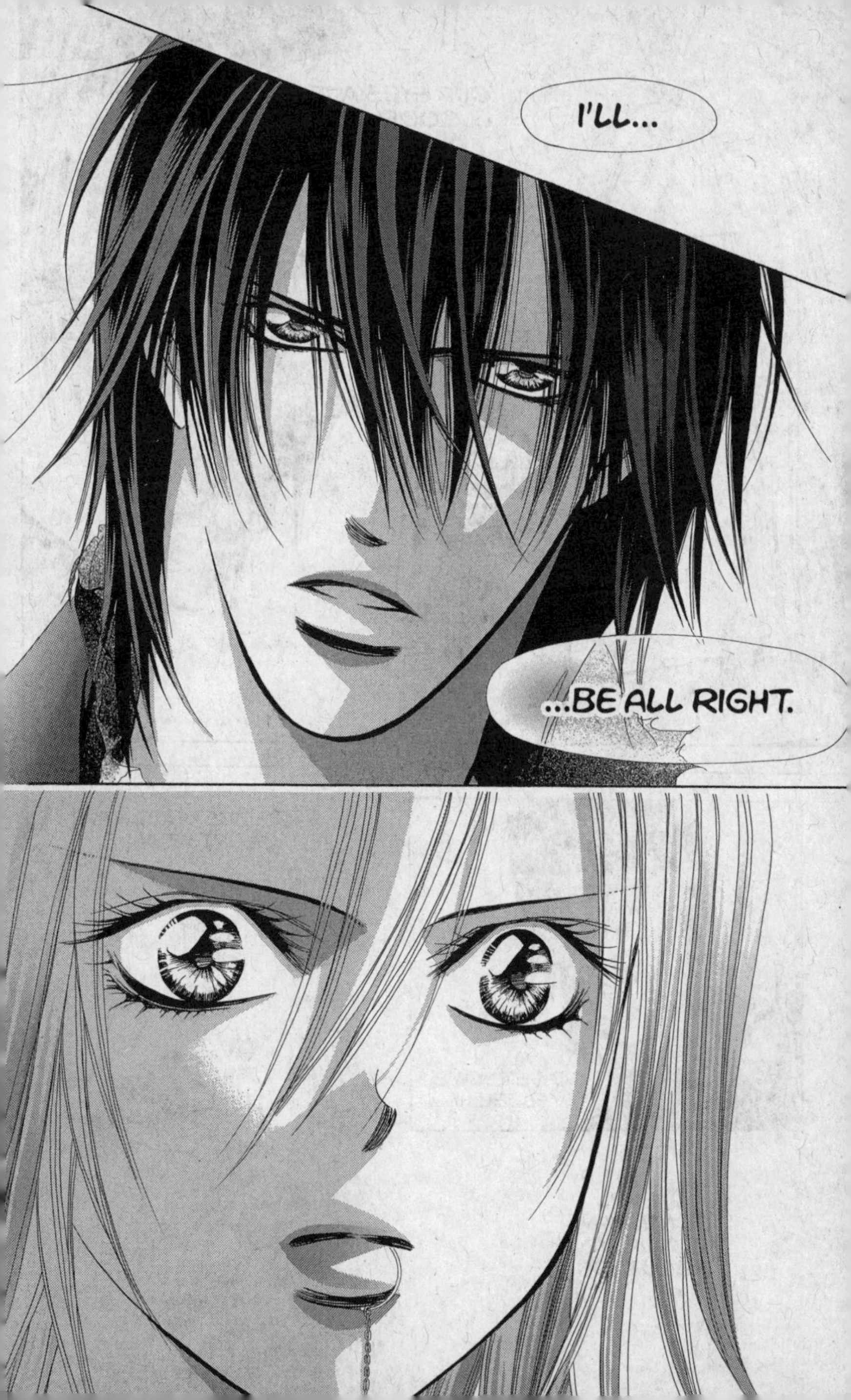
I'LL...
...BE ALL RIGHT.

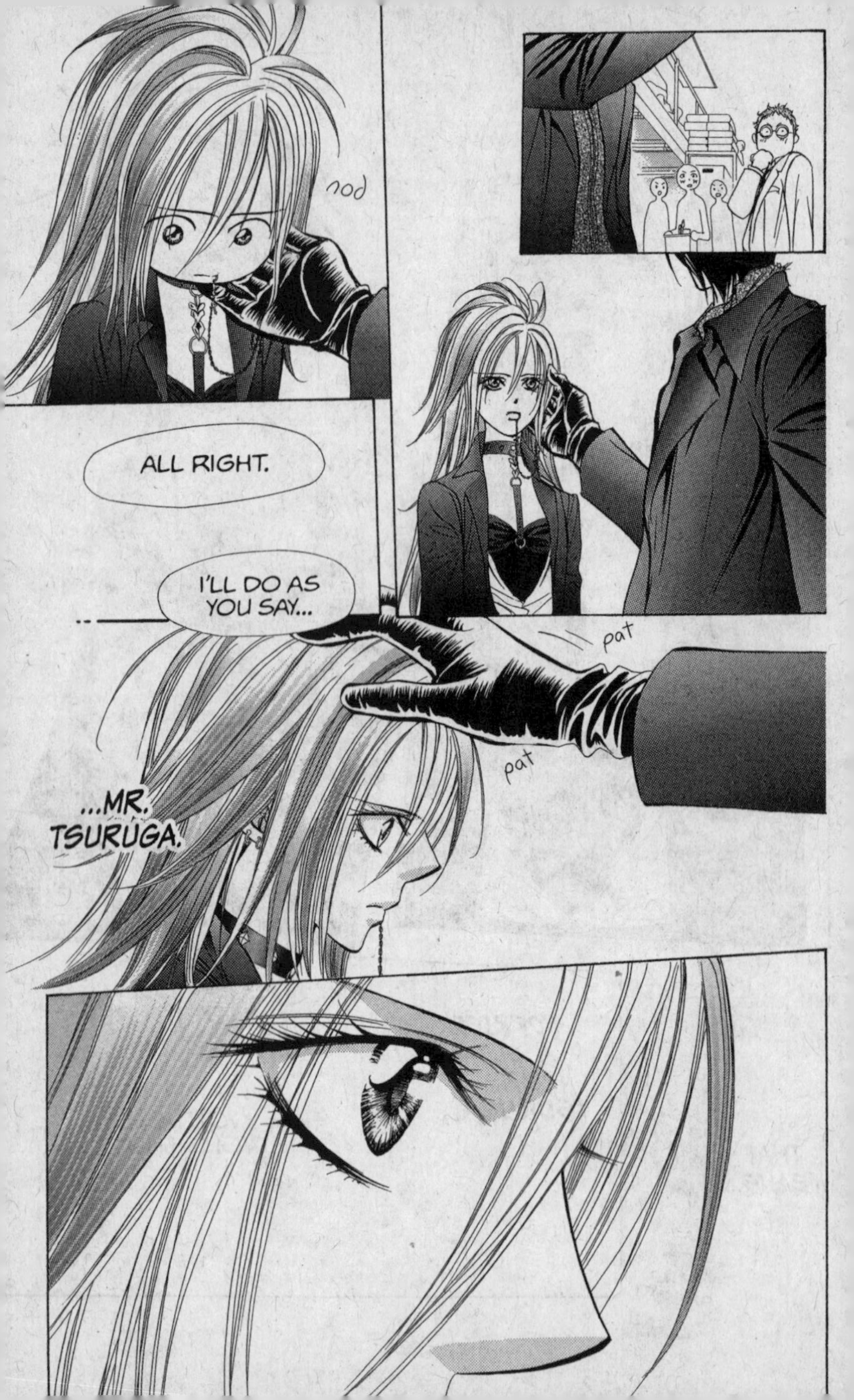
nod
ALL RIGHT.
I'LL DO AS YOU SAY...
pat
pat
...MR. TSURUGA.

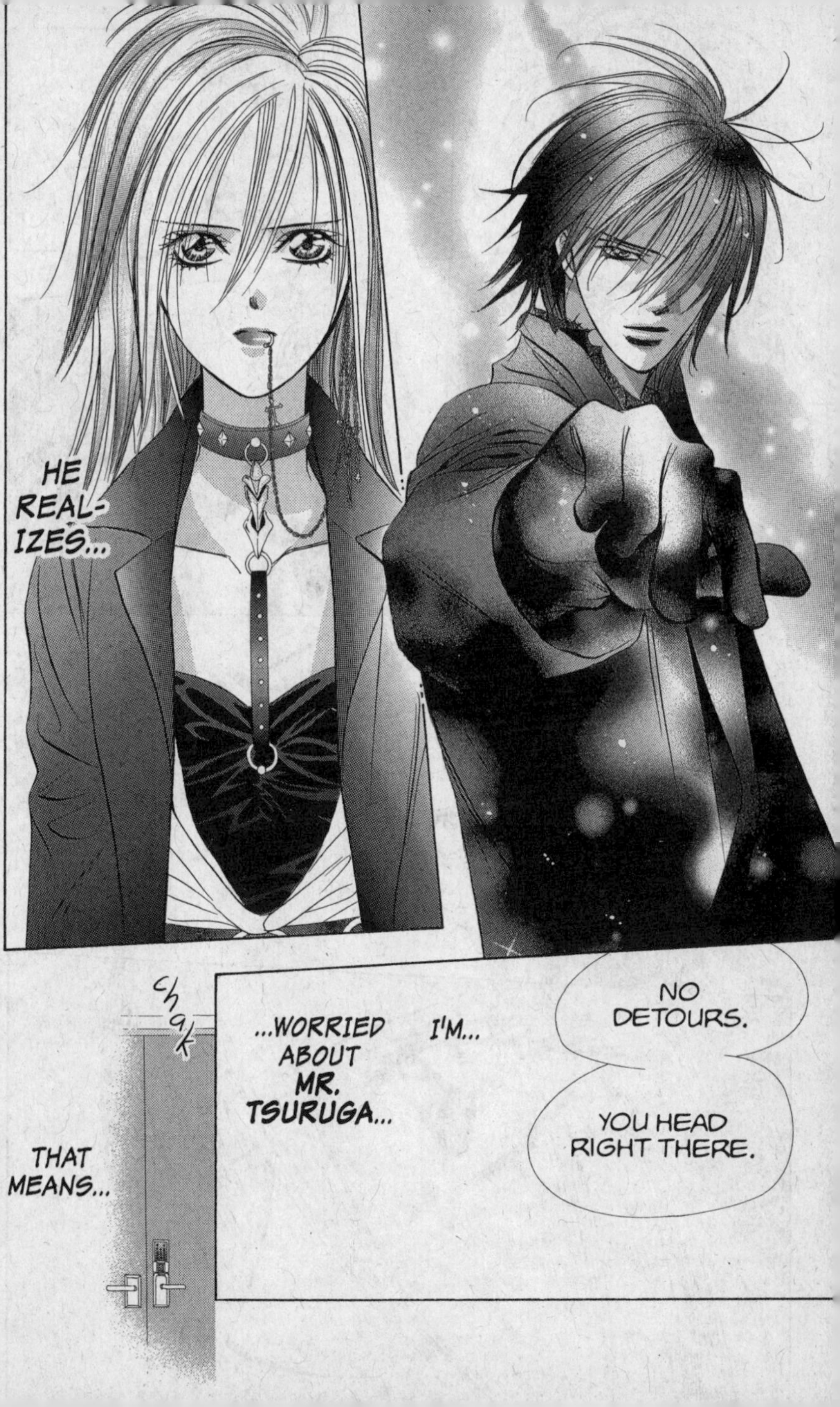
HE REAL-IZES...
NO DETOURS.
YOU HEAD RIGHT THERE.
I'M...
...WORRIED ABOUT MR. TSURUGA...
chak
THAT MEANS...

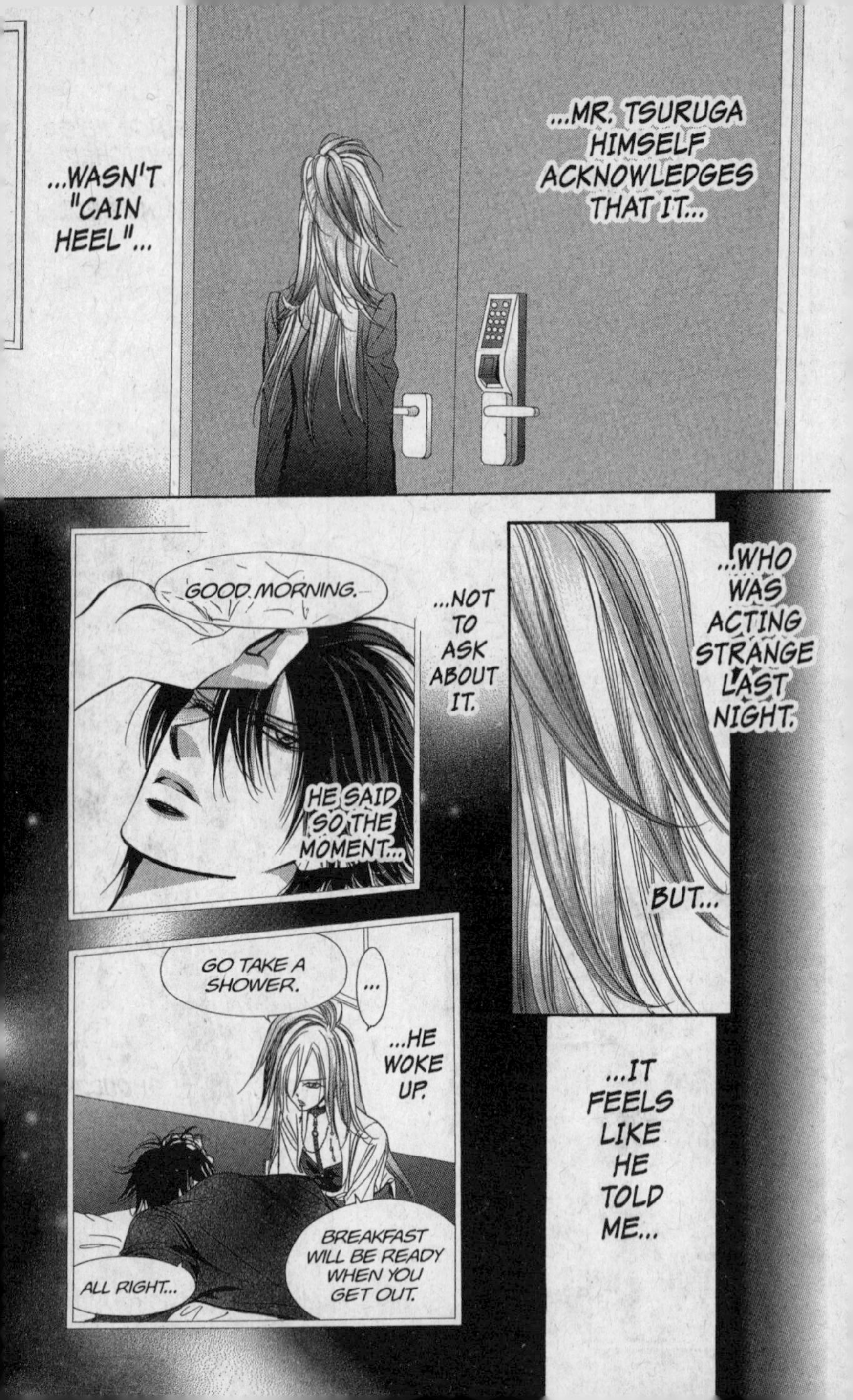
...MR. TSURUGA HIMSELF ACKNOWLEDGES THAT IT...
...WASN'T "CAIN HEEL"...
...WHO WAS ACTING STRANGE LAST NIGHT.
BUT...
...IT FEELS LIKE HE TOLD ME...
...NOT TO ASK ABOUT IT.
GOOD MORNING.
HE SAID SO THE MOMENT...
GO TAKE A SHOWER.
...
...HE WOKE UP.
BREAKFAST WILL BE READY WHEN YOU GET OUT.
ALL RIGHT...

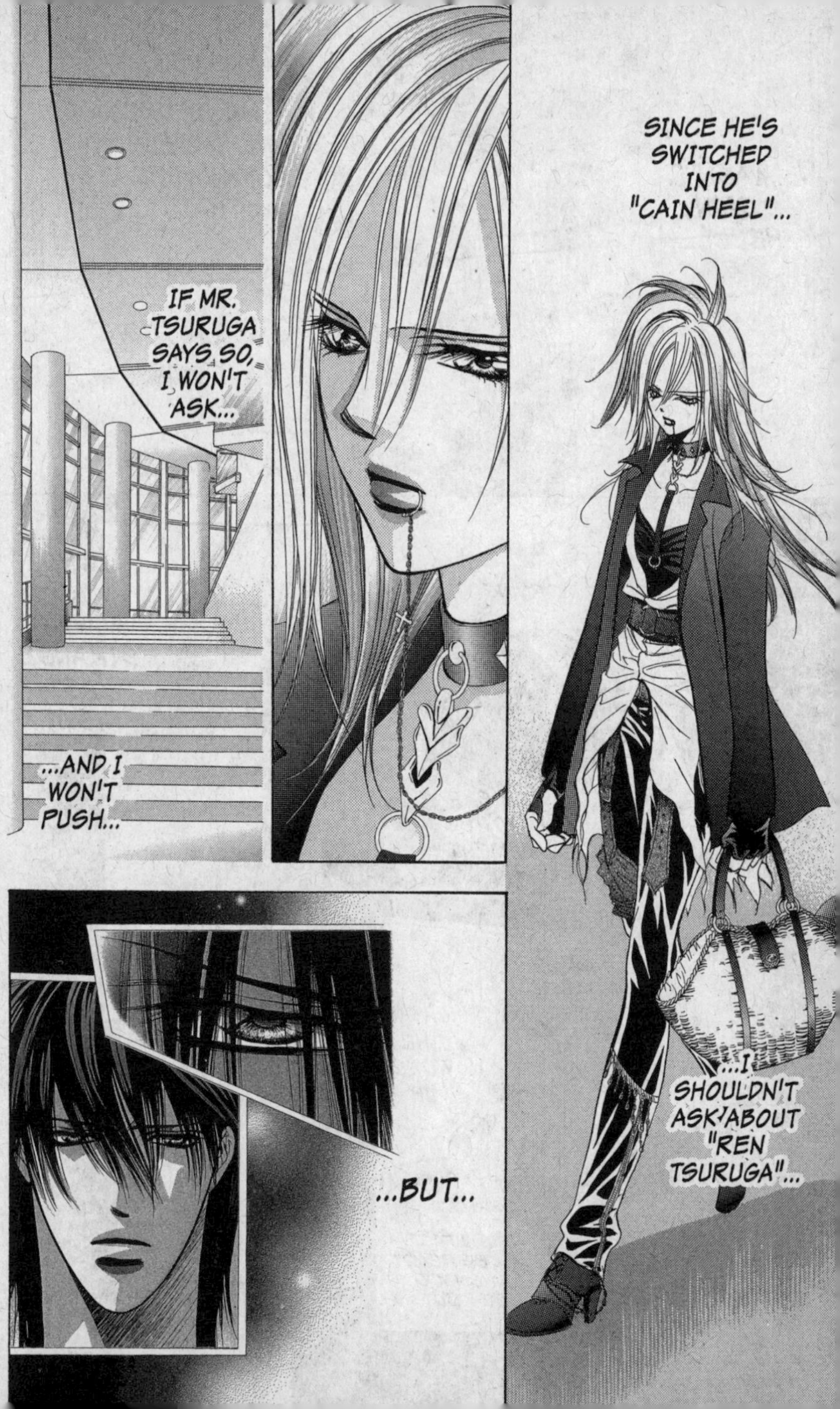
SINCE HE'S SWITCHED INTO "CAIN HEEL"...
...I SHOULDN'T ASK ABOUT "REN TSURUGA"...
IF MR. TSURUGA SAYS SO, I WON'T ASK...
...AND I WON'T PUSH...
...BUT...

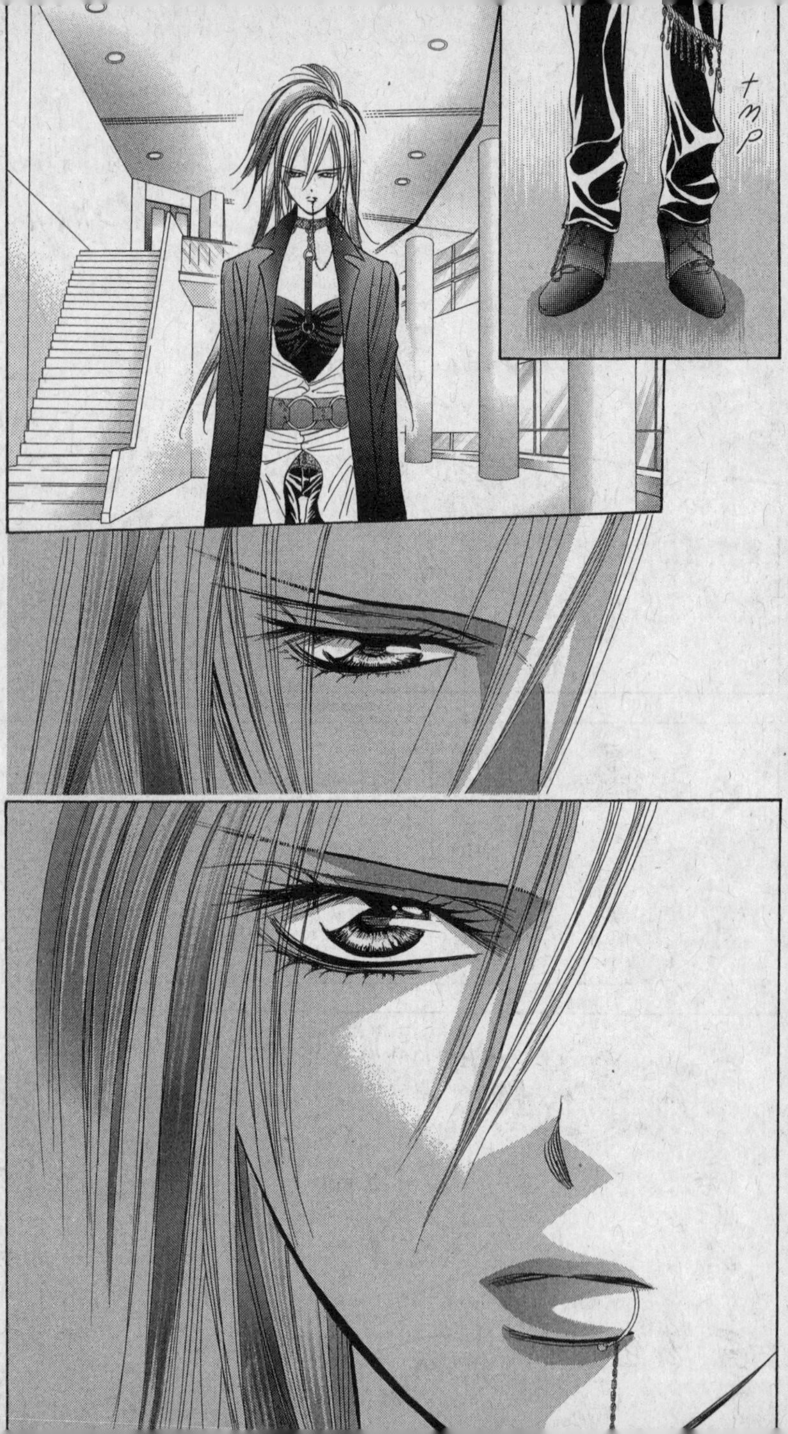
tmp

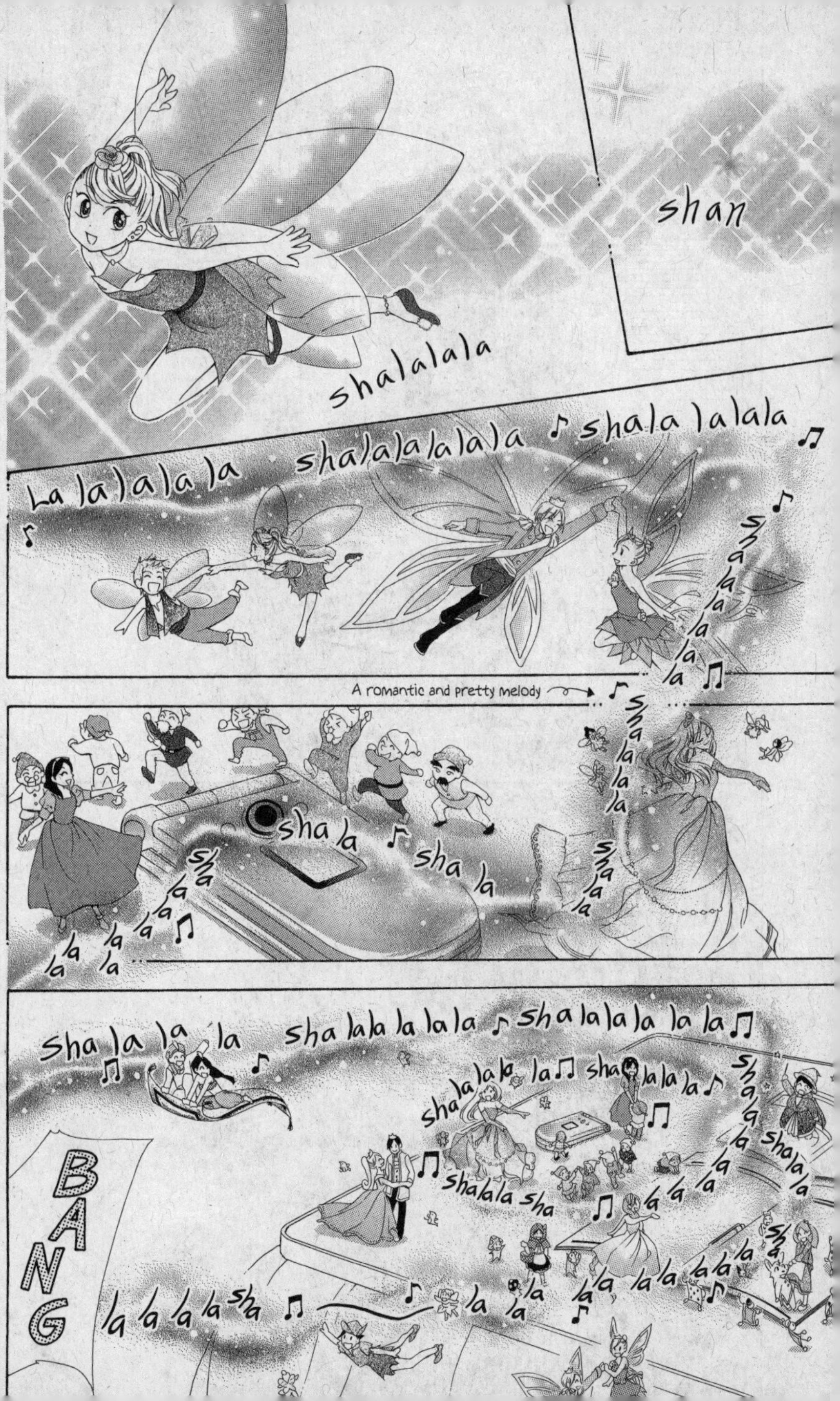
shan
shalalala
La la la la la la shalalalalala ♪ shala lalala ♫
sha la la la la la la la la ♫
A romantic and pretty melody
sha la la la la la
shalalala
sha la ♪ sha la
sha la la la la ♫ la la la la
Sha la la la sha lalalalala ♪ sha la la la la la la ♫
sha la la la la ♫ sha la la la la ♪
shala la la la la shalala
shalala sha
la la la la sha ♫ ♪ la la la la la la la la la la sha ♪
BANG

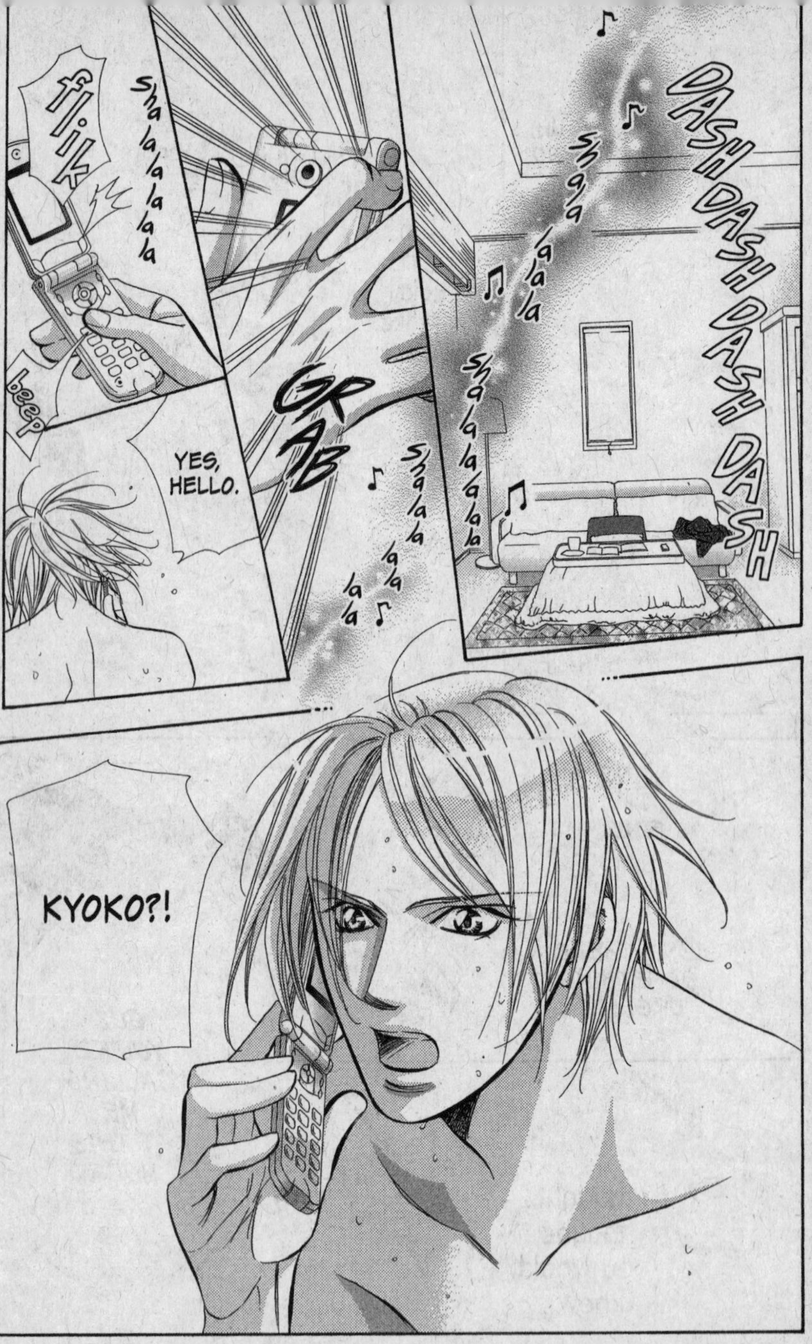
DASH DASH DASH DASH
sha la la la la la
sha la la la la la la
GRAB
sha la la la la la la
flik
sha la la la la la la
beep
YES, HELLO.
...
...
KYOKO?!

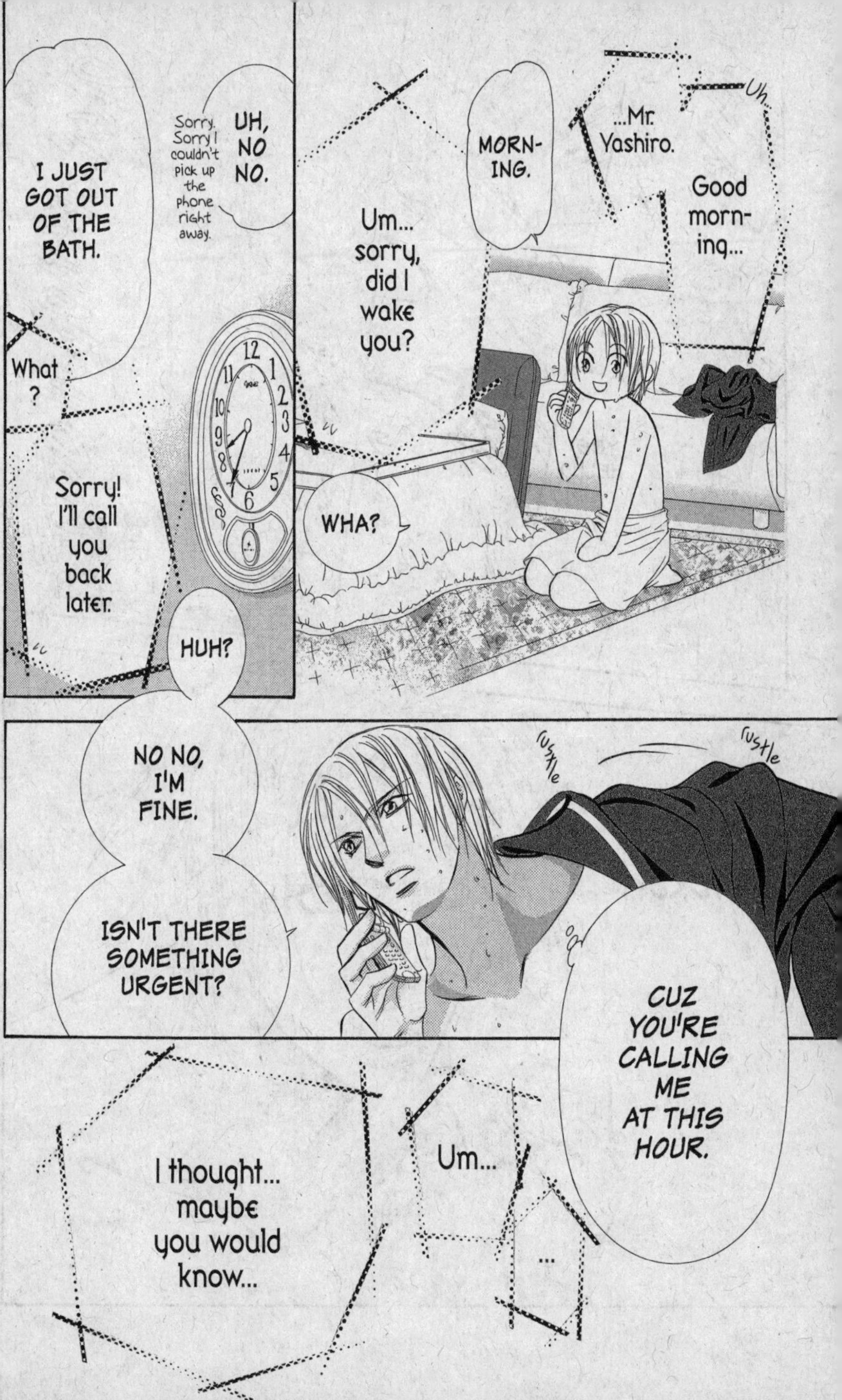
Uh...
Good morn-ing...
...Mr. Yashiro.
MORN-ING.
Um... sorry, did I wake you?
WHA?
UH, NO NO.
Sorry. Sorry I couldn't pick up the phone right away.
I JUST GOT OUT OF THE BATH.
What?
Sorry! I'll call you back later.
rustle
rustle
HUH?
NO NO, I'M FINE.
ISN'T THERE SOMETHING URGENT?
CUZ YOU'RE CALLING ME AT THIS HOUR.
...
Um...
I thought... maybe you would know...

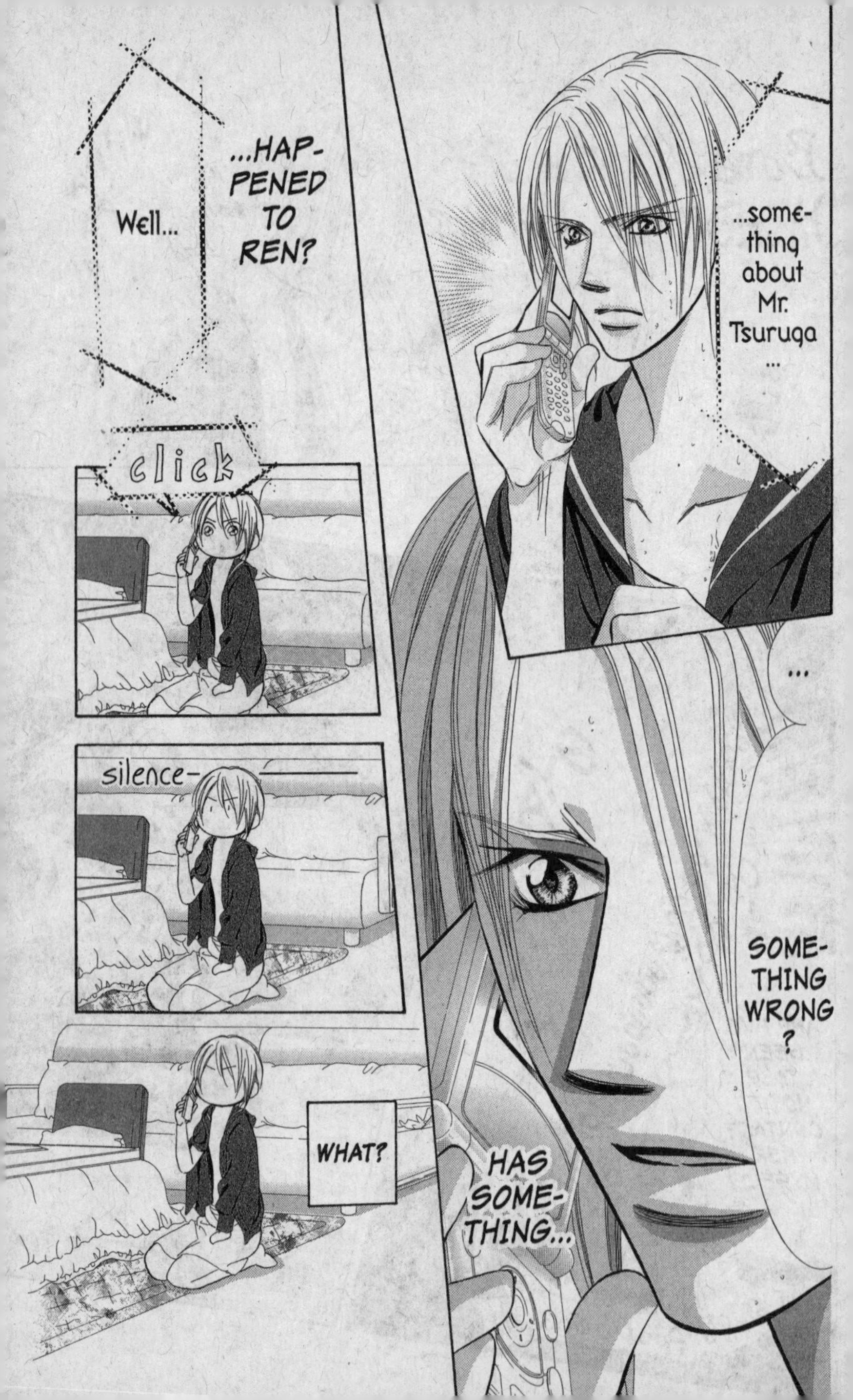
...something about Mr. Tsuruga...
...
SOMETHING WRONG?
HAS SOMETHING...
...HAPPENED TO REN?
Well...
click
silence-
WHAT?

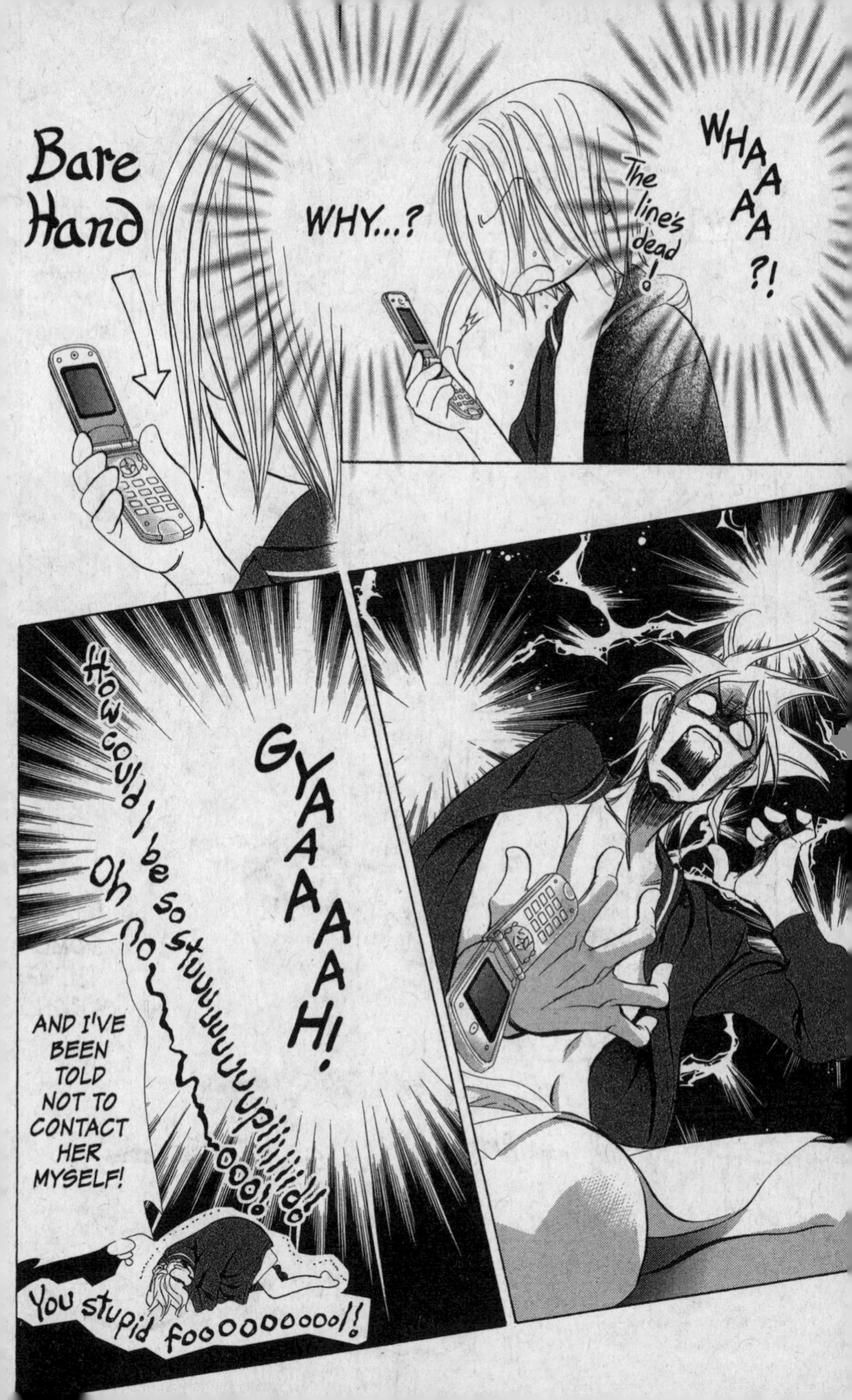
WHAAAA?!
The line's dead!
WHY...?
Bare Hand
GYAAAAAH!
How could I be so stuuuuuuupiiiiid!!
Oh no~~ooo!
AND I'VE BEEN TOLD NOT TO CONTACT HER MYSELF!
You stupid fooooooool!!

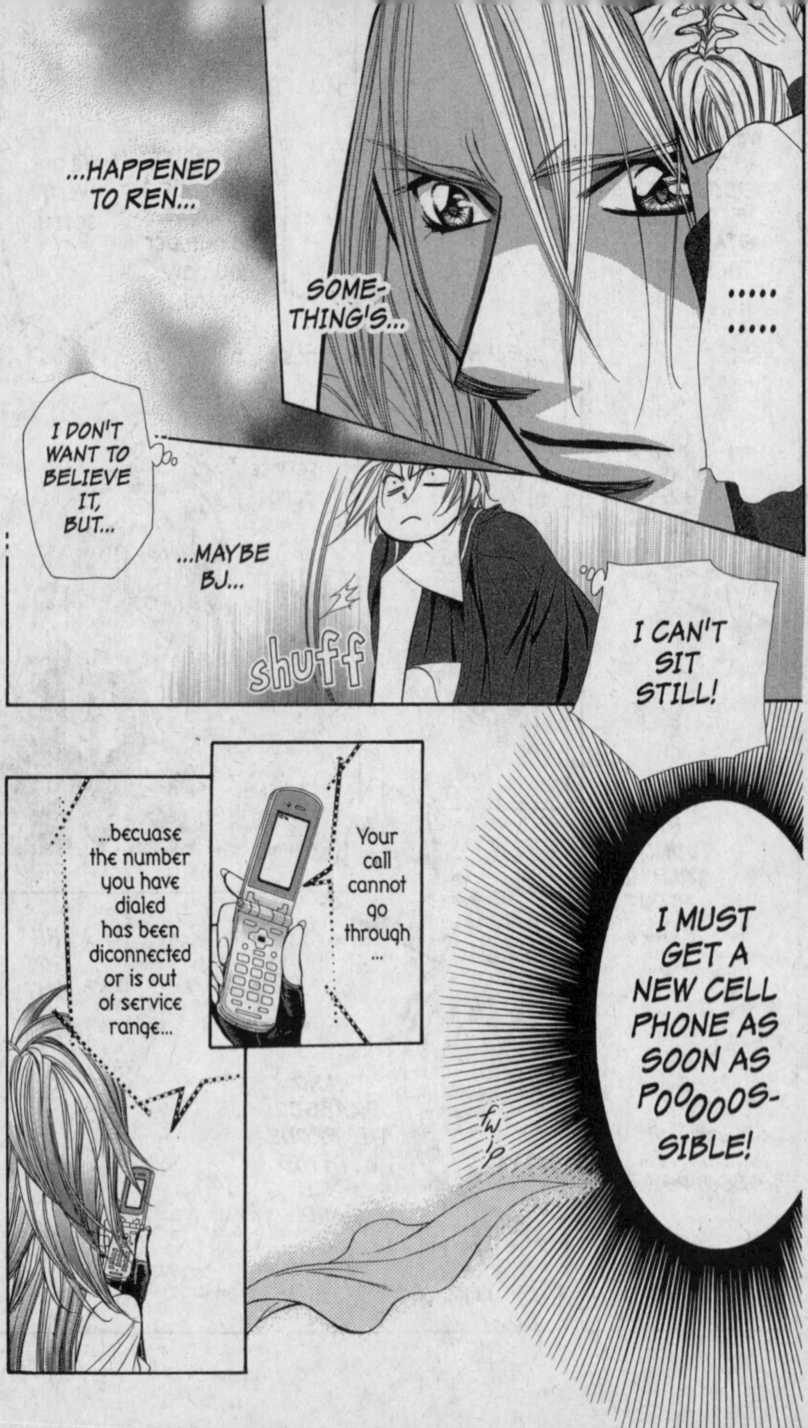
.....
.....
SOME-THING'S...
...HAPPENED TO REN...
I CAN'T SIT STILL!
...MAYBE BJ...
I DON'T WANT TO BELIEVE IT, BUT...
shuff
I MUST GET A NEW CELL PHONE AS SOON AS POOOOOS-SIBLE!
fwip
Your call cannot go through ...
...becuase the number you have dialed has been diconnected or is out of service range...

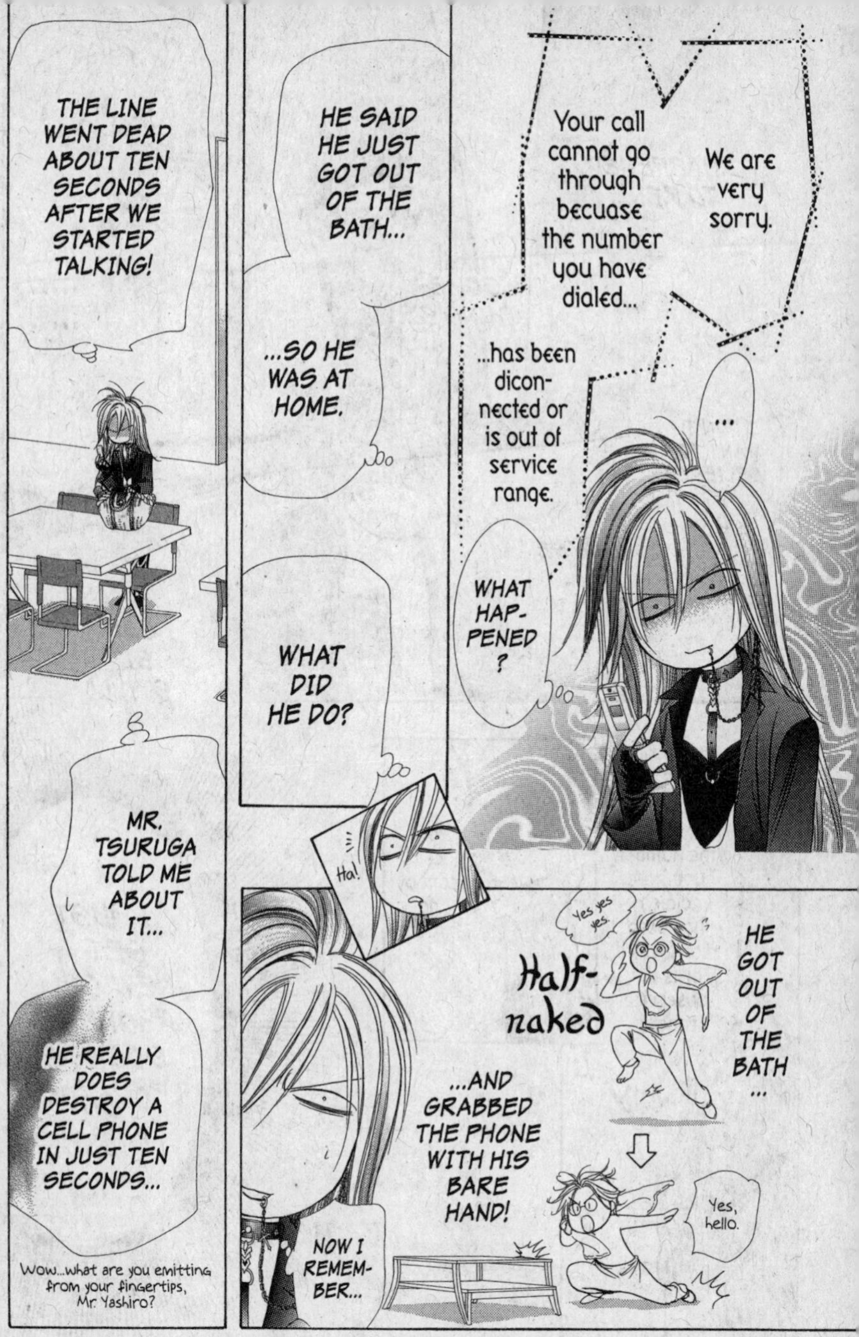
Your call cannot go through becuase the number you have dialed...
We are very sorry.
...has been dicon-nected or is out of service range.
...
WHAT HAP-PENED?
HE SAID HE JUST GOT OUT OF THE BATH...
...SO HE WAS AT HOME.
WHAT DID HE DO?
Ha!
HE GOT OUT OF THE BATH...
Yes yes yes.
Half-naked
...AND GRABBED THE PHONE WITH HIS BARE HAND!
Yes, hello.
NOW I REMEM-BER...
THE LINE WENT DEAD ABOUT TEN SECONDS AFTER WE STARTED TALKING!
MR. TSURUGA TOLD ME ABOUT IT...
HE REALLY DOES DESTROY A CELL PHONE IN JUST TEN SECONDS...
Wow...what are you emitting from your fingertips, Mr. Yashiro?

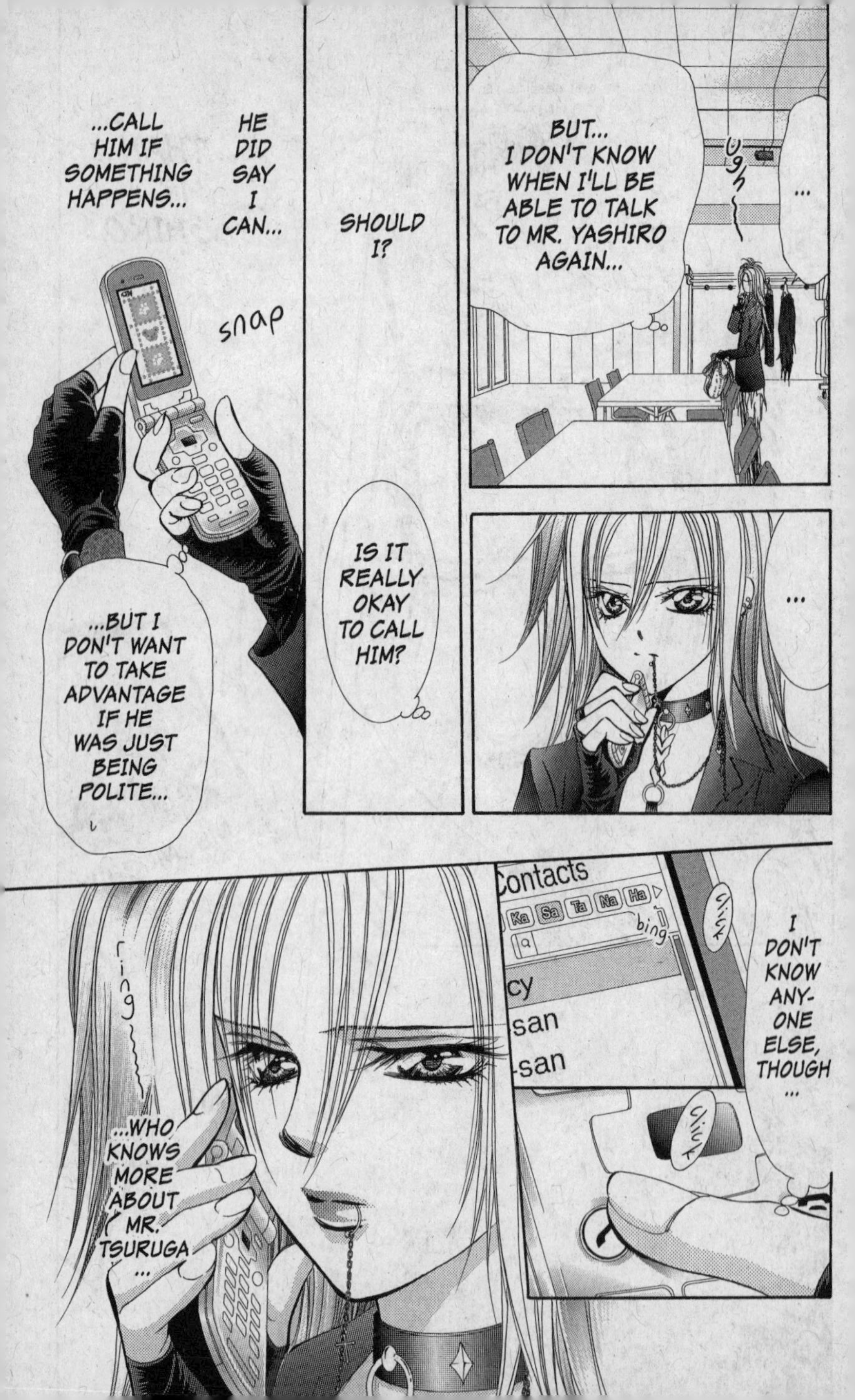
...
ugh~
BUT... I DON'T KNOW WHEN I'LL BE ABLE TO TALK TO MR. YASHIRO AGAIN...
...
SHOULD I?
IS IT REALLY OKAY TO CALL HIM?
HE DID SAY I CAN...
...CALL HIM IF SOMETHING HAPPENS...
snap
...BUT I DON'T WANT TO TAKE ADVANTAGE IF HE WAS JUST BEING POLITE...
I DON'T KNOW ANYONE ELSE, THOUGH...
click
Contacts
Ka Sa Ta Na Ha
bing
cy
san
-san
click
ring~
...WHO KNOWS MORE ABOUT MR. TSURUGA...

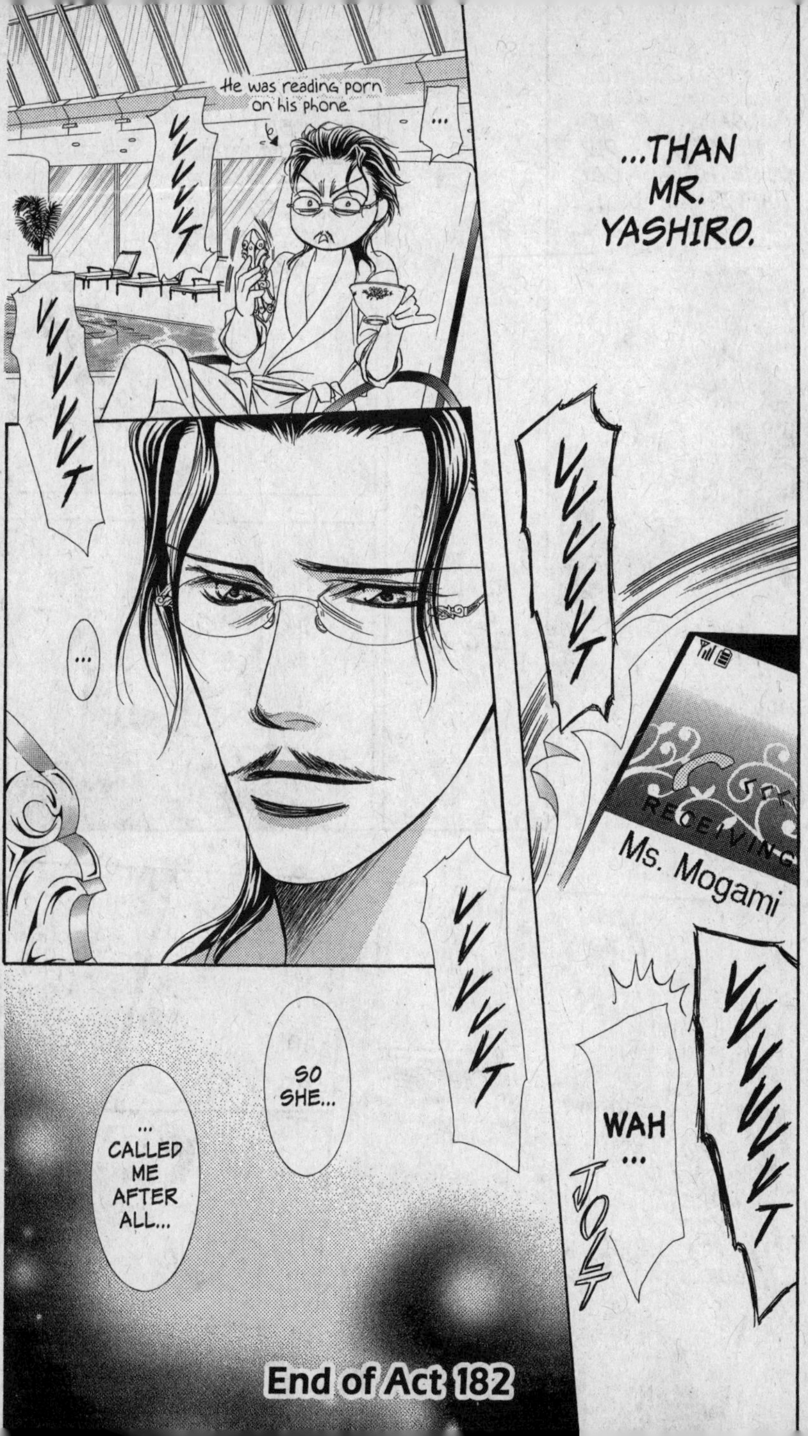
...THAN MR. YASHIRO.
VVVVVT
RECEIVING
Ms. Mogami
VVVVVVT
WAH ...
JOLT
...
He was reading porn on his phone.
VVVVVT
VVVVVVT
...
VVVVVT
SO SHE...
... CALLED ME AFTER ALL...
End of Act 182

Skip-Beat! End Notes

Everyone knows how to be a fan, but sometimes cool things from other cultures need a little help crossing the language barrier.

Page 392, panel 1: Murasame's jacket
The long jacket with kanji inscription is a typical style for *yanki*, a type of Japanese delinquent.

Yoshiki Nakamura is
originally from Tokushima Prefecture.
She started drawing manga in elementary
school, which eventually led to her 1993 debut of
Yume de Au yori Suteki (Better than Seeing in
a Dream) in *Hana to Yume* magazine. Her other
works include the basketball series *Saint Love*,
MVP wa Yuzurenai (Can't Give Up MVP),
Blue Wars and *Tokyo Crazy Paradise*, a
series about a female bodyguard
in 2020 Tokyo.

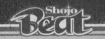

SKIP·BEAT!
3-in-1 Edition
Vol. 10
A compilation of graphic novel volumes 28–30

STORY AND ART BY YOSHIKI NAKAMURA

English Translation & Adaptation/Tomo Kimura
Touch-up Art & Lettering/Sabrina Heep
Design/Yukiko Whitley
Editor/Pancha Diaz

First published in Japan in 2011, 2012 by HAKUSENSHA, Inc., Tokyo.
English language translation rights arranged with HAKUSENSHA, Inc., Tokyo.

Printed in the U.S.A.

Published by VIZ Media, LLC
P.O. Box 77010
San Francisco, CA 94107

www.viz.com www.shojobeat.com

10 9 8 7 6 5 4 3 2 1
3-in-1 edition first printing, March 2015

RATED T FOR TEEN
PARENTAL ADVISORY
SKIP·BEAT! is rated T for Teen and is recommended for ages 13 and up. This volume contains a grudge.
ratings.viz.com

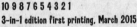

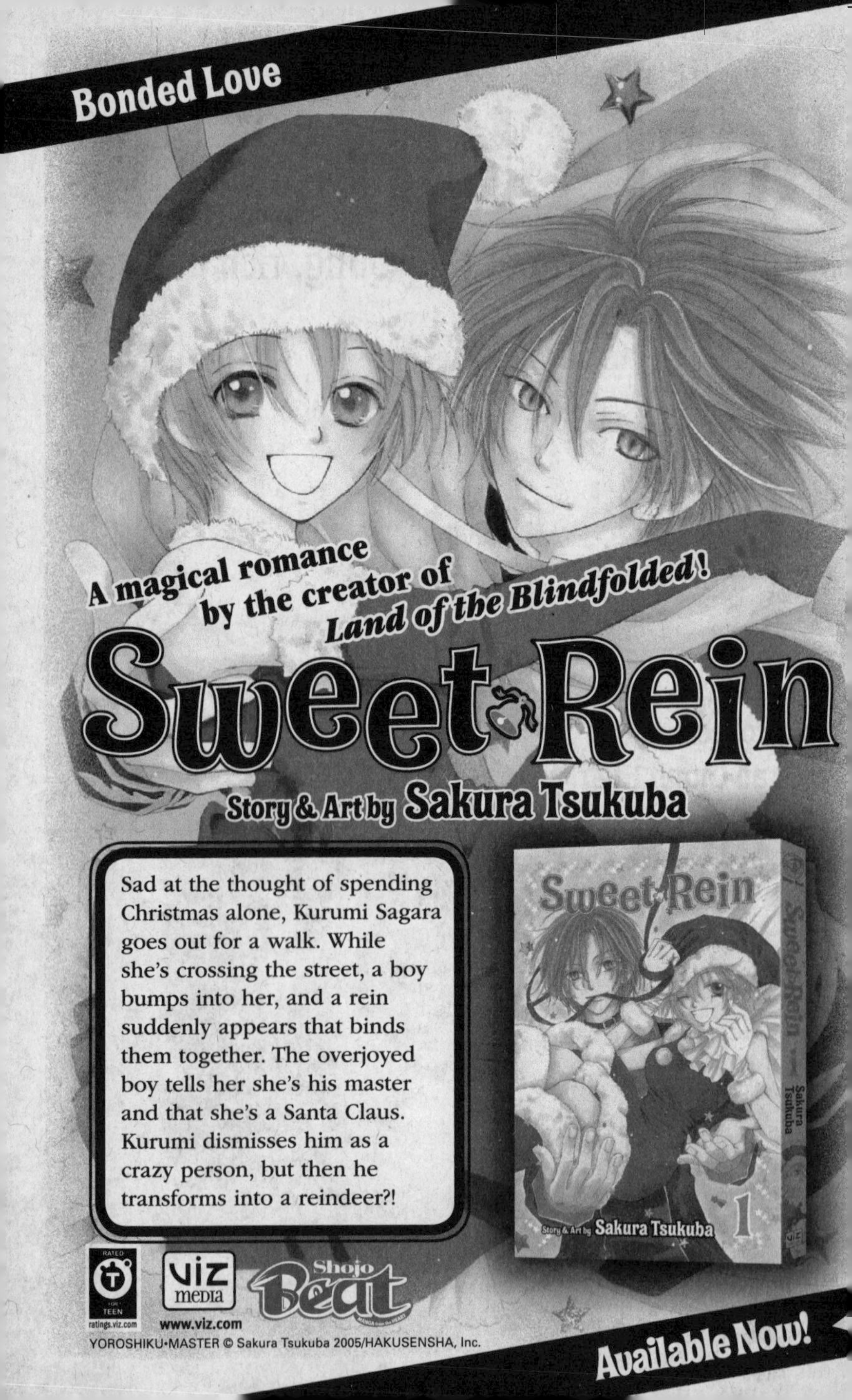
Bonded Love
A magical romance by the creator of Land of the Blindfolded!
Sweet Rein
Story & Art by Sakura Tsukuba
Sad at the thought of spending Christmas alone, Kurumi Sagara goes out for a walk. While she's crossing the street, a boy bumps into her, and a rein suddenly appears that binds them together. The overjoyed boy tells her she's his master and that she's a Santa Claus. Kurumi dismisses him as a crazy person, but then he transforms into a reindeer?!
Sweet Rein
Story & Art by Sakura Tsukuba
1
Sakura Tsukuba
RATED T FOR TEEN
ratings.viz.com
viz media
Shojo Beat
www.viz.com
YOROSHIKU•MASTER © Sakura Tsukuba 2005/HAKUSENSHA, Inc.
Available Now!

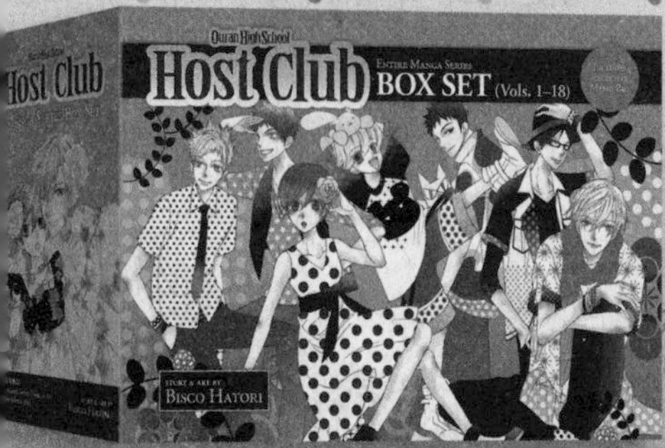
Ouran High School
Host Club
Entire Manga Series
BOX SET (Vols. 1–18)
Story & Art by
Bisco Hatori

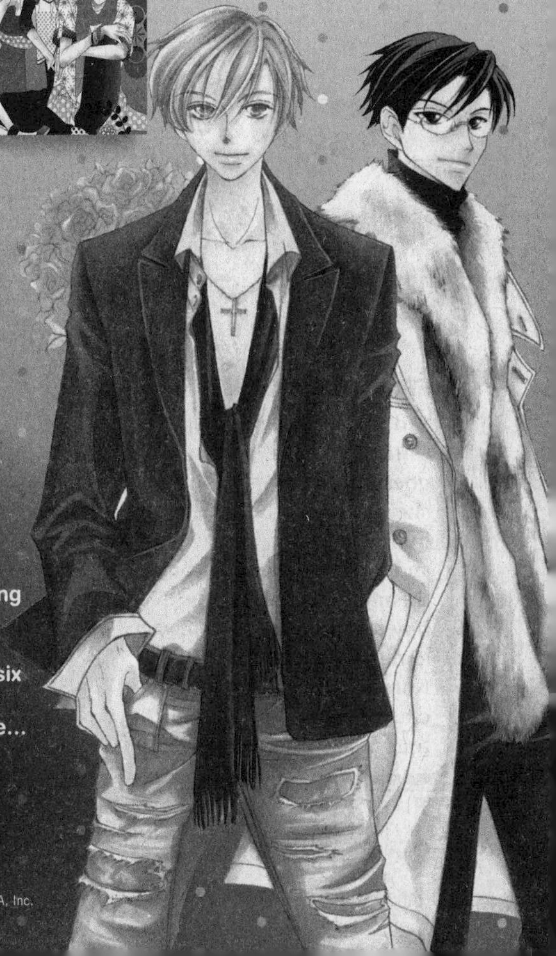

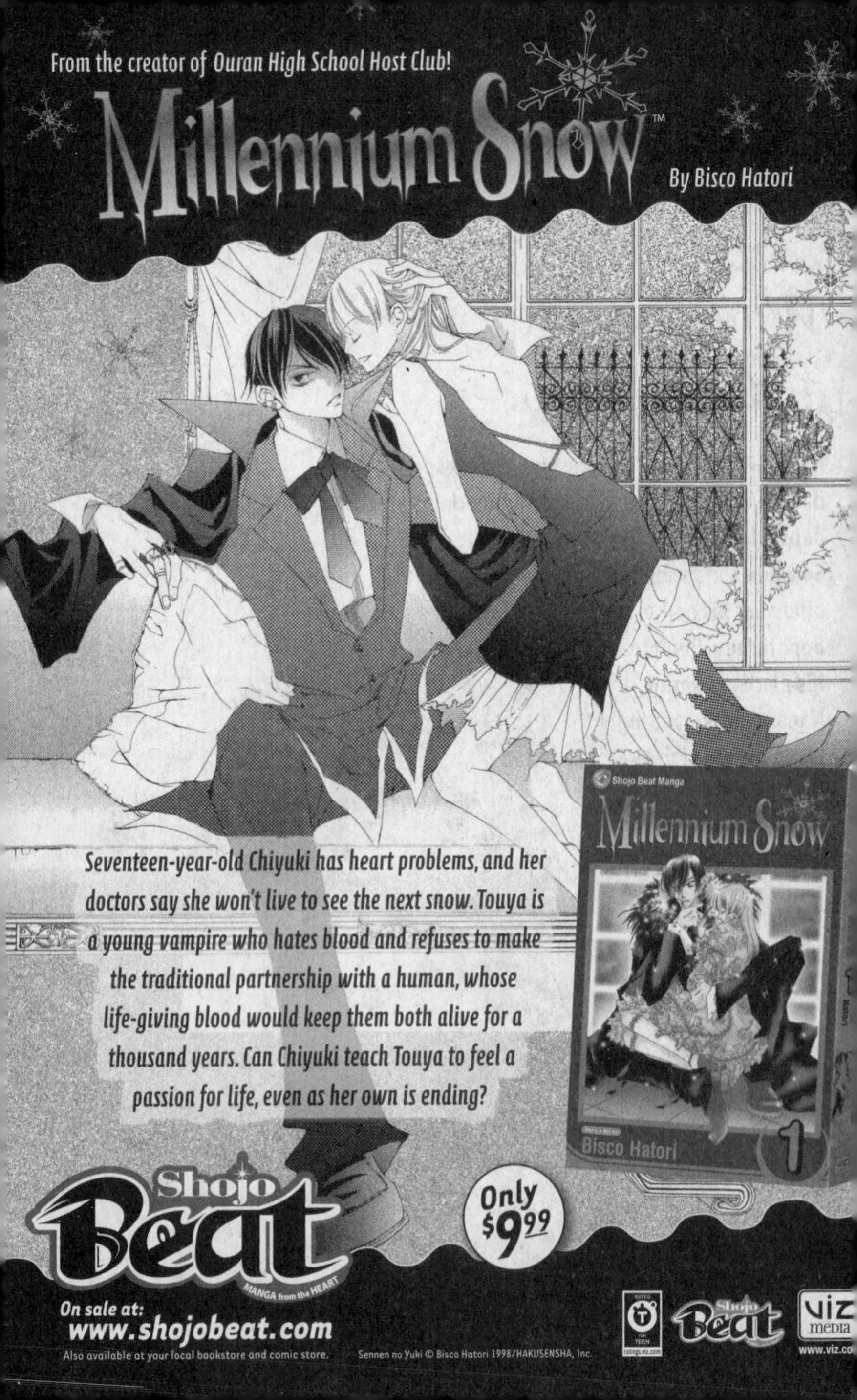
From the creator of Ouran High School Host Club!
Millennium Snow™
By Bisco Hatori
Shojo Beat Manga
Millennium Snow
Bisco Hatori
1
Seventeen-year-old Chiyuki has heart problems, and her doctors say she won't live to see the next snow. Touya is a young vampire who hates blood and refuses to make the traditional partnership with a human, whose life-giving blood would keep them both alive for a thousand years. Can Chiyuki teach Touya to feel a passion for life, even as her own is ending?
Shojo Beat
MANGA from the HEART
Only $9.99
On sale at:
www.shojobeat.com
Also available at your local bookstore and comic store.
Sennen no Yuki © Bisco Hatori 1998/HAKUSENSHA, Inc.
RATED T FOR TEEN
ratings.viz.com
Shojo Beat
VIZ media
www.viz.com

SURPRISE!

You may be reading the wrong way!

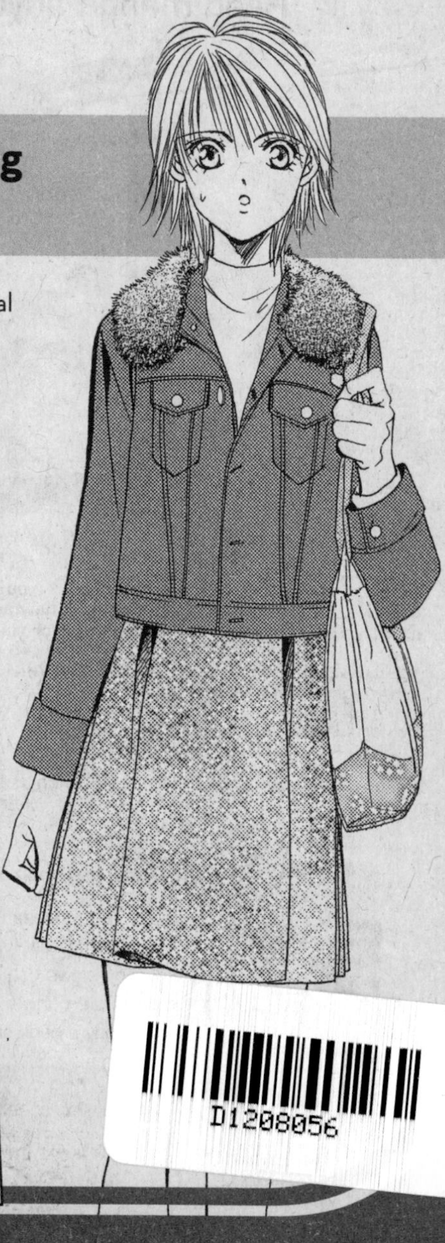

It's true: In keeping with the original Japanese comic format, this book reads from right to left—so action, sound effects, and word balloons are completely reversed. This preserves the orientation of the original artwork—plus, it's fun! Check out the diagram shown here to get the hang of things, and then turn to the other side of the book to get started!

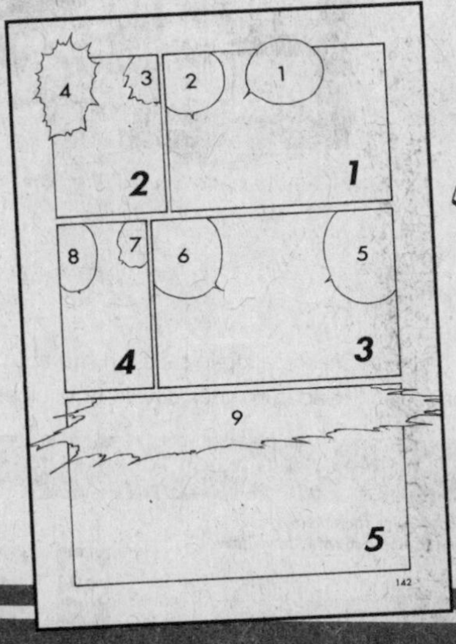

1
2
1
3
4
2
5
6
3
7
8
4
9
5
142